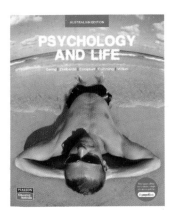

W9-AOR-059

# Welcome to

**To start using MyPsychLab you will need a valid email address, that you check on a regular basis, and the access code that is printed beneath the scratch-off panel below.**

Your access code is:

ASSGPL-CROSS-STAND-NEAGH-LOBBY-FLEES

If the access code above has been revealed and redeemed and you wish to purchase access to this resource, go to: **http://www.pearsoned.com.au/AccessCodes/**

## Register for MyPsychLab

To access MyPsychLab, you must complete an easy, one-time registration process.

1. Go to www.pearsoned.com.au/mypsychlab and click the register button for students.
2. Follow the on-screen instructions to enter your student access code, your instructor supplied course ID, contact information, and create a login code and password.

If you need help during the online registration click help

**After you have registered you are ready to log in to MyPsychLab anytime**

## Logging in to MyPsychLab

You can log in to MyPsychLab anytime after you register, by using the login name and password you created during registration

1. Go to www.pearsoned.com.au/mypsychlab and click the login button for students
2. Enter the login name and password you created during registration
3. Select the book

## Begin exploring MyPsychLab

  **Need help?**

**Visit http://247.global.pearsoned.com**

ISBN 978-14425-0193-5

# PSYCHOLOGY AND LIFE

Gerrig | Zimbardo | Campbell | Cumming | Wilkes

PEARSON

Education
Australia

Copyright © Pearson Education Australia (a division of Pearson Australia Group Pty Ltd) 2009

Pearson Education Australia
Unit 4, Level 3
14 Aquatic Drive
Frenchs Forest NSW 2086

www.pearsoned.com.au

Senior Editor & Development Manager: Alison Green
Development Editor: Michael Stone
Project Editor: Sandra Goodall
Production Coordinator: Chris Richardson
Copy Editor: Jane Tyrrell
Copyright and Pictures Editors: Louise Burke/Emma Gaulton
Indexer: Garry Cousins
Cover design by Couch Creative
Cover photograph from Getty Images, Fredrik Skold
Typeset by Midland Typesetters, Australia

Printed in China(GCC)

3 4 5 13 12 11 10

National Library of Australia
Cataloguing-in-Publication Data

Psychology and life / Richard J. Gerrig ... [et al.].
Frenchs Forest, N.S.W. : Pearson Education Australia, 2008.
9781442500891 (pbk.)
Psychology.
Gerrig, Richard J.
150

An imprint of Pearson Education Australia (a division of Pearson Australia Group Pty Ltd)

# BRIEF CONTENTS

# CONTENTS

Teaching introductory psychology is one of the greatest challenges facing any academic psychologist. Indeed, because of the range of our subject matter, it is probably the most difficult course to teach effectively in all of academia. We must cover both the micro-level analyses of nerve cell processes and the macro-level analyses of cultural systems: both the vitality of health psychology and the tragedy of lives blighted by mental illness. Our challenge in writing this text—like your challenge in teaching—is to give form and substance to all this information: to bring it to life for our students.

More often than not, students come into our course filled with misconceptions about psychology that they have picked up from the infusion of 'pop psychology' into our society. They also bring with them high expectations about what they want to get out of a course in psychology—they want to learn much that will be personally valuable, that will help them improve their everyday lives. Indeed, that is a tall order for any teacher to fill. But we believe that *Psychology and Life* can help you to fill it.

Our goal has been to design a text that students will enjoy reading as they learn what is so exciting and special about the many fields of psychology. In every chapter, in every sentence, we have tried to make sure that students will want to go on reading. At the same time, we have focused on how our text will work within the syllabi of instructors who value a research-centred, applications-relevant approach to psychology.

This 1st Australian edition of *Psychology and Life* is the debut collaboration between Andrew Campbell, Steven Cumming and Fiona Wilkes. This partnership has brought together the best experience of Australian social, developmental, cognitive, health and sensory perception psychology. Each of us have brought our research and teaching experience to a text which has set exemplary standards for scientific rigor with psychology's relevance to contemporary life concerns. Andrew utilises his experience of social and developmental psychology, especially from a contemporary psychological viewpoint that incorporates culture, education and cyberspace. Steven's expertise in cognitive and health psychology is wide reaching in Australia, and Fiona also brings a strong background in cutting-edge sensory and perception research to the text. In the fashion of conversational and relatable examples set by the U.S. authors, Richard Gerrig and Philip Zimbardo, *Psychology and Life* remains a collaboration of like minds: together, we celebrate both an ongoing tradition and a continued vision of bringing the most important psychological insights to bear on students' lives.

# TEXT THEME: THE SCIENCE OF PSYCHOLOGY

The aim of *Psychology and Life* is to use solid scientific research to combat psychological misconceptions. In our experience as teachers, one of the most reliable occurrences on the first day of introductory psychology is the throng of students who push forward at the end of class to ask, in essence, 'Will this class teach me what I need to know?':

My mother is taking Prozac: Will we learn what it does?

Are you going to teach us how to study better?

I need to put my son in daycare to come back to school. Is that going to be all right for him?

What should I do if I have a friend talking about suicide?

We take comfort that each of these questions has been addressed by rigorous empirical research. *Psychology and Life* is devoted to providing students with scientific analyses of their foremost concerns. As a result, the features of *Psychology and Life* support a central theme: psychology as a science, with a focus on applying that science to real life experiences.

## NEW! CRITICAL THINKING IN YOUR LIFE

An important goal of *Psychology and Life* is to teach the scientific basis of psychological reasoning. When our students ask us questions—what they need to know—they quite often have acquired partial answers based on the types of information that are available in the popular media. Some of that information is accurate, but often students do not know how to make sense of it. How do they learn to interpret and evaluate what they hear in the media? How can they become wiser consumers of the overabundance of research studies and surveys cited? How can they judge the credibility of these sources? To counteract this infusion of so-called

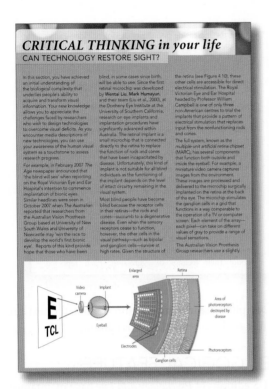
reliable research, we provide students with the scientific tools to think critically about the information with which they are surrounded and to draw generalisations appropriate to the goals and methods of research.

With a new feature we call **Critical Thinking in Your Life**, we seek to confront students directly with the experimental basis of critical conclusions. Our intention is not to maintain that each of these boxes has the definitive answer to a particular research area, but to invite critical thinking and open the door for further questions.

Critical Thinking in Your Life topics, by chapter:
- Why do friendships end? (Chapter 1)
- How can you evaluate psychological information on the web? (Chapter 2)
- What does 'it's genetic' mean? (Chapter 3)
- Can technology restore sight? (Chapter 4)
- Does ecstasy harm the brain? (Chapter 5)
- To smack or not to smack? (Chapter 6)
- How can memory research help you prepare for exams? (Chapter 7)
- Can political experts predict the future? (Chapter 8)
- Are breastfed children smarter? (Chapter 9)
- How does child care affect children's development? (Chapter 10)

- How does motivation affect academic achievement? (Chapter 11)
- Can health psychology help you be a healthy person? (Chapter 12)
- Who are you on the internet? (Chapter 13)
- Is 'insanity' really a defence? (Chapter 14)
- Does therapy affect brain activity? (Chapter 15)
- Do late-night TV ads really work? (Chapter 16)
- How can you get people to volunteer? (Chapter 17)

## PSYCHOLOGY IN YOUR LIFE

The questions we cited earlier are real questions from real students, and students will find the answers throughout the book. These questions represent data we collected from students over the years. We asked them, 'Tell us what you need to know about psychology', and we have placed those questions—the students' own voices—directly into the text in the form of the popular **Psychology in Your Life** sections. Our hope is that students will see, in each instance, exactly why psychological knowledge is directly relevant to the decisions they make every day of their lives.

Psychology in Your Life topics, by chapter:

- Can psychology help me find a career? (Chapter 1)
- Can survey research affect your attitudes? (Chapter 2)
- Why does music have an impact on how you feel?(Chapter 3)
- Why is eating 'hot' food painful? (Chapter 4)
- Do you get enough sleep? (Chapter 5)
- How does classical conditioning affect cancer treatment? (Chapter 6)
- Why does Alzheimer's disease affect memory? (Chapter 7)
- Why and how do people lie? (Chapter 8)
- Do theories of intelligence matter? (Chapter 9)
- Will your brain work differently as you age? (Chapter 10)
- How does genetics contribute to obesity? (Chapter 11)
- Why are some people happier than others? (Chapter 12)
- Why are some people shy? (Chapter 13)
- How can we pinpoint interactions of nature and nurture? (Chapter 14)
- How has mental illness been portrayed in Australian and New Zealand films? (Chapter 14)
- Are lives haunted by repressed memories? (Chapter 15)
- Can lasting relationships form on the internet? (Chapter 16)
- How might reconciliation be possible? (Chapter 17)

## RESEARCH STUDIES

These major studies showcase the how and why behind key psychological research, with particular reference to Australian-based research where applicable. These studies have been expertly integrated into the text itself, allowing students to understand their full impact within the context of their reading. Example topics include plasticity in the visual cortex of adult rats, the impact of meditation on brain structure, the impact of culture on judgments of which category members are typical, the impact of emotions on memory for visual details, individual differences in intimacy goals, family therapy for children's anxiety disorders, cross-cultural differences in cognitive dissonance, and genetic influences on physical and social aggression. Many of

With the increasing popularity of violent video games across all cultures, aggression theories suggest that interactive violent media (violent video games) are perhaps more impacting on increasing aggressive behaviour than non-interactive aggressive media (e.g. TV and movies). An Australian study investigated this hypothesis by inviting 150 University of Sydney students to watch a 2-hour episode of the war mini-series *Band of Brothers* which depicted 6 June 1944 D-Day invasion of Normandy, France. Subjects were asked to rate how they felt about the violence they witnessed in the program at the end of the viewing, with most showing feelings of heightened aggression, but also reporting feelings of sadness and empathy for casualties they saw on film. One week later, subjects were asked to play a violent video game that was similar to the episode they watched on TV. After playing the game for more than 1 hour, both male and female participants were asked the same questions about their feelings of aggression. Each reported

the 200 plus research studies throughout the text are new or have been revised for this edition.

## PEDAGOGICAL FEATURES

The US editions of *Psychology and Life* have maintained a reputation for presenting the science of psychology in a way that is challenging, yet accessible, to a broad range of students, and the first Australian edition is no exception. To enhance students' experience with the book, we include several pedagogical features in this edition:

- **Recap checkpoints.** This feature appears at the end of every major section and provides students

### RECAP CHECKPOINT
**Psychological measurement**

- Researchers strive to produce measures that are both reliable and valid.
- Psychological measurements include self-reports and behavioural measures.

### CONCEPT QUESTIONS

1. Why can some measures be reliable but not valid?

2. Why is it important for interviewers to establish rapport?

3. Suppose a researcher spends time observing children's behaviour in a playground. What kind of measure would that be?

with a brief interim summary of the main points just covered.

- **Concept questions**. Accompanying the *Recap checkpoints* at the end of each main section are thought-provoking questions to test students' mastery of material before moving on.
- **Key terms definitions**. Key terms are boldfaced in the text as they appear and definitions are provided in the margins.
- **Practice test**. Each chapter concludes with a practice test with multiple-choice questions based on the material in both the main text and feature boxes. In addition, we've provided sample essay questions that allow students to think more broadly about the content of each chapter. Multiple-choice answers can be found in MyPsychLab, and essay question suggested answers can be found in the Instructor's Manual.

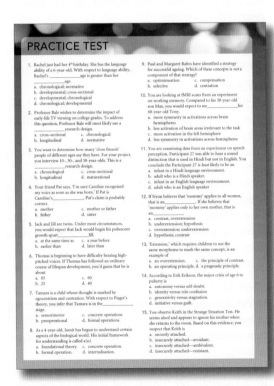

# NEW IN THE AUSTRALIAN EDITION

In addition to the new features mentioned earlier, the Australian edition of *Psychology and Life* is fresh with the most up-to-date coverage and brimming with new references. Our goal is to be the most current, most accurate, and most accessible treatment of our discipline today, within a context applicable to Australian students. *Psychology and Life* also incorporates new research, much of it locally-based, on the diversity of people's life experiences. We intend this book to have meaning for the whole range of students who enrol in introductory psychology—men and women, members of diverse cultural and racial groups, traditional and non-traditional students. Wherever possible, we have brought new research to bear on cultural issues, particularly those relevant to Australia's vast multicultural landscape.

## CHAPTER 1

- The beginnings of Australian psychology in the 1890s with Henry Laurie, Francis Anderson and William Mitchell
- The role of women in the development of psychology in Australia
- Section on careers in psychology in Australia, courtesy of APS

## CHAPTER 2

- Subliminal influence: a section on Media Watch investigation into subliminal advertising used during the 2007 ARIA Awards
- Ethical issues in human and animal research: reference to APS code of ethics
- New section on research with Aboriginal and Torres Strait Islander peoples
- Section on prevalence of animal testing in Australia

## CHAPTER 4

- Statistics on the prevalence of hearing problems in Australia, with particular reference to ATSI peoples
- Extended and new section on smell, incorporating Australian-based research
- Expansion of content on taste and taste adaptation, incorporating Australian-based research

- Inclusion of content on Sydney's Pain Management Research Institute in the 'Pain' section
- New *Psychology in Your Life* box focusing on the development of the bionic eye in Australia

CHAPTER 5
- Section on the meaning of The Dreamtime and 'Story Places' in Indigenous communities
- Cultural constructions of reality in Aboriginal and migrant communities
- Section on Australian sleep studies

CHAPTER 6
- Integration of Australian-based research (by Barry, 2000) on habituation
- Discussion of 'blocking' in humans, with reference to studies by Lovibond et al. 2003
- Reference to Mazurski et al. (1996) and McNally & Westbrook (2006) studies of fear
- New section on evaluative conditioning, with reference to studies undertaken by Lipp, Oughten, & LeLievre (2003)
- Discussion of Australian research in the 'discriminative stimuli and generalisation' section
- Inclusion of the Positive Parenting Program, led by Matt Sanders of UQ
- Australia/NZ studies into taste aversion learning in native fauna

CHAPTER 7
- Australian research on head injury and implicit memory
- Australian research by Kearins into differences in visual recall between white and Indigenous Australians

CHAPTER 8
- Discussion of Australia's multicultural landscape and statistics highlighting the number of different languages spoken
- Integration of research from ANU on 'key words' that typify languages, and how those words are related to culture and understanding
- Extension of section on 'inductive reasoning' to include research undertaken by UNSW
- Expansion of section on 'Availability heuristic' to include discussion of Australian crime statistics
- Inclusion of an Australian-centric example in the 'Representativeness heuristic' section

CHAPTER 9
- Australian examples (Pauline Hanson, HSC/UAI) in the 'History of assessment' introduction
- Discussion of the White Australia Policy in the 'History of Group Comparisons' section
- Section on the classic 1975 Kearins study of the effect of the environment of the intelligence of indigenous Australians

CHAPTER 10
- Reference to the RHEF (2005) studies in general development of Aboriginal children
- Discussion of development of motor skills in Indigenous children
- Expansion of current *Critical Thinking in Your Life* box to incorporate Australian research by Sims et al (2005) on the effects of child care on development
- Introduction of statistics on abuse and neglect in Indigenous communities, accompanied by discussion of underlying reasons, in the 'Human deprivation' section
- Discussion of Aboriginal and Torres Strait Islander people and non-English speaking background community in 'Adolescence' section

CHAPTER 11
- Inclusion of Australian example (AFL player Jason McCartney) in 'Sources of motivation' section
- Discussion of Aboriginal food rules and laws in the 'Cultural impact on eating' section
- Incorporation of Australian research by George Muscat and his colleagues at the University of Queensland (Muscat et al. 2003) into the link between genetics and obesity in the *Psychology in Your Life* box
- Statistics on the prevalence of obesity in Australia

CHAPTER 12
- Integration of Joseph Forgas' (UNSW) pioneering research on the impact of emotion on social functioning in the 'Social functions of emotion' section
- Inclusion of studies by Harris & Cumming (2003) in the section on 'Emotional effects of cognitive functioning'
- Discussion of the Healthy Weight 2008 government initiative in *Critical Thinking in Your Life*

- Aboriginal traditional medicine and health systems in the 'Health Psychology' section
- Statistics on the leading causes of death in Australia
- Discussion of eating habits and their effects (including statistics) on Australians

## CHAPTER 13
- Discussion of 'the self' and differences between Aboriginal teenagers in rural and urban settings in 'The cultural construction of self' section

## CHAPTER 14
- Integration of study by Creamer et al. (2001) into PTSD in woman
- Inclusion of research by Barney et al. (2006) into depression in rural Australia
- Discussion of statistics indicating Aboriginal and Torris Strait Islander suicide rates are 3 times higher than the general Australian population
- Replacement of US example with the case of Derek Percy in the 'Is insanity really a defence' *Critical Thinking in Your Life* box, with inclusion of Australian statistics on the number of defendants who enter an insanity plea
- Discussion of the 'Stigma of mental illness' in NESB and Indigenous communities, based primarily on research by Rooney et al. (1997)
- Australian statistics relating to the stigma of mental illness and reasons behind it (e.g. negative reporting in the media)
- New *Psychology in Your Life* boxed feature about the history of mental illness in Australian and New Zealand films
- Inclusion of a study on the effects of posttraumatic stress disorder in asylum seekers in mandatory detention
- Discussion of the Tiwi Mental Health Program in Northern Territory
- Statistics on Australians suffering from various forms of mental illness
- New *Psychology in Your Life* boxed feature on nature vs nurture based on UNSW research

## CHAPTER 15
- Statistics on the number of Australians suffering from various mental illnesses
- Australian case on repressed memory in *Psychology in Your Life* box

- Australian-based research project, D.I.R.T., by Govender et al. (2006) in the section on 'Counter-conditioning'
- Expansion of section on 'Community support groups' to include discussion of Australian groups such as *beyondblue*

## CHAPTER 16
- Expansion of the 'Fundamental Attribution Error' section to include discussion of 'going walkabout' in Aboriginal and Torres Strait Islander and Pacific Island communities
- Discussion of approaches to reducing the number of negative alcohol-related incidents in Indigenous communities, with reference to research by Gray (2000)
- Inclusion of a study by Hill and Augoustimos (2001) of ATSI communities in the section on 'Reducing Prejudice'
- Expansion of the *Psychology in Your Life* box to include studies by Campbell et al. (2006) into relationships on the internet
- Links to research on the prejudicial attitudes of Australians

## CHAPTER 17
- Section detailing research undertaken by Campbell et al into violent video games
- New section on 'Peace psychology' referencing the recent history of Reconciliation between Australians and Aboriginals
- Research on the attitudes of young Australians towards Muslims under 'Concepts and images of the enemy'

# INSTRUCTOR SUPPLEMENTS

## MYPSYCHLAB
This interactive and instructive multimedia resource can be used to supplement a traditional lecture course or to administer a course entirely online. It is an all-inclusive tool, a text-specific e-book plus multimedia tutorials, audio, video, simulations, animations, and controlled assessments to completely engage students

and reinforce learning. Fully customisable and easy to use, *MyPsychLab* for introductory psychology meets the individual teaching and learning needs of every instructor and every student. Visit the site at **www. pearsoned.com.au/mypsychlab**.

## INSTRUCTOR'S MANUAL

This thoroughly revised Instructor's Manual provides a wonderful tool for classroom preparation and management for first-time or experienced instructors. For each chapter, the Instructor's Manual includes a Chapter-at-a-Glance grid linking chapter topics to other available supplements and resources, learning objectives targeting specific goals for the chapter, detailed chapter outlines, a comprehensive list of discussion questions, lecture extensions, biographical profiles of key figures, a timeline placing important psychological discoveries in historical context, suggestions for further reading, case study lecture launchers, demonstrations and activities for classroom use, updated video, media and web resources, and other detailed pedagogical information.

## COMPUTERISED TEST BANK

The Test Bank is also available in TestGen 7.4 computerised version, for use in personalising tests. TestGen 7.4 is an integrated suite of testing and assessment tools for Windows and Macintosh. You can use TestGen to create professional-looking exams in just minutes by building tests from the existing database of questions, editing questions, or adding your own. TestGen also allows you to prepare printed, network and online tests.

## POWERPOINT PRESENTATION AND MEDIA LIBRARY

An exciting interactive tool for use in the classroom, this dynamic, multimedia resource pairs key points covered in the chapters with images from the textbook to encourage effective lectures and classroom discussions.

## INSIGHTS INTO PSYCHOLOGY VIDEO OR DVD, VOLS. I–IV

These video programs include two or three short clips per topic, covering such topics as animal research, parapsychology, health and stress, Alzheimer's disease, bilingual education, genetics and IQ, and much more. A Video Guide containing critical thinking questions accompanies each video. Also available on DVD.

## THE BLOCKBUSTER APPROACH: A GUIDE TO TEACHING INTRODUCTORY PSYCHOLOGY WITH VIDEO

The Blockbuster Approach is a unique print resource for instructors who enjoy enhancing their classroom presentations with film. With heavy coverage of general, abnormal, social, and developmental psychology, this guide suggests a wide range of films to use in class, and provides questions for reflection and other pedagogical tools to make the use of film more effective in the classroom.

## INTERACTIVE LECTURE QUESTIONS FOR CLICKERS FOR INTRODUCTORY PSYCHOLOGY

These lecture questions will jumpstart exciting classroom discussions.

## ALLYN & BACON DIGITAL MEDIA ARCHIVE FOR PSYCHOLOGY

This comprehensive source includes still images, audio clips, web links, animation and video clips. Highlights include classic Psychology experimental footage from Stanley Milgrim's *Invitation to Social Psychology*, biology animations, and more—with coverage of such topics as eating disorders, aggression, therapy, intelligence, and sensation and perception.

## DISCOVERING PSYCHOLOGY TELECOURSE VIDEOS

Written, designed, and hosted by US author Philip Zimbardo, this set of 26 half-hour videos is available for class use from the Annenberg/CPB collection. The collection includes two completely new programs and more than 15 new sequences that bring students up-to-date on some of the latest developments in the field. A perfect complement to *Psychology and Life*, this course supplement has won numerous prizes and is widely used internationally.

# STUDENT SUPPLEMENTS

## MYPSYCHLAB

This online all-in-one study resource offers a dynamic, electronic version of the Australian *Psychology and Life* textbook with over 200 embedded video clips (2 to 4 minutes in length, close-captioned and with post-viewing activities) and over 100 embedded animations and simulations that dynamically illustrate chapter concepts. With over 100 text-specific practice test questions per chapter, *MyPsychLab* helps students master the concepts and prepare for exams. After a student completes a chapter pre-test, *MyPsychLab* generates a customised Study Plan for that student that helps them focus their study efforts where they need it the most. *MyPsychLab* is available in both course management and website versions, and can be used as an instructor-driven assessment program and/or a student self-study learning program. Visit the site at **www.pearsoned.com.au/mypsychlab**

## GRADE AID WITH PRACTICE TESTS

A comprehensive and interactive study guide filled with in-depth activities. Each chapter includes 'Before You Read', with a brief chapter summary and chapter learning objectives; 'As You Read', a collection of demonstrations, activities, and exercises; 'After You Read', containing three short practice quizzes and one comprehensive practice test; 'When You Have Finished', with web links for further information; and

crossword puzzles using key terms from the text. An appendix includes answers to all practice tests and crossword puzzles.

## DISCOVERING PSYCHOLOGY TELECOURSE STUDY GUIDE

In this Telecourse Study Guide, each chapter corresponds to one program, expands upon the material covered in the program, specifies appropriate reading assignments, and reviews material covered in the text. In addition, the study guide includes learning objectives; reading assignments; key people and terms; video program summaries and test questions with answer key; textbook test questions with answer key; essay questions; student activities; additional book, article, and film resources; and annotated websites. All vocabulary and review questions are keyed to *Psychology and Life*.

## STUDY CARD FOR INTRODUCTORY PSYCHOLOGY

Colourful, affordable, and packed with useful information, Allyn & Bacon/Longman's Study Cards make studying easier, more efficient, and more enjoyable. Course information is distilled down to the basics, helping students quickly master the fundamentals, review a subject for understanding, or prepare for an exam.

## RESEARCH NAVIGATOR GUIDE: PSYCHOLOGY, WITH ACCESS TO RESEARCH NAVIGATORTM

Allyn & Bacon's new Research Navigator™ is the easiest way for students to start a research assignment or research paper. Complete with extensive help on the research process and three exclusive databases of credible and reliable source material including EBSCO's ContentSelect Academic Journal Database, New York Times Search by Subject Archive, and 'Best of the Web' Link Library, Research Navigator™ helps students quickly and efficiently make the most of their research time. The booklet contains a practical and to-the-point discussion of search engines; detailed information on evaluating online sources and citation guidelines for web resources; web links for Psychology; and a complete guide to Research Navigator.

# ACKNOWLEDGMENTS

We scoured the country looking for lecturers and students to assist in the development of this first Australian edition of *Psychology and Life*. Pearson Education Australia would like to thank the following people for providing invaluable feedback, and directly contributing to this fine publication:

## REVIEWERS

**Expert reviewer, Chapters 5 and 6:** Stephen Provost, Southern Cross University
*Other reviewers*
Julie Robinson, Flinders University
Andrew Talk, University of New England
Tom Edwards, Monash University
Kate Mulgrew, Australian Catholic University (McAuley)
Tania Signal, Central Queensland University
Jason Lodge, James Cook University
Lyn Courtney, James Cook University
Kathryn Pozzebon, University of Sunshine Coast
Lynnelle Watts, Edith Cowan University
Julie Fitness, Macquarie University
Tunde Meikle, Australian Catholic University (McAuley)
Lynette Leaney, University of South Australia
Natalie Gasson, Curtin University

## PERSONAL ACKOWLEDGEMENTS

The enormous task of writing a book of this scope was possible only with the expert assistance of all these friends and colleagues and that of the editorial and production staff of Pearson Education Australia. We gratefully acknowledge their invaluable contributions at every stage of this project, collectively and, now, individually. We thank the following people at Pearson Education: Alison Green, Senior Acquisitions Editor; Michael Stone, Development Editor; Sandra Goodall, Project Editor; Louise Burke, Copyright and Pictures Editor.

# ABOUT THE ORIGINATING AUTHORS

## RICHARD J. GERRIG

Richard J. Gerrig is a professor of psychology at Stony Brook University. Before joining the Stony Brook faculty, Gerrig taught at Yale University, where he was awarded the Lex Hixon Prize for teaching excellence in the social sciences. Gerrig's research on cognitive psychological aspects of language use has been widely published. One line of work examines the mental processes that underlie efficient communication. A second research program considers the cognitive and emotional changes readers experience when they are transported to the worlds of stories. His book Experiencing Narrative Worlds was published by Yale University Press. Gerrig is a Fellow of both the American Psychological Association and the Association for Psychological Science. He is also an associate editor of *Psychonomic Bulletin & Review*. Gerrig is the proud father of Alexandra, who at age 16 provides substantial and valuable advice about many aspects of psychology and life in the 21st century. Life on Long Island is greatly enhanced by the guidance and support of Timothy Peterson.

## PHILIP G. ZIMBARDO

Philip G. Zimbardo is an emeritus professor of psychology at Stanford University, where he has taught since 1968, after earlier teaching at Yale University, New York University, and Columbia University. He also continues to teach at the Naval Post Graduate School in Monterey. Zimbardo is internationally recognised as the 'voice and face of contemporary psychology' through his widely seen PBS-TV series, *Discovering Psychology*, his media appearances, best-selling trade books on shyness, and his classic research, The Stanford Prison Experiment. His current research interests are in the domain of experimental social psychology, with a scattered emphasis on everything interesting to study from shyness to time perspective, persuasion, cults, madness, violence, vandalism, political psychology and terrorism.

Zimbardo has been a prolific, innovative researcher across a number of fields in social and general psychology, with more than 300 professional articles and chapters and 50 books to his credit. To recognise the breadth of his research achievements, the American Psychological Association presented Zimbardo with the Ernest Hilgard Award for lifetime contributions to general psychology. He has also won the Vaclav Havel Foundation Award for his body of research on the human condition. Zimbardo has been President of the Western Psychological Association (twice), President of the American Psychological Association, Chair of the Council of Scientific Society Presidents (CSSP), and now Chair of the Western Psychological Foundation and Director of the Center for Interdisciplinary Policy, Education, and Research on Terrorism.

He is most excited about the publication of his new trade book in March 2007 (Random House), which he has been working on intensely for the past several years. Its domain is the psychology of evil; its provocative title: 'The Lucifer Effect: Understanding How Good People Turn Evil'.

# ABOUT THE AUSTRALIAN AUTHORS

ANDREW J. CAMPBELL

Andrew J. Campbell is a lecturer in psychology at The University of Sydney and has been conducting research into the use of the internet, computer games and multimedia in regards to its impact and influence on human behaviour.

Andrew is the Director of Prometheus (www.prometheus.net.au) a unique research group located in the Faculty of Health Sciences at The University of Sydney. Prometheus is dedicated to the research and application of technology towards the advancement of mental health treatments in such disorders as attention deficit/ hyperactivity disorder (AD/HD), depression, anxiety, stress, self-esteem and identity formation of children and adolescents. He is also a registered psychologist in New South Wales and runs a clinic at the Brain and Mind Research Institute in Sydney. This clinic specialises in established psychological disorders such as AD/HD, depression and anxiety, as well as emerging problems with youth, such as computer game obsession behaviour (a.k.a computer game addiction).

STEVEN R. CUMMING

Steven R. Cumming is currently Associate Dean and Director, Learning and Teaching in the Faculty of Health Sciences at the University of Sydney. He has worked as a clinical psychologist and neuropsychologist in Tasmania and New South Wales, and still practices in the areas of anxiety disorders and relationship counselling. His research interests lie in the overlap between cognitive processes, brain function and emotional states, such as the impact of anxiety on memory. In his current role, Steven has extended his research into areas concerning learning and instructional styles, interprofessional learning and curriculum design.

His teaching interests are in introductory biological psychology, and advanced cognition and neuropsychology units, as well as specialist topics in counselling and assessment.

FIONA J. WILKES

Fiona J. Wilkes has been working and researching in the field of psychology for the past 14 years. She worked at Griffith University and Macquarie University before moving to the University of Western Sydney in 2000, where she completed her PhD. Fiona currently teaches in the areas of sensation, perception, research methods and statistics as part of the undergraduate program in the School of Psychology at the University of Western Sydney.

Her research interests are predominantly in the domain of perception with specific focus on chemosensory function and assessment and sensory analysis. She is particularly excited about her recent collaborative publication on *olfactory function* in *Australian Aboriginal children and chronic otitis media*.

Psychology and Life

CHAPTER

1

# CHAPTER FOCUS POINTS

After studying this chapter you will have a better understanding of:

1. What psychology is and the goals of psychological study

2. The history of psychology and the legacy of structuralism and functionalism

3. The seven contemporary theoretical approaches to studying psychology

4. The role of psychologists, where they work and the questions they address

5. Strategies for effective study

## CHAPTER CONTENTS

psychology The scientific study of the behaviour of individuals and their mental processes.

scientific method The set of procedures used for gathering and interpreting objective information in a way that minimises error and yields dependable generalisations.

behaviour The actions by which an organism adjusts to its environment.

Why should you study psychology? Our answer to that question is quite straightforward: We believe that psychological research has immediate and crucial applications to important issues of everyday experience: your physical and mental health, your ability to form and sustain close relationships, and your capacity for learning and personal growth. One of the foremost goals of *Psychology and Life* is to highlight the personal relevance and social significance of psychological expertise.

Every semester when we begin to teach, we are faced with students who enter an introductory psychology class with some very specific questions in mind. Sometimes those questions emerge from their own experience ('What should I do if I think my mother is mentally ill?' 'Will this course teach me how to improve my grades?'); sometimes those questions emerge from the type of psychological information that is communicated through the popular press ('Is it true that oldest children are the most conservative?' 'Are women really always better parents than men?'). The challenge for us as we teach the course is to bring the products of scientific research to bear on questions that matter to our students.

Research in psychology provides a continuous stream of new information about the basic mechanisms that govern mental and behavioural processes. As new ideas replace or modify old ideas, we are continually intrigued and challenged by the many fascinating pieces of the puzzle of human nature. We hope that, by the end of this journey through psychology, you too will cherish your store of psychological knowledge.

Foremost in the journey will be a scientific quest for understanding. We will inquire about the how, what, when and why of human behaviour and about the causes and consequences of behaviours you observe in yourself, in other people and in animals. We will explain why you think, feel and behave as you do. What makes you uniquely different from all other people? Yet why do you often behave so much like others? Are you moulded by heredity, or are you shaped more by personal experiences? How can aggression and altruism, love and hate, and madness and creativity exist side by side in this complex creature—the human animal? In this opening chapter, we consider how and why all these types of questions have become relevant to psychology's goals as a discipline.

# WHAT MAKES PSYCHOLOGY UNIQUE?

To appreciate the uniqueness and unity of psychology, you must consider the way psychologists define the field and the goals they bring to their research and applications. By the end of the book, we hope you will think like a psychologist. In this first section, we'll give you a strong idea of what that might mean.

## DEFINITIONS

Many psychologists seek answers to this fundamental question: What is human nature? Psychology answers this question by looking at processes that occur within individuals as well as forces that arise within the physical and social environment. In this light, we formally define **psychology** as the scientific study of the behaviour of individuals and their mental processes. Let's explore the critical parts of this definition: *scientific, behaviour, individual* and *mental*.

The scientific aspect of psychology requires that psychological conclusions be based on evidence collected according to the principles of the scientific method. The **scientific method** consists of a set of orderly steps used to analyse and solve problems. This method uses objectively collected information as the factual basis for drawing conclusions. We will elaborate on the features of the scientific method more fully in Chapter 2, when we consider how psychologists conduct their research.

**Behaviour** is the means by which organisms adjust to their environment. Behaviour is action. The subject matter of psychology largely consists of the observable behaviour of humans and other species of animals. Smiling, crying, running, hitting, talking and touching are some obvious examples of behaviour you can observe. Psychologists examine what the individual does and how the individual goes about doing it within a given behavioural setting and in the broader social or cultural context.

The subject of psychological analysis is most often an *individual*—a newborn infant, a teenage athlete, a university student adjusting to living on campus, a woman facing a midlife career change, or a man coping with the stress of his wife's deterioration from Alzheimer's disease. However, the subject might also be a chimpanzee learning to use symbols to communicate, a white rat navigating a maze, or a sea slug responding to a danger signal. An individual might be studied in its natural habitat or in the controlled conditions of a research laboratory.

Many researchers in psychology also recognise that they cannot understand human actions without also understanding *mental processes,* the workings of the human mind. Much human activity takes place as private, internal events—thinking, planning, reasoning, creating and dreaming. Many psychologists believe that mental processes represent the most important aspect of psychological inquiry. As you shall soon see, psychological investigators have devised ingenious techniques to study mental events and processes—to make these private experiences public.

The combination of these concerns defines psychology as a unique field. Within the *social sciences,* psychologists focus largely on behaviour in individuals, whereas sociologists study the behaviour of people in groups or institutions, and anthropologists focus on the broader context of behaviour in different cultures. Even so, psychologists draw broadly from the insights of other scholars. Psychologists share many interests with researchers in *biological sciences,* especially with those who study brain

Most psychological study focuses on individuals—usually human ones, but sometimes those of other species. What aspects of your own life would you like psychologists to study?

processes and the biochemical bases of behaviour. As part of the emerging area of *cognitive science,* psychologists' questions about how the human mind works are related to research and theory in computer science, artificial intelligence, and applied mathematics. As a *health science*—with links to medicine, education, law and environmental studies—psychology seeks to improve the quality of each individual's and the collective's wellbeing.

Although the remarkable breadth and depth of modern psychology are a source of delight to those who become psychologists, these same attributes make the field a challenge to the student exploring it for the first time. There is so much more to the study of psychology than you might expect initially—and, because of that, there will also be much of value that you can take away from this introduction to psychology. The best way to learn about the field is to learn to share psychologists' goals. Let's consider those goals.

## THE GOALS OF PSYCHOLOGY

The goals of the psychologist conducting basic research are to describe, explain, predict and control behaviour. These goals form the basis of the psychological enterprise. What is involved in trying to achieve each of them?

### Describing what happens
The first task in psychology is to make accurate observations about

behaviour. Psychologists typically refer to such observations as their *data* (*data* is the plural, *datum* the singular). **Behavioural data** are reports of observations about the behaviour of organisms and the conditions under which the behaviour occurs. When researchers undertake data collection, they must choose an appropriate *level of analysis* and devise measures of behaviour that ensure *objectivity*.

In order to investigate an individual's behaviour, researchers may use different *levels of analysis*—from the broadest, most global level down to the most minute, specific level. Suppose, for example, you were trying to describe a painting you saw at an art gallery (see **Figure 1.1**). At a global level, you might describe it by title, *Bathers,* and by artist, Georges Seurat. At a more specific level, you might recount features of the painting: Some people are sunning themselves on a riverbank while others are enjoying the water, and so on. At a very specific level, you might describe the technique Seurat used—tiny points of paint—to create the scene. The description at each level would answer different questions about the painting.

Different levels of psychological description also address different questions. At the broadest level of psychological analysis, researchers investigate the behaviour of the whole person within complex social and cultural contexts. At this level, researchers might study cross-cultural differences in violence, the origins of

**behavioural data**
Observational reports about the behaviour of organisms and the conditions under which the behaviour occurs or changes.

Figure 1.1

Levels of analysis
Suppose you wanted a friend to meet you in front of this painting. How would you describe it? Suppose your friend wanted to make an exact copy of the painting. How would you describe it?

prejudice, and the consequences of mental illness. At the next level, psychologists focus on narrower, finer units of behaviour, such as speed of reaction to a stoplight, eye movements during reading, and grammatical errors made by children acquiring language. Researchers can study even smaller units of behaviour. They might work to discover the biological bases of behaviour by identifying the places in the brain where different types of memories are stored, the biochemical changes that occur during learning, and the sensory paths responsible for vision or hearing. Each level of analysis yields information essential to the final composite portrait of human nature that psychologists hope ultimately to develop.

However tight or broad the focus of the observation, psychologists strive to describe behaviour *objectively*. Collecting the facts as they exist, and not as the researcher expects or hopes them to be, is of utmost importance. Because every observer brings to each observation his or her *subjective* point of view—biases, prejudices and expectations—it is essential to prevent these personal factors from creeping in and distorting the data. As you will see in the next chapter, psychological researchers have developed a variety of techniques to maintain objectivity.

### Explaining what happens

Whereas *descriptions* must stick to perceivable information, *explanations* deliberately go beyond what can be observed. In many areas of psychology, the central goal is to find regular patterns in behavioural and mental processes. Psychologists want to discover *how* behaviour works. Why do you laugh at situations that differ from your expectations of what is coming next? What conditions could lead someone to attempt suicide or commit rape?

Explanations in psychology usually recognise that most behaviour is influenced by a combination of factors. Some factors operate within the individual, such as genetic makeup, motivation, intelligence level or self-esteem.

These inner determinants tell something special about the organism. Other factors, however, operate externally. Suppose, for example, that a child tries to please a teacher in order to win a prize or that a motorist stuck in a traffic jam becomes frustrated and hostile. These behaviours are largely influenced by events outside the person. When psychologists seek to explain behaviour, they almost always consider both types of explanations. Suppose, for example, psychologists want to explain why some people start smoking. Researchers might examine the possibility that some individuals are particularly prone to risk taking (an internal explanation) or that some individuals experience a lot of peer pressure (an external explanation)—or that both a disposition toward risk taking and situational peer pressure are necessary (a combined explanation).

Often a psychologist's goal is to explain a wide variety of behaviour in terms of one underlying cause. Consider a situation in which your lecturer says that to earn a good grade, each student must participate regularly in class discussions. Your friend, who is always well prepared for class, never raises his hand to answer questions or volunteer information. The lecturer chides him for being unmotivated and perhaps assumes he is not bright. That same friend also goes to parties but never asks anyone to dance, doesn't openly defend his point of view when it is challenged by someone less informed, and rarely engages in small talk at the dinner table. What is your diagnosis? What underlying cause might account for this range of behaviour? How about *shyness?* Like many other people who suffer from intense feelings of shyness, your friend

What causes people to smoke? Can psychologists create conditions under which people will be less likely to engage in this behaviour?

is unable to behave in desired ways (Zimbardo & Radl, 1999). We can use the concept of shyness to explain the full pattern of your friend's behaviour.

To forge such causal explanations, researchers must often engage in a creative process of examining a diverse collection of data. Master detective Sherlock Holmes drew shrewd conclusions from scraps of evidence. In a similar fashion, every researcher must use an informed imagination, which creatively *synthesises* what is known and what is not yet known. A well-trained psychologist can explain observations by using her or his insight into the human experience along with the facts previous researchers have uncovered about the phenomenon in question. Much psychological research attempts to determine which of several explanations most accurately accounts for a given behavioural pattern.

## Predicting what will happen
Predictions in psychology are statements about the likelihood that a certain behaviour will occur or that a given relationship will be found. Often an accurate explanation of the causes underlying some form of behaviour will allow a researcher to make accurate predictions about future behaviour. Thus, if we believe your friend to be shy, we could confidently predict that he would be uncomfortable when asked to have a conversation with a stranger. When different explanations are put forward to account for some behaviour or relationship, they are usually judged by how well they can make accurate and comprehensive predictions. If your friend was to blossom in contact with a stranger, we would be forced to rethink our diagnosis.

Just as observations must be made objectively, scientific predictions must be worded precisely enough to enable them to be tested and then rejected if the evidence does not support them. Suppose, for example, a researcher predicts that the presence of a stranger will reliably cause human and monkey babies, beyond a certain age, to respond with signs of anxiety. We might want to bring more precision to this prediction by examining the dimension of 'stranger'. Would fewer

signs of anxiety appear in a human or a monkey baby if the stranger were also a baby rather than an adult, or if the stranger were of the same species rather than of a different one? To improve future predictions, a researcher would create systematic variations in environmental conditions and observe their influence on the baby's response.

## Controlling what happens
For many psychologists, control is the central, most powerful goal. Control means making behaviour happen or not happen—starting it, maintaining it, stopping it, and influencing its form, strength or rate of occurrence. A causal explanation of behaviour is convincing if it can create conditions under which the behaviour can be controlled.

The ability to control behaviour is important because it gives psychologists ways of helping people improve the quality of their lives. Throughout *Psychology and Life*, you will see examples of the types of *interventions* psychologists have devised to help people gain control over problematic aspects of their lives. Chapter 15, for example, discusses treatments for mental illness. We also describe how people can harness psychological forces to eliminate unhealthy behaviours like smoking and initiate healthy behaviours like regular exercise (see Chapter 12). You will learn what types of parenting practices can help parents maintain solid bonds with their children (Chapter 10); you will learn what forces make strangers reluctant to offer assistance in emergency situations and how those forces can be overcome (Chapter 17). These are just a few examples of the broad range of circumstances in which psychologists use their knowledge to control and improve people's lives. In this respect, psychologists are a rather optimistic group; many believe that virtually any undesired behaviour pattern can be modified by the proper intervention. *Psychology and Life* shares that optimism.

A psychological prediction

For answers go to MyPsychLab!

### RECAP CHECKPOINT
#### What makes psychology unique?

- Psychology is the scientific study of the behaviour and the mental processes of individuals.

- The goals of psychology are to describe, explain, predict and help control behaviour.

### CONCEPT QUESTIONS
1. What are the four components of the definition of psychology?

2. What four goals apply to psychologists who conduct research?

3. Why is there often a close relationship between the goals of explanation and prediction?

If you've ever had a job you didn't like, you probably know a lot about what it means to suffer from a lack of motivation: You can hardly stand the idea of reporting to work; every minute seems like an hour. An important part of having a successful career is finding a work setting that provides the types of challenges and rewards that fit your motivational needs. It probably will not surprise you that researchers have studied the match between vocations and people's individual personalities, values and needs.

To remain motivated for career success, you would like to have a job that suits your interests and serves goals that you consider worthwhile. A widely used test for measuring vocational interests is the *Strong Interest Inventory*, which was originated in 1927 by psychologist **Edward Strong**. To construct the test, Strong first asked groups of men in different occupations to answer items about activities they liked or disliked. Then the answers given by those who were successful in particular occupations were compared with

the responses of men in general to create a scale. Subsequent versions of the test, including a 2004 update, have added scales relevant to women and to newer occupations. The Strong Interest Inventory is quite successful at relating people's likes and dislikes to appropriate occupations (Hansen & Dik, 2005). If you take this test, a vocational counsellor could tell you what types of jobs are typically held by people with interests such as yours because these are the jobs that are likely to appeal to you.

Suppose you have received this sort of advice about what career to pursue. How do you select a particular company to join—and how does that company select you? Researchers in *personnel psychology* have focused a good deal of attention on the concept of *person–organisation fit*—the goal is to maximise the compatibility between people and the organisations that employ them (Dineen et al., 2002; Van Vianen, 2000). One research project has focused on the match between people's personalities and the

'culture' of organisations. Consider the personality factor called 'Agreeableness', which encodes a continuum from 'sympathetic and kind' to 'cold and quarrelsome' (see Chapter 13). Consider, also, a continuum of organisational cultures from those that are supportive and team oriented to those that are aggressive and outcome oriented. Do you see how these dimensions line up? Research suggests that job seekers who score high on Agreeableness will prefer organisations that are culturally supportive and team oriented (Judge & Cable, 1997). Research of this type suggests why it is not just your own motivational states that matter for career success: The extent to which your preferences for achieving goals match the organisation's preferences matters as well.

So, what career path will keep you motivated for success? As with so many of life's dilemmas, psychologists have carried out research that can help you make this important decision.

## THE EVOLUTION OF MODERN PSYCHOLOGY

In the 21st century, it is relatively easy to define psychology and to state the goals of psychological research. As you begin to study psychology, however, it is important to understand the many forces that led to the emergence of modern psychology. At the core of this historical review is one simple principle: *Ideas matter*. Much of the history of psychology has been characterised by heated debates about what constitutes the appropriate subject matter and methodologies for a science of mind and behaviour.

Our historical review will be carried out at two levels of analysis. In the first section, we will consider the period of history in which some of the critical groundwork for

modern psychology was laid down. This focus will enable you to witness at close range the battle of ideas. In the second section, we describe in a broader fashion seven perspectives that have emerged in the modern day. For both levels of focus, you should allow yourself to imagine the intellectual passion with which the theories evolved.

## PSYCHOLOGY'S HISTORICAL FOUNDATIONS

'Psychology has a long past, but only a short history', wrote one of the first experimental psychologists, **Hermann Ebbinghaus** (1908/1973). Scholars had long asked important questions about human nature—about how people perceive reality, the nature of consciousness, and the origins of madness—but they did not possess the means to answer them. Consider the fundamental questions posed in the fourth and fifth centuries B.C. by the classical Greek philosophers Socrates, Plato and Aristotle. Although forms of psychology existed in ancient Indian Yogic traditions, Western psychology traces its origin to these great thinkers' dialogues about how the mind works, the nature of free will, and the relationship of individual citizens to their community or state. Towards the end of the 19th century, psychology began to emerge as a discipline when researchers applied the laboratory techniques from other sciences—such as physiology and physics—to the study of these fundamental questions from philosophy.

A critical figure in the evolution of modern psychology was **Wilhelm Wundt**, who, in 1879 in Leipzig, Germany, founded the first formal laboratory devoted to experimental psychology. Although Wundt had been trained as a physiologist, over his research career his interest shifted from questions of body to questions of mind: he wished to understand basic processes of sensation and perception as well as the speed of simple mental processes. By the time he established his psychology laboratory, Wundt had already accomplished a range of research and published the first of several editions of *Principles of Physiological Psychology* (Kendler, 1987). Once Wundt's laboratory was established at Leipzig, he began to train the first graduate students specifically devoted to the emerging field of psychology. Those students often became founders of their own psychology laboratories around the world.

As psychology became established as a separate discipline, psychology laboratories began to appear in universities outside Europe, one of the first at Johns Hopkins University in 1883. These early laboratories often bore Wundt's impact. For example, after studying with Wundt, **Edward Titchener** became one of the first psychologists in the United States, founding a laboratory at Cornell University in 1892. However, at around the same time, a young Harvard philosophy professor who had studied medicine and had strong interests in literature and religion developed a uniquely American perspective. **William James**, brother of the great novelist Henry James, wrote a two-volume work, *The Principles of Psychology* (1890/1950), which many experts consider to be the most important psychology text ever written. Shortly after, in 1892, G. Stanley Hall founded the American Psychological Association (APA) (Hilgard, 1986). The APA remains arguably one of the most influential psychological societies in the world today.

In Australia, as in Europe and America, psychological study had it beginnings in philosophy. In the 1890s, Henry Laurie (Melbourne), Francis Anderson (Sydney) and William Mitchell (Adelaide) were the first to be appointed a chair in 'Mental Philosophy' in Australia (Taft & Day, 1988). All three were educated in the United Kingdom and brought the British empiricist perspective emphasising experience in relation to reality to their new positions within Australia. In 1903, John Smyth, who had visited Wundt's Leipzig laboratory, founded the first Australian experimental psychology laboratory at Melbourne Teachers College (Taft & Day, 1988). Yet

In 1879, Wilhelm Wundt founded the first formal laboratory devoted to experimental psychology. Suppose you decided to found your own psychology laboratory. What types of issues would you study?

despite these early movements towards establishing psychology in Australia, it wasn't until 1913 that Philip Ridgeway Le Couteur was appointed as the first university lecturer specialising in psychology (University of Western Australia). A further 12 years passed before the first undergraduate major in psychology was offered through the Philosophy Department at Sydney University in 1925, shortly followed by the psychology major through education at the University of Western Australia (Taft & Day, 1988). The Australian Psychological Society (APS) was founded in 1966 and replaced the Australian Branch of the British Psychological Society (BPS) established in 1945 (Taft & Day, 1988).

Almost as soon as psychology emerged, and well before psychology courses were established around the world, a debate arose about the proper subject matter and methods for the new discipline. This debate isolated some issues that still loom large in psychology. We will describe, specifically, the tension between structuralism and functionalism.

## Structuralism: the contents of the mind

Psychology's potential to make a unique contribution to knowledge became apparent when psychology became a laboratory science organised around experiments. In Wundt's laboratory, experimental participants made simple responses (saying yes or no, pressing a button) to stimuli they perceived under conditions varied by laboratory instruments. Because the data were collected through systematic, objective procedures, independent observers could replicate the results of these experiments. Emphasis on the scientific method (see Chapter 2), concern for precise measurement, and statistical analysis of data characterised Wundt's psychological tradition.

When Titchener brought Wundt's psychology to the United States, he advocated that such scientific methods be used to study consciousness. His method for examining the elements of conscious mental life was *introspection*, the systematic examination by individuals of their own thoughts and feelings about specific sensory experiences. Titchener emphasised the 'what' of mental contents rather than the 'why' or 'how' of thinking. His approach came to be known as **structuralism**, the study of the structure of mind and behaviour.

Structuralism was based on the presumption that all human mental experience could be understood as the combination of basic components. The goal of this approach was to reveal the underlying structure of the human mind by analysing the component elements of sensation and other experiences that form an individual's mental life. Many psychologists attacked structuralism on three fronts: (1) It was *reductionistic* because it reduced all complex human experience to simple sensations; (2) it was *elemental* because it sought to combine parts, or elements, into a whole rather than study complex, or whole, behaviours directly; and (3) it was *mentalistic* because it studied only verbal reports of human conscious awareness, ignoring the study of individuals who could not describe their introspections, including animals, children, and the mentally disturbed.

One important alternative to structuralism, pioneered by the German psychologist **Max Wertheimer**, focused on the way in which the mind understands many experiences as *gestalts*—organised wholes—rather than as the sums of simple parts: Your experience of a painting, for example, is more than the sum of the individual daubs of paint. As we

Classroom practices were changed through the efforts of the functionalist John Dewey. What can teachers do to encourage 'intellectual curiosity'?

will see in Chapter 4, *Gestalt psychology* continues to have an impact on the study of perception.

A second major opposition to structuralism came under the banner of *functionalism.*

### Functionalism: minds with a purpose
William James agreed with Titchener that consciousness was central to the study of psychology, but for James, the study of consciousness was not reduced to elements, contents, and structures. Instead, consciousness was an ongoing stream, a property of mind in continual interaction with the environment. Human consciousness facilitated one's adjustment to the environment; thus the acts and functions of mental processes were of significance, not the contents of the mind.

**Functionalism** gave primary importance to learned habits that enable organisms to adapt to their environment and to function effectively. For functionalists, the key question to be answered by research was 'What is the function or purpose of any behavioural act?' The founder of the school of functionalism was the American philosopher **John Dewey**. His concern for the practical uses of mental processes led to important advances in education. Dewey's theorising provided the impetus for *progressive education*: 'Rote learning was abandoned in favour of learning by doing, in expectation that intellectual curiosity would be encouraged and understanding would be enhanced' (Kendler, 1987, p. 124).

Although James believed in careful observation, he put little value on the rigorous laboratory methods of Wundt. In James's psychology, there was a place for emotions, self, will, values, and even religious and mystical experience. His 'warm-blooded' psychology recognised a uniqueness in each individual that could not be reduced to formulas or numbers from test results. For James, explanation rather than experimental control was the goal of psychology (Arkin, 1990).

### The legacy of these approaches
Despite their differences, the insights of the practitioners of both structuralism and functionalism created an intellectual context in which contemporary psychology could flourish. Psychologists currently examine *both* the structure and the function of behaviour. Consider the process of speech production. Suppose you want to invite a friend to watch the Boxing Day Ashes Test Match. To do so, the words you speak must serve the right function—*Ashes Test Match, with me, Boxing day*—but also have the right structure: It wouldn't do to say, 'Would watch Ashes Test Match me the with Boxing day you to like?' To understand how speech production works, researchers study the way that speakers fit meanings (functions) to the grammatical structures of their languages (Bock, 1990). (We will describe some of the processes of language production in Chapter 8.) Throughout *Psychology and Life*, we emphasise both structure and function as we review both classic and contemporary research. Psychologists continue to employ a great variety of methodologies to study the general forces that apply to all humans as well as the unique aspects of each individual.

Sigmund Freud, photographed with his daughter, Anna, on a trip to the Italian Alps in 1913. Freud suggested that behaviour is often driven by motives outside of conscious awareness. What implications does that perspective have for the ways in which you make life choices?

## CURRENT PSYCHOLOGICAL PERSPECTIVES

Suppose your friend accepts the invitation to watch the Boxing Day Ashes Test Match. What *perspective* does each of you bring to your viewing of the match? Suppose one of you played cricket in high school whereas the other did not. Or suppose one of you is a staunch supporter of the English team, whereas the other has no prior commitments to the Australian or English teams. You can see how these different perspectives would affect the way in which you evaluate the match as it unfolds.

In a similar fashion, psychologists' perspectives determine the way in which they examine behaviour and mental processes. The perspectives influence what psychologists look for, where they look, and what research methods they use. In this section, we define seven perspectives—psychodynamic, behaviourist, humanistic, cognitive, biological, evolutionary and sociocultural. As you read the section, note how each perspective defines the causes and consequences of behaviour.

A word of caution: although each perspective represents a different approach to the central issues of psychology, you should come to appreciate why most psychologists borrow and blend concepts from more than one of these perspectives. Each perspective enhances the understanding of the entirety of human experience. In the chapters that follow, we will elaborate in some detail on the contributions of each approach because, taken together, they represent what contemporary psychology is all about.

**The psychodynamic perspective** According to the **psychodynamic perspective**, behaviour is driven, or motivated, by powerful inner forces. In this view, human actions stem from inherited instincts, biological drives, and attempts to resolve conflicts between personal needs and society's demands. Deprivation states, physiological arousal and conflicts provide the power for behaviour just as coal fuels a steam locomotive. According to this model, the organism stops reacting when its needs are satisfied and its drives reduced. The main purpose of action is to reduce tension.

Psychodynamic principles of motivation were most fully developed by the Viennese physician **Sigmund Freud** (1856–1939) in the late 19th and early 20th centuries. Freud's ideas grew out of his work with mentally disturbed patients, but he believed that the principles he observed applied to both normal and abnormal behaviour. Freud's psychodynamic theory views a person as pulled and pushed by a complex network of inner and outer forces. Freud's model was the first to recognise that human nature is not always rational and that actions may be driven by motives that are not in conscious awareness.

Many psychologists since Freud have taken the psychodynamic model in new directions. Freud himself emphasised early childhood as the stage in which personality is formed. Neo-Freudian theorists have broadened psychodynamic theory to include social influences and interactions that occur over the individual's entire lifetime. Psychodynamic ideas have had a great influence on many areas of psychology. You will encounter different aspects of Freud's contributions as you read about child development, dreaming, forgetting, unconscious motivation, personality and psychoanalytic therapy.

**The behaviourist perspective** Those who take the **behaviourist perspective** seek to understand how particular environmental stimuli control particular kinds of behaviour. First, behaviourists analyse the *antecedent* environmental conditions—those that precede the behaviour and set the stage for an organism to make a response or withhold a response. Next, they look at the *behavioural response*, which is the main object of study— the action to be understood, predicted and controlled. Finally, they examine the observable *consequences* that follow from the response. A behaviourist, for example, might be interested in the way in which speeding tickets of varying penalties (the consequences of speeding) change the likelihood that motorists will drive with caution or abandon (behavioural responses).

The behaviourist perspective was pioneered by **John Watson** (1878–1958), who argued that psychological research should seek the laws that govern observable behaviour across species. **B. F. Skinner** (1904–1990) extended the influence of behaviourism by expanding its analyses to the consequences of behaviours. Both researchers insisted on precise definitions of the phenomena studied and on rigorous standards of evidence. Both Watson and Skinner believed that the basic processes they investigated

**psychodynamic perspective** A psychological model in which behaviour is explained in terms of past experiences and motivational forces.

**behaviourist perspective** The psychological perspective concerned with observable behaviour that can be objectively recorded and with the relationships of observable behaviour to environmental stimuli.

John Watson was an important pioneer of the behaviourist perspective. Why did Watson seek laws of behaviour that applied across species?

with nonhuman animals represented general principles that would hold true for humans as well.

**Behaviourism** has yielded a critical practical legacy. Its emphasis on the need for rigorous experimentation and carefully defined variables has influenced most areas of psychology. Although behaviourists have conducted much basic research with nonhuman animals, the principles of behaviourism have been widely applied to human problems. Behaviourist principles have yielded a more humane approach to educating children (through the use of positive reinforcement rather than punishment), new therapies for modifying behaviour disorders, and guidelines for creating model utopian communities.

**The humanistic perspective** Humanistic psychology emerged in the 1950s as an alternative to the psychodynamic and the behaviourist models. According to the **humanistic perspective**, people are neither driven by the powerful, instinctive forces postulated by the Freudians nor manipulated by their environments, as proposed by the behaviourists. Instead, people are active creatures who are innately good and capable of choice. Humanistic psychologists study behaviour, but not by reducing it to components, elements, and variables in laboratory experiments. Instead, they look for patterns in people's life histories.

According to the humanistic perspective, the main task for humans is to strive for positive development.

For example, **Carl Rogers** (1902–1987) emphasised that individuals have a natural tendency toward psychological growth and health—a process that is aided by the positive regard of those who surround them. **Abraham Maslow** (1908–1970) coined the term *self-actualisation* to refer to each individual's drive toward the fullest development of his or her potential. In addition, Rogers, Maslow and their colleagues defined a perspective that strives to deal with the whole person, practising a *holistic* approach to human psychology. They believed that true understanding requires integrating knowledge of the individual's mind, body and behaviour with an awareness of social and cultural forces.

The humanistic approach expands the realm of psychology to include valuable lessons from the study of literature, history and the arts. In this manner, psychology becomes a more complete discipline. Humanists suggest that their view is the yeast that helps psychology rise above its focus on negative forces and on the animal-like aspects of humanity. As we shall see in Chapter 15, the humanistic perspective had a major impact on the development of new approaches to psychotherapy.

**The cognitive perspective** The cognitive revolution in psychology emerged as another challenge to the limits of behaviourism. The centrepiece of the **cognitive perspective** is human thought and all the processes of knowing—attending, thinking, remembering and understanding. From the cognitive perspective, people act because they think, and people think because they are human beings, exquisitely equipped to do so.

Carl Rogers provided foundational ideas for the humanistic perspective. Why did Rogers place an emphasis on positive regard?

According to the cognitive model, behaviour is only partly determined by preceding environmental events and past behavioural consequences, as behaviourists believe. Some of the most significant behaviour emerges from totally novel ways of thinking, not from predictable ways used in the past. The ability to imagine options and alternatives that are totally different from what is or was enables people to work toward futures that transcend current circumstances. An individual responds to reality not as it is in the objective world of matter, but as it is in the *subjective reality* of the individual's inner world of thoughts and imagination. Cognitive psychologists view thoughts as both results and causes of overt actions. Feeling regret when you've hurt someone is an example of thought as a result. But apologising for your actions after feeling regret is an example of thought as a cause of behaviour.

Cognitive psychologists study higher mental processes such as perception, memory, language use, problem solving and decision making at a variety of levels. They may examine patterns of blood flow in the brain during different types of cognitive tasks, a student's recollection of an early childhood event, or changes in memory abilities across the life span. Because of its focus on mental processes, many researchers see the cognitive perspective as the dominant one in psychology today.

## The biological perspective

The **biological perspective** guides psychologists who search for the causes of behaviour in the functioning of genes, the brain, the nervous system and the endocrine system. An organism's functioning is explained in terms of underlying physical structures and biochemical processes. Experience and behaviours are largely understood as the result of chemical and electrical activities taking place within and between nerve cells.

Researchers who take the biological perspective generally assume that psychological and social phenomena can be ultimately understood in terms of biochemical processes: even the most complex phenomena can be understood by analysis, or reduction, into ever smaller, more specific units. They might, for example, try to explain how you are reading the words of this sentence with respect to the exact physical processes in cells in your brain. According to this perspective, behaviour is determined by physical structures and hereditary processes. Experience can modify behaviour by altering these underlying biological structures and processes. Researchers might ask, 'What changes in your brain occurred while you learned to read?' The task of psychobiological researchers is to understand behaviour at the most precise level of analysis.

Many researchers who take the biological perspective contribute to the multidisciplinary field of **behavioural neuroscience**. Neuroscience is the study of brain function; behavioural neuroscience attempts to understand the brain processes underlying behaviours such as sensation, learning and emotion. The advances in the brain imaging techniques that we describe in Chapter 3 have led to dramatic breakthroughs in the field of **cognitive neuroscience**. Cognitive neuroscience trains a multidisciplinary research focus on the brain bases of higher cognitive functions such

as memory and language. As we shall see, brain-imaging techniques allow the biological perspective to be extended into a broad range of human experience.

## The evolutionary perspective

The **evolutionary perspective** seeks to connect contemporary psychology to a central idea of the life sciences, Charles Darwin's theory of evolution by natural selection. The idea of natural selection is quite simple: those organisms that are better suited to their environments tend to produce offspring (and pass on their genes) more successfully than those organisms with poorer adaptations. Over many generations, the species changes in the direction of the privileged adaptation. The evolutionary perspective in psychology suggests that *mental abilities* evolved over millions of years to serve particular adaptive purposes, just as physical abilities did.

To practice evolutionary psychology, researchers focus on the environmental conditions in which the human brain evolved. Humans spent 99 percent of their evolutionary history as hunter–gatherers living in small groups during the Pleistocene era (the roughly 2-million-year period ending 10,000 years ago). Evolutionary psychology uses the rich theoretical framework of evolutionary biology to identify the central adaptive problems that faced this species: avoiding predators and parasites, gathering and exchanging food, finding and retaining mates, and raising healthy children. After identifying the adaptive problems that these early humans faced, evolutionary psychologists generate inferences about the sorts of mental mechanisms, or psychological adaptations, that might have evolved to solve those problems.

Evolutionary psychology differs from other perspectives most fundamentally in its focus on the extremely long process of evolution as a central explanatory principle. Evolutionary psychologists, for example, attempt to understand the different sex roles assumed by men and women as products of evolution, rather than as products of contemporary societal pressures. Because evolutionary psychologists cannot carry out experiments that vary the course of evolution, they must be particularly inventive to provide evidence in favour of their theories.

What mental abilities were needed by the *Australo-pithecus Africanus* of 2 to 3 million years ago, and how might these abilities have evolved to the present day?

**The sociocultural perspective** Psychologists who take a **sociocultural perspective** study *cross-cultural* differences in the causes and consequences of behaviour. The sociocultural perspective is an important response to the criticism that psychological research has too often been based on a Western conception of human nature and had as its subject population only white middle-class Americans (Gergen et al., 1996). A proper consideration of cultural forces may involve comparisons of groups within the same national boundaries. For example, researchers may compare the prevalence of eating disorders for white American versus African American teenagers within the United States (see Chapter 11). Cultural forces may also be assessed across nationalities, as in comparisons of moral judgments in the United States and India (see Chapter 10). Cross-cultural psychologists want to determine whether the theories researchers have developed apply to all humans, or only to more narrow, specific populations.

A cross-cultural perspective can be brought to bear on almost every topic of psychological research: Are people's perceptions of the world affected by culture? Do the languages people speak affect the way they experience the world? How does culture affect the way children develop toward adulthood? How do cultural attitudes shape the experience of old age? How does culture affect our sense of self? Does culture influence an individual's likelihood to engage in particular behaviours? Does culture affect the way individuals express emotions? Does culture affect the rates at which people suffer from psychological disorders?

By asking these types of questions, the sociocultural perspective often yields conclusions that directly challenge those generated from the other perspectives. Researchers have claimed, for example, that many aspects of Freud's psycho-dynamic theories cannot apply to cultures that are very different from Freud's Vienna. This concern was raised as early as 1927 by the anthropologist Bronislaw Malinowski (1927), who soundly critiqued Freud's father-centred theory by describing the family practices of the

Bronislaw Malinowski documented the important roles women play in the culture of the Trobiand Islands. Why is cross-cultural research critical to the search for universal psychological principles?

Trobriand Islanders of New Guinea, for whom family authority resided with mothers rather than with fathers. The sociocultural perspective, therefore, suggests that some universal claims of the psychodynamic perspective are incorrect. The sociocultural perspective poses a continual, important challenge to generalisations about human experience that ignore the diversity and richness of culture.

## Comparing perspectives: focus on aggression

Each of the seven perspectives rests on a different set of assumptions and leads to a different way of looking for answers to questions about behaviour. **Table 1.1** summarises the perspectives. As an example, let's briefly compare how psychologists using these models might deal with the question of why people act aggressively. All of the approaches have been used in the effort to understand the nature of aggression and violence. For each perspective, we give examples of the types of claims researchers might make and experiments they might undertake.

### Table 1.1

Comparison of seven perspectives in contemporary psychology

| Perspective | Focus of study | Primary research topics |
|---|---|---|
| Psychodynamic | Unconscious drives<br>Conflicts | Behaviour as overt expression of unconscious motives |
| Behaviourist | Specific overt responses | Behaviour and its stimulus causes and consequences |
| Humanistic | Human experience and potentials | Life patterns<br>Values<br>Goals |
| Cognitive | Mental processes<br>Language | Inferred mental processes through behavioural indicators |
| Biological | Brain and nervous system processes | Biochemical basis of behaviour and mental processes |
| Evolutionary | Evolved psychological adaptations | Mental mechanisms in terms of evolved adaptive functions |
| Sociocultural | Cross-cultural patterns of attitudes and behaviours | Universal and culture-specific aspects of human experience |

- *Psychodynamic.* Analyse aggression as a reaction to frustrations caused by barriers to pleasure, such as unjust authority. View aggression as an adult's displacement of hostility originally felt as a child against his or her parents.

- *Behaviourist.* Identify reinforcements of past aggressive responses, such as extra attention given to a child who hits classmates or siblings. Assert that children learn from physically abusive parents to be abusive with their own children.

- *Humanistic.* Look for personal values and social conditions that foster self-limiting, aggressive perspectives instead of growth-enhancing, shared experiences.

- *Cognitive.* Explore the hostile thoughts and fantasies people experience while witnessing violent acts, noting both aggressive imagery and intentions to harm others. Study the impact of violence in films and videos, including pornographic violence, on attitudes toward gun control, rape and war.

- *Biological.* Study the role of specific brain systems in aggression by stimulating different regions and then recording any destructive actions that are elicited. Also analyse the brains of mass murderers for abnormalities; examine female aggression as related to phases of the menstrual cycle.

- *Evolutionary.* Consider what conditions would have made aggression an adaptive behaviour for early humans. Identify psychological mechanisms capable of selectively generating aggressive behaviour under those conditions.

- *Sociocultural.* Consider how members of different cultures display and interpret aggression. Identify how cultural forces affect the likelihood of different types of aggressive behaviour.

From this example of aggression, you can see how the different perspectives conspire to provide a full understanding of particular domains of psychological research. In contemporary psychology, most research is informed by multiple perspectives. Throughout *Psychology and Life* you will see how new theories often emerge from combinations of different perspectives. In addition, technological advances have made it easier for researchers to combine perspectives. For example, the innovative brain-imaging techniques you'll learn about in Chapter 3 allow researchers to bring a biological perspective to topics as varied as personality differences (Chapter 13) and therapeutic outcomes (Chapter 15). Moreover, developments such as the Internet have made it easier for researchers to collaborate across the globe. They can bring a sociocultural perspective to topics as diverse as moral reasoning (Chapter 10) and people's body images (Chapter 11). Psychology's diversity of perspectives helps researchers think creatively about core topics of human experience.

## RECAP CHECKPOINT
### The evolution of modern psychology

- Structuralism emerged from the work of Wundt and Titchener. It emphasised the structure of the mind and behaviour built from elemental sensations.

- Functionalism, developed by James and Dewey, emphasised the purpose behind behaviour.

- Taken together, these theories created the agenda for modern psychology.

- Each of the seven contemporary approaches to studying psychology differs in its view of human nature, the determinants of behaviour, the focus of study, and the primary research approach.

- The psychodynamic perspective looks at behaviour as driven by instinctive forces, inner conflicts, and conscious and unconscious motivations.

- The behaviourist perspective views behaviour as determined by external stimulus conditions.

- The humanistic perspective emphasises an individual's inherent capacity to make rational choices.

- The cognitive perspective stresses mental processes that affect behavioural responses.

- The biological perspective studies relationships between behaviour and brain mechanisms.

- The evolutionary perspective looks at behaviour as having evolved as an adaptation for survival in the environment.

- The sociocultural perspective examines behaviour and its interpretation in cultural context.

## CONCEPT QUESTIONS

For answers go to MyPsychLab!

**mypsychlab**
where learning comes to life!

1. What are the central concerns of the structuralist and functionalist approaches?

2. How do the psychodynamic and behaviourist perspectives conceptualise the forces that shape people's actions?

3. Which perspective suggests that people are active creatures who strive for positive development?

4. What is the purpose of cognitive neuroscience?

5. How do the evolutionary perspective and sociocultural perspective complement each other?

# CRITICAL THINKING *in your life*

## WHY DO FRIENDSHIPS END?

An important goal of *Psychology and Life* is to improve your ability to think critically about the world around you: We want to help you 'reach intelligent decisions about what [you] should believe and how [you] should act' (Appleby, 2006, p. 61). Let's consider that aim with respect to a question that has often seemed urgent for the students who enrol in our classes: Why do friendships end?

Try to think back to circumstances in which a valued friendship has dissolved. Were you able to understand what had gone wrong? Psychology can provide theoretical analyses to help you understand what goes on in your life. In fact, researchers have studied the types of events that cause friendships to come to an end (Sheets & Lugar, 2005).

People report such incidents as romantic competition ('she slept with my boyfriend'), disrespectful behaviour ('he let his friends destroy my room'), and betrayals of confidence ('he blabbed all my secrets'). If you understand these different categories, you now have a framework to assess any tensions in your own friendships. The research provides even more specific conclusions: Among about 400 students from the Midwest of the United States of America, the most common sources of conflicts—the causes of arguments that ended friendships—were romantic competition and disrespectful behaviour. Can you use this information to look more critically at the state of your friendships? This research illustrates how psychology can help you perceive and apply appropriate distinctions for your life experiences.

But there's another aspect of critical thinking you can engage here: You should try to ask yourself how broadly you should apply the information you learn. For example, we asserted that the results about friendship emerged from U.S. students from the Midwest of the USA. In this chapter, we've already identified the sociocultural perspective that prompts contemporary researchers always to be mindful of the impact of culture on research results. To assess the cross-cultural generality of the U.S. findings, the researchers collected data from a group of students in Russia. Unlike students in the U.S., the Russian students collectively reported that the greatest source of conflict with their friends centred on betrayals of confidence. Why might that be the case? The researchers speculated that Russians are more sensitive to these circumstances because of 'Russia's totalitarian history, during which a friend's breach of confidence could threaten one's life' (Sheets & Lugar, 2005, p. 391).

Thinking now again about the circumstances in which your own friendships may have broken down, are the reasons more like those reported by Russian or U.S. students? Can you think of any cultural similarities or differences between Australia, the USA and Russia that might explain why your own friendship experiences are more closely aligned with those in either the U.S. or Russia?

There are a couple of noteworthy implications for the cultural differences in friendship conflict reported between U.S. and Russian university students. First, this result reminds you that an important component of critical thinking is to test a conclusion for its soundness and generality. In Chapter 2, we will focus on the scientific method. That discussion will give you an indication of the standards researchers must meet before we report their research in *Psychology and Life*. In addition, throughout the text we will be mindful of how important it is to consider the ways in which culture can affect basic aspects of human existence. The second implication of this difference between U.S. and Russian students refers to how you might behave toward the people around you. Most people in Australia and around the world, now live and work in settings with cultural diversity. Let your education in psychology make you more sensitive to the domains in which culture does and does not matter. Remember, the goal is to have your psychological knowledge help you make more intelligent decisions with respect to your everyday experiences.

In the study, could it matter that the U.S.A. sample came from the Midwest rather than say, the east coast of America?

What aspects of Australian culture and history might have an impact on the psychology of Australian citizens and their friendships?

# WHAT PSYCHOLOGISTS DO

You now know enough about psychology to formulate questions that span the full range of psychological inquiry. If you prepared such a list of questions, you would be likely to touch on the areas of expertise of the great variety of individuals who call themselves psychologists. In **Table 1.2**, we provide our own version of such questions and indicate what sort of psychologist might address each one.

As you examine the table, you will note the great many subdivisions within the profession of psychology. Some of the labels the field uses tell you about the major content of a psychologist's expertise. For example, *cognitive psychologists* focus on basic cognitive processes such as memory and language; *social psychologists* focus on the social forces that shape people's attitudes and behaviour. Some of the labels identify the domains in which psychologists apply their expertise. For example, *industrial–organisational psychologists* focus their efforts on improving people's adjustment in the workplace; *school psychologists* focus on students' adjustment in educational settings.

Each type of psychologist achieves a balance between *research*—seeking new insights—and *application*—putting those insights to use in the world. There's a necessary relationship between those two types of activities. For example, we often think of *clinical psychologists* largely as individuals who apply psychological knowledge to better people's lives. However, as we will see in Chapters 14

## Table 1.2

The diversity of psychological inquiry

| The question | Who addresses it? | Focus of research and practice |
|---|---|---|
| How can people cope better with day-to-day problems? | Clinical psychologists<br>Counselling psychologists<br>Community psychologists<br>Psychiatrists | Study the origins of psychological disorders and evaluate treatment options; provide diagnosis and treatment of psychological disorders and other issues of personal adjustment. |
| How can I cope with the after effects of a stroke? | Rehabilitation psychologists | Provide assessment and counselling for people with illnesses or disabilities; offer coping strategies and education to affected individuals, caretakers, employers and community members. |
| How do memories get stored in the brain? | Biological psychologists<br>Psychopharmacologists | Study the biochemical bases of behaviour, feelings and mental processes. |
| How can you teach a dog to follow commands? | Experimental psychologists<br>Behaviour analysts | Use laboratory experiments, often with nonhuman participants, to study basic processes of learning, sensation, perception, emotion and motivation. |
| Why can't I always recall information I'm sure I know? | Cognitive psychologists<br>Cognitive scientists | Study mental processes such as memory, perception, reasoning, problem solving, decision making and language use. |
| What makes people different from one another? | Personality psychologists<br>Behavioural geneticists | Develop tests and theories to understand differences in personalities and behaviours; study the influence of genetics and environments on those differences. |
| How does peer pressure work? | Social psychologists | Study how people function in social groups as well as the processes by which people select, interpret and remember social information. |
| What do babies know about the world? | Developmental psychologists | Study the changes that occur in the physical, cognitive and social functioning of individuals across the life span; study the influence of genetics and environments on those changes. |
| Why does my job make me feel so depressed? | Industrial–organisational psychologists<br>Human factors psychologists | Study the factors that influence performance and morale in the general workplace or on particular tasks; apply those insights in the workplace. |
| How should teachers deal with disruptive students? | Educational psychologists<br>School psychologists | Study how to improve aspects of the learning process; help design school curricular, teaching-training programs and child-care programs. |
| Why do I get sick before every exam? | Health psychologists | Study how different lifestyles affect physical health; design and evaluate prevention programs to help people change unhealthy behaviours and cope with stress. |
| Was the defendant insane when she committed the crime? | Forensic psychologists | Apply psychological knowledge to human problems in the field of law enforcement. |
| Why do I always choke during important basketball games? | Sports psychologists | Assess the performance of athletes and use motivational, cognitive and behavioural principles to help them achieve peak performance levels. |

and 15, clinical psychologists also have important research functions. Contemporary research continues to improve our understanding of the distinctions among psychological disorders and the treatments that best ease patients' distress.

Take a look back at Table 1.2. We intended the list of questions to demonstrate why psychology has so many divisions. Did we manage to capture your own concerns? If you have the time, make a list of your own questions. Cross off each question as *Psychology and Life* answers it.

Have you begun to wonder exactly how many practising psychologists there are in the world and how many of these psychologists identify as specialists? Worldwide surveys suggest the number is well over 500,000 and within Australia around a third of psychologists identify as having a specialty area (Hosking & Rachiger, 2006). A breakdown of these specialisations, indicating clinical psychology as the dominant specialty area, can be seen in **Figure 1.2**.

Although the percentage of psychologists in the population is greatest in Western industrialised nations, interest in psychology continues to increase in many countries. The International Union of Psychological Science draws together member organisations from 70 countries

Developmental psychologists may use puppets or other toys in their study of how children behave, think, or feel. Why might it be easier for a child to express his or her thoughts to a puppet than to an adult?

(Ritchie, 2004). The Australian Psychological Society (APS) has more than 15,500 members and is the largest professional psychological organisation in Australia. The British Psychological Society (BPS) currently has over 45,000 members, and as you might remember from your earlier reading in this chapter, prior to 1966 the BPS included an Australian Branch. The American Psychological Association (APA), one of the most influential psychological societies, is an organisation that includes psychologists from all over the world and has over 150,000 members.

It probably won't surprise you to learn that, early in its history, research and practice in psychology were dominated by men. Even when they were still few in numbers, however, women made substantial contributions to the field (Russo & Denmark, 1987; Scarborough & Forumoto, 1987). In 1894, Margaret Washburn graduated from Cornell University to become the first woman to receive a PhD in psychology. She went on to write an influential early textbook, *The Animal Mind.* In 1895, Mary Calkins completed all the requirements for a Harvard PhD with an exceptional record. Even so, the Harvard administration refused to grant a PhD to a woman. Despite this insult, Calkins became a successful researcher and the first woman president of the American Psychological Association. Anna Freud, whom we pictured earlier vacationing with her father, brought about important advances in the practice of *psychoanalysis,* a form of therapy based on the psychodynamic perspective.

As psychology was developing in Australia, women were also contributing to psychological research and practice. Ethel Turner Stoneman commenced her BA in 1913 at the University of Western Australia and then studied abnormal psychology and intelligence testing at Stanford University. She returned to Perth and established a State Psychological Clinic in 1926 and lectured part-time in experimental and abnormal psychology at the University of Western Australia (Wilson 1990). Constance Davey received her doctorate from the University of London in 1924. She was the first psychologist appointed to the Education Department in South Australia and had the responsibility of providing services to all children with special needs. Davey also taught

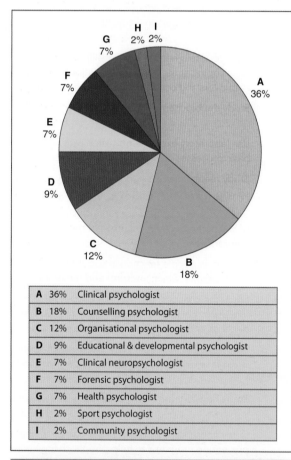

| A | 36% | Clinical psychologist |
|---|-----|----------------------|
| B | 18% | Counselling psychologist |
| C | 12% | Organisational psychologist |
| D | 9%  | Educational & developmental psychologist |
| E | 7%  | Clinical neuropsychologist |
| F | 7%  | Forensic psychologist |
| G | 7%  | Health psychologist |
| H | 2%  | Sport psychologist |
| I | 2%  | Community psychologist |

Figure 1.2

**Breakdown of specialisations**
Shown are percentages of psychologists working in particular settings, according to a survey of Australian Psychological Society (APS) members holding doctoral degrees in psychology.

In 1894, Margaret Washburn became the first woman to receive a PhD in psychology. She went on to write an influential textbook, *The Animal Mind* (1908). What challenges might she have faced as a pioneer woman researcher?

part-time at the University of Adelaide, helping to establish the social work program (Healy, 2001). Born in 1924, Jacqueline Jarret Goodnow completed her honours degree in psychology at Sydney University and her dissertation at Harvard. Concentrating on cognitive and developmental psychology, early in her career she wrote the well received book *A Study of Thinking,* a text that reportedly contributed to changing the course of psychological study towards cognitive science (Walk 1990). Goodnow was awarded the prestigious American Psychological Association's G. Stanley Hall Award for Distinguished Contributions to Developmental Psychology in 1989 and in 1997 she was awarded the Inaugural APS Presidents Award for Distinguished Contributions to Research in Psychology in Australia. Throughout her internationally recognised career Goodnow's worked centred on the 'understanding of cognitive processes, of thinking in a broad sense, with a focus on children' (Walk 1990, p134).

We will highlight the work of pioneering women researchers throughout *Psychology and Life.* As psychology continues to contribute to the scientific and human enterprise, more people—women and men, and members of all segments of society—are being drawn to it as a career.

# HOW TO USE THIS BOOK

You are about to embark with us on an intellectual journey through the many areas of modern psychology. Before we start, we want to share with you some important information that will help guide your adventures. 'The journey' is a metaphor used throughout *Psychology and Life*; your lecturer serves as the tour director, the text as your tour book, and we, your authors, as your personal tour guides. The goal of this journey is for you to discover what is known about the most incredible phenomena in the entire universe: the brain, the human mind and the behaviour of all living creatures. Psychology is about understanding the seemingly mysterious processes that give rise to your thoughts, feelings and actions.

This guide offers general strategies and specific suggestions about how to use this book to get the quality grade you deserve for your performance and to get the most from your introduction to psychology.

## STUDY STRATEGIES

1. **Set aside sufficient time** for your reading assignments and review of class notes. This text contains much new technical information, many principles to learn, and a new glossary of terms to memorise. To master this material, you will need at least three hours of reading time per chapter.

2. **Keep a record of your study time** for this course. Plot the number of hours (in half-hour intervals) you study at each reading session. Chart your time investment on a cumulative graph. Add each new study time to the previous total on the left-hand axis

For answers go to MyPsychLab!

**mypsychlab** where learning comes to life!

of the graph and each study session on the baseline axis. The chart will provide visual feedback of your progress and show you when you have not been hitting the books as you should.

3. **Be an active participant.** Optimal learning occurs when you are actively involved with the learning materials. That means reading attentively, listening to lectures mindfully, paraphrasing in your own words what you are reading or hearing, and taking good notes. In the text, underline key sections, write notes to yourself in the margins, and summarise points that you think might be included on class tests.

4. **Space out your studying.** Research in psychology tells us that it is more effective to do your studying regularly rather than cramming just before exams. If you let yourself fall behind, it will be difficult to catch up with all the information included in your Introductory Psychology course at last-minute panic time.

5. **Get study-centred.** Find a place with minimal distractions for studying. Reserve that place for studying, reading and writing course assignments— and do nothing else there. The place will come to be associated with study activities, and you will find it easier to work whenever you are seated at your study centre.

Take the lecturer's and tutor's perspective, anticipating the kinds of questions she or he is likely to ask, and then making sure you can answer them. Find out what kinds of tests you will be given in this course—essay, short answer questions, multiple choice or true/false. That form will affect the extent to which you focus on the big ideas and/or on details. Essays and short answer questions ask for recall-type memory; multiple-choice and true/false tests ask for recognition-type memory.

## STUDY TECHNIQUES

In this section, we give you specific advice about a technique you can use to learn the material for this course and your other courses. The technique emerged from the principles of human memory we will discuss in Chapter 7. It is called *PQ4R* from the initials of the six phases it suggests for effective study: Preview, Questions, Read, Reflect, Recite, and Review (Thomas & Robinson, 1972).

1. *Preview.* Skim through the chapter to get a general sense of the topics the chapter will discuss. Make yourself aware of the organisation and major topics. Read the section headings and scan the photos and figures. In fact, your first stop for each chapter should be the 'Recap Checkpoint' sections. There you will find the main ideas of each section within the chapter, these sections will give you a clear sense of what the chapter covers.

2. *Questions.* For each section, make up questions. You should use the section headings and key terms to help you. For example, you might transform the heading 'The Goals of Psychology' into the question 'What are the goals of psychology?' You might use the key term *biological perspective* to generate the question, 'What is the major focus of the biological perspective?' These questions will help direct your attention as you read.

3. *Read.* Read the material carefully so that you are able to answer the questions you invented.

4. *Reflect.* As you read the text, reflect on it to relate the material to your prior knowledge about the topics. Think of extra examples to enrich the text. Try to link the ideas together across the subsections.

5. *Recite.* After you have read and reflected on a section, try to demonstrate your recall of the material as concretely as possible. For example, answer the questions you invented earlier by producing the material out loud. For later review, write down the ideas you find difficult to remember.

6. *Review.* After you have read the entire chapter, review the key points. If you are unable to recall important points, or you cannot answer the questions you invented, consult the book and repeat the earlier phases (read, reflect and recite).

Take a moment now to use PQ4R for one of the earlier sections of this chapter to see how each phase works. It will take you some time to master the flow of PQ4R. Make that investment at the beginning of the semester.

## SPECIAL FEATURES

*Psychology and Life* has several features that will help you acquire psychological knowledge.

1. The 'Psychology in Your Life' boxes present applications of psychological research to your everyday life. Each of these boxes presents an answer to questions that we have been asked in class by our own students and we imagine you might ask us.

2. The 'Critical Thinking in Your Life' boxes illustrate how you can put your psychological knowledge to use to improve the quality of your thinking. The boxes provide you with tools for evaluating conclusions and seeing where they apply in your day-to-day experiences. We complete each box with questions to help you deepen your understanding.

3. The chapters feature several research studies that help you see the direct link between the experiments researchers conduct and the conclusions they draw. Researchers in psychology seek rigorous answers to questions that are often urgent. We include specific research studies so you have abundant opportunities to experience the concrete details of that type of rigorous research.

4. The 'Concept questions' refer to the key points you should know before going ahead to the next section. Think of these questions as supplements to those you generated by using PQ4R. Try to answer the questions as you finish your reading of each main section. If

any of the questions stumps you, plunge back into the text and reread the appropriate material until you feel you can provide a good answer. Similarly, use these questions as a starting point for your studying before exams. You will find answers to the questions in MyPsychLab. On some occasions, we will also include more open-ended questions intended to improve your critical thinking with respect to research studies. We leave those questions unanswered, to allow you to discuss them with your lecturer, tutor or classmates.

5. Each chapter concludes with a *Practice test* with multiple-choice questions based on the material in both the main text and the boxes. In addition, we've provided sample essay questions that allow you to think more broadly about the content of each chapter.

6. *Key terms* and *Major contributors* are highlighted in **bold typeface** so they stand out. When you use PQ4R and study for tests, be sure you can define each term and identify each major researcher. Key terms can be found as margin notes and are listed alphabetically at the end of the chapter.

7. The key terms are also gathered together in the *glossary*, found at the end of the text. The glossary provides formal definitions of all key terms that appear in the text. Use it to refresh your memory while studying for tests.

You're on your way. We hope *Psychology and Life* will be a worthwhile journey, full of memorable moments and unexpected pleasures. Let's go, or, as the Italians say, '*Andiamo!*'

## RECAP CHECKPOINT
### How to use this book

- Devise concrete strategies for determining how much study time you need and how to distribute the time most efficiently.

- Take an active approach to your lectures and the text. The PQ4R method provides six phases — Preview, Questions, Read, Reflect, Recite, and Review — for enhanced learning.

- The text includes several special features to help you learn psychological information and apply it to your everyday experiences.

## CONCEPT QUESTIONS

1. What does it mean to be an active participant in a course?

2. What is the relationship between the Questions and Read phases of PQ4R?

3. What is the purpose of the Recite phase of PQ4R?

For answers go to MyPsychLab!

# SUMMARY

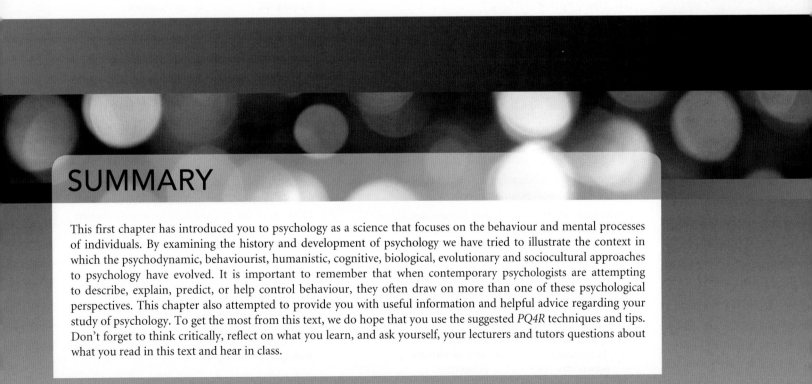

This first chapter has introduced you to psychology as a science that focuses on the behaviour and mental processes of individuals. By examining the history and development of psychology we have tried to illustrate the context in which the psychodynamic, behaviourist, humanistic, cognitive, biological, evolutionary and sociocultural approaches to psychology have evolved. It is important to remember that when contemporary psychologists are attempting to describe, explain, predict, or help control behaviour, they often draw on more than one of these psychological perspectives. This chapter also attempted to provide you with useful information and helpful advice regarding your study of psychology. To get the most from this text, we do hope that you use the suggested *PQ4R* techniques and tips. Don't forget to think critically, reflect on what you learn, and ask yourself, your lecturers and tutors questions about what you read in this text and hear in class.

# KEY TERMS

behaviour (p. 4)
behavioural data (p. 5)
behavioural neuroscience (p. 13)
behaviourism (p. 12)
behaviourist perspective (p. 11)
biological perspective (p. 13)

cognitive neuroscience (p. 13)
cognitive perspective (p. 12)
evolutionary perspective (p. 13)
functionalism (p. 10)
humanistic perspective (p. 12)
psychodynamic perspective (p. 11)

psychology (p. 4)
scientific method (p. 4)
sociocultural perspective (p. 14)
structuralism (p. 10)

# PRACTICE TEST

1. The definition of psychology focuses on both ____ and ____
   a. behaviours; structures
   b. behaviours; mental processes
   c. mental processes; functions
   d. mental processes; structures

2. To what goal of psychology is 'level of analysis' most relevant?
   a. Explaining what happens
   b. Describing what happens
   c. Predicting what will happen
   d. Controlling what happens

3. If you want to ____ what will happen, you first must be able to ____ what will happen.
   a. describe; explain       c. control; predict
   b. describe; control       d. explain; predict

4. The Strong Interest Inventory has been successful at helping
   a. researchers choose the behaviours they will study.
   b. researchers carry out work engaging the biological perspective.
   c. people assess the degree of person-to-organisation fit.
   d. people choose appropriate occupations.

5. Who founded the first laboratory that was devoted to experimental psychology?
   a. William James       c. Max Wertheimer
   b. Wilhelm Wundt       d. John Dewey

6. A researcher tells you that her main goal is to understand mental experiences as the combination of basic components. It is most likely that she finds the historical roots of her research in
   a. functionalism.       c. structuralism.
   b. the humanist         d. the evolutionary
      perspective.            perspective.

7. Two professors at universities in Brisbane and Bombay are collaborating on a research project to determine how their students in Australia and India respond to the same reasoning problems. It's likely that they take a ____ perspective in their research.
   a. humanistic          c. biological
   b. sociocultural       d. psychodynamic

8. The ____ perspective draws on the ways in which human mental abilities serve adaptive purposes.
   a. cognitive           c. evolutionary
   b. humanistic          d. sociocultural

9. When you're home with the flu, you spend a lot of time watching criminal investigation programs on television. You weren't surprised to see a ____ psychologist testifying during a trial.
   a. health              c. forensic
   b. social              d. developmental

10. What type of question would a cognitive psychologist be likely to ask?
    a. Why do children sometimes have imaginary friends?
    b. Why do some students get sick every time they have a major exam?
    c. How can we design a keyboard for a computer that allows people to type more quickly?
    d. How are bilingual individuals able to switch between their two languages?

11. Which type of psychologist is *least* likely to focus on genetic aspects of human psychology?
    a. Industrial–organisational psychologists
    b. Developmental psychologists
    c. Personality psychologists
    d. Biological psychologists

12. Experiences with totalitarian regimes may have made Russian students more sensitive to their friends' ____
    a. betrayals of confidence
    b. romantic competition
    c. disrespectful behaviour
    d. jealousy

13. Who founded the first Australian experimental psychology laboratory?
    a. Henry Laurie
    b. Ethel Turner Stoneman
    c. John Smyth
    d. Philip Ridgeway Le Couteur

14. Individuals employed as psychologists in Australia are most likely to be working in _____
    a. educational settings
    b. health and community services
    c. industry and government
    d. defence

15. What is the proper order of phases for PQ4R?
    a. Questions, Recite, Reflect
    b. Read, Reflect, Recite
    c. Preview, Review, Read
    d. Reflect, Review, Recite

16. In what phase of P4QR should you try to relate the textbook material to your prior knowledge about a topic?
    a. Reflect          c. Review
    b. Recite           d. Questions

## Essay questions

1. With respect to the goals of psychology, why is it appropriate to characterise psychologists as 'rather optimistic'?

2. Why is it often good to consider the same research question from several of psychology's seven contemporary perspectives?

3. Why does the field of psychology include both research and application?

# WEB LINKS

http://www.psychology.org.au
    Australian Psychological Society homepage

Are you ready for the test? MyPsychLab offers dozens of ways to deepen your understanding and test your recall of the material in this chapter—including video and audio clips, simulations and activities, self-assessments, practice tests and other study materials. Specific resources available for this chapter include:

 Psychologists at work

 Branches of psychology
The animal research controversy

To access MyPsychLab, please visit **www.pearsoned.com.au/mypsychlab**

# Who has time to study?

## NOW YOU HAVE READ CHAPTER 1—ARE YOU PREPARED FOR THE EXAM?

Do you understand the key concepts covered in Chapter 1?

- The historical foundations of the psychology discipline
- Current psychological perspectives
- Career opportunities that are available once you have finished your degree

To find out what content you might need help with before your next exam, go to MyPsychLab (MPL) at **www.pearsoned.com.au/mypsychlab**. You will need an access code for the site—use the one packaged with your text or you can purchase one online. Check with your instructor for your course ID number. If your instructor hasn't set up a course yet, you can use the self-assessment mode of MPL. Registration and login are straightforward and there is a lot of help on the site to talk you through.

MyPsychLab gives you access to study materials that directly apply to your trouble spots, including eBook, exercises, simulations, videos, web activities, flash cards and additional quiz questions

'There is not enough time to cover everything in lectures and tutorials. Using MyPsychLab helps me to understand the material without my tutor.'

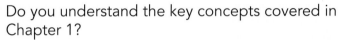

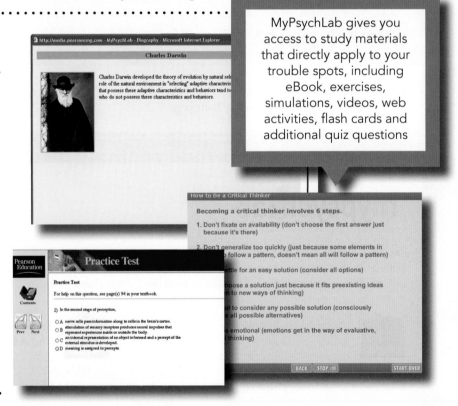

**Charles Darwin**

Charles Darwin developed the theory of evolution by natural selection role of the natural environment in "selecting" adaptive characteristics that possess these adaptive characteristics and behaviors tend to who do not possess these characteristics and behaviors.

**How to Be a Critical Thinker**

**Becoming a critical thinker involves 6 steps.**

1. Don't fixate on availability (don't choose the first answer just because it's there)
2. Don't generalize too quickly (just because some elements in follow a pattern, doesn't mean all will follow a pattern)
   ettle for an easy solution (consider all options)
   oose a solution just because it fits preexisting ideas to new ways of thinking)
   l to consider any possible solution (consciously all possible alternatives)
   emotional (emotions get in the way of evaluative, thinking)

**Practice Test**

Pearson Education

**Practice Test**

For help on this question, see page(s) 94 in your textbook.

2) In the second stage of perception,

- A  nerve cells pass information along to cells in the brain's cortex.
- B  stimulation of sensory receptors produces neural impulses that represent experiences inside or outside the body.
- C  an internal representation of an object is formed and a percept of the external stimulus is developed.
- D  meaning is assigned to percepts.

BACK    STOP    START OVER

**eBook**

An online version of each chapter's *Psychology and Life* from your textbook by Gerrig, Zimbardo, Campbell, Cumming & Wilkes is available in **MyPsychLab**. Go to the **Chapter contents** of MPL to select Chapter 1 and the related section you want to view. It will help you review key concepts before and after taking pre- and post-tests.

## STUDY TIP

**Create your own individualised STUDY PLAN for Chapter 1!**

By taking the pre- and post-tests, MyPsychLab will create a personalised study plan suited to your specific understanding of the topics.

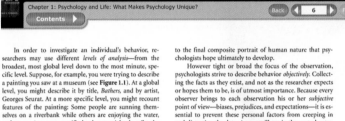

Chapter 1: Psychology and Life: What Makes Psychology Unique?

Contents ►  Back ◄ 6 ► Forward

In order to investigate an individual's behavior, researchers may use different *levels of analysis*—from the broadest, most global level down to the most minute, specific level. Suppose, for example, you were trying to describe a painting you saw at a museum (see **Figure 1.1**). At a global level, you might describe it by title, *Bathers*, and by artist, Georges Seurat. At a more specific level, you might recount features of the painting: Some people are sunning themselves on a riverbank while others are enjoying the water, and so on. At a very specific level, you might describe the technique Seurat used—tiny points of paint—to create the scene. The description at each level would answer different questions about the painting.

Different levels of psychological description also address different questions. At the broadest level of psychological analysis, researchers investigate the behavior of the whole person within complex social and cultural contexts. At this level, researchers might study cross-cultural differences in violence, the origins of prejudice, and the consequences of mental illness. At the next level, psychologists focus on narrower, finer units of behavior, such as speed of reaction to a stop light, eye movements during reading, and grammatical errors made by children acquiring language. Researchers can study even smaller units of behavior. They might work to discover the biological bases of behavior by identifying the places in the brain where different types of memories are stored, the biochemical changes that occur

to the final composite portrait of human nature that psychologists hope ultimately to develop.

However tight or broad the focus of the observation, psychologists strive to describe behavior *objectively*. Collecting the facts as they exist, and not as the researcher expects or hopes them to be, is of utmost importance. Because every observer brings to each observation his or her *subjective* point of view—biases, prejudices, and expectations—it is essential to prevent these personal factors from creeping in and distorting the data. As you will see in the next chapter, psychological researchers have developed a variety of techniques to maintain objectivity.

**Explaining What Happens** Whereas *descriptions* must stick to perceivable information, *explanations* deliberately go beyond what can be observed. In many areas of psychology, the central goal is to find regular patterns in behavioral and mental processes. Psychologists want to discover *how* behavior works. Why do you laugh at situations that differ from your expectations of what is coming next? What conditions could lead someone to attempt suicide or commit rape?

Explanations in psychology usually recognize that most behavior is influenced by a combination of factors. Some factors operate within the individual, such as genetic makeup, motivation, intelligence level, or self-esteem. These

PEARSON

STUDY PLAN

| Chapter: | Chapter 5 - Mind, Consciousness, and Alternate States ▾ |
|---|---|

TOTAL TIME SPENT: 0 HR. 0 MIN.    ► Print Study Plan    ► Email Study Plan

**Study Plan** (Click section link below to go to the multimedia textbook)

| Sections | Pre-Test | Post-Test |
|---|---|---|
| Chapter Opener | | |
| The Contents of Consciousness | | |
| The Functions of Consciousness | | |
| Sleep and Dreams | | |
| Altered States of Consciousness | | |
| Mind-Altering Drugs | | |
| Chapter Summary | | |

✔ excellent    ● needs improvement    ✗ poor

**Tests Taken** (Your study plan is based on the results of the following tests.)

| Test | Date/Time | Time Spent | Correct/Total |
|---|---|---|---|
| No test taken yet. | | | |

'I clearly earned a better grade on my test after studying with MyPsychLab.'

**What can you find in MyPsychLab?**

Self-directed tests * Videos * Simulations * eBook * Biographies * Audio glossary * Web links … and more—organised by chapter, section and learning objective.

mypsych lab™
*where learning comes to life!*

Research Methods in
Psychology

CHAPTER

# CHAPTER FOCUS POINTS

After studying this chapter you will have a better understanding of:

1. The process of psychological research, generating theories and testing hypotheses

2. How to determine causal relationships and correlate between variables

3. The different types of psychological measurement

4. The need for valid and reliable measures

5. The guidelines and procedures for conducting ethical psychological research

6. How to evaluate research claims and think critically

7. The analysis of data and drawing conclusions (found in the Statistical Supplement in MyPsychLab)

## CHAPTER CONTENTS

You may recall that in Chapter 1 we asked you to compose a list of questions that you would like to have answered by the end of *Psychology and Life*. Students who have used the book in the past responded to this request with a range of interesting concerns. Here are some of their questions:

- Why is eating 'hot' food painful?
- Is it bad to smack your children?
- Can psychology help me find a career?
- Do late-night TV ads really work?

In this chapter, we describe how psychologists generate answers to questions that matter most to students. We focus on the special way in which psychology applies the scientific method to its domain of inquiry. We want you to understand how psychologists design their research: How can solid conclusions ever be drawn from the complex and often fuzzy phenomena that psychologists study—how people think, feel, and behave? Even if you never do any scientific research in your life, mastering the information in this section will be useful. The underlying purpose here is to help improve your *critical thinking skills* by teaching you how to ask the right questions and evaluate the answers about the causes, consequences and correlates of psychological phenomena. The mass media constantly release stories that begin with, 'Research shows that . . .' By sharpening your intelligent scepticism, we will help you become a more sophisticated consumer of the research-based conclusions that confront you in everyday life.

## THE PROCESS OF RESEARCH

The research process in psychology can be divided into several steps that usually occur in sequence (see **Figure 2.1**). The process typically begins with a first step in which observations, beliefs, information and general knowledge lead someone to come up with a new idea or a different way of thinking about a phenomenon. Where do researchers' questions originate? Some come from direct observations of events, humans, and nonhumans in the environment. Other research addresses traditional parts of the field: some issues are considered to be 'great unanswered questions' that have been passed down from earlier scholars. Researchers often combine old ideas in unique ways that offer an original perspective. The hallmark of the truly creative thinker is the discovery of a new truth that moves science and society in a better direction.

As psychologists accumulate information about phenomena, they create theories that become an important context to formulate research questions. A **theory** is an organised set of concepts that *explains* a phenomenon or set of phenomena. At the common core of most psychological theories is the assumption of **determinism**; the idea that

all events—physical, mental, and behavioural—are the result of, or determined by, specific causal factors. These causal factors are limited to those in the individual's environment or within the person. Researchers also assume that behaviour and mental processes follow *lawful patterns* of relationships, patterns that can be discovered and revealed through research. Psychological theories are typically claims about the causal forces that underlie such lawful patterns.

When a theory is proposed in psychology, it is generally expected both to account for known facts and, as a second step in the research process, generate new hypotheses. A **hypothesis** is a tentative and testable statement about the relationship between causes and consequences. Hypotheses are often stated as if–then predictions, specifying certain outcomes from specific conditions. We might predict, for example, that *if* children view a lot of violence on television, *then* they will engage in more aggressive acts toward their peers. Research is required to verify the if–then link.

As a third step, researchers rely on the *scientific method* to put their hypotheses to the test. The scientific method is a general set of procedures for gathering and interpreting evidence in ways that limit sources of errors and yield dependable conclusions. Psychology is considered a science to the extent that it follows the rules established by the scientific method. Much of this chapter is devoted to describing the scientific method.

Once researchers have collected their data, they proceed to a fourth step in which they analyse those data and generate conclusions. If they believe that those conclusions will have an impact on the field, researchers will take a fifth step and submit the paper for publication in a journal. For publication to be possible, researchers must keep complete records of observations and data analyses in a form that other researchers can understand and

Scientific theories undergo rigorous testing. Their results must be replicated by independent investigators before the theories are recognised as proven.

**hypothesis** A tentative and testable explanation of the relationship between two (or more) events or variables.

**theory** An organised set of concepts that explains a phenomenon or set of phenomena.

**determinism** The doctrine that all events—physical, behavioural and mental—are determined by specific causal factors that are potentially knowable.

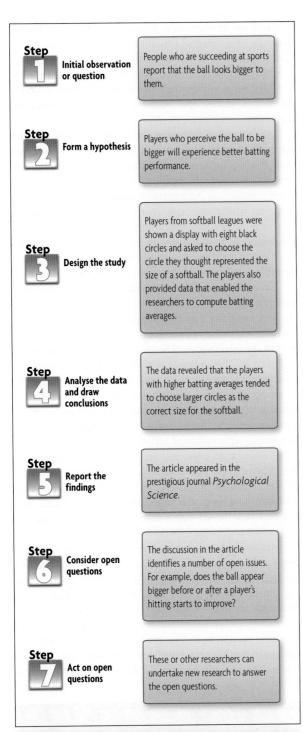

| Step | | |
|---|---|---|
| **1** | Initial observation or question | People who are succeeding at sports report that the ball looks bigger to them. |
| **2** | Form a hypothesis | Players who perceive the ball to be bigger will experience better batting performance. |
| **3** | Design the study | Players from softball leagues were shown a display with eight black circles and asked to choose the circle they thought represented the size of a softball. The players also provided data that enabled the researchers to compute batting averages. |
| **4** | Analyse the data and draw conclusions | The data revealed that the players with higher batting averages tended to choose larger circles as the correct size for the softball. |
| **5** | Report the findings | The article appeared in the prestigious journal *Psychological Science*. |
| **6** | Consider open questions | The discussion in the article identifies a number of open issues. For example, does the ball appear bigger before or after a player's hitting starts to improve? |
| **7** | Act on open questions | These or other researchers can undertake new research to answer the open questions. |

## Figure 2.1

**Steps in the process of conducting and reporting research**
To illustrate the steps in the scientific process, we use a project that sought a relationship between softball players' perceptions of the size of the ball and their actual batting averages (Witt & Proffitt, 2005).

evaluate. Secrecy is banned from the research procedure because all data and methods must eventually be open for *public verifiability*; that is, other researchers must have the opportunity to inspect, criticise, replicate or disprove the data and methods. (We will have more to say on the publication process in the 'Critical Thinking in Your Life' box on p. 46).

At the sixth step of the research process, the scientific community reflects on the research and identifies questions the work leaves unresolved. Most research articles start this process in a *discussion* section in which the researchers lay out the implications and limitations of their work. They might explicitly describe the type of future research they consider desirable. When the data do not fully support a hypothesis, researchers must rethink aspects of their theories. Thus there is continual interaction between theory and research. At a seventh step, the original researchers or their peers might act on open questions and begin the research cycle again.

This research process is centred around appropriate uses of the scientific method. The goal of the scientific method is to allow researchers to draw conclusions with maximum objectivity. Conclusions are *objective* when they are uninfluenced by researchers' emotions or personal biases. Each of the next two sections begins with a *challenge to objectivity* and then describes the *remedy* prescribed by the scientific method.

## OBSERVER BIASES AND OPERATIONAL DEFINITIONS

When different people observe the same events, they don't always 'see' the same thing. In this section, we describe the problem of *observer bias* and the steps researchers take as remedies.

**The challenge to objectivity** An **observer bias** is an error due to the personal motives and expectations of the viewer. At times, people see and hear what they expect rather than what is. Consider a rather dramatic example of observer bias. Around the beginning of the 20th century, a leading psychologist, Hugo Munsterberg, gave a speech on peace to a large audience that included many reporters. He summarised the news accounts of what they heard and saw in this way:

> *The reporters sat immediately in front of the platform. One man wrote that the audience was so surprised by my speech that it received it in complete silence; another wrote that I was constantly interrupted by loud applause and that at the end of my address the applause continued for minutes. The one wrote that during my opponent's speech I was constantly smiling; the other noticed that my face remained grave and without a smile. The one said that I grew purple-red from excitement; and the other found that I grew chalk-white. (1908, pp. 35–36)*

It would be interesting to go back to the original newspapers, to see how the reporters' accounts were related to their political views—then we might be able to understand why the reporters supposedly saw what they did.

**observer bias** The distortion of evidence because of the personal motives and expectations of the viewer.

Look at the glass in this illustration. How would you answer the classic question: Is the glass half empty or half full?

Now suppose you watched this sequence in which water is poured into the glass. Wouldn't you be likely to describe the glass as half full?

Suppose you watched the sequence in which water is removed. Now doesn't the glass seem half empty?

**Figure 2.2**

Observer bias
Is the glass half empty or half full?

In a psychology experiment, we wouldn't expect differences between observers to be quite as radical as those reported by Munsterberg. Nonetheless, the example demonstrates how the same evidence can lead different observers to different conclusions. The biases of the observers act as *filters* through which some things are noticed as relevant and significant and others are ignored as irrelevant and not meaningful.

We'd like you now to try the demonstration in **Figure 2.2**, to illustrate how easy it is to create an observer bias. This quick demonstration gives an idea of how the experiences you have prior to making an observation can influence how you interpret what you see.

Let's apply this lesson to what happens in psychology experiments. Researchers are often in the business of making observations. Given that every observer brings a different set of prior experiences to making those observations—and often those experiences include a commitment to a particular theory—you can see why observer biases could pose a problem. What can researchers do to ensure that their observations are minimally affected by prior expectations?

**The remedy** To minimise observer biases, researchers rely on standardisation and operational definitions. **Standardisation** means using uniform, consistent procedures in all phases of data collection. All features of the test or experimental situation should be sufficiently

standardised so all research participants experience exactly the same experimental conditions. Standardisation means asking questions in the same way and scoring responses according to pre-established rules. Having results printed or recorded helps ensure their comparability across different times and places and with different participants and researchers.

Observations themselves must also be standardised: scientists must solve the problem of how to translate their theories into concepts with consistent meaning. The strategy for standardising the meaning of concepts is called *operationalisation*. An **operational definition** standardises meaning within an experiment, by defining a concept in terms of specific operations or procedures used to measure it or to determine its presence. All the variables in an experiment must be given operational definitions. A **variable** is any factor that varies in amount or kind.

In experimental settings, researchers most often wish to demonstrate a cause-and-effect relationship between two types of variables. The **independent variable** is the factor that the researcher manipulates; it functions as the causal part of the relationship. The effect part of the relationship is served by the **dependent variable**, which is what the experimenter measures. If the researcher's claims about cause and effect are correct, the value of the dependent variable will *depend* on the value of the independent variable. Imagine, for example, that you wished to test the hypothesis we mentioned earlier: that children who view a lot of violence on television will engage in more aggressive acts toward their peers. You could devise an experiment in which you manipulated the amount of violence each participant viewed (the independent variable) and then assessed how much aggression he or she displayed (the dependent variable).

Let's take a moment to put these new concepts to use in the context of a real experiment. The research project we will describe begins with the observation that the world can be sorted into people who claim to be 'morning people'—they feel best performing tasks in the morning—versus others who are most definitely not morning people. Most university students fall into the *not* category! Researchers have demonstrated that people's self-judgments are correct: in laboratory tests, people

Participants, as well as spectators and broadcast viewers, are subject to observer bias. How can you determine what really happened?

most often perform best at those times of day they say they prefer (Yoon et al., 1999). But why? One theory is that performance is worse at the 'wrong' time of day because the individuals suffer from a general decrease in the level of physiological arousal or alertness. This leads to a hypothesis: If you can do something to increase alertness at the wrong time of day, you should be able to lessen or eliminate performance problems.

In **Figure 2.3**, we present an experiment that tested that hypothesis (Ryan et al., 2002). The experiment focused on *older adults*, those age 65 and older. Unlike their younger selves, most older adults are morning people. In this study, the researchers wished to know that all their participants were morning people. For that reason, they had each potential participant fill out the Morningness–Eveningness Questionnaire—a measurement device that categorises people on a scale ranging from 'definitely morning' to 'definitely evening' (Horne & Ostberg, 1976). The experiment used participants who were at least 'moderately' morning people.

Next, the researchers needed a procedure to manipulate the independent variable—physiological arousal. As shown in Figure 2.3, the researchers used a procedure that will be quite familiar to most of you. One group consumed coffee with caffeine and the other group got decaf. The participants didn't know which type of coffee they had. The researchers predicted that the caffeine would produce physiological arousal that would, in turn, have an impact on the participants' ability to perform

at the 'wrong' time of day. To measure the dependent variable—performance—the researchers challenged the participants to memorise a 16-word list. A memory test occurred 20 minutes later. The participants received lists and memory tests once in the morning (8 a.m.) and once in the afternoon (4 p.m.) in sessions separated by 5 to 11 days.

As you can see in Figure 2.3, the independent variable had the effect on the dependent variable that the researchers expected. In circumstances of high physiological arousal—when participants consumed the coffee with caffeine—performance was more or less equal at the two times of day. However, without the caffeine, memory performance was worse in the afternoon. As with all research results, we need to take stock of what we now know. The theory is stated in general terms: There is a relationship between physiological arousal and performance. However, the experiment uses the specific independent variable of caffeine consumption and the specific dependent variable of memory performance to stand in for 'physiological arousal' and 'performance'. Take a moment to think about other ways in which you might operationalise these two concepts, to test the same hypothesis in different fashions. You might, for example, want to manipulate physiological arousal without using caffeine, to show that it is not the caffeine itself having magical effects. This type of concern provides a transition to our exploration of experimental methods.

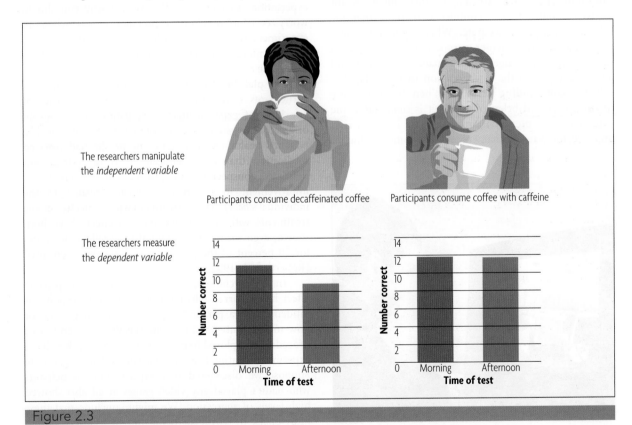

## Figure 2.3

### Elements of an experiment
To test their hypotheses, researchers create operational definitions for the independent and dependent variables.

# EXPERIMENTAL METHODS: ALTERNATIVE EXPLANATIONS AND THE NEED FOR CONTROLS

You know from day-to-day experience that people can suggest many causes for the same outcome. Psychologists face this same problem when they try to make exact claims about causality. To overcome causal ambiguity, researchers use **experimental methods**: they manipulate an independent variable to look for an effect on a dependent variable. The goal of this method is to make strong causal claims about the impact of one variable on the other. In this section, we describe the problem of *alternative explanations* and some steps researchers take to counter the problem.

## The challenge to objectivity

When psychologists test a hypothesis, they most often have in mind an explanation for why change in the independent variable should affect the dependent variable in a particular way. For example, you might predict, and demonstrate experimentally, that playing violent video games leads to high levels of aggression. But how can you know that it was precisely the playing with *violence* that produced aggression? To make the strongest possible case for their hypotheses, psychologists must be very sensitive to the existence of possible *alternative explanations*. The more alternative explanations there might be for a given result, the less confidence there is that the initial hypothesis is accurate. When something other than what an experimenter purposely introduces into a research setting changes a participant's behaviour and adds confusion to the interpretation of the data, it is called a **confounding variable**. When the real cause of some observed behavioural effect is *confounded,* the experimenter's interpretation of the data is put at risk. Suppose, for example, that violent video games are louder

Is violent behaviour caused by playing violent video games? How could you find out?

and involve more movement than do most nonviolent games. In that case, the violent and the superficial aspects of the games are confounded. The researcher is unable to specify which factor uniquely produces aggressive behaviour.

Although each different experimental method potentially gives rise to a unique set of alternative explanations, we can identify two types of confounds that apply to almost all experiments, which we will call *expectancy effects* and *placebo effects*. Unintentional **expectancy effects** occur when a researcher or observer subtly communicates to the research participants the behaviours he or she expects to find, thereby producing the desired reaction. Under these circumstances, the experimenter's expectations, rather than the independent variable, actually help trigger the observed reactions.

> In an experiment, 12 students were given groups of rats that were going to be trained to run a maze. Half of the students were told their rats were from a special *maze-bright* breed. The other students were told their rats were bred to be *maze-dull*. As you might guess, their rats were actually all the same. Nonetheless, the students' results corresponded with their expectations for their rats. The rats labelled bright were found to be much better learners than those that had been labelled as dull (Rosenthal & Fode, 1963).

How do you suppose the students communicated their expectations to their rats? Do you see why you should worry even more about expectancy effects when an experiment is carried out within species—with a human experimenter and human participants? Expectation effects distort the content of discovery.

A **placebo effect** occurs when experimental participants change their behaviour in the *absence* of any kind of experimental manipulation. This concept originated in medicine to account for cases in which a patient's health improved after he or she had received medication that was chemically inert or a treatment that was nonspecific. The placebo effect refers to an improvement in health or wellbeing related to the individual's *belief* that the treatment will be effective. Some treatments with no genuine medical effects have been shown, even so, to produce good or excellent outcomes for 70 percent of the patients on whom they were used (Roberts et al., 1993).

In a psychological research setting, a placebo effect has occurred whenever a behavioural response is influenced by a person's expectation of what to do or how to feel, rather than by the specific intervention or procedures employed to produce that response. Recall the experiment relating television viewing to later aggression. Suppose we discovered that experimental participants who hadn't played any video games at all also showed high levels of aggression. We might conclude that these individuals, by virtue of being put in a situation that allowed them to display aggression, would expect they were *supposed* to behave aggressively and would go

**experimental methods** Research methodologies that involve the manipulation of independent variables in order to determine their effects on the dependent variables.

**expectancy effects** Results that occur when a researcher or observer subtly communicates to participants the kind of behaviour he or she expects to find, thereby creating that expected reaction.

**confounding variable** A stimulus other than the variable an experimenter explicitly introduces into a research setting that affects a participant's behaviour.

**placebo effect** A change in behaviour in the absence of an experimental manipulation.

on to do so. Experimenters must always be aware that participants change the way they behave simply because they are aware of being observed or tested. For example, participants may feel special about being chosen to take part in a study and thus act differently than they would ordinarily. Such effects can compromise an experiment's results.

The remedy Because human and animal behaviours are complex and often have multiple causes, good research design involves anticipating possible confounds and devising strategies for eliminating them. Similar to defensive strategies in sports, good research designs anticipate what the other team might do and make plans to counteract it. Researchers' strategies are called **control procedures**—methods that attempt to hold constant all variables and conditions other than those related to the hypothesis being tested. In an experiment, instructions, room temperature, tasks, the way the researcher is dressed, time allotted, the way the responses are recorded, and many other details of the situation must be similar for all participants, to ensure that their experience is the same. The only differences in participants' experiences should be those introduced by the independent variable. Let's look at remedies for the specific confounding variables, expectancy and placebo effects.

Imagine, for example, that you enriched the aggression experiment to include a treatment group that played nonviolent comical games. You'd want to be careful not to treat your comical and violence participants in different ways based on your expectations. Thus, in your experiment, we would want the research assistant who greeted the participants and later assessed their aggression to be unaware of whether they had played a violent game or a comical nonviolent game. In the best circumstances, bias can be eliminated by keeping *both* experimental assistants and participants unaware of, or *blind* to, which participants get which treatment. This technique is called a **double-blind control**. Recall that in the coffee study (Figure 2.3), we specifically noted that the participants didn't know whether the beverage they were asked to consume contained caffeine or not. In fact, the design was double blind because the experimenters administering the memory tests also did not know which participants had each kind of drink. To provide further reassurance that expectations were not responsible for the memory effects, the experimenters asked the participants to guess which type of coffee they had consumed. Participants were unable to guess correctly (Ryan et al., 2002). This result provides strong evidence that the memory findings did not depend on the participants' expectations about the relationship between caffeine and memory performance.

To account for placebo effects, researchers generally include an experimental condition in which the treatment is not administered. We call this a **placebo control**. Placebo controls fall into the general category of controls by which experimenters assure themselves they are making appropriate comparisons. Consider the story

of a young girl who, when asked if she loved her older sister, replied, 'Compared to what?' That question is one that must be asked—and satisfactorily answered—before you can really understand what a research finding means.

Suppose you see a late-night TV commercial that celebrates the herbal supplement ginkgo biloba as an answer to all your memory problems. What might you expect if you buy a supply of ginkgo and take it weekly? One study demonstrated that university students who took ginkgo every morning for 6 weeks did, in fact, show improvements in their performance on cognitive tasks (Elsabagh et al., 2005). On one task, people were asked to view a series of 20 pictures on a computer screen, name them, and later recall those names. The participants were 14 percent better at this task after 6 weeks of ginkgo. However, participants who took a placebo—a pill with no active ingredients—also improved by 14 percent. The placebo control suggests that improvement on the task was the result of practice from the initial session. The data from control conditions provide an important baseline against which the experimental effect is evaluated.

In some research designs, which are referred to as **between-groups designs** (also called between-subjects designs), different groups of participants are *randomly assigned*, by chance procedures, to an experimental condition (exposed to one or more experimental treatments) or to a control condition (not exposed to an experimental treatment). Random assignment is one of the major steps researchers take to eliminate confounding variables that relate to individual differences among potential research participants. This is the design we had in mind for the aggression experiment. The random assignment to experimental and control conditions makes it quite likely that the two groups will be similar in important ways at the start of an experiment because each participant has the same probability of being in a treatment condition as in a control condition. We shouldn't have to worry, for example, that everyone in the experimental group loves violent video games and everyone in the control group hates them. Random assignment should mix both types of people together in each group. If outcome differences are found between conditions, we can be more confident that the differences were caused by a treatment or intervention rather than by pre-existing differences.

Researchers also try to approximate randomness in the way they bring participants into the laboratory. Typically, psychology experiments use from 20 to 100 participants, but experimenters would often like to generalise from this **sample** to the full **population** from which the sample is drawn. Suppose you would like to test the hypothesis that 6-year-old children are more likely to lie than 4-year-old children. You can bring only a very small subset of all of the world's 4- and 6-year-olds into your laboratory. To generalise beyond your samples, you need to have confidence that your particular 4- and 6-year-olds are comparable to any other randomly selected groups of children. A sample is a **representative sample** of a population if it closely matches the overall characteristics of the population with respect, for example, to the distribution of males and females, racial and ethnic groups, and so on. You can generalise from your sample only to the population it adequately represents. If you had only boys as participants in your lying study, you'd be incorrect to draw conclusions about girls' probable behaviour.

Another type of experimental design, a **within-groups design** (also called within-subjects or repeated measures design), uses each participant as his or her own control. For example, the behaviour of an experimental participant before getting the treatment might be compared with behaviour after. Consider an experiment that assessed 12-month-old infants' ability to learn from emotional responses they witnessed on a television screen.

> How do children learn which objects in their environments are *nice* and which are *nasty*? Researchers tested the idea that children acquire some of this positive and negative information from passive observation of other individuals (Mumme & Fernald, 2003). In one study, 12-month-old infants had the opportunity to interact with novel objects such as a bumpy ball and a plastic valve. As shown in **Figure 2.4**, the children were seated in front of a television screen, with the objects in easy reach. The children viewed two video presentations of an actress describing one of the two objects. In the initial presentation, the actress mentioned the *target* object with a neutral tone of voice and a neutral facial expression. But in the second presentation, the actress used a negative tone of voice and a negative expression while mentioning the same object. The actress never discussed the *distracter* object. Figure 2.4 shows the within-groups (repeated measures) comparison of the extent to which the infants touched each object. As you can see, when the actress's emotion became negative, the infants tended to shy away from the target object. The infants weren't just getting bored. Their behaviour did not vary with respect to touching the object the actress hadn't mentioned.

Because the study was within groups, the experimenters could draw the strong conclusion that the infants' observation of the actress's negative emotions *changed* their willingness to interact with the object. By the way, the experimenters repeated the experiment with 10-month-old infants and discovered that those younger participants did not change their behaviour based on the actress's expressed emotions (Mumme & Fernald, 2003). Thus it's somewhere in that 2-month window between 10 and 12 months that children begin to let their behaviour be guided by their observation of other people's emotional reactions.

The research methodologies we have described so far all involve the manipulation of an independent variable

to look for an effect on a dependent variable. Although this experimental method often allows researchers to make the strongest claims about causal relations among variables, several conditions can make this method less desirable. First, during an experiment, behaviour is frequently studied in an artificial environment, one in which situational factors are controlled so heavily that the environment may itself distort the behaviour from the way it would occur naturally. Critics claim that much of the richness and complexity of natural behaviour patterns is lost in controlled experiments, sacrificed to the simplicity of dealing with only one or a few variables and responses. Second, research participants typically know they are in an experiment and are being tested and measured.

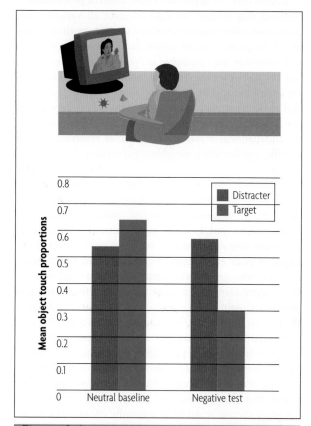

**Figure 2.4**

**Infants learn emotional responses**
The 12-month-olds were seated so that they could interact with the same objects that appeared on the television screen. In two video presentations, an actress mentioned the target object and ignored the *distracter* object. The first video presentation provided a neutral baseline to measure the children's initial preference to interact with each object. In the second video presentation, the actress expressed negative emotions related to the target object. The bar graphs plot the proportion of time the infants spent touching each object. The researchers calculated this measure by dividing the amount of time the infants touched each object into the total duration of the play period. As you can see, when the actress expressed negative emotions towards an object, children touched it much less often.

They may react to this awareness by trying to please the researcher, attempting to 'psych out' the research purpose, or changing their behaviour from what it would be if they were unaware of being monitored. Third, some important research problems are not amenable to ethical experimental treatment. We could not, for example, try to discover whether the tendency toward child abuse is transmitted from generation to generation by creating an experimental group of children who would be abused and a control group of children who would not be. In the next section, we turn to a type of research method that often addresses these concerns.

## CORRELATIONAL METHODS

Is intelligence associated with creativity? Are optimistic people healthier than pessimists? Is there a relationship between experiencing child abuse and later mental illness? These questions involve variables that a psychologist could not easily or ethically manipulate. To answer these questions, as we do in later chapters, requires research based on **correlational methods**. Psychologists use correlational methods when they want to determine to what extent two variables, traits or attributes are related.

To determine the precise degree of correlation that exists between two variables, psychologists compute a statistical measure known as the **correlation coefficient (r)**. This value can vary between +1.0 and −1.0, where +1.0 indicates a perfect positive correlation, −1.0 indicates a perfect negative correlation, and 0.0 indicates no correlation at all. A positive correlation coefficient means that as one set of scores increases, a second set also increases. The reverse is true with negative correlations; the second set of scores goes in the opposite direction to the values of the first scores (see **Figure 2.5**).

Correlations that are closer to zero mean that there is a weak relationship or no relationship between scores on two measures. As the correlation coefficient gets stronger, closer to the ±1.0 maximum, predictions about one variable based on information about the other variable become increasingly more accurate.

Suppose, for example, researchers were interested in determining the relationship between students' sleep habits and their success in university. They might operationally define *sleep habits* as the average amount of sleep per night. *Success in university* could be defined as cumulative grade-point average (GPA). The researchers could assess each variable for an appropriate sample of students and compute the correlation coefficient between them. A strongly positive score would mean that the more a student sleeps, the higher his or her GPA is likely to be. Knowing a student's 'hours per night' would then allow the researchers to make a reasonable prediction about the student's GPA.

The researchers might want to take the next step and say that the way to improve students' GPAs would be to force them to sleep more. This intervention is misguided. A strong correlation indicates only that two sets of data are related in a systematic way; the correlation does not ensure that one causes the other. *Correlation does not imply causation.* The correlation could reflect any one of several cause-and-effect possibilities, or none. For example, a positive correlation between sleep and GPA might mean that (1) people who study more efficiently get to bed sooner, (2) people who experience anxiety about schoolwork cannot fall asleep, or (3) people sleep better when they are taking easy courses. You can see from this example that correlations most often require researchers to probe for deeper explanations.

We don't want to leave you with the impression that correlational methods aren't valuable research tools. Throughout *Psychology and Life*, we will see many correlational studies that have led to important insights. We'll offer just one example here to whet your appetite:

**correlational methods**
Research methodologies that determine to what extent two variables, traits or attributes are related.

**correlational coefficient**
(r) A statistic that indicates the degree of relationship between two variables.

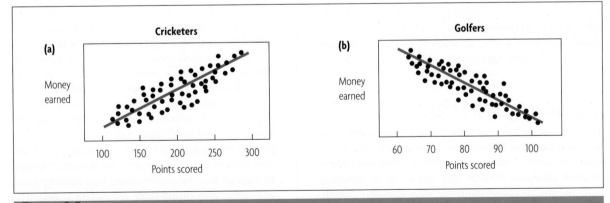

## Figure 2.5

### Positive and negative correlations
These imaginary data display the difference between positive and negative correlations. Each point represents a single cricketer or golfer. (a) In general, the more points (or runs) a professional cricketer scores, the more money he or she will earn. Thus, there is a positive correlation between those two variables. (b) The correlation for golf is negative, because golfers earn more money when they score fewer points.

What procedures might you follow to determine the correlation between students' sleep habits and their success in university? How would you evaluate potential causal relationships underlying any correlation?

What environmental factors explain why, even by age 5, some boys are displaying conduct problems and others are not? A team of researchers sought to demonstrate that this difference among boys arises, in part, from the varying amount of *destructive sibling conflict* the boys experience with their brothers and sisters (Garcia et al., 2000). The researchers reasoned that high levels of conflict with siblings might reinforce the boys' tendency toward aggressive or inappropriate responses to life situations. To measure destructive sibling conflict, the researchers videotaped hour-long play sessions between each of 180 boys and his sibling while they were playing together with different sets of toys. The videotaped play sessions were evaluated on dimensions such as the number of conflicts between the children and the intensity of those conflicts. Correlational analyses strongly supported the prediction that boys who experienced high levels of sibling conflict would also be most likely to display aggressive and delinquent behaviours.

Can you see why a correlational design is required to address this prediction? You can't randomly assign children to have a little or a lot of conflict with their siblings. You must wait to see what differences emerge after children are in one situation or the other.

## SUBLIMINAL INFLUENCE?

To close this section, we offer one concrete example of how psychological research has been used to assess the vigorous claims of advertisers anxious to make you believe in their products. Perhaps you are aware of products that promise to change your life with messages outside conscious awareness—*subliminal* messages: It's magic! It is not unusual for these products to guarantee a better sex life; provide a quick cure for low self-esteem; or promise safe and effective weight loss. How? All you have to do is *listen*—in bed, while walking the dog, when doing your homework—to the 'restful splash of ocean waves breaking on sandy shores.' If you are a fan of *The Simpsons*, you may recall an episode in which Marge purchased Homer a subliminal weight-loss audio tape to listen to while he slept, but he was sent a vocabulary building tape instead. Homer didn't lose any weight, he simply started using 'big words' that no-one could understand (Kogen, Wolodarsky & Reardon, 1992).

Subliminal influence has a long history. Although it was almost certainly a hoax, a 1957 study made headlines when the 'inventor' of subliminal advertising claimed that the message 'Buy Popcorn' flashed on the screen during a movie yielded a 58 percent increase in popcorn sales (Rogers, 1993)! A telephone survey conducted in the U.S.A., showed that nearly 75 percent of the 400 adults surveyed were familiar with subliminal advertising (Rogers & Smith, 1993). Of that group, again, nearly 75 percent believed subliminal advertising was used successfully by marketers. In general, the better educated the respondents were, the more likely they were to believe in the effectiveness of subliminal advertising. In November 2007, there was controversy when the Australian Broadcasting Corporation's program Media Watch questioned the advertising methods used during the television broadcast of the Australian Recording Industry Association (ARIA) awards. It was suggested that sponsor logos and information were presented so briefly onscreen that it may have been at or below the awareness threshold (Palmer, 2007). This type of subliminal advertising is prohibited in Australia under the Commercial Television Industry Code of Practice (Free TV, 2004). Such controversy and prohibition suggests that as consumers we should be wary of subliminal information. But, do subliminal messages really influence mental states and behaviour as their advocates claim? Given your reading so far, you now have the knowledge to address this critical question. Our answer comes from an application of the experimental methods we have described (see **Figure 2.6**).

A team of experimenters set out to determine the effectiveness of listening to commercially available audio-tapes designed to improve self-esteem or memory. The participants were 237 men and women volunteers, ranging from 18 to 60 years of age.

After a pretest session in which their initial self-esteem and memory were measured on standard psychological tests and questionnaires, the participants were randomly assigned to two conditions. Half of them received subliminal memory tapes, and the others received subliminal self-esteem tapes. They listened regularly to the tapes for a 5-week period and then returned to the laboratory for a posttest session to evaluate their memories (using four memory tests) and self-esteem (using three self-esteem scales). The researchers were blind to which participants received which treatment (Greenwald et al., 1991).

Did the tapes boost self-esteem and enhance memory? The results from this controlled experiment indicate no significant improvement was shown on any of the objective measures of either self-esteem

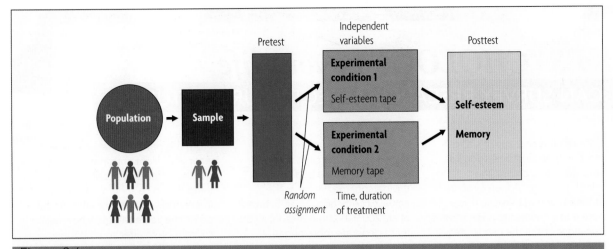

Figure 2.6

**Experimental design for testing hypotheses about the effectiveness of subliminal messages**
In this simplified version of the experiment, a sample of people is drawn from a larger, general population. They are given pretest measures and randomly assigned to receive subliminal tapes. They are then given posttests that objectively assess any changes in the dependent variables: memory and self-esteem.

or memory. However, one very powerful effect did emerge: the placebo effect of expecting to be helped. Anticipating this placebo effect, the researchers had added another independent variable. Half the participants in each group received memory tapes that were mismarked 'self-esteem' and the others received self-esteem tapes in 'memory boxes'. Participants *believed* their self-esteem improved if they received tapes with that label or felt their memory improved if their tapes were labelled 'memory'—even when they had been listening to the other tape!

This rigorous experiment allows for some very concrete advice: Save your money; subliminal self-help programs offer nothing more than placebo effects. An important goal of *Psychology and Life* is to provide you with such concrete conclusions based on solid experimental methods.

This experiment also gives you a specific example of the types of variables that psychologists measure. In this case, it was participants' beliefs about improvements in self-esteem and memory as well as objective measures of self-esteem and memory. In the next section, we discuss more generally the way in which psychologists measure important processes and dimensions of experience.

For answers go to MyPsychLab!

- To test their ideas, researchers use the scientific method, a set of procedures for gathering and interpreting evidence in ways that limit errors.
- Researchers combat observer biases by standardising procedures and using operational definitions.
- Experimental research methods determine whether causal relationships exist between variables specified by the hypothesis being tested.
- Researchers rule out alternative explanations by using appropriate control procedures.
- Correlational research methods determine if and how much two variables are related. Correlations do not imply causation.

## CONCEPT QUESTIONS

1. What is the relationship between theories and hypotheses?
2. What steps can researchers take to overcome observer biases?
3. Why do researchers use double-blind controls?
4. What is meant by a within-groups design?
5. Why does correlation not imply causation?

## CRITICAL THINKING

Consider the study in which 12-month-olds learned emotions toward objects from TV. Why was it important that the children had no prior experience with the objects?

## RECAP CHECKPOINT

### The process of research

- In the initial phase of research, observations, beliefs, information and general knowledge lead to a new way of thinking about a phenomenon. The researcher formulates a theory and generates hypotheses to be tested.

# PSYCHOLOGY *in your life*

## CAN SURVEY RESEARCH AFFECT YOUR ATTITUDES?

Consider this scenario. It's about election time. Just when you've finished eating dinner, the telephone rings. A friendly voice at the other end asks you if you have a few minutes to answer some questions about the candidates. You say, 'Why not?' This is an opportunity for you to be a research participant outside the laboratory. But here's an answer to your question, 'Why not?' The questions on the survey can have a strong impact on your attitudes.

Let's look at a laboratory study that illustrates this principle. The study took place in England, and it focused on participants' attitudes toward their then prime minister, Tony Blair (Haddock, 2002). Participants filled out a questionnaire that began with the question, 'How interested are you in British politics?' After that, the questionnaire continued in one of four ways. One version asked participants to list two positive characteristics for Blair; a second asked participants for five positive characteristics. The remaining two versions of the questionnaires asked for two or five negative characteristics. The next questions on each questionnaire asked the participants to provide favourability ratings towards Blair on 7-point scales with higher scores reflecting more positive attitudes.

From this description, you can see that one important component of the experiment was the number of characteristics each participant attempted to list. Why might that matter? Suppose you were asked to list negative attributes for a politician such as the Australian prime minister or your state's premier. You would probably find it easy to generate two negative attributes but relatively hard to generate five. After trying

to generate five, you might be thinking, 'Hey, if I can't think of five things that are bad about this person, maybe he or she is actually pretty good' (see Schwarz et al., 2003). For that reason, if you try to generate more negative characteristics, you might actually come to like the politician better; if you try to generate more positive characteristics, that effort can have a negative impact on your attitudes.

The results presented in the figure support these predictions for the subset of participants who were relatively uninterested in British politics. For example, those participants' ratings of Blair were relatively more positive when they attempted to recall more negative characteristics. For those participants who were already interested in British politics— presumably because they had sufficient knowledge and strong attitudes—the ease with which they could retrieve information about Blair did not have a similar impact on their attitudes.

From this pattern of results, here's what you might anticipate when you get that after-dinner call: The first thing the voice should ask is how interested you are in politics. At that point, the voice will know how easy it might be to alter your attitudes with questions that, on the surface, seem quite reasonable. Would you have anticipated that having people focus at length on Blair's negative characteristics would make them like him more?

So when you answer 'research' questions out in the real world, be wary of the true purposes of the enterprise. In the laboratory, researchers must provide you with debriefing information (see p. 43) that helps you understand how research participation might have influenced how you think or feel. Those people who catch you after dinner have no similar responsibilities towards full disclosure. Their major hope is that they can change your attitudes in a way that will affect your behaviour when you find yourself in the polling booth.

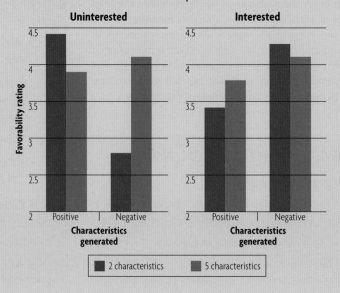

# PSYCHOLOGICAL MEASUREMENT

Because psychological processes are so varied and complex, they pose major challenges to researchers who want to measure them. Although some actions and processes are easily seen, many, such as anxiety or dreaming, are not. Thus one task for a psychological researcher is to make the unseen visible, to make internal events and processes external, and to make private experiences public. You have already seen how important it is for researchers to provide operational definitions of the phenomena they wish to study. Those definitions generally provide some procedure for assigning numbers to, or *quantifying*, different levels, sizes, intensities or amounts of a variable. Many measurement methods are available, each with its particular advantages and disadvantages.

Our review of psychological measurement begins with a discussion of the distinction between two ways of gauging the accuracy of a measure: reliability and validity. We then review different measurement techniques for data collection. By whatever means psychologists collect their data, they must use appropriate statistical methods to verify their hypotheses. A description of how psychologists analyse their data is given in the Statistical Supplement, which can be found in MyPsychLab. Read it in conjunction with this chapter.

## ACHIEVING RELIABILITY AND VALIDITY

The goal of psychological measurement is to generate findings that are both reliable and valid. **Reliability** refers to the consistency or dependability of behavioural data resulting from psychological testing or experimental research. A reliable result is one that will be repeated under similar conditions of testing at different times. A reliable measuring instrument yields comparable scores when employed repeatedly (and when the thing being measured does not change). Consider the experiment we just described (page 36), which showed that subliminal audiotapes generate only placebo effects. That experiment used 237 participants. The experimenters' claim that the result was 'reliable' means that they should be able to repeat the experiment with any new group of participants of comparable size and generate the same pattern of data.

**Validity** means that the information produced by research or testing accurately measures the psychological variable or quality it is intended to measure. A valid measure of *happiness,* for example, should allow us to predict how happy you are likely to be in particular situations. A valid experiment means that the researcher can generalise to broader circumstances, often from the laboratory to the real world. When we gave you advice based on the audiotapes experiment, we were accepting the researchers' claim that the results are valid. Tests and experiments can be reliable without being valid. We could, for example, use your shoe size as an index of your happiness. This would be reliable (we'd always get the same answer), but not valid (we'd learn very little about your day-to-day happiness level).

As you now read about different types of measures, try to evaluate them in terms of reliability and validity.

## SELF-REPORT MEASURES

Often researchers are interested in obtaining data about experiences they cannot directly observe. Sometimes these experiences are internal psychological states, such as beliefs, attitudes and feelings. At other times, these experiences are external behaviours but—like sexual activities or criminal acts—not generally appropriate for psychologists to witness. In these cases, investigations rely on self-reports. **Self-report measures** are verbal answers, either written or spoken, to questions the researcher poses. Researchers devise reliable ways to quantify these self-reports so they can make meaningful comparisons between different individuals' responses.

Self-reports include responses made on questionnaires and during interviews. A *questionnaire* or *survey* is a written set of questions, ranging in content from questions of fact ('Are you a registered voter?'), to questions about past or present behaviour ('How much do you smoke?'), to questions about attitudes and feelings ('How satisfied are you with your present job?'). *Open-ended* questions allow respondents to answer freely in their own words. Questions may also have a number of *fixed alternatives* such as *yes, no,* and *undecided.*

An *interview* is a dialogue between a researcher and an individual for the purpose of obtaining detailed information. Instead of being completely standardised, like a questionnaire, an interview is *interactive.* An interviewer may vary the questioning to follow up on something the respondent said. Good interviewers are also sensitive to the process of the social interaction as well as to the information revealed. They are trained to establish *rapport,* i.e. a positive social relationship with the respondent that encourages trust and the sharing of personal information.

Although researchers rely on a wide variety of self-report measures, there are limits to their usefulness. Obviously, many forms of self-report cannot be used with preverbal children, illiterate adults, speakers of other languages, some psychologically disturbed people, and nonhuman animals. Even when self-reports can be used, they may not be reliable or valid. Participants may misunderstand the questions or not remember clearly what they actually experienced. Furthermore, self-reports may be influenced by social desirability. People may give false or misleading answers to create a favourable (or, sometimes, unfavourable) impression of themselves. They may be embarrassed to report their true experiences or feelings. If respondents are aware of a questionnaire's or interview's purpose, they may lie or alter the truth to get a job, to get paroled from jail, or to accomplish any other

**self-report measures** The self-behaviours that are identified through a participant's own observations and reports.

**reliability** The degree to which a test produces similar scores each time it is used; stability or consistency of the scores produced by an instrument.

**validity** The extent to which a test measures what it was intended to measure.

goal. An interview situation also allows personal biases and prejudices to affect how the interviewer asks questions and how the respondent answers them.

## BEHAVIOURAL MEASURES AND OBSERVATIONS

As a group, psychological researchers are interested in a wide range of behaviours. They may study a rat running a maze, a child drawing a picture, a student memorising a poem, or a worker repeatedly performing a task. **Behavioural measures** are ways to study overt actions and observable and recordable reactions.

One of the primary ways to study what people do is *observation*. Researchers use observation in a planned, precise and systematic manner. Observations focus on either the *process* or the *products* of behaviour. In an experiment on learning, for instance, a researcher might observe how many times a research participant rehearsed a list of words (process) and then how many words the participant remembered on a final test (product). For *direct observations,* the behaviour under investigation must be clearly visible and overt and easily recorded. For example, in a laboratory experiment on emotions, a researcher could observe a participant's facial expressions as the individual looked at emotionally arousing stimuli.

A researcher's direct observations are often augmented by technology. For example, contemporary psychologists often rely on computers to provide very precise measures of the time it takes for research participants to perform various tasks, such as reading a sentence or solving a problem. Although some forms of exact measurement were available before the computer age, computers now provide extraordinary flexibility in collecting and analysing precise information. In Chapter 3, we will describe the newest types of technologies that allow researchers to produce behavioural measures of a remarkable kind: pictures of the brain at work.

By watching from behind a one-way mirror, a researcher can record observations of a child without influencing or interfering with the child's behaviour. Have you ever changed your behaviour when you knew you were being watched?

In *naturalistic observations,* some naturally occurring behaviour is viewed by a researcher, who makes no attempt to change or interfere with it. For instance, a researcher behind a one-way mirror might observe the play of children who are not aware of being observed. Some kinds of human behaviour can be studied only through naturalistic observation because it would be unethical or impractical to do otherwise. For example, it would be unethical to experiment with severe deprivation in early life to see its effects on a child's later development.

When studying behaviour in a laboratory setting, a researcher is unable to observe the long-term effects of one's natural habitat in shaping complex patterns of behaviour. One of the most valuable examples of naturalistic observation conducted in the field is the work of **Jane Goodall** (1986, 1990; Peterson & Goodall, 1993). Goodall has spent more than 30 years studying patterns of behaviour among chimpanzees in Gombe, on Lake Tanganyika in Africa. Goodall notes that had she ended her research after 10 years—as she originally planned—she would not have drawn the correct conclusions:

> We would have observed many similarities in their behavior and ours, but we would have been left with the impression that chimpanzees were far more peaceable than humans. Because we were able to continue beyond the first decade, we could document the division of a social group and observe the violent aggression that broke out between newly separated factions. We discovered that in certain circumstances the chimpanzees may kill and even cannibalize individuals of their own kind. On the other side of the coin, we have learned of the extraordinarily enduring affectionate bonds between family members . . . advanced cognitive abilities, [and the development of] cultural traditions. (Goodall, 1986, pp. 3–4)

In the early stages of an investigation, naturalistic observation is especially useful. It helps researchers discover the extent of a phenomenon or to get an idea of what the important variables and relationships might be. The data from naturalistic observation often provide clues for an investigator to use in formulating a specific hypothesis or research plan.

When they wish to test hypotheses with behavioural measures, researchers sometimes turn to *archival data.* Imagine all the types of information you might find in a library or on the Web: birth and death records, weather reports, movie attendance figures, electoral voting patterns, and so on. Any of those types of information could become valuable to test the right hypothesis. Consider a study that examined whether men and women differ in their level of *heroism* (Becker & Eagly, 2004). To address this question, the researchers couldn't create a laboratory test; they couldn't set a building on fire to see whether more men or women rushed in. Instead, they defined behaviours out in the world that were arguably heroic and then looked to archival records to assess the relative contributions of men and women. For example, the researchers examined participation in 'Doctors of the

Jane Goodall has spent most of her adult life making naturalistic observations of chimpanzees. What has she discovered that she couldn't have discovered if the animals were not in their natural habitat?

World', an organisation that sends medical personnel to all corners of the globe. Personnel in this program assume a 'non-negligible risk [by] delivering health and medical services in environments marked by local violence and unsanitary conditions' (Becker & Eagly, 2004, p. 173). What did the archival data show? More than half of the participants in Doctors of the World (65.8 percent) were women. You can see why archival data are essential to address certain types of questions.

Before we leave the topic of psychological measurement, we must emphasise that many research projects combine both self-report measures and behavioural observations. Researchers may, for example, specifically look for a relationship between how people report they will behave and how they actually behave. In addition, rather than involving large numbers of participants, some research projects will focus all their measures on a single individual or small group in a **case study**. Intensive analyses of particular individuals can sometimes yield important insights into general features of human experience. For example, in Chapter 3 you will learn that careful observations of single patients with brain damage provided the basis for important theories of the localisation of language functions in the brain.

We have now described several types of procedures and measures that researchers use. Before we move on, we want to give you an opportunity to see how the same issue can be addressed in different research designs. Consider Shakespeare's question, 'What's in a name?' In *Romeo and Juliet*, Juliet asserts, 'That which we call a rose by any other name would smell as sweet'. But is that correct? Do you think your name has an impact on the way other people treat you? Is it better to have a common, familiar name or a rare, distinctive one? Or does your name not matter at all?

In **Table 2.1** we give examples of combinations of measures and methods that researchers might use to answer those questions. As you read through Table 2.1,

**case study** Intensive observation of a particular individual or small group of individuals.

## Table 2.1

### What's in a name? Methods and measures

| Research goal | | Dependent measure | |
|---|---|---|---|
| | | Self-report | Observation |
| **Correlational methods** | To assess the correlation between the frequency of people's names and their experience of happiness. | Each participant's assessment of his or her own happiness. | |
| | To assess the correlation between the frequency of children's names and their acceptance by peers. | | Children's amount of social interaction on the playground. |
| **Experimental methods** | To determine if people judge identical photos differently when different names are assigned to them. | Participants' ratings of baby pictures to which random names have been assigned. | |
| | To determine if people's actual social interactions change because of name-based expectations. | | The number of positive facial expressions people produce in conversation with a stranger who has introduced himself as Mark or Marcus. |

ask yourself how willing you would be to participate in each type of study. In the next section, we consider the ethical standards that govern psychological research.

## RECAP CHECKPOINT

### Psychological measurement

- Researchers strive to produce measures that are both reliable and valid.

- Psychological measurements include self-reports and behavioural measures.

## CONCEPT QUESTIONS

1. Why can some measures be reliable but not valid?

2. Why is it important for interviewers to establish rapport?

3. Suppose a researcher spends time observing children's behaviour in a playground. What kind of measure would that be?

# ETHICAL ISSUES IN HUMAN AND ANIMAL RESEARCH

In the study that tested the effectiveness of subliminal messages, the researchers deceived the participants by mislabelling the tapes. They did so to see if the participants' expectations would lead them to believe that the messages were helpful even if objective measures of memory and self-esteem showed no improvement. Deception is always ethically suspect, but in this case, how else could researchers assess the placebo effect of false beliefs held by the participants? How should the *potential gains* of a research project be weighed against the *costs* it incurs to those who are subjected to procedures that are risky, painful, stressful or deceptive? Psychologists ask themselves these questions all the time (Rosenthal, 1994).

Respect for the basic rights of humans and animals is a fundamental obligation of all researchers. The Australian Psychological Society (APS) has a code of ethics setting out principles and ethical standards for researchers. Current research practice is governed by the October 2003 revision of the code (Australian Psychological Society, 2003). Consider the issue of deception in research. The 2003 code asserts, that 'When necessary for scientific reasons to conduct a study without fully informing the participants of its true purpose prior to the commencement of the study…[the psychologist] must ensure that participants do not suffer distress from the research procedure'

(Australian Psychological Society, 2003, p.9). Guidelines of this sort were not always in force. For example, in Chapter 16 we describe classic experiments on *obedience to authority*. In these experiments, participants were deceived into believing that they were giving dangerous electric shocks to total strangers. Evidence from the experiments suggests that the participants were, in fact, experiencing severe emotional 'distress'. For that reason—although the research is quite important to an understanding of human nature—no responsible psychologist could advocate replicating the studies today. In fact, researchers no longer make decisions about issues like the use of deception in isolation. To guarantee that ethical principles are honoured, special committees oversee every research proposal, imposing strict guidelines detailed in the Australian code for the responsible conduct of research set down by the National Health and Medical Research Council and the Australian Research Council (NHMRC & ARC, 2007). Universities, hospitals, and research institutes each have *review boards* that approve and reject proposals for human and animal research. Let's review some of the factors those review boards consider.

## INFORMED CONSENT

At the start of nearly all laboratory research with human subjects, participants are given a description of the procedures, potential risks and expected benefits they will experience. Participants are assured that their privacy is protected: all records of their behaviour are kept strictly confidential; they must approve any public sharing of them. Participants are asked to sign statements indicating that they have been *informed* about these matters and *consent* to continue. The participants are assured in advance that they may leave an experiment any time they wish, without penalty, and are given the names and phone numbers of officials to contact if they have any grievances.

## RISK/GAIN ASSESSMENT

Most psychology experiments carry little risk to the participants, especially where participants are merely asked to perform routine tasks. However, some experiments that study more personal aspects of human nature—such as emotional reactions, self-images, conformity, stress or aggression—can be upsetting or psychologically disturbing. Therefore, whenever a researcher conducts such a study, risks must be minimised, participants must be informed of the risks, and suitable precautions must be taken to deal with strong reactions. Where any risk is involved, it is carefully weighed by each institutional review board in terms of its necessity for achieving the benefits to the participants of the study, to science and to society.

## INTENTIONAL DECEPTION

For some kinds of research, it is not possible to tell the participants the whole story in advance without biasing the results. If you were studying the effects of violence on television on aggression, for example, you would not want your participants to know your purpose in advance. But is your hypothesis enough to justify the deception?

We already noted that the Australian Psychological Society (2003) ethical code gives explicit instructions about the use of deception. In addition to the guideline that participants not be misled about the probability of physical or emotional distress, the Australian Psychological Society and National Health and Medical Research Council provides other restrictions:

(1) the study must have sufficient scientific and educational importance to warrant deception,

(2) researchers must demonstrate that no equally effective procedures excluding deception are available,

(3) the deception must be explained to the participants by the conclusion of the research, and

(4) participants must have the opportunity to withdraw any data provided by them once the deception is explained (APS, 2003; NHMRC, ARC & AVCC, 2007).

In experiments involving deception, an ethics review committee may impose constraints, insist on monitoring initial demonstrations of the procedure, or deny approval.

## DEBRIEFING

Participation in psychological research should always be a mutual exchange of information between researcher and participant. The researcher may learn something new about a behavioural phenomenon from the participant's responses, and the participant should be informed of the purpose, hypothesis, anticipated results, and expected benefits of the study. At the end of an experiment, each participant must be given a careful **debriefing**, in which the researcher provides as much information about the study as possible and makes sure that no-one leaves feeling confused, upset or embarrassed. If it was necessary to mislead the participants during any stage of the research, the experimenter carefully explains the reasons for the deception. Finally, participants have the right to withdraw their data if they feel they have been misused or their rights abused in any way.

## RESEARCH WITH ABORIGINAL AND TORRES STRAIT ISLANDER PEOPLES

For the most part, studies of Indigenous peoples have been conducted by researchers from outside those Indigenous communities. This has meant that research conclusions have been formulated by individuals who do not necessarily share the same values, experiences, spirituality or teachings as Aboriginal and Torres Strait Islanders. In these circumstances, the conclusions may be considered more a reflection of preconceived expectations of Indigenous values (Davidson, Sanson & Gridley, 2000) and the cultural perspectives of non-indigenous Australians, rather than those of Aboriginal and Torres

Strait Islander cultures. In recent times, efforts have been made to redress this bias by incorporating Indigenous perspectives and values in to the research guidelines and codes of practice by which researchers are bound.

The guidelines for ethical conduct in Aboriginal and Torres Strait Islander health research published by the National Health and Medical Research Council (2003) were developed in consultation with Aboriginal and Torres Strait Islander peoples. Central to these guidelines are the following six values:

1. *Spirit and integrity*
   Seen as the overarching and binding value, it represents the continuity and inseparability of past, present and future, and places importance on behaving in ways that maintain the coherence of Aboriginal and Torres Strait Islander cultures.

2. *Reciprocity*
   The researcher is required to respect the cultures and values of the people and, as part of mutual obligation, provide outcomes that are valued by the community and are of benefit to the Aboriginal and Torres Strait Islander peoples.

3. *Respect*
   Respect is closely linked with dignity, and requires the recognition of peoples' contributions and the possible consequences of that contribution. The researcher is also required to acknowledge peoples' right to have differing values, objectives and traditions.

4. *Equality*
   The researcher must treat all participants as equals whilst respecting and appreciating their wisdom and knowledge of their own culture.

5. *Survival and protection*
   The research must contribute to the social and cultural bonds between families and their community; it must respect their right to cultural distinctiveness, and protect the individuals and community from discrimination.

6. *Responsibility*
   The researcher must establish their accountability to individuals and communities and has a responsibility to do no harm to participants, their families or communities.

The relationships between, and the interactions of, these six values are represented in **Figure 2.7**. Adherence to these guidelines will mean that the values and principles of Aboriginal and Torres Strait Islander communities are recognised and reconciled with the interests of research and researchers within Australian society.

## ISSUES IN ANIMAL RESEARCH

Should animals be used in psychological and medical research? This question has often produced very polarised responses. On one side are researchers who point to the very important breakthroughs research with animals has allowed in several areas of science (Domjan & Purdy, 1995;

**debriefing** A procedure at the end of an experiment in which the researcher provides the participant with as much information about the study as possible and ensures that no participant leaves feeling confused or upset.

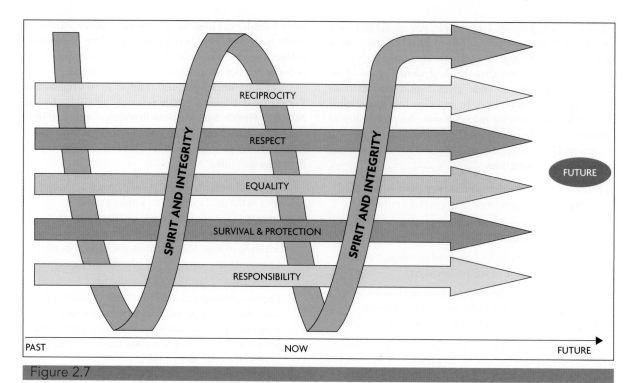

Figure 2.7

Aboriginal and Torres Strait Islander Peoples' values relevant to health research ethics

Petrinovich, 1998). The benefits of animal research have included discovery and testing of drugs that treat anxiety and mental illnesses as well as important knowledge about drug addiction (Miller, 1985). Animal research benefits animals as well. For example, psychological researchers have shown how to alleviate the stresses of confinement experienced by zoo animals. Their studies of animal learning and social organisation have led to the improved design of enclosures and animal facilities that promote good health (Nicoll et al., 1988).

To defenders of animal rights, this list of achievements does not undercut the deep error of believing that there is a 'morally relevant difference separating *Homo sapiens* from other creatures' (Bowd & Shapiro, 1993, p. 136; see also Shapiro, 1998). To remedy this error, ethicists argue for 'a shift from laboratory-based invasive research to minimally manipulative research conducted in naturalistic and semi-naturalistic settings' (Bowd & Shapiro, 1993, p. 140). Each animal researcher must judge his or her work with heightened scrutiny. As provided for research with human participants, the Australian Psychological Society and National Health and Medical Research Council provide ethical guidelines for the care and use of animals for scientific purposes (APS, 2003; NHMRC, 2004).

In terms of human use of animals, it is estimated that only 0.25% of that use is for experimental purposes (Brennan, 1997), and a very small proportion of all experiments conducted within psychology involve animal experimentation. A survey of attitudes towards animal experimentation among school teachers, medical students and the general public in Australia, New Zealand and Japan reported that the majority of respondents agreed

that 'animals have rights that humans should not violate' (Tsuzuki et al. 1998, p. 125). Of the Australian respondents 53 to 63 percent of biology and social science teachers, 62 percent of medical students, and 69 percent of the general public either agreed or strongly agreed with the statement (Tsuziko et al., 1998). As such, although the proportion of animals used for experimental purposes may seem small, to reflect public concern and opinion, it is important to ensure research with animals is conducted in an ethical manner and that all animals receive appropriate care before, during and after the experiment.

The protection and care of animals is always considered in conjunction with the importance and/or potential benefits of the research. In the USA, extensive surveys of 1,188 psychology students and 3,982 American Psychological Association members on their attitudes toward animal research support a criterion of heightened scrutiny (Plous, 1996a, 1996b) and also indicate circumstances in which animal use in research may be considered appropriate:

Roughly 80 percent of the people surveyed believed that observational studies in naturalistic settings were appropriate. Smaller numbers (30 to 70 percent) supported studies involving caging or confinement, depending in part on the type of animal (e.g., rats, pigeons, dogs or primates). Both students and their lecturers disapproved of studies involving physical pain or death.

A majority of both groups (roughly 60 percent) supported the use of animals in undergraduate psychology courses, but only about a third of each group felt that laboratory work with animals should be a required part of an undergraduate psychology major.

Researchers who use animal subjects are required to provide a humane environment. Do you think scientific gains justify the use of nonhuman animals in research?

How do your beliefs compare to these described above and to those of your peers? How would you make decisions about the costs and benefits of animal research?

# BECOMING A WISER RESEARCH CONSUMER

In the final section of this chapter, we will focus on the kinds of critical thinking skills you need to become a wiser consumer of psychological knowledge. Honing these thinking tools is essential for any responsible person in a dynamic society such as ours—one so filled with claims of truth, with false, supposedly commonsense myths, and with biased conclusions that serve special interests. To be a *critical thinker* is to go beyond the information as given and to delve beneath slick appearances, with the goal of understanding the substance without being seduced by style and image.

Psychological claims are an ever-present aspect of the daily life of any thinking, feeling and acting person in this psychologically sophisticated society. Unfortunately, not much information on psychology comes from the books, articles and reports of accredited practitioners. Rather, this information comes from newspaper and magazine articles, TV and radio shows, pop psychology and self-help books. Return to the idea of subliminal mind control. Although it began as a hoax propagated by profit-minded marketing consultant James M. Vicary (Rogers, 1993)—and, as we have seen, has been rigorously discredited in the laboratory—the idea of subliminal influences on overt behaviour continues to exert a pull on people's beliefs—and their wallets!

Studying psychology will help you make wiser decisions based on evidence gathered either by you or by others. Always try to apply the insights you derive from your formal study of psychology to the informal psychology that surrounds you: ask questions about your own behaviour or that of other people, seek answers to these questions with respect to rational psychological theories, and check out the answers against the evidence available to you.

Here are some general rules to keep in mind in order to be a more sophisticated shopper as you travel through the 'supermarket' of knowledge:

- Avoid the inference that correlation is causation.

- Ask that critical terms and key concepts be defined operationally so that there can be consensus about their meanings.

- Consider first how to disprove a theory, hypothesis or belief before seeking confirming evidence, which is easy to find when you're looking for a justification.

- Always search for alternative explanations to the obvious ones proposed, especially when the explanations benefit the proposer.

- Recognise how personal biases can distort perceptions of reality.

- Be suspicious of simple answers to complex questions or single causes and cures for complex effects and problems.

- Question any statement about the effectiveness of some treatment, intervention or product by finding the comparative basis for the effect: compared to what?

For answers go to MyPsychLab!

- Be open-minded yet sceptical: Recognise that most conclusions are tentative and not certain; seek new evidence that decreases your uncertainty while keeping yourself open to change and revision.

- Challenge authority that uses personal opinion in place of evidence for conclusions and is not open to constructive criticism.

We want you to apply open-minded scepticism while you read *Psychology and Life*. We don't want you to view your study of psychology as the acquisition of a list of facts. Instead, we hope you will participate in the joy of observing and discovering and putting ideas to the test.

A news interview with an expert may include misleading sound bites taken out of context or oversimplified 'nutshell' descriptions. How could you become a wiser consumer of media reports?

# CRITICAL THINKING *in your life*

## HOW CAN YOU EVALUATE PSYCHOLOGICAL INFORMATION ON THE WEB?

If you access the World Wide Web, you will discover an amazing range of sites devoted to topics in psychology. For example, for several years we have been trying the simple experiment of typing the word *schizophrenia* (see Chapter 14) into our preferred search engine. Here's some sample data. Six years ago, the search turned up 83,760 pages. Three years ago the search engine found 'about 764,000' pages. Today the search retrieved 'about 17,300,000' pages. That's some increase! No doubt the numbers will grow even higher during the short interval the publisher needs to turn our paragraphs into your textbook. These two data points make it clear why many people characterise the time in which we live as a time of *information explosion*. The challenge for all of us is to become wise consumers of all that information. How can you determine which information posted on the Web arises from legitimate sources and which does not?

In a physical library, it's much easier to determine the source of information. Most psychological

research appears in *journals* that are published by organisations such as the Australian Psychological Society or the American Psychological Association. When research manuscripts are submitted to most journals, they undergo a process of *peer review*. Each manuscript is typically sent to two to five experts in the field. Those experts provide detailed analyses of the manuscript's rationale, methodology and results. Only when those experts have been sufficiently satisfied do manuscripts become journal articles. This is a rigorous process. For example, in 2005, journals published by the American Psychological Association (2006) rejected, on average, 69 percent of the manuscripts submitted to them. The process of peer review isn't perfect—no doubt some worthy research projects are overlooked and some uneven ones slip through—but, in general, this process ensures that the research you read in the vast majority of journals has met high standards.

In this context, it's easy to identify the problem with much of the information on the Web: You

often can't tell who, if anyone, has evaluated the advice a webpage offers or the claims it makes. When you accept information from a webpage, you need to assure yourself that the source is legitimate. One good approach is to look for online versions of the journals available in the library. Also, look for the webpages researchers now often maintain that summarise their projects and list relevant publications. If the information you find on those or any other webpages interests you, try to find the references and publications they list. In general, you should have the greatest confidence in the information provided on a website when the authors of the site are able to point you toward the research sources for that information. You can have confidence in the conclusions we draw throughout *Psychology and Life* because we provide research citations for each of our claims. Make sure to hold web pages to the same standard!

Why does so much information about psychological topic get posted to the Web?

Why do journals request reviews from more than one expert?

# SUMMARY

Chapter 2 introduced the processes of conducting psychological experiments and reporting the results. Research conducted in psychology follows the procedures set out in the scientific method thus ensuring psychology is treated as a science. Psychologists use a variety of methods including self-report and observations and install experimental controls to make sure biases and expectation do not unduly influence the collected data or interpretation of results. It is important to remember that psychologists are bound by ethical guidelines, they must respect the rights of all human and animal research participants, guaranteeing their safety and humane treatment.

# KEY TERMS

behavioural measures (p. 40)
between-groups designs (p. 33)
case study (p. 41)
confounding variable (p. 32)
control procedures (p. 33)
correlation coefficient (r) (p. 35)
correlational methods (p. 35)
debriefing (p. 43)
dependent variable (p. 30)
determinism (p. 28)

double-blind control (p. 33)
expectancy effects (p. 32)
experimental methods (p. 32)
hypothesis (p. 28)
independent variable (p. 30)
observer bias (p. 29)
operational definition (p. 30)
placebo control (p. 33)
placebo effect (p. 32)
population (p. 33)

reliability (p. 39)
representative sample (p. 34)
sample (p. 33)
self-report measures (p. 39)
standardisation (p. 30)
theory (p. 28)
validity (p. 39)
variable (p. 30)
within-groups design (p. 34)

# PRACTICE TEST

1. A(n) _____ is an organised set of concepts that explains a phenomenon or set of phenomena.
   a. theory
   b. hypothesis
   c. operational definition
   d. correlation

2. Dr Peterson is testing the hypothesis that people will cooperate less when a lot of people are in a group. In the experiment she plans, she will vary the number of people in each group. That will be her
   a. placebo control
   b. independent variable
   c. double-blind control
   d. dependent variable

3. Rahul is serving as a research assistant. In the first phase of the experiment, Rahul gives each participant a can of cola or a can of caffeine-free cola. In the second phase of the experiment, Rahul times the participants with a stopwatch while they play a video game. It sounds like this study is lacking a(n)
   a. placebo control
   b. correlational design
   c. operational definition
   d. double-blind control

4. Shirley visits an antique store. The owner explains to her that the smaller an object is, the more he can charge for it. This is an example of a
   a. correlation coefficient
   b. negative correlation
   c. positive correlation
   d. placebo effect

5. Sally isn't very interested in movies. Her friend Rob wants to get her attitude to be more favourable toward his all-time favourite, *Rock 'n' Roll High School*. Rob might be best off asking Sally to generate _____ characteristics for the movie.
   a. two negative
   b. five positive
   c. ten positive
   d. five negative

6. Dr Paul is developing a new measure of hunger. He says, 'I need a measure that will accurately predict how much food people will eat in their next meal'. Dr. Paul's statement is about the _____ of the measure.
   a. operational definition
   b. standardisation
   c. validity
   d. reliability

7. Giovanna is worried that the results of her experiment may be affected by her participants' desire to provide favourable impressions of themselves. It sounds like she might be using _____ measures.
   a. valid
   b. self-report
   c. reliable
   d. operational

8. Andrew wishes to test the hypothesis that people give more freely to charities when the weather is pleasant. To test this hypothesis, Andrew is likely to make use of
   a. double-blind controls.
   b. expectancy effects.
   c. laboratory observation.
   d. archival data.

9. Before you participate in an experiment, the researcher should provide you with information about procedures, potential risks, and expected benefits. This allows you to give
   a. a risk/gain assessment.
   b. informed debriefing.
   c. informed consent.
   d. operational definitions.

10. When school teachers, medical students and the general public from Australia, New Zealand and Japan were surveyed about the uses of nonhuman animals in research, the majority believed that
    a. observational studies in naturalistic settings were appropriate.
    b. nonhuman animals should never be used as replacements for human participants.

c. intentional deception is unethical for experiments with nonhuman animals.
d. animals have rights that humans should not violate.

11. Always search for _____ explanations to the obvious ones proposed.
    a. optimistic
    b. alternative
    c. negative
    d. opposite

12. When articles are submitted to most journals, they are sent out to experts for detailed analyses. This process is known as
    a. debriefing
    b. informed consent
    c. peer review
    d. control procedures

## Essay Questions

1. Why is it so important that research procedures be open for public verifiability?

2. Suppose you wanted to measure 'happiness'. What might you do to assess the validity of your measure?

3. With respect to ethical principles, how are risks and gains defined in the context of psychological research?

# WEB LINKS

http://www.freetv.com.au/Content_Common/pg-Code-of-Practice.seo
   Commercial Television Industry Code of Practice

http://www.psychology.org.au/about/ethics/
   APS Revised Code of Ethics

http://www.nhmrc.gov.au
   National Health and Medical Research Council
   See:  * Code for the Responsible Conduct of Research
         * Guidelines for ethical conduct in Aboriginal and Torres Strait Islander health research

**where learning comes to life!**

Are you ready for the test? MyPsychLab offers dozens of ways to deepen your understanding and test your recall of the material in this chapter—including video and audio clips, simulations and activities, self-assessments, practice tests and other study materials. Specific resources available for this chapter include:

Correlations do not show causation
How to be a Critical Thinker

Distinguishing independent and dependent
  variables
Ethics in psychological research
Doing simple statistics

Naturalistic observation

To access MyPsychLab, please visit **www.pearsoned.com.au/mypsychlab**

# How does this apply to me?

## NOW YOU HAVE READ CHAPTER 2—ARE YOU PREPARED FOR THE EXAM?

To enhance your understanding of any of the material in your *Psychology and Life* textbook, go to **MyPsychLab: www.pearsoned.com.au/mypsychlab**.

Complete pre- and post-tests, create your own individualised study plan, watch videos and animations, and listen to audio glossaries—all of which will help you to understand the themes of this chapter:

- The processes of research
- Psychological measurement
- Ethical issues in human and animal research
- Becoming a wiser research consumer

Check out definitions for key terms, such as EXPECTANCY EFFORTS, PLACEBO EFFECT and DOUBLE-BLIND CONTROL.

Read an online version of Chapter 2, complete with interactive activities and practice tests.

Create a PERSONALISED STUDY PLAN for Chapter 2 by taking the pre- and post-tests.

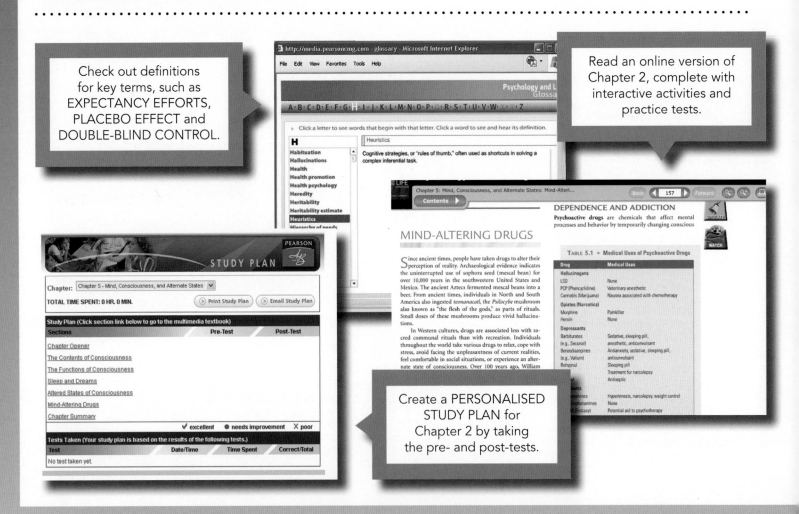

**READ THE STATISTICAL SUPPLEMENT**
Statistics are a vital part of the study of psychology. By reading the online **Statistical Supplement** you will develop a greater appreciation of how psychological knowledge is enhanced by the study of statistics. This will also ensure that you have at least a basic understanding of statistics yourself.

# STATISTICAL SUPPLEMENT
UNDERSTANDING STATISTICS: ANALYSING DATA
AND FORMING CONCLUSIONS

As we noted in Chapter 2, psychologists use statistics to make sense of the data they collect. They also use statistics to provide a quantitative basis for the conclusions they draw. Knowing something about statistics, therefore, can help you appreciate the process by which psychological knowledge is developed. On a more personal level, having a basic understanding of statistics will help you make better decisions when people use data to try to sway your opinions and actions.

Most students perceive statistics as a dry, uninteresting topic. However, statistics have many vital applications in your life. To demonstrate this point, we will follow a single project from its real-world inspiration to the statistical arguments that were used to bolster general conclusions. The project began in response to the types of stories that appear on newspaper front pages, about shy individuals who became *sudden murderers*. Here are examples from newspapers at the time of the Port Arthur massacre in Tasmania:

*When asked about Martin Bryant, Scott Goldsmith 'who lives opposite Bryant on a wide avenue in a middle-class section of Hobart [recalled]…I always said hello to him, and he always said hello back. I would stroll over the road to have a chat to him, and he was very lonely and had few visitors. I always felt sorry for him. He was just shy, quiet and withdrawn.' (Bendeich, 1996, April 30). 'Yvonne Briggs, who used to live nearby' and had dated Bryant said that 'He was a simple person, very polite and always friendly.' Bryant, was much younger than her and he, '…approached her and asked her to go out with him.' 'I couldn't understand it. I thought he was joking', she said. 'He said: I am very lonely. It's awful to be lonely and to have no-one.'…'He came and picked me up. We went dancing one night at a place down Elizabeth Street in Hobart and the second time we went to the Wrest Point Casino…He only kissed me on the cheek and that sort of thing,' Mrs Briggs said. 'Thank you for taking me out.' 'He didn't seem like he'd harm anyone. He seemed very genuine. He would open the car door and things like that." (McGeough & Simpson, 1996, April 30).*

Although he was later described as disturbed and possibly schizophrenic, these initial descriptions of a shy, quiet and lonely man seem incongruous with the Martin Bryant who shot and killed 35 people and injured many more at and around the Port Arthur historical site in Tasmania on April 28, 1996. Yet, this story has a common plot: A shy, quiet person suddenly becomes violent, shocking those who know him. What did Martin Bryant have in common with other people who are suddenly transformed from shy and quiet into violent and ruthless? What personal attributes might distinguish them from us?

Well before Martin Bryant perpetrated his crimes, a team of researchers in the USA had a hunch that there might be a link between shyness and other personal characteristics and violent behaviour (Lee et al., 1977). They began to collect some data that might reveal such a connection. The researchers reasoned that seemingly nonviolent people who suddenly commit murders are probably typically shy, nonaggressive individuals who keep their passions in check and their impulses under tight control. For most of their lives, they suffer many silent injuries. Seldom, if ever, do they express anger, regardless of how angry they really feel. On the outside, they appear unbothered, but on the inside they may be fighting to control furious rages. They give the impression that they are quiet and passive people, both as children and as adults. Because they are shy, they probably do not let others get close to them, so no one knows how they really feel. Then, suddenly, something explodes. At the slightest provocation—one more small insult, one more little rejection, one more bit of social pressure—the fuse is lit, and they release the suppressed violence that has been building up for so long. Because they did not learn to deal with interpersonal conflicts through discussion and verbal negotiation, these sudden murderers act out their anger physically.

The researchers' reasoning led them to the hypothesis that shyness would be more characteristic of *sudden murderers*—people who had engaged in homicide without any prior history of violence or antisocial behaviour—than it would of *habitual criminal murderers*—those who had committed homicide but had a previous record of violent criminal behaviour. In addition, sudden murderers should have higher levels of control over their impulses than habitually violent people. Finally, their passivity and dependence would be manifested in more feminine and

UNDERSTANDING STATISTICS: ANALYSING DATA AND FORMING CONCLUSIONS

'The pre- and post-tests in MPL really helped me to understand what I already knew, and what I still need to learn.'

**What can you find in MyPsychLab?**
Self-directed tests \* Videos \* Simulations \* eBook \* Biographies \* Audio glossary
\* Web links … and more—organised by chapter, section and learning objective.

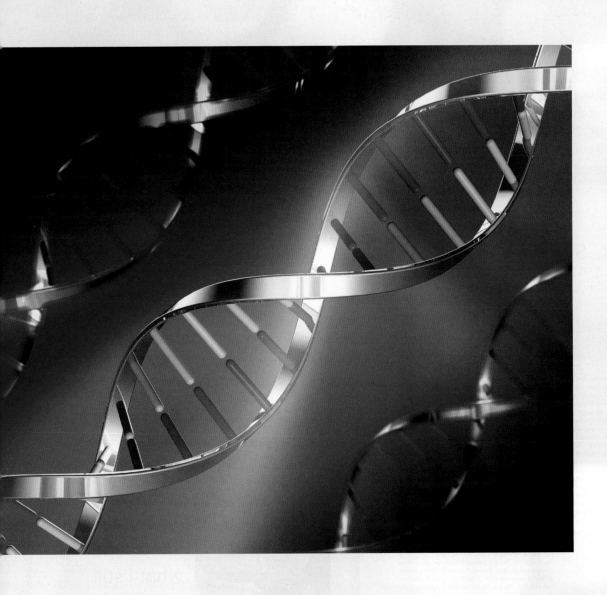

The Biological and Evolutionary
Bases of Behaviour

CHAPTER

3

# CHAPTER
# FOCUS POINTS

After studying this chapter you will have a better understanding of:

1. The contribution of genetic and environmental factors to your physical and psychological attributes

2. The mechanisms of neural transmission and nerve action

3. The organisation and function of the nervous system

4. The major neurotransmitters and their roles

5. Brain structure and function

## CHAPTER CONTENTS

What makes you a unique individual? *Psychology and Life* provides many answers to this question, but in this chapter we will focus on the biological aspects of your individuality. To help you understand what makes you different from the people around you, we will describe the role that heredity plays in shaping your life and in forming the brain that controls your experiences. Of course, you can appreciate these differences only against the background of what you have in common with all other people. You might, therefore, think of this as a chapter about biological potential: What possibilities for behaviour define the human species, and how do those possibilities emerge for particular members of that species?

In a way, this chapter stands as proof of one remarkable aspect of your biological potential: your brain is sufficiently complex to carry out a systematic examination of its own functions. Why is this so remarkable? The human brain is sometimes likened to a spectacular computer: At only one and a half kilograms, your brain contains more cells than there are stars in our entire galaxy—over 100 billion cells that communicate and store information with astonishing efficiency. But even the world's mightiest computer is incapable of reflecting on the rules that guide its own operation. Thus you are much more than a computer; your consciousness allows you to put your vast computational power to work, trying to determine your species' own rules for operation. The research we describe in this chapter arose from the special human desire for self-understanding.

For many students, this chapter will pose a greater challenge than the rest of *Psychology and Life*. It requires that you learn some anatomy and many new terms that seem far removed from the information you may have expected to get from an introduction to psychology. However, understanding your biological nature will enable you to appreciate more fully the complex interplay among the brain, mind, behaviour and environment that creates the unique experience of being human.

Our goal for this chapter is to help you to understand how biology contributes to the creation of unique individuals against a shared background potential. To approach this goal, we first describe how evolution and heredity determine your biology and behaviour. We then see how laboratory and clinical research provide a view into the workings of the brain, the nervous system, and the endocrine system. Finally, we describe the basic mechanisms of communication among cells in your nervous system that produce the full range of complex human behaviours.

## HEREDITY AND BEHAVIOUR

In Chapter 1, we defined one of the major goals of psychology to be the discovery of the causes underlying the variety of human behaviour. An important dimension

Psychologists often wish to understand the separate impact of nature and nurture on individuals' courses through life. Why might it be easier to observe the impact of environments versus the impact of heredity?

of causal explanation within psychology is defined by the end points of *nature* versus *nurture*, or *heredity* versus *environment*. Consider, as we did in Chapter 1, the question of the roots of aggressive behaviour. You might imagine that individuals are aggressive by virtue of some aspect of their biological makeup: they may have inherited a tendency toward violence from one of their parents. Alternatively, you might imagine that all humans are about equally predisposed to aggression and that the degree of aggression individuals display arises in response to features of the environment in which they are raised. The correct answer to this question has a profound impact on how society treats individuals who are overly aggressive—by focusing resources on changing certain environments or on changing aspects of the people themselves. You need to be able to discriminate the forces of heredity from the forces of environment.

Because the features of environments can be directly observed, it is often easier to understand how they affect people's behaviour. You can, for example, actually watch a parent acting aggressively toward a child and wonder what consequences such treatment might have on the child's later tendency toward aggression; you can observe the overcrowded and impoverished settings in which some children grow up and wonder whether these features of the environment lead to aggressive behaviours. The biological forces that shape behaviour, by comparison, are never plainly visible to the naked eye. To make the biology of behaviour more understandable to you, we will begin by describing some of the basic principles that shape a species' potential repertory of behaviours—elements of the theory of evolution—and then describe how behavioural variation is passed from generation to generation.

## EVOLUTION AND NATURAL SELECTION

In 1831, **Charles Darwin**, fresh out of college with a degree in theology, set sail from England on HMS *Beagle*, an ocean research vessel, for a 5-year cruise to survey the coast of

What observations ultimately led Charles Darwin to propose the theory of evolution?

South America. During the trip, Darwin collected everything that crossed his path: marine animals, birds, insects, plants, fossils, seashells and rocks. His extensive notes became the foundation for his books on topics ranging from geology to emotion to zoology. The book for which he is most remembered is *The Origin of Species*, published in 1859. In this work, Darwin set forth science's grandest theory: the evolution of life on planet Earth.

Natural selection Darwin developed his theory of evolution by reflecting on the species of animals he had encountered while on his voyage. One of the many places the *Beagle* visited was the Galápagos Islands, a volcanic archipelago off the west coast of South America. These islands are a haven for diverse forms of wildlife, including 13 species of finches, now known as Darwin's finches. Darwin wondered how so many different species of finches could have come to inhabit the islands. He reasoned that they couldn't have migrated from the mainland because those species didn't exist there. He suggested, therefore, that the variety of species reflected the operation of a process he came to call **natural selection**.

Darwin's theory suggests that each species of finch emerged from a common set of ancestors. Originally, a small flock of finches found their way to one of the islands; they mated among themselves and eventually their number multiplied. Over time, some finches migrated to different islands in the archipelago. What happened next was the process of natural selection. Food resources and living conditions—*habitats*—vary considerably from island to island. Some of the islands are lush with berries and seeds, others are covered with cacti, and others have plenty of insects. At first, the populations on different islands were similar—there was *variation* among the groups of finches

on each island. However, because food resources on the islands were limited, birds were more likely to survive and reproduce if the shape of their beak was well suited to the food sources available on the island. For example, birds that migrated to islands rich in berries and seeds were more likely to survive and reproduce if they had thick beaks. On those islands, birds with thinner, more pointed beaks, unsuitable for crushing or breaking open seeds, died. The environment of each island determined which among the original population of finches would live and reproduce and which would more likely perish, leaving no offspring. Over time, this led to very different populations on each island and permitted the different species of Darwin's finches to evolve from the original ancestral group.

In general, the theory of natural selection suggests that organisms well adapted to their environment, whatever it happens to be, will produce more offspring than those less well adapted. Over time, those organisms possessing traits more favourable for survival will become more numerous than those not possessing those traits. In evolutionary terms, an individual's success is measured by the number of offspring he or she produces.

Contemporary research has shown that natural selection can have dramatic effects, even in the short run. In a series of studies by **Peter** and **Rosemary Grant** (Grant & Grant, 1989, 2002; Weiner, 1994), involving several species of Darwin's finches, records were kept of rainfall, food supply and the population size of these finches on one of the Galápagos Islands. In 1976, the population numbered well over 1,000 birds. The following year brought a murderous drought that wiped out most of the food supply. The smallest seeds were the first to be depleted, leaving only larger and tougher seeds. That year the finch population decreased by more than 80 percent. However, smaller finches with smaller beaks died at a higher frequency than larger finches with thicker beaks. Consequently, as Darwin would have predicted, the larger birds became more numerous in the following years. Why? Because only they, with their larger bodies and thicker

**natural selection** Darwin's theory that favourable adaptations to features of the environment allow some members of a species to reproduce more successfully than others.

beaks, were fit enough to respond to the environmental change caused by the drought. Interestingly, in 1983, rain was plentiful, and seeds, especially the smaller ones, became abundant. As a result, smaller birds outsurvived larger birds, probably because their beaks were better suited for pecking the smaller seeds. The Grants' study shows that natural selection can have noticeable effects even over short periods. Researchers continue to document the impact of environments on natural selection in diverse species, including the European fruit fly (Huey et al., 2000) and the stickleback fish (Rundle et al., 2000).

Although Darwin provided the foundation for evolutionary theory, researchers continue to study mechanisms of evolutionary change that fall beyond the bounds of Darwin's ideas (Gould, 2002). For example, one important question that Darwin was unable to address fully was how populations with common ancestors evolve so that one species becomes two. As you have already seen in the Grants' research with Darwin's finches, species can change rapidly in response to local environments. One explanation for the appearance of new species is that they emerge when two populations from an original species become geographically separate—and therefore evolve in response to different environmental events. Marsupials are now found only in Australia, but earlier 'versions' of marsupials were once more widespread were previously widespread

> Nor can it be pretended that it is an immutable law that marsupials should have been chiefly or solely produced in Australia; or that Edentata and other American types should have been solely produced in South America. For we know that Europe in ancient times was peopled by numerous marsupials; and I have shown in the publications above alluded to, that in America the law of distribution of terrestrial mammals was formerly different from what it now is. (Darwin, 1856)

However, contemporary research on evolution has uncovered many examples of new species that have emerged without that type of geographic isolation (Barton, 2000). Researchers are pursuing a variety of explanations for how species arise under those circumstances. These explanations focus, for example, on how subgroups within a species evolve different cues—such as the chemical signals fruit flies use—to recognise appropriate mates (Higgie et al., 2000). If, over time, those cues become distinct, separate species may emerge.

### Genotypes and phenotypes

Let's return our focus to the forces that bring about change within an existing species.

The example of the ebb and flow of finch populations demonstrates why Darwin characterised the course of evolution as *survival of the fittest*. Imagine that each environment poses some range of difficulties for each species of living beings. Those members of the species who possess the range of physical and psychological attributes best adapted to the environment are most likely to survive. To the extent that the attributes that foster survival can be passed from one generation to another—and stresses in

the environment endure over time—the species is likely to evolve.

To examine the process of natural selection in more detail, we must introduce some of the vocabulary of evolutionary theory. Let us focus on an individual finch. At conception, that finch inherited a **genotype**, or genetic structure, from its parents. In the context of a particular environment, this genotype determined the finch's development and behaviour. The outward appearance and repertory of behaviours of the finch are known as its **phenotype**. For our finch, its genotype may have interacted with the environment to yield the phenotype of *small beak* and *ability to peck smaller seeds*.

If seeds of all types were plentiful, this phenotype would have no particular bearing on the finch's survival. Suppose, however, that the environment provided insufficient seeds to feed the whole population of finches. In that case, the individual finches would be in *competition* for resources. When species function in circumstances of competition, phenotypes help determine which individual members are better adapted to ensure survival. Recall our finch with a small beak. If only small seeds were available, our finch would be at a *selective advantage* with respect to finches with large beaks. If only large seeds were available, our finch would be at a disadvantage.

Only finches that survive can reproduce. Only those animals that reproduce can pass on their genotypes. Therefore, if the environment continued to provide only small seeds, over several generations the finches would probably come to have almost exclusively small beaks—with the consequence that they would be almost exclusively capable of eating only small seeds. In this way, forces in the environment can shape a species' repertory of possible behaviours. **Figure 3.1** provides a simplified model of the process of natural selection. Let us now apply these ideas to human evolution.

### Human evolution

By looking backward to the circumstances in which the human species evolved, you can begin to understand why certain physical and behavioural features are part of the biological endowment of the entire human species. In the evolution of our species, natural selection favoured two major adaptations—bipedalism and encephalisation. Together, they made possible the rise of human civilisation. *Bipedalism* refers to the ability to walk upright, and *encephalisation* refers to increases in brain size. These two adaptations are responsible for most, if not all, of the other major advances in human evolution, including cultural development (see **Figure 3.2**). As our ancestors evolved the ability to walk upright, they were able to explore new environments and exploit new resources. As brain size increased, our ancestors became more intelligent and developed capacities for complex thinking, reasoning, remembering and planning. However, the evolution of a bigger brain did not guarantee that humans would become more intelligent—what was important was the kind of tissue that developed and expanded within the brain (Gibbons, 2002). The genotype coding for mobile and intelligent phenotypes slowly squeezed out other, less

**genotype** The genetic structure an organism inherits from its parents.

**phenotype** The observable characteristics of an organism resulting from the interaction between the organism's genotype and its environment.

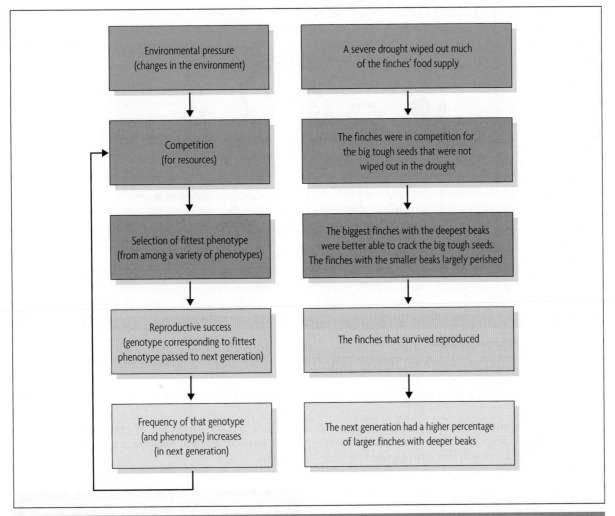

Figure 3.1

**How natural selection works**

Environmental changes create competition for resources among species members. Only those individuals possessing characteristics instrumental in coping with these changes will survive and reproduce. The next generation will have a greater number of individuals possessing these genetically based traits.

well-adapted genotypes from the human gene pool, affording only intelligent bipeds the opportunity to reproduce.

After bipedalism and encephalisation, perhaps the most important evolutionary milestone for our species was the advent of *language* (Bickerton, 1990; Holden, 1998). Think of the tremendous adaptive advantages that language conferred on early humans. Simple instructions for making tools, finding a good hunting or fishing spot, and avoiding danger would save time, effort and lives. Instead of learning every one of life's lessons firsthand, by trial and error, humans could benefit from experiences shared by others. Conversation, even humour, would strengthen the social bonds among members of a naturally gregarious species. Most important, the advent of language would provide for the transmission of accumulated wisdom from one generation to future generations.

Language is the basis for *cultural evolution,* which is the tendency of cultures to respond adaptively, through learning, to environmental change. Cultural evolution has given rise to major advances in toolmaking, improved agricultural practices, and the development and refinement of industry and technology. Cultural evolution allows our species to make very rapid adjustments to changes in environmental conditions. Adaptations to the use of personal computers, for example, have arisen in only the past 20 years. Even so, cultural evolution could not occur without genotype coding for the capacities to learn and to think abstractly. Culture—including art, literature, music, scientific knowledge and philanthropic activities—is possible only because of the potential of the human genotype.

## VARIATION IN THE HUMAN GENOTYPE

You have seen that the conditions in which humans evolved favoured the evolution of important shared biological

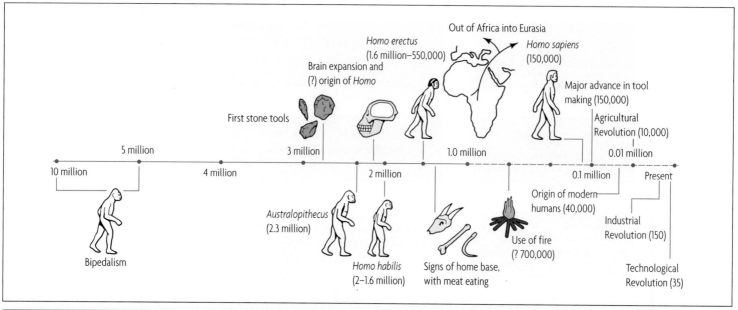

Figure 3.2

**Approximate time line for the major events in human evolution**
Bipedalism freed the hands for grasping and tool use. Encephalisation provided the capacity for higher cognitive processes such as abstract thinking and reasoning. These two adaptations probably led to the other major advances in human evolution.

From Robert Lewin from Human *Evolution: An Illustrated Introduction.* Copyright © 1984 by Blackwell Science Ltd. Reprinted by permission.

**heredity** The biological transmission of traits from parents to offspring.

**genetics** The study of the inheritance of physical and psychological traits from ancestors.

potential: for example, bipedalism and the capacity for thought and language. There remains, however, considerable variation within that shared potential. Your mother and father have endowed you with a part of what their parents, grandparents, and all past generations of their family lines have given them, resulting in a unique biological blueprint and timetable for your development. The study of the mechanisms of **heredity**—the inheritance of physical and psychological traits from ancestors—is called **genetics**.

The earliest systematic research exploring the relationship between parents and their offspring was published in 1866 by **Gregor Mendel** (1822–1884). Mendel's studies were carried out on the humble garden pea. He was able to demonstrate that the physical features of peas that emerged from different seeds—for example, whether the peas appeared *round* or *wrinkled*—could be predicted from the physical features of the plants from which the seeds had been obtained. Based on his observations, Mendel suggested that pairs of 'factors'—one inherited from each parent—determined the properties of the offspring (Lander & Weinberg, 2000). Although Mendel's work originally received little attention from other scientists, modern techniques have allowed researchers to visualise and study Mendel's 'factors,' which we now call *genes.*

**DNA** (deoxyribonucleic acid) The physical basis for the transmission of genetic information.

**genes** The biological units of heredity; discrete sections of chromosomes responsible for transmission of traits.

**Basic genetics** In the nucleus of each of your cells is genetic material called **DNA** (deoxyribonucleic acid; see **Figure 3.3**). DNA is organised into tiny units, called **genes.** Genes contain the instructions for the production of proteins. These proteins regulate the body's physiological

processes and the expression of phenotypic traits: body build, physical strength, intelligence and many behaviour patterns.

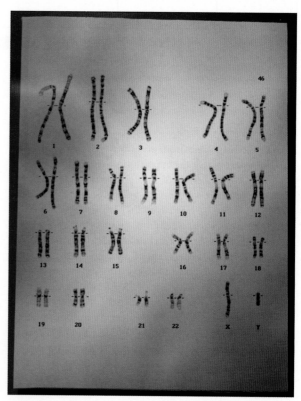

Human chromosomes—at the moment of conception, you inherited 23 from your mother and 23 from your father.

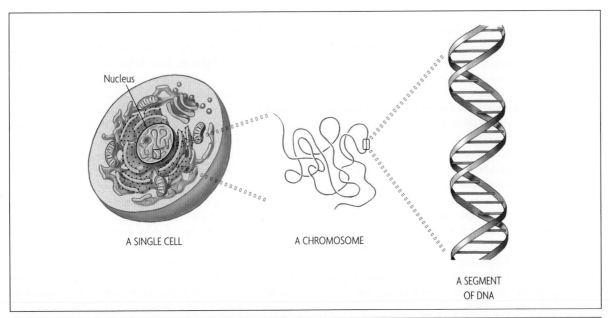

**Figure 3.3**

**Genetic material**

The nucleus of each cell in your body contains a copy of the chromosomes that transmit your genetic inheritance. Each chromosome contains a long strand of DNA arranged in a double helix. Genes are segments of the DNA that contain instructions for the production of the proteins that guide your individual development.

From Lester A. Lefton & Linda Brannon p. 39. *Psychology* 8e. Published by Allyn & Bacon, Boston, MA. Copyright © 2003 by Pearson Education. Reprinted by permission of the publisher.

Genes are found on rodlike structures known as *chromosomes*. At the very instant you were conceived, you inherited from your parents 46 chromosomes— 23 from your mother and 23 from your father. Each of these chromosomes contains thousands of genes— the union of a sperm and an egg results in only one of many billion possible gene combinations. The **sex chromosomes** are those that contain genes coding for development of male or female physical characteristics. You inherited an X chromosome from your mother and either an X or a Y chromosome from your father. An XX combination codes for development of female characteristics; an XY combination codes for development of male characteristics.

In 1990, an international research endeavour called the called the *Human Genome Project* (HGP) was launched. The **genome** of an organism is the full sequence of genes found on the chromosomes with the associated DNA. In 2003, the HGP achieved the goal of providing a complete sequencing of the human genome. With that information in hand, researchers have now turned their attention to identifying all 20,000 to 25,000 human genes. The ultimate goal is to provide a complete account of the location and functions of that full set of genes.

**Genes and behaviour** We have seen that evolutionary processes have allowed a considerable amount of variation to remain in human genotypes; the interactions of these genotypes with particular environments produce variation in human phenotypes. Researchers in the field of **human behaviour genetics** unite genetics and psychology to explore the causal link between inheritance and behaviour (Plomin et al., 2003).

Research in human behaviour genetics often focuses on estimating the **heritability** of particular human traits and behaviours. Heritability is measured on a scale of 0 to 1. If an estimate is near 0, that suggests that the attribute is largely a product of environmental influences; if an estimate is near 1, that suggests that the attribute is largely a product of genetic influences. To tease apart environment and genes, researchers often use *adoption studies* or *twin studies*. For adoption studies, researchers obtain as much information as possible about the birth parents of children who are raised in adoptive homes. As the children develop, researchers assess the relative similarity of children to their birth families—representing genetics—and their adoptive families—representing environment.

In twin studies, researchers examine the extent to which *monozygotic (MZ)* twins and *dizygotic (DZ)* twins show similarity within pairs on particular traits or behaviours. MZ twins share 100 percent of their genetic material, whereas DZ twins share roughly 50 percent. (DZ twins are no more genetically alike than any other pair of brothers and sisters.) Researchers compute heritability estimates by determining how much more alike MZ twins are than DZ twins on a particular attribute. Consider a twin study that estimated the extent to which people inherit their ability to perceive distortions in simple melodies.

**human behaviour genetics** The area of study that evaluates the genetic component of individual differences in behaviours and traits.

**heritability** The relative influence of genetics—versus environment—in determining patterns of behaviour.

**sex chromosomes** Chromosomes that contain the genes that code for the development of male or female characteristics.

**genome** The genetic information for an organism stored in the DNA of its chromosomes.

Do your neighbours complain when you sing in the shower? To what extent is your musical ability, or lack thereof, a product of your genetic makeup? Researchers sought to answer this question for one aspect of musical expertise—the ability to perceive distortions in simple tunes (Drayna et al., 2001). Consider the example in **Figure 3.4**. Even if you can't read music, you can see that the notes toward the end of the musical phrase have been distorted. But would you *hear* the distortion?

In this experiment, 136 pairs of MZ twins and 148 pairs of DZ twins heard 26 brief tunes and indicated whether each melody was correct or incorrect. The scores of the MZ twins—the number correct out of 26—were more similar, with a correlation of 0.67, than the scores of the DZ twins, with a correlation of 0.44. Based on these data, the researchers obtained a heritability estimate of 0.71. This estimate suggests a large genetic component to pitch perception.

Note that this high heritability estimate does not mean that everyone in a family is going to have the same pitch perception abilities. Just as the same parents will produce some children with blue eyes and some with brown eyes, the same parents will produce some children with exceptional musical ability and some children without. Instead, the high heritability suggests that, with respect to pitch perception, there's relatively little room for life experiences to have an impact on how talented you may or may not become.

This example of the heritability of pitch perception points to some of the ethical issues that have arisen in the wake of the Human Genome Project's successes. Suppose the HGP is able to determine which genes are responsible for the differences in pitch perception? If you were to become a parent, would you choose only to have children who were likely to be superior in musical ability? Although this question might not seem urgent in the context of musicianship, ethicists have already begun to ponder the consequences of genetic knowledge (Bostrom, 2005; Liao, 2005). For example, a variety of techniques already allow prospective parents to choose to have a boy or a girl. Should they be willing and able to make that choice? How about choices with respect to a child's intelligence level, sports ability or criminal inclinations? As the HGP and related efforts continue to yield new insights, such ethical questions will become increasingly prominent in debates over public policy.

Still, it's important to remember that—except in cases such as a child's sex—genes are not destiny. In fact, researchers have begun to document important instances in which both genetics and environments play critical roles to determine organisms' behaviours. Consider a study that looked at the nature and nurture of aggression among male rhesus macaques (Newman et al., 2005). Let's start with nature. Within the population of 45 monkeys, there was variation with respect to a gene that affected the levels of neurotransmitters (see p. 66) in the brain—some monkeys had the *high-activity* variation of the gene, whereas other monkeys had the *low-activity* variation. With respect to nurture, roughly half of the monkeys were raised with their own or a foster mother; the others were raised without early maternal care. The experimenters measured the monkeys' aggression by observing, for example, how effectively they competed for food. These observations suggested that the monkeys' levels of aggression depended on both genetics and environment: the monkeys who had the low-activity variation of the gene and who also had been raised by mothers showed the most aggressive behaviour. Monkeys with the same gene variation but who had not experienced maternal contact did not show higher levels of aggression. From this example you can see

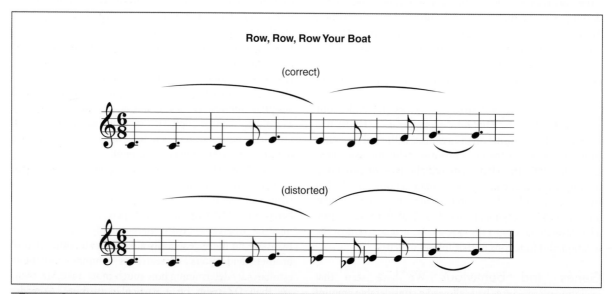

Figure 3.4

Using distorted tunes to study the heritability of pitch perception
If you heard these two melodies played, could you tell which was correct and which was distorted?

why researchers seek to understand how and why certain environments allow genes to be expressed.

The study of human behaviour genetics most often focuses on the origins of individual differences: What factors in your individual genetic inheritance help to explain the way you think and behave? To complement human behaviour genetics, two other fields have emerged that take a broader focus on how forces of natural selection affect the behavioural repertory of humans and other species. Researchers in the field of **sociobiology** provide evolutionary explanations for the social behaviour and social systems of humans and other animal species. Researchers in **evolutionary psychology** extend those evolutionary explanations to include other aspects of human experience, such as how the mind functions.

Consider the question of happiness: How might an evolutionary perspective explain the human species' general ability to experience happiness? Buss (2000) suggested that some limits are placed on human happiness by the 'discrepancies between modern and ancestral environments' (p. 15). For example, although humans evolved in the context of small groups, many people now live in large urban environments in which they are mostly surrounded by large numbers of total strangers. We might no longer have close bonds to the group of individuals that share our space—the types of bonds that could help us weather crises to experience happy lives. What can be done? Although you cannot turn back the tide of cultural evolution that has brought about these changes, you can try to counteract their negative effects by increasing your closeness to your family members and to your friends (Buss, 2000). This example reveals the contrast between the sociobiological emphasis on the human species in a particular environment versus the behaviour genetic emphasis on variation within the general pattern for a species. In the remainder of *Psychology and Life,* we will present several more instances in which the evolutionary perspective sheds light on human experience. These examples range from partner choices in relationships (Chapter 11), to emotional expression (Chapter 12), to patterns of aggression (Chapter 17).

For answers go to MyPsychLab!

## CONCEPT QUESTIONS

1. How does the Grants' research on finches illustrate the role of genetic variation in the process of evolution?

2. What is the difference between a genotype and a phenotype?

3. What were two evolutionary advances most critical in human evolution?

4. What is meant by heritability?

## CRITICAL THINKING

Consider the study on pitch perception. Why did the researchers use familiar melodies such as 'Row, Row, Row Your Boat'?

**sociobiology** A field of research that focuses on evolutionary explanations for the social behaviour and social systems of humans and other animal species.

**evolutionary psychology** The study of behaviour and mind using the principles of evolutionary theory.

# THE NERVOUS SYSTEM IN ACTION

We turn our attention now to the remarkable products of the human genotype: the biological systems that make possible the full range of thought and performance. Long before Darwin made preparations for his trip aboard the *Beagle,* scientists, philosophers, and others debated the role that biological processes play in everyday life. An important figure in the history of brain studies was the French philosopher **René Descartes** (1596–1650). Descartes proposed what at that time was a very new and very radical idea: the human body is an 'animal machine' that can be understood scientifically by discovering natural laws through empirical observation.

Researchers who pursue these natural laws are called *neuroscientists.* Today, **neuroscience** is one of the most rapidly growing areas of research. Important discoveries come with astonishing regularity. Our objective for the remainder of this chapter is to explore how the information available to your senses is ultimately communicated throughout your body and brain by nerve impulses. In this section, we begin that exploration by discussing the properties of the basic unit of the nervous system, the neuron.

**neuroscience** The scientific study of the brain and of the links between brain activity and behaviour.

## THE NEURON

A **neuron** is a cell specialised to receive, process and/or transmit information to other cells within the body. Neurons vary in shape, size, chemical composition and function—over 200 different types have been identified in mammal brains—but all neurons have the same basic structure (see **Figure 3.5**). There are from 100 billion to 1 trillion neurons in your brain.

**neuron** A cell in the nervous system specialised to receive, process and/or transmit information to other cells.

## RECAP CHECKPOINT

### Heredity and behaviour

● Species originate and change over time because of natural selection.

● In the evolution of humans, bipedalism and encephalisation were responsible for subsequent advances, including language and culture.

● The basic unit of heredity is the gene. Genes determine the range of effects that environmental factors can have in influencing the expression of phenotypic traits.

**soma** The cell body of a neuron, containing the nucleus and cytoplasm.

**axon** The extended fibre of a neuron through which nerve impulses travel from the soma to the terminal buttons.

**terminal buttons** The bulblike structures at the branched endings of axons that contain vesicles filled with neurotransmitters.

**sensory neurons** The neurons that carry messages from sense receptors towards the central nervous system.

**motor neurons** The neurons that carry messages away from the central nervous system towards the muscles and glands.

**interneurons** Brain neurons that relay messages from sensory neurons to other interneurons or to motor neurons.

**dendrites** The branched fibres of neurons that receive incoming signals.

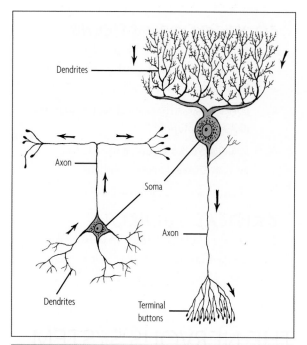

### Figure 3.5

**Two types of neurons**
Note the differences in shape and dendritic branching. Arrows indicate directions in which information flows. Both cells are types of interneurons.

Neurons typically take in information at one end and send out messages from the other. The part of the cell that receives incoming signals is a set of branched fibres called **dendrites**, which extend outward from the cell body. The basic job of the dendrites is to receive stimulation from sense receptors or other neurons. The cell body, or **soma**, contains the nucleus of the cell and the cytoplasm that sustains its life. The soma integrates information about the stimulation received from the dendrites (or in some cases received directly from another neuron) and passes it on to a single, extended fibre, the **axon**. In turn, the axon conducts this information along its length—which, in the spinal cord, can be several feet and, in the brain, less than a millimetre. At the other end of axons are swollen, bulblike structures called **terminal buttons**, through which the neuron is able to stimulate nearby glands, muscles or other neurons. Neurons generally transmit information in only one direction: from the dendrites through the soma to the axon to the terminal buttons (see **Figure 3.6**).

There are three major classes of neurons. **Sensory neurons** carry messages from sense receptor cells *towards* the central nervous system. Receptor cells are highly specialised cells that are sensitive, for example, to light, sound, and body position. **Motor neurons** carry messages *away* from the central nervous system towards the muscles and glands. The bulk of the neurons in the brain are **interneurons**, which relay messages from sensory neurons to other interneurons or to motor neurons. For every motor neuron in the body there are as many as 5,000 interneurons in the great intermediate network that forms the computational system of the brain.

As an example of how these three kinds of neurons work together, consider the pain withdrawal reflex (see **Figure 3.7**). When pain receptors near the skin's surface are stimulated by a sharp object, they send messages via

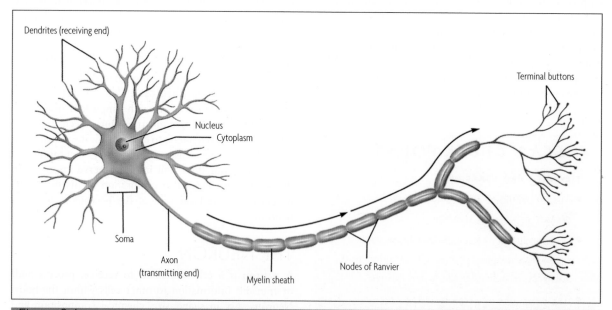

### Figure 3.6

**The major structures of the neuron**
The neuron receives nerve impulses through its dendrites. It then sends the nerve impulses through its axon to the terminal buttons, where neurotransmitters are released to stimulate other neurons.

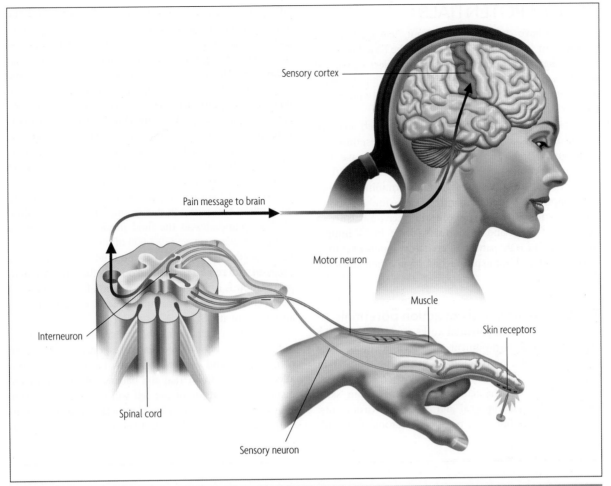

Sensory cortex

Pain message to brain

Motor neuron

Muscle

Skin receptors

Interneuron

Spinal cord

Sensory neuron

**Figure 3.7**

**The pain withdrawal reflex**
The pain withdrawal reflex shown here involves only three neurons: a sensory neuron, a motor neuron and an interneuron.

sensory neurons to an interneuron in the spinal cord. The interneuron responds by stimulating motor neurons, which, in turn, excite muscles in the appropriate area of the body to pull away from the pain-producing object. It is only *after* this sequence of neuronal events has taken place, and the body has been moved away from the stimulating object, that the brain receives information about the situation. In cases such as this, where survival depends on swift action, your perception of pain often occurs after you have physically responded to the danger. Of course, then the information from the incident is stored in the brain's memory system so that the next time you will avoid the potentially dangerous object altogether, before it can hurt you.

Interspersed among the brain's vast web of neurons are about five to ten times as many glial cells (**glia**). The word *glia* is derived from the Greek word for *glue*, which gives you a hint of one of the major duties performed by these cells: They hold neurons in place. In vertebrates, glial cells have several other important functions. A first function applies during development. Glial cells help guide newborn neurons to appropriate locations in the brain. A second function is housekeeping. When neurons are damaged and die, glial cells in the area multiply and clean up the cellular junk left behind; they can also take up excess neurotransmitters and other substances at the gaps between neurons. A third function is insulation. Glial cells form an insulating cover, called a *myelin sheath*, around some types of axons. This fatty insulation greatly increases the speed of nerve signal conduction. A fourth function of glial cells is to prevent toxic substances in the blood from reaching the delicate cells of the brain. Specialised glial cells, called astrocytes, make up a *blood–brain barrier*, forming a continuous envelope of fatty material around the blood vessels in the brain. Substances that are not soluble in fat do not dissolve through this barrier, and because many poisons and other harmful substances are not fat soluble, they cannot penetrate the barrier to reach the brain. Finally, neuroscientists have come to believe that glia may play an active role in neural communication by affecting the concentrations of ions that allow for the transmission of nerve impulses (Fields & Stevens-Graham, 2002).

**glia** The cells that hold neurons together and facilitate neural transmission, remove damaged and dead neurons and prevent poisonous substances in the blood from reaching the brain.

# ACTION POTENTIALS

So far, we have spoken loosely about neurons 'sending messages' or 'stimulating' each other. The time has come to describe more formally the kinds of electrochemical signals used by the nervous system to process and transmit information. These signals are the basis of all you know, feel, desire and create.

This is the basic question asked of each neuron: Should it or should it not *fire*—produce a response—at some given time? In loose terms, neurons make this decision by combining the information arriving at their dendrites and soma (cell body) and determining whether those inputs are predominantly saying 'fire' or 'don't fire'. More formally, each neuron will receive a balance of **excitatory**—fire!—and **inhibitory**—don't fire!—**inputs**. In neurons, the right pattern of excitatory inputs over time or space will lead to the production of an *action potential*: the neuron fires.

**The biochemical basis of action potentials** To explain how an **action potential** works, we need to describe the biochemical environment in which neurons draw together incoming information. All neural communication is produced by the flow of electrically charged particles, called *ions,* through the neuron's membrane, a thin 'skin' separating the cell's internal and external environments. Think of a nerve fibre as a piece of macaroni, filled with salt water, floating in a salty soup. The soup and the fluid in the macaroni both contain ions—atoms of sodium ($Na^+$), chloride ($Cl^-$), calcium ($Ca^+$), and potassium ($K^+$)—that have either positive (+) or negative (−) charges (see **Figure 3.8**). The membrane, or the surface of the macaroni, plays a critical role in keeping the ingredients of the two fluids in an appropriate balance. When a cell is inactive, or in a *resting state,* there are about 10 times as many potassium ions inside as there are sodium ions outside. The membrane is not a perfect barrier; it 'leaks' a little, allowing some sodium ions to slip in while some potassium ions slip out. To correct for this, nature has provided transport mechanisms within the membrane that pump out sodium and pump in potassium. Successful operation of these pumps leaves the fluid inside a neuron with a slightly negative voltage (70/1,000 of a volt) relative to the fluid outside. This means that the fluid inside the cell is *polarised* with respect to the fluid outside the cell. This slight polarisation is called the **resting potential**. It provides the electrochemical context in which a nerve cell can produce an action potential.

The nerve cell begins the transition from a resting potential to an action potential in response to the pattern of inhibitory and excitatory inputs. Each kind of input affects the likelihood that the balance of ions from the inside to the outside of the cell will change. They cause changes in the function of **ion channels**, excitable portions of the cell membrane that selectively permit certain ions to

**excitatory inputs** Information entering a neuron that signals it to fire.

**inhibitory inputs** Information entering a neuron that signals it not to fire.

**action potential** The nerve impulse activated in a neuron that travels down the axon and causes neurotransmitters to be released into a synapse.

**resting potential** The polarisation of cellular fluid within a neuron, which provides the capability to produce an action potential.

**ion channels** The portions of neurons' cell membranes that selectively permit certain ions to flow in and out.

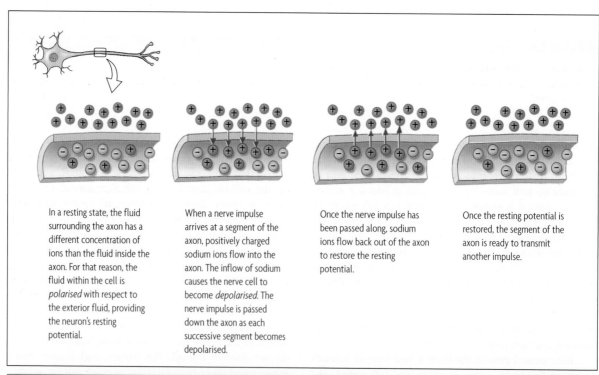

In a resting state, the fluid surrounding the axon has a different concentration of ions than the fluid inside the axon. For that reason, the fluid within the cell is *polarised* with respect to the exterior fluid, providing the neuron's resting potential.

When a nerve impulse arrives at a segment of the axon, positively charged sodium ions flow into the axon. The inflow of sodium causes the nerve cell to become *depolarised.* The nerve impulse is passed down the axon as each successive segment becomes depolarised.

Once the nerve impulse has been passed along, sodium ions flow back out of the axon to restore the resting potential.

Once the resting potential is restored, the segment of the axon is ready to transmit another impulse.

## Figure 3.8

**The biochemical basis of action potentials**
Action potentials rely on an imbalance of the electrical charge of the ions present inside and outside of axons.

From Lester A. Lefton & Linda Brannon p. 49. *Psychology.* 8e. Published by Allyn and Bacon, Boston, MA. Copyright © 2002 by Pearson Education. Reprinted by permission of the publisher.

flow in and out. Inhibitory inputs cause the ion channels to work harder to keep the inside of the cell negatively charged—this will keep the cell from firing. Excitatory inputs cause the ion channels to begin to allow sodium ions to flow in—this will allow the cell to fire. Because sodium ions have a positive charge, their influx can begin to change the relative balance of positive and negative charges across the cell membrane. An action potential begins when the excitatory inputs are sufficiently strong with respect to inhibitory inputs to *depolarise* the cell from –70 millivolts to –55 millivolts: sufficient sodium has entered the cell to effect this change.

Once the action potential begins, sodium rushes into the neuron. As a result, the inside of the neuron becomes positive relative to the outside, meaning the neuron has become fully depolarised. A domino effect now propels the action potential down the axon. The leading edge of depolarisation causes ion channels in the adjacent region of the axon to open and allow sodium to rush in. In this way—through successive depolarisation—the signal passes down the axon (see Figure 3.8).

How does the neuron return to its original resting state of polarisation after it fires? When the inside of the neuron becomes positive, the channels that allow sodium to flow in close and the channels that allow potassium to flow out open. The outflow of potassium ions restores the negative charge of the neuron. Thus, even while the signal is reaching the far end of the axon, the portions of the cell in which the action potential originated are being returned to their resting balance, so that they can be ready for their next stimulation.

## Properties of the action potential

The biochemical manner in which the action potential is transmitted leads to several important properties. The action potential obeys the **all-or-none law**: the size of the action potential is unaffected by increases in the intensity of stimulation beyond the threshold level. Once excitatory inputs sum to reach the threshold level, a uniform action potential is generated. If the threshold is not reached, no action potential occurs. An added consequence of the all-or-none property is that the size of the action potential does not diminish along the length of the axon. In this sense, the action potential is said to be *self-propagating*; once started, it needs no outside stimulation to keep itself moving. It's similar to a lit fuse on a firecracker.

Different neurons conduct action potentials along their axons at different speeds; the fastest have signals that move at the rate of 200 metres per second, the slowest plod along at 10 centimetres per second. The axons of the faster neurons are covered with a tightly wrapped myelin sheath—consisting, as we explained earlier, of glial cells—making this part of the neuron resemble short tubes on a string. The tiny breaks between the tubes are called *nodes of Ranvier* (see Figure 3.6). In neurons having myelinated axons, the action potential literally skips along from one node to the next—saving the time and energy required to open and close ion channels at every location on the axon. Damage to the myelin sheath throws off

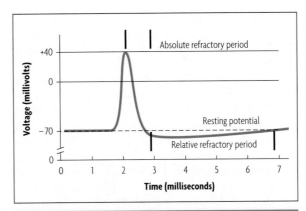

### Figure 3.9

Timetable for electrical changes in the neuron during an action potential
Sodium ions entering the neuron cause its electrical potential to change from slightly negative during its polarised, or resting, state to slightly positive during depolarisation. Once the neuron is depolarised, it enters a brief refractory period during which further stimulation will not produce another action potential. Another action potential can occur only after the ionic balance between the inside and the outside of the cell is restored.

the delicate timing of the action potential and causes serious problems. Multiple sclerosis (MS) is a devastating disorder caused by deterioration of the myelin sheath. It is characterised by double vision, tremors, and eventually paralysis. In MS, specialised cells from the body's immune system actually attack myelinated neurons, exposing the axon and disrupting normal synaptic transmission (Joyce, 1990).

After an action potential has passed down a segment of the axon, that region of the neuron enters a **refractory period** (see **Figure 3.9**). During the *absolute refractory period*, further stimulation, no matter how intense, cannot cause another action potential to be generated; during the *relative refractory period*, the neuron will fire only in response to a stimulus stronger than what is ordinarily necessary. Have you ever tried to flush the toilet while it is filling back up with water? There must be a critical level of water for the toilet to flush again. Similarly, for a neuron to be able to generate another action potential, it must 'reset' itself and await stimulation beyond its threshold. The refractory period ensures, in part, that the action potential will only travel in one direction down the axon; it cannot move backward because 'earlier' parts of the axon are in a refractory state.

## SYNAPTIC TRANSMISSION

When the action potential completes its leapfrog journey down the axon to a terminal button, it must pass its information along to the next neuron. But no two neurons ever touch: they are joined at a **synapse**, with a small gap between the *presynaptic membrane* (the terminal button of the sending neuron) and the *postsynaptic membrane*

**all-or-none law** The rule that the size of the action potential is unaffected by increases in the intensity of stimulation beyond the threshold level.

**refractory period** The period of rest during which a new nerve impulse cannot be activated in a segment of an axon.

**synapse** The gap between one neuron and another.

(the surface of a dendrite or soma of a receiving neuron). When the action potential reaches the terminal button, it sets in motion a series of events called **synaptic transmission**, which is the relaying of information from one neuron to another across the synaptic gap (see **Figure 3.10**). Synaptic transmission begins when the arrival of the action potential at the terminal button causes small round packets, called *synaptic vesicles,* to move toward and affix themselves to the interior membrane of the terminal button. Inside each vesicle are **neurotransmitters**, biochemical substances that stimulate other neurons. The action potential also causes ion channels to open that admit calcium ions into the terminal button. The influx of calcium ions causes the rupture of the synaptic vesicles and the release of whatever neurotransmitters they contain. Once the synaptic vesicles rupture, the neurotransmitters are dispersed rapidly across the *synaptic cleft*, the gap between the terminal button of one neuron and the cell membrane of the next. To complete synaptic transmission, the neurotransmitters attach to *receptor molecules* embedded in the postsynaptic membrane.

The neurotransmitters will bind to the receptor molecules under two conditions. First, no other neurotransmitters or other chemical substances can be attached to the receptor molecule. Second, the shape of the neurotransmitter must match the shape of the receptor molecule—as precisely as a key fits into a keyhole. If either condition is not met, the neurotransmitter will not attach to the receptor molecule. This means that it will not be able to stimulate the postsynaptic membrane. If the neurotransmitter does become attached to the receptor molecule, then it may provide 'fire' or 'don't fire' information to this next neuron. Once the neurotransmitter has completed its job, it detaches from the receptor molecule and drifts back into the synaptic gap. There it is either decomposed through the action of enzymes or reabsorbed into the presynaptic terminal button for quick reuse.

Depending on the receptor molecule, a neurotransmitter will have either an excitatory or an inhibitory effect. That is, the same neurotransmitter may be excitatory at one synapse but inhibitory at another. Each neuron integrates the information it obtains at synapses with between 1,000 and 10,000 other neurons to decide whether it ought to initiate another action potential. It is the integration of these thousands of inhibitory and excitatory inputs that allows all-or-none action potentials to provide the foundation for all human experience.

You may be wondering why we have taken you so deep into the nervous system. After all, this is a psychology course, and psychology is supposed to be about behaviour and thinking and emotion. In fact, synapses are the biological medium in which all these activities occur. If you change the normal activity of the synapse, you change how people behave, how they think, and how they feel. Understanding the functioning of the synapse has led to tremendous advances in the understanding of learning and memory, emotion, psychological disorders, drug addiction and, in general, the chemical formula for mental health. You will use the knowledge you have acquired in this chapter throughout *Psychology and Life.*

## NEUROTRANSMITTERS AND THEIR FUNCTIONS

Dozens of chemical substances are known or suspected to function as neurotransmitters in the brain. The neurotransmitters that have been studied most intensively meet a set of technical criteria. Each is manufactured in the presynaptic terminal button and is released when an action potential reaches that terminal. The neurotransmitter's presence in the synaptic cleft produces a biological response in the post-synaptic membrane, and if its release is prevented, no subsequent responses can occur. To give you a sense of the effects different neurotransmitters have on the regulation of behaviour, we will discuss a set that has been found to play an important role in the daily functioning of the brain. This brief discussion will also enable you to understand many of the ways in which neural transmission can go awry.

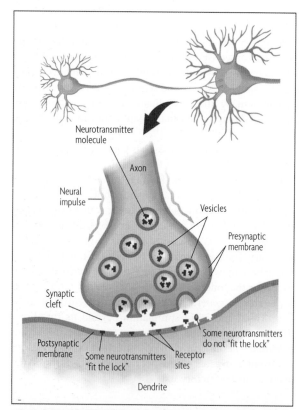

### Figure 3.10

**Synaptic transmission**

The action potential in the presynaptic neuron causes neurotransmitters to be released into the synaptic gap. Once across the gap, they stimulate receptor molecules embedded in the membrane of the postsynaptic neuron. Multiple neurotransmitters can exist within the same cell.

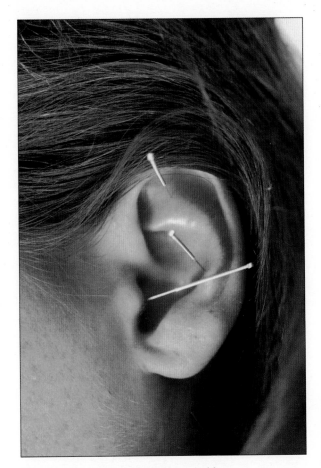

Why do patients experience pain relief from acupuncture?

**Acetylcholine** *Acetylcholine* is found in both the central and peripheral nervous systems. Memory loss among patients suffering from Alzheimer's disease, a degenerative disease that is increasingly common among older persons, is believed to be caused by the deterioration of neurons that secrete acetylcholine. Acetylcholine is also excitatory at junctions between nerves and muscles, where it causes muscles to contract. A number of toxins affect the synaptic actions of acetylcholine. For example, botulinum toxin, often found in food that has been preserved incorrectly, poisons an individual by preventing release of acetylcholine in the respiratory system. This poisoning, known as *botulism*, can cause death by suffocation. Curare, a poison Amazon Indians use on the tips of their blowgun darts, paralyses lung muscles by occupying critical acetylcholine receptors, preventing the normal activity of the transmitter.

**GABA** *GABA* (gamma-aminobutyric acid) is the most common inhibitory neurotransmitter in the brain. GABA may be used as a messenger in as many as a third of all brain synapses. Neurons that are sensitive to GABA are particularly concentrated in brain regions such as the thalamus, hypothalamus and occipital lobes (see pp. 75–78). GABA appears to play a critical role in some forms of psychopathology by inhibiting neural activity; when levels of this neurotransmitter in the brain become low, people may experience the extra neural activity as feelings of anxiety. Anxiety disorders are often treated with *benzodiazepine* drugs, such as *Valium* or *Xanax*, that increase GABA activity (Ballenger, 1999). The *benzodiazepine* drugs do not attach directly to GABA receptors. Instead they allow GABA itself to bind more effectively to postsynaptic receptor molecules.

**Dopamine, noradrenaline and serotonin** The *catecholamines* are a class of chemical substances that include two important neurotransmitters, *dopamine* and *noradrenaline*. Both have been shown to play prominent roles in psychological disorders such as mood disturbances and schizophrenia. Noradrenaline appears to be involved in some forms of depression: Drugs that increase brain levels of this neurotransmitter elevate mood and relieve depression. Conversely, higher-than-normal levels of dopamine have been found in persons with schizophrenia. As you might expect, one way to treat people with this disorder is to give them a drug that decreases brain levels of

Roughly 4.5 million people worldwide, including the actor Michael J. Fox and the former Australian Governor-General Sir Zelman Cowan, are impaired by Parkinson's disease. Research on the neurotransmitter dopamine has led to advances in understanding this disease. How does basic research in neuroscience allow for improved treatments?

dopamine. In the early days of drug therapy, an interesting but unfortunate problem arose. High doses of the drug used to treat schizophrenia produced symptoms of Parkinson's disease, a progressive and ultimately fatal disorder involving disruption of motor functioning. (Parkinson's disease is caused by deterioration of neurons that manufacture most of the brain's dopamine.) This finding led to research that improved drug therapy for schizophrenia and to research that focused on drugs that could be used in the treatment of Parkinson's disease.

All the neurons that produce *serotonin* are located in the brain stem, (see p. 76) which is involved in arousal and many autonomic processes. The hallucinogenic drug LSD (lysergic acid diethylamide) appears to produce its effects by suppressing the effects of serotonin neurons. These serotonin neurons normally inhibit other neurons, but the lack of inhibition produced by LSD creates vivid and bizarre sensory experiences, some of which last for hours. Many antidepressant drugs, such as *Prozac,* enhance the action of serotonin by preventing it from being removed from the synaptic cleft (Barondes, 1994).

**Endorphins** The *endorphins* are a group of chemicals that are usually classified as neuromodulators. A **neuromodulator** is any substance that modifies or modulates the activities of the postsynaptic neuron. Endorphins (short for *endogenous morphines*) play an important role in the control of emotional behaviours (anxiety, fear, tension, pleasure) and pain—drugs like opium and morphine bind to the same receptor sites in the brain. Endorphins have been called the 'keys to paradise' because of their pleasure–pain controlling properties. Researchers have examined the possibility that endorphins are at least partially responsible for the pain-reducing effects of acupuncture and placebos (Benedetti et al., 2005; Han, 2004). Such tests rely on the drug *naloxone,* whose only known effect is to block morphine and endorphins from binding to receptors. Any procedure that reduces pain by stimulating release of endorphins becomes ineffective when naloxone is administered. With the injection of naloxone, acupuncture and placebos do, in fact, lose their power—suggesting that, ordinarily, endorphins help them do their work.

Researchers have also documented that gases like *carbon monoxide* and *nitric oxide* can function as neurotransmitters (Barinaga, 1993). What is most surprising about this new class of neurotransmitters is that they violate many of the normal expectations about synaptic transmission. For example, rather than binding to receptor molecules, as do the other neurotransmitters we have discussed, these gaseous transmitters appear to pass directly through the receptor cell's outer membrane. This surprising discovery should reinforce your impression that the brain possesses many secrets yet to be revealed.

**neuromodulator** Any substance that modifies or modulates the activities of the postsynaptic neuron.

For answers go to MyPsychLab!

# BIOLOGY AND BEHAVIOUR

You now have an understanding of the basic mechanisms that allow nerve cells to communicate. The time has come to assemble those neurons into the larger systems that guide your body and mind. We begin this discussion with an overview of the techniques researchers use to hasten new discoveries. We then offer a general description of the structure of the nervous system, followed by a more detailed look at the brain itself. We discuss the activity of the endocrine system, a second biological control system that works in cooperation with your nervous system and brain. Finally, we describe ways in which your life experiences continue to modify your brain.

## EAVESDROPPING ON THE BRAIN

Neuroscientists seek to understand how the brain works at a number of different levels—from the operation of large structures visible to the naked eye to the properties of individual nerve cells visible only under powerful microscopes. The techniques researchers use are suited

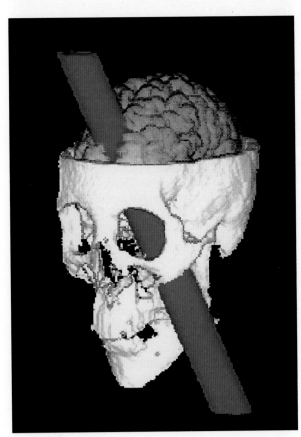

Phineas Gage's skull is preserved in the collections of the Warren Anatomical Museum, Harvard University Medical School. Why were doctors so fascinated by Gage's changes in personality?

to their level of analysis. Here, we discuss the techniques that have been used most often to attribute functions and behaviours to particular regions of the brain.

**Interventions in the brain** Several research methods in neuroscience involve direct intervention with structures in the brain. These methods find their historical roots in circumstances like the story of railroad foreman Phineas Gage, who in September 1848 suffered an accident in which a 3-foot, 7-inch-long pole was blown, as the result of an unexpected explosion, clear through his head. Gage's physical impairment was remarkably slight: He lost vision in his left eye, and the left side of his face was partially paralysed, but his posture, movement, and speech were all unimpaired. Yet, psychologically, he was a changed man, as his doctor's account made clear:

> The equilibrium or balance, so to speak, between his intellectual faculties and animal propensities seems to have been destroyed. He is fitful, irreverent, indulging at times in the grossest profanity (which was not previously his custom), manifesting but little deference for his fellows, impatient of restraint or advice when it conflicts with his desires. . . . Previous to his injury, though untrained in schools, he possessed a well-balanced mind, and was looked upon by those who knew him as a shrewd, smart businessman, very energetic and persistent in executing all his plans of operation. In this regard his mind was radically changed, so decidedly that his friends and acquaintances said he was 'no longer Gage.' (Harlow, 1868, pp. 339–340)

Gage's injury came at a time when scientists were just beginning to form hypotheses about the links between brain functions and complex behaviour. The behavioural changes following the dramatic piercing of his brain prompted his doctor to hypothesise brain bases for aspects of personality and rational behaviour.

At about the same time that Gage was convalescing from his injury, **Paul Broca** was studying the brain's role in language. His first research in this area involved an autopsy of a man whose name was derived from the only word he had been able to speak, 'Tan.' Broca found that the left front portion of Tan's brain had been severely damaged. This finding led Broca to study the brains of other persons who suffered from language impairments. In each case, Broca's work revealed similar damage to the same area of the brain, a region now known as **Broca's area**. As you will see as *Psychology and Life* unfolds, contemporary researchers still attempt to correlate patterns of behaviour change or impairment with the sites of brain damage.

The problem with studying accidentally damaged brains, of course, is that researchers have no control over the location and extent of the damage. To produce a well-founded understanding of the brain and its relationship to behavioural and cognitive functioning, scientists need methods that allow them to specify precisely the brain tissue that has been incapacitated. Researchers have developed a variety of techniques to

**Broca's area** The region of the brain that translates thoughts into speech or signs.

# CRITICAL THINKING *in your life*

## WHAT DOES 'IT'S GENETIC' MEAN?

The Human Genome Project has put the study of genetics very much in the public eye. The media routinely reports on the progress researchers have made in understanding genetic contributions to important aspects of human experience such as obesity, sexuality, and mental illness. We want to give you a framework that should help you evaluate those media reports. We are going to focus our discussion on the behavioural trait of *impulsivity*. Researchers have been interested in this dimension because high levels of impulsivity put people at risk for problems such as drug and alcohol addiction (Sher et al., 2000).

Suppose you see a newspaper headline that reads, 'Scientists Find Impulsivity Gene.' What information should the newspaper article provide? First, it's important to understand exactly what 'impulsivity' means in the context of the article. Take a moment to consider how you might define or apply the term: You probably know some people who you would label as impulsive and others for whom you wouldn't use this label. But what exactly does that mean? Are your acquaintances impulsive because they never plan ahead? Because they can't stop themselves from acting out? Because they take too many risks? If you see the claim 'Scientists Find Impulsivity Gene,' you need to understand exactly how the

researchers are using the term. This level of specificity is important because it's quite possible that the different behaviours associated with the one concept 'impulsivity' could have different genetic bases (Congdon & Canli, 2006). If the newspaper article doesn't offer a careful description of what is meant by 'impulsivity,' you should be cautious about uncritically accepting its conclusions.

The next information you need to find is an explanation for why the researchers believe the gene they have identified plays a causal role in producing impulsive behaviour. Sometimes, this information will be given as a statement of fact: 'People who have variation A of this gene are impulsive; those who have variation B are not'. However, in contemporary research, scientists most often want to provide some sense of the mechanism that allows the gene to influence behaviour. What you'll often learn from those accounts is that the gene in question only indirectly has an influence on a trait.

For example, analyses of impulsive behaviour have recently focused on the neurotransmitter dopamine. Dopamine functions in regions of the brain that are critical to tasks such as planning—it is the neurotransmitter that helps achieve cognitive stability and flexibility (Bilder et al., 2004). From this characterisation, you can see why disruptions in the function of dopamine could lead

people to engage in behaviours that are impulsive or unstable. The implication here is that if you want to find a genetic basis for impulsivity, what you might really seek is a genetic basis for differences in individual brain's uses of dopamine. In fact, researchers have begun to document variations in more than one gene—genes with names such as *DRD4* and *COMT*—that affect the use of dopamine (Congdon & Canli, 2006).

You can start to see how all the pieces fit together. Researchers start with a trait or behaviour such as impulsivity that shows variability among individuals. Over time, they begin to have an understanding of what processes in the brain might produce that variability. Then, they can look for genetic variations that might explain why brains perform differently. Thus, although the headline would read 'Scientists Find Impulsivity Gene,' the real news might be that scientists have discovered how a particular gene—perhaps one of many—has an impact on the brain's use of dopamine. That's a less tidy headline, but it would go closer to the heart of the discovery.

- With respect to genetic research, why is it important to give precise definitions of traits or behaviours?

- Why might the genes that influence impulsivity also have an impact on other behavioural traits?

---

**lesions** Injuries to or destruction of brain tissue.

produce **lesions**, highly localised brain injuries. They may, for example, surgically remove specific brain areas, cut the neural connections to those areas, or destroy those areas through application of intense heat, cold or electricity. As you would guess, experimental work with permanent lesions is carried out exclusively with nonhuman animals. (Recall our discussion in Chapter 2

that the ethics of this type of animal research has now come under heightened scrutiny.) Our conception of the brain has been radically changed as researchers have repeatedly compared and coordinated the results of lesioning experiments on animals with the growing body of clinical findings on the effects of brain damage on human behaviour.

In recent years, scientists have developed a procedure called **repetitive transcranial magnetic stimulation (rTMS)**, which uses pulses of magnetic stimulation to create temporary, reversible 'lesions' in human participants—without any damage being done to tissue, brain regions can be briefly inactivated. This new technique enables researchers to address a range of questions that would not have been possible with nonhuman experiments. Consider an application of rTMS to study the brain bases of visual imagery.

Take a moment to fix your eyes on an object in your environment, perhaps a tree outside the nearest window. Now close your eyes and form a mental image of that same object. What happened in your brain during these two activities? How likely do you think it is that some of the same brain regions are involved in both real acts of perception and in visual imagination? To answer this question, researchers asked participants to memorise displays with four quadrants (see **Figure 3.11**) and then visualise the displays with their eyes closed (Kosslyn et al., 1999). The participants' task was to answer questions about, for example, the relative length or width of the stripes in the different quadrants. This task was designed so that participants were obliged to form visual images. The researchers then used rTMS to 'lesion' the parts of the brain participants use for ordinary vision (which we will discuss in Chapter 4). Just as in the cases in which participants made the quadrant comparisons with their eyes wide open, performance was consistently disrupted in circumstances of visual imagery. This finding strongly suggests that the same brain areas are at work when you look at a tree as when you form a visual image of a tree.

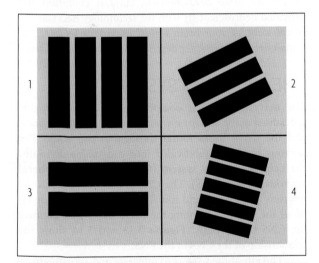

## Figure 3.11

### Test for visual imagery

Try to memorise this figure, quadrant by quadrant, until you can form a mental image of all four quadrants. Now cover the display with your hand. Answer this question by creating a mental visual image: Are the lines longer in quadrant 1 or quadrant 2? Confirm your answer by looking back at the figure.

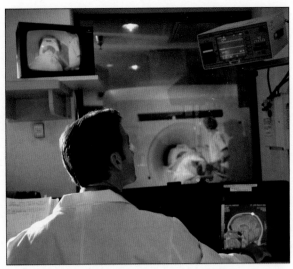

How have new imaging techniques expanded the range of questions researchers can ask?

**repetitive transcranial magnetic stimulation (rTMS)**
A technique for producing temporary inactivation of brain areas using repeated pulses of magnetic stimulation.

You can see why this experiment would not be possible with nonhuman participants: How could we be certain that a rat had formed a visual image? This study illustrates why an ability to create reversible 'lesions' has great potential for improving our understanding of how the brain functions.

On other occasions, neuroscientists learn about the function of brain regions by directly *stimulating* them. For example, in the mid-1950s, **Walter Hess** pioneered the use of electrical stimulation to probe structures deep in the brain. For example, Hess put electrodes into the brains of freely moving cats. By pressing a button, he could then send a small electrical current to the point of the electrode. Hess carefully recorded the behavioural consequences of stimulating each of 4,500 brain sites in nearly 500 cats. Hess discovered that, depending on the location of the electrode, sleep, sexual arousal, anxiety or terror could be provoked by the flick of the switch—and turned off just as abruptly. For example, electrical stimulation of certain regions of the brain led the otherwise gentle cats to bristle with rage and hurl themselves upon a nearby object.

**Recording and imaging brain activity** Other neuroscientists map brain function by using electrodes to record the electrical activity of the brain in response to environmental stimulation. The brain's electrical output can be monitored at different levels of precision. At the most specific, researchers can insert ultrasensitive microelectrodes into the brain to record the electrical activity of a single brain cell. Such recordings can illuminate changes in the activity of individual cells in response to stimuli in the environment.

For human subjects, researchers often place a number of electrodes on the surface of the scalp to record larger, integrated patterns of electrical activity. These electrodes provide the data for an **electroencephalogram (EEG)**, or an amplified tracing of the brain activity. EEGs can be used to study the relationship between psychological activities and brain response. For example, in one experiment,

**electroencephalogram (EEG)**
A recording of the electrical activity of the brain.

participants were asked to view a series of faces and make judgments about whether they thought they would be able to recognise each face in a later memory task. The EEGs revealed a distinctive pattern of brain activity, at the time the participants made their judgments, that predicted those instances in which the participants were, in fact, later able to recognise the faces (Sommer et al., 1995).

Some of the most exciting technological innovations for studying the brain are machines originally developed to help neurosurgeons detect brain abnormalities, such as damage caused by strokes or diseases. These devices produce images of the living brain without invasive procedures that risk damaging brain tissue.

In research with positron emission tomography, or **PET scans**, subjects are given different kinds of radioactive (but safe) substances that eventually travel to the brain, where they are taken up by active brain cells. Recording instruments outside the skull can detect the radioactivity emitted by cells that are active during different cognitive or behavioural activities. This information is then fed into a computer that constructs a dynamic portrait of the brain, showing where different types of psychological activities are actually occurring (see **Figure 3.12**).

**Magnetic resonance imaging**, or **MRI**, uses magnetic fields and radio waves to generate pulses of energy within the brain. As the pulse is tuned to different frequencies, some atoms line up with the magnetic field. When the magnetic pulse is turned off, the atoms vibrate (resonate) as they return to their original positions. Special radio receivers detect this resonance and channel information to a computer, which generates images of the locations of different atoms in areas of the brain. By looking at the image, researchers can link brain structures to psychological processes.

MRI is most useful for providing clear images of anatomical details; PET scans provide better information

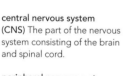

Magnetic resonance imaging (MRI) produces this colour-enhanced profile of a normal brain. What is the purpose of trying to identify brain regions that underlie particular functions?

about function. A newer technique called **functional MRI**, or **fMRI**, combines some of the benefits of both techniques by detecting magnetic changes in the flow of blood to cells in the brain; fMRI allows more precise claims about both structure and function. Researchers have begun to use fMRI to discover the distributions of brain regions responsible for many of your most important cognitive abilities, such as attention, perception, language processing and memory (Cabeza & Nyberg, 2000).

More than 300 years have passed since Descartes sat in his candlelit study and mused about the brain; over 100 years have passed since Broca discovered that brain regions seem to be linked to specific functions. In the time since these developments, cultural evolution has provided neuroscientists with the technology necessary to reveal some of your brain's most important secrets. The remainder of this chapter describes some of those secrets.

## THE NERVOUS SYSTEM

The nervous system is composed of billions of highly specialised nerve cells, or *neurons*, that constitute the brain and the nerve fibres found throughout the body. The nervous system is subdivided into two major divisions: the **central nervous system (CNS)** and the **peripheral nervous system (PNS)**. The CNS is composed of all the neurons in the brain and spinal cord; the PNS is made up of all the neurons forming the nerve fibres that connect the CNS to the body. **Figures 3.13** and **3.14** show the relationship of the CNS to the PNS.

The job of the CNS is to integrate and coordinate all bodily functions, process all incoming neural messages, and send out commands to different parts of the body. The CNS sends and receives neural messages through the *spinal cord,* a trunk line of neurons that connects the brain to the PNS. The trunk line itself is housed in a hollow portion of the vertebral column called the spinal column. Spinal nerves branch out from the spinal cord between each pair of vertebrae in the spinal column,

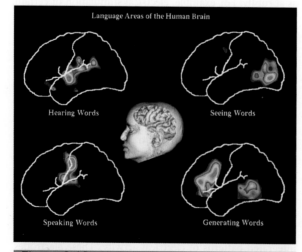

Figure 3.12

**PET scans of the brain at work**
These PET scans show that different tasks stimulate neural activity in distinct regions of the brain.

**PET scans** Brain images produced by a device that obtains detailed pictures of activity in the living brain by recording the radioactivity emitted by cells during different cognitive or behavioural activities.

**functional MRI (fMRI)** A brain-imaging technique that combines benefits of both MRI and PET scans by detecting magnetic changes in the flow of blood to cells in the brain.

**magnetic resonance imaging (MRI)** A technique for brain imaging that scans the brain using magnetic fields and radio waves.

**central nervous system (CNS)** The part of the nervous system consisting of the brain and spinal cord.

**peripheral nervous system (PNS)** The part of the nervous system composed of the spinal and cranial nerves that connect the body's sensory receptors to the CNS and the CNS to the muscles and glands.

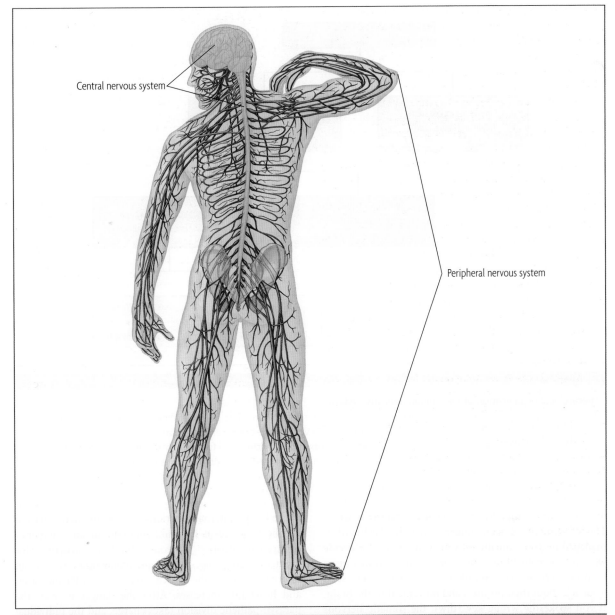

Central nervous system

Peripheral nervous system

**Figure 3.13**

**Divisions of the central and peripheral nervous systems**
The sensory and motor nerve fibres that constitute the peripheral nervous system are linked to the brain by the spinal cord.

From Richard D. McAnulty and M. Michele Burnette. *Fundamentals of Human Sexuality* p. 87. Published by Allyn and Bacon, Boston, MA. Copyright © 2003 by Pearson Education. Reprinted by permission of the publisher.

eventually connecting with sensory receptors throughout the body and with muscles and glands. The spinal cord coordinates the activity of the left and right sides of the body and is responsible for simple fast-action reflexes that do not involve the brain. For example, an organism whose spinal cord has been severed from its brain can still withdraw its limb from a painful stimulus. Although an intact brain would normally be notified of such action, the organism can complete the action without directions from above. Damage to the nerves of the spinal cord can result in paralysis of the legs or trunk, as seen in paraplegic individuals. The extent of paralysis depends on how high up on the spinal cord the damage occurred; higher damage produces greater paralysis.

Despite its commanding position, the CNS is isolated from any direct contact with the outside world. It is the role of the PNS to provide the CNS with information from sensory receptors, such as those found in the eyes and ears, and to relay commands from the brain to the body's organs and muscles. The PNS is actually composed of two sets of nerve fibres (see Figure 3.14). The **somatic nervous system** regulates the actions of the body's skeletal

**somatic nervous system** The subdivision of the peripheral nervous system that connects the central nervous system to the skeletal muscles and skin.

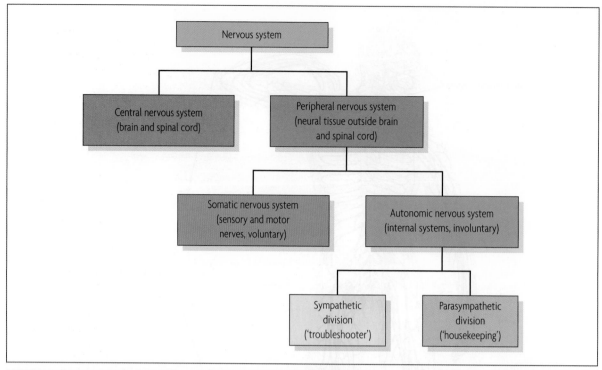

Figure 3.14

**Hierarchical organisation of the human nervous system**
The central nervous system is composed of the brain and the spinal cord. The peripheral nervous system is divided according to function: The somatic nervous system controls voluntary actions, and the autonomic nervous system regulates internal processes. The autonomic nervous system is subdivided into two systems: The sympathetic nervous system governs behaviour in emergency situations, and the parasympathetic nervous system regulates behaviour and internal processes in routine circumstances.

muscles. For example, imagine you are typing a letter. The movement of your fingers over the keyboard is managed by your somatic nervous system. As you decide what to say, your brain sends commands to your fingers to press certain keys. Simultaneously, the fingers send feedback about their position and movement to the brain. If you strike the wrong key (th**w**), the somatic nervous system informs the brain, which then issues the necessary correction, and, in a fraction of a second, you delete the mistake and hit the right key (th**e**).

The other branch of the PNS is the **autonomic nervous system (ANS)**, which sustains basic life processes. This system is on the job 24 hours a day, regulating bodily functions that you usually don't consciously control, such as respiration, digestion and arousal. The ANS must work even when you are asleep, and it sustains life processes during anaesthesia and prolonged coma states.

The autonomic nervous system deals with survival matters of two kinds: those involving threats to the organism and those involving bodily maintenance. To carry out these functions, the autonomic nervous system is further subdivided into the sympathetic and parasympathetic nervous systems (see Figure 3.14). These divisions work in opposition to accomplish their tasks. The **sympathetic division** governs responses to emergency situations; the **parasympathetic division** monitors the routine operation of the body's internal functions. The sympathetic division can be regarded as a troubleshooter—in an emergency or stressful situation, it arouses the brain structures for 'fight or flight.' Digestion stops, blood flows away from internal organs to the muscles, oxygen transfer increases, and heart rate increases. After the danger is over, the parasympathetic division takes charge, and the individual begins to calm down. Digestion resumes, heartbeat slows and breathing is relaxed. The parasympathetic division carries out the body's nonemergency housekeeping chores, such as elimination of bodily wastes, protection of the visual system (through tears and pupil constriction), and long-term conservation of body energy. The separate duties of the sympathetic and parasympathetic nervous systems are illustrated in **Figure 3.15**.

## BRAIN STRUCTURES AND THEIR FUNCTIONS

The brain is the most important component of your central nervous system. The brains of human beings have three interconnected layers. In the deepest recesses of the brain, in a region called the *brain stem*, are structures involved primarily with autonomic processes such as heart rate, breathing, swallowing and digestion. Enveloping this central core is the *limbic system*, which is involved with motivation,

**autonomic nervous system (ANS)** The subdivision of the peripheral nervous system that controls the body's involuntary motor responses.

**sympathetic division** The subdivision of the autonomic nervous system that deals with emergency response and the mobilisation of energy.

**parasympathetic division** The subdivision of the autonomic nervous system that monitors the routine operation of the body's internal functions and conserves and restores body energy.

**CHAPTER 3** THE BIOLOGICAL AND EVOLUTIONARY BASES OF BEHAVIOUR

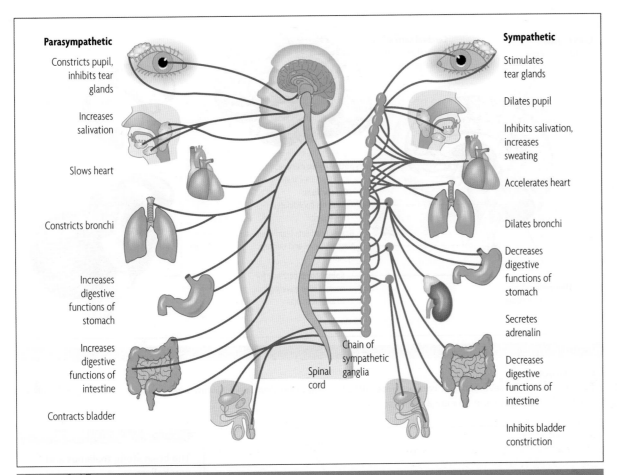

**Parasympathetic**

Constricts pupil, inhibits tear glands

Increases salivation

Slows heart

Constricts bronchi

Increases digestive functions of stomach

Increases digestive functions of intestine

Contracts bladder

**Sympathetic**

Stimulates tear glands

Dilates pupil

Inhibits salivation, increases sweating

Accelerates heart

Dilates bronchi

Decreases digestive functions of stomach

Secretes adrenalin

Decreases digestive functions of intestine

Inhibits bladder constriction

Spinal cord

Chain of sympathetic ganglia

**Figure 3.15**

**The autonomic nervous system**

The parasympathetic nervous system, which regulates day-to-day internal processes and behavior, is shown on the left. The sympathetic nervous system, which regulates internal processes and behaviour in stressful situations, is shown on the right. Note that on their way to and from the spinal cord, the nerve fibres of the sympathetic nervous system innervate, or make connections with, ganglia, which are specialised clusters of neuron chains.

emotion and memory processes. Wrapped around these two regions is the *cerebrum*. The universe of the human mind exists in this region. The cerebrum, and its surface layer, the *cerebral cortex*, integrates sensory information, coordinates your movements, and facilitates abstract thinking and reasoning (see **Figure 3.16**). Let's look more closely at the functions of the three major brain regions, beginning with the brain stem, thalamus, and cerebellum.

**The brain stem, thalamus and cerebellum**
The brain stem is found in all vertebrate species. It contains structures that collectively regulate the internal state of the body (see **Figure 3.17**). The **medulla**, located at the very top of the spinal cord, is the centre for breathing, blood pressure and the beating of the heart. Because these processes are essential for life, damage to the medulla can be fatal. Nerve fibres ascending from the body and descending from the brain cross over at the medulla, which means that the left side of the body is linked to the right side of the brain and the right side of the body is connected to the left side of the brain.

Directly above the medulla is the **pons**, which provides inputs to other structures in the brain stem and to the cerebellum (*pons* is the Latin word for *bridge*). The **reticular formation** is a dense network of nerve cells that serves as the brain's sentinel. It arouses the cerebral cortex to attend to new stimulation and keeps the brain alert even during sleep. Massive damage to this area often results in a coma.

The reticular formation has long tracts of fibres that run to the **thalamus**, which channels incoming sensory information to the appropriate area of the cerebral cortex, where that information is processed. For example, the thalamus relays information from the eyes to cortical areas for vision.

Neuroscientists have long known that the **cerebellum**, attached to the brain stem at the base of the skull, coordinates bodily movements, controls posture, and maintains equilibrium. Damage to the cerebellum interrupts the flow of otherwise smooth movement, causing it to appear uncoordinated and jerky. More recent research suggests that the cerebellum also plays an important role in the

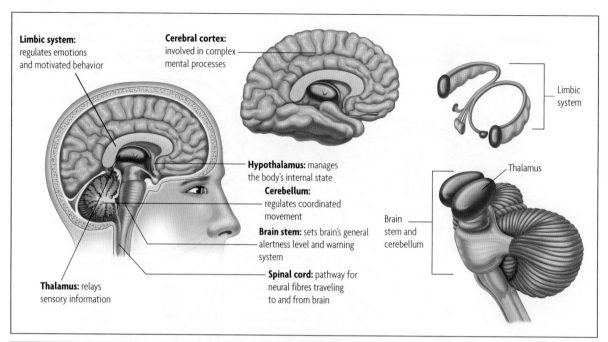

Limbic system: regulates emotions and motivated behavior

Cerebral cortex: involved in complex mental processes

Limbic system

Hypothalamus: manages the body's internal state

Cerebellum: regulates coordinated movement

Brain stem: sets brain's general alertness level and warning system

Spinal cord: pathway for neural fibres traveling to and from brain

Thalamus: relays sensory information

Thalamus

Brain stem and cerebellum

Figure 3.16

**Brain structures**
The brain contains several major components, including the brain stem, cerebellum, limbic system, and cerebral cortex, all of which fit together in an intricate design.

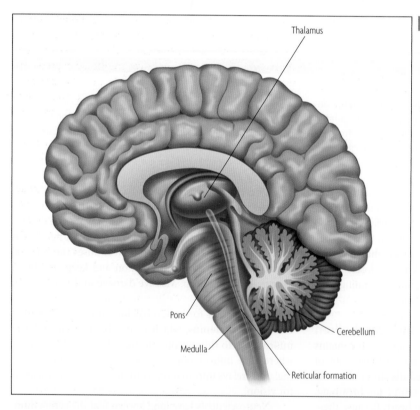

Thalamus

Pons

Medulla

Cerebellum

Reticular formation

Figure 3.17

**The brain stem, thalamus and cerebellum**
These structures are primarily involved in basic life processes: breathing, pulse, arousal, movement, balance, and simple processing of sensory information.

**limbic system** The region of the brain that regulates emotional behaviour, basic motivational urges and memory, as well as major physiological functions.

**hippocampus** The part of the limbic system that is involved in the acquisition of explicit memory.

ability to learn and perform sequences of body movements (Hazeltine & Ivry, 2002; Seidler et al., 2002).

**The limbic system** The **limbic system** mediates motivated behaviours, emotional states and memory processes. It also regulates body temperature, blood pressure and blood-sugar level and performs other housekeeping activities. The limbic system comprises three structures: the hippocampus, amygdala and hypothalamus (see **Figure 3.18**).

The **hippocampus**, which is the largest of the limbic system structures, plays an important role in the acquisition

**CHAPTER 3** THE BIOLOGICAL AND EVOLUTIONARY BASES OF BEHAVIOUR

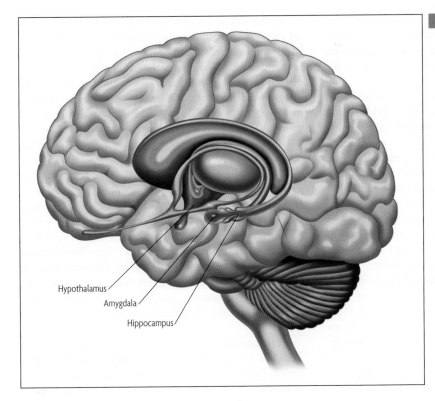

Figure 3.18

**The limbic system**
The structures of the limbic system, which are present only in mammals, are involved in motivated behaviour, emotional states and memory processes.

Hypothalamus

Amygdala

Hippocampus

of memories. Considerable clinical evidence supports this conclusion, including the notable studies of a patient, H.M., perhaps psychology's most famous subject.

> When he was 27, H.M. underwent surgery in an attempt to reduce the frequency and severity of his epileptic seizures. During the operation, parts of his hippocampus were removed. As a result, H.M. could recall only the very distant past; his ability to put new information into long-term memory was gone. Long after his surgery, he continued to believe he was living in 1953, which was the year the operation was performed.

Some types of new memories can still be formed after damage to the hippocampus, however. For example, H.M. was able to acquire new skills. This pattern suggests that if you were in an accident and sustained damage to your hippocampus, you would still be able to learn some new tasks, but you would not be able to remember having done so! As researchers have continued to focus attention on the hippocampus, they have come to a more detailed understanding of how even different regions of the structure play roles in the acquisition of different types of memories (Zeineh et al., 2003). In Chapter 7, we will return to the functions of the hippocampus for memory acquisition.

The **amygdala** plays a role in emotional control and the formation of emotional memories. Because of this control function, damage to areas of the amygdala may have a calming effect on otherwise mean-spirited individuals. (We discuss *psychosurgery* in Chapter 15.) However, damage to some areas of the amygdala also impairs the ability to recognise the emotional content of facial expressions (Adolphs et al., 1994). Those individuals who have suffered amygdala damage are most impaired with respect to negative emotional expressions, especially fear. Researchers speculate that the amygdala may play a special role in people's acquisition and use of knowledge related to threat and danger (Adolphs et al., 1999).

The **hypothalamus** is one of the smallest structures in the brain, yet it plays a vital role in many of your most important daily actions. It is actually composed of several nuclei, small bundles of neurons that regulate physiological processes involved in motivated behaviour (including eating, drinking, temperature regulation and sexual arousal). The hypothalamus maintains the body's internal equilibrium, or **homeostasis**. When the body's energy reserves are low, the hypothalamus is involved in stimulating the organism to find food and to eat. When body temperature drops, the hypothalamus causes blood-vessel constriction, or minute involuntary movements you commonly refer to as the 'shivers'. The hypothalamus also regulates the activities of the endocrine system.

**The cerebrum** In humans, the **cerebrum** dwarfs the rest of the brain, occupying two-thirds of its total mass. Its role is to regulate the brain's higher cognitive and emotional functions. The outer surface of the cerebrum, made up of billions of cells in a layer about a tenth of an inch thick, is called the **cerebral cortex**. The cerebrum is also divided into two almost symmetrical halves, the **cerebral hemispheres** (we discuss the two hemispheres

**hypothalamus** The brain structure that regulates motivated behaviour (such as eating and drinking) and homeostasis.

**homeostasis** Constancy or equilibrium of the internal conditions of the body.

**amygdala** The part of the limbic system that controls emotion, aggression and the formation of emotional memory.

**cerebrum** The region of the brain that regulates higher cognitive and emotional functions.

**cerebral cortex** The outer surface of the cerebrum.

**cerebral hemispheres** The two halves of the cerebrum, connected by the corpus callosum.

**corpus callosum** The mass of nerve fibres connecting the two hemispheres of the cerebrum.

**frontal lobe** Region of the brain located above the lateral fissure and in front of the central sulcus; involved in motor control and cognitive activities.

**parietal lobe** Region of the brain behind the frontal lobe and above the lateral fissure; contains somatosensory cortex.

**occipital lobe** Rearmost region of the brain; contains primary visual cortex.

**temporal lobe** Region of the brain found below the lateral fissure.

**motor cortex** The region of the cerebral cortex that controls the action of the body's voluntary muscles.

at length in a later section of this chapter). The two hemispheres are connected by a thick mass of nerve fibres, collectively referred to as the **corpus callosum**. This pathway sends messages back and forth between the hemispheres.

Neuroscientists have mapped each hemisphere, using two important landmarks as their guides. One groove, called the *central sulcus,* divides each hemisphere vertically, and a second similar groove, called the *lateral fissure,* divides each hemisphere horizontally (see **Figure 3.19**). These vertical and horizontal divisions help define four areas, or brain lobes, in each hemisphere. The **frontal lobe**, involved in motor control and cognitive activities, such as planning, making decisions and setting goals, is located above the lateral fissure and in front of the central sulcus. Accidents that damage the frontal lobes can have devastating effects on human action and personality. This was the location of the injury that brought about such a dramatic change in Phineas Gage (Damasio et al., 1994). The frontal lobe also includes *Broca's area,* the region of the brain that Paul Broca identified from his research on patients with language disorders.

The **parietal lobe**, responsible for sensations of touch, pain and temperature, is located directly behind the central sulcus. The **occipital lobe**, the final destination for visual information, is located at the back of the head. The **temporal lobe**, responsible for the processes of hearing, is found below the lateral fissure, on the sides of each cerebral hemisphere. The temporal lobe includes a region called *Wernicke's area.* In 1874, Carl Wernicke discovered that patients who had damage to this region showed a disruption of their language comprehension.

It would be misleading to say that any lobe alone controls any one specific function. The structures of the brain perform their duties in concert, working smoothly as an integrated unit, similar to a symphony orchestra. Whether you are doing the dishes, solving a calculus problem, or carrying on a conversation with a friend, your brain works as a unified whole, each lobe interacting and cooperating with the others. Nevertheless, neuroscientists can identify areas of the four lobes of the cerebrum that are necessary for specific functions, such as vision, hearing, language and memory. When they are damaged, their functions are disrupted or lost entirely.

The actions of the body's voluntary muscles, of which there are more than 600, are controlled by the **motor cortex**, located just in front of the central sulcus in the frontal lobes. Recall that commands from one side of

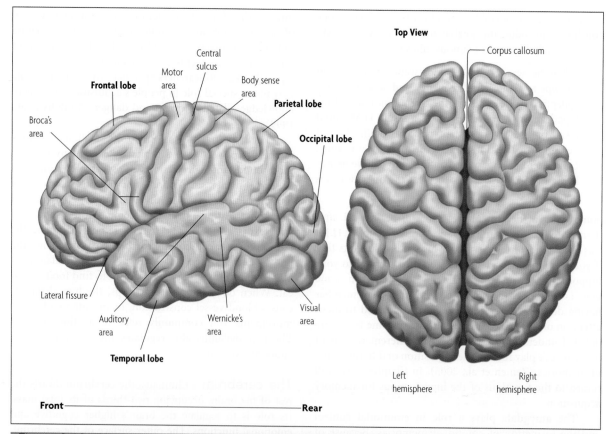

Figure 3.19

The cerebral cortex
Each of the two hemispheres of the cerebral cortex has four lobes. Different sensory and motor functions are associated with specific parts of each lobe.

the brain are directed to muscles on the opposite side of the body. Also, muscles in the lower part of the body—for example, the toes—are controlled by neurons in the top part of the motor cortex. Muscles in the upper part of the body, such as the throat, are controlled by neurons in the lower part of the motor cortex. As you can see in **Figure 3.20**, the upper parts of the body receive far more detailed motor instructions than the lower parts. In fact, the two largest areas of the motor cortex are devoted to the fingers—especially the thumb—and to the muscles involved in speech. Their greater brain area reflects the importance in human activity of manipulating objects, using tools, eating and talking.

The **somatosensory cortex** is located just behind the central sulcus in the left and right parietal lobes. This part of the cortex processes information about temperature, touch, body position and pain. Similar to the motor cortex, the upper part of the sensory cortex relates to the lower parts of the body, and the lower part to the upper parts of the body. Most of the area of the sensory cortex is devoted to the lips, tongue, thumb and index fingers—the parts of the body that provide the most important sensory input (see Figure 3.20). And like the motor cortex, the right half of the somatosensory cortex communicates with the left side of the body, and the left half communicates with the right side of the body.

Auditory information is processed in the **auditory cortex**, which is in the two temporal lobes. The auditory cortex in each hemisphere receives information from *both* ears. One area of the auditory cortex is involved in the

**auditory cortex** The area of the temporal lobes that receives and processes auditory information.

**somatosensory cortex** The region of the parietal lobes that processes sensory input from various body areas.

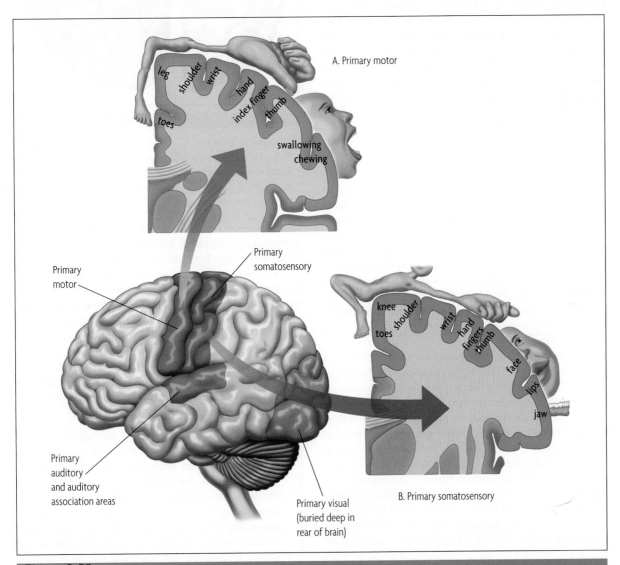

Figure 3.20

Motor and somatosensory cortex
Different parts of the body are more or less sensitive to environmental stimulation and brain control. Sensitivity in a particular region of the body is related to the amount of space in the cerebral cortex devoted to that region. In this figure, the body is drawn so that the size of body parts is relative to the cortical space devoted to them. The larger the body part in the drawing, the greater its sensitivity to environmental stimulation and the greater the brain's control over its movement.

production of language, and a different area is involved in language comprehension. Visual input is processed at the back of the brain in the **visual cortex**, located in the occipital lobes. Here the greatest area is devoted to input from the centre part of the retina, at the back of the eye, the area that transmits the most detailed visual information.

Not all of the cerebral cortex is devoted to processing sensory information and commanding the muscles to action. In fact, the majority of it is involved in *interpreting* and *integrating* information. Processes such as planning and decision making are believed to occur in the **association cortex**. Association areas are distributed to several areas of the cortex—one region is labelled in Figure 3.20. The association cortex allows you to combine information from various sensory modalities to plan appropriate responses to stimuli in the environment.

We have now reviewed the many important structures in your nervous system. When we began to talk about the cerebrum, we noted that each cerebral structure is represented in both hemispheres of your brain. However, the structures in those two hemispheres play somewhat different functions with respect to many types of behaviours. We turn now to those differences between your brain's two hemispheres.

## HEMISPHERIC LATERALISATION

What types of information originally led researchers to suspect that the functions of the brain's two hemispheres differed? Recall that when Paul Broca carried out his autopsy on Tan, he discovered damage in the left hemisphere. As he followed up this original discovery, Broca found that other patients who showed similar disruption of their language abilities—a pattern now known as *Broca's aphasia*—also had damage on the *left* side of their brains. Damage to the same areas on the *right* side of the brain did not have the same effect. What should one conclude?

The chance to investigate hemispheric differences first arose in the context of a treatment for severe epilepsy in which surgeons sever the corpus callosum—the bundle of about 200 million nerve fibres that transfers information back and forth between the two hemispheres (see **Figure 3.21**). The goal of this surgery is to prevent the violent electrical activity that accompanies epileptic seizures from crossing between the hemispheres. The operation is usually successful, and a patient's subsequent behaviour in most circumstances appears normal. Patients who undergo this type of surgery are often referred to as *split-brain* patients.

To test the capabilities of the separated hemispheres of epileptic patients, **Roger Sperry** (1968) and **Michael Gazzaniga** (1970) devised situations that could allow visual information to be presented separately to each hemisphere. Sperry and Gazzaniga's methodology relies on the anatomy of the visual system (see **Figure 3.22**). For each eye, information from the *right visual field* goes to the left hemisphere, and information from the *left visual field* goes to the right hemisphere. Ordinarily, information arriving from both hemispheres is shared very quickly across the corpus callosum. But because these pathways

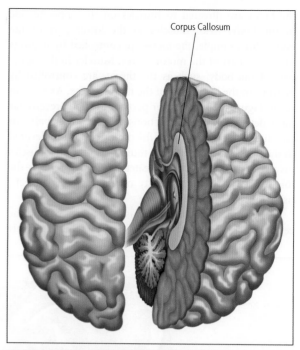

Corpus Callosum

**Figure 3.21**

**The corpus callosum**
The corpus callosum is a massive network of nerve fibres that channels information between the two hemispheres. Severing the corpus callosum impairs this communication process.

have been severed in split-brain patients, information presented to the right or left visual field may remain only in the left or right hemisphere (see **Figure 3.23**).

Because for most people speech is controlled by the left hemisphere, the left hemisphere could 'talk back' to the researchers whereas the right hemisphere could not. Communication with the right hemisphere was achieved by confronting it with manual tasks involving identification, matching or assembly of objects—tasks that did not require the use of words. Consider the following demonstration of a split-brain subject using his left half brain to account for the activity of his left hand, which was being guided by his right half brain.

A snow scene was presented to the right hemisphere and a picture of a chicken claw was simultaneously presented to the left hemisphere. The subject selected, from an array of objects, those that 'went with' each of the two scenes. With his right hand, the patient pointed to a chicken head; with his left hand, he pointed to a shovel. The patient reported that the shovel was needed to clean out the chicken shed (rather than to shovel snow). Because the left brain was not privy to what the right brain 'saw' because of the severed corpus callosum, it needed to explain why the left hand was pointing at a shovel when the only picture the left hemisphere was aware of seeing was a chicken claw. The left brain's cognitive system provided a theory to make sense of the behaviour of different parts of its body (Gazzaniga, 1985).

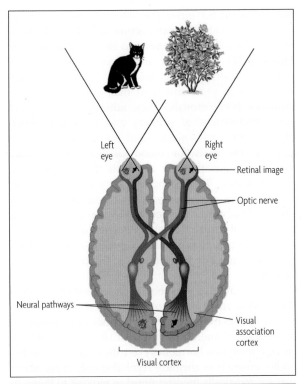

## Figure 3.22

**The neural pathways for visual information**
The neural pathways for visual information coming from the inside portions of each eye cross from one side of the brain to the other at the corpus callosum. The pathways carrying information from the outside portions of each eye do not cross over. Severing the corpus callosum prevents information selectively displayed in the right visual field from entering the right hemisphere, and left visual field information cannot enter the left hemisphere.

From a variety of research methods in addition to split-brain studies, we now know that, for most people, many language-related functions are *lateralised* to the left hemisphere. A function is considered lateralised when one cerebral hemisphere plays the primary role in accomplishing that function. Speech—the ability to produce coherent spoken language—is perhaps the most highly lateralised of all functions. Neuroscientists have found that only about 5 percent of right-handers and 15 percent of left-handers have speech controlled by the right hemisphere; another 15 percent of left-handers have speech processes occurring in both sides of the brain (Rasmussen & Milner, 1977). For most people, therefore, speech is a left-hemisphere function. As a consequence, damage to the left side of most people's brains can cause speech disorders. What is interesting is that for users of languages like American Sign Language—which use systems of intricate hand positions and movements to convey meaning—left-brain damage is similarly disruptive (Corina & McBurney, 2001; Hickok et al., 2002). What is lateralised, therefore, is not speech as such, but rather, the ability to produce the sequences of gestures—either vocal or manual—that encode communicative meaning.

You should not conclude that the right hemisphere therefore has no role in language at all. The right hemisphere does appear to be capable of producing simple, unsophisticated phrases. One of your authors was involved in postsurgical neuropsychological assessment of a patient who had had his corpus callosum resectioned to control intractable epilepsy. At one stage, the pen was placed in his left hand (under the control of the right hemisphere) and he was asked to write his name. He wrote the word 'name'. His right hemisphere 'knew' it was being asked a question and knew it had to produce a written response, but was unable to interpret the question completely, so wrote the

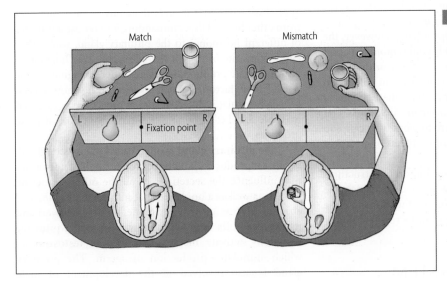

## Figure 3.23

**Coordination between eye and hand**
Coordination between eye and hand is normal if a split-brain patient uses the left hand to find and match an object that appears in the left visual field because both are registered in the right hemisphere. However, when asked to use the right hand to match an object seen in the left visual field, the patient cannot do so because sensory messages from the right hand are going to the left cerebral hemisphere, and there is no longer a connection between the two hemispheres. Here the cup is misperceived as matching the pear.

How have studies with individuals who use sign language influenced researchers' beliefs about the lateralisation of brain function?

last word of the question. Of course, on another occasion with the pen in his right hand, he wrote his name normally in response to the same question. The right hemisphere also has an important role in processing the emotional tone, rather than the literal meaning, of language and in some aspects of reading.

As well as differing in the information that they process, the hemispheres differ in *how* they understand the material that they are processing. The left hemisphere tends to be more *analytical:* It processes information bit by bit. This may explain the left hemisphere's dominance for language. The only way to distinguish between the words 'top' and 'pot' is to keep an accurate record of the *order* in which the sounds come in. The right hemisphere tends to be more *holistic:* it processes information with respect to global patterns. It is the combined action of the right and left hemispheres—each with its particular processing style—that gives fullness to your experiences. For example, you wouldn't be surprised to learn that the left hemisphere, with its attention to fine detail, plays a key role in most forms of problem solving. However, the function of the right hemisphere becomes more apparent when problems require creative solutions or bursts of insight—the right hemisphere helps problem solvers do the broader searches of memory that these types of problems require (Bowden & Beeman, 1998). (If you want to put your right hemisphere to work, you can skip ahead to try some of these types of problems on p. 268 in Chapter 8.)

We have reviewed the many important structures of your nervous system. Now we will consider the endocrine system, a bodily system that functions in close cooperation with the nervous system to regulate bodily functions.

## THE ENDOCRINE SYSTEM

The human genotype specifies a second highly complex regulatory system, the **endocrine system**, to supplement the work of the nervous system. The endocrine system is a network of glands that manufacture and secrete chemical messengers called **hormones** into the bloodstream (see **Figure 3.24**). Hormones are important in everyday functioning, although they are more vital at some stages of life and in some situations than others. Hormones influence body growth. They initiate, maintain and stop development of primary and secondary sexual characteristics; influence levels of arousal and awareness; serve as the basis for mood changes; and regulate metabolism, i.e. the rate at which the body uses its energy stores. The endocrine system promotes the survival of an *organism* by helping fight infections and disease. It advances the survival of the *species* through regulation of sexual arousal, production of reproductive cells and production of milk in nursing mothers. Thus you could not survive without an effective endocrine system.

Endocrine glands respond to the levels of chemicals in the bloodstream or are stimulated by other hormones or by nerve impulses from the brain. Hormones are then secreted into the blood and travel to distant target cells that have specific receptors; hormones exert their influence on the body's program of chemical regulation only at the places that are genetically predetermined to respond to them. In influencing diverse, but specific, target organs or tissue, hormones regulate an enormous range of biochemical processes. This multiple-action communication system allows for control of slow continuous processes such as maintenance of blood-sugar levels and calcium levels, metabolism of carbohydrates, and general body growth. But what happens during crises? The endocrine system also releases the hormone adrenaline into the bloodstream; adrenaline energises your body so that you can respond quickly to challenges.

As we mentioned earlier, the brain structure known as the *hypothalamus* serves as a relay station between the endocrine system and the central nervous system. Specialised cells in the hypothalamus receive messages from other brain cells, commanding it to release a number of different hormones to the pituitary gland, where they either stimulate or inhibit the release of other hormones. Hormones are produced in several different regions of the body. These 'factories' make a variety of hormones, each of which regulates different bodily processes, as outlined in **Table 3.1**. Let's examine the most significant of these processes.

The **pituitary gland** is often called the master gland, because it produces about ten different kinds of hormones that influence the secretions of all the other endocrine glands, as well as a hormone that influences growth. The absence of this growth hormone results in dwarfism; its excess results in gigantic growth. In males, pituitary secretions activate the testes to secrete **testosterone**, which stimulates production of sperm. The pituitary gland is also involved in the development of male secondary sexual characteristics, such as facial hair, voice change and physical maturation. Testosterone may even increase aggression and sexual desire. In females, a

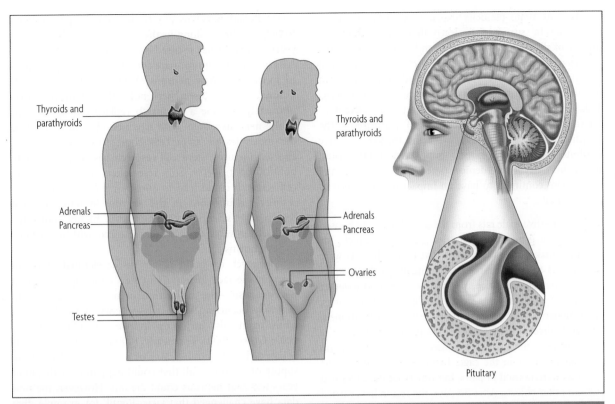

**Figure 3.24**

Endocrine glands in males and females
The pituitary gland is shown at the far right; it is the master gland that regulates the glands shown at the left. The pituitary gland is under the control of the hypothalamus, an important structure in the limbic system.

**Table 3.1**

Major endocrine glands and the functions of the hormones they produce

| These glands: | Produce hormones that regulate: |
|---|---|
| Hypothalamus | Release of pituitary hormones |
| Anterior pituitary | Testes and ovaries |
| | Breast milk production |
| | Metabolism |
| | Reactions to stress |
| Posterior pituitary | Water conservation |
| | Breast milk excretion |
| | Uterus contraction |
| Thyroid | Metabolism |
| | Growth and development |
| Parathyroid | Calcium levels |
| Gut | Digestion |
| Pancreas | Glucose metabolism |
| Adrenals | Fight-or-flight responses |
| | Metabolism |
| | Sexual desire in women |
| Ovaries | Development of female sexual traits |
| | Ova production |
| Testes | Development of male sexual traits |
| | Sperm production |
| | Sexual desire in men |

pituitary hormone stimulates production of **oestrogen**, which is essential to the hormonal chain reaction that triggers the release of ova from a woman's ovaries, making her fertile. Certain birth control pills work by blocking the mechanism in the pituitary gland that controls this hormone flow, thus preventing the ova from being released.

## PLASTICITY AND NEUROGENESIS: OUR CHANGING BRAINS

You now have a good basic idea of your nervous system at work: at all times, millions of neurons are communicating to do the essential work of your body and mind. What makes the brain even more interesting, however, is one consequence of all that neural communication: The brain itself changes over time. Do you want to take a moment to change your brain? Go back a few pages and memorise the definition of *action potential*. If you are successful at learning that definition—or any other new information—you will have brought about a modification of your brain. Researchers refer to changes in the performance of the brain as **plasticity**. A good deal of research in neuroscience focuses on the physical bases for plasticity. For example, researchers examine how learning arises from the formation of new synapses or from changes in communication across existing synapses (Baudry et al., 1999).

**oestrogen** The female sex hormone, produced by the ovaries, that is responsible for the release of eggs from the ovaries and for the development and maintenance of female reproductive structures and secondary sex characteristics.

**plasticity** Changes in the performance of the brain; may involve the creation of new synapses or changes in the function of existing synapses.

Because brain plasticity depends on life experiences, you won't be surprised to learn that brains show the impact of different environments and activities. One line of research, pioneered by **Mark Rosenzweig**, demonstrated the consequences for rats of being raised in impoverished or enriched environments (for reviews, see Rosenzweig, 1996, 1999). Early research demonstrated an advantage for young animals: the average cortex of rats reared in the enriched environments was heavier and thicker—positive attributes—than that of their impoverished littermates. Researchers have now demonstrated that environmental enrichment continues to have an impact on the brains of adult animals.

> Twenty-five male rats from the same litter were housed in small groups for their first 120 days—which, for rats, makes them adults. At that point, the rats were moved to one of three environments. In the *complex environment condition,* the rats were housed together in a cage 'filled with a variety of objects such as swings, wooden blocks, plastic cars and trucks, plastic tunnels, and mirrors' (Briones et al., 2004, p. 131). In the *inactive condition,* the rats were housed individually with no other objects in the cage. In the *social condition,* the rats were housed in pairs, but otherwise the cages had no other objects. After 30 days, the researchers carried out analyses to determine the environments' impact on neurons in visual cortex. Those analyses demonstrated that the complex environment rats had 21 percent more synapses for each neuron than the social rats; they had 27 percent more synapses for each neuron than the isolated rats. These results confirm that enriched environments continue to bring about changes in the brains of adult rats.

With brain-imaging techniques, it is possible to measure very specific brain differences related to individuals' life experiences. Consider those musicians who play the violin. They are required to control the fingers of their left hands with an extremely delicate touch. If you refer back to Figure 3.20, you'll see that a good deal of sensory cortex is devoted to the fingers. Brain scans reveal that the representation of fingers of the left hand is even more enhanced for violin players, as compared to nonplayers (Elbert et al., 1995). No such increase is found for fingers of the right hand, which do not have as great a sensory role in violin playing. The extra representation of the left fingers was greatest for violinists who took up the instrument before age 12.

One important aspect of research on plasticity concerns circumstances in which humans or animals have sustained injuries to the brain or spinal cord through strokes, degenerative diseases or accidents. A good deal of clinical evidence confirms that the brain is sometimes able to heal itself. For example, patients who suffer from strokes that cause disruptions in language often recover over time. In some instances, the damaged brain areas themselves have enough lingering function that recovery is possible; in other cases other brain areas take over the functions of those that were damaged (Kuest & Karbe,

2002). Researchers have also begun to develop techniques to help the brain along in the healing process. In recent years, attention has focused on *stem cells*—unspecialised cells that, under appropriate conditions, can be prompted to function as new neurons (Kintner, 2002; Wilson & Edlund, 2001). Researchers hope that stem cells may ultimately provide a means to replace damaged tissue in the nervous system with new neural growth. Because the most flexible stem cells come from embryos and aborted foetuses, stem cell research has been subject to political controversy. Still, researchers believe that stem cell research could lead to cures for paralysis and other serious malfunctions in the nervous system. For that reason, the scientific community is highly motivated to discover ways to continue research within accepted societal norms.

Research on brain repair has accelerated in recent years in the face of important new data suggesting that **neurogenesis**—the production of new brain cells from naturally occurring stem cells—occurs in the brains of adult mammals, including humans (Gould & Gross, 2002; Gross, 2000). For nearly 100 years, neuroscientists believed that the adult brains of mammals had their full supply of neurons—all that could happen over the adult years was that neurons could die out. However, the new data have challenged that view. Recall, for example, that we identified the hippocampus as an important structure for the formation of certain types of memories. Now that researchers have documented neurogenesis in the adult hippocampus, they are trying to understand the role newly born neurons play in allowing memories to remain accessible over time (Kempermann, 2002).

In this chapter, we have taken a brief peek at the marvellous kilo-and-a-half universe that is your brain. It is one thing to recognise that the brain controls behaviour and your mental processes but quite another to understand how the brain serves all those functions. Neuroscientists are engaged in the fascinating quest to understand the interplay among brain, behaviour and environment. You now have the type of background that will allow you to appreciate new knowledge as it unfolds.

**neurogenesis** The creation of new neurons.

## RECAP CHECKPOINT
### Biology and behaviour

- Neuroscientists use several methods to research the relation between brain and behaviour: studying brain-damaged patients, producing lesions at specific brain sites, electrically stimulating the brain, recording brain activity, and imaging the brain with computerised devices.

- The brain and the spinal cord make up the central nervous system (CNS).

- The peripheral nervous system (PNS) is composed of all neurons connecting the CNS to the body. The PNS consists of the somatic nervous system, which regulates the body's skeletal muscles, and the autonomic nervous system (ANS), which regulates life-support processes.
- The brain consists of three integrated layers: the brain stem, limbic system and cerebrum.
- The brain stem is responsible for breathing, digestion, and heart rate.
- The limbic system is involved in long-term memory, aggression, eating, drinking and sexual behaviour.
- The cerebrum controls higher mental functions.
- Some functions are lateralised to one hemisphere of the brain. For example, most individuals have speech localised in the left hemisphere.
- Although the two hemispheres of the brain work smoothly in concert, they typically embody different styles of processing: The left hemisphere is more analytic; the right hemisphere is more holistic.

- The endocrine system produces and secretes hormones into the bloodstream.
- Hormones help regulate growth, primary and secondary sexual characteristics, metabolism, digestion and arousal.
- New cell growth and life experiences reshape the brain after birth.

## CONCEPT QUESTIONS

1. What are the advantages of fMRI over other brain-imaging techniques?
2. What are the two major divisions of the autonomic nervous system?
3. What are some of the major functions of the amygdala?
4. What processing styles are reflected by the two hemispheres of the brain?
5. Why is the pituitary gland often called the master gland?
6. What is neurogenesis?

## CRITICAL THINKING

Consider the study on plasticity in adult rats. Why did the researchers use both the inactive and social controls?

For answers go to MyPsychLab!

mypsych lab
where learning comes to life!

# PSYCHOLOGY *in your life*

## WHY DOES MUSIC HAVE AN IMPACT ON HOW YOU FEEL?

Suppose you're sitting in a movie theatre watching a comedy. It's likely that the soundtrack will feature music that's upbeat and lively—music you might describe as 'happy.' In Theatre 2, a dramatic movie features 'sad' music. The horror flick in Theatre 3 uses music to try to build up feelings of fear. Does music really have an impact on your emotions? Researchers have turned to the brain to address this question.

As we will see in Chapter 12, solid advances have been made in understanding the relationship between brain states and the emotions you experience. That work provides a context for examining the impact of music in the brain. We know, for example, that pleasant and unpleasant images cause different patterns of brain activity (Davidson et al., 2000a). When you view pleasant stimuli, your brain produces relatively more activity in the prefrontal cortex (the forward region of your frontal lobes) of your left hemisphere; unpleasant stimuli produce relatively more activity in the same region of your right hemisphere.

Does music yield the same pattern? To find out, researchers gathered EEG recordings from students while they listened to pleasant (joyful or happy) music

and unpleasant (fearful and sad) music (Schmidt & Trainor, 2001). The musical passages produced the same asymmetries in brain activity found for other types of stimuli. These results suggest that, for example, happy music makes you feel happy because it involves the same brain regions as other experiences that evoke happy feelings.

But what components of music make it seem happy or sad? One important difference is *tempo*: On the whole, faster music strikes people as happier than slower music. To determine how the brain responds to tempo differences, researchers once again recorded EEGs while students listened to music. In this case, the musical passages were relatively fast or relatively slow (Tsang et al., 2001). Once again the brain revealed an asymmetry in activation. Parallel to the earlier results, 'happier' tempos produced relatively more activity in the left frontal cortex, whereas 'sadder' tempos produced relatively more activity on the right side of the brain.

Let's consider one more aspect of emotion and music. Have you ever had the experience of listening to music so pleasurable, it gives you 'chills'? To study this phenomenon, researchers invited ten students to bring

their own chill-inducing music to the laboratory (Blood & Zatorre, 2001). While the students listened to their personal favourites and neutral musical passages, the researchers monitored both physiological arousal (e.g., heart rate and respiration) as well as brain activity (using PET scans). The physiological data verified the reality of the chills. The students experienced increased heart and respiration rates when listening to their favourite music with respect to neutral music. The PET scans revealed that the chills were accompanied by increased brain activity in regions that signal pleasurable emotional arousal— the more intense the chills, the more these regions became active. The researchers explained the importance of these results: 'Music recruits neural systems of reward and emotion similar to those known to respond specifically to biologically relevant stimuli, such as food and sex, and those that are artificially activated by drugs of abuse. This is quite remarkable, because music is neither strictly necessary for biological survival or reproduction, nor is it a pharmacological substance' (p. 11823).

Next time music sends shivers down your spine, think about exactly how your brain is being engaged.

# SUMMARY

This chapter has explored the ralationship between biology and psychology. In order to fully understand psychology, it is important to understand the biological principles that underpin psychological processes. We have discussed how you are the product of both your genetic legacy and your learning experiences, and tracked the function of your nervous system from the level of an action potential along a single nerve to the complex functions of your two hemispheres.

# KEY TERMS

action potential (p. 64)
all-or-none law (p. 65)
amygdala (p. 77)
association cortex (p. 80)
auditory cortex (p. 79)
autonomic nervous system (ANS) (p. 74)
axon (p. 62)
brain stem (p. 75)
Broca's area (p. 69)
central nervous system (CNS) (p. 72)
cerebellum (p. 75)
cerebral cortex (p. 77)
cerebral hemispheres (p. 77)
cerebrum (p. 77)
corpus callosum (p. 78)
dendrites (p. 62)
DNA (deoxyribonucleic acid) (p. 58)
electroencephalogram (EEG) (p. 71)
endocrine system (p. 82)
evolutionary psychology (p. 61)
excitatory inputs (p. 64)
frontal lobe (p. 78)
functional MRI (fMRI) (p. 72)
genes (p. 58)
genetics (p. 58)
genome (p. 59)
genotype (p. 56)

glia (p. 63)
heredity (p. 58)
heritability (p. 59)
hippocampus (p. 76)
homeostasis (p. 77)
hormones (p. 82)
human behaviour genetics (p. 59)
hypothalamus (p. 77)
inhibitory inputs (p. 64)
interneurons (p. 62)
ion channels (p. 64)
lesions (p. 70)
limbic system (p. 76)
magnetic resonance imaging (MRI) (p. 72)
medulla (p. 75)
motor cortex (p. 78)
motor neurons (p. 62)
natural selection (p. 55)
neurogenesis (p. 84)
neuromodulator (p. 68)
neuron (p. 61)
neuroscience (p. 61)
neurotransmitters (p. 66)
occipital lobe (p. 78)
oestrogen (p. 83)
parasympathetic division (p. 74)

parietal lobe (p. 78)
peripheral nervous system (PNS) (p. 72)
PET scans (p. 72)
phenotype (p. 56)
pituitary gland (p. 82)
plasticity (p. 83)
pons (p. 75)
refractory period (p. 65)
repetitive transcranial magnetic stimulation (rTMS) (p. 71)
resting potential (p. 64)
reticular formation (p. 75)
sensory neurons (p. 62)
sex chromosomes (p. 59)
sociobiology (p. 61)
soma (p. 62)
somatic nervous system (p. 73)
somatosensory cortex (p. 79)
sympathetic division (p. 74)
synapse (p. 65)
synaptic transmission (p. 66)
temporal lobe (p. 78)
terminal buttons (p. 62)
testosterone (p. 82)
thalamus (p. 75)
visual cortex (p. 80)

# PRACTICE TEST

1. When Peter and Rosemary Grant studied several species of Darwin's finches, they discovered that major climate changes affected which populations of finches survived. This is an example of
   a. heritability.
   c. natural selection.
   b. the all-or-none law.
   d. nature versus nurture.

2. Sharon is involved in a project in which she observes the behaviours of young children. She is most able to directly observe their
   a. genotypes.
   c. chromosomes.
   b. phenotypes.
   d. DNA.

3. Suppose you carried out a study to assess whether there is a genetic component to 'sense of humour'. To conclude that genetics plays a role, you would want to find that
   a. DZ twins are more similar in their sense of humour than MZ twins.
   b. DZ twins always have better senses of humour than MZ twins.
   c. MZ twins always have better senses of humour than DZ twins.
   d. MZ twins are more similar in their sense of humour than DZ twins.

4. One of the jobs of_____ is to receive stimulation from other neurons.
   a. axons
   c. synapses
   b. terminal buttons
   d. dendrites

5. After Jonas withdraws money from the bank, he has to wait 2 minutes before his card will work again. This sounds a lot like the _____ in neural transmission.
   a. all-or-none law
   c. refractory period
   b. action potential
   d. ion channels

6. Wilma is creating an illustration of neural transmission. She leaves a small gap between a terminal button on one neuron and the dendrite of the next. She should label that gap the
   a. ion channel.
   c. node of Ranvier.
   b. glia.
   d. synapse.

7. Bea has decided to undergo an acupuncture treatment to help her with her back pain. You explain that researchers believe that acupuncture leads to the release of_____ in the brain.
   a. GABA
   c. endorphins
   b. acetylcholine
   d. dopamine

8. Suppose you want to understand the genetics of impulsivity. You might concentrate your research on variations in genes that affect the brain's use of
   a. glia.
   c. GABA.
   b. dopamine.
   d. ion channels.

9. Which technique allows researchers to create reversible 'lesions'?
   a. fMRI
   c. PET scans
   b. rTMS
   d. EEG

10. The _____ nervous system processes incoming neural messages and sends commands to different parts of the body.
    a. central
    c. somatic
    b. autonomic
    d. peripheral

11. After he experienced damage to his _____, H.M. had difficulties acquiring new information.
    a. reticular formation
    c. hippocampus
    b. thalamus
    d. Broca's area

12. As you are chatting with Tejus, you noticed that she is right-handed. You think that it's most likely that her ability to produce speech is controlled by
    a. her left hemisphere.
    b. her right hemisphere.
    c. both the left and right hemispheres.
    d. neither the left nor the right hemisphere.

13. Which brain structure serves as a relay station between the brain and the endocrine system?
    a. The hippocampus
    c. The pons
    b. The hypothalamus
    d. The amygdala

14. Brain-imaging techniques reveal that the brain representation of the fingers of the left hand is enhanced for people who play the violin versus nonplayers. This result provides an example of
    a. neurogenesis.
    c. lateralisation.
    b. heritability.
    d. brain plasticity.

15. When people listen to _____ music, they are likely to experience relatively more activity in the _____ hemispheres of their brains.
    a. happy; left
    c. sad; left
    b. happy; right
    d. upbeat tempo; right

## Essay questions

1. What important contrasts exist between research in human behaviour genetics and research in evolutionary psychology?

2. Why does a neuron's behaviour depend on the balance of excitatory and inhibitory inputs it receives?

3. Why are the two hemispheres of the brain often characterised as having distinctive processing styles?

# WEB LINKS

http://www.genetics.com.au
   [Australian] Centre for Genetics Education

http://www.genome.gov
   The Human Genome Project

Are you ready for the test? MyPsychLab offers dozens of ways to deepen your understanding and test your recall of the material in this chapter—including video and audio clips, simulations and activities, self-assessments, practice tests and other study materials. Specific resources available for this chapter include:

Heritable information: DNA
Neuronal transmission

How the human genome map
   affects you
Twin studies
Brain imaging
The forebrain
The hindbrain
The midbrain

Split brain

To access MyPsychLab, please visit **www.pearsoned.com.au/mypsychlab**

# Can you think of the answers?

## NOW YOU HAVE READ CHAPTER 3—ARE YOU PREPARED FOR THE EXAM?

To enhance your understanding of any of the material in your *Psychology and Life* textbook, go to **MyPsychLab: www.pearsoned.com.au/ mypsychlab**.

Complete pre- and post-tests, create your own individualised study plan, watch videos and animations and listen to audio glossaries, all of which will help you understand the themes of this chapter.

- Heredity and behaviour
- The nervous system in action
- Biology and behaviour

Read articles from *The New York Times* about Israeli Prime Minister Ariel Sharon's stroke, and the potential contribution made by poorly prescribed drugs

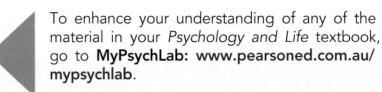

'MyPsychLab was a fantastic asset in preparing for exams.'

EXPLORE
neural transmissions!

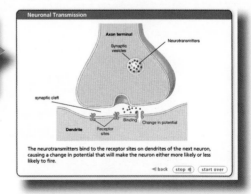

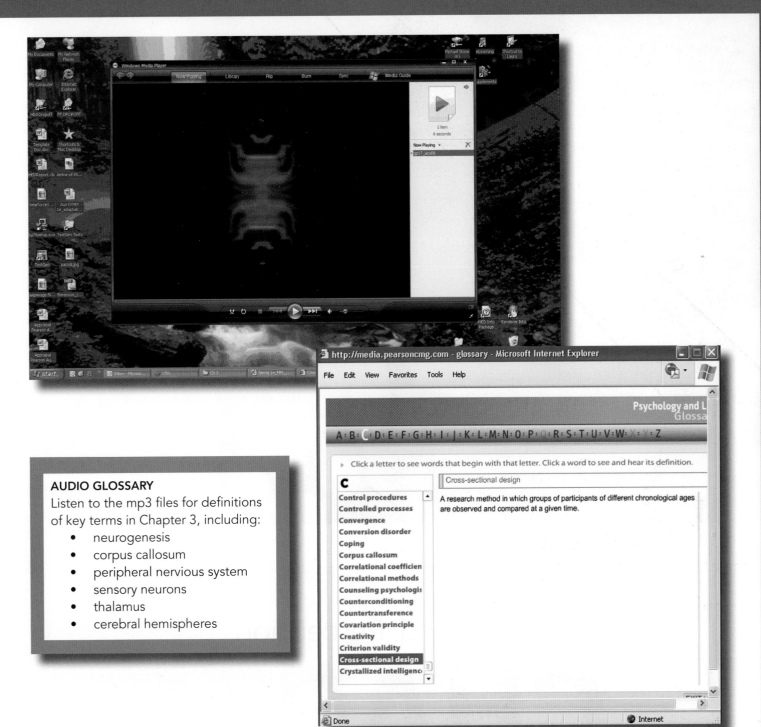

**AUDIO GLOSSARY**

Listen to the mp3 files for definitions of key terms in Chapter 3, including:
- neurogenesis
- corpus callosum
- peripheral nervous system
- sensory neurons
- thalamus
- cerebral hemispheres

**What can you find in MyPsychLab?**

Self-directed tests * Videos * Simulations * eBook * Biographies * Audio glossary * Web links … and more—organised by chapter, section and learning objective.

Sensation and Perception

CHAPTER

4

# CHAPTER FOCUS POINTS

After studying this chapter you will have a better understanding of:

1. The three stages of perception

2. The process of translating physical energy into neural signals

3. The structure of the eye and how we 'see' colour

4. Auditory structures and the psychological dimensions of sound

5. The interaction and function of tastes and smells

6. The functions of touch, vestibular and kinaesthetic systems

7. The active and changeable nature of perception

8. The principles by which we organise and interpret sensations

## CHAPTER CONTENTS

Have you ever wondered how your brain—locked in the dark, silent chamber of the skull—experiences the blaze of colour in a van Gogh painting, the driving melodies and rhythms of rock 'n' roll, the refreshing taste of watermelon on a hot day, the soft touch of a child's kiss, or the fragrance of wildflowers in the springtime? Our task in this chapter is to explain how your body and brain make sense of the buzz of stimulation—sights, sounds, and so on—constantly around you. You will see how evolution has equipped you with the capability to detect many different dimensions of experience.

In this chapter, we will describe how your experience of the world relies on processes of *sensation* and *perception*. We will discover that these processes serve the dual functions of *survival* and *sensuality*. Your sensory and perceptual processes help you survive by sounding alarms of danger, priming you to take swift action to ward off hazards, and directing you toward agreeable experiences. These processes also provide you with sensuality. Sensuality is the quality of being devoted to the gratification of the senses; it entails enjoying the experiences that appeal to your various senses of sight, sound, touch, taste and smell.

We begin with an overview of sensory and perceptual processes—and some challenges the physical world provides to them.

What senses are involved in the enjoyment of a slice of watermelon?

## SENSING, ORGANISING, IDENTIFYING AND RECOGNISING

The term **perception,** in its broad usage, refers to the overall process of apprehending objects and events in the environment—to sense them, understand them, identify and label them, and prepare to react to them. A *percept* is what is perceived—the phenomenological, or experienced, outcome of the process of perception. The process of perception is best understood when we divide it into three stages: sensation, perceptual organisation and identification/recognition of objects.

**Sensation** is the process by which stimulation of *sensory receptors*—the structures in our eyes, ears, and so on—produces neural impulses that represent experiences inside or outside the body. For example, sensation provides the basic facts of the visual field. Nerve cells in your eye pass information along to cells in your brain's cortex, which extract preliminary features from this input.

**Perceptual organisation** refers to the stage in which an internal representation of an object is formed and a percept of the external stimulus is developed. The representation provides a working description of the perceiver's external environment. With respect to vision, perceptual processes provide estimates of an object's likely size, shape, movement, distance and orientation. Those estimates are based on mental computations that integrate your past knowledge with the present evidence received from your senses and with the stimulus within its perceptual context. Perception involves *synthesis* (integration and combination) of simple sensory features, such as colours, edges and lines, into the percept of an object that can be recognised later. These mental activities most often occur swiftly and efficiently, without conscious awareness.

**Identification and recognition**, the third stage in this sequence, assigns meaning to percepts. Circular objects 'become' baseballs, coins, clocks, oranges and moons; people may be identified as male or female, friend or foe, relative or rock star. At this stage, the perceptual question 'What does the object look like?' changes to a question of identification—'What is this object?'—and to a question of recognition—'What is the object's function?' To identify and recognise what something is, what it is called, and how best to respond to it involves higher-level cognitive processes, which include your theories, memories, values, beliefs and attitudes concerning the object.

We have briefly introduced the stages of processing that enable you to arrive at a meaningful understanding of the perceptual world around you. In everyday life, perception seems to be entirely effortless. We will try to convince you that you actually do quite a bit of sophisticated processing, a lot of mental work, to arrive at this 'illusion of ease'.

**perception** The processes that organise information in the sensory image and interpret it as having been produced by properties of objects or events in the external, three-dimensional world.

**sensation** The process by which stimulation of a sensory receptor gives rise to neutral impulses that result in an experience or awareness of conditions inside or outside the body.

**perceptual organisation** The processes that put sensory information together to give the perception of a coherent scene over the whole visual field.

**identification and recognition** Two ways of attaching meaning to percepts.

# THE PROXIMAL AND DISTAL STIMULI

Imagine you are the person in Figure 4.1A, surveying a room from an easy chair. Some of the light reflected from the objects in the room enters your eyes and forms images on your retinas. Figure 4.1B shows what would appear to your left eye as you sit in the room. (The bump on the right is your nose, and the hand and knee at the bottom are your own.) How does this retinal image compare with the environment that produced it?

One very important difference is that the retinal image is *two dimensional*, whereas the environment is *three dimensional*. This difference has many consequences. For instance, compare the shapes of the physical objects in Figure 4.1A with the shapes of their corresponding retinal images (**Figure 4.1C**). The table, rug, window and picture in the real-world scene are all rectangular, but only the image of the window actually produces a rectangle in your retinal image. The image of the picture is a trapezoid, the image of the tabletop is an irregular four-sided figure, and the image of the rug is actually three separate regions with more than 20 different sides! Here's our first perceptual puzzle: How do you manage to perceive all of these objects as simple standard rectangles?

The situation, however, is even a bit more complicated. You can also notice that many parts of what you perceive in the room are not actually present in your retinal image. For instance, you perceive the vertical edge between the two walls as going all the way to the floor, but your retinal image of that edge stops at the tabletop. Similarly, in your retinal image parts of the rug are hidden behind the table; yet this does not keep you from correctly perceiving the rug as a single unbroken rectangle. In fact, when you

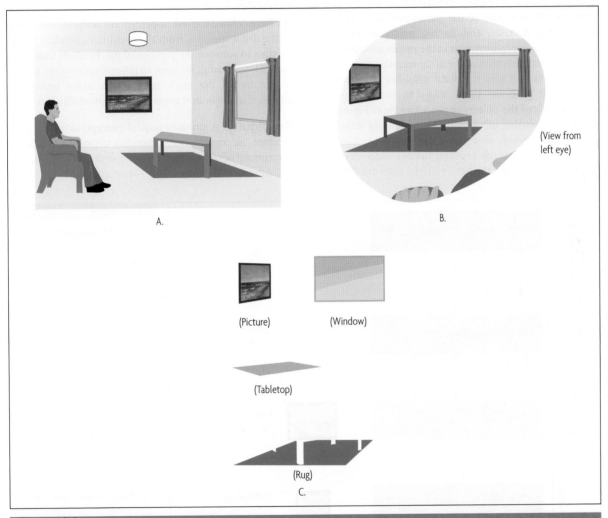

A.

B.

(View from left eye)

(Picture)  (Window)

(Tabletop)

(Rug)

C.

## Figure 4.1

**Interpreting retinal images**
Suppose you are sitting in an easy chair, looking around a room (A). The light reflected from objects in the room forms images on your retina. Consider the information that arrives at your left eye (B). When you see that information out of context (C), you can appreciate the task that faces your visual system: your visual perception must interpret or identify distal stimulus, the actual object in the environment, using the information from the proximal stimulus, the retinal image produced by the object.

consider all the differences between the environmental objects and the images of them on your retina, you may be surprised that you perceive the scene as well as you do.

The differences between a physical object in the world and its optical image on your retina are so profound and important that psychologists distinguish carefully between them as two different stimuli for perception. The physical object in the world is called the **distal stimulus** (distant from the observer) and the optical image on the retina is called the **proximal stimulus** (proximate, or near, to the observer).

The critical point of our discussion can now be restated more concisely: what you wish to *perceive* is the *distal stimulus*—the 'real' object in the environment—whereas the stimulus from which you must derive your information is the *proximal stimulus*—the image on the retina. You can think of the major computational task of perception as the process of determining the distal stimulus from information contained in the proximal stimulus. This is true across perceptual domains. For hearing, touch, taste, and so on, perception involves processes that use information in the proximal stimulus to tell you about properties of the distal stimulus.

To show you how the distal stimulus and proximal stimulus fit with the three stages in perceiving, let's examine one of the objects in the scene from Figure 4.1: the picture hanging on the wall. In the sensory stage, this picture corresponds to a two-dimensional trapezoid in your retinal image; the top and bottom sides converge toward the right, and the left and right sides are different

in length. This is the proximal stimulus. In the perceptual organisation stage, you see this trapezoid as a rectangle turned away from you in three-dimensional space. You perceive the top and bottom sides as parallel but receding into the distance toward the right: you perceive the left and right sides as equal in length. Your perceptual processes have developed a strong *hypothesis* about the physical properties of the distal stimulus; now it needs an identity. In the recognition stage, you identify this rectangular object as a picture. **Figure 4.2** is a flow-chart illustrating this sequence of events. The processes that take information from one stage to the next are shown as arrows between the boxes. By the end of this chapter, we will explain the interactions represented in this figure.

# REALITY, AMBIGUITY, AND ILLUSIONS

We have defined the task of perception as the identification of the distal stimulus from the proximal stimulus. Before we turn to some of the perceptual mechanisms that make this task successful, we want to discuss some other aspects of stimuli in the environment that make perception complex: *ambiguous* stimuli and perceptual *illusions*.

**Ambiguity** A primary goal of perception is to get an accurate 'fix' on the world. Survival depends on accurate perceptions of objects and events in your environment—Is that motion in the trees a tiger?—that are not always easy to

**distal stimulus** In the processes of perception, the physical object in the world, as contrasted with the proximal stimulus, the optical image on the retina.

**proximal stimulus** The optical image on the retina; contrasted with the distal stimulus, the physical object in the world.

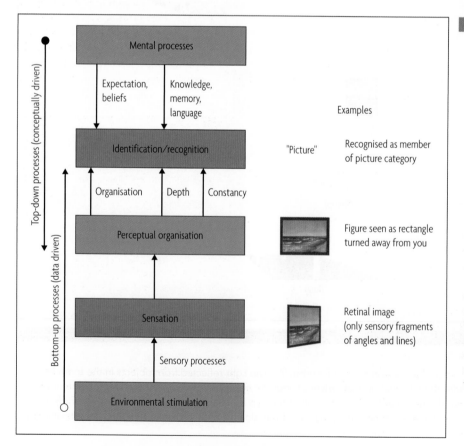

Figure 4.2

Sensation, perceptual organisation, and identification/recognition stages
The diagram outlines the processes that give rise to the transformation of incoming information at the stages of sensation, perceptual organisation, and identification/recognition. Bottom-up processing occurs when the perceptual representation is derived from the information available in the sensory input. Top-down processing occurs when the perceptual representation is affected by an individual's prior knowledge, motivations, expectations, and other aspects of higher mental functioning.

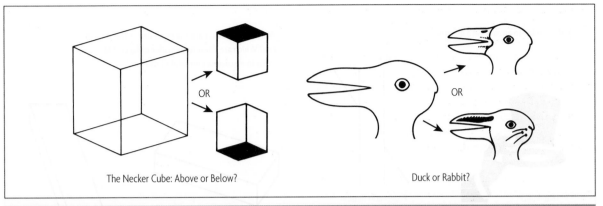

The Necker Cube: Above or Below?

Duck or Rabbit?

## Figure 4.3

Perceptual ambiguities
Each example allows two interpretations, but you cannot experience both at the same time. Do you notice your perception flipping back and forth between each pair of possibilities?

read. **Ambiguity** is an important concept in understanding perception because it shows that a single image at the sensory level can result in *multiple interpretations* at the perceptual and identification levels.

**Figure 4.3** shows two examples of ambiguous figures. Each example permits two unambiguous but conflicting interpretations. Look at each image until you can see the two alternative interpretations. Notice that once you have seen both of them, your perception flips back and forth between them as you look at the ambiguous figure. This perceptual *instability* of ambiguous figures is one of their most important characteristics.

The Necker Cube presents an ambiguity in the perceptual organisation stage. You have two different perceptions of the same objects in the environment. The Necker Cube can be seen as a three-dimensional hollow cube either below you and angled to your left or above you and angled toward your right. The ambiguous alternatives are different physical arrangements of the object in three-dimensional space, both resulting from the same stimulus image.

The duck/rabbit figure is an example of ambiguity in the recognition stage. It is perceived as the same physical shape in both interpretations. The ambiguity arises in determining the kind of object it represents and in how best to classify it, given the mixed set of information available.

Many prominent artists have used perceptual ambiguity as a central creative device in their works. **Figure 4.4** presents *Slave Market with the Disappearing Bust of Voltaire* by Salvador Dali. This work reveals a complex ambiguity in which a whole section of the picture must be radically reorganised and reinterpreted to allow perception of the 'hidden' bust of the French philosopher-writer Voltaire. The white sky under the lower arch is Voltaire's forehead and hair; the white portions of the two ladies' dresses are his cheeks, nose, and chin. (If you have trouble seeing him, try squinting, holding the book at arm's length, or taking off your glasses.) Once you have seen the bust of Voltaire in this picture, however, you will

never be able to look at it without knowing where this Frenchman is hiding.

One of the most fundamental properties of normal human perception is the tendency to transform ambiguity and uncertainty about the environment into a clear interpretation that you can act on with confidence. In a world filled with variability and change, your perceptual system must meet the challenges of discovering invariance and stability.

Illusions Ambiguous stimuli present your perceptual systems with the challenge of recognising one unique figure out of several possibilities. One or another interpretation of the stimulus is correct or incorrect with respect to a particular context. When your perceptual systems actually deceive you into experiencing a stimulus pattern in a manner that is demonstrably incorrect, you are experiencing

**ambiguity** Property of perceptual object that may have more than one interpretation.

## Figure 4.4

Ambiguity in art
This painting by Salvador Dali is called 'Slave Market with the Disappearing Bust of Voltaire'. Can you find Voltaire? Dali is one of a large number of modern and contemporary artists who have exploited ambiguity in their work.

SENSING, ORGANISING, IDENTIFYING AND RECOGNISING

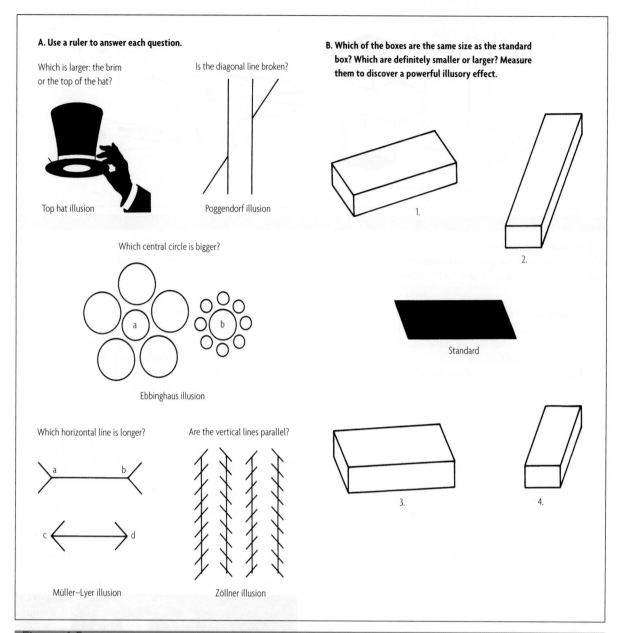

A. Use a ruler to answer each question.

Which is larger: the brim or the top of the hat?

Top hat illusion

Is the diagonal line broken?

Poggendorf illusion

Which central circle is bigger?

a

b

Ebbinghaus illusion

Which horizontal line is longer?

a          b

c          d

Müller–Lyer illusion

Are the vertical lines parallel?

Zöllner illusion

B. Which of the boxes are the same size as the standard box? Which are definitely smaller or larger? Measure them to discover a powerful illusory effect.

1.

2.

Standard

3.

4.

## Figure 4.5

Five illusions to tease your brain
Each of these illusions represents circumstances in which perception is demonstrably incorrect. Researchers often use illusions to test their theories. These theories explain why perceptual systems that generally function quite accurately yield illusions in special circumstances.

**illusion** An experience of a stimulus pattern in a manner that is demonstrably incorrect but shared by others in the same perceptual environment.

an **illusion**. The word *illusion* shares the same root as *ludicrous*—both stem from the Latin *illudere,* which means 'to mock at'. Illusions are shared by most people in the same perceptual situation because of shared physiology in sensory systems and overlapping experiences of the world. (As we will explain in Chapter 5, this sets illusions apart from hallucinations. Hallucinations are nonshared perceptual distortions that individuals experience as a result of unusual physical or mental states.) Examine the classic illusions in **Figure 4.5**. Although it is most convenient for us to present you with visual illusions, illusions also exist in other sensory modalities such as hearing (Russo & Thompson, 2005;

Sonnadara & Trainor, 2005), taste (Todrank & Bartoshuk, 1991), and touch (Heller et al., 2003).

**Illusions in everyday life** Illusions are also a basic part of your everyday life. Consider your day-to-day experience of your home planet, Earth. You've seen the sun 'rise' and 'set' even though you know that the sun is sitting out there in the centre of the solar system as decisively as ever. You can appreciate why it was such an extraordinary feat of courage for Portuguese explorer Ferdinand Magellan and other voyagers to deny the obvious illusion that Earth was flat and sail off toward one of its apparent edges.

Similarly, when a full moon is overhead, it seems to follow you wherever you go even though you know the moon isn't chasing you. What you are experiencing is an illusion created by the great distance of the moon from your eye. When they reach Earth, the moon's light rays are essentially parallel and perpendicular to your direction of travel, no matter where you go.

People can control illusions to achieve desired effects. Architects and interior designers use principles of perception to create objects in space that seem larger or smaller than they really are. A small apartment becomes more spacious when it is painted with light colours and sparsely furnished with low small couches, chairs and tables in the centre of the room instead of against the walls. Psychologists have researched the effects of isolated and confined environments such as space capsules and polar huts on perception in order to design living and working surrounds that have pleasant sensory qualities (Suedfeld & Steel, 2000). Set and lighting directors of movies and theatrical productions purposely create illusions on film and on stage.

Despite all of these illusions—some more useful than others—you generally do pretty well getting around the environment. That is why researchers typically study illusions to help explain how perception ordinarily works so well. The illusions themselves suggest, however, that your perceptual systems cannot perfectly carry out the task of recovering the distal stimulus from the proximal stimulus.

You now have an overview of your sensory and perceptual processes and some of the challenges those processes face. Let's begin to consider those processes in more detail.

## RECAP CHECKPOINT

### Sensing, organising, identifying and recognising

- Perception is a three-stage process consisting of a sensory stage, a perceptual organisation stage, and an identification and recognition stage.

- At the sensory level of processing, physical energy is detected and transformed into neural energy and sensory experience

- At the level of identification and recognition, percepts of objects are compared with memory representations to be recognised as familiar and meaningful objects.

- The task of perception is to determine what the distal (external) stimulus is from the information contained in the proximal (sensory) stimulus.

- Ambiguity may arise when the same sensory information can be organised into different percepts.

- Knowledge about perceptual illusions can provide constraints on ordinary perceptual processes.

## CONCEPT QUESTIONS

1. What are some stages within the overall process of perception?

2. What is the proximal stimulus?

3. What makes a stimulus ambiguous?

For answers go to MyPsychLab!

# SENSORY KNOWLEDGE OF THE WORLD

Your experience of external reality must be relatively accurate and error free. If not, you couldn't survive. You need food to sustain you, shelter to protect you, interactions with other people to fulfil social needs, and awareness of danger to keep out of harm's way. To meet these needs, you must get reliable information about the world. The earliest psychological research on sensation examined the relationship between events in the environment and people's experience of those events.

## PSYCHOPHYSICS

How loud must a fire alarm at a factory be for workers to hear it over the din of the machinery? How bright does a warning light on a pilot's control panel have to be to appear twice as bright as the other lights? How much sugar do you need to put in a cup of coffee before it begins to taste sweet? To answer these questions, we must be able to measure the intensity of sensory experiences. This is the central task of **psychophysics**, the study of the relationship between physical stimuli and the behaviour or mental experiences the stimuli evoke.

The most significant figure in the history of psychophysics was the German physicist **Gustav Fechner** (1801–1887). Fechner coined the term *psychophysics* and provided a set of procedures to relate the intensity of a physical stimulus—measured in physical units—to the magnitude of the sensory experience—measured in psychological units (Fechner, 1860/1966). Fechner's techniques are the same whether the stimuli are for light, sound, taste, odour, or touch: Researchers determine thresholds and construct psychophysical scales relating strength of sensation to strength of stimuli.

### Absolute thresholds and sensory adaptation
What is the smallest, weakest stimulus energy that an organism can detect? How soft can a tone be, for instance,

**psychophysics** The study of the correspondence between physical stimulation and psychological experience.

Can you hear the tone? Hearing evaluation is usually done with an absolute threshold test. Why do these tests require multiple trials?

and still be heard? These questions refer to the **absolute threshold** for stimulation—the minimum amount of physical energy needed to produce a sensory experience. Researchers measure absolute thresholds by asking vigilant observers to perform detection tasks, such as trying to see a dim light in a dark room or trying to hear a soft sound in a quiet room. During a series of many trials the stimulus is presented at varying intensities, and on each trial the observers indicate whether they were aware of it. (If you've ever had your hearing evaluated, you participated in an absolute threshold test.)

The results of an absolute threshold study can be summarised in a **psychometric function**: a graph that shows the percentage of detections (plotted on the vertical axis) at each stimulus intensity (plotted on the horizontal axis). A typical psychometric function is shown in **Figure 4.6**. For very dim lights, detection is at 0 percent; for bright lights, detection is at 100 percent. If there were

a single, true absolute threshold, you would expect the transition from 0 to 100 percent detection to be very sharp, occurring right at the point where the intensity reached the threshold. But this does not happen, for at least two reasons: Viewers themselves change slightly each time they try to detect a stimulus (because of changes in attention, fatigue, and so on), and viewers sometimes respond even in the absence of a stimulus (the type of false alarm we will discuss shortly when we describe signal detection theory). Thus the psychometric curve is usually a smooth S-shaped curve, in which there is a region of transition from no detection to occasional detection to detection all the time.

Because a stimulus does not suddenly become clearly detectable at all times at a specific intensity, the operational definition of absolute threshold is *the stimulus level at which a sensory signal is detected half the time.* Thresholds for different senses can be measured using the same procedure, simply by changing the stimulus dimension. **Table 4.1** shows absolute threshold levels for several familiar natural stimuli.

## Table 4.1

### Approximate thresholds of familiar events

| Sense modality | Detection threshold |
| --- | --- |
| Light | A candle flame seen at 48 kilometres on a dark clear night |
| Sound | The tick of a watch under quiet conditions at 6 metres |
| Taste | One teaspoon of sugar in 7 litres of water |
| Smell | One drop of perfume diffused into the entire volume of a three-room apartment |
| Touch | The wing of a bee falling on your cheek from a distance of 1 centimetre |

Although it is possible to identify absolute thresholds for detection, it is also important to note that your sensory systems are more sensitive to *changes* in the sensory environment than to steady states. The systems have evolved so that they favour new environmental inputs over old through a process called adaptation. **Sensory adaptation** is the diminishing responsiveness of sensory systems to prolonged stimulus input. You may have noticed, for example, that sunshine seems less blinding after a while outdoors. People often have their most fortunate experiences of adaptation in the domain of smell: you walk into a room, and something really has a rank odour; over time, however, as your smell system adapts, the odour fades out of awareness. Your environment is always full of a great diversity of sensory stimulation. The mechanism of adaptation allows you to notice, and react, more quickly to the challenges of new sources of information.

## Figure 4.6

**Calculation of absolute thresholds**
Because a stimulus does not become suddenly detectable at a certain point, absolute threshold is defined as the intensity at which the stimulus is detected half of the time over many trials.

## Response bias and signal detection theory

In our discussion so far, we have assumed that all observers are created equal. However, threshold measurements can also be affected by **response bias**, the systematic tendency for an observer to favour responding in a particular way because of factors unrelated to the sensory features of the stimulus. Suppose, for example, you are in an experiment in which you must detect a weak light. In the first phase of the experiment, the researcher gives you $5 when you are correct in saying, 'Yes, a light was there.' In the second phase, the researcher gives you $5 when you are correct in saying, 'No, there wasn't any light.' In each phase, you are penalised $2 any time you are incorrect. Can you see how this reward structure would create a shift in response bias from phase 1 to phase 2? Wouldn't you say yes more often in the first phase—with the same amount of certainty that the stimulus was present?

**Signal detection theory (SDT)** is a systematic approach to the problem of response bias (Green & Swets, 1966). Instead of focusing strictly on sensory processes, SDT emphasises the process of making a *judgment* about the presence or absence of stimulus events. Whereas classical psychophysics conceptualised a single absolute threshold, SDT identifies two distinct processes in sensory detection: (1) an initial *sensory process,* which reflects the observer's sensitivity to the strength of the stimulus; and (2) a subsequent separate *decision process,* which reflects the observer's response biases.

SDT offers a procedure for evaluating both the sensory process and the decision processes at once. The basic design is given in **Figure 4.7**. A weak stimulus is presented in half the trials; no stimulus is presented in the other half. In each trial, observers respond by saying *yes* if they think the signal was present and *no* if they think it wasn't. As shown in the figure, each response is scored in one of four ways:

- a response is a *hit* when the signal is present and the observer says 'yes';
- a response is a *miss* when the signal is present and the observer says 'no';

If you decline a dinner invitation, will you be avoiding a dull evening (a correct rejection) or sacrificing the chance for a lifetime of love (a miss)?

- a response is a *false alarm* when the signal is absent and the observer says 'yes';
- a response is a *correct rejection* when the signal is absent and the observer says 'no.'

How can we see the impact of the perceivers' decision processes? If Carol is a yea-sayer (she chronically answers yes), she will almost inevitably say yes when the stimulus was present so she'll have a large number of hits. However, she'll also have a high number of false alarms because she'll also say yes quite often when the stimulus was absent. If Bob is a naysayer (he chronically answers no), he will give a lower number of hits but also a lower number of false alarms.

Working with the percentages of hits and false alarms, researchers use mathematical procedures to calculate separate measures of observers' sensitivity and response biases. This procedure makes it possible to find out whether two observers have the same sensitivity despite large differences in response criterion. By providing a way of separating sensory process from response bias, the theory of signal detection allows an experimenter to identify and separate the roles of the sensory stimulus and the individual's criterion level in producing the final response.

### Difference thresholds

Imagine you have been employed by a soft drink company that wants to produce a cola product that tastes noticeably sweeter than existing colas, but (to save money) the firm wants to put as little extra sugar in the cola as possible. You are being asked to measure a **difference threshold**, the smallest physical difference between two stimuli that can still be recognised as a difference. To measure a difference threshold, you use pairs of stimuli and ask your observers whether they believe the two stimuli to be the same or different.

For the beverage problem, you would give your observers two colas on each trial, one of some standard recipe and one just a bit sweeter. For each pair, the individual would say *same* or *different*. After many such trials, you would plot a psychometric function by graphing the percent of *different* responses on the vertical axis

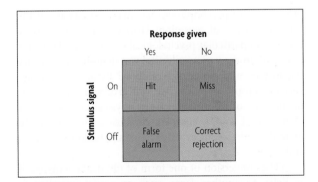

**Figure 4.7**

**The theory of signal detection**
The matrix shows the possible outcomes when a subject is asked if a target stimulus occurred on a given trial.

as a function of the actual differences, plotted on the horizontal axis. The difference threshold is operationally defined as *the point at which the stimuli are recognised as different half of the time.* This difference threshold value is known as a **just noticeable difference**, or **JND**. The JND is a quantitative unit for measuring the magnitude of the psychological difference between any two sensations.

In 1834, **Ernst Weber** pioneered the study of JNDs and discovered the important relationship that we illustrate in **Figure 4.8**. This relationship is summarised as **Weber's law:** *The JND between stimuli is a constant fraction of the intensity of the standard stimulus.* Thus, the bigger or more intense the standard stimulus, the larger the increment needed to get a just noticeable difference. The formula for Weber's law is $\Delta I/I = k$, where $I$ is the intensity of the standard; $\Delta I$, or delta I, is the size of the increase that produces a JND. Weber found that each stimulus dimension has a characteristic value for this ratio. In this formula, $k$ is that ratio, or *Weber's constant*, for the particular stimulus dimension. Weber's law provides a good approximation, but not a perfect fit to experimental data, of how the size of JND increases with intensity (most problems with the law arise when stimulus intensities become extremely high).

You see in **Table 4.2** that Weber's constant ($k$) has different values for different sensory dimensions—smaller values mean that people can detect smaller differences. So this table tells you that you can differentiate two sound frequencies more precisely than light intensities, which, in turn, are detectable with a smaller JND than odour or taste differences are. Your beverage company would need a relatively large amount of extra sugar to produce a noticeably sweeter cola!

**just noticeable difference (JND)** The smallest difference between two sensations that allows them to be discriminated.

**Weber's law** An assertion that the size of a difference threshold is proportional to the intensity of the standard stimulus.

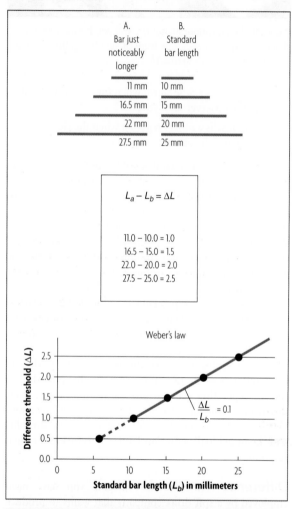

### Figure 4.8

**Just noticeable differences and Weber's Law**

Suppose you are conducting an experiment in which you challenge participants to detect whether two bars are the same or different in length. The longer the standard bar, the greater the amount you must add (ΔL) to see a just noticeable difference. The difference threshold is the added length detected on half the trials. When these increments are plotted against standard bars of increasing length, the proportions stay the same—the amount added is always one-tenth of the standard length. The relationship is linear, producing a straight line on the graph. We can predict that the ΔL for a bar length of 5 will be 0.5.

### Table 4.2

Weber's constant values for selected stimulus dimensions

| Stimulus dimension | Weber's constant ($k$) |
| --- | --- |
| Sound frequency | 0.003 |
| Light intensity | 0.01 |
| Odour concentration | 0.07 |
| Pressure intensity | 0.14 |
| Sound intensity | 0.15 |
| Taste concentration | 0.20 |

Figure from *Introduction to Psychology*, 10th ed. by Atkinson. © 1989 Reprinted with permission of Wadsworth, a division of Thomson Learning.

## FROM PHYSICAL EVENTS TO MENTAL EVENTS

Our review of psychophysics has made you aware of the central mystery of sensation: How do physical energies give rise to particular psychological experiences? How, for example, do the various physical wavelengths of light give rise to your experience of a rainbow? Before we consider specific sensory domains, we will give you an overview of the flow of information from physical events—waves of light and sound, complex chemicals, and so on—to mental events—your experiences of sights, sounds, tastes, and smells.

The conversion of one form of physical energy, such as light, to another form, such as neural impulses, is called **transduction**. Because all sensory information is transduced into identical types of neural impulses, your brain differentiates sensory experiences by devoting special areas of cortex to each sensory domain. For each

**transduction** Transformation of one form of energy into another; for example, light is transformed into neutral impulses.

domain, researchers try to discover how the transduction of physical energy into the electrochemical activity of the nervous system gives rise to sensations of different quality (red rather than green) and different quantity (loud rather than soft).

Sensory systems share the same basic flow of information. The trigger for any sensing system is the detection of an environmental event, or *stimulus*. Environmental stimuli are detected by specialised **sensory receptors**. Sensory receptors convert the physical form of the sensory signal into cellular signals that can be processed by the nervous system. These cellular signals contribute information to higher-level neurons that integrate information across different detector units. At this stage, neurons extract information about the basic qualities of the stimulus, such as its size, intensity, shape and distance. Deeper into the sensory systems, information is combined into even more complex codes that are passed on to specific areas of the sensory and association cortex of the brain.

We move now to specific sensory domains.

## RECAP CHECKPOINT
### Sensory knowledge of the world

- Psychophysics investigates psychological responses to physical stimuli. Researchers measure absolute thresholds and just noticeable differences between stimuli.

- Signal detection allows researchers to separate sensory acuity from response biases.

- Researchers in psychophysics have captured the relationship between physical intensity and psychological effect with mathematical functions.

- Sensation translates the physical energy of stimuli into neural codes via transduction.

### CONCEPT QUESTIONS

1. What is the subject matter of psychophysics?

2. What is the operational definition of an absolute threshold?

3. In signal detection theory, what two processes contribute to observers' judgments?

4. What is a difference threshold?

5. What is transduction?

# THE VISUAL SYSTEM

Vision is the most complex, highly developed and important sense for humans and most other mobile creatures. Animals with good vision have an enormous evolutionary advantage. Good vision helps animals detect their prey or predators from a distance. Vision enables humans to be aware of changing features in the physical environment and to adapt their behaviour accordingly. Vision is also the most studied of all the senses.

## THE HUMAN EYE

The eye is the camera for the brain's motion pictures of the world (see **Figure 4.9**). A camera views the world through a lens that gathers and focuses light. The eye also gathers and focuses light—light enters the *cornea*, a transparent bulge on the front of the eye. Next it passes through the *anterior chamber*, which is filled with a clear liquid called the *aqueous humour*. The light then passes through the *pupil*, an opening in the opaque *iris*. To focus a camera, you move its lens closer to or farther from the object viewed. To focus light in the eye, a bean-shaped crystalline *lens* changes its shape, thinning to focus on distant objects and thickening to focus on near ones. To control the amount of light coming into a camera, you vary the opening of the lens. In the eye, the muscular disk of the iris changes the size of the pupil, the opening through which light passes into the eyeball. At the back of a camera body is the photosensitive film that records the variations in light that have come through the lens. Similarly, in the eye, light travels through the *vitreous*

**sensory receptors** Special cells that convert physical signals into cellular signals that are processed by the nervous system.

For answers go to MyPsychLab!

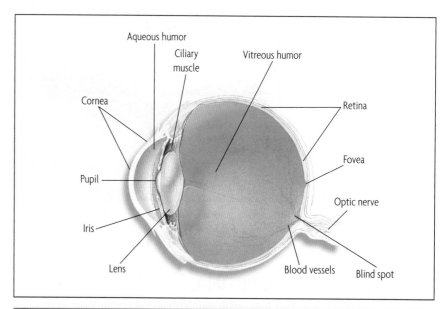

**Figure 4.9**

**Structure of the human eye**
The cornea, pupil and lens focus light onto the retina. Nerve signals from the retina are carried to the brain by the optic nerve.

*humour*, finally striking the *retina*, a thin sheet that lines the rear wall of the eyeball.

As you can see, the features of a camera and the eye are very similar. Now let's examine the components of the vision process in more detail.

## THE PUPIL AND THE LENS

The pupil is the opening in the iris through which light passes. The iris makes the pupil dilate or constrict to control the amount of light entering the eyeball. Light passing through the pupil is focused by the lens on the retina; the lens reverses and inverts the light pattern as it does so. The lens is particularly important because of its variable focusing ability for near and far objects. The ciliary muscles can change the thickness of the lens and hence its optical properties in a process called **accommodation.**

People with normal accommodation have a range of focus from about 7 centimetres in front of their nose to as far as they can see. However, many people suffer from accommodation problems. For example, people who are nearsighted have their range of accommodation shifted closer to them with the consequence that they cannot focus well on distant objects; those who are farsighted have their range of accommodation shifted farther away from them so that they cannot focus normally on nearby objects. Ageing also leads to problems in accommodation. The lens starts off as clear, transparent and convex. As people age, however, the lens becomes more amber tinted, opaque and flattened, and it loses its elasticity. The effect of some of these changes is that the lens cannot become thick enough for close vision. When people age past the 45-year mark, the *near point*—the closest point at which they can focus clearly—gets progressively farther away.

Visual acuity enables predatory animals to detect potential prey from a distance. What range of functions did evolution provide for the human visual system?

## THE RETINA

You look with your eyes but see with your brain. The eye gathers light, focuses it, and starts a neural signal on its way toward the brain. The eye's critical function, therefore, is to convert information about the world from light waves into neural signals. This happens in the **retina,**

at the back of the eye. Under the microscope, you can see that the retina has several highly organised layers of different types of neurons.

The basic conversion from light energy to neural responses is performed in your retina by *rods* and *cones*—receptor cells sensitive to light. These **photoreceptors** are uniquely placed in the visual system between the outer world, ablaze with light, and the inner world of neural processing. Because you sometimes operate in near darkness and sometimes in bright light, nature has provided two ways of processing light—rods and cones (see **Figure 4.10**). The 120 million thin **rods** operate best in near darkness. The 7 million fat **cones** are specialised for the bright, colour-filled day.

You experience differences between the functions of your rods and cones each time you turn off the lights to go to sleep at night. You have noticed many times that at first it seems as though you can't see much of anything in the dim light that remains, but over time your visual sensitivity improves again. You are undergoing the process of **dark adaptation**—the gradual improvement of the eyes' sensitivity after a shift in illumination from light to near darkness. Dark adaptation occurs because, as time passes in the dark, your rods become more sensitive than your cones; over time, your rods are able to respond to less light from the environment than your cones are.

Near the centre of the retina is a small region called the **fovea**, which contains nothing but densely packed cones—it is rod free. The fovea is the area of your sharpest vision—both colour and spatial detail are most accurately detected there. Other cells in your retina are responsible for integrating information across regions of rods and cones. The **bipolar cells** are nerve cells that combine impulses from many receptors and send the results to ganglion cells. Each **ganglion cell** then integrates the impulses from one or more bipolar cells into a single firing rate. The cones in the central fovea send their impulses to the ganglion cells in that region while, farther out on the periphery of the retina, rods and cones converge on the same bipolar and ganglion cells. The axons of the ganglion cells make up the optic nerve, which carries this visual information out of the eye and back toward the brain.

Your **horizontal cells** and **amacrine cells** integrate information across the retina. Rather than send signals toward the brain, horizontal cells connect receptors to each other, and amacrine cells link bipolar cells to other bipolar cells and ganglion cells to other ganglion cells.

An interesting curiosity in the anatomical design of the retina exists where the optic nerve leaves each eye. This region, called the optic disk, or *blind spot*, contains no receptor cells at all. You do not experience blindness there, except under very special circumstances, for two reasons: First, the blind spots of the two eyes are positioned so that receptors in each eye register what is missed in the other; second, the brain fills in this region with appropriate sensory information from the surrounding area.

To find your blind spot, you will have to look at **Figure 4.11** under special viewing conditions. Hold this book at arm's length, close your right eye and fixate on

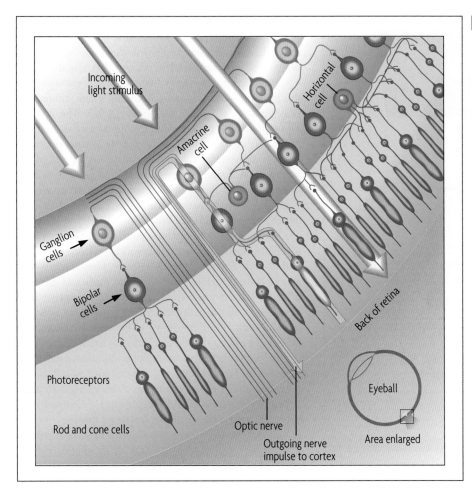

Figure 4.10

**Retinal pathways**
This is a stylised and greatly simplified diagram showing the pathways that connect three of the layers of nerve cells in the retina. Incoming light passes through all these layers to reach the receptors at the back of the eyeball which are pointed away from the source of light. Note that the bipolar cells gather impulses from more than one receptor cell and send the results to ganglion cells. Nerve impulses (blue arrow) from the ganglion cells leave the eye via the optic nerve and travel to the next relay point.

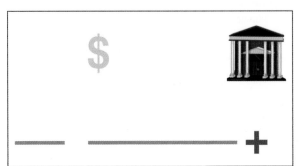

Figure 4.11

**Find your blind spot**
To find your blind spot, hold this book at arm's length, close your right eye, and fixate on the bank figure with your left eye as you bring the book slowly closer. When the dollar sign is in your blind spot, it will disappear, but you will experience no gaping hole in your visual field. Similarly, if you use the same procedure to focus on the plus sign, the line will appear whole when the gap is in your blind spot. In both cases, your visual system fills in the background whiteness of the surrounding area so you "see" the whiteness, which isn't there.

the bank figure with your left eye as you bring the book slowly closer. When the dollar sign is in your blind spot, it will disappear, but you will experience no gaping hole

in your visual field. Instead, your visual system fills in this area with the background whiteness of the surrounding area so you 'see' the whiteness, which isn't there, while failing to see your money, which you should have put in the bank before you lost it!

For a second demonstration of your blind spot, use the same procedure to focus on the plus sign in Figure 4.11. As you pull the book closer to you, do you see the gap disappear and the line become whole?

## PROCESSES IN THE BRAIN

The ultimate destination of much visual information is the part of the occipital lobe of the brain known as primary *visual cortex*. However, most information leaving the retinas passes through other brain regions before it arrives at the visual cortex. Let's trace the pathways visual information takes.

The million axons of the ganglion cells that form each **optic nerve** come together in the *optic chiasma*, which resembles the Greek letter χ (*chi*, pronounced *kye*). The axons in each optic nerve are divided into two bundles at the optic chiasma. Half of the fibres from each retina remain on the side of the body from which they originated. The axons from the inner half of each eye cross over the midline as they continue their journey toward the back of the brain (see **Figure 4.12**).

**optic nerve** The axons of the ganglion cells that carry information from the eye towards the brain.

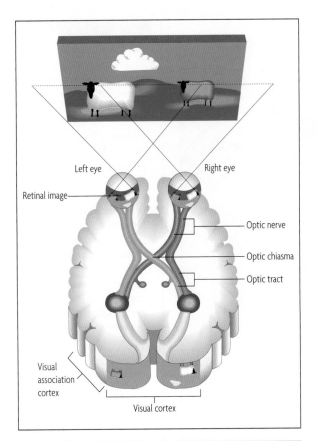

**Figure 4.12**

**Pathways in the human visual system**
The diagram shows the way light from the visual field projects onto the two retinas and the routes by which neural messages from the retina are sent to the two visual centres of each hemisphere.

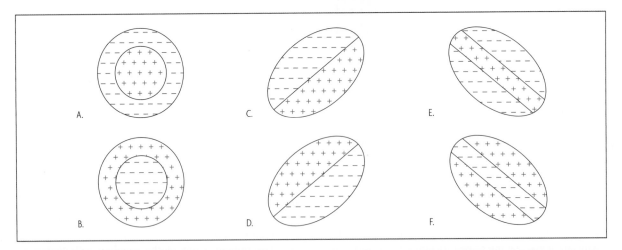

**Figure 4.13**

**Receptive fields of ganglion and cortical cells**
The receptive field of a cell in the visual pathway is the area in the visual field from which it receives stimulation. The receptive fields of the ganglion cells in the retina are circular (A, B); those of the simplest cells in the visual cortex are elongated in a particular orientation (C, D, E, F). In both cases, the cell responding to the receptive field is excited by light in the regions marked with plus signs and inhibited by light in the regions marked with minus signs. In addition, the stimulus that most excites the cell is the one in which areas where light is excitatory (marked with plus signs) are illuminated, but areas where light is inhibitory (marked by minus signs) are in darkness.

**receptive field** The area of the visual field to which a neuron in the visual system responds.

These two bundles of fibres, which now contain axons from both eyes, are renamed *optic tracts*. The optic tracts deliver information to two clusters of cells in the brain. Research supports the theory that visual analysis is separated into pathways for *pattern recognition*—how things look—and *place recognition*—where things are (Pasternak et al., 2003; Rao et al., 1997). The division into pattern and place recognition gives you an example of the way in which your visual system consists of several separate subsystems that analyse different aspects of the same retinal image. Although your final perception is of a unified visual scene, your vision of it is accomplished through a host of pathways in your visual system that, under normal conditions, are exquisitely coordinated.

Pioneering work on how your visual system pieces together information from the world was done by **David Hubel** and **Torsten Wiesel**, sensory physiologists who won a Nobel Prize in 1981 for their studies of *receptive fields* of cells in the visual cortex. The **receptive field** of a cell is the area in the visual field from which it receives stimulation. As shown in **Figure 4.13**, Hubel and Wiesel discovered that cells at different levels of the visual system responded most strongly to different patterns of stimulation. For example, one type of cortical cell, *simple* cells, responded most strongly to bars of light in their 'favourite' orientation (see Figure 4.13). *Complex* cells also each have a 'favourite' orientation, but they require as well that the bar be moving. *Hypercomplex* cells require moving bars of a particular length or moving corners or angles. The cells provide types of information to higher visual centres in the brain that ultimately allow the brain to recognise objects in the visual world.

The advances in imaging techniques we described in Chapter 3 have enabled researchers to discover regions of the cortex that are specially responsive to even more complex environmental images.

Take a moment to look at your hand. Now focus on any other object in the room. If a team of researchers is correct, one particular region of your brain just turned on and off as you shifted your focus from your hand—a body part—to an object from a different category (Downing et al., 2001). To test this hypothesis, the researchers collected fMRI data with the range of pictures shown in **Figure 4.14**. The fMRI images of the brain demonstrated that a region of the cortex on the boundary between the occipital and temporal lobes was selectively active to depictions of the human body (A–F). The exceptions to this finding were faces (G) and parts of faces (M). Other brain regions appear to handle the processing of human faces.

Humans are particularly important to other humans—that probably explains why particular brain regions are devoted to the processing of human faces and bodies. However, researchers still do not know if those regions have those special functions at birth or if those functions are the product of a lifetime of experience.

You have now learned the basics of how visual information is distributed from the eyes to various parts of the brain. Researchers still have more to learn: There are roughly 30 anatomical subdivisions of primate visual cortex, and theories vary about the pattern of communication among those areas (Hilgetag et al., 1996). For now, we turn to particular aspects of the visual world. One of the most remarkable features of the human visual system is that your experiences of form, colour, position and depth are based on processing the same sensory information in different ways. How do the transformations occur that enable you to see these different features of the visual world?

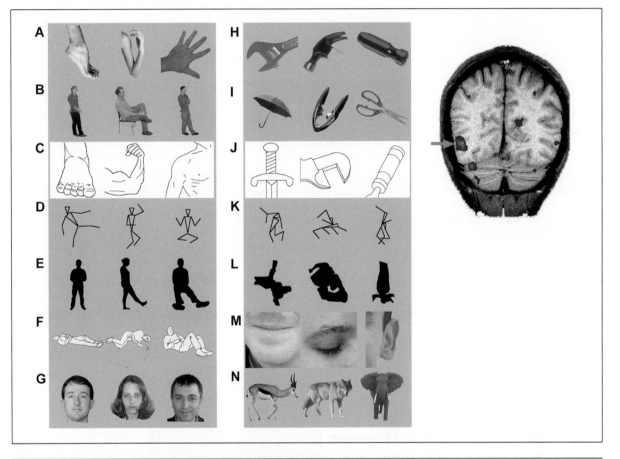

Figure 4.14

Cortical regions for the visual processing of the human body
Researchers used fMRI to assess participants' brain responses to 19 different types of stimuli. The stimuli represent body parts and visual controls for those body parts. Note, for example, how the tools in panel J echo the body parts in panel C. The brain scan shows the region of the cortex on the boundary between the occipital and temporal lobes that became selectively active in response to all depictions of the human body (A–F). This region was not activated when participants viewed whole faces (G), objects (H–J) or scrambled bodies (K–L). The region became active at an intermediate level in response to face parts (M) and mammals (N).

Reprinted with permission from Downing, P.E., Jiang, Y., Shurman, M. & Kanwisher, N. (2001). A cortical area selective for visual processing of the human body. *Science*, 293, 2470–2473. Copyright © 2001 AAAS.

# CRITICAL THINKING *in your life*

## CAN TECHNOLOGY RESTORE SIGHT?

In this section, you have achieved an initial understanding of the biological complexity that underlies people's ability to acquire and transform visual information. Your new knowledge allows you to appreciate the challenges faced by researchers who wish to design technologies to overcome visual deficits. As you encounter media descriptions of new technologies, you can use your awareness of the human visual system as a touchstone to assess research progress. For example, in February 2007 *The Age* newspaper announced that 'the blind will see' when reporting on the Royal Victorian Eye and Ear Hospital's intention to commence implantation of bionic eyes. Similar headlines were seen in October 2007 when *The Australian* reported that researchers from the Australian Vision Prosthesis Group based at University of New South Wales and University of Newcastle may 'win the race to develop the world's first bionic eye'. Reports of this kind provide hope that those who have been blind, in some cases since birth, will be able to see.

Since the first retinal microchip was developed by **Wentai Liu**, **Mark Humayun**, and their team (Liu et al., 2000), at the Donheny Eye Institute at the University of Southern California, research on eye implants and implantation procedures have significantly advanced within Australia. The retinal implant is a small microchip that is connected directly to the retina to replace the function of rods and cones that have been incapacitated by disease. Unfortunately, this kind of implant is not suitable for all blind individuals as the functioning of the implant depends on the level of intact circuitry remaining in the visual system.

Most blind people have become blind because the receptor cells in their retinas—the rods and cones—succumb to a degenerative disease. Even when the sensory receptors cease to function, however, the other cells in the visual pathway—such as bipolar and ganglion cells—survive at high rates. Given the structure of the retina (see Figure 4.10), these other cells are accessible for direct electrical stimulation. The Royal Victorian Eye and Ear Hospital headed by Professor William Campbell is one of only three non-American centres to trial the implants that provide a pattern of electrical stimulation that replaces input from the nonfunctioning rods and cones.

The full system, known as the *multiple-unit artificial retina chipset* (MARC), has several components that function both outside and inside the eyeball. For example, a miniature video camera captures images from the environment. These images are processed and delivered to the microchip surgically implanted on the retina at the back of the eye. The microchip stimulates the ganglion cells in a grid that functions in a way comparable to the operation of a TV or computer screen: Each element of the array— each *pixel*—can take on different values of gray to provide a range of visual sensations.

The Australian Vision Prosthesis Group researchers use a slightly

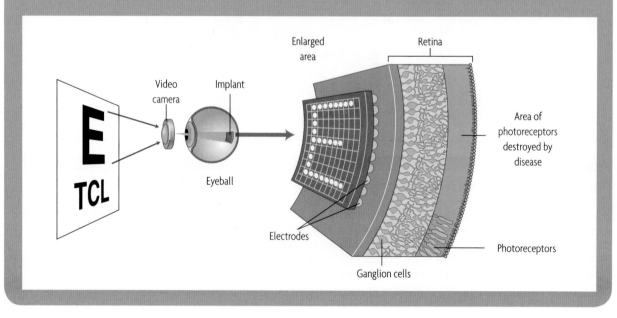

different and potentially less invasive approach to bionic vision. Instead of stimulating the cells by implanting electrodes on the retina, the signals sent from the camera are sent to electrodes on the outer wall of the eye. The resulting signals may then be projected along the optic nerve to the brain.

As you might infer, irrespective of whether eye implants use the MARC procedure or an external wall placement, neither procedure will restore full sight in the way implied by the newspaper headlines about bionic eyes. The amount of information such devices provide is quite limited compared to what you ordinarily obtain through your vast number of rods and cones. However, participants in experimental trials of the MARC have been able to identify simple images and shapes. The hope is that these kinds of implants would restore visual function at least to the point at which people could navigate through their environment and read large-print texts. For the millions of people worldwide affected by diseases that cause degeneration of rods and cones, evolving technologies like bionic eyes may very well provide an ingenious means to help preserve visual function.

- Why would the degeneration of rods and cones lead to blindness?
- In the MARC system, why is the microchip implanted directly on the retina?

## SEEING COLOUR

Physical objects seem to have the marvellous property of being painted with colour. You most often have the impression of brightly coloured objects—the red rock of central Australian deserts, green eucalypt trees or clear blue oceans—but your vivid experience of colour relies on the rays of light these objects reflect onto your sensory receptors. Colour is created when your brain processes the information coded in the light source.

Wavelengths and hues The light you see is just a small portion of a physical dimension called the *electromagnetic spectrum* (see **Figure 4.15**). Your visual system is not equipped to detect other types of waves in this spectrum, such as X-rays, microwaves and radio waves. The physical property that distinguishes types of

What three dimensions underlie experiences of colour?

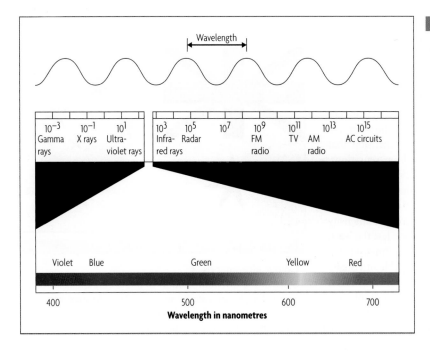

Figure 4.15

**The electromagnetic spectrum**
Your visual system can sense only a small range of wavelengths in the electromagnetic spectrum. You experience that range of wavelengths, which is enlarged in the figure, as the colors violet through red.

From "The Electromagnetic Spectrum," *Perception*, 3e by R. Sekular et al., pp. 27, 221, copyright © 1994 by the McGraw-Hill Companies. Reprinted by permission of the McGraw-Hill Companies.

THE VISUAL SYSTEM

## Figure 4.16

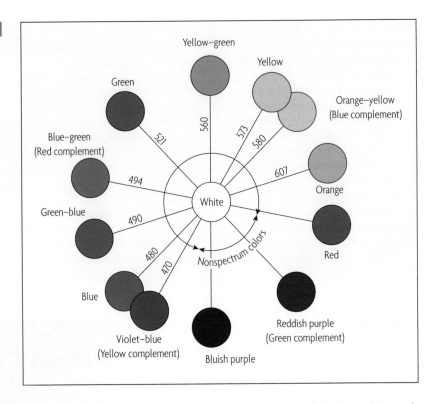

**The colour circle**
Colours are arranged based on similarity. Complementary colours are placed directly opposite each other. Mixing complementary colours yields a neutral grey or white light at the centre. The numbers next to each hue are the wavelength values for spectral colours, i.e. those colours within the regions of visual sensitivity. Nonspectral hues are obtained by mixing short and long spectral wavelengths.

Reprinted with permission from R. Sekular & Blake, *Perception*, 3rd edn, pp. 27, 221. Copyright © 1994 by McGraw-Hill Companies, Inc.

**complementary colours** Colours opposite each other on the colour circle; when additively mixed, they create the sensation of white light.

**hue** The dimension of colour space that captures the qualitative experience of the colour of light.

**saturation** The dimension of colour space that captures the purity and vividness of colour sensations.

**brightness** The dimension of colour space that captures the intensity of light.

electromagnetic energy, including light, is *wavelength*, the distance between the crests of two adjacent waves. Wavelengths of visible light are measured in *nanometres* (billionths of a metre). What you see as light is the range of wavelengths from 400 to about 700 nanometres. Light rays of particular physical wavelengths give rise to experiences of particular colours—for example, violet–blue at the lower end and red–orange at the higher end. Thus light is described physically in terms of wavelengths, not colours; colours exist only in your sensory system's interpretation of the wavelengths.

All experiences of colour can be described in terms of three basic dimensions: hue, saturation and brightness. **Hue** is the dimension that captures the qualitative experience of the colour of a light. In pure lights that contain only one wavelength (such as a laser beam), the psychological experience of hue corresponds directly to the physical dimension of the light's wavelength. **Figure 4.16** presents the hues arranged in a colour circle. Those hues perceived to be most similar are in adjacent positions. This order mirrors the order of hues in the spectrum. **Saturation** is the psychological dimension that captures the purity and vividness of colour sensations. Undiluted colours have the most saturation; muted, muddy, and pastel colours have intermediate amounts of saturation; and greys have zero saturation. **Brightness** is the dimension of colour experience that captures the intensity of light. White has the most brightness; black has the least. When colours are analysed along these three dimensions, a remarkable finding emerges: humans are capable of visually discriminating about 7 million different colours! However, most people can label only a small number of those colours.

Let's explain some facts about your everyday experience of colour. At some point in your science education, you may have repeated Sir Isaac Newton's discovery that sunlight combines all wavelengths of light: you repeated Newton's proof by using a prism to separate sunlight into the full rainbow of colours. The prism shows that the right combination of wavelengths yields white light. The combination of wavelengths is called *additive colour mixture*. Take another look at Figure 4.16. Wavelengths that appear directly across from each other on the colour circle—called **complementary colours**—will create the sensation of white light when mixed. Do you want to prove to yourself the existence of complementary colours? Consider **Figure 4.17**. The green–yellow–black flag should give you the experience of a *negative afterimage* (the afterimage is called 'negative'

## Figure 4.17

**Colour afterimages**
Stare at the dot in the centre of the green, black, and yellow flag for at least 30 seconds. Then fixate on the centre of a sheet of white paper or a blank wall. Try this after-effect illusion on your friends.

because it is the opposite of the original colour). For reasons that we will explain when we consider theories of colour vision, when you stare at any colour long enough to partially fatigue your photoreceptors, looking at a white surface will allow you to experience the complement of the original colour.

You have probably noticed afterimages from time to time in your everyday exposure to colours. Most of your experience with colours, however, does not come from complementary lights. Instead, you have probably spent your time at play with colours by combining crayons or paints of different hues. The colours you see when you look at a crayon mark, or any other coloured surface, are the wavelengths of light that are not absorbed by the surface. Although yellow crayon looks mostly yellow, it lets some wavelengths escape that give rise to the sensation of green. Similarly, blue crayon lets wavelengths escape that give rise to the sensations of blue and some green. When yellow and blue crayon are combined, yellow absorbs blue and blue absorbs yellow— the only wavelengths that are not absorbed look green! This phenomenon is called *subtractive colour mixture*. The remaining wavelengths that are not absorbed—the wavelengths that are reflected—give the crayon mixture the colour you perceive.

Some of these rules about the experience of colour do not apply to those people born with a colour deficiency. *Colour blindness* is the partial or total inability to distinguish colours. The negative afterimage effect of viewing the green, yellow and black flag will not work if you are colour blind. Colour blindness is usually a sex-linked hereditary defect associated with a gene on the X chromosome. Because males have a single X chromosome, they are more likely than females to show this recessive trait. Females would need to have a defective gene on both X chromosomes to be colour blind. An estimate for colour blindness among white males is about 8 percent, but less than 0.5 percent among females (Wolfe et al., 2006).

Most colour blindness involves difficulty distinguishing red from green, especially at weak saturations. More rare are people who confuse yellows and blues. Rarest of all are those who see no colour at all, only variations in brightness. **Figure 4.18** provides an example of the figures researchers use to test for colour blindness. Individuals who have appropriate deficiencies in their red–green system will not see the number. Let's see next how scientists have explained facts about colour vision such as complementary colours and colour blindness.

## Theories of colour vision

The first scientific theory of colour vision was proposed by **Sir Thomas Young** around 1800. He suggested that there were three types of colour receptors in the normal human eye that produced psychologically primary sensations: red, green and blue. All other colours, he believed, were additive or subtractive combinations of these three primaries. Young's theory was later refined and extended by **Hermann von Helmholtz** and came to be known as the Young-Helmholtz **trichromatic theory**.

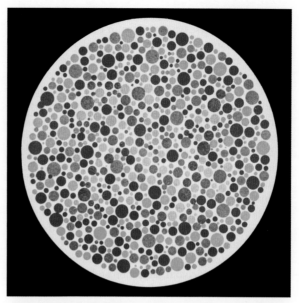

Figure 4.18

A colour blindness test
Individuals who cannot see a number in this display are unable to discriminate red and green.

Trichromatic theory provided a plausible explanation for people's colour sensations and for colour blindness (according to the theory, colour blind people had only one or two kinds of receptors). However, other facts and observations were not as well explained by the theory. Why did adaptation to one colour produce colour afterimages that had the complementary hue? Why did colour blind people always fail to distinguish pairs of colours: red and green or blue and yellow?

Answers to these questions became the cornerstones for a second theory of colour vision proposed by **Ewald Hering** in the late 1800s. According to his **opponent-process theory**, all colour experiences arise from three underlying systems, each of which includes two opponent elements: red versus green, blue versus yellow or black (no colour) versus white (all colours). Hering theorised that colours produced complementary afterimages because one element of the system became fatigued (from overstimulation) and thus increased the relative contribution of its opponent element. According to Hering's theory, types of colour blindness came in pairs because the colour system was actually built from pairs of opposites, not from single primary colours.

For many years, scientists debated the merits of the theories. Eventually, scientists recognised that the theories were not really in conflict; they simply described two different stages of processing that corresponded to successive physiological structures in the visual system (Hurvich & Jameson, 1974). We now know, for example, that there are, indeed, three types of cones. Although the three types each respond to a range of wavelengths, they are each *most* sensitive to light at a particular wavelength. The responses of these cone types confirm Young and Helmholtz's prediction that colour vision relies on three

**opponent-process theory** The theory that all colour experiences arise from three systems, each of which includes two 'opponent' elements (red v green, blue v yellow and black v white).

**trichromatic theory** The theory that there are three types of colour receptors that produce the primary colour sensations of red, green and blue.

types of colour receptors. People who are colourblind lack one or more of these types of receptor cones.

We also now know that the retinal ganglion cells combine the outputs of these three cone types in accordance with Hering's opponent-process theory (De Valois & Jacobs, 1968). According to the contemporary version of opponent-process theory, as supported by **Leo Hurvich** and **Dorothea Jameson** (1974), the two members of each colour pair work in opposition (are opponents) by means of neural inhibition. Some ganglion cells receive excitatory input from lights that appear red and inhibitory input from lights that appear green. Other cells in the system have the opposite arrangement of excitation and inhibition. Together, these two types of ganglion cells form the physiological basis of the red/green opponent-process system. Other ganglion cells make up the blue/yellow opponent system. The black/white system contributes to your perception of colour saturation and brightness.

We turn now from the world of sight to the world of sound.

# HEARING

Hearing and vision play complementary functions in your experience of the world. You often hear stimuli before you see them, particularly if they take place behind you or on the other side of opaque objects such as walls. Although vision is better than hearing for identifying an object once it is in the field of view, you often see the object only because you have used your ears to point your eyes in the right direction. To begin our discussion of hearing, we describe the types of physical energy that arrive at your ears.

## THE PHYSICS OF SOUND

Clap your hands. Whistle. Tap your pencil on the table. Why do these actions create sounds? The reason is that they cause objects to vibrate. The vibrational energy is transmitted to the surrounding medium—usually air—as the vibrating objects push molecules of the medium back and forth. The resulting slight changes in pressure spread outward from the vibrating objects in the form of a combination of *sine waves* travelling at a rate of about 340 metres per second (see **Figure 4.19**). Sound cannot be created in a true vacuum (such as outer space) because there are no air molecules in a vacuum for vibrating objects to move.

A sine wave has two basic physical properties that determine how it sounds to you: frequency and amplitude. *Frequency* measures the number of cycles the wave completes in a given amount of time. A cycle, as indicated in Figure 4.19, is the left-to-right distance from the peak in one wave to the peak in the next wave. Sound frequency is usually expressed in *hertz* (Hz), which measures cycles per second. *Amplitude* measures the physical property of strength of the sound wave, as shown in its peak-to-valley height. Amplitude is defined in units of sound pressure or energy.

## PSYCHOLOGICAL DIMENSIONS OF SOUND

The physical properties of frequency and amplitude give rise to the three psychological dimensions of sound: pitch, loudness, and timbre. Let's see how these phenomena work.

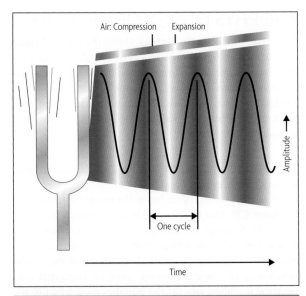

Figure 4.19

**An idealised sine wave**
The two basic properties of sine waves are their *frequency*—the number of cycles in a fixed unit of time—and their *amplitude*—the vertical range of their cycles.

**Pitch** **Pitch** is the highness or lowness of a sound determined by the sound's frequency; high frequencies produce high pitch and low frequencies produce low pitch. The full range of human sensitivity to pure tones extends from frequencies as low as 20 Hz to frequencies as high as 20,000 Hz. (Frequencies below 20 Hz may be experienced through touch as vibrations rather than as sound.) You can get a sense of how big this range is by noting that the 88 keys on a piano cover only the range from about 30 to 4,000 Hz.

As you might expect from our earlier discussion of psychophysics, the relationship between frequency (the physical reality) and pitch (the psychological effect) is not a linear one. At the low end of the frequency scale, increasing the frequency by just a few hertz raises the pitch quite noticeably. At the high end of frequency, you require a much bigger increase in order to hear the difference in pitch. For example, the two lowest notes on a piano differ by only 1.6 Hz, whereas the two highest ones differ by 235 Hz. This is another example of the psychophysics of just noticeable differences.

**Loudness** The **loudness**, or physical intensity, of a sound is determined by its amplitude; sound waves with large amplitudes are experienced as loud and those with small amplitudes as soft. The human auditory system is sensitive to an enormous range of physical intensities. At one limit, you can hear the tick of a wristwatch at 6 metres. This is the system's absolute threshold—if it were more sensitive, you would hear the blood flowing in your ears. At the other extreme, a jetliner taking off 90–100 metres away is so loud that the sound is painful. In terms of physical units of sound pressure, the jet produces a

sound wave with more than a billion times the energy of the ticking watch.

Because the range of hearing is so great, physical intensities of sound are usually expressed in ratios rather than absolute amounts; sound pressure—the index of amplitude level that gives rise to the experience of loudness—is measured in units called decibels (dB). **Figure 4.20** shows the decibel measures of some representative natural sounds. It also shows the corresponding sound pressures for comparison. You can see that two sounds differing by 20 dB have sound pressures in a ratio of 10 to 1. Note that sounds louder than about 90 dB can produce hearing loss, depending on how long a person is exposed to them.

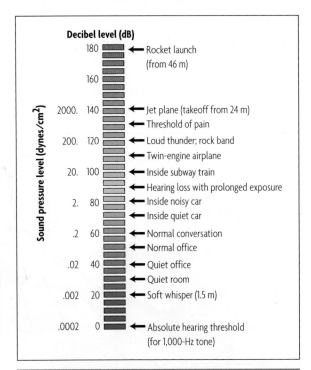

Figure 4.20

**Decibel levels of familiar sounds**
This figure shows the range in decibels of the sounds to which you respond from the absolute threshold for hearing to the noise of a rocket launch. Decibels are calculated from sound pressure, which is a measure of a sound wave's amplitude level and generally corresponds to what you experience as loudness.

**Timbre** The **timbre** of a sound reflects the components of its complex sound wave. Timbre is what sets apart, for example, the sound of a piano from the sound of a flute. A small number of physical stimuli, such as a tuning fork, produce pure tones consisting of a single sine wave. A *pure tone* has only one frequency and one amplitude. Most sounds in the real world are not pure tones. They are complex waves, containing a combination of frequencies and amplitudes.

The sounds that you call *noise* do not have the clear simple structures of frequencies. Noise contains many

**pitch** Sound quality of highness or lowness primarily dependent on the frequency of the sound wave.

**timbre** The dimension of auditory sensation that reflects the complexity of a sound wave.

**loudness** A perceptual dimension of sound influenced by the amplitude of a sound wave.

What physical properties of sounds allow you to pick out the timbres of individual instruments from a musical ensemble?

frequencies that are not systematically related. For instance, the static noise you hear between radio stations contains energy at all audible frequencies; you perceive it as having no pitch because it has no fundamental frequency.

# THE PHYSIOLOGY OF HEARING

Now that you know something about the physical bases of your psychological experiences of sound, let's see how those experiences arise from physiological activity in the auditory system. First, we will look at the way the ear works. Then we will consider some theories about how pitch experiences are coded in the auditory system and how sounds are localised.

**The auditory system** You have already learned that sensory processes transform forms of external energy into forms of energy within your brain. For you to hear, as shown in **Figure 4.21**, four basic energy transformations must take place: (1) Airborne sound waves must get translated into *fluid* waves within the *cochlea* of the ear, (2) the fluid waves must then stimulate mechanical vibrations of the *basilar membrane*, (3) these vibrations must be converted into electrical impulses, and (4) the impulses must travel to the *auditory cortex*. Let's examine each of these transformations in detail.

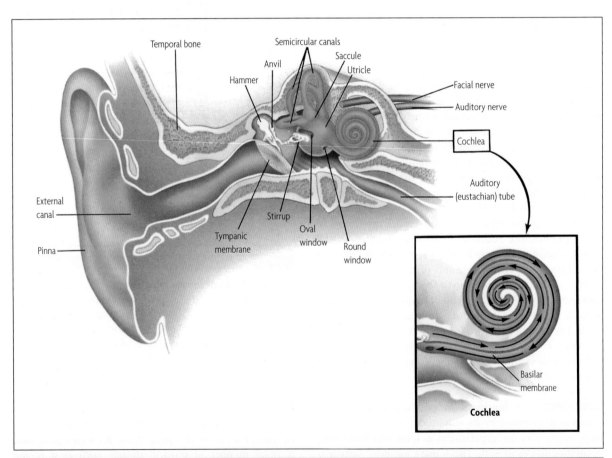

Figure 4.21

**Structure of the human ear**
Sound waves are channelled by the external ear, or pinna, through the external canal, causing the tympanic membrane to vibrate. This vibration activates the tiny bones of the inner ear—the hammer, anvil and stirrup. Their mechanical vibrations are passed along from the oval window to the cochlea, where they set in motion the fluid in its canal. Tiny hair cells lining the coiled basilar membrane within the cochlea bend as the fluid moves, stimulating nerve endings attached to them. The mechanical energy is then transformed into neural energy and sent to the brain via the auditory nerve.

In the first transformation, vibrating air molecules enter the ears (see Figure 4.21). Some sound enters the external canal of the ear directly and some enters after having been reflected off the *external ear*, or *pinna*. The sound wave travels along the canal through the outer ear until it reaches the end of the canal. There it encounters a thin membrane called the eardrum, or *tympanic membrane*. The sound wave's pressure variations set the eardrum into motion. The eardrum transmits the vibrations from the outer ear into the middle ear, a chamber that contains the three smallest bones in the human body: the *hammer*, the *anvil* and the *stirrup*. These bones form a mechanical chain that transmits and concentrates the vibrations from the eardrum to the primary organ of hearing, the *cochlea*, which is located in the *inner ear*.

In the second transformation, which occurs in the cochlea, the airborne sound wave becomes 'seaborne'. The **cochlea** is a fluid-filled coiled tube that has a membrane, known as the **basilar membrane**, running down its middle along its length. When the stirrup vibrates against the oval window at the base of the cochlea, the fluid in the cochlea causes the basilar membrane to move in a wavelike motion (hence 'seaborne'). Researchers speculate that the cochlea's distinctive spiral shape provides greater sensitivity to low-frequency sounds than would be possible without the spiral (Manoussaki et al., 2006).

In the third transformation, the wavelike motion of the basilar membrane bends the tiny hair cells connected to the membrane. The hair cells are the receptor cells for the auditory system. As the hair cells bend, they stimulate nerve endings, transforming the mechanical vibrations of the basilar membrane into neural activity.

Finally, in the fourth transformation, nerve impulses leave the cochlea in a bundle of fibres called the **auditory nerve**. These fibres meet in the *cochlear nucleus* of the brain stem. Similar to the crossing over of nerves in the visual system, stimulation from one ear goes to both sides of the brain. Auditory signals pass through a series of other nuclei on their way to the *auditory cortex*, in the temporal lobes of the cerebral hemispheres. Higher-order processing of these signals begins in the auditory cortex. (As you will learn shortly, other parts of the ear labelled in Figure 4.21 play roles in your other senses.)

The four transformations occur in fully functioning auditory systems. However, the Australian Institute of Health and Welfare found that around 10 percent of Australians reported to be suffering from some form of hearing impairment (AIHW 2004). The two general types of hearing impairment are each caused by a defect in one or more of the components of the auditory system. The less serious type of impairment is *conduction deafness*, a problem in the conduction of the air vibrations to the cochlea. Often in this type of impairment, the bones in the middle ear are not functioning properly, a problem that may be corrected in microsurgery by insertion of an artificial anvil or stirrup. The more serious type of impairment is *nerve deafness*, a defect in the neural mechanisms that create nerve impulses in the ear or relay them to the auditory cortex. Damage to the auditory

Sustained exposure to loud noise can lead to hearing loss. What can people do to avoid such losses?

cortex can also create nerve deafness. Aboriginal and Torres Straight Islanders are significantly more likely than non-indigenous Australians to experience hearing loss of some kind. One contributing factor to this imbalance is the higher prevalence of *otitis media* (a middle-ear infection) in Indigenous communities (Zubrick et al., 2004; DEST 2000). Chronic otitis media can lead to long-term damage of the hearing mechanisms.

You may recall from our earlier discussion of the visual system that damaged or degenerated visual receptors may potentially be replaced by bionic eye implants. These visual system implants were actually developed using the technology of the bionic ear—cochlear implants. Cochlear implants replace, or act in place of non-functioning receptors in the cochlear to produce sound signals. Cochlear implant technology is a direct result of the groundbreaking research conducted in Australia by **Professor Graeme Clark** and his colleagues (Clark, 2003) at The Royal Victorian Eye and Ear Hospital. They were able to analyse complex sound signals, like speech, and transform the information into signals in the auditory nerve, using an implant, allowing the signals to be projected along the auditory nerve to the sound processing regions of the brain.

Specifically, speech signals are transformed into radio waves by a speech processor on the outside of the ear. These radio waves are passed through the skin and detected by the coil implanted in the cochlear. The implant decodes the signal and sends the information to one or more of the 22 implant electrodes that replace the receptor hair cells. The signal sent to each electrode depends on the sound qualities of the original input. It is important to note that the implant does not make sounds louder in the way that hearing aids do. Instead the implant selectively amplifies certain aspects of the speech input, taking into account the theories of pitch perception (we will shortly discuss these theories in detail), and this determines which electrodes receive the signals. The electrodes stimulate nerves ending in the cochlear and the resulting signal is sent to the brain for processing (Clark, 2003).

Since the world's first prototype was implanted by Professor Clark and his team in 1978, more than 50,000 people from around the world have received cochlear

**cochlea** The primary organ of hearing; a fluid-filled coiled tube located in the inner ear.

**basilar membrane** A membrane in the cochlea that when set into motion stimulates hair cells that produce the neural effects of auditory stimulation.

**auditory nerve** The nerve that carries impulses from the cochlea to the cochlear nucleus of the brain.

implants (Bionic Ear Institute, 2006, History section). As with the bionic eye, cochlear implants do not produce signals with the same level of complexity as normally functioning receptors. This is because humans have many thousands of hair cells in the cochlear and 22 electrodes can not reproduce that same complexity of signals. The cochlear implant must also be tuned differently for each person since not all people have the same extent of cochlear damage or have damage in the same locations. Let us now examine how the auditory system contributes to pitch perception.

### Theories of pitch perception

To explain how the auditory system converts sound waves into sensations of pitch, researchers have outlined two distinct theories: place theory and frequency theory.

**Place theory** was initially proposed by Hermann von Helmholtz in the 1800s and was later modified, elaborated and tested by **Georg von Békésy**, who won a Nobel Prize for this work in 1961. Place theory is based on the fact that the basilar membrane moves when sound waves are conducted through the inner ear. Different frequencies produce their most movement at particular locations along the basilar membrane. For high-frequency tones, the wave motion is greatest at the base of the cochlea, where the oval and round windows are located. For low-frequency tones, the greatest wave motion of the basilar membrane is at the opposite end. So place theory suggests that perception of pitch depends on the specific location on the basilar membrane at which the greatest stimulation occurs.

The second theory, **frequency theory**, explains pitch by the rate of vibration of the basilar membrane. This theory predicts that a sound wave with a frequency of 100 Hz will set the basilar membrane vibrating 100 times per second. The frequency theory also predicts that the vibrations of the basilar membrane will cause neurons to fire at the same rate, so that rate of firing is the neural code for pitch. One problem with this theory is that individual neurons cannot fire rapidly enough to represent high-pitched sounds because none of them can fire more than 1,000 times per second. This limitation makes it impossible for one neuron to distinguish sounds above 1,000 Hz—which, of course, your auditory system can do quite well. The limitation might be overcome by the **volley principle**, which explains what might happen at such high frequencies. This principle suggests that several neurons in a combined action, or volley, fire at the frequency that matches a stimulus tone of 2,000 Hz, 3,000 Hz, and so on (Wever, 1949).

As with the trichromatic and opponent-process theories of colour vision, the place and frequency theories each successfully account for different aspects of your experience of pitch. Frequency theory accounts well for coding frequencies below about 5,000 Hz. At higher frequencies, neurons cannot fire quickly and precisely enough to code a signal adequately, even in volley. Place theory accounts well for perception of pitch at frequencies above 1,000 Hz. Below 1,000 Hz, the entire basilar membrane vibrates so broadly that it cannot provide a signal distinctive enough for the neural receptors to use as a means of distinguishing pitch. Between 1,000 and 5,000 Hz, both mechanisms can operate. Thus a complex sensory task is divided between two systems that, together, offer greater sensory precision than either system alone could provide. We see next that you also possess two converging neural systems to help you localise sounds in the environment.

### Sound localisation

Suppose you are walking across campus and you hear someone call your name. In most cases, you can readily locate the spatial location of the speaker. This example suggests how efficiently your auditory system carries out the task of **sound localisation**—you are able to determine the spatial origins of auditory events. You do so through two mechanisms: assessments of the relative timing and relative intensity of the sounds that arrive at each ear (Middlebrooks & Green, 1991; Phillips, 1993).

The first mechanism involves neurons that compare the relative times at which incoming sound reaches each ear. A sound occurring off to your right side, for example, reaches your right ear before your left (see point B in **Figure 4.22**). Neurons in your auditory system are specialised to fire most actively for specific time delays between the two ears. Your brain uses this information about disparities in arrival time to make precise estimates for the likely origins of a sound in space.

The second mechanism relies on the principle that a sound has a slightly greater intensity in the first ear at which it arrives—because your head itself casts a *sound shadow* that weakens the signal. These intensity differences depend on the relative size of the wavelength of a tone with respect to your head. Large-wavelength, low-frequency tones show virtually no intensity differences,

**sound localisation** The auditory processes that allow the spatial origins of environmental sounds.

**place theory** The theory that different frequency tones produce maximum activation at different locations along the basilar membrane, with the result that pitch can be coded by the place at which activation occurs.

**frequency theory** The theory that a tone produces a rate of vibration in the basilar membrane equal to its frequency; pitch can be coded by the frequency of the neural response.

**volley principle** A theory which proposes that when peaks in a sound wave come too frequently for a single neuron to fire at each peak, several neurons fire as a group at the frequency of the stimulus tone.

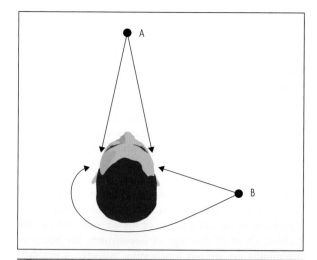

Figure 4.22

**Time disparity and sound localisation**
The brain uses differences in the time course with which sounds arrive at the two ears to localise the sounds in space.

Why might bats have evolved the ability to use echolocation to navigate through their environment?

whereas small-wavelength, high-frequency tones show measurable intensity differences. Your brain, once again, has specialised cells that detect intensity differences in the signals arriving at your two ears.

But what happens when a sound creates neither a timing nor an intensity difference? In Figure 4.22, a sound originating at point A would have this property. With your eyes closed, you cannot tell its exact location. So you must move your head—to reposition your ears—to break the symmetry and provide the necessary information for sound localisation.

It's interesting to note that porpoises and bats use their auditory systems rather than their visual systems to locate objects in dark waters or dark caves. These species use *echolocation*—they emit high-pitched sounds that bounce off objects, giving them feedback about the objects' distances, locations, sizes, textures and movements. In fact, one species of bat is able to use echolocation to differentiate between objects that are just 0.3 millimetres apart (Simmons et al., 1998).

## RECAP CHECKPOINT
### Hearing

- Hearing is produced by sound waves that vary in frequency, amplitude and complexity.

- In the cochlea, sound waves are transformed into fluid waves that move the basilar membrane. Hairs on the basilar membrane stimulate neural impulses that are sent to the auditory cortex.

- Place theory best explains the coding of high frequencies, and frequency theory best explains the coding of low frequencies.

- To compute the direction from which the sound is arriving, two types of neural mechanisms

compute the relative intensity and timing of sounds coming to each ear.

### CONCEPT QUESTIONS

1. What physical property of a sound produces the perception of pitch?

2. What role do hair cells play in the auditory system?

3. Which theory suggests that the perception of pitch depends on the location on the basilar membrane at which the greatest stimulation occurs?

4. What timing difference would you expect if a sound originated off to your right side?

For answers go to MyPsychLab!

# YOUR OTHER SENSES

We have devoted the most attention to vision and hearing because scientists have studied them most thoroughly. However, your ability both to survive in and to enjoy the external environment relies on your full repertoire of senses. We close our discussion of sensation with brief analyses of several of your other senses.

## SMELL

You can probably imagine circumstances in which you'd be just as happy to give up your sense of smell: Have you ever been driving in traffic and found yourself travelling behind a garbage truck? But to avoid that garbage experience, you'd also have to give up the smells of fresh roses, mangoes and sea breezes. Odours—both good and bad—first make their presence known by interacting with receptor proteins on the membranes of *olfactory cilia* (see **Figure 4.23**). It takes only 8 molecules of a substance to initiate one of these nerve impulses, but at least 40 nerve endings must be stimulated before you can smell the substance. Once initiated, these nerve impulses convey odour information to the **olfactory bulb**, located just above the receptors and just below the frontal lobes of the cerebrum. Odour stimuli start the process of smell by stimulating an influx of chemical substances into ion channels in olfactory neurons, an event that, as you may recall from Chapter 3, triggers an action potential. From the olfactory bulbs the signal is projected to a number of higher brain structures including the olfactory cortex, located in the temporal lobe, and the amygdala and hippocampus, which if you again remember from Chapter 3, are important structures of the limbic system and are involved in many aspects of emotion and memory. Olfactory signals are also projected to the thalamus, however, unlike all other sensory systems, olfactory signals

**olfactory bulb** The centre where odour-sensitive receptors send their signals, located just below the frontal lobes of the cortex.

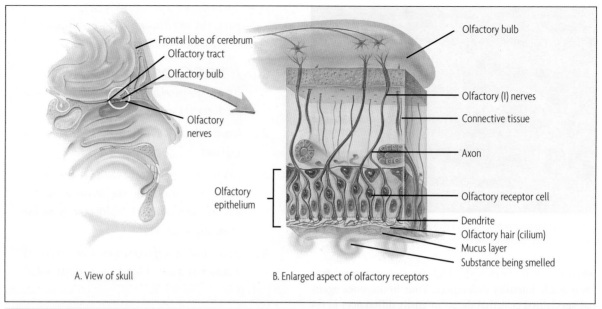

**Figure 4.23**

Receptors for smell
The olfactory receptor cells in your nasal cavities are stimulated by chemicals in the environment. They send information to the olfactory bulb in your brain.

are not relayed through the thalamus before reaching the primary processing cortex.

The significance of the sense of smell varies greatly across species. Smell presumably evolved as a system for detecting and locating food (Moncrieff, 1951). Humans seem to use the sense of smell primarily in conjunction with taste, to seek and sample food. However, for many species smell is also used to detect potential sources of danger. Dogs, rats, insects and many other creatures for whom smell is central to survival have a far keener sense of smell than humans do. Relatively more of their brain is devoted to smell. Smell serves these species well because organisms do not have to come into direct contact with other organisms in order to smell them.

In addition, smell can be a powerful form of active communication. Members of many species communicate by secreting and detecting chemical signals called **pheromones**; chemical substances used within a given species to signal sexual receptivity, danger, territorial boundaries and food sources (Luo et al., 2003). For example, females of various insect species produce sex pheromones to signal that they are available for mating (Carazo et al., 2004; De Cock & Matthysen, 2005). We revisit the topic of pheromones when we discuss both human and nonhuman sexual behaviours in Chapter 11.

**Can you smell that?** Have you ever noticed a foul odour that made you screw up your nose, yet when you complained to a friend about it, they shrugged and asked 'what smell'? Maybe they even said you must be imagining things? It seems strange, but it is possible that your friend may not be able to smell some odours that to you seem impossible to miss!

There are only around 350 functional receptors types (Glusman et al., 2001) that make up the 6 million or so odour receptors in your nose. Given that humans can distinguish around 10,000 different odours, each receptor type must be involved in signalling more than one odour. So although some of the odours humans perceive may be signalled by one receptor, most odours are probably signalled by the combined activation of a number of receptors. It is currently thought that the particular pattern of receptors that are activated by odour molecules form a unique code that higher brain regions use to identify and interpret the odour qualities (Wolfe et al., 2006).

You may remember from your reading of Chapter 3 that genes have a significant impact on human traits and behaviour, and the olfactory system is no exception. The distribution, number and types of receptors that are present in the nose are dependent upon individual genetics. So, although there are around 350 functional receptors expressed by human genes, not all people express the same receptors, and some people are missing certain receptor types all together. This means that if a person is presented with an odour that relies on only one type of receptor to signal its identity, and the person does not have that type of receptor in their nose, they will not be able to smell the odour! The inability to smell one particular odour while having normal sensitivity to all other odours is called *specific anosmia*. **Anosmia** is the inability to smell any odours at all.

Scientists have identified more than 70 different specific anosmias in humans (Coren et al., 2004) and most are believed to have a genetic basis. This type of smell dysfunction is more common that you might expect with about 3 percent of people being unable to smell certain

**pheromones** Chemical signals released by organisms to communicate with other members of the species that often serve as long-distance sexual attractors.

**anosmia** The complete lack of ability to smell; can be permanent or temporary and most often the result of head trauma or nasal and sinus diseases.

components of sweat, and 12 percent are less sensitive to musk odours (Amoore, 1991). Some 40 to 50 percent of people are thought to be anosmic to androstenone, a chemical found in pig meat and sweat. Of those who can smell androstenone, about half describe it as sweet and musky while the other half say it smells like stale urine or sweat (Wysocki, Dorries & Beauchamp, 1989).

So, next time you notice a foul odour and your friend says that they can't smell it, you probably aren't imagining things. It may be that your friend just doesn't have the right receptors for that odour, and if the odour is particularly disgusting, you might wish you didn't have the right receptors as well!

## TASTE

Although food and wine gourmets are capable of making remarkably subtle and complex taste distinctions, many of their sensations are really smells, not tastes. Confusing tastes and smells is very common particularly when eating or drinking, as this is when tastes and smells are working most closely together. Some of the confusion may be due to the mouth-centric nature of eating and drinking—food and beverages go into the mouth—so it is assumed the sensations arise only from the mouth. Another reason for confusion is that when tastes and smells are presented at the same time, in food, it results in the simultaneous activity of the taste and smell systems. The simultaneous activity is integrated in the orbitofrontal cortex (a region of the frontal lobe) and contributes to the perception of a flavour as a whole rather than the perception of separate taste and smell components (Rolls & Baylis, 1994).

Why would a man with a cold be ill-advised to take up wine tasting?

The importance of taste and smell working together to produce flavour is easily noticed when you have a cold. Your food can seem tasteless because your nasal passages are blocked and you can't smell the food. When you recover from your cold and your nasal passages are clear, your food seems tasty once again. Demonstrate this principle for yourself: hold your nose and try to tell the difference between foods of similar texture but different tastes, such as pieces of apple and raw potato. Some students living on campuses with notoriously bad food have reported that wearing nose plugs to meals makes everything taste uniformly bland—which is better than the usual taste!

The surface of your tongue is covered with *papillae*, which give it a bumpy appearance. Many of these papillae contain clusters of taste receptor cells called the *taste buds* (see **Figure 4.24**). Single-cell recordings of taste receptors

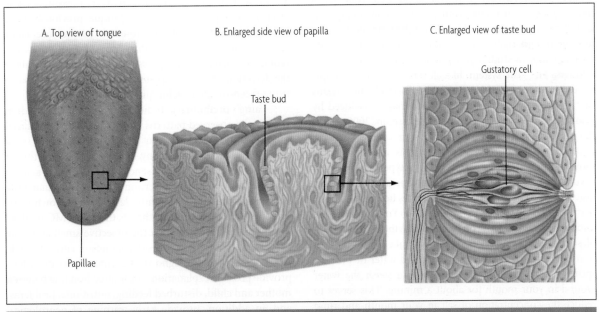

A. Top view of tongue        B. Enlarged side view of papilla        C. Enlarged view of taste bud

Gustatory cell

Taste bud

Papillae

### Figure 4.24

**Receptors for taste**
Part A shows the distribution of the papillae on the upper side of the tongue. Part B shows a single papilla enlarged so that the individual taste buds are visible. Part C shows one of the taste buds enlarged.

show that individual receptor cells respond best to one of the four primary taste qualities: sweet, sour, bitter, and saline (salty) (Frank & Nowlis, 1989). In recent years, researchers have found receptors for a fifth basic taste quality, *umami* (Chaudhari, Landin, & Roper, 2000). Umami is often described as a savoury taste and is the taste of monosodium glutamate (MSG). MSG is a chemical that is commonly added to Asian foods and occurs naturally in foods rich in protein, such as meat, seafood and aged cheese. Although receptor cells for the five qualities may produce small responses to other tastes, the 'best' response most directly encodes quality. This type of coding is different to what is seen in the olfactory system which may use a large number of receptor signals in combination to encode the qualities. There appear to be separate transduction systems for each of the basic classes of taste (Bartoshuk & Beauchamp, 1994).

Taste receptors can be damaged by many things you put in your mouth, such as alcohol, cigarette smoke and acids. Fortunately, your taste receptors get replaced every few days—even more frequently than smell receptors. Indeed, the taste system is the most resistant to damage of all your sensory systems; it is extremely rare for anyone to suffer a total, permanent taste loss (Bartoshuk, 1990).

When a taste molecule stimulates the receptor the signal is sent along a number of nerves including the vagus, facial and glossopharyngeal. The signal projects to the brainstem and on to the thalamus. From the thalamus the signal travels to the limbic system, the somatosensory cortex and to two regions in the frontal lobe, the insula and frontal operculum, that together form the primary taste processing cortex (Finger & Simon, 2000; Finger, 1987).

## Taste adaptation

Did you know that your saliva has a salty taste? It is true, your saliva contains many ions including salts, but if you think about the taste of the saliva in your mouth right now (assuming you aren't snacking on chips as you study), you probably can not detect any saltiness. The taste system, like all sensory systems, adapts to sustained presentation of stimuli. Put simply, this means that the perceived intensity of a taste may be reduced by prior exposure to that particular taste (Breslin, 2000). Thus the perceived intensity of the salt in your saliva is reduced, or becomes unnoticeable, because it is always in your mouth stimulating the receptors. This type of adaptation occurs for all primary tastes. To become aware of a salty taste, the concentration of salty molecules need to be higher than that already present in your saliva. You can taste the saltiness of your saliva if you briefly dilute the concentration of salts in your mouth. For example, take a mouthful of pure water (not tap water, use deionised water or purified spring water with no traces of salt) and swish the water around in your mouth for about a minute. This serves to reduce the concentration of salt in your mouth and rinse away your saliva. After you swallow or spit out the water, saliva will begin to flow back into your mouth, and just for a short while you should be able to taste the salts that are present in saliva—until you adapt once again.

## Taste and smell testing

In Australia, it is becoming common practice for newborns to undergo screening for hearing impairment using otoacoustic emission screeners or automated brainstem evoked response audiometry (Coates, 2003). Similarly, neonate visual functions are tested with techniques such as corneal reflection, blink responses to light, target tracking and pupil dilation (NSW Statewide Ophthalmology Service, 2006). However, as yet, newborns are not tested for taste and smell functioning. One of the reasons for this may be that the roles of taste and smell as possible indicators of neurological dysfunction (Smutzer et al., 2003) and the important relationship between taste and smell, nutritional intake and physiological development have only recently become the focus of intense research. Another reason is that, unlike in vision and hearing, currently there are no established clinical methods for assessing taste and smell function in newborns (Armstrong et al., 2007).

Recently, a group of researchers, lead by **David Laing** at Sydney Children's Hospital and the University of New South Wales, have commenced research to establish methods that may rectify the current deficit in clinical taste and smell assessment. Newborns display distinctive facial expressions shortly after birth (Oster, 1997) and using video-imaging the specific facial expressions made in response to taste and smell stimulation can be recorded and then later analysed (Steiner et al., 2001). The difficulty with these methods is that the data capture and coding procedures are extremely complex, expensive and time-consuming. Thus making them unsuitable for use in hospital and clinical settings where the majority of neonate screening occurs. To overcome these problems, Laing and his team are focusing on the electrical activity that occurs in the facial muscles when tastes or smells are presented. This electrical activity is measured using electromyography (EMG), a technique previously used in cognitive and emotional research to measure facial responses to visual and auditory stimuli. EMG does not require specialist facial expression training and may allow the detection of micro-expressions that are not observable using video-imaging techniques.

Laing's preliminary studies with 6–9 year old children suggest the observed patterns of electrical activity in facial muscles differ depending on the specific taste and smell stimuli presented (Armstrong et al., 2007). From this, it could be inferred that an absence of facial muscle activity indicates an inability to discriminate that particular taste or smell. If the same facial muscle activity is shown to be present in children younger than 6, this new EMG method has the potential to become the objective smell and taste assessment tool for newborns that clinicians currently lack. It would allow early diagnosis of chemosensory disorders, provide possible explanations for limited bonding between mother and child, disturbed feeding, nutritional problems, and, in addition, provide early warning of neurological disorders or disease. If Laing and his team are successful in establishing method, in the future, smell and taste testing may be carried out in Australia alongside the now commonplace vision and hearing tests.

## TOUCH AND SKIN SENSES

The skin is a remarkably versatile organ. In addition to protecting you against surface injury, holding in body fluids and helping regulate body temperature, it contains nerve endings that produce sensations of pressure, warmth, and cold. These sensations are called the **cutaneous senses** (skin senses).

Consider how you become aware that a stimulus is creating *pressure* on your skin. Because you receive so much sensory information through your skin, different types of receptor cells operate close to the surface of the body. Each type of receptor responds to somewhat different patterns of contact with the skin (Blake & Sekuler, 2006). As two examples, *Meissner corpuscles* respond best when something rubs against the skin, and *Merkel disks* are most active when a small object exerts steady pressure against the skin.

The skin's sensitivity to pressure varies tremendously over the body. For example, you are 10 times more accurate in sensing the position of stimulation on your fingertips than on your back. The variation in sensitivity of different body regions is shown by the greater density of nerve endings in these regions and also by the greater amount of sensory cortex devoted to them. In Chapter 3, you learned that your sensitivity is greatest where you need it most—on your face, tongue and hands. Precise sensory feedback from these parts of the body permits effective eating, speaking and grasping.

Suppose someone rubs an ice cube along your arm. You now have some ideas about how you would feel the pressure of the ice cube. But how would you sense that the *temperature* is cold? You may be surprised to learn that you have separate receptors for warmth and coolness. Rather than having one type of receptor that works like a thermometer, your brain integrates separate signals from *cold fibres* and *warm fibres* to monitor changes in environmental temperature.

One aspect of cutaneous sensitivity plays a central role in human relationships: touch. Through touch, you communicate to others your desire to give or receive comfort, support, love and passion. However, where you get touched or touch someone else makes a difference; those areas of the skin surface that give rise to erotic, or sexual, sensations are called *erogenous zones*. Other touch-sensitive erotic areas vary in their arousal potential for different individuals, depending on learned associations and the concentration of sensory receptors in the areas.

## THE VESTIBULAR AND KINESTHETIC SENSES

The next pair of senses we will describe may be entirely new to you because they do not have receptors you can see directly, like eyes, ears or noses. Your **vestibular sense** tells you how your body—especially your head—is oriented in the world with respect to gravity. The receptors for this information are tiny hairs in fluid-filled sacs and canals in the inner ear. The hairs bend when the fluid moves and presses on them, which is what happens when

Why would riding in the front seat of a roller coaster be less likely to make you nauseated than riding in the rear?

**cutaneous senses** The skin senses that register sensations or pressure, warmth and cold.

you turn your head quickly. The *saccule* and *utricle* (shown in Figure 4.21) tell you about acceleration or deceleration in a straight line. The three canals, called the *semicircular canals,* are at right angles to each other and thus can tell you about motion in any direction. They inform you how your head is moving when you turn, nod or tilt it.

People who lose their vestibular sense because of accidents or disease are initially quite disoriented and prone to falls and dizziness. However, most of these people eventually compensate by relying more heavily on visual information. *Motion sickness* can occur when the signals from the visual system conflict with those from the vestibular system. People feel nauseated when reading in a moving car because the visual signal is of a stationary object while the vestibular signal is of movement. Drivers rarely get motion sickness because they are both seeing and feeling motion.

Whether you are standing upright, drawing pictures or making love, your brain needs to have accurate information about the current positions and movement of your body parts relative to one another. The **kinaesthetic sense** (also called *kinesthaesis*) provides constant sensory feedback about what the body is doing during motor activities. Without it, you would be unable to coordinate most voluntary movements.

You have two sources of kinaesthetic information: receptors in the joints and receptors in the muscles and tendons. Receptors that lie in the joints respond to pressures that accompany different positions of the limbs and to pressure changes that accompany movements of the joints. Receptors in the muscles and tendons respond to changes in tension that accompany muscle shortening and lengthening.

**kinaesthetic sense** The sense concerned with bodily position and movement of the body parts relative to one another.

What role does the kinaesthetic sense play in the performance of skilled dancers?

**vestibular sense** The sense that tells how one's own body is oriented in the world with respect to gravity.

The brain often integrates information from your kinaesthetic sense with information from touch senses. Your brain, for example, can't grasp the full meaning of the signals coming from each of your fingers if it doesn't know exactly where your fingers are in relation to one another. Imagine that you pick up an object with your eyes closed. Your sense of touch may allow you to guess that the object is a stone, but your kinaesthetic sense will enable you to know how large it is.

## PAIN

**Pain** is the body's response to stimulation from harmful stimuli—those that are intense enough to cause tissue damage or threaten to do so. Are you entirely happy that you have such a well-developed pain sense? Your answer probably should be 'yes and no'. On the yes side, your pain sense is critical for survival. People born with congenital insensitivity to pain feel no hurt, but their bodies often become scarred and their limbs deformed from injuries that they could have avoided, had their brains been able to warn them of danger (Larner et al., 1994). Their experience shows that pain serves as an essential defence signal—it warns you of potential harm. On the no side, there are certainly times when you would be happy to be able to turn off your pain sense. Researchers from the Pain Management Research Institute in Sydney estimate that chronic pain effects 1 in 6 working Australians (Blyth et al., 2001). The lost and reduced productivity costs Australian employers approximately $5.1 billion each year (van Leeuwen et al., 2006). When medical costs are included, this figure balloons to more than $10 billion annually.

Scientists have begun to identify the specific sets of receptors that respond to pain-producing stimuli. They have learned that some receptors respond only to temperature, others to chemicals, others to mechanical stimuli, and still others to combinations of pain-producing stimuli. This network of pain fibres is a fine meshwork that covers your entire body. Peripheral nerve fibres send pain signals to the central nervous system by two pathways: a fast-conducting set of nerve fibres that are covered with myelin and slower, smaller nerve fibres without any myelin coating. Starting at the spinal cord, the impulses are relayed to the thalamus and then to the cerebral cortex, where the location and intensity of the pain are identified, the significance of the injury is evaluated, and action plans are formulated.

Within your brain, *endorphins* have an impact on your experience of pain. Recall from Chapter 3 that pain-killing drugs such as morphine bind to the same receptor sites in the brain—the term *endorphin* comes from *endogenous* (self-produced) *morphines*. The release of endorphins within the brain controls your experience of pain. Researchers believe that endorphins are at least partially responsible for the pain-reducing effects of acupuncture and placebos (Benedetti et al., 2005; Han, 2004).

Your emotional responses, context factors, and your interpretation of the situation can be as important as actual physical stimuli in determining how much pain you experience (Price, 2000; Turk & Okifuji, 2003). How are pain sensations affected by the psychological context? One theory about the way pain may be modulated is known as the **gate-control theory**, developed by Ronald Melzack (1973, 1980). This theory suggests that cells in the spinal cord act as neurological gates, interrupting and blocking some pain signals and letting others get through to the brain. Receptors in the skin and the brain send messages to the spinal cord to open or close those gates. Suppose, for example, you bump your shin on a table while running to answer the telephone. As you rub the skin around the bump, you send inhibitory messages to your spinal cord—closing the gates. Messages descending from the brain also can close the gates. If, for example, the phone call includes urgent news, your brain might close the gates to prevent you from experiencing the distraction of pain. Melzack (1999) has proposed an updated *neuromatrix theory* of pain that incorporates the reality that people often experience pain with little or no physical cause. In these cases, the experience of pain originates wholly in the brain.

We've just seen that the way you perceive pain may reveal more about your psychological state than about the intensity of the pain stimulus: what you perceive may be different from, and even independent of, what you sense. This discussion of pain prepares you for the rest of the chapter, in which we discuss the perceptual processes that allow you to organise and label your experiences of the world.

## RECAP CHECKPOINT
### Your other senses

- Smell and taste respond to the chemical properties of substances and work together when people are seeking and sampling food.
- Olfaction is accomplished by odour-sensitive cells deep in the nasal passages.
- The specific pattern of olfactory receptor activation is thought to represent the odour qualities.
- Specific anosmia is the inability to smell one particular odour while having normal sensitivity to all other odours.
- Taste receptors are taste buds embedded in papillae, mostly in the tongue.
- Prolonged exposure to a particular taste will result in adaptation, decreasing the perceived intensity of that taste.
- The cutaneous (skin) senses give sensations of pressure and temperature.
- The vestibular sense gives information about the direction and rate of body motion.

- The kinaesthetic sense gives information about the position of body parts and helps coordinate motion.
- Pain is the body's response to potentially harmful stimuli.
- The physiological response to pain involves sensory signals from the site of the pain stimulus being sent to the spinal cord, and nerve impulses moving between the brain and the spinal cord.

## CONCEPT QUESTIONS

1. What is an important brain structure involved in the sense of smell?
2. To what basic taste qualities do your taste buds respond?
3. How does your skin sense temperature?
4. What is the purpose of the vestibular sense?
5. What is the goal of gate-control theory?

Individuals taking part in religious rituals, such as walking on a bed of hot coals, are able to block out pain. What does that tell you about the relationship between the physiology and psychology of pain?

# ORGANISATIONAL PROCESSES IN PERCEPTION

Imagine how confusing the world would be if you were unable to put together and organise the information available from the output of your millions of retinal receptors. You would experience a kaleidoscope of disconnected bits of colour moving and swirling before your eyes. The processes that put sensory information together to give you the perception of coherence are referred to collectively as processes of perceptual organisation.

We begin our discussion of perceptual organisation with a description of the processes of *attention* that prompt you to focus on a subset of stimuli from your kaleidoscope of experience. We then examine the organisational processes first described by *Gestalt* theorists, who argued that what you perceive depends on laws of organisation, or simple rules by which you perceive shapes and forms.

## ATTENTIONAL PROCESSES

Take a moment now to find ten things in your environment that had not been, so far, in your immediate awareness. Had you noticed a spot on the wall? Had you noticed the ticking of a clock? If you start to examine your surroundings very carefully, you will discover that there are literally thousands of things on which you could focus your **attention**. Generally, the more closely you attend to some object or event in the environment, the more you can perceive and learn about it.

**Determining the focus of attention** What forces determine the objects that become the focus of your attention? The answer to this question has two components, which we will call goal-directed selection and stimulus-driven capture (Yantis, 1993). **Goal-directed selection** reflects the choices that you make about the objects to which you'd like to attend, as a function of your own goals. If, for example, you are contemplating a case full of pastries, you might direct your attention only to those desserts covered in chocolate. You are probably already comfortable with the idea that you can explicitly choose objects for particular scrutiny. **Stimulus-driven capture** occurs when features of the stimuli—objects in the environment—themselves automatically capture your attention, independent of your local goals as a perceiver. You've experienced stimulus-driven capture, for example, if you've ever been day-dreaming at a stoplight while out for a drive. The stoplight's abrupt change from red to green will often capture your attention even if you were not particularly focused on it.

You might wonder what the relationship is between these two processes: research suggests that, at least under some circumstances, stimulus-driven capture wins out over goal-directed selection.

For answers go to MyPsychLab!

**attention** A state of focused awareness on a subset of the available perceptual information.

**goal-directed selection** A determinant of why people select some parts of sensory input for further processing; it reflects the choices made as a function of one's own goals.

**stimulus-driven capture** A determinant of why people select some parts of sensory input for further processing.

Researchers created visual displays that put goal-directed selection and stimulus-driven capture into competition (Theeuwes et al., 1998). As shown in Part A of **Figure 4.25**, each trial of an experiment began with a visual display of six grey circles filled with six dim figure eights. After 1 second, the display changed. In half the trials, as shown in Part B, all but one of the circles changed from grey to red. The participants' task was to shift their eyes to the remaining grey circle and respond whether the character inside was either a forward or a backward letter c. When they carry out this task, participants are using goal-directed selection: They are purposely shifting their attention to the remaining grey circle.

Now consider Part C of Figure 4.25. In this instance, which represents the remaining half of the trials, a new element is added to the visual array—a new red circle. New objects are the type of visual stimulus that typically engage stimulus-driven capture. Under ordinary circumstances, we'd expect participants to shift their eyes to that new object. However, in this particular experiment, the participants don't want their eyes to be pulled to that object: they are still asked to report only the contents of the single grey circle. So what happens? Can the participants stop themselves from moving their attention to the new red circle? In fact, on most occasions, the new object automatically drew the participants' attention—even though it was entirely irrelevant to the goal the experimenters had set for them.

You can recognise this phenomenon as stimulus-driven capture because it works in the opposite direction of the perceiver's goals. Because, that is, the participants would perform the task better if they ignored the new red circle, they must be unable to ignore it (because experimental participants almost always prefer to perform as well as possible on the tasks researchers assign them). The important general conclusion is that your perceptual system is organised so that your attention is automatically drawn to objects that are new to an environment (Yantis & Jonides, 1996).

### The fate of unattended information

If you have selectively attended to some subset of a perceptual display—by virtue of your own goals or of properties of the stimuli—what is the fate of the information to which you did *not* attend? Imagine listening to a lecture while people on both sides of you are engaged in conversations. How are you able to keep track of the lecture? What do you notice about the conversations? Could anything appear in the content of one or the other conversation to divert your attention from the lecture?

This constellation of questions was first explored by **Donald Broadbent** (1958), who suggested that the mind has only *limited capacity* to carry out complete processing. This limit requires that attention strictly regulate the flow of information from sensory input to consciousness. The *filter theory* of attention asserted that the selection occurs early on in the process, before the input's meaning is accessed.

To test the filter theory, researchers recreated the real-life situation of multiple sources of input in the laboratory with a technique called **dichotic listening**. In this paradigm, a participant wearing earphones listens to

**dichotic listening** An experimental technique in which a different auditory stimulus is simultaneously presented to each ear.

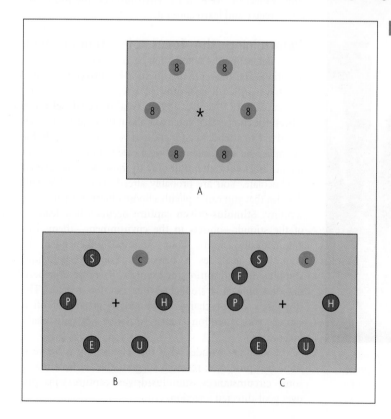

**Figure 4.25**

**Processes that select attention**
At the beginning of each trial of this experiment, participants viewed a display with six grey circles (Part A). When the display changed, the participants' task was to report whether the 'c' in the one remaining grey circle was forward or backward. On half of the trials, the displays did not introduce new objects (Part B); on the other half of the trials, they did (Part C). Although the participants' goal was to attend to the single grey circle, the new objects—when they occurred—automatically drew their attention.

Have you ever had this experience? You are eating a very 'hot' dish in a Chinese or Mexican restaurant and you accidentally bite directly into a chilli pepper. In just moments you go from enjoyment to intense pain. If this has happened, then you know that, in the realm of taste, there is a fine line between what gives pleasure and what gives pain. Let's explore this relationship.

Physiologically, it's easy to explain why hot chilli can cause you pain. On your tongue, your taste buds have associated with them pain fibres (Bartoshuk, 1993). Thus the very same chemical that can stimulate the receptors in your taste buds can stimulate the closely allied pain fibres (Caterina et al., 2000). In the case of hot chilli, this chemical is *capsaicin*. If you want to enjoy a spicy meal, you have to keep the concentration of capsaicin in your meal sufficiently low so that your taste receptors are more active than your pain receptors.

But why, you might wonder, do different people have such obvious differences in their preferences for hot food? People often find it very difficult to understand how their friends can or cannot eat food that is very spicy. Again, we can look to physiology to explain these differences. The figure shows photographs of tongues from two individuals studied by **Linda Bartoshuk** and her colleagues. You can see that one tongue has considerably more taste buds than the other. If there are more

taste buds, there will be more pain receptors. Therefore, people with more taste buds are more likely to get a strong pain response from capsaicin. The group of individuals who have more taste buds have been dubbed *supertasters* (Bartoshuk, 1993). They form a sharp contrast, in the extremes of their sensory experiences, to *non tasters*. For many taste sensations, these two groups are equivalent— you wouldn't know at most times whether you were a supertaster, a nontaster, or somewhere in between. The differences arise only for certain chemicals— capsaicin is an excellent example.

The variations in the density of taste buds on different people's tongues appear to be genetic (Bartoshuk & Beauchamp, 1994). Women are much more likely than men to be supertasters. Supertasters generally have more sensitivity to bitter chemicals—a sensory quality shared by most poisons. You can imagine that if women generally were responsible for nurturing and feeding offspring over the course

of evolution, the children of women with greater taste sensitivity would be more likely to survive. Because taster status is genetic, you can find preference differences among children at very young ages (Anliker et al., 1991). Five- to seven-year-old supertasters preferred milk to cheddar cheese. This preference was reversed for nontasters. Why? The supertasters may perceive the milk as sweeter and the cheese as more bitter than do the nontasters. Thus genetic differences may help explain why some young children have such strong (and vocal) taste preferences.

But let's return to the restaurant meal at which you have had your painful accident. What you might have noticed is that the sensation of pain fades over time. In this respect, the pain receptors in your mouth act like other sensory receptors: Over time, you adapt to a constant stimulus. That's good news! You should be glad that your sensory processes offer built-in relief.

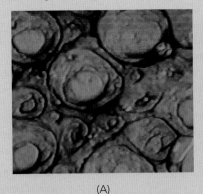

(A)

(A) The tongue of a supertaster.

(B)

(B) The tongue of a nontaster.

two taped messages played at the same time—a different message is played into each ear. The participant is instructed to repeat only one of the two messages to the experimenter while ignoring whatever is presented to the other ear. This procedure is called *shadowing* the attended message (see **Figure 4.26**).

The strongest form of filter theory was challenged when it was discovered that some listeners were recalling

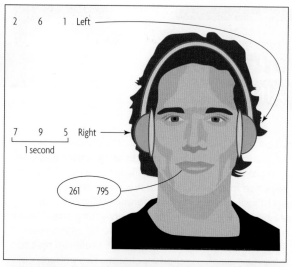

Figure 4.26

### Dichotic listening task

A subject hears different digits presented simultaneously to each ear: 2 (left), 7 (right), 6 (left), 9 (right), 1 (left), and 5 (right). He reports hearing the correct sets—261 and 795. However, when instructed to attend only to the right-ear input, the subject reports hearing only 795.

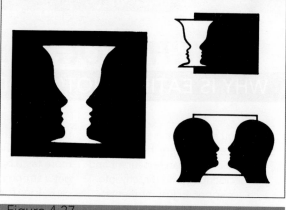

Figure 4.27

### Figure and ground

An initial step in perceptual grouping is for your perceptual processes to interpret part of a scene as a figure standing out against a ground.

**figure** Object like regions of the visual field that are distinguished from background.

**ground** The backdrop of background areas of the visual field against which figures stand out.

**Gestalt psychology** A school of psychology that maintains that psychological phenomena can be understood only when viewed as organised, structured wholes, not when broken down into primitive perceptual elements.

things they would not have been able to recall if attention had been totally filtering all ignored material (Cherry, 1953). Consider, for example, your own name. People often report that they hear their name being mentioned in a noisy room, even when they are engaged in their own conversation. This is often called the *cocktail party phenomenon*. Laboratory research has confirmed that people are especially likely to notice their own names among unattended information (Wood & Cowan, 1995a).

Researchers now believe that information in the unattended channel is processed to some extent but not sufficiently to reach conscious awareness (Wood & Cowan, 1995b). Only if properties of the unattended information are sufficiently distinctive—by virtue, for example, of being a listener's name—will the information become the focus of conscious attention. (We will return to the relationship between attention and consciousness in Chapter 5.) The general rule is that unattended information will not make its presence known. You can see, therefore, why it's dangerous to let yourself become distracted from your immediate task or goal. If you fail to pay attention to some body of information—your psychology lecture, perhaps—the material won't just sink in of its own accord!

Let's suppose that you have focused your attention on some stimulus in the environment. It's time for your processes of perceptual organisation to go to work.

## PRINCIPLES OF PERCEPTUAL GROUPING

Consider the image on the left in **Figure 4.27**. If you're like most people, you'll see a vase as *figure* against a black

*ground*. A **figure** is seen as an object-like region in the forefront, and **ground** is seen as the backdrop against which the figures stand out. As you can see on the right of Figure 4.27, it's possible to change the relationship between figure and ground—to see two faces rather than one vase. One of the first tasks your perceptual processes carry out is to decide what in a scene counts as figure and what as ground.

How do your perceptual processes determine what should be gathered together into the figure? The principles of perceptual grouping were studied extensively by proponents of **Gestalt psychology**, such as **Kurt Koffka** (1935), **Wolfgang Köhler** (1947), and Max Wertheimer (1923). Members of this group maintained that psychological phenomena could be understood only when viewed as organised, structured *wholes* and not when broken down into primitive perceptual elements. The term *gestalt* roughly means 'form', 'whole', 'configuration', or 'essence'. In their experiments, the Gestalt psychologists studied how perceptual arrays give rise to gestalts: They demonstrated that the whole is often quite different from the sum of its parts. By varying a single factor and observing how it affected the way people perceived the structure of the array, they were able to formulate a set of laws:

1. *The law of proximity*. People group together the nearest (most proximal) elements. That's why you see this display as five columns of objects instead of four rows.

**CHAPTER 4** SENSATION AND PERCEPTION

2. *The law of similarity.* People group together the most similar elements. That's why you see a square of Os against a field of Xs rather than columns of mixed Xs and Os.

3. *The law of good continuation.* People experience lines as continuous even when they are interrupted. That's why you interpret this display as an arrow piercing the heart rather than as a design with three separate pieces.

4. *The law of closure.* People tend to fill in small gaps to experience objects as wholes. That's why you fill in the missing piece to perceive a whole circle.

**O**

5. *The law of common fate.* People tend to group together objects that appear to be moving in the same direction. That's why you experience this figure as alternating rows moving apart.

# SPATIAL AND TEMPORAL INTEGRATION

All the Gestalt laws we have presented to you so far should have convinced you that a lot of perception consists of putting the pieces of your world together in the 'right way.' Often, however, you can't perceive an entire scene in one glance or *fixation* (recall our discussion of attention). What you perceive at a given time is often a restricted glimpse of a large visual world extending in all directions to unseen areas of the environment. To get a complete idea of what is around you, you must combine information from fixations of different spatial locations—*spatial integration*—at different moments in time—*temporal integration*.

What may surprise you is that your visual system does not work very hard to create a moment-by-moment, integrated picture of the environment. Research suggests

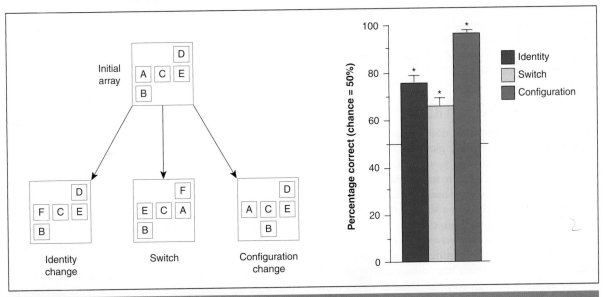

Figure 4.28

**Change blindness**
(A) Schematic illustration of potential changes in the experimental arrays (objects represented by letters). Experimental participants were asked to respond whether a second display was the 'same as' or 'different from' the initial array.
(B) When the identity of the object was changed or two objects were switched, participants often were unable to detect the difference. Only when the whole configuration changed were participants nearly always correct. Mean percentage correct (with standard error bar) for each condition. Asterisks indicate a significant different ($P < .05$>) from change performance of 50% correct.

Reprinted with permission from D.J. Simons & M.S. Ambinder (2005). Change blindness: Theory and consequences. *Current Directions in Psychological Science*, 14, 44–48.

that your visual memory for each fixation on the world does not preserve precise details (Simons & Ambinder, 2005). In fact, viewers are sometimes unable to detect when a whole object has changed from one fixation to the next.

> In one of a series of experiments, participants viewed for 2 seconds an array showing pictures of five familiar objects. Roughly 4 seconds later, the participants viewed a second array. In half of the trials, the second array was identical to the first. However, as shown in Part A of **Figure 4.28**, on the other half of the trials the second array differed from the first in one of three ways: one of the objects had changed identity (e.g., a *stapler* in the first array might be replaced by a *staple remover* in the second array); two of the objects had switched their spatial position; or the whole set of objects was placed in a new configuration. Participants were challenged to judge whether the arrays were the *same* or *different*. You might imagine, on brief reflection, that this would be an easy task: How could you not notice that a *stapler* had turned into a *staple remover*? However, as shown in Part B of Figure 4.28, performance for *identity* and *switch* changes was well below 100 percent correct. Participants were 'blind' to a number of *very* obvious changes (Simons, 1996)!

Many people find this result surprising. How could it be that you have so few processing resources devoted to preserving the details of a scene over time—so that you wouldn't notice that a stapler has turned into a set of keys? Part of the answer might be that the world itself is generally a stable source of information (O'Regan, 1992). It is simply unnecessary to commit to memory information that remains steadily available in the external environment—and so you don't have processes that ordinarily allow you to do so.

## MOTION PERCEPTION

One type of perception that does require you to make comparisons across different glimpses of the world is motion perception. Suppose you see a friend across a classroom. If he stands still, the size of his image on your retina will expand as you draw near. The rate at which this image has expanded gives you a sense of how quickly you have been approaching (Gibson, 1979).

As we noted, motion perception requires you to combine information from difference glimpses of the world. You can appreciate the consequences of how your perceptual processes combine those glimpses quite strongly when you experience the **phi phenomenon**. This phenomenon occurs when two stationary spots of light in different positions in the visual field are turned on and off alternately at a rate of about four to five times per second. This effect occurs on outdoor advertising signs and in disco light displays. Even at this relatively slow rate of alternation, it appears that a single light is moving back and forth between the two spots. There are multiple ways to conceive of the path that leads from the location of the first dot to the location of the second

What makes you aware that the 'protagonist' in this photo is moving—and in what direction is the motion?

dot. Yet human observers normally see only the simplest path, a straight line (Cutting & Proffitt, 1982; Shepard, 1984). This straight-line rule is violated, however, when viewers are shown alternating views of a human body in motion. Then the visual system fills in the paths of normal biological motion (Shiffrar, 1994; Stevens et al., 2000).

## DEPTH PERCEPTION

Until now, we have considered only two-dimensional patterns on flat surfaces. Everyday perceiving, however, involves objects in three-dimensional space. Perceiving all three spatial dimensions is absolutely vital for you to approach what you want, such as interesting people and good food, and avoid what is dangerous, such as speeding cars and falling pianos. This perception requires accurate information about *depth* (the distance from you to an object) as well as about its *direction* from you. Your ears can help in determining direction, but they are not much help in determining depth. Your interpretation of depth relies on many different information sources about distance (often called *depth cues*)—among them binocular cues, motion cues and pictorial cues.

Binocular and motion cues Have you ever wondered why you have two eyes instead of just one? The second eye is more than just a spare—it provides some of the best, most compelling information about depth. The two sources of binocular depth information are *retinal disparity* and *convergence*. Because the eyes are about 5 to 8 centimetres apart horizontally, they receive slightly different views of the world. To convince yourself of this, try the following experiment. First, close your left eye and use the right one to line up your two index fingers with some small object in the distance, holding one finger at arm's length and the other about 30 centimetres in front of your face. Now, keeping your fingers stationary, close your right eye and open the left one while continuing to fixate on the distant object. What happened to the position of your two fingers? The second eye does not see them lined up with the distant object because it gets a slightly different view.

This displacement between the horizontal positions of corresponding images in your two eyes is called

**phi phenomenon** The simplest form of apparent motion, the movement illusion in which one or more stationary lights going on and off in succession are perceived as a single moving light.

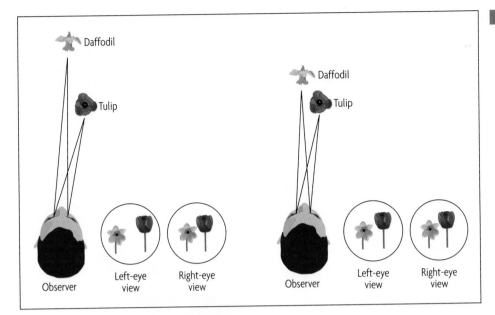

Figure 4.29

Retinal disparity
Retinal disparity
increases with the
distance in depth
between two objects.

**retinal disparity**. It provides depth information because the amount of disparity, or difference, depends on the relative distance of objects from you (see **Figure 4.29**). For instance, when you switched eyes, the closer finger was displaced farther to the side than was the distant finger.

When you look at the world with both eyes open, most objects that you see stimulate different positions on your two retinas. If the disparity between corresponding images in the two retinas is small enough, the visual system is able to fuse them into a perception of a single object in depth. (However, if the images are too far apart, you actually see the double images, as when you cross your eyes.) When you stop to think about it, what your visual system does is pretty amazing: it takes two different retinal images, compares them for horizontal displacement of corresponding parts (binocular disparity), and produces a unitary perception of a single object in depth. In effect, the visual system interprets horizontal displacement between the two images as depth in the three-dimensional world.

Other binocular information about depth comes from **convergence**. The two eyes turn inward to some extent whenever they are fixated on an object (see **Figure 4.30**). When the object is very close—a few centimetres in front of your face—the eyes must turn toward each other quite a bit for the same image to fall on both foveae. You can actually see the eyes converge if you watch a friend focus first on a distant object and then on one about 30 centimetres away. Your brain uses information from your eye muscles to make judgments about depth. However, convergence information from the eye muscles is useful for depth perception only up to about 3 metres. At greater distances, the angular differences are too small to detect because the eyes are nearly parallel when you fixate on a distant object.

To see how *motion* is another source for depth information, try the following demonstration. As you did before, close one eye and line up your two index fingers with some distant object. Then move your head to the side while fixating on the distant object and keeping your fingers still. As you move your head, you see both your fingers move, but the close finger seems to move farther and faster than the more distant one. The fixated object does not move at all. This source of information about depth is called **relative motion parallax**. Motion parallax provides information about depth because, as you move, the relative

retinal disparity The
displacement between
the horizontal positions of
corresponding images in the
two eyes.

relative motion parallax
A source of information about
depth in which the relative
distances of objects from a
viewer determine the amount
and direction of their relative
motion in the retinal image.

Angle of convergence (small)

Angle of convergence
(large)

Fovea        Fovea        Fovea        Fovea

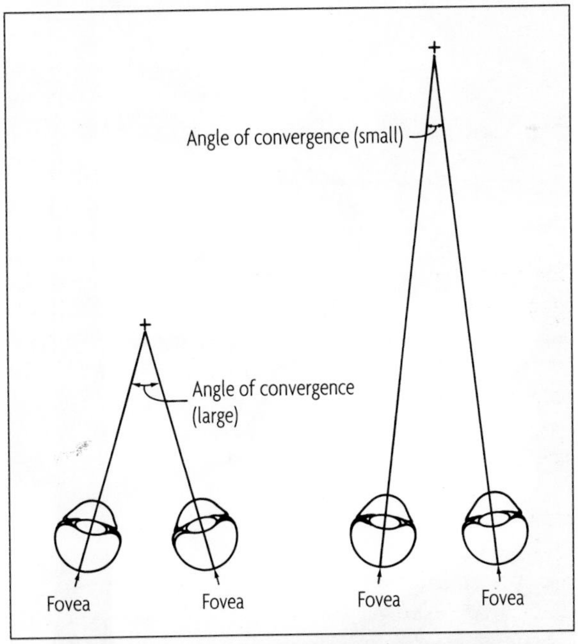

Figure 4.30

Convergence cues to depth
When an object is close to you, your eyes must converge more than when an object is at a greater distance. Your brain uses information from your eye muscles to use convergence as a cue to depth.

convergence The degree to
which the eyes turn inward
to fixate on an object.

distances of objects in the world determine the amount and direction of their relative motion in your retinal image of the scene. Next time you are a passenger on a car trip, keep a watch out the window for motion parallax at work. Objects at a distance from the moving car will appear much more stationary than those closer to you.

Pictorial cues But suppose you had vision in only one eye. Would you not be able to perceive depth? In fact, further information about depth is available from just one eye. These sources are called pictorial cues because they include the kinds of depth information found in pictures. Artists who create images in what appear to be three dimensions (on the two dimensions of a piece of paper or canvas) make skilled use of pictorial cues.

*Interposition*, or *occlusion*, arises when an opaque object blocks out part of a second object (see **Figure 4.31**). Interposition gives you depth information indicating that the occluded object is farther away than the occluding one. Occluding surfaces also block out light, creating shadows that can be used as an additional source of depth information.

Figure 4.31

Interposition cues to depth
What visual cues tell you whether this woman is behind the bars?

Three more sources of pictorial information are all related to the way light projects from a three-dimensional world onto a two-dimensional surface such as the retina: relative size, linear perspective and texture gradients. *Relative size* involves a basic rule of light projection: Objects of the same size at different distances project images of different sizes on the retina. The closest object projects the largest image and the farthest object the smallest image. This rule is called the *size/distance relation*. As you can see in **Figure 4.32**, if you look at an array with identical objects, you interpret the smaller ones to be farther away.

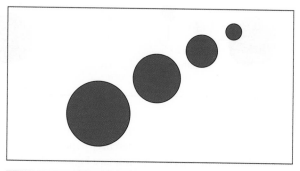

Figure 4.32

**Relative size as a depth cue**
Objects that are closer project larger images on the retina. As a consequence, when you look at an array with identical objects, you interpret the smaller ones to be at a greater distance.

*Linear perspective* is a depth cue that also depends on the size/distance relation. When parallel lines (by definition separated along their lengths by the same distance) recede into the distance, they converge toward a point on the horizon in your retinal image (see **Figure 4.33**). Your visual system's interpretation of converging lines gives rise to the Ponzo illusion. The upper line looks longer because you interpret the converging sides according to linear perspective as parallel lines receding into the distance. In this context, you interpret the upper line as though it were farther away, so you see it as longer—a farther object would have to be longer than a nearer one for both to produce retinal images of the same size.

*Texture gradients* provide depth cues because the density of a texture becomes greater as a surface recedes in depth. The wheat field in **Figure 4.34** is an example of the way texture is used as a depth cue. You can think of this as another consequence of the size/distance relation. In this case, the units that make up the texture become smaller

Figure 4.33

**The Ponzo illusion**
The converging lines add a dimension of depth, and therefore the distance cue makes the top line appear larger than the bottom line, even though they are actually the same length.

as they recede into the distance, and your visual system interprets this diminishing grain as greater distance in three-dimensional space.

By now, it should be clear that there are many sources of depth information. Under normal viewing conditions, however, information from these sources comes together in a single, coherent three-dimensional interpretation of the environment. You experience depth, not the different cues to depth that existed in the proximal stimulus. In other words, your visual system uses cues such as differential motion, interposition and relative size automatically, without your conscious awareness, to make the complex computations that give you a perception of depth in the three-dimensional environment.

## PERCEPTUAL CONSTANCIES

To help you discover another important property of visual perception, we are going to ask you to play with your textbook. Put your book down on a table, then move your head closer to it so that it's about 5 centimetres away. Then move your head back to a normal reading distance. Although the book stimulated a much larger part of your retina when it was up close than when it was far away, didn't you perceive the book's size to remain the same? Now set the book upright and try tilting your head clockwise. When you do this, the image of the book rotates counterclockwise on your retina, but didn't you still perceive the book to be upright?

In general, you see the world as *invariant*, *constant*, and *stable* despite changes in the stimulation of your sensory receptors. Psychologists refer to this phenomenon as **perceptual constancy**. Roughly speaking, it means that you perceive the properties of the distal stimuli, which are usually constant, rather than the properties of proximal stimuli, which change every time you move your eyes or head. For survival, it is critical that you perceive constant and stable properties of objects in the

Figure 4.34

**Examples of texture as a depth cue**
The wheat field is a natural example of the way texture can be used as a depth cue. Notice the way the wheat slants.

world despite the enormous variations in the properties of the light patterns that stimulate your eyes. The critical task of perception is to discover *invariant* properties of your environment despite the variations in your retinal impressions of them. We see next how this works for size, shape and orientation.

**Size and shape constancy** What determines your perception of the size of an object? In part, you perceive an object's actual size on the basis of the size of its retinal image. However, the demonstration with your book shows that the size of the retinal image depends on both the actual size of the book and its distance from the eye. As you now know, information about distance is available from a variety of depth cues. Your visual system combines that information with retinal information about image size to yield a perception of an object size that usually corresponds to the actual size of the distal stimulus. **Size constancy** refers to your ability to perceive the true size of an object despite variations in the size of its retinal image.

If the size of an object is perceived by taking distance cues into account, then you should be fooled about size whenever you are fooled about distance. One such

**size constancy** The ability to perceive the true size of an object despite variations in the size of its retinal image.

**perceptual constancy**
The ability to retain an unchanging percept of an object despite variations in the retinal image.

Figure 4.35

### The Ames room

The Ames room is designed to be viewed through a peephole with one eye—that is the vantage point from which these photographs were taken. The Ames room is constructed from nonrectangular surfaces at odd angles in depth and height. However, with only the view from the peephole, your visual system interprets it as an ordinary room and makes some unusual guesses about the relative heights of the occupants.

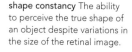

shape constancy The ability to perceive the true shape of an object despite variations in the size of the retinal image.

illusion occurs in the Ames room shown in **Figure 4.35**. In comparison to the child, the adult, looks quite short in the left corner of this room, but he looks enormous in the right corner. The reason for this illusion is that you perceive the room to be rectangular, with the two back corners equally distant from you. Thus you perceive the child's actual size as being consistent with the size of the images on your retina in both cases. In fact, the child is not at the same distance because the Ames room creates a clever illusion. It appears to be a rectangular room, but it is actually made from nonrectangular surfaces at odd angles in depth and height, as you can see in the drawings that accompany the photos. Any person on the right will make a larger retinal image, because he or she is twice as close to the observer. (By the way, to get the illusion you must view the display with a single eye through a peephole—that's the vantage point of the photographs in Figure 4.35. If you could move around while viewing the room, your visual system would acquire information about the unusual structure of the room.)

Another way that the perceptual system can infer objective size is by using prior knowledge about the characteristic size of similarly shaped objects. For instance, once you recognise the shape of a house, a tree or a dog, you have a good idea of how big each is, even without knowing its distance from you. When past experience does not give you knowledge of what familiar objects look like at extreme distances, size constancy may break down. You have experienced this problem if you have looked down at people from the top of a skyscraper and thought that they resembled ants.

**Shape constancy** is closely related to size constancy. You perceive an object's actual shape correctly even when the object is slanted away from you, making the shape of the retinal image substantially different from that of the object itself. For instance, a rectangle tipped away projects a trapezoidal image onto your retina; a circle tipped away from you projects an elliptical image (see **Figure 4.36**). Yet you usually perceive the shapes accurately as a circle and a rectangle slanted away in

Figure 4.36

### Shape constancy

As a coin is rotated, its image becomes an ellipse that grows narrower and narrower until it becomes a thin rectangle, an ellipse again, and then a circle. At each orientation, however, it is still perceived as a circular coin.

space. When there is good depth information available, your visual system can determine an object's true shape simply by taking into account your distance from its different parts.

Lightness constancy Consider the photograph in **Figure 4.37**. When you look at the brick wall in this picture, you don't perceive some of the bricks to be light red and some of them to be dark red—instead, you perceive this as a wall in which all the bricks are equally light or dark but some of them are in shadow (Goldstein, 2007). This is an example of lightness constancy: **lightness constancy** is your tendency to perceive the whiteness, greyness, or blackness of objects as constant across changing levels of illumination.

As with the other constancies we have described, you experience lightness constancy quite frequently in everyday life. Suppose, for example, you are wearing a white T-shirt and walk from a dimly lit room outside into a bright sunny day. In bright sunshine, the T-shirt reflects far more light into your eyes than it does in the dim room, yet it looks about equally light to you in both contexts. In fact, lightness constancy works because the *percentage* of light an object reflects remains about the same even as the *absolute* amount of light changes. Your bright white T-shirt is going to reflect 80 to 90 percent of whatever light is available; your black jeans are going to reflect only about 5 percent of the available light. That's why—when you see them in the same context—the T-shirt will always look lighter than the jeans.

Figure 4.37

**Lightness constancy**
Lightness constancy helps explain why you perceive all the bricks in the wall to be made of the same material.

**lightness constancy** The tendency to perceive the whiteness, greyness or blackness of objects as constant across changing levels of illuminations.

For answers go to MyPsychLab!

In this section, we have described a number of organisational processes in perception. In the final section of the chapter, we consider the identification and recognition processes that give meaning to objects and events in the environment.

# IDENTIFICATION AND RECOGNITION PROCESSES

You can think of all the perceptual processes described so far as providing reasonably accurate knowledge about physical properties of the distal stimulus—the position, size, shape, texture and colour of objects in a three-dimensional environment. However, you would not know what the objects were or whether you had seen them before. Your experience would resemble a visit to an alien planet where everything was new to you; you wouldn't know what to eat, what to put on your head, what to run away from, or what to date. Your environment appears nonalien because you are able to recognise and identify most objects as things you have seen before and as members of the meaningful categories that you know about from experience. Identification and recognition attach meaning to what you perceive.

## BOTTOM-UP AND TOP-DOWN PROCESSES

When you identify an object, you must match what you see to your stored knowledge. Taking sensory data in from the environment and sending it toward the brain for extraction and analysis of relevant information is called bottom-up processing. **Bottom-up processing** is anchored in empirical reality and deals with bits of information and the transformation of concrete, physical features of stimuli into abstract representations. This type of processing is also called *data-driven processing* because your starting point for identification is the sensory evidence you obtain from the environment—the data.

In many cases, however, you can use information you already have about the environment to help you make a perceptual identification. If you visit a zoo, for example, you might be a little more ready to recognise some types of animals than you otherwise would be. You are more likely to hypothesise that you are seeing a tiger there than you would be in your own backyard. When your expectations affect perception, the phenomenon is called top-down processing. **Top-down processing** involves your past experiences, knowledge, motivations and cultural background in perceiving the world. With top-down processing, higher mental functioning influences how you understand objects and events. Top-down processing is also known as conceptually driven (or hypothesis-driven) processing because the concepts you have stored in memory affect interpretation of the sensory data. The importance of top-down processing can be illustrated by drawings known as droodles (Price, 1953/1980). Without the labels, these drawings are meaningless. However, once the drawings are identified, you can easily find meaning in them (see **Figure 4.38**).

For a more detailed example of top-down versus bottom-up processing, we turn to the domain of speech perception. You have undoubtedly had the experience of trying to carry on a conversation at a very loud party. Under those circumstances, it's probably true that not all of the physical signal you are producing arrives unambiguously at your acquaintance's ears: some of what you had to say was almost certainly obscured by coughs, thumping music, or peals of laughter. Even so, people rarely realise that there are gaps in the physical signal they are experiencing. This phenomenon

**bottom-up processing**
Perceptual analyses based on the sensory data available in the environment; results of analysis are passed upward toward more abstract representations.

**top-down processing**
Perceptual processes in which information from an individual's past experience, knowledge, expectations, motivations and background influence the way a perceived object is interpreted.

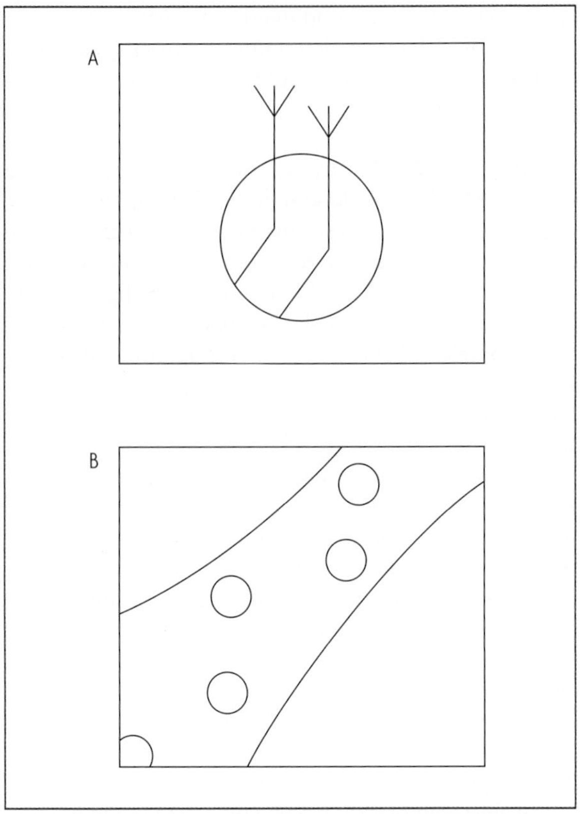

Figure 4.38

**Droodles**
What are these animals? Do you see in (A) an early bird who caught a very strong worm and in (B) a giraffe's neck? Each figure can be seen as representing something familiar to you, although this perceptual recognition usually does not occur until some identifying information is provided.

is known as *phonemic restoration* (Warren, 1970). As we explain more fully in Chapter 10, *phonemes* are the minimal, meaningful units of sound in a language; phonemic restoration occurs when people use top-down processes to fill in missing phonemes. Listeners often find it difficult to tell whether they are hearing a word that has a noise replacing part of the original speech signal or whether they are hearing a word with a noise just superimposed on the intact signal (see part A of **Figure 4.39**) (Samuel, 1981, 1991).

Part B of Figure 4.39 shows how bottom-up and top-down processes could interact to produce phonemic restoration (McClelland & Elman, 1986). Suppose part of what your friend says at a noisy party is obscured so the signal that arrives at your ears is 'I have to go home to walk my (noise)og.' If noise covers the /d/, you are likely to think that you actually heard the full word *dog*. But why? In Figure 4.39, you see two of the types of information relevant to speech perception. We have the individual sounds that make up words and the words themselves. When the sounds /o/ and /g/ arrive in this system, they provide information—in a

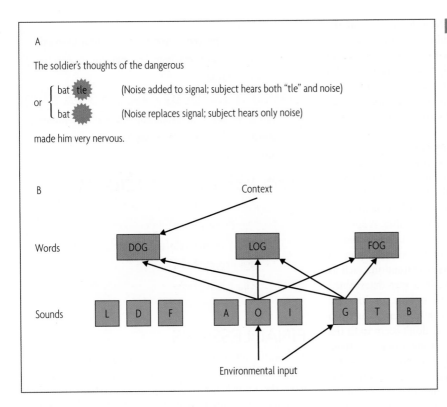

A

The soldier's thoughts of the dangerous

bat tle    (Noise added to signal; subject hears both "tle" and noise)

or

bat    (Noise replaces signal; subject hears only noise)

made him very nervous.

B

Context

Words   DOG   LOG   FOG

Sounds   L  D  F  A  O  I  G  T  B

Environmental input

**Figure 4.39**

**Phonemic restoration**

(A) Listeners are challenged to say whether noise has been added on top of a syllable or used to replace a syllable. Because of phonemic restoration, they often can't tell. They 'hear' the missing information even when the sound is replaced by noise. (B) In this example, noise obscured the /d/ when your friend said 'dog.' Based only on the environmental input, your perceptual system can come up with several hypotheses: dog, log, fog, and so on. However, top-down information from the context—'I have to go home and walk my . . .'—supports the hypothesis that your friend said 'dog.'

Reprinted with permission from Irwin Rock, *The Logic of Perception*. Cambridge, MA, The MIT Press. Copyright © 1983.

bottom-up fashion—to the word level (we have given only a subset of the words in English that end with /og/). This provides you with a range of candidates for what your friend might have said. Now top-down processes go to work—the context helps you select *dog* as the most likely word to appear in this utterance. When all of this happens swiftly enough—bottom-up identification of a set of candidate words and top-down selection of the likely correct candidate—you'll never know that the /d/ was missing. Your perceptual processes believe that the word was intact (Samuel, 1997). The next time you're in a noisy environment, you'll be glad your perceptual processes fill sounds in so efficiently!

## THE INFLUENCE OF CONTEXTS AND EXPECTATIONS

Early in the chapter, we noted that the world often gives you ambiguous information to perceive. Consider **Figure 4.40**. What do you make of it? Suppose we tell you that it's a view into our neighbour's backyard, showing a tree around which his dalmatian routinely sniffs? Now can you see a dog? (The dog's nose is roughly in the middle of the figure.) This is another top-down aspect of perception: Contexts and expectations can influence your hypotheses about what is out there in the world. Have you ever had the experience of seeing people you knew in places where you didn't expect to see them, such as in a different city or a different social group? It takes much longer to recognise them in such situations, and sometimes you aren't even sure that you really know them. The problem is not that they look any different but that the *context* is wrong; you didn't *expect* them to be there. The spatial and

temporal context in which objects are recognised provides an important source of information because from the context you generate expectations about what objects you are and are not likely to see nearby.

Perceptual identification depends on your expectations as well as on the physical properties of the objects you see—object identification is a constructive, interpretive process. Depending on what you already know, where you are, and what else you see around you, your identification may vary. Read the following words:

## THE CAT

**Figure 4.40**

**An ambiguous picture**
What do you see in this picture?

For answers go to MyPsychLab!

mypsychlab
where learning comes to life!

**set** A temporary readiness to perceive or react to a stimulus in a particular way.

They say THE CAT, right? Now look again at the middle letter of each word. Physically, these two letters are exactly the same, yet you perceived the first as an H and the second as an A. Why? Clearly, your perception was affected by what you know about words in English. The context provided by T_E makes an H highly likely and an A unlikely, whereas the reverse is true of the context of C_T (Selfridge, 1955).

Researchers have often documented the effects of context and expectation on perception (and response) by studying set. **Set** is a temporary readiness to perceive or react to a stimulus in a particular way. There are three types of set: motor, mental and perceptual. A *motor set* is a readiness to make a quick, prepared response. A sprinter trains by perfecting a motor set to come out of the blocks as fast as possible at the sound of the starting gun. A *mental set* is a readiness to deal with a situation, such as a problem-solving task or a game, in a way determined by learned rules, instructions, expectations, or habitual tendencies. A *mental set* can actually prevent you from solving a problem when the old rules don't seem to fit the new situation, as we'll see when we study problem solving in Chapter 9. A *perceptual set* is a readiness to detect a particular stimulus in a given context. A new mother, for example, is perceptually set to hear the cries of her child.

Often a set leads you to change your interpretation of an ambiguous stimulus. Consider these two series of words:

FOX; OWL; SNAKE; TURKEY; SWAN; D?VE

BOB; RAY; TONY; BILL; HENRY; D?VE

Did you read through the lists? What word came to mind for D?VE in each case? If you thought DOVE and DAVE, it's because the list of words created a set that directed your search of memory in a particular way.

All the effects of context on perception clearly require that your memory be organised in such a fashion that information relevant to particular situations becomes available at the right times. In other words, to generate appropriate (or inappropriate) expectations, you must be able to make use of prior knowledge stored in memory. Sometimes you 'see' with your memory as much as you see with your eyes. In Chapter 7, we discuss the properties of memory that make context effects on perception possible.

## RECAP CHECKPOINT

### Identification and recognition processes

- During the final stage of perceptual processing — identification and recognition of objects — percepts are given meaning through processes that combine bottom-up and top-down influences.

- Context, expectations and perceptual sets may guide recognition of incomplete or ambiguous data in one direction rather than another equally possible one.

## CONCEPT QUESTIONS

1. Why is phonemic restoration an example of top-down processing?

2. What is the relationship between contexts and expectations?

3. What is a set?

## FINAL LESSONS

To solidify all that you have learned in this chapter, we suggest that you take a look back at Figure 4.2—you now have the knowledge necessary to understand the whole flowchart. Examination of Figure 4.2 will also confirm that the important lesson to be learned from the study of perception is that a perceptual experience in response to a stimulus event is a response of the whole person. In addition to the information provided when your sensory receptors are stimulated, your final perception depends on who you are, whom you are with, and what you expect, want and value. A perceiver often plays two different roles that we can compare to gambling and interior design. As a gambler, a perceiver is willing to bet that the present input can be understood in terms of past knowledge and personal theories. As a compulsive interior decorator, a perceiver is constantly rearranging the stimuli so that they fit better and are more coherent. Incongruity and messy perceptions are rejected in favour of those with clear, clean, consistent lines.

If perceiving were completely bottom-up, you would be bound to the same mundane, concrete reality of the here and now. You could register experience but not profit from it on later occasions, nor would you see the world differently under different circumstances. If perceptual processing were completely top-down, however, you could become lost in your own fantasy world of what you expect and hope to perceive. A proper balance between the two extremes achieves the basic goal of perception: to experience what is out there in a way that optimally serves your needs as a biological and social being, moving about and adapting to your physical and social environment.

# SUMMARY

Chapter 4 has examined how reception, transduction and coding are common to all human senses. We have discussed how humans sense, organise, identify and recognise their physical environments and have established that we apply learned perceptual rules to assist in these processes. However, it is important to remember that while there is a direct correspondence between the physical environmental stimulus and psychological experience, perception is an active and changeable process. Perception is influenced by your past experiences, your knowledge, your motivations and your cultural background. The interaction of these individual factors and perceptual rules can give rise to sensory illusions.

# KEY TERMS

absolute threshold (p. 100)
accommodation (p. 104)
amacrine cells (p. 104)
ambiguity (p. 97)
anosmia (p. 118)
attention (p. 123)
auditory nerve (p. 115)
basilar membrane (p. 115)
bipolar cells (p. 104)
bottom-up processing (p. 134)
brightness (p. 110)
cochlea (p. 115)
complementary colours (p. 110)
cones (p. 104)
convergence (p. 129)
cutaneous senses (p. 121)
dark adaptation (p. 104)
dichotic listening (p. 124)
difference threshold (p. 101)
distal stimulus (p. 96)
figure (p. 126)
fovea (p. 104)
frequency theory (p. 116)
ganglion cells (p. 104)
gate-control theory (p. 122)

Gestalt psychology (p. 126)
goal-directed selection (p. 123)
ground (p. 126)
horizontal cells (p. 104)
hue (p. 110)
identification and recognition (p. 94)
illusion (p. 98)
just noticeable difference (JND)
    (p. 102)
kinaesthetic sense (p. 121)
lightness constancy (p. 133)
loudness (p. 113)
olfactory bulb (p. 117)
opponent-process theory (p. 111)
optic nerve (p. 105)
pain (p. 122)
perception (p. 94)
perceptual constancy (p. 131)
perceptual organisation (p. 94)
pheromones (p. 118)
phi phenomenon (p. 128)
photoreceptors (p. 104)
pitch (p. 113)
place theory (p. 116)
proximal stimulus (p. 96)

psychometric function (p. 100)
psychophysics (p. 99)
receptive field (p. 106)
relative motion parallax (p. 129)
response bias (p. 101)
retina (p. 104)
retinal disparity (p. 129)
rods (p. 104)
saturation (p. 110)
sensation (p. 94)
sensory adaptation (p. 100)
sensory receptors (p. 103)
set (p. 136)
shape constancy (p. 132)
signal detection theory (p. 101)
size constancy (p. 131)
sound localisation (p. 116)
stimulus-driven capture (p. 123)
timbre (p. 113)
top-down processing (p. 134)
transduction (p. 102)
trichromatic theory (p. 111)
vestibular sense (p. 121)
volley principle (p. 116)
Weber's law (p. 102)

# PRACTICE TEST

1. At what stage of perception does meaning get assigned to a percept?
   a. Identification and recognition
   b. Sensation
   c. Perceptual organisation
   d. Sensory adaptation

2. Suppose you are looking at a globe of the world. Although the_____ is a sphere, you'd expect the_____ to be a circle.
   a. distal; absolute
   b. distal; proximal
   c. threshold; distal
   d. proximal; distal

3. In a museum, you are fascinated by a painting. From one angle, you see two faces. From another angle, you see a vase. This is an example of an
   a. illusion.
   b. absolute threshold.
   c. opponent process.
   d. ambiguity.

4. When you first walked into a room, you were overwhelmed by the smell of someone's perfume. Over time, you become less aware of the smell. This is an example of
   a. a psychometric function.
   b. sensory adaptation.
   c. an illusion.
   d. transduction.

5. You are carrying out an experiment in which you want to find a difference threshold for soft drinks that vary in their sugar concentration. You want to find the point at which the stimuli are recognised as different_____percent of the time.
   a. 50
   b. 25
   c. 100
   d. 75

6. The conversion of one form of physical energy into another is called
   a. sensory adaptation.
   b. transduction.
   c. sensory reception.
   d. photoreception.

7. If you walk into a room that has very low illumination, your _____ are likely to contribute more than your_____ to your visual experience.
   a. rods; amacrine cells
   b. horizontal cells; rods
   c. cones; rods
   d. rods; cones

8. In a lecture on the visual system, Mohammad learns about complex cells and hypercomplex cells. The lecture was probably about
   a. dark adaptation.
   b. receptive fields.
   c. accommodation.
   d. absolute thresholds.

9. Which of these pairs does not play a role in opponent-process theory?
   a. red versus green
   b. white versus black
   c. yellow versus blue
   d. blue versus green

10. The MARC device attempts to replace some of the function of the
    a. ganglion cells.
    b. bipolar cells.
    c. rods and cones.
    d. retina.

11. The_____of a sound is determined by its frequency; the_____of a sound is determined by its amplitude.
    a. timbre; pitch
    b. loudness; timbre
    c. loudness; pitch
    d. pitch; loudness

12. The airborne sound wave becomes 'seaborne' when the auditory information reaches the
    a. auditory nerve.
    b. cochlea.
    c. tympanic membrane.
    d. fovea.

13. Teresa is building a robot. She provides the robot with software that allows it to detect when the same sound arrives at slightly different times at its two artificial ears. It appears that Teresa wants the robot to succeed at
    a. pitch perception.
    b. timbre detection.
    c. sound localisation.
    d. sound discrimination.

14. Which of these statements are not true of the olfactory system?
    a. The receptors are located high up in the nasal cavity.
    b. Signals are relayed to the primary cortex via the thalamus.
    c. It most likely evolved for detecting and locating food.
    d. the unique code of activated receptors are interpreted by higher brain regions to identify odour qualities.

15. As Ali eats his dinner he shakes some salt on to each mouthful. Towards the end of the meal he finds he needs to put more and more salt on his food to reach the desired saltiness. Ali is experiencing
    a. taste intensification.
    b. taste-smell confusion.
    c. odour adaptation.
    d. taste adaptation.

16. Which of these is *not* a primary taste quality?
    a. bitter
    b. sweet
    c. tangy
    d. sour

17. Which of these statements is *not* true of the skin senses?
    a. The skin's sensitivity to pressure varies over the body.
    b. The skin senses warmth and coolness with the same receptors.
    c. The skin has several different types of sensory receptors.
    d. Some regions of the skin have more sensory cortex devoted to them.

18. The purpose of_____theory is to explain some aspects of the relationship between physical and psychological experiences of pain.
    a. gate-control
    b. volley
    c. frequency
    d. place

19. In general, you would predict that people with_____taste buds would experience_____pain when they eat spicy food.
    a. fewer; more
    b. fewer; no
    c. more; more
    d. more; less

20. When Shirley walks into a party, she looks around the room to find her husband Paul. This is an example of
    a. goal-driven attention.
    b. stimulus-driven capture.
    c. temporal integration.
    d. sensory adaptation.

21. Tomas owns a ring with a very small gap in it. The law of _____explains why most people perceive his ring to be intact.
    a. similarity
    b. good continuation
    c. common fate
    d. closure

22. You ask a friend to hold both hands up in the air with one hand about 15 centimetres behind the other. You point out to him that the nearer hand covers some parts of the more distant hand. This provides a demonstration of_____as a cue to depth.
    a. relative motion parallax  c. occlusion
    b. convergence               d. texture

23. As someone walks toward you, the person's image on your retina expands. However, you don't perceive the person to be actually getting larger. This is an example of
    a. sensory adaptation.   c. motion constancy.
    b. the phi phenomenon.   d. size constancy.

24. When you engage in_____, you begin with sensory data from the environment.
    a. bottom-up processing   c. pictorial cues
    b. top-down processing    d. hypothesis-driven processing

25. Just as Chris says, 'I love you', a truck sounds its horn. Although the horn covered the 'l' sound in 'love', Pat still perceives 'love' as intact. This is an example of
    a. bottom-up processing.   c. top-down processing.
    b. perceptual constancy.   d. good continuation.

26. For a short while after seeing a horror movie, Christos perceives every shadow as a monster. It sounds like he is experiencing
    a. a perceptual set.    c. the phi phenomenon.
    b. shape constancy.     d. the law of common fate.

## Essay Questions

1. How do ambiguous stimuli demonstrate some of the challenges your sensory and perceptual processes face as they help you interpret the world?

2. How do trichromatic theory and opponent-process theory fit together to explain important aspects of colour vision?

3. Why do different contexts give you different expectations of what you might perceive?

# WEB LINKS

Are you ready for the test? MyPsychLab offers dozens of ways to deepen your understanding and test your recall of the material in this chapter—including video and audio clips, simulations and activities, self-assessments, practice tests and other study materials. Specific resources available for this chapter include:

Normal vision, nearsightedness
Major structures of the ear receptive fields
Top-down processing
Five well-known illusions

Distinguishing figure-ground relationships

About the olfactory and hearing senses
Cochlea

To access MyPsychLab, please visit **www.pearsoned.com.au/mypsychlab**

# How does this apply to me?
## NOW YOU HAVE READ CHAPTER 4—ARE YOU PREPARED FOR THE EXAM?

To enhance your understanding of any of the material in your Psychology and Life textbook, go to **MyPsychLab: www.pearsoned.com.au/mypsychlab**.

Complete pre- and post-tests, create your own individualised study plan, watch videos and animations, and listen to audio glossaries, all of which will help you to understand the themes of this chapter:

- Sensing, organising, identifying and recognising
- Sensory knowledge of the world
- The visual system
- Hearing
- Your other senses
- Organisational processes in perception
- Identification and recognition processes

Complete multiple-choice PRACTICE TEST questions on sensing, organising, identifying, and recognising

EXPLORE the visual cortex!

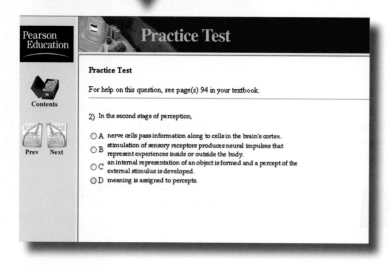

### Practice Test

**Pearson Education**

Contents

Prev   Next

**Practice Test**

For help on this question, see page(s) 94 in your textbook.

2) In the second stage of perception,

○ A   nerve cells pass information along to cells in the brain's cortex.
○ B   stimulation of sensory receptors produces neural impulses that represent experiences inside or outside the body.
○ C   an internal representation of an object is formed and a percept of the external stimulus is developed.
○ D   meaning is assigned to percepts.

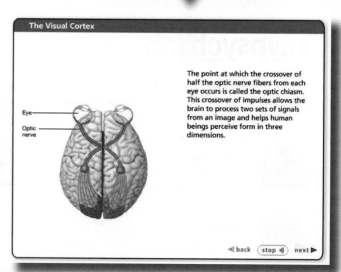

**The Visual Cortex**

The point at which the crossover of half the optic nerve fibers from each eye occurs is called the optic chiasm. This crossover of impulses allows the brain to process two sets of signals from an image and helps human beings perceive form in three dimensions.

Eye

Optic nerve

◄ back   ( stop ◄ )   next ►

**Read the BIOGRAPHIES of Ewald Herring, Thomas Young and Hermann von Helmholtz**
Enjoy a greater appreciation of the men and women who have made significant contributions to the discipline of psychology.

'The diagnostic tests helped me to know what topics I needed to study further and helped me prepare for my exam.'

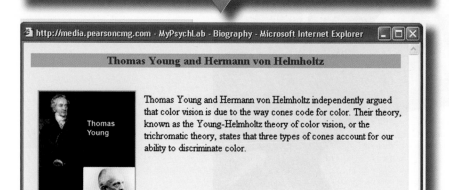

http://media.pearsoncmg.com - MyPsychLab - Biography - Microsoft Internet Explorer

**Thomas Young and Hermann von Helmholtz**

Thomas Young

Hermann von Helmholtz

Thomas Young and Hermann von Helmholtz independently argued that color vision is due to the way cones code for color. Their theory, known as the Young-Helmholtz theory of color vision, or the trichromatic theory, states that three types of cones account for our ability to discriminate color.

Done

View and listen to SIMULATIONS on the *Gestalt Laws of Perceptions*

Gestalt Laws of Perception

key definitions ◄ back  mute  next ►

**Five Gestalt Laws of Perception**

The Law of Proximity:

Objects that are close together are seen as belonging to the same group. Example: Vehicles in a full parking lot will be seen as a group, regardless of type.

Although these dandelions are indeed similar, the distance between the two flowers at the top and the cluster at the bottom causes them to appear as not part of the group.

Each of the simulations in Chapter 4:
- Methods of Constant Stimuli
- Distinguishing Figure-Ground Relationships
- Gestalt Laws of Perception
- Experiencing the Stroop Effect,

allow you to experience significant psychological phenomena first-hand in a fun, interactive way through simulations based on classic psychological studies.

**What can you find in MyPsychLab?**

Self-directed tests * Videos * Simulations * eBook * Biographies * Audio glossary * Web links … and more—organised by chapter, section and learning objective.

mypsych lab ™
where learning comes to life!

# Mind, Consciousness and Alternate States

CHAPTER

**5**

# CHAPTER FOCUS POINTS

After studying this chapter you will have a better understanding of:

1. The nature of consciousness

2. How consciousness has been studied in psychology

3. What function consciousness serves

4. The nature of sleep and dreams, and their importance to our lives and cultures

5. Altered states of consciousness, and how they come about

6. Drugs which affect our consciousness.

## CHAPTER CONTENTS

As you begin reading this chapter, take a moment to think about a favourite past event. Now think about what you'd like to have happen tomorrow or the next day. Where did these memories of the past and projections into the future *come* from and when did they *arrive*? Although you obviously have a vast body of information stored in your brain, it is very unlikely that the thoughts we asked you to have were 'in mind' just as you were sitting down to read your psychology text. Therefore, you might feel comfortable saying that the thoughts arrived in your consciousness—and that they came from some part of your brain that was not then conscious. But how did these particular thoughts come to mind? Did you actually consider several different memories or options for the future? That is, were you consciously aware of making a choice? Or did thoughts somehow just emerge—by virtue of some set of unconscious operations—into your consciousness?

This series of questions provides a preview of the major topics of Chapter 5. In this chapter, we will address a series of questions: What is ordinary conscious awareness? What determines the contents of your consciousness? Why do you need consciousness? Can unconscious mental events really influence your thoughts, emotions and behaviour? How does consciousness change over the course of a day–night cycle, and how can you intentionally alter your state of consciousness? The budding psychologist in you will also want to know how aspects of mind can be studied scientifically. How can you externalise the internal, make public the private, and measure precisely subjective experiences?

Our analysis will begin with an exploration of the contents and functions of consciousness. Then we will shift to the regular mental changes experienced during daydreaming, fantasising, sleeping and night dreaming. Finally, we will look at how consciousness is altered dramatically by hypnosis, meditation, religious rituals and drugs.

# THE CONTENTS OF CONSCIOUSNESS

**consciousness** A state of awareness of internal events and the external environment.

We must start by admitting that the term **consciousness** is ambiguous. We can use the term to refer to a general state of mind *or* to its specific contents: Sometimes you say you were 'conscious' in contrast to being 'unconscious' (for example, being under anaesthesia or asleep); at other times, you say you were conscious—*aware*—of certain information or actions. There is, in fact, a certain consistency here—to be conscious of any particular information, you must be conscious. In this chapter, when we speak of the *contents* of consciousness, we mean the body of information of which you are aware.

Why is self-awareness considered such an important aspect of consciousness?

## AWARENESS AND CONSCIOUSNESS

Some of the earliest research in psychology concerned the contents of consciousness. As psychology gradually diverged from philosophy in the 1800s, it became the science of the mind. Wundt and Titchener used introspection to explore the contents of the conscious mind, and William James observed his own stream of consciousness (see Chapter 1). In fact, on the very first page of his classic 1892 text, *Psychology*, James endorsed as a definition of psychology 'the description and explanation of states of consciousness as such.'

Your ordinary waking consciousness includes your perceptions, thoughts, feelings, images and desires at a given moment—all the mental activity on which you are focusing your attention. You are conscious of both what you are doing and also of the fact that you are doing it. At times, you are conscious of the realisation that others are observing, evaluating and reacting to what you are doing. A *sense of self* comes out of the experience of watching yourself from this privileged 'insider' position. Taken together, these various mental activities form the contents of consciousness—all the experiences you are consciously aware of at a particular time (Natsoulas, 1998).

We have defined the general types of information that *might* be conscious at a particular place and time, but what determines what is conscious right now? Were you, for example, aware of your breathing just now? Probably not; its control is part of *nonconscious processes*. Were you thinking about your last vacation or about the author of *Hamlet*? Again, probably not; control of such thoughts are part of *preconscious memories*. Were you aware of background noises, such as the ticking of a clock, the hum of traffic, or the buzzing of a fluorescent light? It would be difficult to be aware of all this and still pay full attention to the meaning of the material in this chapter; these stimuli are part of *unattended information*. Finally, there may be types of information that are *unconscious*—not readily accessible to conscious awareness—such as the set of grammatical rules that enable you to understand this sentence. Let's examine each of these types of awareness.

Nonconscious processes  There is a range of **nonconscious** bodily activities that rarely, if ever, impinge on consciousness. An example of nonconscious processes at work is the regulation of blood pressure. Your nervous system monitors physiological information to detect and act on changes continually, without your awareness. At certain times, some ordinarily nonconscious activities can be made conscious: You can, for example, choose to exercise conscious control over your pattern of breathing. Even so, your nervous system takes care of many important functions without requiring conscious resources.

Preconscious memories  Memories accessible to consciousness only after something calls your attention to them are known as **preconscious memories**. The storehouse of memory is filled with an incredible amount of information, such as your general knowledge of language, sports or geography and recollections of your personally experienced events. Preconscious memories function silently in the background of your mind until a situation arises in which they are consciously necessary (as when we asked you to call to mind a favourite past event). Memory will be discussed in detail in Chapter 7.

Unattended information  At any given time, you are surrounded by a vast amount of stimulation. As we described in Chapter 4, you can focus your attention only on a small part of it. What you focus on, in combination with the memories it evokes, will determine, to a large extent, what is in consciousness. Nevertheless, you sometimes have an unconscious representation of information that is not the focus of your attention. Recall this scenario from Chapter 4: At a noisy party, you try to focus attention on your attractive date and remain seemingly oblivious to a nearby conversation—until you overhear your name mentioned. Suddenly you are aware that you must have been monitoring the conversation—in some unconscious way—to detect that special signal amid the noise (Wood & Cowan, 1995a).

**nonconscious** Not typically available to consciousness or memory.

**preconscious memories** Memories that are not currently conscious but that can easily be called into consciousness when necessary.

At any given time, thoughts about your job, your parents, or your hungry pet may flow below the level of consciousness until something occurs to focus your attention on one of these topics. Why are these memories considered preconscious, not unconscious?

**The unconscious** You typically recognise the existence of *unconscious* information when you cannot explain some behaviour by virtue of forces that were conscious at the time of the behaviour. An initial theory of unconscious forces was developed by Sigmund Freud, who argued that certain life experiences—traumatic memories and taboo desires—are sufficiently threatening that special mental processes (that we will describe in Chapter 13) permanently banish them from consciousness. Freud believed that when the content of unacceptable ideas or motives is *repressed*—put out of consciousness—the strong feelings associated with the thoughts still remain and influence behaviour. Freud's 'discovery' of the unconscious contradicted a long tradition of Western thought. From the time the English philosopher John Locke (1690/1975) wrote his classic text on the mind, *An Essay Concerning Human Understanding*, most thinkers firmly believed that rational beings had access to all the activities of their own minds. Freud's initial hypothesis about the existence of unconscious mental processes was considered outrageous by his contemporaries (Dennett, 1987). (We will revisit Freud's ideas when we discuss the origin of your unique personality in Chapter 13.)

Many psychologists now use the term *unconscious* to refer to information and processes that are more benign than the types of thoughts Freud suggested must be repressed (Baars & McGovern, 1996; Westen, 1998). For example, many types of ordinary language processing rely on unconscious processes. Consider this sentence (Vu et al., 2000):

*She investigated the bark.*

How did you interpret this sentence? Did you picture some woman looking after a dog or examining a tree? Because the word *bark* is ambiguous—and the sentence context provides little help—you can only guess at what the writer meant. Now consider the same sentence in a slightly larger context:

*The botanist looked for a fungus. She investigated the bark.*

Did you find the sentence easier to understand in this context? If you did, it's because your unconscious language processes used the extra context to make a very swift choice between the two meanings of *bark*.

With this example, we demonstrate that processes that operate below the level of consciousness often affect your behaviour—in this case, the ease with which you came to a clear understanding of the sentence. We have thus shifted subtly from discussing the contents of consciousness to discussing the functions of consciousness. Before we take up that topic in detail, however, we will briefly describe two ways in which the contents of consciousness can be studied.

## STUDYING THE CONTENTS OF CONSCIOUSNESS

To study consciousness, researchers have had to devise methodologies to make deeply private experiences overtly measurable. One method is a new variation on Wundt and Titchener's practice of introspection. Experimental participants are asked to speak aloud as they work through a variety of complex tasks. They report, in as much detail as possible, the sequence of thoughts they experience while they complete the tasks. The participants' reports, called **think-aloud protocols**, are used to document the mental strategies and representations of knowledge that the participants employ to do the task. These protocols also allow researchers to analyse the discrepancies between task performance and awareness of how it is carried out (Ericsson & Simon, 1993).

In the **experience-sampling method**, participants wear devices that signal them when they should provide reports about what they are feeling and thinking. For example, in one methodology, participants wear electronic pagers. A radio transmitter activates the pager at various random times each day for a week or more. Whenever the pager signals, participants may be asked to respond to questions such as 'How well were you concentrating?' In this way, researchers can keep a running record of participants' thoughts, awareness, and focuses of attention as they go about their everyday lives (Hektner & Csikszentmihalyi, 2002). Consider an experiment that used palm-top computers to obtain experience samples.

A researcher provided 15 European American and 21 Asian (Japanese and Korean) students with palm-top computers (Oishi, 2003). At five random times during the day, the computers signalled the students to complete a survey that measured their sense of emotional wellbeing. These random samples allowed the researcher to calculate the proportion of time that each participant was experiencing overall positive moods while actually experiencing the day-to-day variations of life. At the end of the week-long experiment, the participants provided retrospective ratings by looking back over the week and noting the extent to which they had experienced positive moods. Mood ratings were combined so that higher numbers, on an 8-point scale, reflected more positive evaluations. **Figure 5.1** shows that the experience-sampling and retrospective measures yielded different conclusions. Whereas the Asians reported more positive moods while immersed in day-to-day experiences, they reported less positive moods when looking back on the week. Why might that be? The researcher suggested that European Americans and Asians have different cultural expectations of how satisfied they should be with their lives. Those cultural expectations had an impact on the retrospective judgments.

You can see from this example how important the experience-sampling measures were. If you just looked at the retrospective data, you might conclude that Asians have less happy lives. The day-to-day data argue strongly against that conclusion.

If you take a quick look around the room in which you are reading, you appreciate once more how many objects in your environment are readily available

**think-aloud protocols** Reports made by experimental participants of the mental processes and strategies they use while working on a task.

**experience-sampling method** An experimental method describing the typical contents of consciousness; participants are asked to record what they are feeling and thinking whenever signalled to do so.

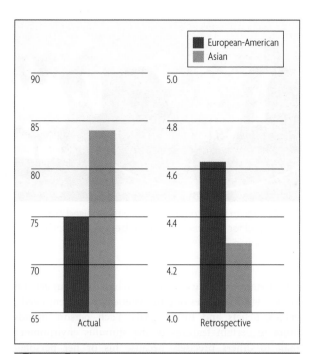

**Figure 5.1**

**Cross-cultural measures of wellbeing**
European Americans and Asians provided evaluations of their actual experiences of positive moods, based on random samples of their ongoing experience and retrospective reports looking back over a week's time. The Asians reported higher actual experiences of positive moods but were less positive when looking back on the week.

but are not (until you inspect the room) part of the contents of your consciousness. You can carry out the same quick review of your memory to demonstrate how much you have stored beyond the information that is the particular focus of your conscious attention. Techniques such as think-aloud protocols and experience sampling allow researchers to determine—for particular tasks and for particular times—which subset of all the information individuals have available is present in consciousness.

# THE FUNCTIONS OF CONSCIOUSNESS

When we address the question of the *functions* of consciousness, we are trying to understand why we *need* consciousness—what does it add to our human experience? In this section, we describe the importance of consciousness to human survival and social function.

## THE USES OF CONSCIOUSNESS

The most important evolutionary force leading to the emergence of human consciousness was, of course, competition with other humans. The human mind may have evolved as a consequence of the extreme *sociability* of human ancestors, which was perhaps originally a group defence against predators and a means to exploit resources more efficiently. However, close group living then created new demands for cooperative as well as competitive abilities with other humans. Natural selection favoured those who could think, plan, and imagine alternative realities that could promote both bonding with kin and victory over adversaries. Those who developed language and tools won the grand prize of survival of the fittest mind—and, fortunately, passed it on to us (Terrace & Metcalfe, 2005).

Because consciousness evolved, you should not be surprised that it provides a range of functions that aid in the survival of the species (Baars, 1997; Baars & McGovern, 1994; Cheney & Seyfarth, 1990; Ornstein, 1991). Consciousness also plays an important role in allowing for the construction of both personal and culturally shared realities.

**Aiding survival** From a biological perspective, consciousness probably evolved because it helped individuals make sense of environmental information and use that information in planning the most appropriate and effective actions. Usually, you are faced with a sensory-information overload. William James described the massive amount of information that strikes the sensory receptors as a 'blooming, buzzing confusion' assailing you from all sides. Consciousness helps you adapt to your environment by making sense of this profusion of confusion in three ways.

First, consciousness reduces the flow of stimulus input by restricting what you notice and what you focus on. You might recognise this *restrictive* function of consciousness from the discussion of *attention* in Chapter 4. Consciousness helps you tune out much of the information that is not relevant to your immediate goals and purposes. Suppose you decide to take a walk to enjoy a spring day. You notice trees blooming, birds singing and children playing. If, all at once, a snarling dog appears on the scene, you use consciousness to restrict your attention to that dog and assess the level of danger. The restrictive function also applies to information you draw from your internal storehouse of information. When, at the outset of this chapter, we asked you to think about a favourite past event, we were asking you to use your consciousness to restrict your mental attention to a single past memory.

A second function of consciousness is *selective storage*. Even within the category of information to which you consciously attend, not all of it has continuing relevance to your ongoing concerns. After your encounter with the snarling dog, you might stop yourself and think, 'I want to remember not to walk down this block'. Consciousness allows you to selectively store—commit to memory—information that you want to analyse, interpret and act on in the future; consciousness allows you to classify events and experiences as relevant or irrelevant to personal needs by selecting some and ignoring others. When we consider memory processes in Chapter 7, we will see that not all the information you add to memory requires conscious processing. Still, conscious memories have different properties—and involve different brain regions—than other types of memories.

A third function of consciousness is to make you stop, think and consider alternatives based on past knowledge and imagine various consequences. This *planning* function enables you to suppress strong desires when they conflict with moral, ethical or practical concerns. With this kind of consciousness you can plan a route for your next walk that avoids that snarling dog. Because consciousness gives you a broad time perspective in which to frame potential actions, you can call on knowledge of the past and expectations for the future to influence your current decisions. For all these reasons, consciousness gives you great potential for flexible, appropriate responses to the changing demands in your life.

## Personal and cultural constructions of reality

No two people interpret a situation in exactly the same way. Your *personal construction of reality* is your unique

The Australian Government formally recognised and apologised for hurt caused to members of the Stolen Generation in 2008.

interpretation of a current situation based on your general knowledge, memories of past experiences, current needs, values, beliefs and future goals. Each person attends more to certain features of the stimulus environment than to others precisely because his or her personal construction of reality has been formed from a selection of unique inputs. When your personal construction of reality remains relatively stable, your *sense of self* has continuity over time.

Because the people of a given culture share many of the same experiences, they often have similar constructions of reality. *Cultural constructions of reality* are ways of thinking about the world that are shared by most members of a particular group of people. When a member of a society develops a personal construction of reality that fits in with the cultural construction, it is affirmed by the culture and, at the same time, it affirms the cultural construction. You already saw one example of the impact of culture on the construction of reality: recall that Asian students reported retrospectively that their moods had been less positive than did their European American peers, despite their day-to-day experiences.

Individual differences in personal constructions of reality are increased when people have grown up in different cultures, lived in different environments within a culture, or faced different survival tasks. One of the most significant challenges to Australian Aboriginal identity in the recent past was the removal of Aboriginal children from their families to create a 'stolen generation'. Clark (2000) interviewed a number of Indigenous individuals having experienced this event, and found that most had suffered some degree of confusion in their identity formation, particularly when younger.

Simon Correy of the University of Sydney argues that in the era prior to the landmark *Mabo* case in 1993, Aboriginal social life was 'characterised by a degree of commonality of experience and a shared framework of understanding through which they became aware of their own and other's experiences' (Correy, 2005). Correy goes on to say that during this period, Aboriginal communities could take it for granted that they shared a common history as well as common experiences and understanding of those experiences. Following the *Mabo* decision and subsequent Native Title legislation (see *Native Title Act 1993*, *Native Title Amendment Act 1998*), the identification of traditional owners directed the reflection of conscious life on itself and compelled Aboriginal claimants to, in effect, thematise intersubjectivity.

Migrants to Australia also face the need to reconcile differing cultural constructions of reality, which can lead to rather unexpected results. For example, Chinese women entering Australia under schemes designed to increase the numbers of skilled professionals have been found to shift towards more domestic occupations, leaving the paid workforce in a process which Ho (2006) describes as the 'feminisation' of their roles. In Chapter 13, we will describe more fully the relationship between the personal and the cultural sense of self.

## STUDYING THE FUNCTIONS OF CONSCIOUSNESS

Many functions of consciousness include implicit comparisons with what remains unconscious. That is, conscious processes often affect or are affected by unconscious processes. To study the functions of consciousness, researchers often study the relationship between conscious and unconscious influences on behaviour. Researchers have developed a variety of ways to demonstrate that unconscious processes can affect conscious behaviour (Nelson, 1996; Westen, 1998).

For example, researchers have used the *SLIP* (*Spoonerisms of Laboratory-Induced Predisposition*) technique to determine the way in which unconscious forces affect the probability of making a speech error (Baars et al., 1992). The SLIP procedure enables an experimenter to induce slips of the tongue by setting up expectations for certain patterns of sound. Thus, after pronouncing a series of word pairs like *ball doze*, *bell dark*, and *bean deck*, a participant might mispronounce *darn bore* as *barn door*. Experimenters can assess conscious or unconscious influences on the probability of such sound exchanges by altering circumstances external to the task. For instance, participants were more likely to make the error *bad shock* (from *shad bock*) when they believed they might receive a painful electric shock sometime during an experiment (Motley & Baars, 1979). Similarly, male participants who performed the SLIP task in the presence of a provocative female experimenter were more likely to err in producing *good legs* (from *lood gegs*). These results suggest an unconscious contribution to the production of speech errors.

Another way to study the functions of consciousness is to determine which of the many tasks you carry out on a day-to-day basis require conscious intervention. To give you an example, we want you to put your book down for a moment and try to find an object in the room that is *red*. Let's assume that there is, in fact, a red object in your room. Under most circumstances, you should

have felt as if your eyes were drawn to that object without any conscious effort. Research confirms that people can carry out search for certain basic features of objects such as colour, shape, and size, with little or no conscious attention (Wolfe, 2003). Suppose, now, that you try to find an object that is both *blue* and *red*. If you take a moment to carry out that task, you should have a very different sense of how much conscious effort is involved. Under most circumstances, you'll have to use conscious attention to find an object that has a combination of two features.

We provide another example of the uses of conscious attention in **Figure 5.2**. In Part A, try to find the yellow and blue item. In Part B, try to find the yellow house with blue windows. Wasn't this second task much easier? Performance is much less affected by all the extra objects in the picture when the two colours are organised into *parts* and *wholes* (Wolfe et al., 1994). Could you feel your conscious attention being more engaged when we asked you to find the yellow and blue item? From results of this sort, researchers are assembling a global view of the circumstances in which consciousness functions.

We have seen how the contents and functions of consciousness are defined and studied. We turn now to ordinary and then extraordinary alterations in consciousness.

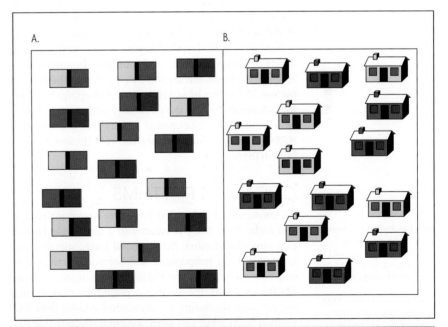

Figure 5.2

**Search for the conjunction of two colours**
(A) Find the yellow and blue item. (B) Find the yellow house with blue windows. (A) Search is very inefficient when the conjunction is between the colours of two parts of a target. (B) However, search is much easier when the conjunction is between the colour of the whole item and the colour of one of its parts.

Adapted with permission from Jerome Kuhl, from 'Features and Objects in Visual Processing,' by Anne Triesman, *Scientific American*, November 1986, p. 116.

## RECAP CHECKPOINT
### The functions of consciousness

- Consciousness aids your survival and enables you to construct both personal and culturally shared realities.

- Researchers have studied the relationship between conscious and unconscious processes.

## CONCEPT QUESTIONS

1. What is the selective storage function of consciousness?

2. What is a cultural construction of reality?

3. Why does the SLIP procedure provide information about the functions of consciousness?

# SLEEP AND DREAMS

Almost every day of your life you experience a rather profound change in consciousness: When you decide it's time to end your day, you surrender yourself to sleep—and while you sleep you will undoubtedly dream. A third of your life is spent sleeping, with your muscles in a state of 'benign paralysis' and your brain humming with activity. We begin this section by considering the general biological rhythms of wakefulness and sleeping. We then focus more directly on the physiology of sleeping. Finally, we examine the major mental activity that accompanies sleep—dreaming—and explore the role dreams play in human psychology.

## CIRCADIAN RHYTHMS

All creatures are influenced by nature's rhythms of day and night. Your body is attuned to a time cycle known as a **circadian rhythm**: Your arousal levels, metabolism, heart rate, body temperature and hormonal activity ebb and flow according to the ticking of your internal clock. For the most part, these activities reach their peak during the day—usually during the afternoon—and hit their low point at night while you sleep. Research suggests that the clock your body uses is not exactly in synchrony with the clock on the wall: Without the corrective effects of external time cues, the human internal 'pacemaker' establishes a 24.18-hour cycle (Czeisler et al., 1999). The exposure to sunlight that you get each day helps you make the small adjustment to a 24-hour cycle. Information about sunlight is gathered through your eyes, but receptors for regulation of circadian rhythms are not the same receptors as allow

you to see the world (Menaker, 2003). For example, animals without rods and cones (see Chapter 4) still sense light in a way that enables them to maintain their circadian rhythms (Freedman et al., 1999).

Changes that cause a mismatch between your biological clock and environmental clocks affect how you feel and act (Moore-Ede, 1993). Perhaps the most dramatic example of how such mismatches arise comes from long-distance air travel. When people fly across time zones, they may experience *jet lag*, a condition whose symptoms include fatigue, irresistible sleepiness and subsequent unusual sleep-wake schedules. Jet lag occurs because the internal circadian rhythm is out of phase with the normal temporal environment (Redfern et al., 1994). For example, your body says it's 2 a.m.—and thus is at a low point on many physiological measures—when local time requires you to act as if it is noon.

What variables influence jet lag? The direction of travel and the number of time zones passed through are the most important variables. Travelling eastbound creates greater jet lag than westbound flight because your biological clock can be more readily extended than shortened, as required on eastbound trips (it is easier to stay awake longer than it is to fall asleep sooner). When healthy volunteers were flown back and forth between Europe and the United States, their peak performance on standard tasks was reached within 2 to 4 days after westbound flights but 9 days after eastbound travel (Klein & Wegmann, 1974).

## THE SLEEP CYCLE

About a third of your circadian rhythm is devoted to that period of behavioural quiescence called *sleep*. Most of what is known about sleep concerns the electrical activities of the brain. The methodological breakthrough for the study of sleep came in 1937 with the application of a technology that records brain wave activity of the sleeper in the form of an electroencephalogram (EEG). The EEG provided an objective, ongoing measure of the way brain activity varies when people are awake or asleep. With the EEG, researchers discovered that brain waves change in form at the onset of sleep and show further systematic, predictable changes during the entire sleep period (Loomis et al., 1937). The next significant discovery in sleep research was that bursts of **rapid eye movements (REM)** occur at periodic intervals during sleep (Aserinsky & Kleitman, 1953). The time when a sleeper is not showing REM is known as **non-REM (NREM) sleep**. We will see in a later section that REM and NREM sleep have significance for one of the night's major activities—dreaming.

Let us track your brain waves through the night. As you prepare to go to bed, an EEG records that your brain waves are moving along at a rate of about 14 cycles per second (cps). Once you are comfortably in bed, you begin to relax, and your brain waves slow down to a rate of about 8 to 12 cps. When you fall asleep, you enter your *sleep cycle*, each of whose stages shows a distinct EEG pattern. In stage 1 sleep, the EEG shows brain waves of

---

**circadian rhythm** A consistent pattern of cyclical body activities, usually lasting 24 to 25 hours and determined by an internal biological clock.

**rapid eye movements (REM)** A behavioural sign of the phase of sleep during which the sleeper is likely to be experiencing dreamlike mental activity.

**non-REM (NREM) sleep** The period during which a sleeper does not show rapid eye movement; characterised by less dream activity than during REM sleep.

about 3 to 7 cps. During stage 2, the EEG is characterised by *sleep spindles*, minute bursts of electrical activity of 12 to 16 cps. In the next two stages (3 and 4) of sleep, you enter into a very deep state of relaxed sleep. Your brain waves slow to about 1 to 2 cps, and your breathing and heart rate decrease. In a final stage, the electrical activity of your brain increases; your EEG looks very similar to those recorded during stages 1 and 2. It is during this stage that you will experience REM sleep, and you will begin to dream (see **Figure 5.3**). (Because the EEG pattern during REM sleep resembles that of an awake person, REM sleep was originally termed *paradoxical sleep*.)

Cycling through the first four stages of sleep, which are NREM sleep, requires about 90 minutes. REM sleep lasts for about 10 minutes. Over the course of a night's sleep, you pass through this 100-minute cycle four to six times (see **Figure 5.4**). With each cycle, the amount of time you spend in deep sleep (stages 3 and 4) decreases, and the amount of time you spend in REM sleep increases. During the last cycle, you may spend as much time as an hour in REM sleep. NREM sleep accounts for 75 to 80 percent of total sleep time, and REM sleep makes up 20 to 25 percent of sleep time.

Not all individuals sleep for the same amount of time. Although a genetic sleep need is programmed into the human species, the actual amount of sleep each individual obtains is highly affected by conscious actions. People actively control sleep length in a number of ways, such as by staying up late or using alarm clocks. Sleep duration is also controlled by circadian rhythms; that is, when one goes to sleep influences sleep duration. Getting adequate amounts of NREM and REM sleep is only likely when you standardise your bedtime and rising time across the entire

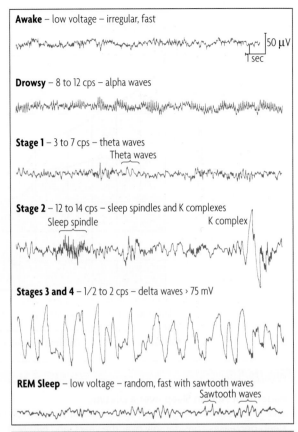

**Figure 5.3**

**EEG patterns reflecting the stages of a regular night's sleep**

Each sleep stage is defined by characteristic patterns of brain activity.

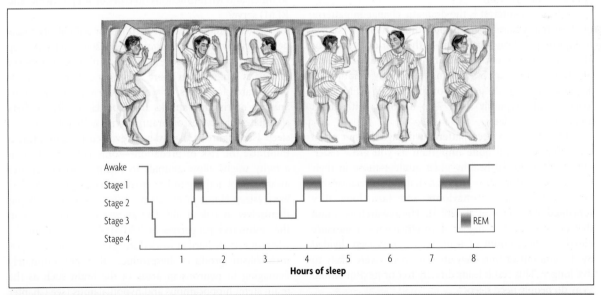

**Figure 5.4**

**The stages of sleep**

A typical pattern of the stages of sleep during a single night includes deeper sleep in the early cycles but more time in REM in the later cycles.

From "The March of Sleep Cycles" from *Sleep* by J. Allan Hobson. Copyright © 1989 by J. Allan Hobson, M.D. Reprinted by permission of Henry Holt and Company, LLC.

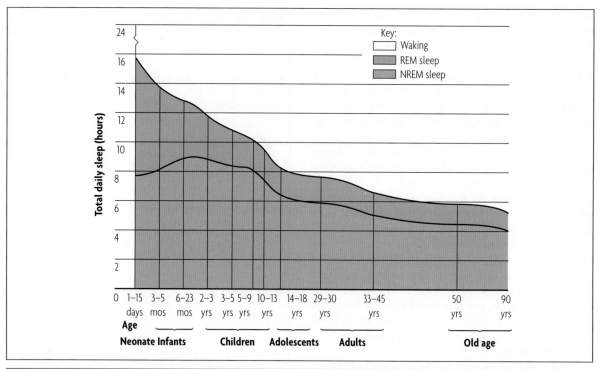

Figure 5.5

**Patterns of Human Sleep over a Lifetime**
The graph shows changes with age in total amounts of daily REM sleep and NREM sleep. Note that the amount of REM sleep decreases considerably over the years, and NREM diminishes less sharply.

Reprinted with permission from Roffwarg et al., "Ontogenetic Development of the Human Sleep-Dream Cycle," *Science, 152*, 604–619, 1966. Copyright ©1966 AAAs.

week, including weekends. In that way, the time you spend in bed is likely to correspond closely to the sleepy phase of your circadian rhythm.

Of further interest is the dramatic change in patterns of sleep that occurs over an individual's lifetime (shown in **Figure 5.5**). You started out in this world sleeping for about 16 hours a day, with nearly half of that time spent in REM sleep. By age 50, you may sleep only 6 hours and spend only about 20 percent of the time in REM sleep. Young adults typically sleep 7 to 8 hours, with about 20 percent REM sleep.

The change in sleep patterns with age doesn't mean that sleep isn't still quite important as you grow older. One study followed healthy older adults—those in their 60s through to their 80s—to see if there was a relationship between their sleep behaviours and how long they remained alive (Dew et al., 2003). The researchers found that people who had higher sleep efficiency—a measure based on the amount of time they were asleep divided by the amount of time they spent in bed—were likely to live longer. This result leads directly to our next question: Why do people need sleep?

## WHY SLEEP?

The orderly progression of stages of sleep in humans and other animals suggests that there is an evolutionary basis and a biological need for sleep. People function quite well

when they get the time-honoured 7 to 8 hours of sleep a night (Harrison & Horne, 1996). Why do humans sleep so much and what functions do types of sleep (NREM and REM) serve?

The two most general functions for NREM sleep may be *conservation* and *restoration* (Siegel, 2005). NREM sleep may have evolved because it enabled animals to conserve energy at times when there was no need to forage for food, search for mates, or work. However, sleep also puts animals at risk for attacks from predators. Researchers speculate that cycles of brain activity across a period of sleep (see Figure 5.3) may have evolved to help animals minimise the risk of predation—some patterns of brain activity might allow animals to retain relatively greater awareness of activity in the environment even while they were asleep (Lima et al., 2005). Why would animals put themselves at risk at all? The answer quite likely lies in the restorative properties of NREM sleep. For example, when brains are hard at work during waking states, oxygen metabolism produces by-products that are ultimately damaging to neurons in areas of the brain such as the brain stem, hippocampus and hypothalamus (see Chapter 3). NREM sleep provides the brain with an opportunity to interrupt that damage and undertake repairs of brain cells (Siegel, 2005).

If you were to be deprived of REM sleep for a night, you would have more REM sleep than usual the next night, suggesting that REM sleep also serves some necessary functions. For example, it appears that, during infancy, the brain activity that defines REM sleep is necessary for the development of normal function in the visual system and perhaps other sensory and motor systems (Siegel, 2005). For adults, research has focused on the role REM sleep plays in learning and memory (Paller & Voss, 2004; Walker & Stickgold, 2006). Consider an experiment that asked participants to learn a new task.

> At the beginning of the experiment, 24 participants spent a night in a sleep lab, so that the researchers could obtain a baseline measure for the amount of REM sleep they experienced in a night (Smith et al., 2004). The next evening, 6 participants were assigned to a control group. They spent the evening in the lab, but they carried out no special activities. The other 18 participants were asked to learn a new task—a problem-solving task called the Tower of Hanoi. Participants' REM sleep was then assessed for a second time. On this second night, participants in the task-learning group had more intense REM sleep compared to their baseline—they experienced both more rapid eye movements as a percentage of the number of minutes of REM sleep. Members of the control group did not show any comparable changes in their REM sleep. After a week had passed, participants in the training group returned to attempt the Tower of Hanoi once again. The participants generally showed improvement on the task from the initial test to this retest. However, those individuals who showed the greatest intensity of REM sleep after the training session also showed the greatest improvement on the Tower of Hanoi.

This experiment suggests that REM sleep provides a context in which the brain solidifies its attainment of new tasks. It's important to note that NREM sleep also plays a role in the consolidation of learning and memory.

Researchers have demonstrated that performance on some tasks is marked by increases in stage 3 and stage 4 sleep early in the night and REM sleep late in the night (Walker & Stickgold, 2006).

What is the relationship between actual sleep patterns and people's perceptions of insomnia?

## SLEEP DISORDERS

It would be great if you could always take a good night's sleep for granted. Unfortunately, many people suffer from sleep disorders that pose a serious burden on their personal lives and careers. Disordered sleep can also have societal consequences. Of those individuals whose work schedules include night shifts, more than half nod off at least once a week on the job. Some of the world's most serious industrial accidents—Three Mile Island, Chernobyl, Bhopal and the *Exxon Valdez* disaster—have occurred during late evening hours. People have speculated that these accidents happened because key personnel failed to function optimally as a result of insufficient sleep. Because sleep disorders are important in many students' lives, we review them here. As you read, remember that sleep disorders vary in severity. Similarly, their origins involve biological, environmental and psychological forces.

Insomnia When people are dissatisfied with their amount or quality of sleep, they are suffering from **insomnia**. This chronic failure to get adequate sleep is characterised by an inability to fall asleep quickly, frequent arousals during sleep or early-morning awakening. In a recent poll, 54 percent of adults ages 18 and older reported that, in the past year, they experienced insomnia a few nights or more each week (National Sleep Foundation, 2005).

Insomnia is a complex disorder caused by a variety of psychological, environmental, and biological factors

insomnia The chronic inability to sleep normally.

What is the relationship between actual sleep patterns and people's perceptions of insomnia?

(Spielman & Glovinsky, 1997). However, when insomniacs are studied in sleep laboratories, the objective quantity and quality of their actual sleep vary considerably, from disturbed sleep to normal sleep. Research has revealed that many insomniacs who complain of lack of sleep actually show completely normal physiological patterns of sleep—a condition described as subjective insomnia. For example, in one study 38 percent of the participants who reported that they suffered from insomnia actually had normal sleep (Edinger et al., 2000). Equally interesting, the same study showed detectable sleep disturbances in 43 percent of the participants who had no complaints of insomnia. The discrepancies may result from differences in the cognitions and emotions that surround sleep (Espie, 2002). People who experience insomnia—or those who only think they do—may be less able to banish intrusive thoughts and feelings from consciousness even while they are trying to sleep.

## Narcolepsy

**Narcolepsy** is a sleep disorder characterised by periodic sleep during the daytime. It is often combined with *cataplexy*, muscle weakness or a loss of muscle control brought on by emotional excitement (such as laughing, anger, fear, surprise or hunger) that causes the afflicted person to fall down suddenly. When they fall asleep, narcoleptics enter REM sleep almost immediately. This rush to REM causes them to experience—and be consciously aware of—vivid dream images or sometimes terrifying hallucinations. Narcolepsy affects about 1 of every 2,000 individuals. Because narcolepsy runs in families, scientists believe the disease has a genetic basis (Mahowald & Schenck, 2005). Narcolepsy often has a negative social and psychological impact on sufferers because of their desire to avoid the embarrassment caused by sudden bouts of sleep (Broughton & Broughton, 1994).

## Sleep apnoea

**Sleep apnoea** is an upper-respiratory sleep disorder in which the person stops breathing while asleep. When this happens, the blood's oxygen level drops and emergency hormones are secreted, causing the sleeper to awaken and begin breathing again. Although most people have a few such apnoea episodes a night, someone with sleep apnoea disorder can have hundreds of such cycles every night. Sometimes apnoea episodes frighten the sleeper, but often they are so brief that the sleeper fails to attribute accumulating sleepiness to them (Orr, 1997). Sleep apnoea affects roughly 2 percent of adults (Sonnad et al., 2003).

Sleep apnoea also occurs frequently among premature infants, who sometimes need physical stimulation to start breathing again. Because of their underdeveloped respiratory system, these infants must remain attached to monitors in intensive care nurseries as long as the problem continues.

## Somnambulism

Individuals who suffer from **somnambulism**, or *sleepwalking*, leave their beds and wander while still remaining asleep. Sleepwalking is more frequent among children than among adults. For example, studies have found that about 7 percent of children sleepwalk (Nevéus et al., 2001) but only about 2 percent of adults do so (Ohayon et al., 1999). Sleepwalking is associated with NREM sleep. When monitored in a sleep laboratory, adult sleepwalkers demonstrated abrupt arousal—involving movement or speech—during stage 3 and stage 4 sleep (see Figure 5.3) in the first third of their night's sleep (Guilleminault et al., 2001). Contrary to popular conceptions, it is not particularly dangerous to wake sleepwalkers—they're just likely to be confused by the sudden awakening. Still, sleepwalking in itself can be dangerous because individuals are navigating in their environments without conscious awareness.

**Sleep disorder research in Australia** The website for the Australasian Sleep Association (**www.sleepaus.on.net**) contains a wealth of information regarding sleep and the costs associated with sleep disorders. According to the report by Access Economics, 'Wake up Australia: The Value of Health Sleep', over 1.2 million Australians suffer from sleep disorders. This is estimated to have cost the nation more than $10 billion in 1994. Sleep disorders are implicated in 9 percent of workplace accidents, 8 percent of cases of depression, and 8 percent of motor vehicle accidents. Not surprisingly, then, Australian researchers have been among those leading the way in understanding the psychology of sleep and its disorders.

The economic costs of fatigue may well be even greater than the estimate given above, if some of the 'hidden' costs revealed by Dorrian, Hussey and Dawson (2007) are taken into account. They analysed train drivers' work histories to estimate levels of fatigue. Fatigue impacted on the driver's ability to plan ahead, causing them to use more heavy braking and less throttle, and consequently to burn up to 9 percent more fuel. Even moderate fatigue more than doubled the amount of time at which the trains were travelling in excess of the maximum speed allowed, suggesting that safety was also compromised. These results are not surprising, since Dawson and Reid (1997) showed that fatigue operates very much like alcohol consumption. A person who has been sleep deprived for 24 hours performs very like a person who has a blood alcohol concentration of .01% (twice the legal limit for driving in most of Australia).

The development of an effective behavioural treatment for insomnia would thus have significant benefits both for individuals and for the community. One innovative, and somewhat counter-intuitive, treatment showing great promise is described by Harris, Lack, Wright, Grandisar and Brooks (2007). (This program is certainly not something that the reader should try at home!) Participants in their study were allowed to fall asleep for between 90 seconds and four minutes every half hour for an entire day. The treatment commenced one evening and terminated the following evening with enough time for them to get home at their normal bedtime. Over the next two weeks there was a dramatic improvement in both the time taken to fall asleep and the total amount of sleep experienced.

**narcolepsy** A sleep disorder characterised by an irresistible compulsion to sleep during the daytime.

**sleep apnoea** A sleep disorder of the upper respiratory system that causes the person to stop breathing while asleep.

**somnambulism** A disorder that causes sleepers to leave their beds and wander while still remaining asleep; also known as sleepwalking.

# PSYCHOLOGY *in your life*

## DO YOU GET ENOUGH SLEEP?

Ten or twenty years ago there was very little to do after midnight. When students had finished with their homework, they could pretty much choose between watching late-night television or rolling into bed. By contrast, there are now ample opportunities for you to maintain a 24/7 life style. Consider the World Wide Web and its constant supply of new information. At any time of day or night, you can cruise the Web or join a chat room. You can finish your midnight snack in Newcastle, New South Wales, at the same time you chat with someone eating an early breakfast in Newcastle on Tyne in the U.K.

Easy access to 24/7 stimulation has amplified what we might characterise as many people's love–hate relationship with sleep. People love to sleep because being rested feels good (and being sleepy feels awful). As we've seen in this chapter, your body needs sleep to function effectively. However, people hate to sleep because there are so many enjoyable things to do while they are awake.

From the point of view of many researchers, the 21st century's

enticements have only made a bad situation worse. They have been worried for several years that adolescents and university students do not get nearly enough sleep (Dement & Vaughan, 1999; Wolfson & Carskadon, 1998). Although experts recommend that everyone gets 8 hours of sleep, a 2004 poll carried out by the U.S. National Sleep Foundation (2005) suggests that the average 18- to 29-year-old rarely meets this standard. On weekdays, the average duration of sleep for individuals in this age range is 6.8 hours. In this age range, 55 percent of the individuals reported that they experienced daytime sleepiness at least one day a week; 44 percent reported that they have missed days of work or events because of lack of sleep. In addition, 46 percent reported having driven while drowsy at least once a month in the past year.

How concerned are you about the amount of sleep you get? Research suggests that university students underestimate the negative consequences of sleep deprivation on their cognitive performance (Pilcher & Walters, 1997). Take a moment to consider the reality

that chronic sleep loss is likely to be quite unfortunate for your college performance (Buboltz et al., 2002). No doubt many college students lose sleep because of the stresses associated with studying for exams and writing papers (Murphy & Archer, 1996). However, 55 percent of poll participants in the 18-to-29 range agreed to the statement that they 'often stay up later than they should because they are watching TV or are on the Internet' (National Sleep Foundation, 2000). Does this apply to you?

We are not trying to discourage you from taking leading an exciting and varied life. We are simply offering the observation that progress often seems to bring with it new reasons for people to lose sleep. Sleepiness has many serious consequences: lower marks, work problems and car accidents are just a few. So far, scientists have been able to invent pills that can stop you from sleeping—but none that can stop you from needing sleep. As you make plans to fill up the whole 24 hours in a day, research strongly suggests that you should still put aside 8 hours for sleep.

## DREAMS: THEATRE OF THE MIND

During every ordinary night of your life, you enter into the complex world of dreams. Once the province only of prophets, psychics and psychoanalysts, dreams have become a vital area of study for scientific researchers. Much dream research begins in sleep laboratories, where experimenters can monitor sleepers for REM and NREM sleep. Although individuals report more dreams when they are awakened from REM periods—on about 82 percent of their awakenings—dreaming also takes place during NREM periods—on about 54 percent of awakenings (Foulkes, 1962). Dreaming associated with NREM states is less likely to contain story content that is emotionally

involving. It is more akin to daytime thought, with less sensory imagery.

Because dreams have such prominence in people's mental lives, virtually every culture has arrived at the same question: Do dreams have significance? The answer that has almost always emerged is yes. That is, most cultures encode the belief that, in one way or another, dreams have important personal and cultural meaning. We now review some of the ways in which cultures attach meaning to dreams.

Freudian dream analysis The most prominent dream theory in modern Western culture was originated by Sigmund Freud. Freud called dreams 'transient psychoses' and models of 'everynight madness'. He also called them 'the royal road to the unconscious'. He made the analysis of dreams the cornerstone of psychoanalysis with his classic book *The Interpretation of Dreams* (1900/1965). Freud saw dream images as symbolic expressions of powerful unconscious, repressed wishes. These wishes appear in disguised form because they harbour forbidden desires, such as sexual yearning for the parent of the opposite sex. The two dynamic forces operating in dreams are thus the *wish* and the *censorship*, a defence against the wish. The censor transforms the hidden meaning, or **latent content**, of the dream into **manifest content**, which appears to the dreamer after a distortion process that Freud referred to as **dream work**. The manifest content is the acceptable version of the story; the latent content represents the socially or personally unacceptable version but also the true, 'uncut' one.

According to Freud, the interpretation of dreams requires working backward from the manifest content to the latent content. To the psychoanalyst who uses dream analysis to understand and treat a patient's problems, dreams reveal the patient's unconscious wishes, the fears attached to those wishes, and the characteristic defences the patient employs to handle the resulting psychic conflict between the wishes and the fears. Freud believed in both idiosyncratic—special to particular individuals—and universal meanings—many of a sexual nature—for the symbols and metaphors in dreams:

> *Boxes, cases, chests, cupboards and ovens represent the uterus, and also hollow objects, ships, and vessels of all kinds. Rooms in dreams are usually women; if the various ways in and out of them are represented, this interpretation is scarcely open to doubt. . . . A dream of going through a suite of rooms is a brothel or harem dream. . . . It is highly probable that all complicated machinery and apparatus occurring in dreams stand for the genitals (and as a rule male ones) . . . (Freud, 1900/1965, pp. 389–391)*

Freud's theory of dream interpretation related dream symbols to his explicit theory of human psychology. Freud's emphasis on the psychological importance of dreams has pointed the way to contemporary examinations of dream content (Domhoff, 1996; Fisher & Greenberg, 1996).

## Non-Western approaches to dream interpretation

Many people in Western societies may never think seriously about their dreams until they become students of psychology or enter therapy. By contrast, in many non-Western cultures, dream sharing and interpretation is part of the very fabric of the culture (Wax, 2004). Consider the daily practice of the Archur Indians of Ecuador (Schlitz, 1997, p. 2):

> *Like every other morning, the men [of the village] sit together in a small circle. . . . They share their dreams from the night before. This daily ritual of dream-sharing is vital to the life of the Archur.*

> *It is their belief that each individual dreams, not for themselves, but for the community as a whole. Individual experience serves collective action.*

During these morning gatherings, each dreamer tells his dream story and the others offer their interpretations, hoping to arrive at some consensus understanding of the meaning of the dream. Contrast the belief that individuals dream 'for the community as a whole' with the view articulated by Freud, that dreams are the 'royal road' to the individual unconscious.

In many cultures, specific groups of individuals are designated as possessing special powers to assist with dream interpretation. Consider the practices of Mayan Indians who live in various parts of Mexico, Guatemala, Belize and Honduras. In the Mayan culture, *shamans* function as dream interpreters. In fact, among some subgroups of Mayans, the shamans are selected for these roles when they have dreams in which they are visited by deities who announce the shaman's calling. Formal instruction about religious rituals is also provided to these newly selected shamans by way of dream revelation. Although the shamans, and other religious figures, have special knowledge relevant to dream interpretation, ordinary individuals also recount and discuss dreams. Dreamers commonly wake their bed partners in the middle of the night to narrate dreams; mothers in some communities ask their children each morning to talk about their dreams. In contemporary times, the Mayan people have been the victims of civil war in their homelands; many people have been killed or forced to flee. One important response, according to anthropologist **Barbara Tedlock**, has been 'an increased emphasis on dreams and visions that enable them to stay in touch with their ancestors and the sacred earth on which they live' (Tedlock, 1992, p.471).

## Dreams and the Dreamtime

The Dreamtime is a central cultural construct for Indigenous Australians, but it is important to understand there are fundamental differences between the physical state of sleeping and dreaming as opposed to the *Dreamtime*, which, as a term of reference, is actually a construct of colonial settlers.

The *Dreamtime* corresponds to a word or phrase in many Aboriginal languages, e.g. the Yolngu Wangarr, the Warlpiri Tjukurrpa, and the Arrernte Altyerrenge (Morphy 1999:265). To these we can add Kuwalkujin or Mirndiyan in Lardil and Yuujbanda for the Kaiadilt. The Dreamtime refers to the ancient past during which Indigenous people and other fauna and flora were adapting and evolving in a continent of changing environmental conditions. It provides an explanation of how the world was created and how individuals now should behave. It is thought that the concept of Dreaming was first reported by Baldwin Spencer during the 1894 Horn Expedition into the McDonnell Ranges of South Australia. It 'signifies a diverse set of narratives which, as 'lore and law', still connect thousands of contemporary Australians of Aboriginal descent with all other entities that are part of the world' (Findlay, 2007).

**latent content** In Freudian dream analysis, the hidden meaning of a dream.

**manifest content** In Freudian dream analysis, the surface content of a dream which is assumed to mask the dream's actual meaning.

**dream work** In Freudian dream analysis, the process by which the internal censor transforms the latent content of a dream into manifest content.

Indigenous Australians believe information about their environment and local laws is imparted in dreams. What can you learn about yourself and your surroundings from your own dreams?

sky to better observe the world below. These traditional Aboriginal healers say they were taught to do this by their grandparents who took them on dream journeys and passed onto them the secrets of healing.

This forward-thinking time perspective can be seen in other non-Western groups views of dreaming. Freud's theory had dream interpretation looking backward in time, toward childhood experiences and repressed wishes. In many other cultures, dreams are believed instead to present a vision of the future (Basso, 1987). For example, among the people of the Ingessana Hills, a region along the border of Ethiopia and the Sudan, the timing of festivals is determined by dream visions (Jedrej, 1995). The keepers of religious shrines are visited in their dreams by their fathers and other ancestors who instruct them to 'announce the festival'. Other groups have culturally given systems of relationships between dream symbols and meanings. Consider these interpretations from the Kalapalo Indians of central Brazil (Basso, 1987, p. 104):

> When we dream we are burnt by fire, later we will be bitten by a wild thing, by a spider or a stinging ant, for example.
> When [we dream] we are making love to women, we will be very successful when we go fishing.
> When a boy is in seclusion and he dreams of climbing a tall tree, or another one sees a long path, they will live long. This would also be true if we dreamt of crossing a wide stream in a forest.

Note how each interpretation looks to the future. The future orientation of dream interpretation is an important component of a rich cultural tradition.

## Contemporary theories of dream content

The cornerstone of both Western and non-Western approaches to dream interpretation is that dreams provide information that is of genuine value to the person or community. When researchers first began to consider the biological underpinnings of dream they challenged this view. For example, the *activation-synthesis model* suggested that signals emerged from the brain stem that stimulated the forebrain and association areas of the cortex to produce random memories and connections with the dreamer's past experiences (Hobson, 1988; Hobson & McCarley, 1977). According to this view, there are no logical connections, no intrinsic meaning, and no coherent patterns to these random bursts of electrical 'signals.'

However, contemporary research on dreams contradicts the view that the content emerges from random signals. Brain-imaging studies suggest that the hippocampus—a brain structure critical to the acquisition of certain types of memories (see Chapter 7)—is active during REM sleep (Nielsen & Stenstrom, 2005). Another brain structure that plays an important role for emotional memories—the amygdala—is also quite active during REM sleep. This deeper understanding of the physiological aspects of dreams supports the assertion that one of the functions of sleep is to draw together 'an individual's

Aboriginals believe that the Dreamtime coexists with the natural environment, but they are separated by a space dimension, and is inhabited by spiritual forms of deceased ancestors ('unseen people'). Aboriginals believe that connections can occur between these two dimensions via dreams, also known as Story Places. By frequenting a Story Place, individuals may receive gifts of knowledge usually encoded in songs. The particular knowledge imparted is likely to deal with the nature of the local Story Place inhabitants—the processes of nature and the interrelation of plants and animals, including humans, and laws for their behaviour. It is also believed that pieces of knowledge will be communicated to people whom the unseen people know to properly observe the behavioural traditions and rules of the tribe ('the Law').

The type of knowledge that is transmitted varies, and includes trivial and lighthearted stories about animal behaviour, but the most important communications concern cosmology and cosmogony—the creation and origin of the parts of the universe.

The Lardil tribe of Mornington Island believe that to maintain a balanced system of communal knowledge, it is essential to have contributions of knowledge imparted in dreams in the vicinity of each and every Story Place.

It is also said that during the night the spirit of the *ngangkari* (a word for Indigenous practitioner or healer in Central Australia) leaves the body and soars into the recent experiences of the past few days along with their goals, desires, and problems' (Paller & Voss, 2004, p. 667). According to this view, the story of the dream reflects the brain's attempt to weave a narrative around the recent fragments of a person's life that become most prominent during REM sleep.

Studies of dream content confirm that content of dreams shows a good deal of continuity with dreamers' waking concerns (Domhoff, 2005). For example, research using experience-sampling methods suggested that girls were more likely than boys to be thinking about friends of both sexes, rather than just friends of their own sex (Richards et al., 1998). Dream studies with 9- to 15-year-olds demonstrate similar gender differences in dream content about peers (Strauch, 2005; Strauch & Lederbogen, 1999). In addition, across adulthood, the overall content of each individual's dreams stays very much the same over years or even decades (Domhoff, 1999).

You might consider keeping your own dream log—try to write your dreams as soon as you wake up each morning—to see both how your own dreams relate to daily concerns and how your dream content changes or remains stable over time. Still, we should warn you that some people have more difficulty recalling dreams than other people do (Wolcott & Strapp, 2002). For example, it's easier to recall dreams if you wake up during a REM period or close to one. If you want to recall your dreams, you might consider changing the time you set your alarm. Also, people who have more positive attitudes toward dreaming appear to find it easier to recall their dreams. In that sense, the interest you show in your dreams by undertaking a dream log might help increase your ability to recall them.

For answers go to MyPsychLab!

**Nightmares** When a dream frightens you by making you feel helpless or out of control, you are having a *nightmare*. For most people nightmares are relatively infrequent. In one sample of 89 undergraduates who kept dream logs daily for one month, the average number of nightmares reported in the month was 0.48. That monthly average corresponds to a rate of 5.76 nightmares each year (Zadra & Donderi, 2000). However, some people experience nightmares more frequently, sometimes as often as every night. Children, for example, are more likely than adults to experience nightmares (Mindell, 1997). Also, people who have experienced traumatic events, such as rape or war, may have repetitive nightmares that force them to relive some aspects of their trauma. College students who experienced a major earthquake in the San Francisco Bay area were about twice as likely to experience nightmares as were a matched group of students who hadn't experienced an earthquake—and, as you might imagine, many of the nightmares were about the devastating effects of earthquakes (Wood et al., 1992).

We can consider nightmares to be at the outer limit of ordinary consciousness. We turn now to circumstances in which individuals deliberately seek to go beyond those everyday experiences.

## RECAP CHECKPOINT
### Sleep and dreams

- Circadian rhythms reflect the operation of a biological clock.

- Patterns of brain activity change over the course of a night's sleep. REM sleep is signalled by rapid eye movements.

- The amount of sleep and relative proportion of REM to NREM sleep change with age.

- REM and NREM sleep serve different functions, including conservation and restoration.

- Sleep disorders such as insomnia, narcolepsy and sleep apnoea have a negative impact on people's ability to function during waking time.

- Freud proposed that the content of dreams is unconscious material slipped by a sleeping censor.

- In other cultures, dreams are interpreted regularly, often by people with special cultural roles.

- Some dream theories have focused on biological explanations for the origins of dreams.

## CONCEPT QUESTIONS

1. Why do you experience jet lag?
2. How does the balance of NREM and REM sleep change over the course of a night?
3. What two functions might NREM sleep serve?
4. What happens to a person who suffers from sleep apnoea?
5. What did Freud mean by the latent content of a dream?

## CRITICAL THINKING
Consider the study that documented the impact of new task learning on REM sleep. Why was it important to have the control group?

# ALTERED STATES OF CONSCIOUSNESS

In every culture, some people have been dissatisfied with ordinary transformations of their waking consciousness. They have developed practices that take them beyond familiar forms of consciousness to experiences of altered states of consciousness. Some of these practices are individual, such as meditation. Others, such as certain religious practices, are shared attempts to transcend the normal boundaries of conscious experience. We survey a variety of such practices in which altered states of consciousness are induced by a range of procedures.

## LUCID DREAMING

Is it possible to be aware that you are dreaming while you are dreaming? Proponents of the theory of **lucid dreaming** have demonstrated that being consciously aware that one is dreaming is a learnable skill—perfected with regular practice—that enables dreamers to control the direction of their dreams (Gackenbach & LaBerge, 1988; LaBerge & DeGracia, 2000).

> **Stephen LaBerge** and his colleagues devised a methodology that enabled them to test the reality of reports of lucid dreaming. The demonstration relied on previous research that had shown that some of the eye movements of REM sleep correspond to the reported direction of the dreamer's gaze. The researchers therefore asked experienced lucid dreamers to execute distinctive patterns of *voluntary* eye movements when they realised that they were dreaming. The prearranged eye movement signals appeared on the polygraph records during REM, thus demonstrating that the participants had indeed been lucid during REM sleep (LaBerge et al., 1981).

A variety of methods have been used to induce lucid dreaming. For example, in some lucid dreaming research, sleepers wear specially designed goggles that flash a red light when they detect REM sleep. The participants have learned previously that the red light is a cue for becoming consciously aware that they are dreaming (LaBerge & Levitan, 1995). Once aware of dreaming, yet still not awake, sleepers move into a state of lucid dreaming in which they can take control of their dreams, directing them according to their personal goals and making the dreams' outcomes fit their current needs. The ability to have lucid dreams reportedly increases when sleepers firmly believe that such dreams are possible and regularly practise the induction techniques (LaBerge & Rheingold, 1990). Researchers such as Stephen LaBerge argue that gaining control over the 'uncontrollable' events of dreams is healthy because it enhances self-confidence and generates positive experiences for the individual. However, some therapists who use dream analysis as part of their understanding of a patient's problems oppose

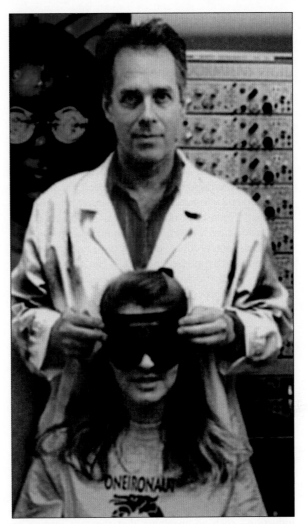

Researcher Stephen LaBerge adjusts the special goggles that will alert the sleeping participant that REM sleep is occurring. The individual is trained to enter into a state of lucid dreaming, being aware of the process and content of dream activity. If you had the ability to experience lucid dreaming, in what ways would you shape your dreams?

**lucid dreaming** The theory that conscious awareness of dreaming is a learnable skill that enables dreamers to control the direction and content of their dreams.

such procedures because they feel that they distort the natural process of dreaming.

## HYPNOSIS

As portrayed in popular culture, hypnotists wield vast power over their witting or unwitting participants. Is this view of hypnotists accurate? What is hypnosis, what are its important features, and what are some of its valid psychological uses? The term **hypnosis** is derived from Hypnos, the name of the Greek god of sleep. Sleep, however, plays no part in hypnosis, except that people may in some cases give the *appearance* of being in a deeply relaxed, sleeplike state. (If people were really asleep, they could not respond to hypnosis.) A broad definition of hypnosis is that it is an alternative state of awareness characterised by the special ability some people have of responding to suggestion with changes in perception, memory, motivation and sense of self-control. In the

**hypnosis** An altered state of awareness characterised by deep relaxation, susceptibility to suggestions and changes in perception, memory, motivation and self-control.

hypnotic state, participants experience heightened responsiveness to the hypnotist's suggestions—they often feel that their behaviour is performed without intention or any conscious effort.

Researchers have often disagreed about the psychological mechanisms involved in hypnosis (Lynn & Kirsch, 2006). Some early theorists suggested that hypnotised individuals enter into a *trance* state, far different from waking consciousness. Others argued that hypnosis was nothing more than heightened motivation. Still others believed it to be a type of social role playing, a kind of *placebo* response of trying to please the hypnotist (see Chapter 2). In fact, research has largely ruled out the idea that hypnosis involves a special trancelike change in consciousness. However, even though nonhypnotised individuals can produce some of the same patterns of behaviour that hypnotised individuals can, there appear to be some added effects of hypnosis—beyond motivational or placebo processes. After we discuss hypnotic induction and hypnotisability, we describe some of those effects.

## Hypnotic induction and hypnotisability

Hypnosis begins with a *hypnotic induction*, a preliminary set of activities that minimises external distractions and encourages participants to concentrate only on suggested stimuli and believe that they are about to enter a special state of consciousness. Induction activities involve suggestions to imagine certain experiences or to visualise events and reactions. When practised repeatedly, the induction procedure functions as a learned signal so that participants can quickly enter the hypnotic state. The typical induction procedure uses suggestions for deep relaxation, but some people can become hypnotised with an active, alert induction—such as imagining that they are jogging or riding a bicycle (Banyai & Hilgard, 1976).

**Hypnotisability** represents the degree to which an individual is responsive to standardised suggestions to experience hypnotic reactions. There are wide individual differences in susceptibility, varying from a complete lack of responsiveness to total responsiveness. **Figure 5.6** shows the percentage of university-age individuals who presented various levels of hypnotisability the first time they were given a hypnotic induction test. What does it mean to have scored 'high' or 'very high' on this scale? When the test is administered, the hypnotist makes a series of posthypnotic suggestions, dictating the experiences each individual might have. When the hypnotist suggested that their extended arms had turned into bars of iron, highly hypnotisable individuals were likely to find themselves unable to bend those arms. With the appropriate suggestion, they were likely to brush away a nonexistent fly. As a third example, highly hypnotisable individuals probably couldn't nod their heads 'no' when the hypnotist suggested they had lost that ability. Students who scored 'low' on the hypnotisability scale experienced few if any of these reactions.

Hypnotisability is a relatively stable attribute. When 50 men and women were retested 25 years after their college hypnotisability assessment, the results

**hypnotisability** The degree to which an individual is responsive to standardised hypnotic suggestion.

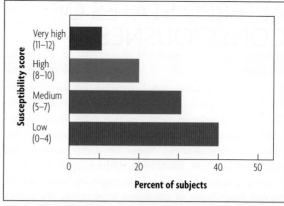

### Figure 5.6

**Level of hypnosis at first induction**
The graph shows the results for 533 individuals hypnotised for the first time. Hypnotisability was measured on the Stanford Hypnotic Susceptibility Scale, which consists of 12 items.

indicated a remarkably high correlation coefficient of .71 (Piccione et al., 1989). Children tend to be more suggestible than adults; hypnotic responsiveness peaks just before adolescence and declines thereafter. Although hypnotisability is relatively stable, it is not correlated with any personality trait such as gullibility or conformity (Fromm & Shor, 1979; Kirsch & Lynn, 1995). In fact, the personality trait that has the highest positive correlation with hypnotisability is *absorption*, which is an individual's 'predisposition to become highly involved in imaginative or sensory experiences' (Council & Green, 2004, p. 364). If, for example, you often find yourself losing track of the 'real' world while you watch a movie, you might also be highly hypnotisable.

Some evidence indicates genetic determinants of hypnotisability. Early research demonstrated that hypnotisability scores of identical twins are more similar than are those of fraternal twins (Morgan et al., 1970). More recently, studies have begun to focus on the particular genes that underlie individual differences. For example, researchers have identified a gene known as *COMT* that influences the brain's use of the neurotransmitter dopamine. Variations in this gene are related to individual differences in hypnotisability (Raz, 2005).

**Effects of hypnosis** In describing the way in which hypnotisability is measured, we already mentioned some of the standard effects of hypnosis: while under hypnosis, individuals respond to suggestions about motor abilities (for example, their arms become unbendable) and perceptual experiences (for example, they hallucinate a fly). How can we be sure, however, that these behaviours arise from special properties of hypnosis and not just a strong willingness on participants' part to please the hypnotist? To address this important question, researchers have often conducted experiments that contrast the performance of truly hypnotised individuals to that of *simulators*.

Two groups of students participated in an experiment. One group was truly hypnotised. The other group was instructed to *simulate* hypnosis: they were instructed by a first experimenter that it was their task to fool a second experimenter into believing that they were, in fact, hypnotised. Both groups were then exposed to a series of tones and asked to judge their loudness. An important part of the experiment was a *demand* instruction, in which the participants were told what they *should* experience (Reed et al., 1996, p. 143):

*People who are exposed to the tone more than once tend to drift back into hypnosis, and this greatly reduces the intensity of the sound that they hear. You probably drifted back into hypnosis on this last trial, and for this reason, heard very little of the tone. Perhaps you didn't hear it at all.*

If all the effects of hypnosis can be attributed to participants' desire to respond correctly to experimenter demands, we would expect hypnotised and simulating participants to respond in the same way to this demand. In fact, they do not. Truly hypnotised individuals gave a wider variety of reports: They told something closer to their true experiences rather than inventing something they thought the experimenter wanted to hear (Reed et al., 1996).

In this case, simulators presumably guess incorrectly what they would be experiencing were they truly hypnotised. From experiments of this type, we can learn exactly what independent contribution hypnosis makes to people's experiences.

An undisputed value of hypnosis is its ability to reduce pain (*hypnotic analgesia*). Your mind can amplify pain stimuli through anticipation and fear; you can diminish this psychological effect with hypnosis (Chaves, 1999). Pain control is accomplished through a variety of hypnotic suggestions: imagining the part of the body in pain as nonorganic (made of wood or plastic) or as separate from the rest of the body, thus taking one's mind on a vacation from the body and distorting time in various ways. People can control pain through hypnosis even when they banish all thoughts and images from consciousness (Hargadon et al., 1995).

You probably won't be surprised to learn that people who are high in hypnotisability are able to obtain greater pain relief through hypnosis. Researchers are trying to understand the brain bases for this difference. For example, a brain-imaging study demonstrated that people who were higher in hypnotisability also had larger regions at the front of the corpus callosum (see Chapter 3) (Horton et al., 2004). This area of the corpus callosum plays a role in attention and the inhibition of unwanted stimuli, suggesting that people who are highly hypnotisable may have more brain tissue that allows them to use hypnosis to inhibit pain. Studies with EEG measures also demonstrate—in the context of hypnotic pain reduction—differences in the brain responses of low and high hypnotisable individuals (Ray et al., 2002).

Hypnosis has also been shown to have effects on psychological wellbeing. Barling and Raine (2005) compared progressive muscle relaxation, guided imagery and deep trance on measures of depression, anxiety, stress and immune system competence. Deep trance was found to produce improvements in burnout, depression and anxiety, as well as in immunocompetence, measured by the biological marker salivary immunoglobulin A.

One final note on hypnosis: the power of hypnosis does *not* reside in some special ability or skill of the hypnotist, but rather it resides in the relative hypnotisability of the person or persons being hypnotised. Being hypnotised does not involve giving up one's personal control; instead, the experience of being hypnotised allows an individual to learn new ways to exercise control that the hypnotist—as coach—can train the subject—as performer—to enact. Keep all of this in mind if you watch a stage show in which people perform outlandish acts under hypnosis: stage hypnotists make a living entertaining audiences by getting highly exhibitionist people to do things in public that most others could never be made to do. As used by researchers and therapists, hypnosis is a technique with the potential to allow you to explore and modify your sense of consciousness.

## MEDITATION

Many religions and traditional psychologies of the East work to direct consciousness away from immediate worldly concerns. They seek to achieve an inner focus on the mental and spiritual self. **Meditation** is a form of consciousness change designed to enhance self-knowledge and wellbeing by achieving a deep state of tranquility. During *concentrative* meditation, a person may focus on and regulate breathing, assume certain body positions (yogic positions), minimise external stimulation, generate specific mental images, or free the mind of all thought. By contrast, during *mindfulness* meditation, a person learns to let thoughts and memories pass freely through the mind without reacting to them.

meditation A form of consciousness alteration designed to enhance self-knowledge and wellbeing through reduced self-awareness.

How does meditation create an altered state of consciousness?

Research has often focused on the ability of meditation to relieve the anxiety of those who must function in stress-filled environments (Anderson et al., 1999; Shapiro et al., 1998). For example, mindfulness meditation has served as the basis for mindfulness-based stress reduction (Kabat-Zinn, 1990). In one study, women suffering from heart disease were given 8 weeks of training on mindfulness meditation; at the end of this intervention, the women reported consistently lower feelings of anxiety than they did before the study (Tacon et al., 2003). Women in the control group didn't experience improvement in their anxiety reports. Because feelings of anxiety play a role in the development of heart disease, this result provides evidence that the mind can help to heal the body. (We will return to this theme when we discuss health psychology in Chapter 12.)

Brain-imaging techniques have begun to reveal the ways in which the practice of meditation affects patterns of brain activity (Cahn & Polich, 2006). In fact, recent evidence suggests that, over time, the practice of meditation might have a positive impact on the brain itself.

> The researchers reasoned that the activities associated with meditation—focused attention on internal and external sensations—would bring about positive changes in the brain regions associated with these activities (Lazar et al., 2005). To test this hypothesis, the researchers recruited two groups of participants: twenty individuals with extensive meditation experience and 15 control individuals with no meditation experience. All the participants underwent MRI scans to provide measures of the thickness of relevant areas of cortex. As the researchers had predicted, these scans revealed that the meditation groups had thicker cortex in areas of auditory and somatosensory cortex (see Chapter 3). The two groups did not differ in areas of the cortex that were not directly relevant to meditation. The researchers carried out further analyses that indicated that those individuals who had the most meditation experience also had the greatest extra thickness in relevant areas of cortex.

As people grow older, they typically lose cortical thickness. Based on their findings, the researchers speculated that meditation could help slow this natural loss of neurons. Practisers of meditation have suggested that, when practised regularly, some forms of meditation can heighten your consciousness and help you achieve enlightenment by enabling you to see familiar things in new ways. This recent research suggests that meditation might also literally be good for your brain.

## RELIGIOUS ECSTASY

Meditation, prayer, fasting and spiritual communication all contribute to intense *religious experiences*. For William James (1902), religious experiences constituted unique psychological experiences characterised by a sense of oneness and relatedness of events, of realness and vividness of experiences, and an inability to communicate, in ordinary language, the nature of the whole experience. For many people, religious experiences are clearly not part of their ordinary consciousness.

Few religious experiences are more intense than those of the Holy Ghost people of Georgia. Their beliefs and practices create a unique form of consciousness that enables them to do some remarkable things. At church services, they handle deadly poisonous snakes, drink strychnine poison, and handle fire. To prepare for these experiences, they listen to long sermons and participate in loud insistent singing and wild spinning and dancing:

> The enthusiasm may verge on violence. . . . Members wail and shake and lapse into the unintelligible, ecstatic 'new tongues' ofglossolalia [artificial speech with no linguistic content]. . . . The ecstasy spreads like contagion . . . Their hands are definitely cold, even after handling fire. This would correspond with research in trance states involved in other religious cultures. It would also account for the vagueness of memory, almost sensory amnesia, that researchers have reported in serpent handlers as well as fire handlers. (Watterlond, 1983, pp. 53, 55)

Psychological research on serpent-handling religious-group members has found them to be generally well-adjusted people who receive powerful social and psychological support from being part of the group. Participating in the 'signs of the spirits' gives them a 'personal reward equalled in no other aspect of their lives' (Watterlond, 1983).

In this section, we have reviewed several ways in which people achieve altered states of consciousness in their dreaming and waking lives. We conclude this chapter with a discussion of what might be the most common means people use to affect their consciousness: mind-altering drugs.

## RECAP CHECKPOINT
### Altered states of consciousness

- Lucid dreaming is an awareness that one is dreaming, in an attempt to control the dream.

- Hypnosis is an alternate state of consciousness characterised by the ability of hypnotisable people to change perception, motivation, memory and self-control in response to suggestions.

- Meditation changes conscious functioning by ritual practices that focus attention away from external concerns to inner experience.

- In some cultural groups, people undergo intense religious experiences.

# MIND-ALTERING DRUGS

Since ancient times, people have taken drugs to alter their perception of reality. Archaeological evidence indicates the uninterrupted use of sophora seed (mescal bean) for over 10,000 years in the southwestern United States and Mexico. The ancient Aztecs fermented mescal beans into a beer. From ancient times, individuals in North and South America also ingested *teonanacatl*, the *Psilocybe* mushroom also known as 'the flesh of the gods,' as parts of rituals. Small doses of these mushrooms produce vivid hallucinations.

In Western cultures, drugs are associated less with sacred communal rituals than with recreation. Individuals throughout the world take various drugs to relax, cope with stress, avoid facing the unpleasantness of current realities, feel comfortable in social situations, or experience an alternate state of consciousness. Over 100 years ago, William James reported on his experiments with a mind-altering drug. After inhaling nitrous oxide, James explained that 'the keynote of the experience is the tremendously exciting sense of intense metaphysical illumination. Truth lies open to the view in depth beneath depth of almost blinding evidence. The mind sees all the logical relations of being with an apparent subtlety and instantaneity to which its normal consciousness offer no parallel' (James, 1882, p. 186). Thus James's interest in the study of consciousness extended to the study of self-induced alternate states.

As we see in Chapter 15, drugs that have an impact on individual's psychological states are often a critical aspect of the treatment of psychological disorders. In fact, as we indicate in **Table 5.1**, many types of drugs have important medical uses. Still, many individuals use drugs that are not prescribed to enhance physical or psychological health. According to the 2004 National Drug Strategy Household Survey (NDSHS), 38 percent of Australians more than 14 years of age had used illicit drugs, and 15 percent had done so at least once in the previous year. The most common illicit drug used was marijuana, with a third of all those surveyed having reported at least one use in their lifetime. The use of alcohol was unchanged across the period from 1991 to 2004, with 85 percent of respondents having reported drinking at least once in the last year. Smoking rates had declined between 1991 and 2004, but still 17 percent of Australians smoked daily. These figures support the importance of understanding the physiological and psychological consequences of drug use.

For answers go to MyPsychLab!

## Table 5.1

### Medical uses of psychoactive drugs

| Drug | Medical uses |
| --- | --- |
| **Hallucinogens** | |
| LSD | None |
| PCP (Phencyclidine) | Veterinary anesthetic |
| Cannabis (Marijuana) | Nausea associated with chemotherapy |
| **Opiates (Narcotics)** | |
| Morphine | Painkiller |
| Heroin | None |
| **Depressants** | |
| Barbiturates (e.g., Seconal) | Sedative, sleeping pill, anesthetic, anticonvulsant |
| Benzodiazepines | Antianxiety, sedative, sleeping pill, |
| (e.g., Valium) | anticonvulsant |
| Rohypnol | Sleeping pill |
| GHB | Treatment for narcolepsy |
| Alcohol | Antiseptic |
| **Stimulants** | |
| Amphetamines | Hyperkinesis, narcolepsy, weight control |
| Methamphetamines | None |
| MDMA (Ecstasy) | Potential aid to psychotherapy |
| Cocaine | Local anesthetic |
| Nicotine | Nicotine gum for cessation of smoking habit |
| Caffeine | Weight control, stimulant in acute respiratory failure, analgesic |

## DEPENDENCE AND ADDICTION

**Psychoactive drugs** are chemicals that affect mental processes and behaviour by temporarily changing conscious awareness. Once in the brain, they attach themselves to synaptic receptors, blocking or stimulating certain

**psychoactive drugs**
Chemicals that affect mental processes and behaviour by temporarily changing conscious awareness of reality.

**tolerance** A situation that occurs with continued use of a drug in which an individual requires greater dosages to achieve the same effect.

**physiological dependence** The process by which the body becomes adjusted to or dependent on a drug.

**addiction** A condition in which the body requires a drug in order to function without physical and psychological reactions to its absence.

**psychological dependence** The psychological need or craving for a drug.

**hallucinations** False perceptions that occur in the absence of objective stimulation.

reactions. By doing so, they profoundly alter the brain's communication system, affecting perception, memory, mood and behaviour. However, continued use of a given drug creates **tolerance**—greater dosages are required to achieve the same effect. (We describe some of the psychological roots of tolerance in Chapter 6.) Hand-in-hand with tolerance is **physiological dependence**, a process in which the body becomes adjusted to and dependent on the substance, in part because neurotransmitters are depleted by the frequent presence of the drug. The tragic outcome of tolerance and dependence is **addiction**. A person who is addicted requires the drug in his or her body and suffers painful withdrawal symptoms (shakes, sweats, nausea, and, in the case of alcohol withdrawal, even death) if the drug is not present.

When an individual finds the use of a drug so desirable or pleasurable that a *craving* develops, with or without addiction, the condition is known as **psychological dependence**, which can occur with any drug. The result of drug dependence is that a person's lifestyle comes to revolve around drug use so wholly that his or her capacity to function is limited or impaired. In addition, the expense involved in maintaining a drug habit of daily—and increasing—amounts often drives an addict to robbery, assault, prostitution or drug peddling.

## VARIETIES OF PSYCHOACTIVE DRUGS

Table 5.1 lists common psychoactive drugs. (In Chapter 15, we discuss other types of psychoactive drugs used to relieve mental illness.) We briefly describe how each class of drugs achieves its physiological and psychological impact. We also note the personal and societal consequences of drug use.

**Hallucinogens** The most dramatic changes in consciousness are produced by drugs known as *hallucinogens* or *psychedelics;* these drugs alter both perceptions of the external environment and inner awareness. As the name implies, these drugs often create **hallucinations**—vivid perceptions that occur in the absence of objective stimulation. The hallucinations may lead to a loss of boundary between self and nonself. *LSD* and *PCP* are two common hallucinogens that are synthesised in laboratories. Hallucinogenic drugs typically act in the brain by affecting the use of the chemical neurotransmitter serotonin (Aghajanian & Marek, 1999). For example, LSD binds very tightly to serotonin receptors so that neurons produce prolonged activation.

*Cannabis* is a plant with psychoactive effects. Its active ingredient is THC, found in both *hashish* (the solidified resin of the plant) and *marijuana* (the dried leaves and flowers of the plant). The experience derived from inhaling THC depends on its dose—small doses create mild, pleasurable high, and large doses result in long hallucinogenic reactions. Regular users report euphoria, feelings of wellbeing, distortions of space and time, and, occasionally, out-of-body experiences. However,

How does marijuana have an impact in the brain?

depending on the context, the effects may be negative—fear, anxiety and confusion.

Researchers have known for several years that *cannabinoids,* the active chemicals in marijuana, bind to specific receptors in the brain—these cannabinoid receptors are particularly common in the hippocampus, the brain region involved in memory. More recent research has led to the discovery of *anandamide,* a neurotransmitter that binds to the same receptors (Di Marzo et al., 1994; Stahl, 1998). That is, cannabinoids achieve their mind-altering effects at brain sites sensitive to anandamide, a naturally occurring substance in the brain. These naturally occurring cannabinoids function as neuromodulators. For example, they suppress the release of the neurotransmitter GABA (Wilson & Nicoll, 2002). These brain cannabinoids appear to play an important role in regulating appetite and feeding behaviours (Kirkham, 2005). This normal function may help explain why marijuana users often find themselves intensely hungry.

**Opiates** *Opiates,* such as *heroin* and *morphine,* suppress physical sensation and response to stimulation. In Chapter 3, we noted that the brain contains endorphins (short for *endogenous morphines)* that generate powerful effects on mood, pain, and pleasure. These endogenous opiates play a critical role in the brain's response to both physical and psychological stressors (Ribeiro et al., 2005). Drugs like opium and morphine bind to the same receptor sites in the brain as the endorphins (Harrison et al., 1998). Thus both opiates and, as we described in the previous section, marijuana achieve their effects because they have active components that have similar chemical properties to substances that naturally occur in the brain.

The initial effect of an intravenous injection of heroin is a rush of pleasure. Feelings of euphoria supplant all worries and awareness of bodily needs. However, heroin use often leads to addiction. When the neural receptors in the endogenous opiate system are artificially stimulated, the brain loses its subtle balance. People who try to withdraw from opiates often experience harsh physical symptoms (e.g., vomiting, pain and insomnia) as well as intense craving for the drug. When people undertake medical assistance to help with withdrawal, they often

Why does heroin use often lead to addiction?

receive treatments that block the opiates' ability to create pleasure responses in the brain (Grüsser et al., 2006).

Depressants The *depressants* include *barbiturates* and, most notably, *alcohol*. These substances tend to depress (slow down) the mental and physical activity of the body by inhibiting or decreasing the transmission of nerve impulses in the central nervous system. Depressants achieve this effect, in part, by facilitating neural communication at synapses that use the neurotransmitter GABA (Delaney & Sah, 1999; Malizia & Nutt, 1995). GABA often functions to inhibit neural transmission, which explains depressants' inhibiting outcomes. In recent years, two depressants, *Rohypnol* (more commonly known as *roofies*) and *GHB*, have achieved reputations as 'date rape drugs'. Both substances can be manufactured as colourless liquids so that they can be added to alcohol or other beverages without detection. In that way, victims can be sedated and raped. In addition, Rohypnol causes amnesia, so that victims may not remember events that occurred while they were under the drug's influence.

Alcohol was apparently one of the first psychoactive substances used extensively by early humans. Under its influence, some people become silly, boisterous, friendly and talkative; others become abusive and violent; still others become quietly depressed. Alcohol appears to stimulate the release of dopamine, which enhances feelings of pleasure. Also, as with other depressants, it appears to affect GABA activity (Pierucci-Lagha et al., 2005). At small dosages, alcohol can induce relaxation and slightly improve an adult's speed of reaction. However, the body can break down alcohol only at a slow rate, and large amounts consumed in a short time period overtax the central nervous system. Driving accidents and fatalities occur six times more often to individuals with 0.10 percent alcohol in their bloodstream than to those with half that amount. Another way alcohol intoxication contributes to accidents is by dilating the pupils of the eyes, thereby causing night vision problems. When the level of alcohol in the blood reaches 0.15 percent, there are gross negative effects on thinking, memory and judgment, along with emotional instability and loss of motor coordination.

Excess consumption of alcohol is a major social problem in Australia. When the amount and frequency of drinking interfere with job performance, impair social and family relationships, and create serious health problems, the diagnosis of *alcoholism* is appropriate. Physical dependence, tolerance and addiction all develop with prolonged heavy drinking. For some individuals, alcoholism is associated with an inability to abstain from drinking. For others, alcoholism manifests itself as an inability to stop drinking once the person takes a few drinks. In a 2004 survey, 10 percent of 14- to 19-year-olds reported drinking in a manner that would be defined as risky (NDSHS). Given the relationship between alcohol use and road traffic accidents these young Australians place themselves at greater risk when drinking is combined with driving. The Australian Institute of Health and Welfare has found that approximately 1 in 45 Australians have an acquired brain injury, and that younger men were much more likely to be affected than any other group. The two most likely causes of these injuries were traffic accidents and blows to the head.

Stimulants *Stimulants*, such as *amphetamines*, *meth-amphetamines* and *cocaine*, keep the drug user aroused and induce states of euphoria. Stimulants achieve their effects by increasing the brain levels of neurotransmitters such as norepinephrine, serotonin and dopamine. For example, stimulants act in the brain to prevent the action of molecules that ordinarily remove dopamine from synapses (Martin-Fardon et al., 2005). The serious addition that often accompanies stimulant use may arise because of long-term changes in the neurotransmitter systems (Ahmed & Koob, 2004). *MDMA*—more commonly known as *ecstasy*—is a stimulant but also produces hallucinogen like distortions of time and perception. As with other stimulants, ecstasy causes nerve cells to release greater amounts of norepinephrine, serotonin and dopamine. In the *Critical Thinking in Your Life* box, we explore the question of whether ecstasy use leads to long-term brain damage.

Stimulants have three major effects that users seek: increased self-confidence, greater energy and hyperalertness, and mood alterations approaching euphoria. Heavy users experience frightening hallucinations and develop beliefs

Why does alcohol remain the most popular way in which university students alter their consciousness?

# CRITICAL THINKING *in your life*

## DOES ECSTASY HARM THE BRAIN?

Over the last several years, *ecstasy (MDMA)* has emerged as a party drug of choice. According to National Drug and Alcohol Research Centre at the University of NSW about 90,000 people will consume an estimated three-quarters of a million ecstasy tablets in Sydney alone this year. The stimulant properties of the drug gives users feelings of boundless energy; the hallucinogenic properties makes sounds, colours, and emotions more intense. As we noted in the text, ecstasy brings about these effects by altering the functioning of neurotransmitters such as dopamine, serotonin, and norepinephrine. Here's an important question: Given these powerful effects on neurotransmitters, does ecstasy have a long-term impact on the brain? We want to help you think critically about the evidence researchers have brought to bear on this question.

At first, it might seem that it would be relatively easy to assess the impact of ecstasy on the brain: As a scientist, you administer some appropriate amount of the drug and then measure its impact. What are the problems with this simple design? The most prominent problem is that the starting position is that ecstasy is *bad* for the brain. For that reason, researchers couldn't carry out experiments with humans as participants. Instead, they must use animal models—typically rats and mice. Much of that research has demonstrated that ecstasy causes damage to neural function. However, the type of damage hasn't always been consistent among species (Colado et al.,

2004). The implication is that ecstasy use is almost certainly dangerous to human brains—but based on research with other species it's hard to be sure exactly what the negative consequences will be.

Another important issue is to what extent the studies accurately reflect human norms of drug use. For particular studies, it's important to know how the doses and frequency of MDMA presentation correspond to the amount of the drug a human might ingest over time. For example, researchers indicate whether they are studying the consequences of a single dose, occasional use, or heavy use. But there's more than that to the human consumption of ecstasy. Researchers recognise, for example, that ecstasy users often ingest the drug at the same time that they have consumed alcohol. This leads to the question of how alcohol and ecstasy jointly affect the brain. Recent research suggests that the combination of ecstasy and alcohol produces negative effects in rats' brains that would not have occurred with ecstasy alone (Cassel et al., 2005).

Researchers also recognise that people often take ecstasy in hot, crowded settings. This is a particular concern because one of the effects of ecstasy can be *hyperthermia*— overheating of the body. In the worst cases, hyperthermia can be fatal. One study contrasted the impact of ecstasy on rats who were housed in rooms that were either normal temperature (about 19° C) or quite hot (about 30° C). Those rats who were housed in the hot rooms had consistently higher

peak body temperatures after they ingested ecstasy (Green et al., 2004). The rats that were given ecstasy repeatedly had even greater problems regulating body temperatures than did the rats that ingested a single dose. The researchers speculated that repeated ecstasy use damaged the neurons that would ordinarily help the body to regulate temperature.

Dr Iain McGregor, Associate Professor at the University of Sydney's School of Psychology is recognised as a leading researcher into the long-term effects of ecstasy use. The most far-reaching aspect of his research is the finding that lab rats, given modest amounts of MDMA, still show effects three to six months later. One of the effects is increased anxiety, even after small doses of the drug. It is almost like the social circuit of the brain is overactivated in the short term by ecstasy, but in the long term may become damaged or burnt out.

You can see that the research on ecstasy points to a negative impact on the brain. That conclusion may not surprise you. Still, it's important for you to understand the ways in which scientists plan research that has maximal implications for human experience. Over the last few years, research on ecstasy has shown reasonable sensitivity to the circumstances in which people are most likely to ingest the drug.

- How might you determine what pattern of ecstasy use is most typical for human users?
- Why is it important to test the impact of ecstasy in both normal and hot temperature rooms?

Evidence suggests that ecstasy use and higher temperatures is a dangerous combination.

that others are out to harm them. These beliefs are known as *paranoid delusions*. A special danger with cocaine use is the contrast between euphoric highs and very depressive lows. This leads users to increase uncontrollably the frequency of drug use and the dosage. *Crack,* a crystallised form of cocaine, increases these dangers. Crack produces a swift high that wears off quickly; craving for the drug is intense.

Two stimulants that you may often overlook as psychoactive drugs are *caffeine* and *nicotine*. As you may know from experience, two cups of strong coffee or tea administer enough caffeine to have a profound effect on heart, blood and circulatory functions and make it difficult for you to sleep. Nicotine, a chemical found in tobacco, is a sufficiently strong stimulant to have been used in high concentrations by Native American shamans to attain mystical states or trances. Unlike some modern users, however, the shamans knew that nicotine is addictive, and they carefully chose when to be under its influence. Like other addictive drugs, nicotine mimics natural chemicals released by the brain. In fact, research has uncovered common regions of brain activation for addiction to nicotine and cocaine (Pich et al., 1997).

Chemicals in nicotine stimulate receptors that make you feel good whenever you have done something right—a phenomenon that aids survival. Unfortunately, nicotine teases those same brain receptors into responding as if it were good for you to be smoking. It's not. As you know, smoking is far from good for your health.

We began this chapter by asking you to remember your past and plan for your future. These ordinary activities allowed us nonetheless to pose some interesting questions about consciousness: Where did your thoughts come from? How did they emerge? When did they arrive? You've now learned some of the theories that apply to these questions and how it has been possible to test those theories. You've seen that consciousness ultimately allows you to have the full range of experiences that define you as human.

We also asked you to consider some increasingly less ordinary uses of consciousness. Why, we asked, do people become dissatisfied with their everyday working minds and seek to alter their consciousness in so many ways? Ordinarily, your primary focus is on meeting the immediate demands of tasks and situations facing you. However, you are aware of these reality-based constraints on your consciousness. You realise they limit the range and depth of your experience and do not allow you to fulfil your potential. Perhaps, at times, you long to reach beyond the confines of ordinary reality. You may seek the uncertainty of freedom instead of settling for the security

## RECAP CHECKPOINT
### Mind-Altering Drugs

- Psychoactive drugs affect mental processes by temporarily changing consciousness as they modify nervous system activity.

- Among psychoactive drugs that alter consciousness are hallucinogens, opiates, depressants and stimulants.

## CONCEPT QUESTIONS

1. What is the definition of drug tolerance?

2. How do drugs like heroin work in the brain?

3. To what category of drugs does nicotine belong?

For answers go to MyPsychLab!

# SUMMARY

Chapter 5 has introduced the notion of consciousness and has outlined some of the scientific analysis in this complex area of investigation. The general concept of consciousness has been a topic of some controversy in Western thought, but is now an accepted area for scholarly investigation. A considerable proportion of our life is spent in sleep and our understanding of the importance of this behaviour has increased greatly in the last few years. Altered states of consciousness are employed by many individuals and groups, and their study has led to increased understanding of normal states of consciousness. The impact of differing psychoactive substances on consciousness seems to be involved in their ability to control behaviour, but carries with it considerable risk of harm.

# KEY TERMS

addiction (p. 164)
circadian rhythm (p. 150)
consciousness (p. 144)
dream work (p. 156)
experience-sampling method
   (p. 146)
hallucinations (p. 164)
hypnosis (p. 159)
hypnotisability (p. 160)

insomnia (p. 153)
latent content (p. 156)
lucid dreaming (p. 159)
manifest content (p. 156)
meditation (p. 161)
narcolepsy (p. 154)
nonconscious (p. 145)
non-REM (NREM) sleep (p. 150)
physiological dependence (p. 164)

preconscious memories (p. 145)
psychoactive drugs (p. 163)
psychological dependence (p. 164)
rapid eye movements (REM)
   (p. 150)
sleep apnoea (p. 154)
somnambulism (p. 154)
think-aloud protocols (p. 146)
tolerance (p. 164)

# PRACTICE TEST

1. Freud suggested that some memories are sufficiently threatening that they are forced to reside in
   a. the unconscious.
   c. consciousness.
   b. the preconscious.
   d. manifest content.

2. You have a group of men and women watch the same TV commercial for a new car. If you want to determine what type of information the commercial brings to mind, you could use
   a. the SLIP technique.
   c. lucid dreaming.
   b. a visual search experiment.
   d. think-aloud protocols.

3. Which of these is an example of the selective storage function of consciousness?
   a. Rob kept his eye on the hoop while he shot the basketball.
   b. Laura decided to get chocolate ice cream instead of vanilla.
   c. Mel hit the gas pedal as soon as the light turned green.
   d. Salvatore committed to memory the address of his new girlfriend.

4. Because it requires more conscious attention, it is harder to find a _____ object than a _____ object.

   a. red; large and red
   b. green; green and yellow
   c. red and blue; green and yellow
   d. red and blue; red

5. You would probably experience the most jet lag if you travelled from _____ to _____.
   a. Darwin/Brisbane
   b. Sydney/Melbourne
   c. Sydney/Perth
   d. Melbourne/Adelaide

6. Both NREM and REM sleep may be important for
   a. conservation.
   c. latent and manifest content.
   b. restoration.
   d. learning and memory.

7. Several times a night, Carolyn stops breathing and then she wakes up. It sounds like Carolyn suffers from
   a. insomnia.
   c. somnambulism.
   b. sleep apnoea.
   d. narcolepsy.

8. The activation-synthesis model claimed that
   a. dreams arise from random brain activity.
   b. manifest content is synthesised from latent content.
   c. dream content reflects people's day-to-day concerns.
   d. girls and boys have different dream content.

9. Experts recommend that people get _____ hours of sleep; 18- to 29-year-olds typically get _____ sleep than that.
   a. 8; more
   b. 7; less
   c. 8; less
   d. 6; more

10. To demonstrate that _____ is possible, researchers had participants perform distinctive patterns of voluntary eye movements while they were asleep.
    a. lucid dreaming
    b. hypnosis
    c. meditation
    d. activation and synthesis

11. Which of these individuals would you expect to be most responsive to hypnosis?
    a. 19-year-old Paula
    b. 11-year-old Ralph
    c. 24-year-old Jeannine
    d. 46-year-old George

12. Research suggests that people who practise _____ have thicker areas of cortex than individuals who do not.
    a. hypnosis
    b. lucid dreaming
    c. somnambulism
    d. meditation

13. Craving for a drug in the absence of a physical need is the definition of
    a. addiction.
    b. drug tolerance.
    c. psychological dependence.
    d. physiological dependence.

14. Hallucinogens act in the brain by _____ the activation of _____ neurons.
    a. inhibiting; GABA
    b. prolonging; dopamine
    c. prolonging; serotonin
    d. inhibiting; dopamine

15. Heavy use of _____ may lead to paranoid delusions.
    a. stimulants
    b. depressants
    c. opiates
    d. hallucinogens

16. To simulate circumstances in which humans take ecstasy, researchers tested rats who were housed in rooms with different temperatures. The study demonstrated a more _____ impact of ecstasy when the rats ingested the drug in a _____ temperature room.
    a. positive; high
    b. negative; normal
    c. positive; low
    d. negative; high

## Essay Questions

1. How has the concept of the unconscious been modified in the time since Freud's theory?

2. What practices of dream interpretation are carried out in non-Western cultures?

3. What physiological mechanisms explain why drug use often leads to addiction?

# WEB LINKS

http://www.sleepaus.on.net
   Australasian Sleep Association

http://aboriginalart.com.au/culture/dreamtime.html
   Aboriginal Art and Culture Centre: The Dreamtime

http://ndarc.med.unsw.edu.au
   National Drug and Alcohol Research Centre

Are you ready for the test? MyPsychLab offers dozens of ways to deepen your understanding and test your recall of the material in this chapter—including video and audio clips, simulations and activities, self-assessments, practice tests and other study materials. Specific resources available for this chapter include:

Gestalt laws of perception
General model of drug addiction

Drinking behaviour
How cocaine works
Hypnosis
Lucid dreaming

To access MyPsychLab, please visit **www.pearsoned.com.au/mypsychlab**

# Did you get it?

## NOW YOU HAVE READ CHAPTER 5—ARE YOU PREPARED FOR THE EXAM?

To enhance your understanding of any of the material in your *Psychology and Life* textbook, go to **MyPsychLab: www.pearsoned.com.au/mypsychlab**.

Complete pre- and post-tests, create your own individualised study plan, watch videos and animations and listen to audio glossaries—all of which will help you to understand the themes of this chapter:

- The contents of consciousness
- The functions of consciousness
- Sleep and dreams
- Altered states of consciousness
- Mind-altering

Watch SIMULATIONS on the General Model of Drug Addiction

**How Pleasure Centers Function**                                      screen 4 of 19

Human brains are designed by evolution to find some activities pleasant (rewarding) and others unpleasant (punishing). When the brain interprets an event or sensory input as rewarding, it provides the individual with a sensation of pleasure or reward by firing neurons in the VTA, the brain's midbrain. This center, in turn, fires the NA and several other brain centers by releasing the neurotransmitter Dopamine (DA).

One of the other centers that is fired is called the amygdala, which attaches the experience of pleasure or reward to the memory of the event just experienced.

An Allyn & Bacon product. Copyright © 2007 Pearson Education, Inc.

Take a PRACTICE TEST via your eBOOK

**Read Chapter 5 of your *Psychology and Life* eBook!**
Learn all about *mind-altering drugs* and a range
of other topics from this chapter in an online
version of your textbook. The eBook matches
your text word-for-word, page-by-page.

Multimedia activities are placed in context
throughout the eBook through the use of icons.
It will help you review key concepts before and
after taking pre- and post-tests.

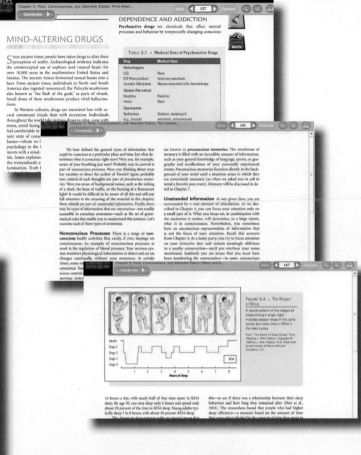

Watch a VIDEO on
*hypnosis*

View streaming video clips that directly relate to the concepts covered in the chapter. Chapter 5 has videos on:

- Infancy: habituation
- Chronic fatigue syndrome
- Insomnia
- Hypnosis

- Lucid dreaming
- Alcohol withdrawal
- Alcoholism

- Is the sun a drug?
- Teen alcoholism
- Teen drinking

Page references for the textbook chapter are also provided so you know exactly what concept the video is referring to!

**What can you find in MyPsychLab?**

Self-directed tests * Videos * Simulations * eBook * Biographies * Audio glossary
* Web links … and more—organised by chapter, section and learning objective.

Learning and Behaviour Analysis

CHAPTER

6

# CHAPTER
# FOCUS POINTS

After studying this chapter you will have a better understanding of:

1. How learning and behaviour have been studied in the laboratory

2. Classical conditioning and how we learn about relations between events in our environment

3. Applications of classical conditioning to understanding human psychopathology

4. Operant conditioning and how we learn about the consequences of our behaviour

5. The use of operant conditioning in everyday life

6. Biological constraints on learning

7. How learning is related to cognition

## CHAPTER CONTENTS

Imagine that you are in a movie theatre, watching a horror film. As the hero approaches a closed door, the music on the movie's sound track grows dark and menacing. You suddenly feel the urge to yell, 'Don't go through that door!' Meanwhile, you find that your heart is racing. But why? If you think about this question formally, you might come to the answer, 'I have learned an association between movie music and movie events—and that's what's making me nervous!' But had you ever thought about this relationship before? Probably not. Somehow, by virtue of sitting in enough movie theatres, you have learned the association without any particular thought. The main topic of Chapter 6 is the types of associations that you acquire effortlessly in your day-to-day experience.

Psychologists have long been interested in *learning*, the ways in which organisms learn from experiences in the world. In just a moment, we will offer a more precise definition of learning. We then consider particular types of learning: classical conditioning and operant conditioning. As you will see, each of these types of learning represents a different way in which organisms acquire and use information about the structure of their environments. For each of these types of learning, we will describe both the basic mechanisms that govern its operation in the laboratory and applications to real-life situations.

In this chapter, we also reflect on the way learning is similar and dissimilar across species. You will see that basic processes of conditioning are the same across a wide variety of species. However, we will note that some aspects of learning are constrained by species' particular genetic endowments. In particular, we will see how the techniques used to study learning in animals have been developed to investigate more complex cognitive processes which influence behaviour in both animals and humans.

# THE STUDY OF LEARNING

To begin our exploration of learning, we will first define learning itself and then offer a brief sketch of the history of psychological research on the topic.

## WHAT IS LEARNING?

**Learning**, a process that results in a relatively consistent change in behaviour or behaviour potential, is based on experience. Let's look more closely at the three critical parts of this definition.

### A change in behaviour or behaviour potential
It is obvious that learning has taken place when you are able to demonstrate the results, such as when you drive a car or use a microwave oven. You can't directly observe learning itself—you can't ordinarily see the changes in your brain—but learning is apparent from improvements in your *performance*. Often, however, your performance doesn't show everything that you have learned. Sometimes,

too, you have acquired general attitudes, such as an *appreciation* of modern art or an *understanding* of Eastern philosophy, that may not be apparent in your measurable actions. In such instances, you have achieved a potential for behaviour change because you have learned attitudes and values that can influence the kinds of books you read or the way you spend your leisure time. This is an example of the **learning-performance distinction**—the difference between what has been learned and what is expressed, or performed, in overt behaviour.

### A relatively consistent change
To qualify as learned, a change in behaviour or behaviour potential must be relatively consistent over different occasions. Thus once you learn to swim, you will probably always be able to do so. Note that consistent changes are not always permanent changes. You may, for example, have become quite a consistent dart thrower when you practised every day. If you gave up the sport, however, your skills might have deteriorated toward their original level. But if you have learned once to be a champion dart thrower, it ought to be easier for you to learn a second time. Something has been 'saved' from your prior experience. In that sense, the change may be permanent.

### A process based on experience
Learning can take place only through experience. Experience includes taking in information (and evaluating and transforming it) and making responses that affect the environment. Learning consists of a response influenced by the lessons of memory. Learned behaviour does not include changes that come about because of physical maturation or brain development as the organism ages, nor those caused by illness or brain damage. Some lasting changes in behaviour require experience following maturational readiness. For example, consider the timetable that determines when an infant is ready to crawl, stand, walk, run and be toilet trained. No amount of training or practice will produce those behaviours before the child has matured sufficiently. Psychologists are especially interested in discovering what

How does consistent form in ballet dancers fit the definition of learning?

aspects of behaviour can be changed through experience and how such changes come about.

**Habituation** Before we move on, we want to help you master this definition of learning. To do so, we will describe a basic form of learning: *habituation*. Suppose you hear a balloon pop in the back yard at a five-year-old's birthday party. The first time it pops, you will respond with a strong startle reflex. However, over the course of the day, as balloons continue to pop regularly, the strength of the reflex decreases. This is an example of **habituation**: You show a decrease in reflexive response when a stimulus is presented repeatedly. Habituation helps keep your focus on novel events in the environment—you don't expend behavioural effort to respond repeatedly to old stimuli.

One way of thinking about this, proposed by Sokolov (1963) is that when our internal 'model' of the world corresponds to what is observed we essentially stop processing new information about it. The process of habituation can be modulated under certain circumstances, however. Sometimes information is too important for us to ignore. So, for example, if I had asked you to count the number of times a phone rang in the room the level of habituation would have been diminished greatly (Barry, 2004).

Note how habituation fits the definition of learning. There's a change in behaviour (you are no longer startled by the balloons popping) that is based on experience (you realise that it is likely that balloons will pop), and that behaviour change is consistent (you are no longer startled for a period of time). Suppose you move inside the house where there are more balloons. At least once or twice, you might find yourself startled when they pop. Thus we see that habituation can produce consistent changes in behaviour that are not, at the same time, permanent. Further experience in the environment will once again change your behaviour.

# BEHAVIOURISM AND BEHAVIOUR ANALYSIS

Much of modern psychology's view of learning finds its roots in the work of John Watson (1878–1958). Watson founded the school of psychology known as *behaviourism*. For nearly 50 years, American psychology was dominated by the behaviourist tradition expressed in Watson's 1919 book, *Psychology from the Standpoint of a Behaviourist*. Watson argued that introspection—people's verbal reports of sensations, images and feelings—was *not* an acceptable basis for a science of psychology because it was too subjective. How could scientists verify the accuracy of such private experiences? But once introspection has been rejected, what should the subject matter of psychology be? Watson's answer was *observable behaviour*. In Watson's words, 'States of consciousness, like the so-called phenomenon of spiritualism, are not objectively verifiable and for that reason can never become data for science'

B. F. Skinner expanded on Watson's ideas and applied them to a wide spectrum of behaviour. Why did Skinner's psychology focus on environmental events rather than internal states?

**habituation** A decrease in a behavioural response when a stimulus is presented repeatedly.

(Watson, 1919, p. 1). Watson also defined the chief goal of psychology as 'the prediction and control of behaviour' (Watson, 1913, p. 158).

B.F. Skinner (1904–1990) adopted Watson's cause and expanded his agenda. Skinner began the research that would lead him to formulate this position when, after reading Watson's 1924 book *Behaviourism*, he began his graduate study in psychology at Harvard. Over time, Skinner formulated a position known as *radical behaviourism*. Skinner embraced Watson's complaint against internal states and mental events. However, Skinner focused not so much on their legitimacy as data as on their legitimacy as causes of behaviour (Skinner, 1990). In Skinner's view, private events, such as thinking and imagining, do not *cause* behaviour. Rather, they are examples *of* behaviour that are themselves caused by environmental stimuli.

Suppose that we deprive a pigeon of food for 24 hours, place it in an apparatus where it can obtain food by pecking a small disk, and find that it soon does so. Skinner would argue that the animal's behaviour can be fully explained by environmental events—deprivation and the use of food as reinforcement. The subjective feeling of hunger, which cannot be directly observed or measured, is not a cause of the behaviour but the result of deprivation. It adds nothing to our account to say that the bird pecked the disk because it was hungry or because it wanted to get the food. To explain what the bird does, you need not understand anything about its inner psychological states—you need only to understand the simple principles of learning that allow the bird to acquire the association between behaviour and reward. This is the essence of Skinner's brand of behaviourism (Delprato & Midgley, 1992).

This brand of behaviourism originated by Skinner served as the original philosophical cornerstone of **behaviour analysis**, the area of psychology that focuses on discovering environmental determinants of learning and

**behaviour analysis** The area of psychology that focuses on the environmental determinants of learning and behaviour.

behaviour (Grant & Evans, 1994). In general, behaviour analysts attempt to discover regularities in learning that are universal, occurring in all types of animal species, including humans, under comparable situations. That is why studies with nonhuman animals have been so critical to progress in this area. Complex forms of learning represent combinations and elaborations of simpler processes and not qualitatively different phenomena. In the sections that follow, we describe classical conditioning and operant conditioning—two simple forms of learning that give rise to quite complex behaviours.

For answers go to MyPsychLab!

## RECAP CHECKPOINT
### The study of learning

- Learning entails a relatively consistent change in behaviour or behaviour potential based on experience.

- Behaviourists believe that much behaviour can be explained by simple learning processes.

- They also believe that many of the same principles of learning apply to all organisms.

## CONCEPT QUESTIONS

1. What is meant by the learning–performance distinction?

2. Why did Watson emphasise the study of observable behaviour?

3. What is a major goal of behaviour analysis?

4. What is the definition of habituation?

# CLASSICAL CONDITIONING: LEARNING PREDICTABLE SIGNALS

Imagine once more that you are watching that horror movie. Why does your heart race when the sound track signals trouble for the hero? Somehow your body has learned to produce a physiological response (a racing heart) when one environmental event (for example, scary music) is associated with another (scary visual events). This type of learning is known as **classical conditioning**, a basic form of learning in which one stimulus or event predicts the occurrence of another stimulus or event. The organism learns a new *association* between two stimuli—a stimulus that did not previously elicit the response and one

**classical conditioning**
Learning in which a behaviour (conditioned response) is elicited by a conditioned stimulus whose power is acquired through an association with a biologically significant unconditioned stimulus.

that naturally elicited the response. As you shall see, the innate capacity to quickly associate pairs of events in your environment has profound behavioural implications.

## PAVLOV'S SURPRISING OBSERVATION

The first rigorous study of classical conditioning was the result of what may well be psychology's most famous accident. The Russian physiologist **Ivan Pavlov** (1849–1936) did not set out to study classical conditioning or any other psychological phenomenon. He happened on classical conditioning while conducting research on digestion, for which he won a Nobel Prize in 1904.

Pavlov had devised a technique to study digestive processes in dogs by implanting tubes in their glands and digestive organs to divert bodily secretions to containers outside their bodies so that the secretions could be measured and analysed. To produce these secretions, Pavlov's assistants put meat powder into the dogs' mouths. After repeating this procedure a number of times, Pavlov observed an unexpected behaviour in his dogs—they salivated *before* the powder was put in their mouths! They would start salivating at the mere sight of the food and, later, at the sight of the assistant who brought the food or even at the sound of the assistant's footsteps. Indeed, any stimulus that regularly preceded the presentation of food came to elicit salivation. Quite by accident, Pavlov had observed that learning may result from two stimuli becoming associated with each other.

Fortunately, Pavlov had the scientific skills and curiosity to begin a rigorous attack on this surprising phenomenon. He ignored the advice of the great physiologist of the time, Sir Charles Sherrington, that he should give up his foolish investigation of 'psychic' secretions. Instead, Pavlov abandoned his work on digestion and, in so doing, changed the course of psychology forever (Pavlov, 1928). For the remainder of Pavlov's life, he continued to search for the variables that influence classically conditioned behaviour. Classical conditioning is also called *Pavlovian conditioning* because of Pavlov's discovery of the major phenomena

Physiologist Ivan Pavlov (shown here with his research team) observed classical conditioning while conducting research on digestion. What were some of Pavlov's major contributions to the study of this form of learning?

of conditioning and his dedication to tracking down the variables that influence it.

Pavlov's considerable research experience allowed him to follow a simple and elegant strategy to discover the conditions necessary for his dogs to be conditioned to salivate. As shown in **Figure 6.1**, dogs in his experiments were first placed in a restraining harness. At regular intervals, a stimulus such as a tone was presented, and a dog was given a bit of food. Importantly, the tone had no prior meaning for the dog with respect to food or salivation. As you might imagine, the dog's first reaction to the tone was only an *orienting response*—the dog pricked its ears and moved its head to locate the source of the sound. However, with *repeated pairings* of the tone and the food, the orienting response **habituated** and salivation began. What Pavlov had observed in his earlier research was no accident: the phenomenon could be replicated under controlled conditions. Pavlov demonstrated the generality of this effect by using a variety of other stimuli ordinarily neutral with respect to salivation, such as lights and ticking metronomes.

The main features of Pavlov's classical conditioning procedure are illustrated in **Figure 6.2**. At the core of classical conditioning are *reflex* responses such as salivation, pupil contraction, knee jerks or eye blinking. A **reflex** is a response that is naturally triggered—*elicited*—by specific stimuli that are biologically relevant for the organism. Any stimulus, such as the food powder used in Pavlov's experiments, that naturally elicits a reflexive behaviour is called an **unconditioned stimulus (UCS)** because learning is not a necessary condition for the stimulus to control the behaviour. The behaviour elicited by the unconditioned stimulus is called the **unconditioned response (UCR)**.

In Pavlov's experiments, the stimuli such as lights and tones did not originally trigger the reflex response of salivation. However, over time each neutral stimulus was repeatedly paired with the unconditioned stimulus. This neutral stimulus is called the **conditioned stimulus (CS)**: Its power to elicit behaviour is *conditioned* on its association with the UCS. After several trials, the CS will produce a response called the **conditioned response (CR)**. The conditioned response is whatever response the conditioned stimulus elicits as a product of learning—we will provide several examples as this section unfolds. Let's review. Nature provides the UCS–UCR connections, but the learning produced by classical conditioning creates the CS–CR connection. The conditioned stimulus acquires some of the power to influence behaviour that was originally limited to the unconditioned stimulus. Let's now look in more detail at the basic processes of classical conditioning.

## PROCESSES OF CONDITIONING

Pavlov's original experiments inspired extensive study of how classically conditioned responses appear and disappear. In this section, we describe several important conclusions researchers have reached about the basic processes of classical conditioning. These conclusions have emerged from hundreds of different studies across a wide range of animal species.

### Acquisition and extinction

**Figure 6.3** displays a hypothetical classical conditioning experiment. The first panel displays **acquisition**, the process by which the CR is first elicited and gradually increases in frequency over repeated trials. In general, the CS and UCS must be paired several times before the CS reliably elicits a CR. With systematic CS–UCS pairings, the CR is elicited with increasing frequency, and the organism may be said to have acquired a conditioned response.

In classical conditioning, as in telling a good joke, *timing* is critical. The CS and UCS must be presented closely enough in time to be perceived by the organism as being related. (We will describe an exception to this rule in a later section on *taste-aversion learning*.) Researchers have studied at least four temporal patterns between the two stimuli, as shown in **Figure 6.4** (Hearst, 1988).

**conditioned response (CR)** In classical conditioning, a response elicited by some previously neutral stimulus that occurs as a result of pairing the neutral stimulus with an unconditioned stimulus.

**reflex** An unlearned response elicited by specific stimuli that have biological relevance for an organism.

**acquisition** The stage in a classical conditioning experiment during which the conditioned response is first elicited by the conditioned stimulus.

**unconditioned stimulus (UCS)** In classical conditioning, the stimulus that elicits an unconditioned response.

**unconditioned response (UCR)** In classical conditioning, the response elicited by an unconditioned stimulus without prior training or learning.

**conditioned stimulus (CS)** In classical conditioning, a previously neutral stimulus that comes to elicit a conditioned response.

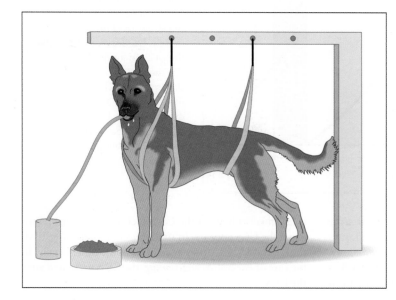

Figure 6.1

**Pavlov's original procedure**
In his original experiments, Pavlov used a variety of stimuli such as tones, bells, lights and metronomes to serve as neutral stimuli. The experimenter presented one of these neutral stimuli and then the food powder. The dog's saliva was collected through a tube.

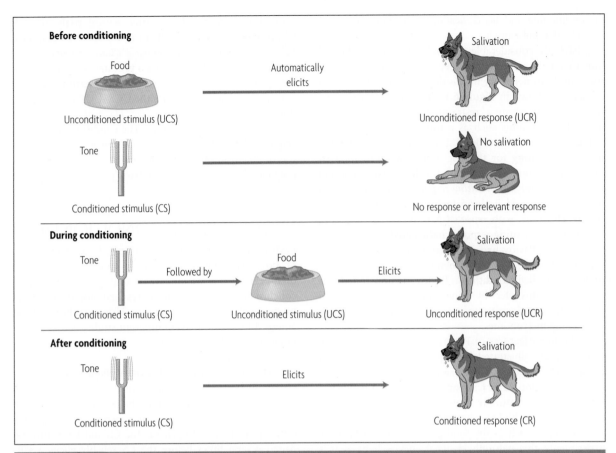

**Figure 6.2**

**Basic features of classical conditioning**
Before conditioning, the unconditioned stimulus (UCS) naturally elicits the unconditioned response (UCR). A neutral stimulus, such as a tone, has no eliciting effect. During conditioning, the neutral stimulus is paired with the UCS. Through its association with the UCS, the neutral stimulus becomes a conditioned stimulus (CS) and elicits a conditioned response (CR) that is similar to the UCR.

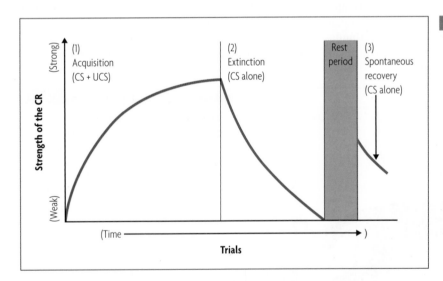

**Figure 6.3**

**Acquisition, extinction and spontaneous recovery in classical conditioning**
During acquisition (CS + UCS), the strength of the CR increases rapidly. During extinction, when the UCS no longer follows the CS, the strength of the CR drops to zero. The CR may reappear after a brief rest period, even when the UCS is still not presented. The reappearance of the CR is called spontaneous recovery.

The most widely used type of conditioning is called *delay conditioning*, in which the CS comes on prior to and stays on at least until the UCS is presented. In *trace conditioning*, the CS is discontinued or turned off before the UCS is presented. *Trace* refers to the memory that the organism is assumed to have of the CS, which is no longer present when the UCS appears. In *simultaneous conditioning*, both the CS and UCS are presented at the same time. Finally, in the case of *backward conditioning*, the CS is presented after the UCS.

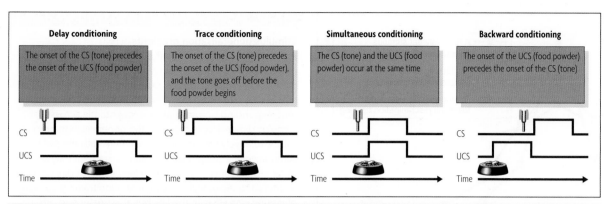

| Delay conditioning | Trace conditioning | Simultaneous conditioning | Backward conditioning |
|---|---|---|---|
| The onset of the CS (tone) precedes the onset of the UCS (food powder) | The onset of the CS (tone) precedes the onset of the UCS (food powder), and the tone goes off before the food powder begins | The CS (tone) and the UCS (food powder) occur at the same time | The onset of the UCS (food powder) precedes the onset of the CS (tone) |

= tuning fork

= food bowl/ food powder

## Figure 6.4

**Four variations of the CS–UCS temporal arrangement in classical conditioning**
Researchers have explored the four possible timing arrangements between the CS and UCS. Conditioning is generally most effective in a delay conditioning paradigm with a short interval between the onsets of the CS and UCS.

From Robert A. Baron, *Psychology*, 5/e, p. 172. Published by Allyn and Bacon, Boston, MA. Copyright © 2001 by Pearson Education. Reprinted by permission of the publisher.

Conditioning is usually most effective in a delayed conditioning paradigm, with a short interval between the onsets of the CS and UCS. However, the exact time interval between the CS and the UCS that will produce optimal conditioning depends on several factors, including the intensity of the CS and the response being conditioned. Let's focus on the response being conditioned. For muscular responses, such as eye blinks, a short interval of a second or less is best. For visceral responses, such as heart rate and salivation, however, longer intervals of 5 to 15 seconds work best.

Conditioning is generally poor with a simultaneous procedure and very poor with a backward procedure. Evidence of backward conditioning may appear after a few pairings of the UCS and CS but disappear with extended training as the animal learns that the CS is followed by a period free of the UCS. In both cases, conditioning is weak because the CS does not actually predict the onset of the UCS. (We will return to the importance of predictability, or *contingency*, in the next section.)

But what happens when the CS (for example, the tone) no longer predicts the UCS (the food powder)? Under those circumstances, the CR (salivation) becomes weaker over time and eventually stops occurring. When the CR no longer appears in the presence of the CS (and the absence of the UCS), the process of **extinction** is said to have occurred (see Figure 6.3, panel 2). Conditioned responses, then, are not necessarily a permanent aspect of the organism's behavioural repertoire. However, the CR will reappear in a weak form when the CS is presented alone again after extinction (see Figure 6.3, panel 3). Pavlov referred to this sudden reappearance of the CR after a rest period, or time-out, without further exposure to the UCS as **spontaneous recovery** after extinction.

When the original pairing is renewed, post extinction, the CR becomes rapidly stronger. This more rapid relearning is an instance of *savings:* Less time is necessary to reacquire the response than to acquire it originally. Thus

some of the original conditioning must be retained by the organism even after experimental extinction appears to have eliminated the CR. In other words, extinction has only weakened performance, not wiped out the original learning. This is why we made a distinction between learning and performance in our original definition of learning.

**Stimulus generalisation** Suppose we have taught a dog that presentation of a tone of a certain frequency predicts food powder. Is the dog's response specific to only that stimulus? If you think about this question for a moment, you will probably not be surprised that the answer is no. In general, once a CR has been conditioned to a particular CS, similar stimuli may also elicit the

Why might a child who has been frightened by one dog develop a fear response to all dogs?

**extinction** In conditioning, the weakening of a conditioned association in the absence of a reinforcer or unconditioned stimulus.

**spontaneous recovery** The reappearance of an extinguished conditioned response after a rest period.

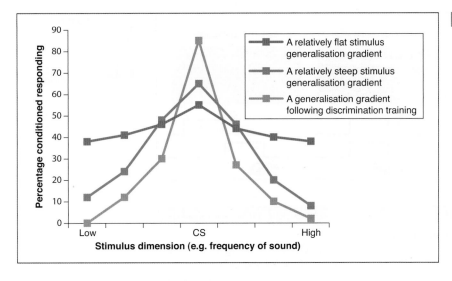

Figure 6.5

**Stimulus generalisation gradients**
After pairing a particular CS (for example a tone of a specific pitch) with a US, conditioned responding to other more or less similar stimuli can be examined. If tones of lower and higher pitch (frequency) are tested, it may be found that responding occurs relatively consistently across that stimulus dimension. In this case the generalisation gradient will be relatively flat, as can be seen here with the red line. Alternatively, a steeper generalisation gradient may be obtained, as shown by the green line, if responding is more restricted to the actual CS. Discrimination training consists of pairing one CS with the US, but also presenting other stimuli without the US. This typically produces the very steep generalisation gradient shown by the blue line.

response. For example, if conditioning was to a high-frequency tone, a slightly lower tone could also elicit the response. A child bitten by a big dog is likely to respond with fear even to smaller dogs. This automatic extension of responding to stimuli that have never been paired with the original UCS is called **stimulus generalisation**. The more similar the new stimulus is to the original CS, the stronger the response will be. When response strength is measured for each of a series of increasingly dissimilar stimuli along a given dimension, as shown in **Figure 6.5**, a *generalisation gradient* is found.

The existence of generalisation gradients should suggest to you the way classical conditioning serves its function in everyday experience. Because important stimuli rarely occur in exactly the same form every time in nature, stimulus generalisation builds in a similarity safety factor by extending the range of learning beyond the original specific experience. With this feature, new but comparable events can be recognised as having the same meaning, or behavioural significance, despite apparent differences. For example, even when a predator makes a slightly different sound or is seen from a different angle, its prey can still recognise and respond to it quickly.

**Stimulus discrimination** In some circumstances, however, it is important that a response be made to only a very small range of stimuli. An organism should not, for example, exhaust itself by fleeing too often from animals that are only superficially similar to its natural predators. **Stimulus discrimination** is the process by which an organism learns to respond differently to stimuli that are distinct from the CS on some dimension (for example, differences in hue or in pitch). An organism's discrimination among similar stimuli (tones of 1,000, 1,200, and 1,500 Hz, for example) is sharpened with discrimination training in which only one of them (1,200 Hz, for example) predicts the UCS and in which the others are repeatedly presented without it. Early in conditioning, stimuli similar to the CS will elicit a similar response, although not quite as strong. As discrimination training proceeds, the responses to the other, dissimilar stimuli weaken: The organism gradually

learns which event-signal predicts the onset of the UCS and which signals do not.

For an organism to perform optimally in an environment, the processes of generalisation and discrimination must strike a balance. You don't want to be over selective—it can be quite costly to miss the presence of a predator. You also don't want to be over responsive—if you are fearful of every shadow, you will waste time and energy to dispel your worry. Classical conditioning provides a mechanism that allows creatures to react efficiently to the structure of their environments (Garcia, 1990).

## FOCUS ON ACQUISITION

In this section, we will examine more closely the conditions that are necessary for classical conditioning to take place. So far, we have *described* the acquisition of classically conditioned responses, but we have not yet *explained* it. Pavlov believed that classical conditioning resulted from the mere pairing of the CS and the UCS. In his view, if a response is to be classically conditioned, the CS and the UCS must occur close together in time—that is, be *temporally contiguous*. But as we will see next, contemporary research has modified that view.

Pavlov's theory dominated classical conditioning until the mid-1960s, when **Robert Rescorla** (1966) conducted a very telling experiment using dogs as subjects. Rescorla designed an experiment using a tone (the CS) and a shock (the UCS). For one group of animals the CS and UCS were merely contiguous—which, if Pavlov were correct, would be sufficient to produce classical conditioning. For the other group of animals, the tone reliably predicted the presence of the shock.

In the first phase of the experiment, Rescorla trained dogs to jump a barrier from one side of a shuttle box to the other to avoid an electric shock delivered through the grid floor (see **Figure 6.6**). If the dogs did not jump, they received a shock; if they did jump, the shock was postponed. Rescorla used the frequency

**stimulus generalisation**
The automatic extension of conditioned responding to similar stimuli that have never been paired with the unconditioned stimulus.

**stimulus discrimination** A conditioning process in which an organism learns to respond differently to stimuli that differ from the conditioned stimulus on some dimension.

with which dogs jumped the barrier as a measure of fear conditioning.

When the dogs were jumping across the barrier regularly, Rescorla divided his subjects into two groups and subjected them to another training procedure. To the random group, the UCS (the shock) was delivered randomly and independently of the CS (the tone) (see **Figure 6.7**). Although the CS and the UCS often occurred close together in time—they were, by chance, temporally contiguous—the UCS was as likely to be delivered in the absence of the CS as it was in its presence. Thus the CS had no predictive value. For the contingency group, however, the UCS always followed the CS. Thus, for this group, the sounding of the tone was a reliable predictor of the delivery of the shock.

Once this training was complete, the dogs were put back into the shuttle box, but this time with a twist. Now the tone used in the second training procedure occasionally sounded, signalling shock. What happened? **Figure 6.8** indicates that dogs exposed to the *contingent* (predictable) CS–UCS relation jumped more frequently in the presence of the tone than did dogs exposed only to the *contiguous* (associated) CS–UCS relation. Contingency was critical for the signal to serve the dogs as a successful cue for the shock.

Thus, in addition to the CS being contiguous—occurring close in time—with the UCS, the CS must also *reliably predict* the occurrence of the UCS in order for classical conditioning to occur (Rescorla, 1988). This finding makes considerable sense. After all, in natural situations, where learning enables organisms to adapt to changes in their environment, stimuli come in clusters and not in neat, simple units, as they do in laboratory experiments.

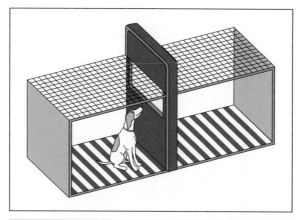

## Figure 6.6

**A shuttlebox**
Rescorla used the frequency with which dogs jumped over a barrier as a measure of fear conditioning.

There's one last requirement for a stimulus to serve as a basis for classical conditioning: It must be *informative* in the environment. Consider an experimental situation in which rats have learned that a tone predicts a shock. Now, a light is added into the situation so that both the light and tone precede the shock. However, when the light is subsequently presented alone, the rats do not appear to have learned that the light predicts the shock (Kamin, 1969). For these rats, the previous conditioning to the tone in the first phase of the experiment *blocked* any subsequent conditioning that could occur to the light. From the rat's point of view, the light may as well not have existed; it provided no additional information beyond that already given by the tone. And, lest you should think that all this is only relevant if you are a rat, evidence for blocking can certainly be found in human learning tasks,

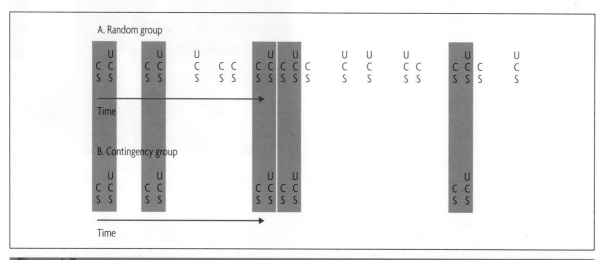

## Figure 6.7

**Rescorla's procedure for demonstrating the importance of contingency**
For the random group, 5-second tones (the CS) and 5-second shocks (the UCS) were distributed randomly through the experimental period. For the contingency group, the dogs experienced only the subset of tones and shocks that occurred in a predictive relationship (the onset of the CS preceded the onset of the UCS by 30 seconds or less). Only the dogs in the contingency group learned to associate the CS with the UCS.

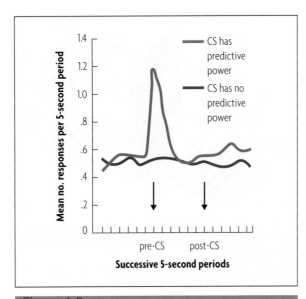

**Figure 6.8**

**A shuttlebox**
Rescorla used the frequency with which dogs jumped over a barrier as a measure of fear conditioning.

and its analysis is the focus of considerable contemporary attention (Lovibond, Been, Mitchell, Bouton, & Froghardt, 2003; Mitchell & Lovibond, 2002).

The requirement of informativeness explains why conditioning occurs most rapidly when the CS stands out against the many other stimuli that may also be present in an environment. A stimulus is more readily noticed the more *intense* it is and the more it *contrasts* with other stimuli. To generate good conditioning, you must present either a strong, novel stimulus in an unfamiliar situation or a strong, familiar stimulus in a novel context.

You can see that classical conditioning is more complex than even Pavlov originally realised. A neutral stimulus will become an effective CS only if it is both appropriately contingent and informative. But now let's shift your attention a bit. We want to identify real-life situations in which classical conditioning plays a role.

## APPLICATIONS OF CLASSICAL CONDITIONING

Your knowledge of classical conditioning can help you understand significant everyday behaviour. In this section, we help you recognise some real-world instances of emotions and preferences as the products of this form of learning. We also explore the role classical conditioning plays in the unfolding of drug addiction.

**Emotions and preferences** Earlier we asked you to think about your experience at a horror movie. In that case, you (unconsciously) learned an association between scary music (the CS) and certain likely events (the UCS—the kinds of things that happen in horror movies that cause reflexive revulsion). If you pay careful attention to events in your life, you will discover that there are many

circumstances in which you can't quite explain why you are having such a strong emotional reaction or why you have such a strong preference about something. You might take a step back and ask yourself, Is this the product of classical conditioning?

Consider these situations (Rozin et al., 1986; Rozin & Fallon, 1987):

- Do you think you'd be willing to eat fudge that had been formed into the shape of dog faeces?
- Do you think you'd be willing to drink a sugar-water solution if the sugar was drawn from a container that you knew was incorrectly labelled poison?
- Do you think you would be willing to drink apple juice into which a sterilised cockroach had been dipped?

If each of these situations makes you say 'No way!' you are not alone. The classically conditioned response—feelings of disgust or danger—wins out over the knowledge that the stimulus is really okay. Because classically conditioned responses are not built up through conscious thought, they are also hard to eliminate through conscious reasoning!

One of the most extensively studied real-world products of classical conditioning is *fear conditioning*. In the earliest days of behaviourism, John Watson and his colleague Rosalie Rayners sought to prove that many fear responses could be understood as the pairing of a neutral stimulus with something naturally fear provoking. To test their idea, they experimented on an infant who came to be called Little Albert.

How do processes of classical conditioning help explain people's fear responses at horror movies?

Watson and Rayner (1920) trained Albert to fear a white rat he had initially liked, by pairing its appearance with an aversive UCS—a loud noise just behind him created by striking a large steel bar with a hammer. The unconditioned startle response and the emotional distress to the noxious noise formed the basis of Albert's learning to react with fear to the appearance of the white rat. His fear was developed in just seven conditioning trials. The emotional conditioning was then extended to behavioural conditioning when Albert learned to escape from the feared stimulus. The infant's learned fear then generalised to other furry objects, such as a rabbit, a dog and even a Santa Claus mask! (Albert's mother, a wet nurse at the hospital where the study was conducted, took him away before the researchers could try to treat the experimentally conditioned fear. So we don't know what happened to Little Albert [Harris, 1979; Schwartz, 1987].)

How did John Watson and Rosalie Rayner condition Little Albert to fear small, furry objects?

As you'll recall from Chapter 2, researchers in psychology are guided by important ethical principles. Those principles make them look back at Watson and Rayner's experiment with grave discomfort: no ethical researcher would ever replicate an experiment of this type. However, it is known from better controlled experiments that people can acquire mild conditioned fear to stimuli paired with aversive events (Ohman & Mineka, 2001). Conditioned fear is most rapidly acquired to stimuli such as pictures of spiders and snakes, which seems to 'make sense' in terms of evolutionary pressure for this kind of conditioning. Mazurski, Bond, Siddle & Lovibond (1996) showed that aversive conditioning was greater to when the CS was an angry face displayed by an adult, than a happy face, and that this difference did not occur if the face was displayed by a child. Although an evolutionary advantage for learning about the expression of anger and painful subsequent events is not the only explanation for this difference, the demonstration that emotional responding can be conditioned in the laboratory with relatively mild stimuli, strongly suggests that this is a very potent mechanism which could play an important role in controlling behaviour in the real world when strongly aversive events are experienced (McNally & Westbrook, 2006).

The potency and evolutionary importance of fear conditioning may mean that even a single traumatic event can condition you to respond with strong physical, emotional and cognitive reactions—perhaps for a lifetime. For example, one of our friends was in a bad car accident during a rainstorm. Now every time it begins to rain while he is driving, he becomes panic-stricken, sometimes to the extent that he has to pull over and wait out the storm. On one occasion, this rational, sensible man even crawled into the back seat and lay on the floor, face down, until the rain subsided. We will see in Chapter 15 that therapists have designed treatments for these types of fears that are intended to counter the effects of classical conditioning.

We don't want to leave you with the impression that only negative responses are classically conditioned. In fact, we suspect that you will also be able to interpret responses of happiness or excitement as instances of classical conditioning. Certainly workers in the advertising industry hope that classical conditioning works as a positive force. They strive, for example, to create associations in your mind between their products (for example, jeans, sports cars, and soft drinks) and passion. They expect that elements of their advertisements—'sexy' individuals or situations—will serve as the UCS to bring about the UCR—feelings of sexual arousal. The hope then is that the product itself will be the CS, so that the feelings of arousal will become associated with it.

One form of conditioning which may have particular relevance here is known as 'evaluative' conditioning. Evaluative conditioning is sometimes referred to as the process by which we acquire 'likes and dislikes'. The original demonstration of evaluative conditioning by Martin and Levy (1978) showed that simply pairing pictures which were rated positively with others that were not could result in the neutral pictures becoming more liked than they had been. This process appears to have taken place without conscious awareness on the part of the participants. Evaluative conditioning has even been applied to learning in social situations, such that it is possible that one reason we like particular individuals may simple be that on our first meeting they were in the presence of another person we liked already (Walther, 2002). There is also some evidence that evaluative conditioning may be very difficult to extinguish, meaning that although the conditioned response may be relatively subtle its unconscious nature and persistence may make it extremely influential in our behaviour. The nature of evaluative conditioning and the parameters of its operation have thus been of considerable interest, and Australian researchers have made important contributions to this debate (e.g., Lipp, Ougten, & LeLievre, 2003).

Why do we like these people? Could it be evaluative conditioning?

**Learning to be a drug addict** Consider this scenario. A man's body lies in a Kings Cross alley, a half-empty syringe dangling from his arm. Cause of death? The coroner called it an overdose, but the man had ordinarily shot up far greater doses than the one that had supposedly killed him. This sort of incident baffled investigators. How could an addict with high drug tolerance die of an overdose when he didn't even get a full hit?

Some time ago, Pavlov (1927) and later his colleague Bykov (1957) pointed out that tolerance to opiates can develop when an individual anticipates the pharmacological action of a drug. Contemporary researcher **Shepard Siegel** refined these ideas. Siegel suggested that the setting in which drug use occurs acts as a conditioned stimulus for a situation in which the body learns to protect itself by preventing the drug from having its usual effect. When people take drugs, the drug (UCS) brings about certain physiological responses to which the body responds with countermeasures intended to re-establish homeostasis (see Chapter 3). The body's countermeasures to the drug are the unconditioned response (UCR). Over time, this *compensatory response* also becomes the conditioned response. That is, in settings ordinarily associated with drug use (the CS), the body physiologically prepares itself (the CR) for the drug's expected effects. Tolerance arises because, in that setting, the individual must consume an amount of the drug that overcomes the compensatory response before starting to get any 'positive' effect. Increasingly larger doses are needed as the conditioned compensatory response itself grows.

Siegel tested these ideas in his laboratory by creating tolerance to heroin in laboratory rats.

> In one study, Siegel and his colleagues classically conditioned rats to expect heroin injections (UCS) in one setting ($CS_1$) and dextrose (sweet sugar) solution injections in a different setting ($CS_2$) (Siegel et al., 1982). In the first phase of training, all rats developed heroin tolerance. On the test day, all animals received a larger than-usual dose of heroin—nearly twice the previous amount. Half of them received it in the setting where heroin had previously been administered; the other half received it in the setting where dextrose solutions had been given during conditioning. Twice as many rats died in the dextrose-solution setting as in the usual heroin setting: 64 percent versus 32 percent!

Presumably, those receiving heroin in the usual setting were more prepared for this potentially dangerous situation because the context ($CS_1$) brought about a physiological response (CR) that countered the drug's typical effects (Poulos & Cappell, 1991).

To find out if a similar process might operate in humans, Siegel and a colleague interviewed heroin addicts who had come close to death from supposed overdoses. In 7 out of 10 cases, the addicts had been shooting up in a new and unfamiliar setting (Siegel, 1984). Although this natural experiment provides no conclusive data, it suggests that a dose for which an addict has developed tolerance in one setting may become an overdose in an unfamiliar setting. This analysis allows us to suggest that the addict we invoked at the beginning of this section died because he had never shot up before in that alley.

Although we have mentioned research with heroin, classical conditioning is an important component to tolerance for a variety of drugs including alcohol (Siegel, 2005). Thus the same principles Pavlov observed for dogs, bells and salivation help explain some of the mechanisms underlying human drug addiction.

For answers go to MyPsychLab!

## RECAP CHECKPOINT

### Classical conditioning: learning predictable signals

- In classical conditioning, first investigated by Pavlov, an unconditioned stimulus (UCS) elicits an unconditioned response (UCR). A neutral stimulus paired with the UCS becomes a conditioned stimulus (CS) which elicits a response called the conditioned response (CR).

- Extinction occurs when the UCS no longer follows the CS.

- Stimulus generalisation is the phenomenon whereby stimuli similar to the CS elicit the CR.

- Discrimination learning narrows the range of CSs to which an organism responds.

- For classical conditioning to occur, a contingent and informative relationship must exist between the CS and UCS.

- Classical conditioning explains many emotional responses and drug tolerance.

## CONCEPT QUESTIONS

1. What is the role of reflexive behaviours in classical conditioning?

2. What is the difference between the UCS and the CS?

3. What is meant by stimulus discrimination?

4. Why is contingency so important in classical conditioning?

5. What is the conditioned response when classical conditioning plays a role in drug addiction?

## CRITICAL THINKING

Consider the experiment that demonstrated conditioned heroin tolerance in rats. Why were the rats given twice the normal dose of heroin on the test day?

# PSYCHOLOGY *in your life*

## HOW DOES CLASSICAL CONDITIONING AFFECT CANCER TREATMENT?

Medical researchers have made great strides in developing more effective treatments to combat cancers. Many of those treatments involve chemotherapy: drug treatments that kill or greatly weaken cancer cells. People who undergo chemotherapy often experience negative consequences such as fatigue and nausea. You might assume that those side effects would arise from the direct action of the chemotherapy drugs. Although that is partially the case, research suggests that processes of classical conditioning contribute greatly to the persistence of those side effects over time.

Consider a study that looked at cancer patients' experiences of fatigue. Patients undergoing chemotherapy often report experiencing fatigue and note that the fatigue prevents them from continuing a 'normal life' (Curt et al., 2000). To explain the origins of some of those feelings of fatigue, researchers tested a model based on classical conditioning (Bovbjerg et al., 2005). The 82 women in the study repeatedly visited the same outpatient clinic to undergo treatment for breast cancer. In each session, the women received infusions of chemotherapy.

Let's evaluate this situation in terms of classical conditioning. The chemotherapy drugs serve as the unconditioned stimulus (UCS) producing post treatment fatigue as an unconditioned response (UCR). Then, the researchers suggested that the clinic environment served as a conditioned stimulus (CS).

Over the visits to the clinic—as the CS became paired with the UCS—this model suggests that the women would begin to experience anticipatory fatigue as a conditioned response (CR) as soon as they arrived at the clinic.

To test this idea, the researchers measured how the women's fatigue changed over time. They measured both how the women felt before each session of chemotherapy—their level of preinfusion anticipatory fatigue—and how they felt after each session—their level of postinfusion fatigue. The data showed a clear pattern: Over visits to the clinic, the women experienced increasing levels of anticipatory fatigue. You might think that the fatigue was getting worse just because of the cumulative effect of chemotherapy. However, the women did not report higher levels of postinfusion fatigue. Consistent with the model based on classical conditioning, the greater levels of anticipatory fatigue seemed to have as one important source conditioned associations with the clinic environment. In fact, researchers have produced evidence to support a classical conditioning analysis of other aspects of chemotherapy. Many patients, for example, begin to experience nausea before the chemotherapy sessions—the clinic settings in which they receive treatment begin to function as a conditioned stimulus (Tomoyasu et al., 1996).

This classical conditioning model might help explain why some of the aftereffects of chemotherapy endure well after the end of treatment. Researchers surveyed a group of 273 Hodgkin's disease survivors who ranged from 1 to 20 years beyond treatment (Cameron et al., 2001). The participants were asked to reflect over the past 6 months to indicate whether they 'had noticed any smell or odour (anything [they had] seen/places [they had] gone to; any foods or drinks)' that had reminded them of treatment and made them 'feel good or bad emotionally or physically' (p. 72). More than half of the participants—55 percent—reported lingering bad responses that were triggered by stimuli associated with their chemotherapy. The researchers suggest that these persistent responses were the result of classically conditioned associations between various aspects of the chemotherapy experience (the CS) and the drug infusions (the UCS).

These studies provide strong evidence for the role of classical conditioning to amplify the negative effects of chemotherapy. The studies also give researchers a context in which they can begin to design treatments. For example, researchers could devise ways to change contextual cues to decrease the likelihood that a clinic environment would become a conditioned stimulus. Interventions of that sort couldn't eliminate negative effects of chemotherapy but they could help stop those negative effects from enduring over time.

# OPERANT CONDITIONING: LEARNING ABOUT CONSEQUENCES

**law of effect** A law of learning where the power of a stimulus to evoke a response is strengthened when the response is followed by a reward and weakened when it is not followed by a reward.

Let's return to the movie theatre. The horror film is now over, and you peel yourself off your seat. Your companion asks you if you're hoping that a sequel will be made. You respond, 'I've learned that I shouldn't go to horror films'. You're probably right, but what kind of learning is this? Once again our answer begins around the turn of the 20th century.

## THE LAW OF EFFECT

At about the same time that Pavlov was using classical conditioning to induce Russian dogs to salivate to the sound of a bell, **Edward L. Thorndike** (1898) was watching American cats trying to escape from puzzle boxes (see **Figure 6.9**). Thorndike reported his observations and inferences about the kind of learning he believed was taking place in his subjects. The cats at first only struggled against their confinement, but once some 'impulsive' action allowed them to open the door 'all the other unsuccessful impulses [were] stamped out and the particular impulse leading to the successful act [was] stamped in by the resulting pleasure' (Thorndike, 1898, p. 13).

What had Thorndike's cats learned? According to Thorndike's analysis, learning was an association between stimuli in the situation and a response that an animal learned to make: a *stimulus–response (S–R) connection.* Thus the cats had learned to produce an appropriate response (for example, clawing at a button or loop) that in these stimulus circumstances (confinement in

**operant conditioning** Learning in which the probability of a response is changed by a change in its consequences.

**operant** Behaviour emitted by an organism that can be characterised in terms of the observable effects it has on the environment.

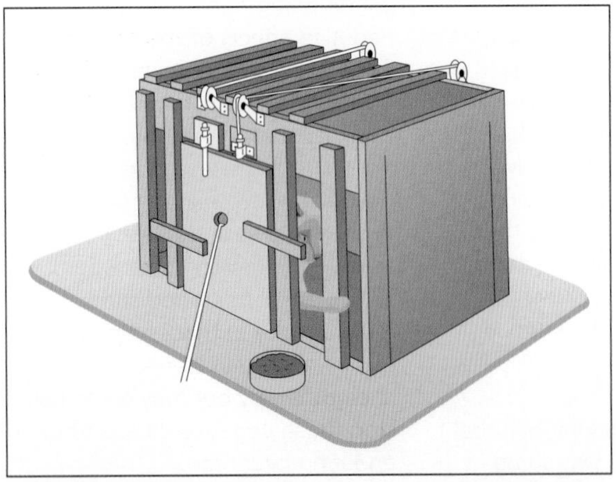

Figure 6.9

**A thorndike puzzle box**
To get out of the puzzle box and obtain food, Thorndike's cat had to manipulate a mechanism to release a weight that would then pull the door open.

the puzzle box) led to a desired outcome (momentary freedom). Note that the learning of these S–R connections occurred gradually and automatically in a mechanistic way as the animal experienced the consequences of its actions through blind *trial and error.* Gradually, the behaviours that had satisfying consequences increased in frequency; they eventually became the dominant response when the animal was placed in the puzzle box. Thorndike referred to this relationship between behaviour and its consequences as the **law of effect**: A response that is followed by satisfying consequences becomes more probable in that situation and a response that is followed by dissatisfying consequences becomes less probable.

## EXPERIMENTAL ANALYSIS OF BEHAVIOUR

B. F. Skinner embraced Thorndike's view that environmental consequences exert a powerful effect on behaviour. Skinner outlined a program of research whose purpose was to discover, by systematic variation of stimulus conditions, the ways that various environmental conditions affect the likelihood that a given response will occur:

> *A natural datum in a science of behavior is the probability that a given bit of behavior will occur at a given time. An experimental analysis deals with that probability in terms of frequency or rate of responding. . . . The task of an experimental analysis is to discover all the variables of which probability of response is a function. (Skinner, 1966, pp. 213–214)*

Skinner's analysis was experimental rather than theoretical—theorists are guided by derivations and predictions about behaviour from their theories, but empiricists, such as Skinner, advocate the bottom-up approach. They start with the collection and evaluation of data within the context of an experiment and are not theory driven.

To analyse behaviour experimentally, Skinner developed **operant conditioning** procedures, in which he manipulated the *consequences* of an organism's behaviour in order to see what effect they had on subsequent behaviour. An **operant** is any behaviour that is *emitted* by an organism and can be characterised in terms of the observable effects it has on the environment. Literally, *operant* means *affecting the environment,* or operating on it (Skinner, 1938). Operants are *not elicited* by specific stimuli as classically conditioned behaviours are. Pigeons peck, rats search for food, babies cry and coo, some people gesture while talking, and others stutter. The probability of these behaviours occurring in the future can be increased or decreased by manipulating the effects they have on the environment. If, for example, a baby's coo prompts desirable parental contact, the baby will coo more in the future. Operant conditioning, then, modifies the probability of different types of operant behaviour as a function of the environmental consequences they produce.

What environmental contingencies might cause babies to smile more often?

To carry out his new experimental analysis, Skinner invented an apparatus that allowed him to manipulate the consequences of behaviour, the *operant chamber*. **Figure 6.10** shows how the operant chamber works. When, after having produced an appropriate behaviour defined by the experimenter, a rat presses a lever, the mechanism delivers a food pellet. This device allows experimenters to study the variables that allow rats to learn—or not to learn—the behaviours they define. For example, if a lever press produces a food pellet only after a rat has turned a circle in the chamber, the rat will swiftly learn (through a process called *shaping* that we will consider shortly) to turn a circle before pressing the lever.

In many operant experiments, the measure of interest is how much of a particular behaviour an animal carries out in a period of time. Researchers record the pattern and total amount of behaviour emitted in the course of an experiment. This methodology allowed Skinner to study the effect of reinforcement contingencies on animals' behaviour.

## REINFORCEMENT CONTINGENCIES

A **reinforcement contingency** is a consistent relationship between a response and the changes in the environment that it produces. Imagine, for example, an experiment in which a pigeon's pecking a disk (the response) is generally followed by the presentation of grain (the corresponding change in the environment). This consistent relationship, or reinforcement contingency, will usually be accompanied by an increase in the rate of pecking. For delivery of grain to increase *only* the probability of pecking, it must be contingent *only* on the pecking response—the delivery must occur regularly after that response but not after other responses, such as turning or bowing. Based on Skinner's work, modern behaviour analysts seek to understand behaviour in terms of reinforcement contingencies. Let's take a closer look at what has been discovered about these contingencies.

**reinforcement contingency** A consistent relationship between a response and the changes in the environment that it produces.

**Positive and negative reinforcers** Suppose you are now captivated by the idea of getting your pet rat to turn a circle in its cage. To increase the probability of circle-turning behaviour, you would want to use a **reinforcer**, any stimulus that—when made contingent on a behaviour—increases the probability of that behaviour over time. *Reinforcement* is the delivery of a reinforcer following a response.

**reinforcer** Any stimulus that when made contingent upon a response increases the probability of that response.

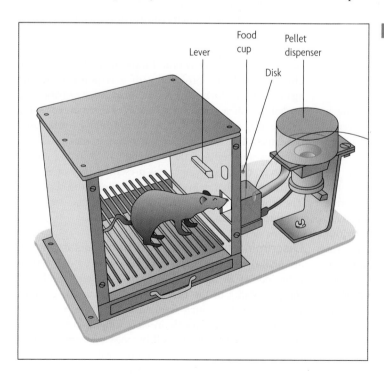

Lever    Food cup    Pellet dispenser

Disk

### Figure 6.10

**Operant chamber**
In this specially designed apparatus, typical of those used with rats, a press on the lever may be followed by delivery of a food pellet.

Reinforcers are always defined empirically, in terms of their effects on changing the probability of a response. If you look out at the world, you can probably find three classes of stimuli: those toward which you are neutral, those that you find *appetitive* (you have an 'appetite' for them), and those that you find *aversive* (you seek to avoid them). The compositions of these classes of stimuli clearly are not the same for all individuals: what is appetitive or aversive is defined by the behaviour of the individual organism. Consider the strawberry. Although many people find strawberries quite delicious, one of your authors finds strawberries virtually inedible. If you intend to use strawberries to change that author's behaviour, it's important to know that—for him—they are aversive rather than appetitive.

When a behaviour is followed by the delivery of an appetitive stimulus, the event is called **positive reinforcement**. Your pet rat will turn circles if a consequence of circle turning is the delivery of desirable food. Humans will tell jokes if a consequence of their joke telling is a type of laughter they find pleasurable.

When a behaviour is followed by the removal of an aversive stimulus, the event is called **negative reinforcement**. Your author, for example, would be more likely to perform a behaviour if it would allow him to cease eating strawberries. There are two general types of learning circumstances in which negative reinforcement applies. In *escape conditioning*, animals learn that a response will allow them to escape from an aversive stimulus. Raising an umbrella during a downpour is a common example of escape conditioning. You learn to use an umbrella to escape the aversive stimulus of getting wet. In *avoidance conditioning*, animals learn responses that allow them to avoid aversive stimuli before they begin. Suppose your car has a buzzer that sounds when you fail to buckle your seat belt. You will learn to buckle up to avoid the aversive noise.

To distinguish clearly between positive and negative reinforcement, remember the following: both positive reinforcement and negative reinforcement *increase* the probability of the response that precedes them. Positive reinforcement increases response probability by the presentation of an appetitive stimulus following a response; negative reinforcement does the same in reverse, through the removal, reduction or prevention of an aversive stimulus following a response.

Recall that for classical conditioning, when the unconditioned stimulus is no longer delivered, the conditioned response suffers extinction. The same rule holds for operant conditioning—if reinforcement is withheld, **operant extinction** occurs. Thus, if a behaviour no longer produces predictable consequences, it returns to the level it was at before operant conditioning—it is extinguished. You can probably catch your own behaviours being reinforced and then *extinguished*. Have you ever had the experience of dropping a few coins into a drinks dispenser and getting nothing in return? If you kicked the machine one time and your can of drink came out, the act of kicking would be reinforced. However, if the next few times your kicking produced no cans, kicking would quickly be extinguished.

As with classical conditioning, *spontaneous recovery* is also a feature of operant conditioning. Suppose you had reinforced a pigeon by providing food pellets when it pecked a key in the presence of a green light. If you discontinued the reinforcement, the pecking behaviour would extinguish. However, the next time you put the pigeon back in the apparatus with the green light on, the pigeon would likely spontaneously peck again. That's spontaneous recovery. In human terms, you might kick the drinks machine again with a time lag after your initial extinction experiences.

**Positive and negative punishment** You are probably familiar with another technique for decreasing the probability of a response—punishment. A **punisher** is any stimulus that—when it is made contingent on a response—decreases the probability of that response over time. *Punishment* is the delivery of a punisher following a response. Just as we could identify positive and negative reinforcement, we can identify positive punishment and negative punishment. When a behaviour is followed by the delivery of an aversive stimulus, the event is called **positive punishment** (you can remember *positive* because something is added to the situation). Touching a hot stove, for example, produces pain that punishes the preceding response so that you are less likely next time to touch the stove. When a behaviour is followed by the removal of an appetitive stimulus, the event is referred to as **negative punishment** (you can remember *negative* because something is subtracted from the situation). Thus when a parent withdraws a child's allowance after she hits her baby brother, the child learns not to hit her brother in the future. Which kind of punishment explains why you might stay away from horror movies?

Although punishment and reinforcement are closely related operations, they differ in important ways. A good way to differentiate them is to think of each in terms of its effects on behaviour. Punishment, by definition, always *reduces* the probability of a response occurring again; reinforcement, by definition, always *increases* the probability of a response recurring. For example, some people get severe headaches after drinking caffeinated beverages. The headache is the stimulus that positively punishes and reduces the behaviour of drinking coffee. However, once the headache is present, people often take aspirin or another pain reliever to eliminate the headache. The aspirin's analgesic effect is the stimulus that negatively reinforces the behaviour of ingesting aspirin.

**Discriminative stimuli and generalisation** You are unlikely to want to change the probability of a certain behaviour at all times. Rather, you may want to change the probability of the behaviour in a particular context. For example, you often want to increase the probability that a child will sit quietly in class without changing the probability that he or she will be noisy and active during recess. Through their associations with reinforcement

---

**positive reinforcement** A behaviour is followed by the presentation of an appetitive stimulus, increasing the probability of that behaviour.

**punisher** Any stimulus that when made contingent upon a response decreases the probability of that response.

**negative reinforcement** A behaviour is followed by the removal of an aversive stimulus, increasing the probability of that behaviour.

**positive punishment** A behaviour is followed by the presentation of an aversive stimulus, decreasing the probability of that behaviour.

**negative punishment** A behaviour is followed by the removal of an appetitive stimulus, decreasing the probability of that behaviour.

**operant extinction** When a behaviour no longer produces predictable consequences, its return to the level of occurrence it had before operant conditioning.

or punishment, certain stimuli that precede a particular response—**discriminative stimuli**—come to set the context for that behaviour. Organisms learn that, in the presence of some stimuli but not of others, their behaviour is likely to have a particular effect on the environment. For example, in the presence of a green traffic light, the act of crossing an intersection in a motor vehicle is reinforced. When the light is red, however, such behaviour may be punished—it may result in a traffic ticket or an accident. Skinner referred to the sequence of discriminative stimulus–behaviour–consequence as the **three-term contingency** and believed that it could explain most human action (Skinner, 1953). **Table 6.1** describes how the three-term contingency might explain several different kinds of human behaviour.

Under laboratory conditions, manipulating the consequences of behaviour in the presence of discriminative stimuli can exert powerful control over that behaviour. For example, a pigeon might be given grain after pecking a disk in the presence of a green light but not a red light. The green light is a discriminative stimulus that sets the occasion for pecking; the red is a discriminative stimulus that sets the occasion for not pecking. Organisms learn quickly to discriminate between these conditions, responding regularly in the presence of one stimulus and not responding in the presence of the other. By manipulating the components of the three-term contingency, you can constrain a behaviour to a particular context.

Organisms also generalise responses to other stimuli that resemble the discriminative stimulus. Once a response has been reinforced in the presence of one discriminative stimulus, a similar stimulus can become a discriminative stimulus for that same response. For example, pigeons trained to peck a disk in the presence of a green light will also peck the disk in the presence of lights that are lighter or darker shades of green than the original discriminative stimulus. Similarly, you generalise to different shades of green on traffic lights as a discriminative stimulus for your 'resume driving' behaviour.

Of course colour is not the only stimulus dimension allowing discrimination to occur. One of the most important features of a stimulus is it's duration, and temporal discrimination is critical for many important human behaviours. Consider a sport such as cricket, for example. Simply increasing the rate at which a bat is swung each time the bowler approaches is unlikely to lead to success. What matters is the discrimination of very subtle differences in timing of, for example, the bowler's action, to allow the instrumental response to meet with success and the ball to be dispatched for four. Both pigeons (Spetch & Cheng, 1998) and humans (Bizo & McMahon, 2007) are capable of discriminating very slight differences in time of stimulus presentation, although there is some debate whether the pattern of results are identical to those obtained for other stimulus dimensions.

## Using reinforcement contingencies

Are you ready to put your new knowledge of reinforcement contingencies to work? Here are some considerations you might have:

- *How can you define the behaviour that you would like to reinforce or eliminate?* You must always carefully target the specific behaviour whose probability you would like to change. Reinforcement should be contingent on exactly that behaviour. When reinforcers are presented noncontingently, their

**discriminative stimuli** Stimuli that act as predictors of reinforcement, signalling when particular behaviours will result in positive reinforcement.

**three-term contingency** The means by which organisms learn that, in the presence of some stimuli but not others, their behaviour is likely to have a particular effect on the environment.

## Table 6.1

The three-term contingency: relationships among discriminative stimuli, behaviour and consequences

|  | Discriminative stimulus | Emitted response | Stimulus consequence |
|---|---|---|---|
| 1. Positive reinforcement: A response in the presence of an effective signal produces the desired consequence. This response Increases. | Soft-drink machine | Put coin in slot | Get drink |
| 2. Negative reinforcement (escape): An aversive situation is escaped from by an operant response. This escape response increases. | Heat | Fan oneself | Escape from heat |
| 3. Positive punishment: A response is followed by an aversive stimulus. The response is eliminated or suppressed. | Attractive matchbox | Play with matches | Get burned or get caught and spanked |
| 4. Negative punishment: A response is followed by the removal of an appetitive stimulus. The response is eliminated or suppressed. | Brussels sprouts | Refusal to eat them | No dessert |

presence has little effect on behaviour. For example, if a parent praises bad work as well as good efforts, a child will not learn to work harder in school—but because of the positive reinforcement, other behaviours are likely to increase. (What might those be?)

- *How can you define the contexts in which a behaviour is appropriate or inappropriate?* Remember that you rarely want to allow or disallow every instance of a behaviour. We suggested earlier, for example, that you might want to increase the probability that a child will sit quietly in class without changing the probability that he or she will be noisy and active during recess. You must define the discriminative stimuli and investigate how broadly the desired response will be generalised to similar stimuli. If, for example, the child learned to sit quietly in class, would that behaviour generalise to other 'serious' settings?

- *Have you unknowingly been reinforcing some behaviours?* Suppose you want to eliminate a behaviour. Before you turn to punishment as a way of reducing its probability (more on that in the Critical Thinking in Your Life box), try to determine whether you can identify reinforcers for that behaviour. If so, you can try to extinguish the behaviour by eliminating those reinforcers. Imagine, for example, that a young boy throws a large number of tantrums. You might ask yourself, 'Have I been reinforcing those tantrums by paying the boy extra attention when he screams?' If so, you can try to eliminate the tantrums by eliminating the reinforcement. Even better, you can combine extinction with positive reinforcement of more socially approved behaviours.

It's important to be aware that the reinforcers parents produce can make children's conduct problems, such as tantrums, more likely. In fact, parenting research has identified unknowing reinforcement as one cause of serious behaviour problems in children. For example, Gerald Patterson and his colleagues (Patterson, 2002; Reid et al., 2002) have outlined a *coercion model* for antisocial behaviour. Family observations suggest that children are put at risk when their parents issue threats in response to small misbehaviours (e.g., whining, teasing or yelling) without following through. At some moments, however, these parents would issue harsh or explosive discipline toward the same behaviours. The children appear to learn the lesson that relatively large acts of aggressive and coercive behaviour are appropriate and necessary for achieving goals—leading to a cycle of increase in the severity of the children's antisocial behaviour.

Behaviour analysts assume that any behaviour that persists does so because it results in reinforcement. Any behaviour, they argue—even irrational or bizarre behaviour—can be understood by discovering what the reinforcement or payoff is. For example, symptoms of mental or physical disorders are sometimes maintained because the person gets attention and sympathy and is excused from normal responsibilities. These *secondary gains* reinforce irrational and sometimes self-destructive behaviour. Can you see how shy behaviours can be maintained through reinforcement, even though the shy person would prefer not to be shy? Of course, it is not always possible to know what reinforcers are at work in an environment. However, as a behaviour becomes more or less probable, you might try to carry out a bit of behaviour analysis.

One final thought. It's often the case that real-life situations will involve intricate combinations of reinforcement and punishment. Suppose, for example, parents use negative punishment by grounding a teenager for two weeks when he stays out past curfew. To soften up his parents, the teen helps more than usual around the house. Assuming his helping behaviour appeals to the parents, the teen is trying to reinforce his parents' 'reducing the sentence' behaviour. If this strategy succeeds in changing the punishment to only one week, the teen's helping behaviour will have been negatively reinforced—because helping led to the removal of the aversive stimulus of being grounded. Whenever the teen is grounded again (a discriminative stimulus), his helping behaviour should be more likely. Do you see how all the contingencies fit together to change both the teen's and the parents' behaviours? The principles described here form the basis for an extremely effective Positive Parenting Program (Triple P) led by Professor Matt Sanders at the University of Queensland <http://www.pfsc.uq.edu.au/>.

Let's now take a look at the ways in which various objects and activities may come to function as reinforcers.

## PROPERTIES OF REINFORCERS

Reinforcers are the power brokers of operant conditioning: They change or maintain behaviour. Reinforcers have a number of interesting and complex properties. They can be learned through experience rather than be biologically determined and can be activities rather than objects. In some situations, even ordinarily powerful reinforcers may not be enough to change a dominant behaviour pattern (in this case, we would say that the consequences were not actually reinforcers).

### Conditioned reinforcers
When you came into the world, there were a handful of **primary reinforcers**, such as food and water, whose reinforcing properties were biologically determined. Over time, however, otherwise neutral stimuli have become associated with primary reinforcers and now function as **conditioned reinforcers** for operant responses. Conditioned reinforcers can come to serve as ends in themselves. In fact, a great deal of human behaviour is influenced less by biologically significant primary reinforcers than by a wide variety of conditioned reinforcers. Money, grades, smiles of approval, gold stars and various kinds of status symbols are among the many potent conditioned reinforcers that influence much of your behaviour.

**primary reinforcers**
Biologically determined reinforcers such as food and water.

**conditioned reinforcers**
In classical conditioning, formerly neutral stimuli that have become reinforcers.

How can parents use reinforcement contingencies to affect their children's behaviour?

Virtually any stimulus can become a conditioned reinforcer by being paired with a primary reinforcer. In one experiment, simple tokens were used with animal learners.

> With raisins as primary reinforcers, chimps were trained to solve problems. Then tokens were delivered along with the raisins. When only the tokens were presented, the chimps continued working for their 'money' because they could later deposit the hard-earned tokens in a 'chimp-o-mat' designed to exchange tokens for the raisins (Cowles, 1937).

Teachers and experimenters often find conditioned reinforcers more effective and easier to use than primary reinforcers because (1) few primary reinforcers are available in the classroom, whereas almost any stimulus event that is under control of a teacher can be used as a conditioned reinforcer; (2) they can be dispensed rapidly; (3) they are portable; and (4) their reinforcing effect may be more immediate because it depends only on the perception of receiving them and not on biological processing, as in the case of primary reinforcers.

In some institutions, such as psychiatric hospitals or drug treatment programs, *token economies* are set up based on these principles. Desired behaviours (grooming or taking medication, for example) are explicitly defined, and token payoffs are given by the staff when the behaviours are performed. These tokens can later be exchanged by the patients for a wide array of rewards and privileges (Kazdin, 1994; Martin & Pear, 1999). These systems of reinforcement are especially effective in modifying patients' behaviours regarding self-care, upkeep of their environment, and, most important, frequency of their positive social interactions.

## Response deprivation and positive reinforcers

Suppose you need to get a child to do something. You don't want to pay her or give her a gold star, so instead you strike this bargain: 'When you finish your homework, you can play with your video game.' Why might this tactic work? According to *response deprivation theory*, behaviours become preferred and, therefore, reinforcing when an animal is prevented from engaging in them (Timberlake & Allison, 1974). For example, water-deprived rats learned to increase their running in an exercise wheel when their running was followed by an opportunity to drink. Conversely, exercise-deprived rats learned to increase their drinking when that response was followed by a chance to run (Premack, 1965). Can you see how the promise of video games after homework follows this same pattern? For a period of time, the child is video game–deprived—the rate at which the child would ordinarily play the video game is restricted below normal. To overcome that deprivation, she will learn to work on her homework.

This analysis suggests two important lessons. First, these examples remind you why you shouldn't assume that the same activity will function as a reinforcer for an animal at all times. You need to know, for example, whether the animal is food-deprived before you attempt to use food as a reinforcer. Second, these examples suggest why virtually any activity can come to serve as a reinforcer. You can experience deprivation along any number of dimensions.

Inedible tokens can be used as conditioned reinforcers. In one study, chimps deposited tokens in a 'chimp-o-mat' in exchange for raisins. What types of conditioned reinforcers function in your life?

In fact, if you didn't allow a child to do homework for a period of time, she would learn other behaviours to overcome homework-doing deprivation.

# SCHEDULES OF REINFORCEMENT

What happens when you cannot, or do not want to, reinforce your pet on every occasion when it performs a special behaviour? Consider a story about the young B. F. Skinner. It seems that one weekend he was secluded in his laboratory with not enough of a food-reward supply for his hardworking rats. He economised by giving the rats pellets only after a certain interval of time—no matter how many times they pressed in between, they couldn't get any more pellets. Even so, the rats responded as much with this *partial reinforcement schedule* as they had with continuous reinforcement. And what do you predict happened when these animals underwent extinction training and their responses were followed by no pellets at all? The rats whose lever pressing had been partially reinforced continued to respond longer and more vigorously than did the rats who had been reinforced after every response. Skinner was on to something important!

The discovery of the effectiveness of partial reinforcement led to extensive study of the effects of different **schedules of reinforcement** on behaviour (see **Figure 6.11**). You have experienced different schedules of reinforcement in your daily life. When you raise your hand in class, the teacher sometimes calls on you and sometimes does not; some poker machine players continue to play even though the reinforcers are delivered only rarely. In real life or in the laboratory, reinforcers can be delivered according to either a *ratio schedule*, after a certain number of responses, or an *interval schedule*, after the first response following a specified interval of time. In each case, there can be either a constant, or *fixed*, pattern of reinforcement or an irregular, or *variable*, pattern of reinforcement, making four major types of schedules in all. So far you've learned about the **partial reinforcement effect**: Responses acquired under schedules of partial reinforcement are more resistant to extinction than those acquired with continuous reinforcement. Let's see what else researchers have discovered about different schedules of reinforcement.

## Fixed-ratio schedules
In **fixed-ratio (FR) schedules**, the reinforcer comes after the organism has emitted a fixed number of responses. When reinforcement follows one response, the schedule is called an FR-1 schedule (this is the original continuous reinforcement schedule). When reinforcement follows only every 25th response, the schedule is an FR-25 schedule. FR schedules generate high rates of responding because there is a direct correlation between responding and reinforcement. A pigeon can get as much food as it wants in a period of time if it pecks often enough. Figure 6.11 shows that FR schedules produce a pause after each reinforcer. The higher the ratio, the longer the pause after each reinforcement. Stretching

**schedules of reinforcement**
In operant conditioning, the patterns of delivering and withholding reinforcement.

**partial reinforcement effect**
The behavioural principle that states that responses acquired under intermittent reinforcement are more difficult to extinguish than those acquired with continuous reinforcement.

**fixed-ratio (FR) schedule**
A schedule of reinforcement in which a reinforcer is delivered for the first response made after a fixed number of responses.

**variable-ratio (VR) schedule**
A schedule of reinforcement in which a reinforcer is delivered for the first response made after a variable number of responses whose average is predetermined.

Figure 6.11

**Reinforcement schedules**
These different patterns of behavior are produced by four simple schedules of reinforcement. The hash marks indicate when reinforcement is delivered.

the ratio too thin by requiring a great many responses for reinforcement without first training the animal to emit that many responses may lead to extinction. Many salespeople are on FR schedules: They must sell a certain number of units before they can get paid.

## Variable-ratio schedules
In a **variable-ratio (VR) schedule**, the average number of responses between reinforcers is predetermined. A VR-10 schedule means that, on average, reinforcement follows every 10th response, but it might come after only 1 response or after 20 responses. Variable-ratio schedules generate the highest rate of responding and the greatest resistance to extinction, especially when the VR value is large. Suppose you start a pigeon with a low VR value (for example, VR-5) and then move it toward a higher value. A pigeon on a VR-110 schedule will respond with up to 12,000 pecks per hour and will continue responding for hours even with no reinforcement. Gambling is maintained by variable (in fact random) ratio schedules built into the poker machine by which there are different fixed probabilities of a play being

# CRITICAL THINKING *in your life*

## TO SMACK OR NOT TO SMACK?

If you plan to become a parent (or if you already are one), you have almost certainly considered the question 'To smack or not to smack?' In fact, most mothers in Australia believe smacking is acceptable. A 2006 Morgan poll commissioned by insurance program MumsCover found that 80% of Australian mothers wanted to retain the right to smack. In fact, in 2007 the Australian Family First party responded by putting forward the *Criminal Law Consolidation (Reasonable Chastisement of Children) Amendment Bill* which sought to 'enshrine in legislation a parent's or guardian's choice to discipline their child' (Family First 2007). But what are the consequences for children who are smacked?

Why is that a difficult question to answer? First, no researchers could ethically conduct an experiment in which they expose children to physical punishment. For that reason, all research on punishment relies on correlational analyses: Researchers try to assess whether a relationship exists between the amount of physical punishment children have experienced and negative aspects of their behaviour. This leads to a second problem with research on smacking. Parents may be unwilling or unable to give accurate indications of how often they smacked their children. Researchers can ask the children, but they might also misremember or misrepresent the past. A third problem is getting accurate data on the child behaviours that led parents to smack them: How 'bad' were the children before they were smacked? A final problem with research on smacking is understanding its impact as an element of a larger environment (Kazdin & Benjet, 2003). The households in which parents smack their children the most also tend, for example, to be households with more marital discord. Perhaps it's other factors of that sort that lead children whose parents smacked them to

have problems later in life. The smacking itself might have played no causal role.

Despite all these obstacles, researchers have been able to reach important conclusions. For example, we know that physical punishment beyond smacking leads to negative child outcomes (Benjet & Kazdin, 2003; Gershoff, 2002). Consider one study involving 273 kindergarten children in Indiana and Tennessee. Mothers were asked to fill out self-reports about the types of physical punishment they used with their children (Strassberg et al., 1994). About 6 percent of the mothers did not use physical punishment. Sixty-eight percent of the children were smacked by their mothers. The remaining 26 percent received more intense forms of physical punishment: Their mothers hit them with fists or closed hands or beat them up.

About 6 months after the mothers reported on their forms of physical punishment, the children were observed interacting with peers in school. The researchers recorded the children's acts of aggression toward their peers—instances, for example, in which they bullied or became angry and hit another child. Based on these observations, each child earned a score for aggressive acts per hour. The accompanying figure presents the results. As you can see, the more intense the form of the mother's physical punishment, the more aggressive the child.

But what can we say about mild smacking? Given the difficulties of coming to clear research conclusions, you should consider the question of 'To smack or not to smack?' with respect to your goals as a parent (Benjet & Kazdin, 2003). People

usually turn to physical punishment to stop children from performing unwanted behaviours. However, experts suggest that parents instead use positive reinforcement: 'Many undesirable behaviours can be completely suppressed by positive reinforcement of alternative and incompatible behaviours' (Benjet & Kazdin, p. 215). For example, you can praise a child for sitting quietly rather than smacking him for running around. Thus reinforcing children for behaving well is often a better long-term strategy than punishing them for behaving poorly.

For the reasons we have explored, researchers might never be able to provide definitive evidence that mild smacking has negative outcomes for children. However, as you saw in the figure, at least certain types of physical punishments are strongly associated with negative child outcomes. As a parent, you presumably want to avoid putting your children at risk. To meet that goal, consider using other strategies besides physical punishment to modify your children's behaviour.

Why would parents be 'unwilling or unable' to provide accurate information about their smacking practices?

Why did the researchers observe children's school behaviour to document the impact of corporal punishment?

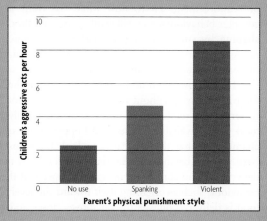

reinforced by different monetary outcomes. VR schedules leave you guessing when the reward will come—you gamble that it will be after the next response, not many responses later (Rachlin, 1990).

**Fixed-interval schedules** On a **fixed-interval (FI) schedule**, a reinforcer is delivered for the first response made after a fixed period of time. On an FI-10 schedule, the subject, after receiving reinforcement, has to wait 10 seconds before another response can be reinforced irrespective of the number of responses. Response rates under FI schedules show a scalloped pattern. Immediately after each reinforced response, the animal makes few if any responses. As the payoff time approaches, the animal responds more and more. You experience a FI schedule when you reheat a slice of pizza. Suppose you set the oven's timer for 2 minutes. You probably won't check very much for the first 90 seconds, but in the last 30 seconds, you'll peek in more often.

**Variable-interval schedules** For **variable-interval (VI) schedules**, the average interval is predetermined. For example, on a VI-20 schedule, reinforcers are delivered at an average rate of 1 every 20 seconds. This schedule generates a moderate but very stable response rate. Extinction under VI schedules is gradual and much slower than under fixed-interval schedules. In one case, a pigeon pecked 18,000 times during the first 4 hours after reinforcement stopped and required 168 hours before its responding extinguished completely (Ferster & Skinner, 1957). Checking your email is on a VI schedule, since you can never be quite sure when the next message you want to read will come in, ensuring that you do this regularly while you are logged on.

## SHAPING

As parts of experiments, we have spoken of rats pressing levers to get food. However, even lever pressing is a learned behaviour. When a rat is introduced to an operant chamber, it is quite unlikely it will ever press the lever spontaneously; the rat has learned to use its paws in many ways, but it probably has never pressed a lever before. How should you go about training the rat to perform a behaviour that it would rarely, if ever, produce on its own? You've settled on a reinforcer, food, and a schedule of reinforcement, FR-1—now what? To train new or complex behaviours, you will want to use a method called **shaping by successive approximations**—in which you reinforce any responses that successively approximate and ultimately match the desired response.

Here's how you'd do it. First, you deprive the rat of food for a day. (Without deprivation, food is not likely to serve as a reinforcer.) Then you systematically make food pellets available in the food hopper in an operant chamber so that the rat learns to look there for food. Now you can begin the actual shaping process by making delivery of food contingent on specific aspects of the rat's behaviour, such as orienting itself toward the lever. Next, food is delivered only as the rat moves closer and closer

This quadriplegic, Craig Cook, is assisted by a monkey who had been operantly shaped to comb his hair, feed him, turn book pages, and make other responses he cannot do for himself. For each of these behaviours, can you think through the successive approximations you would reinforce to arrive at the end point?

to the lever. Soon the requirement for reinforcement is actually to touch the lever. Finally, the rat must depress the lever for food to be delivered. In small increments, the rat has learned that a lever press will produce food. Thus, for *shaping* to work, you must define what constitutes progress toward the target behaviour and use *differential reinforcement* to refine each step along the way.

Let's look at another example, in which shaping was used to improve the performance of a Canadian pole vaulter who was an international competitor.

> A 21-year-old university pole vaulter sought a research team's assistance to help him correct a technical problem with his vaulting technique (Scott et al., 1997). The vaulter's particular problem was that he didn't sufficiently extend his arms (holding the pole) above his head before he planted the pole to lift himself off. At the beginning of the intervention, the vaulter's average hand-height at takeoff was calculated as 2.25 metres. The goal was set to use a shaping procedure to help him achieve his physical potential of 2.54 metres. A photoelectric beam was set up so that, when the vaulter achieved a desired extension, the beam was broken and equipment produced a beep. The beep served as a conditioned positive reinforcer. At first, the beam was set at 2.30 metres, but once the vaulter was able to reach that height with 90 percent success, the beam was moved to 2.35 metres. Further success brought further increments of 2.40, 2.45, 2.50, and 2.52 metres. In that way, the vaulter's behaviour was successfully shaped toward the desired goal.

You can imagine how difficult it would have been for the vaulter to show spontaneous improvement of 0.27 metres. The shaping procedure allowed him to achieve that gain through successive approximations to the desired behaviour.

Let's return to your rat. Recall that we suggested you might wish to teach it to turn circles in its cage. Can you devise a plan, using shaping, to bring about

**fixed-interval (FI) schedule** A schedule of reinforcement in which a reinforcer is delivered for the first response made after a fixed period of time.

**variable-interval (VI) schedule** A schedule of reinforcement in which a reinforcer is delivered for the first response made after a variable period of time whose average is predetermined.

**shaping by successive approximations** A behavioural method that reinforces responses that successively approximate and ultimately match the desired response.

this behaviour? Think about what each successive approximation would be. At the beginning, for example, you might reinforce the rat if it just turned its head in a particular direction. Next, you would let the rat obtain a food pellet only if it turned its whole body in the right direction. What might you do after that?

The two forms of learning we have examined so far—classical conditioning and operant conditioning—have most often been studied with the assumption that processes of learning are consistent across all animals. In fact, we have cited examples from dogs, cats, rats, mice, pigeons and humans to show exactly such consistency. However, researchers have come to understand that learning is modified in many situations by the particular biological and cognitive capabilities of individual species. We turn now to the processes that limit the generality of the laws of learning.

## RECAP CHECKPOINT

### Operant conditioning: learning about consequences

- Thorndike demonstrated that behaviours which bring about satisfying outcomes tend to be repeated.

- Behaviours are made more likely by positive and negative reinforcement. They are made less likely by positive and negative punishment.

- Contextually appropriate behaviour is explained by the three-term contingency of discriminative stimulus—behaviour—consequence.

- Primary reinforcers are stimuli that function as reinforcers even when an organism has not had previous experience with them. Conditioned reinforcers are acquired by association with primary reinforcers.

- Probable activities function as positive reinforcers.

- Behaviour is affected by schedules of reinforcement that may be varied or fixed and delivered in intervals or in ratios.

- Complex responses may be learned through shaping.

### CONCEPT QUESTIONS

1. What is the law of effect?

2. How do reinforcement and punishment affect the probability of behaviours?

3. What is the role of discriminative stimuli in operant conditioning?

4. What is the difference between fixed-ratio and fixed-interval schedules of reinforcement?

5. What is meant by shaping?

### CRITICAL THINKING

In the experiment with chimps, why did the researcher start the training with raisins before moving to tokens?

# BIOLOGY AND LEARNING

The contemporary view that a single, general account of the associationist principles of learning is common to humans and all animals was first proposed by English philosopher **David Hume** in 1748. Hume reasoned that 'any theory by which we explain the operations of the understanding, or the origin and connexion of the passions in man, will acquire additional authority, if we find that the same theory is requisite to explain the same phenomena in all other animals' (Hume, 1748/1951, p. 104).

The appealing simplicity of such a view has come under scrutiny since the 1960s as psychologists have discovered certain constraints, or limitations, on the generality of the findings regarding conditioning (Bailey & Bailey, 1993; Garcia, 1993; Todd & Morris, 1992, 1993). In Chapter 3, we suggested that animals have evolved in response to the need for survival: we can explain many of the differences among species as adaptations to the demands of their particular environmental niches. The same evolutionary perspective applies to a species' capacity for learning (Leger, 1992). **Biological constraints on learning** are any limitations on learning imposed by a species' genetic endowment. These constraints can apply to the animal's sensory, behavioural and cognitive capacities. we will examine two areas of research that show how behaviour–environment relations can be biased by an organism's genotype: instinctual drift and taste-aversion learning.

**biological constraints on learning** Any limitations on an organism's capacity to learn caused by the inherited sensory, response, or cognitive capabilities of members of a given species.

## INSTINCTUAL DRIFT

You have no doubt seen animals performing tricks on television or in the circus: animals that have been trained to play ping-pong, water-ski or even surf. For years, **Keller Breland** and **Marion Breland** used operant conditioning techniques to train thousands of animals from many different species to perform a remarkable array of behaviours. The Brelands had believed that general principles derived from laboratory research using virtually any type of response or reward could be directly applied to the control of animal behaviour outside the laboratory.

At some point after training, though, some of the animals began to 'misbehave'. For example, a raccoon was trained to pick up a coin, put it into a toy bank and collect an edible reinforcer. The raccoon, however, would not immediately deposit the coin. Even worse, when there were two coins to be deposited, conditioning broke down completely—the raccoon would not give up the coins at all. Instead, it would rub the coins together, dip them into the bank, and then pull them back out. But is this really so strange? Raccoons often engage in rubbing and washing behaviours as they remove the outer shells of a favourite food, crayfish. Similarly, when pigs were given the task of putting their hard-earned tokens into a large piggy bank, they instead would drop the coins onto the floor, poke at them with their snouts, and toss them into the air. Again, should you consider this strange? These behaviours are all part of the pig's natural food-gathering repertory.

These experiences convinced the Brelands that, even when animals have learned to make operant responses perfectly, the 'learned behaviour drifts toward instinctual behaviour' over time. They called this tendency **instinctual drift** (Breland & Breland, 1951, 1961). The behaviour of their animals is not explainable by ordinary operant principles, but it is understandable if you consider the species-specific tendencies imposed by an inherited genotype. These tendencies override the changes in behaviour brought about by operant conditioning.

The bulk of traditional research on animal learning focused on arbitrarily chosen responses to conveniently available stimuli. The Brelands' theory and demonstration of instinctual drift makes it evident that not all aspects of learning are under the control of the experimenters' reinforcers. Behaviours will be more or less easy to change as a function of an animal's normal, genetically programmed responses in its environment. Conditioning will be particularly efficient when you can frame a target response as biologically relevant. For example, what change might you make to get the pigs to place their tokens in a bank? If the token was paired with a water reward for a thirsty pig, it would then not be treated as if it were food but would be deposited in the bank as a valuable commodity—dare we say a liquid asset?

## TASTE-AVERSION LEARNING

Your authors have a pair of confessions to make: One of us still gets a bit queasy at the thought of eating oysters kilpatrick; the other has the same response, alas, to bourbon and coke. Why? In each case we became violently ill after consuming these items. The oysters were probably not to blame for the illness, since they were consumed just before the author came down with a serious bout of the flu. And it is probably safe to drink bourbon and coke, as long as sensible limits are imposed. It makes no difference to how we feel, however: we dislike the smell and taste of these items, and avoid them entirely. Why does our knowledge of the cause of our illness have no effect on our behaviour? We can look to nonhuman animals for a clue to why this is so.

Suppose we asked you to devise a strategy for tasting a variety of unfamiliar substances. If you had the genetic endowment of rats, you would be very cautious in doing so. When presented with a new food or flavour, rats take only a very small sample. Only if it fails to make them sick will they go back for more. To flip that around, suppose we include a substance with the new flavour that does make the rats ill—they'll never consume that flavour again. This phenomenon is known as **taste-aversion learning**. You can see why having this genetic capacity to sample and learn which foods are safe and which are toxic could have great survival value. One contemporary example is the great difficulties being faced in New Zealand, where an introduced pest, the possum, is proving difficult to control using poison baits due to its demonstrable ability to learn about, and avoid, the flavour following sub-lethal exposure (Clapperton, Mathews, Fawkes & Pearson, 1996).

Taste-aversion learning is an enormously powerful mechanism. Unlike most other instances of classical conditioning, taste aversion is learned with only one pairing of a CS (the novel flavour) and its consequences (the result of the underlying UCS—the element that actually brings about the illness). This is true even with a long interval, 12 hours or more, between the time the rat consumes the substance

How could you use operant conditioning techniques to teach an animal friend to waterski?

**CHAPTER 6** LEARNING AND BEHAVIOUR ANALYSIS

and the time it becomes ill. Finally, unlike many classically conditioned associations that are quite fragile, this one is permanent after one experience. Again, to understand these violations of the norms of classical conditioning, consider how dramatically this mechanism aids survival.

**John Garcia**, the psychologist who first documented taste-aversion learning in the laboratory, and his colleague Robert Koelling used this phenomenon to demonstrate that, in general, animals are biologically prepared to learn certain associations. The researchers discovered that some CS–UCS combinations can be classically conditioned in particular species of animals, but others cannot.

In phase 1 of Garcia and Koelling's experiment, thirsty rats were first familiarised with the experimental situation in which licking a tube produced three CSs: saccharin-flavoured water, noise and bright light. In phase 2, when the rats licked the tube, half of them received only the sweet water and half received only the noise, light, and plain water. Each of these two groups was again divided: half of each group was given electric shocks that produced pain, and half was given X-ray radiation that produced nausea and illness.

The amount of water drunk by the rats in phase 1 was compared with the amount drunk in phase 2, when pain and illness were involved (see **Figure 6.12**). Big reductions in drinking occurred when flavour was associated with illness (taste aversion) and when noise and light were associated with pain. However, there was little change in behaviour under the other two conditions—when flavour predicted pain or when the 'bright-noisy water' predicted illness.

The pattern of results suggests that rats have an inborn bias to associate particular stimuli with particular consequences (Garcia & Koelling, 1966). Some instances of conditioning, then, depend not only on the relationship between stimuli and behaviour but also on the way an organism is genetically predisposed toward stimuli in its environment (Barker et al., 1978). Animals appear to have encoded, within their genetic inheritance, the types of sensory cues—taste, smell, or appearance—that are most

How does instinctual drift affect the behaviours possums can learn to perform?

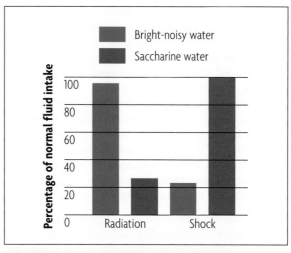

Figure 6.12

**Inborn bias**
Results from Garcia and Koelling's study (1966) showed that rats possess an inborn bias to associate certain cues with certain outcomes. Rats avoided saccharin-flavoured water when it predicted illness but not when it predicted shock. Conversely, rats avoided the 'bright-noisy water' when it predicted shock but not when it predicted illness.

likely to signal dimensions of reward or danger. Taste-aversion learning is an example of what researchers call *biological preparedness*: A particular species has evolved so that the members of the species require less learning experience than normal to acquire a conditioned response. Experimenters who try arbitrarily to break these genetic links will look forward to little success. (In Chapter 14, we will see that researchers believe humans are biologically prepared to acquire intense fears—known as *phobias*—to stimuli such as snakes and spiders that provided dangers over the course of human evolution.)

Researchers have put knowledge of the mechanisms of taste-aversion learning to practical use. To stop coyotes from killing sheep (and sheep ranchers from shooting coyotes), John Garcia and colleagues put toxic lamb burgers wrapped in sheep fur on the outskirts of fenced-in areas of sheep ranches. The coyotes who eat these lamb burgers get sick, vomit and develop an instant distaste for lamb meat. Their subsequent disgust at the mere sight of sheep makes them back away from the animals instead of attacking.

In this chapter's Psychology in Your Life box, we described for you the role that classical conditioning plays in people's experiences of chemotherapy. Classical conditioning also explains why cancer patients become unable to tolerate normal foods in their diets. Their aversions are, in part, a consequence of their chemotherapy treatments, which often follow meals and produce nausea.

A group of 22 women undergoing treatments for breast cancer provided reports on their food preferences over the course of eight sessions of chemotherapy, each separated by 3 weeks. The women reported everything they had eaten in the 24-hour periods before and after chemotherapy. They rated each type of food and beverage on a scale from 1 (dislike very much) to 9 (like very much). The researchers considered an aversion to have formed if a participant's rating dropped by 4 points over the course of chemotherapy. Overall, 46 percent of the women developed an aversion to at least one food. However, those aversions formed in the first two sessions of therapy were short lived. The researchers speculated that, unlike rats and other animals that acquire taste aversions, these women were able to reason that 'the chemotherapy caused nausea, not the food'. If they tried the food again, the women provided themselves with extinction trials that extinguished the conditioned aversion (Jacobsen et al., 1993).

By showing that aversions are acquired through the mechanisms of classical conditioning, researchers can devise means to counteract them (Bernstein, 1991). Researchers have arranged, for example, for children with cancer not to be given meals just before chemotherapy. They've also created 'scapegoat' aversions. The children are given candies or ice cream of unusual flavours to eat before the treatments so the taste aversion becomes conditioned only to those special flavours and not to the flavours they generally like.

You have now seen why modern behaviour analysts must be attentive to the types of responses each species is best suited to learn (Todd & Morris, 1992). If you want to teach an old dog new tricks, you're best off adapting the tricks to the dog's genetic behavioural repertory! Our survey of learning is not complete, however, because we have not yet dealt with types of learning that might require more complex cognitive processes. We turn now to those types of learning.

## LEARNING AND BEHAVIOUR IN AUSTRALIAN ANIMAL SPECIES

Laboratory research into the principles of learning has been dominated by the study of two species: the rat and the pigeon. Comparative psychology is concerned with how differences in phylogeny and habitat may influence the nature of learning across different species. The existence of differences between species reflecting different evolutionary histories has been the subject of quite intense debate. One of the most influential contributors to this debate, Bitterman (1960, 1965) claimed to have demonstrated qualitative differences in learning across a number of species, including the rat, fish and turtle. MacPhail (1992) reviewed much of this evidence and other work, but came to a different conclusion. MacPhail argued that the 'null-hypothesis' of no qualitative difference in learning across all infra-human vertebrate species had not been disproved. Rather, MacPhail concluded that any differences observed could most probably be attributed to differences in such things as sensory processing or motivational states. For the time being the 'jury is out' on this question, but this is largely because a great deal more needs to be known about learning in species other than the rat and pigeon before any firm conclusions may be drawn.

There have been some attempts to investigate questions of a comparative nature employing Australian fauna. One of the first of these was an ingenious study of schedules of reinforcement in *Octopus cyaneus* Gray conducted by Crancher, King, Bennett and Montgomery (1972). Six octopuses, plucked from the waters of Sydney Harbour, were shaped to insert their arm into a plastic tube protruding above the water surface in their tank in order to break a photo-electric beam, and thus have pieces of prawn dropped into the tank. Crancher et al then compared performance under different schedules of reinforcement. They found that different animals varied in rate of responding, that variable ratio performance produced the greatest rate of responding with little evidence for post-reinforcement pauses, and that extinction was rather slow and characterised by spontaneous recovery at the commencement of sessions. In other words, although response rates were not as great as that expected from a rat or pigeon, the general pattern of behaviour to schedules of reinforcement was not greatly different to that which would have been expected from a vertebrate. Research into learning in marine species is difficult and resource intensive, but the similarity of octopus behaviour to terrestrial vertebrates, despite very great differences in phylogenetic history, continues to excite scientific interest and promises to be an important area for comparative study in the near future (Hochner, Shomrat & Fiorito, 2006).

More recent research on Australian native species has focused upon marsupials. The American opossum has received more attention than any other marsupial species (Wynne & McLean, 1999) and appears to be as 'smart' as any other non-human species according to these authors. Bonney and Wynne (2004) compared two Australian marsupials, the quokka and the fat tailed dunnart, in a variety of operant tasks such as discrimination, learning sets and configural discriminations. Both species were able to acquire basic discriminations and set learning, but the dunnart proved to be capable of solving configural discriminations and exhibited superior performance in reversal sets. Hudson, Foster and Temple (1999) trained brushtail possums to press a response key for chips of carob, their preferred food. They went on to compare responding under a variety of FR schedules. The possums' behaviour was very similar to that exhibited by other species such as the rat. In New Zealand the brushtail possum is an introduced pest, which destroys native fauna and flora, and carries bovine tuberculosis. Hudson et al make the point that much more needs to be known about the learning capabilities of these species for effective controls to be developed.

More naturalistic efforts have been made to understand the role of learning in a variety of important ecological areas of concern. For example, Griffin and Evans (2003) found that pairing a model of a predator with simulated capture allowed predator-naive tammar wallabies to acquire an avoidance response. They also found that this response generalised strongly to another model predator (a cat). These results suggest potential procedures which could be employed to reduce predation when captive-bred animals are released in the wild, or when animals are moved into areas of greater risk. Australia's own introduced pest, the cane toad (*Bufo marinus*), impacts on fauna by virtue of its high toxicity which tends to kill any creature foolish enough to eat it. But recent media reports (e.g. http://www.abc.net.au/news/stories/2007/09/15/2033759.htm) suggest that crows have learned to eat only that part of the toad which is non-poisonous (its underside). Just how this has been achieved is somewhat mysterious, but it seems possible that taste-aversion learning is involved. For fish, the tadpoles of *B. marinus* are the problem. Crossland (2001) described how barramundi and sooty grunter learned to avoid tadpoles, apparently because of their taste. Future integration of laboratory and naturalistic studies may help to determine more precisely the mechanisms at play in these important phenomena, opening up new opportunities to understand and protect our environment and the other species we share it with.

## RECAP CHECKPOINT

### Biology and learning

- Research suggests that learning may be constrained by the species-specific repertoires of different organisms.
- Instinctual drift may overwhelm some response—reinforcement learning.
- Taste-aversion learning suggests that species are genetically prepared for some forms of associations.
- The principles of learning established in the laboratory seem to apply to native species in the natural environment.

### CONCEPT QUESTIONS

1. What is instinctual drift?
2. What makes taste-aversion learning unusual as a conditioned response?
3. How does knowledge of the principles of learning help biologists to design ways of limiting the effects of introduced predators?

### CRITICAL THINKING

Recall the study of taste aversions in cancer patients. What data might the researchers have collected to test their speculation about extinction?

# COGNITIVE INFLUENCES ON LEARNING

Our reviews of classical and operant conditioning have demonstrated that a wide variety of behaviours can be understood as the products of simple learning processes. You might wonder, however, if certain classes of learning require more complex, more cognitive types of processes. *Cognition* is any mental activity involved in the representation and processing of knowledge, such as thinking, remembering, perceiving and language use. In this section, we look at forms of learning in animals and humans that cannot be explained only by principles of classical or operant conditioning. We suggest, therefore, that the behaviours are partially the product of cognitive processes.

## ANIMAL COGNITION

In this chapter, we have emphasised that, species-specific constraints aside, rules of learning acquired from research on rats and pigeons apply as well to dogs, monkeys and humans. Researchers who study **animal cognition** have demonstrated that it is not only classical and operant conditioning that generalises across species (Wasserman, 1993, 1994). In his original formulation of the theory of evolution, Charles Darwin suggested that cognitive abilities evolved along with the physical forms of animals. In this section, we will describe two impressive types of animal performance that indicate further continuity in the cognitive capabilities of nonhuman and human animals.

**animal cognition** The cognitive capabilities of nonhuman animals.

**Cognitive maps** Edward C. Tolman (1886–1959) pioneered the study of cognitive processes in learning by inventing experimental circumstances in which mechanical one-to-one associations between specific stimuli and responses could not explain animals' observed behaviour. Consider the maze shown in **Figure 6.13**. Tolman and his students demonstrated that, when an original goal path is

For answers go to MyPsychLab!

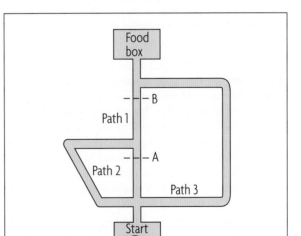

### Figure 6.13

**Use of cognitive maps in maze learning**
Subjects preferred the direct path (Path 1) when it was open. With a block at A, they preferred Path 2. When a block was placed at B, the rats usually chose Path 3. Their behaviour seemed to indicate that they had a cognitive map of the best way to get the food.

blocked in a maze, a rat with prior experience in the maze will take the shortest detour around the barrier, even though that particular response was never previously reinforced (Tolman & Honzik, 1930). The rats, therefore, behaved as if they were responding to an internal **cognitive map**—a representation of the overall layout of the maze—rather than blindly exploring different parts of the maze through trial and error (Tolman, 1948). Tolman's results showed that conditioning involves more than the simple formation of associations between sets of stimuli or between responses and reinforcers. It includes learning and representing other facets of the total behavioural context.

Research in Tolman's tradition has consistently demonstrated an impressive capacity for spatial memory in birds, bees, rats, humans, and other animals (Benhamou & Poucet, 1996; Olton, 1992). To understand the efficiency of spatial cognitive maps, consider the functions they serve (Poucet, 1993):

- Animals use spatial memory to recognise and identify features of their environments.
- Animals use spatial memory to find important goal objects in their environments.
- Animals use spatial memory to plan their route through an environment.

You can see these different functions of cognitive maps at work in the many species of birds that store food over a dispersed area but are able to recover that food with great accuracy when they need it:

> Clark's nutcracker is the champion among food storers that have been studied. In the late summer, these birds bury up to 6,000 caches of pine seeds on mountainsides in the American Southwest. They recover the seeds as late as the next spring, when the cached food supports exceptionally early breeding. (Shettleworth, 1993, p. 180)

The birds are not just roaming their environment and coming on the seeds through good fortune. They return, with up to 84 percent accuracy, to the thousands of locations at which they buried their seeds (Kamil & Balda, 1990). They are also able to discriminate sites that still have seeds from those that have been emptied (Kamil et al., 1993). Bird species that depend heavily on cached seeds for their food supply outperform other, even closely related, species on laboratory spatial memory tasks (Balda et al., 1997; Olson et al., 1995). No differences correlated with caching behaviour are found when the species are compared on nonspatial memory tasks. Note that these birds' caching behaviours are not reinforced when they initially bury their seeds. Only if their cognitive maps remained accurate over the winter can they later recover the seeds and survive to reproduce.

**Conceptual behaviour** We have seen that cognitive maps, in part, help animals preserve details of the spatial locations of objects in their environments. But what other cognitive processes can animals use to find structure, or categories of experiences, in the diverse stimuli they encounter in their environments? In Chapter 10, we will suggest that one of the challenges of language acquisition is for children to form generalisations about new *concepts* and *categories* they are learning, like the words *dog* and *tree*. Human children, however, are not the only animals capable of facing this challenge. Researchers have demonstrated that pigeons also have the cognitive ability to make use of *conceptual* distinctions.

We have seen that cognitive maps, in part, help animals preserve details of the spatial locations of objects in their environments. But what other cognitive processes can animals use to find structure, or categories of experiences, in the diverse stimuli they encounter in their environments? In Chapter 7, we will describe some of the ways in which humans carve up the world. For example, people can think about objects like *chairs* and *cars* both as their own basic categories but also understand that both chairs and cars belong to the higher-order category of artificial, human-made stimuli, whereas *flowers* and *people* belong to the higher-order category of natural stimuli. Humans, however, are not the only animals capable of showing flexibility in the way they carve up the world. Researchers have demonstrated that pigeons as well have the cognitive ability to categorise objects in different ways.

> Pigeons viewed colour photographs of people, flowers, cars, and chairs (see **Figure 6.14**). For each photograph, the pigeons need to make one of two types of correct responses to obtain food. On half of the trials, the pigeons pecked one of four keys that represented the four basic categories of people, flowers, cars and chairs. On the other half of the trials, the pigeons pecked one of two keys that represented the higher-order categories of natural stimuli (people and flowers) versus artificial stimuli (cars and chairs). The two types of trials were randomly intermingled: the pigeons could see the same photo and have to categorise it as a 'flower' and then as a 'natural stimulus' in back-to-back trials. In fact, the pigeons were readily able to learn to respond correctly for both types of category judgments. At the end of the experiment, the researchers tested the pigeons with new photographs—photographs from the same categories that had not been part of the original training set. The pigeons were able to provide correct responses to these new photographs at a level well above chance. The test with novel photographs strongly suggests that the pigeons had learned general categories rather than individual responses to particular stimuli (Lazareva et al., 2004).

We will devote Chapters 7 and 8 to an analysis of cognitive processes in humans. However, this experiment that demonstrates flexible categorisation in pigeons should convince you that humans are not the only species with impressive and useful cognitive capabilities. Before we conclude this chapter, let's move to another type of learning that requires cognitive processes.

cognitive map A mental representation of physical space.

Figure 6.14

**Categorisation in pigeons**

Pigeons viewed photographs that fit into four basic categories (chairs, cars, flowers and people) as well as two higher-order categories (artificial stimuli and natural stimuli).

Reprinted with permission from Edward Wasserman, *Categorisation in Pigeons*, Department of Psychology, University of Iowa.

## OBSERVATIONAL LEARNING

To introduce this further type of learning, we'd like you to return for a moment to the comparison of rats' and humans' approaches to sampling new foods. The rats are almost certainly more cautious than you are, but that's largely because they are missing an invaluable source of information—input from other rats. When you try a new food, it's almost always in a context in which you have good reason to believe that other people have eaten and enjoyed the food. The probability of your 'food-eating behaviour' is thus influenced by your knowledge of patterns of reinforcement for other individuals. This example illustrates your capacity to learn via *vicarious reinforcement* and *vicarious punishment*. You can use your cognitive capacities for memory and reasoning to change your own behaviours in light of the experience of others.

In fact, much *social learning* occurs in situations where learning would not be predicted by traditional conditioning theory because a learner has made no active response and has received no tangible reinforcer. The individual, after simply watching another person exhibiting behaviour that was reinforced or punished, later behaves in much the same way, or refrains from doing so. This is known as **observational learning**. Cognition often enters into observational learning in the form of expectations. In essence, after observing a model, you may think, 'If I do exactly what she does, I will get the same reinforcer or avoid the same punisher'. A younger child may be better

behaved than his older sister because he has learned from the sister's mistakes.

This capacity to learn from watching as well as from doing is extremely useful. It enables you to acquire large integrated patterns of behaviour without going through the tedious trial-and-error process of gradually eliminating wrong responses and acquiring the right ones. You can profit immediately from the mistakes and successes of others. Researchers have demonstrated that observational learning is not special to humans. Among other species, pigeons (Zentall et al., 1996), zebra danio fish (Hall & Suboski, 1995), and even octopuses (Fiorito & Scotto, 1992) are capable of changing their behaviour after observing the performance of another member of their species.

A classic demonstration of human observational learning occurred in the laboratory of **Albert Bandura**. After watching adult models punching, hitting and kicking a large plastic BoBo doll, the children in the experiment later showed a greater frequency of the same behaviours than did children in control conditions who had not observed the aggressive models (Bandura et al., 1963). Subsequent studies showed that children imitated such behaviours just from watching filmed sequences of models, even when the models were cartoon characters.

There is little question now that we learn much—both prosocial (helping) and antisocial (hurting) behaviours—through observation of models, but there are many possible models in the world. What variables are important in determining which models will be most likely to influence you? Research has yielded the following general conclusions (Baldwin & Baldwin, 1973; Bandura, 1977). A model's observed behaviour will be most influential when

- it is seen as having reinforcing consequences.
- the model is perceived positively, liked and respected.
- there are perceived similarities between features and traits of the model and the observer.
- the observer is rewarded for paying attention to the model's behaviour.
- the model's behaviour is visible and salient—it stands out as a clear figure against the background of competing models.
- it is within the observer's range of competence to imitate the behaviour.

To understand this list of findings, imagine yourself in modelling situations and see how each item in the list would apply. Imagine, for example, you are watching someone who is learning how to parachute jump. Or consider how someone might learn to be a 'good' gang member by observing his or her friends.

Because people learn so efficiently from models, you can understand why a good deal of psychological research has been directed at the behavioural impact of television: Are viewers affected by what they see being rewarded and punished on TV? Attention has focused on the link between televised acts of violence—murder, rape, assault, robbery, terrorism and suicide—and children's and adolescents' subsequent behaviour. Does exposure to acts of violence

**observational learning** The process of learning new responses by watching the behaviour of another.

foster imitation? The conclusion from psychological research is yes—it does for some people, and particularly in the United States (Comstock & Scharrer, 1999).

The project began in 1977 when a team of researchers measured 2 years of television viewing for 557 children starting in either first or third grade. In particular, the researchers obtained measures of the extent to which the children watched TV shows with violent content. Fifteen years later, the researchers were able to conduct interviews with 329 of those children, who were now 20 to 22 years old (Huesmann et al., 2003). The researchers sought to determine whether there would be a relationship between the amount of television violence the individuals viewed in childhood and their level of aggression as young adults. Their adult level of aggression was measured both through their own self-reports and through the reports of others, such as spouses. As shown in **Figure 6.15**, the men and women who had watched the most violent TV as children also displayed the highest adult levels of aggression. These data suggest that early TV viewing of violence causes later aggression. You might wonder, however, if the causality works in the opposite direction: Could it be that the children destined to be aggressive were already more interested in violent content as children? Fortunately, the researchers collected data that allowed them to argue against this possibility. For example, the data found only a small relationship between childhood aggression and the individuals' viewing of TV violence as adults.

This study argues strongly that children who watch violent TV are at risk to become overly aggressive as adults.

Several decades of research have demonstrated three ways in which television violence has a negative impact on viewers' lives (Smith & Donnerstein, 1998). First, as we have just seen, the viewing of television violence brings about, through the mechanisms of observational learning, increases in aggressive behaviour. This causal association has particularly important implications for children: aggressive habits born of heavy television viewing early in life may serve as the basis for antisocial behaviour later in life; second, the viewing of television violence leads viewers to overestimate the occurrences of violence in the everyday world. Television viewers may be unduly afraid of becoming victims of real-world violence; third, the viewing of television violence may bring about *desensitisation,* a reduction in both emotional arousal and distress at viewing violent behaviour.

Note that research has also shown that children can learn prosocial, helping behaviours when they watch television programs that provide prosocial behavioural models (Rosenkoetter, 1999; Singer & Singer, 1990). You should take seriously the idea that children learn from the television they watch. As a parent or child minder you may want to help children select appropriate televised models.

An analysis of observational learning acknowledges both that principles of reinforcement influence behaviour and that humans have the capacity to use their cognitive processes to change behaviours with vicarious rewards and punishment. This approach to the understanding of human behaviour has proven very powerful. In Chapter 15, we will look at successful programs of therapy that have emerged from the cognitive modification of maladaptive patterns of behaviour.

Let's close this chapter by calling back to mind a visit to a horror movie. How can behaviour analysis explain your experiences? If you went to the movie because of a friend's recommendation, you have succumbed to vicarious reinforcement. If you made it to the theatre, despite having to forgo your normal route, you have shown evidence of a cognitive map. If the sound of scary music made you fear for the hero's wellbeing, you felt the effects of classical conditioning. If your failure to enjoy the film made you vow never to see a horror movie again, you have discovered the effect a punisher has on your subsequent behaviour.

Are you ready to return to the theatre?

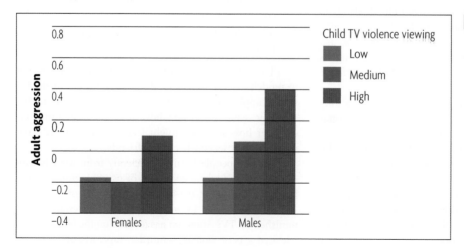

### Figure 6.15

**TV violence and aggression**
For both men and women, those individuals who had viewed the most violent TV as children also displayed the most aggression as adults. The measure of aggression is a composite score that reflects the individuals' self-ratings and ratings of them by others. Higher scores indicate higher levels of aggression.

## RECAP CHECKPOINT
### Cognitive influences on learning

- Some forms of learning reflect more complex processes than those of classical or operant conditioning.

- Animals develop cognitive maps to enable them to function in a complex environment.

- Conceptual behaviour allows animals to form generalisations about the structure of the environment.

- Behaviours can be vicariously reinforced or punished. Humans and other animals can learn through observation.

## CONCEPT QUESTIONS

1. What conclusions did Tolman draw from his pioneering work?

2. What evidence suggests that pigeons are able to categorise stimuli with some flexibility?

3. What is meant by vicarious reinforcement?

4. Why is it important to evaluate children's TV viewing in the context of observational learning?

## CRITICAL THINKING

Consider the TV viewing study. What steps did the researchers take to assert that they had given the right causal explanation for the correlation revealed in their data?

# SUMMARY

Chapter 6 provided an overview of the major ways in which learning has been investigated. The laboratory study of Pavlovian and operant conditioning has revealed a rich set of principles for understanding how the environment influences behaviour. These ideas have proved to be extraordinarily valuable as they have been translated into practical applications in areas such as the treatment of phobias, drug addiction and parenting. Social processes are also involved in learning, and these must be understood for a more complete picture of human behaviour to be obtained. The laws of learning provide the starting point for understanding cognition in animals and humans and will be explored more fully in later chapters.

# KEY TERMS

acquisition (p. 177)
animal cognition (p. 199)
behaviour analysis (p. 175)
biological constraints on learning (p. 195)
classical conditioning (p. 176)
cognitive map (p. 200)
conditioned reinforcers (p. 190)
conditioned response (CR) (p. 177)

conditioned stimulus (CS) (p. 177)
discriminative stimuli (p. 189)
extinction (p. 179)
fixed-interval (FI) schedule (p. 194)
fixed-ratio (FR) schedule (p. 192)
habituation (p. 175)
instinctual drift (p. 196)
law of effect (p. 186)
learning (p. 174)

learning-performance distinction (p. 174)
negative punishment (p. 188)
negative reinforcement (p. 188)
observational learning (p. 201)
operant (p. 186)
operant conditioning (p. 186)
operant extinction (p. 188)
partial reinforcement effect (p. 192)
positive punishment (p. 188)

# PRACTICE TEST

1. You are watching the Olympics and see a young skater fall down several times during a practice session on a jump that is usually easy for her. This provides a good example of
   a. classical conditioning.
   c. the law of effect.
   b negative reinforcement.
   d. the learning-performance distinction.

2. When Joan first moved to the city 6 months ago, she couldn't sleep at night because of the traffic noise. Now she hardly hears the traffic at all. This is an example of
   a. sensitisation.
   c. consistency.
   b. habituation.
   d. classical conditioning.

3. If a researcher told you he was a close adherent to Skinner's ideas, you would *not* expect his research to focus on
   a. internal states as causes of behaviour.
   b. forms of learning conserved across species.
   c. associations between behaviours and rewards.
   d. the environmental stimuli that cause behaviours.

4. In Pavlov's experiments,_____served as the unconditioned stimulus.
   a. salivation
   c. the sight of the assistant
   b. food powder
   d. tones

5. A dog has undergone a classical conditioning procedure so that on day 1 it salivates when it hears a tone. On day 3, the dog no longer salivates to the tone. You might guess that on day 2 the dog went through the process of
   a. acquisition.
   c. extinction.
   b. habituation.
   d. sensitisation.

6. Six-year-old Pavel has a neighbour with a small dog who barks at him every time he walks by the house. Over time, Pavel has become frightened of all the dogs he sees. This is an example of
   a. stimulus discrimination.
   c. spontaneous recovery.
   b. backward conditioning.
   d. stimulus generalisation.

7. Peter wishes to use classical conditioning in which a light will be the CS and an electric shock will be the UCS. You tell him that the light must_____the shock.
   a. be temporally contiguous with
   c. be in a blocking relationship with
   b. reliably predict
   d. occur after

8. When classical conditioning contributes to drug tolerance, the conditioned stimulus is
   a. the setting in which individuals take the drugs.
   b. the body's compensatory reaction to the drug.
   c. the high the drugs give when individuals take them.
   d. the individual's fear of an overdose.

9. For people undergoing chemotherapy, an unconditioned response would be
   a. anticipatory fatigue.
   b. the setting in which the individual receives the treatment.
   c. their body's reaction to the drugs.
   d. the infusion of drugs into their bodies.

10. Before you start an operant conditioning experiment, you buy some very expensive chocolate. When people perform a desired behaviour, you will ask them to eat some of the chocolate. You think it's likely that the chocolate will be a_____of the people.
    a. reinforcer for all
    c. punisher for all
    b. reinforcer for none
    d. reinforcer for some

11. Which of these concepts is not an element of the three-term contingency?
    a. discriminative stimulus
    c. emitted response
    b. operant extinction
    d. stimulus consequence

12. Carlotta's parents haven't allowed her to watch television for 3 days. At dinner, she eats her brussels sprouts on the promise that she'll be allowed to watch TV that night. It sounds like Carlotta's parents might be familiar with
    a. operant extinction.
    c. token economies.
    b. conditioned reinforcement theory.
    d. response deprivation theory.

13. Which statement is best supported by current research?
    a. Researchers have demonstrated that mild smack leads to negative outcomes.
    b. Researchers have demonstrated that mild smack leads to positive outcomes.
    c. Researchers do not know how mild smack affects children.
    d. Researchers cannot assess the intensity of physical punishment.

14. In your new job, you get paid $2 every time you finish polishing 20 apples. This situation puts you on a_____schedule.
    a. variable-interval
    b. fixed-interval
    c. variable-ratio
    d. fixed-ratio

15. In one experiment, raccoons began to rub two coins together rather than learning the target behaviour, which was to deposit the coins into a toy bank. This is an example of
    a. operant extinction.
    b. conditioned reinforcers.
    c. instinctual drift.
    d. shaping by successive approximations.

16. In taste-aversion learning, a novel flavour often serves as the
    a. UCS.
    b. CS.
    c. CR.
    d. UCR.

17. One night after eating a kebab you get very sick. Now you shudder at the idea of eating a kebab. You want to overcome this aversion to kebabs. A friend suggests that you allow yourself to experience some extinction trials. This means that you should
    a. associate kebabs with foods you like.
    b. eat some more kebabs.
    c. make yourself sick eating something else.
    d. use kebabs as a reward.

18. Birds like Clark's nutcrackers are very successful at finding the seeds they have buried. This provides evidence for species-specific
    a. conditioning processes.
    b. applications of classical conditioning.
    c. spatial memory.
    d. shaping processes.

19. Suppose you showed a pigeon a photograph of a car. As a human, you can categorise the photograph as both a *car* and an *artificial stimulus*. You believe that you can train a pigeon to categorise the photograph
    a. as both a *car* and an *artificial stimulus*.
    b. only as a *car*.
    c. only as an *artificial stimulus*.
    d. as neither a *car* nor an *artificial stimulus*.

20. Zoe watches her older sister slip on a newly polished kitchen floor and bruise her arm. After that, Zoe is very careful when she walks on a newly polished kitchen floor. This is an example of
    a. observational learning.
    b. classical conditioning.
    c. operant extinction.
    d. sensitisation.

## Essay Questions

1. Given what you've learned about classical conditioning, what information might you share with someone who is about to undergo chemotherapy?

2. Why might you choose one schedule of reinforcement (e.g., fixed-interval vs. variable-interval) over another?

3. What mechanisms explain why viewing of TV violence might be a cause of aggressive behaviour?

# WEB LINKS

http://raisingchildren.net.au/articles/smacking_video.html
    Raising children: smacking

Are you ready for the test? MyPsychLab offers dozens of ways to deepen your understanding and test your recall of the material in this chapter—including video and audio clips, simulations and activities, self-assessments, practice tests and other study materials. Specific resources available for this chapter include:

 Schedules of reinforcement
Forms of learning

 Process of stimulus generalisation and stimulus discrimination in classical conditioning
Process of extinction and spontaneous recovery
Bandura's Bobo Doll experiment
Classical conditioning of Little Albert

 Pigeon in the Skinner Box
Television violence

To access MyPsychLab, please visit **www.pearsoned.com.au/mypsychlab**

# How much do you remember?

## NOW YOU HAVE READ CHAPTER 6—ARE YOU PREPARED FOR THE EXAM?

To enhance your understanding of any of the material in your *Psychology and Life* textbook, go to **MyPsychLab: www.pearsoned.com.au/mypsychlab**.

Complete pre- and post-tests, create your own individualised study plan, watch videos and animations and listen to audio glossaries—all of which will help you to understand the themes of this chapter:

- The study of learning
- Classical conditioning: learning predictable signals
- Operant conditioning: learning about consequences
- Biology and learning
- Cognitive influences on learning

EXPLORE the dolphins at Sea World!

Read a section about *classical conditioning* in your eBook!

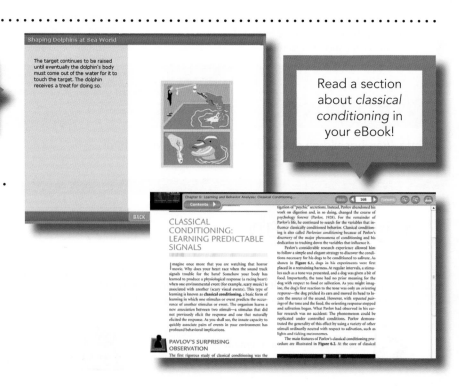

'MPL was a wonderful asset in exam preparation.'

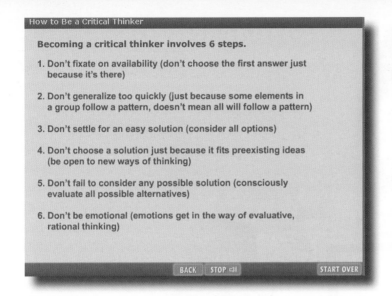

**How to Be a Critical Thinker**

Becoming a critical thinker involves 6 steps.

1. Don't fixate on availability (don't choose the first answer just because it's there)

2. Don't generalize too quickly (just because some elements in a group follow a pattern, doesn't mean all will follow a pattern)

3. Don't settle for an easy solution (consider all options)

4. Don't choose a solution just because it fits preexisting ideas (be open to new ways of thinking)

5. Don't fail to consider any possible solution (consciously evaluate all possible alternatives)

6. Don't be emotional (emotions get in the way of evaluative, rational thinking)

BACK   STOP ◁))   START OVER

'There is not enough time to cover everything in lectures and tutorials. Using MyPsychLab helps me to understand the material without my tutor.'

Take a MyPsychLab EXAM on content covered in Chapter 6!

COURSES > GERRIG > CONTROL PANEL > PREVIEW ASSESSMENT CHAPTER 6 EXAM

📖 **Preview Assessment Chapter 6 Exam**

Announcements
Chapter Contents
E-Book
Multimedia Library
eThemes
Writing Resources
External Links
Course Map

─ INSTRUCTORS ─
Control Panel

| | |
|---|---|
| **Name:** | Chapter 6 Exam |
| **Instructions:** | Your results will be recorded in the Course Compass grade book. |
| **Multiple Attempts:** | Not allowed. This Test can only be taken once. |
| **Force Completion:** | This Test can be saved and resumed later. |

**Question 1   Multiple Choice**                                                                            5 p[oints]

_____ is the process that results in a relatively consistent change in behavior or behavior potential and is based on experience.

○ Learning
○ Conditioning
○ Pairing
○ Approximation
○ Habituation

**Question 2   Multiple Choice**                                                                            5 p[oints]

_____ is a decrease in behavioral response when a stimulus is presented repeatedly.

○ Learning
○ Conditioning
○ Pairing
○ Approximation
○ Habituation

**What can you find in MyPsychLab?**

Self-directed tests ∗ Videos ∗ Simulations ∗ eBook ∗ Biographies ∗ Audio glossary ∗ Web links … and more—organised by chapter, section and learning objective.

mypsych lab ™
where learning comes to life!

Memory

# CHAPTER
## 7

# CHAPTER
# FOCUS POINTS

After studying this chapter you will have a better understanding of:

1. The processes of encoding, storage and retrieval in human memory.

2. The major distinctions that are described in theories of memory—implicit vs explicit, semantic vs episodic and declarative vs procedural memory.

3. How to organise your own study time to maximise the likelihood of successful test performance.

4. How to describe the differences between sensory memory, short-term memory and long-term memory.

5. How to explain the 'levels of processing' approach to long term memory.

6. How to describe why we forget things, and the different types of interference that effect long-term memory.

7. Why it takes longer to answer the question 'Is a sparrow a bird?' than 'Does a sparrow have wings?'

8. How schemas influence the way incoming information is organised.

# CHAPTER CONTENTS

As you begin this chapter on memory processes, we'd like you to take a moment to retrieve your own earliest memory. How long ago did the memory originate? How vivid a scene do you recall? Has your memory been influenced by other people's recollections of the same event?

Now, a slightly different exercise. We'd like you to imagine what it would be like if you suddenly had no memory of your past—of the people you have known or of events that have happened to you. You wouldn't remember your mother's face, or your 10th birthday, or your Year 12 formal. Without such time anchors, how would you maintain a sense of who you are—of your identity? Or suppose you lost the ability to form any new memories. What would happen to your most recent experiences? Could you follow a conversation or untangle the plot of a TV show? Everything would vanish, as if events had never existed, as if you had never had any thoughts in mind. Is there any activity you can think of that is not influenced by memory?

If you have never given much thought to your memory, it's probably because it tends to do its job reasonably well—you take it for granted, alongside other bodily processes, like digestion or breathing. But as with stomach aches or allergies, the times you notice your memory are likely to be the times when something goes wrong: you forget your car keys, an important date, lines in a play, or the answer to an examination question that you know you 'really knew'. These occasions are irritating, but keep in mind that the average human brain can store an estimated 100 trillion bits of information. The task of managing such a vast array of information is a formidable one. Perhaps you shouldn't be too surprised when an answer is sometimes not available when you need it!

**memory** The mental capacity to encode, store and retrieve information.

How are actors and actresses able to remember all the different aspects—movements, expressions and words—of their performances?

**explicit uses of memory** Conscious effort to encode or recover information through memory processes.

**implicit uses of memory** Availability of information through memory processes without conscious effort to encode or recover information.

Our goal in this chapter is to explain how you usually remember so much and why you forget some of what you have known. We will explore how you get your everyday experiences into and out of memory. You will learn what psychology has discovered about different types of memories and about how those memories work. We hope that in the course of learning the many facts of memory, you will gain an appreciation for how wonderful memory is.

One last thing: because this is a chapter on memory, we're going to put your memory immediately to work. We'd like you to remember the number 46. Do whatever you need to do to remember 46. And yes, there will be a test!

# WHAT IS MEMORY?

To begin, we will define **memory** as the capacity to store and retrieve information. In this chapter, we will describe memory as a type of *information processing*. We will therefore focus on the flow of information in and out of your memory systems. Our examination of the processes that guide the acquisition and retrieval of information will enable you to refine your sense of what *memory* means.

## TYPES OF MEMORIES

When you think about memory, what is most likely to come to mind at first are situations in which you use your memory to recall (or try to recall) specific events or information: your favourite movie, the dates of World War II, or your student ID number. In fact, one of the important functions of memory is to allow you to have conscious access to the personal and collective past. But memory does much more for you than that. It also enables you to have effortless continuity of experience from one day to the next. When you drive in a car, for example, it is this second function of memory that makes the landmarks along the roadside seem familiar. In defining types of memories, we will make plain to you how hard your memory works to fulfil these functions, often outside of conscious awareness.

Implicit and explicit memory Imagine you are travelling on a bus. As soon as you sit down you realise that you know the person sitting next to you, but you have no idea *how* you know her. Is she the newsagent from around the corner? Your Introductory Psychology lecturer? The neighbour from three doors down who you never see much? You know that the face is familiar, but no amount of searching through your memories of people helps you place her. Hours later, it pops into your head—she's the florist from the shopping centre, and you probably saw her yesterday when you were catching up with friends for a muffin and a coffee at the café near her shop.

This simple example allows you to understand the difference between **explicit** and **implicit uses of memory**.

Implicit memory is associated with a sense of familiarity: something about the woman on the bus' face automatically triggers a sense that you know you have seen her before. But no amount of conscious thought can bring to mind who she is, or where you last saw her. Explicit memory refers to the conscious, deliberate retrieval of information from memory. In the example from the bus, you had a strong implicit memory of who she was, but you were unable to retrieve the explicit memory to go with that.

Thus, when it comes to using knowledge stored in memory, sometimes the use will be implicit—the information becomes available without any conscious effort—and sometimes it will be explicit—you make a conscious effort to recover the information.

We can make a similar distinction when it comes to the initial acquisition of memories. What shape is a *Give Way* sign? If you think about it, you probably know that they are triangular. Did you ever memorise a list of road sign shapes? Probably not. Rather, it's likely that you acquired this knowledge incidentally, without conscious effort. By contrast, you probably learned the rules of the road intentionally—that is, at some point you practised the rules, or wrote them down, or otherwise used some conscious effort to learn them,. As we shall see in Chapter 10, to learn the association between words and experiences, your younger self needed to engage in explicit memory processes. You learned the word *refrigerator* because someone called your attention to the name of that object.

The distinction between implicit and explicit memory greatly expands the range of questions researchers must address about memory processes (Bowers & Marsolek, 2003; Buchner & Wippich, 2000). Most early memory research concerned explicit memory for intentionally acquired information. Experimenters most frequently provided participants with new information to retain, and theories of memory were directed to explaining what participants could and could not remember under those circumstances. However, as you will see in this chapter, researchers have now devised methods for studying implicit memory as well. Thus we can give you a more complete account of the variety of uses to which you put your memory. We can acknowledge that most circumstances in which you encode or retrieve information represent a mix of implicit and explicit uses of memory. Let's turn now to a second dimension along which memories are distributed.

### Declarative and procedural memory
Can you whistle, or ride a bicycle, or use chopsticks? What kind of memory allows you to do these sorts of things? You probably remember having to learn these skills, but now they seem effortless. The examples we gave before of both implicit and explicit memories all involved the recollection of *facts* and *events*, which is called **declarative memory**. Now we see that you also have memories for *how to do things*, which is called **procedural memory**. Because the bulk of this chapter will be focused on how you acquire and use facts, let's take a moment now to consider how you acquire the ability to do things.

*Procedural memory* refers to the way you remember how things get done. It is used to acquire, retain and employ perceptual, cognitive and motor skills. Theories of procedural memory most often concern themselves with the time course of learning (Anderson, 1996; Anderson et al., 1999): How do you go from a conscious list of declarative facts about some activity to an unconscious, automatic performance of that same activity? And why is it that after learning a skill, you often find it difficult to go back and talk about the component declarative facts?

We can see these phenomena at work in even the very simple activity of dialling a phone number that, over time, has become highly familiar. At first, you probably had to think your way through each digit, one at a time. You had to work through a list of declarative facts:

First, I must dial 2,

Next, I must dial 0,

Then I dial 7,

and so on.

However, when you began to dial the number often enough, you could start to produce it as one unit—a swift sequence of actions on the touch-tone pad. The process at work is called *knowledge compilation* (Anderson, 1987). As a consequence of practice, you are able to carry out longer sequences of the activity without conscious intervention. But you also don't have conscious access to the content of these compiled units: Back at the telephone, it's not uncommon to find someone who can't actually remember the phone number without pretending to dial it. In general, knowledge compilation makes it hard to share your procedural knowledge with others. You may have noticed this if your parents tried to teach you to drive. Although they may be good drivers themselves, they may not have been very good at communicating the content of compiled good-driving procedures.

You may also have noticed that knowledge compilation can lead to errors. If you are a skilled typist, you've probably suffered from the *the* problem: As soon as you hit the *t* and the *h* keys, your finger may fly to the *e*, even if you're really trying to type *throne* or *thistle*. Once you have sufficiently committed the execution of

Why does pretending to dial a number help you to remember it?

**declarative memory** Memory for information such as facts and events.

**procedural memory** Memory for how things get done; the way perceptual, cognitive, and motor skills are acquired, retained and used.

*the* to procedural memory, you can do little else but finish the sequence. Without procedural memory, life would be extremely laborious—you would be doomed to go step by step through every activity. However, each time you mistakenly type *the*, you can reflect on the trade-off between efficiency and potential error. Let's continue now to an overview of the basic processes that apply to all these different types of memory.

## AN OVERVIEW OF MEMORY PROCESSES

For any memory system to work, it must do at least three things: information has to get into it; it has to be kept somewhere; and it has to be able to be extracted from it. **Encoding** is the initial processing of information that leads to a representation in memory. **Storage** is the retention over time of encoded material. **Retrieval** is the recovery at a later time of the stored information. Simply put, encoding gets information in, storage holds it until you need it, and retrieval gets it out. Let's now expand on these ideas.

*Encoding* requires that you form *mental representations* of information from the external world. You can understand the idea of mental representations if we draw an analogy to representations outside your head. Imagine we wanted to know something about the best gift you got at your last birthday party. (Let's suppose it's not something you have with you.) What could you do to inform us about the gift? You might describe the properties of the object. Or you might draw us a picture. Or you might pretend that you're using the object. These are all different representations of the original object. Although none of the representations is likely to be quite as good as having the real thing present, they should allow us to acquire knowledge of the most important aspects of the gift. Mental representations work much the same way. They preserve important features of past experiences in a way that enables you to *re-present* those experiences to yourself. There are no absolute rules about how 'best' to encode information. You may have friends who can only remember things if they've drawn a diagram of them, or who need to write things out in dot points, or who can only play their piano pieces if they are sitting at their piano. All these are examples of the individuality of encoding.

Similarly, cultural and historical factors also serve to define the 'best' encoding strategy. Australians of English and European backgrounds tend to encode things verbally—their sense of 'self' is a narrative. For many Indigenous Australian groups, identity is defined by place. In a study of Aboriginal and white Australian children of different age groups, Kearins (1976, 1981) determined that the Aboriginal children had superior visual recall. As they encode information using predominantly visual strategies, they tend to show superior skill in spatial and visual recall, and are more likely to process information simultaneously rather than successively (Klich & Davidson, 1983). It has been suggested that the differences in visual memory in Indigenous people are a result of living conditions in the bush and desert regions of Australia (Klekamp et al., 1987). Later in the chapter we will explore the relationship between how you encode information and how it is eventually retrieved.

If information is properly encoded, it will be retained in *storage* over some period of time. Storage requires both short- and long-term changes in the structures of your brain. At the end of the chapter, we will see how researchers are attempting to locate the brain

*Retrieval* is the payoff for all your earlier effort. When it works, it enables you to gain access—often in a split second—to information you stored earlier. Can you remember what comes before storage: decoding or encoding? The answer is simple to retrieve now, but will you still be able to retrieve the concept of encoding as swiftly and with as much confidence when you are tested on this chapter's contents days or weeks from now? Discovering how you are able to retrieve one specific bit of information from the vast quantity of information in your memory storehouse is a challenge facing psychologists who want to know how memory works and how it can be improved.

Although it is easy to define encoding, storage and retrieval as separate memory processes, the interaction among the three processes is quite complex. For example, to be able to encode the information that you have seen a tiger, you must first retrieve from memory information about the concept *tiger*. Similarly, to commit to memory the meaning of a sentence such as 'He's got the heart of Phar Lap', you must retrieve the meanings of each individual word, retrieve the rules of grammar that specify how word meanings should be combined in English, and retrieve cultural information that specifies exactly how brave and strong Phar Lap—the best horse never to win a Melbourne Cup—was.

We are now ready to look in more detail at the encoding, storage and retrieval of information. Our

**encoding** The process by which a mental representation is formed in memory.

**storage** The retention of encoded material over time.

**retrieval** The recovery of stored information from memory.

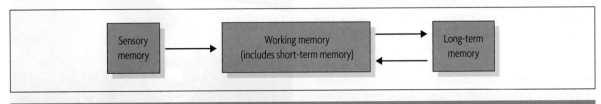

### Figure 7.1

#### The flow of information in and out of long-term memory

Memory theories describe the flow of information to and from long-term memory. The theories address initial encodings of information in sensory and working memory, the transfer of information into long-term memory for storage and the transfer of information from long-term memory to working memory for retrieval.

discussion will start with short-lived types of memories, beginning with sensory memory, and then move to the more permanent forms of long-term memory (see **Figure 7.1**). We will give you an account of how you remember and why you forget. Our plan is to make you forever self-conscious about all the ways in which you use your capacity for memory. We hope this will even allow you to improve some aspects of your memory skills.

# MEMORY USE FOR THE SHORT TERM

Let's begin with a demonstration of the impermanence of some memories. In **Figure 7.2** we have provided you with a reasonably busy visual scene. We'd like you to take a quick look at it—about 10 seconds—and then cover it up. Suppose we now ask you a series of questions about the scene:

1. What tool is the little boy at the bottom holding?

2. What is the middle man at the top doing?

3. In the lower right-hand corner, does the woman's umbrella handle hook to the left or to the right?

To answer these questions, wouldn't you be more comfortable if you could go back and have an extra peek at the picture?

This quick demonstration reminds you that much of the information you experience never lodges itself securely in your memory. Instead, you possess and use the information only for the short term. In this section, we examine properties of three less permanent uses of memory: *sensory memory*, *short-term memory* and *working memory*.

## SENSORY MEMORY

Imagine you are reading this book in an electrical storm. You glance at Figure 7.2 during a flash of lightning. Although the lightning lasts only a fraction of a second, you might have the impression that you could briefly still 'see' the whole picture, but that the image you have 'fades' very quickly. This extra peek at the picture is provided by your **iconic memory**—a **sensory** memory system in the visual domain that allows large amounts of information to be stored for very brief durations (Neisser, 1967). There is some evidence that similar memory systems exist in other sensory systems; however, iconic memory is the best understood example, so we will focus on that here. Iconic memory allows very large amounts of information to be stored for very brief durations. A visual memory, or icon, lasts about half a second. Iconic memory was first revealed in experiments that required participants to retrieve information from visual displays that were exposed for only one-twentieth of a second.

George Sperling (1960, 1963) presented participants with arrays of three rows of letters and numbers.

| 7 | 1 | V | F |
| X | L | 5 | 3 |
| B | 4 | W | 7 |

Participants were asked to perform two different tasks. In a *whole-report procedure,* they tried to recall as many of the items in the display as possible. Typically, they could report only about four of twelve, or one-third of the available items. Other participants underwent a *partial-report procedure,* which required them to report only one row rather than the whole pattern. The trick was that they didn't know *which* row they had to report until after the display was presented. A signal of a high, medium, or low tone was sounded immediately after the presentation to indicate which row the participants were to report. Sperling found that regardless of which row he asked for, the participants' recall was well above the roughly 33% accuracy of the whole report condition.

Because participants could accurately report any of the three rows in response to a tone, Sperling concluded that all of the information in the display must have been stored,

**iconic memory** Memory system in the visual domain that allows large amounts of information to be stored for very brief durations.

For answers go to MyPsychLab!

**mypsychlab** where learning comes to life!

Figure 7.2

**How much can you remember from this scene?**
After viewing this scene for about 10 seconds, cover it up and try to answer the questions in the text. Under ordinary circumstances, iconic memory preserves a glimpse of the visual world for a brief time after the scene has been removed.

albeit briefly, in iconic memory. The difference between whole- and partial-report is that the image is fading so quickly that there isn't time to 'read out' all 12 items in whole report, but the fact that people can remember any three suggests that they are all available for a short period of time. That is evidence for the large capacity of iconic memory. At the same time, the difference between the whole- and partial-report procedures suggests that the information fades rapidly: The participants in the whole-report procedure were unable to recall all the information present in the icon. This second point was reinforced by experiments in which the identification signal was slightly delayed. **Figure 7.3** shows that as the delay interval increases from 0 seconds to 1 second, the number of items accurately reported declines steadily. Researchers have measured quite accurately the time course with which information must be transferred from the fading icon (Becker et al., 2000; Gegenfurtner & Sperling, 1993). To take advantage of the 'extra peek' at the visual world, your memory processes must very quickly transfer information to more durable stores.

Note that iconic memory is not the same as the 'photographic memory' that some people claim to have. The technical term for 'photographic memory' is *eidetic imagery*: people who experience eidetic imagery are able to recall the details of a picture, for periods of time considerably longer than iconic memory, as if they were still looking at a photograph. 'People' in this case really means children: researchers have estimated that roughly 8 percent of preadolescent children are eidetickers, but virtually no adults (Neath & Surprenant, 2003). No satisfactory theory has been proposed for why eidetic imagery fades over time (Crowder, 1992). However, if you are reading this book as a high school or university student, you almost certainly have iconic memory but not eidetic images.

## SHORT-TERM MEMORY

Before you began to read this chapter, you may not have been aware that you had iconic memory. It is very likely, however, that you were aware that there are some memories that you possess only for the short term. Consider the common occurrence of consulting a telephone book to find the number of a plumber or a shop and then remembering the number just long enough to dial it. If the number is engaged, you often have to go back to the phone book and look it up again. When you consider this experience, it's easy to understand why researchers have hypothesised

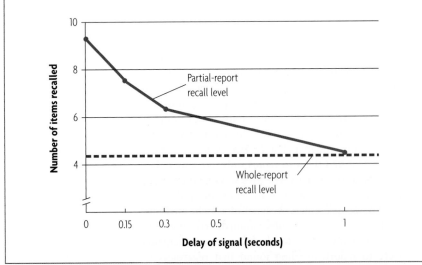

Figure 7.3

**Recall by the partial-report method**
The solid line shows the average number of items recalled using the partial-report method, both immediately after presentation and at four later times. For comparison, the dotted line shows the number of items recalled by the whole-report method. (Adapted from Sperling, 1960.)

a special type of memory called **short-term memory (STM)**.

You shouldn't think of short-term memory as a particular place that memories go to, but rather as a built-in mechanism for focusing cognitive resources on some small set of mental representations (Shiffrin, 2003). But the resources of STM are fickle. As even your experience with phone numbers shows, you have to take some special care to ensure that memories become encoded into more permanent forms.

**The capacity limitations of STM** In Chapter 4, we described how your attentional resources are devoted to selecting the objects and events in the external world on which you will expend your mental resources. Just as there are limits on your capacity to attend to more than a small sample of the available information, there are limits on your ability to keep more than a small sample of information active in STM. The limited capacity of STM enforces a sharp focus of mental attention.

To estimate the capacity of STM, researchers at first turned to tests of *memory span*. At some point in your life, you have probably been asked to carry out a task like this one:

> Read the following list of random numbers once, cover them, and write down as many as you can in the order they appear.
>
> 8  1  7  3  4  9  4  2  8  5
>
> How many did you get correct?
> Now read the next list of random letters and perform the same memory test.
>
> J  M  R  S  O  F  L  P  T  Z  B

How many did you get correct

If you are like most individuals, you probably could recall somewhere in the range of five to nine items. **George Miller** (1956) suggested that seven (plus or minus two) was the 'magic number' that characterised people's memory performance on random lists of letters, words, numbers, or almost any kind of meaningful, familiar item.

Tests of memory span, however, overestimate the true capacity of STM because participants are able to use other sources of information to carry out the task. When other sources of memory are factored out, researchers have estimated the pure contribution of STM to your seven (or so) item memory span to be only between three and five items (Cowan, 2001). But if that's all the capacity you have to commence the acquisition of new memories, why don't you notice your limitations more often? Despite the capacity limitations of STM, you function efficiently for at least two reasons. As we will see in the next two sections, the encoding of information in STM can be enhanced through rehearsal and chunking.

**Rehearsal** You probably know that a good way to keep the plumber's telephone number in mind is to keep repeating the digits in a cycle in your head. This memorisation technique is called *maintenance rehearsal*. The fate of unrehearsed information was demonstrated in an ingenious experiment.

Participants heard three consonants, such as F, C and V. They had to recall those consonants when given a signal after a variable interval of time, ranging from 3 to 18 seconds. To prevent rehearsal, a *distractor task* was put between the stimulus input and the recall signal—the participants were given a three-digit number and told to count backward from it by 3's until the recall signal was presented. Many different consonant sets were given, and several short delays were used over a series of trials with a number of participants.

As shown in **Figure 7.4**, recall became increasingly poorer as the time required to retain the information became longer. After even 3 seconds, there was considerable memory loss, and by 18 seconds, loss was nearly total. In the absence of an opportunity to rehearse the information, short-term recall was impaired with the passage of time (Peterson & Peterson, 1959).

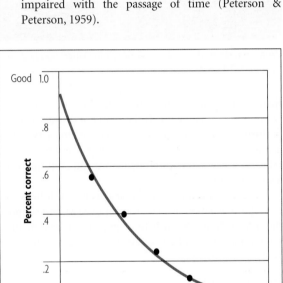

**Figure 7.4**

**Short-term memory recall without rehearsal**
When the interval between stimulus presentation and recall was filled with a distracting task, recall became poorer as the interval grew longer.

Performance suffered because information could not be rehearsed. It also suffered because of interference from the competing information of the distractor task. (We will discuss interference as a cause of forgetting later in this chapter.) You may have noticed that often a new acquaintance says his or her name—and

**short-term memory (STM)**
Memory processes associated with preservation of recent experiences and with retrieval of information from long-term memory.

What role does short-term memory play when you punch in your ATM password?

down the sequence into the well-known acronyms—FBI, CSIRO and UNICEF. If you do the latter, it's easy for you to recall all the letters in proper sequence after one quick glance. It would be impossible for you to remember them all from a short exposure if you saw them as 14 unrelated items.

Your memory span can always be greatly increased if you can discover ways to organise an available body of information into smaller chunks. A famous subject, S. F., was able to memorise 84 digits by grouping them as racing times (S. F. was an avid runner):

> S. F.'s memory protocols provided the key to his mental wizardry. Because he was a long-distance runner, S. F. noticed that many of the random numbers could be grouped into running times for different distances. For instance, he would recode the sequence 3, 4, 9, 2, 5, 6, 1, 4, 9, 3, 5 as 3:49.2, near record mile; 56:14, 10-mile time; 9:35, slow 2 miles. Later, S. F. also used ages, years of memorable events, and special numerical patterns to chunk the random digits. In this way, he was able to use his long-term memory to convert long strings of random input into manageable and meaningful chunks. S. F.'s memory for letters was still about average, however, because he had not developed any chunking strategies to recall alphabet strings (Chase & Ericsson, 1981; Ericsson & Chase, 1982).

Like S. F., you can structure incoming information according to its personal meaning to you (linking it to the ages of friends and relatives, for example); or you can match new stimuli with various codes that have been stored in your long-term memory. Even if you can't link new stimuli to rules, meanings or codes in your long-term memory, you can still use chunking. You can simply group the items in a rhythmical pattern or temporal group (181379256460 could become 181, pause, 379, pause, 256, pause, 460). You know from everyday experience that this grouping principle works well for remembering telephone numbers.

then you immediately forget it. One of the most common reasons for this is that you are distracted from performing the type of rehearsal you need to carry out to acquire a new memory. As a remedy, try to encode and rehearse a new name carefully before you continue with a conversation.

Our conclusion so far is that rehearsal will help you to keep information from fading out of STM. But suppose the information you wish to acquire is, at least at first, too cumbersome to be rehearsed? You might turn to the strategy of chunking.

Chunking A *chunk* is a meaningful unit of information (Anderson, 1996). A chunk can be a single letter or number, a group of letters or other items, or even a group of words or an entire sentence. For example, the letter sequence B-D-O-P-G consists of five letters that could exhaust your STM capacity. However, another five-letter sequence, A-N-Z-A-C is probably easier to remember, as it is the acronym for the Australian and New Zealand Army Corps which is associated with the ANZAC Day public holiday and other events. While both are five-letter sequences, ANZAC constitutes only one chunk, leaving you much more capacity for other chunks of information. **Chunking** is the process of reconfiguring items by grouping them on the basis of similarity or some other organising principle, or by combining them into larger patterns based on information stored in long-term memory (Baddeley, 1994).

See how many chunks you find in this sequence of 14 letters:. FBICSIROUNICEF You can answer '14' if you see the sequence as a list of unrelated letters, or '3' if you break

chunking The process of taking single items of information and recoding them on the basis of similarity or other organising principle.

How can you put chunking to good use while listening to a lecture?

# WORKING MEMORY

Our focus so far has been on short-term memory, and specifically the role that STM plays in the explicit acquisition of new memories. However, you need more memory resources on a moment-by-moment basis than those that allow you to acquire facts. For example, you also need to be able to retrieve pre-existing memories. At the start of this chapter, we asked you to commit a number to memory. Can you remember now what it was? If you can remember (if not, peek), you have made your mental representation of that memory active once more—that's another memory function. If we ask you to do something more complicated— suppose we ask you to toss a ball from hand to hand while you count backward by 3s from 132—you'll put even more demands on your memory resources.

Based on an analysis of the memory functions you require to navigate through life, researchers have articulated theories of **working memory**—the memory resource that you use to accomplish tasks such as reasoning and language comprehension. Suppose you are trying to remember a phone number while you search for a pencil and pad to write it down. Whereas your short-term memory processes allow you to keep the number in mind, your more general working memory resource allows you to execute the mental operations to accomplish an efficient search. Working memory provides a foundation for the moment-by-moment fluidity of thought and action.

Theories of working memory often have as one component the 'classic' short-term memory. **Alan Baddeley** and his colleagues (Baddeley, 1986, 1992; Baddeley & Andrade, 2000) have provided evidence for three components of working memory:

- A *phonological loop*. This resource holds and manipulates speech-based information. The phonological loop overlaps most with short-term memory, as we have described it in the earlier sections. When you rehearse a telephone number by 'listening' to it as you run it through your head, you are making use of the phonological loop.

- A *visuospatial sketchpad*. This resource performs the same types of functions as the phonological loop for visual and spatial information. If, for example, someone asked you how many desks there are in your psychology classroom, you might use the resources of the visuospatial sketchpad to form a mental picture of the classroom and then estimate the number of desks from that picture.

- The *central executive*. This resource is responsible for controlling attention and coordinating information from the phonological loop and the visuospatial sketchpad. Any time you carry out a task that requires a combination of mental processes—imagine, for example, you are asked to describe a picture from memory—you rely on the central executive function to apportion your mental resources to different aspects of the task (we return to this idea in Chapter 8).

For a storage system to work efficiently, information has to be encoded, stored and retrieved. There also needs to be an 'executive' system that supervises and integrates all the other processes.

The incorporation of short-term memory into the broader context of working memory should help reinforce the idea that STM is not a place but a process. To do the work of cognition—to carry out cognitive activities like language processing or problem solving—you must bring a lot of different elements together in quick succession. You can think of working memory as short-term special focus on the necessary elements. If you wish to get a better look at a physical object, you can shine a brighter light on it; working memory shines a brighter mental light on your mental objects—your memory representations. Working memory also coordinates the activities required to take action with respect to those objects.

Researchers have demonstrated that working memory capacity differs among individuals. They have devised several procedures to measure those differences (Conway et al., 2005). We will give you an example of one of those measures, which is called *working memory span*. Unlike standard short-term memory tasks, your working memory span is measured by asking you to remember something while doing something else with your cognitive processes. For example, researchers may ask participants to read aloud a series of sentences and then recall the final words. We've given you some sentences to try in **Table 7.1**. It's really not so easy! People are usually considered to be *high span* if they can recall 4 or more words and *low span* if they recall 2.5 or fewer—notice this is much smaller than the usual estimate of short-term memory capacity, as the task is much harder. These are averages across several trials and sets of sentences, so you shouldn't take too seriously your results from one attempt at Table 7.1.

Read these sentences aloud, and then (without looking back) try to recall the final words of each sentence.

Because working memory span is a measure of the resources individuals have available to carry out short-term cognitive processes, researchers can use it to predict performance on a variety of tasks. For example, working memory allows individuals to bring together pieces of information and combine them into more complex memory representations. In general, the greater

**working memory** A memory resource that is used to accomplish tasks such as reasoning and language comprehension.

**Table 7.1**

A test for working memory span

> Read these sentences aloud and then (without looking back) try to recall the final words of each sentence.
>
> He had patronised her when she was a schoolgirl and teased her when she was a student.
>
> He had an elongated skull which sat on his shoulders like a pear on a dish.
>
> The products of digital electronics will play an important role in your future.
>
> The taxi turned up Michigan Avenue where they had a clear view of the lake.
>
> When at last his eyes opened, there was no gleam of triumph, no shade of anger.

Daneman & Carpenter, 1980.

For answers go to MyPsychLab!

the working memory capacity, the more information individuals should be able to integrate.

Researchers identified groups of individuals with low and high working memory capacity (von Hecker & Dutke, 2004). Each participant was asked to carry out a task in which they tried to piece together the overall social structure of a group—they tried to determine, for example, how many cliques there were within the group. The information participants used to find this structure were reports of pairwise relationships such as 'Bob has a positive relationship with Paul.' Participants were given 7 seconds to consider each relationship. After viewing all the information, participants attempted to provide a graph representing what they understood the structure of the groups to be. The researchers measured how often those graphs represented correct relationships—the highest possible score on this measure was 60. On average, individuals with high working memory capacity recalled about 48 pairs correctly; individuals with low working memory capacity recalled 38 pairs correctly.

This experiment confirmed the expectation that higher working memory capacity allows individuals more ability to integrate separate pieces of information. Experiments that measure working memory capacity help define the ways in which different individuals expend their memory resources.

A final note on working memory: working memory helps maintain your psychological present. It is what sets a context for new events and links separate episodes together into a continuing story. It enables you to maintain and continually update your representation of a changing situation and to keep track of topics during a conversation. All of this is true because working memory serves as a conduit for information coming and going to long-term memory. Let's turn our attention now to the types of memories that can last a lifetime.

# LONG-TERM MEMORY: ENCODING AND RETRIEVAL

How long can memories last? At the chapter's outset, we asked you to recall your own earliest memory. How old is that memory? Fifteen years? Twenty years? Longer? When psychologists speak of *long-term memory*, it is with the knowledge that memories often last a lifetime. Therefore, whatever theory explains how memories are acquired for the long term must also explain how they can remain accessible over the life course. **Long-term memory (LTM)** is the storehouse of all the experiences, events, information, emotions, skills, words, categories, rules and judgments that have been acquired from sensory and short-term memories. LTM constitutes each person's total knowledge of the world and of the self.

You may have noticed that it is easier to understand a class if the teacher tells you in advance what the main objectives are for the session. This is because you have a framework for understanding the incoming information. In this section of the book, our objective is to explain that your ability to remember will be greatest when there is a good match between the circumstances in which you encoded information and the circumstances in which you attempt to retrieve it. We will see over the next several sections what it means to have a 'good match'.

## RETRIEVAL CUES

To begin our exploration between encoding and retrieval, let's consider this general question: How do you 'find' a memory? The basic answer is that you use retrieval cues. **Retrieval cues** are the stimuli available as you search for a particular memory. These cues may be provided externally, such as questions on a quiz ('What memory principles do you associate with the research of Sternberg and Sperling?'), or generated internally ('Where have I met her before?').

Each time you attempt to retrieve an explicit memory, you do so for some purpose, and that purpose often supplies the retrieval cue. It won't surprise you that memories can be easier or harder to retrieve depending on the quality of the retrieval cue. If a friend asks you, 'Who's the one Roman emperor I can't remember?' you're likely to be involved in a guessing game. If she asks instead, 'Who was the emperor after Claudius?' you can immediately respond 'Nero'.

To give you a full sense of the importance of retrieval cues, we will attempt to replicate classic memory experiments by asking you to learn some word pairs. Keep working at it until you can go through the six pairs three times in a row without an error.

Apple–Boat

Hat–Bone

Bicycle–Clock

Mouse–Tree

Ball–House

Ear–Blanket

Now that you've committed the pairs to memory, we want to make the test more interesting. We need to do something to give you a *retention interval*—a period of time over which you must keep the information in memory. Let's spend a moment, therefore, discussing some of the procedures we might use to test your memory.

You might assume that you either know something or you don't and that any method of testing what you know will give the same results. Not so. Let's consider two tests for explicit memory, recall and recognition.

**Recall and recognition** When you **recall**, you reproduce the information to which you were previously exposed. 'What is an axon?' is a recall question. **Recognition** refers to the realisation that a certain stimulus event is one you have seen or heard before. 'Which is the term for a visual sensory memory: (1) echo; (2) engram; (3) icon; or (4) abstract code?' is a recognition question, as the correct answer is available to you, you only have to choose it. You can relate recall and recognition to your day-to-day experiences of explicit memory. When trying to identify a criminal, the police would be using a recall method if they asked the victim to describe, from memory, some of the perpetrator's distinguishing features: 'Did you notice anything unusual about the attacker?' They would be using the recognition method if they showed the victim photos, one at a time, from a file of criminal suspects or if they asked the victim to identify the perpetrator in a police lineup.

Let's now use these two procedures to test you on the word pairs you learned a few moments ago. What words finished the pairs?

Hat–?          Bicycle–?          Ear–?

Can you select the correct pair from these possibilities?

| Apple–Baby | Mouse–Tree | Ball–House |
|---|---|---|
| Apple–Boat | Mouse–Tongue | Ball–Hill |
| Apple–Bottle | Mouse–Tent | Ball–Horn |

Was the recognition test easier than the recall test? It should be. Let's try to explain this result with respect to retrieval cues.

Both recall and recognition require a search using cues. The cues for recognition, however, are much more useful. For recall, you have to hope that the cue alone will help you locate the information. For recognition, part of the work has been done for you. When you look at the pair *Mouse–Tree*, you only have to answer yes or no to 'Did I have this experience?' rather than, in response to *Mouse—?* 'What was the experience I had?' In this light, you can see that we made the recognition test reasonably easy for you. Suppose we had given you, instead, recombinations of the original pairs. Which of these are correct?

Hat–Clock          Ear–Boat

Hat–Bone          Ear–Blanket

Now you must recognise not just that you saw the word before, but that you saw it in a particular context. (We will return to the idea of context shortly.) If you are a veteran of difficult multiple-choice exams, you have come to learn how tough even recognition situations can be. However, in most cases, your recognition performance will be better than your recall because retrieval cues are more straightforward for recognition. Let's look at some other aspects of retrieval cues.

**long-term memory (LTM)** Memory processes associated with the preservation of information for retrieval at any later time.

**recall** A method of retrieval in which an individual is required to reproduce the information previously presented.

**recognition** A method of retrieval in which an individual is required to identify stimuli as having been experienced before.

**retrieval cues** Internally or externally generated stimuli available to help with the retrieval of a memory.

**Episodic and semantic memories** We have already made a pair of distinctions about types of memories. You have implicit and explicit memories and declarative and procedural memories. We can define another dimension along which declarative memories differ with respect to the cues that are necessary to retrieve them from memory. Canadian psychologist **Endel Tulving** (1972) first proposed the distinction between *episodic* and *semantic* types of declarative memories.

**Episodic memories** preserve, individually, the specific events or episodes that you have experienced. For example, memories of your happiest birthday or of your first kiss are stored in episodic memory. To recover such memories, you need retrieval cues that specify something about the time at which the event occurred and something about the content of the events. If you were asked what you had for breakfast yesterday, you would probably retrieve the answer by thinking about what you were doing: whether you ate at the table or on the train, whether you had to be at uni early or not, and any number of other things that are not about breakfast itself, but about the events and experiences surrounding yesterday's breakfast, Depending on how the information has been encoded, you may or may not be able to produce a specific memory representation for an event. For example, do you have any specific memories to differentiate the tenth time ago you brushed your teeth from the eleventh time ago?

Everything you know, you began to acquire in some particular context. However, there are large classes of information that, over time, you encounter in many different contexts. These classes of information come to be available for retrieval without reference to their multiple times and places of experience. These **semantic memories** are generic, categorical memories, such as the meanings of words and concepts. For most people, facts like the formula $E = MC^2$ and the capital of France don't require retrieval cues that make reference to the episodes, the original learning contexts, in which the memory was acquired.

Of course, this doesn't mean that your recall of semantic memories is foolproof. You know perfectly well that you can forget many facts that have become dissociated from the contexts in which you learned them. A good strategy when you can't recover a semantic memory is to treat it like an episodic memory again. You will have been in examinations when an item of semantic knowledge has been hard to retrieve, and you might have gone back to episodic cues to attempt to retrieve it, thinking things like 'I studied it last week—after band practice and before Rob came over. It's in my yellow study notebook, near the bottom of the page…'

## CONTEXT AND ENCODING

To continue our exploration of encoding and retrieval, we want you to consider a phenomenon that you might call 'context shock'. You see someone across a crowded room, and you know that you know the person but you just can't place her. Finally, after staring for longer than is entirely polite, you remember who it is—and you realise that the difficulty is that the person is in the wrong context. What is the woman who delivers your mail doing at your best friend's party? Whenever you have this type of experience, you have rediscovered the principle of **encoding specificity**: memories emerge most efficiently when the context of retrieval matches the context of encoding. Let's see how researchers have demonstrated that principle.

### Encoding specificity
What are the consequences of learning information in a particular context? Endel Tulving and Donald Thomson (1973) first demonstrated the power of encoding specificity by reversing the usual performance relationship between recall and recognition.

Participants were asked to learn pairs of words like *train–black*, but they were told that they would be responsible for remembering only the second word of the pair. In a subsequent phase of the experiment, participants were asked to generate four free associates to words like *white*. Those words were chosen so that it was likely that the original to-be-remembered words (like *black*) would be among the associates. The participants were then asked to check off any words on their associates lists that they recognised as to-be-remembered words from the first phase of the experiment. They were able to do so 54 percent of the time. However, when the participants were later

Events of personal importance, like seeing a relative or good friend for the first time after a year's separation, are retained in *episodic* memory. What types of information from *semantic* memory might contribute to a reunion?

semantic memories Generic, categorical memories, such as the meanings of words and concepts.

episodic memories Long-term memories for autobiographical events and the contexts in which they occurred.

encoding specificity The principle that subsequent retrieval of information is enhanced if cues received at the time of recall are consistent with those present at the time of encoding.

given the first words of the pair, like *train*, and asked to recall the associate, they were 61 percent accurate. In other words, directly contrary to what we have said above, this experiment seemed to produce conditions where participants were more able to recall the words than to recognise them.

Why was recall better than recognition? Tulving and Thomson suggested that what mattered was the change in context. After the participants had studied the word *black* in the context of *train*, it was hard to recover the memory representation when the context was changed to *white*. Given the significant effect of even these minimal contexts, you can anticipate that richly organised real-life contexts would have an even greater effect on your memory.

Researchers have been able to demonstrate rather remarkable effects of context on memory. In one experiment, scuba divers learned lists of words either on a beach or underwater. They were then tested for retention of those words, again in one of those two contexts. Performance was nearly 50 percent better when the context at encoding and recall matched—even though the material had nothing at all to do with water or diving (Gooden & Baddeley, 1975). Similarly, people performed better on memory tasks when the tempo of background music remained the same between encoding and recall (Balch & Lewis, 1996).

> ### Your secret weapons for success at university
> It is because we know that recall is better when there is a match of conditions between study and test, that most school and university student counsellors advise students to study under conditions that come close to matching the conditions of testing— that is, you should study, if possible, in a quiet, well-lit room, sitting at an uncluttered desk on a firm upright chair. This maximises the potential overlap between study conditions and examination conditions, and therefore allows you to use encoding specificity to your advantage.

Memory performance has also been shown to be much improved when the smell of chocolate was present at both encoding and recall (Schab, 1990). This research on context-dependent memory with odours has been extended to suggest that the odour must be *distinctive* in the environment.

What odours are sufficiently distinctive to foster context-dependent memories? A pair of experiments used a scent *novel* for the participants (*osmanthus*, 'an unusual, Asian, floral-fruity scent'; Herz, 1997, p. 375), a familiar scent that was *inappropriate* for a research laboratory (*peppermint)*, and a familiar scent *appropriate* for the laboratory (*clean fresh pine*). The hypothesis tested was that only the two odours that called attention to themselves in the environment—by virtue of being novel or inappropriate—would be used for encoding. The results supported this prediction.

Although the encoding and retrieval sessions were 48 hours apart, participants were able to remember reliably more words (from a 20-item list) when the odour in the laboratory room was the same at retrieval as at encoding—but only for osmanthus and peppermint (Herz, 1997).

These studies suggest that not all environmental odours are sufficiently distinctive to provide context for memory encoding. What is distinctive, of course, will vary from context to context. In a candy shop, peppermint might lose its power as a distinctive element of the context.

**The serial position effect** We can also use changes in context to explain one of the classic effects in memory research: the **serial position effect**. Suppose we required you to learn a list of unrelated words. If we asked you to recall those words in order, your data would almost certainly conform to the pattern shown in **Figure 7.5**: you would do very well on the first few words (the **primacy effect**) and very well on the last few words (the **recency effect**) but rather poorly on the middle part of the list. Figure 7.5 shows the generality of this pattern when students are asked to try to remember word lists of varying lengths (6, 10 and 15 words) using either *serial recall* ('Recite the words in the order you heard them') or *free recall* ('Recite as many words as you can') (Jahnke, 1965). Researchers have found primacy and recency in a wide variety of test situations (Neath & Surprenant, 2003). What day is it today? Do you believe that you would be almost a second faster to answer

After receiving a traffic infringement warning from these officers, why might you not recognise them if you ran into them at a party?

**serial position effect** A characteristic of memory retrieval in which the recall of beginning and end items on a list is often better than recall of items appearing in the middle.

**primacy effect** Improved memory for items at the start of a list.

**recency effect** Improved memory for items at the end of a list.

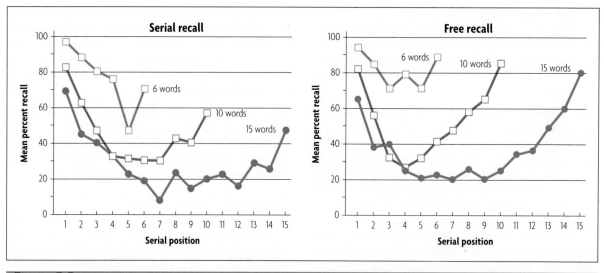

**Figure 7.5**

**The serial position effect**
This figure shows the generality of the serial position effect. Students were asked to try to remember word lists of varying lengths (6, 10 and 15 words) using either *serial recall* ('Recite the words in the order you heard them') or *free recall* ('Recite as many words as you can'). Each curve shows better memory for both the beginning (the *primacy* effect) and end (the *recency* effect) of the list.

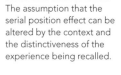

**contextual distinctiveness**
The assumption that the serial position effect can be altered by the context and the distinctiveness of the experience being recalled.

this question at the beginning or end of the week than in the middle (Koriat & Fischoff, 1974)?

The role context plays in producing the shape of the serial position curve has to do with the **contextual distinctiveness** of different items on a list, different experiences in your life, and so on (Neath et al., 2006). To understand contextual distinctiveness, you can ask the question, 'How different were the contexts in which I learned this information from the context in which I will

try to recall it?' Let's focus on recency. **Figure 7.6** is a visual representation of distinctiveness. Imagine, in part A, that you are looking at train tracks. What you can see is that they look as if they clump together at the horizon—even though they are equally spaced apart. We could say that the nearest tracks stand out most—are most distinctive— from your context. Imagine now that you are trying to remember the last 10 movies you've seen. The movies are like the train tracks. Under most circumstances, you

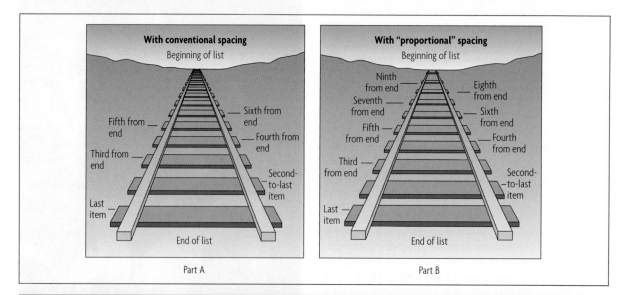

**Figure 7.6**

**Contextual distinctiveness**
You can think of items you put into memory as train tracks. In part A, you can imagine that memories farther back in time become blurred together, just like train tracks in the distance.

In part B, you see that one way to combat this effect is to make the earlier tracks physically farther apart, so the distances look proportional. Similarly, you can make early memories more distinctive by moving them apart psychologically.

should remember the last movie best because you share the most overlapping context with the experience—it is 'closest' to the context of your current experiences. This logic suggests that 'middle' information will become more memorable if it is made more distinctive. The idea with respect to our analogy, as shown in part B of Figure 7.6, is to make the train tracks seem equally far apart.

> To make the train tracks seem evenly spaced, engineers would have to make the more distant ones actually be farther apart. Researchers have used the same logic for a memory test, by exploiting the analogy between space and time. They had participants try to learn lists of letters, but they manipulated how far apart in time the letters were made to seem. This manipulation was accomplished by asking participants to read out some number of random digits that appeared on a computer screen between the letters. In the *conventional* condition (like part A of Figure 7.6), each pair of letters was separated by two digits. In the *proportional* condition (like part B), the first pair had four digits and the last pair had zero digits; this should have the effect of making the early digits more distinctive, just like moving distant train tracks farther apart. Participants, in fact, showed better memory for early items on the list when those items had been made more separate (Neath & Crowder, 1990).

This experiment suggests that the standard recency effect arises because the last few items are almost automatically distinctive. The same principle may explain primacy—each time you begin something new, your activity establishes a new context. In that new context, the first few experiences are particularly distinctive. Thus you can think of primacy and recency as two views of the same set of train tracks—one from each end!

## THE PROCESSES OF ENCODING AND RETRIEVAL

We have seen so far that a match between the context of encoding and of retrieval is beneficial to good memory performance. We will now refine this conclusion somewhat by considering the actual processes that are used to get information to and from long-term memory. We will see that memory functions best when encoding and retrieval processes make a good match as well.

Levels of processing Let's begin with the idea that the type of processing you perform on information—the type of attention you pay to information at time of encoding—will have an influence on your memory for the information. **Levels-of-processing theory** suggests that the deeper the level at which information was processed, the more likely it is to be committed to memory (Craik & Lockhart, 1972; Lockhart & Craik, 1990). If processing involves more analysis, interpretation, comparison and elaboration, it should result in better memory. This is advice that we often give to students—they should read for meaning and understanding, rather than just skimming the words on the page.

The depth of processing is often defined by the judgments participants are required to make when they first process material to be remembered. Consider the word *GRAPE*. We could ask you to make a physical judgment—is the word in capital letters? Or a rhyme judgment—does the word rhyme with *tape*? Or a meaning judgment—does the word represent a type of fruit? Do you see how each of these questions requires you to think a little bit more deeply about *GRAPE*? In fact, the deeper the original processing participants carry out, the more words they remember (Lockhart & Craik, 1990).

A difficulty of the levels-of-processing theory, however, is that researchers have not always been able to specify exactly what makes certain processes 'shallow' or 'deep.' Even so, results of this sort confirm that the way in which information is committed to memory—the mental processes that you use to encode information—has an effect on whether you can retrieve that information later. However, so far we have discussed only explicit memory. We will now see that the match between processes at encoding and retrieval is particularly critical for implicit memory.

Processes and implicit memory Earlier, we defined the explicit versus implicit dimension for memories as a distinction that applies both at encoding and at retrieval (Bowers & Marsolek, 2003). Under many circumstances, for example, you will retrieve implicit memories that you originally encoded intentionally. This is true when you greet your best friend by name without having to expend any particular mental effort. Even so, implicit memories are often most robust when there is a strong match between the processes at implicit encoding and the processes at implicit retrieval. This perspective is called **transfer-appropriate processing**: Memory is best when the type of processing carried out at encoding *transfers* to the processes required at retrieval (Roediger et al., 2002). To support this perspective, we will first describe some of the methodologies that are used to demonstrate implicit memories. Then we will show how the match between encoding and retrieval processes matters.

Let's consider a typical experiment in which implicit memory is assessed. The researchers presented students with lists of concrete nouns and asked them to judge the pleasantness of each word on a 1 (least pleasant) to 5 (most pleasant) scale (Rajaram & Roediger, 1993). The pleasantness ratings required participants to think about the meaning of a word without explicitly committing it to memory. After this study phase, participants' memory was assessed using one of four implicit memory tasks (suppose that a word on one list was *unicorn*):

- *Word fragment completion.* The participant is given fragments of a word, like___ni___or___, and asked to complete the fragments with the first word that comes to mind.
- *Word stem completion.* The participant is asked to complete a stem, like *uni_____*, with the first word that comes to mind.

**transfer-appropriate processing** The perspective that suggests that memory is best when the type of processing carried out at encoding matches the processes carried out at retrieval.

**levels-of-processing theory** A theory that suggests that the deeper the level at which information was processed the more likely it is to be retained in memory.

- *Word identification.* Words are flashed on a computer screen in such a fashion that participants cannot see them clearly. They must try to guess each word that is flashed. In this case, one of the words would be *unicorn.*

- *Anagrams.* Participants are given a scrambled word, like *corunni,* and asked to give the first unscrambled word that comes to mind.

Just like our example with *unicorn,* correct responses to each of the tasks can be provided by words from the earlier lists. What is critical, however, is that the experimenters have not called attention to the relationship between the words on the earlier list and appropriate responses on these new tasks—that's why the use of memory is implicit.

To assess the degree of implicit memory, the researchers compared the performance of participants who had seen a particular word, like *unicorn,* on the pleasantness lists with those who had not. **Figure 7.7** plots the improvement brought about by implicit memory for a word—percentage correct when the word had appeared on the participant's list minus percentage correct when it had not. (Different participants experienced different word lists.) You can see that for each task there was an advantage to having seen a word before, even though participants had been asked only to say whether the word had a pleasant meaning. This advantage is known as **priming** because the first experience of the word *primes* memory for later experiences. For some memory tasks, like word fragment completion, researchers have found priming effects lasting a week and beyond (Sloman et al., 1988).

**priming** In the assessment of implicit memory, the advantage conferred by prior exposure to a word or situation.

Let's turn now to the nature of the match between encoding and retrieval. The four implicit memory tests we've mentioned so far all rely on a *physical* match between the original stimulus and the information given at test. In a sense, whatever processes allow you to encode *unicorn* also make that word available when you are asked to complete the stem *uni_____,* and so on. We can, however, introduce another test, *general knowledge,* that relies on *meaning* or *concepts* instead of on a physical match. Imagine we gave you the question, 'What mythological creature had a single horn?' You might very well say *unicorn.* However, if you became more likely to say unicorn because you had seen the word on an earlier list, in a different context, that would be evidence of implicit memory.

Using two different types of implicit memory tests based on priming—by physical features or by meaning—we can look for a relationship between encoding and retrieval.

Memory researchers designed a levels-of-processing experiment to demonstrate that different implicit memories rely on different types of processes. Participants were asked to respond to each word on a list. For *deep* judgments, they responded to the words' meanings—for example, 'Can you buy this?' For *shallow* judgments, they responded to the words' physical features—for example, 'Does this word contain a 'c'?' The researchers assessed implicit memory by using general knowledge questions and word fragment completion. Let's examine the tasks with an eye to transfer-appropriate processing. The deep judgments engage conceptual processes at encoding, but the shallow judgments do not. The general knowledge questions engage conceptual processes at retrieval, but word fragment completion does not. Accordingly, the researchers predicted that they should find a priming advantage for deep judgments when processes at encoding and retrieval matched (deep judgments with general knowledge questions) than when they mismatched (deep judgments with fragment completion). The results confirmed the prediction (Hamilton & Rajaram, 2001).

This type of research supports the idea of transfer-appropriate processing: if you use a certain type of processing—for example, physical or meaning analysis—to encode information, you will retrieve that information most efficiently when the processing uses the same type of analysis.

Earlier we made this assertion: your ability to remember will be greatest when there is a good match between the circumstances in which you encode information and the circumstances in which you attempt to retrieve it. This section provided the research evidence for this assertion. Note that this analysis defines both when your memory processes will function relatively well (i.e., when circumstances of encoding and retrieval match) and when those processes will function relatively less well (i.e., when there is a mismatch). In that sense, we've already provided you with some initial ideas about why you might

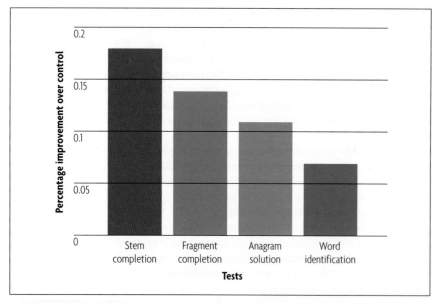

Figure 7.7

Priming on implicit memory tests

Priming indicates improvement on the various tasks over performance on control words. Some implicit memory tests demonstrate that priming can last a week or more.

Adapted with permission from Table 1 in 'Direct Comparison of Four Implicit Memory Tests' by Suparna Rajaram & H.L. Roediger III.

not be capable of retrieving memories when you need them. Let's now look more generally at circumstances in which your memory processes fall short.

## WHY WE FORGET

Much of the time, your memory works just fine. You see a new acquaintance walking toward you, and you retrieve her name from memory without hesitation. Unfortunately, every once in a while, you end up greeting her in awkward silence—with that awful realisation that you can't remember her name. How does that happen? Sometimes the answer can be provided by the processes we've already discussed. It could be the case, for example, that you're trying to recall the name in a context that's very different from the one in which you learned it. However, researchers have studied other explanations for forgetting. In fact, the earliest formal body of research on memory, published in 1885, focused directly on that topic. Let's begin with that work.

### Ebbinghaus quantifies forgetting

See if this statement rings true: 'Facts crammed at examination time soon vanish, if they were not sufficiently grounded by other study and later subjected to a sufficient review.' In other words, if you cram for a test, you're not likely to remember very much a few days later. This astute, and very contemporary, observation was made in 1885 by the German psychologist Hermann Ebbinghaus who outlined a series of such phenomena to motivate his new science of memory. Ebbinghaus's observations added up to a convincing argument in favour of an empirical investigation of memory. What was needed was a methodology, and Ebbinghaus invented a brilliant one. Ebbinghaus used nonsense syllables—meaningless three-letter units consisting of a vowel between two consonants, such as *CEG* or *DAX*. He used nonsense syllables, rather than meaningful words, like DOG, because he hoped to obtain a 'pure' measure of memory—one uncontaminated by previous learning or associations that a person might bring to the experimental memory task. Not only was Ebbinghaus the researcher, he was also his own subject. He performed the research tasks himself and measured his own performance. The task he assigned himself was memorisation of lists of varying length. Ebbinghaus chose to use *rote learning*, memorisation by mechanical repetition, to perform the task.

Ebbinghaus started his studies by reading through the items one at a time until he finished the list. Then he read through the list again in the same order, and again, until he could recite all the items in the correct order—the *criterion performance*. Then he distracted himself from rehearsing the original list by forcing himself to learn many other lists. After this interval, Ebbinghaus measured his memory by seeing how many trials it took him to *relearn* the original list. If he needed fewer trials to relearn it than he had needed to learn it initially, information had been *saved* from his original study. (This concept should be familiar from Chapter 6. Recall that there is often a savings when animals relearn a conditioned response.)

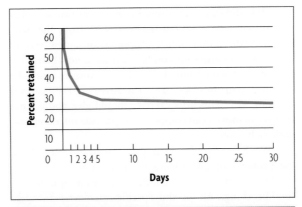

### Figure 7.8

Ebbinghaus's forgetting curve
The curve shows how many nonsense syllables are remembered by individuals using the savings method when tested over a 30-day period. The curve decreases rapidly and then reaches a plateau of little change.

For example, if Ebbinghaus took 12 trials to learn a list and 9 trials to relearn it several days later, his savings score for that elapsed time would be 25 percent (12 trials − 9 trials = 3 trials; 3 trials ÷ 12 trials = 0.25, or 25 percent). Using savings as his measure, Ebbinghaus recorded the degree of memory retained after different time intervals. The curve he obtained is shown in **Figure 7.8**. As you can see, he found a rapid initial loss of memory, followed by a gradually declining rate of loss.

You have experienced the pattern revealed in Ebbinghaus's forgetting curve countless times in your life. Consider, for example, how you'd feel about taking an exam a week, or a fortnight, or a month after you studied for it. You know from experience that much of what you learned will no longer be accessible. Similarly, you might find it easy to recall a name right after you've learned it, but if a week goes by when you don't use it, you might find yourself thinking, 'I know I knew her name!'

### Interference

Why else might you forget a name that you knew a week ago? One important answer is that you didn't learn that name in isolation. Before you learned it, you had lots of other names in your head; after you learned it, you probably acquired a few more new ones. All those other names can have a negative impact on your ability to retrieve the one name you need in the moment. To make this point more formally, we want you to try to learn some new word pairs. Once again, keep working on these word pairs until you can repeat them three times in a row without an error.

Apple–Robe

Hat–Circle

Bicycle–Roof

Mouse–Magazine

Ball–Baby

Ear–coin

How did it go? Examine the list. You can see what we've done—we've paired the first word from the pairs we gave you earlier in the chapter with a new second word. Was it harder for you to learn these new pairs? Do you think it would now be harder for you to recall the old ones? (Go ahead and try.) The answer in both cases is typically 'yes'. This brief exercise should give you a sense of how memories can compete—or provide *interference*—with each other.

We have already given you a real-life example of the problem of interference when we asked you to try to differentiate your recollections of your episodes of toothbrushing. All of the specific memories interfere with each other. **Proactive interference** (*proactive* means 'forward acting') occurs when information you have acquired in the past makes it more difficult to acquire new information (see **Figure 7.9**). **Retroactive interference** (*retroactive* means 'backward acting') occurs when the acquisition of new information makes it harder for you to remember older information. The word lists we've provided demonstrate both of these types of interference. You've also experienced both proactive and retroactive interference if you've ever changed your phone number. At first, you probably found it hard to remember the new number—the old one kept popping out (proactive interference). However, after finally being able to reliably reproduce the new one, you may have found yourself unable to remember the old number—even if you had used it for years (retroactive interference).

**proactive interference**
Circumstances in which past memories make it more difficult to encode and retrieve new information.

**retroactive interference**
Circumstances in which the formation of new memories makes it more difficult to recover older memories.

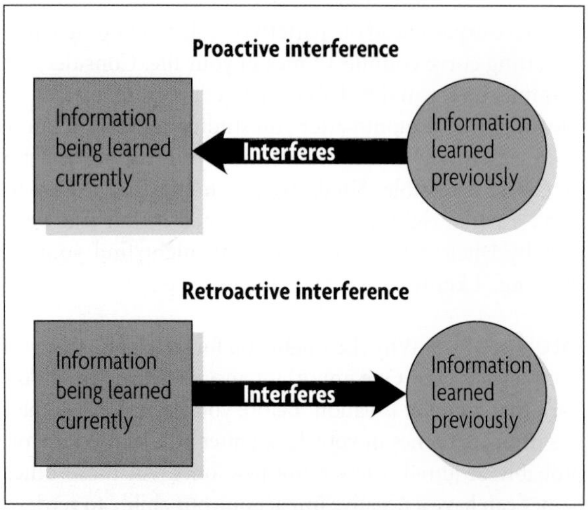

As with many other memory phenomena, Hermann Ebbinghaus was the first researcher to document interference rigorously through experiments. Ebbinghaus, after learning dozens of lists of nonsense syllables, found himself forgetting about 65 percent of the new ones he was learning. Fifty years later, students at Northwestern University who studied Ebbinghaus's lists had the same experience—after many trials with many lists, what the students had learned earlier interfered proactively with their recall of current lists (Underwood, 1948, 1949).

In this section, we've suggested some reasons why you might forget information. It seems fitting that we move now to research that gives advice on how to make memory function better.

# IMPROVING MEMORY FOR UNSTRUCTURED INFORMATION

After reading this whole section, you should have some concrete ideas about how you could improve your everyday memory performance—how you can remember more and forget less. (The Critical Thinking in Your Life box, later in the chapter, will help you solidify those ideas with respect to school work.) You know, especially, that you're best off trying to recover a piece of information in the same context, or by performing the same types of mental tasks, as when you first acquired it. But there's a slightly different problem with which we still must give you some help. It has to do with encoding unstructured or arbitrary collections of information.

For example, imagine that you are working as a sales assistant in a store. You must try to commit to memory the several items that each customer wants: 'The woman in the green blouse wants hedge clippers and a garden hose. The man in the blue shirt wants a pair of pliers, six quarter-inch screws, and a paint scraper.' This scenario, in fact, comes very close to the types of experiments in which researchers ask you to memorise paired associates. How did you go about learning the word pairs we presented earlier? The task probably was somewhat of a chore because the pairs were not particularly meaningful for you—and information that isn't meaningful is hard to remember. To find a way to get the right items to the right customer, you need to make associations seem less arbitrary. Let's explore *elaborative rehearsal* and *mnemonics*.

**Elaborative rehearsal** A general strategy for improving encoding is called **elaborative rehearsal**. The basic idea of this technique is that while you are rehearsing information—while you are first committing it to memory—you elaborate on the material to enrich the encoding. One way to do this is to invent a relationship that makes an association seem less arbitrary. For example, if you wanted to remember the pair *Mouse–Tree*, you might conjure up an image of a mouse scurrying up a tree to look for cheese. Recall is enhanced when you encode separate bits of information into this type of miniature story line. Can you imagine, in the sales assistant situation, swiftly making up a story to link each customer with the appropriate items?

## Figure 7.9

**Proactive and retroactive interference**
Proactive and retroactive interference help explain why it can be difficult to encode and retrieve memories. What you have learned in the past can make it more difficult for you to encode new information (proactive interference). What you are learning now can make it more difficult for you to retrieve old information (retroactive interference).

From Robert A. Baron, *Psychology*, 5e, p. 225. Published by Allyn & Bacon, Boston, MA. Copyright © 2001 by Pearson Education. Reprinted by permission of the publisher.

**elaborative rehearsal**
A technique for improving memory by enriching the encoding of information.

How might a waiter or waitress use elaborative rehearsal or mnemonics to get the right meals to the right customers?

The *peg-word method* is similar to the method of loci, except that you associate the items on a list with a series of cues rather than with familiar locations. Typically, the cues for the peg-word method are a series of rhymes that associate numbers with words. For example, you might memorise 'one is a *bun*,' 'two is a *shoe*,' 'three is a *tree*,' and so on. Then you would associate each item on your list interacting with the appropriate cue. Suppose a history lecturer asked you to memorise, in order, the rulers of the Roman Empire. You might have Augustus eating a platter of buns, Tiberius wearing oversized shoes, Caligula sitting in a tree, and so on. You can see that the key to learning arbitrary information is to encode the information in such a fashion that you provide yourself with efficient retrieval cues.

**mnemonics** Strategies or devices that use familiar information during the encoding of new information to enhance subsequent access to the information in memory.

(It will work with practice.) You may have already guessed that it is also often helpful to supplement your story line with a mental picture—a visual image—of the scene you are trying to remember. Visual imagery can enhance your recall because it gives you codes for both verbal and visual memories simultaneously (Paivio, 1995).

Elaborative rehearsal can also help save you from what has been called the *next-in-line effect*: when, for example, people are next in line to speak, they often can't remember what the person directly before them said. If you've ever had a circle of people each give his or her name, you're probably well acquainted with this effect. What was the name of the person directly in front of you? The origin of this effect appears to be a shift in attention toward preparing to make your own remarks or to say your own name (Bond et al., 1991). To counter this shift, you should use elaborative rehearsal. Keep your attention focused on the person in front of you and enrich your encoding of his or her name: '*Erin*—I can't help st-*erin* at her'.

**Mnemonics** Another memory-enhancing option is to draw on special mental strategies called *mnemonics* (from the Greek word meaning 'to remember'). **Mnemonics** are devices that encode a long series of facts by associating them with familiar and previously encoded information. Many mnemonics work by giving you ready-made retrieval cues that help organise otherwise arbitrary information.

Consider the *method of loci*, first practised by ancient Greek orators. The singular of *loci* is *locus*, and it means 'place'. The method of loci is a means of remembering the order of a list of names or objects—or, for the orators, the individual sections of a long speech—by associating them with some sequence of places with which you are familiar. To remember a grocery list, you might mentally put each item sequentially along the route you take to get from home to school. To remember the list later, you mentally go through your route and find the item associated with each spot (see **Figure 7.10**).

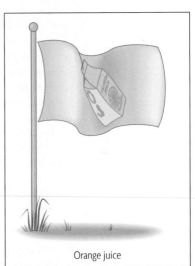

Bread

Orange juice

Ice cream

Bananas

**Figure 7.10**

**The method of loci**

In the method of loci, you associate the items you wish to remember (such as the items on a grocery list) with locations along a familiar path (such as your route to and from school).

# CRITICAL THINKING *in your life*

## HOW CAN MEMORY RESEARCH HELP YOU PREPARE FOR EXAMS?

One important use of critical thinking is to apply new knowledge to your life's important tasks. As you read about memory, you should ask yourself questions of this sort: 'How can I put the information to immediate use? How will this research help me prepare for my next exam?' Let's see what advice can be generated from this type of critical thinking:

- *Encoding specificity*. As you'll recall, the principle of encoding specificity suggests that the context of retrieval should match the context of encoding. In school settings, 'context' often will mean 'the context of other information'. If you always study material in the same context, you may find it difficult to retrieve it in a different context—so, if a lecturer's questions approach a topic in a slightly unusual way, you might be entirely at a loss. As a remedy, you should change contexts even while you study. Rearrange the order of your notes. Ask yourself questions that mix different topics together. Try to make your own novel combinations. But if you get stuck while you're taking an exam, try to generate as many retrieval cues as you can that reinstate the original context: 'Let's see. We heard about this in the same lecture we learned about short-term memory . . .'

- *Serial position*. You know from the serial position curve that, under very broad circumstances, information presented in the 'middle' is least well remembered. In fact, students fail more exam items on material from the middle of a lecture than on material from the start or end of the lecture (Holen & Oaster, 1976; Jensen, 1962). When you're listening to a lecture, you should remind yourself to pay special attention in the middle of the session. When it comes time to study, you should devote some extra time and effort to that material—and make sure not to study the material in the same order each time. You might also note that the chapter you're reading now is about at the middle of *Psychology and Life*. If you have a final examination that covers all the course material, you're going to want to make an especially careful review of this chapter.

- *Elaborative rehearsal and mnemonics*. Sometimes when you study for exams, you will feel as if you are trying to acquire 'unstructured information'. You might, for example, be asked to memorise the functions of different parts of the brain. Under these circumstances, you need to find ways to provide the structure yourself. Try to form visual images or make up sentences or stories that use the concepts in creative ways. One of your authors still remembers his mnemonic from Introductory Psychology to remember the function of the *ventromedial hypothalamus*, which is often abbreviated VMH: Very Much Hungry (however, as you will learn in Chapter 11, research in the 30 intervening years has made that mnemonic less accurate). Elaborative rehearsal allows you to use what you know already to make new material more memorable.

- *Metamemory*. Research on metamemory suggests that people generally have good intuitions about what they know and what they don't know. If you are in an exam situation in which there is time pressure, you should allow those intuitions to guide how you allocate your time. You might, for example, read the whole test over quickly and see which questions give you the strongest feelings-of-knowing. If you are taking an exam on which you lose points for giving wrong answers, you should be particularly attentive to your metamemory intuitions, so you can avoid answering those questions on which you 'sense' you are most likely to be incorrect.

As you read the basic facts from memory research, you might not have immediately seen how to put the information to use. We've given you these concrete ideas so you can see how critical thinking will allow you to apply psychological knowledge directly to your life.

- Why might it be a good idea to shuffle your notes before you study for an exam?

- What could a lecturer do to help students overcome the impact of serial position on lecture material?

# METAMEMORY

Suppose you're in a situation in which you'd really like to remember something. You're doing your best to use retrieval cues that reflect the circumstances of encoding, but you just can't get the bit of information to emerge. Part of the reason you're expending so much effort is that you're sure that you are in possession of the information. But are you correct to be so confident about the contents of your memory? Questions like this one—about how your memory works or how you know what information you possess—are questions of **metamemory**. One major question on metamemory has been when and why *feelings-of-knowing*—the subjective sensations that you do have information stored in memory—are accurate.

Research on feelings-of-knowing was pioneered by **J. T. Hart** (1965), who began his studies by asking students a series of general knowledge questions. Suppose, for example, we asked you, 'What planet is the largest in our solar system?' Do you know the answer? If you don't, how would you respond to this question: 'Even though I don't remember the answer now, do I know the answer to the extent that I could pick the correct answer from among several wrong answers?' This was the question Hart put to his participants. He allowed them to give ratings from 1, to say they were quite sure they wouldn't choose correctly on the multiple choice, to 6, to say they were quite sure they would choose correctly. What would your rating be? Now here are your alternatives:

a. Pluto
b. Venus
c. Earth
d. Jupiter

If you made an accurate feeling-of-knowing judgment, you should have been less likely to get the correct answer, d, if you gave a 1 rating than if you gave a 6. (Of course, to have a fair test, we'd want to give you a long series of questions.) Hart found that when participants gave 1 ratings, they answered the questions correctly only 30 percent of the time, whereas 6 ratings predicted 75 percent success. That's pretty impressive evidence that feelings-of-knowing can be accurate.

Research on metamemory focuses on both the processes that give rise to feelings-of-knowing and on how their accuracy is ensured (Benjamin, 2005; Koriat & Levy-Sadot, 2001; Metcalfe, 2000):

- The *cue familiarity hypothesis* suggests that people base their feelings-of-knowing on their familiarity with the retrieval cue. Suppose you were asked, 'What is the last name of the poet who wrote 'I love a sunburnt country…?' If you have prior familiarity with the poem 'My Country' you might think that you probably would be able to recognise the correct alternative when given the multiple choice.
- The *accessibility hypothesis* suggests that people base their judgments on the accessibility, or availability, of partial information from memory. Thus, if the question 'poet who wrote, "I love a sunburnt country…"?' calls quite easily to mind information you believe to be related to the correct answer, you are likely to think that you will be able to recognise the correct answer as well.

Both of these theories have obtained empirical support—and both suggest that you can generally trust your instincts when you believe that you know something. (Later in the chapter, we will describe research on eyewitness testimony, which provides some exceptions to this general rule.)

You have now learned quite a bit about how you get information in and out of memory. You know what we mean by a 'good match' between the circumstances of encoding and of retrieval. In the next section, we will shift our focus from your memory processes to the content of your memories.

**metamemory** Implicit or explicit knowledge about memory abilities and effective memory strategies; cognition about memory.

## RECAP CHECKPOINT

### Long-term memory: encoding and retrieval

- Long-term memory (LTM) constitutes your total knowledge of the world and of yourself. It is nearly unlimited in capacity.
- Your ability to remember information relies on the match between circumstances of encoding and retrieval.
- Retrieval cues allow you to access information in LTM.
- Episodic memory is concerned with memory for events that have been personally experienced. Semantic memory is memory for the basic meaning of words and concepts.
- Similarity in context between learning and retrieval aids retrieval.
- The serial position curve is explained by distinctiveness in context.
- Information processed more deeply is typically remembered better.
- For implicit memories, it is important that the processes of encoding and retrieval be similar.
- Ebbinghaus studied the time course of forgetting.
- Interference occurs when retrieval cues do not lead uniquely to specific memories.
- Memory performance can be improved through elaborative rehearsal and mnemonics.

- In general, feelings-of-knowing accurately predict the availability of information in memory.

## CONCEPT QUESTIONS

1. Do circumstances of recall or recognition generally provide more retrieval cues?

2. At a party, why might you have the best recall of the first person to whom you spoke?

3. What does the perspective known as transfer-appropriate processing suggest?

4. For your English class, you memorise Hamlet's soliloquy. When you're done, you can no longer recite the poem you learned last week. Is this an example of proactive or retroactive interference?

5. How could you use the method of loci to remember the order of elements in the periodic table?

6. What two types of information contribute to feelings of knowing?

## CRITICAL THINKING

Recall the experiment in which odours served as memory cues. How could the experimenter know which odours were novel, appropriate and inappropriate?

**concepts** Mental representations of kinds or categories of items and ideas.

For answers go to MyPsychLab!

# STRUCTURES IN LONG-TERM MEMORY

In most of our examples so far, we have asked you to try to acquire and retrieve isolated or unrelated bits of information. What you mostly have represented in memory, however, are large bodies of *organised knowledge*. Recall, for example, that we asked you to consider whether *grape* is a fruit. You could say *yes* very quickly. How about *porcupine*? Is it a fruit? How about *tomato*? In this section, we will examine how the difficulty of these types of judgments relates to the way information is structured in memory. We will also discuss how memory organisation allows you to make a best guess at the content of experiences you can't remember exactly.

## MEMORY STRUCTURES

An essential function of memory is to draw together similar experiences, to enable you to discover patterns in your interactions with the environment. (Recall a similar description, in Chapter 4, on the functions of perception.) You live in a world filled with countless individual events, from which you must continually extract information to combine them into a smaller, simpler set that you can manage mentally. But apparently you don't need to expend any particular conscious effort to find structure in the world. Just as we suggested when we defined the incidental acquisition of memories, it's unlikely that you ever formally thought to yourself something like, 'Here's the shape of a Give Way sign'. It is through ordinary experience in the world that you have acquired mental structures to mirror environmental structures. Let's look at the types of memory structures you have formed in your moment-by-moment experience of the world.

**Categories and concepts** We will begin by previewing one of the topics we will discuss in Chapter 10—the mental effort a child must go through to acquire the meaning of a word, such as *doggie*. For this word to have meaning, the child must be able to store each instance in which the word *doggie* is used, as well as information about the context. In this way, the child finds out what common core experience—a furry creature with four legs—is meant by *doggie*. The child must acquire the knowledge that *doggie* applies not just to one particular animal, but to a *whole category* of creatures. This ability to categorise individual experiences—to take the same action toward them or give them the same label—is one of the most basic abilities of thinking organisms (Murphy, 2002).

The mental representations of the categories you form are called **concepts**. The concept *doggie*, for example, names the set of mental representations of experiences of dogs that a young child has gathered together in memory. (As we will see in Chapter 10, if the child hasn't yet refined his or her meaning for *doggie*, the concept might also include features that adults wouldn't consider to be appropriate.) You have acquired a vast array of concepts. You have categories for *objects* and *activities*, such as *sheds* and *cricket*. Concepts may also represent *properties*, such as *red* or *large*; *abstract ideas*, such as *truth* or *love*; and *relations*, such as *smarter than* or *sister of*. Each concept represents a summary unit for your experience of the world.

As you consider the many categories you experience in the world, you will recognise that some category members are more or less typical. You can develop this intuition if you think about a category like *bird*. You would probably agree that a robin is a typical bird, whereas an emu or a penguin is atypical. The degree of typicality of a category member has real-life consequences. Classic research has shown, for example, that people respond more quickly to typical members of a category than to its more unusual ones. Your reaction time to determine that a robin is a bird would be quicker than your reaction time to determine that a penguin is a bird (Rosch et al., 1976). But what makes people consider a robin to be a typical bird, rather than an emu? Answers to this question have often focused on *family resemblance*—typical category members have attributes that overlap with many other members of the category (Rosch & Mervis, 1975). Robins have most of the attributes you associate with birds—they are about the right size, they fly, and so on. Emus, by contrast, are unusually large and they do not fly. These examples suggest that family resemblance plays a role in judgments of typicality. However, recent research suggests that the most typical category members are also the *ideal* category members.

A team of researchers recruited individuals from two communities who had several decades of fishing experience: One group was Native American Menominee Indians from northern central Wisconsin; the second group was European Americans from roughly the same geographical location (Burnett et al., 2005). The experiment used these two groups because they differ with respect to the species of fish they consider to be most desirable or ideal. For example, the Menominee people consider sturgeon to be sacred. The researchers presented the participants with a group of 44 cards printed with the names of local fish. Participants sorted these cards into groups—the researchers used the participants' verbal justifications (e.g., 'good eating') for which fish they grouped together as an index of desirability. Also, the participants rated the extent to which each species was a good example of the 'fish' category. The researchers found a 0.80 correlation between desirability and typicality. (Recall from Chapter 2 that correlations range from —1.0 to + 1.0.) That's impressive evidence that the participants' notions of the 'ideal' fish played a role in their judgments of typicality. In addition, the ratings were influenced by cultural differences in desirability. For example, the Menominee group rated sturgeon as even more typical than did the European–American group.

If you don't have a lot of fishing experience, you might have less of a sense than these participants did about which fish are desirable. However, you can think about

How does the formation of categories—such as what constitutes a healthy head of lettuce, a sweet strawberry, or a tasty tomato—help you make daily decisions such as what to buy for dinner?

categories with which you have a lot of experience to see how your notions of what is ideal inform your judgments about what is typical.

**Basic levels and hierarchies** Concepts, and their prototypes, do not exist in isolation. As shown in **Figure 7.11**, concepts can often be arranged into meaningful organisations. A broad category like *animal* has several subcategories, such as *bird* and *fish*, which in turn contain exemplars such as *canary, ostrich, shark* and *salmon*. The animal category is itself a subcategory of the still larger category of *living beings*. Concepts are also linked to other types of information: You store the knowledge that some birds are *edible*, some are *endangered*, some are *birds of prey*.

There seems to be a level in such hierarchies at which people best categorise and think about objects. This has been called the **basic level** (Rosch, 1973, 1978). For example, when you buy an apple at the grocery store, you could think of it as a *piece of fruit*—but that seems imprecise—or a *Golden Delicious*—but that seems too specific or narrow. The basic level is just *apple*. If you were shown a picture of such an object, that's what you'd be likely to call it. You would also be faster to say that it was an apple than that it was a piece of fruit (Rosch, 1978). The basic level emerges through your experience of the world. You are more likely to encounter the term *apple* than its more or less specific alternatives. If you became an apple grower, however, you might find yourself having daily conversations about *Pink Ladies* or *Granny Smiths*. With those experiences, your basic level would probably shift lower in the hierarchy.

**Schemas** We have seen that concepts are the building blocks of memory hierarchies. They also serve as building blocks for more complex mental structures. Imagine that you are staying in a holiday house that you have never been in before. You want to make a sandwich and you need to look for bread, margarine, jam and the like. You probably wouldn't start looking in the laundry—you'd go straight to the kitchen. Then, when you were in the kitchen, you'd look for the margarine in the fridge, not the microwave. This is because, even though this house is new to you, you have been in enough houses to have in mind a general idea of a house. Nested within that general idea of a house, you have a general idea of a kitchen. An important task of our memory system is to generalise from millions of isolated examples into a single organising concept that 'makes sense' of particular experiences or events. In this example, you have developed a single representation that combines the individual concepts of a kitchen—your knowledge about ovens, sinks and refrigerators—into a larger unit. We call that larger unit a schema. **Schemas** are conceptual frameworks, or clusters of knowledge, regarding objects, people and situations. Schemas are 'knowledge packages' that encode complex generalisations about your experience of the structure of the environment. You have schemas for kitchens and bedrooms, race car drivers and teachers, surprise parties and formals. In later chapters, we'll provide

**basic level** The level of categorization that can be retrieved from memory most quickly and used most efficiently.

**schemas** General conceptual frameworks or clusters of knowledge regarding objects, people and situations.

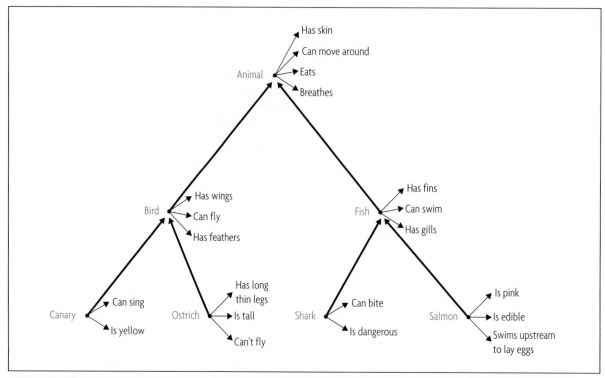

**Figure 7.11**

**Hierarchically organised structure of concepts**
The category *animal* can be divided into subcategories such as *bird* and *fish*; similarly, each subcategory can be further divided. Some information (such as '*has skin*') applies to all concepts in the hierarchy; other information (such as '*can sing*') applies only to concepts at lower levels (for example, a *canary*).

more illustrations of the types of schemas that shape your day-to-day experiences. For example, in Chapter 10 we'll see that the attachment relationships children form with their parents provide schemas for later social interactions. In Chapter 13, we'll see that you possess a *self-schema*—a memory structure that allows you to organise information about yourself.

One thing you may have guessed is that your schemas do not include all the individual details of all your varied experiences. A schema represents your average experience of situations in the environment. Thus your schemas are not permanent but shift with your changing life events. Your schemas also include only those details in the world to which you have devoted sufficient attention. For example, what appears on the *tails* side of a five-cent coin? You may have thought 'An echidna', but is there anything else? You probably didn't think to mention the number 5, because that has not been the focus of your attention since you were very young and had no other way of knowing the value of coins. Similarly American students appeared to 'forget' the word *Liberty*, which appears on every coin (Rubin & Kontis, 1983). Thus your schemas provide an accurate reflection of what you've *noticed* about the world. Let's now look at all the ways in which you use your concepts and schemas.

**Using memory structures** Let's consider some instances of memory structures in action. To begin, consider

the picture in part A of **Figure 7.12**. What is it? Although we purposely chose an unusual member of the category, you probably reached the conclusion 'It's a chair' with reasonable ease. However, to do so, you needed to draw on your memory representations of members of that category. You can say 'It's a chair' because the object in the figure calls to mind your past experiences of chairs.

Researchers have provided two theories of how people use concepts in memory to categorise the objects they encounter in the world. One theory suggests that, for each concept in memory, you encode a **prototype**—a representation of the most central or average member of a category (Rosch, 1978). On this view, you recognise objects by comparing them to prototypes in memory. Because the picture in part A of Figure 7.12 matches many of the important attributes of the prototype in part B, you can recognise the picture as a chair.

An alternative theory suggests that people retain memories of the many different **exemplars** they experience for each category. In part C of Figure 7.12, we give you a subset of the exemplars of chairs you might have seen. On the exemplar view, you recognise an object by comparing it to the exemplars you have stored in memory. You recognise the picture as a chair because it is similar to several of those exemplars. Researchers have conducted a large number of studies to test between prototype and exemplar accounts of categorisation. The data largely support the exemplar view: people appear to categorise

**prototype** The most representative example of a category.

**exemplars** Members of categories that people have encountered.

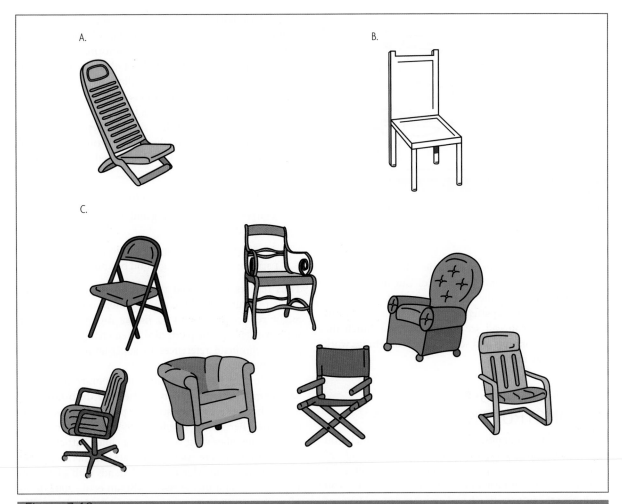

Figure 7.12

**Theories of categorisation**
A. What is this unusual object? B. One theory suggests that you categorise this object as a chair by comparing it to a single prototype stored in memory. C. An alternative theory suggests that you categorise this object by comparing it to the many exemplars you have in memory.

the objects they encounter by comparing them to multiple representations in memory (Nosofsky & Stanton, 2005; Smits et al., 2002).

We intended the picture in Figure 7.12 to be an unusual chair but clearly a chair nonetheless. However, as we saw in Chapter 4, sometimes the world provides ambiguous stimuli—and you use prior knowledge to help interpret those stimuli. Do you remember **Figure 7.13**? Do you see a duck or a rabbit? Let's suppose we give you the expectation that you're going to see a duck. If you match the features of the picture against the features of a duck present in exemplars in memory, you're likely to be reasonably content. The same thing would happen if we told you to expect a rabbit. You use information from memory to generate—and confirm—expectations.

As we've previously noted, memory representations also allow you to understand when something is unusual in the world. Suppose that in the holiday house example from earlier the fridge did happen to be in the laundry. You would have to learn to override your 'house' schema

and look in the laundry for margarine. You would probably also remember the house as 'the house with the fridge in the laundry' and that unusual fact would make this house memorable even after many holidays at more 'schema-consistent' houses. In one study, researchers illustrated that schema-inconsistent information is more memorable by filling a graduate student office with both typical objects (e.g., notebook, pencil) and atypical objects (e.g., harmonica, toothbrush) (Lampinen et al., 2001). Participants spent 1 minute in the room. In a later phase of the experiment, participants indicated which items on a list had been present in the room. Their memory was consistently more accurate for the atypical items than for the typical items. In addition, the participants were likely to have more specific memories of having seen the atypical items, whereas their memories for the typical items were based more on a general sense of familiarity. This study illustrates how memory structures direct your attention to unusual aspects of a scene.

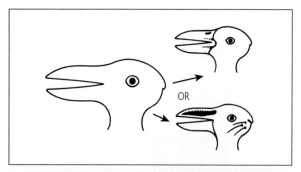

**Figure 7.13**

Recognition illusion
Duck or rabbit?

Taken together, these examples demonstrate that the availability of memory structures can influence the way you think about the world. Your past experiences colour your present experiences and provide expectations for the future. You will see shortly that, for much the same reasons, concepts and schemas can sometimes work against accurate memory.

## REMEMBERING AS A RECONSTRUCTIVE PROCESS

Let's turn now to another important way in which you use memory structures. In many cases, when you are asked to remember a piece of information, you can't remember the information directly. Instead, you *reconstruct* the information based on more general types of stored knowledge. To experience **reconstructive memory**, consider this trio of questions:

- Did Chapter 3 have the word *the* in it?
- Did 1991 contain the day July 7?
- Did you breathe yesterday between 2:05 and 2:10 p.m.?

You probably were willing to answer 'Yes!' to each of these questions without much hesitation, but you almost certainly don't have specific, episodic memories to help you (unless, of course, something happened to fix these events in memory—perhaps July 7 is your birthday or you crossed out all the *the*'s in Chapter 3 to curb your boredom). To answer these questions, you must use more general memories to reconstruct what is likely to have happened. Let's examine this process of reconstruction in a bit more detail.

**The accuracy of reconstructive memory** If people reconstruct some memories, rather than recovering a specific memory representation for what happened, then you might expect distortions—or occasions on which the reconstructed memory differed from the real occurrence. One of the most impressive demonstrations of memory distortions is also the oldest. In his classic book *Remembering: A Study in Experimental and Social Psychology* (1932),

**Sir Frederic Bartlett** undertook a program of research to demonstrate how individuals' prior knowledge influenced the way they remembered new information. Bartlett studied the way British undergraduates remembered stories whose themes and wording were taken from another culture. His most famous story was 'The War of the Ghosts', an American Indian tale.

Bartlett found that his readers' reproductions of the story were often greatly altered from the original. The distortions Bartlett found involved three kinds of reconstructive processes:

- *Levelling*—simplifying the story.
- *Sharpening*—highlighting and overemphasising certain details.
- *Assimilating*—changing the details to better fit the participant's own background or knowledge.

Thus readers reproduced the story with words familiar in their culture taking the place of those unfamiliar: *Boat* might replace *canoe* and *go fishing* might replace *hunt seals*. Bartlett's participants also often changed the story's plot to eliminate references to supernatural forces that were unfamiliar in their culture.

Following Bartlett's lead, contemporary researchers have demonstrated a variety of memory distortions that occur when people use constructive processes to reproduce memories (Bergman & Roediger, 1999). How, for example, do you remember what you did as a child? Participants in one experiment were asked to indicate whether, before the age of 10, they had 'Met and shook hands with a favourite TV character at a theme resort' (Braun et al., 2002, p. 7). After answering that question—as part of a larger life-experiences inventory—some of the participants read an advertisement for Disneyland that evoked the idea of a family visit: 'Go back to your childhood . . . and remember the characters of your youth, Mickey, Goofy, and Daffy Duck'. Later the ad described circumstances in which the visitor was able to shake hands with a childhood hero: 'Bugs Bunny, the character you've idolised on TV, is only

Suppose, while you were at this dinner party, someone told you the man in the middle was a millionaire. How would this affect your memories of his actions at the party? What if you had been told he only had delusions of being a millionaire?

**reconstructive memory**
The process of putting information together based on general types of stored knowledge in the absence of a specific memory representation.

234 **CHAPTER 7** MEMORY

several feet away. . . . You [reach up] to grab his hand' (p. 6). After reading this type of ad, participants were now more likely to indicate—though they hadn't before—that they shook a character's hand. Moreover, they were more likely to report a specific memory that they had shaken Bugs Bunny's hand at Disneyland: 16 percent of the participants in this advertisement group remembered having done so versus 7 percent of the participants in a group that hadn't read the autobiographical ad. Of course, none of these memories can be accurate: Bugs Bunny isn't a Disney character!

This study suggests how even memories for your own life events are reconstructed from various sources. The study also illustrates the fact that people with no reason to consciously distort or misrepresent their recollection are not always accurate at recalling the original sources for various components of their memories (Mitchell & Johnson, 2000). In fact, researchers have demonstrated that individuals will sometimes come to believe that they actually carried out actions that they, in fact, only accomplished in their imaginations.

A group of 210 students participated in an experiment that had three sessions. In session 1, the students sat at a table that was covered with an array of objects. The researcher read statements to the students that described actions that could be carried out with the objects. Some of those actions were ordinary (e.g., flip the coin) and some were bizarre (e.g., sit on the dice). The students were asked actually to perform half of the actions (both ordinary and bizarre), but they were asked only to imagine performing the rest. Session 2 took place 24 hours later. In that second session, the students were asked only to imagine performing actions—including some from the day before—up to five times. In session 3, which took place two weeks after session 2, the students were asked to think back to the first session. They were asked to recall whether they had actually performed each action or only imagined doing it. For both ordinary and bizarre actions, the same rule held true: the more times in session 2 the students had imagined carrying out an action, the more likely they were to remember actually having performed the action—even when they never had done so (Thomas & Loftus, 2002).

Can you find applications of this result in your own life? Suppose you keep reminding yourself to set your alarm clock before you go to bed. Each time you remind yourself, you form a picture in your head of the steps you must go through. If you imagine setting the clock often enough, you might mistakenly come to believe that you actually did so! Of course, the opposite can also happen: have you ever been away from the house and suddenly wondered if you *really* turned off the iron, or just *thought* about doing it before you left? Sometimes that worry can be so strong that you might have gone all the way home, only to find that you really had turned it off. In this case, you have incorrectly 'forgotten' something that you have actually

very recently done. It is important to keep in mind, however, that just as in Chapter 4, when we discussed perceptual illusions, psychologists often infer the normal operation of processes by demonstrating circumstances in which the processes lead to errors. You can think of these memory distortions as the consequences of processes that usually work pretty well. In fact, a lot of the time, you don't need to remember the exact details of a particular episode. Reconstructing the gist of events will serve just fine. There is, however, at least one real-life domain in which you are always held responsible for *exactly* what happened. Let's turn now to eyewitness memory.

Eyewitness memory A witness in a courtroom swears 'to tell the truth and nothing but the truth'. Throughout this chapter, however, we have seen that whether a memory is accurate or inaccurate depends on the care with which it was encoded and the match of the circumstances of encoding and retrieval. Consider the cartoon of a crowd scene we asked you to examine earlier in the chapter. Without looking back, try to write down or think through as much as you can about the scene. Now turn back to p. 214. How did you do? Was everything you recalled accurate? Because researchers understand that people may not be able to report 'the truth', even when they genuinely wish to do so, they have focused a good deal of attention on the topic of *eyewitness memory*. The goal is to help the legal system discover the best methods for ensuring the accuracy of witnesses' memories.

Influential studies on eyewitness memory were carried out by **Elizabeth Loftus** (1979; Wells & Loftus, 2003) and her colleagues. The general conclusion from their research was that eyewitnesses' memories for what they had seen were quite vulnerable to distortion from *post event information*. For example, participants in one study were shown a film of an automobile accident and were asked to estimate the speeds of the cars involved (Loftus & Palmer, 1974). However, some participants were asked, 'How fast were the cars going when they smashed into each other?' while others were asked, 'How fast were the cars going when they contacted each other?' *Smash*

Why might the different words eyewitnesses use to describe an accident affect their later recall?

participants estimated the cars' speed to have been over 40 miles per hour [60 kilometres]; *contact* participants estimated the speed at 30 miles per hour [almost 50 kilometres]. About a week later, all the eyewitnesses were asked, 'Did you see any broken glass?' In fact, no broken glass had appeared in the film. However, about a third of the *smash* participants reported that there had been glass, whereas only 14 percent of the *contact* eyewitnesses did so. Thus post event information had a substantial effect on what eyewitnesses reported they had experienced.

This experiment represents what is probably the real-life experience of most eyewitnesses: After the events, they have a lot of opportunities to acquire new information that can interact with their original memories. In fact, Loftus and her colleagues demonstrated that participants often succumb to a *misinformation effect* (Loftus, 2005). For example, in one study participants watched a slide show of a traffic accident. They were then asked a series of questions. For half of the participants, one question was 'Did another car pass the red Datsun while it was stopped at the stop sign?' For the other half, the question read, 'Did another car pass the red Datsun while it was stopped at the yield sign?' The original slide show displayed a stop sign. Still, when participants were asked to recognise the original slide between options with a stop sign or a yield (Give Way) sign, those who had been asked about the stop sign were 75 percent correct, whereas those who had been asked about a yield sign were only 41 percent correct (Loftus et al., 1978). That's a large impact of misinformation.

> In one experiment, participants viewed a slide show of an office theft. The slide show was accompanied by a tape recording of a woman's voice describing the sequence of events. Immediately after the slide show, the participants heard the woman describe the events again. However, this post event narrative contained misinformation. For example, for participants who had seen *Glamour* magazine, the tape mentioned *Vogue* instead. Forty-eight hours later, the researcher tested his participants' memory for the information pictured in the slides, but he explicitly informed them that there was no question on the memory test for which the correct answer was mentioned in the post event narrative. Thus, if participants were able to make a clear distinction in memory between the original events and the post event information, they should have remained unaffected by that post event information. That was not the case. Even with fair warning, participants often recalled post event misinformation rather than real memories (Lindsay, 1990, reproduced with permission).

The participants had been unable to discriminate between the original sources—event or post event—of the memory representations. Researchers continue to refine their understanding of circumstances that lead eyewitnesses astray. They have demonstrated, for example, that misinformation has a greater impact when the source seems similar to the source of the original events—when sources are dissimilar, people can keep better track of what information emerged from each source (Lindsay et al., 2004). This type of result puts a limit on the extent to which eyewitness memories might be contaminated by other information.

We have now considered several important features of the encoding, storage and retrieval of information. In the final section of the chapter, we discuss the brain bases of these memory functions.

## RECAP CHECKPOINT
### Structures in long-term memory

- Concepts are the memory building blocks of thinking. They are formed when memory processes gather together classes of objects or ideas with common properties.
- Concepts are often organised in hierarchies, ranging from general, to basic level, to specific.
- Schemas are more complex cognitive clusters.
- All these memory structures are used to provide expectations and a context for interpreting new information.
- Remembering is not simply recording but is a constructive process.
- Past experiences affect what you remember.
- New information can bias your recall, making eyewitness memory unreliable when contaminated by post event input.

## CONCEPT QUESTIONS

1. What is the relationship between categories and concepts?

2. What claim is made by the exemplar theory of categorisation?

3. On Frederic Bartlett's account, what three processes create distortions in reconstructive memory?

4. How did Elizabeth Loftus and her colleagues demonstrate misinformation effects?

## CRITICAL THINKING

Recall the study that investigated the typicality of fish. Why might the researchers have used two groups from the same geographical region?

# BIOLOGICAL ASPECTS OF MEMORY

The time has come, once again, for us to ask you to recall the number you committed to memory at the beginning of the chapter. Can you still remember it? What was the point of this exercise? Think for a minute about biological aspects of your ability to look at an arbitrary piece of information and commit it instantly to memory. How can you do that? To encode a memory requires that you instantly change something inside your brain. If you wish to retain that memory for at least the length of a chapter, the change must have the potential to become permanent. Have you ever wondered how this is possible? Our excuse for having you recall an arbitrary number was

## PSYCHOLOGY in your life

### WHY DOES ALZHEIMER'S DISEASE AFFECT MEMORY?

In recent years, researchers have acquired a deeper understanding of how memories are formed in the brain. This knowledge has allowed for focused attention on *Alzheimer's disease*—a biological condition in which memory function gradually breaks down. This disease afflicts about 5 percent of Americans aged 65 to 74. Beyond age 65, the risk of the disease doubles every 5 years—it affects nearly 50 percent of individuals over 85 (National Institute on Aging, 2005). Alzheimer's disease onset is deceptively mild—in early stages the only observable symptom may be memory impairment. However, its course is one of steady deterioration. Individuals with Alzheimer's disease may show gradual personality changes, such as apathy, lack of spontaneity, and withdrawal from social interactions. In advanced stages, people with Alzheimer's disease may become completely mute and inattentive, even forgetting the names of their spouse and children.

The symptoms of Alzheimer's disease were first described in 1906 by the German psychiatrist Alois Alzheimer. In those earliest investigations, Alzheimer noted that the brains of individuals who had died from the disease contained unusual tangles of neural tissue and sticky deposits called plaques. Still, Alzheimer could not determine whether those brain changes were the cause of the disease or its products. (As you might recall from Chapter 2, correlation does not necessarily imply causation.) Only in the past 10 to 15 years have researchers been able to assemble the evidence that the plaques themselves cause the brain to deteriorate (Esler & Wolfe, 2001; Hardy & Selkoe, 2002). The plaques are formed from a substance called *amyloid β-peptide (Aβ)*. Ordinary processes in the human brain that aid in the growth and maintenance of neurons create $A\beta$ as a by-product. Normally, $A\beta$ dissolves in the fluid surrounding neurons, without any consequences. However, in Alzheimer's disease, $A\beta$ becomes deadly to neurons: $A\beta$ forms plaques and causes brain cells to self-destruct (Marx, 2001).

This understanding of the role of $A\beta$ in the progress of Alzheimer's disease has led to important recent breakthroughs. For example, researchers are beginning to improve their ability to diagnose the disease. As we will see in Chapter 10, human ageing is accompanied by some ordinary changes in memory function. To make a timely diagnosis of Alzheimer's disease, doctors need a way to determine whether older adults' memory impairments are something more than ordinary change. For most of the past 100 years that was a difficult task. Alzheimer's disease could be definitively diagnosed only when doctors could see the patients' brains—something that was not possible while the patients were living. However, researchers have begun to develop applications of PET scans (see Chapter 3) that enable them to detect the presence of $A\beta$ in the living brain (Helmuth, 2002). The key advance was the manufacture of a radioactive marker that attaches itself to the $A\beta$ plaques. This radioactive marker becomes visible through PET scans—providing a mechanism for early diagnosis of ominous patterns of $A\beta$ in the brain.

Early diagnosis would allow early treatment, with the goal of minimising the negative impact of the disease. Although scientists are pursuing a number of preventive measures and treatments, several lines of research once again focus on $A\beta$ (Travis, 2005). For example, researchers are seeking methods to interrupt the biochemical processes that produce $A\beta$ in the first place. They are also exploring techniques to destroy the $A\beta$ plaques once they have begun to form. Taken together, these approaches hold out great hope that Alzheimer's disease will be less devastating for future generations.

so that we could ask you to reflect on how remarkable the biology of memory really is. Let's take a closer look inside the brain.

## SEARCHING FOR THE ENGRAM

Let's consider your memory for the number 46 or, more specifically, your memory that the number 46 was the number we asked you to remember. How could we determine where in your brain that memory resides? **Karl Lashley** (1929, 1950), who performed pioneering work on the anatomy of memory, referred to this question as the search for the **engram**, the physical memory representation. Lashley trained rats to learn mazes, removed varying-size portions of their cortexes, and then retested their memories for the mazes. Lashley found that memory impairment from brain lesioning was proportional to the amount of tissue removed. The impairment grew worse as more of the cortex was damaged. However, memory was not affected by *where* in the cortex the tissue was removed. Lashley concluded that the elusive engram did not exist in any localised regions but was widely distributed throughout the entire cortex.

Perhaps Lashley could not localise the engram partly because of the variety of types of memories that are called into play even in an apparently simple situation. Remember that rats are trained to run mazes for a food reward, so maze learning, in fact, involves complex interactions of spatial, visual, and olfactory signals. Neuroscientists now believe that memory for complex sets of information is distributed across many neural systems, even though discrete types of knowledge are separately processed and localised in limited regions of the brain (Markowitsch, 2000; Rolls, 2000).

Four major brain structures are involved in memory:

- The *cerebellum*, essential for procedural memory, memories acquired by repetition, and classically conditioned responses.
- The *striatum*, a complex of structures in the forebrain; the likely basis for habit formation and for stimulus-response connections.
- The *cerebral cortex*, responsible for sensory memories and associations between sensations.
- The *amygdala* and *hippocampus*, largely responsible for declarative memory of facts, dates and names and also for memories of emotional significance.

Other parts of the brain, such as the thalamus, the basal forebrain and the prefrontal cortex, are involved also as way stations for the formation of particular types of memories (see **Figure 7.14**).

In Chapter 3, we focused directly on brain anatomy. Here, let's take a look at the methods that neuroscientists use to draw conclusions about the role of specific brain structures for memory. We will examine two types of research. First, we consider the insights generated by 'experiments of nature'—circumstances in which individuals who have suffered brain damage volunteer to further memory research. Second, we describe the ways in which researchers are applying new

**engram** The physical memory trace for information in the brain.

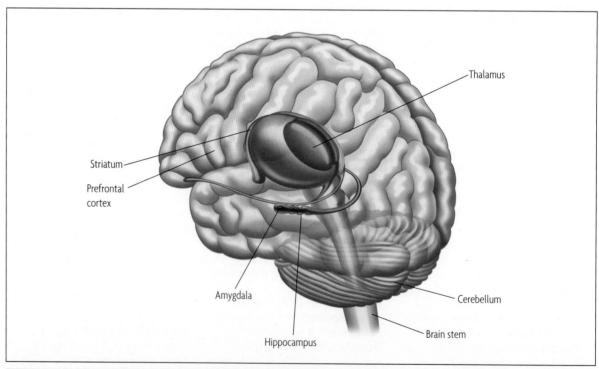

**Figure 7.14**

**Brain structures involved in memory**
This simplified diagram shows some of the main structures of the brain that are involved in the formation, storage and retrieval of memories.

brain-imaging techniques to improve their understanding of memory processes in the brain.

## AMNESIA

In 1960, Nick A., a young air force radar technician, experienced a freak injury that permanently changed his life. Nick had been sitting at his desk while his roommate played with a miniature fencing foil. Then, suddenly, Nick stood up and turned around—just as his buddy happened to lunge with the miniature sword. The foil pierced Nick's right nostril and continued to cut upwards and backwards into the left side of his brain. The accident left Nick seriously disoriented. His worst problem was **amnesia,** the failure of memory over a prolonged period. Because of Nick's amnesia, he forgets many events immediately after they happen. After he reads a few paragraphs of writing, the first sentences slip from his memory. He cannot remember the plot of a television show unless, during commercials, he actively thinks about and rehearses what he was just watching. However, Nick has perfectly normal recall of events up to, and including, his brain injury. His memory problem is marked by an almost total inability to learn any **new** information—existing memories, acquired before the injury, are still well preserved.

The particular type of amnesia from which Nick suffers is called *anterograde* amnesia. This means that Nick can no longer form explicit memories for events that occur after the time at which he suffered physical damage. Other patients suffer from *retrograde* amnesia. In those cases, brain damage prevents access to memories that preceded the moment of injury. If you've ever had the misfortune of receiving a sharp blow to the head (during, for example, a car crash), you're likely to have experienced retrograde amnesia for the events leading up to the accident.

Researchers are grateful to patients like Nick for allowing themselves to be studied as 'experiments of nature'. By relating the locus of brain injuries like Nick's to patterns of performance deficit, researchers have begun to understand the mapping between the types of memories we have introduced you to in this chapter and regions of the brain (O'Connor & Lafleche, 2005). Nick still remembers how to do things—his procedural knowledge appears to be intact even in the absence of declarative knowledge. So, for example, he remembers how to mix, stir and bake the ingredients in a recipe, but he forgets what the ingredients are.

The selective impairment of explicit memory of the sort demonstrated by Nick strongly suggests that different regions of the brain are involved for different types of encoding and retrieval. For that reason, damage to a single brain region may impair one memory process but not another. Researchers have demonstrated this type of dissociation by contrasting explicit and implicit uses of memory.

Fifteen amnesic and 12 control individuals participated in a study that assessed their explicit and implicit memory ability (Goshen-Gottstein et al.,

2000). In the experiment, the participants viewed word pairs such as *purse–sauce*. Their task was to create a meaningful sentence for each pair that kept the words in their original order (e.g., a participant might think, 'I filled the purse with sauce'). Later, the participants performed explicit and implicit memory tasks. For the explicit task, participants were again presented with pairs of words. They were asked to indicate whether they had previously seen both words from the pair. By comparison with the control individuals, the amnesiacs performed quite poorly on this explicit task. For the implicit memory task, the participants also saw pairs of words. However, in this case they were asked to indicate whether both letter strings were legitimate words in the English language. On this implicit task, amnesiacs performed as well as the controls. Although the amnesiacs couldn't explicitly remember that they had seen words like *purse* and *sauce* paired together, their earlier experience of creating sentences with the words still improved performance on the implicit task.

The knowledge that certain forms of brain damage selectively impair explicit but not implicit memory allows researchers to isolate the specific contributions of the two types of memory to encoding and retrieval. Consider, for example, the ways in which people form new verbal associations of the type conveyed in a sentence such as '*medicine* cured *hiccup*'. We know, because of the type of research we just described, that individuals with amnesia can acquire knowledge of individual words outside of explicit awareness—but can they also acquire knowledge of associations between words? One answer, from research with an individual known as C. V., whose amnesia stems from damage to the part of his temporal lobe called the medial temporal lobe, is no (Rajaram & Coslett, 2000). Although C. V. provided evidence of *perceptual* implicit memory, he provided no evidence of *conceptual* implicit memory (see page 223). This result suggests that, without explicit memory function, you cannot encode certain types of associations. Studies of this type allow researchers to gain a better understanding of both the brain bases of memory and the organisation of memory processes.

## BRAIN IMAGING

Psychologists have gained a great deal of knowledge about the relationship between anatomy and memory from the amnesic patients who generously serve as participants in these experiments. However, the advent of brain-imaging techniques has enabled researchers to study memory processes in individuals without brain damage (Nyberg & Cabeza, 2000). (You may want to review the section on imaging techniques in Chapter 3.) For example, using positron emission tomography (PET), Endel Tulving and his colleagues (Habib et al., 2003) have identified a difference in activation between the two brain hemispheres in the encoding and retrieval of episodic information. Their studies parallel standard memory studies, except that the participants' cerebral blood flow is monitored through PET scans during encoding or

**amnesia** A failure of memory caused by physical injury, disease, drug use, or psychological trauma.

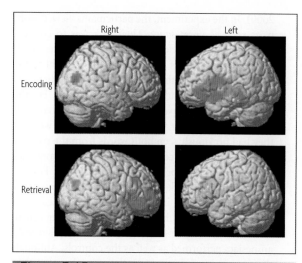

| | Right | Left |
|---|---|---|
| Encoding | | |
| Retrieval | | |

**Figure 7.15**

**Brain activity for encoding and retrieval**
The figure displays the regions of the brain that were most highly activated for encoding versus retrieval. The PET scans display disproportionately high brain activity in the left prefrontal cortex for the encoding of episodic information and in the right prefrontal cortex for the retrieval of episodic information.

Reprinted from *Trends in Cognitive Sciences*, 7(6), Reza Habib, Lars Nyberg, and Endel Tulving, 'Brain activity for encoding versus retrieval,' p. 241, Copyright © 2003, with permission from Elsevier.

retrieval. As you can see in **Figure 7.15**, these researchers discovered disproportionately high brain activity in the left prefrontal cortex for encoding of episodic information and in the right prefrontal cortex for retrieval of episodic information. Thus the processes show some anatomical distinctions in addition to the conceptual distinctions made by cognitive psychologists.

Research with functional magnetic resonance imaging (fMRI) has also provided remarkable detail about the way that memory operations are distributed in the brain. For example, studies with fMRI have begun to identify the specific brain regions that are activated when new memories are formed.

> One project examined the transfer of information from working memory to long-term memory (Ranganath et al., 2005). In the study, participants received 1-second views of line drawings of complex shapes. The researchers instructed the participants to form a vivid image of the shape so they could keep it in working memory across an interval of 7 to 13 seconds. At the end of that interval, participants were shown a second object and had to say whether it was a match or mismatch to the first. Throughout this period, participants were undergoing fMRI scans. After 128 trials, participants received a surprise test of long-term memory. They viewed a series of line drawings and attempted to say which had appeared in the matching trials and which had not. As you would expect, the participants got some items correct and some incorrect. The fMRI scans uncovered a fascinating pattern: when areas in the prefrontal cortex and hippocampus were more active at the time particular line drawings were initially encoded into working memory, participants were better able to recognise those line drawings; when those areas were relatively inactive at encoding, participants failed to recognise those line drawings.

We don't know exactly what participants did while viewing some of the line drawings that caused the brain to respond in a certain way. However, that type of brain response successfully predicted what participants would remember. This research captures the biological basis for the birth of new memories.

Historically, it has been difficult for researchers to obtain brain images of some of the most important subcortical regions involved in memory processes. For example, as you can see in Figure 7.15, the hippocampus is rolled into a small tight spiral deep within the brain. However, recent breakthroughs in fMRI have provided some of the first images of the particular regions of the hippocampus that are at work while people learn and recall new associations.

> While lying in an MRI device, participants took part in a memory experiment. The participants viewed pictures of strangers' faces paired with names (e.g., Janet). This task was meant to reflect the types of new associations between faces and names people need to learn in everyday life. The brain scans showed a remarkable pattern of activity (see **Figure 7.16**). One pair of regions within the hippocampus-areas two and three of the *cornu ammonis* (abbreviated CA23) and the *dentate gyrus* (DG)—showed a high level of activity during initial encoding. Once, however, the participants had learned the associations, these subregions became less active. Another subregion—known as the *subiculum*—became active just for the retrieval of the new associations between faces and names rather than for their encoding (Zeineh et al., 2003).

Unless you pursue studies in cognitive neuroscience, you needn't worry why it is that the *dentate gyrus* handles encoding and the *subiculum* handles retrieval. Instead, studies of this sort should give you a strong sense of the link between the memory processes labelled in cognitive psychological models (e.g., encoding and retrieval) and comparable operations in the brain.

The results from imaging studies illustrate why researchers from different disciplines must work closely together in the quest for a full understanding of memory processes. Psychologists provide the data on human performance that become fuel for neurophysiologists' detection of specialised brain structures. At the same time, the realities of physiology constrain psychologists' theories of the mechanisms of encoding, storage, and retrieval. Through shared effort, scientists in these fields of research provide great insight into the operation of memory processes.

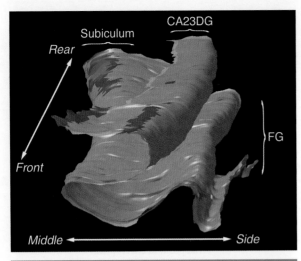

**Figure 7.16**

**Regions of the hippocampus involved in encoding and retrieval**

The regions shown in red—areas two and three of the *cornu ammonis* (CA23) and the *dentate gyrus* (DG)—are particularly active during encoding of new associations. The region shown in blue—the *subiculum*—is particularly active during recall. The region shown in purple—the *fusiform gyrus* (FG)—is active for both encoding and retrieval, which suggests that the activation is not related to learning or recall in particular.

Adapted with permission from M.M. Zeineh et al., 'Regions of the Hippocampus Involved in Encoding and Retrieval' *Science, 299,* 577–580, 2003. Copyright © 2003 AAAS.

## RECAP CHECKPOINT
### Biological aspects of memory

- Different brain structures (including the hippocampus, the amygdala, the cerebellum and the cerebral cortex) have been shown to be involved in different types of memories.

- Experiments with individuals with amnesia have helped investigators understand how different types of memories are acquired and represented in the brain.

- Brain-imaging techniques have extended knowledge about the brain bases of memory encoding and retrieval.

## CONCEPT QUESTIONS

1. What did Karl Lashley conclude about the location of the engram?

2. What has been learned about the impairment of implicit memory for individuals with amnesia?

3. What have PET studies indicated about the brain bases of encoding and retrieval of episodic information?

## CRITICAL THINKING

Recall the study that examined memory for line drawings. Why was it important that the test of long-term memory be a surprise to the participants?

For answers go to MyPsychLab!

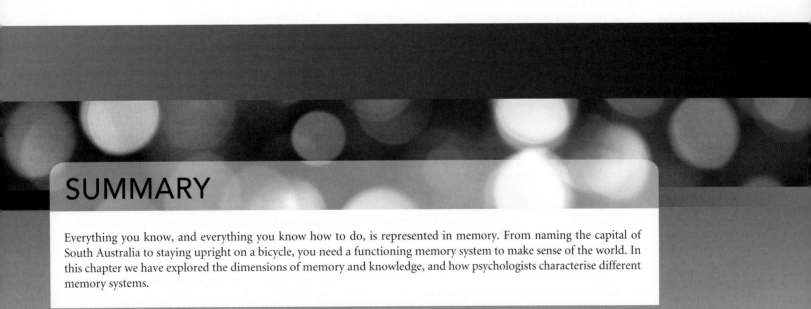

# SUMMARY

Everything you know, and everything you know how to do, is represented in memory. From naming the capital of South Australia to staying upright on a bicycle, you need a functioning memory system to make sense of the world. In this chapter we have explored the dimensions of memory and knowledge, and how psychologists characterise different memory systems.

# KEY TERMS

amnesia (p. 239)
basic level (p. 231)
chunking (p. 216)
concepts (p. 230)
contextual distinctiveness (p. 222)
declarative memory (p. 211)
elaborative rehearsal (p. 226)
encoding (p. 212)
encoding specificity (p. 220)
engram (p. 238)
episodic memories (p. 220)
exemplars (p. 232)
explicit uses of memory (p. 210)

iconic memory (p. 213)
implicit uses of memory (p. 210)
levels-of-processing theory (p. 223)
long-term memory (LTM) (p. 219)
memory (p. 210)
metamemory (p. 229)
mnemonics (p. 227)
primacy effect (p. 221)
priming (p. 224)
proactive interference (p. 226)
procedural memory (p. 211)
prototype (p. 232)
recall (p. 219)

recency effect (p. 221)
recognition (p. 219)
reconstructive memory (p. 234)
retrieval (p. 212)
retrieval cues (p. 219)
retroactive interference (p. 226)
schemas (p. 231)
semantic memories (p. 220)
serial position effect (p. 221)
short-term memory (STM) (p. 215)
storage (p. 212)
transfer-appropriate processing (p. 223)
working memory (p. 217)

# PRACTICE TEST

1. Early in the day, Toby passes a man selling oranges. Later, his mother asks him what he'd like to have as a snack. He says, 'I'd like an orange.' She asks him, 'Why an orange?' Toby replies, 'It's just what came to mind.' It sounds like this is a(n) _____ use of memory.
   a. explicit
   b. implicit
   c. procedural
   d. iconic

2. At her school's talent show, Noa answers questions about politics while spinning basketballs on her fingers. The question and answering mostly require _____memory, whereas the ball spinning mostly requires_____memory.
   a. implicit; procedural
   b. declarative; procedural
   c. procedural; declarative
   d. implicit; declarative

3. Which is the correct order of these processes?
   a. retrieval, encoding, storage
   b. encoding, retrieval, storage
   c. encoding, storage, retrieval
   d. storage, encoding, retrieval

4. To demonstrate the capacity of iconic memory, George Sperling showed that participants performed better with the _____procedure.
   a. whole-report
   b. procedural memory
   c. partial-report
   d. implicit memory

5. Mark looks a number up in a phone book but he forgets it before he has a chance to make the call. It sounds like Mark should have spent more effort on          .
   a. rehearsal
   b. chunking
   c. memory span
   d. iconic memory

6. Which of these is not a component of working memory?
   a. The iconic memory buffer
   b. The phonological loop
   c. The central executive
   d. The visuospatial sketchpad

7. Because of the usefulness of the retrieval cues, _____is usually easier than_____.
   a. recall; episodic memory
   b. recognition; recall
   c. semantic memory; recognition
   d. recall; recognition

8. After Meghan meets a group of people, she can only remember the name of the last person she met. This is an example of a(n) _____effect.
   a. primacy
   b. contextual distinctiveness
   c. encoding specificity
   d. recency

9. Consider the word *Wooloomooloo*. Which of these questions asks you to process that word at the deepest level of processing?
   a. How many times does the letter 'o' appear in the word?
   b. Is this word the name of a suburb?
   c. How many syllables does the word have?
   d. What is the word's first letter?

10. You've just memorised a list of nonsense words. You are going to try to recall the words every day for the next 30 days (without looking back at the list). You would expect to show the most forgetting between _____.
    a. day 1 and day 2
    b. day 3 and day 5
    c. day 5 and day 10
    d. day 10 and day 30

11. Pavel needs to learn the order of the planets with respect to their distance from the sun. To begin, he imagines Mercury as a giant bun and Venus shaped like a shoe. It sounds like Pavel is using
    a. the method of loci.
    b. the peg-word method.
    c. metamemory.
    d. iconic memory.

12. At the start of each exam, Sarah reads over the full set of questions to determine which ones she feels pretty sure she'll get right. To make these judgments, Sarah is using
    a. encoding specificity.
    b. mnemonics.
    c. elaborative rehearsal.
    d. metamemory.

13. Which of these is a term at the basic level of the category?
    a. animal
    b. shark
    c. fish
    d. canary

14. At the children's zoo, Tabitha sees a lamb and a platypus. When she gets home, Tabitha will probably find it easier to remember the_____because it was schema_____.
    a. platypus; inconsistent    c. platypus; consistent
    b. lamb; inconsistent    d. lamb; inconsistent

15. Which of these is *not* one of the reconstructive processes Sir Frederic Bartlett identified?
    a. sharpening    c. levelling
    b. assimilating    d. localising

16. In an experiment, participants watch a movie of a teenager driving through a orange light and swerving into a parked car. Which of these questions might the researcher use to demonstrate a misinformation effect?
    a. How fast was the car going when it went through the orange light?
    b. How fast was the car going when it hit the parked car?
    c. How fast was the car going when it went through the green light?
    d. How fast was the car going when it swerved into the parked car?

17. Karl Lashley carried out his search for the engram by training rats on mazes and then removing different amounts of the _____.
    a. cortex    c. striatum
    b. cerebellum    d. amygdala

18. Constantine suffers from amnesia. You would expect to find that his ability to acquire_____ memories is more impaired than his ability to acquire _____memories.
    a. declarative; explicit    c. implicit; procedural
    b. explicit; implicit    d. implicit; declarative

19. If you were asked to identify the brain bases of the encoding and retrieval of episodic memories, you should point to
    a. the striatum.    c. prefrontal cortex.
    b. the cerebellum.    d. the amygdala.

20. Alois Alzheimer was able to demonstrate that
    a. plaques in the brain caused Alzheimer's disease.
    b. amyloid -peptide caused Alzheimer's disease.
    c. plaques in the brain could be used to prevent Alzheimer's disease.
    d. people who died of Alzheimer's disease had plaques in their brains.

## Essay Questions

1. What are the relationships among encoding, storage, and retrieval?
2. What are the primary functions of working memory?
3. In what ways have brain-imaging techniques helped confirm some of the theoretical distinctions made by memory researchers?

# WEB LINKS

www.alzheimers.org.au/
Alzheimer's Australia

www.amnesia.com.au
Amnesia Group

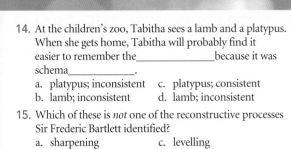

Are you ready for the test? MyPsychLab offers dozens of ways to deepen your understanding and test your recall of the material in this chapter—including video and audio clips, simulations and activities, self-assessments, practice tests and other study materials. Specific resources available for this chapter include:

Encoding, storage, and retrieval in memory
Key processes in stages of memory

Serial position curve
How good is your memory for stories?

Alzheimer's and dementia
Estrogen and memory
Memory hazards

To access MyPsychLab, please visit **www.pearsoned.com.au/mypsychlab**

# Can you think of the answers?

## NOW YOU HAVE READ CHAPTER 7—ARE YOU PREPARED FOR THE EXAM?

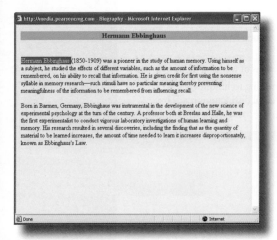

To enhance your understanding of any of the material in your *Psychology and Life* textbook, go to **MyPsychLab: www.pearsoned.com.au/mypsychlab**.

Complete pre- and post-tests, create your own individualised study plan, watch videos and animations and listen to audio glossaries—all of which will help you to understand the themes of this chapter:

- What is memory?
- Memory use for the short-term?
- Long-term memory: encoding and retrieval
- Structures in long-term memory
- Biological aspects of memory

Read all about Hermann Ebbinghaus in the BIOGRAPHY section

Take the pre- and post-tests and create your own Chapter 7 STUDY PLAN

'Using MyPsychLab was like having my own personal tutor.'

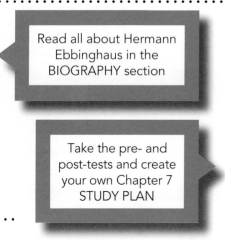

EXPLORE the *Key Processes in Stages of Memory*

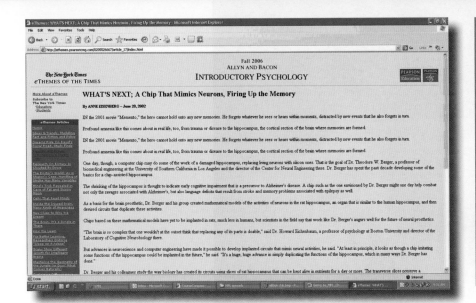

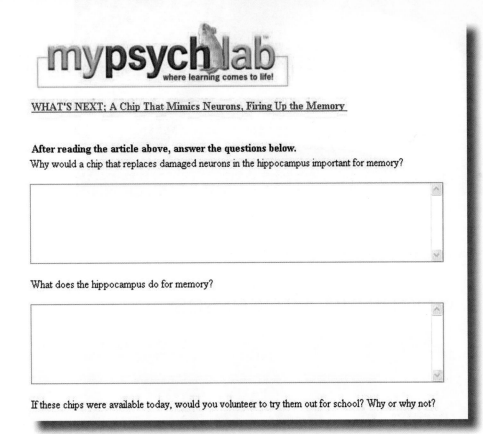

## WHAT'S NEXT; A Chip That Mimics Neurons, Firing Up the Memory

**After reading the article above, answer the questions below.**

Why would a chip that replaces damaged neurons in the hippocampus important for memory?

What does the hippocampus do for memory?

If these chips were available today, would you volunteer to try them out for school? Why or why not?

### What can you find in MyPsychLab?

Self-directed tests * Videos * Simulations * eBook * Biographies * Audio glossary * Web links … and more—organised by chapter, section and learning objective.

Cognitive Processes

CHAPTER

8

# CHAPTER FOCUS POINTS

After studying this chapter you will have a better understanding of:

1. The terms 'cognition' and 'cognitive psychology'.

2. How to describe the processes of attention, and give examples of the ways in which attention is limited.

3. How to reflect upon the processes supporting human language—both at the cognitive level and at the communicative level.

4. How to be aware of the 'Whorfian hypothesis' and the relationship between language, culture and knowledge.

5. Definitions of the term 'representation' and be able to describe visual and verbal representations, and their impact upon cognitive processes.

6. How to describe cultural differences in cognitive processes.

7. How to compare algorithmic and heuristic approaches to problem solving.

8. The evolutionary origin of human reason and problem solving.

# CHAPTER CONTENTS

I t is midnight. There's a knock on your door. When you answer, no one is there, but you see an envelope on the floor. Inside the envelope is a single sheet of paper with a handwritten message: 'The cat is on the mat.' What do you make of this?

You must now begin to engage a variety of cognitive processes. You will need language processes to put together some basic meanings for the words, but what then? Can you find any episode in memory to which these words are relevant? (Recall that in Chapter 7 we discussed memory as a type of cognitive processing.) If you can't, you'll have to give other types of thought to the matter. Is the message a code? What kind of code? Whom do you know who might encode a message? Does the fate of civilisation rest in your hands?

Perhaps we're getting a bit carried away, but we want to make plain to you what kinds of activities count as **cognitive processes** and why they might interest you. The capacity to use language and to think in abstract ways has often been cited as the essence of the human experience. You tend to take cognition for granted because it's an activity you do continually during your waking hours. Even so, when a carefully crafted speech wins your vote or when you read a detective story in which the sleuth combines a few scraps of apparently trivial clues into a brilliant solution to a crime, you are forced to acknowledge the intellectual triumph of cognitive processes.

**Cognition** is a general term for all the things we do with information: As shown in **Figure 8.1**, the study of cognition is the study of your mental life. (Note that Chapter 4 already discussed some of the topics shown in Figure 8.1.) Cognition includes both contents and

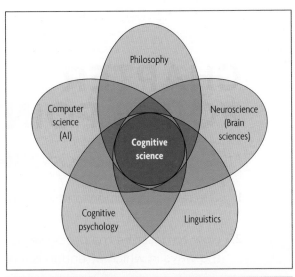

### Figure 8.2

**The domain of cognitive science**
The domain of cognitive science occupies the intersection of philosophy, neuroscience, linguistics, cognitive psychology and computer science (artificial intelligence).

processes. The *contents* of cognition are *what* you know—concepts, facts, propositions, rules and memories: 'A dog is a mammal.' 'A red light means stop.' 'I first left home at age 18.' Cognitive *processes* are *how* you manipulate these mental contents—in ways that enable you to interpret the world around you and to find creative solutions to your life's dilemmas.

Within psychology, the study of cognition is carried out by researchers in the field of **cognitive psychology**. Although scientists and philosophers have been interested in the contents of human thought for millennia, the term 'Cognitive Psychology' was first used by Ulric Neisser in the mid-1960s. Neisser's definition of cognitive psychology—all processes by which the sensory input is transformed, reduced, elaborated, stored, recovered and used—suggests the complexity of the topic we are about to discuss (Neisser, 1967). Over the past three decades, the field of cognitive psychology has been supplemented by the interdisciplinary field of **cognitive science** (see **Figure 8.2**). Cognitive science focuses the collected knowledge of several academic specialties on the same theoretical issues. It benefits the practitioners of each of these fields to share their data and insights. You saw this cognitive science philosophy at work in Chapter 7, when we described how studies of the biology of memory can be used to constrain—limit and refine—theories of memory processes. Many of the theories we will describe in this chapter have similarly been shaped through the interactions of researchers from a number of disciplinary perspectives.

We will begin our study of cognition with a brief description of the ways in which researchers try to measure the inner, private processes involved in cognitive functioning. Then we will examine, at some length, topics

**cognitive psychology** The study of higher mental processes, such as attention, language use, memory, perception, problem solving and thinking.

**cognitive processes** Higher mental processes, such as perception, memory, language, problem solving and abstract thinking.

**cognitive science** The interdisciplinary field of study of the approach systems and processes that manipulate information.

**cognition** Processes of knowing, including attending, remembering and reasoning; also the content of the processes, such as concepts and memories.

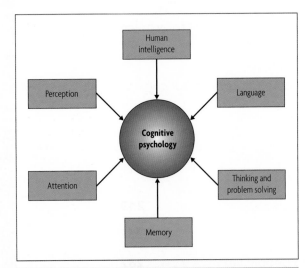

### Figure 8.1

**The domain of cognitive psychology**
Cognitive psychologists study higher mental functions with particular emphasis on the ways in which people acquire knowledge and use it to shape and understand their experiences in the world.

From Solso, Robert L., *Cognitive Psychology*, 3e, pp. 7, 289, 290. © 1991. Published by Allyn & Bacon, Boston, MA. Copyright © 2003 by Pearson Education. Reprinted by permission of the publisher.

in cognitive psychology that generate much basic research and practical application: language use, visual cognition, problem solving, reasoning, and judging and decision making.

# STUDYING COGNITION

How can you study cognition? The challenge, of course, is everything we are interested in is invisible! It all goes on inside the head. You can see the input—for example, a note that says, 'Call me'—and experience the output—you make a phone call—but how can you determine the series of mental steps that connected the note to your response? How, that is, can you reveal what happened in the middle—the cognitive processes and the mental representations on which your action relies? In this section, we describe the types of logical analyses that have made possible the scientific study of cognitive psychology.

## DISCOVERING THE PROCESSES OF MIND

One of the fundamental methodologies for studying mental processes was devised, in 1868, by the Dutch physiologist **F. C. Donders**. To study the 'speed of mental processes,' Donders invented a series of experimental tasks that he believed were differentiated by the mental steps involved for successful performance (Lachman et al., 1979). **Table 8.1** provides a paper-and-pencil experiment that follows Donders's logic. Before reading on, please take a moment to complete each task.

How long did you take to do task 1? Suppose you wanted to give a list of the steps you carried out to perform the task. It might look something like this:

a. Determine whether a character is a capital letter or a small letter.

b. If it is a capital letter, draw a C on top.

How long did you take for task 2? When we have used this exercise, students have often taken an additional half minute or more. You can understand why, once we spell out the necessary steps:

a. Determine whether a character is a capital letter or a small letter.

b. Determine whether each capital letter is a vowel or a consonant.

c. If it is a consonant, draw a C on top. If it is a vowel, draw a V.

Thus, going from task 1 to task 2, we add two mental steps, which we can call *stimulus categorisation* (vowel or consonant?) and *response selection* (draw a C or draw a V). Task 1 requires one stimulus categorisation step. Task 2 requires two such categorisations. Task 2 also requires selecting between two responses. Because task 2 requires you to do everything you did for task 1 and more, it

## Table 8.1

Donders' analysis of mental processes

Note how long (in seconds) it takes you to complete each of these three tasks. Try to complete each task accurately, but as quickly as possible.

*Task 1:* Draw a C on top of all the capitalised letters:
TO Be, oR noT To BE: tHAT Is thE qUestioN: WhETher 'Tis noBlEr In tHE MINd tO SuFfER tHe SLings AnD ARroWS Of OUtrAgeOUs forTUNe, or To TAke ARmS agaINST a sEa Of tROUBleS, AnD by oPPOsinG END theM.          TIME: _____

*Task 2:* Draw a V on top of the capitalised vowels and a C on top of the capitalized consonants:
TO Be, oR noT To BE: tHAT Is thE qUestioN: WhETher 'Tis noBlEr In tHE MINd tO SuFfER tHe SLings AnD ARroWS Of OUtrAgeOUs forTUNe, or To TAke ARmS agaINST a sEa Of tROUBleS, AnD by oPPOsinG END theM.          TIME: _____

*Task 3:* Draw a V on top of all the capitalised letters:
TO Be, oR noT To BE: tHAT Is thE qUestioN: WhETher 'Tis noBlEr In tHE MINd tO SuFfER tHe SLings AnD ARroWS Of OUtrAgeOUs forTUNe, or To TAke ARmS agaINST a sEa Of tROUBleS, AnD by oPPOsinG END theM.          TIME: _____

takes you more time. That was Donders's fundamental insight: extra mental steps will often result in more time to perform a task.

You may be wondering why we included task 3. This is a necessary procedural control for the experiment. We have to ensure that the time difference between tasks 1 and 2 does not stem from the fact that it takes much longer to draw Vs than to draw Cs. Task 3 should still be much swifter than task 2. Was it?

Researchers still follow Donders's basic logic. They frequently use *reaction time*—the amount of time it takes experimental participants to perform particular tasks—as a way of testing specific accounts of how some cognitive process is carried out. Donders's basic premise that extra mental steps will result in extra time is still fundamental to a great deal of cognitive psychological research. Let's see how this successful idea has been developed over the past 135 years.

## MENTAL PROCESSES AND MENTAL RESOURCES

When cognitive psychologists break down high-level activities, like language use or problem solving, into their component processes, they often act as if they are playing a game with blocks. Each block represents a different component that must be carried out. The goal is to determine the shape and size of each block and to see how the blocks fit together to form the whole activity. For the Donders tasks, you see that the blocks can be laid out in a row (see **Figure 8.3**, part A). Each step comes directly after another. The block metaphor allows you to see that we could also stack the blocks so more than one process occurs simultaneously (part B). These two pictures illustrate the distinction between **serial** and **parallel processes**. Processes are *serial* when they take place one after the other. Suppose you're in a restaurant and you need to decide what to order. You focus on entries one at a time and then judge whether they qualify as 'yes', 'no', or 'maybe'. For each entry, your judgment processes follow your reading processes. Processes are *parallel* when they overlap in time. When it comes time to place your order, the language processes that enable you to understand the waiter's question (e.g., 'What can I get for you?') are likely to operate at the same time as the

processes that allow you to formulate your reply (e.g., 'I'd like the osso buco'). That's why you're ready to respond as soon as the waiter finishes his question. We know that some mental processes are serial, some are parallel, and some can be either serial parallel depending on what other things are going on.

Cognitive psychologists often use reaction times to determine whether processes are carried out in parallel or serially. However, the examples in part C of Figure 8.3 should convince you that this is a tricky business. Imagine that we have a task that we believe can be broken down into two processes, *X* and *Y*. If the only information we have is the total time needed to complete the process, we can never be sure if processes *X* and *Y* happen side by side or one after the other. Much of the challenge of research in cognitive psychology is to invent task circumstances that allow the experimenter to determine which of many possible configurations of blocks is correct. In task 2 of the exercise you just did, we could be reasonably certain that the processes were serial because some activities logically required others. For example, you couldn't execute your response (prepare to draw a C or a V) until you had determined what the response might be.

In many cases, theorists try to determine if processes are serial or parallel by assessing the extent to which the processes place demands on *mental resources*. Suppose, for example, you are driving with a friend and chatting. You also have the car stereo on. Ordinarily, when the road is clear and the traffic is light, you can easily do all these things at once—driving, talking and listening to music. However, imagine now that a huge electrical storm suddenly opens up overhead: the road is suddenly wet and it is hard to see ahead. What would you do in these circumstances? Many people would turn the stereo

**serial processes** Two or more mental processes that are carried out in order one after the other.

**parallel processes** Two or more mental processes that are carried out simultaneously.

A. The Donders Task

| CAPITAL LETTER? | → | CONSONANT OR VOWEL? | → | WRITE C OR V? |

——————— Time ———————→

B. Serial versus parallel processes

| PROCESS A | → | PROCESS B | → | PROCESS C |

| PROCESS A |

| PROCESS B |

| PROCESS C |

——————— Time ———————→

C. Time equivalence of serial and parallel processes

| PROCESS X | → | PROCESS Y |

| PROCESS X |

| PROCESS Y |

——————— Time ———————→

### Figure 8.3

**Breaking down high-level cognitive activities**

a. Cognitive psychologists attempt to determine the identity and organisation of the mental processes that are the building blocks of high-level cognitive activities.

b. Our version of the Donders task requires that at least three processes be carried out one after the other.

c. Some processes are carried out serially, in sequence; others are carried out in parallel, all at the same time. (C) The time taken to perform a task does not always allow researchers to conclude whether serial or parallel processes were used.

Why is it difficult to carry on a conversation while you are trying to avoid puddles?

off and tell their friend to be quiet. This is because, with the addition of the storm, the task of driving the car has suddenly become more difficult and has demanded greater attention. As we will discuss later, some aspects of attention are limited, so as the demand of driving increases, something else has to be sacrificed. Driving a car in a storm makes more demand on mental resources than driving along an open road on a clear day.

A key assumption in this example is that you have *limited* processing resources that must be spread over different mental tasks (Logan, 2002). Your *attentional processes* are responsible for distributing these resources. In Chapter 4, we discussed attention as the set of processes that allow you to select, for particular scrutiny, some small subset of available perceptual information. Our use of *attention* here preserves the idea of selectivity. The decision now, however, concerns which mental processes will be selected as the recipients of processing resources.

We have one more complication to add: not all processes put the same demands on resources. We can, in fact, define a dimension that goes from processes that are *controlled* to those that are *automatic* (Shiffrin & Schneider, 1977). **Controlled processes** require attention; **automatic processes** generally do not. It is often difficult to carry out more than one controlled process at a time because they require more resources; automatic processes can often be performed alongside other tasks without interference.

We want to give you an example of an automatic process. To get started, take a moment to carry out the task in **Table 8.2**. Did you find List A somewhat harder than List B?

Experimental participants were asked to make the types of judgments illustrated in Table 8.2. The pattern of results suggested that people find it harder to respond *different* when the numbers are close together (for example, 1–2) than when they are far apart (for example, eight–one) irrespective of whether the numbers are rendered as arabic numerals or written out. Note that list A had 'close' different pairs and list B had 'far' different pairs, so you should have found it somewhat harder to complete list A. But why should the closeness of the numbers matter for a judgment of *physical* similarity? *One–two* and *one–nine* are about equal on the dimension of *physical* dissimilarity. The researchers suggested that when you look at *2* or *two*, you can't help but think of the quantity it represents—even when the quantity, in this case, impairs performance on the task you've been asked to carry out. That is, you *automatically* access the meaning of a number, even when you don't need (or want) to do so (Dehaene & Akhavein, 1995).

This number task illustrates that automatic processes rely heavily on the efficient use of memory (Barrett et al., 2004). Whether the object in the environment is *2* or *two*, your memory processes swiftly provide information about quantity.

## Table 8.2

### Number processing

Your task is to put a check mark on top of the pairs of numbers that are physically different, in either numbers or words (that is, you would check both 4–6 and four–six). Try to judge which list is harder.

**List A**

| | | | |
|---|---|---|---|
| 8–8 | nine–eight | 1–2 | eight–eight |
| 2–1 | 8–9 | 9–9 | 2–2 |
| two–two | one–two | nine–nine | eight–nine |
| one–one | 1–1 | two–one | 9–8 |

**List B**

| | | | |
|---|---|---|---|
| 1–1 | nine–two | one–one | nine–nine |
| 2–9 | eight–two | 9–9 | 1–9 |
| eight–one | 8–8 | eight–eight | nine–one |
| 2–2 | 1–8 | 2–8 | two–two |

The number task also illustrates the way in which tasks that first involved controlled processes can become automatic with sufficient practice. You probably remember, as a small child, having to learn how numbers work. Now, the association between numbers and the quantities they represent has become so automatic, you can't shut off the association. You can probably think of other instances in which you've practised enough to make tasks automatic. Did you learn to play an instrument? Can you type without looking at the keyboard?

Let's apply this knowledge of controlled and automatic processes back to the situation of driving, listening to the stereo and talking. When you are driving on a clear day, you feel little interference between the three activities, suggesting that maintaining your direction, following the Hilltop Hoods CD and planning your utterances are each relatively automatic activities. The situation changes, however, when the storm forces you to devote attention to watching the road and carefully steering the car. Now you must select where to go and what to say. Because you can't make all of these choices simultaneously, you have come up against the limits of your processing resources (Tombu & Jolicœur, 2005). This example shows why controlled and automatic processes are defined along a dimension, rather than constituting strict categories. When circumstances become challenging, what before seemed automatic now requires controlled attention. Thus processes may require more or less attention, depending on the context.

You now know a lot about the logic of mental processes. To explain how complex mental tasks are carried out, theorists propose models that combine serial and parallel and controlled and automatic processes. The goal of much cognitive psychological research is to invent experiments that confirm each of the components of such models. Now that you understand some of the logic behind cognitive psychological research into mental processes, it is time to move to more specific domains in which you put cognitive processes to work. We begin with language use.

**controlled processes**
Processes that require attention; it is difficult to carry out more than one controlled process at a time.

**automatic processes**
Processes that do not require attention.

For answers go to MyPsychLab!

**mypsychlab** where learning comes to life!

**language production** What people say, sign, and write, as well as the processes they go through to produce these messages.

**audience design** The process of shaping a message depending on the audience for which it is intended.

# LANGUAGE USE

Let's return to the message you received at midnight, 'The cat is on the mat'. What could we do to change the situation so that this message immediately made sense to you? The easiest step we could take would be to introduce appropriate background knowledge. Suppose you are a secret agent who always gets instructions in this curious fashion. You might know that 'the cat' is your contact and that 'on the mat' means in the wrestling arena. Off you go.

But you don't have to be a spy for 'The cat is on the mat' to take on a variety of meanings:

- Suppose your cat waits on a mat by the door when she wants to be let out. When you say to your room mate, 'The cat is on the mat', you use those words to communicate, 'Could you get up and let the cat out?'

- Suppose your friend is worried about pulling the car out of the driveway because she's uncertain where the cat is. When you say, 'The cat is on the mat', you use those words to communicate, 'It's safe to pull out of the driveway.'

- Suppose you are trying to have a race between your cat and your friend's dog. When you say, 'The cat is on the mat', you use those words to communicate, 'My cat won't race!'

These examples illustrate the difference between *sentence meaning*—the generally simple meaning of the combined words of a sentence—and *speaker's meaning*—the unlimited number of meanings a speaker can communicate by putting a sentence to good use (Grice, 1968). When psychologists study language use, they want to comprehend both the *production* and the *understanding* of speakers' meaning:

- How do speakers produce the right words to communicate the meaning they intend?

- How do listeners recover the messages the speakers wished to communicate?

- We will examine each of these questions in turn. We also consider the evolutionary and cultural context of language use.

## LANGUAGE PRODUCTION

Look at **Figure 8.4**. Try to formulate a few sentences about this picture. What did you think to say? Suppose now we asked you to redescribe the person for someone who is blind. How would your description change? Does this second description seem to require more mental effort? The study of **language production** concerns both what people say—what they choose to say at a given time—and the processes they go through to produce the message. Note that language users need not produce language out loud. Language production also includes both signing and writing. For convenience, however, we will call language producers *speakers* and language understanders *listeners*.

Audience design We asked you to imagine the different descriptions you'd give of Figure 8.4 to a sighted and a blind person as a way of getting you to think about **audience design** in language production. Each time you produce an utterance, you must have in mind the audience to whom the utterance will be directed, and what knowledge you share with members of that audience (Clark, 1996; Clark & Van Der Wege, 2002). For example, it won't do you the least bit of good to say, 'The cat is on the mat' if your listener does not know that the cat sits on the mat only when she wishes to be let out. An overarching rule of audience design, the *cooperative principle,* was first proposed by the philosopher **H. Paul Grice** (1975). Grice phrased the cooperative principle as an instruction to speakers that they should produce utterances appropriate to the setting and meaning of the ongoing conversation. To expand on this instruction, Grice defined four maxims that cooperative speakers live by. In **Table 8.3**, we present each of those maxims, as well as an invented conversation that illustrates the effect the maxims have on moment-by-moment choices in language production.

Figure 8.4

**Language production**
How would you describe this character to a friend? How might your description change if your friend were blind?

As you can see from Table 8.3, being a cooperative speaker depends, in large part, on having accurate expectations about what your listener is likely to know and understand. Thus you certainly wouldn't tell a friend 'I'm having lunch with Alex' if you didn't have good reason to believe that your friend knew who Alex was. You also must assure yourself that, of all the Alexes your friend might know and that she knows that you know, only one would come to mind as the specific Alex you would mention in these circumstances. More formally, we can say that there must be some Alex who is prominent in the *common ground*—common knowledge—you share with your friend.

**Herbert Clark** (1996) suggested that language users have different bases for their judgments of common ground:

- *Community membership.* Language producers often make strong assumptions about what is likely to be mutually known based on shared membership in communities of various sizes.

- *Copresence for actions.* Language producers often assume that the actions and events they have shared with other conversationalists become part of common ground. This includes information discussed in earlier parts of a conversation (or in past conversations).

- *Perceptual copresence.* Perceptual copresence exists when a speaker and a listener share the same perceptual events (sights, sounds, and so on).

Thus your use of Alex in 'I'm having lunch with Alex' might succeed because your friend and you are part of a small community (for example, room-mates) that includes only one Alex (community membership). Or it might succeed because you've introduced the existence of Alex earlier in the conversation (copresence for actions). Or Alex might be standing right there in the room (perceptual copresence). You can see from this example why judgments of common ground often rely on the ability of your memory processes to provide information about individuals and communities (Horton & Gerrig, 2005a, 2005b). For you to say 'I'm having lunch with Alex', you must be reasonably certain that 'Alex' will be sufficiently memorable for your particular listener.

Let's focus a bit more on community membership. Take a moment to think about this question: What information would you expect the community members of your college or university to know? What information would you expect students to know—but not the professors? Researchers have examined the extent to which people's estimates of community knowledge are accurate and useful.

> In a first experiment, undergraduates in Hong Kong viewed a series of slides of 30 landmarks from Hong Kong, Macau and New York City (Lau et al., 2001). The participants were asked whether they recognised each landmark and whether they could name it. In addition, the participants tried to estimate what percentage of their classmates would recognise each landmark. The results from this experiment indicated that the students were pretty accurate at guessing what members of their own communities were likely to know: their estimates were reasonably close to the actual percentages of students who got the landmarks correct. However, the students also tended to err in the direction of believing other people knew the same things they did: they gave higher estimates for those landmarks they themselves knew. In a second experiment, a new group of participants were asked to provide descriptions of each of the 30 landmarks. Their goal was to provide a description that would allow one of their classmates to choose correctly each landmark from among the 30 pictures. The researchers demonstrated that the length of the descriptions was related to community knowledge: Participants generally used more words to describe the landmarks that the first experiment showed to be the least recognisable.

You can think about these results with respect to your own day-to-day experiences. If you are talking to a classmate, you can probably say something like 'Meet me at the Union for lunch'. If you're expecting a visit from a friend

## Table 8.3

Grice's maxims in language production

1. *Quantity:* Make your contribution as informative as is required (for the current purposes of the exchange). Do not make your contribution more informative than is required.

   *The consequence for the speaker:* You must try to judge how much information your audience really needs. Often this judgment will require you to assess what your listener is likely to know already.

2. *Quality:* Try to make your contribution one that is true. Do not say what you believe to be false. Do not say that for which you lack adequate evidence.

   *The consequence for the speaker:* When you speak, listeners will assume that you can back up your assertions with appropriate evidence. As you plan each utterance, you must have in mind the evidence on which it is based.

3. *Relation:* Be relevant.

   *The consequence for the speaker:* You must make sure that your listeners will see how what you are saying is relevant to what has come before. If you wish to shift the topic of conversation—so that your utterance is not directly relevant—you must make that clear.

4. *Manner:* Be perspicacious. Avoid obscurity of expression. Avoid ambiguity. Be brief. Be orderly.

   *The consequence for the speaker:* It is your responsibility to speak in as clear a manner as possible. Although you will inevitably make errors, as a cooperative speaker you must ensure that your listeners can understand your message.

   In this conversation, can you see how Chris follows (or violates) Grice's maxims?

| What is said | What Chris might be thinking |
| --- | --- |
| Pat: *Have you ever been to New York City?*<br>Chris: *I was there once in 2002.* | I don't know why Pat is asking me this question, so I probably should say a little more than just 'yes'. |
| Pat: *I'm supposed to visit, but I'm worried about being mugged.*<br>Chris: *I think a lot of areas are safe.* | I can't say that he shouldn't worry because he won't believe me. What can I say that will sound true but make him feel okay? |
| Pat: *How was your hotel?*<br>Chris: *We didn't stay overnight.* | If I say, 'We didn't stay in a hotel,' that might suggest we stayed somewhere else. I need to say something relevant that will make clear why I can't answer the question. |
| Pat: *Would you like to go to New York with me?*<br>Chris: *I'd have to find a way to see if it would be possible for me to leave without it being too impossible.* | I don't want to go, but I don't want to seem rude. Will Pat notice that I'm being evasive in my response? |
| Pat: *Huh?*<br>Chris: *Well . . .* | Trapped. |

for whom the campus is new, you would probably say something more, like, 'It's the red building on the left, about 100 metres beyond the fountain'. The comparative lengths of your descriptions suggest that you're using community membership to plan your utterances.

Our discussion so far has focused on language production at the level of the message. How you shape what you wish to say will depend on the audience to whom you are speaking. Let's turn now to a discussion of the mental processes that allow you to produce these messages.

Speech execution and speech errors Would you like to be famous for tripping over your tongue? Consider the Reverend W. A. Spooner of Oxford University, who lent his name to the term *spoonerism*: an

exchange of the initial sounds of two or more words in a phrase or sentence. For example, when he was tongue-lashing a lazy student for wasting the term, Reverend Spooner said, 'You have tasted the whole worm!' It is not clear how many 'spoonerisms' Spooner actually uttered, and it now seems likely that many of them were made up as jokes by his students. Nonetheless, his name has become synonymous with a particular type of language production error. A spoonerism is one of the limited types of speech errors that language producers make. These errors give researchers insight into the planning that goes on as speakers produce utterances. As you can see in **Table 8.4**, you need to plan an utterance at a number of different levels, and speech errors give evidence for each of those levels (Bock & Levelt, 1994; Rapp & Goldrick, 2000). What should impress you about all these examples

## Table 8.4

**Errors in planning speech production**

Types of planning:

- Speakers must choose the content words that best fit their ideas.

  If the speaker has two words in mind, such as *grizzly* and *ghastly*, a blend like grastly might result.

- Speakers must put the chosen words in the right places in the utterance.

  Because speakers plan whole units of their utterances while they produce them, content words will sometimes become misplaced.

  a tank of gas → a gas of tank

  wine is being served at dinner → dinner is being served at wine

- Speakers must fill in the sounds that make up the words they wish to utter.

  Once again, because speakers plan ahead, sounds will sometimes get misplaced.

  left hemisphere → heft lemisphere

  pass out → pat ous

of errors is that they are not just random—they make sense given the structure of spoken English. Thus a speaker might exchange initial consonants—'tips of the slung' for 'slips of the tongue'—but would never say, 'tlips of the sung,' which would violate the rule of English that 'tl' does not occur as an initial sound (Fromkin, 1980).

Given the importance of speech errors to developing theoretical models of speech production, researchers have not always been content just to wait around for errors to happen naturally. Instead, researchers have explored a number of ways to produce artificial errors in controlled experimental settings (e.g., Hartsuiker et al., 2003; Warker & Dell, 2006). Those techniques have yielded insights into both the processes and representations that underlie fluent speech production:

- *Processes.* Recall, from Chapter 5, the SLIP (for 'spoonerisms of laboratory-induced predisposition') technique that encourages participants to produce spoonerisms (Baars, 1992). In this procedure, participants are asked to read silently lists of word pairs that provide models for the phonetic structure of a target spoonerism: *ball doze, bash door, bean deck, bell dark.* They then are required to pronounce out loud a word pair like *darn bore*, but under the influence of the earlier pairs it will sometimes come out *barn door*.

  With this technique, researchers can study the factors that affect the likelihood that speakers will produce errors. For example, a spoonerism is more likely when the error will still result in real words

(Baars et al., 1975; Hartsuiker et al., 2005). Thus an error on *darn bore* (to produce *barn door*) is more likely than an error on *dart board* (to produce *bart doard*). Findings like this one suggest that while you are producing utterances, some of your cognitive processes are devoted to detecting and editing potential errors. Those processes are reluctant to let you pronounce sounds like *doard*, which are not real English words.

- *Representations.* Another procedure required participants to read pairs of idioms (like *shoot the breeze* and *raise the roof*). After a 2-second interval, they were asked to produce one of the idioms from memory, as swiftly as possible. Under this time pressure, participants sometimes produced *blends* of the two idioms, such as *kick the maker* (from *kick the bucket* and *meet your maker*). These blend errors were most likely when the two idioms shared the same underlying meaning (as with *kick the bucket* and *meet your maker*) rather than when they differed in meaning (as with *shoot the breeze* and *raise the roof*). This result suggests that representations of idioms with similar meanings are linked in memory: as you begin to produce one idiom, a representational link to another with similar meaning may lead to a blend error (Cutting & Bock, 1997). That's the way the cookie bounces!

We have now looked at some of the forces that lead speakers to produce particular utterances and at some of the processes that allow them to do so. We turn next to the listeners, who are responsible for understanding what speakers intend to communicate.

## LANGUAGE UNDERSTANDING

Suppose a speaker has produced the utterance 'The cat is on the mat'. You already know that, depending on the context, this utterance can be used to communicate any number of different meanings. How, as a listener, do you settle on just one meaning? We will begin this discussion of language understanding by considering more fully the problem of the ambiguity of meaning.

Among ichthyologists, this is a *Choerodon fasciatus*. What would you call it if you were talking or writing about it to a friend?

**Resolving ambiguity** What does the word *bank* mean? You can probably think of at least two meanings, one having to do with rivers and the other having to do with money. Suppose you hear the utterance 'He came from the bank.' How do you know which meaning is intended? You need to be able to resolve the *lexical ambiguity* between the two meanings. (*Lexical* is related to *lexicon*, a synonym for *dictionary*.) If you think about this problem, you'll realise that you have some cognitive processes that allow you to use surrounding context to eliminate the ambiguity—to *disambiguate*—the word. Have you been talking about rivers or about money? That broader context should enable you to choose between the two meanings. But how?

Before we answer that question, we'd like to introduce another type of ambiguity. What does this sentence mean: 'The mother of the boy and the girl will arrive soon?' You may detect only one meaning right off, but there is a *structural ambiguity* here (Akmajian et al., 1990). Take a look at **Figure 8.5**. Linguists often represent the structure of sentences with tree diagrams to show how the various words are gathered together into grammatical units. In part A, we've shown you an analysis of 'The cat is on the mat'. The structure is pretty simple: a noun phrase made up of an article and a noun, plus a verb phrase made up of a verb and a prepositional phrase. In the other two parts, you see the more complex structures for the two different meanings of 'The mother . . .' In part B, the analysis shows that the whole phrase 'of the boy and the girl' applies to the mother. One person—the mother of two children—will arrive soon. In part C, the analysis shows that there are two noun phrases, 'the mother of the boy' and 'the girl.' There are two people, both of whom will arrive soon. Which understanding of the sentence did you come to when you first read it? Now that you can see that two meanings are possible, we arrive at the same question we did for lexical ambiguity: How does prior context enable you to settle on one meaning when more than one is possible?

Let's return to lexical ambiguity (an ambiguity of word meaning). Consider this sentence: 'Nancy watched the ball'.

When you read this sentence, how do you interpret the word *ball*? If you imagine that you have a dictionary in your head, your entry for ball might look something like this:

*Definition 1.* A round object used in a game or sport
*Definition 2.* A large formal event for dancing

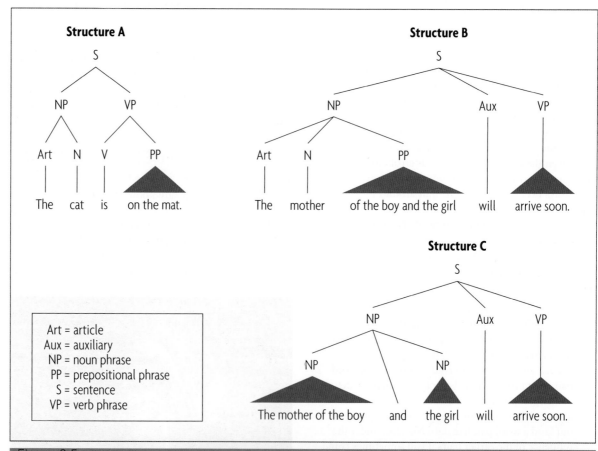

Figure 8.5

**Sentence structures**

Linguists use tree diagrams to display the grammatical structure of sentences. Part A shows the structure of 'The cat is on the mat'. Parts B and C show that the sentence 'The mother of the boy and the girl will arrive soon' can be represented by two different structural analyses. Who will arrive soon, one person (structure B) or two (structure C)?

Now that you are looking at a picture of dancing couples, what comes to mind when you think of the word *ball*?

The sentence 'Nancy watched the ball' contains no information that allows you to choose between these two definitions. In fact, research suggests that both definitions become accessible in memory after you read this type of sentence (Vu et al., 1998). You need help from surrounding context to determine which ball is which. But how does context help you decide among meanings? Research suggests that context provides a variety of types of evidence (Vu et al., 1998, 2000). Consider these examples:

1. She catered the ball.
2. The juggler watched the ball.
3. The debutante sat by the door. She watched the ball.

In example 1, the verb *catered* helps specify which definition of *ball* is appropriate; in example 2, the noun *juggler* does the work. In example 3, the first sentence evokes a scenario that creates a storylike context for the second sentence, 'She watched the ball'.

These examples suggest that you put various types of evidence to swift and efficient use each time you encounter an ambiguous word: Context immediately affects listeners' consideration of the meanings of ambiguous words (Gorfein, 2001). Context wields a similar influence on structural ambiguities (Filik et al., 2005; Spivey et al., 2002). Contextual information speeds decisions when you must choose among different possible grammatical structures.

In recent years, researchers have begun to study the brain bases of ambiguity resolution. Consider these two sentences:

The lock on the chest had been broken with the poker.

The picture on the wall had been chosen by his girlfriend.

You may not have been aware of it, but that first sentence had three ambiguous words: *lock*, *chest* and *poker*. Even though you probably weren't aware of these ambiguities, your brain will have processed the two sentences differently (Rodd et al., 2005). In an experiment, participants underwent fMRI scans while listening to noise (the nonlinguistic control condition), low ambiguity sentences and high ambiguity sentences. **Figure 8.6** shows regions of the brain that were more active for each type of sentence. The areas in blue and yellow indicate brain regions that were involved for comprehending low ambiguity sentences or both types of sentences with respect to noise. The regions in blue indicate that extra regions of the brain were active when the sentences were high in ambiguity. These regions are, presumably, the brain bases of the processes that allow context to resolve ambiguities.

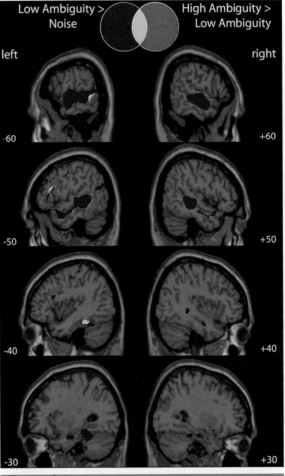

Figure 8.6

**The brain bases of ambiguity resolution**
Participants underwent fMRI scans while understanding low and high ambiguity sentences. The brain regions indicated in blue are those areas that were more active during the low ambiguity sentences than during the control noise condition. The regions in yellow were more active (with respect to the control) for both types of ambiguous sentences. The regions in red were more active for high ambiguity sentences than for low ambiguity sentences.

From J.M. Rodd, M.H. Davis, & I.S. Johnsrude, 'The neural mechanisms of speech comprehension: fMRI studies of semantic ambiguity,' *Cerebral Cortex, 15,* 1261-1269, 2005. By permission of Oxford University Press.

The overall conclusion you can draw is that your language processes use context powerfully and efficiently to resolve ambiguities. In a way, this shows that there is a good match between production and understanding. When we discussed language production, we emphasised audience design—the processes by which speakers try to make their utterances appropriate in the current context. Our analysis of understanding suggests that listeners expect speakers to have done their jobs well. Under those circumstances, it makes sense for listeners to let context guide their expectations about what speakers will have meant.

**The products of understanding** Our discussion of ambiguity resolution focused on the *processes* of understanding. In this section, we shift our attention to the *products* of understanding. The question now is: What *representations* result in memory when listeners understand utterances or texts? What, for example, would be stored in memory when you hear our old standby 'The cat is on the mat'? Research has suggested that meaning representation begins with basic units called *propositions* (Clark & Clark, 1977; Kintsch, 1974). Propositions are the main ideas of utterances. For 'The cat is on the mat', the main idea is that something is on something else. When you read the utterance, you will extract the proposition *on* and understand the relationship that it expresses between *the cat* and *the mat*. Often propositions are written like this: *ON (cat, mat)*. Many utterances contain more than one proposition. Consider 'The cat watched the mouse run under the sofa'. We have as the first component proposition *UNDER (mouse, sofa)*. From that, we build up *RUN (mouse, UNDER (mouse, sofa))*. Finally, we get to *WATCH (cat, RUN (mouse, UNDER (mouse, sofa)))*.

How can we test whether your mental representations of meaning really work this way? Some of the earliest experiments in the psychology of language were devoted to showing the importance of propositional representations in understanding (Kintsch, 1974). Research has shown that if two words in an utterance belong to the same proposition, they will be represented together in memory even if they are not close together in the actual sentence.

Consider the sentence, 'The mausoleum that enshrined the tzar overlooked the square.' Although *mausoleum* and *square* are far apart in the sentence, a propositional analysis suggests that they should be gathered together in memory in the proposition *OVERLOOKED (mausoleum, square)*. To test this analysis, researchers asked participants to read lists of words and say whether each had appeared in the sentence. Some participants saw *mausoleum* directly after *square* on the list. Other participants saw *mausoleum* after a word from another proposition. The response 'Yes, I saw *mausoleum*' was swifter when *mausoleum* came directly after *square* than when its predecessor came from another proposition. This finding suggests that the concepts *mausoleum* and *square* had been represented together in memory (Ratcliff & McKoon, 1978).

Have you ever noticed how hard it is to remember *exactly* what someone said? You might, for example, have tried to remember a line from a movie word-for-word—but you realised when you got home that you could only remember the general sense of what was said. This experiment indicates why word-for-word memory isn't so good: because one of the main operations your language processes carry out is the extraction of propositions, the exact form with which those propositions were rendered gets lost pretty quickly (for example, 'The cat chased the mouse' versus 'The mouse was chased by the cat').

Not all the propositions listeners store in memory are made up of information directly stated by the speaker. Often listeners fill gaps with **inferences**—logical assumptions made possible by information in memory. Consider this pair of utterances:

'I'm heading to the deli to meet Jessica.

'She promised to buy me a sandwich for lunch.'

To understand how these sentences go together, you must draw at least two important inferences. You must figure out both who *she* is in the second sentence and how going to a deli is related to a promise to buy a sandwich. Note that a friend who actually uttered this pair of sentences would be confident you could figure these things out. You'd never expect to hear this:

'I'm heading to the deli to meet Jessica. She—and by *she* I mean Jessica—promised to buy me a sandwich—and a *deli* is a place where you can buy a sandwich—for lunch.'

Speakers count on listeners to draw inferences of this sort.

A great deal of research has been directed towards determining what types of inferences listeners draw on a regular basis (Gerrig & O'Brien, 2005). The number of potential inferences after any utterance is unlimited. For example, because you know that Jessica is likely to be a human, you could infer that she has a heart, a liver, a pair of lungs, and so on (and on), but it's unlikely that you would feel compelled to call any of those (perfectly valid) inferences to mind when you heard 'I'm heading to the deli to meet Jessica.'

Research suggests, in fact, that the models readers develop for the whole situation of a text affects which inferences they encode. For example, read the text numbered 1 in **Table 8.5**. At the end of this text, did you encode the inference that Carol is likely to dump the spaghetti on the customer? Research suggests that readers consistently draw that inference (Peracchi & O'Brien, 2004). Now read the text numbered 2. In this latter case, readers appear to be much less likely to envision an ending in which Carol dumps the spaghetti. They use information from the broader situation—Carol's general pacifism—to imagine a different ending.

Our discussion of language use has demonstrated how much work a speaker does to produce the right sentence at the right time and how much work a listener does to figure out exactly what the speaker meant. You

**inferences** Missing information filled in on the basis of a sample of evidence or on the basis of prior beliefs and theories.

## Table 8.5

Text situations and inferences

1. Carol was a single mother with two young children. She had to work two jobs to make ends meet. She worked full-time as a teacher and part-time as a waitress. She hated not having much free time. Carol was known for her short temper and her tendency to act without thinking. She never thought about the consequences of her actions, so she often suffered negative repercussions. She refused to let people walk all over her. In fact, she had just been given a ticket for road rage. She decided she would never put up with anyone that was not nice to her. One particular night, Carol had an extremely rude customer. He complained about the spaghetti, and he yelled at Carol as if it were her fault. Carol lifted the spaghetti above his head.

2. Carol was a single mother with two young children. She had to work two jobs to make ends meet. She worked full-time as a teacher and part-time as a waitress. She hated not having much free time. Carol was known for her ability to peacefully settle any confrontation. She would never even think to solve her problems with physical violence. She taught her students and her own children how to solve problems through conversation. She believed this was an effective way to stop the increasing violence in the schools. Carol also helped other parents learn to deal with their anger. One particular night, Carol had an extremely rude customer. He complained about the spaghetti, and he yelled a Carol as if it were her fault. Carol lifted the spaghetti above his head.

usually aren't aware of all this work! Does this give you a greater appreciation for the elegant efficiency of your cognitive processes?

## LANGUAGE AND EVOLUTION

We just concluded you have a range of processes that are working diligently in the background to help you produce and understand language. A question that has long fascinated researchers is whether any other species possesses the same range of processes. We know of no other species that uses a language as complex as any human language. That observation raises an interesting question: What processes did humans evolve that make human language possible? To answer that question, researchers have largely turned to research with other species: They attempt to define what makes humans and human languages special. We will focus on *language structure* and *audience design.*

One property that makes human language special is that people can produce an unlimited number of messages with a limited number of words: You follow the grammatical rules of your language—of the types represented by the structures in Figure 8.5—to produce as many sentences as you'll ever need from the set of words you know. Researchers have suggested that humans are the only species that can apply rules of the complexity found in human languages (Fitch & Hauser, 2004; Hauser et al., 2002). This conclusion has been reached after several decades of research in which people have tried to teach nonhuman species languages with humanlike structure.

Beginning as early as the 1920s, psychologists tried to address this question by attempting to teach language to chimpanzees. Chimps don't have the appropriate vocal apparatus to produce spoken language, so researchers had to devise other methods of communication. For example, a chimp named Washoe was taught a highly simplified version of American Sign Language (Gardner & Gardner, 1969); a chimp named Sarah was taught to manipulate symbols (which stood for concepts like *apple* and *give*) on a magnetic board (Premack, 1971). The results of these experiments inspired great controversy (Seidenberg & Petitto, 1979). Sceptics asked whether the chimps' occasional combinations of gestures or symbols (for example, *Washoe sorry, You more drink*) constituted any meaningful kind of language use. They also wondered whether most of the meaning attributed to the chimps' utterances wasn't arising in the heads of the humans rather than in the heads of the chimps.

**Sue Savage-Rumbaugh** and her colleagues (Savage-Rumbaugh et al., 1998) have conducted research that has provided more solid insights into the language capabilities of chimps. Savage-Rumbaugh works primarily with *bonobos,* a species of great ape that is evolutionarily more similar to humans even than common chimpanzees. Rather remarkably, two of the bonobos in her studies, Kanzi and Mulika, acquired the meanings of plastic symbols *spontaneously:* They received no explicit training; rather, they acquired the symbols by observing others (humans and bonobos) using them to communicate. Moreover, Kanzi and Mulika were able to understand some *spoken* English. For example, when Kanzi heard a spoken word, he was able to locate either the symbol for the word or a photograph of the object. Kanzi was also able to follow simple commands such as 'Take off Sue's shoe'. Kanzi's performance strongly suggests that some aspects of human language performance can be found in other species. However, Kanzi still falls short of human abilities: He wasn't able to acquire the type of rule system that would allow him to produce an unlimited number of utterances. Other cross-species research reinforces the conclusion that humans alone evolved the processes to produce and understand appropriately complex grammatical structures (Fitch & Hauser, 2004).

Another focus of cross-species comparison has been on what we earlier called *audience design.* When you are successful at audience design, you take into account what your listener does and doesn't know. Are nonhuman animals able to modify their messages based on what members of their audience know? Researchers have set out to answer this question. For example, **Dorothy Cheney** and **Robert Seyfarth** (1990) have done extensive research on the communicative capabilities of *vervet monkeys.* Vervet monkeys make distinct *calls* to signal the presence

LANGUAGE USE       259

Some bonobos have learned the meanings of words without explicit training. What other abilities must these animals demonstrate before it can be said that they have genuinely acquired a human language?

of different dangers, such as leopards, eagles, and snakes. These monkeys are able to modify their calls depending on their audience: Female monkeys gave alarms at much higher rates when they were with their own offspring than when they were with monkeys unrelated to them. However, the vervets do not modify their calls based on what their audience knows: in an experimental setting, mother vervets produced the same calls irrespective of whether their offspring had also witnessed the events that evoked the calls.

Researchers continue to try to understand exactly what sets humans apart from other species with respect to their ability to engage in audience design (Karin-D'Arcy & Povinelli, 2002; Povinelli & Prince, 1998). For example, in one study *pileated gibbons* viewed experimental displays that had, as their central elements, photographs of either a human or another gibbon looking either to the left or to the right (Horton & Caldwell, 2006). As another part of the display, a toy was placed either to the right or to the left of the photographs. The gibbons were able to use the direction of gaze in the photographs to find their way to the toys. This ability to use another individual as a source of information about the world is a step in the direction of audience design. Studies of this sort allow researchers to understand at exactly what step human abilities evolved beyond nonhuman abilities.

An evolutionary perspective on language examines the critical processes humans evolved to make language possible. However, that general set of processes allows a wide variety of languages to emerge. In the next section, we discuss some potential consequences of the differences among languages.

## LANGUAGE, THOUGHT AND CULTURE

Have you had the opportunity to learn more than one language? If so, do you believe that you *think* differently in the two languages? Does language affect thought? This question is one that researchers have addressed in a variety

of ways. Let us give you a cross-linguistic example to make this question more concrete. Imagine a scene in which a child has watched her father throw a ball. If the child were an English speaker, she might utter the sentence, 'Daddy threw the ball'. If, by contrast, the child were a Turkish speaker, she would say, 'Topu babam atti'. Is this just a different collection of words for the same idea? Not entirely: the *-ti* suffix at the end of the Turkish sentence indicates that the event was witnessed by the speaker; if the event hadn't been witnessed by the speaker, a different suffix (*mi s*) would be added to *at* (which is the equivalent of *threw*) to form *atmi s*. As an English speaker, you are not required to divide the world into events you witnessed yourself versus those you learned about through other sources; as a Turkish speaker, you would be (Slobin, 1982; Slobin & Aksu, 1982). Could it be the case that the different grammatical requirements of these two languages would affect, in very basic ways, the manner in which people think about the world? No one knows the answer to this specific question about English and Turkish— Would you like to carry out appropriate research?—but this distinction provides a good example of why people have so often been intrigued by the question of language's potential influence on thought.

Scholarly work on this question was originated by **Edward Sapir** and his student **Benjamin Lee Whorf**, whose cross-linguistic explorations led them to the somewhat radical conclusion that differences in language would create differences in thought. Here's how Sapir put it:

> *We see and hear and otherwise experience very largely as we do because the language habits of our community predispose certain choices of interpretation. (Sapir, 1941 /1964, p. 69)*

For Sapir and Whorf, this conclusion emerged directly from relationships they believed to exist in their own data. From the hypotheses that Sapir and Whorf proposed, the one that has received the most attention is called *linguistic relativity* (Brown, 1976). According to this hypothesis, the structure of the language an individual speaks has an impact on the way in which that individual thinks about the world. Contemporary researchers in psychology, linguistics and anthropology have attempted to create rigorous tests of these ideas (Gentner & Goldin-Meadow, 2003). Let's look at a particular domain in which researchers have demonstrated an impact of language on thought.

You may be surprised to learn that languages of the world differ with respect to the number of basic colour terms they use. As determined by linguistic analysis, English has 11 *(black, white, red, yellow, green, blue, brown, purple, pink, orange,* and *gray);* some languages of the world, such as the language spoken by the Dani people of Papua New Guinea, have only 2, a simple distinction between *black* and *white* (or *light* and *dark*) (Berlin & Kay, 1969). Other cultures have intermediate numbers of colours, such as some Indigenous Australian groups that have names for the colours that we know as black, white, red and yellow, but no word for green. Whorf had suggested that language users 'dissect nature

Some Indigenous Australian groups have names for black, white, red and yellow, but not for green. Could language differences such as this affect the way people experience the world?

along the lines laid down by [their] native languages' (1956, p. 213). Researchers speculated that the category structure implied by colour terms might influence the ways in which speakers of different languages were able to think about colours:

> Researchers asked 12 speakers of Himba from northern Namibia to examine triads of colour chips all taken from the blue-green continuum. The participants' task was to indicate 'which of these three colours look most like each other, in the way that brothers look like each other?' (Roberson et al., 2005, p. 395). Unlike English, the Himba language doesn't make a lexical distinction between *blue* and *green*. Instead, Himba speakers use the term *borou* that covers most green and blue hues. The researchers looked for evidence of *categorical perception:* they assessed the extent to which Himba speakers perceived hues to be more similar within the categories marked by the language than between categories. Indeed, the Himba participants' similarity judgments showed a clear impact of the categorical structure of their language

The results provide support for the claim of linguistic relativity—that language may, in some circumstances, have an impact on thought.

There are thousands of languages in the world, which provide many interesting distinctions: As we indicated for the English–Turkish example with which we started, many interesting hypotheses about the link between language and thought have yet to be tested (Slobin, 2003).

Most research investigating the Whorfian hypothesis has been conducted by examining the relationship between language and thought *across* different languages, but of course if the principle is correct, it should also apply *within* languages. Consider Australian English compared with English as it is spoken in the U.K. or the U.S. As well as the difference in accent, Australians have words that do not appear in other languages. Does this mean that Australians conceptualise the world slightly differently from our English or American cousins?

Anna Wierzbicka from the Australian National University is interested in 'key words' that typify languages, and how those words are related to culture and understanding. Words like 'dob' and 'whinge' are peculiarly Australian, and both have strongly negative associations in our culture. (Have you ever known anybody to happily identify themselves as a 'dobber' or 'whinger'?) Of course other English language cultures do have a concept of 'a person who whines a lot' or 'a person who tells on someone else', but perhaps in Australia, where the first European settlers were prisoners who endured many months of hardship at sea in order to arrive in another prison, there is perhaps an especially vitriolic and hostile attitude surrounding complaining about your circumstances and reporting others to figures of authority.

It is likely to be the case that very many of the lexical and grammatical differences—differences in words and structures—between languages will have no effect on thought. Even so, as we describe cultural differences throughout *Psychology and Life*, it is worth keeping an open mind about linguistic relativity. This is particularly important in a multicultural society like Australia, where there are over 400 different languages spoken at home, according to the 2006 Census. In societies such as Australia's, where members of different cultures speak very different languages, we can wonder to what extent language plays a causal role in bringing about cultural differences.

Let's turn now from circumstances in which meaning is communicated through words to those in which meaning relies also on pictures.

## RECAP CHECKPOINT

### Language use

- Language users both produce and understand language.
- Speakers design their utterances to suit particular audiences
- Speech errors reveal many of the processes that go into speech planning.
- Much of language understanding consists of using context to resolve ambiguities.
- Memory representations of meaning begin with propositions supplemented with inferences.
- Studies of language evolution have focused on grammatical structure and audience design.
- The language individuals speak may play a role in determining how they think.

## CONCEPT QUESTIONS

1. What is the relationship between the cooperative principle and audience design?

2. Suppose you are trying to pronounce 'big pet' and 'bird pen'. Why would you be more likely to commit the speech error 'pig bet' than 'pird ben'?

3. How would you detect inferences in people's representations?

4. What are two language abilities that researchers suggest might set humans apart from other species?

5. What does the linguistic relativity hypothesis suggest?

## CRITICAL THINKING

Recall the study on community membership. Why might the researchers have used landmarks from three different cities?

# PSYCHOLOGY *in your life*
## WHY AND HOW DO PEOPLE LIE?

In this section on language use, we have emphasised that people aspire to be cooperative conversationalists. For example, we suggested that people follow the principle, 'Try to make your contribution one that is true'. However, we know that people often fall away from this standard. When people were asked to keep diaries of the lies they told, most averaged one or two a day (DePaulo et al., 2003). But why do people lie? When the lies are relatively mild, more people lie for psychological reasons (e.g., they wish to spare themselves embarrassment) than for personal advantage (e.g., they wish to avoid an unpleasant chore). However, when lies become more serious, the motives for lying shift in the direction of personal advantage. In one study, participants were asked to reveal the most serious lie that they had ever told (DePaulo et al., 2004). People quite frequently committed serious lies to conceal affairs or other forbidden forms of social contact. People felt that they were entitled to cheat on their partners and lied in service to that sense of entitlement. Thus the lies worked for personal advantage.

Let's focus on the mental processes that people use to lie. Should it be easier or harder to tell a lie than to tell the truth? The answer is: It depends (DePaulo et al., 2003).

Suppose you are asked, 'What did you do last night?' If you choose to lie spontaneously, it might be harder for you to formulate a lie than to tell the truth. However, if you have prepared your lie in advance—because you anticipate the awkward question—you might produce your lie with great fluency. Still, lies and truths differ from each other in some consistent ways. A study that reviewed the literature on the content of lies reported that liars provide fewer details in their accounts than do people who are telling the truth (DePaulo et al., 2003). In addition, liars' accounts were consistently less plausible and less fluent than truthful accounts.

These results suggest that speakers may engage different mental processes to produce their lies. To test this hypothesis, researchers have begun analyse patterns of brain activity that underlie truth-telling and lying. In one study, participants were asked to lie or tell the truth about their participation in an incident in which a gun was fired in a hospital (Mohamed et al., 2006). To make the experience of lying as real as possible, participants in the *guilty* condition actually fired a starter pistol (loaded with blanks) in the testing room. Participants in both the *guilty* and *not-guilty* conditions answered a series of questions while undergoing fMRI scans. Participants in the guilty condition received instructions to lie about their role in the incident. The fMRI scans revealed that several areas of the brain were more active for lying than for truth-telling. For example, brain regions responsible for planning and emotion were harder at work when participants prepared their lies.

Another study looked into the brains of people who qualify as *pathological liars*—these are individuals who lie with sufficient regularity that the behaviour is considered abnormal (by the types of *DSM-IV* criteria we describe in Chapter 14). The overall structure of brains of the pathological liars were compared using MRI to the brains of matched controls (Yang et al., 2005). Those brain comparisons revealed consistent differences in the prefrontal cortex. The pathological liars, for example, had more of the type of brain tissue that allows neurons to communicate with each other. Prefrontal cortex is a region of the brain that plays an important role in planning—suggesting that the pathological liars are particularly well equipped to plan their lies. These results, however, leave open the question of cause and effect: Did pathological liars start life with brains of this type (which, perhaps, caused or allowed them to lie frequently) or did frequent lying change their brains?

# VISUAL COGNITION

In **Figure 8.7**, we give you two choices for visual representations of the sentence 'The cat is on the mat'. Which one seems right? If you think in terms of language-based propositions, each alternative captures the right meaning—the cat *is* on the mat. Even so, you're probably happy only with option A because it matches the scene you likely called to mind when you first read the sentence (Searle, 1979). How about option B? It probably makes you somewhat nervous because it seems as if the cat is going to tip right over. This anxious feeling must arise because you can think with pictures. In a sense, you can *see* exactly what's going to happen. In this section, we will explore some of the ways in which visual images and visual processes contribute to the way you think.

Figure 8.7

**Visual representations**
Are both of these cats on the mat?

## USING VISUAL REPRESENTATIONS

History is full of examples of famous discoveries apparently made on the basis of mental imagery (Shepard, 1978). Frederich Kekulé, the discoverer of the chemical structure of benzene, often conjured up mental images of dancing atoms that fastened themselves into chains of molecules. His discovery of the benzene ring occurred in a dream in which a snakelike molecule chain suddenly grabbed its own tail, thus forming a ring. Michael Faraday, who discovered many properties of magnetism, knew little about mathematics, but he had vivid mental images of the properties of magnetic fields. Albert Einstein claimed to have thought entirely in terms of visual images, translating his findings into mathematical symbols and words only after the work of visually based discovery was finished.

We have given you these examples to encourage you to try to indulge in visual thinking. But even without trying, you regularly use your capabilities for manipulating visual images. Consider a classic experiment in which participants were asked to transform images in their heads.

> Researchers presented students with examples of the letter R and its mirror image that had been rotated various amounts, from 0 to 180 degrees (see **Figure 8.8**). As the letter appeared, the student had to identify it as either the normal R or its mirror image. The reaction time taken to make that decision was longer in direct proportion to the amount the figure had been rotated. This finding indicated that a subject was imagining the figure in his or her 'mind's eye' and rotating the image into an upright position at some fixed rate before deciding whether the figure was an R or a mirror image. The consistency of the rate of rotation suggested that the process of mental rotation was very similar to the process of physical rotation (Shepard & Cooper, 1982).

You put this ability for mental rotation to very good use. You often see objects in the environment from unfamiliar points of view. Mental rotation allows you to transform the

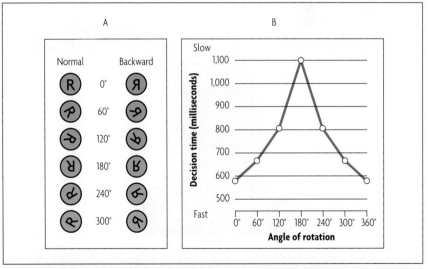

Figure 8.8

**Rotated R used to assess mental imagery**
Participants presented with these figures in random order were asked to say, as quickly as possible, whether each figure was a normal R or a mirror image. The more the figure was rotated from upright, the longer the reaction time was.

image to one that matches representations stored in memory (Lloyd-Jones & Luckhurst, 2002). For example, in Figure 8.7, you almost certainly had to rotate the image (or did you just tilt your head?) to recognise the object as a cat on a mat.

You can also use visual images to answer certain types of questions about the world. Suppose, for example, we asked you whether a golf ball is bigger than a ping-pong ball. If you can't retrieve that fact directly from memory, you might find it convenient to form a visual image of them side by side. This use of an image, once again, has much in common with the properties of real visual perception.

In one study, participants first memorised pictures of complex objects, such as a motorboat (see **Figure 8.9**). Then they were asked to recall their visual images of the boat and focus on one spot—for example, the motor. When asked if the picture contained another object—a windshield or an anchor, for example (both were present)—they took longer to 'see' the anchor than the windshield, which was closer to the motor than the anchor was. The reaction time difference provides evidence that people scan visual images as if they were scanning real objects (Kosslyn, 1980).

There are, of course, limits to the use of your visual imagination. Consider this problem:

*Imagine that you have a large piece of blank paper. In your mind, fold it in half (making two layers), fold it in half again (four layers), and continue folding it over 50 times. About how thick is the paper when you have finished? (Adams, 1986)*

The actual answer is about 79 million kilometres ($2^{50} \times 0.7$mm, the thickness of a piece of paper),

approximately half the distance between Earth and the sun. Your estimate was probably considerably lower. Your mind's eye was overwhelmed by the information you asked it to represent.

We want you to try one last exercise using visual imagery. Find any object in your environment and examine it for a few seconds. Now, close your eyes and try to create a visual image of the same object. Consider this question: How much overlap was there in the brain regions that were active when you engaged in visual perception versus visual imagery?

To answer this question, researchers had participants learn a series of line drawings of common objects such as a tree (Ganis et al., 2004). In the next phase of the experiment, participants underwent fMRI scans while they either inspected the same drawings on a computer screen or generated visual images of the drawings. For each drawing, they answered a simple question such as whether the object contained circular parts. **Figure 8.10** presents the results of the fMRI scans from different regions of the brain. The left and middle columns show the regions of the brain that differed for each task from the baseline condition (i.e., when participants were not engaged in a task). The right column shows the brain regions that were particular to the perception task. These data support two important conclusions. First, there was substantial overlap between brain processes for perception and imagery. Second, brain regions for imagery were a subset of those for perception—participants didn't use any special regions to create a visual image. With respect to brain activity, you use much the same resources to encode the visual world as to recreate a visual representation.

## COMBINING VERBAL AND VISUAL REPRESENTATIONS

Our discussion so far has largely focused on the types of visual representations that you form by committing to memory—or in the case of imagery, retrieving from memory—visual stimuli from the environment. However, you often form visual images based on verbal descriptions. You can, for example, create a mental picture of a cat with three tails, although you've almost certainly never seen one. The verbal description enables you to form a visual representation. Your ability to produce a mental image of a verbal scene is particularly useful when you read works of fiction that involve spatial details. Consider this passage from the James Bond short story 'From a View to a Kill':

*The clearing was about as big as two tennis courts and floored in thick grass and moss. There was one large patch of lilies of the valley and, under the bordering trees, a scattering of bluebells. To one side there was a low mound . . . completely surrounded and covered with brambles and briar roses now thickly in bloom. Bond walked round this and gazed in among the roots, but there was nothing to see except the earthy shape of the mound. (Fleming, 1959, pp. 19–20)*

Figure 8.9

Visual scanning of mental images

After studying a picture of a boat, subjects were asked to 'look at' the motor in their own mental images. They were then asked whether the boat had a windshield or an anchor. The faster response to the windshield, which was closer to the motor than was the anchor, indicated that the subjects were scanning their visual images.

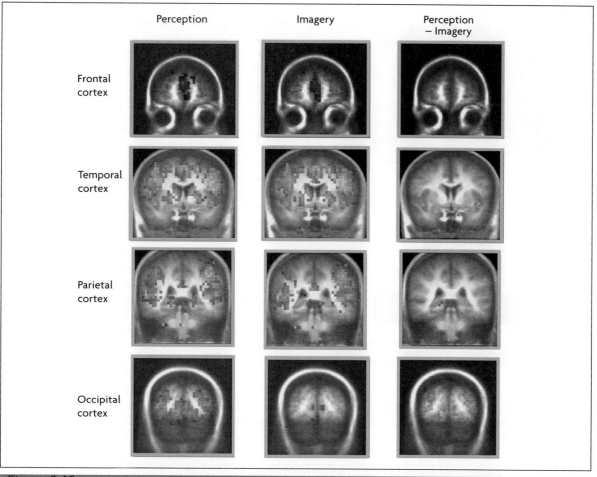

|  | Perception | Imagery | Perception – Imagery |
|---|---|---|---|
| Frontal cortex | | | |
| Temporal cortex | | | |
| Parietal cortex | | | |
| Occipital cortex | | | |

Figure 8.10

**The brain bases of visual imagery**

The figure shows the results of fMRI scans when participants were engaged in either a perception task or an imagery task. The left and middle columns show brain activity for each task: regions marked with red, orange and yellow were more active with respect to a no-task baseline; regions marked in blues were less active. The right column shows the brain regions that were affected by the perception task but not the imagery task. These fMRI scans demonstrate that much the same brain regions are used for perception and imagery.

Reprinted from *Cognitive Brain Research, 20*, G. Ganis et al., 'Brain areas underlying visual mental imagery and visual perception: An fMRI study,' pp. 226–241, copyright © 2004, with permission from Elsevier.

Did you try to imagine the scene—and help Bond search for danger? (He will find it.) When you read, you can form a *spatial mental model* to keep track of the whereabouts of characters (Zwaan & Radvansky, 1998). Researchers have often focused on the ways in which spatial mental models capture properties of real spatial experiences (Rinck et al., 1997).

Suppose, for example, you read a passage of a text that places you in the middle of an interesting environment.

*You are hob-nobbing at the opera. You came tonight to meet and chat with interesting members of the upper class. At the moment, you are standing next to the railing of a wide, elegant balcony overlooking the first floor. Directly behind you, at your eye level, is an ornate lamp attached to the balcony wall. The base of the lamp, which is attached to the wall, is gilded in gold. (Franklin & Tversky, 1990, p. 65)*

In a series of experiments, readers studied descriptions of this sort that vividly described the layout of objects around the viewer (Franklin & Tversky, 1990). The researchers wished to show that readers were faster or slower to access information about the scene, depending on where the objects were in the mental space around them. Readers, for example, were quicker to say what object was in front of them in the scene than what object was behind them, even though all objects were introduced equally carefully in the stories (see **Figure 8.11**). It's easiest to understand this result if you believe that the representation you form while reading actually places you, in some sense, in the scene. You are able to transform a verbal experience into a visual, spatial experience.

In general, when you think about the world around you, you are almost always combining visual and verbal representations of information. To prove that to yourself, you can take a minute to draw a map of the world. Go ahead—

Figure 8.11

**Spatial mental models**
You can use imagination to project yourself into the middle of a scene. Just as if you were really standing in the room, you would take less time to say what is in front of you (the lamp) than what is behind you (the bust).

make a sketch! How do you go about doing this? Some of the things you draw in are probably based on visual experiences—you know the overall shape of Africa only because you have seen it represented in the past. Other features of your drawing will probably rely on verbal information—you are likely to remember that Japan is made up of several islands, even if you don't have a visual representation of quite where they go. In one study, nearly 4,000 students from 71 cities in 49 countries were asked to carry out the task of drawing a world map (Saarinen, 1987). The goal of the study was to broaden understanding of cultural differences in the way the world is visualised and to promote world peace. The study found that the majority of maps had a Eurocentric worldview. Europe was placed in the centre of the map and the other countries were arranged around it, probably due to the dominance for many centuries of Eurocentric representations in geography books. For example, the common Mercator projection, 'stretches' the poles to occupy the whole of the top and bottom of the page. This results in countries closer to the poles being larger on the map, relative to their real size, than those closer to the equator. Europe, especially northern Europe, therefore appears proportionally larger than more equatorial Asia, Africa and Australia,

However, the study also yielded many instances of culture-biased maps, such as the one by a Chicago student, in **Figure 8.12**, and that of an Australian student, in **Figure 8.13**. These maps show what happens when a verbal perspective—My home should be in the middle!—is imposed on a visual representation.

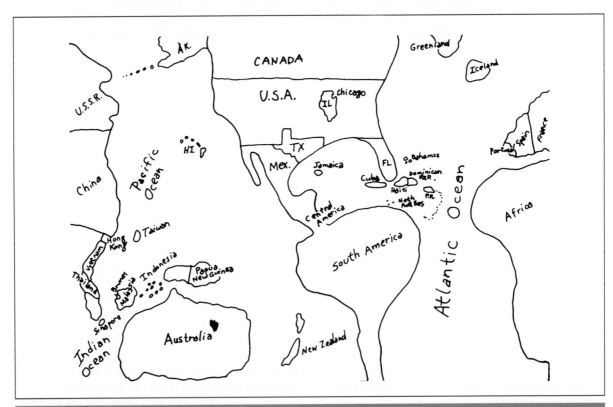

Figure 8.12

**A Chicagocentric view of the world**
How does this view of the world compare with yours?

**CHAPTER 8** COGNITIVE PROCESSES

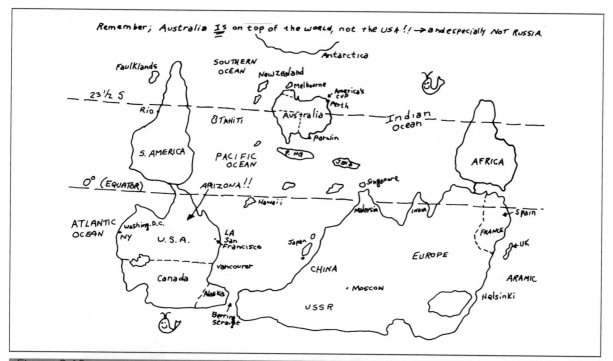

Remember; Australia **IS** on top of the world, not the USA !! → and especially NOT RUSSIA.

Figure 8.13

An Australocentric view of the world
Down Under is back on top!

Both figures from Robert L. Solso, *Cognitive Psychology*, 3e, pp. 7, 289, 290. Published by Allyn and Bacon, Boston, MA. Copyright © 1991 by Pearson Education. Reprinted by permission of the publisher.

In this section, we have seen that you have visual processes and representations to complement your verbal abilities. These two types of access to information give you extra help in dealing with the demands and tasks of your life. We turn now to domains in which you put both visual and verbal representations to use in coping with your life's complexities: *problem solving* and *reasoning*.

For answers go to MyPsychLab!

## RECAP CHECKPOINT

### Visual cognition

- Visual representations can be used to supplement propositional representations.
- Visual representations allow you to think about visual aspects of your environment.
- People form visual representations that combine verbal and visual information.

## CONCEPT QUESTIONS

1. How similar are the processes of physical rotation and mental rotation?

2. What has research shown about the brain bases of visual images?

3. If you're imagining yourself in a scene, does it matter how you place yourself in the room?

## CRITICAL THINKING

Consider the experiment on scanning of mental images. Why was it important for participants to memorise the pictures in advance?

# PROBLEM SOLVING AND REASONING

Let's return for a minute to your mysterious message, 'The cat is on the mat'. If you've come to understand the message, what do you do next? For those of you whose lives are less filled with mystery, consider a more common situation: You've accidentally locked yourself out of your home, room or car. Again, what do you do next? For both situations, reflect on the types of mental steps you might take to overcome your difficulty. Those mental steps will almost certainly include the cognitive processes that

**problem solving** Thinking that is directed toward solving specific problems and that moves from an initial state to a goal state by means of a set of mental operations.

**reasoning** The process of thinking in which conclusions are drawn from a set of facts.

make up **problem solving** and **reasoning**. Both of these activities require you to combine current information with information stored in memory to work toward some particular goal: a conclusion or a solution. We will look at aspects of problem solving and at two types of reasoning: *deductive* and *inductive*.

## PROBLEM SOLVING

*What goes on four legs in the morning, on two legs at noon, and on three legs in the twilight?* According to Greek mythology, this was the riddle posed by the Sphinx, an evil creature who threatened to hold the people of Thebes in tyranny until someone could solve the riddle. To break the code, Oedipus had to recognise elements of the riddle as metaphors. Morning, noon and twilight represented different periods in a human life. A baby crawls and so (effectively) has four legs, an adult walks on two legs, and

an older person walks on two legs but uses a cane, making a total of three legs. Oedipus's solution to the riddle was *humans.*

Although your daily problems may not seem as monumental as the one faced by young Oedipus, problem-solving activity is a basic part of your everyday existence. You continually come up against problems that require solutions: how to manage work and tasks within a limited time frame, how to succeed at a job interview, how to break off a relationship, and so on. Many problems involve discrepancies between what you know and what you need to know. When you solve a problem, you reduce that discrepancy by finding a way to get the missing information. To get into the spirit of problem solving, try the problems in **Figures 8.14** and **8.15**. After you're finished, we'll see how psychological research can shed light on your performance—and, perhaps, provide some suggestions about how to improve it.

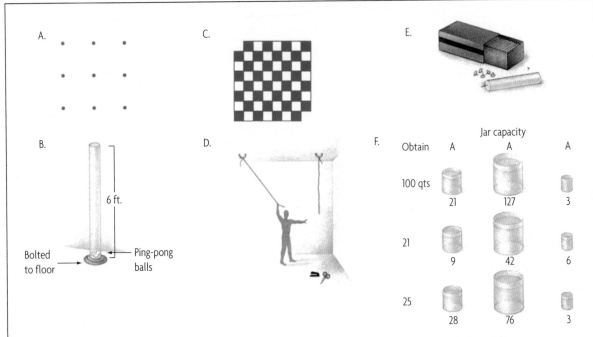

(A) Can you connect all the dots in the pattern by drawing four straight, connected lines without lifting your pen from the paper?
(B) A prankster has put 3 ping-pong balls into a 6-foot-long pipe that is standing vertically in the corner of the physics lab, fastened to the floor. How would you get the ping-pong balls out?
(C) The checkerboard shown has had 2 corner pieces cut out, leaving 62 squares. You have 31 dominoes, each of which covers exactly 2 checkerboard squares. Can you use them to cover the whole checkerboard?
(D) You are in the situation depicted and given the task of tying the 2 strings together. If you hold one string, the other is out of reach. Can you do it?
(E) You are given the objects shown (a candle, tacks, matches in a matchbox). The task is to mount a lighted candle on a door. Can you do it?
(F) You are given 3 'water-jar' problems. Using only the 3 containers (water supply is unlimited), can you obtain the exact amount specified in each case?

Figure 8.14

**Can you solve it? (Part I)**
Try to solve each of these problems (the answers are given in Figure 8.15 on page 270, but don't look until you try to solve them all).

CHAPTER 8 COGNITIVE PROCESSES

**Problem spaces and processes** How do you define a problem in real-life circumstances? You usually perceive the difference between your current state and a desired goal: For example, you are broke, and you'd like to have some money. You are also usually aware of some of the steps you would be able (or willing) to take to bridge the gap: You will try to get a part-time job, but you won't become a pickpocket. The formal definition of a *problem* captures these three elements (Newell & Simon, 1972). A problem is defined by (1) an *initial state*—the incomplete information or unsatisfactory conditions you start with; (2) a *goal state*—the information or state of the world you hope to obtain; and (3) a *set of operations*—the steps you may take to move from an initial state to a goal state. Together, these three parts define the **problem space**. You can think of solving a problem as walking through a maze (the problem space) from where you are (the initial state) to where you want to be (the goal state), making a series of turns (the allowable operations).

Much of the initial difficulty in solving a problem will arise if any of these elements are not well defined (Simon, 1973). A *well-defined problem* is similar to a textbook problem in which the initial state, the goal state, and the operations are all clearly specified. Your task is to discover how to use allowable, known operations to get the answer. In contrast, an *ill-defined problem* is similar to designing a home, writing a novel, or finding a cure for AIDS. The initial state, the goal state, and/or the operations may be unclear and vaguely specified. In such cases, the problem solver's first task is to work out, as much as possible, exactly what the problem is—to make explicit a beginning, an ideal solution, and the possible means to achieve it.

As you know from your own experience, even when the initial and goal states are well defined, it can still be difficult to find the right set of operations to get from the beginning to the end. If you think back to your experience in maths classes, you know that this is true. Your teacher gave you a formula like $x^2 + x - 12 = 0$ and asked you to solve for possible values of $x$. What do you do next? To solve this algebra problem, you can use an **algorithm**: a step-by-step procedure that always provides the right answer for a particular type of problem. If you apply the rules of algebra correctly, you are guaranteed to obtain the correct values of $x$ (i.e., 3 and −4). If you've ever forgotten the combination to a lock, you may also have engaged in behaviour guided by an algorithm. If you try solutions systematically (e.g., 1, 2, 3; 1, 2, 4) you will definitely arrive at the right combination—though you may be at it for a good long while! Because well-defined problems have clear initial states and goal states, algorithms are more likely to be available for them than for ill-defined problems. When algorithms are unavailable, problem solvers often rely on **heuristics**, which are strategies or 'rules of thumb.' Suppose, for example, you are reading a mystery and you'd like to solve the problem of who murdered an e-commerce tycoon. You might rule out the possibility that 'the butler did it' because you use the heuristic that authors wouldn't use such a trite plot line. As we shall see

How do scientists approach the ill-defined problem of curing AIDS?

**problem space** The elements that make up a problem.

shortly, heuristics are also a critical aspect of *judgment* and *decision making*.

Researchers have been interested in understanding the way people apply both algorithms and heuristics as they make their way through a problem space. To study the steps problem solvers take, researchers have often turned to **think-aloud protocols**. In this procedure, participants are asked to verbalise their ongoing thoughts (Ericsson & Simon, 1993). For example, a pair of researchers were interested in capturing the mental processes that enable participants to solve the mutilated checkerboard problem that is part C of Figure 8.14 (Kaplan & Simon, 1990). Here is one of their participants having the crucial breakthrough that the problem cannot be solved with only horizontal and vertical placement of pieces (the checkerboard was pink and black):

> *So you're leaving . . . it's short—how many, you're leaving uhhhh . . . there's more pinks than black, and in order to complete it you'd have to connect two pinks but you can't because they are diagonally . . . is that getting close? (Kaplan & Simon, 1990, p. 388)*

The solver has just realised that the goal cannot be accomplished if the dominoes can just be placed horizontally or vertically. Researchers have often used participants' own accounts of their thinking as the starting point for more formal models of problem solving (Simon, 1979, 1989).

**think-aloud protocols** Reports made by experimental participants of the mental processes and strategies they use while working on a task.

**algorithm** A step-by-step procedure that always provides the right answer for a particular type of problem.

**heuristics** Cognitive strategies, or 'rules of thumb', often used as shortcuts in solving a complex inferential task.

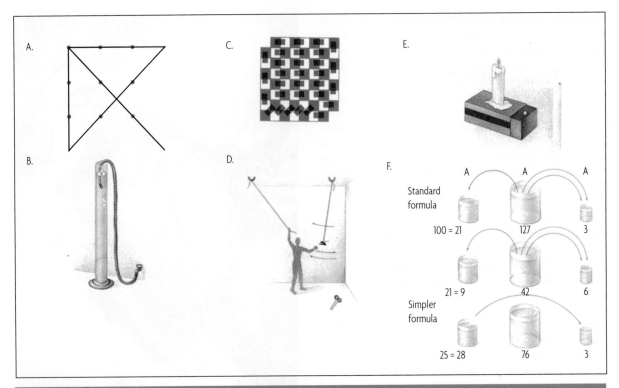

Figure 8.15

Can you solve it? (Part II)

Here are the solutions to the problems. How did you do? As the section on problem solving and reasoning unfolds, we will talk about what makes these problems hard.

Reprinted with permission from *How to Solve Problems* by Wayne A. Wickelgren, p. 31. Copyright ©1974 by W.H. Freeman and Company.

**Improving your problem solving** What makes problem solving hard? If you reflect on your day-to-day experience, you might come up with the answer 'There are too many things to consider all at once.' Research on problem solving has led to much the same conclusion. What often makes a problem difficult to solve is that the mental requirements for solving a particular problem overwhelm processing resources (Kotovsky & Simon, 1990; MacGregor et al., 2001). To solve a problem, you need to plan the series of operations you will take. If that series becomes too complex, or if each operation itself is too complex, you may be unable to see your way through from the initial state to the goal state. How might you overcome this potential limitation?

An important step in improving problem solving is to find a way to represent a problem so that each operation is possible, given your processing resources. If you must habitually solve similar problems, a useful procedure is to practise each of the components of the solution so that, over time, those components require fewer resources (Kotovsky et al., 1985). Suppose, for example, you were a cab driver in New York City and were faced with daily traffic jams. You might mentally practise your responses to jams at various points in the city, so that you'd have ready solutions to components of the overall problem of getting your fare from a pickup spot to a destination. By practising these component solutions, you could keep more of your attention on the road!

Sometimes, finding a useful representation means finding a whole new way to think about the problem (Novick & Bassok, 2005). Read the puzzle given in **Table 8.6**. How would you go about offering this proof? Think about it for a few minutes before you read on. How well did you do? If the word *proof* suggested to you something mathematical, you probably didn't make much progress. A better way to think about the problem is to imagine two monks, one starting at the top and another starting at the bottom (Adams, 1986). As one climbs and one descends, it's clear that they will pass at some point along the mountain, right (see **Figure 8.16**)? Now replace the pair of monks with just the one—conceptually it's the same—and there's your proof. What makes this problem suddenly very easy is using the right sort of representation: visual rather than verbal or mathematical.

If you go back to the problems in Figure 8.14 you have other good examples of the importance of an appropriate representation of the problem space. To get the ping-pong balls out of the pipe, you had to realise that the solution did not involve reaching into the pipe. To connect the two strings, you had to see one of the tools on the floor as a weight. To mount the candle on the door, you had to alter your usual perspective and perceive the matchbox as a platform instead of as a container, and you had to perceive the candle as a tool as well as the object to be mounted on the door. The last two problems show a phenomenon called functional fixedness (Duncker, 1945; Maier, 1931). **Functional fixedness** is a mental block that adversely affects problem solving by inhibiting the perception of a new function for an object that was previously associated with some other purpose. Whenever you are stuck on a problem, you should ask yourself, 'How am I representing the problem? Are there different or better ways that I can think about the problem or components of its solution?' If words don't work, try drawing a picture. Or try examining your assumptions, and see what 'rules' you can break by making novel combinations.

Often, when you try to solve problems, you engage in special forms of thinking that are called reasoning. Let's turn now to a first type of reasoning you use to solve problems, *deductive reasoning*.

## DEDUCTIVE REASONING

Suppose you are on your way to a restaurant and you want to pay for your meal with your only credit card, American Express. You call the restaurant and ask, 'Do you accept American Express?' The restaurant's hostess replies, 'We accept all major credit cards.' You can now safely conclude that they accept American Express. To see why, we can reformulate your interchange to fit the structure of the *syllogism*, introduced by the Greek philosopher Aristotle over 2,000 years ago:

> *Premise 1. The restaurant accepts all major credit cards. Premise 2. American Express is a major credit card. Conclusion. The restaurant accepts American Express.*

Aristotle was concerned with defining the logical relationships between statements that would lead to *valid* conclusions. **Deductive reasoning** involves the correct application of such logical rules. We gave the credit card example to show that you are quite capable of drawing conclusions that have the form of logical, deductive proofs. Even so, psychological research has focused on the question of whether you actually have the formal rules of deductive reasoning represented in your mind (Schaeken et al., 2000). This body of research suggests that you may have some general, abstract sense of formal logic, but your real-world deductive reasoning is affected both by the specific knowledge you possess about the world and the representational resources you can bring to bear on a particular reasoning problem. Let's expand on these conclusions.

> *How does knowledge influence deductive reasoning? Consider this syllogism:*

> *Premise 1. All things that have a motor need oil. Premise 2. Automobiles need oil.*

> *Conclusion. Automobiles have motors.*

Is this a valid conclusion? According to the rules of logic, it is *not* because Premise 1 leaves open the possibility that some things that don't have motors will also need oil. The difficulty is that what is invalid in a logic problem is not

See a 'proof' for the monk puzzle in Figure 8.16.

| Table 8.6 |
| --- |
| **The monk puzzle** |
| One morning, exactly at sunrise, a Buddhist monk began to climb a tall mountain. A narrow path, no more than a foot or two wide, spiralled around the mountain to a glittering temple at the summit. The monk ascended at varying rates of speed, stopping many times along the way to rest and eat dried fruit he carried with him. He reached the temple shortly before sunset. After several days of fasting and meditation, he began his journey back along the same path, starting at sunrise and again walking at variable speeds with many pauses along the way. His average speed descending was, of course, greater than his average climbing speed. Prove that there is a spot along the path that the monk will occupy on both trips at precisely the same time of day. |

'The Monk Puzzle' from *Conceptual Blockbusting: A Guide to Better Ideas* by James L. Adams. © 1974.

necessarily untrue in real life. That is, if you take Premises 1 and 2 to be all the information in your possession—as you should if you accept this simply as an exercise in formal logic—the conclusion is not valid. Even so, when participants judge whether the conclusion 'follows logically from the premises', they are much more inclined to say yes when the conclusion considers *automobiles* than they are when the nonsense term *oppobines* is substituted (Markovitz & Nantel, 1989).

This result illustrates a general **belief-bias effect**: People tend to judge as valid those conclusions that they find believable and judge as invalid those conclusions they find unbelievable (Janis & Frick, 1943). Research suggests that the belief bias emerges because of the type of processing in which people engage in response to believable versus unbelievable conclusions (Ball et al., 2006). When you see a conclusion you believe such as 'automobiles have motors', you are likely to engage in *confirmatory* testing so that you try to find a mental model of circumstances that match the conclusion. If you can find that confirmatory evidence, you're through. That explains why you don't settle in long enough to see the possibility that—with respect to the logical structure of the premises—automobiles might need oil for reasons other than having a motor. When you see a conclusion you disbelieve, you're likely to engage in *disconfirmatory* testing—you work harder to find circumstances that invalidate the conclusion. When you try to assess the logic of conclusions, try not to let yourself be biased in favour of the beliefs you hold in advance. You might be happy to learn that formal instruction on logical reasoning, of the sort you are obtaining now, helps reduce belief bias (Evans et al., 1994).

In some cases, your ability to apply real-world knowledge helps you to perform better on reasoning tasks. Imagine that you are given the array of four cards pictured in **Figure 8.17**, which have printed on them *A, D, 4*

**functional fixedness** An inability to perceive a new use for an object previously associated with some other purpose.

**belief-bias effect** A situation that occurs when a person's prior knowledge, attitudes or values distort the reasoning process by influencing the person to accept invalid arguments.

**deductive reasoning** A form of thinking in which one draws a conclusion that is intended to follow logically from two or more statements or premises.

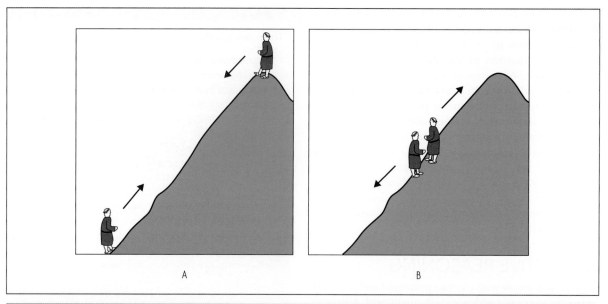

## Figure 8.16

**A 'proof' for the monk puzzle**
Panel A shows two monks, one who starts at the bottom of the mountain and one who starts at the top. Panel B shows that they must meet at some time during the day. Replace the two monks with a single monk, and you have your proof!

Reprinted with permission from *How to Solve Problems* by Wayne A. Wickelgren, p. 31. Copyright © 1974 by W.H. Freeman and Company.

and *7*. Your task is to determine which cards you must turn over to test the rule 'If a card has a vowel on one side, then it has an even number on the other side' (Johnson-Laird & Wason, 1977). What would you do? Most people say that they would turn over the *A*, which is correct, and the *4*—which is incorrect. No matter what character appears on the flip side of the *4*, the rule will not be invalidated. (Can you see why that is true?) Instead, you must flip the *7*. If you were to find a vowel there, you would have invalidated the rule.

The original research on this task, which is often called the *Wason selection task*, prompted doubts about people's ability to reason effectively. This negative view, however, has been modified in two ways. First, researchers have suggested that participants may follow a nondeductive strategy of examining the cards that will allow them to *confirm* rather than *disconfirm* the generality of the relationship stated in the rule. Although this strategy may lead to the appearance of faulty deductive reasoning, it is a reasonable real-world strategy for learning about associations and making decisions (Oaksford & Chater, 1994; Oaksford et al., 1997).

Second, deductive reasoning is improved when participants are able to apply their real-world knowledge to the Wason task (Holyoak & Spellman, 1993). Suppose you were asked to perform what is a logically comparable task, on the lower set of cards in Figure 8.17. In this case, however, you are asked to evaluate the rule 'If a customer is to drink an alcoholic beverage, then she *must* be at least 18' (Cheng & Holyoak, 1985). Now you can probably see immediately which are the correct cards to turn over: *17* and *drinking beer*. If you look at Figure 8.17, you'll see

that 7 and 17 have the same logical function. You need to turn 17 over for the same reasons of logic you need to turn 7 over. However, your real-world experience helps you appreciate why turning 17 over is logically necessary.

This example of age and alcohol comes from the more general category of permission situations. You probably have a good deal of experience with these sorts of situations—recall all the times you were given conditions like, 'You can't watch television unless you do your homework.' You most likely never recognised that

## Figure 8.17

**Abstract versus real-world reasoning**
In the top row, you are required to say which cards you must turn over to test the rule 'If a card has a vowel on one side, then it has an even number on the other side.' In the bottom row, you must say which cards you need to turn over to test the rule 'If a customer is to drink an alcoholic beverage, then she *must* be at least 18.' People typically do better on the second task, which allows them to use real-world strategies.

deductive inference was involved in such circumstances! Some researchers suggest that people encode a *pragmatic reasoning schema* based on early life experiences with permission situations (Chao & Cheng, 2000). This schema allows individuals to reason effectively in the types of permissions situations that have occurred in their environments. The real-life situation linking age to drinking calls to mind this schema; the arbitrary situation linking even numbers and vowels does not. As a consequence, the arbitrary reasoning task underestimates your ability to make correct deductions.

Note that researchers who take an evolutionary perspective on human cognition have proposed an alternative to the view that people *acquire* a schema with respect to permissions. In a version of the card-turning task adapted for children, participants as young as 3 years old could reason successfully about what was and was not permitted by a rule. This result suggests that reasoning about permission situations may be innate (Cummins, 1996). That is, the ability to determine when actions do not follow social norms may be part of the genetic package you inherited as a member of the highly social human species (Cummins, 1999).

To begin this section on deductive reasoning, we described a situation in which you drew a valid deductive inference about your ability to use your American Express card to buy a meal. Unfortunately, life provides many occasions on which you cannot be so certain that you have drawn valid inferences from valid premises. We turn now to a version of the restaurant scenario that requires you to use a different form of reasoning.

## INDUCTIVE REASONING

Let's suppose that you have arrived outside the restaurant and only then think to check to see if you have enough cash. Once again you find that you'll want to use your American Express card, but there's no helpful sign on the outside. You peek through the restaurant's windows and see well-dressed clientele. You look at the expensive prices on the menu. You consider the upscale quality of the neighbourhood. All these observations lead you to believe that the restaurant is likely to take your credit card. This is not deductive reasoning because your conclusion is based on probabilities rather than logical certainties. Instead, this is **inductive reasoning**—a form of reasoning that uses available evidence to generate likely, but not certain, conclusions.

Although the name might be new, we have already described to you several examples of inductive reasoning. We saw repeatedly, in Chapters 4 and 7, that people use past information stored as schemas to generate expectations about the present and future. You are using inductive reasoning, for example, if you decide that a certain odour in the air indicates that someone is making popcorn; you are using inductive reasoning if you agree that the words on this page are unlikely to suddenly become invisible (and that, if you study, your knowledge of this material won't become invisible on exam day). Finally, earlier in this chapter, we discussed the types of inferences people

draw when they use language. Your belief that *she* must be *Jessica* in the sequence of utterances we gave you relies on inductive inference.

In real-life circumstances, much of your problem-solving ability relies on inductive reasoning. Return to our earlier example: You have accidentally locked yourself out of your home, room, or car. What should you do? A good first step is to call up from memory solutions that worked in the past. This process is called *analogical problem solving*: You establish an analogy between the features of the current situation and the features of previous situations (Chen et al., 2004; Holyoak & Thagard, 1997). In this case, your past experiences of 'being locked out' may have allowed you to form the *generalisation* 'find other people with keys' (Ross & Kennedy, 1990). With that generalisation in hand, you can start to figure out who those individuals might be and how to find them. This task might require you to retrieve the method you developed for tracking down your room-mates at their afternoon classes. If this problem seems easy to you, it's because you have grown accustomed to letting your past inform your present: inductive reasoning allows you to access tried-and-true methods that speed current problem solving.

We have one caution to add about inductive reasoning. Often a solution that has worked in the past can be reused for a successful solution. But sometimes you must recognise that reliance on the past can hamper your problem-solving ability when there is a critical difference between the old and current situations. The water-jar problem given in Figure 8.14 is a classic example of circumstances in which reliance on the past may cause you to miss a solution to a problem (Luchins, 1942). If you had discovered, in the first two problems in part F, the conceptual rule that $B - A - 2(C) = answer$, you probably tried the same formula for the third problem and found it didn't work. Actually, simply filling jar $A$ and pouring off enough to fill jar $C$ would have left you with the right amount. If you were using your initial formula, you probably did not notice this simpler possibility—your previous success with the other rule would have given you a mental set. A **mental set** is a pre-existing state of mind, habit or attitude that can enhance the quality and speed of perceiving and problem solving under some conditions. However, the same set may inhibit or distort the quality of your mental activities at times when old ways of thinking and acting are non-productive in new situations. When you find yourself frustrated in a problem-solving situation, you might take a step back and ask yourself, 'Am I allowing past successes to narrow my focus too much?' Try to make your problem solving more creative by considering a broader spectrum of past situations and past solutions.

Unlike deductive reasoning, which is based upon logic and argument structure, inductive reasoning also relies upon one's experiences and understanding of the world. As we have more experiences in life, our ability to inductively reason to an acceptable solution also changes. John Taplin, Brett Hayes and colleagues at the University of New South Wales have conducted a series of studies relevant to changes in the process of inductive

**mental set** The tendency to respond to a new problem in the manner used to respond to a previous problem.

**inductive reasoning** A form of reasoning in which a conclusion is made about the probability of some state of affairs, based on the available evidence and past experience.

reasoning as a child grows older (Hayes et al., 2002). In general, as children age they are less likely to draw conclusions from specific observations—*if an animal is woolly then it is probably a sheep*—to more general and abstract features—*if an animal is woolly then it probably lives somewhere cold*. This change in inductive reasoning style also reflects the development of more sophisticated concepts and more complex and general schemata (see Chapter 7 for a discussion of schema theory). The accumulation of experiences both broadens and informs the inductive reasoning process.

Before we leave this discussion of reasoning, we're going to turn once more to your brain. In this section, we've made a rather strong distinction between deductive and inductive reasoning. Research suggests that separation also exists in the way your brain accomplishes the two types of reasoning.

Participants carried out two types of reasoning tasks while their brains were undergoing PET scans. As shown in the top portion of **Figure 8.18**, one type of problem required deduction. Participants viewed classic syllogisms and assessed whether the conclusions were valid or not. A second type of problem provided premises that left conclusions uncertain. For that reason, the problems required participants to engage in inductive reasoning. Participants indicated whether the arguments were likely to be true than false. As shown in the bottom portion of Figure 8.18, the two types of reasoning brought about different patterns of activation. The data are easy to summarise: deductive reasoning

produced greater activation in the right hemisphere; inductive reasoning produced greater activation in the left hemisphere (Parsons & Osherson, 2001).

To make sense of this result, think back to Chapter 3. Recall that your left hemisphere plays a large role in language processing whereas your right hemisphere does not. The results of this study on reasoning suggest that deductive reasoning involves a type of logical analysis that is relatively independent of language. Inductive reasoning calls upon the language-based comprehension and inferencing processes we described earlier in the chapter.

In this section, we have examined a range of types of problem solving and reasoning—and have suggested, in each case, concrete steps you can take to improve your performance in real-world circumstances. We follow the same strategy in the final section of the chapter. We describe some major research findings on the processes of *judgment* and *decision making* and then suggest how you can apply those findings to important situations in your life.

## RECAP CHECKPOINT
### Problem solving and reasoning

- Problem solvers must define initial state, goal state, and the operations that get them from the initial to the goal state.

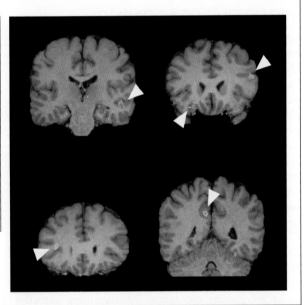

| Deductive reasoning: | Inductive reasoning: |
|---|---|
| Either he likes country music or he listens to opera. | If he is either an accountant or a librarian he listens to opera. |
| He does not like country music. | He listens to opera. |
| He listens to opera. | He is an accountant. |
| **Is the conclusion valid?** | **Is the conclusion more likely to be true than false?** |

## Figure 8.18

### Reasoning in the brain
When students were asked to carry out deductive reasoning, brain structures on the right sides of their brain were relatively more active. (Those areas are shown in green.) When students were asked to carry out inductive reasoning, brain structures on the left sides of their brain were relatively more active. (Those areas are shown in yellow.)

From Parsons & Osherson, 2001, p. 959.

- Deductive reasoning involves drawing conclusions from premises based on rules of logic.
- Inductive reasoning involves inferring a conclusion from evidence based on its likelihood or probability.

## CONCEPT QUESTIONS

1. With respect to problem solving, what is an algorithm?

2. What does it mean to overcome functional fixedness?

3. What happens when people succumb to the belief-bias effect?

4. What role does memory play in inductive reasoning?

## CRITICAL THINKING

Consider the experiment on the brain bases of reasoning processes. For the inductive reasoning problems, why did participants judge likely rather than absolute truth or falsehood?

# JUDGMENT AND DECISION MAKING

For a final time, we're back to 'The cat is on the mat.' Let's engage the processes of *judgment* and *decision making*. How likely is it that the message was just a prank? How likely is it that the message has some real importance that has eluded you? Should you just give up and go to sleep?

This series of questions illustrates one of the great truths of your day-to-day experience: you live in a world filled with *uncertainty*. Here are some more questions, of a sort that will be entirely familiar. Should you spend $10 on a movie you may or may not enjoy? Before an exam, would you be better off studying your notes or rereading the chapter? Are you ready to commit yourself to a long-term relationship? Because you can only guess at the future, and because you almost never have full knowledge of the past, very rarely can you be completely certain that you have made a correct judgment or decision. Thus the processes of judgment and decision making must operate in a way that allows you to deal efficiently with uncertainty. As **Herbert Simon**, one of the founding figures of cognitive psychology, put it: because 'human thinking powers are very modest when compared with the complexities of the environments in which human beings live' they must

be content 'to find "good enough" solutions to their problems and "good enough" courses of action' (1979, p. 3). In this light, Simon suggested that thought processes are guided by *bounded rationality*. Your judgments or decisions might not be as good—as 'rational'—as they always could be, but you should be able to see how they result from your applying limited resources to situations that require swift action.

Despite what politicians may say, the world has not become 'more uncertain' since the 9/11 hijackings or the Bali bombing, nor indeed since the last rise in housing interest rates. It is sometimes useful in politics to present uncertainty as a new and special problem (and of course to say that the party you favour can somehow offer less uncertainty!). The future has been uncertain throughout our evolutionary history, and in order to survive we have to develop methods of making 'best guesses' about what might happen from a range of possibilities. From the perspective of an evolutionary psychologist our species would have developed its way of making decisions in an uncertain world because it was adaptive—individuals who could respond quickly WITHOUT always having to reason everything through were more likely to survive.

Before we move to a closer analysis of the products of bounded rationality, let's quickly distinguish between the two processes of judgment and decision making. **Judgment** is the process by which you form opinions, reach conclusions, and make critical evaluations of events and people. You often make judgments spontaneously, without prompting. **Decision making** is the process of choosing between alternatives, selecting and rejecting available options. Judgment and decision making are interrelated processes. For example, you might meet someone at a party and, after a brief discussion and a dance together, *judge* the person to be intelligent, interesting, honest and sincere. You might then *decide* to spend most of your party time with that person and to arrange a date for the next weekend; decision making is more closely linked to behavioural actions. Let's turn now to research on these two types of thinking.

## HEURISTICS AND JUDGMENT

What's the best way to make a judgment? Suppose, for example, you are asked whether you enjoyed a movie. To answer this question, you could fill out a chart with two columns, 'What I liked about the movie' and 'What I didn't like about the movie,' and see which column came out longer. To be a bit more accurate, perhaps you'd weight the entries in each list according to their importance (thus you might weight 'the actors' performances' as more important on the plus side than 'the blaring sound track' on the minus side). If you went through this whole procedure, you'd probably be pretty confident of your judgment—but you know already that this is an exercise you rarely undertake. In real-life circumstances, you have to make judgments frequently and rapidly. You don't have the time—and often you don't have sufficient

For answers go to MyPsychLab!

**judgment** The process by which people form opinions, reach conclusions and make critical evaluations of events and people based on available material.

**decision making** The process of choosing between alternatives; selecting or rejecting available options.

If you were in a happy mood, would you be more likely to remember good times from your younger days?

availability heurisitic A judgment based on the information readily available in memory.

information—to use such a formal procedure. What do you do instead? An answer to this question was pioneered by **Amos Tversky** and **Daniel Kahneman**, who argued that people's judgments rely on heuristics rather than on formal methods of analysis. As we noted in our discussion of problem solving, heuristics are informal rules of thumb that provide shortcuts, reducing the complexity of making judgments.

How do you demonstrate that people are using these mental rules of thumb? As you will soon see, researchers have most often opted to show the circumstances in which the shortcuts lead people to make errors. The logic of these experiments should sound familiar to you by now: just as you can understand perception by studying perceptual illusion and memory by studying memory failures, you can understand judgment processes by studying judgment errors (Kahneman, 1991). As in those other domains, you have to be careful not to mistake the method for the conclusion. Even though there is a wide range of situations in which psychologists can show that your perceptual processes can be fooled, you rarely walk into walls. Similarly, despite the errors that arise because your judgment making is implemented by heuristics, you rarely bump against the wall of cognitive limitations. As we said above, we have developed these heuristics because they work more often that not.

Does this mean you should be entirely comfortable with these types of errors? Here the analogy to perception breaks down to some extent. Most perceptual illusions are immune to learning. You're always going to perceive the lengths of the lines of the Müller-Lyer illusion (see Chapter 4) to be different, no matter how much you learn about it. By comparison, knowing about judgmental heuristics can enable you to avoid some types of errors. Although general intellectual skills provide no defence against these errors—even the most gifted judgment makers err under some circumstances—specific training can help. Throughout this section, we will point out the ways in which you can improve your judgment making. Let's turn now to three heuristics: *availability*, *representativeness* and *anchoring*.

**Availability heuristic** We'll begin by asking you to make a rather trivial judgment. (We know you're likely to give the wrong answer, and we don't want to embarrass you about something important.) Think about the entirety of the English language. Do you think there are more words in English that start with *k* (for example, *kangaroo*) or have *k* in third position (for example, *duke*)? If you are like the participants in a study by Tversky and Kahneman (1973), then you probably judged that *k* is found more often at the beginning of words. In fact, *k* appears about twice as often in the third position.

Why do most people believe that *k* is more likely to appear in first position? The answer has to do with the *availability* of information from memory. When we are asked to answer a question like that, we go into our mental dictionary (called the *lexicon*). We have had such practice at grouping words alphabetically that all the words starting with a particular letter line themselves up neatly—*kangaroo, kindness, king*, etc. There is no equivalent way to 'capture' the words with *k* as the third letter. Your decision about which word was more common was based upon the fact that words starting with *k* are more easily available to you. Your judgment, thus, arises from use of the **availability heuristic**: You base your judgment on information that is readily available in memory. This heuristic makes sense because much of the time what is available from memory will lead to accurate judgments. If, for example, you judge bowling to be a less dangerous sport than hang-gliding, availability is serving you well. Trouble only arises either when (1) memory processes give rise to a biased sample of information, or (2) the information you've stored in memory is not accurate. Let's look at an example of each of these potential problems.

The *k* question is a good example of circumstances in which your memory processes can make an availability-based judgment inaccurate. Given the way words are organised in memory, it's simply easier to find words that begin with a particular letter. Let's consider another case that is closer to the judgments you make in everyday life. Suppose we asked you to look into your future: Do you predict that you will experience more happy or unhappy events? It turns out that your answer to this question will depend, in part, on your current mood. Consider a study in which the researchers asked participants to think of past instances of happy or unhappy events—for example, a welcome invitation or a painful injury—and to estimate how likely it would be that events of this type would happen to them again in the next six months (Macleod & Campbell, 1992). The participants' ability to recall past events was strongly predicted by their mood—and the availability of mood-congruent memories predicted judgments about the future. Thus participants in a happy mood found it easier to recall happy events. But, also, the availability of those happy events led participants to judge that more happy events, and fewer unhappy events, would occur in the future. This experiment demonstrates how easily judgments can be affected by the type of information that is—for whatever reasons—easily available from memory. You see the implications for your day-to-day life. If you are making important judgments about your future, you should factor in the way mood affects the information available to you. More generally, when it's time to make an important judgment, you can ask yourself, 'Is there anything special about my frame of mind that will bias the information coming out of memory?'

A second difficulty with availability as a judgement heuristic arises when the information you have stored in memory has a bias to it. We see examples of this in our everyday behaviour, including some very important safety behaviours. All of us behave as if we are safe at home, or among people we know, and at risk out of home among strangers. Yet Australian crime statistics consistently report that about two-thirds of murder victims, and over half of all assault victims, know their attacker (ABC Radio National, 1 Sept, 1996). If we were really responding to the statistical risk of crime, we'd be out in the streets chatting to strangers night and day! Why do we overestimate the risk of 'stranger' crime and underestimate the likelihood of 'domestic' crime in this way? Probably because, as a result of film, television and news presentations of crime, the unsolved, random street crime has become easier for us to imagine—more available to us—than the ideas of domestic and peer crime.

Many students show a bias in the way they commit information to memory that has a negative impact on exam performance. Suppose you are taking a multiple-choice exam. You answer a question, but then, after giving it some additional thought, you decide to change your answer. Are you more likely to change from wrong to right or right to wrong? If you are like most students, you probably believe that you should stick with your first answer—it probably makes you nervous to change your answer. But should it?

Researchers inspected the multiple-choice exams of a group of 1,561 students to determine the consequences of answer changes (Kruger et al., 2005). Of the 3,291 answers those students changed, 23 percent were from one wrong answer to another wrong answer. Of the remaining changes, 51 percent made a wrong answer right; 25 percent made a right answer wrong. This pattern suggests that you shouldn't be reluctant to consider changing an answer. However, when a subset of this group were asked about the wisdom of changing answers, 75 percent indicated that it's a better idea to stick with one's original answer. The researchers argued that students' prejudice against changing answers comes from a memory bias: they suggested that students find more memorable instances in which changed answers led to negative outcomes then when they led to positive outcomes. How many times have you complained to yourself, 'I had that one right!' Now, how many times have you complained, 'I had that one wrong!' To test the hypothesis that students are more likely to commit negative outcomes to memory, the researchers carried out a second experiment. In this case, the researchers gave students feedback on correct and incorrect answers shortly after they completed a multiple-choice exam. Four to six weeks later, the researchers asked the participants to try to recall the instances in which they had considered changing their answers, what they had decided, and the consequences of those decisions. A student might, for example, have reported that she had deliberated on three problems and always stuck with her original answer. The memory data showed a consistent bias: participants *overestimated* how often they switched an answer and then got the question wrong; they *underestimated* how often they switched an answer and then got the question right.

Put yourself in a classroom while you are sitting a multiple choice exam. You get to a moment at which you're trying to decide whether to change an answer. These data suggest that you make this judgment with respect to a biased database: you have committed more negative outcomes to memory than positive outcomes—those are the outcomes that are available. This analysis certainly doesn't mean that you should *always* change your answers. However, you should be aware now of why your feelings of distress arise when you contemplate a change.

Representativeness heuristic When you make judgments based on the **representativeness heuristic**, you assume that if something has the characteristics considered typical of members of a category, it is, in fact, a member of that category. This heuristic will seem familiar to you because it captures the idea that people use past information to make judgments about similar circumstances in the present. That is the essence of inductive reasoning. Under most circumstances—as long as you have unbiased ideas about the features and categories that go together—making judgments along the lines of similarity will be quite reasonable. Thus, if you are deciding whether to begin a new activity like hang-gliding, it makes sense to determine how representative that sport is of the category of activities you have previously enjoyed.

Representativeness will lead you astray, however, when it causes you to ignore other types of relevant information, as you will now see. Let's imagine a woman called Julia, and give you some facts about her. Julia is 37 years old; she has never married, but is in a stable long-term relationship; she is deeply committed to social justice issues and joined the Labor Party at university, but let the membership lapse. Julia has, however, kept up an active interested in left-wing politics. Which of the following is more likely to be true of Julia?

1. Julia is an academic

2. Julia is a feminist academic.

If you answered 2, think carefully. All feminist academics are academics. Even if there were NO academics who were not feminists, Julia would be exactly as likely to be

representativeness heuristic
A cognitive strategy that assigns an object to a category on the basis of a few characteristics regarded as representative of that category.

an academic as a feminist academic (and that is probably still a fair way off!). It is not possible for the likelihood of being in a subgroup to exceed the likelihood of being in the larger group.

Kahneman and colleagues (Kahneman & Frederick, 2002; Kahneman & Tversky, 1973) have investigated why it is that people sometimes estimate a greater probability for subgroup membership than for the larger, superordinate group. They provided their participants with a list of options, including those in **Figure 8.19**, and gave them the chance to win $45—real money—by ranking the correct option as number 1. Which option seems correct to you? If you're like a majority of the original participants, you'll lose the $45 because you'll say *tennis* rather than *a ball game*. The lower part of Figure 8.19 shows why *tennis* could never be as good a bet: it is included within the category *a ball game*. Participants judge *tennis* to be a better answer because it seems to have all the features of the sport the attorney is likely to play. However, this judgment by representativeness causes participants to neglect another sort of information— category structure. In this case, the measurable cost is $45 (Bar-Hillel & Neter, 1993).

The implication for your day-to-day life is that you should not be fooled into grabbing at a representative alternative before you consider the structure of all the alternatives.

Let's look at a second representativeness example that also might affect the bets you make. Suppose you

A successful Jerusalem attorney. Colleagues say his whims prevent him from being a team worker, attributing his success to competitiveness and drive. Slim and not tall, he watches his body and is vain. Spends several hours a week on his favorite sport. What sport is that?

a. Fast walking
b. A ball game
c. Tennis
d. A track and field sport

A ball game

Tennis

The more inclusive category <u>must</u> be more probable.

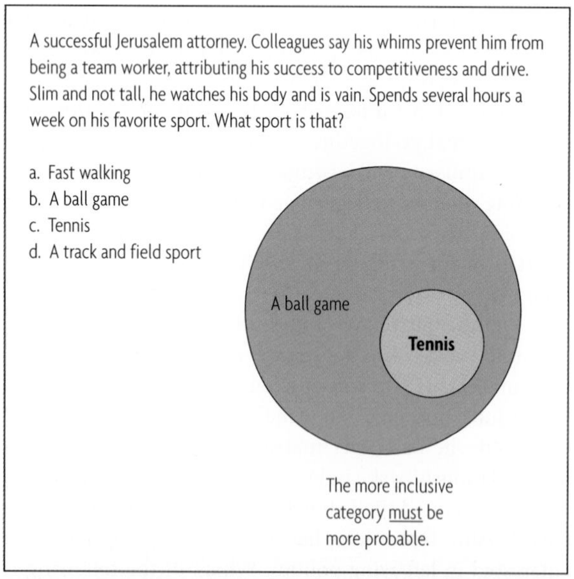

## Figure 8.19

### Using the representativeness heuristic

When asked to choose the attorney's favorite sport, the representativeness heuristic leads most people to choose 'tennis'. However, as shown in the bottom part of the figure, the more probable answer is 'a ball game', because that includes within it 'tennis'.

**anchoring heuristic** An insufficient adjustment up or down from an original starting value when judging the probable value of some event or outcome.

were given the opportunity to play in a simple lottery. To win, you must match three numbers in exact order. Which of these numbers would you feel most comfortable betting on?

| 859 | 101 | 333 |
| 574 | 948 | 772 |

The question we are really asking you is: Which of these numbers strikes you as most representative of the numbers that win these kinds of lotteries? If you are like most bettors, you will avoid number series that have repeated digits—because those numbers do not seem representative of a random sequence. In fact, 27 percent of the time a three-digit number—with each digit drawn randomly from the pool 0 to 9—will have a repeated numeral. Nevertheless, among individuals who took part in almost exactly the lottery described above, only 12.6 percent chose to play a number with a repeated digit (Holtgraves & Skeel, 1992). You should be wary, in general, of the way that most gambling situations are constructed. Most often the hope is that you will be guided by representativeness—so you'll choose the options that look like they're more likely to win—rather than by a careful consideration of the odds.

**Anchors aweigh!** To introduce you to a third heuristic, we need you to try a thought experiment. First take 5 seconds to estimate the following mathematical product and write down your answer:

$$1 \times 2 \times 3 \times 4 \times 5 \times 6 \times 7 \times 8 = \underline{\hspace{2em}}$$

In 5 seconds, you can probably make only a couple of calculations. You get a partial answer, perhaps 24, and then adjust up from there. Now try this series of numbers:

$$8 \times 7 \times 6 \times 5 \times 4 \times 3 \times 2 \times 1 = \underline{\hspace{2em}}$$

Even if you notice that this is the same list in reverse, you can see how the experience of carrying out the multiplication would feel quite different. You'd start with $8 \times 7$, which is 56, and then attempt $56 \times 6$, which already feels quite large. Once again, you can only make a partial guess and then adjust upward. When Tversky and Kahneman (1974) gave these two arrangements of the identical problem to experimental participants, the 1 to 8 order produced median estimates of 512, and the 8 to 1 group produced estimates of 2,250 (*the real answer is 40,320*). Apparently, when participants adjusted up from their 5-second estimates, the higher partial solutions led to higher estimates.

Performance on this simple multiplication task provides evidence for the **anchoring heuristic**: People's judgments of the probable value of some event or outcome represent insufficient adjustments—either up or down—from an original starting value. In other words, your judgment is 'anchored' too firmly to an original guess. People show a strong tendency to be influenced by an anchor, even when the information is clearly of little or no use. For example, in one study students were given an arbitrary identification number (in the range 1,928 to 1,935) that they were instructed to copy onto their questionnaires. Subsequently, the students estimated the number of doctors listed in the local Yellow Pages. Students in the control group—who hadn't received an ID anchor—produced an average estimate of 219 physicians. Students with the ID anchors produced an estimate of 539—even though they had been specifically warned that the ID number might affect their judgments (Wilson et al., 1996). You can see how hard it is not to let an anchor have an impact.

Why do people make insufficient adjustments from anchors? Researchers have begun to address this question in real-life circumstances—in which people produce their own anchors before beginning the adjustment process. Consider this question: What is the duration of Mars's orbit around the sun? How might you answer that question? Research suggests that you start with the duration of the earth's orbit of 365 days as an anchor. What next? You might use the knowledge that Mars is further from the sun than the earth is to adjust away from the 365-day anchor toward a larger value. In fact, participants in an experiment estimated Mars's orbit to be about 492 days (Epley & Giovich, 2006). This estimate is still short of the actual value, which is 869 days. What people appeared to do in the experiment was to start with a reasonable anchor (i.e. 365 days) and keep adjusting until they reached a value that seemed *plausible*. When you find yourself in situations of anchoring and adjustment, put this result to use: you should expend some extra effort to confirm that a plausible value is, in fact, the right answer.

You employ judgmental heuristics like availability, representativeness, and anchoring because, in most situations, they allow you to make efficient, acceptable judgments. In a sense, you are doing the best you can, given the uncertainties of situations and constraints on your processing resources. We have shown you, however, that heuristics can lead to errors. Try to use this knowledge to examine your own thought processes when the time comes to make important judgments. Be especially critical when you feel others might be trying to bias your judgments. Let's move now to the decisions you make, often on the basis of those judgments.

## THE PSYCHOLOGY OF DECISION MAKING

Let us begin with a powerful example of the way that psychological factors affect the decisions people make. Consider the problem given in part 1 of **Table 8.7**. Read the instructions, and then make your choice between Spot A and Spot B. Now read the version of the problem given in part 2. Would you like to change your choice?

In an experiment, students read one version of this problem (Shafir, 1993). When they were asked in part 1 which option they preferred, 67 percent of the students opted for Spot B. However, when students were asked in part 2 to cancel an option, this figure fell to 52 percent (that is, 48 percent said they would cancel Spot B). Why is this change odd? If you take a close look at the 'prefer' and 'cancel' versions of the problem, you will see that there is no difference in the information available in the two cases. On first pass, you might expect that the same information would lead to the same decision. But that's not what people do. It seems that the 'prefer' question focuses people's attention on positive features of options—you're gathering evidence in favour of something—whereas the 'cancel' question focuses attention on negative features of

---

### Table 8.7

The effect of psychological factors on decision making

| Part 1: Prefer version | Part 2: Cancel version |
|---|---|
| 1. Imagine that you are planning a week's vacation in a warm spot in spring. You currently have two options that are reasonably priced, The travel brochure gives only a limited amount of information about the two options. Given the information available, which vacation spot would you prefer? | 2. Imagine that you are planning a week's vacation in a warm spot in spring. You currently have two options that are reasonably priced, but you can no longer retain your reservation for both. The travel brochure gives only a limited amount of information about the two options. Given the information available, which reservation do you decide to cancel? |
| Spot A  average weather<br>average beaches<br>medium-quality hotel<br>medium-temperature water<br>average nightlife | Spot A  average weather<br>average beaches<br>medium-quality hotel<br>medium-temperature water<br>average nightlife |
| Spot B  lots of sunshine<br>gorgeous beaches and coral reefs<br>ultramodern hotel<br>very cold water<br>very strong winds<br>no nightlife | Spot B  lots of sunshine<br>gorgeous beaches and coral reefs<br>ultramodern hotel<br>very cold water<br>very strong winds<br>no nightlife |

options—you're gathering evidence against something. Your decision may shift.

This straightforward example demonstrates that the way in which a question is phrased can have great consequences for the decision you will make (Slovic, 1995). This is why you need to understand the psychological aspects of decision making: You need to be able to test your own decisions to see whether they hold up under careful analysis. In this case, you might ask yourself, 'How would my choice change if I were asked to reject an option rather than to choose one?' If you find that your top preference is also your top candidate for rejection, you will have learned that the option has both many positive and many negative features. Now ask, 'Is that acceptable?' This is a key step in developing your critical thinking skills.

### The framing of decisions

One of the most natural ways to make a decision is to judge which option will bring about the biggest gain or which option will bring about the smallest loss. Thus, if we offer you $5 or $10, you will feel very little uncertainty that the better option is $10. What makes the situation a bit more complicated, however, is that the perception of a gain or a loss often depends on the way in which a decision is *framed*. A **frame** is a particular description of a choice. Suppose, for example, you were asked how happy you would be to get a $1,000 pay rise. If you were expecting no increase at all, this would seem like a great gain, and you'd probably be quite happy. But suppose you'd been told several times to expect a raise of $10,000. Now how do you feel? Suddenly, you may feel as if you've lost money because the $1,000 is less than what you had expected. You're not happy at all! In either case, you'd be getting $1,000 more a year—objectively, you'd be in exactly the same position—but the psychological effect is very different. That's why *reference points* are important in decision making (Kahneman, 1992). What seems like a gain or a loss will be determined in part by the expectations—a $0 raise or a $10,000 raise—to which a decision maker refers. (The decision, in this case, might be whether to stay in the job!)

Let's now take a look at a slightly more complex example in which framing has a sizeable impact on the decisions people make. In **Table 8.8**, you are asked to imagine making a choice between surgery and radiation for treatment of lung cancer. First, read the *survival* frame for the problem and choose your preferred treatment; then read the *mortality* frame and see if you feel like changing your preference. Note that the data are objectively the same in the two frames. The only difference is whether statistical information about the consequences of each treatment is presented in terms of survival rates or of mortality rates. When this decision was presented to participants, the focus on relative gains and losses had a marked effect on choice of treatment. Radiation therapy was chosen by only 18 percent of the participants who were given the survival frame, but by 44 percent of those given the mortality frame. This framing effect held equally for a group of clinic patients, statistically sophisticated

**frame** The perspective from which a choice is described or framed. It affects how a decision is made and which option is ultimately exercised.

**Table 8.8**

**The effect of framing**

**Survival frame**

*Surgery.* Of 100 people having surgery, 90 live through the postoperative period, 68 are alive at the end of the first year, and 34 are alive at the end of five years.

*Radiation therapy.* Of 100 people having radiation therapy, all live through the treatment, 77 are alive at the end of one year, and 22 are alive at the end of five years.

*What do you choose:* surgery or radiation?

**Mortality frame**

*Surgery.* Of 100 people having surgery, 10 die during surgery or the postoperative period, 32 die by the end of one year, and 66 die by the end of five years.

*Radiation therapy.* Of 100 people having radiation therapy, none dies during treatment, 23 die by the end of one year, and 78 die by the end of five years.

*What do you choose:* surgery or radiation?

business students, and experienced physicians (McNeil et al., 1982).

What makes this example important is that it mirrors the uncertainty you frequently have in real life.

> Suppose you have been in a relationship for 6 months. How do you decide whether the relationship has a healthy future? Researchers demonstrated that framing has an impact on students' level of relationship optimism (Knee & Boon, 2001). At the outset of the study, the participants were informed that most undergraduates value partners who have honesty, humour and intelligence. The participants were then asked to imagine a hypothetical partner who embodied a subset of those features. In the *gain* version of the description, the students were told that their partners possessed two of the three features (e.g., honesty and humour). In the *loss* version of the description, the students were told their partners lacked one of the three features (e.g., intelligence). You can see that these two descriptions yield the same individual (e.g., in either case he or she is honest and funny but not intelligent). Still, when students rated their impressions of the future success of the relationship, they were consistently less optimistic with the *loss* description than with the *gain* description.

You can see how a small change in framing could have a large impact on how you think about your future. This result should encourage you to try to think about important decisions with *both* a gain frame and a loss frame. Suppose, for example, you are going to buy a new car. The salesperson will be inclined to frame everything as a gain: 'Seventy-eight percent of Subarus require no repairs in the first year!' You can reframe that to 'Twenty-two percent require some repairs in the first year!' Would the new frame change how you feel about the situation? It's an exercise worth trying in real life.

The car salesperson is a good example of a situation in which someone is trying to frame information in a fashion that will have a desired effect on your decision. This, of course, is a regular part of your life. For example, as each election approaches, the opposing candidates compete to have their framings of themselves and of the issues prevail among the voters. One candidate might say, 'I believe in sticking with policies that have been successful'. His opponent might counter, 'He is afraid of new ideas'. One candidate might say, 'That policy will bring about economic growth'. Her opponent might counter, 'That policy will bring about environmental destruction'. Often both claims are true—the same policy often will bring about both economic good and environmental harm. In this light, whichever frame seems more compelling may be largely a matter of personal history (Tversky & Kahneman, 1981; Vaughan & Seifert, 1992). Thus your knowledge of framing effects can help you understand how people can come to such radically different decisions when they are faced with exactly the same evidence. If you want to understand other people's actions, try to think about how those individuals have framed a decision.

**Consequences of decision making** What happens when you make a decision? In the best of all possible worlds, everything goes well—and you never look back. However, as you likely know, not all decisions yield the best of all possible worlds. When decisions turn out

In what ways can salespeople frame their products to get prospective customers to consider them in a positive light?

badly, you will likely experience *regret*. Studies suggest that the categories in which people express the greatest regret is their decisions with respect to their education and careers (Roese & Summerville, 2005). To explain this finding, researchers point to the fact that these two domains provide a particularly wide range of opportunities: There are many ways to pursue an education and many careers to which someone might aspire. That range of opportunities makes it quite easy for people to wonder, 'Did I make the right decision?'

People also experience more regret when they are clear on the costs associated with particular decisions (van Dijk & Zeelenberg, 2005). Consider a moment on a game show when a contestant must choose between *Box A* and *Box B*. If the contestant chooses the box with $10 instead of $10,000, it's easy to understand why he would experience regret. Some decisions in life are like the game show. You have the lemon gelato. Your friend has the tiramisu. After you each take one bite, you know that you made the wrong decision. You experience regret because you have a clear grasp on what you gave up. In other cases, you have a much vaguer grasp on the consequences of your decision. If you choose a poodle as a pet, you'll never know exactly how different your life would have been had you gone for a bulldog. In that type of situation, it's less likely that you will experience regret.

The possibility of regret provides one explanation for why you might experience **decision aversion**: You might find that you will try hard to avoid making any decision at all. In **Table 8.9**, we provide an example of circumstances that can bring about an increasing unwillingness to make a decision. Consider the scenario in part A. Which would you choose? Researchers found that only 34 percent of their participants said they would wait for more information (Tversky & Shafir, 1992). Now consider the slightly altered scenario given in part B. Do you want to change your choice? In fact, 46 percent of the participants who read this version said they would wait for new information. How could this be? Ordinarily, you would expect that adding an option would decrease the share of the other options. If, for example, a third candidate enters a political race, you would expect that candidate to pull votes away from the original pair. Here, however, the addition of a third possibility increases the share of one of the original choices by 12 percent. What's going on?

The key to obtaining this effect is to make the decision hard. When the researchers tested participants on a version of the problem that provided a low-quality CD player as an extra option, only 24 percent said they would wait for more information—a decrease rather than an increase—which reflects the ease of choosing the Sony. The decision between the less expensive Sony model and the top-quality Aiwa, however, is hard. It's convenient to put the hard decision off, to wait for more information.

One final observation: Not all decision makers are created equal. Suppose you go to a video store to choose a DVD for a Saturday night rental. If you are a *satisficer*, you would likely browse the DVDs until you got to one that struck you as interesting enough. If you are a

**decision aversion** The tendency to avoid decision-making; the tougher the decision, the greater the likelihood of decision aversion.

## Table 8.9

Decision aversion

> A. Suppose you are considering buying a compact disk (CD) player, and have not yet decided what model to buy. You pass by a store that is having a 1-day clearance sale. They offer a popular Sony player for just $99, well below the list price. Do you
>
>   1. buy the Sony player
>   2. wait until you learn more about the various models
>
> B. Suppose you are considering buying a compact disk (CD) player, and have not yet decided what model to buy. You pass by a store that is having a 1-day clearance sale. They offer a popular Sony player for just $99, and a top-of-the-line Aiwa player for just $159, both well below the list price. Do you
>
>   1. buy the Aiwa player
>   2. buy the Sony player
>   3. wait until you learn more about the various models

From Amos Tversky & Eldar Shafir (1992) Choice under confict: The dynamics of deferred decision, *Psychological Science*, 3(6). © 1992 by Blackwell Publishing. Reprinted with permission.

*maximiser*, you would likely browse all the DVDs until you had convinced yourself that you'd found exactly the best one. Researchers have demonstrated that there are both satisficers and maximisers in the world—and that the style of decision making has important consequences (Schwartz et al., 2002).

One study followed a group of 548 students as they went onto the job market (Iyengar et al., 2006). The students completed a questionnaire that revealed the extent to which they were satisficers or maximisers: They indicated their agreement with statements such as, 'When shopping, I have a hard time finding clothes that I really love'. The researchers contacted the students 3 months and 6 months after they completed the initial questionnaire—at those points in time, the students were interviewing and then accepting jobs. The researchers collected a variety of data to determine how the students experienced the process. Those data showed a clear pattern: the maximisers had accepted jobs that, on average, provided 20% higher salaries—yet they were miserable. As the researchers put it, 'Despite their relative success, maximisers [were] less satisfied with the outcomes of the job search, and more pessimistic, stressed, tired, anxious, worried, overwhelmed and depressed throughout the process' (Iyengar et al., 2006, p. 147). Apparently, the quest for an elusive 'best' outcome provided the maximisers with a substantial psychological burden.

For answers go to MyPsychLab!

**mypsychlab** where learning comes to life!

We imagine that most people would like to have a good job without making themselves miserable. As you undertake your own job searches, you might think back to this distinction between maximisers and satisficers—to consider how you might achieve a decision that affords your life a sense of balance.

Throughout this chapter, we've asked you to imagine the mysterious midnight message, 'The cat is on the mat'. Our goal has been to get you to consider your many types of cognitive processing—language use, visual cognition, problem solving, reasoning, judging and deciding. Now that this chapter has come to an end, we hope that the example will stick with you—so that you'll never take your cognitive processes for granted. Every chance you get, give some thought to your thought, reason about your reasoning, and so on. You will be reflecting on the essence of the human experience.

## RECAP CHECKPOINT

### Judgment and decision making

- Much of judgment and decision making is guided by heuristics — mental shortcuts that can help individuals reach solutions quickly.

- Availability, representativeness and anchoring can all lead to errors when they are misapplied.

- Decision making is affected by the way in which different options are framed.

- The possibility of regret makes some decisions hard, particularly for individuals who are maximisers rather than satisficers.

## CONCEPT QUESTIONS

1. Why do people rely on heuristics when they are making judgements?

2. What heuristic might you use to answer the question, 'What is the age of the oldest living human being?'

3. Why do frames play such a large role in the psychology of decision making?

4. What is the distinction between satisficers and maximisers?

## CRITICAL THINKING

Recall the study on representativeness. Why did the researchers offer participants $45 if they got the right answer?

# CRITICAL THINKING *in your life*
## CAN POLITICAL EXPERTS PREDICT THE FUTURE?

Here's an exercise you might try: Spend about 15 minutes on the Web gathering experts' predictions about what lies in the political future: Will one party gain a new majority in the next election? Will the Middle East become more democratic? You are likely to find a diversity of opinions on every issue. So, who should you believe? According to a long-term study conducted by psychologist **Philip Tetlock** (2005), the safest answer is that you shouldn't believe anyone—or, more exactly, you can't know whom to believe. Let's see why.

To study the collective wisdom of experts, Tetlock recruited a sample of 284 individuals who had strong credentials for making political predictions with respect to certain countries or regions of the world. (Tetlock assured his participants anonymity, so he was unable to reveal exactly who any of his experts were.) He asked individuals to make predictions of this sort: 'How likely is it that after the next election, the party that currently has the most representatives in the legislative branch of government will *retain this status. . . , will lose this status, or will strengthen this position*' (p. 46)? The questions were made concrete for different countries and regions. The participants were officially experts for some of the questions, whereas for other questions they had to rely on more general knowledge. For example, one participant might be an expert on questions about Russia but

not for questions about Italy. The participants were asked to rate each of the three options (e.g., retain this status, lose this status, strengthen this position) on a scale from a likelihood of 0 percent ('impossible') to a likelihood of 100 percent ('certainty'). Tetlock examined the accuracy of 27,451 political forecasts by waiting long enough to see, in each case, what actually happened.

Because there were three options for each question, participants should have been right one-third of the time just by chance. If they had true expertise, they should have been right much more often than that. But they weren't. In fact, in some comparisons experts did worse than chance. Moreover, the participants overall did no better in their official areas of expertise than when they just used their general knowledge to answer questions. That is, in general, experts on Russia and experts on Italy did just about as well answering questions on Russia (and Italy). You might wonder if fame played a role. Did better known experts outperform their lesser known peers? The answer is decidedly no. As Tetlock put it, 'experts in demand were more overconfident than their colleagues who eked out existences far from the limelight' (p. 63).

If experts fare so poorly in their predictions, why does anyone still listen to them? An important reason is that experts aren't generally held accountable for their predictions: The media rarely

tracks down the expert who made the confident prediction that Smith would win, to ask her why Jones is now president. But Tetlock *did* ask his experts to explain why they had been wrong. The experts provided explanations in categories that will likely be familiar to you from your own life. They explained, for example, why they were 'almost right' or why they were 'wrong for the right reasons.' They identified 'out of the blue' forces that no one could have foreseen in advance of the outcome they had predicted.

Here's a safe conclusion from Tetlock's research: With respect to politics, no one can routinely predict the future. Some people do a bit better than others, but you can't use their confidence or fame to know who those people are. Still, it's important to note that this research is about a particular type of expert and a particular type of prediction. You shouldn't discount all experts. For example, when you consult medical doctors, they should be able to make their predictions—'Here's the likely impact of treatment'—based on years of education and prior experience. Also, they are regularly held accountable for the accuracy of those predictions!

- Why might Tetlock have given the participants three explicit options for each prediction?

- Why might overconfidence help people become or stay famous, even if their predictions are incorrect?

# SUMMARY

'Cognition' refers to everything associated with information processing in the human mind. In this chapter, we have particularly focused upon attention, language processing, reasoning and problem solving. We have learned that cognition is heavily influenced by forces such as education and training, culture and background, and that we cannot really talk about 'cognition' without reference to cultural and social processes.

# KEY TERMS

algorithm (p. 269)
anchoring heuristic (p. 278)
audience design (p. 252)
automatic processes (p. 251)
availability heuristic (p. 276)
belief-bias effect (p. 271)
cognition (p. 248)
cognitive processes (p. 248)

cognitive psychology
  (p. 248)
cognitive science (p. 248)
controlled processes (p. 251)
decision aversion (p. 281)
decision making (p. 275)
deductive reasoning (p. 271)
frame (p. 280)

functional fixedness (p. 271)
heuristics (p. 269)
inductive reasoning (p. 273)
inferences (p. 258)
judgment (p. 275)
language production (p. 252)
mental set (p. 273)
parallel processes (p. 250)

problem solving (p. 268)
problem space (p. 269)
reasoning (p. 268)
representativeness heuristic
  (p. 277)
serial processes (p. 250)
think-aloud protocols
  (p. 269)

# PRACTICE TEST

1. According to the logic of Donders's analysis,
   a. categorisation is among the hardest mental processes.
   b. it should always take longer to draw a capital C than a capital V.
   c. extra mental steps often result in more time to complete a task.
   d. reaction time is useful for understanding the order of mental processes.

2. When Jerry goes with friends to a fast-food restaurant, they each wait in a different line to see who gets to the counter first. That's a good example of_____processing.
   a. serial          c. parallel
   b. automatic       d. ambiguity

3. Lauren can juggle and talk at the same time. Warren cannot. It sounds like juggling is more of a(n)_____process for Lauren than for Warren.
   a. controlled      c. parallel
   b. automatic       d. serial

4. A friend walks up to you and says, 'Remember what I said yesterday? Well, forget about it.' If you understand all of this, it's because your friend has made an appropriate assessment of common ground based on
   a. copresence for actions.  c. community membership.
   b. perceptual copresence.   d. linguistic membership.

5. Which of these sentences would likely produce a different pattern of brain activity than the other three?
   a. There was sugar in Tom's coffee.
   b. Melissa was hoping to discover the name and address of the criminal.
   c. Lisa was making many enemies.
   d. As Aileen walked into the bank, she pulled a muscle in her calf.

6. Research has demonstrated that_____can learn the meanings of plastic symbols without any explicit training.
   a. vervet monkeys       c. chimpanzees
   b. pileated gibbons      d. bonobos

7. The hypothesis of linguistic relativity suggests that
   a. languages can carve up the colour spectrum in any way they choose.
   b. the languages individuals speak affect the way they think about the world.
   c. people have evolved to use languages with greater complexity than other species.
   d. some languages do not allow people to engage in audience design.

8. People's motive for mild lies is more likely to be_____, whereas for serious lies the motive is more likely to be_____.
   a. selfishness; psychological reasons
   b. personal advantage; vanity
   c. psychological reasons; personal advantage
   d. personal advantage; selfishness

9. You are lying on your side when a friend walks up to say hello. To recognise your friend, you might have to use
   a. mental rotation.      c. a spatial mental model.
   b. mental scanning.      d. a problem space.

10. Take a moment to form a visual image of the Australian Coat of Arms. Focus on the animals that are depicted. Which of these questions should take the longest for you to answer?
    a. Is there an emu?
    b. Does the kangaroo have all its paws on the ground?
    c. Does the emu have long toenails?
    d. Can you see both eyes of either animal?

11. Suppose you study a text that inserts you into the middle of a room with objects around you. It should take you the least time to verify that object that is
    a. in front of you.
    c. on your left side.
    b. behind you.
    d. on your right side.

12. A(n)_____is *not* one component of the definition of a problem space.
    a. algorithm
    c. goal state
    b. set of operations
    d. initial state

13. You are asked to enforce the rule, 'If a card has a vowel on one side, it has an even number on the other side.' Which of these cards should you turn over to see if the rule has been violated?
    a. F
    c. 9
    b. H
    d. 16

14. When you are engaging in_____reasoning, you should be wary of a_____.
    a. inductive reasoning; algorithm
    b. inductive reasoning; mental set
    c. deductive reasoning; premise
    d. deductive reasoning; think-aloud protocol

15. Suppose you are asked to estimate whether Hollywood releases more comedies or horror flicks each year. To answer this question, you are most likely to use the_____ heuristic.
    a. anchoring
    c. representativeness
    b. adjustment
    d. availability

16. You ask a friend whether you should stick with your current romantic partner. The friend suggests that you focus on the ways in which the partner improves your life. Your friend is trying to use_____to influence your decision making.
    a. reference points
    c. an algorithm
    b. decision aversion
    d. a frame

17. Because Paul is a satisficer, you would expect him to
    a. watch the first TV channel that catches his interest.
    b. be unhappy even though he recently obtained a high-paying job.
    c. test drive dozens of new cars before making a purchase.
    d. try every flavour of coffee at the new corner market.

18. Suppose you asked an expert on Australia and an expert on New Zealand to make predictions about an upcoming election in New Zealand. According to Philip Tetlock's research, you would expect that
    a. their predictions would be about equally accurate.
    b. the predictions of the Australian expert would be better.
    c. the predictions of the New Zealand expert would be better.
    d. only one of them would be correct.

## Essay Questions

1. Why is ambiguity an important problem for language comprehension?

2. What factors affect your ability to engage in accurate deductive reasoning?

3. Under what circumstances are decisions most likely to cause people regret?

# WEB LINKS

http://www.vaclang.org.au/
Victorian Aboriginal Corporation for Languages

http://www.ethnologue.com/
Ethnologue Languages of the World

Are you ready for the test? MyPsychLab offers dozens of ways to deepen your understanding and test your recall of the material in this chapter—including video and audio clips, simulations and activities, self-assessments, practice tests and other study materials. Specific resources available for this chapter include:

The two-string problem

Explore your mental space
Intuition and discovery in problem solving
Anchoring and adjustment

Computer brains
Language learning

To access MyPsychLab, please visit **www.pearsoned.com.au/mypsychlab**

# Very interesting ...

## NOW YOU HAVE READ CHAPTER 8—ARE YOU PREPARED FOR THE EXAM?

To enhance your understanding of any of the material in your *Psychology and Life* textbook, go to **MyPsychLab: www.pearsoned.com.au/mypsychlab**.

Complete pre- and post-tests, create your own individualised study plan, watch videos and animations and listen to audio glossaries—all of which will help you to understand the themes of this chapter:

- Discovering cognition
- Language use
- Visual cognition
- Problem solving and reasoning
- Judgment and decision making

Read Erica Goodes article on *Mastering the Geometry of the Jungle* in the RESEARCH NAVIGATOR for an expert perspective on cognitive processes

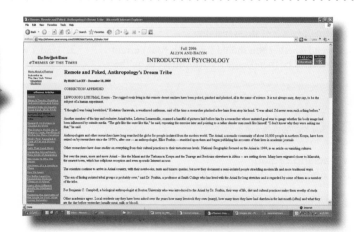

'MyPsychLab gave me the principles to focus on when I was studying.'

Watch SIMULATIONS of anchoring and adjustment and answer questions to test your comprehension

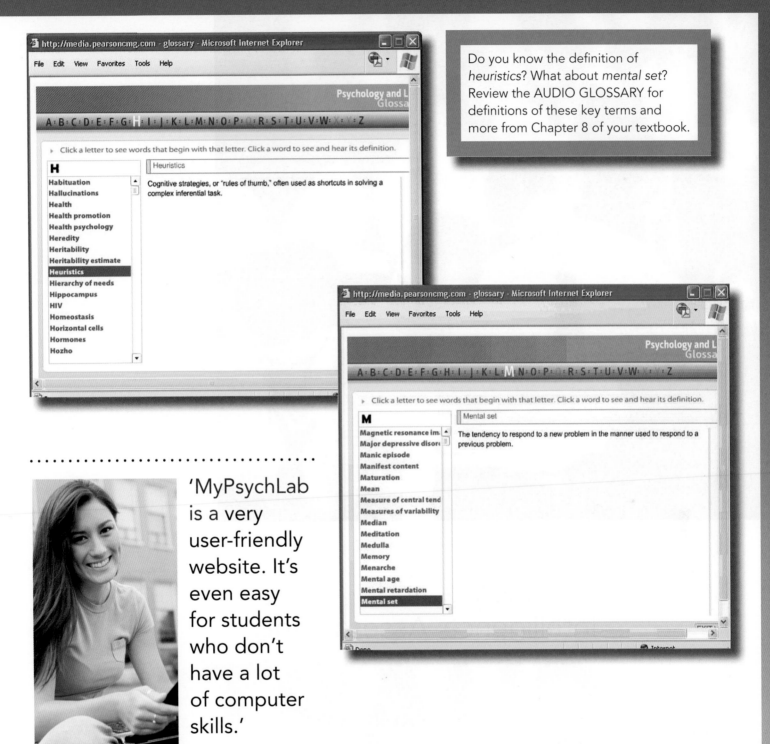

Do you know the definition of *heuristics*? What about *mental set*? Review the AUDIO GLOSSARY for definitions of these key terms and more from Chapter 8 of your textbook.

'MyPsychLab is a very user-friendly website. It's even easy for students who don't have a lot of computer skills.'

### What can you find in MyPsychLab?

Self-directed tests * Videos * Simulations * eBook * Biographies * Audio glossary * Web links … and more—organised by chapter, section and learning objective.

# Intelligence and
# Intelligence Assessment

## CHAPTER

## 9

# CHAPTER FOCUS POINTS

After studying this chapter you will have a better understanding of:

1.  The definition and history of the concept of intelligence

2.  How to distinguish a 'good' from a 'bad' test of intelligence on the basis of the psychometric properties of validity and reliability

3.  How to discuss, in an informed way, the impact of cultural and social background on measures of intelligence

4.  The extent to which both genetic endowment and educational opportunity influence measured intelligence

5.  The relationship between intelligence, creativity and mental illness.

# CHAPTER CONTENTS

Suppose you were asked to define the word intelligence. What types of behaviours or skills would you include in your definition? Think back on your own experiences. What was it like when you first started school? What was it like when you started your first job? It's very likely that all through life you have heard about behaviours that are smart or not so smart, and from all of those comments you have formed your definition of intelligence. When those labels are applied to behaviours in casual conversation, they have relatively few consequences. However, there are many settings in which it matters whether your behaviours are considered intelligent or not. For example, schools in most states of Australia have some form of 'streaming', so that children with similar abilities are placed together in class. Before entering high school you may have done a scholarship test, designed to predict your potential ability as a senior student. While all of these tests are designed to measure skills, such as literacy, numeracy and problem solving, rather than intelligence itself, you will see later that there is considerable controversy about whether intelligence is something different from all of these skills, or whether it is just the average of all of these intellectual abilities

In this chapter, we examine the foundations and uses of intelligence assessment. We review the contributions psychologists have made to the understanding of individual differences in the areas of intelligence. We also discuss the types of controversies that almost inevitably arise when people begin to interpret these differences. Our focus will be on how intelligence tests work, what makes any test useful, and why they do not always do the job they were intended to do. Finally, we will conclude on a personal note, by considering the role of psychological assessment in society.

We begin now with a brief overview of the general practice of psychological assessment.

## WHAT IS ASSESSMENT?

**psychological assessment**
The use of specified procedures to evaluate the abilities, behaviours and personal qualities of people.

**P**sychological assessment is the use of specified testing procedures to evaluate the abilities, behaviours and personal qualities of people. Psychological assessment is often referred to as the measurement of *individual differences* because the majority of assessments specifies how an individual is different from or similar to other people on a given dimension. Before we examine in detail the basic features of psychological testing, let's outline the history of assessment. This historical overview will help you to understand both the uses and limitations of assessment, as well as prepare you to appreciate some current controversies.

### HISTORY OF ASSESSMENT

The development of formal tests and procedures for assessment is a relatively new enterprise in Western psychology, coming into wide use only in the early 1900s. However, long before Western psychology began to devise tests to evaluate people, assessment techniques were commonplace in ancient China. In fact, China employed a sophisticated program of civil service testing over 4,000 years ago—officials were required to demonstrate their competence every third year at an oral examination. Two thousand years later, during the Han Dynasty, written civil service tests were used to measure competence in the areas of law, the military, agriculture and geography. During the Ming Dynasty (A.D. 1368–1644), public officials were chosen on the basis of their performance at three stages of an objective selection procedure. During the first stage, examinations were given at the local level. The 4 percent who passed these tests had to endure the second stage: 9 days and nights of essay examinations on the classics. The 5 percent who passed the essay exams were allowed to complete a final stage of tests conducted at the nation's capital. China's selection procedures were observed and described by British diplomats, missionaries and traders in the early 1800s. Modified versions of China's system were soon adopted by the British and spread from there to the United States and more widely (Wiggins, 1973).

The key figure in the development of Western intelligence testing was a half-cousin to Charles Darwin, **Sir Francis Galton**. His book *Hereditary Genius*, published in 1869, greatly influenced subsequent thinking on the methods, theories, and practices of testing. While Darwin, a deeply religious and humanitarian man, had been careful not to extend his Evolutionary Theory into an explanation of the organisation of human society, Galton attempted

What important ideas about the assessment of intelligence are credited to Sir Francis Galton (1822–1911)?

to apply Darwinian evolutionary theory to the study of human abilities. He was interested in how and why people differ in their abilities. He wondered why some people were gifted and successful—like him—while many others were not. You will sometimes hear the term 'social Darwinism' used to describe programs designed to change some aspect of society. Ironically, Galton was far more of a 'social Darwinist' that Darwin was.

Galton was the first to postulate four important ideas about the assessment of intelligence. First, differences in intelligence were *quantifiable* in terms of degrees of intelligence. In other words, numerical values could be assigned to distinguish among different people's levels of intelligence. Second, differences among people formed a *bell-shaped curve*, or *normal distribution*. On a bell-shaped curve, most people's scores cluster in the middle and fewer are found toward the two extremes of genius and mental deficiency (we return to the bell-shaped curve later in the chapter). Third, intelligence, or mental ability, could be measured by objective tests, tests on which each question had only one 'right' answer. And fourth, the precise extent to which two sets of test scores were related could be determined by a statistical procedure he called *co-relations*, now known as *correlations*. These ideas proved to be of lasting value.

Unfortunately, Galton postulated a number of ideas that proved considerably more controversial. He believed, for example, that genius was inherited. In his view, talent or eminence, ran in families; nurture had only a minimal effect on intelligence. In his view, intelligence was related to Darwinian species' fitness and, somehow, ultimately to one's moral worth. Galton attempted to base public policy on the concept of genetically superior and inferior people. He started the eugenics movement, which advocated improving the human species by applying evolutionary theory to encouraging biologically superior people to interbreed while discouraging biologically inferior people from having offspring. In a heavily class-based social system such as 19th century Britain, Galton's belief that intelligence was inherited and predicted social success and prestige amounted to a 'rallying cry' for the upper- and middle classes to multiply—to increase their social and political power at the expense of the working classes. Galton wrote, 'There exists a sentiment, for the most part quite unreasonable, against the gradual extinction of an inferior race' (Galton, 1883/1907, p. 200). As we will discuss later, it is impossible to separate discussion of the inheritance of intelligence from other fundamental social, political and economic values.

These controversial ideas were endorsed and extended later by many who argued forcefully that the intellectually superior race should propagate at the expense of those with inferior minds. Among the proponents of these ideas were American psychologists Goddard and Terman, whose theories we review later, and, of course, Nazi dictator Adolf Hitler. We will also see later in the chapter that remnants of these elitist ideas are still being proposed today. Even in modern, liberal democracies such as the United States and Australia, there are still individuals who argue that the social welfare and health care systems should be organised so that it is easier for some 'types'

of people (e.g. heterosexuals and Australian citizens) to live comfortably and have children than it is for other 'types' of people. While this is not always to do with intelligence, it still reflects 'Galtonian' views in that that some individuals, due to their intrinsic properties should be allowed preferential access to resources. In the 1998 Australian federal election, Pauline Hanson's One Nation Party ran on a platform which, among other things, suggested reform to reduce the provision of welfare to migrants, particularly Asian immigrants.

Sir Francis Galton's work created a context for contemporary intelligence assessment. Let's now see what features define the circumstances of formal assessment.

## BASIC FEATURES OF FORMAL ASSESSMENT

To be useful for classifying individuals or for selecting those with particular qualities, a **formal assessment** procedure should meet three requirements. The assessment instrument should be: (1) reliable, (2) valid, and (3) standardised. If it fails to meet these requirements, we cannot be sure whether the conclusions of the assessment can be trusted. Although this chapter focuses on intelligence assessment, formal assessment procedures apply to all types of psychological testing. To ensure that you'll understand the broad application of these principles, we will draw on examples both from intelligence testing and other domains of psychological assessment.

**formal assessment** The systematic procedures and measurement instruments used by trained professionals to assess an individual's functioning, aptitudes, abilities or mental states.

Reliability As you'll recall from Chapter 2, *reliability* is the extent to which an assessment instrument can be trusted to give consistent scores. If you stepped on your bathroom scale three times in the same morning and it gave you a different reading each time, the scale would not be doing its job. You would call it *unreliable* because you could not count on it to give consistent results. Of course, if you ate a big meal in between two weighings, you wouldn't expect the scale to produce the same result. That is, a measurement device can be considered reliable or unreliable only to the extent that the underlying concept it is measuring remains unchanged.

One straightforward way to test if your bathroom scales are working would be to weigh the same object—say a brick—twice on the same scales. There may well be a small difference between the two measurements—ambient temperature might have a slight but measurable effect on the action of the scales, or the battery charge might have changed a little between weighings. However, as the difference in score between the two weighings gets bigger, the more worried you would be that the scales are not working properly. This is the logic behind calculating the **test–retest reliability** of any psychological measurement instrument—it is a measure of the correlation between the scores of the same people, on the same test, given on two different occasions. A perfectly reliable test will yield a correlation coefficient of +1.00. This means that the identical pattern of scores emerges both times. The same people who got the highest and lowest scores the first

**test-retest reliability** A measure of correlation between the scores of the same people on the same test given on two different occasions.

time do so again. A totally unreliable test results in a 0.00 correlation coefficient. That means there is no relationship between the first set of scores and the second set. Someone who initially got the top score gets a completely different score the second time. As the correlation coefficient moves higher (toward the ideal of +1.00), the test is increasingly reliable. However, as with the bathroom scales, it is actually very rare that test–retest reliability will reach **exactly** 1.00. Even a very good test—like a very good set of scales—will almost always show a small difference between two occasions of measurement. In general, in psychological measurement, reliability coefficients above 0.8 indicate good levels of reliability.

There are two other ways to assess reliability. One is to administer alternate, **parallel forms** of a test instead of giving the same test twice. Using parallel forms reduces the effects of direct practice of the test questions, memory of the test questions, and the desire of an individual to appear consistent from one test to the next. Reliable tests yield comparable scores on parallel forms of the test. The other measure of reliability is the **internal consistency** of responses on a single test. For example, we can compare a person's score on the odd-numbered items of a test with the score on the even-numbered items. A reliable test yields the same score for each of its halves. It is then said to have high internal consistency on this measure of **split-half reliability**.

In most circumstances, not only should the measurement device itself be reliable, but so should the method for using the device. Suppose researchers wished to observe children in a classroom in order to assess different levels of aggressive play. The researchers might develop a *coding scheme* that would allow them to make appropriate distinctions. The scheme would be reliable to the extent that all the people who viewed the same behaviour would give highly similar ratings to the same children. This is one of the reasons that quite a lot of training is required before individuals can carry out accurate psychological assessment. They must learn to apply systems of distinctions in a reliable fashion.

It is very likely that you will have a multiple choice examination at the end of this semester—maybe for

The wrong way to measure split-half reliability.

Psychology or for another subject. As you probably know, multiple choice tests are scored using scanners and computer scoring software. The most important output from this process, as far as you are concerned, is your result and the results of your friends. This is important to your teaching staff as well; however we also use the software to extract information about the test itself. For example, we know the reliability of the exam overall, we know about how every question 'performs'. Do the students who generally perform more strongly tend to get a particular question right? Is there a 'too clever' incorrect alternative in a question that 'tricks' the stronger students but not the weaker ones? If so, we would change that alternative before using the question again in future years. We also use some 'anchor' questions—a small group of questions that may appear a few years running. These provide us with a way to check that the exam questions are behaving in the same way year after year, despite changes in the group of students or the teaching staff. On the basis of all of this data, we continuously aim to improve the reliability of the assessment.

Validity Recall from Chapter 2 that the *validity* of a test is the degree to which it measures what an assessor intends it to measure. A valid test of intelligence measures that trait and predicts performance in situations where intelligence is important. Scores on a valid measure of creativity reflect actual creativity, not drawing ability or moods. A Psychology examination should test what you have learned form our studies in Psychology, not your general knowledge of current affairs. It should allow you and your lecturers to predict your suitability to higher level study and make informed decisions about future academic options In general, then, validity reflects a test's ability to make accurate predictions about behaviours or outcomes related to the purpose or design of the test. Three important types of validity are *face validity*, *criterion validity* and *construct validity*.

The first type of validity is based on the surface *content* of a test. When test items appear to be directly related to the attribute of interest, the test has **face validity**. 'What is the square root of nine?' is a face valid item for a mathematics test—it is clear to any reader of the question that their mathematics knowledge is being assessed. Face-valid tests are very straightforward—they simply ask what the test-maker needs to know: 'How anxious do you feel?' 'Are you creative?' The person taking the test is expected to answer accurately and honestly. Unfortunately, face validity is often not sufficient to ensure accurate measurement. First, people's perceptions of themselves may not be accurate, or they may not know how they should rate themselves in comparison to other people. Second, a test that too obviously measures some attribute may allow test takers to manipulate the impression they make. Consider the classic case of institutionalised mental patients who did not want to be released from their familiar, structured environment.

These long-term schizophrenic patients were interviewed by the staff about how disturbed they were. When they were given a *transfer* interview to assess if they were well enough to be moved to an open ward,

**parallel forms** Different versions of a test to assess test reliability; the change of forms reduces effects of direct practice, memory or the individual's desire to appear consistent on the same items.

**internal consistency** A measure of reliability; the degree to which a test yields similar scores across its different parts, such as odd versus even items.

**split-half reliability** A measure of the correlation between test takers' performance on different halves (e.g., odd- and even-numbered items) of a test.

**face validity** The degree to which test items appear to be directly related to the attribute the researcher wishes to measure.

these patients gave generally positive self-references. However, when the purpose of the interview was to assess their suitability for *discharge,* the patients gave more negative self-references because they did not want to be discharged. Psychiatrists who rated the interview data, without awareness of this experimental variation in the purpose of the interview, judged those who gave more negative self-references as more severely disturbed and recommended against their discharge. So the patients achieved the assessment outcome they wanted. The psychiatrists' assessment may also have been influenced by their perspective that anyone who wanted to stay in a mental hospital must be very disturbed (Braginsky & Braginsky, 1967).

This example makes it particularly clear that test givers cannot rely only on measures that have face validity. Let's consider other types of validity that overcome some of these limitations.

To assess the **criterion validity** (also known as predictive validity) of a test, psychologists compare a person's score on the test with his or her score on some other standard, or *criterion,* associated with what the test measures. For example, your final Year 12 result (such as a TER, UAI or ENTER score) may have been used as the basis for admission to the university you are currently studying at. To assess the criterion validity of the final Year 12 score as a predictor of university success, we might keep track of a group of students through their HSC and university lives and examine the relationship between their final Year 12 score and a measure of university performance, such as their average mark on university subjects. When this has been done, it has been found that Year 12 results are a good predictor of performance at university especially at first year level (e.g. Evans & Farley, 1998). For many personal qualities of interest to psychologists, no ideal criterion exists. No single behaviour or objective measure of performance can indicate, for example, how anxious, depressed or aggressive a person is overall. Psychologists have theories, or *constructs*, about these abstract qualities— what causes them, how they affect behaviour, and how they relate to other variables. The **construct validity** of a test is the degree to which it adequately measures the underlying construct. For example, a new measure of depression has construct validity if the scores it produces correlate highly with valid measures of the features that define the construct of depression. In addition, the new measure should not show relationships with features that fall outside the construct of depression.

The conditions under which a test is valid may be very specific, so it is always important to ask about a test, 'For what purpose is it valid?' Knowing which other measures a test does and does not correlate with may reveal something new about the measures, the construct or the complexity of human behaviour. For example, suppose you design a test to measure the ability of medical students to cope with stress. You then find that scores on that test correlate well with students' ability to cope with classroom stress. You presume your test will also correlate with students'

ability to deal with stressful hospital emergencies, but you discover it does not. Because you have demonstrated some validity, you have learned something both about your test—the circumstances in which it is valid—and about your construct—different categories of stressors have different consequences. You would then modify your test to take account of the kinds of special stressors found in hospital emergencies.

Consider for a moment the relationship between validity and reliability. Whereas reliability is measured by the degree to which a test correlates with itself (administered at different times or using different items), validity is measured by the degree to which the test correlates with something external to it (another test, a behavioural criterion, or judges' ratings). Usually, a test that is not reliable is also not valid because a test that cannot predict itself will be unable to predict anything else. For example, if your class took a test of aggressiveness today and scores were uncorrelated with scores from a parallel form of the test tomorrow (demonstrating unreliability), it is unlikely that the scores from either day would predict which students had fought or argued most frequently over a week's time: after all, the two sets of test scores would not even make the same prediction! Conversely, it is quite possible for a test to be highly reliable without being valid. Suppose, for example, we decided to use your adult height as a measure of intelligence. Do you see why that would be reliable but not valid?

Norms and standardisation So we have a reliable and valid test, but we still need *norms* to provide a context for interpreting different test scores. Suppose, for example, you get a score of 18 on a test designed to reveal how depressed you are. What does that mean? Are you a little depressed, not at all depressed, or about averagely depressed? To find out what your score means, you would want to compare your individual score with typical scores, or statistical **norms**, of other students. You would check the test norms to see what the usual range of scores is and what the average is for students of your age and sex. That would provide you with a context for interpreting your depression score.

You might have encountered test norms when you received your scores on state-wide tests at primary and high school. You would have seen what your score was on, say, literacy. You would also have seen how that score compared with the average score of other students at your year level. The norms told you how your scores compared with those of other students and helped you interpret how well you had done relative to that *normative population.* Group norms are most useful for interpreting individual scores when the comparison group shares important qualities with the individuals tested, such as age, social class, culture and experience.

For norms to be meaningful, everyone must take the same test under standardised circumstances. **Standardisation** is the administration of a testing device to all persons, in the same way, under the same conditions. There is little point in comparing the score of a student who performed a literacy test in a quiet room with 15 other students in the

**criterion validity** The degree to which test scores indicate a result on a specific measure that is consistent with some other criterion of the characteristic being assessed; also known as predictive validity.

**norms** Standards based on measurements of a large group of people; used for comparing the scores of an individual with those of others within a well-defined group.

**construct validity** The degree to which a test adequately measures an underlying construct.

**standardisation** A set of uniform procedures for treating each participant in a test, interview or experiment, or for recording data.

fourth week of term 2 with a group who performed the test in a town hall with 400 other students on the last day of school in December. The need for standardisation sounds obvious, but it does not always occur in practice. Some people may be allowed more time than others, be given clearer or more detailed instructions, be permitted to ask questions, or be motivated by a tester to perform better. Consider the experience of one of your authors:

> As a graduate student at Yale, I administered a scale to assess children's degree of test anxiety in grade-school classes. Before starting, one teacher told her class, 'We're going to have some fun with this new kind of question game this nice man will play with you.' A teacher in another classroom prepared her class for the same assessment by cautioning, 'This psychologist from Yale University is going to give you a test to see what you are thinking; I hope you will do well and show how good our class is!' (Zimbardo, personal communication, 1958)

Could you directly compare the scores of the children in these two classes on this 'same' test? The answer is no because the test was not administered in a standardised way. In this case, the children in the second class scored higher on test anxiety. (You're probably not surprised!) When procedures do not include explicit instructions about the way to administer the test or the way to score the results, it is difficult to interpret what a given test score means or how it relates to any comparison group.

We have now reviewed some of the concerns researchers have when they construct a test and find out whether it is indeed testing what they wish to test. They must assure themselves that the test is reliable and valid. They must also specify the standard conditions under which it should be administered, so that resulting norms have meaning. Therefore, you should evaluate any test score you get in terms of the test's reliability and validity, the norms of performance, and the degree of standardisation of the circumstances in which you took the test.

We are now ready to turn to the measurement of intelligence.

For answers go to MyPsychLab!

**mypsychlab** where learning comes to life!

**intelligence** The global capacity to profit from experience and to go beyond given information about the environment.

How would you feel if someone used your adult height to assess intelligence? The measure would be reliable, but would it be valid?

### What is assessment?

- Psychological assessment has a long history, beginning in ancient China. Many important contributions were made by Sir Francis Galton

- A useful assessment tool must be reliable, valid and standardised. A reliable measure gives consistent results. A valid measure assesses the attributes for which the test was designed.

- A standardised test is always administered and scored in the same way; norms allow a person's score to be compared with the averages of others of the same age, sex and culture.

## CONCEPT QUESTIONS

1. What overarching ideas did Sir Francis Galton contribute to the study of intelligence?

2. What is meant by split-half reliability?

3. How would a research determine whether a measure has predictive validity?

4. Why is it important to have norms for measures?

## CRITICAL THINKING

Recall the study that looked at psychiatrists' assessments of patients. What might the psychiatrists do to mask the purpose of the assessment?

# INTELLIGENCE ASSESSMENT

How intelligent are you or your friends? To answer this question, you must begin by defining **intelligence**. Doing so is not an easy task, but a group of 52 intelligence researchers concurred on this general definition: 'Intelligence is a very general mental capability that, among other things, involves the ability to reason, plan, solve problems, think abstractly, comprehend complex ideas, learn quickly and learn from experience' (Gottfredson, 1997, p. 13). Given this range of capabilities, it should be clear immediately why controversy has almost always surrounded how intelligence is measured. The way in which theorists conceptualise intelligence and higher mental functioning greatly influences the way they try to assess it (Sternberg, 1994). Some psychologists believe that human intelligence can be quantified and reduced to a single score. Others argue that intelligence has many components that should be separately assessed. Still others say that there are actually several distinct kinds of intelligence, across different domains of experience.

In this section, we will describe how tests of intelligence mesh with these different conceptions of intelligence. Let's begin by considering the historical context in which interest in intelligence and intelligence testing first arose.

## THE ORIGINS OF INTELLIGENCE TESTING

As discussed earlier, Sir Francis Galton had very particular views about the origin and importance of intelligence. He believed that intelligence could be reduced to fundamental sensory and intellectual processes, and used a laboratory to measure functions such as people's ability to distinguish between the size or weight of a range of objects—abilities that seem removed from our modern conception of intelligence. Galton assessed over 10,000 people in this way, and therefore developed a comprehensive norming sample for his tasks. However, there was little standardisation in Galton's approach, and it was impossible for testing to occur anywhere but in his very specifically designed laboratories. To identify the first 'modern' intelligence test, we need to move from Britain to France, and to the year 1905. The year 1905 marked the first published account of a workable intelligence test. **Alfred Binet** had responded to the call of the French minister of public instruction for the creation of more effective teaching methods for developmentally disabled children. Binet and his colleague **Théophile Simon** believed that measuring a child's intellectual ability was necessary for planning an instructional program. Binet attempted to devise an objective test of intellectual performance that could be used to classify and separate developmentally disabled from normal schoolchildren. He hoped that such a test would reduce the school's reliance on the more subjective, and perhaps biased, evaluations of teachers.

To *quantify*—measure—intellectual performance, Binet designed age-appropriate problems or test items on which many children's responses could be compared. The problems on the test were chosen so that they could be scored objectively as correct or incorrect, could vary in content, were not heavily influenced by differences in children's environments, and assessed judgment and reasoning rather than rote memory (Binet, 1911).

Children of various ages were tested, and the average score for normal children at each age was computed. Then each individual child's performance was compared with the average for other children of his or her age. Test results were expressed in terms of the average age at which normal children achieved a particular score. This measure was called the **mental age**. For instance, when a child's score equalled the average score of a group of 5-year-olds, the child was said to have a *mental age* of 5, regardless of his or her actual **chronological age**, the number of years since birth.

Binet's successful development of an intelligence test had great impact in the United States. A unique combination of historical events and social-political forces had prepared the United States for an explosion of interest in assessing mental ability. At the beginning of the 20th century, the United States was a nation in turmoil. As a result of global economic, social and political conditions, millions of immigrants entered the country. New universal education laws flooded schools with students. Some form of assessment was needed to identify, document and classify immigrant adults and schoolchildren (Chapman, 1988). When World War I began, millions of volunteers marched into recruiting stations. Recruiters needed to determine who of these many people had the ability to learn quickly and benefit from special leadership training. New non-verbal, group-administered tests of mental ability were used to evaluate over 1.7 million recruits. A group of prominent psychologists, including Lewis Terman, Edward Thorndike and Robert Yerkes, responded to the wartime emergency and designed these tests in only one month's time (Lennon, 1985).

One consequence of this large-scale testing program was that the American public came to accept the idea that intelligence tests could differentiate people in terms of leadership ability and other socially important characteristics. This acceptance led to the widespread use of tests in schools and industry. Assessment was seen as a way to inject order into a chaotic society and as an inexpensive, democratic way to separate those who could benefit from education or military leadership training from those who could not. To facilitate the wide-scale use of intelligence testing, researchers strove for more broadly applicable testing procedures.

## IQ TESTS

Although Binet began the standardised assessment of intellectual ability in France, U.S. psychologists soon took the lead. They also developed the **IQ**, or **intelligence quotient**. The IQ was a numerical, standardised measure of intelligence. Two families of individually administered IQ tests are used widely today: the Stanford–Binet scales and the Wechsler scales.

### The Stanford–Binet Intelligence Scale

Stanford University's **Lewis Terman**, a former public school administrator, appreciated the importance of Binet's method for assessing intelligence. He adapted Binet's test questions for U.S. schoolchildren, he standardised the administration of the test, and he developed age-level norms by giving the test to thousands of children. In 1916, he published the Stanford Revision of the Binet Tests, commonly referred to as the *Stanford–Binet Intelligence Scale* (Terman, 1916).

**mental age** In Binet's measure of intelligence, the age at which a child is performing intellectually, expressed in terms of the average age at which normal children achieve a particular score.

**chronological age** The number of months or years since an individual's birth.

**intelligence quotient (IQ)** An index derived from standardised tests of intelligence; obtained by dividing an individual's mental age by chronological age and then multiplying by 100.

With his new test, Terman provided a base for the concept of the intelligence quotient, or IQ (a term coined by William Stern, 1914). The IQ was the ratio of mental age to chronological age multiplied by 100 to eliminate decimals:

$$IQ = \text{mental age} \div \text{chronological age} \times 100$$

A child with a chronological age of 8 whose test scores revealed a mental age of 10 had an IQ of 125 (10 ÷ 8 × 100 = 125), whereas a child of that same chronological age who performed at the level of a 6-year-old had an IQ of 75 (6 ÷ 8 × 100 = 75). Individuals who performed at the mental age equivalent to their chronological age had IQs of 100. Thus the score of 100 was considered to be the average IQ.

The new Stanford–Binet test soon became a standard instrument in clinical psychology, psychiatry and educational counselling. The Stanford–Binet contains a series of subtests, each tailored for a particular mental age. Since it was first introduced, the Stanford–Binet has undergone a series of revisions (Terman & Merrill, 1937, 1960, 1972; Thorndike et al., 1986). Through those revisions, the range of the test has been extended to measure the IQ of very young children and very intelligent adults. In addition, the revisions have provided updated norms for age-appropriate average scores. The most recent, fifth edition of the Stanford–Binet test provides IQ estimates for individuals in the normal range of performance as well as for those individuals who are either mentally impaired or mentally gifted (Roid, 2003).

### The Wechsler Intelligence Scales

**David Wechsler** of Bellevue Hospital in New York set out to correct the dependence on verbal items in the assessment of adult intelligence. In 1939, he published the Wechsler–Bellevue Intelligence Scale, which combined verbal subtests with nonverbal, or performance, subtests. Thus, in addition to an overall IQ score, people were given separate estimates of verbal IQ and nonverbal IQ. After a few changes, the test was retitled the *Wechsler Adult Intelligence Scale—* the WAIS—in 1955. Today, you would take the WAIS-III (Wechsler, 1997).

The WAIS-III has 14 subtests that span *verbal* and *performance* aspects of IQ. **Table 9.1** provides examples of the types of questions you would find on the test. The verbal subtests cover areas such as vocabulary and comprehension. The performance subtests involve manipulation of materials and have little or no verbal content. If you were to take the WAIS-III, you would perform the full range of subtests, and receive 3 scores: a Verbal IQ, a Performance IQ, and an overall, or Full Scale, IQ.

The WAIS-III is designed for people age 16 years and older, but similar tests have been developed for children (see **Figure 9.1**). *The Wechsler Intelligence Scale for Children— Fourth Edition* (WISC-IV; Wechsler, 2003) is suited for children ages 6 to 16, and the *Wechsler*

### Table 9.1

Questions and problems similar to those on the WAIS-III

| Verbal subtests | |
|---|---|
| Information | Who wrote *The Great Gatsby*? |
| Comprehension | What does it mean when people say "Birds of a feather flock together"? |
| Arithmetic | If you paid $8.50 for a movie ticket and $2.75 for a bucket of popcorn, how much change would you have left from a $20 bill? |
| Similarities | In what ways are airplanes and submarines alike? |
| Digit span | Repeat the following numbers: 3 2 7 5 9. |
| Vocabulary | What does *emulate* mean? |

| Performance subtests | |
|---|---|
| Digit symbol-coding | The examiner presents a key that matches digits (e.g., 1, 2, 3) with symbols (e.g., Φ, Θ, ∀). The test taker uses the key to complete a chart that gives just digits or symbols. |
| Picture completion | The test taker examines a picture and says what is missing (e.g., a horse without a mane). |
| Block design | The test taker uses patterned blocks to reproduce designs provided by the examiner. |
| Picture arrangement | The test taker puts a series of cartoonlike pictures into order so that they tell a story. |
| Object assembly | The examiner gives the test taker a set of cardboard puzzle pieces. The test taker arranges the pieces to form a picture of a common object. |

*Preschool and Primary Scale of Intelligence—Third Edition* (WPPSI-III; Wechsler, 2002) for children ages 2½ to 7¼ years. The recent revisions of both of these tests have made the materials more colourful, more contemporary and more enjoyable for children.

The WAIS-III, the WISC-IV, and the WPPSI-III form a family of intelligence tests that yield a Verbal IQ, a Performance IQ, and a Full Scale IQ at all age levels. In addition, they provide comparable subtest scores that allow researchers to track the development over time of more

**Figure 9.1**

Intelligence testing

A psychologist administers an intelligence test to a 4-year-old child. The performance part of the test includes sorting an array of coloured lollies. Why is performance an important component of an IQ assessment?

specific intellectual abilities. For this reason, the Wechsler scales are particularly valuable when the same individual is to be tested at different ages—for example, when a child's progress in response to different educational programs is monitored.

## EXTREMES OF INTELLIGENCE

IQ scores are no longer derived by dividing mental age by chronological age. If you took the test today, your score would be added up and directly compared with the scores of other people your age. An IQ of 100 is 'average' and would indicate that 50 percent of those your age had earned lower scores. As you can see in **Figure 9.2**, scores between 90 and 110 are labelled 'normal.' In this section, we consider the individuals whose IQ scores fall on either side of this range.

Intellectual disability **Intellectual disability** is typically classified according to two main criteria: the existence of a significantly sub-average level of general intelligence, and deficits in adaptive behaviour, manifestation of which occurs in the developmental years (generally taken as being from birth to 18 years).

The assessment of intelligence and adaptive behaviour is usually done by using standardised tests. An inherent difficulty in assessment is that the criteria for determining low levels of intelligence and adaptive behaviour have varied over time, and from place to place. For example, the American Association on Intellectual and Developmental Disabilities (formerly the American Association on Mental Retardation) has continuously changed the criterion for the intelligence level. It has variously been specified in terms of standard deviations below the mean (either 1 or 2), or in terms of a particular IQ score (either 70 or 75) (Macmillan, Gresham, & Siperstein, 1993). Similarly, the criterion for required low level of adaptive behaviour has changed.

'Intellectual disability' is the term most widely used and accepted in Australia. It is used in legislation (for example, the *Victorian Intellectually Disabled Persons' Services Act [1986]*), as well as in the title of the key organisations which serve as the scientific and service/advocacy bodies in Australia:

**intellectual disability**
Condition in which individuals have IQ scores of 70 to 75 or below and also demonstrate limitations in the ability to bring adaptive skills to bear on life tasks.

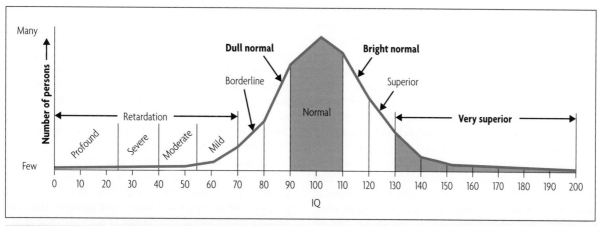

**Figure 9.2**

Distribution of IQ scores among a large sample

IQ scores are normed so that a score of 100 is the population average (as many people score below 100 as score above 100). Scores between 90 and 110 are labeled normal. Scores above 120 are considered to be superior or very superior; scores below 70 represent increasing levels of mental disability.

From *Wechsler's Measurement and Appraisal of Adult Intelligence*, 5e by Joseph D. Matarazzo, copyright © 1978 by Oxford University Press, Inc. Used by permission of Oxford University Press, Inc.

- The Australasian Society for the Study of Intellectual Disability (ASSID)
- The National Council on Intellectual Disability (NCID)

Former terms, no longer used in Australia and also rapidly becoming obsolete elsewhere, are *mental retardation, mental deficiency* and *subnormality*.

Intellectual disability can be brought about by a number of genetic and environmental factors. For example, individuals with *Down syndrome*—a disorder caused by extra genetic material on the 21st chromosome—often have low IQs. Another genetic disorder, known as *phenylketonuria* (PKU), also has a potential negative impact on IQ (Gassió et al., 2005). However, through strict adherence to a special diet, people can control the negative effects of PKU if it is diagnosed in infancy. Family studies suggest that genetic inheritance likely plays a role only in the range of what historically would have been called mild retardation (see Figure 9.2) (Plomin & Spinath, 2004).

The more severe forms of intellectual disability appear to be caused by the occurrence of spontaneous genetic abnormalities in an individual's development that are not heritable. The environment that is most often critical for disability is the prenatal environment. Pregnant women who suffer diseases such as rubella and syphilis are at risk for having children with intellectual disabilities. In addition, pregnant women who consume alcohol or other drugs, particularly during the early weeks of pregnancy, also increase the likelihood of having children with cognitive deficits (Mattson et al., 2001).

Historically, schools first existed for children who were deaf or blind, but it was not until the 1920s that schools for children with intellectual disabilities were established. These were privately operated by voluntary organisations or associations. In the same period, special classes were created in a number of 'regular' schools to cater for the needs of these children. During this period, only 11 percent of the estimated 22,000 children with intellectual disabilities received school education. These were mostly children with lower levels of disability. This trend continued well into the 1970s. During the 1970s state governments began to take a more active role in the education of children with disabilities, and by the end of the decade, the number of children being educated in special schools rose to around 25,000.

IQ scores give general information about how well people are able to perform—with respect to age-appropriate norms—on a variety of verbal and nonverbal tasks. In some instances, there is cause for concern when IQ scores and performance fail to match up. People who present a sufficiently large discrepancy between their achievement and their measured IQ might be diagnosed with a learning disability. Before clinicians diagnose a learning disability they need to rule out other factors that can lead to poor performance such as low motivation, mediocre teaching, or physical problems (e.g., visual deficits). Many schools now provide special assistance to students who have been diagnosed with intellectual disabilities.

**Giftedness** Individuals are most likely to be labelled as *gifted* if they have an IQ score above 130. However, as with the definition of intellectual disability, researchers have suggested that the conception of giftedness is not adequately captured just by IQ. For example, **Joseph Renzulli** (2005) has argued in favour of a 'three-ring' conception of giftedness that characterises giftedness along the dimensions of ability, creativity and task commitment. On this view, individuals can be considered gifted with IQs that are above average but not necessarily superior. In addition, they need to show high levels of creativity and exert high levels of commitment to particular problems or domains of performance. This expanded definition of giftedness explains why people often are not gifted across the academic spectrum (Winner, 2000). Abilities, creativity, and task commitment may all differ, for example, between verbal and mathematical domains.

What qualities do gifted children generally possess? The formal study of gifted children began in 1921 when Lewis Terman (1925) began a long-term study of a group of over 1,500 boys and girls who tested in the top 1 percent of their school populations. This group of individuals was followed all the way into their 80s (Holahan & Sears, 1995). Terman and his successors wanted to see how these children fared as they made their way through life. The questions Terman asked continue to shape the research agenda. For example, Terman explored the myth that gifted children have problems with social and emotional adjustment. Terman concluded just the opposite: he found his sample to be better adjusted than their less gifted peers. However, more contemporary studies support the conclusion that gifted children are more introverted—more internally oriented (see pp. 448–449)—than their peers (Sak, 2004). That orientation toward their own inner lives supports, in part, the task commitment that helps define giftedness. Still, gifted students report a reasonable level of participation in school activities. For example, a sample of 230 students attending a summer gifted program reported sports as their most frequent extracurricular or out-of-school activity (Olszewski-Kubilius & Lee, 2004). They were also involved in many academic clubs and competitions, with particular emphasis on mathematics.

Terman also documented that the children were largely successful in life. This is not surprising because, as we'll note again later in the chapter, IQ is a good predictor of occupational status and income. Thus the concern about gifted individuals is not that they aren't doing well. The concern, instead, is that they don't receive sufficient educational support to allow them to develop their gifts fully (Sternberg & Grigorenko, 2003; Winner, 2000). When giftedness is recognised as a multidimensional construct, gifted education must also have the flexibility to address individual students' particular talents.

# THEORIES OF INTELLIGENCE

So far, we have seen some of the ways in which intelligence has been measured. It is important to keep in mind that intelligence, the test and IQ are three difference concepts, like length, a ruler and centimetres. Intelligence, like length, is the property that we wish to measure, a test, like a ruler, is the instrument we use to measure it, and IQ, like centimetres, is the unit that it is measured in. You are now in a position to ask yourself: Do these tests capture everything that is meant by the word *intelligence*? Do these tests capture all abilities you believe constitute your own intelligence? To help you to think about those questions, we now review theories of intelligence. As you read about each theory, ask yourself whether its proponents would be comfortable using IQ as a measure of intelligence.

## PSYCHOMETRIC THEORIES OF INTELLIGENCE

Psychometric theories of intelligence originated in much the same philosophical atmosphere that gave rise to IQ tests. **Psychometrics** is the field of psychology that specialises in mental testing in any of its facets, including personality assessment, intelligence evaluation and aptitude measurement. Thus psychometric approaches are intimately related to methods of testing. These theories examine the *statistical relationships* between different measures of ability, such as the 14 subtests of the WAIS-III, and then make inferences about the nature of human intelligence on the basis of those relationships. The technique used most frequently is called *factor analysis,* a statistical procedure that takes a large number of responses to individual items and extracts an overall pattern of responses that represents. The goal of factor analysis is to identify the basic psychological dimensions of the concept being investigated. Of course, a statistical procedure only identifies statistical regularities; it is up to psychologists to suggest and defend interpretations of those regularities.

**Charles Spearman** carried out an early and influential application of factor analysis in the domain of intelligence. Spearman discovered that if people are given a number of ability tests, there will be an overall correlation between their scores on different tests. This does not mean that everybody is equally good or bad at everything, but it does mean that, in general, a person who is above average on, say, mathematics, is likely to also be above average on another ability, say, literacy. While we all know individuals for whom this is not the case, it is true that there is usually a relationship between different abilities. From this pattern he concluded that there is a factor of *general intelligence*, or **g**, underlying all intelligent performance (Spearman, 1927). Each individual domain also has associated with it specific skills that Spearman called *s*. For example, a person's performance on tests of vocabulary or arithmetic depends both on his or her general intelligence and on domain-specific abilities. Researchers have used MRI scans to identify the basis for *g* in the brain. **Figure 9.3** displays some of the regions of the brain in which people who were relatively high on general intelligence had more brain tissue than people who were lower on general intelligence (Haier et al., 2004).

**Raymond Cattell** (1963), using more advanced factor analytic techniques, determined that general intelligence can be broken down into two relatively independent components, which he called crystallised and fluid intelligence. **Crystallised intelligence** involves the knowledge a person has already acquired and the ability to access that knowledge; it is measured by tests of vocabulary, arithmetic and general information. **Fluid intelligence** is the ability to see complex relationships and solve new problems; it is measured by tests using unusual or novel objects or problems. Because the tests involve situations that are relatively new to everybody

**psychometrics** The field of psychology that specialises in mental testing.

For answers go to MyPsychLab!

**g** The factor of general intelligence underlying all intelligent performance.

**crystallised intelligence** The facet of intelligence involving the knowledge a person has already acquired and the ability to access that knowledge.

**fluid intelligence** The aspect of intelligence that involves the ability to see complex relationships and solve problems.

who takes the test, previously acquired knowledge—crystallised intelligence—provides little assistance in these tasks. Examples of tests of fluid intelligence include block designs, spatial visualisation and some abstract reasoning tasks. Crystallised intelligence allows you to cope well with your life's recurring, concrete challenges; fluid intelligence helps you attack novel, abstract problems.

**J. P. Guilford** (1961) used factor analysis to examine the demands of many intelligence-related tasks. His *structure of intellect* model specifies three features of intellectual tasks: the *content*, or type of information; the *product*, or form in which information is represented; and the *operation*, or type of mental activity performed.

As shown in **Figure 9.4**, there are five kinds of content in this model—visual, auditory, symbolic, semantic and behavioural; six kinds of products—units, classes, relations, systems, transformations and implications; and five kinds of operations—evaluation, convergent production, divergent production, memory and cognition. Each task performed by the intellect can be identified according to the particular types of content, products and operations involved. Further, Guilford believes that each content-product-operation combination (each small cube in the model) represents a distinct mental ability. For example, as Figure 9.4 shows, a test of vocabulary would assess your ability for *cognition* of *units* with *semantic content*. Learning a dance routine, in contrast, requires *memory* for *behavioural systems*.

This theoretical model is analogous to a chemist's periodic table of elements. By means of such a systematic framework, intellectual factors, like chemical elements, may be postulated before they are discovered. In 1961, when Guilford proposed his model, nearly 40 intellectual abilities had been identified. Researchers have since accounted for over 100, which shows the predictive value of Guilford's conception of intelligence (Guilford, 1985).

Since Guilford, many psychologists have broadened their conceptions of intelligence to include much more than performance on traditional IQ tests. We now examine two types of theories that go beyond IQ.

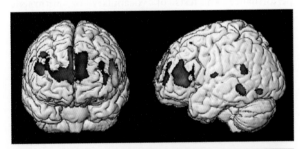

Figure 9.3

### The brain bases of general intelligence

After completing the WAIS to measure general intelligence, individuals underwent MRI scans to reveal the structure of their brains. The coloured regions are areas in which individuals with relatively higher general intelligence had more brain tissue.

Reprinted from *NeuroImage, 23*, R.J. Haier et al., "Structural brain variation and general intelligence," pp. 425–433, copyright © 2004, with permission of Elsevier.

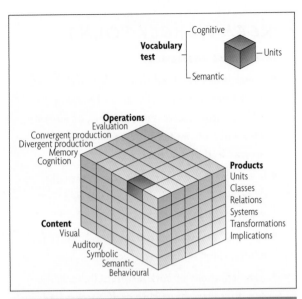

Figure 9.4

### The structure of intellect

In his structure of intellect model, J. P. Guilford specified three features of intellectual tasks: the content, or type of information; the product, or form in which information is represented; and the operation, or type of mental activity performed. Each task performed by the intellect can be identified according to the particular types of content, products and operations involved. For example, a test of vocabulary would assess your ability for cognition of units with semantic content.

Reprinted with permission from J.P. Guilford, "The Structure of the Intellect" from *Way Beyond the IQ*, 1977, p. 161. Copyright © 1977 Creative Education Foundation.

## STERNBERG'S TRIARCHIC THEORY OF INTELLIGENCE

**Robert Sternberg** (1999) also stresses the importance of cognitive processes in problem solving as part of his more general theory of intelligence. Sternberg outlines a triarchic—three-part—theory. His three types of intelligence, analytical, creative and practical, all represent different ways of characterising effective performance.

*Analytical intelligence* provides the basic information-processing skills that people apply to life's many familiar tasks. This type of intelligence is defined by the components, or mental processes, that underlie thinking and problem solving. Sternberg identifies three types of components that are central to information processing: (1) knowledge acquisition components, for learning new facts; (2) performance components, for problem-solving strategies and techniques; and (3) metacognitive components, for selecting strategies and monitoring progress toward success. To put some of your analytical intelligence to work, we'd like you now to try the exercise in **Table 9.2**.

# CRITICAL THINKING *in your life*

## ARE BREASTFED CHILDREN SMARTER?

Breastfed children are more intelligent, according study of almost 4000 Brisbane-born children. Researchers in the joint Mater–University of Queensland Study of Pregnancy tested the intellectual abilities of 3880, five-year-old children after establishing breastfeeding patterns when the same group of children was aged just six-months-old.

At this time, mothers were asked to categorise the period they had breastfed as either: never breastfed; less than three weeks; three weeks to less than seven weeks; seven weeks to less than four months; four months to less than six months; or still breastfeeding at six months.

The Peabody Picture Vocabulary Test Revised (PPVT-R)—a test that is know to correlate with intelligence among children was given to all children in the study and higher PPVT-R scores were found to be correlated with increased durations of breastfeeding, in addition to other factors such as maternal age, social class, income etc.

After adjustment for other factors, the average test result for those children breastfed for six months or more was 8.2 points higher for females and 5.8 points higher for males when compared with those who were never breastfed.

One of the authors, Professor Jake Najman, noted the study's findings could be explained by psychological influences such as a stronger attachment being facilitated between mother and child through the act of breastfeeding, thereby encouraging cognitive development. A second factor could be a unique, nutritional component of breast milk, possibly a lipid, essential for optimal brain development.

---

How did you do on the anagrams? To solve these anagrams, you mostly needed to use performance components and metacognitive components. The performance components are what allowed you to manipulate the letters in your head; the metacognitive components are what allowed you to have strategies for finding solutions. Consider T-R-H-O-S. How did you mentally transform that into SHORT? A good strategy to get started is to try consonant clusters that are probable in English—such as S-H and T-H. Selecting strategies requires metacognitive components; carrying them out requires performance components. Note that a good strategy will sometimes fail. Consider T-N-K-H-G-I. What makes this anagram hard for many people is that K-N is not a very likely combination to start a word, whereas T-H is. Did you stare at this anagram for a while, trying to turn it into a word beginning with T-H?

By breaking down various tasks into their components, researchers can pinpoint the processes that differentiate the performance outcomes of individuals with different IQs. For example, researchers might discover that the metacognitive components of high-IQ students prompt them to select different strategies to solve a particular type of problem than do their lower-IQ peers. The difference in strategy selection accounts for the high-IQ students' greater problem-solving success.

*Creative intelligence* captures people's ability to deal with two extremes: novel versus very routine problems. Suppose, for example, a group of individuals found themselves stranded after an accident. You would credit with intelligence the person in the group who could most quickly help the group find its way home. In other circumstances, you would recognise as intelligent the behaviour of someone who was able to perform routine tasks automatically. If, for example, a group of people carried out the same tasks day after day, you would be most impressed by the individual who could complete the tasks successfully with the least amount of 'new' thought.

## Table 9.2

### Using analytical intelligence

The following is a list of anagrams—scrambled words. As quickly as possible, try to find a solution for each anagram (Sternberg, 1986).

1. H-U-L-A-G _____
2. P-T-T-M-E _____
3. T-R-H-O-S _____
4. T-N-K-H-G-I _____
5. T-E-W-I-R _____
6. L-L-A-O-W _____
7. R-I-D-E-V _____
8. O-C-C-H-U _____
9. T-E-N-R-E _____
10. C-I-B-A-S _____

Turn to page 319 for the solutions.

*Source:* Adapted from American Association on Mental Retardation, 1992, pp. 24, 40–41.

*Practical intelligence* is reflected in the management of day-to-day affairs. It involves your ability to *adapt* to new and different contexts, *select* appropriate contexts, and effectively *shape* your environment to suit your needs. Practical intelligence is bound to particular contexts. To measure practical intelligence, researchers must immerse themselves in those contexts.

A team of researchers set the goal of measuring practical intelligence among adolescents from the Yup'ik Eskimo group in Alaska (Grigorenko et al., 2004). Although the Yup'ik people live in modern houses with electricity, oil and telephones, many communities can only be reached by airplane during the long harsh winters. For that reason, the measure of practical intelligence focused on the types of knowledge that remain relevant to survival in Yup'ik communities. Consider this question:

Uncle Markus knows a lot about hunting wolverines. He is most likely to catch a wolverine when he sets his trap:

(a) on a slanted tree.  (b) in the hollow of a dead tree.
(c) far from any water.  (d) near a frozen river.

Did you choose (a) as the correct answer? The practical intelligence test consisted of 36 items of this sort. The adolescent students in the sample completed this test. In addition, the researchers gathered evaluations from other members of the group, including adults and elders, about which adolescents they thought could be best described as, for example, *umyuartuli*— 'a good thinker, one who comes up with novel solu-

tions to problems and uses the mind to survive' (p. 191). The Yup'ik adolescents produced a range of scores on the measure of practical intelligence. In general, those who lived in urban environments had less practical intelligence than those who lived in rural environments. In addition, the adolescents who had the highest levels of practical intelligence also earned the most positive evaluation for traits such as *umyuartuli*.

You can see from this example why the concept of practical intelligence has different meanings in different contexts. However, the general idea remains the same: people can bring more or less practical intelligence to bear on their day-to-day tasks.

## GARDNER'S MULTIPLE INTELLIGENCES AND EMOTIONAL INTELLIGENCE

**Howard Gardner** (1983, 1999) has also proposed a theory that expands the definition of intelligence beyond those skills covered on an IQ test. Gardner identifies numerous intelligences that cover a range of human experience. The value of any of the abilities differs across human societies, according to what is needed by, useful to, and prized by a given society. As shown in **Table 9.3**, Gardner identified eight intelligences.

Gardner argues that Western society promotes the first two intelligences, whereas non-Western societies often value others. For example, in the Caroline Island of Micronesia, sailors must be able to navigate long

### Table 9.3

Gardner's eight intelligences

| Intelligence | End states | Core components |
|---|---|---|
| Logical–mathematical | Scientist Mathematician | Sensitivity to, and capacity to discern, logical or numerical patterns; ability to handle long chains of reasoning. |
| Linguistic | Poet Journalist | Sensitivity to the sounds, rhythms and meanings of words; sensitivity to the different functions of language. |
| Naturalist | Biologist Environmentalist | Sensitivity to the differences among diverse species; abilities to interact subtly with living creatures. |
| Musical | Composer Violinist | Abilities to produce and appreciate rhythm, pitch and timbre; appreciation of the forms of musical expressiveness. |
| Spatial | Navigator Sculptor | Capacities to perceive the visual-spatial world accurately and to perform transformations on one's initial perceptions. |
| Bodily kinaesthetic | Dancer Athlete | Abilities to control one's body movements and to handle objects skillfully. |
| Interpersonal | Therapist Salesperson | Capacities to discern and respond appropriately to the moods, temperaments, motivations and desires of other people. |
| Intrapersonal | Person with detailed, accurate self-knowledge | Access to one's own feelings and the ability to discriminate among them and draw upon them to guide behaviour; knowledge of one's own strengths, weaknesses, desires and intelligences. |

From *Multiple Intelligences* by Howard Gardner. © 1993 by Howard Gardner. Reprinted by permission of Basic Books, a member of Perseus Books, L.L.C.

distances without maps, using only their spatial intelligence and bodily kinaesthetic intelligence. Such abilities count more in that society than the ability to write a term paper. In Bali, where artistic performance is part of everyday life, musical intelligence and talents involved in coordinating intricate dance steps are highly valued. Interpersonal intelligence is more central to collectivist societies such as Japan, where cooperative action and communal life are emphasised, than it is in individualistic societies such as the United States (Triandis, 1990).

Assessing these kinds of intelligence demands more than paper-and-pencil tests and simple quantified measures. Gardner's theory of intelligence requires that the individual be observed and assessed in a variety of life situations as well as in the small slices of life depicted in traditional intelligence tests.

In recent years, researchers have begun to explore a type of intelligence—*emotional intelligence*—that is related to Gardner's concepts of *interpersonal* and *intrapersonal* intelligence (see Table 9.3). **Emotional intelligence** is defined as having four major components (Mayer & Salovey, 1997; Mayer et al., 2004):

- The ability to perceive, appraise and express emotions accurately and appropriately
- The ability to use emotions to facilitate thinking
- The ability to understand and analyse emotions and to use emotional knowledge effectively
- The ability to regulate one's emotions to promote both emotional and intellectual growth.

This definition reflects a new view of the positive role of emotion as it relates to intellectual functioning—emotions can make thinking more intelligent, and people can think intelligently about their emotions and those of others.

Researchers have begun to demonstrate that emotional intelligence has important consequences for everyday life.

Take a moment to review the components of the definition of emotional intelligence. Can you see how people who have more of these abilities would also be better able to cope with day-to-day hassles? A pair of researchers tested the hypothesis that people high in emotional intelligence would cope better and therefore have a greater sense of psychological wellbeing (Slaski & Cartwright, 2002). The sample they used were middle managers working for a major retailer in England. These men and women had jobs that were reasonably demanding. Each manager completed an assessment device that measured emotional intelligence—EQ. They also reported on aspects of wellbeing, such as their level of psychological distress, their morale, and their quality of working life. Finally, each manager's supervisor rated his or her job performance. The researchers divided the managers into a low-EQ group and a high-EQ group. The results were quite dramatic. By comparison to the low-EQ group, the high-EQ managers reported less psychological distress, higher morale, and better quality of working life. Their bosses also rated the high-EQ group as better managers.

You can probably see how all the pieces fit together. People whose emotional intelligence allows them to experience low distress and good morale are also more likely to be effective in their jobs. The same researchers are now trying to implement a training program to improve the emotional intelligence of the low-**EQ** managers.

Our review of intelligence testing and theories of intelligence sets the stage for a discussion of the societal circumstances that make the topic of intelligence so controversial.

**EQ** The emotional intelligence counterpart of IQ.

**emotional intelligence** The abilities to perceive, appraise and express emotions accurately; to use emotions to facilitate thinking and analysis; to use emotional knowledge effectively and regulate emotions to promote emotional and intellectual growth.

## RECAP CHECKPOINT
### Theories of intelligence

- Psychometric analyses of IQ suggest that several basic abilities, such as fluid and crystallised aspects of intelligence, contribute to IQ scores.

- Contemporary theories conceive of and measure intelligence very broadly by considering the skills and insights people use to solve the types of problems they encounter.

- Sternberg differentiates analytical, creative and practical aspects of intelligence.

- Garner identifies eight types of intelligence that both include and go beyond the types of intelligence assessed by standard IQ measures. Recent research has focused on emotional intelligence.

## CONCEPT QUESTIONS

1. Why did Spearman come to believe in g, general intelligence?

2. What are the three types of intelligence in Sternberg's triarchic theory?

3. In Gardner's theory, what kind of intelligence might determine whether someone could be a successful sculptor?

## CRITICAL THINKING
Consider the study relating emotional intelligence to everyday wellbeing. Why is it important to obtain measures of the participants' success from their bosses?

For answers go to MyPsychLab!

# PSYCHOLOGY *in your life*

## DO THEORIES OF INTELLIGENCE MATTER?

When students learn about Sternberg's triarchic intelligences and Gardner's multiple intelligence, they often have this response: It's nice to say that other things matter besides classic academic intelligence, but do these theories really have an impact beyond an introductory psychology textbook? In fact, both Gardner (1999a) and Sternberg (Stemler et al., 2006; Sternberg & Grigorenko, 2000) are heavily involved with the reform of educational practice. Their quest is to export their insights about intelligence from research settings directly into classrooms.

Let's focus on a classroom study that grew out of both Gardner's and Sternberg's theories (Williams et al., 2002). The study involved several hundred fifth- and sixth-graders in schools in Connecticut and Massachusetts. The purpose of the study was to improve the students' school performance by providing them with a special curriculum—the *practical intelligence for school* (PI FS) curriculum—that emphasised practical intelligence. Recall that practical intelligence relates to people's ability to manage their day-to-day tasks. The curriculum embodied five themes that helped students acquire practical intelligence for school:

- *Knowing why.* Students were asked to consider the purposes of schoolwork (e.g., What is the point of homework?) and the relationship of schoolwork to life outside school (e.g., How do tests in school help prepare you

for the tests adults face in their work?).

- *Knowing self.* Students were encouraged to think about their strengths and weaknesses with respect to schoolwork and other aspects of life; they were encouraged to imagine how they would take advantage of their strengths and work around their weaknesses.

- *Knowing differences.* Students were encouraged to consider why different working styles might be necessary for different types of assignments (e.g., completing maths problems versus writing an essay).

- *Knowing process.* Students were encouraged to develop an awareness of the types of problems that arise in academic settings and the processes and resources that are available to overcome those problems.

- *Revisiting.* Students were encouraged to consider the benefits of reviewing their work by rereading texts, revising writing, reworking problems, and so on.

Can you see how each of these themes could help students develop practical intelligence with respect to school success?

The students received pre-tests of their abilities in October and post-tests of their abilities in June.

Those pre- and post-tests assessed improvement in a variety of

domains, such as reading, writing and homework quality. Students who had been exposed to the PIFS curriculum showed considerable improvement across the year. You might wonder if the improvement came about just because of ordinary classroom activities unrelated to the PIFS curriculum. To address that issue, the research team also assessed the progress of a control group who hadn't experienced the PIFS curriculum. The students in the control group also showed improvement, but not to the same extent as the PIFS students. For example, in the Connecticut sample one group of PIFS students showed a 17 percent greater improvement in a measure of reading and writing ability than did the control-group students. Similarly, in the Massachusetts sample a PIFS group showed 18 percent greater improvement in writing than did the control-group students. The curriculum that focused on practical intelligence allowed students to show greater improvement on classic academic tasks such as reading and writing.

Take a look back at the five themes embodied in the PIFS curriculum. How much have you thought about each of these themes? Can you see how ideas from a theory of intelligence—*practical* intelligence is different from *analytical* intelligence—generate a successful approach to lessons in the classroom?

## THE POLITICS OF INTELLIGENCE

We have seen that contemporary conceptions of intelligence reject the narrow linking of a score on an IQ test with a person's intelligence. Even so, IQ tests remain the most frequent measure of 'intelligence' in Western society. Because of the prevalence of IQ testing and the availability of IQ scores, it becomes easy to compare different groups according to their 'average' IQ. Such ethnic and racial group comparisons have often been used as evidence for the innate, genetic inferiority of members of certain racial groups. We will briefly examine the history of this practice of using IQ test scores to index the alleged mental inferiority of certain groups. Then we will look at current evidence on the nature and nurture of intelligence and IQ test performance. You will see that this is one of the most politically volatile issues in psychology because public policies about immigration quotas, educational resources, and more may be based on how group IQ data are interpreted.

## THE HISTORY OF GROUP COMPARISONS

In the early 1900s, psychologist Henry Goddard advocated mental testing of all immigrants into the United States and in 1924 the US Congress passed the Immigration Restriction Act, which made it national policy to administer intelligence tests to immigrants as they arrived in New York. This policy was not necessarily racially based—the testing was to be done regardless of the country of origin of the immigrant, but its consequence was that was that a large database of IQ test results of people from different countries was built very quickly. It was observed that some groups tended to achieve lower scores than others, and large numbers of Jewish, Italian, Russian, and immigrants of other nationalities, were classified as 'morons' on the basis of IQ tests. Some psychologists interpreted these statistical findings as evidence that immigrants from southern and eastern Europe were genetically inferior to those from the hardy northern and western European stock (see Ruch, 1937). However, you can probably think of several reasons why these groups of immigrants may have performed more poorly on IQ tests developed in the U.S. First of all, the groups that performed comparatively poorly were also the least familiar with the dominant language and culture embedded in the IQ tests, because they had immigrated most recently. (Within a few decades, these group differences completely disappeared from IQ tests, but the theory of racially inherited differences in intelligence persisted.) It should also be kept in mind that the people who were being tested were not a random sample of the population that they came from. People do not migrate at random, so a sample of migrants cannot be assumed to be typical of the population as a whole. It is impossible to draw conclusions about, say, the Irish people on the basis of the attributes of those Irish people who are seeking a better life in another country. Suppose we based our opinions about the English on our observations of backpackers at Bondi Beach?

Goddard (1917) and others then went beyond merely associating low IQ with hereditary racial and ethnic origins. They added moral worthlessness, mental deficiency and immoral social behaviour to the mix of negatives related to low IQ. Evidence for their view came from case studies of infamous families. Consider the *Kallikak* family, a family with one 'good seed' side and one 'bad seed' side to its family tree. (In his study, Goddard renamed the family Kallikak, which means good–bad in Greek.) Martin Kallikak was a Revolutionary War soldier who had an illegitimate son with a woman described as developmentally disabled. Their union eventually produced 480 descendants. Goddard classified 143 of them as 'defective' and only 46 as normal. He found crime, alcoholism, mental disorders and illegitimacy common among the rest of the family members. By contrast, when Martin Kallikak later married a 'good woman', their union produced 496 descendants, only three of whom were classified as 'defective'. Goddard also found that many offspring from this high-quality union had become 'eminent' (Goddard, 1914). Goddard came to believe that heredity determined intelligence, genius and eminence on the positive side. On the negative side, he arrayed delinquency, alcoholism, sexual immorality, developmental disability and maybe even poverty (McPherson, 1985).

The situation for migrants in Australia at the same time was not very different. Our *Immigration Restriction Act* was passed in 1901, as one of the group of immigration rules that became known as the 'White Australia Policy'. Although it did not have a mandatory IQ test, it prevented people from entering the country if they could be considered to be insane; if they might become a burden to the public or any person suffering from an infectious or contagious disease or 'of a loathsome or dangerous character' (Commonwealth of Australia, 2007). Immigrants were also asked to complete a dictation test, which could be conducted in any European language, not necessarily the migrant's native language.

Goddard's genetic inferiority argument was further reinforced by the fact that, on the World War I Army Intelligence tests, African-Americans and other racial minorities scored lower than the white majority. Lewis Terman, who as we saw promoted IQ testing in the United States, commented in this unscientific manner on the data he had helped collect on U.S. racial minorities:

> Their dullness seems to be racial. . . . There seems no possibility at present of convincing society that they should not be allowed to reproduce, although from a eugenics point of view, they constitute a grave problem because of their unusually prolific breeding. (Terman, 1916, pp. 91–92)

The names have changed, but the problem remains the same. In the United States today, African Americans and Latinos score, on average, lower than Asian Americans

A 1906 badge supporting a 'White Australia'. Museum Victoria Collection: www.museumvictoria.com.au.

and whites on standardised intelligence tests. Of course, there are individuals in all groups who score at the highest (and the lowest) extremes of the IQ scale. How should these group differences in IQ scores be interpreted? One tradition has been to attribute these differences to genetic inferiority (nature). After we discuss the evidence for genetic differences in IQ, we will consider a second possibility, that differences in environments (nurture) exert a significant impact on IQ. The validity of either explanation, or some combination of them, has important social, economic and political consequences.

**heritability estimate** A statistical estimate of the degree of inheritance of a given trait or behaviour, assessed by the degree of similarity between individuals who vary in their extent of genetic similarity.

## HEREDITY AND IQ

How can researchers assess the extent to which intelligence is genetically determined? Any answer to this question requires that the researcher choose some measure as an index of intelligence. Thus the question becomes not whether 'intelligence', in the abstract, is influenced by heredity but, in most cases, whether IQs are similar within family trees. To answer this more limited question, researchers need to tease apart the effects of shared genes and shared environment. One method is to compare functioning in identical twins (monozygotic), fraternal twins (dizygotic), and relatives with other degrees of genetic overlap. **Figure 9.5** presents correlations between

IQ scores of individuals on the basis of their degree of genetic relationship (Plomin & Petrill, 1997). As you can see, the greater the genetic similarity, the greater the IQ similarity. (Note in these data that the impact of environment is also revealed in the greater IQ similarities among those who have been reared together.)

Researchers use results of this sort to try to estimate the *heritability* of IQ. A **heritability estimate** of a particular trait, such as intelligence, is based on the proportion of the variability in test scores on that trait that can be traced to genetic factors. The estimate is found by computing the variation in all the test scores for a given population (university students or psychiatric patients, for example) and then identifying what portion of the total variance is due to genetic or inherited factors. This is done by comparing individuals who have different degrees of genetic overlap. Researchers who have reviewed the variety of studies on heritability of IQ conclude that about 50 percent of the variance in IQ scores is due to genetic makeup (Grigorenko, 2000).

What is perhaps even more interesting, however, is that heritability *increases* across the life span: Heritability is about 40 percent for 4- to 6-year-olds but increases to about 60 percent in early adulthood and to about 80 percent in older adults! Many people are surprised by this result, because it seems that environments should have

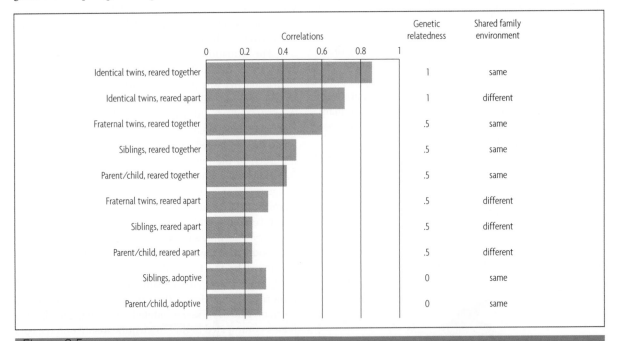

**Figure 9.5**

### IQ and genetic relationship

This figure presents the correlations between the IQ scores of identical (monozygotic) and fraternal (dizygotic) twins reared together (in the same home environments) or reared apart (in different home environments). For comparison, it also includes data for siblings (brothers and sisters) and parents and children, both biological and adoptive. The data demonstrate the importance of both genetic factors (the numbers under "genetic relatedness" specify the overlap of genetic material) and environmental factors. For example, identical twins show higher correlations between their IQs than do fraternal twins—a genetic influence. However, both types of twins show higher correlations when raised together—an environmental influence.

Reprinted from *Intelligence, 24*, R. Plomin & S.A. Petrill, "Genetics and Intelligence: What's New?" pp. 53–77, copyright © 1997, with permission from Elsevier.

This photo shows Nobel Prize winning chemist Marie Curie posing with her daughters Eve (on the left) and Irene (on the right) in their home garden. Irene also won a Nobel Prize in chemistry and Eve became a famous author. Why do families like this one encourage researchers to attempt to understand the impact of heredity and environment on IQ?

more, not less, of an effect as people get older. Here's how researchers explain this counterintuitive finding: 'It is possible that genetic dispositions nudge us toward environments that accentuate our genetic propensities, thus leading to increased heritability throughout the life span' (Plomin & Petrill, 1997, p. 61).

Let's return now to the point at which genetic analysis becomes controversial: test score differences between African Americans and white Americans. Although several decades ago, the gap was 15 IQ points, the scores of whites and blacks have been converging over time, so that on a number of contemporary indicators the gap is between 7 and 10 points (Nisbett, 1995, 1998; Williams & Ceci, 1997). Although the close in the gap suggests environmental influences, the lingering difference has prompted many people to suggest that there are unbridgeable genetic differences between the races (Hernnstein & Murray, 1994). However, even if IQ is highly heritable, does this difference reflect genetic inferiority of individuals in the lower-scoring group? The answer is no. Heritability is based on an estimate *within* one given group. It cannot be used to interpret differences *between* groups, no matter how large those differences are on an objective test. Heritability estimates pertain only to the average in a given population of individuals. Even though we know that height, for instance, has a high heritability estimate (about 90 percent), you cannot determine how much of your height is due to genetic influences. The same argument is true for IQ; despite high heritability estimates, we cannot determine

the specific genetic contribution to any individual's IQ or to mean IQ scores among groups. The fact that on an IQ test one racial or ethnic group scores lower than another group does not mean that the difference between these groups is genetic in origin, even if the heritability estimate for IQ scores is high as assessed within a group.

Another reason that genetic makeup cannot be wholly responsible for group differences in IQ has to do with the *relative* sizes of the differences. There is much overlapping in the distribution of each group's scores despite mean differences: The difference between groups is small compared with the differences among the scores of individuals within each group (Loehlin, 2000; Suzuki & Valencia, 1997). In general, the differences between the gene pools of different racial groups are minute compared with the genetic differences among individual members of the same group. Furthermore, in Australia, race is often more of a *social* construct than a *biological* construct. Consider the purple 'Wiggle', Jeff Fatt. Jeff's family ran a department store in Casino (northern NSW) called the Kwong Sing Emporium. After getting his Bachelor of Arts degree in Industrial Design, Jeff moved to Sydney to help his brother Hilton set up PA systems for the local bands. Through his involvement in the music scene he met Anthony Field, joined the popular Australian band called 'The Cockroaches' and was asked by Anthony to join in a new musical project, a children's album, which became 'The Wiggles'. Jeff provides an excellent example of multicultural Australia and a good migrant experience.

The family of 'The Wiggles' member, Jeff Fatt, ran a department store in country NSW called the Kwong Sing Emporium. What does that suggest about the construct of race in Australia?

THE POLITICS OF INTELLIGENCE

307

As such, there is great danger in treating IQ differences among socially distinct groups as if those differences conform to underlying biology (Sternberg et al., 2005).

Researchers have found ways to put this perspective to a test in a series of studies in which the degree of white or European parentage among blacks is determined. In the United States, the 'black' population is estimated to be about 20 to 30 percent European through intermarriages. Does it make a difference in IQ if a 'black' person has more or less European genetic stock? The genetic argument holds that it does, but the data suggest the correlation of degree of European ancestry with IQ is very low (on the order of only .15 across many studies). This is true whether skin colour or blood groups are used as the index of racial mixture. Comparisons of German children fathered by African American GI fathers and white GI fathers show no difference in their IQ scores (Loehlin, 2000; Nisbett, 1998).

Surely genetics plays a sizable role in influencing individuals' scores on IQ tests, as it does on many other traits and abilities. We have argued, however, that heredity does not constitute an adequate explanation for IQ differences between racial and ethnic groups. It has a necessary, but not sufficient, role in our understanding of such performance effects. Let's turn now to the role the environment may play in creating the IQ gap.

## ENVIRONMENTS AND IQ

In 1975 Judith Kearins published the first of a series of studies that would change the way that we understand the contribution of environment to intelligence in Australia. Kearins noted that Indigenous Australian children typically score slightly below their year level on conventional ability tests. Rather than assuming that this might be due to a difference in intelligence between Indigenous and non-indigenous children, Kearins decided to explore how different groups of children perform different sorts of tasks. She developed a cognitive task resembling a common children's party game—sometimes called 'Kim's Game'. Objects are placed on a grid pattern and hidden under a cover. After the cover has been removed, the child has 30 seconds to examine the array before the cover is replaced. Some of the objects are then moved, unseen by the child. When the cover is removed again, the child has to replace the objects to the to where they were in at the previous viewing.

The important thing about Kearins' (1975) study was not the task itself, but rather the objects that she used in the task. She used four versions of the task. In two versions, the objects were natural (e.g. rock, twig etc), whereas in two they were man-made or 'artefactual'. One of the natural and one of the artefactual groups consisted of objects with different names (e.g. matchbox, pencil, hairpin), whereas in the other condition the children saw a number of objects with the same name (e.g. several different feathers). **Table 9.4** provides a summary of the how the objects were arranged in the different conditions.

Kearins found that in all four conditions, the Indigenous children performed better than the white children overall.

## Table 9.4

Summary of how objects were selected and presented in the Kearins (1975, 1978) studies

|  | Natural | Artefactual |
| --- | --- | --- |
| Different name | Twig, seed-pod, feather | Matchbox, ring, eraser |
| Same name | Many different seed-pods | Many different rings |

Adapted from American Association on Mental Retardation, 1992, pp. 24, 40–41.

Importantly, the Indigenous children performed equally well regardless of whether the objects had the same or different names, whereas the white children always showed an advantage for objects that had different names.

How can these differences be explained? Kearins suggested that the two groups of children were doing different things when they were shown the objects to remember. The white children, coming from a culture where language is vital to understanding, attempted to store the objects verbally, remembering them as a word list. That is why these children showed an advantage for objects with different names. However, they could not effectively remember all the words in the 30 seconds available (there were 12 – 20 object arrays). Kearins thought that the Indigenous children and adolescents, in contrast, understood the world more visually. Because they encoded the items visually, they were able to do it in the time available, and the 'name-ability' of the objects made less difference to their memory.

While this is an interesting interpretation of what the children did when they were remembering the objects, Kearins also attempted to explain *why* the children did the task so differently. Her first explanation was in terms of evolutionary biology. She observed in a subsequent study that the effects were replicated regardless of whether the Indigenous children were living on the desert fringe, or in suburban Perth. She reasoned that there are certain visual processing skills that would have helped Australian Indigenous people survive in the desert environment, and that these may have been encoded genetically, to emerge no matter where a child finished up living. However, after interviews and discussion, Kearins realised that there was an alternative, environmental explanation to do with differences in child rearing practices. She noted that Indigenous mothers are less likely to support the heads of their infants at around 20 weeks of age than white mothers. As the children are therefore more likely to be 'sitting up' than 'lying down' at the same developmental stage, Kearins proposed that they develop an accurate sense of vertical and horizontal space earlier. For the same reason, as they are less likely to be nestled against their mothers, they also observe the 'external' world more often. As we know from Chapter 8 these early experiences influence both brain development and intellectual abilities, resulting in children who approach these memory tasks in quite a different way from the white children.

Kearins' studies, and a related study by Drinkwater (1976) provide an interesting insight into the scientific process surrounding issues such as IQ and race, and highlight how we should not always settle for a single explanation of any behaviour Through critical reflection and careful follow up research, Kearins modified her own position, rather than becoming entrenched in a single world view.

Because heritability estimates are less than 1.0, we know that genetic inheritance is not solely responsible for anyone's IQ. Environments must also affect IQ. But how can we assess what aspects of the environment are important influences on IQ? What features of your environment affect your potential to score well on an IQ test (Beiser & Gotowiec, 2000; Ceci, 1999; Rowe, 1997; Suzuki & Valencia, 1997)? Environments are complex stimulus packages that vary on many dimensions, both physical and social, and may be experienced in different ways by those within them. Even children in the same family setting do not necessarily share the same critical, psychological environment. Think back to growing up in your family. If you had siblings, did they all get the same attention from parents, did conditions of stress change over the course of time, did the family's financial resources change, did your parents' marital status change? It is obvious that environments are made up of many components that are in a dynamic relationship and that change over time. So it becomes difficult for psychologists to say what kinds of environmental conditions— attention, stress, poverty, health, war, and so on—actually have an impact on IQ.

Researchers have most often focused on more global measures of environment, like the socioeconomic status of the family. For example, in a large-scale longitudinal study of more than 26,000 children, the best predictors of a child's IQ at age 4 were the family's socioeconomic status and the level of the mother's education. This was equally true for African American and white children (Broman et al., 1975). Similarly, **Figure 9.6** shows an overall impact of social class on IQ.

Why does social class affect IQ? Wealth versus poverty can affect intellectual functioning in many ways, health and educational resources being two of the most obvious. Poor health during pregnancy and low birth weight are solid predictors of a child's lowered mental ability. Children born into impoverished families often suffer from poor nutrition, many going to school hungry, thus less able to concentrate on learning tasks. Furthermore, impoverished homes may suffer from a lack of books, written media, computers, and other materials that add to one's mental stimulation. The 'survival orientation' of poor parents, especially in single-parent families, that leaves parents little time or energy to play with and intellectually stimulate their children is detrimental to performance on tasks such as those on standard IQ tests.

Researchers have spent the past 40 years developing programs intended to counteract the effects of impoverished environments. The Head Start program was first funded by the U.S. federal government in 1965 to address the 'physical health, developmental, social, educational, and emotional needs of low-income children and to increase the capacity of the families to care for their children, through

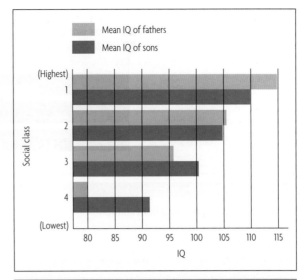

Figure 9.6

**The relationship among heredity, environment and IQ**
This chart shows evidence for the contribution of heredity and environment to IQ scores. There are similar IQs for fathers and sons (influence of heredity), but the IQs of both fathers and sons are related to social class (influence of environment).

empowerment and supportive services' (Kassebaum, 1994, p. 123). The idea of Head Start and similar programs in Australia such as Best Start and Good Beginnings was not to move children to privileged environments but to improve the environments into which they were born. Children are exposed to special preschool education, they receive decent daily meals, and their parents are given advice on health and other aspects of child rearing.

Consider a program started in 1962 at the High/Scope Perry preschool in Ypsilanti, Michigan (Schweinhart, 2004). The program focused on a group of 3- and 4-year-old low-income African American children who had been evaluated as being at risk for school failure. The High/Scope Perry program provided the children with a classroom environment that focused on *participatory education*—children were encouraged to initiate and plan their own activities and activities for the classroom group. In addition, the program involved parents in the children's educations through home visits and parent group meetings. The researchers followed the students who participated in the program for the next 40 years. **Figure 9.7** compares the outcomes of participants to a group of students from the same population who did not. As you can see, High/Scope Perry students had higher IQs at age 5 than their peers outside the program. They were also considerably more likely to graduate from a regular high school and have higher paying jobs at age 40.

Similar data have emerged from an early intervention program in Chicago: Fifteen years after participating in a preschool program, students saw many of the same advantages as the High/Scope Perry group including much higher rates of high school graduation (Reynolds et al., 2001). These studies provide strong evidence for the importance

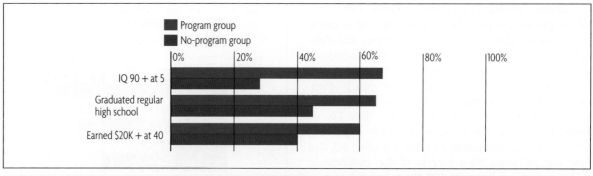

**Figure 9.7**

The impact of a preschool intervention
Students who participated in the High/Scope Perry preschool program had better outcomes than students who were not participants.

From Lawrence J. Scheinhart, "The High/Scope Perry Preschool Study Through Age 40."

of the environment for intellectual development. They also provide concrete models for programs that can change the lives of children who are at risk.

## CULTURE AND THE VALIDITY OF IQ TESTS

People would probably care much less about IQ scores if they didn't allow for such useful predictions: Extensive research shows that IQ scores are valid predictors of school grades from elementary school through college, of occupational status, and of performance in many jobs (Gottfredson, 2002; Nettlebeck & Wilson, 2005). These patterns of results suggest that IQ tests validly measure intellectual abilities that are very basic and important toward the types of success that are valued in Western cultures—intelligence, as measured by IQ, directly affects success. IQ distinctions can also affect academic and job performance indirectly by changing one's motives and beliefs. Those with higher IQ scores are likely to have had more success experiences in school, become more motivated to study, develop an achievement orientation, and become optimistic about their chances of doing well. Also, children scoring low on IQ tests may get 'tracked' into schools, classes, or programs that are inferior and may even be stigmatising to the students' sense of self-competence. In this way, IQ can be affected by environment and, in turn, can create new environments for the child—some better, some worse. IQ assessment may thus become destiny—whatever the child's underlying genetic endowment for intelligence.

Even though IQ tests have proven to be valid for mainstream uses, many observers still question their validity for comparisons among different cultural and racial groups (Greenfield, 1997; Samuda, 1998; Serpell, 2000). Kearins' series of studies—outlined earlier in the chapter—caution us against overemphasising a single score in the attempt to understand how people think. We need to think about HOW people go about responding to the test, or Sternberg's 'metacomponents' of intelligence, if we are going to really make sense of intellectual ability.

For years Dr. Graham Chaffey of the University of New England has observed the cycle of underachievement in the performance of children of Aboriginal and Torres Strait Islander backgrounds in gifted programs (Chaffey 2002). He coined the phrase 'invisible underachievers' to describe this underachievement, and identified reasons behind it:

- culturally biased identification tools
- peer pressure
- low teacher expectations
- underachievement/loss of talent through lack of use
- feeling isolated from non-indigenous/minority classmates
- feeling misunderstood by teachers who often lack substantial training in multicultural education
- feeling misunderstood by teachers who often lack substantial training in gifted education
- feeling misunderstood by members of their families who often lack understanding of their giftedness. (Cooper, 2003)

Chaffey argues that for Aboriginal and Torres Strait Islander children to be able to develop their gifts to full potential there needs to be systematic and effective education, learning and practice, through an inclusive constructivist curriculum. He developed the **Coolabah Dynamic Assessment Method**. This method aims to meet the needs of gifted Aboriginal and Torres Strait Islander students, as well as those from non-English speaking backgrounds by:

- addressing the mismatch between learning and teaching styles
- using mentors (community involvement is paramount to success)
- helping students to develop questioning, introspective attitudes

**Coolabah Dynamic Assessment Method** A tool for identifying the learning potential of gifted Aboriginal students who underperform in the classroom.

- helping students to understand and explore the problems they may face (i.e. as they try to align their cultural values with those of the dominant culture)
- helping students to cope with peer pressures not to succeed
- helping students to remediate any areas of skill that are lacking especially limited language skills
- providing opportunities to explore a variety of career options
- helping students to learn the strengths of each culture and the unity of all people. (Clark 1992, p. 520)

In a PhD study involving 79 Aboriginal students from years 3 to 5 in schools in Armidale, using the Coolibath method, there were significant improvements in students' scores. One student's score skyrocketed from 18 to 91. Chaffey's method of assessment is currently being trialled at 10 schools in New South Wales with the support of Sydney Archdiocese Catholic Education Office

One of the standard concerns about IQ tests is that they are biased toward or against members of different cultures. Critics have argued that group differences in IQ scores are caused by systematic bias in the test questions, making them invalid and unfair for minorities. But even when tests are made more 'culture-fair,' there remains a racial gap (Neisser et al., 1996). In fact, the issue may be more a problem of the *context* of the test rather than the *content* of the test. **Claude Steele** (1997; Steele & Aronson, 1995, 1998) has argued that people's performance on ability tests is influenced by **stereotype threat** (also known as *stereotype vulnerability*)—the threat of being at risk for confirming a negative stereotype of one's group. Steele's research suggests that the belief that a negative stereotype is relevant in a situation can function to bring about the poor performance encoded in the stereotype.

> In one study, black and white undergraduates tried to answer very difficult verbal questions of the type found on the Graduate Record Exam. Half of the students were led to believe that performance on the questions was *diagnostic* of their intellectual ability; the other half were only told that the experiment concerned psychological factors involved in solving problems. The theory of stereotype threat suggests that only students for whom the threat of the stereotype is called into action by the situation—the black students in the *diagnostic* condition—will perform less well on the questions. As you can see in part A of **Figure 9.8**, the results confirmed this prediction. When the black students believed performance could be used to diagnose their intelligence, they performed less well (Steele & Aronson, 1995). The logic of stereotype threat applies to any group for whom there is a stereotype of inferior performance. For example, stereotypes suggest that women are less able at maths than are men. As shown in part B of Figure 9.8, a difficult maths test produced gender differences only when students had been told that it would (Steele, 1997). That is, prior to attempting the problems,

students in the *gender-difference* condition had been told that the test had, in the past, produced gender differences—and so it did, for them.

Note that in each of these studies what matters is how the test takers define the situation. Only when people believe the situation is relevant to the stereotype—because, for example, they believe that the test measures intelligence—does knowledge of the stereotype impair performance. Do you think it would be possible to measure IQ without invoking stereotype threat? If not, researchers may never be able to determine 'real' performance.

One final thought on intelligence and culture. Taken as a whole, Australia and other developed countries like the United States demonstrate a cultural bias toward genetic explanations of individual differences. **Harold Stevenson** and his colleagues (1993) spent several years tracking the mathematics achievement of Chinese, Japanese and U.S. children. In 1980, Asian children on the average vastly outperformed their U.S. peers. In 1990, the gap remained: 'Only 4.1% of the Chinese children and 10.3% of the Japanese children . . . had scores as low as those of the average American child' (p. 54). Are Asian children genetically superior? In fact, people in the United States are more likely to answer yes. When Stevenson and his colleagues asked Asian and U.S. students, teachers and parents to contrast the importance of 'studying hard' versus 'innate intelligence', Asian respondents emphasised hard work. U.S. respondents emphasised innate ability. Do you see how this perspective could lead to the conclusion by Americans

**stereotype threat** The threat associated with being at risk for confirming a negative stereotype of one's group.

Model, Michelle Leslie, whose Eurasian looks are becoming more popular in representing the multicultural world in which we live.

that Asians must be genetically superior in mathematics? Because such beliefs have public policy implications—how much money should be expended on teaching mathematics if Americans cannot learn maths anyway? It is important to examine rigorous research to sort out what can and cannot be changed with respect to intellectual performance.

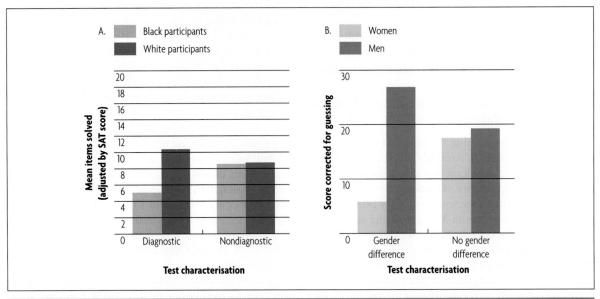

Figure 9.8

Stereotype threat

Stereotype threat occurs when people believe a negative stereotype is relevant to the current testing situation. (A) One study examined the stereotype that African Americans score poorly on intelligence tests. Half of a sample of black and white students were led to believe that a test was diagnostic of their intellectual ability; the other half did not receive this information. When black students believed that the test was diagnostic, their performance was impaired. (Participants' SAT scores were used to eliminate preexisting differences between their expected performance.) (B) A second study examined the stereotype that women score poorly on mathematics exams. Half of a sample of male and female students were told that a maths test had previously produced gender differences; the other half did not receive this information. When women believed that the test would produce gender differences, their performance was impaired.

From Claude M. Steele, "A Threat in the Air: How Stereotypes Shape Intellectual Identity and Performance," *American Psychologist, 52,* 613–629, 1997. Copyright © 1997 by the American Psychological Association. Reprinted with permission.

For answers go to MyPsychLab!

## RECAP CHECKPOINT

### The politics of intelligence

- Almost from the outset, intelligence tests have been used to make negative claims about ethnic and racial groups.

- Because of the reasonably high heritability of IQ, some researchers have attributed the lower scores of some racial and cultural groups to innate inferiority.

- Environmental disadvantages and stereotype threat appear to explain the lower scores of certain groups. Research shows that group differences can be affected through environmental interventions.

## CONCEPT QUESTIONS

1. Under what circumstances did Goddard and others begin to make IQ comparisons among groups?

2. Why is it inappropriate to use heritability estimates to make claims about racial differences in IQ?

3. What aspects of people's lives are affected by preschool interventions?

4. What did Harold Stevenson's research reveal about cross-cultural views of academic achievements?

## CRITICAL THINKING

Consider the study on stereotype threat. In what ways do real-life circumstances of testing make stereotypes seem relevant?

# CREATIVITY

**B**efore we leave the area of intelligence and its assessment, we turn to the topic of creativity. **Creativity** is an individual's ability to generate ideas or products that are both *novel* and *appropriate* to the circumstances in which they were generated (Sternberg & Lubart, 1999). Consider the invention of the wheel. The device was novel because no one before its unknown inventor had seen the application of rolling objects. It was appropriate because the use to which the novel object could be put was very clear. Without appropriateness, new ideas or objects are often considered strange or irrelevant.

Our discussion of creativity falls within a chapter on intelligence because many people believe that there is a strong relationship between intelligence and creativity. To determine if this is the case, we need to be able first to test creativity and then to determine the relationship between creativity and intelligence. Thus we first discuss methods for judging ideas or products to be creative and then look at the link to intelligence. Next, we look at situations of exceptional creativity and evaluate the relationship between creativity and madness. We will see what lessons you can learn from people who are possessed with exceptional creative abilities.

## ASSESSING CREATIVITY AND THE LINK TO INTELLIGENCE

How might you go about rating individuals as (relatively) creative or uncreative? Many approaches focus on **divergent thinking**, which is defined as the ability to generate a variety of unusual solutions to a problem. Questions that test divergent thinking give the test taker the opportunity to demonstrate *fluid* (swift) and *flexible* thinking (Torrance, 1974; Wallach & Kogan, 1965):

- Name all the things you can think of that are square.
- List as many white edible things as you can in 3 minutes.
- List all the uses that you can think of for a *brick*.

Responses are scored along such dimensions as *fluency*, the overall number of distinct ideas; *uniqueness*, the number of ideas that were given by no other person in an appropriate sample; and *unusualness*, the number of ideas that were given by, for example, less than 5 percent of a sample (Runco, 1991).

When creativity is assessed in this fashion, the test provides a performance index that can be correlated with other measures. On many occasions, researchers have evaluated the relationship between measures of divergent thinking and IQ. A common pattern has emerged: there is a weak or moderate correlation between the two measures up to an IQ level of about 120; above 120, the correlation

decreases (Sternberg & O'Hara, 1999). Why might this be so? One researcher suggests that 'intelligence appears to enable creativity to some extent but not to promote it' (Perkins, 1988, p. 319). In other words, a certain level of intelligence gives a person the opportunity to be creative, but the person may not avail himself or herself of that opportunity.

Creativity researchers have often been concerned that divergent-thinking tests are too closely tied to the tradition of intelligence testing and to IQ tests themselves (which may explain the correlations up into the 120 IQ range) (Lubart, 1994). A different approach to judging some individuals as creative or uncreative is to ask them specifically to generate a creative product—a drawing, a poem or a short story. Judges then rate the creativity of each of the products. Consider the two photographs shown in **Figure 9.9**. Which do you think is more creative? Could you explain why you think so? Do you think your friends would agree? Research has shown that agreement is quite high when judges rank products for creativity (Amabile, 1983). People can be reliably identified across judges as being high or low in creativity.

## EXTREMES OF CREATIVITY

There are some exceptional individuals who would emerge from assessments of creativity as almost off the scale. Whom do you think of when you are asked to name someone who is exceptionally creative? Your answer is likely to depend partly on your own areas of expertise and your

Art historians have often speculated that Vincent van Gogh's creativity as an artist was influenced by mental illness. What, in general, have researchers discovered about the link between creativity and madness?

**creativity** The ability to generate ideas or products that are both novel and appropriate to the circumstances.

**divergent thinking** An aspect of creativity characterised by an ability to produce unusual but appropriate responses to problems.

**Figure 9.9**

Making judgments about creativity

Hypothetical photography class assignment: Take the best picture you can of (A) a noncreative response. (B) A creative response.

own preferences. Psychologists might nominate Sigmund Freud. Those people interested in fine art, music or dance might mention Pablo Picasso, Igor Stravinsky, or Graham Murphy. Is it possible to detect the commonalities in the personalities or backgrounds of such individuals that could be predictive of exceptional creativity? Howard Gardner (1993) chose a selection of individuals whose extraordinary abilities were relevant to the eight types of intelligence we described earlier, including Freud, Picasso, Stravinsky and Murphy. Gardner's analysis allows him to yield a portrait of the life experiences of the *exemplary creator*, whom he dubs E.C.:

> E.G. discovers a problem area or realm of special interest, one that promises to [lead] into uncharted waters. This is a highly charged moment. At this point E.G. becomes isolated from her peers and must work mostly on her own. She senses that she is on the verge of a breakthrough that is as yet little understood, even by her. Surprisingly, at this crucial moment, E.G. craves both cognitive and affective support, so that she can retain her bearings. Without such support, she might well experience some kind of breakdown. (Gardner, 1993, p. 361)

What lessons are there for you in tales of exceptional creativity that would allow you to be more creative? You can emulate a pattern of *risk taking*. Highly creative individuals are willing to go into 'uncharted waters' (Gardner, 1993; Sternberg & Lubart, 1996). There is a pattern of *preparation*. Highly creative individuals typically have spent years acquiring expertise in the domains in which they will excel (Weisberg, 1986). There is a pattern of *intrinsic motivation*. Highly creative individuals pursue their tasks because of the enjoyment and satisfaction they take in the products they generate (Collins & Amabile, 1999). If you can bring all these factors together in your own life, you should be able to increase your personal level of creative performance.

Before we leave the topic of creativity, we want to consider one of the most common stereotypes of exemplary creators: Their life experiences border on—or include the experience of—madness. The idea that great creativity is intimately related to madness has a history that has been traced as far back as Plato (Kessel, 1989). In more modern times, Kraepelin (1921) argued that the manic phases of individuals who suffer from 'manic-depressive insanity,' or bipolar disorder, provide a context of free-flowing thought processes that facilitate great creativity. Mania, as we will see in Chapter 15, is characterised by periods of enduring excitedness; the person generally acts and feels elated and expansive.

There is little doubt that many great figures in the arts and humanities have suffered from such mood disorders. You may have encountered the story of David Helfcott depicted in the movie *Shine*—a talented musician who has suffered for many years with severe mental illness. But is there really a relationship between creativity and mental illness? After all, nearly 20 percent of the Australian population will suffer from some form of mental illness throughout our lives, and not all of us are creative geniuses. However, to establish a link between creativity and mental illness, researchers have attempted to go beyond those anecdotal reports. A review of the literature suggests that there is at least a weak association between some forms of mental illness—such as bipolar disorder—and creativity (Lauronen et al., 2004). However, as always, a correlation doesn't indicate whether there is a causal relationship. It could be the case that some forms of mental illness allow people to be more creative; it could be the case that the effort to be highly creative increases the likelihood that people will experience mental illness. There could also be some features of people's brains that make them highly creative and also more prone to mental illness—with no causal link between the two phenomena (Dietrich, 2004).

You have now learned some of the ways in which psychologists assess and interpret individual differences in intelligence and creativity. You have a good understanding of how researchers have tried to measure and understand these difficult concepts. In this chapter's final section, we consider why psychological assessment can sometimes generate controversy.

## RECAP CHECKPOINT
### Creativity

- Creativity is often assessed using tests of divergent thinking.
- Exceptionally creative people take risks, prepare and are highly motivated.
- Although there is an association between creativity and some forms of mental illness, a causal link has not been established.

## CONCEPT QUESTIONS

1. How is creativity measured?
2. What is the relationship between IQ and creativity?
3. What three factors appear to play a role in exceptional creativity?

# ASSESSMENT AND SOCIETY

The primary goal of psychological assessment is to make accurate assessments of people that are as free as possible of errors of assessors' judgments. This goal is achieved by replacing subjective judgments of teachers, employers and other evaluators with more objective measures that have been carefully constructed and are open to critical evaluation. This is the goal that motivated Alfred Binet in his pioneering work. Binet and others hoped that testing would help democratise society and minimise decisions based on arbitrary criteria of sex, race, nationality, privilege or physical appearance. However, despite these lofty goals, there is no area of psychology more controversial than assessment. Three ethical concerns that are central to the controversy are the fairness of test-based decisions, the utility of tests for evaluating education, and the implications of using test scores as labels to categorise individuals.

Critics concerned with the fairness of testing practices argue that the costs or negative consequences may be higher for some test takers than for others (Bond, 1995). The costs are quite high, for example, when tests on which minority groups receive low scores are used to keep them out of certain jobs. In some cities, applicants for civil service cleaning jobs must pass a verbal test, rather than a more appropriate test of manual skills. According to researcher William Banks, this is a strategy unions use to keep minorities from access to jobs (1990). Sometimes, minority group members test poorly because their scores are evaluated relative to inappropriate norms. In addition, arbitrary cut-off scores that favour applicants from one group may be used to make selection decisions, when, in reality, a lower cut-off score that is fairer would produce just as many correct hiring decisions. In addition, over reliance on testing may make personnel selection an automatic attempt to fit people into available jobs. Instead, sometimes society might benefit more by changing job descriptions to fit the needs and abilities of people.

A second ethical concern is that testing not only helps evaluate students; it may also play a role in the shaping of education. The quality of school systems and the effectiveness of teachers are frequently judged on the basis of how well their students score on standardised achievement tests. Local support of the schools through tax levies, and even individual teacher salaries, may ride on test scores. The high stakes associated with test scores have led to cheating scandals in several North American school districts (Kantrowitz & McGinn, 2000). For example, in Potomac, Maryland, an elementary school principal resigned when strong evidence suggested that fifth-graders at her school had been given several types of assistance, including extra time and second chances, to improve their test scores (Thomas & Wingert, 2000). The evidence against the school had come from the students themselves. The 10-year-olds reported to their parents that they had been asked or allowed to cheat: they wondered why the adults at the school had insisted that they do so. These circumstances illustrate how damaging it can be when test scores are taken to matter more than education.

A third ethical concern is that test outcomes can take on the status of unchangeable labels. People too often think of themselves as being an IQ of 110 or a B student,

For answers go to MyPsychLab!

**mypsychlab** where learning comes to life!

When schools are rewarded for high scores on standardised tests, are teachers likely to place more emphasis on test-taking skills than on broader learning goals?

as if the scores were labels stamped on their foreheads. Such labels may become barriers to advancement as people come to believe that their mental and personal qualities are fixed and unchangeable—that they cannot improve their lot in life. For those who are negatively assessed, the scores can become self-imposed motivational limits that lower their sense of self-efficacy and restrict the challenges they are willing to tackle. That is another insidious consequence of pronouncements about group deficiencies in IQ. Those stigmatised publicly in this way come to believe what the 'experts' are saying about them, and so disidentify with schools and education as means to improve their lives.

This tendency to give test scores a sacred status has societal as well as personal implications. When test scores become labels that identify traits, states, maladjustment, conflict and pathology within an individual, people begin to think about the 'abnormality' of individual children rather than about educational systems that need to modify programs to accommodate all learners. Labels put the spotlight on deviant personalities rather than on dysfunctional aspects of their environment. In societies that have an individualistic orientation, like the United States, people are all too ready to misattribute success and failure to the person, while underestimating the impact of the behavioural setting. We blame the victim for failure and thereby take society off the hook; we give credit to the person for success and thereby do not recognise the many societal influences that made it possible. We need to recognise that what people are now is a product of where they've been, where they think they are headed, and what situation is currently influencing their behaviour.

We'd like to conclude this chapter on a personal note from Phil Zimbardo, one that may have some inspirational value to students who do not do well on objective tests:

*Although I have gone on to have a successful career as a professional psychologist, the relevant tests I took many years ago would have predicted otherwise. Despite being an Honors undergraduate student, who graduated Summa Cum Laude, I got my only C grade in Introductory Psychology, where grades were based solely on multiple-choice exams. I was initially rejected for graduate training at Yale University; then I became an alternate, and finally, I was accepted reluctantly. This was in part because my GRE math scores were below the psychology department's*

*criterion cutoff level. But I later discovered that it was also due in part to the false assumption of some faculty that I must be Negro—on the basis of the pattern of my answers and other 'evidence' revealed in my application and tests. Such data negatively colored their judgments of my potential for a career in psychology. Fortunately, some others were willing to give me a chance when one of their respectable admits (Gordon Bower, now a famous psychologist) went elsewhere to start his graduate training.*

*Successful performance in a career and in life requires much more than the skills, abilities, and traits measured by standardized tests. While the best tests perform the valuable function of predicting how well people will do on the average, there may be decisional error for any given individual. People can override the pessimistic predictions of their tests scores when ambition, imagination, hope, personal pride, and intense effort empower their performance. Perhaps it is vital to know when you should believe more in yourself than in the results of a test.*

## RECAP CHECKPOINT
### Assessment and society

- Though often useful for prediction and as an indication of current performance, test results should not be used to limit an individual's opportunities for development and change

- When the results of an assessment will affect an individual's life, the techniques used must be reliable and valid for that individual and for the purpose in question.

## CONCEPT QUESTIONS

1. Why might assessment have negative consequences for particular groups of individuals?

2. Why might assessment play a role in shaping education?

3. Why might test scores become labels that have broad consequences?

# SUMMARY

Think of yourself and your three best friends. Can you line them up in order of 'intelligence'? You probably find that some people are 'smart' at some things—perhaps music, or listening to others, or maths—and others are 'smart' at other things. The more we understand about intelligence, the more difficult it becomes to capture it with a single number on a single test. Modern concepts of intelligence focus upon the many complex things that help an individual find a happy and successful pathway through life, without focusing on particular skills.

# KEY TERMS

chronological age (p. 295)
Coolabah Dynamic Assessment Method (p. 310)
construct validity (p. 293)
creativity (p. 313)
criterion validity (p. 293)
crystallised intelligence (p. 299)
divergent thinking (p. 313)
emotional intelligence (p. 303)
EQ (p. 303)

face validity (p. 292)
fluid intelligence (p. 299)
formal assessment (p. 291)
g (p. 299)
heritability estimate (p. 306)
intellectual disability (p. 297)
intelligence (p. 294)
intelligence quotient (IQ) (p. 295)
internal consistency (p. 292)
mental age (p. 295)

norms (p. 293)
parallel forms (p. 292)
psychological assessment (p. 290)
psychometrics (p. 299)
split-half reliability (p. 292)
standardisation (p. 293)
stereotype threat (p. 311)
test–retest reliability (p. 291)

# PRACTICE TEST

1. Which of these was *not* one of the ideas Sir Francis Galton formulated about intelligence assessment?
   a. Differences in intelligence are quantifiable.
   b. Intelligence could be measured by objective tests.
   c. Intelligence scores followed a bell-shaped curve.
   d. Intelligence scores change over the lifespan.

2. To measure the_____of his Latin exam, Caligula compared his score on even-numbered items with his score on odd-numbered items.
   a. test-retest reliability
   b. face validity
   c. internal consistency
   d. criterion validity

3. Martin filled out a test to measure his happiness. He got a score of 72. To interpret that score, Martin needs to consult the_____the test.
   a. norms for
   b. split-half reliability for
   c. standardisation of
   d. predictive validity of

4. Deborah is 10 years old, but she has a mental age of 12. Using the original method for calculating IQ, you conclude that Deborah has an IQ of
   a. 90.
   b. 120.
   c. 150.
   d. 100.

5. Which cause of intellectual disability is easiest to treat?
   a. Down syndrome
   b. The mother's prenatal consumption of alcohol.
   c. The mother's prenatal consumption of cocaine.
   d. PKU

6. Which of these qualities is *not* part of the 'three-ring' conception of giftedness?
   a. creativity
   b. mathematical
   c. task commitment
   d. high ability genius

7. When Poindexter took IQ tests on the Web, he took four tests at the same site and obtained scores of 116, 117, 129, and 130. Given these scores, you conclude that the IQ tests are
   a. both reliable and valid.
   b. neither reliable nor valid.
   c. reliable but not valid.
   d. valid but not reliable.

8. _____intelligence is defined as the knowledge a person has already acquired.
   a. Fluid
   b. Analytical
   c. Crystallised
   d. Creative

9. Felix is applying for chef school. He takes an entrance exam that poses a series of questions on food preparation. This sounds most like a test of_____intelligence.
   a. practical
   b. analytic
   c. fluid
   d. creative

10. Julian is rarely aware when the people around him are upset. You suspect that Julian is not very high on_____intelligence.
   a. naturalist
   b. spatial
   c. emotional
   d. bodily kinaesthetic

11. Which of these ideas was *not* part of the Practical Intelligence for School curriculum?
   a. Knowing when
   b. Knowing self
   c. Knowing process
   d. Knowing differences

12. Goneril and Regan are sisters. You would expect them to have the most similar IQs if they
   a. are fraternal twins.
   b. are identical twins.
   c. grew up in the same home.
   d. were adopted before age 2.

13. Studies of the impact of socioeconomic status (SES) on IQ suggests that
   a. individuals with higher SES generally have higher IQs.
   b. SES only has an impact on IQ scores for specific racial groups.
   c. SES has no overall impact on IQ scores.
   d. Individuals with lower SES do not benefit from preschool programs.

14. Stereotype threat has an impact on people's test performance when they believe that
   a. the testing situation is relevant to the stereotype.
   b. the stereotype is widespread in a culture.
   c. the testing situation is unfair to certain ethnic groups.
   d. stereotypes change over time.

15. A test of _____ might include a question like, 'Name all the things you can think of that are round'.
   a. analytic intelligence
   b. crystallised intelligence
   c. convergent thinking
   d. divergent thinking

16. If you want to understand the origins of 'Exceptional Creators', you *don't* need to focus on
   a. preparation.
   b. intrinsic motivation.
   c. IQ.
   d. risk taking.

17. Which of these statements best captures the relationship between mental illness and creativity?
   a. Researchers have demonstrated that the hard work of being creative causes people to become mentally ill.
   b. Researchers have demonstrated that people who are mentally ill are more creative.
   c. Researchers have demonstrated that people who are highly creative experience less mental illness than other individuals.
   d. Researchers have not demonstrated that there is a causal relationship between mental illness and creativity.

18. The goal of psychological assessment is often to replace _____ with _____.
   a. objective measures; verifiable labels
   b. reliable measures; valid measures
   c. valid measures; subjective impressions
   d. subjective impressions; objective measures

19. Children at a Maryland school reported to their parents that they had been allowed to cheat on standardised exams. To what societal concern about assessment does that incident relate?
   a. The consequences of assessment may be worse for some groups than for others.
   b. Assessment can yield outcomes that become unchangeable labels.
   c. Assessment plays a role in the shaping of educational practices.
   d. People may have to work harder to overcome negative assessments.

20. When Cyrus was 12, he was told he was a genius. As an adult, he never feels as if he is living up to his potential. This is a good example of circumstances in which assessment has
   a. generated an incorrect outcome.
   b. yielded a label that has personal implications.
   c. shaped the educational experiences of an individual.
   d. had negative consequences for Cyrus's group.

## Essay Questions

1. What is the goal of Howard Gardner's theory of multiple intelligences?

2. How have Head Start and other early intervention programs demonstrated the impact of environments on IQ?

3. Why is it difficult to establish a causal link between mental illness and creativity?

# WEB LINKS

http://www.qagtc.org.au/assess.htm
    The Queensland Association for Gifted and Talented Children Inc

http://www.racismnoway.com.au/classroom/factsheets/59.html
    The 'White Australia' Policy Fact Sheet

http://www.mensa.org.au
    Australian Mensa

www.intelligenceltd.com
    IntelligenceLTD

## Solutions to the anagrams in Table 9.2

1. laugh          6. allow

2. tempt          7. drive

3. short          8. couch

4. knight          9. enter

5. write          10. basic

Are you ready for the test? MyPsychLab offers dozens of ways to deepen your understanding and test your recall of the material in this chapter—including video and audio clips, simulations and activities, self-assessments, practice tests and other study materials. Specific resources available for this chapter include:

 Gardner's Theory of Intelligence

 Sternberg's Triarchic Theory of Intelligence
Correlations between IQ scores of persons
    of varying relationships

 A mother's IQ

To access MyPsychLab, please visit **www.pearsoned.com.au/mypsychlab**

# Will it be on the test?

## NOW YOU HAVE READ CHAPTER 9—ARE YOU PREPARED FOR THE EXAM?

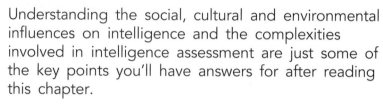

Understanding the social, cultural and environmental influences on intelligence and the complexities involved in intelligence assessment are just some of the key points you'll have answers for after reading this chapter.

To enhance your understanding of any of the material in your *Psychology and Life* textbook, go to **MyPsychLab: www.pearsoned.com.au/ mypsychlab**. Complete pre- and post-tests, create your own individualised study plan, watch videos and animations and listen to audio glossaries, all of which will help you to understand the themes of this chapter.

Watch VIDEOS on intelligence and grading in schools

See how much you know about mental illness and creativity by taking PRACTICE TEST

EXPLORE Gardner's multiple theories of intelligence

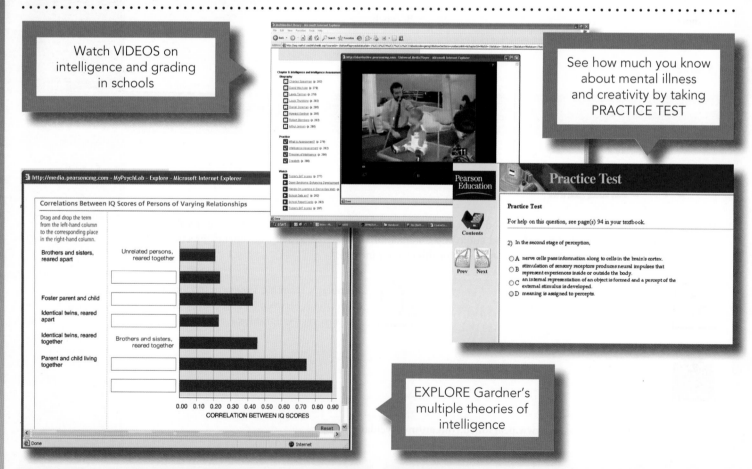

Watch SIMULATIONS of classical experiments, such as *Gardner's Theory of Intelligence*

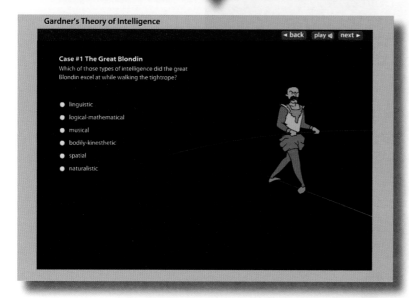

**Gardner's Theory of Intelligence**

◄ back    play ◄))    next ►

**Case #1 The Great Blondin**
Which of those types of intelligence did the great
Blondin excel at while walking the tightrope?

- linguistic
- logical-mathematical
- musical
- bodily-kinesthetic
- spatial
- naturalistic

'MyPsychLab was easy to sign up, easy to figure out, easy to use, and always available, so I could work on any chapter at any time.'

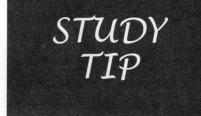

# STUDY TIP

**Review the definitions of key terms for each chapter**

An entire list of key terms and their definitions are available via the audio glossary. Simply click a word to see and hear its definition. Some of the definitions you will find in Chapter 9 include:

- Fluid intelligence
- Split-half reliability
- Predictive validity
- Stereotype threat

http://media.pearsoncmg.com - glossary - Microsoft Internet Explorer

File    Edit    View    Favorites    Tools    Help

Psychology and L
Glossa

A · B · C · D · E · F · G · H · I · J · K · L · M · N · O · P · Q · R · S · T · U · V · W · X · Y · Z

▸  Click a letter to see words that begin with that letter. Click a word to see and hear its definition.

**C**

Control procedures
Controlled processes
Convergence
Conversion disorder
Coping
Corpus callosum
Correlational coefficien
Correlational methods
Counseling psychologis
Counterconditioning
Countertransference
Covariation principle
Creativity
Criterion validity
Cross-sectional design
Crystallized intelligenc

Cross-sectional design

A research method in which groups of participants of different chronological ages are observed and compared at a given time.

Done                                      Internet

## What can you find in MyPsychLab?

Self-directed tests * Videos * Simulations * eBook * Biographies * Audio glossary * Web links … and more—organised by chapter, section and learning objective.

mypsych lab
*where learning comes to life!*

## Human Development
## Across the Lifespan

# CHAPTER FOCUS POINTS

After studying this chapter you will have a better understanding of:

1. How to use research approaches in developmental psychology

2. The pre and post-natal developmental stages

3. The process of psychosocial, cognitive and physical development in children

4. The process of physical change in adulthood

5. How language is learnt and develops as we grow

6. How cognition develops across the lifespan

7. How we obtain and use social skills across the lifespan

8. Understanding of sex and gender development

9. How we obtain moral development.

## CHAPTER CONTENTS

Imagine you are holding a newborn baby. How might you predict what this child will be like as a 1-year-old? At 5 years? At 15? At 50? At 70? At 90? Your predictions would almost certainly consist of a mixture of the general and the specific—the child is extremely likely to learn a language but might or might not be a gifted author. Your predictions would also rely on considerations of heredity and of environment—if both of the child's parents were gifted authors, you might be willing to guess that the child would also show literary talent; if the child was educated in an enriched environment, you might predict that the child's accomplishments would exceed those of the parents. In this chapter, we describe the theories of developmental psychology that enable us to think systematically about the types of predictions we can make for the life course of a newborn child.

**Developmental psychology** is the area of psychology that is concerned with changes in physical and psychological functioning that occur from conception across the entire life span. The task of developmental psychologists is to find out how and why organisms change over time—to document and explain development. Investigators study the time periods in which different abilities and functions first appear and observe how those abilities are modified. The basic premise is that mental functioning, social relationships and other vital aspects of human nature develop and change throughout the entire life cycle. **Table 10.1** presents a rough guide to the major periods of the life span.

In this chapter we will provide a general account of how researchers document development and the theories they use to explain patterns of change over time. We will then divide your life experiences into different domains and trace development in each domain. Early in the chapter, we focus on physical, cognitive and language development. We then shift our attention to the changing nature of social relationships over the life span as well as the specific tasks individuals face at different moments in their lives. Let's begin now with the question of what it means to study development.

## STUDYING DEVELOPMENT

Suppose we ask you to make a list of all the ways in which you believe you have changed in the last year. What sorts of things would you put on the list? Have you undertaken a new physical fitness program? Or have you let an injury heal? Have you developed a range of new hobbies? Or have you decided to focus on just one interest? Have you developed a new circle of friends? Or have you become particularly close to one individual? When we describe development, we will conceptualise it in terms of *change*. We have asked you to perform this exercise of thinking about your own changes to make the point that change almost always involves trade-offs.

Often people conceptualise the life span as mostly *gains*—changes for the better—in childhood and mostly *losses*—changes for the worse—over the course of adulthood. However, the perspective on development we will take here emphasises that *options*, and therefore gains and losses, are features of all development (Dixon, 2003; Lachman, 2004). When, for example, people choose a lifetime companion, they give up variety but gain security. When people retire, they give up status but gain leisure time.

It is also important that you not think of development as a *passive* process. You will see that many developmental changes require an individual's *active* engagement with his or her environment (Bronfenbrenner, 1999; Bronfenbrenner & Ceci, 1994).

To document change, a good first step is to determine what an average person is like—in physical appearance, cognitive abilities, and so on—at a particular age. **Normative investigations** seek to describe a characteristic of a specific age or developmental stage. By systematically testing individuals of different ages, researchers can determine developmental landmarks. These data provide *norms*, standard patterns of development or achievement, based on observation of many people.

Normative standards allow psychologists to make a distinction between chronological age—the number of months or years since a person's birth—and **developmental age**—the chronological age at which most people show the particular level of physical or mental development demonstrated by that child. A 3-year-old child who has verbal skills typical of most 5-year-olds is said to have a developmental age of 5 for verbal skills. Norms provide a standard basis for comparison both between individuals and between groups.

Developmental psychologists use several types of research designs to understand possible mechanisms of change. In a **longitudinal design**, the same individuals are repeatedly observed and tested over time, often for many years (see **Figure 10.1**). Recall the study on the effectiveness of the Hope/Perry preschool program described in Chapter 9. The researchers first collected data on a group of children when they were 3 and 4 years

### Table 10.1

Stages in life span development

| Stage | Age period |
| --- | --- |
| Prenatal | Conception to birth |
| Infancy | Birth at full term to about 18 months |
| Early childhood | About 18 months to about 6 years |
| Middle childhood | About 6 years to about 11 years |
| Adolescence | About 11 years to about 20 years |
| Early adulthood | About 20 years to about 40 years |
| Middle adulthood | About 40 years to about 65 years |
| Late adulthood | About 65 years and older |

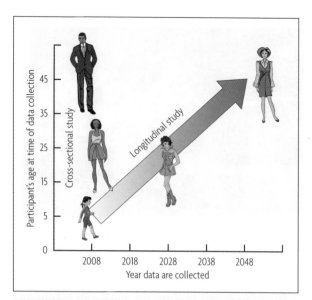

Participant's age at time of data collection

Cross-sectional study

Longitudinal study

Year data are collected

## Figure 10.1

**Longitudinal and cross-sectional research**

In longitudinal studies, researchers follow the same group of individuals over days, months or years. In cross-sectional studies, researchers test individuals of different ages at the same moment in time.

old (Schweinhart, 2004). To assess the long-term impact of the preschool program, the researchers studied the children every year until age 11, and then again at ages 14, 15, 19, 27, and 40. This longitudinal data collection allowed the researchers to draw strong conclusions about the program's lifelong benefits. Researchers also often use longitudinal designs to study *individual differences*. To understand the life outcomes of different people, researchers may assess a range of potential causal factors early in life and see how those factors influence each individual's life course.

A general advantage of longitudinal research is that because the participants have lived through the same socioeconomic period, age-related changes cannot be confused with variations in differing societal circumstances. A disadvantage, however, is that some types of generalisations can be made only to the same *cohort*, the group of individuals born in the same time period as the research participants. Also, longitudinal studies are costly because it is difficult to keep track of the participants over extended time, and data are easily lost because participants quit or disappear.

Much research on development uses a **cross-sectional design**, in which groups of participants, of different chronological ages, are observed and compared at one and the same time. A researcher can then draw conclusions about behavioural differences that may be related to age changes. For example, researchers who wanted to determine how children learn to walk without falling down tested children of ages 15, 21, 27, 33, and 39 months on the same laboratory task (Joh & Adolph, 2006). A disadvantage of cross-sectional design comes from comparing individuals who differ by year of birth as well as by chronological age. Age-related changes are confounded by differences in the social or political conditions experienced by different birth cohorts. Thus a study comparing samples of 10- and 18-year-olds now might find that the participants differ from 10- and 18-year-olds who grew up in the 1970s, in ways related to their different eras as well as to their developmental stages.

Each methodology gives researchers the opportunity to document change from one age to another. Researchers use these methodologies to study development in each of several domains. As we now consider some of those domains—physical, cognitive and social development— you'll come to appreciate and understand some of the vast changes you've already experienced.

**cross-sectional design**
A research method in which groups of participants of different chronological ages are observed and compared at a given time.

In a longitudinal design, observations are made of the same individual at different ages, often for many years. This well-known woman might be part of a longitudinal study of British children born in 1926. How might she be similar to and different from other children in that cohort?

A drawback of cross-sectional research is the cohort effect. What differences might exist between these two groups of females as a result of the eras in which they lived?

**zygote** The single cell that results when a sperm fertilises an egg.

For answers go to MyPsychLab!

# PHYSICAL DEVELOPMENT ACROSS THE LIFESPAN

Many of the types of development we describe in this chapter require some special knowledge to detect. For example, you might not notice landmarks in social development until you read about them here. We will begin, however, with a realm of development in which changes are often plainly visible to the untrained eye: **physical development**. There is no doubt that you have undergone enormous physical change since you were born. Such changes will continue until the end of your life. Because physical changes are so numerous, we will focus on the types that have an impact on psychological development.

## PRENATAL AND CHILDHOOD DEVELOPMENT

You began life with unique genetic potential: At the moment of conception a male's sperm cell fertilised a female's egg cell to form the single-cell **zygote**; you received half of the 46 chromosomes found in all normal human body cells from your mother and half from your father. In this section, we outline physical development in the *prenatal period*, from the moment of conception until the moment of birth. We also describe some of the sensory abilities children have obtained even before birth. Finally, we describe the important physical changes that you experienced during childhood.

**Physical development in the womb** The earliest behaviour of any kind is the heartbeat. It begins in the *prenatal period*, before birth, when the embryo is about 3 weeks old and 15 mm long. Responses to stimulation have been observed as early as the sixth week, when the embryo is not yet an inch long. Spontaneous movements are observed by the eighth week (Kisilevsky & Low, 1998).

After the eighth week, the developing embryo is called a *foetus*. The mother feels foetal movements in about the sixteenth week after conception. At this point, the foetus is about 18 centimetres (the average length at birth is 50 centimetres). As the brain grows in utero, it generates new neurons at the rate of 250,000 per minute, reaching

**physical development** The bodily changes, maturation and growth that occur in an organism, starting with conception and continuing across the life span.

As the brain grows in the developing foetus, it generates 250,000 new neurons per minute. What must the brain be prepared to do, as soon as the child enters the world?

a full complement of over 100 billion neurons by birth (Cowan, 1979). In humans and many other mammals, most of this cell proliferation and migration of neurons to their correct locations take place prenatally; the development of the branching processes of axons and dendrites largely occurs after birth (Kolb, 1989). The sequence of brain development, from 30 days to 9 months, is shown in **Figure 10.2**.

During the first months of pregnancy, environmental factors such as malnutrition, infection, radiation or drugs can prevent the normal formation of organs and body structures. For example, when mothers are infected with rubella (German measles) 2 to 4 weeks after conception, the probability is roughly 50 percent that the child will suffer negative consequences such as mental retardation, eye damage, deafness or heart defects. If exposure occurs at other times, the probability of adverse effects is much lower (e.g., 22 percent in the second month; 8 percent in the third month) (Murata et al., 1992). Similarly, mothers who consume certain substances, like alcohol, during sensitive periods put their unborn children at risk for brain damage and other impairments (Mattson et al., 2001; Randall, 2001). Facial abnormalities, for example, are most likely to arise from mothers' drinking in the first two months of pregnancy (Coles, 1994). Pregnant women who smoke also put their children at risk, particularly in the second half of pregnancy. Smoking during pregnancy increases the risk of miscarriage, premature births, and low-birth-weight babies. In fact, women who are exposed to second-hand smoke during pregnancy are also more likely to have babies with low birth weights (Dejin-Karlsson et al., 1998).

Some substances may bring about damage at virtually any time during pregnancy. Cocaine, for example, travels through the placenta and can affect foetal development directly. In adults, cocaine causes blood vessels to constrict; in pregnant women, cocaine restricts placental blood flow and oxygen supply to the foetus. If severe oxygen deprivation results, blood vessels in the foetus's brain may burst. Such prenatal strokes can lead to lifelong mental handicaps (Koren et al., 1998; Singer et al., 2002). Research suggests that the brain systems most damaged by cocaine are those responsible for controlling attention: children exposed

When something touches a newborn's cheek, the rooting reflex prompts the baby to seek something to suck. In what other ways are children prewired for survival?

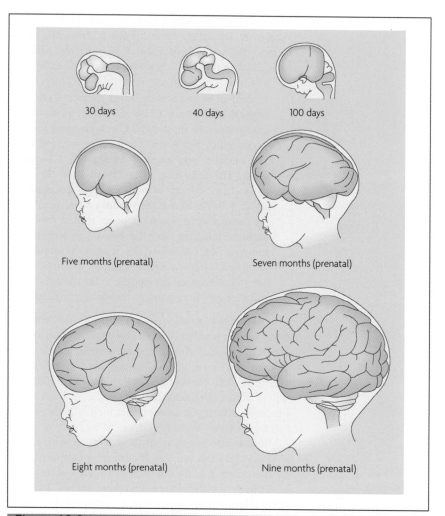

## Figure 10.2

**The development of the human brain**
During the nine months before birth, the brain reaches its complement of over 100 billion neurons.

Adapted from *The Brain* by W.M. Cowan. Copyright © 1979 W.M. Cowan.

to cocaine in the womb may spend their lives overcome by the distractions of irrelevant sights and sounds.

We use these examples to emphasise that nature and nurture interact to shape body and brain even before a child is born.

**Babies prewired for survival** What capabilities are programmed into this body and brain at birth? We are accustomed to thinking about newborns as entirely helpless. John Watson, the founder of behaviourism, described the human infant as 'a lively, squirming bit of flesh, capable of making a few simple responses'. If that sounds right, you might be surprised to learn that, moments out of the womb, infants reveal remarkable abilities to obtain information through their senses and react to it. They might be thought of as *prewired for survival*, well suited to respond to adult caregivers and to influence their social environments.

For example, infants can hear even before birth. Researchers have demonstrated that what infants hear while in the womb has consequences. Newborns prefer to listen to their mothers' voices rather than the voices of other women (Spence & DeCasper, 1987; Spence & Freeman, 1996). In fact, the most recent research suggests that children recognise their mothers' voices even before they are born.

A team of researchers recruited mothers-to-be at a hospital in southeast China (Kisilevsky et al., 2003). On average, the mothers had been pregnant for 38.4 weeks, which meant that the foetuses were full term. The mothers were asked to tape-record a 2-minute poem. The recordings of the poem were played to the foetuses through a loudspeaker that was poised about 4 inches above the mothers' abdomens. Half the foetuses were played the poem read in their own mothers' voice; the other half heard the poem read by someone else's mother. The researchers monitored foetal heart rate. The results were quite dramatic: foetal heart rate increased in response to the mothers' voice and decreased in response to the strangers' voices!

Given these strong results favouring mothers, you might wonder whether children also respond more to their fathers' voices. Unfortunately, research so far indicates that children don't seem to have enough auditory experience with their dads. Newborns show no preference for their fathers' voices (DeCasper & Prescott, 1984). Even at age 4 months, infants still do not prefer their father's voice to a stranger's voice (Ward & Cooper, 1999).

Infants also put their visual systems to work almost immediately: a few minutes after birth, a newborn's eyes are alert, turning in the direction of a voice and searching inquisitively for the source of certain sounds. Even so, vision is less well developed than the other senses at birth. The visual acuity of adults is roughly 40 times better than the visual acuity of newborns (Sireteanu, 1999). Visual acuity improves rapidly over the first 6 months of a baby's life. Newborns also are ill equipped to experience the world in three dimensions: it is only at about 4 months of age that children are able to combine information from their two eyes to perceive depth. Good vision—sensitivity to contrast, visual acuity and colour discrimination— requires that a great many photoreceptor cells function in the centre of the eye's receptive area and that the optics

of the eye develop appropriately (see Chapter 4). Many of these components have yet to mature in the infant's visual system. Good vision also requires that numerous connections between neurons in the brain's visual cortex be made in response to visual experience (Maurer et al., 1999). At birth, not enough of these connections are laid down.

Even without perfect vision, however, children have visual preferences. Pioneering researcher **Robert Fantz** (1963) observed that babies as young as 4 months old preferred looking at objects with contours rather than those that were plain, complex ones rather than simple ones, and whole faces rather than faces with features in disarray. More recent research suggests that—by the age of 3 days— infants have a preference for *top-heavy patterns* (Macchi Cassia et al., 2004). To experience a top-heavy pattern, take a look at your face in a mirror—your eyes, eyebrows, and so on, take up much more space than your lips. The fact that faces are top heavy might explain why infants prefer to look at human faces versus other types of visual displays.

Once children start to move around in their environment, they quickly acquire other perceptual capabilities. For example, classic research by **Eleanor Gibson** and **Richard Walk** (1960) examined how children respond to depth information. This research used an apparatus called a *visual cliff.* The visual cliff had a board running across the middle of a solid glass surface. As shown in **Figure 10.3**, checkerboard cloth was used to create a deep end and a shallow end. In their original research, Gibson and Walk demonstrated that children would readily leave the centre board to crawl across the shallow end, but they were reluctant to crawl across the deep end. Subsequent research has demonstrated that fear of the deep end depends on crawling experience: Children who have begun to crawl experience fear of the deep end, whereas their non-crawling same-age peers do not (Campos et al., 1992). Thus wariness of heights is not quite 'prewired,' but it develops quickly as children begin to explore the world under their own power.

**Growth and maturation in childhood** Newborn infants change at an astonishing rate but, as shown in **Figure 10.4**, physical growth is not equal across all physical structures. You've probably noticed that babies seem to be all head. At birth, a baby's head is already about 60 percent of its adult size and measures a quarter of the whole body length (Bayley, 1956). An infant's body weight doubles in the first 6 months and triples by the first birthday; by the age of 2, a child's trunk is about half of its adult length. Genital tissue shows little change until the teenage years and then develops rapidly to adult proportions.

For most children, physical growth is accompanied by the maturation of motor ability. **Maturation** refers to the process of growth typical of all members of a species who are reared in the species' usual habitat. The characteristic maturational sequences newborns experience are determined by the interaction of inherited biological boundaries and environmental inputs. For

**maturation** The continuing influence of heredity throughout development, the age-related physical and behavioural changes characteristic of a species.

Early on, infants can perceive large objects that display a great deal of contrast. What visual experiences do newborns find particularly appealing?

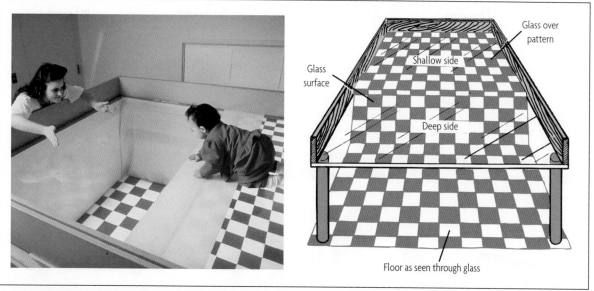

**Figure 10.3**

The visual cliff
Once children have gained experience crawling around their environment, they show fear of the deep side of the visual cliff.

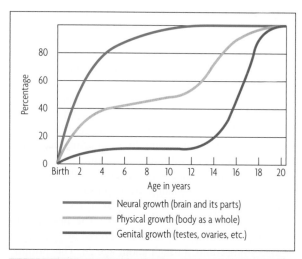

**Figure 10.4**

**Growth patterns across the first two decades of life**
Neural growth occurs very rapidly in the first year of life. It is much faster than overall physical growth. By contrast, genital maturation does not occur until adolescence.

example, in the sequence for locomotion, as shown in **Figure 10.5**, a child learns to sit up without special training. This sequence applies to the great majority of babies; a minority of children skip a step or develop their own original sequences. Even so, in cultures in which there is less physical stimulation, children begin to walk later. In typical Anglo-Australian society, most babies are pushed in strollers during their early infant years. This is not the case in Aboriginal culture, where most babies are carried about on a relative's back or hip. The difference between these two cultural groups is that Aboriginal children tend

to develop faster motor skills due to their having exposure to more exercise in their environment their most Anglo children. Although it is believed that Aboriginal children tend to develop faster in motor skill development, it is still important to note that infants across all cultural groups will develop their full potential of motor skills. Having said this, some infants are likely to excel in development over certain stages.

There has been a call for culturally relevant national legislation relating to Aboriginal and Torres Strait Islander child development for more than a decade, without this resulting. As such, research has tended to learn more about specific health development rather than psychological and motor development in Aboriginal children. This is perhaps due to there being a higher rate of immunity problems, asthma and nutritional problems in Aboriginal communities that more often than not lead to increased problems with normal physical and intellectual development (RHEF, 2005).

## PHYSICAL DEVELOPMENT IN ADOLESCENCE

The first concrete indicator of the end of childhood is the *pubescent growth spurt*. At around age 10 for girls and age 12 for boys, growth hormones flow into the bloodstream. For several years, the adolescent may grow 3 to 6 inches a year and gain weight rapidly as well. The adolescent's body does not reach adult proportions all at once. Hands and feet grow to full adult size first. The arms and legs come next, with the torso developing most slowly. Thus an individual's overall shape changes several times over the teenage years.

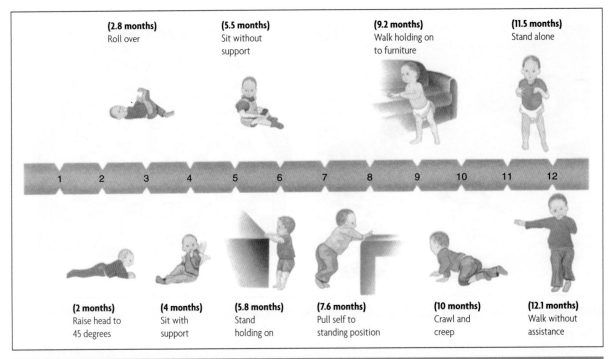

**(2.8 months)**
Roll over

**(5.5 months)**
Sit without
support

**(9.2 months)**
Walk holding on
to furniture

**(11.5 months)**
Stand alone

1 2 3 4 5 6 7 8 9 10 11 12

**(2 months)**
Raise head to
45 degrees

**(4 months)**
Sit with
support

**(5.8 months)**
Stand
holding on

**(7.6 months)**
Pull self to
standing position

**(10 months)**
Crawl and
creep

**(12.1 months)**
Walk without
assistance

Figure 10.5

Maturational timetable for locomotion
The development of walking requires no special teaching. It follows a fixed, time-ordered sequence that is typical of all physically capable members of our species.

Another important process that occurs during adolescence is **puberty**, which brings about sexual maturity. (The Latin word *pubertas* means 'covered with hair' and signifies the growth of hair on the arms and legs, under the arms, and in the genital area.) Puberty for males brings about the production of live sperm; for girls it leads to **menarche**, the onset of menstruation. In Australia, the average time for menarche is between the ages of 12 and 13, although the normal range extends from 11 to 15. For boys, the production of live sperm first occurs, on average, between the ages of 12 and 14, but again there is considerable variation in this timing. These physical changes often bring about an awareness of sexual

feelings. In Chapter 11, we will discuss the onset of sexual motivation.

Some other important physical changes happen inside adolescents' brains. Researchers once thought that most brain growth was over within the first few years of life. However, recent studies using brain imaging techniques have demonstrated continuing development within the adolescent brain (Paus, 2005). The areas of the brain that undergo the greatest change from puberty into young adulthood are the *frontal lobes*—the areas responsible for planning and regulation of emotions. The new growth beginning around ages 10 to 12 is followed by pruning of unused connections through about age 20. This pruning process leaves individuals with efficient and well-organised adult brains.

With the passing of adolescence, your body once again reaches a period of the life span in which biological change is comparatively minimal. You may affect your body in a variety of ways—by diet and exercise, for example—but the next striking set of changes that are consistent consequences of ageing occurs in middle and late adulthood.

## PHYSICAL CHANGES IN ADULTHOOD

Some of the most obvious changes that occur with age concern your physical appearance and abilities. As you grow older, you can expect your skin to wrinkle, your hair to thin and gray, and your height to decrease by up to

**puberty** The process through which sexual maturity is attained.

**menarche** The onset of menstruation.

Aboriginal children learn fine motor skills at an earlier age than their Anglo peers.

Why do researchers give the advice 'Use it or lose it'?

5 centimetres. You can also expect some of your senses to become less acute. These changes do not appear suddenly at age 65. They occur gradually, beginning as soon as early adulthood. However, before we describe some common age-related changes, we want to make a more general point: Many physical changes arise not from ageing but from *disuse*; research supports a general belief in the maxim, 'Use it or lose it'. Older adults who maintain (or renew) a program of physical fitness may experience fewer of the difficulties that are often thought to be inevitable consequences of ageing. (Note that we will reach exactly the same conclusion when we discuss cognitive and social aspects of middle and late adulthood.) Let's now look, however, at some changes that are largely unavoidable and frequently have an impact on the way adults think about their lives.

Vision The vast majority of people over 65 experience some loss of visual function (Carter, 1982; Pitts, 1982). With age, the lenses of people's eyes become yellowed and less flexible. The yellowing of the lens is thought to be responsible for diminished colour vision experienced by some older people. Colours of lower wavelengths—violets, blues and greens—are particularly hard for some older adults to discriminate. The rigidity of the lens can make seeing objects at close range difficult. Lens rigidity also affects dark adaptation, making night vision a problem for older people. Many normal visual changes can be aided with corrective lenses.

Hearing Hearing loss is common among those 60 and older. The average older adult has difficulty hearing high-frequency sounds (Corso, 1977). This impairment is usually greater for men than for women. Older adults can have a

hard time understanding speech—particularly that spoken by high-pitched voices. (Oddly enough, with age, people's speaking voices increase in pitch due to stiffening of the vocal cords.) Deficits in hearing can be gradual and hard for an individual to notice until they are extreme. In addition, even when individuals become aware of hearing loss, they may deny it because it is perceived as an undesirable sign of ageing. Some of the physiological aspects of hearing loss can be overcome with the help of hearing aids. You should also be aware, as you grow older or interact with older adults, that it helps to speak in low tones, enunciate clearly and reduce background noise.

Reproductive and sexual functioning We saw that puberty marks the onset of reproductive functioning. In middle and late adulthood, reproductive capacity diminishes. Around age 50, most women experience *menopause*, the cessation of menstruation and ovulation. For men, changes are less abrupt, but the quantity of viable sperm falls off after age 40, and the volume of seminal fluid declines after age 60. Of course, these changes are relevant primarily to reproduction. Increasing age and physical change do not necessarily impair other aspects of sexual experience (Levine, 1998; Levy, 1994). Indeed, sex is one of life's healthy pleasures that can enhance successful ageing because it is arousing, provides aerobic exercise, stimulates fantasy, and is a vital form of social interaction.

You have had a brief review of the landmarks of physical development. Against that background, let's turn now to the ways in which you developed an understanding of the world around you.

Older adults can and do enjoy the many benefits of intimacy and sexual relationships. Why does this image clash with stereotypes of late adulthood?

- Environmental factors can affect physical development while a child is still in the womb.

- Newborns and infants possess a remarkable range of capabilities: they are prewired for survival.

- Through puberty, adolescents achieve sexual maturity.

- Some physical changes in late adulthood are consequences of disuse, not inevitable deterioration.

For answers go to MyPsychLab!

**mypsychlab** where learning comes to life!

## CONCEPT QUESTIONS

1. How does experience with crawling influence children's performance on the visual cliff?

2. What have recent studies demonstrated with respect to brain development in adolescence?

3. Why does increasing age often have an effect on colour vision?

## CRITICAL THINKING

Consider the study on prenatal voice recognition. Why did the researchers have mothers tape-record the poems rather than having them read them 'live'?

# COGNITIVE DEVELOPMENT ACROSS THE LIFESPAN

**cognitive development** The development of processes of knowing, including imagining, perceiving, reasoning and problem solving.

**schemes** Piaget's term for cognitive structures that develop as infants and young children learn to interpret the world and adapt to their environment.

**assimilation** According to Piaget, the process whereby new cognitive elements are fitted in with old elements or modified to fit more easily.

How does an individual's understanding of physical and social reality change across the life span? **Cognitive development** is the study of the processes and products of the mind as they emerge and change over time. Because researchers have been particularly fascinated by the earliest emergence of cognitive capabilities, we will focus much of our attention on the earliest stages of cognitive development. However, we will also describe some of the discoveries researchers have made about cognitive development across the adult years.

As we begin this discussion of cognitive development, we want to remind you of a distinction we introduced in Chapter 3—*nature versus nurture*. The question is how best to account for the profound differences between a newborn and, for example, a 10-year-old: to what extent is such development determined by heredity (nature), and to what extent is it a product of learned experiences (nurture)? The debate concerning nature and nurture has a long history among philosophers, psychologists and educators. On one side of this debate are those who believe that the human infant is born without knowledge or skills and that experience, in the form of human learning, etches messages on the blank tablet (in Latin, the *tabula rasa*) of the infant's unformed mind. This view, originally proposed by British philosopher **John Locke**, is known as *empiricism*. It credits human development to experience. Empiricists believe that what directs human development is the stimulation people receive as they are *nurtured*. Among the scholars opposing empiricism was French philosopher **Jean-Jacques Rousseau**. He argued the *nativist* view that *nature*, or the evolutionary legacy that each child brings into the world, is the mould that shapes development. Our discussion of cognitive development should lead you to see that there is truth to both sides of the debate. Children have innate preparation to learn from their experiences in the world.

We begin our discussion of cognitive development with the pioneering work of the late Swiss psychologist Jean Piaget.

## PIAGET'S INSIGHTS INTO MENTAL DEVELOPMENT

For nearly 50 years, **Jean Piaget** (1929, 1954, 1965, 1977) developed theories about the ways that children think, reason and solve problems. Perhaps Piaget's interest in cognitive development grew out of his own intellectually active youth: Piaget published his first article at age 10 and was offered a post as a museum curator at age 14 (Brainerd, 1996). Piaget used simple demonstrations and sensitive interviews with his own children and with other children to generate complex theories about early mental development. His interest was not in the amount of information children possessed but in the ways their thinking and inner representations of physical reality changed at different stages in their development.

### Building blocks of developmental change

Piaget gave the name **schemes** to the mental structures that enable individuals to interpret the world. Schemes are the building blocks of developmental change. Piaget characterised the infant's initial schemes as *sensorimotor intelligence*—mental structures or programs that guide sensorimotor sequences, such as sucking, looking, grasping and pushing. With practice, elementary schemes are combined, integrated and differentiated into ever more complex, diverse action patterns, as when a child pushes away undesired objects to seize a desired one behind him or her. According to Piaget, two basic processes work in tandem to achieve cognitive growth—assimilation and accommodation. **Assimilation** modifies new environmental information to fit into what is already known; the child accesses existing schemes to structure incoming sensory data. **Accommodation** restructures or modifies the child's existing schemes so that new information is accounted for more completely.

Consider the transitions a baby must make from sucking at a mother's breast, to sucking the nipple of a bottle, to sipping through a straw, and then to drinking from a cup. The initial sucking response is a reflex action present at birth, but it must be modified somewhat so that the child's mouth fits the shape and size of the mother's nipple. In adapting to a bottle, an infant still uses many parts of the sequence unchanged (assimilation) but must grasp and draw on the rubber nipple somewhat differently from before and learn to hold the bottle at an appropriate angle (accommodation). The steps from bottle to straw to cup require more accommodation but continue to rely on earlier skills. Piaget saw cognitive development as the result of exactly this sort of interweaving of assimilation and accommodation. The balanced application of assimilation and accommodation permits children's behaviour and knowledge to become less dependent on concrete external reality, relying more on abstract thought.

### Stages in cognitive development

Piaget believed that children's cognitive development could be divided into a series of four ordered, discontinuous stages (see **Table 10.2**). All children are assumed to progress through these stages in the same sequence, although one child may take longer to pass through a given stage than another.

**Sensorimotor stage** The sensorimotor stage extends roughly from birth to age 2. In the early months, much of an infant's behaviour is based on a limited array of inborn schemes, like sucking, looking, grasping and pushing. During the first year, sensorimotor sequences are improved, combined, coordinated and integrated (sucking and grasping, looking and manipulating, for example). They become more varied as infants discover that their actions have an effect on external events.

The most important cognitive acquisition of the infancy period is the ability to form mental representations of absent objects—those with which the child is not in direct sensorimotor contact. **Object permanence** refers to children's understanding that objects exist and behave independently of their actions or awareness. In the first months of life, children follow objects with their eyes, but, when the objects disappear from view, they turn away as if the objects had also disappeared from their minds. At around 3 months of age, however, they keep looking at the place where the objects had disappeared. Between 8 and 12 months, children begin to search for those disappearing objects. By age 2 years, children have no remaining uncertainty that 'out of sight' objects continue to exist (Flavell, 1985).

**Preoperational stage** The preoperational stage extends roughly from 2 to 7 years of age. The big cognitive advance in this developmental stage is an improved ability

**Table 10.2**

Piaget's stages of cognitive development

| Stage/Ages | Characteristics and major accomplishments |
|---|---|
| Sensorimotor (0–2) | Child begins life with small number of sensorimotor sequences. Child develops object permanence and the beginnings of symbolic thought. |
| Preoperational (2–7) | Child's thought is marked by egocentrism and centration. Child has improved ability to use symbolic thought. |
| Concrete operations (7–11) | Child achieves understanding of conservation. Child can reason with respect to concrete, physical objects. |
| Formal operations (11→) | Child develops capacity for abstract reasoning and hypothetical thinking. |

accommodation Where existing schemes change to accommodate new information learnt by a child.

object permanence The recognition that objects exist independently of an individual's action or awareness; an important cognitive acquisition of infancy.

sensorimotor stage The period between birth and age 2 during which an infant's knowledge of the world is limited to their sensory perceptions and motor activities.

preoperational stage The period between ages 2 and 7 during which a child learns to use language. During this stage, children do not yet understand concrete logic.

Piaget observed that the typical 6-month-old will attend to an attractive toy (left) but will quickly lose interest if a screen blocks the toy from view (right). What understanding about objects will the child achieve by age 2?

to represent mentally objects that are not physically present. Except for this development, Piaget characterises the preoperational stage according to what the child *cannot* do. For example, Piaget believed that young children's preoperational thought is marked by **egocentrism**, the child's inability to take the perspective of another person. You have probably noticed egocentrism if you've heard a 2-year-old's conversations with other children. Children at this age often seem to be talking to themselves rather than interacting.

Preoperational children also experience **centration**—the tendency to have their attention captured by the more perceptually striking features of objects. Centration is illustrated by Piaget's classic demonstration of a child's inability to understand that the amount of a liquid does not change as a function of the size or shape of its container.

> When an equal amount of lemonade is poured into two identical glasses, children of ages 5 and 7 report that the glasses contain the same amount. When, however, the lemonade from one glass is poured into a tall, thin glass, their opinions diverge. The 5-year-olds know that the lemonade in the tall glass is the same lemonade, but they report that it now is *more*. The 7-year-olds correctly assert that there is no difference between the amounts.

In Piaget's demonstration, the younger children centre on a single, perceptually salient dimension—the height of the lemonade in the glass. The older children take into account both height and width and correctly infer that appearance is not reality.

### Concrete operations stage

The concrete operations stage goes roughly from 7 to 11 years of age. At this stage, the child has become capable of *mental operations*, actions performed in the mind that give rise to logical thinking. The preoperational and concrete operations stages are often put in contrast because children in the concrete operation stage are now capable of what they failed earlier on. Concrete operations allow children to replace physical action with mental action. For example, if a child sees that Adam is taller than Zara and, later, that Zara is taller than Tanya, the child can reason that Adam is the tallest of the three—without physically manipulating the three individuals. However, the child still cannot draw the appropriate inference ('Adam is tallest') if the problem is just stated with a verbal description. This inability to determine relative heights (and solve similar problems) without direct physical observation suggests that abstract thought is still in the offing in the period of concrete operations.

The lemonade study illustrates another hallmark of the concrete operations period. The 7-year-olds have mastered what Piaget called **conservation**: They know that the physical properties of objects do not change when nothing is added or taken away, even though the objects' appearance changes. **Figure 10.6** presents examples of Piaget's tests of conservation for different dimensions. One of the newly acquired operations children can bring to bear on conservation tasks is reversibility. *Reversibility* is the child's understanding that both physical actions and mental operations can be reversed: The child can reason that the amount of lemonade *can't* have changed because when the physical action is reversed—when the lemonade is poured back into the original glass—the two volumes will once again look identical.

**egocentrism** In cognitive development, the inability of a young child at the preoperational stage to take the perspective of another person.

**centration** A thought pattern common during the beginning of the preoperational stage of cognitive development in a child.

**conservation** According to Piaget, the understanding that physical properties do not change when nothing is added or taken away, even though appearances may change.

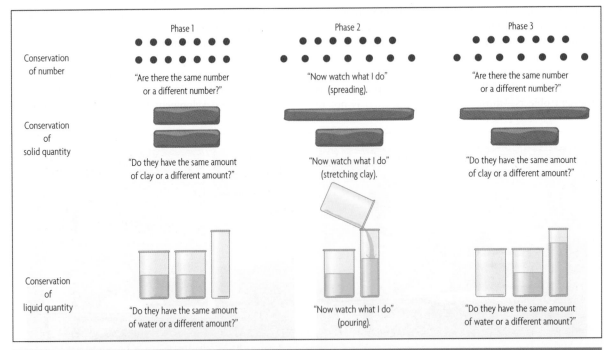

**Figure 10.6**

Tests of conservation

This 5-year-old girl is aware that the two containers have the same amount of coloured liquid. However, when the liquid from one is poured into a taller container, she indicates that there is more liquid in the taller one. She has not yet grasped the concept of conservation, which she will understand by age 6 or 7. Why wouldn't the 5-year-old child understand the concept, even if she were told the right answer?

Formal operations stage The formal operations stage covers a span roughly from age 11 on. In this final stage of cognitive growth, thinking becomes abstract. Adolescents can see how their particular reality is only one of several imaginable realities, and they begin to ponder deep questions of truth, justice and existence. They seek answers to problems in a systematic fashion: once they achieve formal operations, children can start to play the role of scientist, trying each of a series of possibilities in careful order. Adolescents also begin to be able to use the types of advanced deductive logic we described in Chapter 8. Unlike their younger siblings, adolescents have the ability to reason from abstract premises ('If A, then B' and 'not B') to their logical conclusions ('not A').

## CONTEMPORARY PERSPECTIVES ON EARLY COGNITIVE DEVELOPMENT

Piaget's theory remains the classic reference point for the understanding of cognitive development (Flavell, 1996; Lourenço & Machado, 1996; Scholnick et al., 1999). However, contemporary researchers have come up with more flexible ways of studying the development of the child's cognitive abilities.

Infant cognition We've already detailed some of the tasks Piaget used to draw conclusions about cognitive development. However, contemporary researchers have developed innovative techniques that have allowed them to re-evaluate some of Piaget's conclusions. Consider object permanence, which Piaget suggested was the major accomplishment of the 2-year-old child. Contemporary research techniques suggest that infants as young as 3 months old have already developed aspects of this concept. This important finding has been shown with different tasks devised by researcher **Renée Baillargeon** and her colleagues (Wang et al., 2004).

In one study, 4-month-old infants watched while an experimenter lowered a wide rectangular object (see **Figure 10.7**) (Wang et al., 2004). In one condition, the path of the object would put it behind a *wide occluder*—a barrier wide enough to hide the rectangular object completely. In the other condition, the object was destined to pass behind a *narrow occluder*—a barrier too narrow to occlude the object fully. As this event unfolded, a screen appeared that hid the final moment in which the object was lowered. When the screen disappeared, the object was fully hidden. How did the infants respond in the two conditions? If they didn't have object permanence, we would expect them to be equally unbothered in both cases—once the rectangular object was gone, we would expect them to have no recollection that it had ever existed. Suppose they did have some recollection of the object. In that case, we would expect that they—like adults who watched the events—would be rather surprised that a wide object could be hidden by a narrow occluder. To assess the infants' degree of surprise, the researchers recorded how long infants looked at the displays after the screen disappeared. The infants who saw the narrow occluder event looked at the display for about 16 seconds longer than their peers who saw the wide occluder event.

We can't take the infants' surprise as evidence that they have acquired the full concept of object permanence—they may only know that something is wrong without knowing exactly what that something is (Lourenço & Machado, 1996). Even so, the research by Baillargeon and her colleagues suggests that even very young children have acquired important knowledge of the physical world.

The innovative methods researchers have developed to penetrate infants' minds continue to transform our understanding of what infants know and how they know it. Consider the relationship between actions and goals. As an adult, you are accustomed to inferring people's goals

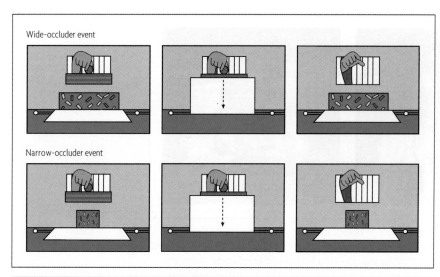

Wide-occluder event

Narrow-occluder event

## Figure 10.7

### Four-month-olds and object permanence

Four-month-olds watched an experimenter lower a rectangular object (shown in brown) behind a wide occluder or a narrow occluder (each shown in patterned green). As the event unfolded, a screen appeared to mask the moment at which the object passed behind the occluder. When the screen disappeared, the experimenter's hand was empty. The infants who saw the narrow-occluder event spent more time looking at the display, suggesting they were surprised that a wide object could be hidden behind a narrow occluder. The infants' surprise suggests they have attained some aspects of object permanence: The rectangular object was out of sight but not out of mind.

From *Cognition, 93*, Su-hua Wang et al., 'Young infants' reasoning about hidden objects: Evidence from violation-of-expectation tasks with test trials only,' pp. 167–198, Copyright © 2004, with permission from Elsevier.

**foundational theories** Frameworks for initial understanding formulated by children to explain their experiences of the world.

**internalisation** According to Vygotsky, the process through which children absorb knowledge from the social context.

separately, in each of several major domains, as children develop **foundational theories**—frameworks for initial understanding—to explain their experiences of the world (Gelman & Raman, 2002; Wellman & Inagaki, 1997). For example, children accumulate their experiences of the properties of mental states into a *theory of mind*, or naive psychology. By doing so, they are better able to understand the thought processes of themselves and others.

Researchers have formally studied the development of scientific concepts, such as the way in which children project biological properties from one species to another. When asked which of a series of animals sleep or have bones, 4-year-old children were inclined to make their judgments based on their perceptions of the similarity of the animal to humans (Carey, 1985). For example, more 4-year-olds attributed these properties (i.e., 'sleep' and 'have bones') to dogs than they did to fish, and attributions to fish were, in turn, greater than those to flies. Over time, children must replace a theory based on similarity to humans with one that acknowledges more structure in the animal kingdom— for example, they must acquire the formal distinction between *vertebrates* and *invertebrates* that defines which types of animals have bones. Similarly, 3- and 4-year-old children understand that what is inside objects affects their functions—although they have no clear idea what those insides are (Gelman, 2003; Gelman & Wellman, 1991). Thus, although 3- and 4-year-olds aren't entirely sure what kinds of things are inside dogs, they are quite certain that a dog would cease to be a dog if you removed whatever is inside. In each domain, you see that children begin to develop a general theory and then use a range of new experiences to provide successive refinements.

### Social and cultural influences on cognitive development

Another focus of contemporary research is on the role of social interactions in cognitive development. Much of this research has its origins in the theories of Russian psychologist **Lev Vygotsky**. Vygotsky argued that children develop through a process of **internalisation**: They absorb knowledge from their social context that has a major impact on how cognition unfolds over time.

when you watch them perform actions. For example, if you see someone pull out a set of keys, you easily infer that he or she needs to unlock something. When did you start to understand how actions relate to goals? Research suggests that 3-month-olds have begun to understand these relationship—but only when they have appropriate experience of their own (Sommerville et al., 2005). To support that claim, researchers outfitted one group of 3-month-olds with special Velcro mittens that allowed them to pick up toys. (Children of this age don't have the manual dexterity to grasp objects without this extra assistance.) A second group of children didn't have that novel experience of picking up toys. Both groups of children watched an experimenter perform a series of events that also involved grasping toys. An adult watching those events would infer that the experimenter had the particular goal, for example, of picking up a teddy bear. The group of children with grasping experience appeared to make that inference, but their inexperienced peers did not. This result brings us full circle to Piaget. Piaget suggested that children's knowledge is built up from active experience in the environment. This study confirms that active experience helps children learn how actions and goals fit together.

### Children's foundational theories

Piaget's theory is built around stages in which landmark changes take place in children's ways of thinking. More recently, researchers have explored the idea that changes occur

How do children begin to form generalisations about the world based on what they have experienced and observed?

The social theory that Vygotsky pioneered has found support in cross-cultural studies of development. As Piaget's theory initially seized the attention of developmental researchers, many of them sought to use his tasks to study the cognitive achievements of children in diverse cultures (Rogoff, 2003; Rogoff & Chavajay, 1995). These studies began to call into question the universality of Piaget's claims because, for example, people in many cultures failed to show evidence that they had acquired formal operations. Late in his life, Piaget himself began to speculate that the specific achievements he characterised as formal operations may rely more on the particular type of science education children obtain rather than on an unfolding of biologically predetermined stages of cognitive development (Lourenço & Machado, 1996).

Vygotsksy's concept of internalisation helps explain the effect culture has on cognitive development. Children's cognition develops to perform culturally valued functions (Serpell, 2000; Serpell & Boykin, 1994). Piaget, for example, invented tasks that reflected his own preconceptions about appropriate and valuable cognitive activities. Other cultures prefer their children to excel in other ways. If Piaget's children had been evaluated with respect to their understanding of the cognitive complexities of weaving, they probably would have appeared to be retarded in their development relative to Mayan children in Guatemala (Rogoff, 1990). Cross-cultural studies of cognitive development have quite often demonstrated that type of schooling plays a large role in determining children's achievement on Piagetian tasks (Rogoff & Chavajay, 1995). Psychologists must use these types of findings to sort out the nature and nurture of cognitive development.

The developmental changes we have documented so far are very dramatic. It's easy to tell that a 12-year-old has all sorts of cognitive capabilities unknown to a 1-year-old. We now shift to the more subtle changes that take place throughout adulthood.

## COGNITIVE DEVELOPMENT IN ADULTHOOD

As we have traced cognitive development across childhood into adolescence, 'change' has usually meant 'change for the better.' When we arrive at the period of late adulthood, though, cultural stereotypes suggest that 'change' means 'change for the worse' (Parr & Siegert, 1993). However, even when people believe that the course of adulthood brings with it general decline, they still anticipate certain types of gains very late into life (Dixon, 1999). We will look at intelligence and memory to see the interplay of losses and gains.

Intelligence There is little evidence to support the notion that general cognitive abilities decline among the healthy elderly. Only about 5 percent of the population experiences major losses in cognitive functioning. When age-related decline in cognitive functioning occurs, it is usually limited to only some abilities. When intelligence is separated into the components that make up your verbal abilities (*crystallised intelligence*) and those that are part

Many prominent figures, such as Gough Whitlam, continue to make important professional contributions through their 70s and beyond. How can some aspects of intellectual performance be kept from decline through late adulthood?

of your ability to learn quickly and thoroughly (*fluid intelligence*), fluid intelligence shows the greater decline with age (Baltes & Staudinger, 1993; Singer et al., 2003). Much of the decrease in fluidity has been attributed to a general slowing down of processing speed: Older adults' performance on intellectual tasks that require many mental processes to occur in small amounts of time is greatly impaired (Salthouse, 1996).

But all change is not in the direction of poorer functioning. For instance, psychologists are now exploring age-related gains in wisdom—expertise in the fundamental practices of life (Baltes & Kunzmann, 2003; Baltes & Staudinger, 2000). **Table 10.3** presents some of the types of knowledge that define wisdom (Smith & Baltes, 1990). You can see that each type of knowledge is best acquired over a long and thoughtful life. Furthermore, individuals vary greatly in their later-life intellectual performance. Research indicates that older adults who pursue high levels of environmental stimulation tend to maintain high levels of cognitive abilities.

### Table 10.3

**Features of wisdom**

- *Rich factual knowledge.* General and specific knowledge about the conditions of life and its variations
- *Rich procedural knowledge.* General and specific knowledge about strategies of judgment and advice concerning life matters
- *Life span contextualism.* Knowledge about the contexts of life and their temporal (developmental) relationships
- *Uncertainty.* Knowledge about the relative indeterminacy and unpredictability of life and ways to manage it

# PSYCHOLOGY in your life

## WILL YOUR BRAIN WORK DIFFERENTLY AS YOU AGE?

If you've spent time with older adults, you've probably heard them make casual claims like, 'My brain just doesn't work as well as it used to work.' Researchers have believed for a long time that older brains function differently from younger brains. However, as brain-making techniques have become more available as research tools, an understanding of those changes has grown. Images of the brain at work reveal consistent differences in patterns of brain activity over the adult years.

Let's consider brain activity related to two tasks that should be roughly familiar from earlier chapters. One task assessed participants' ability to use working memory: they attempted to commit four words to working memory and then indicated whether a subsequent probe word had been among that original group. A second task assessed participants' ability to engage visual attention: they monitored a video display of the letter B to determine whether it had briefly disappeared zero, once, or two times over the course of a trial. The participants for the two tasks were younger adults (with an average age of 22.6 years) and older adults (with an average age of 70.3 years). The two groups were equally accurate on the two tasks, although the younger adults were faster. The figure reveals the results of fMRI scans participants underwent as they performed each task (Cabeza et al., 2004). The coloured areas are the regions that were most active for each task. What you can see, as indicated by the arrows, is that the older adults

showed a pattern of brain activity in which both hemispheres of the brain were more active.

To understand these results, recall from Chapter 3 the finding that the brain's two hemispheres typically carry out different types of processes. The fMRI scans in the figure indicate that the brains of older adults become more symmetrical with respect to the functions in which they play a role (Cabeza, 2002). Researchers have offered two general explanations for this developmental change in the way that processes are distributed to the brain's two hemispheres. Some researchers have argued that when older brains recruit different areas from those used by younger brains, that activity represents *compensations* for other ageing-related changes in the brain. Other researchers have argued that brain activation unique to older adults reflects *distraction*—an inability to inhibit unnecessary brain activity.

In fact, researchers have found evidence suggesting that both compensation and distraction are at work in the ageing brain. To provide evidence for compensation, a study using PET scans examined the

relationship between individual differences in brain activity and recognition memory performance (Grady et al., 2005). As in earlier studies, older adults were likely to show activity in brain areas that were mostly not active for younger adults. Moreover, there was a positive correlation such that the *more* active those areas were, the *better* the older adults performed on recognition memory. That result supports the idea that the use of these brain areas yields an advantage for older adults. However, researchers have also carried out fMRI studies spanning several memory tasks to demonstrate that there are certain areas that older brains appear unable to turn off (Grady et al., 2006). The consistent appearance of brain activity that is not task relevant provides evidence that some age-related differences in brain function result in distraction from the task at hand.

This body of research supports the conclusion that your brain will, in fact, work differently as you age. The changes in function reflect compensation and distraction with respect to day-to-day cognitive tasks.

From R. Cabeza et al., 'Task-independent and task-specific age effects in brain activity during working memory, visual attention, and episodic retrieval,' *Cerebral Cortex*, 14, 372, 2004, by permission of Oxford University Press, Inc.

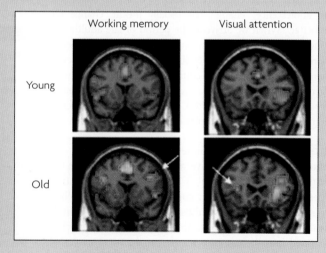

A group of 22 senior professors, ages 60 to 71, from the University of California, Berkeley, were compared in their intellectual functioning to their younger colleagues (ages 30 to 59) and to a control group of older adults in the same age range. The professors performed a variety of tests that tapped different aspects of cognitive functioning. On some of the tests—for example, paired associate learning (see Chapter 7)—the senior professors showed typical patterns of age-related impairment. However, on other measures, the senior professors kept pace with their younger colleagues. For example, they were equally able to listen to tape-recordings of brief stories and recall information from those stories. The control group of older adults showed typical age-related impairment on this task. How can we explain preserved function for the professors? The researchers suggest that the professors' occupation which requires them to maintain a high level of mental activity, may protect them from some typical losses of ageing (Shimamura et al., 1995).

Does this finding make you want to become a college professor? Other studies suggest that you need not go to that extreme. Research using fMRI scans has suggested, for example, that older adults with more education are better able to compensate for natural decline in their ageing brains than are their less educated peers (Springer et al., 2005). There's another good reason to continue your education.

The more general conclusion is that you should keep your mind at work. **Warner Schaie** and his colleagues have even been able to demonstrate that training programs can reverse older adults' decline in some cognitive abilities (Schaie, 2005). It appears that disuse, rather than decay, may be responsible for the deficits in intellectual performance that are not related to processing speed (Hultsch et al., 1999). As promised, we have again arrived at the conclusion that 'Use it or lose it (or seek training to get it back)' is an appropriate motto for the wise older adult.

How can older adults cope successfully with whatever changes inevitably accompany increasing age? Successful ageing might consist of making the most of gains while minimising the impact of the normal losses that accompany ageing. This strategy for successful ageing, proposed by psychologists **Paul Baltes** and **Margaret Baltes**, is called **selective optimisation with compensation** (Baltes et al., 1992; Freund & Baltes, 1998). *Selective* means that people scale down the number and extent of their goals for themselves. *Optimisation* refers to people exercising or training themselves in areas that are of highest priority to them. *Compensation* means that people use alternative ways to deal with losses—for example, choosing age-friendly environments. Let's consider an example:

> When the concert pianist [Arthur] Rubinstein was asked, in a television interview, how he managed to remain such a successful pianist in his old age, he mentioned three strategies: (1) In old age he performed fewer pieces, (2) he now practiced each piece more frequently, and (3) he produced more ritardandos [slowings of the tempo] in his playing

> before fast segments, so that the playing speed sounded faster than it was in reality. These are examples of selection (fewer pieces), optimisation (more practice), and compensation (increased use of contrast in speed). (Baltes, 1993, p. 590)

Memory A common complaint among the elderly is the feeling that their ability to remember things is not as good as it used to be. On a number of tests of memory, adults over 60 *do* perform worse than young adults in their 20s (Hess, 2005). People experience memory deficits with advancing age, even when they have been highly educated and otherwise have good intellectual skills (Zelinski et al., 1993). Ageing does *not* seem to diminish elderly individuals' ability to access their general knowledge store and personal information about events that occurred long ago. In a study of name and face recognition, middle-aged adults could identify 90 percent of their high school classmates in yearbooks 35 years after graduation; older adults were still able to recognise 70 to 80 percent of their classmates some 50 years later (Bahrick et al., 1975). However, ageing affects the processes that allow new information to be effectively organised, stored and retrieved (Craik, 1994; Giambra & Arenberg, 1993).

As yet, researchers have been unable to develop a wholly adequate description of the mechanisms that underlie memory impairment in older adults—perhaps because the impairment has multiple sources. (Hess, 2005). Some theories focus on differences between older and younger people in their efforts to organise and process information. Other theories point to elderly people's reduced ability to pay attention to information. Another type of theory looks to neurobiological changes in the brain systems that produce the physical memory traces. We explore those ideas in the *Psychology in Your Life* box. Note that these brain changes are not the same as the abnormal tangles of neural tissue and plaques that cause the memory loss of Alzheimer's disease (see Chapter 7). Researchers also believe that older adults' performance may be impaired by their very belief that their memory will be poor (Hertzog et al., 1990; Levy & Langer, 1994). Researchers continue to evaluate the relative contributions of each of these factors.

Let's now narrow our focus from general cognitive development to the more specific topic of the acquisition of language.

**selective optimisation with compensation** A strategy for successful ageing in which one makes the most gains while minimising the impact of losses that accompany normal ageing.

## RECAP CHECKPOINT

### Cognitive development across the lifespan

- Piaget's key ideas about cognitive development include development of schemes, assimilation, accommodation, and the four-stage theory of discontinuous development. The four stages are: sensorimotor, preoperational, concrete operational, and formal operational.

- Many of Piaget's theories are now being altered by ingenious research paradigms that reveal infants and young children to be more competent than Piaget had thought.

- Researchers suggest that children develop foundational theories, which change over time, in different psychological and physical domains.

- Cross-cultural research has questioned the universality of cognitive developmental theories.

- Age-related declines in cognitive functioning are typically evident in only some abilities. Research suggests that some cognitive deficits are caused by disuse rather than inevitable decay.

- Successful cognitive ageing can be defined as people optimising their functioning in select domains that are of highest priority to them and compensating for losses by using substitute behaviours.

For answers go to MyPsychLab!

## CONCEPT QUESTIONS

1. In Piaget's theory, what is the relationship between assimilation and accommodation?

2. What does it mean when a child is able to overcome centration?

3. How has contemporary research modified conclusions about object permanence?

4. What was the major emphasis of Lev Vygotsky's theory?

5. What is meant by selective optimisation with compensation?

## CRITICAL THINKING

Recall the experiment that looked at the performance of older professors. Why was it important to use younger professors as the comparison group of younger adults?

# ACQUIRING LANGUAGE

Here's a remarkable fact: by the time they are 6 years old, children can analyse language into its units of sound and meaning; use the rules they have discovered to combine sounds into words and words into meaningful sentences; and take an active part in coherent conversations. Children's remarkable language accomplishments have prompted most researchers to agree that the ability to learn language is biologically based—that you are born with an innate language capacity (Pinker, 1994). Even so, depending on where a child happens to be born, he or she may end up as a native speaker of any one of the world's 4,000 different languages. In addition, children are prepared to learn both spoken languages and gestural languages, like Auslan (Australian Sign Language www.auslan.org.au). This means that the innate predisposition to learn language must be both quite strong and quite flexible (Meier, 1991).

To explain how it is that infants are such expert language learners, we will describe the evidence that supports the claim of an innate language capacity. But we will also discuss the role that the environment plays—after all, children learn the particular languages that are being used in the world around them. **Table 10.4** outlines the various types of knowledge children must acquire for their particular signed or spoken language. You might review the language use section of Chapter 8 (pages 252 to 262) to remind yourself how adults put all these types of knowledge to use in fluent conversation.

| Table 10.4 |
| --- |
| **The structure of language** |
| **Grammar** is the field of study that seeks to describe the way language is structured and used. It includes several domains: |
| **Phonology**—the study of the sounds that are put together to form words. |
| A **phoneme** is the smallest unit of speech that distinguishes between any two utterances. For example, *b* and *p* distinguish *bin* from *pin*. |
| **Phonetics** is the study and classification of speech sounds. |
| **Syntax**—the way in which words are strung together to form sentences. For example, subject *(I)* + verb *(like)* + object *(you)* is standard English word order. |
| A **morpheme** is the minimum distinctive unit of grammar that cannot be divided without losing its meaning. The word *bins* has two morphemes, *bin* and *s*, indicating the plural. |
| **Semantics**—the study of the meanings of words and their changes over time. |
| **Lexical meaning** is the dictionary meaning of a word. Meaning is sometimes conveyed by the *context* of a word in a sentence ('Run *fast*' versus 'Make the knot *fast*') or the *inflection* with which it is spoken (try emphasising different words in *white house cat*). |
| **Pragmatics**—rules for participation in conversations; social conventions for communicating, sequencing sentences and responding appropriately to others. |

# PERCEIVING SPEECH AND PERCEIVING WORDS

Imagine you are a newborn child, hearing a buzz of noise all around you. How do you start to understand that some of those sounds are relevant to communicating with other people? A child's first step in acquiring a particular language is to take note of the sound contrasts that are used meaningfully in that language. (For signed languages, the child must attend to contrasts in hand positions, for example.) Each spoken language samples from the set of possible distinctions that can be produced by the human vocal tract; no language uses all of the speech–sound contrasts that can be made. The minimal meaningful units in a language are known as **phonemes**. There are about 45 distinct phonemes in English. Imagine you heard someone speak the words *right* and *light*. If you are a native speaker of English, you would have no trouble hearing the difference—/r/ and /l/ are different phonemes in English. If your only language experience was with Japanese, however, you would not be able to hear the difference between these two words because /r/ and /l/ are not distinct phonemes in Japanese. Do English speakers acquire the ability to make this distinction, or do Japanese speakers lose it?

To answer this type of question, researchers needed to develop methods to obtain linguistic information from pre-linguistic children.

> Using principles of operant conditioning we described in Chapter 5, researchers condition infants to turn their head toward a sound source when they detect a change from one speech sound to another. The reward that reinforces this behaviour is an illuminated box that contains a clapping and drumming toy animal. The procedure ensures that, if the children detect changes, they are very likely to turn toward the sound source. To measure the children's ability to perceive a distinction, researchers monitor how frequently the children turn their heads when a change is present.
>
> **Janet Werker** and her colleagues (Werker, 1991; Werker & Lalond, 1988) have used this technique to examine the innate basis of speech perception abilities, a version of the /r/–/l/ question we posed earlier. Werker studied sound distinctions that are used in Hindi, but not in English—distinctions that make it difficult for adult English speakers to learn Hindi. Werker and her colleagues measured the ability of infants learning English or Hindi, as well as adults who spoke English or Hindi, to hear the differences between the Hindi phonemes. She found that all the infants, regardless of which language they were learning, could hear the differences until the age of 8 months. However, of the infants older than 8 months and of the adults, only the Hindi speakers or speakers-to-be could hear the Hindi contrasts.

Research of this type strongly suggests that you started out with an innate ability to perceive sound contrasts that are important for spoken languages. However, you swiftly lose the ability to perceive some of the contrasts that are not present in the language you begin to acquire (Werker & Tees, 1999).

Along with this biological headstart for speech perception, many children also get an environmental headstart. When adults in many cultures speak to infants and young children, they use a special form of language that differs from adult speech: an exaggerated, high-pitched intonation known as **child-directed speech**, or less formally as *motherese* or *parentese*. The features that define child-directed speech appear in many but not all cultures (Fernald & Morikawa, 1993; Kitamura et al., 2002). Child-directed speech may help infants acquire language by keeping them interested in and attentive to the things that their parents say to them. The sound patterns of child-directed speech also emphasise emotional content, which might help forge an emotional bond between infants and their caregivers (Trainor et al., 2000).

At what age are children able to perceive the repetition of patterns of sounds—words—within the stream of speech directed to them? This is the first big step toward acquiring language: You can't learn that *doggie* has something to do with the shaggy thing in the corner until you recognise that the sound pattern *doggie* seems to recur in that shaggy thing's presence. Infants, on average, appear to gain the insight that repeated sounds have significance somewhere between ages 6 and 7½ months (Jusczyk, 2003; Jusczyk & Aslin, 1995). For one special word, however, the breakthrough comes a couple of months early: children at age 4½ months already show a recognition preference for their own names (Mandel et al., 1995)!

# LEARNING WORD MEANINGS

Once you could detect the co-occurrence of sounds and experiences, you were prepared to start learning word meanings. There's no denying that children are excellent word learners. At around 18 months, children's word learning often takes off at an amazing rate. Researchers have called this phase the *naming explosion* because children begin to acquire new words, especially names for objects, at a rapidly increasing rate (see **Figure 10.8**). By the age of 6, the average child is estimated to understand 14,000 words (Templin, 1957). Assuming that most of these words are learned between the ages of 18 months and 6 years, this works out to about nine new words a day or almost one word per waking hour (Carey, 1978). How is this possible?

Imagine a straightforward situation in which a child and her father are walking through a park and the father points and says, 'That's a doggie.' The child must decide to which piece of the world *doggie* applies. This is no easy feat (Quine, 1960). Perhaps *doggie* means 'any creature with four legs' or 'the animal's fur' or 'the animal's bark' or any of the other large set of meanings that will be true each time someone points toward a dog. Given all the possibilities, how are children able to fix the meanings of individual words?

child-directed speech A form of speech with an exaggerated and high-pitched intonation that adults use to speak to infants and young children.

phonemes Minimal units of speech in any given language that make a meaningful difference in speech and production and reception.

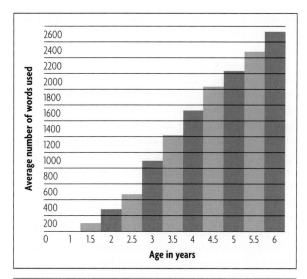

**Figure 10.8**

**Children's growth in vocabulary**
The number of words a child can use increases rapidly between the ages of 18 months and 6 years. This study shows children's average vocabularies at intervals of 6 months.

Researchers suggest that children act like scientists—developing *hypotheses* about what each new word might mean. You can, for example, see children's scientific minds actively at work when they *overextend* words, using them incorrectly to cover a wide range of objects. They may use the word *doggie* to refer to all animals, or the word *moon* to refer to all round objects, including clocks and coins. Other times, children might *underextend* a word—believing, for example, that *doggie* refers only to their own family dog.

The view that children form hypotheses, however, does not explain how children acquire particular meanings in particular contexts. Researchers have suggested that children's hypotheses are guided by expectations such as the principle of contrast. This principle suggests that differences in forms signal differences in meaning: when children hear new words, they should look for meanings that contrast with those for the words they already know (Clark, 2003). Suppose, for example, a father and daughter are watching a TV scene in which a kangaroo is jumping. The child knows the word jump but not the word kangaroo. Suppose the parent says, *Kangaroo!* What might happen next? Because the child knows jump, she supposes that her parent would just say jump if 'kangaroo' just meant 'jump'—different forms should signal contrasts in meaning. The child can now hypothesise that kangaroo must label the object rather than the action. She is on her way to acquiring a meaning for kangaroo. If you've spent time around small children, you've probably noticed the principle of contrast at work. For example, a child will often become upset if his mother calls his fire *engine* a fire *truck!*

**language-making capacity**
The innate guidelines or operating principles that children bring to the task of learning a language.

## ACQUIRING GRAMMAR

To explain how children acquire meanings, we characterised children as scientists whose hypotheses are constrained by innate principles. We can use the same analogy to describe how children acquire the rules by which units of meaning are combined into larger units—in other words, grammar. The challenge for the child is that different languages follow different rules. For example, in English the typical ordering of units in a sentence is subject-verb-object, but in Japanese the ordering is subject-object-verb. Children must discover what order is present in the language being used around them. How do they do that?

Most researchers now believe that a large part of the answer resides in the human genome. Linguist **Noam Chomsky** (1965, 1975), for example, argued that children are born with mental structures that facilitate the comprehension and production of language. Some of the best evidence for such a biological basis for grammar comes from children who acquire complete grammatical structure in the absence of well-formed input. For example, researchers have studied deaf children whose hearing loss was sufficiently severe that they could not acquire spoken language but whose parents did not expose them to full-fledged signed languages such as Australian Sign Language (Goldin-Meadow, 2003). These children began to invent signing systems of their own and—despite the lack of environmental support for these invented languages— the gestural systems came to have regular, grammatical structure: 'With or without an established language as a guide, children appear to be 'ready' to seek structure at least at word and sentence levels when developing systems for communication' (Goldin-Meadow & Mylander, 1990, p. 351).

But how can researchers go about specifying exactly what knowledge is innately given? The most productive approach to this question is to study language acquisition across many languages—*cross-linguistically*. By examining what is hard and what is easy for children to acquire across the world's many languages, researchers can determine what aspects of grammar are most likely to be supported by innate predispositions.

Here we arrive back at the child as scientist. Children bring innate constraints to the task of learning a particular language. **Dan Slobin** has defined these guidelines as a set of *operating principles* that together constitute the child's **language-making capacity**. According to Slobin's (1985) theory, the operating principles take the form of directives to the child. Here, for example, is an operating principle that helps children discover the words that go together to form a grammatical unit: 'store together ordered sequences of word classes and function classes that co-occur in the expression of a particular proposition type, along with a designation of the proposition type' (p. 1252). In simpler language, this operating principle suggests that children must keep track of the relationship between the order in which words appear and the meanings they express. Slobin derived the operating principles by summarising across the data provided by a large number of other researchers, who examined a variety of different languages. We will use English examples to demonstrate the principles at work.

Consider what English-speaking children can do when they begin, at about age 2, to use combinations of words— the *two-word stage*. Children's speech at this point has been characterised as *telegraphic* because it is filled with short, simple sequences using mostly nouns and verbs. Telegraphic speech lacks function words, such as *the*, *and* and *of*, which help express the relationships between words and ideas. For example, 'All gone milk' is a telegraphic message.

For adults to understand two-word utterances, they must know the context in which the words are spoken. 'Tanya ball', for example, could mean, among other things, 'Tanya wants the ball' or 'Tanya throws the ball'. Even so, children at the two-word stage show evidence that they have already acquired some knowledge of the grammar of English. Operating principles allow them to discover that word order is important in English and that the three critical elements are actor-action-object (subject-verb-object), arranged in that order. Evidence for this 'discovery' comes when children misinterpret a sentence such as 'Mary was followed by her little lamb to school' as *Mary* (actor) *followed* (action) *her lamb* (object) (see **Figure 10.9**). Over time, children must apply other operating principles to discover that there are exceptions to the actor-action-object rule.

Consider now an operating principle, which Slobin calls extension, that requires children to try to use the same unit of meaning, or *morpheme*, to mark the same concept.

Examples of such concepts are possession, past tense, and continuing action. In English, each of these concepts is expressed by adding a grammatical morpheme to a content word, such as *'s* (e.g., Maria's), *-ed* (e.g., call*ed*), and *-ing* (e.g., laugh*ing*). Note how the addition of each of these sounds to a noun or verb changes its meaning.

Children use operating principles like extension to form hypotheses about how these morphemes work.

Children develop linguistic fluency by listening to the speech patterns of those around them. What are the roles of nature and nurture in the acquisition of grammar?

## Figure 10.9

**Acquiring grammar**
Many toddlers would interpret 'Mary was followed by the lamb' and 'Mary followed the lamb' to have identical meanings.

Because this principle requires that the child try to mark all cases in the same way, however, the error of **over-regularisation** often results. For example, once children learn the past-tense rule (adding *-ed* to the verb), they add *-ed* to all verbs, forming words such as *doed* and *breaked*. As children learn the rule for plurals (adding the sound *-s* or *-z* to the end of a word), they again overextend the rule, creating words such as *foots* and *mouses*. Over-regularisation is an especially interesting error because it usually appears *after* children have learned and used the correct forms of verbs and nouns. The children first use the correct verb forms (for example, *came* and *went)*, apparently because they learned them as separate vocabulary items; but when they learn the general rule for the past tense, they extend it even to verbs that are exceptions to the rule—words that they previously used correctly. Over time, children use other operating principles to overcome this temporary over-application.

Children's acquisition of language has a major impact on their ability to participate in social interactions. Keep them in mind as we shift our focus now to social development across the life span.

**over-regularisation** A grammatical error, usually appearing during early language development, in which rules of the language are applied too widely, resulting in incorrect linguistic forms.

### RECAP CHECKPOINT
#### Acquiring language
- Many researchers believe that humans have an inborn language-making capacity. Even so, interactions with adult speakers is an essential part of the language acquisition process.

- Like scientists, children develop hypotheses about the meanings and grammar of their language. These hypotheses are often constrained by innate principles

## CONCEPT QUESTIONS

1. What are important functions of child-directed speech?

2. Why do children overextend word meanings?

3. How does research with deaf children support the idea that aspects of grammar are innate?

4. How would you notice when a child is over-regularising English past tense constructions?

## CRITICAL THINKING

Consider the study on children's ability to perceive sound distinctions. Why was it important to compare English-speaking adults with infants who are English speakers-to-be?

# SOCIAL DEVELOPMENT ACROSS THE LIFESPAN

We have seen so far how radically you change as a physical and cognitive being from birth to older adulthood. In this section of the chapter we explore **social development**: how individuals' social interactions and expectations change across the life span. We will see that your social and cultural environment interacts with biological ageing to provide each period of the life span with its own special challenges and rewards.

As we discuss social development, it is particularly important for you to consider the way in which culture and environment affect certain aspects of our lives. For example, people who live in circumstances of economic hardship undergo types of stresses that are absent from the 'normal' course of development (Crockett & Silbereisen, 2000; Leventhal & Brooks-Gunn, 2000). Current trends in Australia and in other countries throughout the world make it imperative for developmental psychologists to consider the difficult circumstances in which many children, adolescents and adults are forced to live—circumstances that continually put their sanity, safety, and survival at risk (Huston, 2005). Australian culture also enforces different outcomes for men and women and for individuals who belong to minority groups. For example, elderly women are more often economically

**social development** The ways in which individuals' social interactions and expectations change across the life span.

disadvantaged than elderly men; in the United States of America elderly African American women are worse off even than elderly white women (Carstensen & Pasupathi, 1993). These differences are direct products of structural inequities in contemporary society.

When we draw conclusions about the 'average' life course, keep in mind that culture dictates that some individuals will depart from this average; as we describe the psychological challenges facing the 'ordinary' individual, bear in mind that many individuals face extraordinary challenges. It is the role of researchers to document the impact of contemporary problems—and to design interventions to alleviate their harshest consequences. Major reforms are clearly needed to institute and coordinate better health care, welfare programs, and social policy. Psychologists will play a role in helping define what is in the best interest of families and their children (Scarr & Eisenberg, 1993). As we discuss social development, we will have several opportunities to revisit the impact of culture.

As you read the remainder of this chapter, keep in mind how the tasks of life are jointly determined by a biological accumulation of years and a social accumulation of cultural experiences. To begin our discussion of social development, we describe Erik Erikson's life span theory, which makes explicit the challenges and rewards in each of life's major periods.

Erik Erikson's psychosocial stage model is a widely used tool for understanding human development over the life span. What crisis did Erikson suggest dominates individuals of your age?

# ERIKSON'S PSYCHOSOCIAL STAGES

**Erik Erikson** (1963), who was trained by Sigmund Freud's daughter, Anna Freud, proposed that every individual must successfully navigate a series of **psychosocial stages**, each of which presented a particular conflict or crisis. Erikson identified eight stages in the life cycle. At each stage, a particular crisis comes into focus, as shown in **Table 10.5**. Although each conflict never completely disappears, it needs to be sufficiently resolved at a given stage if an individual is to cope successfully with the conflicts of later stages.

In Erikson's first stage an infant needs to develop a basic sense of *trust* in the environment through interaction with caregivers. Trust is a natural accompaniment to a strong attachment relationship with a parent who provides food, warmth and the comfort of physical closeness. But a child whose basic needs are not met, who experiences inconsistent handling, lack of physical closeness and warmth, and the frequent absence of a caring adult, may develop a pervasive sense of mistrust, insecurity and anxiety.

With the development of walking and the beginnings of language, there is an expansion of a child's exploration and manipulation of objects (and sometimes people). With these activities should come a comfortable sense of *autonomy* and of being a capable and worthy person. Excessive restriction or criticism at this second stage may lead instead to self-doubts, whereas demands beyond the child's ability, as in too-early or too-severe toilet training, can discourage the child's efforts to persevere in mastering new tasks.

Toward the end of the preschool period, a child who has developed a basic sense of trust, first in the immediate environment and then in himself or herself, can now *initiate* both intellectual and motor activities. The ways that parents respond to the child's self-initiated activities either encourage the sense of freedom and self-confidence needed for the next stage or produce guilt and feelings of being an inept intruder in an adult world.

During the elementary school years, the child who has successfully resolved the crises of the earlier stages is ready to go beyond random exploring and testing to the systematic development of *competencies*. School and sports offer arenas for learning intellectual and motor skills, and interaction with peers offers an arena for developing social skills. Successful efforts in these pursuits lead to feelings of competence. Some youngsters, however, become spectators rather than performers or experience enough failure to give them a sense of inferiority, leaving them unable to meet the demands of the next life stages.

Erikson believed that the essential crisis of adolescence is discovering one's true *identity* amid the confusion created by playing many different roles for the different audiences in an expanding social world. Resolving this crisis helps the individual develop a sense of a coherent self; failing to do so adequately may result in a self-image that lacks a central, stable core.

The essential crisis for the young adult is to resolve the conflict between *intimacy* and *isolation*—to develop the capacity to make full emotional, moral and sexual commitments to other people. Making that kind of commitment requires that the individual compromise some personal preferences, accept some responsibilities, and yield some degree of privacy and independence. Failure to resolve this crisis adequately leads to isolation and the inability to connect to others in psychologically meaningful ways.

The next major opportunity for growth, which occurs during adult midlife, is known as *generativity*. People in their 30s and 40s move beyond a focus on self and

**psychosocial stages**
Proposed by Erik Erikson, successive developmental stages that focus on an individual's orientation toward the self and others.

## Table 10.5

### Erikson's psychosocial stages

| Approximate age | Crisis | Adequate resolution | Inadequate resolution |
|---|---|---|---|
| 0–1½ | Trust vs. mistrust | Basic sense of safety | Insecurity, anxiety |
| 1½–3 | Autonomy vs. self-doubt | Perception of self as agent capable of controlling own body and making things happen | Feelings of inadequacy to control events |
| 3–6 | Initiative vs. guilt | Confidence in oneself as initiator, creator | Feelings of lack of self-worth |
| 6–puberty | Competence vs. inferiority | Adequacy in basic social and intellectual skills | Lack of self-confidence, feelings of failure |
| Adolescent | Identity vs. role confusion | Comfortable sense of self as a person | Sense of self as fragmented; shifting, unclear sense of self |
| Early adult | Intimacy vs. isolation | Capacity for closeness and commitment to another | Feeling of aloneness, separation; denial of need for closeness |
| Middle adult | Generativity vs. stagnation | Focus of concern beyond oneself to family, society, future generations | Self-indulgent concerns; lack of future orientation |
| Later adult | Ego integrity vs. despair | Sense of wholeness, basic satisfaction with life | Feelings of futility, disappointment |

partner to broaden their commitments to family, work, society and future generations. Those people who haven't resolved earlier developmental tasks are still self-indulgent, question past decisions and goals, and pursue freedom at the expense of security.

The crisis in later adulthood is the conflict between *ego integrity* and *despair*. Resolving the crises at each of the earlier stages prepares the older adult to look back without regrets and to enjoy a sense of wholeness. When previous crises are left unresolved, aspirations remain unfulfilled, and the individual experiences futility, despair and self-deprecation.

You will see that Erikson's framework is very useful for tracking individuals' progress across the life span. We begin with childhood.

## SOCIAL DEVELOPMENT IN CHILDHOOD

Children's basic survival depends on forming meaningful, effective relationships with other people. **Socialisation** is the lifelong process through which an individual's behaviour patterns, values, standards, skills, attitudes and motives are shaped to conform to those regarded as desirable in a particular society. This process involves many people—relatives, friends, teachers—and institutions—schools, houses of worship—that exert pressure on the individual to adopt socially approved values and standards of conduct. The family, however, is the most influential shaper and regulator of socialisation. The concept of family itself is being transformed to recognise that many children grow up in circumstances that include either less (a single parent) or more (an extended household) than a mother, father and siblings. Whatever the configuration, though, the family helps the individual form basic patterns of responsiveness to others—and these patterns, in turn, become the basis of the individual's lifelong style of relating to other people.

Temperament  Even as infants begin the process of socialisation, they do not all start at the same place. Children begin life with differences in **temperament**—biologically based levels of emotional and behavioural response to the environment (Thomas & Chess, 1977). Researcher **Jerome Kagan** and his colleagues have demonstrated that some infants are 'born shy' and others are 'born bold' (Kagan & Snidman, 2004). These groups of children differ in sensitivity to physical and social stimulation: the shy or *inhibited* babies are consistently 'cautious and emotionally reserved when they confront unfamiliar persons or contexts'; the bold or *uninhibited* babies are consistently 'sociable, affectively spontaneous, and minimally fearful in the same unfamiliar situations' (Kagan & Snidman, 1991, p. 40). In one sample, about 10 percent of the infants were inhibited and about 25 percent were uninhibited; the rest of the infants fell in between those endpoints (Kagan & Snidman, 1991). Researchers have demonstrated that differences in temperament can be detected even while babies are still in the womb: high levels of foetal activity are

associated with increased difficulty once the children are born (DiPietro et al., 1996).

Longitudinal studies have demonstrated the long-term impact of early temperament. Children who, at age 4 months, displayed inhibited and uninhibited temperaments continue to behave differently as they get older (Kagan & Snidman, 2004). At age 2, the inhibited children generally showed the most fear—and the uninhibited children the least fear—when they were faced with unfamiliar events. At age 4, the uninhibited children were considerably more likely to be sociable when interacting with unfamiliar children. However, not all children who start out at the extreme ends of the dimension of inhibited versus uninhibited remain at those extremes—some children become less shy or more bold as they age (Pfeifer et al., 2002). However, even when children's responses become less extreme, they very rarely shift from one category to the other. For example, a child who started out life as inhibited might become less shy over time, but he or she would rarely switch over to being a bold child. In a large Australian longitudinal study conducted by Prior et al., (2000) where children's temperament development was studied between 1983–2000, it was found that of all children in the study who were found to be extremely shy in their early childhood years (ages 3–7) only 20% of them continued with this level of shyness into their teenage years (ages 13–14). The other 80% of extremely shy children identified in the study were found to be less introverted as they grew older, but still preferred to be less social than outgoing children of their age group due to their shyness.

A study of children's temperament being influenced by parenting styles in both Australia and the United States (Russell et al, 2003), found that between these two westernised countries the child's own temperament dictated as to whether they would be more social or aggressive regardless of their parent's temperament and parenting style. Only in the U.S. sample of parents was it found that an authoritarian father had some minor impact on aggressiveness or social skills in both boys' and girls' social relationships.

Temperament development sets the stage for later aspects of social development. Next, we consider the

Why is it important for a child to develop a secure attachment to a parent or other caregiver?

socialisation The lifelong process whereby an individual's behavioural patterns, values, standards, skills, attitudes and motives are shaped to conform to those regarded as desirable in a particular society.

temperament A child's biologically based level of emotional and behavioural response to environmental events.

**CHAPTER 10**  HUMAN DEVELOPMENT ACROSS THE LIFESPAN

*attachment* bonds children form as their first social relationships.

Attachment    Social development begins with the establishment of a close emotional relationship between a child and a mother, father or other regular caregiver. This intense, enduring, social–emotional relationship is called **attachment**. Because children are incapable of feeding or protecting themselves, the earliest function of attachment is to ensure survival. In some species, the infant automatically becomes *imprinted* on the first moving object it sees or hears (Johnson & Gottlieb, 1981). **Imprinting** occurs rapidly during a critical period of development and cannot easily be modified. The automaticity of imprinting can sometimes be problematic. Ethologist **Konrad Lorenz** demonstrated that young geese raised by a human imprint on the human instead of on one of their own kind. In nature, fortunately, young geese mostly see other geese first.

You won't find human infants imprinting on their parents. Even so, **John Bowlby** (1973), an influential theorist on human attachment, suggested that infants and adults are biologically predisposed to form attachments. That attachment relationship has broad consequences. Beginning with Bowlby (1973), theorists have suggested that the experiences that give rise to an attachment relationship provide individuals with a lifelong schema for social relationships called an *internal working model* (Bretherton, 1996). An internal working model is a memory structure that gathers together a child's history of interactions with his or her caretakers, the interactions that yielded a particular pattern of attachment. The internal working model provides a template that an individual uses to generate expectations about future social interactions.

One of the most widely used research procedures for assessing attachment is the *Strange Situation Test*, developed by **Mary Ainsworth** and her colleagues

Konrad Lorenz, the researcher who pioneered the study of imprinting, graphically demonstrates what can happen when young animals become imprinted on someone other than their mother. Why is imprinting important for many animal species?

(Ainsworth et al., 1978). In the first of several standard episodes, the child is brought into an unfamiliar room filled with toys. With the mother present, the child is encouraged to explore the room and to play. After several minutes, a stranger comes in, talks to the mother, and approaches the child. Next, the mother exits the room. After this brief separation, the mother returns, there is a reunion with her child, and the stranger leaves. The researchers record the child's behaviours at separation and reunion. Researchers have found that children's responses on this test fall into three general categories (Ainsworth et al., 1978):

- *Securely attached* children show some distress when the parent leaves the room; seek proximity, comfort and contact upon reunion; and then gradually return to play.

- *Insecurely attached–avoidant* children seem aloof and may actively avoid and ignore the parent upon her return.

- *Insecurely attached–ambivalent/resistant* children become quite upset and anxious when the parent leaves; at reunion, they cannot be comforted, and they show anger and resistance to the parent but, at the same time, express a desire for contact.

In middle-class North American samples, about 70 percent of babies are classified as securely attached; among the insecurely attached children, about 20 percent are classified as avoidant and 10 percent as resistant. Cross-cultural research on attachment relationships—in countries as diverse as Australia, Sweden, Israel, Japan and China—reveals reasonable consistency in the prevalence of types of attachments (Van IJzendoorn & Kroonenberg, 1988). In every country, the majority of children are securely attached; most of the cultural differences occur with respect to the prevalence of different types of insecure attachments. Researchers also find a high rate of agreement between attachment classifications made in the Strange Situation and those based on naturalistic observation of children and mothers in their homes (Pederson & Moran, 1996).

Categorisations based on the Strange Situation Test have proven to be highly predictive of a child's later behaviour in a wider variety of settings, particularly the overall division between children who are securely and insecurely attached. For example, longitudinal research revealed that children who showed secure or insecure behaviour in the Strange Situation at 15 months differed widely in their school behaviour at age 8 to 9 years (Bohlin et al., 2000). Those children who had been securely attached at 15 months were more popular and less socially anxious than their peers who had been insecurely attached. Similar continuity from the quality of attachment to later years has been demonstrated in 10-year-olds (Urban et al., 1991) and adolescents (Weinfeld et al., 1997). This suggests that the quality of attachment, as revealed in the Strange Situation, really does have long-term importance (Stams et al., 2002). We will see in Chapter 16 that

**attachment** Emotional relationship between a child and the regular caregiver.

**imprinting** A primitive form of learning in which some infant animals physically follow and form an attachment to the first moving object they see and/or hear.

researchers also use attachment measures to predict the quality of adults' loving relationships.

Attachment relationships are quite important in young lives. Secure attachment to adults who offer dependable social support enables the child to learn a variety of pro-social behaviours, to take risks, to venture into novel situations, and to seek and accept intimacy in personal relationships.

# CRITICAL THINKING *in your life*

## HOW DOES CHILD CARE AFFECT CHILDREN'S DEVELOPMENT?

If you plan to have both children and a career, you're likely to face a difficult question: Is it wise to put your children in child care? This is an issue that receives a lot of attention—with highly polarised views—in the popular press. To make this important judgment, you need to get beyond the false dichotomy of 'child care is good' versus 'child care is bad'. Rather, you should formulate the more specific questions that allow you to put the decision in perspective. Let us suggest two of those questions: In what ways is child care better or worse for the developing child? What is the optimal form of child care?

We have already provided the context in which you can interpret the first question: If the attachments between children and mothers are so critical, shouldn't anything that disrupts the formation of those attachments— such as child care—be necessarily bad for the children? The answer to this question is, 'On balance, *no*' (Scarr, 1998). To arrive at this answer, researchers typically made comparisons between children who stayed at home and those who were placed in child care, on measures of both intellectual and social development. Researchers have found that children placed in child care are often at an *advantage* with respect to these measures, primarily because child care provides more opportunities (Burchinal et al., 2000; Clarke-Stewart, 1991, 1993). Intellectual development can benefit from a greater range of educational and play activities; social development can benefit from a wider variety of social interactions than would be available in the home.

There are two reasons, however, that the answer 'no' must be qualified by 'on balance.' One is that there are individual differences in the way children respond to care outside the home. The second is that child care takes many forms. For example, early child development research undertaken in Australia by Sims et al., (2005) states that cortisole levels in some children (an enzyme found in saliva that can indicate stress levels in humans) increases significantly in some children when they are placed in unfamiliar child care settings. Researchers, therefore, have turned their attention away from the 'better or worse' question toward the issue of what constitutes quality care for particular children (Sagi et al., 2002; Zaslow, 1991), but have equally considered the impact of psychosocial influences with the psychophysiological aspects of child care.

**Alison Clarke-Stewart** (1993), an expert on child care, has summarised the research literature to provide a series of guidelines for quality child care. Some of her recommendations relate to the physical comfort of the children:

- The child-care centre should be physically comfortable and safe.
- There should be at least one caretaker for every six or seven children (more for children under age 3).
- Children should be taught social problem-solving skills.

Clarke-Stewart has also suggested that child-care providers should share the qualities of good parents:

- Caregivers should be responsive to the children's needs and actively involved in their activities.
- Caregivers should not put undue restrictions on the children.
- Caregivers should have sufficient flexibility to recognise differences among the needs of individual children.

If these guidelines are followed, quality child care can be provided to all children whose parents work outside the home. As psychologists spread the message that child care does not harm, and may even enhance, children's development, parents should feel less distress about the necessity of a dual-career family. Such a reduction in stress could only improve the child's overall psychological environment.

- If you are trying to compare outcomes for children who do and do not participate in child care, on what dimensions should you try to match the children?
- How might you assess whether child-care providers interact with children in appropriate ways?

## Parenting styles and parenting practices

As we noted earlier, children bring individual temperaments to their interactions with their parents. Children's temperaments may make parents' best (or worst) efforts at parenting have unexpected consequences. Researchers recognise that children's temperaments and parents' behaviours each influence the other to yield developmental outcomes such as the quality of attachment relationships: As much as parents change their children, children change their parents (Collins et al., 2000).

Even so, researchers have located a **parenting style** that is generally most beneficial. This style resides at the intersection of the two dimensions of *demandingness* and *responsiveness* (Maccoby & Martin, 1983): 'Demandingness refers to the parent's willingness to act as a socialising agent, whereas responsiveness refers to the parent's recognition of the child's individuality' (Darling & Steinberg, 1993, p. 492). As shown in **Figure 10.10**, *authoritative* parents make appropriate demands on their children—they demand that their children conform to appropriate rules of behaviour—but are also responsive to their children. They keep channels of communication open to foster their children's ability to regulate themselves (Gray & Steinberg, 1999). This authoritative style is most likely to produce an effective parent–child bond. The contrast, as seen in **Figure 10.10**, is to parenting styles that are *authoritarian*—parents apply discipline with little attention to the child's autonomy—or *indulgent*—parents are responsive, but they fail to help children learn about the structure of social rules in which they must live—or *neglecting*—parents neither apply discipline nor are they responsive to their children's individuality.

| | Parent's responsiveness | |
|---|---|---|
| | *Accepting Responsive Child-centered* | *Rejecting Unresponsive Parent-centered* |
| **Parent's demandingness** *Demanding, controlling* | Authoritative-reciprocal High in bidirectional communication | Authoritarian Power assertive |
| *Undemanding, low in control attempts* | Indulgent | Neglecting, ignoring, indifferent, uninvolved |

Figure 10.10

A classification of parenting styles

Parenting styles can be classi-fied with respect to the two dimensions of demandingness—the parent's willingness to act as a socialising agent—and responsiveness—the parent's recognition of the child's individuality. The authoritative style is most likely to produce an effective parent–child bond.

Even parents with the same overall styles put different priorities on the *socialisation goals* they consider important for the children. **Parenting practices** arise in response to particular goals (Darling & Steinberg, 1993). Thus authoritative parents who wish their children to do well in school may create a home environment in which the children come to understand why their parents value that as a goal—and may strive to do well in school because they are effectively socialised toward that goal (Noack, 2004). However, because not all authoritative parents value school success, you could not predict children's school performance based only on their parents' style (Steinberg et al., 1992). Parents' general attitudes and specific behaviours are both important for charting their children's life course.

A close interactive relationship with loving adults is a child's first step toward healthy physical growth and normal socialisation. As the original attachment to the primary caregiver extends to other family members, they too become models for new ways of thinking and behaving. From these early attachments, children develop the ability to respond to their own needs and to the needs of others.

## Contact comfort and social experience

What do children obtain from the attachment bond? Sigmund Freud and other psychologists argued that babies become attached to their parents because the parents provide them with food—their most basic physical need. This view is called the *cupboard theory* of attachment. If the cupboard theory were correct, children should thrive as long as they are adequately fed. Does this seem right?

**Harry Harlow** (1965) did not believe that the cupboard theory explained the importance of attachment. He set out to test the cupboard theory against his own hypothesis that infants might also attach to those who provide **contact comfort** (Harlow & Zimmerman, 1958). Harlow separated macaque monkeys from their mothers at birth and placed them in cages, where they had access to two artificial 'mothers': a wire one and a terry cloth one. Harlow found that the baby monkeys nestled close to the terry cloth mother and spent little time on the wire one. They did this even when only the wire mother gave milk! The baby monkeys also used the cloth mother as a source of comfort when frightened and as a base of operations when exploring new stimuli. When a fear stimulus (for example, a toy bear beating a drum) was introduced, the baby monkeys would run to the cloth mother. When novel and intriguing stimuli were introduced, the baby monkeys would gradually venture out to explore and then return to the terry cloth mother before exploring further.

Further studies by Harlow and his colleagues found that the monkeys' formation of a strong attachment to the mother substitute was not sufficient for healthy social development. At first, the experimenters thought the young monkeys with terry cloth mothers were developing normally, but a very different picture emerged when it was time for the female monkeys who had been raised in this way to become mothers. Monkeys who had been deprived

**parenting style** The manner in which parents rear their children.

**parenting practices** Specific parenting behaviours that arise in response to particular parental goals.

**contact comfort** Comfort derived from an infant's physical contact with the mother or caregiver.

How did Harlow demonstrate the importance of contact comfort for normal social development?

of chances to interact with other responsive monkeys in their early lives had trouble forming normal social and sexual relationships in adulthood.

Primate researcher **Stephen Suomi** (1999; Champoux et al., 1995) has shown that putting emotionally vulnerable infant monkeys in the foster care of supportive mothers virtually turns their lives around. Suomi notes that monkeys put in the care of mothers known to be particularly loving and attentive are transformed from marginal members of the monkey troop into bold, outgoing young males who are among the first to leave the troop at puberty to work their way into a new troop. This *cross-fostering* gives them coping skills and information essential for recruiting support from other monkeys and for maintaining a high social status in the group. Let's see now what lessons research with monkeys holds for human deprivation.

Human deprivation Tragically, human societies have sometimes created circumstances in which children are deprived of contact comfort. Many studies have shown that a lack of close, loving relationships in infancy affects physical growth and even survival. In 1915, a doctor at Johns Hopkins Hospital reported that, despite adequate physical care, 90 percent of the infants admitted to orphanages in Baltimore died within the first year. Studies of hospitalised infants over the next 30 years found that, despite adequate nutrition, the children often developed respiratory infections and fevers of unknown origin, failed

to gain weight, and showed general signs of physiological deterioration (Bowlby, 1969; Spitz & Wolf, 1946).

Contemporary studies continue to demonstrate patterns of disruption. For example, one study compared attachment outcomes for children raised at home to those for children largely (90 percent of their lives) raised in institutions (Zeanah et al., 2005). The researchers found that 74 percent of the home-reared children had secure attachments; for institution-reared children, only 20 percent had secure attachments. Moreover, a lack of normal social contact may have a long-lasting effect on children's brain development. One study compared a group of children who had spent about their first 1½ years in orphanages to those who had been raised by their biological parents (Wismer Fries et al., 2005). At age 4½, the two groups of children interacted with a stranger. The children who spent their earliest days in orphanages failed to show a normal pattern of brain response—as indicated by brain hormone levels—to the interaction with the stranger.

Unfortunately, no matter what the setting in which children live, there is a potential for abuse. In a recent analysis, the U.S. government found that about 170,000 children experienced physical abuse in a single year, and roughly 90,000 experienced sexual abuse (U.S. Department of Health and Human Services, 2005). In one sample of 375 young adults, nearly 11 percent reported having endured some type of physical or sexual abuse. Of that group, about 80 percent presented symptoms of one or more psychiatric disorders (Silverman et al., 1996). Instances of child abuse provide psychologists with a very important agenda: to determine what types of interventions are in the best interest of the child. In Australia, between the years of 2005 and 2006, 266,745 cases of childhood neglect or abuse were reported (Australian Institute of Health and Welfare, 2007). Causes behind why child abuse occurs in Australia have strong correlations with both community, culture, parenting styles and the levels of parent education in both anglo, multicultural and Aboriginal communities. Child abuse in Australia ranges from physical injuries, sexual abuse, malnourishment, substance abuse, criminal behaviour and, of course, psychological abuse (Cicchetti & Carlson, 1989), In contrast to Australia, roughly 523,000 U.S. children and youths have been removed from their homes and placed in some type of government-funded setting, for example a foster home or group residence (National Clearinghouse on Child Abuse and Neglect Information, 2005). Are these children always happy to be removed from their abusive homes? The answer is complex because even abused children have often formed an attachment to their caretakers: The children may remain loyal to their natural family and hope that everything could be put right if they were allowed to return. This is one reason that much research attention is focused on designing intervention programs to reunite families (Miller et al., 2006).

In this section, you have seen how experiences during childhood have an impact on later social development. We now shift our focus to later periods of life, beginning with adolescence.

# SOCIAL DEVELOPMENT IN ADOLESCENCE

Earlier in the chapter, we defined adolescence by physical and cognitive changes. In this section, those changes will serve as background to social experiences. Because the individual has reached a certain level of physical and mental maturity, new social and personal challenges present themselves. We will first consider the general experience of adolescence and then turn to the individual's changing social world.

**The experience of adolescence** The traditional view of adolescence predicts a uniquely tumultuous period of life, characterised by extreme mood swings and unpredictable, difficult behaviour: 'storm and stress.' This view can be traced back to romantic writers of the late 18th and early 19th centuries, such as Goethe. The storm-and-stress conception of adolescence was strongly propounded by **G. Stanley Hall**, the first psychologist of the modern era to write at length about adolescent development (1904). Following Hall, the major proponents of this view have been psychoanalytic theorists working within the Freudian tradition (for example, Blos, 1965; Freud, 1946, 1958). Some of them have argued that not only is extreme turmoil a normal part of adolescence but that failure to exhibit such turmoil is a sign of arrested development. **Anna Freud** wrote that 'to be normal during the adolescent period is by itself abnormal' (1958, p. 275).

Two early pioneers in cultural anthropology, **Margaret Mead** (1928) and **Ruth Benedict** (1938), argued that the storm-and-stress theory is not applicable to many non-Western cultures. They described cultures in which children gradually take on more and more adult responsibilities without any sudden stressful transition or period of indecision and turmoil. Contemporary research has confirmed that the experience of adolescence differs across cultures (Arnett, 1999). Those cross-cultural differences argue against strictly biological theories of adolescent experience. Instead, researchers focus on the transitions children are expected to make in different cultures.

Recall that in Erikson's description of the life span, the essential task of adolescence is to discover one's true identity. For cultures such as the majority culture in Australia, one consequence is that children attempt to achieve *independence* from their parents. With approximately 1.2 million young people aged 12–24 in New South Wales, Australia, 34,000 of these being aboriginal or Torres Strait Islander, it is not unreasonable to suggest that a good portion of these adolescents are seeking to obtain independence and identity. Across the years of 10–17, part of the struggle teenagers and adolescents have to contend with are stages of puberty which add angst to their battles for independence, as demonstrated in **Table 10.6**. Parents and their adolescent children must weather a transition in their relationship from one in which a parent has unquestioned authority to one in which the adolescent is granted reasonable independence to make important decisions (Allen & Land, 1999; Holmbeck

& O'Donnell, 1991). Consider the results of a study that followed 1,330 adolescents from age 11 to age 14 (McGue et al., 2005). As 14-year-olds, these adolescents reported greater conflict with their parents than they had at age 11. At age 14, the adolescents' parents were less involved in their lives; the adolescents had less positive regard for their parents and they believed that their parents had less positive regard for them. These data illustrate some of the relationship costs that arise when children strive for independence. We don't want to paint an overly negative picture: most adolescents at most times still are able to use their parents as ready sources of practical and emotional support (Smetana et al., 2006). However, against that background, the striving for identity and independence explains why individuals might experience a certain amount of 'storm and stress.'

Now that we've considered the general adolescent experience, let's turn to the increasing importance of peers in adolescents' social experience.

**Peer relationships** Much of the study of social development in adolescence focuses on the changing roles of family (or adult caretakers) and friends (Smetana et al., 2006). We have already seen that attachments to adults form soon after birth. Children also begin to have friends at very young ages. Adolescence, however, marks the first period in which peers appear to compete with parents to shape a person's attitudes and behaviours. Adolescents participate in peer relations at the three levels of friendships, cliques and crowds (Brown & Klute, 2003). Over the course of these years, adolescents come to count increasingly on

## Table 10.6

### Adolescent identity developmental stages

#### Identity development in early adolescence (age 10–14)

- Am I normal?
- Daydreaming
- Vocational goals change frequently
- Begin to develop own value system
- Emerging sexual feelings and sexual exploration
- Imaginary audience
- Desire for privacy
- Magnify own problems: no one understands

#### Identity development in middle adolescence (age 15–17)

- Experimentation with sex, drugs, friends, jobs and risk-taking behaviour

#### Identity development in late adolescence (age 18–21)

- Pursue realistic vocational goals with training or career employment
- Relate to family as an adult
- Realisations of own limitations and mortality
- Establishment of sexual identity; sexual activity is more common
- Establishment of ethical and moral value system
- More capable of intimate, complex relationships

their one-on-one *friendships* to provide them with help and support (Furman & Buhrmester, 1992). *Cliques* are groups that most often consist of 6 to 12 individuals. Membership in these groups may change over time, but they tend to be drawn along lines of, for example, age and race (Smetana et al., 2006). Finally, *crowds* are the larger groups such as sport 'jocks' or 'nerds' that exist more loosely among individuals of this age. Through interaction with peers at these three levels, adolescents gradually define the social component of their developing identities, determining the kinds of people they chose to be and the kinds of relationships they choose to pursue (Berndt, 1992; Hartup, 1996).

The peer relationships that adolescents form are quite important to social development. They give individuals opportunities to learn how to function in what can often be demanding social circumstances. In that sense, peer relationships play a positive role in preparing adolescents for their futures. At the same time, parents often worry—with reasonable cause—about negative aspects of peer influence. For example, research supports the conclusion that adolescents are more likely to engage in risky behaviours when they are under the influence of their peers.

To study developmental changes in peer influence, researchers recruited three groups of participants: Adolescents (age 13 to 16), young adults (ages 18 to 22), and adults (ages 24 and older) (Gardner & Steinberg, 2005). Participants in each age range played a video game called 'Chicken'. In this game, players act as drivers. They must decide how soon to stop their car when a light changes from green to orange. Their goal is to achieve as much distance as they can before the light turns red and a wall pops up. If they don't stop in time, they'll crash into the wall. About half of the participants played the game alone. The other half played in groups of three—each participant played in turn while the other two watched. **Figure 10.11** presents the results of the experiment. As you can see, adolescents were far more likely to engage in risky driving (within the context of the video game) when in the presence of their peers.

This study confirms a general tendency for adolescents to demonstrate peer influence as a shift toward riskier behaviours. However, some adolescents are more susceptible to peer influence than others—and that susceptibility has consequences. In a longitudinal study, students who were more susceptible to their close friends' influence at the study's outset were more likely to have problems with drugs and alcohol 1 year later (Allen et al., 2006). We note, once again, that adolescence need not be a time of storm and stress. However, research of this type indicates the patterns of behaviour that indicate some adolescents are at risk.

## SOCIAL DEVELOPMENT IN ADULTHOOD

Erikson defined two tasks of adulthood as intimacy and generativity. Freud identified the needs of adulthood as *Lieben und Arbeiten*, or love and work. Abraham Maslow (1968, 1970) described the needs of this period of life as love and belonging, which, when satisfied, develop into the needs for success and esteem. Other theorists label these needs as affiliation or social acceptance and achievement or competence needs. The shared core of these theories is that adulthood is a time in which both social relationships and personal accomplishments take on special priority. In this section, we track these themes across the breadth of adulthood.

Intimacy Erikson described **intimacy** as the capacity to make a full commitment—sexual, emotional and moral—to another person. Intimacy, which can occur in both friendships and romantic relationships, requires openness, courage, ethical strength and usually some compromise of one's personal preferences. Research has consistently confirmed Erikson's supposition that social intimacy is a prerequisite for a sense of psychological wellbeing across the adult life stages (Fernandez-Ballesteros, 2002; Ishii-Kuntz, 1990). **Figure 10.12** demonstrates that interactions with family and friends trade off over this long span of years to provide a fairly constant level in people's reports of their own wellbeing. The changes in these sources of support reflect, in part, the life events that are typically correlated with each age. Let's examine these correlations.

Young adulthood is the period in which many people enter into marriage or other stable relationships. The group that counts as family thus will ordinarily grow

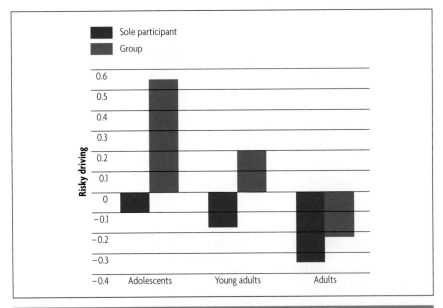

**Figure 10.11**

### Peer influence on risky behavior

Adolescents, young adults, and adults played a video game called 'Chicken' by themselves or in a group setting. The video game allowed participants to take risks while driving. The y-axis plots a measure of risky driving: Larger positive scores indicate higher risk. Adolescents showed the largest impact of the presence of peers.

From Margo Gardner and Laurence Steinberg, 'Peer Influence on Risk Taking, Risk Preference, and Risky Decision Making in Adolescence and Adulthood: An Experimental Study,' *Developmental Psychology*, 41(4), 625–635. Copyright © 1997 by the American Psychological Association. Reprinted with permission.

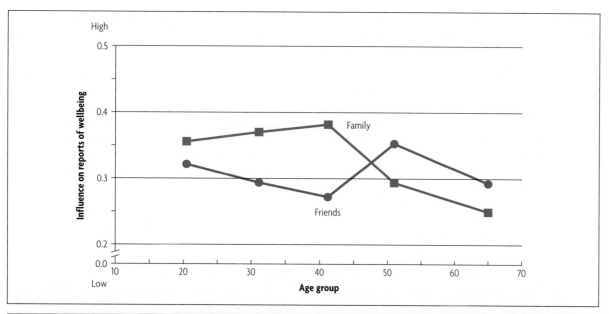

**Figure 10.12**

The effects of social interaction on wellbeing
Across the life span, social interactions with family and friends trade off to provide a fairly constant level of individuals' reports of well-being.

larger. Historically, most research on relationships and families across adulthood focused on the so-called standard configurations of a mother, father and a house full of children. However, as the realities of people's families have changed, researchers have tried to document and understand the consequences of those changes (Mason et al., 1998). For example, studies now focus on the ways in which homosexual couples enter into and sustain long-term relationships (James & Murphy, 1998). Research suggests that the strategies heterosexuals and homosexuals use to maintain relationships over time have much in common: both types of couples try to remain close by, for example, sharing tasks and activities together (Haas, 2003; Haas & Stafford, 1998). However, to combat a lack of social acceptance for gay and lesbian relationships, homosexual couples also need to take special measures to maintain relationships, such as being publicly 'out' as a couple. Some heterosexual couples also must persevere in the face of continuing barriers to social acceptance; research suggests that interracial couples also face types of prejudices that have a negative impact on the ability of relationships to endure (Chan & Wethington, 1998; Gaines & Agnew, 2003).

Each of these types of relationships increases the role of family in adults' social lives. Families also grow when individuals decide to include children in their lives. What may surprise you, however, is that the birth of children can often pose a threat to the overall happiness of a couple. Why might that be? Researchers have focused on differences in the way that men and women make the transition to parenthood in heterosexual relationships (Cowan & Cowan, 1998, 2000). In contemporary Western society, marriages are more often founded on notions of equality between men and women than was true in the past. However, children's births can have the effect of pushing husbands and wives in the direction of more traditional gender roles. The wife may feel too much of the burden of child care; the husband may feel too much pressure to support a family. The net effect may be that, following the birth of a child, the marriage changes in ways that both spouses find to be negative (Cowan et al., 1985). Although research on gay male and lesbian couples raising children is far more limited, that research suggests that, as you might expect, concerns about gender roles with respect to parenting have less of a negative impact on homosexual relationships (Patterson, 2002).

For many heterosexual couples, satisfaction with the marriage continues to decline because of conflicts as the child or children pass through their adolescent years. Contrary to the cultural stereotype, many parents look forward to the time when their youngest child leaves home and leaves them with an 'empty nest' (White & Edwards, 1990). Parents may enjoy their children most when they are no longer under the same roof (Levenson et al., 1993). Have we discouraged you from having children? We certainly hope not! Our goal, as always, is to make you aware of research that can help you anticipate and interpret the patterns in your own life.

If marriages are, on the whole, happier when the spouses reach late adulthood, should everyone try to stay married late into life? In Australia, approximately 40 per cent of marriages end in divorce (ABS researchers would like to be able to determine which couples are fundamentally mismatched—with respect, for example, to their patterns of interactions—and which couple could avoid divorce (Orbuch et al., 2002; Story & Bradbury, 2004)).

In 1983, researchers began a longitudinal study of married couples. After following the couples for 14 years, the researchers were able to form some generalisations about why some of the couples remained married while some had been divorced (Gottman & Levenson, 2000). During the initial data collection in 1983, the couples visited the laboratory to have conversations on a neutral topic (events of the day) and a conflictual topic (each couple's area of continuing disagreement). Trained research assistants viewed tapes of these conversations and evaluated the extent of positive and negative affect—emotional content—the spouses expressed toward each other. Some couples discussed difficult topics with a sense of humour, whereas other couples discussed similar topics with put-downs and complaints. The affective content of their discussions was highly predictive of the couples' fates. From the sample of 79 couples, 11 percent got divorced relatively early—after, on average, 7.4 years after marriage. On the whole, those couples had shown high levels of *negative* affect in their discussions of conflictual topics. There were also 16 percent of the couples who divorced relatively late—after, on average, 13.9 years. On the whole, those who had shown low levels of *positive* affect toward each other.

Why did this pattern emerge? The researchers suggested that 'intense marital conflict likely makes it difficult to stay in the marriage for long, but its absence makes marriage somewhat more acceptable. Nonetheless, the absence of positive affect takes its toll' (Gottman & Levenson, 2000, p. 743). You can probably find both types of relationships around you: those in which couples fight constantly and those in which couples are calm but do not respond positively to each other.

When individuals stay together late into life, one member of the couple most often must cope with the death of a spouse. When we contemplate the death of a spouse or partner, we have come back to one reason that the balance of social interactions shifts somewhat from family to friends late in life (see **Figure 10.12**). A stereotype about late adulthood is that individuals become more socially isolated. Although it is true that older individuals may interact socially with fewer people, the nature of those

Statistically speaking, which spouse is likely to outlive the other? What effect might the quality of the marriage have on this outcome?

interactions changes so that intimacy needs continue to be met. This trade-off is captured by the **selective social interaction theory**. This view suggests that, as people age, they become more selective in choosing social partners who satisfy their emotional needs. According to **Laura Carstensen** (1991, 1998), selective interaction may be a practical means by which people can regulate their emotional experiences and conserve their physical energy. Older adults remain vitally involved with some people—particularly family members and long time friends.

Let's conclude this section where we began, with the idea that social intimacy is a prerequisite for psychological well-being. What matters most is not the quantity of social interaction but the quality (particularly, in Australian culture, for women). As you grow into older adulthood, you will begin to protect your need for intimacy by selecting those individuals who provide the most direct emotional support.

Let's turn now to a second aspect of adult development, generativity.

Generativity Those people who have established an appropriate foundation of intimate relationships are most often able to turn their focus to issues of **generativity**. This is a commitment beyond oneself to family, work, society or future generations—typically a crucial step in development in one's 30s and 40s (McAdams & de St. Aubin, 1998). An orientation toward the greater good allows adults to establish a sense of psychological well-being that offsets any longing for youth.

> **George Vaillant** studied the personality development of 95 highly intelligent men through interviews and observations over a 30-year period following their graduation from college in the mid-1930s. Many of the men showed great changes over time, and their later behaviour was often quite different from their behaviour in college. The interviews covered the topics of physical health, social relationships and career achievement. At the end of the 30-year period, the 30 men with the best outcomes and the 30 with the worst outcomes were identified and compared (see **Table 10.7**). By middle life, the best-outcome men were carrying out generativity tasks, assuming responsibility for others, and contributing in some way to the world. Their maturity even seemed to be associated with the adjustment of their children—the more mature fathers were better able to give children the help they needed in adjusting to the world (Vaillant, 1977).

This study illustrates the prerequisites for generativity: For the best-outcome men, other aspects of their lives were sufficiently stable to allow them to direct their resources outwards, toward generations to come. When asked what it means to be well adjusted, middle-aged adults (average age 52) and older adults (average age 74) gave the same response as their most frequent answer. Both groups suggested that adjustment relies on being 'others oriented'—on being a caring, compassionate person and

## Table 10.7

Differences between best- and worst-outcome subjects on factors related to psychosocial maturity

| | Best outcomes (30 Men) | Worst outcomes (30 Men) |
|---|---|---|
| Personality integration rated in bottom fifth percentile during college | 0% | 33% |
| Dominated by mother in adult life | 0% | 40% |
| Bleak friendship patterns at 50 | 0% | 57% |
| Failure to marry by 30 | 3% | 37% |
| Pessimism, self-doubt, passivity and fear of sex at 50 | 3% | 50% |
| Childhood environment poor | 17% | 47% |
| Current job has little supervisory responsibility | 20% | 93% |
| Subjects whose career choice reflected identification with father | 60% | 27% |
| Children's outcome described as good or excellent | 66% | 23% |

having good relationships (Ryff, 1989). This is the essence of generativity.

Let us also note that most older adults looking back on their lives do so with a degree of wellbeing that is unchanged from earlier years of adulthood (Carstensen & Freund, 1994). As we have seen with respect to social relationships, late adulthood is a time when goals are shifted; priorities change when the future does not apparently flow as freely. Across that change in priorities, however, older adults preserve their sense of the value of their lives. Erikson defined the last crisis of adulthood to be the conflict between ego integrity and despair. The data suggest that few adults look back over their lives with despair. Most older adults review their lives—and look to the future—with a sense of wholeness and satisfaction.

We have worked our way through the life span by considering social and personal aspects of childhood, adolescence, and adulthood. To finish the chapter, we will trace two particular domains in which experience changes over time, the domains of sex and gender differences and moral development.

## RECAP CHECKPOINT
### Social development across the lifespan
- Social development takes place in a particular cultural context.
- Erik Erikson conceptualised the life span as a series of crises with which individuals must cope.

- Children begin the process of social development with different temperaments.
- Socialisation begins with an infant's attachment to a caregiver.
- Failure to make this attachment leads to numerous physical and psychological problems.
- Lack of nurturing relationships in childhood can impair social development.
- Adolescents must develop a personal identity by forming comfortable social relationships with parents and peers.
- The central concerns of adulthood are organised around the needs of intimacy and generativity.
- People become less socially active as they grow older because they selectively maintain only those relationships that matter most to them emotionally.
- People assess their lives, in part, by their ability to contribute positively to the lives of others.

## CONCEPT QUESTIONS
1. At what life stage did Erik Erikson suggest people navigate the crisis of intimacy versus isolation?
2. What long-term consequences have been demonstrated for children's early attachment quality?
3. What dimensions define parenting styles?
4. In what levels of peer relationships do adolescents engage?
5. What is meant by selective social interaction?

## CRITICAL THINKING
Recall the longitudinal study that looked at the precursors to divorce. At the study's outset, why were the couples asked to discuss conflictual topics?

For answers go to MyPsychLab!

# SEX AND GENDER DIFFERENCES

One type of information most children begin to acquire in the first few months in life is that there are two categories of people in their social world: males and females.

Over time, children learn that there are many respects in which the psychological experiences of males and females are quite similar. However, when differences do, in fact, occur children acquire an understanding that some of those differences arise from biology and others arise from cultural expectations. Biologically based characteristics that distinguish males and females are referred to as **sex differences**. These characteristics include different reproductive functions and differences in hormones and anatomy. However, the first differences children perceive are entirely social: they begin to sense differences between males and females well before they understand anything about anatomy. In contrast to biological sex, **gender** is a psychological phenomenon referring to learned sex-related behaviours and attitudes. Cultures vary in how strongly gender is linked to daily activities and in the amount of tolerance for what is perceived as cross-gender behaviour. In this section, we consider both sex differences and gender development: The nature and nurture of children's sense of maleness of femaleness.

## SEX DIFFERENCES

Starting at about 6 weeks after conception, male foetuses begin to diverge from female foetuses', when the male testes develop and begin to produce the hormone *testosterone*. The presence or absence of testosterone plays a critical role in determining whether a child will be born with male or female anatomy. Testosterone also has an impact on brain development: Experiments with non-human animals have demonstrated that sex differences in neural structure are largely brought about by this hormone (Morris et al., 2004).

The exact role of testosterone is less clear for the development of the human brain. However, brain scans have revealed consistent structural differences between men's and women's brains (Goldstein et al., 2001). Men typically have bigger brains than women—appropriate comparisons across the sexes adjust for that overall variation. The differences that remain after those adjustments are intriguing with respect to behavioural dissimilarities between men and women. For example, MRI scans reveal that the regions of the frontal lobe that play an important role in regulating social behaviour and emotional functioning are relatively bigger in women than in men (Gur et al., 2002). Another interesting difference has been found with the levels of testosterone before and after birth and its relation to language development in British infants. At age 18–24 months, girls were found to have a significantly larger vocabulary than boys at their equivalent age. This suggested that foetal testosterone levels may have some impact on neural mechanisms underlying communication development. To confirm that sex differences of this type are biological—rather than the product of a lifetime of experience as men or women in particular cultural roles—researchers have undertaken similar studies with children and adolescents (De Bellis et al., 2001; Suzuki et al., 2005). Those studies confirm that sex differences emerge in the brain as a part of ordinary biological development.

Other analyses of sex differences focus on the distinct ways in which men's and women's brains accomplish cognitive and emotional tasks (Kimura, 1999). Consider the brain processes engaged when the two sexes view emotionally charged pictures.

Twelve men and 12 women underwent fMRI scans while viewing 96 pictures that ranged from neutral (e.g., a book or a fork) to negative (e.g., an autopsy or a gravestone) (Canli et al., 2002). As the participants viewed the pictures, they provided ratings of the intensity of their emotional experience on a scale ranging from 0 ('not emotionally intense at all') to 3 ('extremely emotionally intense'). Three weeks after this initial experience, the participants completed a test of recognition memory for the pictures—they had not been warned when they first viewed the pictures that this test was forthcoming. The researchers assessed the relationship between brain activity at the time of encoding and subsequent memory performance. They found distinct patterns of activity for men and for women. For example, greater activity in the left amygdala (see Chapter 3) preceded recognition success for women; greater activity in the right amygdala preceded success for men.

Further studies of the brain at work confirm sex differences in the encoding and recognition of emotionally arousing stimuli (Cahill et al., 2004). These studies suggest that some of the behavioural differences that set men and women apart can be traced to biological differences rather than to cultural roles.

Most research on the biology of sex differences with human subjects focuses on global differences between men and women. However, researchers have recently begun to look at the biological origins of more fine-grained differences among individuals. These studies turn once again to the impact of the hormone testosterone on later development. In this case, the researchers determined the level of testosterone in the amniotic fluid of each individual participant. The researchers correlated those foetal testosterone levels with, for example, the quality of each boy's or girl's social relationships when they were 4-years-old (Knickmeyer et al., 2005). In general, boys had higher levels of foetal testosterone than girls. Against that background, individuals' higher levels of foetal testosterone were associated with poorer social relationships for both boys and girls. These results suggest that the extent to which individuals conform to expectations for male and female behaviour may depend, in part, on their prenatal hormonal environment (Morris et al., 2004).

## GENDER IDENTITY AND GENDER ROLES

You have just seen that important aspects of men's and women's behaviour are shaped by biological differences. However, cultural expectations also have an important impact on **gender identity**—an individual's sense of maleness or femaleness. Gender identity includes

**sex differences** Biologically based characteristics that distinguish males from females.

**gender** A psychological phenomenon that refers to learned sex-related behaviours and attitudes of males and females.

**gender identity** One's sense of maleness or femaleness; usually includes awareness and acceptance of one's biological sex.

awareness and acceptance of one's sex. This awareness develops at quite a young age: 10- to 14-month-old children already demonstrate a preference for a video showing the abstract movements of a child of the same sex (Kujawski & Bower, 1993). **Gender roles** are patterns of behaviour regarded as appropriate for males and females in a particular society. They provide the basic definitions of masculinity and femininity.

Much of what people consider masculine or feminine is shaped by culture (Leaper, 2000). Many researchers have suggested that gender-role socialisation begins at birth. In one study, parents described their newborn daughters, using words such as *little*, *delicate*, *beautiful* and *weak*. By contrast, parents described their newborn sons as *firm*, *alert*, *strong* and *coordinated*. The babies actually showed no differences in height, weight or health (Rubin et al., 1974). Parents dress their sons and daughters differently, give them different kinds of toys to play with, and communicate with them differently. For children as young as 18 months, parents tend to respond more positively when their children play with sex-appropriate toys. For example, in one experiment fathers gave fewer positive reactions to boys engaging in play with toys typical for girls (Fagot & Hagan, 1991). In general, children receive encouragement from their parents to engage in sex-typed activities (Lytton & Romney, 1991; Witt, 1997).

Parents are not the only socialisers of gender roles. **Eleanor Maccoby** (1998) argues, for example, that parents do not merely stamp in gender roles. She has found

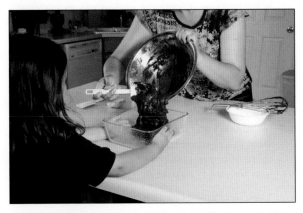

How do parents and peers influence children's acquisition of gender roles?

evidence that play styles and toy preferences are not, in fact, highly correlated with parental preferences or roles. Young children are segregationists—they seek out peers of the same sex even when adults are not supervising them or in spite of adult encouragement for mixed-group play. Maccoby believes that many of the differences in gender behaviour among children are the results of peer relationships.

In fact, boys and girls show consistent differences in their patterns of social interaction. Some differences relate to the structure of those interactions. For example, at least by the age of 6, boys prefer to interact in groups, whereas girls prefer one-on-one interactions (Benenson et al., 1997; Benenson & Heath, 2006). Other differences between boys and girls relate to the content of their play (Rose & Rudolph, 2006). Girls are more likely than boys to engage in social conversations and disclose information about themselves. Boys are more likely than girls to engage in rough-and-tumble play. These differences become more prominent as children grow older—providing evidence for the development of gender roles.

Interactions with their parents and peers provide children with an abundance of opportunities to acquire gender roles. Even so, young children themselves appear to believe that biology is destiny.

> Groups of children ages 4, 5, 8, 9 and 10 were asked to make predictions about a 10-year-old character named Chris or Pat. The children all believed that the character had been brought up on a beautiful island. However, some of the children were told that Chris or Pat was raised on that isolated island entirely by members of the same sex (e.g., Chris was a boy and all of his caretakers were also male) or entirely by members of the opposite sex (e.g., Chris was a boy and all of his caretakers were female). How did the environment affect the 4- to 10-year-olds' predictions about Chris or Pat's sex-stereotyped behaviour? Until age 9, children believed that sex-stereotyped behaviour would emerge regardless of the social context. For example, the younger children thought it was equally likely that boy Chris would want to be a fire fighter and girl Chris would want to be a nurse, no matter who raised him or her. The older children's judgments were, by contrast, sensitive to the context in which the child was raised: Now Chris's career choice was influenced by his or her caretakers' sex as well as his or her own (Taylor, 1996).

These results suggest that children underestimate the effects environments have on the ways in which boys and girls become different. They are also consistent with the finding that children between the ages of 2 and 6 seem to have more extreme and inflexible perceptions of gender than adults do (Stern & Karraker, 1989). When shown infants dressed in neutral clothing, children of this age are much more consistently affected in their judgments about the infant by an arbitrary label of 'male' or 'female' than adults are. Younger children's extreme reactions may be linked to the fact that they are at an age when they are trying to establish their own gender identity. They appear, on the whole, to be much more attuned to the 'scripts' for

**gender roles** Sets of behaviours and attitudes associated by society as being male or female and expressed publicly by the individual.

gender-appropriate behaviour than are their older siblings (Levy & Fivush, 1993).

We have briefly considered how and why it is that boys and girls experience social development in different fashions. In the next section you will see that some researchers believe that gender also has an impact on moral development.

For answers go to MyPsychLab!

## RECAP CHECKPOINT
### Sex and gender differences

- Research has revealed biologically based sex differences between the brains of men and women.

- Beginning at birth, parents and peers help bring about the socialisation of gender roles.

## CONCEPT QUESTIONS

1. What is the distinction between sex differences and gender differences?

2. What does research suggest about differences between men and women for the processing of emotional stimuli?

3. In what ways are young children 'segregationists'?

## CRITICAL THINKING

Recall the experiment that examined children's understanding of sex differences. Why might the researchers have identified Chris or Pat specifically as a 10-year-old?

# MORAL DEVELOPMENT

So far we have seen, across the life span, how important it is to develop close social relationships. Let's now consider another aspect of what it means to live as part of a social group: on many occasions you must judge your behaviour according to the needs of society, rather than just according to your own needs. This is the basis of *moral behaviour*. **Morality** is a system of beliefs, values and underlying judgments about the rightness or wrongness of human acts. Society needs children to become adults who accept a moral value system and whose behaviour is guided by moral principles (Killen & Hart, 1999). As you know, however, what constitutes moral and immoral behaviour in particular situations can become a matter of heated public debate. Perhaps it is no coincidence, therefore, that the study of moral development has also proved to be controversial. The controversy begins with the foundational research of Lawrence Kohlberg.

## KOHLBERG'S STAGES OF MORAL REASONING

**Lawrence Kohlberg** (1964, 1981) founded his theory of moral development by studying *moral reasoning*—the judgments people make about what courses of action are correct or incorrect in particular situations. Kohlberg's theory was shaped by the earlier insights of Jean Piaget (1965), who sought to tie the development of moral judgment to a child's general cognitive development. In Piaget's view, as the child progresses through the stages of cognitive growth, he or she assigns differing relative weights to the *consequences* of an act and to the actor's *intentions*. For example, to the preoperational child, someone who breaks ten cups accidentally is 'naughtier' than someone who breaks one cup intentionally. As the child gets older, the actor's intentions weigh more heavily in the judgment of morality.

> Children aged 3, 4 and 5 years old were asked to make moral judgments about people's behaviour that varied along three dimensions: actions, outcomes and intentions. The *actions* were defined as either positive or negative within a particular scenario (e.g., petting vs. hitting an animal) as were the *outcomes* (e.g., the animal either cried or smiled). To vary *intentions*, the experimenters described some behaviours as intentional and others as accidental (e.g., the actor hit the pet either on purpose or by mistake). The children were asked to rate the *acceptability* of the behaviour by choosing one of a series of five faces that represented values from 'really, really bad' to 'really, really good'. The younger children based their acceptability ratings almost entirely on the outcome; only the 5-year-olds took intention into account. However, when children were asked whether the actor should be *punished*, more younger children took the actor's intention into account (Zelazo et al., 1996).

These results suggest that as children become more sophisticated cognitively, they are able to shift their focus from just outcomes to consideration of both outcomes and intentions together. However, the difference between acceptability judgments and punishment judgments suggests that some types of moral judgments allow children to consider more factors at an earlier age. As we saw earlier in the chapter, what children are specifically asked to do determines, in part, how 'mature' they seem.

Kohlberg expanded Piaget's view to define stages of moral development. Each stage is characterised by a different basis for making moral judgments (see **Table 10.8**). The lowest level of moral reasoning is based on self-interest; higher levels centre on social good, regardless of personal gain. To document these stages, Kohlberg used a series of dilemmas that pit different moral principles against one another:

**morality** A system of beliefs and values that ensures that individuals will keep their obligations to others in society and will behave in ways that do not interfere with the rights and interests of others.

## Table 10.8

Kohlberg's stages of moral reasoning

| Levels and stages | Reasons for moral behaviour |
| --- | --- |
| **I Preconventional morality** | |
| Stage 1  Pleasure/pain orientation | To avoid pain or not to get caught |
| Stage 2  Cost–benefit orientation; reciprocity—an eye for an eye | To get rewards |
| **II Conventional morality** | |
| Stage 3  Good-child orientation | To gain acceptance and avoid disapproval |
| Stage 4  Law and order orientation | To follow rules, avoid censure by authorities |
| **III Principled morality** | |
| Stage 5  Social contract orientation | To promote the society's welfare |
| Stage 6  Ethical principle orientation | To achieve justice and avoid self-condemnation |
| Stage 7  Cosmic orientation | To be true to universal principles and feel oneself part of a cosmic direction that transcends social norms |

*In one dilemma, a man named Heinz is trying to help his wife obtain a certain drug needed to treat her cancer. An unscrupulous druggist will only sell it to Heinz for ten times more than what the druggist paid. This is much more money than Heinz has and more than he can raise. Heinz becomes desperate, breaks into the druggist's store, and steals the drug for his wife. Should Heinz have done that? Why? An interviewer probes the participant for the reasons for the decision and then scores the answers*

The scoring is based on the *reasons* the person gives for the decision, not on the decision itself. For example, someone who says that the man should steal the drug because of his obligation to his dying wife or that he should not steal the drug because of his obligation to uphold the law (despite his personal feelings) is expressing concern about meeting established obligations and is scored at Stage 4.

Four principles govern Kohlberg's stage model: (1) an individual can be at only one stage at a given time; (2) everyone goes through the stages in a fixed order; (3) each stage is more comprehensive and complex than the preceding; and (4) the same stages occur in every culture. Kohlberg inherited much of this stage philosophy from Piaget, and, in fact, the progression from Stages 1 to 3 appears to match the course of normal cognitive development. The stages proceed in order, and each can be seen to be more cognitively sophisticated than the preceding. Almost all children reach Stage 3 by the age of 13.

Much of the controversy with Kohlberg's theory occurs beyond Stage 3. In Kohlberg's original view, people would continue their moral development in a steady progression beyond level 3. However, not all people attain Stages 4 to 7. In fact, many adults never reach Stage 5, and only a few go beyond it. The content of Kohlberg's later stages appears to be subjective, and it is hard to understand each successive stage as more comprehensive and sophisticated than the preceding. For example, 'avoiding self-condemnation,' the basis for moral judgments at

Stage 6, does not seem obviously more sophisticated than 'promoting society's welfare', the basis for Stage 5. Furthermore, the higher stages are not found in all cultures (Eckensberger & Zimba, 1997). We turn now to extended contemporary critiques of Kohlberg's theory that arise from considerations of gender and culture.

## GENDER AND CULTURAL PERSPECTIVES ON MORAL REASONING

Most critiques of Kohlberg's theory take issue with his claims of universality: Kohlberg's later stages have been criticised because they fail to recognise that adult moral judgments may reflect different, but equally moral, principles. In a well-known critique, **Carol Gilligan** (1982) pointed out that Kohlberg's original work was developed from observations only of boys. She argued that this research approach overlooked potential differences between the habitual moral judgments of men and women. Gilligan proposed that women's moral development is based on a standard of *caring for others* and progresses to a stage of self-realisation, whereas men base their reasoning on a standard of *justice*. Thus Gilligan's theory broadens Kohlberg's ideas about the range of considerations that may be relevant to moral judgments beyond childhood. Although we can value this contribution, research has suggested that she is incorrect to identify unique styles of moral reasoning for men and women. Let's examine the evidence.

Some studies have indicated that women mould their moral decisions to maintain harmony in their social relationships, whereas men refer more to fairness (Lyons, 1983). Even so, researchers continue to dispute whether gender differences in moral reasoning really exist at all (Jaffee & Hyde, 2000). Although men and women may arrive at their adult levels of moral development through different processes, the actual judgments they make as adults are highly similar (Boldizar et al., 1989). One possibility is that the gender differences are really consequences of the different types of social situations that arise in the lives of men and women. When asked to reason about the same moral dilemmas, men and women gave highly similar patterns of care and justice responses (Clopton & Sorell, 1993).

We can thus characterise adult reasoning about moral dilemmas as a mix between considerations of justice and considerations of caring. This mix will remain in place over most of the life span. However, as you might expect, moral judgments are affected by general changes in adult cognition. One relevant change of late adulthood is that individuals shift the grounds for their judgments away from the details of specific situations towards the use of general principles. Consequently, moral judgments come to be based more on general societal concerns—for example, 'What is the law?'—than on particular dilemmas—for example, 'Should an exception be made in this case?' (Pratt et al., 1988).

Note that debates about gender differences in moral reasoning have still mostly been carried out with respect to moral reasoning in Western cultures. Cross-cultural research has provided an important critique of this whole body of research: Comparisons between cultures suggest that it is not even possible to make universal claims about the set of situations to which moral judgments are relevant. Consider this situation: You see a stranger at the side of the road with a flat tire. Should you stop to help? Suppose you say no. Is that immoral? If you have grown up in a Western country such as Australia, U.K. or the U.S., you probably think helping, under these circumstances, is a matter of personal choice, so it isn't immoral. But if you had grown up as a Hindu in India, a culture that puts considerably more emphasis on interdependence and mutual assistance, you probably *would* view a failure to help as immoral (Miller et al., 1990).

Let's consider a study that made cross-cultural comparisons of moral reasoning:

Participants for a study on moral judgments were recruited from two locations: New Haven, Connecticut, and Mysore, in southern India. These representatives of Western and Hindu cultures were asked to respond to scenarios that made a contrast between *justice* and *interpersonal responsibility*. Suppose, for example, the only way you could deliver the wedding rings to your best friend's wedding was to steal money for a train ticket. The principle of *justice* suggests that you shouldn't steal; the principle of *interpersonal responsibility* suggests that you should honour your interpersonal commitment. If you grew up in a Western culture, you probably don't think of interpersonal responsibility in moral terms: it would be unfortunate, but not immoral, to fail to deliver the wedding rings. However, we just noted that members of the Hindu culture in India do generally consider interpersonal commitments to have a moral character. As a consequence, the researchers predicted that Indian respondents would be more likely to favour interpersonal responsibility than would U.S. respondents. As shown in **Figure 10.13**, at three different ages Indian respondents were more likely to choose the options that favoured interpersonal responsibility (Miller & Bersoff, 1992).

You can see from this example the role that culture plays in defining what is moral or immoral. If you've grown up in a Western country, you are probably surprised how strongly individuals from India believe that the commitment to the friend must be honoured—it is better to steal than to fail to deliver the rings. Note that this difference in cultural norms most likely applies beyond the two countries of the United States and India. As we will explore more fully in later chapters, the United States, like Australia, and India are typical of Western and non-Western countries with respect to their emphasis on the individual good versus the collective good.

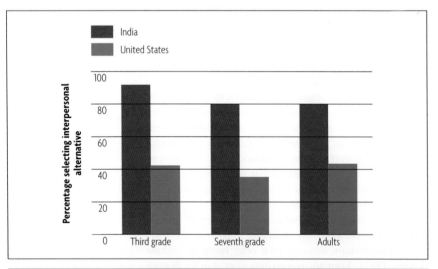

Figure 10.13

**Cross-cultural responses to moral dilemmas**
Schoolchildren and adults in India and the United States were asked to choose which courses of action they thought characters should take to resolve moral dilemmas. The participants from India were much more likely to favour interpersonal responsibility options over justice options.

## RECAP CHECKPOINT
### Moral development
- Kohlberg defined stages of moral development.
- Subsequent research has evaluated gender and cultural differences in moral reasoning.
- Different cultures have different standards for what types of situations and behaviours count as moral or immoral.

## CONCEPT QUESTIONS
1. What are the three major levels of moral reasoning in Kohlberg's theory?

2. What distinction did Carol Gilligan believe separates the moral reasoning of men and women?

3. What cultural difference explains why some moral judgments differ for groups in the United States and India?

## CRITICAL THINKING

Consider the study that examined the affects of actions, outcomes and intentions on children's moral reasoning. Why might children have been more sensitive to intentions when judging punishment versus acceptability?

# LEARNING TO AGE SUCCESSFULLY

Let us now review some of the themes of this chapter, to form a prescription for successful ageing. Early in the chapter, we encouraged you to think of development as a type of change that always brings with it gains and losses. In this light, the trick to prospering across the life span is to solidify one's gains and minimise one's losses. We saw that the rule 'use it or lose it' applies in both physical and cognitive domains of life. Many of the changes that are stereotypically associated with ageing are functions of disuse rather than decay. Our first line of advice is straightforward: Keep at it!

We also suggested that part of successful ageing means to employ *selective optimisation with compensation*

For answers go to MyPsychLab!

(Baltes et al., 1992; Freund & Baltes, 1998). As you may recall, *selective* means that people choose the most appropriate goals for themselves. *Optimisation* refers to people's exercising or training themselves in areas that are of highest priority to them. *Compensation* refers to the alternative ways that people use to deal with losses. In this chapter, we saw another good example of this process when we considered the way in which social relationships change during adulthood. Older adults select the goal of having friends who provide optimal levels of emotional support; the choice of friends must change over time to compensate for deaths or other disruptions (Carstensen, 1998; Lang & Carstensen, 1994). Although the selective optimisation perspective originated in research on the ageing process, it is a good way to characterise the choices you must make throughout your life span. You should always try to select the goals most important to you, optimise your performance with respect to those goals, and compensate when progress toward those goals is blocked. That's our final bit of advice about life span development. We hope you will age wisely and well.

How do friends contribute to successful ageing?

# SUMMARY

Chapter 10 provides a broad overview of developmental theories including how research is carried out using longitudinal designs across the lifespan. Physical, cognitive and sensory perception stages of development are outlined, particularly in childhood and adolescence. The Chapter discusses how language is learnt and develops over time, and highlights how cognitive functions mature rapidly and can be maintained across the lifespan. An overview of social skills development is presented as well as how gender and sex roles are learnt. Moral development is discussed and the chapter concludes with theories and studies on how we can age successfully.

# KEY TERMS

accommodation (p. 333)
assimilation (p. 332)
attachment (p. 347)
centration (p. 334)
child-directed speech (p. 341)
cognitive development (p. 332)
conservation (p. 334)
contact comfort (p. 349)
cross-sectional design (p. 325)
developmental age (p. 324)
developmental psychology (p. 324)
egocentrism (p. 334)
foundational theories (p. 336)
gender (p. 356)
gender identity (p. 356)

gender roles (p. 357)
generativity (p. 354)
imprinting (p. 347)
internalisation (p. 336)
intimacy (p. 352)
language-making capacity (p. 342)
longitudinal design (p. 324)
maturation (p. 328)
menarche (p. 330)
morality (p. 358)
normative investigations (p. 324)
object permanence (p. 333)
over-regularisation (p. 343)
parenting practices (p. 349)
parenting style (p. 349)

physical development (p. 326)
phonemes (p. 341)
preoperational stage (p. 333)
psychosocial stages (p. 345)
puberty (p. 330)
schemes (p. 332)
selective optimisation with
    compensation (p. 339)
selective social interaction theory (p. 354)
sensorimotor stage (p. 333)
sex differences (p. 356)
social development (p. 344)
socialisation (p. 346)
temperament (p. 346)
zygote (p. 326)

# PRACTICE TEST

1. Rachel just had her 4th birthday. She has the language ability of a 6-year-old. With respect to language ability, Rachel's _____ age is greater than her _____ age.
   a. chronological; normative
   b. developmental; cross-sectional
   c. developmental; chronological
   d. chronological; developmental

2. Professor Bale wishes to determine the impact of early-life TV viewing on college grades. To address this question, Professor Bale will most likely use a _____ research design.
   a. cross-sectional    c. chronological
   b. longitudinal    d. normative

3. You want to determine how many 'close friends' people of different ages say they have. For your project, you interview 10-, 30- and 50-year-olds. This is a _____ research design.
   a. chronological    c. cross-sectional
   b. longitudinal    d. maturational

4. Your friend Pat says, 'I'm sure Caroline recognised my voice as soon as she was born.' If Pat is Caroline's_____, Pat's claim is probably correct.
   a. mother    c. mother or father
   b. father    d. sister

5. Jack and Jill are twins. Under most circumstances, you would expect that Jack would begin his pubescent growth spurt_____Jill.
   a. at the same time as    c. a year before
   b. earlier than    d. later than

6. Thomas is beginning to have difficulty hearing high-pitched voices. If Thomas has followed an ordinary course of lifespan development, you'd guess that he is about
   a. 85    c. 60
   b. 25    d. 40

7. Tamara is a child whose thought is marked by egocentrism and centration. With respect to Piaget's theory, you infer that Tamara is in the_____ stage.
   a. sensorimotor    c. concrete operations
   b. preoperational    d. formal operations

8. As a 4-year-old, Jasnit has begun to understand certain aspects of the biological world. His initial framework for understanding is called a(n)
   a. foundational theory.    c. concrete operation.
   b. formal operation.    d. internalisation.

9. Paul and Margaret Baltes have identified a strategy for successful ageing. Which of these concepts is *not* a component of that strategy?
   a. optimimsation    c. compensation
   b. selective    d. centration

10. You are looking at fMRI scans from an experiment on working memory. Compared to his 38-year-old son Max, you would expect to see_____for 68-year-old Tony.
    a. more symmetry in activations across brain hemispheres
    b. less activation of brain areas irrelevant to the task
    c. more activation in the left hemisphere
    d. less symmetry in activations across hemispheres

11. You are examining data from an experiment on speech perception. Participant 27 was able to hear a sound distinction that is used in Hindi but not in English. You conclude the Participant 27 is *least* likely to be an
    a. infant in a Hindi language environment.
    b. adult who is a Hindi speaker.
    c. infant in an English language environment.
    d. adult who is an English speaker

12. If Siyun believes that 'mummy' applies to all women, that is an_____. If she believes that 'mummy' applies only to her own mother, that is an_____
    a. contrast, overextension
    b. underextension; hypothesis
    c. overextension; underextension
    d. hypothesis; contrast

13. 'Extension,' which requires children to use the same morpheme to mark the same concept, is an example of
    a. an overextension.    c. the principle of contrast.
    b. an operating principle.    d. a pragmatic principle.

14. According to Erik Erikson, the major crisis of age 6 to puberty is
    a. autonomy versus self-doubt.
    b. identity versus role confusion
    c. generativity versus stagnation.
    d. initiative versus guilt.

15. You observe Keith in the Strange Situation Test. He seems aloof and appears to ignore his mother when she returns to the room. Based on this evidence, you suspect that Keith is
    a. securely attached.
    b. insecurely attached—avoidant.
    c. insecurely attached—ambivalent.
    d. insecurely attached—resistant.

16. As a mother, Lisbeth is high on the dimension of demandingness and low on the dimension of responsiveness. This combination would be described as a(n) _____style of parenting.
    a. indulgent
    b. authoritative
    c. neglecting
    d. authoritarian

17. You have just made an arrangement to conduct a longitudinal study on Matthew from birth to age 40. You expect to find that Matthew will be most susceptible to peer influence at the age of_____years.
    a. 14
    b. 9
    c. 19
    d. 24

18. As people become older adults, you would generally expect them to have
    a. social interactions with more people.
    b. social interactions with fewer people.
    c. lower quality social interactions with friends.
    d. lower quality social interactions with family members.

19. Which of these statements was *not* mentioned as a recommendation for quality child care?
    a. Children should be taught social problem-solving skills.
    b. Children should have similar levels of intellectual development.
    c. Caregivers should not put undue restrictions on the children.
    d. Children should have a free choice of activities intermixed with explicit lessons.

20. Whereas_____differences are affected by culture, _____differences are affected by biology.
    a. gender; sex
    b. generativity; gender
    c. sex; identity
    d. sex; gender

21. Professor Clark wishes to study sex differences in the rate at which children learn to count from 1 to 10. He might be most interested in the
    a. way in which testosterone influences the developing brain.
    b. rate at which fathers praise their daughters when they count correctly.
    c. number of opportunities boys and girls are given to count in school.
    d. errors that boys and girls make before they learn the adult counting system.

22. You are asked to guess whether 6-year-old Chris is a girl or boy. Which observation would most lead you to believe that Chris is a girl?
    a. Chris enjoys rough-and-tumble play.
    b. Chris doesn't like to engage in social conversations.
    c. Chris most enjoys one-on-one relationships.
    d. Chris prefers to have social interactions in groups.

23. When it comes to moral behaviour, Gracie is most concerned about following rules and avoiding the censure of authorities. She is at the stage of_____morality.
    a. principled
    b. cultural
    c. preconventional
    d. conventional

24. Carol Gilligan criticised Kohlberg's theory by arguing that women are more focused on the standard of_____, whereas men are more focused on the standard of _____.
    a. caring for others; avoiding pain
    b. caring for others; justice
    c. justice; caring for others
    d. avoiding self-condemnation; justice

25. Cross-cultural analyses of moral reasoning suggest that
    a. people in some cultures never achieve preconventional morality.
    b. moral judgments within cultures are rarely consistent.
    c. different features of situations have moral relevance in different cultures.
    d. people's moral judgments across cultures are almost always the same.

## Essay Questions

1. Why do researchers believe that some aspects of cognitive development occur within specific domains of knowledge?

2. Why does deprivation and abuse have consequences for social development?

3. Why is it sometimes difficult to discriminate between sex differences and gender differences?

# WEB LINKS

http://www.chdf.org.au/
   Centre for Health Promotion

http://www.aifs.gov.au/atp/
   Australian Temperament Project

http://www.ncac.gov.au/families_and_children/families_children_index.htm
   National Childcare Accreditation Council Inc

Are you ready for the test? MyPsychLab offers dozens of ways to deepen your understanding and test your recall of the material in this chapter—including video and audio clips, simulations and activities, self-assessments, practice tests and other study materials. Specific resources available for this chapter include:

Ageing and changes in physical appearance: The visual cliff

Cross-sectional and longitudinal research designs
Life stages and approximate ages in human development
Erikson's stages
Different gender stereotypes
Major changes in important domains of adult functioning

The newborn's reflexes
Conservation
The preoperational & concrete operational stage
The sensorimotor stage
Parenting styles
Peer groups in adolescence
Physical development after 40
Gender vs. sex

To access MyPsychLab, please visit **www.pearsoned.com.au/mypsychlab**

# Has your knowledge developed?

## NOW YOU HAVE READ CHAPTER 10—ARE YOU PREPARED FOR THE EXAM?

To enhance your understanding of any of the material in your *Psychology and Life* textbook, go to **MyPsychLab: www.pearsoned.com.au/mypsychlab**.

Complete pre- and post-tests, create your own individualised study plan, watch videos and animations and listen to audio glossaries—all of which will help you understand the themes of this chapter:

- Studying development
- Physical development across the lifespan
- Cognitive development across the lifespan
- Acquiring language
- Social development across the lifespan
- Sex and gender differences
- Moral development
- Learning to age successfully

EXPLORE different gender sterotypes

Answer pre- and post-test questions on *Piaget's Theory*, *Erikson's psychosocial stages* and *physical changes in adulthood* to create your own personalised STUDY PLAN

Read all about Lawrence Kohlberg and his theory of moral development

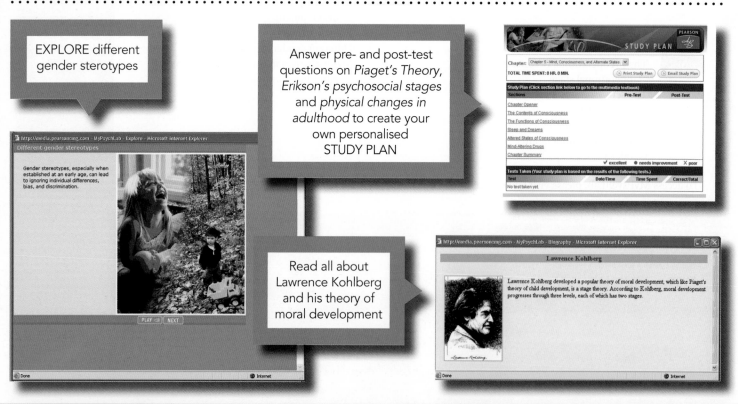

View the online version of *Chapter 10: Human Development Across the Lifespan* via your **eBook**.

It matches your textbook word-for-word, page-for-page!

Multimedia activities are placed in context throughout the eBook through the use of icons. The *Psychology and Life* site is a completely interactive experience.

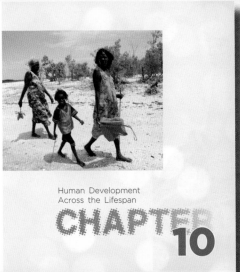

Human Development
Across the Lifespan
CHAPTER
**10**

# STUDY TIP

**Just watch!**
View streaming video clips that directly relate to the concepts covered in the chapter. Chapter 10 has videos on:

- Brain development and nutrition (p. 327)
- Classic: Eleanor Gibson and Richard Walk: Visual cliff (p. 329)
- Cochlear implants (p. 331)
- Effects of prenatal smoking on children's development (p. 327)
- Foetal alcohol damage (p. 327)
- Foetal development (p. 327)
- Infant perception (p. 328)
- Labour and birth (p. 206)
- Male menopause (p. 331)
- Menopause (p. 331)
- Period of the zygote (p. 326)
- Physical development after 40 (p. 331)
- The newborn's reflexes (p. 327)
- The pregnant body (p. 326)
- Classic: Jean Piaget: sensorimotor development (p. 333)
- Cognitive development in middle adulthood (p. 337)
- Conservation (p. 334)
- Reflexes: Babinski (p. 333)
- Reflexes: Moro (p. 333)
- Reflexes: Palmar grasp (p. 333)
- Reflexes: Sucking (p. 333)
- The preoperational & concrete operational stage (p. 333–4)
- The preschool years: egocentrism (p. 333–4)
- The sensorimotor stage (p. 333)
- Theory of mind (p. 336)
- Birds and language (p. 340)
- Child-directed speech (p. 342)
- Hand gesturing study (p. 342)
- Language learning (p. 342)
- Learning language (p. 341)
- Stimulating language development (p. 341)
- Teaching in a bilingual classroom (p. 343)
- Adolescence: identity and role development (p. 351)
- Adolescence: identity and role development and ethnicity (p. 351)
- Adolescence: identity and role development and sexual orientation (p. 351)
- Adolescence: social changes (p. 351)
- Adolescent behaviour: health and lifestyle choices (p. 351)
- Adolescent egocentrism (p. 351)
- Attachment in infants (p. 347)
- Child sexual abuse (p. 350)
- Death and dying (p. 354)
- Divorce and adolescence (p. 351)
- Early adulthood: social and personality development (p. 352)
- Effects of emotional disability on peer interactions (p. 352)
- Parenting styles (p. 349)
- Peer groups in adolescence (p. 351–2)
- Teen pregnancy (p. 352)
- Temperament: difficult (p. 346)
- Temperament: easy (p. 346)
- Temperament: inhibited (p. 346)
- Temperament: uninhibited (p. 346)
- Ageing and culture (p. 361)
- Ageing stereotypes (p. 361)
- Early gender typing (p. 357)
- Kohlberg and the Heinz dilemma (p. 358–9)
- Moral development: conventional (p. 359)
- Moral development: postconventional (p. 359)
- Moral development: preconventional (p. 359)

Page references for the textbook chapter are also provided so you know exactly what concept the video is referring to!

**What can you find in MyPsychLab?**
Self-directed tests ∗ Videos ∗ Simulations ∗ eBook ∗ Biographies ∗ Audio glossary ∗ Web links … and more—organised by chapter, section and learning objective.

# Motivation

# CHAPTER FOCUS POINTS

After studying this chapter you will have a better understanding of:

1. The principle theories behind motivation behaviour

2. How we are motivated to eat

3. The motivation behind sexual behaviour

4. Why we motivate ourselves for personal achievement

## CHAPTER CONTENTS

Your alarm clock went off this morning. You would have loved to hit the snooze button to get a few extra minutes of sleep, but you dragged yourself right out of bed. Why? Were you desperately hungry? Did you have to complete some important assignment? Had you made a date with someone who has captured your heart? When you consider the question 'Why did I get out of bed this morning?' you have arrived directly at the core question of *motivation*: What makes you act as you do? What makes you persistently try to attain some goals despite the high effort, pain and financial costs involved? Why, conversely, do you sometimes procrastinate too long before attempting to achieve other goals or give in and quit too soon?

It is the task of psychological researchers to bring theoretical rigor to such questions of motivation. How might motivational states affect the outcome of a sports competition or an exam? Why do some people become overweight and others starve themselves to death? Are our sexual behaviours determined by our genetic heritage? In this chapter, you will learn that human actions are motivated by a variety of needs—from fundamental physiological needs like hunger and thirst to psychological needs like personal achievement. But you will see that physiology and psychology are often not easy to separate. Even a seemingly biological drive such as hunger competes with an individual's need for personal control and social acceptance to determine patterns of eating.

We begin the chapter by providing you with a framework to understand general issues about the nature and study of motivation. In the second part of the chapter, we will look in depth at three types of motivation, each important in a different way and each varying in the extent to which biological and psychological factors operate. These three are hunger, sex and personal achievement.

# UNDERSTANDING MOTIVATION

**motivation** The process of starting, directing and maintaining physical and psychological activities.

**M**otivation is the general term for all the processes involved in starting, directing and maintaining physical and psychological activities. The word *motivation* comes from the Latin *movere*, which means 'to move'. All organisms move towards some stimuli and activities and away from others, as dictated by their appetites and aversions. Theories of motivation explain both the general patterns of 'movement' of each animal species, including humans, and the personal preferences and performances of the individual members of each species. Let's begin our analysis of motivation by considering the different ways in which motivation has been used to explain and predict species and individual behaviour.

What different motivational questions might be asked of this individual's behaviour?

## FUNCTIONS OF MOTIVATIONAL CONCEPTS

Psychologists have used the concept of motivation for five basic purposes:

- *To relate biology to behaviour.* As a biological organism, you have complex internal mechanisms that regulate your bodily functioning and help you survive. Why did you get out of bed this morning? You may have been hungry, thirsty or cold. In each case, internal states of deprivation trigger bodily responses that motivate you to take action to restore your body's balance.

- *To account for behavioural variability.* Why might you do well on a task one day and poorly on the same task another day? Why does one child do much better at a competitive task than another child with roughly the same ability and knowledge? Psychologists use motivational explanations when the variations in people's performance in a constant situation cannot be traced to differences in ability, skill, practice or chance. If you were willing to get up early this morning to get in some extra studying but your friend was not, we would be comfortable describing you as in a different motivational state than your friend.

- *To infer private states from public acts.* You see someone sitting on a park bench, chuckling. How can you explain this behaviour? Psychologists and laypersons are alike in typically moving from observing some behaviour to inferring some internal cause for it. People are continually interpreting behaviour in terms of likely reasons for why it occurred as it did. The same rule applies to your own behaviours. You often seek to discover whether your own actions are best understood as internally or externally motivated.

- *To assign responsibility for actions.* The concept of personal responsibility is basic in law, religion and ethics. Personal responsibility presupposes inner motivation and the ability to control your actions. People are judged less responsible for their actions when (1) they did not intend negative consequences to occur, (2) external forces were powerful enough to provoke the behaviours, or (3) the actions were influenced by drugs, alcohol or intense emotion. Thus a theory of motivation must be able to discriminate among the different potential causes of behaviour.

- *To explain perseverance despite adversity.* A final reason psychologists study motivation is to explain why organisms perform behaviours when it might be easier not to perform them. Motivation gets you to work or class on time even when you're exhausted. Motivation helps you persist in playing the game to the best of your ability even when you are losing and realise that you can't possibly win.

You now have a general sense of the circumstances in which psychologists might invoke the concept of motivation to explain and predict behaviour. Before we turn to specific domains of experience, let's consider general sources of motivation.

## SOURCES OF MOTIVATION

In 2003, AFL player Jason McCartney scored the winning goal for his team, the Kangaroos, as they defeated the Richmond Tigers. McCartney played in virtually a

What combination of internal and external motivational forces may have helped AFL player Jason McCartney to triumph over adversity and return to the sport he loved?

complete protective body stocking, to protect his body, after suffering severe burns during the 2001 Bali Bombing. Family, friends and fans feared he would not survive, let alone play AFL again, after returning to Australia in an almost unrecognisable state, and lapsing into a week-long coma. Jason fought back though, and not only made a return to AFL football, but also married his fiance in 2003.

Could you do what Jason McCartney did? Could you come back from a serious illness to challenge your body again? Do you think that whatever motivated his behaviour was something *internal* to him? Would it take a special set of life experiences for someone to persevere in this manner? Or was it something *external*, something about the situation? Would many or most people behave in this way if they were put in the same situation? Or does his behaviour represent an *interaction* of aspects of the person and features of the situation? To help you think about the sources of motivation, we will explore this distinction between internal and external forces. Let's begin with theories that explain certain types of behaviour as arising from internal biological drives.

**Drives and incentives** Some forms of motivation seem very basic: If you feel hungry, you eat; if you feel thirsty, you drink. The theory that much important behaviour was motivated by internal drives was most fully developed by theorist **Clark Hull** (1943, 1952). In Hull's view, **drives** are internal states that arise in response to an animal's physiological needs. Organisms seek to maintain a state of equilibrium, or **homeostasis**, with respect to biological conditions such as the body's temperature and energy supply (see Chapter 3, p. 79). Drives are aroused when deprivation creates disequilibrium or *tension*. These drives activate the organism toward *tension reduction*; when the drives are satisfied or reduced—when homeostasis is restored—the organism ceases to act. Thus, according to Hull, when an animal has been deprived of food for many hours, a state of hunger is aroused that motivates food-seeking and eating behaviours. The animal's responses that have led to the food goal will be reinforced because they are associated with the tension reduction that eating produces.

Can tension reduction explain all motivated behaviour? Apparently not. Consider groups of rats that have been deprived of food or water. Tension reduction would predict that they would eat or drink at their first opportunity. However, when such rats were placed in a novel environment with plenty of opportunities everywhere to eat or drink, they chose to explore instead. Only after they had first satisfied their curiosity did they begin to satisfy their hunger and thirst (Berlyne, 1960; Fowler, 1965; Zimbardo & Montgomery, 1957). In another series of studies, young monkeys spent much time and energy manipulating gadgets and new objects in their environment, apparently for the sheer pleasure of 'monkeying around,' without any rewards relevant to physiological needs (Harlow et al., 1950).

These experiments demonstrate that behaviour is not only motivated by internal drives: behaviour is also motivated by **incentives**—external stimuli or rewards that

**drives** Internal states that arise in response to a disequilibrium in an animal's physiological needs.

**homeostasis** The body's ability to maintain internal equilibrium by adjusting it's physiological processes, such as temperature, heart rate and blood pressure.

**incentives** External stimuli or rewards that motivate behaviour although they do not relate directly to biological needs.

do not relate directly to biological needs. When the rats or monkeys were attuned to objects in the environment rather than to their own internal states, they demonstrated that their behaviour was controlled by incentives. Human behaviour is also controlled by a variety of incentives. Why do you stay up late cruising the Web instead of getting a good night's sleep? Why do you watch a movie that you know will make you feel anxious or frightened? Why do you eat junk food at a party even when you're already feeling full? In each case, elements of the environment serve as incentives to motivate your behaviour.

You can see already that behaviours find their origins in a mixture of internal and external sources of motivation. Even though rats might feel biological pressure to eat or drink, they also indulge an impulse to explore a new environment. We turn now to a contemporary approach to motivation that specifically examines competing motivational states, *reversal theory*.

**Reversal theory** Michael Apter (1989, 2001) and his colleagues developed a theory that also rejects the idea of motivation as tension reduction. Instead, the theory hypothesises four pairs of *metamotivational states:* states that give rise to distinct patterns of motivation. As shown in **Table 11.1**, the pairs are placed in opposition. The theory claims that, at any given time, only one of the two states in

**reversal theory** Theory that explains human motivation in terms of reversals from one to the other opposing metamotivational states.

each pair can be operative. If you work your way through the table, you'll see how each pair defines motivational states that are incompatible. For example, imagine you are in some work-related situation. At a given moment, are you motivated to fit in or to be independent? Are you motivated to be focused on your own feelings or focused on others' feelings? This theory is known as **reversal theory** because it seeks to explain human motivation in terms of *reversals* from one to the other of the opposing states. Consider the contrast between the *paratelic* and the *telic states*. You are in a paratelic state when you engage in an activity with no goal beyond enjoying that particular activity; you are in a telic state when you engage in an activity that is important to you beyond the moment. For example, you are probably in a telic state right now as you read your textbook—you wish to acquire the material so you can do well on an exam. If, however, you take a break from studying to eat a snack or listen to a new CD, you have almost certainly gone into a paratelic state. Reversal theory, in fact, suggests that you are always in one or the other state but never both simultaneously.

At times, you have probably become very aware of the types of reversals predicted by this theory. One particularly dramatic form of reversal occurs in people who engage in high-risk activities, such as parachuting.

Why would people voluntarily jump out of airplanes—and claim to do it for fun? It is hard to understand this behaviour with respect to tension reduction because the anticipation of jumping out of an airplane increases, rather than reduces, tension. Reversal theory, however, suggests that the experience of parachuting presents a switch from a telic to a paratelic state. In the telic state, high arousal—of the type that would be experienced as you contemplate jumping out of an airplane—leads to feelings of anxiety; in the paratelic state, high arousal is experienced as great excitement. Thus a reversal from the telic to the paratelic state at the same level of arousal would create an immediate shift from great anxiety to great pleasure. To verify the existence of this immediate shift, researchers gathered data from members of two parachuting clubs. Members of the clubs reported on their feelings of anxiety and excitement in the time before, during, and after their leaps. The data showed a clear reversal: Moments before the leap, they were anxious (but not excited); moments after the parachute opened, they were excited (but not anxious). The arousal did not go away—it took on a different meaning as the parachuter reversed from the telic to the paratelic state (Apter & Batler, 1997).

Do you see how reversal theory explains the self-reports of these parachuters?

Reversal theory provides an interesting general approach to motivation. We move now to a different tradition of research on motivation, one that focuses on species-specific *instinctual* behaviours.

**Instinctual behaviours and learning** Why do organisms behave the way they do? Part of the answer is that some aspects of a species's behaviour are governed by

### Table 11.1

Principal characteristics of the four pairs of metamotivational states

| Telic | Paratelic |
|---|---|
| Serious | Playful |
| Goal-oriented | Activity-oriented |
| Prefers planning ahead | Living for the moment |
| Anxiety-avoiding | Excitement-seeking |
| Desires progress—achievement | Desires fun and enjoyment |

| Conformist | Negativistic |
|---|---|
| Compliant | Rebellious |
| Wants to keep to rules | Wants to break rules |
| Conventional | Unconventional |
| Agreeable | Angry |
| Desires to fit in | Desires to be independent |

| Mastery | Sympathy |
|---|---|
| Power-oriented | Care-oriented |
| Sees life as struggle | Sees life as cooperative |
| Tough-minded | Sensitive |
| Concerned with control | Concerned with kindness |
| Desires dominance | Desires affection |

| Autic | Alloic |
|---|---|
| Primary concern with self | Primary concern with others |
| Self-centered | Identifying with other(s) |
| Focus on own feelings | Focus on others' feelings |

Note: The terms *telic* and *paratelic* are derived from the ancient Greek word *telos*, meaning 'goal'. The terms *autic* and *alloic* are based on Greek words meaning 'self' and 'other'.

Instinctive behaviours, like the nest-building practices of the African Masked Weaver, are motivated by genetic inheritance. What instincts have theorists attributed to human practice?

**instincts**, preprogrammed tendencies that are essential for the survival of their species. Instincts provide repertoires of behaviour that are part of each animal's genetic inheritance. Salmon swim thousands of miles back to the exact stream where they were spawned, leaping up waterfalls until they come to the right spot, where the surviving males and females engage in ritualised courtship and mating. Fertilised eggs are deposited, the parents die, and, in time, their young swim downstream to live in the ocean until, a few years later, it is time for them to return to complete their part in this continuing drama. Similarly remarkable activities can be reported for most species of animals. Bees communicate the location of food to other bees, army ants go on highly synchronised hunting expeditions, birds build nests, and spiders spin complex webs—exactly as their parents and ancestors did.

Early theories of human function tended to overestimate the importance of instincts for humans. William James, writing in 1890, stated his belief that humans rely even more on instinctual behaviours than other animals (although human instincts were generally not carried out with fixed-action patterns). In addition to the biological instincts humans share with animals, a host of social instincts, such as sympathy, modesty, sociability and love, come into play. For James, both human and animal instincts were *purposive*—they served important purposes, or functions, in the organism's adaptation to its environment.

Sigmund Freud (1915) proposed that humans experience drive states arising from life instincts (including sexuality) and death instincts (including aggression). He believed that instinctive urges direct *psychic energy* to satisfy bodily needs. Tension results when this energy cannot be discharged; this tension drives people toward activities or objects that will reduce the tension. For example, Freud believed that the life and death instincts operated largely below the level of consciousness. However, their consequences for conscious thoughts, feelings and actions were profound, because of the way the instincts motivated people to make important life choices (we will expand on these ideas in Chapter 13).

By the 1920s, psychologists had compiled lists of over 10,000 human instincts (Bernard, 1924). At this same time, however, the notion of instincts as universal explanations for human behaviour was beginning to stagger under the weight of critical attacks. Cross-cultural anthropologists, such as Ruth Benedict (1959) and Margaret Mead (1939), found enormous behavioural variation between cultures. Their observations contradicted theories that considered only the universals of inborn instincts.

Most damaging to the early instinct notions, however, were behaviourist empirical demonstrations that important behaviours and emotions were learned rather than inborn. These types of demonstrations should be familiar to you from Chapter 6. We saw there that human and non-human animals alike are highly sensitive to the ways in which stimuli and responses are associated in the environment. If you want to explain why one animal performs a behaviour and another does not, you may need to know nothing more than that one animal's behaviour was reinforced and the other's was not. Under those circumstances, you don't need a separate account of motivation at all (that is, it would be a mistake to say that one animal is 'motivated' and the other is not).

Recall, however, that in Chapter 6 we also saw that the types of behaviours animals will most readily learn are determined in part by species-specific instincts. That is, each animal displays a combination of learned and instinctive behaviours. Thus, if you are asked to explain or predict an animal's behaviour, you will want to know two things: first, something about the history of its species—What adaptive behaviours are part of the organism's genetic inheritance?—and second, something about the personal history of the animal—What unique set of environmental associations has the organism experienced? In these cases, motivation resides in the effects history has on current behaviour.

One final look back to Chapter 6. We saw there that cognitively oriented researchers have challenged the belief that instincts and reinforcement history are sufficient to explain all the details of an animal's behaviour. Let's turn now to the role of expectations and cognition in motivation.

### Expectations and cognitive approaches to motivation

Consider *The Wizard of Oz* as a psychological study of motivation. Dorothy and her three friends work hard to get to the Emerald City, overcoming barriers, persisting against all adversaries. They do so because they expect the Wizard to give them what they are missing. Instead, the wonderful (and wise) Wizard makes them aware that they, not he, always had the power to fulfill their wishes. For Dorothy, *home* is not a place but a feeling of security, of comfort with people she loves; it is wherever her heart is. The courage the Lion wants, the intelligence the Scarecrow longs for, and the emotions the Tin Man dreams of are attributes they already possess. They need

**instincts** Preprogrammed tendencies that are essential to a species' survival.

to think about these attributes not as internal conditions but as positive ways in which they are already relating to others. After all, didn't they demonstrate those qualities on the journey to Oz—a journey motivated by little more than an *expectation*, an idea about the future likelihood of getting something they wanted? The Wizard of Oz was clearly among the first cognitive psychologists because he recognised the importance of people's thought processes in determining their goals and behaviours to reach them!

Contemporary psychologists use cognitive analyses to explore the forces that motivate a variety of personal and social behaviours. These psychologists share the Wizard's point of view that significant human motivation comes not from objective realities in the external world but from subjective interpretations of reality. The reinforcing effect of a reward is lost if you don't perceive that your actions obtained it. What you do now is often controlled by what you think was responsible for your past successes and failures, by what you believe is possible for you to do, and by what you anticipate the outcome of an action will be. Cognitive approaches explain why human beings are often motivated by expectations of future events.

The importance of *expectations* in motivating behaviour was developed by **Julian Rotter** (1954) in his **social-learning theory** (we touched on social learning in our discussion of observational learning in Chapter 6). For Rotter, the probability that you will engage in a given behaviour (studying for an exam instead of partying) is determined by your *expectation* of attaining a goal (getting a good grade) that follows the activity and by the *personal value* of that goal. A *discrepancy* between expectations and reality can motivate an individual to perform corrective behaviours (Festinger, 1957; Lewin, 1939). Suppose you find that your own behaviours do not match the standards or values of a group to which you belong—you might be motivated to change your behaviours to achieve a better fit with the group. You might, for example, be motivated to change your style of dress or the music to which you listen to reduce the discrepancy between expectations and reality.

How do expectations relate to internal and external forces of motivation? **Fritz Heider** (1958) postulated that the outcome of your behaviour (a poor grade, for example) can be attributed to *dispositional forces,* such as lack of effort or insufficient intelligence, or to *situational forces,* such as an unfair test or a biased teacher. These attributions influence the way you will behave. You are likely to try harder next time if you see your poor grade as a result of your lack of effort, but you may give up if you see it as resulting from injustice or lack of ability (Dweck, 1975). Thus the identification of a source of motivation as internal or external may depend, in part, on your own subjective interpretation of reality.

Let's review the various sources of motivation. We began with the observation that researchers can differentiate internal and external factors that bring about behaviours. Drives, instincts and histories of learning are all internal sources of motivation that affect behaviours in the presence of appropriate external stimuli. Once organisms begin to think about their behaviours—something humans are

particularly prone to do—expectations about what should or should not happen also begin to provide motivation. Thinking animals can choose to attribute some motivations to themselves and others to the outside world.

## A HIERARCHY OF NEEDS

We have now reviewed several sources of motivation. As a preview for the rest of the chapter, we want to return to a more global account of the domains in which motivational concepts apply. Our intent is to give you a general sense of the forces that could guide your life.

Humanist psychologist **Abraham Maslow** (1970) formulated the theory that basic motives form a **hierarchy of needs**, as illustrated in **Figure 11.1**. In Maslow's view, the needs at each level of the hierarchy must be satisfied— the needs are arranged in a sequence from primitive to advanced—before the next level can be achieved. At the bottom of this hierarchy are the basic *biological needs*, such as hunger and thirst. They must be met before any other needs can begin to operate. When biological needs are pressing, other needs are put on hold and are unlikely to influence your actions. When they are reasonably well satisfied, the needs at the next level—*safety needs*—motivate you. When you are no longer concerned about danger, you become motivated by *attachment needs*—needs to belong,

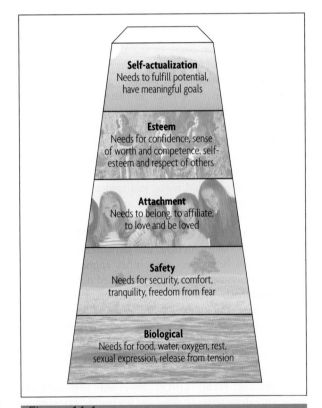

Figure 11.1

**Maslow's Hierarchy of Needs**
According to Maslow, needs at the lower level of the hierarchy dominate an individual's motivation as long as they are unsatisfied. Once these needs are adequately met, the higher needs occupy the individual's attention.

**hierarchy of needs** Maslow's view that basic human motives form a hierarchy and that the needs at each level of the hierarchy must be satisfied before the next level can be achieved.

**social-learning theory** The learning theory that stresses the role of observation and the imitation of behaviours observed in others.

Where does the need to belong, to form attachments and experience love, fit in Maslow's hierarchy?

to affiliate with others, to love, and to be loved. If you are well fed and safe and if you feel a sense of social belonging, you move up to *esteem needs*—to like oneself, to see oneself as competent and effective, and to do what is necessary to earn the esteem of others.

At the top of the hierarchy are people who are nourished, safe, loved and loving, secure, thinking and creating. These people have moved beyond basic human needs in the quest for the fullest development of their potentials, or *self-actualisation*. A self-actualising person is self-aware, self-accepting, socially responsive, creative, spontaneous, and open to novelty and challenge, among other positive attributes.

Maslow's theory is a particularly upbeat view of human motivation. At the core of the theory is the need for each individual to grow and actualise his or her highest potential. However, you know from your own experience that Maslow's strict hierarchy breaks down. You may, for example, have skipped a meal so that you could help out a friend. You may have endured the danger of a wilderness trek to boost your self-esteem. Even so, we hope Maslow's scheme will enable you to bring some order to different aspects of your motivational experiences.

We have now given you a general framework for understanding motivation. In the remainder of the chapter, we will take a closer look at three different types of behaviours that are influenced by interactions of motives: eating, sexual performance and personal achievement.

# RECAP CHECKPOINT
## Understanding motivation

- Motivation is a dynamic concept used to describe the processes directing behaviour.
- Motivational analysis helps explain how biological and behavioural processes are related and why people pursue goals despite obstacles and adversity.
- Drive theory conceptualises motivation as tension reduction.
- People are also motivated by incentives — external stimuli that are not related to physiological needs.
- Reversal theory posits opposing pairs of metamotivational states.
- Instinct theory suggests that motivation often relies on innate stereotypical responses.
- Social and cognitive psychologists emphasise the individual's perception of, interpretation of, and reaction to a situation.
- Abraham Maslow suggested that human needs can be organised hierarchically.
- Although real human motivation is more complex, Maslow's theory provides a useful framework for summarising motivational forces.

# CONCEPT QUESTIONS

For answers go to MyPsychLab!

1. As you're sitting on a bench, you see another student go running by. Which function of motivational concepts applies to how you interpret the situation?

2. What does it mean for an organism to achieve homeostasis?

3. What two major instincts were elements of Sigmund Freud's theory?

4. What distinction did Fritz Heider make with respect to explanations for outcomes?

5. What did Abraham Maslow mean by attachment needs?

# CRITICAL THINKING

Consider the experiment with members of the parachuting clubs. What could happen after they leave the airplane for the paratelic state to reverse back to the telic?

# EATING

We'd like to ask you to make a prediction. We are about to offer a slice of pizza to a student enrolled in an Introductory Psychology course. How likely do you think it is that the student will eat the slice of pizza? Are you willing to make a guess? Your response should probably be, 'I need more information.' In the last section, we gave you a way of organising the extra information you need to acquire before making such a prediction. You would want to know about *internal* information. How much has the student eaten already? Is the student trying to diet? You would also want to know about *external* information. Is the pizza tasty? Are friends there to share the pizza and conversation? You can see already that we have some work to do to explain the types of forces that might influence even a simple outcome, such as whether someone is going to eat a slice of pizza. Let's begin with some of the physiological processes that evolution has provided to regulate eating.

## THE PHYSIOLOGY OF EATING

When does your body tell you it's time to eat? You have been provided with a variety of mechanisms that contribute to your physical sense of hunger or satiety (Logue, 1991). To regulate food intake effectively, organisms must be equipped with mechanisms that accomplish four tasks: (1) detect internal food need, (2) initiate and organise eating behaviour, (3) monitor the quantity and quality of the food eaten, and (4) detect when enough food has been consumed and stop eating. Researchers have tried to understand these processes by relating them either to *peripheral* mechanisms in different parts of the body, such as stomach contractions, or to *central* brain mechanisms, such as the functioning of the hypothalamus. Let's look at these processes in more detail.

Peripheral responses   Where do sensations of hunger come from? Does your stomach send out distress signals to indicate that it is empty? A pioneering physiologist, **Walter Cannon** (1934), believed that gastric activity in an empty stomach was the sole basis for hunger. To test this hypothesis, Cannon's intrepid student A. L. Washburn trained himself to swallow an uninflated balloon attached to a rubber tube. The other end of the tube was attached to a device that recorded changes in air pressure. Cannon then inflated the balloon in Washburn's stomach. As the student's stomach contracted, air was expelled from the balloon and activated the recording device. Reports of Washburn's hunger pangs were correlated with periods when the record showed his stomach was severely contracted but not when the record showed his stomach was distended. Cannon thought he had proved that stomach cramps were responsible for hunger (Cannon & Washburn, 1912).

Although Cannon and Washburn's procedure was ingenious, later research showed that stomach contractions are not even a necessary condition for hunger. Injections of sugar into the bloodstream will stop the stomach contractions but not the hunger of an animal with an empty stomach. Human patients who have had their stomachs entirely removed still experience hunger pangs (Janowitz & Grossman, 1950), and rats without stomachs still learn mazes when rewarded with food (Penick et al., 1963). So, although sensations originating in the stomach may play a role in the way people usually experience hunger, they do not fully explain how the body detects its need for food and is motivated to eat.

Your empty stomach may not be necessary to feel hungry, but does a 'full' stomach terminate eating? Research has shown that gastric distension caused by food—but not by an inflated balloon—will cause an individual to end a meal (Logue, 1991). Thus the body is sensitive to the source of pressure in the stomach. The oral experience of food also provides a peripheral source of *satiety* cues—cues relevant to feelings of satiation or fullness. You may have noticed that you become less enthusiastic about the tastes of even your favourite foods over the course of a meal, a phenomenon called *sensory-specific satiety* (Raynor & Epstein, 2001). Foods high in calories and high in protein produce more satiety than do low-calorie and low-protein food (Johnson & Vickers, 1993; Vandewaters & Vickers, 1996). This immediate reduction in 'liking' for these types of foods may be one way in which your body regulates intake. However, the 'specific' in sensory-specific satiety means that the satiety applies to specific flavours and not to the food itself. In one experiment, participants had reached satiety for particular foods, such as pineapple or cucumber. However, when the flavours of the food were slightly altered—by the addition of vanilla-flavoured whipped cream or salt and pepper—people showed renewed interest in the foods (Romer et al., 2006). This body of research suggests that variety in food tastes—as is common in many multicourse meals—might counteract other bodily indications that you've already had enough to eat.

Why do people tend to eat more food when a variety of tastes are available?

Let's turn now to the brain mechanisms involved in eating behaviours, where information from peripheral sources is gathered together.

Central responses As is often the case, simple theories about the brain centres for the initiation and cessation of eating have given way to more complex theories. The earliest theories of the brain control of eating were built around observations of the *lateral hypothalamus (LH)* and the *ventromedial hypothalamus (VMH)*. (The location of the hypothalamus is shown in Figure 3.18 on page 77.) Research showed that if the VMH was lesioned (or the LH stimulated), the animal consumed more food. If the procedure was reversed, so that the LH was lesioned (or the VMH stimulated), the animal consumed less food. These observations gave rise to the *dual-centre model*, in which the LH was thought to be the 'hunger centre' and the VMH the 'satiety centre'.

Over time, however, the data failed to confirm this theory (Martin et al., 1991; Rolls, 1994). For example, rats with VMH lesions only over-eat foods they find palatable; they strongly avoid foods that don't taste good. Thus the VMH could not just be a simple centre for signalling 'eat more' or 'don't eat more'—the signal depends on the type of food. In fact, destruction of the VMH may, in part, have the effect of exaggerating ordinary reflex responses to food (Powley, 1977). If the rat's reflex response to good-tasting food is to eat it, its exaggerated response will be to overeat. If the rat reflexively avoids bad-tasting food by gagging or vomiting, its exaggerated response could keep the rat from eating altogether.

Let's focus on how the VMH and LH carry out the tasks assigned to them by the brain. Some of the most important information the VMH and LH use to regulate eating comes from your bloodstream (Woods et al., 1998). Sugar (in the form of glucose in the blood) and fat are the energy sources for metabolism. The two basic signals that initiate eating come from receptors that monitor the levels of sugar and fat in the blood. When stored glucose is low or unavailable for metabolism, signals from liver cell receptors are sent to the LH, where neurons acting as glucose detectors change their activity in response to this information. Other hypothalamic neurons may detect changes in free fatty acids and insulin levels in the blood. Together, these neurons appear to activate appetitive systems in the lateral zone of the hypothalamus and initiate eating behaviour. Signals that the blood has a high level of glucose or fatty acids are used by the VMH to terminate eating behaviours.

We have seen so far that you have body systems that are dedicated to getting you to start and to stop eating. You almost certainly know, however, from an enormous amount of personal experience, that your need for food depends on more than just the cues generated by your body. Let's look now at psychological factors that motivate you to eat more food or less food.

# THE PSYCHOLOGY OF EATING

You know now that your body is equipped with a variety of mechanisms that regulate the amount of food you eat. But do you eat only in response to hunger? You are likely to respond, 'Of course not!' If you think back over the last couple of days, you can probably recall several occasions on which when and what you ate had little to do with hunger. In this section on the psychology of eating, we begin by reviewing the impact of culture on what and how much you eat. Next we focus on ways in which people attempt to control their eating to have an impact on body shape and size—we explore some of the roots and consequences of obesity and dieting. We then describe how eating disorders may arise as an extreme response to concerns about body image and weight.

Cultural impact on eating How do you decide when and what you should eat? To answer this question, first think about the impact of culture. For example, people in Australia typically eat three daily meals at set times; the timing of those meals relies more on social norms than on body cues. Moreover, people often choose what to eat based on social or cultural norms. Would you say yes if you were offered a free lobster dinner? Your answer might depend on whether, for example, you are an observant Jew (in which case you would say no) or a vegetarian (in which case your answer would still depend on whether you are the type of vegetarian who eats seafood). These examples suggest immediately why culture can trump your body's cues.

Let's look more closely at the culture of eating in Australia. One important source of information is the Australian federal government, which serves a number of functions. First, the government regulates what counts as a 'serving size' and what types of nutritional information food manufacturers must provide to their customers. Second, the government provides periodic advice on the components of a healthy diet. For example, the Australian Department of Health and Ageing and the Commonwealth Scientific and Industrial Research Organisation (CSIRO) produce regular publications such as *The Total Wellbeing Diet*. This publication provides general advice about weight management and physical exercise as well as specific recommendations about how individuals can maintain a healthy diet. The government's publications reflect the current state of scientific knowledge: recommendations change over time as research advances. You can be quite certain that the dietary guidelines will change again in your lifetime. As with any other type of research-based advice, it's important for you to understand how data support the recommendations as they evolve.

Other aspects of Australian culture work against recommendations for healthy eating. For example, unhealthy food is relatively inexpensive compared to healthy food. People with limited amounts of money might find a healthy diet relatively unaffordable. This observation has led to the suggestion that people's nutrition would improve if the price differential between healthy and unhealthy food changed (Epstein et al., 2006). Consider a study in which U.S. researchers worked with an Alabama deli to decrease prices on healthy foods (Horgen & Brownell, 2002). When the healthy food cost less, people ate more of it. This type of research supports the conclusion that some barriers to healthy eating are the product of economic constraints.

In comparison, it is also important to look at the culture of eating amongst Aboriginal Australians. Aboriginals have cultural laws laid down by 'The Dreamtime' in their history (approximately 40,000 years ago) and these laws affect the types of food eaten, and also who gather or hunt what types of food. Eating habits and the way in which food is prepared or stored is also part of this custom.

Rules and laws differed from one language group to another depending on the environment and the Dreamtime stories that belonged to that area. Due to there being numerous tribes within Aboriginal culture there are countless laws about eating; however, one example is that regardless of the differing languages spoken by Indigenous Australians men and women are to eat separately. In some seasons when food is short, some people have preference over others for various types of food. Heart, liver, kidneys and other animal organs are often saved for the elders in tribal groups.

Some foods often called 'totems' have spiritual significance to some people. These animals and plants need to be protected and were often not eaten or only eaten during ceremonies. Pregnant women, boys prior to initiations and girls prior to puberty would be denied foods for sacred reasons. Certain foods are prepared by women, others by men. Yams, roots, nuts, fruit and shellfish are often prepared by women, while flesh foods such as kangaroo and emu are often prepared by men. These rules are not the same in all Aboriginal tribes. In some tribal groups the men do all the cooking, whilst in others it is the women's job. In other tribes the food prepared by a man is not eaten by a woman, and vice versa. At times of sadness (mourning) or during some ceremonies only certain people could feed particular people. For example in some areas a person who is morning may not touch food until ceremonies for the deceased are over. These examples are important to note because food in indigenous cultures represents other important sacred issues other than just nutrition.

The problem remains, however, that Australian culture provides a strong context for unhealthy eating. The most obvious comparison to other cultures is in the size of the portions we eat. For example, researchers undertook a comparison of the relative portion sizes in France and the United States to try to explain what they called the *French paradox* (Rozin et al., 2003): Although the French typically eat diets with more total fat than do people in the United States, the French are nonetheless considerably less likely to be overweight. To address this paradox, the researchers measured portion sizes in restaurants in Philadelphia and in Paris. On average, the portions in Philadelphia were 25 percent larger. The researchers also looked at ingredients in cookbook recipes. U.S. recipes called for more meat;

French recipes called for more vegetables. Consider this consequence as we move to a discussion of obesity and dieting: There are about a third as many obese people in France as there are in the United States and Australia, which are the two leading countries with increased obesity rates in the Western world (Rozin et al., 2003).

Obesity and dieting Psychologists have spent a good deal of time considering circumstances that have given rise to what has often been labelled an 'epidemic' of obesity. To determine who is overweight and who is obese, researchers often turn to a measure called *body mass index (BMI)*. To calculate BMI, one divides an individual's weight in kilograms by the square of height in metres. For example, someone who weighed 154 lbs and was 5'7" would have a BMI of 24.2. (154 lbs = 69.8 kilograms. 5'7" = 1.70 metres. $69.8/(1.70)^2 = 24.2$. You can also use Google to find a BMI calculator on the Web.) In most instances, individuals who have BMIs between 25 to 29.9 are considered overweight. Those individuals with BMIs 30 and above are considered obese. The 1999-2000 Australian Diabetes, Obesity and Lifestyle Study indicated over 7 million adult Australians aged 25 years and over (60 percent) were overweight. Of these, over 2 million (21 percent) were obese. In comparison, roughly 71 percent of adult men and 62 percent of the adult women in the United States are overweight or obese (Ogden et al., 2006). Among children and adolescents, approximately 18.2 percent of boys and 16.0 percent of girls are overweight or obese in both countries.

These figures suggest why there's a certain urgency to answer the question, Why do people become overweight? It probably will not surprise you, as you have seen throughout *Psychology and Life*, that the answer lies partly in nature and partly in nurture. This chapter's Psychology In Your Life box describes the strong case for 'nature': Some people have a genetic predisposition toward obesity. However, even a biological predisposition may not be enough to 'cause' a particular person to become overweight. What matters, in addition, is the way in which an individual *thinks* about food and eating behaviours. Early research on psychological aspects of eating focused on the extent to which overweight individuals are attentive to their bodies' internal hunger cues versus food in the external environment (Schachter, 1971a). The suggestion was that, when food is available and prominent, overweight individuals ignore the cues their bodies give them. This theory proved to be insufficient, however, because weight itself does not always predict eating patterns. That is, not all people who are overweight have the same psychological makeup with respect to eating behaviours. Let's see why.

**Janet Polivy** and **Peter Herman** have proposed that the critical dimension that underlies the psychology of eating behaviours is *restrained* versus *unrestrained* eating (Polivy & Herman, 1999). *Restrained* eaters put constant limits on the amount of food they will let themselves eat: they are chronically on diets; they constantly worry about food. Although obese people may be more likely to report these kinds of thoughts and behaviours, individuals can be restrained eaters whatever their body size. How

# PSYCHOLOGY *in your life*

## HOW DOES GENETICS CONTRIBUTE TO OBESITY?

Students often wonder whether they are fighting a battle with their genes to maintain a healthy weight. In fact, some of them are correct to believe that they may have a genetic predisposition toward obesity. Researchers have provided ample evidence that people are born with innate tendencies to be lighter or heavier. For example, studies of identical twins have revealed great similarity in their overall weight (Allison et al., 1994; Stunkard et al., 1990). Part of this similarity may be explained by the finding that the rate at which an individual's body burns calories to maintain basic functions, the individual's *resting metabolic rate*, is also highly heritable (Bouchard et al., 1989). Thus some people are innately predisposed to burn a lot of calories just through ordinary day-to-day activities; others are not. Those who are not are more at risk for weight gain.

Recently, researchers have discovered some of the actual genetic mechanisms that may predispose some individuals to obesity (Gura, 2000; Marx, 2003). For example, a gene has been isolated that appears to control signals to the brain that enough fat has been stored in the body in the course of a meal—so the individual should stop eating (Zhang et al., 1994). The gene influences the production of a hormone called *leptin*.

Recall from Chapter 5 that cannabinoids in your brain play a role in stimulating appetite (Kirkham, 2005). Leptin works in opposition to those cannabinoids

to keep appetite under control (Jo et al., 2005). If leptin is not available to balance these cannabinoids, it is likely that individuals will continue to eat. Thus the gene that controls leptin appears to have a critical influence on weight regulation and the potential for obesity. In fact, researchers have discovered small populations of obese individuals with mutations in this gene; the mutation appears to explain their obesity (Jackson et al., 1997; Montague et al., 1997). Because these mutations are extremely rare, they cannot account for the vast majority of cases of obesity. Even so, the confirmation that leptin plays a role in weight regulation has encouraged researchers' efforts to identify and understand other weight-related genes.

Research by Professor George Muscat at The University of Queensland has also found that the activation of the gene, called PPARd, in muscle cells increases fat (lipid) metabolism and the production of HDL or 'good' cholesterol. This is viewed as an important breakthrough for the treatment of obesity because it identifies a 'drugable' gene that plays a key role in increasing metabolic rate and reducing cellular energy stores in muscle cells (Muscat, et al, 2003).

Recent research has also focused on a gene called *GAD2* (Boutin & Frougel, 2005). GAD2 helps regulate the amount of the neurotransmitter GABA that is present in the hypothalamus. In general, when more GABA is available, appetite is increased.

For that reason, people who have a form of GAD2 that allows more GABA to be available may be at risk for overeating. You can see that GAD2 is not directly an *obesity* gene. Rather, it has an indirect influence on obesity through its direct influence on GABA. Researchers expect to find a range of genes that similarly have an indirect impact on obesity.

Genetic research holds out the promise of innovative solutions to obesity. Researchers hope, for example, that an understanding of the link between genes and weight regulation will enable them to provide new drug treatments (Campfield et al., 1998; Gura, 2003). Some of the early efforts have been discouraging: Research manipulating leptin has yet to show a great impact on weight loss. However, given constant leaps forward in genetic understanding, scientists continue to form new hypotheses about how they might intervene in the body's mechanisms for weight regulation (Gura, 2000).

Nonetheless, even the most optimistic researchers provide words of caution: 'Innovative drugs will be most effective when they are used as adjuncts to, rather than substitutes for, lifestyle changes to improve the metabolic fitness, health, and quality of life for obese individuals' (Campfield et al., 1998, p. 1387). Put another way, no matter how much we come to understand *nature*, we must always be aware that *nurture* still plays a critical role in our life outcomes.

---

do people gain weight if they are constantly on a diet? Research suggests that when restrained eaters become *disinhibited*—when life circumstances cause them to let down their restraints—they tend to indulge in high-calorie binges. Unfortunately, many types of life circumstances appear to lead restrained eaters to become disinhibited. Disinhibition will occur, for example, when restrained eaters are made to feel stress about their capabilities and self-esteem (Greeno & Wing, 1994; Tanofsky-Kraff et al., 2000). In fact, one type of stress is the *anticipation* of being on a strict diet.

Based on self-evaluations of their behaviours and thoughts with respect to food and dieting, female university students were classified as either restrained (17 women) or unrestrained (24 women) eaters. The students were told they were taking part in a study 'investigating the effects of food deprivation on taste perception' (Urbszat et al., 2002, p. 398). When they arrived for the experiment, half of the students were asked to undertake a low-calorie diet—approved by 'the Canadian Government and the University of Toronto'—for 1 week. Participants in both the *diet* and *no-diet* conditions were then asked to perform taste tests on three plates of cookies. The participants believed that these taste tests were the baseline data for the study of taste perception. In fact, the researchers were measuring the total grams of cookies each participant consumed. The results of the study are shown in **Figure 11.2**. For unrestrained eaters, it made no difference whether they were anticipating a strict diet. However, for the restrained eaters, anticipation of the diet led them to eat more than twice as many of the cookies.

**anorexia nervosa** An eating disorder in which an individual weighs less than 85% of her or his expected weight but still expresses intense fear of becoming fat.

**bulimia nervosa** An eating disorder characterised by binge eating followed by measures to purge the body of excess calories.

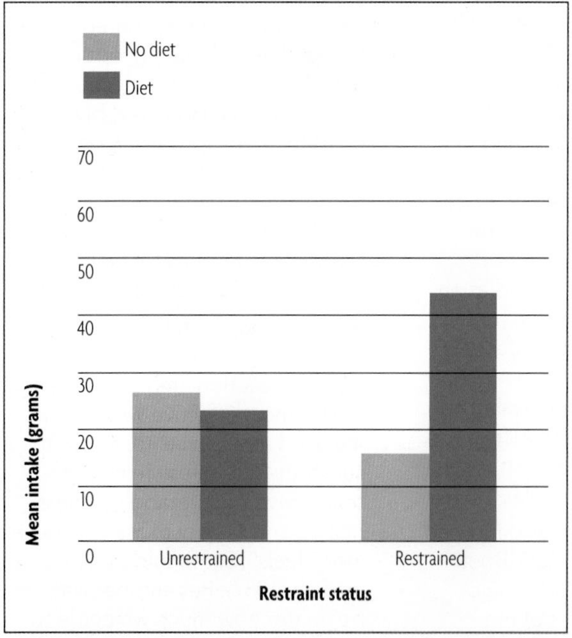

Figure 11.2

**The effects of anticipated diets**
Restrained and unrestrained eaters sampled cookies to rate their taste. Half of the women in each group had agreed to undertake a reduced-calorie diet for 1 week. For unrestrained eaters, the amount of cookies (in grams) they ate while making the taste ratings was unaffected by the anticipation of a diet. However, those restrained eaters who anticipated dieting ate more than twice as much as their no-diet peers.

This result suggests why diets are often unsuccessful for restrained eaters. As the researchers note, their diets can be broken even 'by the prospect of not being able to eat forbidden food' (Urbszat et al., 2002, p. 399).

You see now why it might be difficult for people to lose weight once they have become overweight. Many overweight people report themselves as constantly on diets—they are often restrained eaters. If stressful life events occur that cause these eaters to become disinhibited, binge eating can easily lead to weight gain. Thus the psychological consequences of being constantly on a diet can, paradoxically, create circumstances that are more likely to lead to weight gain than to weight loss. In the next section, we will see how these same psychological forces can lead to health- and life-threatening eating disorders.

**Eating disorders and body image** One finding about body image is that the group of people who believe themselves to be overweight is larger than the group of people who are actually overweight (Brownell & Rodin 1994). When the disparity between people's perceptions of their body image and their actual size becomes too large, they may be at risk for *eating disorders*. **Anorexia nervosa** is diagnosed when an individual weighs less than 85 percent of her or his expected weight but still expresses an intense fear of becoming fat (*DSM-IV-TR*, 2000). The behaviour of people diagnosed with **bulimia nervosa** is characterised by binges—periods of intense, out-of-control eating—followed by measures to purge the body of the excess calories—self-induced vomiting, misuse of laxatives, fasting, and so on (*DSM-IV-TR*, 2000). Sufferers from anorexia nervosa may also binge and then purge as a way of minimising calories absorbed. Both of these syndromes can have serious medical consequences. In the worst cases, sufferers may starve to death.

The prevalence of anorexia among women in late adolescence and early adulthood is about 0.5 percent (*DSM-IVTR*, 2000; Hoek & Van Hoeken, 2003). About 1 percent of the women in this same age group suffer from bulimia (*DSM-IV-TR*, 2000). Women suffer from both diseases at approximately 10 times the rate of men.

Why do people begin to starve themselves to death, and why are most of those people women? There is some evidence that a predilection toward eating disorders may be genetically transmitted (Kortegaard et al., 2001). Much research attention, however, has focused on women's expectations for their ideal weight as generated by society and the media (Durkin & Paxton, 2002; Wertheim et al., 1997). For example, many of the magazines that are marketed specifically to women put great emphasis on weight loss; the same is not true for the magazines that men read (Andersen & DiDomenico, 1992). Thus women may get more cultural support for their belief that they are overweight than do men. The belief that eating disorders follow, in part, from cultural forces has also received support from a number of analyses that have demonstrated important cultural differences.

A sample of 219 students from the University of Vermont and 349 students from the University of Ghana were asked a number of questions about their eating and dieting practices. These surveys revealed, for example, that although roughly the same number of the university-age men in the two countries had ever been on a diet (United States, 5.3 percent; Ghana, 6.1 percent) considerably more U.S. women (43.5 percent) had undertaken diets than had Ghanian women (13.3 percent). The students were also asked to choose which of the figures from **Figure 11.3** best represented what they considered to be the ideal male and female bodies. The students' average ratings are presented in **Figure 11.4**. What you can see is that the ratings for men are pretty consistent across raters (that is, men and women) and countries. Compare the average ratings to those in Figure 11.3. The 'ideal' male lies between M5 and M6, but closer to M5. However, the ratings for the ideal woman's body differed from the United States to Ghana by about a full point. Students in the United States idealised a body a bit slimmer than F5; Ghanians chose something closer to F6 (Cogan et al., 1996).

How might these differences be explained? The researchers suggest that in Ghana, as well as in other African countries, not everyone can *afford* to be overweight: 'fat is associated with wealth and abundance' (Cogan et al., 1996, p. 98). As you can see in Figure 11.4, the positive association between size and prosperity is particularly applied to women, and particularly by Ghanian men.

Within the United States, it is equally easy to find group differences in judgments about body size. For example, in one study, white university students revealed themselves to be less satisfied with their bodies than did their black peers. In addition, when asked to choose a drawing to represent their preferred size, white students chose smaller figures than black students (Aruguete et al., 2005). Similarly, when black and white university women rated photographs of thin, average and large models, only the white women rated the large models lower (compared to the thin and average models) on dimensions such as attractiveness, intelligence and popularity (Hebl & Heatherton, 1998).

Against this background, you will probably not be surprised to learn that white females are also more likely to suffer from eating disorders than are African American females. One study involved 985 white women and 1,061 African American women who were all about 21 years of age (Striegel-Moore et al., 2003). In those groups, 1.5 percent of the white women had suffered from anorexia nervosa at some point in their lives; no African American women had experienced that disorder. Bulimia nervosa had affected 2.3 percent of the white women but only 0.4 percent of the African American women. Fewer studies have examined other racial and ethnic groups, but evidence to date suggests that eating disturbances are also less frequent in Asian Americans than whites but equally common among Hispanic females as among

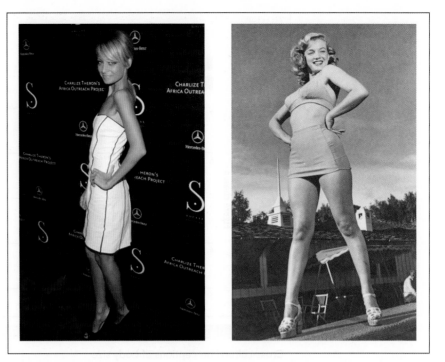

What do these photographs of Nicole Richie and Marilyn Monroe suggest about changes over time in how thin women must be for the media to promote them as sexy?

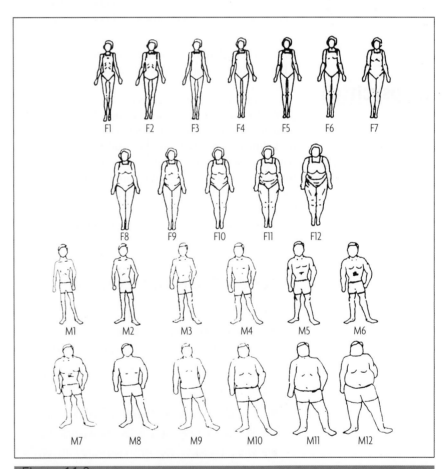

Figure 11.3

**Judgments of body size**
Which picture do you believe best represents the U.S. ideal for a woman? For a man?

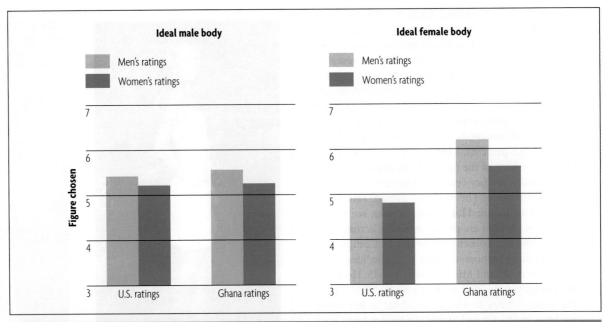

**Figure 11.4**

**Cross-cultural perceptions of body size**
Students from the University of Vermont and the University of Ghana indicated which of the figures from Figure 11.3 best represented what they considered to be the ideal male and female bodies. The students' ratings for male bodies are largely consistent across raters (that is, men and women) and countries. However, the ratings for the ideal woman's body differed from the United States to Ghana by about a full point. Ghanian men gave even higher ratings than Ghanian women.

For answers go to MyPsychLab!

**mypsychlab** *where learning comes to life!*

whites. For each of these findings, researchers try to draw a link between cultural values about body size and dieting behaviours.

A final note: right now, you're likely to be part of a particular culture that promotes eating disorders. Women in high school and university tend to suffer from anorexia or bulimia more than do non-students. In university settings, women may solve the tension between wanting to look attractive and wanting to eat and drink with their friends by bingeing—enjoying the party—and then purging—eliminating the calories (Rand & Kuldau, 1992). You should be aware that university life provides this dangerous potential.

## RECAP CHECKPOINT

### Eating

• The body has a number of mechanisms to regulate the initiation and cessation of eating.

• Cultural norms have an impact on what and how much people eat.

• If individuals become restrained eaters, their diets may result in weight gain rather than weight loss.

• Eating disorders are life-threatening illnesses that may arise from cultural pressure and misperceptions of body image.

## CONCEPT QUESTIONS

1. What is sense-specific satiety?

2. What evidence suggests that the VMH plays a different role in eating from that suggested by the dual-centre model?

3. What pattern of eating do restrained eaters generally follow?

4. What are the symptoms of bulimia nervosa?

## CRITICAL THINKING

Recall the study that demonstrated the impact of anticipated diets on food consumption. Why did the researchers lead the students to believe that the study was focused on taste perception?

# SEXUAL BEHAVIOURS

Your body physiology makes it essential that you think about food every day. But what about sex? It's easy to define the biological function of sex—reproduction—but does that explain the frequency with which you think about sexual behaviours? When asked how often they think about sex, 54 percent of adult men and 19 percent of adult women report they think about sex at least once every day (Michael et al., 1994). How can we explain the frequency with which people think about sex? How do thoughts about sex relate to sexual behaviours?

The question of motivation, once again, is the question of why people carry out certain ranges of behaviour. As we already acknowledged, sexual behaviours are biologically necessary only for reproduction. Thus, although eating is essential to individual survival, sex is not. Some animals and humans remain celibate for a lifetime without apparent detriment to their daily functioning. But reproduction is crucial to the survival of the species as a whole. To ensure that effort will be expended toward reproduction, nature has made sexual stimulation intensely pleasurable. An orgasm serves as the ultimate reinforcer for the energy expended in mating.

This potential for pleasure gives to sexual behaviours motivating power well beyond the need for reproduction. Individuals will perform a great variety of behaviours to achieve sexual gratification. But some sources of sexual motivation are external. Cultures establish norms or standards for what is acceptable or expected sexual behaviour. Whereas most people may be motivated to perform behaviours that accord with those norms, some people achieve their sexual satisfaction primarily by violating them.

In this section, we will first consider some of what is known about the sex drive and mating behaviour in non-human animals. Then we shift our attention to selected issues in human sexuality.

## NON-HUMAN SEXUAL BEHAVIOURS

The primary motivation for sexual behaviours in non-human animals is reproduction. For species that use sex as a means of reproduction, evolution has generally provided two sexual types, males and females. The female produces relatively large eggs (which contain the energy store for the embryo to begin its growth), and the male produces sperm that are specialised for motility (to move into the eggs). The two sexes must synchronise their activity so that sperm and egg meet under the appropriate conditions, resulting in conception.

Sexual arousal is determined primarily by physiological processes. Animals become receptive to mating largely in response to the flow of hormones controlled by the pituitary gland and secreted from the *gonads*, the sex organs. In males, these hormones are known as *androgens*, and they are continuously present in sufficient supply so that males are hormonally ready for mating at almost any time. In the females of many species, however, the sex hormone *oestrogen* is released according to regular time cycles of days or months, or according to seasonal changes. Therefore, the female is not always hormonally receptive to mating.

What factors determine the sexual behaviours of most species?

These hormones act on both the brain and genital tissue and often lead to a pattern of predictable *stereotyped sexual behaviour* for all members of a species. If, for example, you've seen one pair of rats in their mating sequence, you've seen them all. The receptive female rat darts about the male until she gets his attention. Then he chases her as she runs away. She stops suddenly and raises her rear, and he enters her briefly, thrusts and pulls out. She briefly escapes him and the chase resumes—interrupted by 10 to 20 intromissions before he ejaculates, rests awhile, and starts the sex chase again. Apes also copulate only briefly (for about 15 seconds). For sables, copulation is slow and long, lasting for as long as 8 hours. Predators, such as lions, can afford to indulge in long, slow copulatory rituals—as much as every 30 minutes over 4 consecutive days. Their prey, however, such as antelope, copulate for only a few seconds, often on the run (Ford & Beach, 1951).

Sexual arousal is often initiated by stimuli in the external environment. In many species, the sight and sound of ritualised display patterns by potential partners is a necessary condition for sexual response. Furthermore, in species as diverse as sheep, bulls and rats, the novelty of the female partner affects a male animal's behaviour. A male that has reached sexual satiation with one female partner may renew sexual activity when a new female is introduced (Dewsbury, 1981). Touch, taste and smell can also serve as external stimulants for sexual arousal. As we described in Chapter 4, some species secrete chemical signals, called *pheromones,* that attract suitors, sometimes from great distances (Carazo et al., 2004; DeCock & Matthysen 2005). In many species, the female emits pheromones when her fertility is optimal (and hormone level and sexual interest are peaking). These secretions are unconditioned stimuli for arousal and attraction in the males of the species, who have inherited the tendency to be aroused by the stimuli. When captive male rhesus monkeys smell the odour of a sexually receptive female in an adjacent cage, they respond with a variety of sex-related physiological changes, including an increase in the size of their testes (Hopson, 1979).

Although sexual response in non-human animals is largely determined by innate biological forces, this still leaves room for 'cultural' aspects to affect choices of mate. Consider the sailfin molly.

Under most circumstances, the female sailfin mollies from the Comal River in Texas show a mating preference for larger males. However, what happens when a female sailfin molly observes another female showing a preference for a smaller male? To answer this question, researchers arranged a set of tanks so that female sailfin mollies swam in a large tank that had two smaller tanks at each end (Witte & Noltemeier, 2002). In the initial phase of the experiment, a large and a small male fish were put into small tanks at either end. As seen in **Figure 11.5**, the females spent considerably more time swimming in proximity to the larger male. In the second phase of the experiment, a second female was placed in another small tank so that she appeared to be swimming near the smaller of the two males. The original female had 20 minutes to observe the second female fraternising with the smaller male. In the final phase of the experiment, the researchers removed the second female and again observed the original females' preferences. As seen in Figure 11.5, in the second preference test the pattern had largely reversed. The female sailfin mollies were now spending most of their time swimming near the smaller males.

**sexual arousal** The motivational state of excitement and tension brought about by physiological and cognitive reactions to erotic stimuli.

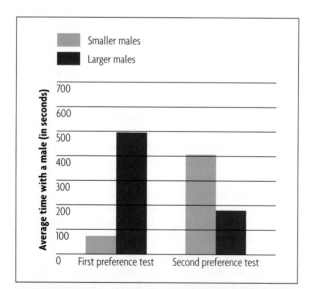

Figure 11.5

**Female sailfin mollies' mate selection**
Researchers calculated how long female sailfin mollies swam in proximity to larger versus smaller male fish. In the first preference test, the females spent much more time swimming near the larger fish. Next, the original females observed a second female swim close to the smaller male for 20 minutes. In the second preference test, which took place after those 20 minutes, the original females reversed their original pattern to spend more time close to the smaller males.

Are you surprised to learn that innocent fish swimming in aquariums are paying attention to which other fish have been judged desirable and undesirable? This experiment sets the stage for our discussion of human sexuality. We will soon see that researchers believe that human sexual response is also shaped both by our evolutionary history and the preferences of those around us.

## HUMAN SEXUAL AROUSAL AND RESPONSE

Hormonal activity, so important in regulating sexual behaviour among other animal species, has little effect on sexual receptiveness or gratification in the majority of men and women (LeVay & Valente, 2002). In women, hormones play an important role in controlling the cycles of ovulation and menstruation. However, individual differences in hormone levels, within normal limits, are not predictive of the frequency or quality of sexual activity. For men, the hormone *testosterone* is necessary for sexual arousal and performance. Most healthy men from ages 18 to at least 60 have sufficient testosterone levels to experience normal sex drives. Once again, individual variation in these levels among men, within normal limits, is not related to sexual performance.

**Sexual arousal** in humans is the motivational state of excitement and tension brought about by physiological and cognitive reactions to erotic stimuli. *Erotic stimuli*, which may be physical or psychological, give rise to sexual excitement or feelings of passion. Sexual arousal induced by erotic stimuli is reduced by sexual activities that are perceived by the individual as satisfying, especially by achieving orgasm.

Researchers have studied sexual practices and sexual responses in non-human animals for several decades, but for many years studies of similar behaviours in humans were off limits. **William Masters** and **Virginia Johnson** (1966, 1970, 1979) broke down this traditional taboo. They legitimised the study of human sexuality by directly observing and recording, under laboratory conditions, the physiological patterns involved in ongoing human sexual performance. By doing so, they explored not what people said about sex but how individuals actually reacted or performed sexually.

For their direct investigation of the human response to sexual stimulation, Masters and Johnson conducted controlled laboratory observations of thousands of volunteer males and females during tens of thousands of sexual response cycles of intercourse and masturbation. Four of the most significant conclusions drawn from this research are that (1) men and women have similar patterns of sexual response; (2) although the sequence of phases of the sexual response cycle is similar in the two sexes, women are more variable, tending to respond more slowly but often remaining aroused longer; (3) many women can have multiple orgasms, whereas men rarely do in a comparable time period; and (4) penis size is generally unrelated to any aspect of sexual performance (except in the male's attitude toward having a large penis).

Four phases were found in the human sexual response cycle: excitement, plateau, orgasm and resolution (see **Figure 11.6**).

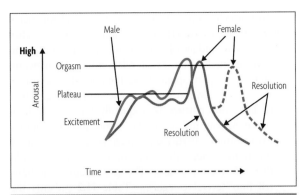

## Figure 11.6

**Phases of human sexual response**
The phases of human sexual response in males and females have similar patterns. The primary differences are in the time it takes for males and females to reach each phase, and in the greater likelihood that females will achieve multiple orgasms.

- In the excitement phase (lasting from a few minutes to more than an hour), there are vascular (blood vessel) changes in the pelvic region. The penis becomes erect and the clitoris swells; blood and other fluids become congested in the testicles and vagina; a reddening of the body, or sex flush, occurs.
- During the plateau phase, a maximum (though varying) level of arousal is reached. There are rapidly increased heartbeat, respiration, and blood pressure, increased glandular secretions, and both voluntary and involuntary muscle tension throughout the body. Vaginal lubrication increases and the breasts swell.
- During the orgasm phase, males and females experience a very intense, pleasurable sense of release from the sexual tension that has been building. Orgasm is characterised by rhythmic contractions that occur approximately every eight-tenths of a second in the genital areas. Respiration and blood pressure reach very high levels in both men and women, and heart rate may double. In men, throbbing contractions lead to ejaculation, an 'explosion' of semen.
- During the resolution phase, the body gradually returns to its normal pre-excitement state, with both blood pressure and heartbeat slowing down. After one orgasm, most men enter a refractory period, lasting anywhere from a few minutes to several hours, during which no further orgasm is possible. With sustained arousal, some women are capable of multiple orgasms in fairly rapid succession.

Although Masters and Johnson's research focused on the physiology of sexual response, perhaps their most important discovery was the central significance of *psychological* processes in both arousal and satisfaction. They demonstrated that problems in sexual response often have psychological, rather than physiological, origins and can be modified or overcome through therapy. Of particular concern is the inability to complete the response cycle and achieve gratification. Often the source of the

How did William Masters and Virginia Johnson legitimise the study of human sexuality?

inability is a preoccupation with personal problems, fear of the consequences of sexual activity, anxiety about a partner's evaluation of one's sexual performance, or unconscious guilt or negative thoughts. However, poor nutrition, fatigue, stress and excessive use of alcohol or drugs can also diminish sexual drive and performance.

We have now reviewed some physiological aspects of human sexuality and sexual arousal. But we have not yet considered the forces that give rise to *differences* in sexual expression. We begin with the idea that the goal of reproduction ensures different patterns of sexual behaviour for men and for women.

## THE EVOLUTION OF SEXUAL BEHAVIOURS

For non-human animals, we have already seen that the pattern of sexual behaviours was largely fixed by evolution. The main goal is reproduction—preservation of the species—and sexual behaviours are highly ritualised and stereotyped. Can the same claim be made for general patterns of human sexual behaviours?

Evolutionary psychologists have explored the idea that men and women have evolved to have different *strategies* that underlie sexual behaviour (Buss, 2004). To describe these strategies, we have to remind you of some of the realities of human reproduction. Human males could reproduce hundreds of times a year if they could find enough willing mates. To produce a child, all they need to invest is a teaspoon of sperm and a few minutes of intercourse. Women can reproduce at most about once a year, and each child then requires a huge investment of time and energy. (Incidentally, the world record for the number of times a woman has given birth falls short of 50, but men have fathered many more children. A Moroccan despot, King Ismail the Blood-Thirsty, had over 700 children, and the first emperor of China is said to have fathered over 3,000; both had large harems.)

Thus, when reproduction is a goal, eggs are the limited resource and males compete for opportunities to fertilise them. The basic problem facing a male animal is to maximise the number of offspring he produces, by mating with the largest number of females possible. But the basic problem facing a female animal is to find a high-quality male to ensure the best, healthiest offspring from her limited store of eggs. Furthermore, human offspring take so long to mature and are so helpless while growing that substantial **parental investment** is required (Bell, 2001; Wright, 1994). Mothers and fathers must spend time and energy raising the children—unlike fish or spiders, which simply lay eggs and depart. Females thus have the problem of selecting not just the biggest, strongest, smartest, highest-status, most thrilling mate but also the most loyal, committed partner to help raise their children.

One evolutionary psychologist, **David Buss** (2004), has suggested that men and women evolved different strategies, emotions and motivations for short-term mating versus long-term mating. The male strategy of seducing and abandoning as many women as possible—showing signs of loyalty and commitment and then leaving—is a short-term strategy. The male strategy of staying committed to the female and investing in the offspring is a long-term strategy. The female strategy of attracting a loyal male who will stay to help raise her children is a long-term strategy. The female strategy of acquiring resources or obtaining men of high status is a short-term strategy. Because these claims about men's and women's differing strategies are based on evolutionary analyses, researchers have sought cross-cultural data to support them. For example, one study involved over 16,000 participants from 52 nations (Schmitt, 2003). The men and women in the study provided information about their interest in short-term sexual relationships. Across the whole sample, men consistently reported greater desire for sexual variety than did women. This result supports the evolutionary claim that men's and women's different reproductive roles has an impact on sexual behaviour.

Researchers have provided a variety of types of evidence to support predictions of evolutionary theory. Consider how men's and women's mating strategies could give rise to different experiences of jealousy. According to evolutionary theory, a woman should experience jealousy when she suspects that her partner might no longer feel committed to providing resources to raise her children—these concerns focus on *emotional involvement*. By contrast, a man should experience jealousy when he suspects that he is being burdened by children with whom he has no genetic relationship—these concerns focus on *sexual infidelity*.

parental investment The time and energy parents must spend raising their offspring.

To test evolutionary theory's predictions about men's and women's experiences of jealousy, a researcher asked male and female participants to recall or imagine a committed heterosexual relationship (Schützwohl, 2006). The participants were then asked to consider this scenario, with sex-appropriate terms: 'Imagine that of late your partner is frequently tardy in coming home. At your insistence, s/he admits meeting another man/woman.' Participants then generated a list of questions—under these circumstances, what would they ask their partners? The participants' questions fell into several categories. **Table 11.2** presents the categories relevant to evolutionary theory: Emotional involvement questions and sexual infidelity questions. **Figure 11.7** shows the percentage of men and women who wished to ask each type of question. As you can see, women were much more likely to devise questions based on emotional involvement; men were much more likely to devise questions based on sexual infidelity.

Does this pattern seem familiar from your own experiences of jealousy? This research illustrates how important aspects of human lives may be guided by our evolutionary history.

## Table 11.2

Questions for an unfaithful partner

| Emotional involvement questions | |
|---|---|
| • Other referent | Do you love him? |
| | Have you fallen in love with her? |
| • Self-referent | Do you still love me? |
| | Don't you love me anymore? |
| Sexual infidelity questions | Did you have sex? |
| | Have you slept with him? |

Adapted from a study by Achim Schützwohl, 'Sex differences in jealousy: Information search and cognitive preoccupation,' *Personality and Individual Differences*, Science Direct online.

Although research supports many of the predictions of the evolutionary account of human sexual behaviours, other theorists believe that the account greatly underestimates the role of culture (Angier, 1999; Baumeister & Twenge, 2002). For example, women demonstrate greater *erotic plasticity* than men: women show greater variation in sexual responses and sexual behaviours than men do (Baumeister, 2000). These variations appear, in large part, to be a consequence of cultural constraints (Hyde & Durik, 2000). Consider the 'sexual revolution' of the 1960s: changes in sexual behaviour were brought about by women's increased willingness to engage in casual sexual relations. What had changed was not, of course, women's evolutionary history but, rather, cultural attitudes toward the expression of sexuality.

Although the evolutionary approach explains some aspects of human sexual behaviour, the critique calls attention to variability imposed by culture. Norms of sexual behaviour are highly sensitive to time and place. We turn now to sexual norms.

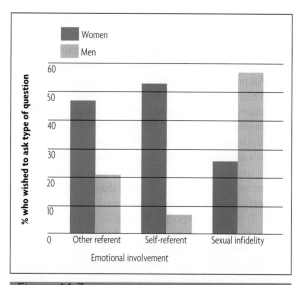

Figure 11.7

**Sex differences in jealousy**
Heterosexual men and women wrote questions they imagined asking if they learned their partners had been unfaithful. Women devised more questions that focused on emotional involvement. Men devised more questions focused on sexual infidelity.

Adapted from a study by Achim Schützwohl, 'Sex differences in jealousy: Information search and cognitive preoccupation,' *Personality and Individual Differences*, Science Direct online.

## SEXUAL NORMS

What is an average sex life like? Scientific investigation of human sexual behaviour was given the first important impetus by the work of **Alfred Kinsey** and his colleagues beginning in the 1940s (1948, 1953). They interviewed some 17,000 Americans about their sexual behaviour and revealed—to a generally shocked public—that certain behaviours, previously considered rare and even abnormal, were actually quite widespread—or at least were reported to be. The norms for sexual behaviour have changed over the years, in part because of scientific advances. For example, the availability of birth control pills in the early 1960s allowed women more sexual freedom because it reduced the likelihood of pregnancy. The arrival of Viagra in 1998 allowed men to prolong their years of sexual activity. Alongside the impact of science, there has been a general trend in many cultures toward more open discourse about sexual issues. **Table 11.3** provides data from a study that surveyed members of the classes of 1950, 1975, and 2000 from the same high school in the northeastern United States with respect to their sexual experiences in high school (Caron & Moskey, 2002). You can see that there have been general trends for people to talk more openly with their families about sexual issues at the same time that actual sexual experiences have increased.

These sexual norms are part of what you acquire as a member of a culture. We already suggested that some general 'male' and 'female' aspects of sexual behaviour may be products of the evolution of the human species. Even so, different cultures define ranges of behaviour that

Table 11.3

Sexual experiences of the classes of 1950, 1975 and 2000

|  | 1950 | 1975 | 2000 | $X^2$ |
|---|---|---|---|---|
| In high school, how much did you discuss sexual intercourse, birth control, sexually transmitted diseases, or pregnancy with your parents/family? |  |  |  | 52.32* |
| We never talked about sex issues | 65% | 50% | 15% | |
| We talked about sex occasionally/a few times | 25% | 41% | 45% | |
| We talked about sex many times/regularly | 10% | 9% | 40% | |
| Which statement *best* describes your sexual experience while in high school? |  |  |  | 88.24* |
| I did not think about sex | 25% | 2% | 6% | |
| I had kissed someone | 41% | 9% | 3% | |
| I had 'made out' with someone | 10% | 24% | 22% | |
| I had sex 1–3 times | 8% | 13% | 11% | |
| I had sex more than 3 times | 16% | 52% | 58% | |

*$p < .001$

Adapted from Sandra L. Caron and Eilean G. Moskey, 'Changes over time in teenage sexual relationships: Comparing the high school class of 1950, 1975 and 2000.' University of Maine.

Although sex fulfils the biological function of reproduction, most humans engage in sex many more times than they reproduce. Even so, how does the evolutionary perspective explain contemporary sexual strategies?

are considered to be appropriate for expressing sexual impulses. **Sexual scripts** are socially learned programs of sexual responsiveness that include prescriptions, usually

**sexual scripts** Socially learned programs of sexual responsiveness.

unspoken, of what to do; when, where, and how to do it; with whom, or with what, to do it; and why it should be done (Laumann & Gagnon, 1995; Mahay et al., 2001). Different aspects of these scripts are assembled through social interaction over your lifetime. The attitudes and values embodied in your sexual script are an external source of sexual motivation: the script suggests the types of behaviours you might or should undertake.

Scripts are combinations of prescriptions generated by social norms (what is proper and accepted), individual expectations and preferred sequences of behaviour from past learning. Your sexual scripts include scenarios not only of what you think is appropriate on your part but also of your expectations for a sexual partner. When they are not recognised, discussed or synchronised, differing scripts can create problems of adjustment between partners.

Let's focus more specifically on the sexual practices of university students. Researchers have often been interested in understanding *sexual risk taking*: circumstances in which individuals engage in sexual practices that ignore the risk of pregnancy or sexually transmitted diseases. Given our discussion of evolution and sex differences, you may not be surprised to learn that, on the whole, men are more likely than women to engage in risky behaviours (Poppen, 1995). In one sample of university students, more men than women report that they have gone to bars to meet prospective sex partners (77 vs. 14 percent) and that they have had sex with someone they have just met (47 vs. 24 percent). In addition, slightly more men than women reported having had sex without some form of contraception (78 vs. 64 percent).

Research into the sexual experience of university students has revealed another area in which male and female sexual scripts come into devastating conflict: *rape*. In one study, researchers asked 4,446 women attending 2- or 4-year technical college and university courses to provide information about their experiences of sexual aggression in 7 months of an academic year (Fisher et al., 2000). In that reference period, 1.1 percent of the women had experienced attempted rape and 1.7 percent had experienced completed rape. The researchers extended those numbers to estimate the likelihood that a woman would experience an attempted or completed rape during her university career: They concluded that the number of victimised women might climb to 20 to 25 percent. The

How might instances of sexual harassment arise from conflicting sexual scripts?

researchers also examined a particular type of rape: **date rape**. Date rape applies to circumstances in which someone is coerced into sexual activity by a social acquaintance. For this sample of women, 12.8 percent of completed rapes and 35.0 percent of attempted rapes occurred on dates.

When asked to say who was responsible for a date rape, males surveyed tend to blame the victim (that is, the woman who was raped) more than females do (Bell et al., 1994; Ryckman et al., 1998). Studies of date rape reveal that women's and men's sexual scripts differ significantly with respect to the incidence of *token resistance*—a woman's mild resistance to sexual advances despite the intention, ultimately, to allow sexual intercourse. Very few women—about 5 percent—report engaging in token resistance, but about 60 percent of men say that they have, at least once, *experienced* token resistance (Marx & Gross, 1995). The difference between those two figures likely includes many incidents of date rape. Research suggests that some men come to believe that token resistance is part of a sexual game; resistance doesn't signal genuine distress on a woman's part. It is important for men to understand that women, in fact, rarely report themselves to be playing that game—resistance is real.

Throughout most of our discussion of sexual motivation, we have been ignoring a major category of sexual experience: homosexuality. We conclude this section on sexual motivation with a discussion of lesbians and gay men. This discussion will give us another opportunity to see how sexual behaviour is controlled by the interplay of internal and external motivational forces.

## HOMOSEXUALITY

Our discussion so far has focused on the motivations that cause people to perform a certain range of sexual behaviours. In this same context we can discuss the existence of homosexuality. That is, rather than presenting homosexuality as a set of behaviours that is 'caused' by a deviation from heterosexuality, our discussion of sexual motivation should allow you to see that all sexual behaviour is 'caused'. In this view, homosexuality and heterosexuality result from similar motivational forces. Neither of them represents a motivated departure from the other.

Most surveys of sexual behaviour have tried to obtain an accurate estimate of the incidence of homosexuality. In his early research, Alfred Kinsey found that 37 percent of men in his sample had had at least some homosexual experience and that about 4 percent were exclusively homosexual (percentages for women were somewhat smaller). One major project found that about 4 percent of women in their sample were sexually attracted to individuals of the same gender, but only 2 percent of the sample had actually had sex with another woman in the past year. Similarly, 6 percent of the men in their survey were sexually attracted to other men, but again only 2 percent of the sample had actually had sex with another man in the past year (Michael et al., 1994). In a 2003 survey of over 20,000 adults in Australia, conducted by the Australian Research Centre in Sex, Health and Society

What evidence suggests that sexual orientation has a genetic component?

(ARCSHS) at La Trobe University, 1.6 percent of men identified as homosexual and 0.8 percent of women as lesbian. Are these figures correct? As long as there is societal hostility directed toward acting on homosexual desires, it may be impossible to get entirely accurate estimates of the incidence of homosexuality because of people's reluctance to confide in researchers.

In this section we consider the origins of homosexuality and heterosexuality. We also review research on societal and personal attitudes toward homosexual behaviour.

## The nature and nurture of homosexuality

After our discussion of evolution and sexual behaviours, it should not surprise you to learn that research evidence suggests that sexual preference has a genetic component. As is often the case, researchers have made this assertion based on studies that compare concordance rates of *monozygotic* (MZ) twins (those who are genetically identical) and *dizygotic* (DZ) twins (those who, like siblings, share only half their genes). When both members of a pair of twins have the same orientation— homosexual or heterosexual—they are concordant. If one twin is homosexual and the other is heterosexual, they are discordant. Studies of both gay men and lesbians have demonstrated considerably higher concordance rates for MZ than for DZ twins (Rahman & Wilson, 2003). For example, in one sample of roughly 750 pairs of twins, 32 percent of the MZ twins were concordant for non-heterosexual orientations versus 8 percent of DZ twins (Kendler et al., 2000). Although MZ twins may also be reared in more similar environments than DZ twins— they may be treated more similarly by their parents—this pattern strongly suggests that sexuality may, in part, be genetically determined. With this knowledge in hand, researchers have started to search for the gene sequences

that might control the emergence of homosexuality or heterosexuality (Hyde, 2005). So, does biology determine your sexual destiny? Further research may strengthen or weaken the case, but it seems clear that some aspects of homosexuality and heterosexuality emerge in response to purely biological forces.

Social psychologist **Daryl Bem** (1996, 2000) has suggested that biology does not affect sexual preference directly, but rather has an indirect impact by influencing the temperaments and activities of young children. Recall from Chapter 10 that researchers have suggested that boys and girls engage in different activities—boys' play, for example, tends to be more rough-and-tumble. According to Bem's theory, depending on whether they engage in sex-typical or sex-atypical play, children come to feel dissimilar to either their same-sex or opposite-sex peers. In Bem's theory, 'exotic becomes erotic': Feelings of dissimilarity lead to emotional arousal; over time this arousal is transformed into erotic attraction. For example, if a young girl feels dissimilar from other girls because she does not wish to engage in girl-typical activities, over time her emotional arousal will be transformed into homosexual feelings. Note that Bem's theory supports the assertion that homosexuality and heterosexuality arise from the same causal forces: in both cases, the gender the child perceives as dissimilar becomes, over time, eroticised.

**Society and homosexuality** Suppose Bem is correct to argue that childhood experiences matter enormously. Does everyone act on the urgings set down in childhood? What, perhaps, most sets homosexuality apart from heterosexuality is the continuing hostility toward homosexual behaviours in many corners of society. In one survey, a sample of 1,335 heterosexual men and women were asked how uncomfortable they would feel being around 'a man who is homosexual' or 'a woman who is a lesbian' (Herek, 2002). **Figure 11.8** presents the percentage who responded that they would be 'somewhat' or 'very' uncomfortable. You can see that both men and women anticipate more discomfort being around homosexuals who match their own sex. Researchers have labelled highly negative attitudes toward gay people *homophobia*.

Most homosexuals come to the realisation that they are motivated toward same-sex relationships in the hostile context of societal homophobia. Even so, research suggests that many individuals begin to recognise those feelings at quite young ages. For example, researchers asked students from the southeastern United States attending a conference for gay, lesbian, bisexual and transgendered youth to indicate the age at which they became aware of their sexual orientation (Maguen et al., 2002). Among the gay men, the mean age was 9.6 years; among the lesbians the mean age was 10.9 years. The men reported having same-sex sexual contact at 14.9 years and the women reported same-sex contact at 16.7 years. These data suggest that many people become aware of their homosexual orientation at a time when they must still function in school environments that are often quite hostile to homosexuality (D'Augelli et al., 2002). In addition, homosexual youths must often make

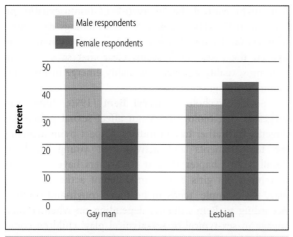

## Figure 11.8

**Attitudes toward homosexuality**

Participants were asked how uncomfortable they would feel being around 'a man who is homosexual' or 'a woman who is a lesbian'. The figure indicates the percentage of men and women who responded that they would be 'somewhat' or 'very' uncomfortable.

From Gregory M. Herek, 'Gender Gaps in Public Opinion About Lesbians and Gay Men,' *Public Opinion Quarterly, 66,* 40-66, by permission of Oxford University Press and the American Association for Public Opinion Research.

the difficult decision of whether to disclose their sexual orientation to their parents. Most adolescents rely on their parents for both emotional and financial support; to disclose their homosexuality puts them at risk of losing both types of sustenance. In fact, parental rejection is related to increases in suicide attempts (D'Augelli et al., 2001).

These findings for adolescents reinforce the point that most gay and lesbian individuals find homophobia more psychologically burdensome than homosexuality itself. In 1973, the American Psychiatric Association voted to remove homosexuality from the list of psychological disorders; the American Psychological Association followed in 1975 (Morin & Rothblum, 1991). These changes are fully supported by the Australian Psychological Society (APA, 2000). Spurring this action were research reports suggesting that, in fact, most gay men and lesbians are happy and productive. Contemporary research suggests that much of the stress associated with homosexuality arises not from the sexual motivation itself—gay people are happy with their orientations—but from the way in which people respond to the revelation of that sexual motivation. Much of lesbians' and gay men's anxiety about homosexuality arises not from being homosexual, but from an ongoing need either to reveal ('come out') to or conceal ('stay in the closet') their sexual identity from family, friends, and coworkers (D'Augelli et al., 2005). More generally, homosexuals experience distress because they can't speak openly about their lives (Lewis et al., 2006). As you might expect, gay men and lesbians also spend time worrying about establishing and maintaining loving relationships, just as heterosexuals do.

The willingness of lesbians and gay men to 'come out' may serve as a first step toward decreasing societal hostility.

Research has shown that people's attitudes toward gay men and lesbians are much less negative when they actually *know* individuals in these groups; in fact, on average the more gay men and lesbians a person knows, the more favourable is his or her attitude (Herek & Capitanio, 1996; Liang & Alimo). (When we turn to the topic of prejudice in Chapter 17, we will see there again how experiences with members of minority groups can lead to more positive attitudes.) Do you have any gay, lesbian or bisexual friends? How have your attitudes been influenced by interactions with gay people? Are you yourself gay, lesbian or bisexual? How have or could have the attitudes of people around you been affected by knowing that you are gay?

This brief review of homosexuality allows us to reinforce our main conclusions about human sexual motivation. Some of the impetus for sexual behaviours is internal—genetic endowment and species evolution provide internal models for both heterosexual and homosexual behaviours. But the external environment also gives rise to sexual motivation. You learn to find some stimuli particularly alluring and some behaviours culturally acceptable. In the case of homosexuality, external societal norms may work against the internal dictates of nature.

Let's move now to our third example of important motivation: the forces that set an individual's course for relative success or failure.

## RECAP CHECKPOINT
### Sexual behaviours

- From an evolutionary perspective, sex is the mechanism for producing offspring.
- In animals, the sex drive is largely controlled by hormones.
- The work of Masters and Johnson provided the first hard data on the sexual response cycles of men and women.
- Evolutionary psychologists suggest that much of human sexual behaviour reflects different mating strategies for men and women.
- Discrepancies in sexual scripts can lead to serious misunderstandings and even date rape.
- Homosexuality and heterosexuality are determined both by genetics and personal and social environments.

## CONCEPT QUESTIONS

1. What is meant by stereotyped sexual behaviour?

2. What four phases did Masters and Johnson identify for human sexual response?

For answers go to MyPsychLab!

**mypsychlab** where learning comes to life!

3. According to evolutionary theories, why do men desire more sexual variety than do women?

4. What are sexual scripts?

5. What does twin research suggest about the genetics of homosexuality?

## CRITICAL THINKING

Recall the study that looked at jealousy in men and women. Why was it important to break the emotional involvement category of questions into smaller categories that referred to the self and to the other?

These men are participating in the semi-final Wheelchair Rugby match between New Zealand and Great Britain at the Athens 2004 Paralympic Games. How can motivation explain variability among individuals—the fact, for example, that some people do better in competition than others?

# MOTIVATION FOR PERSONAL ACHIEVEMENT

Why do some people succeed, whereas other people, relatively speaking, fail? Why, for example, are some people able to swim the English Channel, whereas other people just wave woefully from the shore? You are likely to attribute some of the difference to genetic factors like body type, and you're correct to do so. But you also know that some people are simply much more interested in swimming the English Channel than are others. So we are back at one of our core reasons for studying motivation. We want, in this case, to understand the motivational forces that lead different people to seek different levels of personal achievement. Let's begin with a construct that's actually called the *need for achievement.*

## NEED FOR ACHIEVEMENT

As early as 1938, **Henry Murray** had postulated a need to achieve that varied in strength in different people and influenced their tendency to approach success and evaluate their own performances. **David McClelland** and his colleagues (1953) devised a way to measure the strength of this need and then looked for relationships between strength of achievement motivation in different societies; conditions that had fostered the motivation, and its results in the work world. To gauge the strength of the need for achievement, McClelland used his participants' fantasies. On what is called the **Thematic Apperception Test (TAT)**, participants were asked to generate stories in response to a series of ambiguous drawings. Participants shown TAT pictures were asked to make up stories about them—to say what was happening in the picture and describe probable outcomes. Presumably, they projected into the scene reflections of their own values, interests

and motives. According to McClelland, 'If you want to find out what's on a person's mind, don't ask him, because he can't always tell you accurately. Study his fantasies and dreams. If you do this over a period of time, you will discover the themes to which his mind returns again and again. And these themes can be used to explain his actions' (McClelland, 1971, p. 5).

From participant responses to a series of TAT pictures, McClelland worked out measures of several human needs, including needs for power, affiliation and achievement. The **need for achievement** was designated as *n Ach*. It reflected individual differences in the importance of planning and working toward attaining one's goals. **Figure 11.9** shows an example of how a high *n Ach* individual and a low *n Ach* individual might interpret a TAT picture. Studies in both laboratory and real-life settings have validated the usefulness of this measure.

For example, high-scoring *n Ach* people were found to be more upwardly mobile than those with low scores; sons who had high *n Ach* scores were more likely than sons with low *n Ach* measures to advance above their fathers' occupational status (McClelland et al., 1976). Men and women who measured high on *n Ach* at age 31 tended to have higher salaries than their low *n Ach* peers by age 41 (McClelland & Franz, 1992). Do these findings indicate that high *n Ach* individuals are always willing to work harder? Not really. In the face of a task that they are led to believe will be difficult, high *n Ach* individuals quit early on (Feather, 1961). What, in fact, seems to typify high *n Ach* individuals is a need for *efficiency*—a need to get the same result for less effort. If they out earn their peers, it might be because they also value concrete feedback on how well they are doing. As a measure of progress, salary is very concrete (McClelland, 1961; McClelland & Franz, 1992).

How does a high need for achievement arise? Researchers have considered whether parenting practices can bring about a high or low need for achievement. Data come from a longitudinal analysis of a group of Boston-area children.

**need for achievement (n Ach)** An assumed basic human need to strive for achievement of goals that motivates a wide range of behaviour and thinking.

**Thematic Apperception Test (TAT)** A projective test in which pictures of ambiguous scenes are presented to an individual who is encouraged to generate stories about them.

David McClelland and Carol Franz (1992) compared measures of parenting practice, collected in 1951 when the children were about 5 years old, with measures of *n Ach* and earnings, collected in 1987–1988, when the children were 41. In 1951, the parents were asked to indicate their practices with respect to feeding and toilet training the child. McClelland and Franz considered children to have experienced a high degree of *achievement pressure* when their parents had fed and toilet trained them by strict rules. Overall, there was a positive correlation between early parental achievement pressure and subsequent adult *n Ach*. Furthermore, children who had experienced a high degree of achievement pressure were earning about $10,000 more annually than their peers who had experienced little such pressure.

These data suggest that the degree to which you experience a need to achieve may have been established in the first few years of your life.

## ATTRIBUTIONS FOR SUCCESS AND FAILURE

Need for achievement is not the only variable that affects motivation toward personal success. To see why, let's begin with a hypothetical example. Suppose you have two friends who are taking the same class. On the first mid-semester assessment, each gets a C. Do you think they would be equally motivated to study hard for the second mid-semester assessment? Part of the answer will depend on the way in which they each explained the C to themselves.

Consider, for example, the importance of locus of control (Rotter, 1954). A *locus of control orientation* is a belief about whether the outcomes of your actions are contingent on what you do *(internal control orientation)* or on environmental factors *(external control orientation)*. In the case of the Cs, your friends might *attribute* their performance to either an external cause (construction noise during the exam) or an internal cause (poor memory). **Attributions** are judgments about the causes of outcomes. (We will develop attribution theory at length in Chapter 16.) In this case, the attributions can have an impact on motivation. If your friends believe they can attribute their performance to construction noise, they are likely to study hard for the next mid-semester assessment. If they think the fault lies in their poor memory, they're more likely to slack off.

Locus of control is not the only dimension along which attributions can vary (Peterson & Seligman, 1984). We can also ask: 'To what extent is a causal factor likely to be stable and consistent over time, or unstable and varying?' The answer gives us the dimension of *stability* versus *instability*. Or we can ask: 'To what extent is a causal factor highly specific, limited to a particular task or situation, or global, applying widely across a variety of settings?' This gives us the dimension of *global* versus *specific*.

An example of how locus of control and stability can interact is given in **Figure 11.10**. Let's stay with the example of attributions about exam grades. Your friends can interpret their grades as the result of internal factors, such as ability (a stable personality characteristic) or effort (a varying personal quality). Or they may view the grades as caused primarily by external factors such as the difficulty of the task, the actions of others (a stable situational problem), or luck (an unstable external feature). Depending on the nature of the attribution they make for this success or failure, they are likely to experience one of the emotional responses depicted in **Table 11.4**. What is important here is that the type of interpretation will influence both their emotions and subsequent motivation—to study harder or

**attributions** Judgments about the causes of outcomes.

### Figure 11.9

**Alternative interpretations of a TAT picture**

*Story showing high* n Ach
This boy has just finished his violin lesson. He's happy at the progress he is making and is beginning to believe that all his progress is making the sacrifices worthwhile. To become a concert violinist, he will have to give up much of his social life to practise for many hours each day. Although he knows he could make more money by going into his father's business, he is more interested in being a great violinist and giving people joy with his music. He renews his personal commitment to whatever it takes to make it.

*Story showing low* n ach
This boy is holding his brother's violin and wishes he could play it. But he knows it is not worth the time, energy, and money for lessons. He feels sorry for his brother; he has given up all the enjoyable things in life to practise, practise, practise. It would be great to wake up one day and be a top-notch musician, but it doesn't work that way. The reality is boring practice, no fun, and the strong possibility of becoming just another guy playing a musical instrument in a small-town band.

skip work—regardless of the true reason for the success or failure.

So far we have been considering the possibility that both of your friends will explain their Cs in the same way, but it's very likely that they might arrive at different explanations. One may believe something external ('The professor gave an unfair exam'); the other may believe something internal ('I'm not smart enough for this class'). Researchers have shown that the way people explain events in their lives—from winning at cards to being turned down for a date—can become lifelong, habitual *attributional styles* (Haines et al., 1999). The way you account for your successes and failures can influence your motivation, mood, and even ability to perform appropriately. For several years, researcher **Martin Seligman** has studied the ways in which people's *explanatory style*—their degree of optimism or pessimism—affects activity and passivity, whether they persist or give up easily, take risks, or play it safe (Seligman, 1991).

In Chapter 14, we will see that an internal–global–stable explanatory style ('I never do anything right') puts individuals at risk for depression (and one of the symptoms of depression is impaired motivation). For now, however, let's focus on the way in which explanatory style might lead one of your friends to have an A and the other an F by the end of the semester. Seligman's research team has worked on the problem of explaining one person's ability and another's inability to resist failure. The secret ingredient has turned out to be familiar and seemingly simple: *optimism* versus *pessimism*. These two divergent ways of looking at the world influence motivation, mood and behaviour.

The *pessimistic attributional style* focuses on the causes of failure as internally generated. Furthermore, the bad

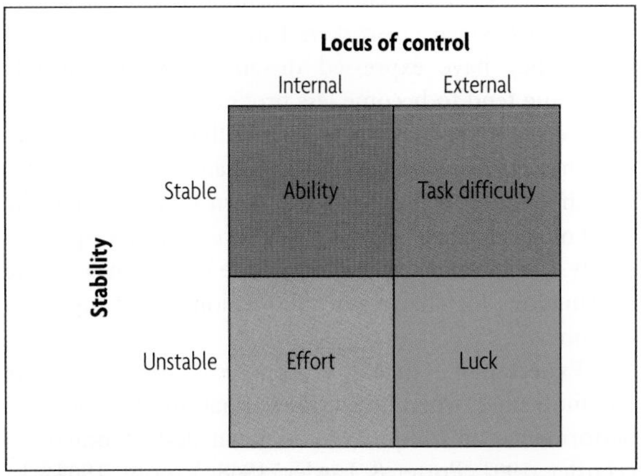

## Figure 11.10

**Attributions regarding causes for behavioural outcomes**
Four possible outcomes are generated with just two sources of attributions about behaviour: the locus of control and the situation in which the behaviour occurs. Ability attributions are made for the internal–stable combination, effort for the internal but unstable combination, a difficult task (test) when external–stable forces are assumed to be operating, and luck for the unstable–external combination.

## Table 11.4

**Attribution-dependent emotional responses**

Your feelings in response to success and failure depend on the kinds of attributions you make regarding the cause of those outcomes. For example, you take pride in success when you attribute it to your ability but are depressed when you perceive lack of ability to cause failure. Or you feel gratitude when you attribute your success to the actions of others but anger when they are seen as contributing to your failure.

| Attribution | Emotional Responses | |
| --- | --- | --- |
| | Success | Failure |
| Ability | Competence | Incompetence |
| | Confidence | Resignation |
| | Pride | Depression |
| Effort | Relief | Guilt |
| | Contentment | Shame |
| | Relaxation | Fear |
| Action of others | Gratitude | Anger |
| | Thankfulness | Fury |
| Luck | Surprise | Surprise |
| | Guilt | Astonishment |

situation and the individual's role in causing it are seen as stable and global—'It won't ever change and it will affect everything.' The *optimistic attributional style* sees failure as the result of external causes—'The test was unfair'—and of events that are unstable or modifiable and specific—'If I put in more effort next time, I'll do better, and this one setback won't affect how I perform any other task that is important to me.'

These causal explanations are reversed when it comes to the question of success. Optimists take full, personal internal–stable–global credit for success. However, pessimists attribute their success to external–unstable–global or specific factors. Because they believe themselves to be doomed to fail, pessimists perform worse than others would expect, given objective measures of their talent. A body of research supports these generalisations about optimists and pessimists. For example, one study measured the explanatory styles of 130 male salespeople in a leading United Kingdom insurance company (Corr & Gray, 1996). In the study, salespeople with more positive attributional styles were also likely to have higher sales. In everyday life, interpretations of events affect both optimists' and pessimists' levels of motivation for future performance.

To close this section, let's look at a research example of the powerful impact of causal attributions in an academic setting.

When you finish university, you're going to want to get the best job possible. But how do you think that's going to happen? Are you going to get a good job because of your own skills and initiative (an internal attribution)? Or because of random circumstances and good luck (an external attribution)? Research suggests that students who believe they have control over career outcomes are more likely to meet their career aspirations. In that context, what can be done to encourage students to change their attributions from external to internal?

A team of researchers developed an intervention that they called *attributional retraining*. Groups of students who indicated that they believed they have little control over their careers viewed a videotaped conversation between a male and female graduate of their university. For the experimental group, part of the graduates' discussion focused on how they made career decisions: 'I realised as I was growing up that anything worthwhile in terms of my career was going to take effort and hard work' (Luzzo et al., 1996, p. 417). The control group did not hear this type of information. After this brief intervention, members of the experimental group now indicated a more internal locus of control for career choices and also, as time passed, engaged in more behaviours related to career exploration. The control group did not show these changes (Luzzo et al., 1996, reproduced with permission).

Because of the way in which attributions affected motivation, a small amount of information about career choices had a profound effect on students' ideas about their futures.

We believe that there is much value to you in this line of psychological research. You can work at developing an optimistic explanatory style for your successes and failures. You can avoid making negative, stable, dispositional attributions for your failures by examining possible causal forces in the situation. Finally, don't let your motivation be undermined by momentary setbacks. You can apply this research-based advice to better your life—a recurring theme of *Psychology and Life*.

## WORK AND ORGANISATIONAL PSYCHOLOGY

Now suppose your positive philosophy has helped you to get a job in a big corporation. Can we predict exactly how motivated you'll be just by knowing about you, as an individual—your *n Ach* score or your explanatory style? Your individual level of motivation will depend, in part, on the overall context of people and rules in which you work. Recognising that work settings are complex social systems, **organisational psychologists** study various aspects of human relations, such as communication among employees, socialisation or enculturation of workers, leadership, attitudes and commitment toward a job and/or an organisation, job satisfaction, stress and burnout, and overall quality of life at work. As consultants to businesses, organisational psychologists may assist in recruitment, selection and training of employees. They also make recommendations about job redesign—tailoring a job to fit the person. Organisational psychologists apply theories

of management, decision making and development to improve work settings.

Let's look at a pair of theories organisational psychologists have developed to understand motivation in the workplace. *Equity theory* and *expectancy theory* attempt to explain and predict how people will respond under different working conditions. These theories assume that workers engage in certain cognitive activities, such as assessing fairness through processes of social comparison with other workers or estimating expected rewards associated with their performance.

**Equity theory** proposes that workers are motivated to maintain fair or equitable relationships with other relevant persons (Adams, 1965). Workers take note of their inputs (investments or contributions they make to their jobs) and their outcomes (what they receive from their jobs), and then they compare these with the inputs and outcomes of other workers. When the ratio of outcomes to inputs for Worker A is equal to the ratio for Worker B (outcome A ÷ input A = outcome B ÷ input B), then Worker A will feel satisfied. Dissatisfaction will result when these ratios are not equal. Because feeling this inequity is aversive, workers will be motivated to restore equity by changing the relevant inputs and outcomes. These changes could be behavioural (for example, reducing input by working less, increasing outcome by asking for a raise). Or they could be psychological (for example, reinterpreting the value of the inputs—'My work isn't really that good'—or the value of the outcome—'I'm lucky to have a weekly paycheck I can count on').

Have you noticed the consequences of equity or inequity in your own work situations? Consider a situation in which a co-worker leaves for a better job. How does that make you feel? Equity theory suggests that you may feel like you have been unfairly left behind in an undesirable job. In fact, when co-workers leave in circumstances in which they have expressed dissatisfaction, the people remaining tend to become less productive in their jobs—they decrease productivity to restore their sense of equity (Sheehan, 1993). If you end up in a management position, you should try to prevent this pattern by addressing the psychological needs of your employees with respect to equity. For example, keep in mind the benefit of adequate explanations for changes in the relationship of inputs to outcomes.

**Expectancy theory** proposes that workers are motivated when they expect that their effort and performance on the job will result in desired outcomes (Harder, 1991; Porter & Lawler, 1968; Vroom, 1964). In other words, people will engage in work they find attractive (leading to favourable consequences) and achievable. Expectancy theory emphasises three components: expectancy, instrumentality and valence. *Expectancy* refers to the perceived likelihood that a worker's efforts will result in a certain level of performance. *Instrumentality* refers to the perception that performance will lead to certain outcomes, such as rewards. *Valence* refers to the perceived attractiveness of particular outcomes. With respect to a particular work situation, you can imagine

How does expectancy theory explain some players' choice to favour hitting 'fours' and 'sixes' over achieving a higher batting average?

you do to change the workplace to restore high values for instrumentality?

As a conclusion to this section, we offer a cautionary note on achievement and motivation in work settings. When you make a personal choice about how hard you can work at a career, keep a careful watch on other aspects of your life. As we will see in the next chapter, aggressive striving for success may, in some respects, work counter to the goal of having a long and healthy life.

We have come a long way since we asked you to consider why you got out of bed this morning. We have described the biology and psychology of hunger and eating, and the evolutionary and social dimensions of human sexuality. We have explored individual differences in people's need to achieve and explain personal success. Throughout this discussion, you have seen the intricate interplay of nature and nurture, at the level of both the species and the individual. So, with all this information in hand, why *did* you get out of bed this morning?

different probabilities for these three components. You might, for example, have a job in which there is a high likelihood of reward if performance is successful (high instrumentality) but a low likelihood that performance will be successful (low expectancy) or a low likelihood that the reward will be worthwhile (low valence). According to expectancy theory, workers assess the probabilities of these three components and combine them by multiplying their individual values. Highest levels of motivation, therefore, result when all three components have high probabilities, whereas lowest levels result when any single component is zero.

Can you see how an expectancy theory analysis might help you if you were in a management position? You should be able to think more clearly about expectancy, instrumentality and valence. You should be able to determine if one piece of the picture is out of kilter. Suppose, for example, your employees came to believe that there wasn't enough of a relationship between their efforts and how much they are rewarded. What could

For answers go to MyPsychLab!

# CRITICAL THINKING *in your life*

## HOW DOES MOTIVATION AFFECT ACADEMIC ACHIEVEMENT?

Suppose you've signed up for your Introductory Psychology course with two friends, Angela and Blake. On the first day of class, Angela says, 'I want to get the top grade in the class.' Blake replies, 'I'll just be happy if I don't get an F.' Can you see how Angela's and Blake's goals would motivate them to engage in very different behaviours? One of them is likely to spend much more time reading this text! We can develop the contrast between Angela and Blake to examine, more generally, what researchers have learned about how students' goals affect their motivation and classroom performance. The purpose of this review is to allow you to think critically about your own goals and motivation.

Analyses of students' performance have identified three general types of achievement goals (Meece et al., 2006). Angela is representative of a student who has *performance-approach goals*. She focuses on appearing more competent than others. Blake is representative of a student who has *performance-avoidance goals*. He focuses on avoiding being judged as less competent than others. The third type of goals is *mastery goals*. Students who are motivated by mastery goals focus on mastering new skills: 'Success is evaluated in terms of self-improvement, and students derive satisfaction from the inherent qualities of the task, such as its interest and challenge' (Meece et al., p. 490). Researchers measure students' goal orientation by asking them to agree with

statements such as 'I desire to completely master the material presented in this class' and 'I just want to avoid doing poorly in this class' (McGregor & Elliott, 2002, p. 381).

In general, students with mastery goals are most highly motivated to engage in the behaviours that help ensure academic achievement. One study assessed students' behaviours 2 weeks before an Introductory Psychology exam and then immediately before the exam (McGregor & Elliott, 2002). Those students with performance-avoidance goals also avoided studying: Two weeks before the exam, they admitted that they hadn't yet done much to prepare; immediately before the exam they admitted that they didn't feel ready. Students with mastery goals and performance-approach goals all started preparing for the exam well in advance. However, students with mastery goals were distinguished by the calm with which they anticipated the exam: From 2 weeks before the exam to immediately before the exam, they became less concerned about avoiding it.

As you examine the goals that underlie your own academic achievement, also think back to your classroom experiences: Teachers differ with respect to the goals they instil (Meece et al., 2006). Teachers can emphasise mastery goals by acknowledging students' effort and enjoyment when acquiring new abilities; teachers can emphasise

performance goals by identifying students whose test scores are highest or ignoring poor students. In general, students' goals tend to mirror their teachers' goals. Students may not always have had opportunities to develop mastery goals.

In addition, teachers observe students' behaviour to make attributions about their motivation. Suppose you do poorly on an exam.

As we noted in the text, you can explain your performance with respect to dimensions such as stability and controllability. Teachers use the same dimensions to respond to their students (Reyna & Weiner, 2001; Weiner, 2006). Consider controllability. Suppose a professor believes that Blake failed an exam because he never works, whereas Angela failed an exam because she transferred late into the class. The professor is likely to be considerably more sympathetic towards Angela than towards Blake. It will be to Blake's advantage to change his professor's attributions!

When students do poorly in our classes, we encourage them to examine the goals they bring to the course and how those goals motivate their behaviour. We hope you can see the importance of undertaking this exercise.

- Why might students with mastery goals grow increasingly calm as an exam approaches?
- What could students do to change professor's attributions about their performance?

# SUMMARY

Chapter 11 provides an overview of motivation and how it impacts across hunger, sex, academic pursuits and mastery over other skills and personal goals in our lives. Reversal theory outlines metamotivational states we experience on a daily basis in regard to productive behaviour for long or short term goals. The biology and psychology of eating behaviour demonstrates why people choose to eat or diet the way they do. Discussion about how sexual motivation and preference for our partners is also highlighted by the work of Johnson and Masters, as well as Kinsey, each of whom outline how sex motivates aspects for certain behaviour in humans. Lastly, a review of personal needs for achievement demonstrate that motivation is also affected by attributional styles such as optimism and pessimism.

# KEY TERMS

anorexia nervosa (p. 380)
attributions (p. 392)
bulimia nervosa (p. 380)
date rape (p. 388)
drives (p. 371)
equity theory (p. 394)
expectancy theory (p. 394)

hierarchy of needs (p. 374)
homeostasis (p. 371)
incentives (p. 371)
instincts (p. 373)
motivation (p. 370)
need for achievement (p. 391)
organisational psychologists (p. 394)

parental investment (p. 386)
reversal theory (p. 372)
sexual arousal (p. 384)
sexual scripts (p. 387)
social-learning theory (p. 374)
Thematic Apperception Test (TAT)
   (p. 391)

# PRACTICE TEST

1.  You are watching your friend Carlos play tennis with little success. At the end of the match, he comes over and says, 'I just couldn't get motivated today.' How is Carlos using the concept of motivation?
    a.  To infer private states from public acts
    b.  To relate biology to behaviour
    c.  To account for behavioural variability
    d.  To explain perseverance despite adversity

2.  Which of these is *not* a pair of metamotivational states?
    a.  ambition versus passivity
    b.  mastery versus sympathy
    c.  autic versus alloic
    d.  conformist versus negativistic

3.  A(n) _____is a preprogrammed tendency that is essential for the survival of a species.
    a.  incentive              c.  metamotivational state
    b.  drive                  d.  instinct

4.  According to Maslow, you should always try to satisfy your _____needs before you satisfy your_____needs.
    a.  attachment; biological    c.  safety; esteem
    b.  esteem; attachment        d.  self-actualisation; esteem

5.  At every meal, Jonah only eats food with one flavour. Because of _____, this should generally _____the amount of food Jonah eats.
    a.  stomach contractions; increase
    b.  lateral hypothalamus stimulation; decrease
    c.  sensory-specific satiety; increase
    d.  sensory-specific satiety; decrease

6.  When restrained eaters become disinhibited, they tend to
    a.  engage in high-calorie binges.
    b.  reduce their food consumption further.
    c.  go off their diets permanently.
    d.  behave more like unrestrained eaters.

7. Which of these statements is *not* true?
   a. Anorexia is diagnosed when people weigh less than 85 percent of their expected body weight.
   b. Men and women suffer from anorexia at the same rate.
   c. Bulimia is characterised by binging and purging.
   d. Bulimia occurs more often than anorexia.

8. Variations in the gene GAD2 influence
   a. production of the hormone leptin.
   b. the amount of GABA available in the hypothalamus.
   c. the action of cannabanoids in the brain to change appetite.
   d. the interaction between brain cannabanoids and leptin.

9. Because of the action of_____, you would expect_____of many species not always to be receptive to mating.
   a. androgens; females      c. androgens; males
   b. estrogen; males          d. estrogen; females

10. According to Masters and Johnson's research on human sexual arousal, the_____phase precedes the_____phase.
    a. resolution; plateau     c. plateau; orgasm
    b. plateau; excitement     d. resolution; orgasm

11. You have a friend who focuses a lot of energy on having brief sexual relationships. This sounds like a_____mating strategy for a_____.
    a. long-term; female       c. long-term; male
    b. short-term; male        d. short-term; female

12. According to research, which pair of siblings should be most likely to share the same sexual orientation?
    a. Larry and John, DZ twins
    b. Deborah and Patty, MZ twins
    c. Rose and Leo, DZ twins
    d. Anne and Charlotte, DZ twins

13. Which of these statements is *not* true for individuals high in need for achievement?
    a. They always complete their tasks.
    b. They like work to go efficiently.
    c. They like to attain their goals.
    d. They spend time on planning.

14. Every day, Victor gets a perfect score on his local newspaper's trivia quiz. Victor thinks this is possible because the trivia questions are really easy. This is an_____for his_____ performance.
    a. internal-stable         c. external-stable
    b. external-unstable       d. external-unstable

15. During a lecture, your professor talks a lot about 'valence' and 'instrumentality.' The lecture most likely concerns
    a. attributions.           c. need for achievement.
    b. equity theory.          d. expectancy theory.

16. On the way into an exam, you overhear Trudy say, 'I'm going to get a perfect score on this exam.' You suspect that Trudy is motivated by_____goals.
    a. performance-approach
    b. mastery
    c. performance-avoidance
    d. equity

## Essay Questions

1. How does culture affect the development of eating disorders?

2. What is the origin of sexual scripts?

3. What impact do optimistic versus pessimistic attributional styles have on people's lives?

# WEB LINKS

http://www.csiro.au/science/Twd.html
  CSIRO Total Wellbeing Diet

http://indigenousaustralia.frogandtoad.com.au/food3.html
  'Frog and Toad', Aboriginal Food Rules and Laws

http://www.fpv.org.au/2_9_1.html
  Sex! Life! Family Planning Victoria

Are you ready for the test? MyPsychLab offers dozens of ways to deepen your understanding and test your recall of the material in this chapter—including video and audio clips, simulations and activities, self-assessments, practice tests and other study materials. Specific resources available for this chapter include:

Internal & external attributions
Maslow's Hierarchy of Needs
Evolutionary drive, arousal, cognitive,
  and humanistic theories of
  motivation

Eating disorders
Food and the brain

To access MyPsychLab, please visit **www.pearsoned.com.au/mypsychlab**

# Are you motivated to succeed?

## NOW YOU HAVE READ CHAPTER 11—ARE YOU PREPARED FOR THE EXAM?

To enhance your understanding of any material in your *Psychology and Life* textbook, go to **MyPsychLab: www.pearsoned.com.au/mypsychlab**.

Complete pre- and post-tests, create your own individualised study plan, watch videos and animations and listen to audio glossaries—all of which will help you understand the themes of this chapter:

- Understanding motivation
- Eating
- Sexual behaviours
- Motivation for personal achievement

Watch VIDEOS on *food and the brain* and other topics related to key concepts covered in Chapter 11

Expand your knowledge and learn more about motivation with RESEARCH NAVIGATOR

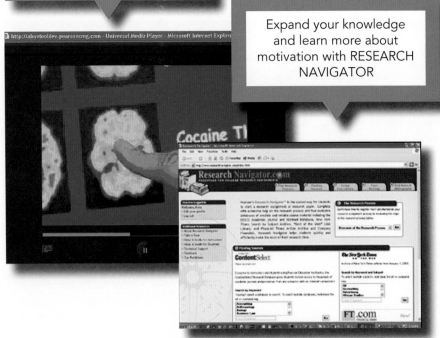

'I wish all texbooks had a site like MyPsychLab.'

**WHICH SCIENTIFIC MINDS FORM THE BASIS FOR THE STUDY OF MOTIVATION?**
View BIOGRAPHIES of *Alfred Kinsey*, *Abraham Maslow* and more, to better understand these men and women who made such significant contributions to the studies you have read about in Chapter 11.

'MyPsychLab was easy to sign up, easy to figure out, easy to use, and always available, so I could work on any chapter at any time.'

Learn more about Maslow's *Hierarchy of Needs*

**Abraham Maslow**

Abraham Maslow (1908–1970) was a humanistic psychologist best known for his development of a hierarchy of needs that must be fulfilled in order for an individual to reach self-actualization--the ability to realize one's unique potential as a human being.

Maslow received his Ph.D. at the University of Wisconsin in 1934 under Harry Harlow. He then taught at Wisconsin for a year, followed by appointments at Teachers College of Columbia University, Brooklyn College, and finally, Brandeis University, where he spent most of his academic career. He moved to Menlo Park, Califor 1969 as a resident fellow of the Laughlin Foundation.

Maslow is considered one of the foremost spokesmen of humanistic psychology was founder of the Journal of Humanistic Psychology. He is particularly known theory of motivation, and the concept of a hierarchy of needs, ranging from bas survival needs to the need for self-actualization. His influential writings include *T a Psychology of Being* (1962) and *Religion, Values and Peak Experiences* (He served in 1968 as president of the American Psychological Association

**Alfred Kinsey**

Alfred Kinsey conducted a series of national studies on human sexual behavior during the 1940s. His research revealed numerous interesting findings in regard to the types and patterns of sexual activities in which people engage.

Read about Kinsey's studies on Human Sexual Behaviour

**What can you find in MyPsychLab?**
Self-directed tests * Videos * Simulations * eBook * Biographies * Audio glossary * Web links … and more—organised by chapter, section and learning objective.

mypsych lab
where learning comes to life!

# Emotion, Stress and Health

# CHAPTER 12

# CHAPTER FOCUS POINTS

After studying this chapter you will have a better understanding of:

1. The psychology and the physiology of human emotional responses

2. How to describe the major theories of emotion and the relationship between thought, emotion and behaviour

3. The main psychological, physiological and health consequences of acute and chronic stress

4. Your own coping resources, and your ability to manage stress

5. The ways in which the concept of 'health' and approaches to prevention and treatment of poor health differ between different cultural groups

6. The prevalence and management of 'lifestyle' diseases in the Australian population.

## CHAPTER CONTENTS

Suppose we asked you right now, 'How are you feeling?' How would you answer that question? There are at least three different types of information you might provide. First, you might reveal to us the mood you are in— the *emotions* you are feeling. Are you happy because you know you can finish reading this chapter in time to go to a party? Are you angry because your boss just yelled at you over the telephone? Second, you might tell us something more general about the amount of *stress* you are experiencing. Do you feel as if you can cope with all the tasks you have to get done? Or are you feeling a bit overwhelmed? Third, you might report on your psychological or physical *health*. Do you feel some illness coming on? Or do you feel an overall sense of wellness?

This chapter will explore interactions among these three ways in which you might answer the question 'How are you feeling?'—in relation to your emotions, stress and health. *Emotions* are the touchstones of human experience. They give richness to your interactions with people and nature and significance to your memories. In this chapter, we will discuss the experience and functions of emotions. But what happens if the emotional demands on your biological and psychological functioning are too great? You may become overwhelmed and unable to deal with the stressors of your life. This chapter will also examine how *stress* affects you and how you can combat it. Finally, we will broaden our focus to consider psychology's contributions to the study of health and illness. *Health psychologists* investigate the ways in which environmental, social and psychological processes contribute to the development of disease. Health psychologists also use psychological processes and principles to help treat and prevent illness while also developing strategies to enhance personal wellness.

We begin now by looking at the content and meaning of emotions.

# EMOTIONS

Just imagine what your life would be like if you could think and act but not feel. Would you be willing to give up the capacity to experience fear if you would also lose the passion of a lover's kiss? Would you give up sadness at the expense of joy? Surely these would be bad bargains, promptly regretted. We will soon see that emotions serve a number of important functions. Let us begin, however, by offering a definition of emotion and by describing the roots of your emotional experiences.

Although you might be tempted to think of emotion as only a feeling—'I feel happy' or 'I feel angry'—we need a more inclusive definition of this important concept that involves both the body and the mind. Contemporary psychologists define **emotion** as a complex pattern of bodily and mental changes that includes physiological arousal, feelings, cognitive processes, visible expressions (including face and posture), and specific behavioural reactions made in response to a situation perceived as

Charles Darwin was one of the first to use photographs in the study of emotion. These plates are from *The Expression of Emotions in Man and Animals* (1872/1965). Why did Darwin believe that emotions were the product of evolution?

personally significant. To see why all of these components are necessary, imagine a situation in which you would feel a surge of happiness. You might notice changes in your physiology, such as a gently beating heart. Your overall mood would be positive. The associated cognitive processes include interpretations, memories and expectations that allow you to label the situation as happy. Your overt behavioural reactions might be expressive (smiling) and/or action-oriented (embracing a loved one). None of these, by itself is happiness—emotions are always a combination of physiological, mood, cognitive and behavioural changes.

Before we provide an account that unites arousal, feelings, thoughts and actions, we need to make a distinction between emotions and moods. We have defined emotions as specific responses to specific events—in that sense, emotions are typically relatively short lived and relatively intense. By contrast, *moods* are often less intense and may last several days. There's often a weaker connection between moods and triggering events. You might be in a good or bad mood without knowing exactly why. Keep this distinction between emotions and moods in mind as we describe the theories that explain them.

## BASIC EMOTIONS AND CULTURE

Suppose you could gather together in one room representatives from a great diversity of human cultures. What would be common in their experiences of emotion? For an initial answer, you might look to Charles Darwin's book *The Expression of Emotions in Man and Animals* (1872/1965). Darwin believed that emotions evolve alongside other important aspects of human and non-human structures and functions. He was interested in the *adaptive* functions of emotions, which he thought of not as vague, unpredictable, personal states, but as highly specific, coordinated modes of operation of the human brain. Darwin viewed emotions as inherited, specialised mental states designed to deal with a certain class of *recurring situations* in the world. Over the history of our

**emotion** A complex pattern of changes, including physiological arousal, feelings, cognitive processes and behavioural reactions, made in response to a situation perceived to be personally significant.

Why do researchers believe that some emotional responses are innate?

species, humans have been attacked by predators, fallen in love, given birth to children, fought each other, confronted their mates' sexual infidelity and witnessed the death of loved ones—innumerable times. We might expect, therefore, that certain types of emotional responses would emerge in all members of the human species. Researchers have tested this claim of the *universality of emotions* by looking at the emotional responses of newborn children as well as the consistency of facial expressions across cultures.

### Are some emotional responses innate?

If the evolutionary perspective is correct, we would expect to find much the same patterns of emotional responses in children all over the world (Izard, 1994). **Silvan Tomkins** (1962, 1981) was one of the first psychologists to emphasise the pervasive role of immediate, unlearned affective (emotional) reactions. He pointed out that, without prior learning, infants respond to loud sounds with fear or with difficulties in breathing. They seem 'prewired' to respond to certain stimuli with an emotional response general enough to fit a wide range of circumstances.

Cross-cultural research has confirmed the expectation that some emotional responses are quite similar in children from very different cultures.

> Five- and 12-month-old children in the United States and Japan were visited in their homes. The experimenters subjected each child to a procedure in which the infant's wrists were grasped and folded across the infant's stomach. The experimenters videotaped each infant's response. Infants from both cultures moved their facial muscles in the same patterns—resulting in highly similar expressions of distress. Japanese and American infants also showed similar rates of negative vocalisation and physical struggling (Camras et al., 1992).

Although this study demonstrates important cross-cultural consistency, more recent research has exposed some differences. In one study, 11-month-old children from China were consistently less emotionally expressive than their age-mates from Japan and the United States

(Camras et al., 1998). These results suggest that culture acts very early in life to have an impact on innate emotional responses.

Note that infants also seem to have an innate ability to interpret the facial expressions of others. In one experiment, 4- to 6-month-old infants habituated—they showed decreasing interest—to repeated presentations of adult faces showing a single emotion drawn from the set of surprise, fear, and anger (see Chapter 10 for examples of habituation procedures with children). When the infants were subsequently shown a photograph with a different emotion, they responded with renewed interest—suggesting that surprise, fear and anger expressions 'looked different' to them, even at these very young ages (Serrano et al., 1992). Infants also produce more positive behaviours (for example, approaching movements and smiles) towards happy expressions and more negative behaviours (for example, avoidance movements and frowns) towards angry expressions. This suggests that they not only recognise but also have a very early understanding of the 'meaning' of these expressions (Serrano et al., 1995).

### Are emotional expressions universal?

We have seen that infants produce and perceive standard emotional expressions. If that is so, we might also expect to find adult members of even vastly different cultures showing reasonable agreement in the way they believe emotion is communicated by facial expressions.

According to **Paul Ekman**, the leading researcher on the nature of facial expressions, all people share an overlap in 'facial language' (Ekman, 1984, 1994). Ekman and his associates have demonstrated what Darwin first proposed— that a set of emotional expressions is universal to the human species, presumably because they are innate components of our evolutionary heritage. Before you read on, take a look at **Figure 12.1** to see how well you can identify these seven universally recognised expressions of emotion (Ekman & Friesen, 1986).

There is considerable evidence that these seven expressions are recognised and produced worldwide in response to the emotions of happiness, surprise, anger, disgust, fear, sadness and contempt. Cross-cultural researchers have asked people from a variety of cultures to identify the emotions associated with expressions in standardised photographs.

Individuals are generally able to identify the expressions associated with the seven emotions.

> In one study, members of a preliterate culture in New Guinea (the Fore culture), who had had almost no exposure to Westerners or to Western culture prior to this experiment, accurately identified the emotions expressed in the white faces shown in Figure 12.1. They did so by referring to situations in which they had experienced the same emotion. For example, photo 5 (fear) suggested being chased by a wild boar when you didn't have your spear, and photo 6 (sadness) suggested your child had died. Their only confusion came in distinguishing surprise, photo 2, from fear,

Figure 12.1

Anger, happiness, surprise, fear, sadness and disgust. But which is which?

perhaps because these people are most fearful when taken by surprise.

Next, researchers asked other members of the culture (who had not participated in the first study) to model the expressions that they used to communicate six of the emotions (excluding contempt). When U.S. college students viewed videotapes of the facial expressions of the Fore people, they were able to identify their emotions accurately—with one exception. Not surprisingly, the Americans had difficulty distinguishing between the Fore poses of fear and surprise, the same emotions that the Fore had confused in the Western poses (Ekman & Friesen, 1971).

More recent research has compared judgments of facial expressions across individuals in Hungary, Japan, Poland, Sumatra, the United States and Vietnam—high agreement was found across these diverse populations (Biehl et al., 1997). The general conclusion is that people

all over the world, regardless of cultural differences, race, sex or education, express basic emotions in much the same way and are able to identify the emotions others are experiencing by reading their facial expressions.

Note that the claim of universality is focused on the basic set of seven emotions. Ekman and his colleagues make no claim that all facial expressions are universal or that cultures express all emotions in the same way (Ekman, 1994).

In fact, Ekman (1972) called his position on universality the *euro-cultural* theory, to reflect the joint contributions of the brain (the product of evolution) and culture in emotional expression. The brain specifies which facial muscles move, to produce a particular expression, when a particular emotion is aroused. Different cultures, however, impose their own constraints beyond universal biology. We reported some cultural effects in the description of the research comparing responses of members of the Fore culture and U.S. college students.

The six-country comparison we cited earlier also produced some differences among the countries, against the general background of agreement (Biehl et al., 1997). For example, Japanese adults were worse at identifying anger than were U.S., Hungarian, Polish and Vietnamese adults. Vietnamese adults were worse at identifying disgust than the participants from all the other countries.

Why might these differences arise? Let's now look directly at cultural influences on emotionality.

**How does culture constrain emotional expression?** We've just seen that some aspects of emotional expression are universal. Even so, different cultures have different standards for how emotion should be managed. Some forms of emotional response, even facial expressions, are unique to each culture. Cultures establish social rules for when people may show certain emotions and for the social appropriateness of certain types of emotional displays by given types of people in particular settings (Mesquita & Frijda, 1992; Ratner, 2000). Let's look at three examples of cultures that express emotions in manners different from the Western norm.

The Wolof people of Senegal live in a society where status and power differences among people are rigidly defined. High-caste members of this culture are expected to show great restraint in their expressions of emotionality; low-caste individuals are expected to be more volatile, particularly a caste called the *griots*. The griots, in fact, are often called upon to express the 'undignified' emotions of the nobility.

> One afternoon, a group of women (some five nobles and two griots) were gathered near a well on the edge of town when another woman strode over to the well and threw herself down it. All the women were shocked at the apparent suicide attempt, but the noblewomen were shocked in silence. Only the griot women screamed, on behalf of all. (Irvine, 1990, p. 146)

Can you imagine how you would respond in this situation? It might be easier to put yourself in the place of the griots rather than in the place of the noblewomen: How could you help but scream? The answer, of course, is

that the noblewomen have acquired cultural norms for emotional expression that require them not to show any overt response.

A second example of cultural variation in emotional expression arose in the life of one of your authors. At the funeral of an American friend of Syrian descent, he was surprised to see and hear a group of women shrieking and wailing when a visitor entered the funeral parlour. They then stopped just as suddenly until the next visitor arrived, when once again they started their group wailing. What is the explanation for this behaviour? Because it is difficult for the family members of the deceased to sustain a high emotional pitch over the three days and nights of such wakes, they hire these professional criers to display, on their behalf, appropriately strong emotions to each newcomer. This is an expected practice among a number of Mediterranean and Near Eastern cultures.

For our third example, we turn to a cross-cultural difference in norms for emotional displays related to pain. Recall from Chapter 4 that psychological context has a major impact on the extent to which people experience pain. Similarly, the cultural context has an impact on the extent to which it is considered appropriate for people to perform behaviours that reveal they are experiencing pain. For example, one study demonstrated a contrast between what people in the United States and Japan consider proper behavioural displays for pain (Hobara, 2005). Participants in both cultures completed the Appropriate Pain Behaviour Questionnaire (APBQ) that includes such items as 'Women should be able to tolerate pain in most circumstances' and 'It is acceptable for men to cry when in pain.' In general, Japanese participants provided lower scores on the APBQ: they indicated less approval for open emotional expressions of pain. In addition, both cultural groups suggested more approval for women's emotional displays than men's displays. The researcher attributed the cultural difference to the 'traditional stoicism . . . of many Asian cultures' (Hobara, 2005, p. 392).

When you think about the types of emotional patterns that may have evolved over the course of human experience, always bear in mind that culture may have the last word. Can you see how different standards for

In what ways do cultures constrain emotional expressions in situations like funerals?

emotional expression could cause misunderstandings between people of different cultural origins?

We have seen so far that some physiological responses to emotional situations—such as smiles and grimaces—may be innate. Let's turn now to theories that consider the link between other physiological responses and their psychological interpretations.

## THEORIES OF EMOTION

Theories of emotion generally attempt to explain the relationship between physiological and psychological aspects of the experience of emotion. We will begin this section by discussing the responses your body gives in emotionally relevant situations. We will then review theories that explore the way these physiological responses contribute to your psychological experience of emotion.

### Physiology of emotion

What happens when you experience a strong emotion? Your heart races, respiration goes up, your mouth dries, your muscles tense, and maybe you even shake. In addition to these noticeable changes, many others occur beneath the surface. All these responses are designed to mobilise your body for action to deal with the source of the emotion. Let's look at their origins.

The *autonomic nervous system* (ANS) prepares the body for emotional responses through the action of both its sympathetic and parasympathetic divisions (see Chapter 3). The balance between the divisions depends on the quality and intensity of the arousing stimulation. With mild, *unpleasant* stimulation, the *sympathetic* division is more active; with mild, *pleasant* stimulation, the *parasympathetic* division is more active. With more intense stimulation of either kind, both divisions are increasingly involved. Physiologically, strong emotions such as fear or anger activate the body's *emergency reaction system*, which swiftly and silently prepares the body for potential danger. The sympathetic nervous system takes charge by directing the release of hormones (adrenaline and noradrenaline) from the adrenal glands, which in turn leads the internal organs to release blood sugar, raise blood pressure, and increase sweating and salivation. To calm you after the emergency has passed, the parasympathetic nervous system inhibits the release of the activating hormones. You may remain aroused for a while after an experience of strong emotional activation because some of the hormones continue to circulate in your bloodstream.

As we will see when we describe specific theories of emotion, researchers have debated the question 'Do particular emotional experiences give rise to distinct patterns of activity in the autonomic nervous system?' Cross-cultural research suggests that the answer to the question is yes. A team of researchers measured autonomic responses such as heart rate and skin temperature while men and women from the United States and Minangkabau men from West Sumatra generated emotions and emotional expressions. Members of the Minangkabau culture are socialised not to display negative emotions. Would they, even so, show the same underlying autonomic

patterns for negative emotions as did the American. participants? The data revealed a high level of similarity across the two cultures, leading the researchers to suggest that patterns of autonomic activity are 'an important part of our common evolved biological heritage' (Levenson et al., 1992, p. 986).

Let's move now from the autonomic nervous system to the central nervous system. Integration of both the hormonal and the neural aspects of arousal is controlled by the *hypothalamus* and the *limbic system*, control systems for emotions and for patterns of attack, defence, and flight. Neuroanatomy research has particularly focused on the *amygdala* as a part of the limbic system that acts as a gateway for emotion and as a filter for memory. The amygdala does this by attaching significance to the information it receives from the senses. It plays an especially strong role in attaching meaning to negative experiences. For example, when people view pictures of fearful facial expressions, the left amygdala (each side of your brain has a separate amygdala) shows increasing activity as the intensity of the expression increases; by contrast, happy facial expressions produce less activity in the same structure the more intensely happy the face becomes (Morris et al., 1996).

In Chapter 10, we described research demonstrating that the left and right amygdala take on different processing roles when men and women encounter and remember emotionally charged pictures (Cahill et al., 2004; Canli et al., 2002). Recent evidence from PET scans suggests that men's and women's brains are organised differently for emotions even when they are not actively engaged with a task (Kilpatrick et al., 2006). Parallelling the results for emotional memories, men show greater resting activity in the right amygdala, whereas women show more activity in the left amygdala. However, men and women also differ with respect to patterns of connections to other brain regions. For men, the right amygdala communicates extensively with brain regions such as areas of the motor and visual cortex that are oriented toward the external environment. For women, the left amygdala communicates extensively with regions such as the hypothalamus that are oriented toward the body's inner environment. These data suggest that men and women may be biologically predisposed to respond differently to emotional events.

The *cortex* is involved in emotional experiences through its internal neural networks and its connections with other parts of the body. The cortex provides the associations, memories, and meanings that integrate psychological experience and biological responses. Research using brain-scanning techniques has begun to map particular responses for different emotions. For example, positive and negative emotions are not just opposite responses in the same portions of the cortex. Rather, opposite emotions lead to greatest activity in quite different parts of the brain. Consider a study in which participants underwent fMRI scans while viewing positive pictures (e.g., puppies, brownies and sunsets) and negative pictures (angry people, spiders and guns). The scans showed greater activity in the brain's

How does the brain respond differently to experiences of puppies and spiders?

left hemisphere for positive pictures and in the right hemisphere for negative pictures (Canli et al., 1998). In fact, researchers have suggested that there are two distinct systems in the brain that handle *approach-related* and *withdrawal-related* emotional responses (Davidson et al., 2000a). Consider puppies and spiders. It is likely that most people would want to approach the puppies but withdraw from the spiders. Research suggests that different brain circuits— apportioned to the different hemispheres of the brain— underlie those responses.

We have seen so far that your body provides many responses to situations in which emotions are relevant. But how do you know which feeling goes with which physiological response? We now review three theories that attempt an answer to this question.

### James–Lange theory of body reaction

You might think, at first, that everyone would agree that emotions precede responses: For example, you yell at someone (response) because you feel angry (emotion). However, over 100 years ago, William James argued, as Aristotle had much earlier, that the sequence was reversed—you feel *after* your body reacts. As James put it, 'We feel sorry because we cry, angry because we strike, afraid because we tremble' (James, 1890/1950, p. 450). This view that emotion stems from *bodily feedback* became known as **James–Lange theory of emotion** (Carl Lange was a Danish scientist who presented similar ideas the same year as James). According to this theory, perceiving a stimulus causes autonomic arousal and other bodily actions that lead to the experience of a specific emotion (see **Figure 12.2**). The James–Lange theory is considered a *peripheralist* theory because it assigns the most prominent role in the emotion chain to visceral reactions, the actions of the autonomic nervous system that are peripheral to the central nervous system.

### Cannon–Bard theory of central neural processes

Physiologist Walter Cannon (1927, 1929) rejected the peripheralist theory in favour of a *centralist* focus on the action of the central nervous system. Cannon (and other critics) raised a number of objections to the James–Lange theory (Leventhal, 1980). They noted, for example, that visceral activity is irrelevant for emotional experience— experimental animals continue to respond emotionally even after their viscera are separated surgically from the CNS. They also argued that ANS responses are typically too slow to be the source of split-second elicited emotions. According to Cannon, emotion requires that the brain intercede between the input stimulation and the output response. Signals from the thalamus get routed to one area of the cortex to produce emotional feeling and to another for emotional expressiveness.

Another physiologist, Philip Bard (1898–1977), also concluded that visceral reactions were not primary in the emotion sequence. Instead, an emotion-arousing stimulus has two simultaneous effects, causing both bodily arousal via the sympathetic nervous system and the subjective experience of emotion via the cortex. The views of these physiologists were combined in the **Cannon–Bard theory of emotion**. This theory states that an emotion stimulus produces two concurrent reactions, arousal and experience of emotion, that do not cause each other (see **Figure 12.2**). If something makes you angry, your heartbeat increases at the same time as you think 'I'm ticked off!'—but neither your body nor your mind dictates the way the other responds.

The Cannon–Bard theory predicts independence between bodily and psychological responses. We will see next that contemporary theories of emotion reject the claim that these responses are necessarily independent.

### Cognitive appraisal theories of emotion

Because arousal symptoms and internal states are similar for many different emotions, it is possible to confuse them at times when they are experienced in ambiguous or novel situations. According to **Stanley Schachter** (1971b), the experience of emotion is the joint effect of physiological arousal and **cognitive appraisal**, with both parts necessary for an emotion to occur. All arousal is assumed to be general and undifferentiated, and arousal is the first step in the emotion sequence. You appraise your physiological arousal in an effort to discover what you are feeling, what emotional label best fits, and what your reaction means in the particular setting in which it is being experienced. **Richard Lazarus** (1991, 1995; Lazarus & Lazarus, 1994),

**Cannon–Bard theory of emotion** A theory stating that an emotional stimulus produces two co-occurring reactions—arousal and experience of emotion—that do not cause each other.

**James–Lange theory of emotion** A peripheral-feedback theory of emotion stating that an eliciting stimulus triggers a behavioural response that sends different sensory and motor feedback to the brain and creates a specific emotion.

**cognitive appraisal** The cognitive interpretation and evaluation of a stressor.

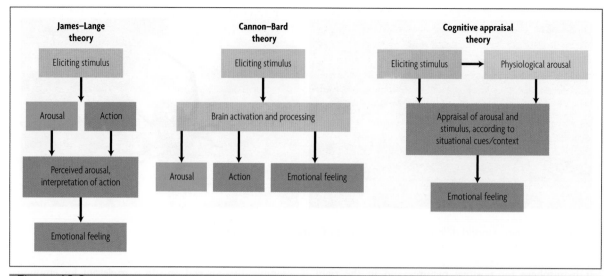

Figure 12.2

**Comparing three theories of emotion**

These classic theories of emotion propose different components of emotion. They also propose different process sequences by which a stimulus event results in the experience of emotion. In the James–Lange theory, events trigger both autonomic arousal and behavioural action, which are perceived and then result in a specific emotional experience. In the Cannon–Bard theory, events are first processed at various centers in the brain, which then direct the simultaneous reactions of arousal, behavioural action and emotional experience. In the cognitive appraisal theory, both stimulus events and physiological arousal are cognitively appraised at the same time according to situational cues and context factors, with the emotional experience resulting from the interaction of the level of arousal and the nature of appraisal.

Figure from Spencer A. Rathus, *Psychology*, 3/e. Copyright © 1987. Reprinted with permission of Wadsworth, a division of Thomson Learning: www.thomsonrights.com

another leading proponent of the cognitive appraisal view, maintains that 'emotional experience cannot be understood solely in terms of what happens in the person or in the brain, but grows out of ongoing transactions with the environment that are evaluated' (Lazarus, 1984a, p. 124). Lazarus also emphasises that appraisal often occurs without conscious thought. When you have past experiences that link emotions to situations—here comes that bully I've clashed with before!—you need not explicitly search the environment for an interpretation of your arousal. This position has become known as the **cognitive appraisal theory of emotion** (see **Figure 12.2**).

To test this theory, experimenters have sometimes created situations in which environmental cues were available to provide a label for an individual's arousal.

A female researcher interviewed male participants who had just crossed one of two bridges in Vancouver, Canada. One bridge was a safe, sturdy bridge; the other was a wobbly, precarious bridge. The researcher pretended to be interested in the effects of scenery on creativity and asked the men to write brief stories about an ambiguous picture that included a woman. She also invited them to call her if they wanted more information about the research. Those men who had just crossed the dangerous bridge wrote stories with more sexual imagery, and four times as many of those men called the female researcher than did those who had crossed the safe bridge. To show that arousal was the independent variable influencing the emotional

misinterpretation, the research team also arranged for another group of men to be interviewed 10 minutes or more after crossing the dangerous bridge, enough time for their physical arousal symptoms to be reduced. These nonaroused men did not show the signs of sexual response that the aroused men did (Dutton & Aron, 1974).

In this situation, the male participants came to an emotional judgment ('I am interested in this woman') based on a *misattribution* of the source of arousal (the woman rather than the danger of the bridge). In a similar experiment, students who performed 2 minutes of aerobic exercise reported less extreme emotions just after the exercise—when they could easily attribute their arousal to the exercise rather than to an emotional state—by comparison to the emotions they reported after a brief delay that made the exercise seem less relevant to continuing arousal (Sinclair et al., 1994).

Some of the specific aspects of the cognitive appraisal theory have been challenged. For example, you learned earlier that arousal states—the activity of the autonomic nervous system—accompanying different emotions are not identical (Levenson et al., 1992). Therefore, interpretations of at least some emotional experiences may not require appraisal. Furthermore, experiencing strong arousal without any obvious cause does not lead to a neutral, undifferentiated state, as the theory assumes. Stop for a moment and imagine that, right now, your heart suddenly starts beating quickly, your breathing becomes fast and

**cognitive appraisal theory of emotion** the theory that emotion is the joint effect of physiological arousal and cognitive appraisal, which determines how an ambiguous inner state of arousal will be labelled.

shallow, your chest muscles tighten, and your palms become drenched with sweat. What interpretation would you put on these symptoms? Are you surprised to learn that people generally interpret *unexplained* physical arousal as *negative*, a sign that something is wrong? In addition, people's search for an explanation tends to be biased toward finding stimuli that will explain or justify this negative interpretation (Marshall & Zimbardo, 1979; Maslach, 1979).

Another critique of the cognitive appraisal theory of emotion comes from researcher **Robert Zajonc** (pronounced Zy-Onts). Zajonc demonstrated conditions under which people have preferences—emotional responses to stimuli—without knowing why (Zajonc, 2000, 2001). In an extensive series of experiments on the *mere exposure effect*, participants were presented with a variety of stimuli, such as foreign words, Chinese characters, sets of numbers and strange faces. These stimuli were flashed so briefly that participants could not consciously recognise the items. Later on, participants were asked how much they liked particular stimuli, some of which were old (i.e., those stimuli had been flashed below the threshold of consciousness) whereas some were new. The participants tended to give higher ratings to the old items. Because participants experienced these positive emotions without conscious awareness of their origins, the emotional response could not emerge from an appraisal process.

The mere exposure effect can work both ways. One of your authors worked for many months in a group home for memory disordered patients in Tasmania. Occasionally members of the group would have arguments, often quite heated. We noticed that the patients became classically conditioned to display anger and hostility when they saw a patient had fought with previously, even though they could not give a reason for their anger as they had forgotten the original argument. In other words they felt a surge of anger towards the person without any cognitive understanding or appraisal.

It is probably safest to conclude that cognitive appraisal is an important process of emotional experience, but not the only one (Izard, 1993). Under some circumstances, you will, in fact, look to the environment (at least unconsciously) to try to interpret why you feel the way you do. Under other circumstances, however, your emotional experiences may be under the control of the innate links provided by evolution. The physiological response will not require any interpretation. These different routes to emotional experiences suggest that emotions serve a range of functions. We turn now to those functions.

## FUNCTIONS OF EMOTION

Why do you have emotions? What functions do emotions serve for you? To think about these questions, it might help to review your day and imagine how different it would have been if you couldn't experience or understand emotions. Let's examine some of the roles researchers have suggested that emotion plays in your life.

### Motivation and attention

The very first time you wear your new jumper, the shoulder seam rips. Why are you likely to storm back to the store and demand a refund? From Chapter 11, you should recognise this as a question about motivation. If you want to answer, 'Because I'd be angry' or 'Because I'd be disappointed', you can see that emotions often provide the impetus for action. Emotions serve a motivational function by *arousing* you to take action with regard to some experienced or imagined event. Emotions then direct and *sustain* your behaviours towards specific goals. For the love of another person, you may do all you can to attract, be near, and protect him or her. For the love of principle or of country, you may sacrifice your life.

Let's consider specific circumstances in which emotional responses have an impact on how you focus your attention. Recall from Chapter 4 that, at any given time, you can attend to only a very small subset of the objects and events available in the environment. Research suggests that emotion focuses your attention in a way that yields better memory.

> Participants viewed photographs that were either neutral (e.g., an airplane or a barometer) or aroused negative emotions (e.g., a grenade or a hypodermic needle) (Kensinger et al., 2006). The presentations lasted either 250 milliseconds (i.e., a quarter second) or 500 milliseconds (i.e., a half second). Participants judged whether the objects in each photograph could fit inside a shoebox—they inspected a reference shoebox in advance of the task. Two days after viewing the photographs, participants returned to the laboratory to complete a memory task they hadn't expected. They were asked to view another series of photographs and say whether each photograph was 'new' (i.e., it was an object they hadn't seen before), 'similar' (i.e., it was a different photograph of an old object—for example, a different airplane), or 'same' (i.e., it was the exact photograph they saw before). When they had viewed the original photographs for 500 milliseconds, participants were better able to discriminate 'same' from 'similar' photographs for the emotionally arousing objects: The emotion evoked by the objects helped focus attention on precise visual details.

What emotions would you be likely to feel if people all around you were wildly cheering your favourite team?

The advantage for emotionally arousing photographs didn't emerge when participants viewed the objects for just 250 milliseconds. This suggests that a certain amount of processing time is necessary before emotions can begin to affect the focus of attention.

Social functions of emotion On a social level, emotions serve the broad function of regulating social interactions. As a positive social glue, they bind you to some people; as a negative social repellent, they distance you from others. You back off when someone is bristling with anger, and you approach when another person signals receptivity with a smile, dilated pupils and a 'come hither' glance. You might suppress strong negative emotions out of respect for another person's status or power. Consider D. R., a woman who lost the function of her amygdala—and with it the ability to perceive anger and fear (Scott et al., 1997). Imagine what life would be like if you couldn't understand when people were trying to communicate negative emotions. For example, what would it be like not to be able to learn from others that a situation was dangerous? Or that your actions had given rise to an angry response? When D. R. lost function in her amygdala, she also lost her ability to function fully in her social world.

The emotions you experience have a strong impact on how you function in social settings. Joseph Forgas from the University of New South Wales has conducted pioneering research on the impact of emotion on social functioning. Consider the consequences of people's positive or negative moods on the ways in which they made requests.

Participants in an experiment watched short films that put them in happy, neutral or sad moods. Once the mood was established, the experimenter asked each participant to perform a favour: Would he or she retrieve a stimulus file from a research assistant in the next room? The words the participants used to make the request were recorded. Raters (who did not know which participant had been in which mood) provided ratings of the politeness of each request. As shown in **Figure 12.3**, mood had a large impact on politeness: sad participants were the most polite. People in sad moods appeared to be cautious about making direct—potentially impolite—demands on other people (Forgas, 1999).

Think about your own life: Are you more risk-taking in social situations when you are in a happy mood? Are you more cautious when you are in a sad mood?

Research also points to the impact of emotion on stimulating prosocial behaviour (Hoffman, 1986; Isen, 1984; Schroeder et al., 1995). When individuals are made to feel good, they are more likely to engage in a variety of helping behaviours (Carlson et al., 1988). When research participants were made to feel guilty about a misdeed, they were more likely to volunteer aid in a future situation, presumably to reduce their guilt (Carlsmith & Gross, 1969). Similarly, how people feel depends on how prosocial they have been. For example, when individuals recalled instances in which they had refused to help another person, their moods became more negative (Williamson et al., 1996). This was particularly true when the person they had refused to help was a good friend, family member or romantic partner. How you feel is greatly affected by how well you are able to carry out your social obligations.

## EMOTIONAL EFFECTS ON COGNITIVE FUNCTIONING

Emotions serve cognitive functions by influencing what you attend to, the way you perceive yourself and others, and the way you interpret and remember various features of life situations. Researchers have demonstrated that emotional states can affect learning, memory, social judgments and creativity (Bradley, 1994; Forgas, 1995, 2000). Your emotional responses play an important role in organising and categorising your life experiences.

Research on the role of emotion in information processing was pioneered by **Gordon Bower** (1981, 1991) and his students. Bower's model proposes that, when a person experiences a given emotion in a particular situation, that emotion is stored in memory along with the ongoing events, as part of the same context. This pattern of memory representation gives rise to mood-congruent processing and mood-dependent memory. *Mood-congruent processing* occurs when people are selectively sensitised to process and retrieve information that agrees with their current mood state. Material that is congruent with one's prevailing mood is more likely to be noticed, attended to and processed more deeply and with greater

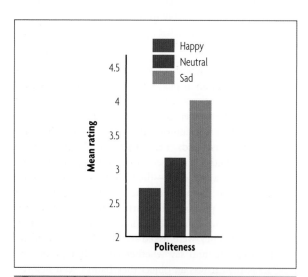

Figure 12.3

**The effects of mood on request politeness**
Participants in happy, neutral or negative moods made requests of a stranger. Raters assessed the politeness of each request on a scale ranging from 1 (impolite) to 7 (polite). Participants in sad moods produced requests that were relatively more polite (e.g., 'Would you mind getting me the stimulus file?' vs. 'I need the stimulus file').

Has a strong emotion, like anger, ever driven you to engage in irrational or destructive behaviour?

**Table 12.1**

Moral reasoning problems

1. A runaway trolley is heading down the tracks toward five workmen who will be killed if the trolley proceeds on its present course. You are on a footbridge over the tracks in between the approaching trolley and the five workmen. Next to you on this footbridge is a stranger who happens to be very large.

   The only way to save the lives of the five workmen is to push this stranger off the bridge and onto the tracks below where his large body will stop the trolley. The stranger will die if you do this, but the five workmen will be saved.

   Is it appropriate for you to push the stranger onto the tracks in order to save the five workmen?

2. You are at the wheel of a runaway trolley quickly approaching a fork in the tracks. On the tracks extending to the left is a group of five railway workmen. On the tracks extending to the right is a single railway workman.

   If you do nothing the trolley will proceed to the left, causing the deaths of the five workmen. The only way to avoid the deaths of these workmen is to hit a switch on your dashboard that will cause the trolley to proceed to the right, causing the death of the single workman.

   Is it appropriate for you to hit the switch in order to avoid the deaths of the five workmen?

elaborative associations (Gilligan & Bower, 1984). *Mood-dependent memory* refers to circumstances in which people find it easier to recall information when their mood at retrieval matches their mood when they first committed the information to memory (Eich, 1995; Eich & Macaulay, 2000). Here's an example of mood congruency you might have noticed: people who are in pleasant moods tend to recall more positive events from their lives than do people who are in unpleasant moods (Eich et al., 1994).

As well as the overall tone, or *valency* of the mood (positive versus negative), the type of emotional state also influences cognitive functions. For example, people who more anxious than others are more likely to have difficulty with prospective memory tasks, or tasks that require you to remember to do something later on (such as to pick up the dry cleaning on the way home) (eg Harris & Menzies, 1999; Harris & Cumming, 2003)

Researchers have also been interested in understanding the circumstances in which emotions have an impact on judgments and reasoning (Adolphs & Damasio, 2001). Consider the two reasoning problems given in **Table 12.1**. How would you answer the question at the end of each problem? If you analyse the situations carefully—trying to stick only to the outcomes—you'll see that in each case one person dies so that five others might live. However, most people respond differently to the scenarios: they believe it is appropriate to flip the switch, but they find it difficult to agree that they would actually push a stranger onto trolley tracks. One hypothesis for this difference is that the first type of problem engages emotional processing. It's hard to be unemotional about the idea of actually *pushing* someone onto the tracks. Evidence in favour of this hypothesis comes directly from the brain. In one study, researchers asked participants to consider moral reasoning problems while undergoing fMRI scans (Greene et al., 2001). As in example 1, some of the problems were *personal*—they asked participants to consider actions that required direct personal involvement. The contrasting problems, as in

example 2, were relatively *impersonal*. The two types of problems led to quite different responses in the brain. In particular, for the personal problems the fMRI scans showed considerably more activity in those brain regions that had been associated, in prior research, with emotional processing. This study provides strong evidence that the content of the problems you face in life determines the way in which cognition and emotion interact to yield solutions.

One final note about the relationship between mood and cognition: Researchers have consistently demonstrated that positive affect—pleasant moods—produces more efficient and more creative thinking and problem solving (Isen et al., 1987). Consider a study in which physicians were asked to solve problems that required a certain level of creativity. Those who had been placed in a mildly pleasant mood (the experimenters gave the doctors a small gift of sweets) performed reliably better on the creativity test than did those doctors in the control group (who got no prior gift) (Estrada et al., 1994). You can see an immediate application of these types of findings: you are likely to carry out your study more efficiently and creatively if you can maintain a happy mood. You might be thinking, 'How am I supposed to stay happy with all the work I have to do?' As we turn now to the topic of stress, and how to cope with it, you will learn how to take cognitive control over how you are 'feeling'.

## RECAP CHECKPOINT
### Emotions

- Emotions are complex patterns of changes made up of physiological arousal, cognitive appraisal, and behavioural and expressive reactions.

- As a product of evolution, all humans may share a basic set of emotional responses.

- Cultures, however, vary in their rules of appropriateness for displaying emotions.

- Classic theories emphasise different parts of emotional response, such as peripheral bodily reactions or central neural processes.

- More contemporary theories emphasise the appraisal of arousal.

- Emotions serve motivational, social and cognitive functions.

## CONCEPT QUESTIONS

1. What has cross-cultural research revealed about the recognition of facial expressions?

2. What role does the autonomous nervous system play in experiences of emotion?

3. What is the main claim of the Cannon-Bard theory of emotion?

4. What is the general relationship between mood and politeness in social situations?

5. What is meant by mood-dependent memory?

## CRITICAL THINKING

How might you confirm that the pairs 'one—two' and 'one—nine' are about equal with respect to the physical similarity of the number names?

# PSYCHOLOGY *in your life*
## WHY ARE SOME PEOPLE HAPPIER THAN OTHERS?

You might think this question has an easy answer: Aren't some people happier than others because better things happen to them? That's true in part, but you might be surprised to learn that genetics has a large impact on how happy people are as they make their way through life.

Consider a study that used the classic methodology of behaviour genetics: the researchers examined the extent to which monozygotic (MZ) twins (who are genetically identical) and dizygotic (DZ) twins (who, like other siblings, share only half their genes) showed similar reports of wellbeing (Lykken & Tellegen, 1996). The twins' happiness levels were measured by questionnaires that asked them to respond to statements such as 'Taking the good with the bad, how happy

and contented are you on the average now, compared with other people?' The researchers examined two sets of responses from MZ and DZ twins, obtained when they were roughly 20 and 30 years old. As shown in the figure, they performed a 'cross-twin, cross-time' analysis: they calculated the extent to which one twin's happiness as a 30-year-old was correlated with his or her brother's or sister's happiness at age 20. The researchers found that there was virtually no relationship for the DZ twins. However, for the MZ twins, 80 percent of the relationship in the ratings from ages 20 to 30 could be explained by this cross-twin analysis.

The researchers suggested that this pattern within the pairs of MZ twins is best explained if baseline happiness—the average

amount of happiness each person will experience across the life span—has a strong genetic component. This doesn't mean, of course, that there is a gene (or genes) specifically for *happiness*. Remember from Chapter 2 that 'correlation is not causation.' It could be the case that some other aspects of an individual's behaviours or experiences mediate the genetic influence on happiness. For example, there might be genes that separately affect people's experiences of positive and negative emotions—with a joint impact on average wellbeing (Hamer, 1996).

Are you surprised by the claim that genetics affects average happiness? As we noted at the outset, you might have thought that your happiness would be more strongly affected by the environment: Are you in a romantic relationship? How hard are your courses? What are the obstacles in your life? The researchers propose that such environmental events cause variation around an average level of happiness that was 'set' at birth. As an analogy, think of the way the thermostat in your home works. Suppose you set it to 20°C—environmental events will cause variation around this temperature, but on average the temperature should be 20°C. The research on happiness suggests that each of us has a set happiness level—analogous, for example, to 9°C, 20°C, or 31°C—which remains our average in the face of life's ups and downs. Of course, just as thermostats may function less well under extremes, some life events (e.g., marriages and the deaths of spouses) will cause people to experience levels of happiness that depart from their set point (Lucas et al., 2003).

Beyond your individual circumstances, your experience of happiness is also influenced by the context in which we now function as a species. David Buss (2000) has suggested that some limits are placed on human happiness by the 'discrepancies between modern and ancestral environments' (p. 15). For example, although humans evolved in the context of small groups, many people now live in large urban environments in which they are mostly surrounded by large numbers of total strangers. We no longer have close bonds to the group of individuals that share our space—the types of bonds that could help us weather crises to experience happy lives. What can be done? Although you cannot turn back the tide of cultural evolution that has brought these changes about, you can try to counteract these changes by increasing your closeness to your family members and to your friends (Buss, 2000).

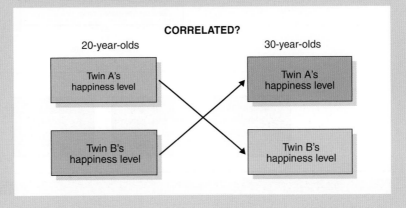

# STRESS OF LIVING

Suppose we asked you to keep track of how you are 'feeling' over the course of a day. You might report that for brief periods, you felt happiness, sadness, anger, astonishment, and so on. There is one feeling, however, that people often report as a kind of background noise for much of their day-to-day experience, and that is stress (Sapolsky, 1994). Modern industrialised society sets a rapid, hectic pace for living. People often have too many demands placed on their time, are worried about uncertain futures, and have little time for family and fun. But would you be better off without stress? A stress-free life would offer no challenge—no difficulties to surmount, no new fields to conquer, and no reasons to sharpen your wits or improve your abilities. Every organism faces challenges from its external environment and from its personal needs. The organism must solve these problems to survive and thrive.

**Stress** is the pattern of responses an organism makes to stimulus events that disturb its equilibrium and tax or exceed its ability to cope. In normal conversation we sometimes use the word stress to refer to both the stimulus ('Parking around campus is a real stress') and the response ('I feel stress when I'm late for a tute'). However,

psychologists tend to use the term 'stress' only to refer to the response, and use 'stressor' to refer to those elements in the environment that are thought to give rise the stress. The stimulus events include a large variety of external and internal conditions that collectively are called stressors. A **stressor** is a stimulus event that places a demand on an organism for some kind of adaptive response: a cyclist swerves in front of your car, your lecturer moves forward the due date of your major assignment, you're asked to run for student representative on the Academic Board. An individual's response to the need for change is made up of a diverse combination of reactions taking place on several levels, including physiological, behavioural, emotional and cognitive. People typically associate stress with *distress*—and assume that all stress is bad. However, you also experience *eustress*. ('*Eu*' is an ancient Greek suffix meaning 'good.') As you'll see by the end of this section, in many circumstances stress can bring about positive changes in your life.

**Figure 12.4** shows the elements of the stress process. Our goal for this section is to give you a clear understanding of all the features represented in this figure. We will begin by considering general physiological responses to stressors. We then describe the particular effects of different categories of stressors. Finally, we explore different methods you can use to cope with the stress in your life.

**stressor** An internal or external event or stimulus that induces stress.

**stress** The pattern of specific and nonspecific responses an organism makes to stimulus events that disturb its equilibrium and tax or exceed its ability to cope.

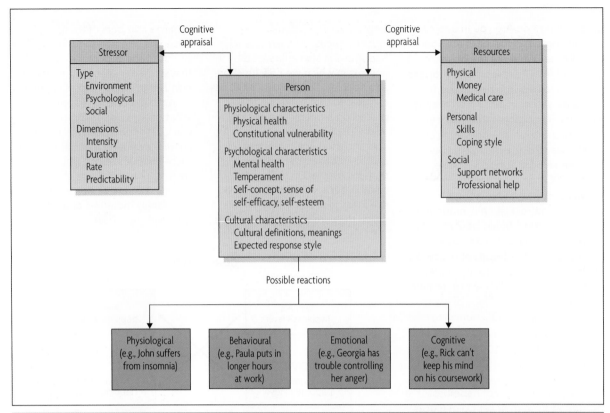

Figure 12.4

**A model of stress**
Cognitive appraisal of the stress situation interacts with the stressor and the physical, social and personal resources available for dealing with the stressor. Individuals respond to threats on various levels: physiological, behavioural, emotional and cognitive. Some responses are adaptive, and others are maladaptive or even lethal.

# PHYSIOLOGICAL STRESS REACTIONS

How would you respond if you arrived at a class and discovered that you were about to have a spot test? You would probably agree that this would cause you some stress, but what does that mean for your body's reactions? Many of the physiological responses we described for emotional situations are also relevant to day-to-day instances of stress. Such transient states of arousal, with typically clear onset and offset patterns, are examples of **acute stress**. **Chronic stress**, in contrast, is a state of enduring arousal, continuing over time, in which demands are perceived as greater than the inner and outer resources available for dealing with them. An example of chronic stress might be a continuous frustration with your inability to find time to do all the things you want to do. Let's see how your body responds to these different types of stresses.

**Emergency reactions to acute threats** In the 1920s, Walter Cannon outlined the first scientific description of the way animals and humans respond to danger. He found that a sequence of activity is triggered in the nerves and glands to prepare the body either to

defend itself and struggle or to run away to safety. Cannon called this dual stress response the **fight-or-flight response**. At the centre of this stress response is the *hypothalamus*, which is involved in a variety of emotional responses. The hypothalamus has sometimes been referred to as the stress centre because of its twin functions in emergencies: (1) It controls the autonomic nervous system (ANS) and (2) it activates the pituitary gland.

The ANS regulates the activities of the body's organs. In stressful conditions, breathing becomes faster and deeper, heart rate increases, blood vessels constrict, and blood pressure rises. In addition to these internal changes, muscles open the passages of the throat and nose to allow more air into the lungs while also producing facial expressions of strong emotion. Messages go to smooth muscles to stop certain bodily functions, such as digestion, that are irrelevant to preparing for the emergency at hand.

Another function of the ANS during stress is to get adrenaline flowing. It signals the inner part of the adrenal glands, the *adrenal medulla*, to release two hormones, *adrenaline* (called *epinephrine* in the US) and *noradrenaline* (*norepinephrine*), which, in turn, signal a number of other organs to perform their specialised functions. The spleen releases more red blood corpuscles (to aid in clotting if there is an injury), and the bone marrow is stimulated

**fight-or-flight response** A sequence of internal activities triggered when an organism is faced with a threat; prepares the body for combat and struggle or for running away to safety.

**acute stress** A transient state of arousal with typically clear onset and offset patterns.

**chronic stress** A continuous state of arousal in which an individual perceives demands as greater than the inner and outer resources available for dealing with them.

Whether at work or play, individuals in contemporary society are likely to encounter a stressful environment. What situations in your life do you find most stressful?

to make more white corpuscles (to combat possible infection). The liver is stimulated to produce more sugar, building up body energy.

The *pituitary gland* responds to signals from the hypothalamus by secreting two hormones vital to the stress reaction. The *thyrotropic hormone* (TTH) stimulates the *thyroid gland*, which makes more energy available to the body. The *adrenocorticotropic hormone* (ACTH), known as the 'stress hormone,' stimulates the outer part of the adrenal glands, the *adrenal cortex*, resulting in the release of hormones that control metabolic processes and the release of sugar from the liver into the blood. ACTH also signals various organs to release about 30 other hormones, each of which plays a role in the body's adjustment to this call to arms. A summary of this physiological stress response is shown in **Figure 12.5**.

An analysis by health psychologist **Shelley Taylor** and her colleagues (2000) suggests that these physiological responses to stress may have different consequences for females than for males. Taylor et al. suggest that females do not experience *fight-or-flight*. Rather, these researchers argue that stressors lead females to experience a **tend-and-befriend response**: in times of stress, females ensure the safety of their offspring by tending to their needs; females befriend other members of their social group with the same goal of reducing the vulnerability of their offspring. You can see how this analysis of sex differences in stress responses fits with our earlier discussions of evolutionary perspectives on human behaviour. For example, when we discussed human sexual behaviours in Chapter 11, we noted that men and women's *mating strategies* differ, in part, because of the relative roles men and women have played—over the course of evolution—in child rearing. The idea here is very much the same: because of men and women's different evolutionary niches with respect to nurturing offspring, the same initial physiological responses to stress ultimately produce quite different behaviours.

Unfortunately, neither the fight-or-flight nor the tend-and-befriend response is entirely useful for contemporary lives. Many of the stressors both men and women experience on a day-to-day basis make the physiological stress responses fairly maladaptive. Suppose, for example, you are taking a difficult exam and the clock is swiftly ticking away. Although you might value the heightened attentiveness brought about by your stress response, the rest of the physiological changes do you no good: there's no one to fight or to tend, and so on. Indeed, increased muscle tension in your arm and hand, shallow breathing and fidgetiness work directly AGAINST what you are trying to do in the exam. Even the increased attention may not help frightened animals scan the environment for an escape path, rather than focusing on one spot. While our overall level of arousal is high when we are under stress, we are often distracted and have difficulty concentrating.

We evolved in an environment where the threats we face posed real and immediate danger to our lives and health. Car parking spaces, relationship difficulties, examinations and mortgage repayments all came along later. Unfortunately, our ability to respond to stress has not changed as quickly as the stressors we face have changed. This is particularly important because, as we will see next, many people live their lives under circumstances of chronic stress.

### The General Adaptation Syndrome (GAS) and chronic stress

The first modern researcher to investigate the effects of continued severe stress on the body was **Hans Selye**, a Canadian endocrinologist. Beginning in the late 1930s, Selye reported on the complex response of laboratory animals to damaging agents such as bacterial infections, toxins, trauma, forced restraint, heat, cold, and so on. According to Selye's theory of stress, many kinds of stressors can trigger the same reaction or general bodily response. All stressors call for *adaptation*: an organism must maintain or regain its integrity and

**tend-and-befriend response**
A response to stressors that is hypothesised to be typical for females.

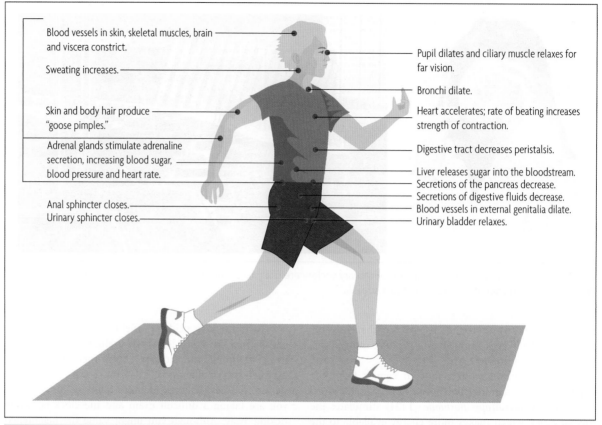

**Figure 12.5**

**The body's reaction to stress**
Stress produces a wide range of physiological changes in your body.

Blood vessels in skin, skeletal muscles, brain and viscera constrict.

Sweating increases.

Skin and body hair produce "goose pimples."

Adrenal glands stimulate adrenaline secretion, increasing blood sugar, blood pressure and heart rate.

Anal sphincter closes.
Urinary sphincter closes.

Pupil dilates and ciliary muscle relaxes for far vision.

Bronchi dilate.

Heart accelerates; rate of beating increases strength of contraction.

Digestive tract decreases peristalsis.

Liver releases sugar into the bloodstream.
Secretions of the pancreas decrease.
Secretions of digestive fluids decrease.
Blood vessels in external genitalia dilate.
Urinary bladder relaxes.

---

**general adaptation syndrome (GAS)** The pattern of nonspecific adaptational physiological mechanisms that occurs in response to continuing threat by almost any serious stressor.

wellbeing by restoring equilibrium, or homeostasis. The response to stressors was described by Selye as the **general adaptation syndrome (GAS)**. It includes three stages: an alarm reaction, a stage of resistance, and a stage of exhaustion (Selye, 1976a, 1976b). *Alarm reactions* are brief periods of bodily arousal that prepare the body for vigorous activity. If a stressor is prolonged, the body enters a stage of *resistance*—a state of moderate arousal. During the stage of resistance, the organism can endure and *resist* further debilitating effects of prolonged stressors. However, if the stressor is sufficiently long lasting or intense, the body's resources become depleted and the organism enters the stage of *exhaustion*. The three stages are diagrammed and explained in **Figure 12.6**.

Selye identified some of the dangers associated with the stage of exhaustion. Recall, for example, that ACTH plays a role in the short-term response to stress. In the long term, however, its action reduces the ability of natural killer cells to destroy cancer cells and other life-threatening infections. When the body is stressed chronically, the increased production of 'stress hormones' compromises the integrity of the immune system. This application of the general adaptation syndrome has proven valuable to explain **psychosomatic disorders**—illnesses that could not be wholly explained by physical causes—that had baffled physicians who had never considered stress as a

**psychosomatic disorders** Physical disorders aggravated by or primarily attributable to prolonged emotional stress or other psychological causes.

cause for illness and disease. What serves the body well in adapting to acute stress impairs the body's response to chronic stress.

Selye's research makes disease seem an inevitable response to stress. We will see, however, that your psychological interpretation of what is stressful and what is not stressful—the way in which you appraise potentially stressful events—has an impact on your body's physiological response. To give a full account of the effect of stress on your body, we will have to combine Selye's foundational physiological theory with later research on psychological factors.

## PSYCHOLOGICAL STRESS REACTIONS

Your physiological stress reactions are automatic, predictable, built-in responses over which you normally have no conscious control. However, many psychological reactions are learned. They depend on perceptions and interpretations of the world. In this section, we discuss psychological responses to different categories of stressors, such as major life changes and traumatic events.

**Major life events** Major *changes* in life situations are at the root of stress for many people. Even events that you

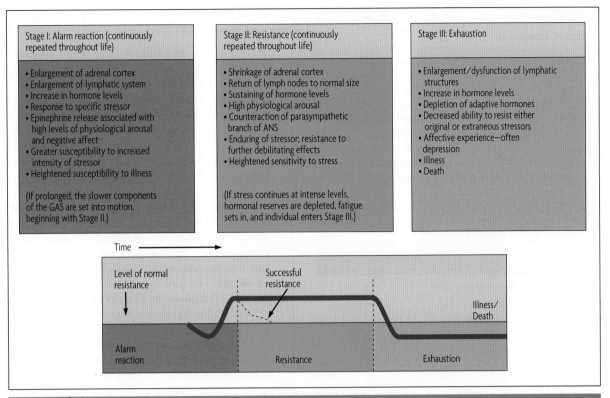

| Stage I: Alarm reaction (continuously repeated throughout life) | Stage II: Resistance (continuously repeated throughout life) | Stage III: Exhaustion |
|---|---|---|
| • Enlargement of adrenal cortex<br>• Enlargement of lymphatic system<br>• Increase in hormone levels<br>• Response to specific stressor<br>• Epinephrine release associated with high levels of physiological arousal and negative affect<br>• Greater susceptibility to increased intensity of stressor<br>• Heightened susceptibility to illness<br><br>(If prolonged, the slower components of the GAS are set into motion, beginning with Stage II.) | • Shrinkage of adrenal cortex<br>• Return of lymph nodes to normal size<br>• Sustaining of hormone levels<br>• High physiological arousal<br>• Counteraction of parasympathetic branch of ANS<br>• Enduring of stressor; resistance to further debilitating effects<br>• Heightened sensitivity to stress<br><br>(If stress continues at intense levels, hormonal reserves are depleted, fatigue sets in, and individual enters Stage III.) | • Enlargement/dysfunction of lymphatic structures<br>• Increase in hormone levels<br>• Depletion of adaptive hormones<br>• Decreased ability to resist either original or extraneous stressors<br>• Affective experience—often depression<br>• Illness<br>• Death |

Time →

Level of normal resistance

Successful resistance

Illness/Death

Alarm reaction

Resistance

Exhaustion

**Figure 12.6**

**The general adaptation syndrome (GAS)**

Following exposure to a stressor, the body's resistance is diminished until the physiological changes of the corresponding alarm reaction bring it back up to the normal level. If the stressor continues, the bodily signs characteristic of the alarm reaction virtually disappear; resistance to the particular stressor rises above normal but drops for other stressors. This adaptive resistance returns the body to its normal level of functioning. Following prolonged exposure to the stressor, adaptation breaks down; signs of alarm reaction reappear, the stressor effects are irreversible, and the individual becomes ill and may die.

welcome, such as winning the lottery or getting promoted, may require major changes in your routines and adaptation to new requirements. Recall, for example, the pattern of marital wellbeing we described in Chapter 10. Although the birth of a child is one of the most sought-after changes in a married couple's life, it is also a source of major stress, contributing to reduced marital satisfaction (Cowan & Cowan, 1988; Levenson et al., 1993). Thus, when you try to relate stress to changes in your life, you should consider both positive and negative changes.

The influence of life events on subsequent mental and physical health has been a target of considerable research. It started in the 1960s with the development of the Social Readjustment Rating Scale (SRRS), a simple measure for rating the degree of adjustment required by the various life changes, both pleasant and unpleasant, that many people experience. The scale was developed from the responses of adults from all walks of life, who were asked to identify from a list those life changes that applied to them. These adults rated the amount of readjustment required for each change by comparing each to marriage, which was arbitrarily assigned a value of 50 life-change units. Researchers then calculated the total number of **life-change units (LCUs)** an individual had undergone, using the units as a measure

of the amount of stress the individual had experienced (Holmes & Rahe, 1967). The SRRS was updated in the 1990s. The researchers used the same procedure of asking participants to rate the stress of life events as compared to marriage (Miller & Rahe, 1997). In this update, the LCU estimates went up 45 percent over the original values—that is, participants in the 1990s reported that they were experiencing overall much higher levels of stress than their peers had in the 1960s. Women in the 1990s also reported experiencing more stress in their lives than did men.

**Table 12.2** provides a modification of this scale for tertiary students. Before reading on, take a moment to test your level of stress on the student stress scale. What is your LCU rating? We have provided room for you to carry out this exercise three times, so that you can chart your level of stress across the semester.

Researchers have found a variety of ways to examine the relationship between life events and health outcomes. In one study, participants volunteered to be exposed to viruses that cause the common cold. Those participants who reported a rate of negative life events above the group's average were about 10 percent more likely to actually come down with a cold (Cohen et al., 1993). Consider another study that should have immediate

**life-change units (LCUs)** In stress research, the measure of the stress levels of different types of change experienced during a given period.

## Table 12.2

### Student stress scale

The Student Stress Scale represents an adaptation of Holmes and Rahe's Social Readjustment Rating Scale. Each event is given a score that represents the amount of readjustment a person has to make in life as a result of the change. People with scores of 300 and higher have a high health risk. People scoring between 150 and 300 points have about a 50–50 chance of serious health change within 2 years. People scoring below 150 have a 1 in 3 chance of serious health change. Calculate your total life-change units (LCUs) three times during the semester and then correlate those scores with any changes in your health status.

| Event | Life-change units |
| --- | --- |
| Death of a close family member | 100 |
| Death of a close friend | 73 |
| Divorce between parents | 65 |
| Jail term | 63 |
| Major personal injury or illness | 63 |
| Marriage | 58 |
| Being fired from job | 50 |
| Failing an important course | 47 |
| Change in health of family member | 45 |
| Pregnancy | 45 |
| Sex problems | 44 |
| Serious argument with close friend | 40 |
| Change in financial status | 39 |
| Change of major | 39 |
| Trouble with parents | 39 |
| New girl- or boyfriend | 38 |
| Increased workload at school | 37 |
| Outstanding personal achievement | 36 |
| First quarter/semester in university | 35 |
| Change in living conditions | 31 |
| Serious argument with instructor | 30 |
| Lower grades than expected | 29 |
| Change in sleeping habits | 29 |
| Change in social activities | 29 |
| Change in eating habits | 28 |
| Chronic car trouble | 26 |
| Change in number of family get-togethers | 26 |
| Too many missed classes | 25 |
| Change of university | 24 |
| Dropping of more than one class | 23 |
| Minor traffic violations | 20 |

My 1st total ☐☐☐ (date:————)

My 2nd total ☐☐☐ (date:————)

My 3rd total ☐☐☐ (date:————)

relevance to the choices you make about how to organise your schoolwork.

When a you are set a difficult assignment—a stressful life event in every student's life—do you try to take care of it as soon as possible or do you put it off to the very last minute? Psychologists have developed a measurement device called the General Procrastination Scale (Lay, 1986) to differentiate those individuals who habitually put things off—*procrastinators*—from those who don't—*nonprocrastinators*. A pair of researchers administered this scale to students in a health psychology course who had a report due late in the semester. The students were also asked to report, early and late in the semester, how many symptoms of physical illness they had experienced. Not surprisingly, procrastinators, on average, handed their reports in later than did nonprocrastinators; procrastinators also, on average, obtained lower grades on those papers. **Figure 12.7** displays the effect of procrastination on physical health. As you can see, early in the semester, procrastinators reported fewer symptoms, but by late in the semester, they were reporting more symptoms than their nonprocrastinating peers (Tice & Baumeister, 1997).

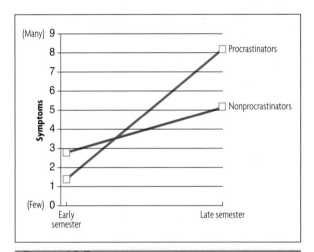

## Figure 12.7

### The health costs of procrastination

Researchers identified students who were, generally, procrastinators and nonprocrastinators. The students were asked to report, early and late in the semester, how many symptoms of physical illness they had experienced. By late in the semester all students showed increases in symptoms. However—as all their work came due—procrastinators were reporting even more symptoms than their nonprocrastinating peers.

You see in this study why not all life events have the same impact on all people. The nonprocrastinators got to work right away and so experienced stress and symptoms early in the semester. However, the consequences for the procrastinators of avoiding the early semester stress was a great increase in physical illness toward the end of the semester. Therefore, they were likely to be feeling ill just at the point in the semester when they needed to be in good health to complete all the work they had put off! Think about these results as you develop your own plan for navigating each semester. If you believe that you habitually procrastinate, consider consulting with a psychologist or university counsellor to modify your behaviour. Your grades and health are at stake!

**Traumatic events** An event that is negative but also uncontrollable, unpredictable or ambiguous is particularly stressful. These conditions hold especially true in the case of *traumatic events*. Some traumatic events, such as rape and car accidents, affect individuals. Others, such as earthquakes and cyclones, have a broader impact. In recent years, no traumatic event has had as widespread consequences as the events of September 11, 2001. On that day, attacks on the World Trade Center and the Pentagon with commercial aircraft led to the deaths of almost 3,000 people. With the goal of providing appropriate mental health care, researchers moved swiftly to assess the psychological aftermath of the attacks.

One particular focus was on the prevalence of **post-traumatic stress disorder (PTSD)**. PTSD is a stress reaction in which individuals suffer from persistent re-experiences of the traumatic event in the form, for example, of flashbacks or nightmares (*DSM-IV*,1994). Sufferers experience an emotional numbing in relation to everyday events and feelings of alienation from other people. Finally, the emotional pain of this reaction can result in an increase in various symptoms, such as sleep problems, guilt about surviving, difficulty in concentrating and an exaggerated startle response.

In October and November 2001, a team of researchers conducted a Web-based survey of 2,273 adults across the United States (Schlenger et al., 2002). The survey assessed both the participants' exposure to the incidents and their mental health symptoms. As seen in **Table 12.3**, greater exposure made it more likely that people would experience PTSD. The group most affected were those who lived in the New York City metropolitan area. Those individuals were most likely to have been personally involved in the

Why might TV viewing have an impact on people's experiences of PTSD?

## Table 12.3

The psychological impact of exposure to the events of September 11, 2001

|  | Probable PTSD |
| --- | --- |
| **PROXIMITY TO CRASH SITES** | |
| New York City metropolitan area | 11.2 |
| District of Columbia metropolitan area | 2.7 |
| Other major metropolitan area | 3.6 |
| Remainder of the United States | 4.0 |
| **TELEVISION VIEWING PER DAY** (in hours) | |
| Less than 4 | 0.8 |
| 4 to 7 | 3.9 |
| 8 to 11 | 4.2 |
| 12 or more | 10.1 |

tragedy. As seen in Table 12.3, the events didn't have extra impact on people in the Washington, DC, area. The researchers suggested that the difference between New York and DC might reflect the difference between attacks on a civilian target (the World Trade Center) and a military target (the Pentagon).

**Table 12.3** also shows that individuals who watched the most television coverage of the events also reported higher levels of symptoms of PTSD. Researchers will continue to assess the mental health consequences of September 11: they attempt to form generalisations from people's responses to catastrophes so that they can alleviate the worst consequences when new circumstances present themselves.

As we noted earlier, people also suffer from individual traumatic events with a negative impact on their psychological health. For example, rape victims often show many of the signs of posttraumatic stress (Kilpatrick et al., 2003). In assessments 2 weeks after being assaulted, 94 percent of rape victims were diagnosed with PTSD; 12 weeks after the assault, 51 percent of the victims still met diagnostic criteria (Foa & Riggs, 1995). The following excerpt of a discussion between two college students about the aftershock of being raped reveals the powerful and enduring emotions.

> *Alice: I was in shock for a pretty long time. I could talk about the fact that I was a rape victim, but the emotions didn't start surfacing until a month later.*
>
> *Beth: During the first two weeks there were people I had chosen to tell who were very, very supportive; but after two weeks, it was like, 'Okay, she's over it, we can go on now.' But the farther along you get, the more support you need, because, as time passes, you become aware of your emotions and the need to deal with them.*
>
> *Alice: There is a point where you deny it happened. You just completely bury it.*
>
> *Beth: It's so unreal that you don't want to believe that it actually happened or that it can happen. Then you go through a long period of fear and anger.*

**post-traumatic stress disorder (PTSD)** An anxiety disorder characterised by the persistent re-experience of traumatic events through distressing recollections, dreams, hallucinations or dissociative flashbacks.

*Alice: I'm terrified of going jogging. [Alice had been jogging when she was raped.] I completely stopped any kind of physical activity after I was raped. I started it again this quarter, but every time I go jogging I have a perpetual fear. My pulse doubles. Of course I don't go jogging alone anymore, but still the fear is there constantly.*

*Beth: There's also a feeling of having all your friends betray you. I had a dream in which I was being assaulted outside my dorm. In the dream, everyone was looking out their windows—the faces were so clear—every one of my friends lined up against the windows watching, and there were even people two feet away from me. They all saw what was happening and none of them did anything. I woke up and had a feeling of extreme loneliness. (Stanford Daily, 1982)*

The emotional responses of posttraumatic stress can occur in an acute form immediately following a disaster and can subside over a period of several months. We will return to the topic of PTSD when we discuss anxiety disorders in Chapter 14.

### Chronic stressors

In our discussion of physiological responses to stress, we made a distinction between stressors that are acute, with clear onsets and offsets, versus those that are chronic—that is, endure over time. With psychological stressors, it's not always easy to draw a sharp distinction. Suppose, for example, your bicycle is stolen. Originally, this is an acute source of stress. However, if you begin to worry constantly that your new bike will also be stolen, the stress associated with this event can become chronic. Researchers have found this pattern in people who suffer from serious illnesses like cancer (Andersen et al., 1994; Kangas et al., 2005). The chronic stress of coping with the anxiety of a cancer diagnosis and treatment may impair health more rapidly than the disease alone would.

For many people, chronic stress arises from conditions in society and the environment. What cumulative effects do overpopulation, crime, economic conditions,

Thousands of people in Melbourne rally against the new federal workchoices legislation. Many of these workers are likely to have experienced chronic stress because of this new legislation. What are some likely consequences for their physical and mental health?

pollution, AIDS, and the threat of terrorism have on you? How do these and other environmental stressors affect your mental wellbeing? Some groups of people suffer chronic stress by virtue of their socioeconomic status or racial identity, with stark consequences for overall well-being (Gallo & Matthews, 2003; Stone, 2000). Consider a U.S. study that measured economic hardships for more than a thousand participants over three decades (Lynch et al., 1997). Economic hardship was defined as household income of less than 200 percent of the federal poverty level. As assessed in 1994, the more periods of economic hardship adults experienced between 1965 and 1983, the more difficulties they had with physical functioning related to basic activities of daily living, such as cooking, shopping, and bathing. Similar effects were found for psychological and cognitive functioning. Compared to those with no period of economic hardship, people with three episodes of poverty were three times more likely to have experienced symptoms of clinical depression, they were more than five times more likely to be assessed as cynically hostile and lacking optimism, and they were more than four times more likely to report difficulties with cognitive functioning. To confirm that these results were caused by economic hardship and not by initial poor health, the researchers demonstrated comparable patterns of disability among those participants whose health at the initial measurement in 1965 had been good or excellent.

Given these research findings, you will not be surprised to learn that chronic stress can also influence children's intellectual development. Consider a study that assessed the level of stress in a group of 6- to 16-year-old children and also measured their intelligence with an IQ test (see Chapter 9). The data revealed a negative correlation between stress and the Verbal/Comprehension measure on the IQ test: on average, the higher the level of stress in the children's lives, the less well they performed on this measure (Plante & Sykora, 1994). Apparently, high levels of chronic stress play a disruptive role in children's cognitive performance. These data echo the findings we reported in Chapter 9 (see page 308) on the impact of environments on intelligence. Researchers understand that the social programs intended to improve children's lives must acknowledge the whole range of chronic stressors associated with poverty.

### Daily hassles

You may agree that the end of a relationship, an earthquake or prejudice might cause stress, but what about the smaller stressors you experience on a day-to-day basis? What happened to you yesterday? You probably didn't get a divorce or survive a plane crash. You're more likely to have lost your notes or textbook. Perhaps you were late for an important appointment, or you got a parking ticket, or a noisy neighbour ruined your sleep. These are the types of recurring day-to-day stressors that confront most people, most of the time.

In a diary study, a group of white middle-class, middle-aged men and women kept track of their daily hassles over a 1-year period (along with a record of major life changes and physical symptoms). A clear relationship emerged between hassles and health problems: The more frequent and intense the hassles people reported, the poorer was their health, both physical and mental (Lazarus, 1981, 1984b). As daily hassles go down, well-being goes up (Chamberlain & Zika, 1990). Consider a study that demonstrated the impact of daily hassles in the workplace.

> Participants in the study worked full time in university administration, with their effort largely focused on the quality of student life (Luong & Rogelberg, 2005). For a period of 5 days, participants kept records of their number of meetings. An interaction counted as a meeting if it involved two or more people and was more than a brief chat or 5-minute phone call. Participants also provided daily accounts of wellbeing: They recorded their levels of *fatigue* (e.g., the extent to which they were worn out at the present moment) and their levels of *subjective workload* (e.g., the extent to which they felt busy or rushed). The results demonstrated positive correlations between the number of meetings and both of these measures: more meetings were associated with greater fatigue and higher subjective workload.

If you've ever worked in an office, these results probably have a familiar ring: the more often you are interrupted for meetings, the less you feel like you're making progress on your work.

We have been focusing largely on day-to-day hassles. It is worth noting, however, that for many people daily hassles may be balanced out by daily positive experiences (Lazarus & Lazarus, 1994). The relative balance of positive and negative experiences may have health consequences. For example, one study asked 96 men to give daily reports of positive and negative events. The men were also tested daily for the strength of their immune response. Results showed that desirable life events were associated with a stronger immune response, undesirable events with a weaker response (Stone et al., 1994). Therefore, if we want to predict your life course based on daily hassles, we also need to know something about the daily pleasures your life provides (Lyubomirsky et al., 2005).

We have just reviewed many sources of stress in people's lives. Psychologists have recognised for quite a long time that the impact of these different types of stressors depends in large part on how effectively people can cope with them. Let's now consider how people cope successfully and unsuccessfully with stress.

## COPING WITH STRESS

If living is inevitably stressful, and if chronic stress can disrupt your life and even kill you, you need to learn how to manage stress. **Coping** refers to the process of dealing with internal or external demands that are perceived as straining or exceeding an individual's resources (Lazarus & Folkman, 1984). Coping may consist of behavioural, emotional or motivational responses and thoughts. We begin this section by describing how cognitive appraisal affects what you experience as stressful. We then consider types of coping responses; we describe both general principles of coping and specific interventions. Finally, we consider some individual differences in individuals' ability to cope with stress.

**Appraisal of stress** Do exams freak you out, or do you find the demands of essays and reports much more stressful? Perhaps you are OK with both exams and other assessment, but find social events stressful. It is clear that not all people find the same things stressful. It is not events themselves that are stressful, but how we interpret or *appraise* those events. *Cognitive appraisal* is the cognitive interpretation and evaluation of a stressor. Cognitive appraisal plays a central role in defining the situation—what the demand is, how big a threat it is, and what resources you have for meeting it (Lazarus, 1993; Lazarus & Lazarus, 1994). Some stressors, such as undergoing bodily injury or finding one's house on fire, are experienced as threats by almost everyone, others are unique to the experiences of an individual. A friend of one of your authors cannot sleep in a room if the wardrobe doors are open. Clearly this is a very specific stressor, related to her experiences as a child with older brothers—decades ago—in suburban Melbourne. Some situations cause you stress but not your friends and family; other events cause them stress but not you. Why?

Richard Lazarus, whose general theory of appraisal we addressed in our discussion of emotions, has distinguished two stages in the cognitive appraisal of demands. *Primary appraisal* describes the initial evaluation of the seriousness of a demand. This evaluation starts with the questions 'What's happening?' and 'Is this thing good for me, stressful or irrelevant?' If the answer to the second question is 'stressful,' you appraise the potential impact of the stressor by determining whether harm has occurred or is likely to and whether action is required (see **Table 12.4**). Once you decide something must be done, *secondary appraisal* begins.

You evaluate the personal and social resources that are available to deal with the stressful circumstance and consider the action options that are needed. Appraisal continues as coping responses are tried; if the first ones don't work and the stress persists, new responses are initiated, and their effectiveness is evaluated.

Cognitive appraisal is an example of a stress moderator variable. **Stress moderator variables** are those variables that change the impact of a stressor on a given type of stress reaction. Moderator variables filter or modify the usual effects of stressors on the individual's reactions. For example, your level of fatigue and general health status are moderator variables influencing your reaction to a given psychological or physical stressor. When you're in good shape, you can deal with a stressor better than when you aren't. You can see how cognitive appraisal also fits the definition of a moderator variable. The way in which you appraise a stressor will determine the types of coping responses you need to bring to it. Let's now consider general types of coping responses.

**stress moderator variables** Variables that change the impact of a stressor on a given type of stress reaction.

**coping** The process of dealing with internal or external demands that are perceived to be threatening or overwhelming.

**Table 12.4**

Stages in stable decision making/cognitive appraisal

| Stage | Key questions |
|---|---|
| 1. Appraising the challenge | Are the risks serious if I don't change? |
| 2. Surveying alternatives | Is this alternative an acceptable means for dealing with the challenge? |
| | Have I sufficiently surveyed the available alternatives? |
| 3. Weighing alternatives | Which alternative is best? |
| | Could the best alternative meet the essential requirements? |
| 4. Deliberating about commitment | Will I implement the best alternative and allow others to know? |
| 5. Adhering despite negative feedback | Are the risks serious if I *don't* change? |
| | Are the risks serious if I *do* change? |

**Types of coping responses** Suppose you have a big exam coming up. You've thought about it—you've appraised the situation—and you're quite sure that this is a stressful situation. What can you do? It's important to note that coping can precede a potentially stressful event in the form of **anticipatory coping** (Folkman, 1984). How do you deal with the stress of the upcoming exam? How do you tell your parents that you are dropping out of school or your lover that you are no longer in love? Anticipating a stressful situation leads to many thoughts and feelings that themselves may be stress inducing, as in the cases of interviews, speeches or blind dates. You need to know how to cope.

**anticipatory coping** Efforts made in advance of a potentially stressful event to overcome, reduce or tolerate the imbalance between perceived demands and available resources.

The two main ways of coping are defined by whether the goal is to confront the problem directly—*problem-directed coping*—or to lessen the discomfort associated with the stress—*emotion-focused coping* (Billings & Moos, 1982; Lazarus & Folkman, 1984). Several subcategories of these two basic approaches are shown in **Table 12.5**.

Let's begin with problem-directed coping. 'Taking the bull by the horns' is how we usually characterise the strategy of facing up to a problem situation. This approach includes all strategies designed to deal *directly* with the stressor, whether through overt action or through realistic problem-solving activities. You face up to a bully or run away; you try to win him or her over with bribes or other incentives. Your focus is on the problem to be dealt with and on the agent that has induced the stress. You acknowledge the call to action, you appraise the situation and your resources for dealing with it, and you undertake a response that is appropriate for removing or lessening the threat. Such problem-solving efforts are useful for managing *controllable stressors*—those stressors that you can change or eliminate through your actions, such as overbearing bosses or underwhelming grades.

The emotion-focused approach is useful for managing the impact of more *uncontrollable stressors*. Suppose you are responsible for the care of a parent with Alzheimer's. In that situation, there is no 'bully' you can eliminate from the environment; you cannot make the disease go away. Even in this situation, some forms of problem-directed coping would be useful. For example, you could modify your work schedule to make it easier to provide care. However, because you cannot eliminate the source of stress, you also can try to change your feelings and thoughts about the disease. For example, you might take part in a support group for Alzheimer's caregivers or learn relaxation techniques. These approaches still constitute a coping strategy because you are acknowledging that there is a threat to your wellbeing and you are taking steps to modify that threat.

**Table 12.5**

Taxonomy of coping strategies

| Type of coping strategy | Example |
|---|---|
| PROBLEM-DIRECTED COPING<br>Change stressor or one's relationship to it through direct actions and/or problem-solving activities | Fight (destroy, remove, or weaken the threat)<br>Flight (distance oneself from the threat)<br>Seek options to fight or flight (negotiating, bargaining, compromising)<br>Prevent future stress (act to increase one's resistance or decrease strength of anticipated stress) |
| EMOTION-FOCUSED COPING<br>Change self through activities that make one feel better but do not change the stressor | Somatically focused activities (use of anti-anxiety medication, relaxation, biofeedback)<br>Cognitively focused activities (planned distractions, fantasies, thoughts about oneself)<br>Therapy to adjust conscious or unconscious processes that lead to additional anxiety |

Why are multiple coping strategies beneficial for individuals such as Alzheimer's caregivers?

You will be better off if you have multiple strategies to help you cope in stressful situations (Tennen et al., 2002). For coping to be successful, your resources need to match the perceived demand. Thus the availability of multiple coping strategies is adaptive because you are more likely to achieve a match and manage the stressful event. Consider a study that examined the ways in which Israeli citizens cope with the chronic threat of terrorism (Bleich et al., 2003). A sample of 742 adults revealed that, on average, they used 6.4 coping strategies. Those coping strategies included checking on the whereabouts of family members, talking to others about what could be done, maintaining faith in God, and avoiding television and radio broadcasts. For many stressful situations, knowing that you possess a variety of coping strategies can help increase your actual ability to meet demands. Self-confidence can insulate you from experiencing the full impact of many stressors; believing you have coping resources readily available short-circuits the stressful, chaotic response 'What am I going to do?'

Researchers who study coping have discovered that some individuals meet stressors with a particular degree of resilience—they are able to achieve positive outcomes despite serious threats to their well-being (Masten, 2001). Research has focused on the types of coping skills that resilient individuals have acquired and how they have acquired them. An important part of the answer is that children who become resilient have been raised by supportive parents with good parenting skills (see Chapter 10). In addition, resilient children appear to

have developed coping skills that relate to their ability to regulate their own behaviour (Smart, Hayes, Sanson & Toumbourou,, 2007; Buckner et al., 2003). They can stay focused on tasks (which allows for problem-directed coping) and control their emotional responses (which allows for emotion-focused coping) in ways that better their life outcomes.

Up to now, we have been discussing general approaches to coping with stressors. Now we review specific cognitive and social approaches to successful coping.

**Modifying cognitive strategies** A powerful way to adapt to stress is to change your evaluations of stressors and your self-defeating cognitions about the way you are dealing with them. You need to find a different way to think about a given situation, your role in it, and the causal attributions you make to explain the undesirable outcome. Two ways of mentally coping with stress are *reappraising* the nature of the stressors themselves and *restructuring* your cognitions about your stress reactions.

We have already described the idea that people control the experience of stress in their lives in part by the way they appraise life events (Lazarus & Lazarus, 1994). Learning to think differently about certain stressors, to relabel them, or to imagine them in a less-threatening (perhaps even funny) context is a form of cognitive reappraisal that can reduce stress. Worried about giving a speech to a large, forbidding audience? One stressor reappraisal technique is to imagine your potential critics sitting there in the nude—this surely takes away a great deal of their fearsome power. Anxious about being shy at a party you must attend? Think about finding someone who is shyer than you and reducing his or her social anxiety by initiating a conversation.

You can also manage stress by changing what you tell yourself about it and by changing your handling of it. Cognitive-behaviour therapist **Donald Meichenbaum** (1977, 1985, 1993) has proposed a three-phase process that allows for such *stress inoculation*. In Phase 1, people work to develop a greater awareness of their actual behaviour, what instigates it, and what its results are. One of the best ways of doing this is to keep daily logs. By helping people redefine their problems in terms of their causes and results, these records can increase their feelings of control. You may discover, for example, that your grades are low (a stressor) because you always leave too little time to do a good job on your class assignments. In Phase 2, people begin to identify new behaviours that negate the maladaptive, self-defeating behaviours. Perhaps you might create a fixed 'study time' or limit your phone calls to 10 minutes each night. In Phase 3, after adaptive behaviours are being emitted, individuals appraise the consequences of their new behaviours, avoiding the former internal dialogue of put-downs. Instead of telling themselves, 'I was lucky the lecturer called on me when I happened to have read the text', they say, 'I'm glad I was prepared for the lecturer's question. It feels great to be able to respond intelligently in that class.'

## Table 12.6

**Examples of coping self-statements**

**Preparation**

I can develop a plan to deal with it.

Just think about what I can do about it. That's better than getting anxious.

No negative self-statements, just think rationally.

**Confrontation**

One step at a time; I can handle this situation.

This anxiety is what the doctor said I would feel; it's a reminder to use my coping exercises.

Relax; I'm in control. Take a slow, deep breath.

**Coping**

When fear comes, just pause.

Keep focused on the present; what is it I have to do?

Don't try to eliminate fear totally; just keep it manageable.

It's not the worst thing that can happen.

Just think about something else.

**Self-reinforcement**

It worked; I was able to do it.

It wasn't as bad as I expected.

I'm really pleased with the progress I'm making.

**perceived control** The belief that one has the ability to make a difference in the course of the consequences of some event or experience; often helpful in dealing with stressors.

**social support** Resources, including material aid, socioemotional support and informational aid, provided by others to help a person cope with stress.

This three-phase approach means initiating responses and self-statements that are incompatible with previous defeatist cognitions. Once started on this path, people realise that they are changing—and can take full credit for the change, which promotes further successes. **Table 12.6** gives examples of the new kinds of self-statements that help in dealing with stressful situations. *Stress inoculation training* has been used successfully in a wide variety of domains.

This study involved 22 students who were beginning their first year of law school (Sheehy & Horan, 2004). The students received stress inoculation training that was specifically geared to the types of stressors that arise in law school. For example, the training focused on the anxiety students experience when they interact with lecturers and compete with peers. In addition, the students learned cognitive restructuring techniques to combat negative self-statements and irrational beliefs. Although all of the students ultimately received the training, roughly half began training immediately at the start of the study, whereas the other half waited several weeks to begin. That research design gave the researchers the opportunity to demonstrate the benefits of the stress inoculation training (by comparing the immediate group to the delayed group) without denying some students those benefits. In fact, participants who completed immediate training reported lower levels of stress at the end of the delay period than their classmates whose training was delayed. In addition, several of the students who completed the training outperformed expectations (based on their LSAT scores) when the semester's grades were posted.

The whole law school class of 158 students had the opportunity to participate in the stress inoculation training. Only this small subset was wise enough to reap the benefits.

Another main component of successful coping is for you to establish **perceived control** over the stressor, a belief that you can make a difference in the course or the consequences of some event or experience (Endler et al., 2000; Roussi, 2002). If you believe that you can affect the course of an illness or the daily symptoms of a disease, you are probably adjusting well to the disorder. However, if you believe that the source of the stress is another person whose behaviour you cannot influence or a situation that you cannot change, chances increase for a poor psychological adjustment to your chronic condition. Those individuals who are able to maintain perceived control even in the face of fatal diseases like full-blown AIDS reap mental and physical health benefits (Thompson et al., 1994).

While you file away these control strategies for future use, we will turn to a final aspect of coping with stress—the social dimension.

## Social support as a coping resource

**Social support** refers to the resources others provide giving the message that one is loved, cared for, esteemed and connected to other people in a network of communication and mutual obligation. In addition to these forms of *emotional support*, other people may provide *tangible support* (money, transportation, housing) and *informational support* (advice, personal feedback, information). Anyone with whom you have a significant social relationship—such as family members, friends, co-workers and neighbours—can be part of your social support network in time of need.

Much research points to the power of social support in moderating the vulnerability to stress (Holahan et al., 1997). When people have other people to whom they can turn, they are better able to handle job stressors, unemployment, marital disruption and serious illness, as well as their everyday problems of living. Consider individuals who serve as peacekeepers in the world's many troubled regions. The traumas associated with life in battle zones often leads to posttraumatic stress disorder. However, a study of Dutch peacekeepers who served in Lebanon demonstrated that those individuals who experienced higher levels of positive social interactions had fewer symptoms of PTSD (Dirkzwager et al., 2003).

Researchers are trying to identify which types of social supports provide the most benefit for specific life events. One study examined the impact of informational support and emotional support for men and women who were undergoing facial surgery (Krohne & Slangen, 2005). Overall, people who had more social support anticipated their surgery with less anxiety, required less anaesthesia during surgery, and had briefer hospital stays. However, the more specific results differed for men and women. Although patients of both sexes obtained an advantage from greater informational support, only women were much affected by the level of emotional support. More

| Support is | wanted | not wanted |
|---|---|---|
| received | positive congruent support | support commission |
| not received | support omission | null support |

## Figure 12.8

**Matches and mismatches for social support**
When people need to cope with difficult situations, there can be matches or mismatches between the social support they want and the social support they need.

From Julie S. Reynolds and Nancy Perrin, 'Matches and Mismatches for Social Support and Psychosocial Adjustment to Breast Cancer,' *Health Psychology*, 23(4), 425-430. Copyright © 2004 by the American Psychological Association. Reprinted with permission.

generally, what appears to matter is the match between the type of support an individual needs and what that individual gets. As shown in **Figure 12.8**, there are four different possibilities for how desires and reality can be related (Reynolds & Perrin, 2004). People are best off when there's a match between what they want and what they get. In an investigation of over 90,000 calls to Lifeline Australia it was found that the majority of those calls were from people who had used the service more than once, and from this and other data it was suggested that Lifeline primarily provides a social support service rather than a specific suicide crisis intervention service. This led the authors to question whether Lifeline Australia should rethink its training and service provision model in order to accommodate this new social support function (Watson, McDonald & Pearce, 2006).

Researchers are also trying to determine when sources of support actually increase anxiety (Holahan et al., 1997). For example, if someone insisted on accompanying you to a doctor's appointment or to a university interview when you preferred to go alone, you might experience additional anxiety about the situation. Similarly, patients with serious diseases may find themselves unable to meet the expectations of those individuals in their social circle.

Why are some forms of social support more welcome than others?

A group of researchers examined the ways in which patients' perceptions of the expectations of the individuals around them affected their adjustment to their illness. The patients were in the final phases of renal disease; all required dialysis. The researchers asked the patients to respond to statements such as 'I sometimes feel that my family and friends expect me to cope much better with my illness than I actually can' and 'I sometimes think that my family and friends expect me to take more responsibility for my treatment than I can manage' on a scale ranging from *strongly disagree* to *strongly agree*. The researchers also obtained measures of how well the patients were coping with their illness. The results revealed consistent positive correlations between expectations and measures of distress. For example, patients who perceived their family and friends' expectations to be excessive were more likely to report depression and low quality of life (Hatchett et al., 1997).

It seems quite likely that these patients' friends and family were doing their best to provide support. Even so, their expectations for the patients increased the patients' distress.

Being part of an effective social support network means that you believe others will be there for you if you need them—even if you don't actually ask for their help when you experience stress. One of the most important take-home messages from *Psychology and Life* is that you should always work at being part of a social support network and never let yourself become socially isolated.

## POSITIVE EFFECTS OF STRESS

In this section, we have focused largely on the potential for stress to bring about negative life outcomes. This focus reflects the great effort researchers have expended to help people prevent and overcome those negative outcomes. However, in recent years, psychologists have turned more attention to the potential for stress to have positive effects in people's lives. This change reflects, in part, the emergence of *positive psychology* as an important movement within the profession of psychology. Positive psychology asks this question, 'Can psychologists take what they have learned about the science and practice of treating mental illness and use it to create a practice of making people lastingly happier?' (Seligman et al., 2005, p. 410). The goal of positive psychology is to provide people with the knowledge and skills that allow them to experience fulfilling lives. Let's consider stress and coping from a positive psychology perspective.

When we first defined stress, we made a distinction between distress and eustress. It's probably easy for you to generate circumstances in which you experienced distress—but what about eustress? Consider the last time you watched any kind of running race. Did you enjoy the experience of seeing who would win? Did you feel your heart race as the runners approached the finish line? Researchers have demonstrated that eustress—the experience of excitement and anxiety—is often an important motivation for people to watch, for example, sporting events (Wann et al., 1999, 2002). If a team or competitor you favour ultimately loses, you may experience some distress. However, along the way, you probably have a more positive emotional experience when competitions stimulate eustress. Search your life for other circumstances in which the experience of stressful events gives you pleasure. We'll offer one more example: Why do you feel happy while you're riding a roller coaster?

For some types of stressful events, it might be hard to anticipate how any positive effects could emerge. However, research has demonstrated that people can experience positive outcomes and personal growth from deeply negative events. One type of research focuses on *benefit finding*—people's ability to identify positive aspects of negative life events (Tennen & Affleck, 2002). Consider a study of women with early-stage breast cancer.

> Researchers recruited a group of women who had been diagnosed with breast cancer, on average, about a half year earlier. The women were asked, 'Have there been any benefits that have resulted from your experience with breast cancer?' (Sears et al., 2003, p. 491). Of the 92 women in the study, 83 percent were able to report benefits. The women provided responses such as 'My husband and I have gotten a lot closer since this happened' and 'When you come close to death, life becomes more real to you.' The researchers followed the women over the course of a year to determine how their mental and physical health evolved. In general, the women who were doing the best were the ones who were able to use perceived benefits to engage in *positive reappraisal coping*. That is, some women were able to cope with the consequences of their illness by attempting to reappraise the situation in terms of its positive impact.

We noted earlier that reappraisal is an important tool for coping with stress. In this case, people's ability to perceive benefits of negative events aids in that process of reappraisal.

People also may experience *posttraumatic growth*—positive psychological change—in response to serious illnesses, accidents, natural disasters and other traumatic events. Post-traumatic growth occurs in five domains (Cryder et al., 2006; Tedeschi & Calhoun, 2004):

- New possibilities: 'I have new things that I like to do.'
- Relating to others: 'I feel closer to other people than I did before.'
- Personal strength: 'I learned I can count on myself.'
- Appreciation of life: 'I learned that life is important.'
- Spiritual change: 'I understand religious ideas more.'

Not everyone who experiences trauma will experience post-traumatic growth. For example, one study focused on a group of 6- to 15-year-old children who had survived Hurricane Floyd in North Carolina (Cryder et al., 2006). The children who experienced the most post-traumatic growth were the ones who perceived themselves to have

the best array of strategies (of the sort we have described in this section) to cope with problems. More generally, people seem likely to experience post-traumatic growth when they frequently turn their thoughts back to the original traumatic events, to help themselves understand and make sense of those events.

At many points in this discussion of stress, we have noted the effect of stress on physical or psychological wellbeing. We will now turn directly to the ways in which psychologists apply their research knowledge to issues of illness and health.

For answers go to MyPsychLab!

## RECAP CHECKPOINT
### Stress of living

- Stress can arise from negative or positive events. At the root of most stress is change and the need to adapt to environmental, biological, physical and social demands.
- Psychological stress reactions are regulated by the hypothalamus and a complex interaction of the hormonal and nervous systems.
- Depending on the type of stressor and its effect over time, stress can be a mild disruption or lead to health-threatening reactions.
- Cognitive appraisal is a primary moderator variable of stress.
- Coping strategies either focus on problems (taking direct actions) or attempt to regulate emotions (indirect or avoidant).
- Cognitive reappraisal and restructuring can be used to cope with stress.
- Social support is also a significant stress moderator, as long as it is appropriate to the circumstances.
- Stress can lead to a positive changes such as post-traumatic growth.

### CONCEPT QUESTIONS

1. What are the three stages of the general adaptation syndrome?
2. How did life-change unit estimates change from the 1960s to the 1990s?
3. How do daily hassles and daily pleasures affect wellbeing?
4. What does it mean to engage in emotion-focused coping?

# HEALTH PSYCHOLOGY

How much do your psychological processes contribute to your experiences of illness and wellness? We have already given you reason to believe that the right answer may be 'quite a bit'. This acknowledgment of the importance of psychological and social factors in health has spurred the growth of a new field, health psychology. **Health psychology** is the branch of psychology that is devoted to understanding the way people stay healthy, the reasons they become ill, and the way they respond when they do get ill. **Health** refers to the general condition of the body and mind in terms of soundness and vigour. It is not simply the absence of illness or injury, but is more a matter of how well all the body's component parts are working together. We will begin our discussion of health psychology by describing how the field's underlying philosophy departs from a traditional Western medical model of illness. We then consider the contributions of health psychology to the prevention and treatment of illness and dysfunction.

## THE BIOPSYCHOSOCIAL MODEL OF HEALTH

Health psychology is guided by a *biopsychosocial model* of health. We can find the roots of this perspective in many non-Western cultures. To arrive at a definition of the biopsychosocial model, we will start with a description of some of these non-Western traditions.

**Traditional medicine—psychological and behavioural approaches** Traditional Australian Aboriginal medicine is a complex system closely linked to the culture and beliefs of the people, and knowledge of their land and its flora and fauna. Its survival is explained by its 'embeddedness' in the social fabric of Aboriginal culture. Reid (1978) has shown that, although Aborigines living at Yirrkala in the Northern Territory choose Western medicine to treat the majority of their sicknesses, they continue to explain the causes of these sicknesses through their traditional beliefs.

Western medicine is primarily interested in the recognition and treatment of disease. Traditional medicine seeks to a provide meaningful explanation for illness and to respond to the personal, family and community issues surrounding illness. Traditional medicine explains not only the 'how' but also the 'why' of sickness.

The Aboriginal approach to health care is a holistic one. It recognises the social, physical and spiritual dimensions of health and life. Their concept of health in many ways is closer than that of Western medicine to the WHO definition of health, 'a state of complete physical, mental and social wellbeing and not merely the absence of disease or infirmity'. The Warlpiri Aboriginal tribe have described health as 'life' or *Wankaru*. Their definition takes in a whole of life cycle. The front of their Health Centre at the Aboriginal settlement of Yuendumu is adorned with a painting showing family life, food, shelter, warmth, water and exercise, all essential for health.

**Traditional health system of the warlpiri Aborigines** The Warlpiri Aborigines comprise one of the largest tribes in the Northern Territory. They are scattered over many Aboriginal communities in the north-west of Central Australia: The main components of the Warlpiri health system are the *ngangkayikirili* or traditional healers, commonly referred to as *ngangkari* or *ngangkayi* (healing power), *Yawulyu* ceremonies; healing songs and herbal medicine. In addition, there are laws governing behaviour that are aimed at preventing sickness.

### Ngangkari
Professor Elkin (1977) referred to the traditional healers as Aboriginal men of high degree. The healers are kindred to Amerindian 'men of power' and shamans. These healers are specially chosen and trained to remove the influence of sorcery and evil spirits and to restore the wellbeing of the soul or spirit. Their role is extremely important because most serious illness is thought to be brought about by loss of a vital substance from the body (soul loss), introduction of a foreign and harmful substance into the body (spirit intrusion or possession), or violation of taboos and sorcery (singing). The traditional healers usually gain the power to heal through inheritance or through special spiritual experiences. They possess a spirit called *mapanpa* which is associated with healing power. This is different from the spirit that every Warlpiri person has, 'like a shadow' (Tynan 1979). The traditional healer carries out a healing ritual which often includes sucking the sick person. After sucking, the healer usually spits out a wooden object called *yarda* which is covered in blood. The *yarda* represents the evil influence. Sometimes, the traditional healer massages the patient, manipulates the body or sings during the ritual. The traditional healer may diagnose the state of the spirit, e.g. *kurrunpa yulangu* (the spirit is sad). Traditional healing methods do not always involve the use of herbal medicine.

**health psychology** The field of psychology devoted to understanding the ways people stay healthy, the reasons they become ill and the ways they respond when they become ill.

**health** A general condition of soundness and vigour of body and mind; not simply the absence of illness or injury.

### Yawulyu ceremonies and healing songs

Warlpiri women frequently perform *Yawulyu* ceremonies. These ceremonies improve the health of sick people but cannot remove the influence of sorcery. The ceremony consists of singing songs and painting designs on the sick person. These designs are derived from the power of the Dreamtime. Each ritual is carried out by the *kirda* (owners) or *kurdungurlu* (managers) of a particular 'Dreaming'. Sometimes the songs and designs appear to the people in their dreams and are thought to be revealed by spirit creatures called *yinawuru* (Munn 1973). During the ceremony the sick person may be massaged with fat and red ochre. These materials derive special potency from the songs. In some cases senior men and women sing songs without the ceremony to strengthen sick people. Songs are sometimes sung to ensure safe childbirth. The *Yawulyu* ceremonies and songs assist in providing strong family support for the sick person.

### Herbal medicine

Herbal medicine and knowledge of plants is not the domain of any particular group in the Warlpiri system. Its knowledge and use are shared by the whole family. The Warlpiri have extensive knowledge of plants and have published their own book which lists several plants and their medicinal uses (Henshall et al., 1980).

Medicinal plants are mainly used symptomatically for coughs and colds, pains and aches. Some are used as dressings for wounds and sores. Herbal medicine was the first component of the Warlpiri health system to be eroded by the introduction of Western medicine. However, the movement of the Warlpiri people back to their traditional land has led to a renewal of interest in the use of herbal medicine.

### The Warlpiri health system

The Warlpiri health system can be represented as follows: (Adapted from Tynan, 1979). When someone falls sick one of the three main components of the health system is tried.

Traditional Aboriginal medicine is linked closely to knowledge of local flora, such as the bloodwood (Eucalyptus terminalis), which the Warlpiri people use to cure certain ailments. How does the Aboriginal approach to health psychology differ from that of the wider Australian community?

If it does not work, another component is used or the same component tried again until there is a definite outcome.

### Preventing sickness

Reid (1982) gives a good description of prevention at the level of personal relationship and religious injunctions.

> *Preventive measures can include avoiding foods prohibited during ceremonies or life crises, obeying ritual proscriptions, taking care not to abuse ones' land or trespass on territories of others, avoiding prohibited sacred sites or approaching them with ritual protection, observing debts and obligations to others, containing anger, violence or jealousy, exercising caution in interactions with strangers and taking steps to avoid sorcery or often conflict with others.*

In summary 'good health' is associated with strict adherence to approved patterns of behaviour and avoidance of inappropriate behaviours, people and sites.

**Toward a biopsychosocial model** We have just seen that healing practices in non-Western cultures often assumed a link between the body and the mind. By contrast, modern Western scientific thinking has relied almost exclusively on a *biomedical model* that has a dualistic conception of body and mind. According to this model, medicine treats the physical body as separate from the psyche; the mind is important only for emotions and beliefs and has little to do with the reality of the body. Over time, however, researchers have begun to document types of interactions that make the strict biomedical model unworkable. You have already seen some of the evidence: good and bad life events can affect immune function; people are more or less resilient with respect to the negative consequences of stress; adequate social support can decrease the probability of death. These realisations yield the three components of the **biopsychosocial model**. The *bio* acknowledges the reality of biological illness. The *psycho* and the *social* acknowledge the psychological and social components of health.

The biopsychosocial model links your physical health to your state of mind and the world around you. Health psychologists view health as a dynamic, multidimensional experience. Optimal health, or **wellness**, incorporates physical, intellectual, emotional, spiritual, social and environmental aspects of your life. When you undertake an activity for the purpose of preventing disease or detecting it in the asymptomatic stage, you are exhibiting health behaviour. The general goal of health psychology is to use psychological knowledge to promote wellness and positive health behaviours. Let's now consider theory and research relevant to this goal.

## HEALTH PROMOTION

**Health promotion** means developing general strategies and specific tactics to eliminate or reduce the risk that people will get sick. The prevention of illness in the 21st century poses a much different challenge than it did at the beginning of the 20th century. In 1900, the primary

**biopsychosocial model** A model of health and illness that suggests links among the nervous system, the immune system, behavioural styles, cognitive processing and environmental domains of health.

**wellness** Optimal health, incorporating the ability to function fully and actively over the physical, intellectual, emotional, spiritual, social and environmental domains of health.

**health promotion** The development and implementation of general strategies and specific tactics to eliminate or reduce the risk that people will become ill.

## Table 12.7

Leading causes of death, Australia, 2005

| Rank | Males | Females | Contributors to cause of death* |
|------|-------|---------|-------------------|
| 1 | Ischaemis | Ischaemic Heart Disease | D, S/ D.S |
| 2 | Lung cancer | Stroke | D, S/D, S |
| 3 | Stroke | Other heart disease | D, S/D, S |
| 4 | Other heart disease | Dementia and related disorders | D, S/ |
| 5 | Prostate cancer | Breast cancer | D, S/D, S |
| 6 | Chronic obstructive pulmonary disease | Lung cancer | D, s/S |
| 7 | Colorectal cancer | Chronic obstructive pulmonary disease | D/DS |
| 8 | Other cancers | Colorectal cancer | |
| 9 | Diabetes | Diabetes | D |
| 10 | Suicide | Influenza and pneumonia | A/DA, S |

*D = diet; S = smoking; A/DA = alcohol/drug abuse

*Source:* Australian Bureau of Statistics, 2005.

cause of death was infectious disease. Health practitioners at that time launched the first revolution in public health. Over time, through the use of research, public education, the development of vaccines and changes in public health standards (such as waste control and sewage), they were able to reduce substantially the deaths associated with such diseases as influenza, tuberculosis, polio, measles, and smallpox.

If researchers wish to contribute to the trend toward improved quality of life, they must attempt to decrease those deaths associated with lifestyle factors (see **Table 12.7**). Smoking, being overweight, eating foods high in fat and cholesterol, drinking too much alcohol, driving without seat belts, and leading stressful lives all play a role in heart disease, cancer, strokes, accidents and suicide. Changing the behaviours associated with these diseases of civilisation will prevent much illness and premature death.

Based on this knowledge, it's easy to make some recommendations. You are more likely to stay well if you practise good health habits, such as those listed in **Table 12.8**. Many of these suggestions probably are

## Table 12.8

Ten steps to personal wellness

1. Exercise regularly.
2. Eat nutritious, balanced meals (high in vegetables, fruits, and grains; low in fat and cholesterol).
3. Maintain proper weight.
4. Sleep 7 to 8 hours nightly; rest/relax daily.
5. Wear seat belts and bike helmets.
6. Do not smoke or use drugs.
7. Use alcohol in moderation, if at all.
8. Engage only in protected, safe sex.
9. Get regular medical/dental checkups; adhere to medical regimens.
10. Develop an optimistic perspective and friendships.

familiar to you already. However, health psychologists would like to use psychological principles to increase the probability that you will actually do the things you know are good for you. To show you how that works, we now consider a pair of concrete domains: smoking and AIDS.

Smoking It would be impossible to imagine that anyone reading this book wouldn't know that smoking is extremely dangerous. Roughly 4.9 million people worldwide die each year from smoking-related illnesses (World Health Organisation, 2002). Even so, 3.1 million people in Australia still smoke cigarettes (National Drug Strategy Household Survey, 2001). Health psychologists would like to understand both why people begin to smoke—so that the psychologists can help prevent it—and how to assist people in quitting—so they can reap the substantial benefits of becoming ex-smokers.

Analyses of why some people start smoking have focused on interactions of nature and nurture. For example, one study compared monozygotic and dizygotic twins for the similarity of their tobacco use (Kendler et al., 2000). (Recall that monozygotic twins share identical genetic material, whereas dizygotic twins are no more genetically alike than other siblings.) The data, obtained from the Swedish Twin Registry, included twins born in several different decades. As shown in **Table 12.9**, birth cohort had a large impact on the estimates of heritability for women but not for men. For men, the genetic impact on smoking was large—the closer the estimate is to 1.0, the more genetic factors predict the behaviour—and steady across groups. However, for the women the estimate increased dramatically over time. Why would this be? The researchers suggested that the 'reduction in social restrictions on smoking in Sweden as the 20th century progressed permitted genetic factors . . . to increasingly express themselves' (p. 891). That is, as social restrictions on women lifted, those women who were genetically inclined to smoke were able to do so.

To understand the link between genes and smoking, researchers have often focused on personality differences

**Table 12.9**

The impact of social restrictions on estimates of heritability for regular tobacco use

| Birth Years | Men | Women |
| --- | --- | --- |
| 1910–1924 | 0.53 | 0.00 |
| 1925–1939 | 0.58 | 0.21 |
| 1940–1958 | 0.51 | 0.64 |

**AIDS** Acronym for acquired immune deficiency syndrome, a syndrome caused by a virus that damages the immune system and weakens the body's ability to fight infection.

**HIV** Human immunodeficiency virus, a virus that attacks white blood cells (T lymphocytes) in human blood, thereby weakening the functioning of the immune system; HIV causes AIDS.

that predict which people will start smoking. One personality type that has been associated with the initiation of smoking is called *sensation seeking* (Zuckerman, 1988). Individuals characterised as sensation seeking are more likely to engage in risky activities. One study compared personality assessments of men and women in the mid-1960s (1964–1967) with their smoking or nonsmoking behaviour in the late 1980s (1987–1991). Both men and women who had revealed themselves to be sensation seeking in the 1960s were more likely to be smoking 20 to 25 years later (Lipkus et al., 1994). Health psychologists understand that successful interventions to prevent the initiation of smoking must address the aspects of individuals' personalities that make smoking attractive to them.

The best approach to smoking is never to start at all. But for those of you who have begun to smoke, what has research revealed about quitting? Although many people who try to quit have relapses, the majority of people who give up do it 'on their own' without professional treatment programs. Researchers have identified stages people pass through that represent increasing readiness to quit (Norman et al., 1998, 2000):

- *Precontemplation.* The smoker is not yet thinking about quitting.
- *Contemplation.* The smoker is thinking about quitting but has not yet undertaken any behavioural changes.
- *Preparation.* The smoker is getting ready to quit.
- *Action.* The smoker takes action toward quitting by setting behavioural goals.
- *Maintenance.* The smoker is now a nonsmoker and is trying to stay that way.

This analysis suggests that not all smokers are psychologically equivalent in terms of readiness to quit. Interventions can be designed that nudge smokers up the scale of readiness, until, finally, they are psychologically prepared to take healthy action.

Successful smoking-cessation treatment requires that both smokers' physiological and psychological needs be met (Tsoh et al., 1997, QUIT Victoria, 2007). On the physiological side, smokers are best off learning an effective form of *nicotine replacement therapy,* such as nicotine patches or nicotine gum. On the psychological side, smokers must understand that there are huge numbers of ex-smokers and realise that it is possible to quit. Furthermore, smokers must learn strategies to cope with the strong temptations that accompany efforts to quit. Treatments often incorporate the types of cognitive

coping techniques we described earlier, which allow people to alleviate the effects of a wide range of stressors. For smoking, people are encouraged to find ways to avoid or escape from situations that may bring on a renewed urge to smoke. At the same time, public health campaigners are working at the political and business level to reduce the availability and accessibility of nicotine products (Hooker & Chapman, 2006)

## AIDS

**AIDS** is an acronym for *acquired immune deficiency syndrome.* Although hundreds of thousands are dying from this virulent disease, many more are now living with HIV infection. **HIV** *(human immunodeficiency virus)* is a virus that attacks the white blood cells (T lymphocytes) in human blood, thus damaging the immune system and weakening the body's ability to fight other diseases. The individual then becomes vulnerable to infection by a host of other viruses and bacteria that can cause such life-threatening illnesses as cancer, meningitis and pneumonia. The period of time from initial infection with the virus until symptoms occur (incubation period) can be 5 years or longer. Although most of the estimated millions of those infected with the HIV virus do not have AIDS (a medical diagnosis), they must live with the continual stress that this life-threatening disease might suddenly emerge. At the present time, there are treatments that delay the onset of full-blown AIDS, but there is neither a cure for AIDS nor a vaccine to prevent its spread.

The HIV virus is not airborne; it requires direct access to the bloodstream to produce an infection. The HIV virus is generally passed from one person to another in one of two ways: (1) the exchange of semen or blood during sexual contact and (2) the sharing of intravenous needles and syringes used for injecting drugs. The virus has also been passed through blood transfusions and medical procedures in which infected blood or organs are unwittingly given to healthy people. Many people suffering from haemophilia have contracted AIDS in this way. However, everyone is at risk for AIDS.

The only way to protect oneself from being infected with the AIDS virus is to change those lifestyle habits that put one at risk. This means making permanent changes in patterns of sexual behaviour and use of drug

Why is regular exercise an important component of a lifelong plan to reduce stress and preserve health?

paraphernalia. Health psychologist **Thomas Coates** is part of a multidisciplinary research team that is using an array of psychological principles in a concerted effort to prevent the further spread of AIDS (Coates & Szekeres, 2004). The team is involved in many aspects of applied psychology, such as assessing psychosocial risk factors, developing behavioural interventions, training community leaders to be effective in educating people toward healthier patterns of sexual and drug behaviour, assisting with the design of media advertisements and community information campaigns, and systematically evaluating changes in relevant attitudes, values and behaviours. Successful AIDS interventions require three components (Starace et al., 2006):

- *Information.* People must be provided with knowledge about how AIDS is transmitted and how its transmission may be prevented; they should be counselled to practise safer sex (for example, use condoms during sexual contact) and use sterile needles.
- *Motivation.* People must be motivated to practise AIDS prevention.
- *Behavioural skills.* People must be taught how to put the knowledge to use.

Why are all three of these components necessary? People might be highly motivated but uninformed, or vice versa. They may have both sufficient knowledge and sufficient motivation but lack requisite skills. They may not, for example, know exactly how to overcome the social barrier of asking a partner to use a condom (Leary et al., 1994). Psychological interventions can provide role-playing experience, or other behavioural skills, to make that barrier seem less significant.

## TREATMENT

Treatment focuses on helping people adjust to their illnesses and recover from them. We will look at three aspects of treatment. First, we consider the role of psychologists in encouraging patients to adhere to the regimens prescribed by health-care practitioners. Next, we look at techniques that allow people to explicitly use psychological techniques to take control over the body's responses. Finally, we examine instances in which the mind can contribute to the body's cure.

### Patient adherence
Patients are often given a *treatment regimen.* This might include medications, dietary changes, prescribed periods of bed rest and exercise, and follow-up procedures such as return checkups, rehabilitation training and chemotherapy. Failing to adhere to treatment regimens is one of the most serious problems in health care (Clark & Becker, 1998). The rate of patient nonadherence is estimated to be as high as 50 percent for some treatment regimens. Recent research has focused on the types of individual differences that lead some individuals to comply whereas others do not.

A team of researchers examined the relevance of *monitoring attentional style* to patient compliance.

When they are ill, some individuals pay close attention to all aspects of the illness—they are called *high monitors.* By contrast, *low monitors* are less likely to focus their attention on their illness. It might not sound dangerous, at first, to be a high monitor. However, because of the tight attentional focus, high monitors tend to overestimate the severity of their illness. As a consequence, high monitors have lower perceived control over their illness—which, the researchers suggested, could undermine their adherence to a treatment regimen. In the current study, the researchers assessed a group of patients for their monitoring attentional style as well as their perceived control and adherence to the regimen. The results fit the pattern the researchers laid out. By comparison to low monitors, high monitors perceived less control over their illness and were also less likely to comply with the regimen specified by their doctors (Christensen et al., 1997).

Prior to reading about this study, you might have thought that people who are very focused on their illness would be more likely to take good care of themselves. Instead, the data suggest that too tight a focus on an illness can make it seem even worse than it really is—and, therefore, beyond hope of a remedy in a way that discourages patients from taking necessary actions.

Research has shown that health-care professionals can take steps to improve patient adherence. Patients are more satisfied with their health care when they trust that the efficacy of the treatment outweighs its costs. They are also more likely to comply with a regimen when practitioners communicate clearly, make sure that their patients understand what has been said, act courteously, and convey a sense of caring and supportiveness. In addition, health professionals must recognise the role of cultural and social norms in the treatment process and involve family and friends where necessary. Some physicians critical of their profession's outdated reliance on the biomedical model argue that doctors must be taught to care in order to cure (Siegel, 1988). Compliance-gaining strategies developed from psychological research are also being used to help overcome the lack of cooperation

Why does relaxation through meditation have health benefits?

between patients and practitioners (Putnam et al., 1994; Zimbardo & Leippe, 1991).

## Harnessing the mind to heal the body

More and more often, the treatments to which patients must adhere involve a psychological component. Many investigators now believe that psychological strategies can improve wellbeing. For example, many people react to stress with tension, resulting in tight muscles and high blood pressure. Fortunately, many tension responses can be controlled by psychological techniques, such as *relaxation* and *biofeedback*.

Relaxation through meditation has ancient roots in many parts of the world. In Eastern cultures, ways to calm the mind and still the body's tensions have been practiced for centuries. Today, Zen discipline and yoga exercises from Japan and India are part of daily life for many people both there and, increasingly, in the West. Growing evidence suggests that complete relaxation is a potent antistress response (Deckro et al., 2002). The **relaxation response** is a condition in which muscle tension, cortical activity, heart rate and blood pressure all decrease and breathing slows (Benson & Stuart, 1992; Friedman et al., 1996). There is reduced electrical activity in the brain, and input to the central nervous system from the outside environment is lowered. In this low level of arousal, recuperation from stress can take place. Four conditions are regarded as necessary to produce the relaxation response: (1) a quiet environment, (2) closed eyes, (3) a comfortable position, and (4) a repetitive mental device such as the chanting of a brief phrase over and over again. The first three conditions lower input to the nervous system, and the fourth lowers its internal stimulation.

**Biofeedback** is a self-regulatory technique used for a variety of special applications, such as control of blood pressure, relaxation of forehead muscles (involved in tension headaches), and even diminishment of extreme blushing. As pioneered by psychologist **Neal Miller** (1978), biofeedback is a procedure that makes an individual aware of ordinarily weak or internal responses by providing clear external signals. The patient is allowed to 'see' his or her own bodily reactions, which are monitored and amplified by equipment that transforms them into lights and sound cues of varying intensity. The patient's task is then to control the level of these external cues.

Let's consider one application of biofeedback. Participants who suffered from either high or low blood pressure were brought into a laboratory (Rau et al., 2003). Feedback from equipment measuring an index of the participants' blood pressure on each heart cycle was delivered to a computer screen so that growing green bars indicated changes in the right direction and growing red bars indicated changes in the wrong direction. In addition, the researchers provided verbal reinforcement: 'You did it the right way!' After three training sessions, the participants were able to raise or lower their blood pressure, as desired. If you ever become concerned about your blood pressure or other physical disorders, results of this sort might encourage you to seek a course of biofeedback to complement a drug regimen.

## Psychoneuroimmunology

In the early 1980s, researchers made a series of discoveries that confirmed another way in which the mind affects the body: psychological states can have an impact on immune function. Historically, scientists had assumed that immunological reactions—rapid production of antibodies to counterattack substances that invade and damage the organism—were automatic biological processes that occurred without any involvement of the central nervous system. However, conditioning experiments of the type we described in Chapter 6 proved that assumption to be incorrect.

Groundbreaking researchers **Robert Ader** and **Nicholas Cohen** (1981) taught one group of rats to associate sweet-tasting saccharin with cyclophosphamide (CY), a drug that weakens immune response. A control group received only the saccharin. Later, when both groups of rats were given only saccharin, the animals that had been conditioned to associate saccharin with CY produced significantly fewer antibodies to foreign cells than those rats in the control group. Thus the learned association alone was sufficient to elicit suppression of the immune system, making the experimental rats vulnerable to a range of diseases. The learning effect was so powerful that, later in the study, some of the rats died after drinking only the saccharin solution.

Results like this strongly suggested that immune function can be modified by psychological states. A new field of study, **psychoneuroimmunology**, has emerged to explore these types of results that involve psychology, the nervous system, and the immune system (Ader & Cohen, 1993; Coe, 1999).

Research over the past 25 years has confirmed that stressors—and how people cope with them—have a consistent impact on the ability of the immune system to function effectively (Kiecolt-Glaser et al., 2002). Consider one of the immune system's basic functions, to heal small wounds in your skin. In one study, a research team led by **Janet Kiecolt-Glaser** gave 13 caretakers for relatives with Alzheimer's disease (see Chapter 7) and 13 control participants standardised small wounds to their skin. On average, the Alzheimer's caretakers, who experience chronic stress, took 9 days longer for their wounds to heal (Kiecolt-Glaser et al., 1995)! Subsequent research examined the physiological mechanisms underlying this effect. For example, as seen in **Figure 12.9**, participants who reported higher levels of perceived stress in their lives had lower levels of the critical substances that regulate healing at the wound site (Glaser et al., 1999). You can see from these data how small differences in stress level may affect the speed with which a person's body can heal even the smallest scratch or scrape. From that basic insight, you can understand why research suggests that stress responses play an even more profound role with respect to the progression of

**relaxation response** A condition in which muscle tension, cortical activity, heart rate, and blood pressure decrease and breathing slows.

**psychoneuroimmunology** The research area that investigates interactions between psychological processes, such as responses to stress, and the functions of the immune system.

**biofeedback** A self-regulatory technique by which an individual acquires voluntary control over nonconscious biological processes.

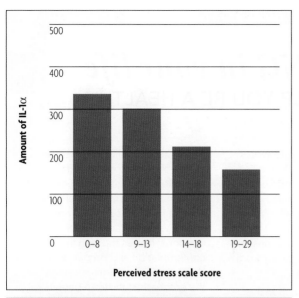

Figure 12.9

**Perceived stress and immune function**
Researchers created standardised wounds on participants' forearms. Twenty-four hours later, participants reported on the stress of their daily life (high scores indicate more perceived stress). The researchers also took samples from the wound sites to assess the levels of the substance IL-1α, which regulates immune function. The data indicated that participants with the highest perceived stress had the lowest levels of IL-1α.

serious medical conditions such as infectious diseases and cancer. Researchers wish to understand how the mind affects immune function so they can harness that power to slow these serious illnesses.

## Psychological impact on health outcomes

The discussion of psychoneuroimmunology allows you to understand the potential for psychological factors to have an impact on physical health. In fact, researchers have designed stress-management programs they hope will provide patients with the coping resources to help change the consequences of disease. Recall our earlier discussion of social support as a coping resource. Some researchers have found that patients who participate in support groups have longer survival times for serious illnesses. For example, in one sample of women suffering from metastatic breast cancer, those patients who participated in group therapy survived for an average of 36.6 months, compared with 18.9 months for the control group (Spiegel et al., 1989). Although not all studies have confirmed that social support leads to increased survival times, participants in stress-management programs consistently have better psychological functioning and better quality of life over the course of their diseases (Claar & Blumenthal, 2003).

One last note on treatment. Have you ever had a secret too shameful to tell anyone? If so, talking about the secret could very well improve your health. That is the conclusion from a large body of research by health psychologist **James Pennebaker** (1990, 1997;

Petrie et al., 1998), who has shown that suppressing thoughts and feelings associated with personal traumas, failures, and guilty or shameful experiences takes a devastating toll on mental and physical health. Such inhibition is psychologically hard work and, over time, it undermines the body's defences against illness. The experience of letting go often is followed by improved physical and psychological health weeks and months later. Consider the effects of emotional disclosure on health outcomes for people with HIV infection.

Thirty-seven adults with HIV infection participated in this study. Roughly half of the patients were assigned to an emotional writing group. In four 30-minute sessions on consecutive days, participants wrote about 'the most traumatic and emotional experiences of their lives' (Petrie et al., 2004, p. 273). The control group spent the same amount of time on a neutral task, writing accounts, for example, about what they had done in the previous day. To assess the impact of emotional writing, the researchers measured *HIV viral load*—the number of HIV copies in a millilitre of blood. **Figure 12.10** displays the dramatic impact of emotional writing. Those participants who had engaged in emotional writing had consistently lower viral loads 2 weeks, 3 months and 6 months after the writing sessions.

This result is consistent with other data indicating that individuals' stress level has an impact on the course of HIV infection. Emotional writing helped participants cope with some negative psychological consequences of the infection.

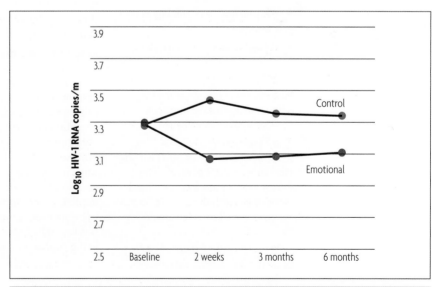

Figure 12.10

**The impact of emotional writing on HIV infection**
Participants engaged in four sessions of either emotional or neutral writing. Their HIV viral load was assessed 2 weeks, 3 months, and 6 months after the writing sessions. Participants who had engaged in emotional writing had consistently lower viral loads.

Figure 1 from 'Effect of Written Emotional Expression on Immune Function in Patients with Human Immunodeficiency Virus Infection: A Randomized Trial' by Petrie, et al.

# CRITICAL THINKING *in your life*

## CAN HEALTH PSYCHOLOGY HELP YOU BE A HEALTHY PERSON?

In November 2002, Australian Health Ministers met and agreed that obesity had become significant public health problem in Australia, and in response established a **National Obesity Taskforce**. The aim of the taskforce was to "develop a national action plan for tackling overweight and obesity, and to identify roles and responsibilities for implementing the national plan".

Since its inception, the Taskforce has implemented a number of plans aimed at improving the health of all Australians. Key initiatives include:

- new physical activity recommendations for children and young people
- redesigned *Physical Activity Guidelines for adults*
- a resource kit for schools to promote healthy eating and physical activity
- the promotion of Healthy School Canteens
- the establishment of a network of Whole-of-Community Healthy Weight Demonstration Sites
- a review of the evidence for actions to reduce obesity in adults and older Australians.

The Taskforce also held an Aboriginal and Torres Strait Islander workshop in 2003 in which 'Ten Principles for Future Actions' were developed, with the overarching recommendation of 'ensur[ing] that the Council of Australian Governments (COAG) endorses,

prioritise and supports actions that will reduce overweight & obesity in Aboriginal and Torres Strait Islander communities'. (URL: <http://www.health.gov.au/internet/healthyactive/publishing.nsf/Content/indigenous_obesity.pdf/$File/indigenous_obesity.pdf> )

Most notably, in 2004 the Taskforce released a **national action plan** entitled *Healthy Weight 2008—Australia's Future: The National Action Agenda for Children and Young People and their Families*. The strategy focused not only on the growing problem of obesity in young people, but also recognised the importance of promoting a healthy lifestyle for their families, notably older Australians, and those identifying themselves as Aboriginal or Torres Strait Islander people.

So, how can your knowledge of health psychology help people reap these benefits of *Healthy Weight 2008* and other such initiatives?

Researchers are exploring the questions of who exercises regularly and why and are trying to determine what programs or strategies are most effective in getting people to start and continue exercising (Dishman & Buckworth, 1997). In fact, much the same model that we outlined for people's readiness to *quit* smoking applies to people's readiness to begin exercising (Marshall & Biddle, 2001; Myers & Roth, 1997). In the *precontemplation* stage,

an individual is still more focused on the barriers to exercise (for example, too little time, no exercise partners) rather than the benefits (for example, helps relaxation, improves appearance). As the individual moves through the *contemplation* and *preparation* stages toward the training stages, the emphasis shifts from barriers to benefits.

If you do not exercise regularly now, how can you get beyond precontemplation? Research suggests that individuals can learn strategies that allow them to overcome obstacles to exercise (Simkin & Gross, 1994). You can treat exercise like any other situation in which you use cognitive appraisal to cope with stress. Try to structure your life so that exercise is a healthy pleasure. You should also be aware that many university students have 'rebounds' in both their eating and exercising: when periods of academic stress have passed, they return from poor eating and minimal exercising to healthy behaviour (Griffin et al., 1993).

How might you structure your thoughts to avoid this pattern? Try to help *Healthy Weight 2008* meet its goals!

- Why might the same stages apply to undertaking healthy behaviours and overcoming unhealthy behaviours?
- Why is it stressful to contemplate healthy behaviours such as regular exercise?

## PERSONALITY AND HEALTH

Do you know a person like this: Someone who is driven to succeed, no matter what obstacles; someone whose high school class voted him or her 'Most likely to have a heart attack before age 20'? Are you that person? As you've observed the way in which some people charge through

life while others take a more relaxed pace, you may have wondered whether these different personalities affect health. Research in health psychology strongly suggests that the answer is yes.

In the 1950s, Meyer Friedman and Ray Rosenman reported what had been suspected since ancient times: There was a relationship between a constellation of personality traits and the probability of illness, specifically coronary heart disease (Friedman & Rosenman, 1974). These researchers identified two behaviour patterns that they labelled Type A and Type B. The **Type A behaviour pattern** is a complex pattern of behaviour and emotions that includes being excessively competitive, aggressive, impatient, time urgent, and hostile. Type A people are often dissatisfied with some central aspect of their lives, are highly competitive and ambitious, and often are loners. The **Type B behaviour pattern** is everything Type A is not—individuals are less competitive, less hostile, and so on. Importantly, these behaviour patterns have an impact on health. In their original discussion, Friedman and Rosenman reported that people who showed Type A behaviour patterns were stricken with coronary heart disease considerably more often than individuals in the general population.

Because the Type A behaviour pattern has many components, researchers have focused their attention on identifying the specific Type A elements that most often put people at risk. The personality trait that has emerged most forcefully as 'toxic' is hostility.

A longitudinal study began in 1986, with 774 men in the sample who were free of any evidence of cardiovascular disease (Niaura et al., 2002). In 1986, each participant's level of hostility was measured (using a set of questions from the Minnesota Multiphasic Personality Inventory, a device we will describe in Chapter 13). Hostility is defined as the consistency with which individuals look at the world and other people in a cynical and negative manner. To display the relationship between hostility and coronary heart disease, the researchers divided the hostility scores into percentile groups. As shown in **Figure 12.11**, those individuals whose hostility scores were in the upper 20 percent had a dramatically larger number of episodes of coronary heart disease in the subsequent years. In this sample of men, hostility was a better predictor of future illness than several behavioural risk factors such as smoking and drinking.

Hostility may affect health for both physiological reasons—by leading to chronic overarousal of the body's stress responses—and psychological reasons—by leading hostile people to practise poor health habits and avoid social support (Smith & Ruiz, 2002).

The good news is that researchers have begun to implement behavioural treatments to reduce hostility and other aspects of the Type A behaviour pattern (Smith & Ruiz, 2002; Thoresen & Powell, 1992). For example, one intervention was directed toward high-hostile men who had been diagnosed with coronary heart disease (Gidron et al., 1999). As part of the intervention, the men were taught how to use problem-focused coping to reduce anger; they were taught how to use cognitive restructuring to reduce cynicism. After 8 weeks, men in the intervention group reported consistently lower levels of hostility than their peers in the control (nonintervention) group. In addition, the men in the intervention group had lower average blood pressure than their control peers. Do you recognise

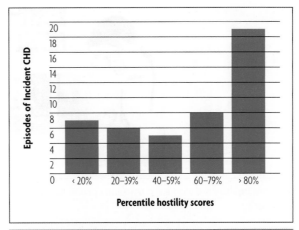

**Figure 12.11**

**Hostility predicts coronary heart disease**
Study participants were divided into percentile groups based on their self-reports of hostility. Men whose scores placed them in the top 20 percent on the measure (i.e., the group greater than 80 percent) had the highest levels of coronary heart disease.

yourself in the definition of hostility? If you do, protect your health by seeking out this type of intervention.

To round out this section on personality and health we want to remind you of the concept of *optimism* we introduced in Chapter 11. We saw there that optimistic individuals attribute failures to external causes and to events that were unstable or modifiable (Seligman, 1991). This style of coping has a strong impact on the optimist's well-being. Researchers have demonstrated that optimism has an impact on the function of the immune system (Segerstrom et al., 1998). Optimistic people have fewer physical symptoms of illness, are faster at recovering from certain illnesses, are generally healthier, and live longer (Hegelson, 2003; Peterson et al., 1988). A positive outlook may both reduce your body's experience of chronic stress and make it more likely that you'll engage in healthy behaviours.

## JOB BURNOUT AND THE HEALTH-CARE SYSTEM

One final focus of health psychology is to make recommendations about the design of the health-care system. Researchers, for example, have examined the stress associated with being a health-care provider. Even the most enthusiastic health-care providers run up against the emotional stresses of working intensely with large numbers of people suffering from a variety of personal, physical and social problems.

The special type of emotional stress experienced by these professional health and welfare practitioners has been termed *burnout* by **Christina Maslach**, a leading researcher on this widespread problem. **Job burnout** is a syndrome of emotional exhaustion, depersonalisation and reduced personal accomplishment that is often experienced by workers in professions that demand

**Type A behaviour pattern**
A complex pattern of behaviours and emotions that includes excessive emphasis on competition, aggression, impatience and hostility; hostility increases the risk of coronary heart disease.

**Type B behaviour pattern**
As compared to Type A behaviour pattern, a less competitive, less aggressive, less hostile pattern of behaviour and emotion.

**job burnout** The syndrome of emotional exhaustion, depersonalisation and reduced personal accomplishment, often experienced by workers in high-stress jobs.

Why are health-care workers particularly prone to job burnout?

high-intensity interpersonal contact with patients, clients or the public. Health practitioners begin to lose their caring and concern for patients and may come to treat them in detached and even dehumanised ways. They feel bad about themselves and worry that they are failures. Burnout is correlated with greater absenteeism and turnover, impaired job performance, poor relations with co-workers, family problems and poor personal health (Maslach et al., 2001; Schaufeli et al., 1993). To give one example, Scutter and Goold (1995) identified symptoms of burnout in over half of their sample of newly qualified phyiotherapists in South Australia.

Job burnout in today's workforce is reaching ever higher levels because of the effects of organisational downsizing, job restructuring and greater concerns for profits than for employee morale and loyalty. Burnout then is not merely a concern of workers and health-caregivers, but it also reveals organisational dysfunction that needs to be corrected by reexamining goals, values, workloads and reward structures (Leiter & Maslach, 2005).

What recommendations can be made? Several social and situational factors affect the occurrence and level of burnout and, by implication, suggest ways of preventing or minimising it (Leiter & Maslach, 2005; Prosser et al., 1997). For example, the quality of the patient–practitioner interaction is greatly influenced by the number of patients for whom a practitioner is providing care—the greater the number, the greater the cognitive, sensory and emotional overload. Another factor in the quality of that interaction is the amount of direct contact with patients. Longer work hours in continuous direct contact with patients are correlated with greater burnout. This is especially true when the nature of the contact is difficult and upsetting, such as contact with patients who are dying (Catalan et al., 1996). The emotional strain of such prolonged contact can be eased by a number of means. For example, practitioners can modify their work schedules in order to withdraw temporarily from such high-stress situations. They can use teams rather than only individual contact. They can arrange opportunities to get positive feedback for their efforts.

## A TOAST TO YOUR HEALTH

It's time for some final advice. Instead of waiting for stress or illness to come and then reacting to it, set goals and structure life in ways that are most likely to forge a healthy foundation. The following nine steps to greater happiness and better mental health are presented as guidelines to encourage you to take a more active role in your own life and to create a more positive psychological environment for yourself and others. Think of the steps as *year-round resolutions*.

1. Never say bad things about yourself. Look for sources of your unhappiness in elements that can be modified by future actions. Give yourself and others only *constructive criticism*—what can be done differently next time to get what you want?

2. Compare your reactions, thoughts and feelings with those of friends, co-workers, family members and others so that you can gauge the appropriateness and relevance of your responses against a suitable social norm.

3. Have several close friends with whom you can share feelings, joys and worries. Work at developing, maintaining and expanding your social support networks.

4. Develop a sense of *balanced time perspective* in which you can flexibly focus on the demands of the task, the situation, and your needs; be future oriented when there is work to be done, present oriented when the goal is achieved and pleasure is at hand, and past oriented to keep you in touch with your roots.

5. Always take full credit for your successes and happiness (and share your positive feelings with other people). Keep an inventory of all the qualities that make you special and unique—those qualities you can offer others. For example, a shy person can provide a talkative person with the gift of attentive listening. Know your sources of personal strength and available coping resources.

6. When you feel you are losing control over your emotions, distance yourself from the situation by physically leaving it, role-playing the position of another person in the situation or conflict, projecting your imagination into the future to gain perspective on what seems an overwhelming problem now, or talking to a sympathetic listener. Allow yourself to feel and express your emotions.

7. Remember that failure and disappointment are sometimes blessings in disguise. They may tell you that your goals are not right for you or may save you from bigger letdowns later on. Learn from every failure. Acknowledge setbacks by saying, 'I made a mistake', and move on. Every accident, misfortune or violation of your expectations is potentially a wonderful opportunity in disguise.

8. If you discover you cannot help yourself or another person in distress, seek the counsel of a trained specialist in your student health department or community. In some cases, a problem that appears to be psychological may really be physical and vice versa. Check out your student mental health services

before you need them, and use them without concern about being stigmatised.

9. Cultivate healthy pleasures. Take time out to relax, to meditate, to get a massage, to fly a kite and to enjoy hobbies and activities you can do alone and that help you get in touch with and better appreciate yourself.

So how are you feeling? If the stressors in your life have the potential to put you in a bad mood, we hope you'll be able to use cognitive reappraisal to minimise their impact. If you are feeling ill, we hope you'll be able to use your mind's healing capacity to speed your way back toward health. Never underestimate the power of these different types of 'feelings' to exercise control over your life. Harness that power!

## RECAP CHECKPOINT

### Health psychology

- Health psychology is devoted to treatment and prevention of illness.

- The biopsychosocial model of health and illness looks at the connections among physical, emotional and environmental factors in illness.

- Illness prevention in the 21st century focuses on lifestyle factors such as smoking and AIDS-risk behaviours.

- Psychological factors influence immune function.

- Psychosocial treatment of illness adds another dimension to patient treatment.

- Individuals who are characterised by Type A (especially hostile), Type B and optimistic behaviour patterns will experience different likelihoods of illness.

- Health-care providers are at risk for burnout, which can be minimised by appropriate situational changes in their helping environment.

## CONCEPT QUESTIONS

1. What has research revealed about the genetics of smoking?

2. What are the three components of successful AIDS interventions?

3. What conditions are necessary to produce the relaxation response?

4. What is the central goal for researchers who study psychoneuroimmunology?

5. What is the 'toxic' aspect of Type A personalities?

6. How is job burnout defined?

## CRITICAL THINKING

Consider the study that examined the health impact of emotional disclosure. Why did the researchers ask participants in the control group to write texts?

For answers go to MyPsychLab!

# SUMMARY

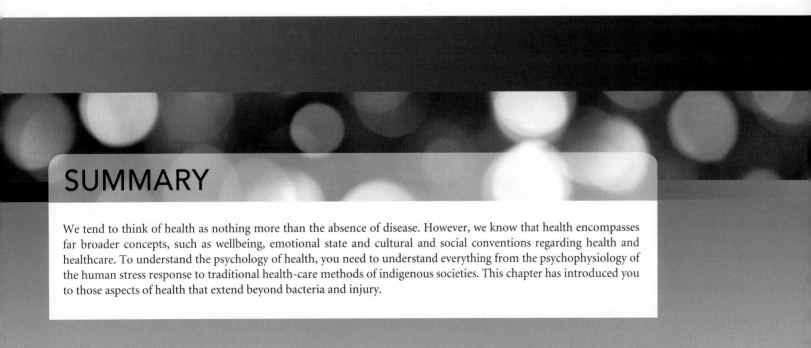

We tend to think of health as nothing more than the absence of disease. However, we know that health encompasses far broader concepts, such as wellbeing, emotional state and cultural and social conventions regarding health and healthcare. To understand the psychology of health, you need to understand everything from the psychophysiology of the human stress response to traditional health-care methods of indigenous societies. This chapter has introduced you to those aspects of health that extend beyond bacteria and injury.

# KEY TERMS

acute stress (p. 416)
AIDS (p. 432)
anticipatory coping (p. 424)
biofeedback (p. 434)
biopsychosocial model (p. 430)
Cannon–Bard theory of emotion (p. 409)
chronic stress (p. 416)
cognitive appraisal (p. 409)
cognitive appraisal theory of emotion
    (p. 410)
coping (p. 423)
emotion (p. 404)
fight-or-flight response (p. 416)

general adaptation syndrome (GAS)
    (p. 418)
health (p. 429)
health promotion (p. 430)
health psychology (p. 429)
HIV (p. 432)
James–Lange theory of emotion
    (p. 409)
job burnout (p. 437)
life-change units (LCUs) (p. 419)
perceived control (p. 426)
post-traumatic stress disorder (PTSD)
    (p. 421)

psychoneuroimmunology (p. 434)
psychosomatic disorders (p. 418)
relaxation response (p. 434)
social support (p. 426)
stress (p. 415)
stress moderator variables (p. 423)
stressor (p. 415)
tend-and-befriend response (p. 417)
Type A behaviour pattern (p. 437)
Type B behaviour pattern (p. 437)
wellness (p. 430)

# PRACTICE TEST

1. Which statement is true of moods, but not emotions?
   a. They may last several days.
   b. They can be either positive or negative.
   c. They may arise from specific events.
   d. They are relatively intense.

2. Which of these facial expressions is *not* among the seven universally recognised expressions of emotion?
   a. concern          c. disgust
   b. contempt         d. happiness

3. The _____ prepares the body for physiological aspects of emotional responses.
   a. hypothalamus     c. autonomous nervous system
   b. amygdala         d. hippocampus

4. According to the _____ theory of emotion, you feel after your body reacts.
   a. Cannon–Bard         c. James–Lange
   b. cognitive appraisal  d. approach-related

5. Which piece of evidence suggests that not all emotional experiences rely on cognitive appraisal?
   a. Across cultures, facial expressions are highly similar.
   b. The cortex has a separate circuit for withdrawal-related emotional responses.
   c. People in some cultures don't express pain.
   d. People experience the mere exposure effect.

6. When Betsy woke up, she was in a terrific mood. She experienced a flood of happy memories. This is an example of
   a. cognitive appraisal.
   b. mood-congruent processing.
   c. mood-dependent processing.
   d. approach-related cognition.

7. Professor Rollins wishes to predict Henrik's level of happiness from Horace's level of happiness. That prediction is likely to be the most accurate if Horace is Henrik's
   a. older brother.       c. MZ twin.
   b. DZ twin.             d. closest friend.

8. The brain structure that plays an important role in the fight-or-flight response is the
   a. pituitary gland.     c. hypothalamus.
   b. amygdala.            d. thyroid gland.

9. For people in the 1990s, reports of life-change events were _____ people's reports in the 1960s.
   a. higher than          c. lower than
   b. the same as          d. predicted by

10. If you are faced by _____ stressors, the type of coping that is likely to be most useful is _____ coping.
    a. uncontrollable; problem-directed
    b. controllable; emotion-focused
    c. controllable; delay-based
    d. uncontrollable; emotion-focused

11. Which type of coping self-statement is this: 'It worked; I was able to do it?'
    a. Coping           c. Confrontation
    b. Preparation      d. Self-reinforcement

12. When May was diagnosed with skin cancer, Al searched the Web to help her learn more about treatment options. This type of social support is _____ support.
    a. tangible          c. emotional
    b. informational     d. inoculation

13. A few months after surviving a cyclone, Judy says, 'I am grateful for every new day.' It sounds like Judy experienced posttraumatic growth in which domain?
    a. Spiritual change      c. Appreciation of life
    b. Relating to others    d. Personal strength

14. Consider the stages people pass through as they attempt to quit smoking. Which of these pairs are in the wrong order?
    a. preparation; contemplation
    b. contemplation; action
    c. action; maintenance
    d. preparation; maintenance

15. Marsea is participating in a laboratory study. Every time her blood pressure goes up, she sees a 'sad face' on a computer display. It seems that Marsea is learning how to use
    a. the relaxation response.
    b. biofeedback.
    c. anticipatory coping.
    d. stress inoculation.

16. Researchers gave caretakers of Alzheimer's patients and control individuals standardised wounds. What was the result of the study?
    a. The wounds of the Alzheimer's caretakers took longer to heal.
    b. The wounds of the control individuals took longer to heal.
    c. There was no difference in the time it took the wounds to heal.
    d. The wounds of the control individuals were larger.

17. The aspect of the _____ behaviour pattern that has the greatest impact on health is _____.
    a. Type B; hostility
    b. Type A; optimism
    c. Type B; pessimism
    d. Type A; hostility

18. Which of these features is *not* part of the definition of job burnout?
    a. depersonalisation
    b. disharmony
    c. emotional exhaustion
    d. reduced personal accomplishment

19. Rhonda takes a fifteen minute break every afternoon to take a walk in a park near her office. Rhonda appears to be heeding the advice to
    a. have a balanced time perspective.
    b. cultivate healthy pleasures.
    c. distance herself from conflicts.
    d. recognise blessings in disguise.

20. Annaliese has had four exams in the last week. If she follows a typical pattern, Annaliese will _____ in the coming week.
    a. eat less healthy food
    b. exercise less
    c. show no changes in food consumption
    d. exercise more

## Essay Questions

1. What evidence suggests that some emotional responses are innate while others are not?

2. Why does perceived control have an impact on people's ability to cope with stress?

3. What factors affect the likelihood that patients will adhere to treatment regimens?

# WEB LINKS

Are you ready for the test? MyPsychLab offers dozens of ways to deepen your understanding and test your recall of the material in this chapter—including video and audio clips, simulations and activities, self-assessments, practice tests and other study materials. Specific resources available for this chapter include:

Recognising facial expressions of emotions
How stressed are you?

Physiological, evolutionary and cognitive theories of emotion
Coping strategies and their effects
Selye's general adaptation syndrome

Coping with stress
9/11 Post-traumatic stress disorder.

To access MyPsychLab, please visit **www.pearsoned.com.au/mypsychlab**

# What is the diagnosis?
## NOW YOU HAVE READ CHAPTER 12—ARE YOU PREPARED FOR THE EXAM?

To enhance your understanding of any of the material in your *Psychology and Life* textbook, go to **MyPsychLab: www.pearsoned.com.au/mypsychlab**.

Complete pre- and post-tests, create your own individualised study plan, watch videos and animations and listen to audio glossaries—all of which will help you understand the themes of this chapter:

- Emotions
- Stress of living
- Health psychology

MyPsychLab gives you access to study materials that directly apply to your trouble spots, including eBook, exercises, simulations, videos, web activities, flash cards and additional quiz questions.

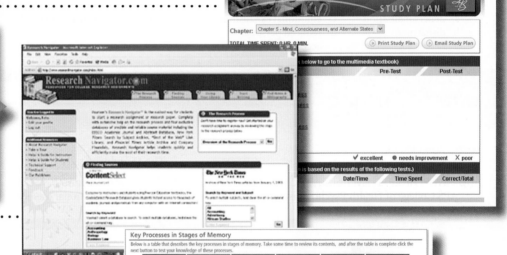

'MyPsychLab was a fantastic asset in preparing for exams.'

**eTHEMES: Health and Stress**

By scrolling down the page you will find articles from *The New York Times* associated with the concepts discussed in Chapter 12.

Read Susan Saulny's article entitled *Goodbye, Therapist. Hello, Anxiety?* Be sure to answer the questions linked to the article.

'The diagnostic tests helped me to know what topics I needed to study further and helped me prepare for my exam.'

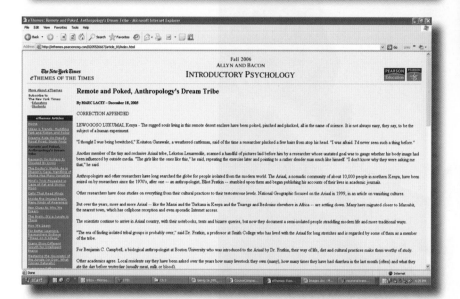

## STUDY TIP

**Develop your own personalised study plan**

Take PRE- and POST-TESTS on *emotional patterns, the Social Readjustment Rating Scale* and other topics covered in Chapter 12. Based on your grades in each test, MyPsychLab will create a STUDY PLAN which will identify your specific areas of weakness and strength.

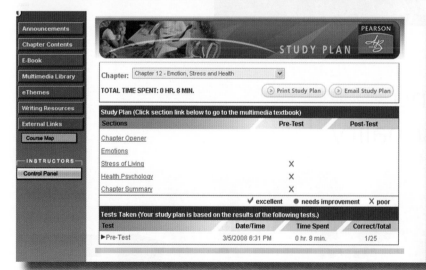

### What can you find in MyPsychLab?

Self-directed tests * Videos * Simulations * eBook * Biographies * Audio glossary * Web links … and more—organised by chapter, section and learning objective.

Understanding
Human Personality

CHAPTER

13

# CHAPTER
# FOCUS POINTS

After studying this chapter you will have a better understanding of:

1. Understanding type and trait personality theories

2. A history of psychodynamic theories of personality

3. A history of humanistic theories of personality

4. Understanding social-learning and cognitive theories of personality

5. Theories of 'The Self' and their relationship to culture

6. The comparison of personality theories

7. How to assess personality.

## CHAPTER CONTENTS

Suppose we asked you to compare and contrast your two closest friends. In what ways are they similar? In what ways are they different? It seems likely that your analysis would very quickly come to focus on your friends' *personalities*. You might, for example, assert that one is friendlier than the other or one has more self-confidence than the other. Assertions of this sort would suggest that you've brought your own personality theory to bear on your relationships—you have your own system for appraising personality. You use your beliefs to determine who in a new class would be friend or foe; you worked out techniques for dealing with your parents or teachers based on the way you read their personalities.

Psychologists define personality in many different ways, but common to all of the ways are two basic concepts: *uniqueness* and *characteristic patterns of behaviour*. We define **personality** as the complex set of psychological qualities that influence an individual's characteristic patterns of behaviour across different situations and over time.

Theories of personality are hypothetical statements about the structure and functioning of individual personalities. They help to achieve two of the major goals of psychology: (1) understanding the structure, origins and correlates of personality; and (2) predicting behaviour and life events based on what we know about personality. Different theories make different predictions about the way people will respond and adapt to certain conditions.

Before we examine some of the major theoretical approaches, we should ask why there are so many different (often competing) theories. Theorists differ in their approaches to personality by varying their starting points and sources of data and by trying to explain different types of phenomena. Some are interested in the structure of individual personality and others in how that personality developed and will continue to grow. Some are interested in what people do, either in terms of specific behaviours or important life events; others study how people feel about their lives. Finally, some theories try to explain the personalities of people with psychological problems, whereas others focus on healthy individuals. Thus each theory can teach something about personality, and together they can teach much about human nature.

Our goal for this chapter is to provide you with a framework for understanding your everyday experience of personality. However, before we begin, consider this series of questions: If psychologists studied *you*, what portrait of your personality would they draw? What early experiences might they identify as contributing to the way you now act and think? What conditions in your current life exert strong influences on your thoughts and behaviours? What makes you different from other individuals who are functioning in many of the same situations as you? This chapter should help you formulate specific answers to these questions.

**personality** The psychological qualities of an individual that influence a variety of characteristic behaviour patterns across difference situations and over time.

**personality types** Distinct patterns of personality characteristics used to assign people to categories; qualitative differences used to discriminate among people.

# TYPE AND TRAIT PERSONALITY THEORIES

Two of the oldest approaches to describing personality involve classifying people into a limited number of *distinct types* and scaling the degree to which they can be described by *different traits*. There seems to be a natural tendency for people to place their own and others' behaviour into different categories. Let's examine the formal theories psychologists have developed to capture these differences in types and traits.

## CATEGORISING BY TYPES

We are always categorising people according to distinguishing features. These include sex and race and, sometimes, more broad issues such as a degree taken at university or what university they attended. Some personality theorists also group people into distinct, non-overlapping categories that are called **personality types**. Personality types are all-or-none phenomena, not matters of degree: if a person is assigned to one type, he or she could not belong to any other type within that system. Many people like to use personality types in everyday life because they help simplify the complex process of understanding other people.

One of the earliest type theories was originated in the fifth century B.C. by **Hippocrates**, the Greek physician who gave medicine the Hippocratic oath. He theorised that the body contained four basic fluids, or *humours*, each associated with a particular *temperament*—a pattern of emotions and behaviours. In the second century A.D., a later Greek physician, **Galen**, suggested that an individual's personality depended on which humour was predominant in his or her body. Galen paired Hippocrates's body humours with personality temperaments according to the following scheme:

- *Blood.* Sanguine temperament: cheerful and active
- *Phlegm.* Phlegmatic temperament: apathetic and sluggish
- *Black bile.* Melancholy temperament: sad and brooding
- *Yellow bile.* Choleric temperament: irritable and excitable

The theory proposed by Galen was believed for centuries, up through the Middle Ages, although it has not held up to modern scrutiny. (We will, however, see a modern echo of these temperaments in Hans Eysenck's trait theory, which we present on p. 448.)

In modern times, **William Sheldon** (1942) originated a type theory that related physique to temperament. He assigned people to three categories based on their body builds: *endomorphic* (fat, soft, round), *mesomorphic* (muscular, rectangular, strong), or *ectomorphic* (thin, long, fragile). Sheldon believed that endomorphs are relaxed,

Hippocrates theorised that the body contained four essential fluids, or humours, each associated with a particular temperament. Clockwise: a melancholy patient suffers from an excess of black bile; blood impassions a sanguine lutenist to play; a maiden, dominated by phlegm, is slow to respond to her lover; choler, too much yellow bile makes an angry master. Do you believe Hippocrates's personality types apply to the people you know?

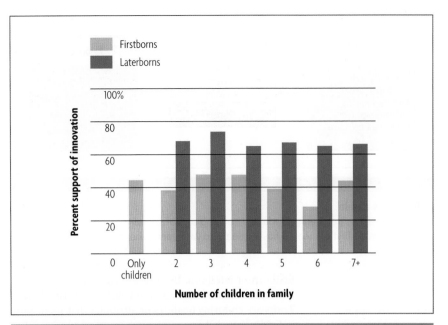

fond of eating and sociable. Mesomorphs are physical people, filled with energy, courage and assertive tendencies. Ectomorphs are brainy, artistic and introverted; they would think about life, rather than consuming it or acting on it. For a period of time, Sheldon's theory was sufficiently influential that nude 'posture' photographs were taken of thousands of students at U.S. universities like Yale and Wellesley to allow researchers to study the relationships between body type and life factors. However, like Hippocrates's much earlier theory, Sheldon's notion of body types has proven to be of very little value in predicting an individual's behaviour (Tyler, 1965).

More recently, **Frank Sulloway** (1996) has proposed a contemporary type theory based on *birth order*. Are you the *firstborn* child (or *only* child) in your family, or are you a *laterborn* child? Because you can take on only one of these birth positions, Sulloway's theory fits the criteria for being a type theory. (For people with unusual family constellations—for example, a very large age gap between two children—Sulloway still provides ways of categorising individuals.) Sulloway makes birth-order predictions based on Darwin's idea that organisms diversify to find niches in which they will survive. According to Sulloway, firstborns have a ready-made niche: they immediately command their parents' love and attention; they seek to maintain that initial attachment by identifying and complying with their parents. By contrast, laterborn children need to find a different niche—one in which they don't so

clearly follow their parents' example. As a consequence, Sulloway characterises laterborns as 'born to rebel': 'they seek to excel in those domains where older siblings have not already established superiority. Laterborns typically cultivate openness to experience—a useful strategy for anyone who wishes to find a novel and successful niche in life' (Sulloway, 1996, p. 353). To test the prediction that later-borns embrace innovation, whereas firstborns prefer the status quo, Sulloway examined scientific, historical, and cultural revolutions and determined the birth position of large numbers of historical and contemporary figures who had supported or opposed those revolutions. **Figure 13.1** presents data on the extent to which firstborn and laterborn scientists supported 23 innovative theories in science. As you can see, for all the family sizes, laterborn children were more likely to support the innovative theory than were firstborns. Do you have brothers or sisters? Can you find this pattern in your own family?

Do you know people whom you would label as particular 'types'? Does the 'type' include all there is to know about the person? Type theories often don't seem to capture more subtle aspects of people's personalities. Let's turn now to theories that allow more flexibility by differentiating individuals according to traits rather than types.

## DESCRIBING WITH TRAITS

Type theories presume that there are separate, discontinuous categories into which people fit, such as

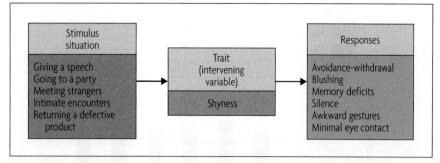

Figure 13.2

**Shyness as a trait**
Traits may act as intervening variables, relating sets of stimuli and responses that might seem, at first glance, to have little to do with each other.

see **Figure 13.2**

**traits** Enduring personal qualities or attributes that influence behaviour across situations.

firstborn or laterborn. By contrast, trait theories propose *continuous dimensions*, such as intelligence or friendliness. **Traits** are enduring qualities or attributes that predispose individuals to behave consistently across situations. For example, you may demonstrate honesty on one day by returning a lost wallet and on another day by not cheating on a test. Some trait theorists think of traits as *predispositions* that cause behaviour, but more conservative theorists use traits only as *descriptive dimensions* that simply summarise patterns of observed behaviour. Let's examine prominent trait theories.

## Allport's trait approach
**Gordon Allport** (1937, 1961, 1966) viewed traits as the building blocks of personality and the source of individuality. According to Allport, traits produce coherence in behaviour because they connect and unify a person's reactions to a variety of stimuli. Traits may act as *intervening variables*, relating sets of stimuli and responses that might seem, at first glance, to have little to do with each other (see **Figure 13.2**).

Allport identified three kinds of traits: cardinal traits, central traits, and secondary traits. *Cardinal traits* are traits around which a person organises his or her life. For Mother Teresa, a cardinal trait might have been self-sacrifice for the good of others. However, not all people develop such overarching cardinal traits. Instead, *central traits* are traits that represent major characteristics of a person, such as honesty or optimism. *Secondary traits* are specific personal features that help predict an individual's behaviour but are less useful for understanding an individual's personality. Food or dress preferences are examples of secondary traits. Allport was interested in discovering the unique combination of these three types of traits that make each person a singular entity and championed the use of case studies to examine these unique traits.

**five-factor model** A comprehensive descriptive personality system that maps out the relationships among common traits, theoretical concepts and personality scales; informally called the Big Five.

Allport saw *personality structures*, rather than *environmental conditions*, as the critical determiners of individual behaviour. 'The same fire that melts the butter hardens the egg' was a phrase he used to show that the same stimuli can have different effects on different individuals. Many contemporary trait theories have followed in Allport's tradition.

**Identifying universal trait dimensions** In 1936, a dictionary search by Gordon Allport and his colleague H. S. Odbert found over 18,000 adjectives in the English language to describe individual differences. Researchers since that time have attempted to identify the fundamental dimensions that underlie that enormous trait vocabulary. They have tried to determine how many dimensions exist and which ones will allow psychologists to give a useful, universal characterisation of all individuals.

**Raymond Cattell** (1979) used Allport and Odbert's list of adjectives as a starting point in his quest to uncover the appropriate small set of basic trait dimensions. His research led him to propose that 16 factors underlie human personality. Cattell called these 16 factors *source traits* because he believed they provide the underlying source for the surface behaviours we think of as personality. Cattell's 16 factors included important behavioural oppositions such as *reserved* versus *outgoing*, *trusting* versus *suspicious*, and *relaxed* versus *tense*. Even so, contemporary trait theorists argue that even fewer dimensions than 16 capture the most important distinctions among people's personalities.

**Hans Eysenck** (1973, 1990) derived just two broad dimensions from personality test data: *extraversion* (internally versus externally oriented) and *neuroticism* (emotionally stable versus emotionally unstable). As shown in **Figure 13.3**, Eysenck plotted the two dimensions of extraversion and neuroticism to form a circular display. He suggested that each quadrant of the display represents one of the four personality types associated by Galen with

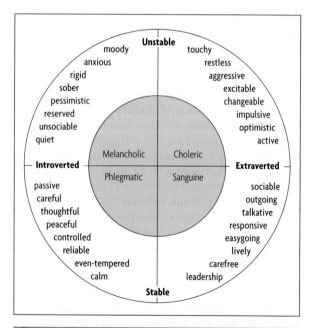

Figure 13.3

**The four quadrants of Eysenck's personality circle**
The two dimensions of extraversion and neuroticism yield a circular display. Eysenck related each quadrant of the display to one of the four personality types defined by Galen. Eysenck's trait theory, however, allows for individual variation within these categories.

In the absence of personality test results, traits can be inferred from observed behaviour. For example, Martin Luther King, Jr. (left) would be thought to have the cardinal trait of peacefully resisting injustice; honesty would be one of Harry Cooper's central traits; and Kylie Minogue's predilection for changeable styles would be a secondary trait. What do you think may be your cardinal, central and secondary traits?

Hippocrates's humours. Eysenck's trait theory, however, allows for individual variation within these categories. Individuals can fall anywhere around the circle, ranging from very introverted to very extraverted and from very unstable (neurotic) to very stable. The traits listed around the circle describe people with combinations of these two dimensions. For example, a person who is very extraverted and somewhat unstable is likely to be impulsive.

**Five-factor model** Research evidence supports many aspects of Eysenck's theory. However, in recent years, a consensus has emerged that five factors, which overlap imperfectly with Eysenck's three dimensions, best characterise personality structure. The five dimensions are very broad because each brings into one large category many traits that have unique connotations but a common theme. These five dimensions of personality are now called the **five-factor model**, or, more informally, the *Big Five* (McCrae & Costa, 1999). The five factors are summarised in **Table 13.1**. You'll notice again that each dimension has two poles—terms that are similar in meaning to the name of the dimension describe the high pole, and terms that are opposite in meaning describe the low pole.

The movement toward the five-factor model represented attempts to find structure among the large list of traits that Allport and Odbert (1936) had extracted from the dictionary. The traits were boiled down into about 200 synonym clusters that were used to form trait dimensions that have a high pole and a low pole, such as *responsible* versus *irresponsible*. Next, people were asked to rate themselves and others on the bipolar dimensions, and the ratings were subjected to statistical procedures to determine how the synonym clusters were interrelated. Using this method, several independent research teams

### Table 13.1

The five-factor model

| Factor | Endpoints of the dimension |
|---|---|
| Extraversion | Talkative, energetic and assertive versus quiet, reserved and shy |
| Agreeableness | Sympathetic, kind and affectionate versus cold, quarrelsome and cruel |
| Conscientiousness | Organised, responsible and cautious versus careless, frivolous and irresponsible |
| Neuroticism | Stable, calm and contented versus anxious, unstable and temperamental |
| Openness to experience | Creative, intellectual and open-minded versus simple, shallow and unintelligent |

came to the same conclusion: that there are only *five basic dimensions* underlying the traits people use to describe themselves and others (Norman, 1963, 1967; Tupes & Christal, 1961).

Since the 1960s, very similar dimensions have also been found in personality questionnaires, interviewer checklists, and other data (Costa & McCrae, 1992; Digman, 1990; Wiggins & Pincus, 1992). To demonstrate the universality of the five-factor model, researchers have broadened their studies beyond the English language: The five-factor structure has been replicated in a number of languages including German, Portuguese, Hebrew, Chinese, Korean and Japanese (McCrae & Costa, 1997). The five factors are not meant to replace the many specific trait terms that carry their own nuances and shades of meaning. Rather, they outline a taxonomy—a classification system—that allows you to give a description of all the people you know in ways that capture the important dimensions on which they differ.

We have emphasised that the five-factor model originally emerged from statistical analyses of clusters of trait terms, rather than from a theory that said, 'These are the factors that must exist' (Ozer & Reise, 1994). However, researchers have started to demonstrate that there are differences in the ways that individuals' brains function that correspond to trait differences in the five-factor model.

Recall from Chapter 12 that a brain structure called the amygdala plays an important role in the processing of emotional stimuli. However, researchers had begun to suspect that not all amygdalas—and, therefore, not all people—responded to stimuli in the same way. To test this idea, a team of researchers recruited 15 participants who differed in their level of extraversion (Canli et al., 2002). The researchers predicted that extraversion would have an impact on emotional processing because that trait captures important aspects of people's emotional lives. To look for individual differences, the researchers had the participants view fearful, happy, and neutral faces while they underwent fMRI scans. **Figure 13.4** displays the correlation between participants' self-reports of extraversion and activity in the left and right amygdalas: The areas in red are those areas for which high levels of extraversion were associated with high levels of brain activity. As you can see, extraversion was not correlated with the brains' responses to fearful faces (i.e., there are no areas in red). In fact, fearful faces activated both the left and right amygdalas, but more or less equally across all levels of extraversion. By contrast, for happy faces the highly extraverted individuals showed abundant activity in their left amygdala.

You might recall from Chapter 12 that researchers have characterised emotions as either *approach-related* or *withdrawal-related*. This study suggests that people who are most content to approach other people—that's what makes them extraverted—have more activation in brain regions that support approach-related emotions.

Supporters of the five-factor model have also tried to explain why exactly these five dimensions emerge by looking to evolution: they try to relate the five dimensions to consistent types of interactions that people had with each other and with the external world over the course of human evolution (Costa & McCrae, 1992; McCrae et al., 2000). An evolutionary basis would help explain the universality of the five factors across diverse cultures. If this explanation is correct, we might also expect that, like other aspects of human experience that have been shaped

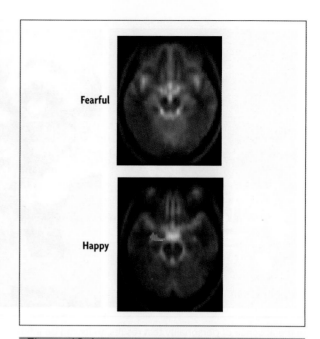

**Figure 13.4**

**Extraversion affects the function of the left amygdala**
Participants viewed fearful and happy faces. The figure displays in red those areas of the brain for which there was a positive correlation between extraversion and amygdala activity. For the fearful faces, there was no correlation. However, for happy faces, the most extraverted participants also showed the highest levels of activity in their left amygdalas.

From Canli et al. (2002), Amygdala response to happy faces as a function of extraversion, *Science*, 296: 2191. Reprinted with permission from AAAS.

by evolution, traits can be passed from one generation to the next. We turn now to that claim.

## TRAITS AND HERITABILITY

You've probably heard people say things such as 'Jim's artistic, like his mother' or 'Mary's as stubborn as her grandfather'. Or maybe you've felt frustrated because the characteristics that you find irritating in your siblings are those you would like to change in yourself. Let's look at the evidence that supports the heritability of personality traits.

Recall that *behavioural genetics* is the study of the degree to which personality traits and behaviour patterns are inherited. To determine the effect of genetics on personality, researchers study the personality traits of family members who share different proportions of genes and who have grown up in the same or different households. For example, if a personality characteristic such as *sociability* is passed on genetically, then sociability should correlate more highly between identical, *monozygotic* twins (who share 100 percent of their genes) than between fraternal, *dizygotic* twins or other siblings (who share, on average, 50 percent of their genes).

Heritability studies show that almost all personality traits are influenced by genetic factors (Loehlin et al., 1998). The findings are the same with many different measurement techniques, whether they measure broad traits, such as extraversion and neuroticism, or specific traits, such as self-control or sociability. Let's consider one sample study.

We just introduced you to the five-factor model of personality. Researchers have turned their attention to the question of whether there is a genetic basis for the factors specified by this model. In one study, a team of researchers from Germany and Poland obtained personality measures for 660 monozygotic twin pairs and 304 dizygotic twin pairs. Data were provided both by self-report (that is, the twins filled out personality inventories of the type we cover later in the chapter) and by peer report (that is, friends and family members made ratings on one or the other twin). Past research has generally only used self-report data. Critics of heritability research have worried that monozygotic and dizygotic twins may have biases in the way they compare themselves to their twins versus other individuals. The inclusion of peer report eliminates the possibility that high heritability estimates are merely consequences of twins' biases in reporting on themselves. In fact, in all cases, the personalities of monozygotic twins were rated as more similar than those of dizygotic twins. The self-ratings, for example, revealed inter-twin correlations of .52 (monozygotic) versus .23 (dizygotic). Using both the self and peer data, these researchers demonstrated substantial heritability estimates for each of the factors defined by the five-factor model (Riemann et al., 1997).

Research with identical twins demonstrates the heritability of personality traits. Are there personality traits you believe run in your family?

Look back to Table 13.1. Which poles of the five factors seem to apply best to you? Can you find similarities between you and your parents?

## DO TRAITS PREDICT BEHAVIOURS?

Suppose we ask you to choose some trait terms that you believe apply particularly well to yourself. You might tell us, for example, that you are *very friendly*. What do we now know? If personality theories allow us to make predictions about behaviours, what can we predict from knowing that you rate yourself as being very friendly? How can we determine the validity of your belief? Let's explore this question.

One idea you might have is that knowing that a person can be characterised by a particular trait would enable you to predict his or her behaviour across different *situations*. Thus, we would expect you to produce friendly behaviours in all situations. However, in the 1920s, several researchers who set out to observe trait-related behaviours in different situations were surprised to find little evidence that behaviour was consistent across situations. For example, two behaviours presumably related to the trait of honesty—lying and cheating on a test—were only weakly correlated among school children (Hartshorne & May, 1928). Similar results were found by other researchers who examined the *cross-situational consistency* for other traits such as introversion or punctuality (Dudycha, 1936; Newcomb, 1929).

If trait-related behaviours are not cross-situationally consistent—that is, if people's behaviour changes in different situations—why do you perceive your own and others' personalities to be relatively stable? Even more puzzling, the personality ratings of observers who know an individual from one situation correlate with the ratings of observers who know the individual from another situation. The observation that personality ratings across time and among different observers *are consistent*, whereas behaviour ratings of a person across situations *are not consistent*, came to be called the **consistency paradox** (Mischel, 1968).

The identification of the consistency paradox led to a great deal of research (Mischel, 2004). Over time, the consensus emerged that the appearance of behavioural inconsistency arose, in large part, because situations had been categorised in the wrong way: The paradox fades away once theorists can provide an appropriate account of the *psychological features* of situations (Mischel & Shoda, 1995, 1999). Suppose, for example, you want to try to assess behavioural consistency by determining if a friend acts in much the same way at every party she attends. You're likely to discover that her behaviour varies widely if your level of analysis is just 'parties'. What you need to determine is what psychologically relevant features separate parties into different categories. Perhaps your friend feels uncomfortable in situations in which she is expected to disclose personal information to strangers. As a consequence, she might seem very unfriendly at

consistency paradox The observation that personality ratings across time and among different observers are consistent while behaviour ratings across situations are not consistent.

Assuming you could afford either one, which of these vacations would you prefer? What might that tell us about the ways in which personality traits interact with features of situations?

some parties (where she is expected to disclose personal information) but quite friendly at others (where she is not). Meanwhile, other situations that require her to be disclosing—such as job interviews—might also bring out negative behaviours. Thus we find consistency in the way that features of situations elicit people's distinctive responses.

Researchers have described the knowledge people have of the relationships between dispositions and situations as *if . . . then . . . personality signatures:* If an individual brings a particular disposition to a specific situation *then* he or she will behave in a particular way (Mischel, 2004). Consider a study that demonstrated the richness of participants' *if . . . then . . .* knowledge.

> The researchers asked participants to imagine a college student named Jane (Kammrath et al., 2005). However, different subsets of the participants imagined that Jane was a friendly person, a yes-person, a flirtatious person, a shy person, or an unfriendly person. After spending a few moments contemplating Jane with that disposition, participants provided judgments of how much warmth they believed Jane would display in six situations: interacting with peers or with professors, with women or with men, with people she was meeting for the first time or with people she has known for a long time. **Figure 13.5** shows participants' warmth predictions for the contrast between new acquaintances (*unfamiliar*) and old acquaintances (*familiar*). You can see that people made very different predictions for different situations. For example, they expected *if* Jane were shy *then* she would be far less warm with unfamiliar than with familiar individuals.

Take a moment to trace through the rest of the data in Figure 13.5. You should be able to convince yourself that you also possess a good deal of knowledge of the *if . . . then . . .* relationships that explain the interactions of dispositions and situations.

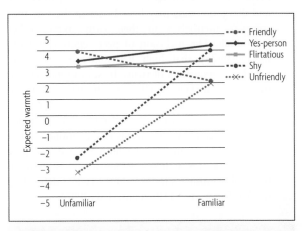

### Figure 13.5

**Students' knowledge of *if . . . then . . .* personality signatures**

Participants imagined a student named Jane as a friendly person, a yes-person, a flirtatious person, a shy person or an unfriendly person. They were asked to imagine how warmly Jane would behave on a scale from 25 (Jane feels basically cold and indifferent) to 15 (Jane feels genuine warmth and caring). The participants' predictions for how warmly each version of Jane would behave differed greatly when they imagined her interacting with unfamiliar versus familiar individuals.

Adapted from L.K. Kammrath, R. Mendoza-Denton, and W. Mischel, "Incorporating *If...Then...*Personality Signatures in Person Perception: Beyond the Person-Situation Dichotomy," *Journal of Personality and Social Psychology, 88*(4), 605–618. Copyright © 2005 by the American Psychological Association. Adapted with permission. The use of APA information does not imply endorsement by APA.

## EVALUATION OF TYPE AND TRAIT THEORIES

We have seen that type and trait theories allow researchers to give concise descriptions of different people's personalities. These theories have been criticised, however, because they do not generally explain how behaviour is generated or how personality develops; they only identify and describe characteristics that are correlated with behaviour. Although contemporary trait theorists have begun to address these concerns, trait theories typically portray a *static*, or at least stabilised, view of *personality structure* as it currently exists. By contrast, psychodynamic theories of personality, to which we next turn, emphasise conflicting forces within the individual that lead to change and development.

## RECAP CHECKPOINT

### Type and trait personality theories

- Some theorists categorise people by all-or-none types, assumed to be related to particular characteristic behaviours.

- Other theorists view traits — attributes along continuous dimensions — as the building blocks of personality.

- The five-factor model is a personality system that maps out the relationships among common trait words, theoretical concepts and personality scales.

- Twin and adoption studies reveal that personality traits are partially inherited.

- Furthermore, people display behavioural consistency when situations are defined with respect to relevant psychological features.

## CONCEPT QUESTIONS

1. How are personality types defined?

2. What are the endpoints of the trait dimension of neuroticism?

3. How have researchers assessed the heritability of traits?

4. What is the consistency paradox?

## CRITICAL THINKING

Recall the study that examined the heritability of the five factors. Why was each peer rater (that is, the friends and family members) only asked to provide information for one twin?

# PSYCHODYNAMIC THEORIES

Common to all **psychodynamic personality theories** is the assumption that powerful inner forces shape personality and motivate behaviour. Sigmund Freud, the originator of psychodynamic theories, was characterised by his biographer Ernest Jones as 'the Darwin of the mind' (1953). Freud's theory of personality boldly attempts to explain the origins and course of personality development, the nature of mind, aspects of abnormal personality and the way personality can be changed by therapy. Here we will focus only on normal personality; Freud's views on psychopathology and treatment will be treated in Chapters 14 and 15. After we explore Freud, we will describe some criticisms and reworkings of his theories.

## FREUDIAN PSYCHOANALYSIS

According to psychoanalytic theory, at the core of personality are events within a person's mind *(intrapsychic events)* that motivate behaviour. Often, people are aware of these motivations; however, some motivation also operates at an unconscious level. The *psychodynamic* nature of this approach comes from its emphasis on these inner wellsprings of behaviour, as well as the clashes among these internal forces. For Freud, *all behaviour was motivated.* No chance or accidental happenings cause behaviour; all acts are determined by motives. Every human action has a cause and a purpose that can be discovered through analysis of thought associations, dreams, errors and other behavioural clues to inner passions. The primary data for Freud's hypotheses about personality came from clinical observations and in-depth case studies of individual patients in therapy. He developed a theory of normal personality from his intense study of those with mental disorders. Let's look at some of the most important aspects of Freud's theory.

**Drives and psychosexual development** Freud's medical training as a neurologist led him to postulate a common biological basis for the behavioural patterns he observed in his patients. He ascribed the source of motivation for human actions to *psychic energy* found within each individual. Each person was assumed to have inborn instincts or drives that were *tension systems* created by the organs of the body. These energy sources, when activated, could be expressed in many different ways.

Freud originally postulated two basic drives. One he saw as involved with *self-preservation* (meeting such needs as hunger and thirst). The other he called *Eros,* the driving force related to sexual urges and preservation of the species. Freud greatly expanded the notion of human sexual desires to include not only the urge for sexual union but all other attempts to seek pleasure or to make physical contact with others. He used the term **libido** to identify the source of energy for sexual urges—a psychic energy that drives us toward sensual pleasures of all types. Sexual urges demand immediate satisfaction, whether through direct actions or through indirect means such as fantasies and dreams.

Clinical observation of patients who had suffered traumatic experiences during World War I led Freud to add the concept of *Thanatos,* or the death instinct, to his collection of drives and instincts. Thanatos was a

For answers go to MyPsychLab!

**libido** The psychic energy that drives individuals toward sensual pleasures of all types, especially sexual ones.

**psychodynamic personality theories** Theories of personality that share the assumption that personality is shaped by and behaviour is motivated by inner forces.

# PSYCHOLOGY *in your life*

## WHY ARE SOME PEOPLE SHY?

Surveys reveal that more than 50 percent of university students consider themselves to be 'currently shy' (Carducci & Zimbardo, 1995). Most of them say that shyness is an undesirable condition that has negative personal and social consequences. Another group of students say that they are 'situationally shy'. They feel 'shy in certain situations that are novel, awkward, or socially pressured, such as blind dates, singles bars, or being put on the spot to perform in public without preparation. Researchers investigating shyness in adults were surprised to discover that it is the 'not shy' person who is the rare, unusual breed in the United States and in every other country surveyed (Zimbardo, 1991).

**Shyness** may be defined as an individual's discomfort and/ or inhibition in interpersonal situations that interferes with pursuing one's interpersonal or professional goals. Shyness can be the mild reticence and social awkwardness many people feel in new situations, but it can escalate into the extreme of a totally inhibiting fear of people (we will discuss this *social phobia* in Chapter 14). Many shy people are also *introverted*; they prefer solitary, nonsocial activities. Others are 'shy extraverts,' publicly outgoing yet privately shy, preferring to engage in social activities, having the social skills to do so effectively, yet doubting that others will really like or respect them (Pilkonis & Zimbardo, 1979).

So why are some people shy and others are not? One explanation may be *nature*. Research evidence suggests that about 10 percent of infants are 'born shy' (Kagan,

1994). From birth, these children are unusually cautious and reserved when they interact with unfamiliar people or situations. A complementary explanation focuses on *nurture*. As children, some individuals are ridiculed, laughed at, or singled out for public shame; others grow up in families that make 'being loved' contingent on competitive success in appearance and performance.

A third explanation focuses on culture. Shyness is highest in some Asian countries, notably Japan and Taiwan, and lowest in Israel, among nine countries studied (Zimbardo, 1991). This difference is attributed in part to cultural emphases on shame for social failure and obedience to authority in these Asian countries versus encouragement for taking risks and externalising blame in Israel (Pines & Zimbardo, 1978). A fourth explanation accounts, in part, for a recent rise in reported prevalence of shyness in western countries such as Australia, United Kingdom and the United States: Young people are intensively involved with electronic technology. Spending long hours, typically alone, watching TV, playing video games, surfing the Web, and doing email is socially isolating and reduces daily face-to-face contact. Heavy use of the Internet has been argued to make people feel lonely, isolated, and shier (Kraut et al., 1998; Nie & Erbring, 2000). In contrast, Australian researchers have found that the Internet can help socially fearful people practise social behaviour that may later improve their shyness in offline social settings (Campbell, et al, 2006).

As shyness gets more extreme,

it intrudes on ever more aspects of one's life to minimise social pleasures and maximise social discomfort and isolation. There are some simple concepts and tactics we suggest for shy students to think about and try out (Zimbardo, 1991):

- Realise that you are not alone in your shyness; every person you see is more like you than different from you in his or her shyness.

- Shyness can be modified, even when there is a genetic component, but it takes dedication and a resolve to change, as with any long-standing habit you want to break.

- Practise smiling and making eye contact with most people you meet.

- Talk up; speak in a loud, clear voice, especially when giving your name or asking for information.

- Be the first to ask a question or make a comment in a new social situation. Be prepared with something interesting to say, and say it first; everyone appreciates an 'ice breaker.'

- Never put yourself down. Instead, think about what you can do next time to gain the outcome you want.

- Focus on making others feel comfortable, especially searching out those other shy people. Doing so lowers your self-consciousness.

If you are shy, we hope you will adopt these suggestions. Other students who have followed them have been released from the prison of shyness into a life filled with newfound liberties.

**shyness** An individual's discomfort and/or inhibition in interpersonal situations that interferes with pursuing an interpersonal professional goal.

Why did Freud believe that eating is motivated not only by the self-preservation drive to satisfy hunger but also by the 'erotic' drive to seek oral gratification?

occurs in the phallic stage. Here, the 4- or 5-year-old child must overcome the *Oedipus complex.* Freud named this complex after the mythical figure Oedipus, who unwittingly killed his father and married his mother. Freud believed that every young boy has an innate impulse to view his father as a sexual rival for his mother's attentions. Because the young boy cannot displace his father, the Oedipus complex is generally resolved when the boy comes to *identify* with his father's power. (Freud was inconsistent with respect to his theoretical account of the experiences of young girls.)

According to Freud, either too much gratification or too much frustration at one of the early stages of psychosexual development leads to **fixation**, an inability to progress normally to the next stage of development. As shown in Table 13.2, fixation at different stages can produce a variety of adult characteristics. The concept of fixation explains why Freud put such emphasis on early experiences in the continuity of personality. He believed that experiences in the early stages of psychosexual development had a profound impact on personality formation and adult behaviour patterns.

**fixation** A state in which a person remains attached to objects or activities more appropriate for an earlier stage of psychosexual development.

### Psychic determinism

The concept of fixation gives us a first look at Freud's belief that early conflicts help *determine* later behaviours. **Psychic determinism** is the assumption that all mental and behavioural reactions (symptoms) are determined by earlier experiences. Freud believed that symptoms were not arbitrary. Rather, symptoms were related in a meaningful way to significant life events.

**psychic determinism** The assumption that mental and behavioural reactions are determined by previous experiences.

Freud's belief in psychic determinism led him to emphasise the **unconscious**—the repository of information that is unavailable to conscious awareness (see **Figure 13.6**). Other writers had discussed this construct, but Freud put the concept of the unconscious determinants of human thought, feeling and action at centre stage in the human drama. According to Freud, behaviour can be motivated by drives of which a person is not aware. You may act without knowing why or without

**unconscious** The domain of the psyche that stores repressed urges and primitive impulses.

negative force that drove people toward aggressive and destructive behaviours. These patients continued to relive their wartime traumas in nightmares and hallucinations, phenomena that Freud could not work into his self-preservation or sexual drive theory. He suggested that this primitive urge was part of the tendency for all living things to seek to return to an inorganic state. However, this death instinct took a back seat in Freud's theoretical vehicle, which was largely driven by Eros.

According to Freud, Eros, as a broadly defined sexual drive, does not suddenly appear at puberty but operates from birth. Eros is evident, he argued, in the pleasure infants derive from physical stimulation of the genitals and other sensitive areas, or *erogenous zones.* Freud's five stages of *psychosexual development* are shown in **Table 13.2**. Freud believed that the physical source of sexual pleasure changed in this orderly progression. One of the major obstacles of psychosexual development, at least for boys,

## Table 13.2

Freud's stages of psychosexual development

| Stage | Age | Erogenous zones | Major developmental task (potential source of conflict) | Some adult characteristics of children who have been fixated at this stage |
|---|---|---|---|---|
| Oral | 0–1 | Mouth, lips, tongue | Weaning | Oral behavior, such as smoking, overeating; passivity and gullibility |
| Anal | 2–3 | Anus | Toilet training | Orderliness, parsimoniousness, obstinacy, or the opposite |
| Phallic | 4–5 | Genitals | Oedipus complex | Vanity, recklessness or the opposite |
| Latency | 6–12 | No specific area | Development of defence mechanisms | None: Fixation does not normally occur at this stage |
| Genital | 13–18 | Genitals | Mature sexual intimacy | Adults who have successfully integrated earlier stages should emerge with a sincere interest in others and a mature sexuality |

Figure 13.6

**Freud's conception of the human mind**
Freudian theory likens the human mind to an iceberg.
The tip of the iceberg, which you can see, represents
consciousness. The unconscious is the vast bulk of the
iceberg which remains hidden beneath the water.

**id** The primitive, unconscious part of the personality that represents the internalisation of society's values, standards and morals.

**superego** The aspect of personality that represents the internalisation of society's values, standards, and morals.

**ego** The aspect of personality involved in self-preservation activities and in directing instinctual drives and urges into appropriate channels.

unconscious desire? The concept of unconscious motivation adds a new dimension to personality by allowing for greater complexity of mental functioning.

We've now reviewed some basic aspects of Freud's theory. Let's see how they contribute to the structure of personality.

**The structure of personality** In Freud's theory, personality differences arise from the different ways in which people deal with their fundamental drives. To explain these differences, Freud pictured a continuing battle between two antagonistic parts of the personality—the *id* and the *superego*—moderated by a third aspect of the self, the *ego*. Although we will refer to these three aspects almost as if they are separate creatures, keep in mind that Freud believed them all to be just different mental *processes*. He did not, for example, identify specific brain locations for the id, ego, and superego.

The **id** is the storehouse of the fundamental drives. It operates irrationally, acting on impulse and pushing for expression and immediate gratification without considering whether what is desired is realistically possible, socially desirable or morally acceptable. The id is governed by the *pleasure principle*, the unregulated search for gratification—especially sexual, physical and emotional pleasures—to be experienced here and now without concern for consequences.

The **superego** is the storehouse of an individual's values, including moral attitudes learned from society. The superego corresponds roughly to the common notion of *conscience*. It develops as a child comes to accept as his or her own values the prohibitions of parents and other adults against socially undesirable actions. It is the inner voice of *oughts* and *should nots*. The superego also includes the *ego ideal*, an individual's view of the kind of person he or she should strive to become. Thus the superego is often in conflict with the id. The id wants to do what feels good, whereas the superego insists on doing what is right.

The **ego** is the reality-based aspect of the self that arbitrates the conflict between id impulses and superego demands. The ego represents an individual's personal view of physical and social reality—his or her conscious beliefs about the causes and consequences of behaviour. Part of the ego's job is to choose actions that will gratify id impulses without undesirable consequences. The ego is governed by the *reality principle*, which puts reasonable choices before pleasurable demands. Thus the ego would block an impulse to cheat on an exam because of concerns about the consequences of getting caught, and it would substitute the resolution to study harder the next time or solicit the teacher's sympathy. When the id and the superego are in conflict, the ego arranges a compromise that at least partially satisfies both. However, as id and superego pressures intensify, it becomes more difficult for the ego to work out optimal compromises.

**Repression and ego defence** Sometimes this compromise between id and superego involves 'putting a lid on the id'. Extreme desires are pushed out of conscious

direct access to the true cause of your actions. There is a *manifest* content to your behaviour—what you say, do, and perceive—of which you are fully aware, but there is also a concealed, *latent* content. The meaning of neurotic (anxiety-based) symptoms dreams, and slips of the pen and tongue is found at the unconscious level of thinking and information processing. Many psychologists today consider this concept of the unconscious to be Freud's most important contribution to the science of psychology. Much modern literature and drama as well explore the implications of unconscious processes for human behaviour.

According to Freud, impulses within you that you find unacceptable still strive for expression. A *Freudian slip* occurs when an unconscious desire is betrayed by your speech or behaviour. For example, one of your authors felt obligated to write a thank-you note although he hadn't much enjoyed the weekend he'd spent at a friend's home. He intended to write, 'I'm glad we got to spend a chunk of time together'. However, in a somewhat testy phone call, the friend informed him that he'd actually written, 'I'm glad we got to spend a *junk* of time together'. Do you see how the substitution of *junk* for *chunk* could be the expression of an

awareness into the privacy of the unconscious. **Repression** is the psychological process that protects an individual from experiencing extreme anxiety or guilt about impulses, ideas or memories that are unacceptable and/or dangerous to express. The ego remains unaware of both the mental content that is censored and the process by which repression keeps information out of consciousness. Repression is considered to be the most basic of the various ways in which the ego defends against being overwhelmed by threatening impulses and ideas.

**Ego defence mechanisms** are mental strategies the ego uses to defend itself in the daily conflict between id impulses that seek expression and the superego's demand to deny them (see **Table 13.3**). In psychoanalytic theory, these mechanisms are considered vital to an individual's psychological coping with powerful inner conflicts. By using them, a person is able to maintain a favourable self-image and to sustain an acceptable social image. For example, if a child has strong feelings of hatred toward his father—which, if acted out, would be dangerous—repression may take over. The hostile impulse is then no longer consciously pressing for satisfaction or even recognised as existing. However, although the impulse is not seen or heard, it is not gone; these feelings continue to play a role in personality functioning. For example, by developing a strong *identification* with his father, the child may increase his sense of self-worth and reduce his unconscious fear of being discovered as a hostile agent.

In Freudian theory, **anxiety** is an intense emotional response triggered when a repressed conflict is about to emerge into consciousness. Anxiety is a danger signal:

Why might a person's enthusiasm for boxing suggest the use of displacement as an ego defence mechanism?

Repression is not working! Red alert! More defences needed! This is the time for a second line of defence, one or more additional ego defence mechanisms that will relieve the anxiety and send the distressing impulses back down into the unconscious. For example, a mother who does not like her son and does not want to care for him might use *reaction formation*, which transforms her unacceptable impulse into its opposite: 'I don't hate my child' becomes 'I love my child. See how I smother the dear little thing with love?' Such defences serve the critical coping function of alleviating anxiety.

If defence mechanisms defend you against anxiety, why might they still have negative consequences for you? Useful as they are, ego mechanisms of defence are ultimately self-deceptive. When overused, they create more

**repression** The basic defence mechanism by which painful or guilt-producing thoughts, feelings or memories are excluded from conscious awareness.

**ego defence mechanisms** Mental strategies (conscious or unconscious) used by the ego to defend itself against conflicts experienced in the normal course of life.

**anxiety** An intense emotional response caused by the preconscious recognition that a repressed conflict is about to emerge into consciousness.

## Table 13.3

Major ego defence mechanisms

| | |
|---|---|
| Denial of reality | Protecting self from unpleasant reality by refusing to perceive it |
| Displacement | Discharging pent-up feelings, usually of hostility, on objects less dangerous than those that initially aroused the emotion |
| Fantasy | Gratifying frustrated desires in imaginary achievements ("daydreaming" is a common form) |
| Identification | Increasing feelings of worth by identifying self with another person or institution, often of illustrious standing |
| Isolation | Cutting off emotional charge from hurtful situations or separating incompatible attitudes into logic-tight compartments (holding conflicting attitudes that are never thought of simultaneously or in relation to each other); also called *compartmentalisation* |
| Projection | Placing blame for one's difficulties on others or attributing one's own "forbidden" desires to others |
| Rationalisation | Attempting to prove that one's behaviour is "rational" and justifiable and thus worthy of the approval of self and others |
| Reaction formation | Preventing dangerous desires from being expressed by endorsing opposing attitudes and types of behaviour and using them as "barriers" |
| Regression | Retreating to earlier developmental levels involving more childish responses and usually a lower level of aspiration |
| Repression | Pushing painful or dangerous thoughts out of consciousness, keeping them unconscious; this is considered to be *the most basic of the defence mechanisms* |
| Sublimation | Gratifying or working off frustrated sexual desires in substitutive nonsexual activities socially accepted by one's culture |

problems than they solve. It is psychologically unhealthy to spend a great deal of time and psychic energy deflecting, disguising and rechannelling unacceptable urges in order to reduce anxiety. Doing so leaves little energy for productive living or satisfying human relationships. Some forms of mental illness result from excessive reliance on defence mechanisms to cope with anxiety, as we will see in a later chapter on mental disorders.

## EVALUATION OF FREUDIAN THEORY

We have devoted a great deal of space to outlining the essentials of psychoanalytic theory because Freud's ideas have had an enormous impact on the way many psychologists think about normal and abnormal aspects of personality. However, there probably are more psychologists who criticise Freudian concepts than who support them. What is the basis of some of their criticisms?

First, psychoanalytic concepts are vague and not operationally defined; thus much of the theory is difficult to evaluate scientifically. Because some of its central hypotheses cannot be disproved, even in principle, Freud's theory remains questionable. How can the concepts of libido, the structure of personality and repression of infantile sexual impulses be studied in any direct fashion?

A second, related criticism is that Freudian theory is good history but bad science. It does not reliably *predict* what will occur; it is applied *retrospectively*—after events have occurred. Using psychoanalytic theory to understand personality typically involves historical reconstruction, not scientific construction of probable actions and predictable outcomes. In addition, by overemphasising historical origins of current behaviour, the theory directs attention away from the current stimuli that may be inducing and maintaining the behaviour.

There are three other major criticisms of Freudian theory. First, it is a developmental theory, but it never included observations or studies of children. Second, it minimises traumatic experiences (such as child abuse) by reinterpreting memories of them as fantasies (based on a child's desire for sexual contact with a parent). Third, it has an *androcentric* (male-centred) bias because it uses a male model as the norm without trying to determine how females might be different.

Some aspects of Freud's theory, however, continue to gain acceptance as they are modified and improved through empirical scrutiny. For example, in Chapter 5, we saw that the concept of the unconscious is being systematically explored by contemporary researchers (Baars & McGovern, 1996; Westen, 1998). This research reveals that much of your day-to-day experience is shaped by processes outside of your awareness. These results support Freud's general concept but weaken the link between unconscious processes and psychopathology: Little of your unconscious knowledge will cause you anxiety or distress. Similarly, researchers have found evidence for some of the habits of mind Freud characterised as defence mechanisms. We suggested earlier that individuals are most likely to use defence mechanisms when they are experiencing anxiety. Researchers have tested this hypothesis in a variety of ways.

> One study focused on a group of 9- to 11-year-old girls (Sandstrom & Cramer, 2003). The researchers carried out interviews with their peers to determine who among the group of 50 girls was relatively popular and who was relatively unpopular. Each of the 50 girls underwent a laboratory experience in which they were rejected by another young girl. The researchers reasoned that—because of their history of negative social interactions—the unpopular girls would experience more anxiety than the popular girls in the face of this rejection. The researchers suggested that, to cope with that anxiety, the unpopular girls would show evidence for more frequent use of defence mechanisms. To test this hypothesis, the researcher asked the girls to tell stories based on cards from the *Thematic Apperception Test*. The stories were analysed for evidence of the defence mechanisms *denial* and *projection* (see Table 13.3). These analyses supported the hypothesis: the unpopular girls used more defence mechanisms than the popular girls after the episode of peer rejection.

Some of the styles for coping with stress we described in Chapter 12 fall within the general category of defence mechanisms. You might recall, for example, that inhibiting the thoughts and feelings associated with personal traumas or guilty or shameful experiences can take a devastating toll on mental and physical health (Pennebaker, 1997; Petrie et al., 2004). These findings echo Freud's beliefs that repressed psychic material can lead to psychological distress.

Freud's theory is the most complex, comprehensive and compelling view of normal and abnormal personality functioning—even when its predictions prove wrong. However, like any other theory, Freud's theory is best treated as one that must be confirmed or disconfirmed element by element. Freud retains his influence on contemporary psychology because some of his ideas have been widely accepted. Others have been abandoned. Some of the earliest revisions of Freud's theory arose from within his own original circle of students. Let's see how they sought to amend Freud's views.

## EXTENDING PSYCHODYNAMIC THEORIES

Some of those who came after Freud retained his basic representation of personality as a battleground on which unconscious primal urges conflict with social values. However, many of Freud's intellectual descendants made major adjustments in the psychoanalytic view of personality. In general, these post-Freudians have made the following changes:

- They put greater emphasis on ego functions, including ego defences, development of the self, conscious thought processes and personal mastery.

- They view social variables (culture, family and peers) as playing a greater role in shaping personality.
- They put less emphasis on the importance of general sexual urges, or libidinal energy.
- They have extended personality development beyond childhood to include the entire life span.

We will now review key features of the theories of Alfred Adler, Karen Horney, and Carl Jung.

**Alfred Adler** (1929) rejected the significance of Eros and the pleasure principle. Adler believed that as helpless, dependent, small children, people all experience feelings of *inferiority*. He argued that all lives are dominated by the search for ways to overcome those feelings. People compensate to achieve feelings of adequacy or, more often, overcompensate in an attempt to become *superior*. Personality is structured around this underlying striving; people develop lifestyles based on particular ways of overcoming their basic, pervasive feelings of inferiority. Personality conflict arises from incompatibility between external environmental pressures and internal strivings for adequacy, rather than from competing urges within the person.

**Karen Horney** was trained in the psychoanalytic school but broke from orthodox Freudian theory in several ways. She challenged Freud's phallocentric emphasis on the importance of the penis, hypothesising that male envy of pregnancy, motherhood, breasts and suckling is a dynamic force in the unconscious of boys and men. This 'womb envy' leads men to devalue women and to overcompensate by unconscious impulses toward creative work. Horney also placed greater emphasis than did Freud on cultural factors and focused on present character structure rather than on infantile sexuality (Horney, 1937, 1939). Because Horney also had influence on the development of humanistic theories, we will return to her ideas in the next section.

**Carl Jung** (1959) greatly expanded the conception of the unconscious. For him, the unconscious was not limited to an individual's unique life experiences but was filled with fundamental psychological truths shared by the whole human race, a **collective unconscious**. The collective unconscious explains your intuitive understanding of primitive myths, art forms, and symbols, which are the universal archetypes of existence. An **archetype** is a primitive symbolic representation of a particular experience or object. Each archetype is associated with an instinctive tendency to feel and think about it or experience it in a special way. Jung postulated many archetypes that give rise to myths and symbols: the sun god, the hero, the earth mother. *Animus* was the male archetype, *anima* was the female archetype, and all men and women experienced both archetypes in varying degrees. The archetype of the self is the *mandala*, or magic circle; it symbolises striving for unity and wholeness (Jung, 1973).

Jung saw the healthy, integrated personality as balancing opposing forces, such as masculine aggressiveness and feminine sensitivity. This view of personality as a

Jung recognised creativity as a means to release images from both the personal and collective unconscious. Why did Jung believe in the two types of unconscious?

constellation of compensating internal forces in dynamic balance was called **analytic psychology**. In addition, Jung rejected the primary importance of libido, so central to Freud's own theory. Jung added two equally powerful unconscious instincts: the need to create and the need to become a coherent, whole individual. In the next section on humanist theories, we will see this second need paralleled in the concept of *self-actualisation*.

**analytic psychology** A branch of psychology that views the person as a constellation of compensatory internal forces in a dynamic balance.

## RECAP CHECKPOINT
### Psychodynamic theories

- Freud's psychodynamic theory emphasises instinctive biological energies as sources of human motivation.
- Basic concepts of Freudian theory include psychic energy as powering and directing behaviour, early experiences as key determinants of lifelong personality, psychic determinism and powerful unconscious processes.
- Personality structure consists of the id, the superego, and the reconciling ego.
- Unacceptable impulses are repressed and ego defence mechanisms are developed to lessen anxiety and bolster self-esteem.
- Post-Freudians like Adler, Horney and Jung put greater emphasis on ego functioning and social variables and less on sexual urges. They saw personality development as a lifelong process.

## CONCEPT QUESTIONS

1. According to Freud's theory, what behaviours might arise if an individual became fixated at the oral stage of development?

**collective unconscious** The part of an individual's unconscious that is inherited, evolutionarily developed, and common to all members of the species.

**archetype** A universal, inherited, primitive, and symbolic representation of a particular experience or object.

For answers go to MyPsychLab!

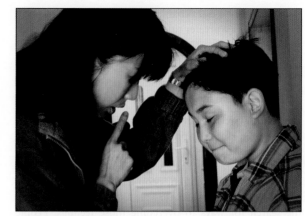

Why did Carl Rogers emphasise parents' unconditional positive regard for their children?

# HUMANISTIC THEORIES

Humanistic approaches to understanding personality are characterised by a concern for the integrity of an individual's personal and conscious experience and growth potential. The key feature of all humanistic theories is an emphasis on the drive toward self-actualisation. **Self-actualisation** is a constant striving to realise one's inherent potential—to fully develop one's capacities and talents. In this section, you will see how humanist theorists have developed this concept of self-actualisation. You will learn, in addition, what additional features set humanistic theories apart from other types of personality theories.

## FEATURES OF HUMANISTIC THEORIES

Humanistic personality theorists, such as Carl Rogers, Abraham Maslow and Karen Horney, believed that the motivation for behaviour comes from a person's unique tendencies, both innate and learned, to develop and change in positive directions toward the goal of self-actualisation. Recall from Chapter 11 that Maslow placed self-actualisation at the pinnacle of his hierarchy of needs. The striving toward self-fulfilment is a constructive, guiding force that moves each person toward generally positive behaviours and enhancement of the self.

The drive for self-actualisation at times comes into conflict with the need for approval from the self and others, especially when the person feels that certain obligations or conditions must be met in order to gain approval. For example, Carl Rogers (1947, 1951, 1977) stressed the importance of **unconditional positive regard** in raising children. By this, he meant that children should feel they will always be loved and approved of, in spite of their mistakes and misbehaviour—that they do not have to earn their parents' love. He recommended that, when a child misbehaves, parents should emphasise that it is the behaviour they disapprove of, not the child. Unconditional positive regard is important in adulthood, too, because worrying about seeking approval interferes with self-actualisation. As an adult, you need to give and receive unconditional positive regard from those to whom you are close. Most important, you need to feel unconditional positive *self-regard*, or acceptance of yourself, in spite of the weaknesses you might be trying to change.

Although not often given due credit, Karen Horney was another major theorist whose ideas created the foundation of humanistic psychology (Frager & Fadiman, 1998). Horney came to believe that people have a 'real self' that requires favourable environmental circumstances to be actualised, such as an atmosphere of warmth, the goodwill of others, and parental love of the child as a 'particular individual' (Horney, 1945, 1950). In the absence of those favourable nurturing conditions, the child develops a basic anxiety that stifles spontaneity of expression of real feelings and prevents effective relations with others. To cope with their basic anxiety, individuals resort to interpersonal or intrapsychic defences. Interpersonal defences produce movement toward others (through excessive compliance and self-effacing actions), against others (by aggressive, arrogant, or narcissistic solutions), and away from others (through detachment). Intrapsychic defences operate to develop for some people an unrealistic idealised self-image that generates a 'search for glory' to justify it and a pride system that operates on rigid rules of conduct to live up to a grandiose self-concept. Such people often live by the 'tyranny of shoulds', self-imposed obligations, such as 'I should be perfect, generous, attractive, brave', and so forth. Horney believed that the goal of a humanistic therapy was to help the individual achieve the joy of self-realisation and promote the inherent constructive forces in human nature that support a striving for self-fulfilment.

An important aspect of each of the theories of Maslow, Rogers and Horney is the emphasis on self-actualisation or progress toward the real self. In addition, humanistic theories have been described as being holistic, dispositional and phenomenological. Let's see why.

**self-actualisation** A concept in personality psychology referring to a person's constant striving to realise his or her potential and to develop inherent talents and capabilities.

**unconditional positive regard** Complete love and acceptance of an individual by another person, such as a parent for a child, with no conditions attached.

Humanistic theories are *holistic* because they explain people's separate acts in terms of their entire personalities; people are not seen as the sum of discrete traits that each influence behaviour in different ways. Maslow believed that people are intrinsically motivated toward the upper levels of the hierarchy of needs (discussed in Chapter 11), unless deficiencies at the lower levels weigh them down.

Humanistic theories are *dispositional* because they focus on the innate qualities within a person that exert a major influence over the direction behaviour will take. Situational factors are seen as constraints and barriers (like the strings that tie down balloons). Once freed from negative situational conditions, the actualising tendency should actively guide people to choose life-enhancing situations. However, humanistic theories are not dispositional in the same sense as trait theories or psychodynamic theories. In those views, personal dispositions are recurrent themes played out in behaviour again and again. Humanistic dispositions are oriented specifically toward creativity and growth. Each time a humanistic disposition is exercised, the person changes a little, so that the disposition is never expressed in the same way twice. Over time, humanistic dispositions guide the individual toward self-actualisation, the purest expression of these motives.

Humanistic theories are *phenomenological* because they emphasise an individual's frame of reference and subjective view of reality—not the objective perspective of an observer or of a therapist. Thus a humanistic psychologist always strives to see each person's unique point of view. This view is also a present-oriented view; past influences are important only to the extent that they have brought the person to the present situation, and the future represents goals to achieve. Thus, unlike psychodynamic theories, humanistic theories do not see people's present behaviours as unconsciously guided by past experiences.

The upbeat humanist view of personality was a welcome treat for many psychologists who had been brought up on a diet of bitter-tasting Freudian medicine. Humanistic approaches focus directly on improvement—on making life more palatable—rather than dredging up painful memories that are sometimes better left repressed. The humanist perspective emphasises each person's ability to realise his or her fullest potential.

## EVALUATION OF HUMANISTIC THEORIES

Freud's theory was often criticised for providing the too-pessimistic view that human nature develops out of conflicts, traumas and anxieties. Humanistic theories arose to celebrate the healthy personality that strives for happiness and self-actualisation. It is difficult to criticise theories that encourage and appreciate people, even for their faults. Even so, critics have complained that humanistic concepts are fuzzy and difficult to explore in research. They ask, 'What exactly is self-actualisation?' 'Is it an inborn tendency, or is it created by the cultural context?' Humanistic theories also do not traditionally focus on the particular characteristics of individuals. They are more theories about human nature and about qualities all people share than about the individual personality or the basis of differences among people. Other psychologists note that, by emphasising the role of the self as a source of experience and action, humanistic psychologists neglect the important environmental variables that also influence behaviour.

Despite these limitations, a type of contemporary research can be traced in part to the humanist tradition that focuses directly on individual *narratives* or *life stories* (McAdams, 2001). The tradition of using psychological theory to understand the details of an individual's life—to produce a *psychobiography*—can be traced back to Freud's analysis of Leonardo da Vinci (Freud, 1910/1957; see Elms, 1988, for a critique of Freud's work). **Psychobiography** is defined as 'the systematic use of psychological (especially personality) theory to transform a life into a coherent and illuminating story' (McAdams, 1988, p. 2). Consider the great artist Pablo Picasso. Picasso suffered a series of traumas as a young child, including being present during a serious earthquake and having a young sister who died. A psychobiography might attempt to explain some of Picasso's vast artistic creativity as the lifelong residue of his responses to these early traumas (Gardner, 1993).

When a well-known or historical figure is the subject of a psychobiography, a researcher may turn to published work, diaries and letters as sources of relevant data. For more ordinary individuals, researchers may directly elicit narratives of life experiences. The request might be, for example, that the participant talk about a recent peak experience: 'What were you thinking and feeling? What might this episode say about who you are, who you were, who you might be, or how you have developed over time?' (McAdams & de St. Aubin, 1992, p. 1010). The characteristic themes that emerge over series of narrative accounts support the holistic and phenomenological version of personality that was put forth by the early humanists: people construct their identities by weaving life stories out of the strands of narrative. Personal accounts provide a window on people's views of themselves and interpersonal relationships.

Humanistic theorists emphasised each individual's drive toward self-actualisation. This group recognised, however, that people's progress toward this goal is determined, in part, by realities of their environments. We turn now to theories that directly examine how individuals' behaviours are shaped by their environments.

**psychobiography** The use of psychological (especially personality) theory to describe and explain an individual's course through life.

### RECAP CHECKPOINT

#### Humanistic theories

- Humanistic theories focus on self-actualisation — the growth potential of the individual.

- These theories are holistic, dispositional and phenomenological.

- Contemporary theories in the humanist tradition focus on individuals' life stories.

## CONCEPT QUESTIONS

1. What is self-actualisation?

2. In what ways are humanistic theories dispositional?

3. What is a psychobiography?

# SOCIAL-LEARNING AND COGNITIVE THEORIES

Common to all the theories we have reviewed so far is an emphasis on hypothesised inner mechanisms—traits, instincts, impulses, tendencies toward self-actualisation— that propel behaviour and form the basis of a functioning personality. What most of these theories lack, however, is a solid link between personality and

If your parents complimented you every time you got a new haircut, would that reinforce your behaviour to return to the same hairdresser each time? Alternatively, what if they were critical of your haircut? Would you change hairdressers or would you believe they were criticising your looks no matter what hairdresser you were going to? What effect could their criticism have over time on the thoughts of your self-image and grooming behaviour?

particular behaviours. Psychodynamic and humanistic theories, for example, provide accounts of the total personality but do not predict specific actions. Another tradition of personality theory emerged from a more direct focus on individual differences in behaviour. Recall from Chapter 6 that much of a person's behaviour can be predicted from contingencies in the environment. Psychologists with a *learning theory* orientation look to the environmental circumstances that control behaviour. Personality is seen as the sum of the overt and covert responses that are reliably elicited by an individual's *reinforcement history*. Learning theory approaches suggest that people are different because they have had different histories of reinforcement.

Consider a behaviourist conception of personality developed by a team of Yale University psychologists headed by **John Dollard** and **Neal Miller** (1950). Dollard and Miller introduced concepts such as learned drives, inhibition of responses, and learned habit patterns. Similar to Freud, they emphasised the roles of the motivating force of tension and the reinforcing (pleasurable) consequences of *tension reduction*. Organisms act to reduce tension produced by unsatisfied drives. Behaviour that successfully reduces such tensions is repeated, eventually becoming a learned habit that is reinforced by repeated tension reduction. Dollard and Miller also showed that one could learn by *social imitation*—by observing the behaviour of others without having to actually perform the response. Suppose a youngster sees his older sister given a lolly when she races to meet their father as he arrives home; the younger brother may begin to carry out the same behaviour. The idea of imitation broadened the ways psychologists understood that effective or destructive habits are learned. Personality emerges as the sum of these learned habits. Contemporary social-learning and cognitive theories often share Dollard and Miller's belief that behaviour is influenced by environmental contingencies. These theories, however, go one step further to emphasise the importance of cognitive processes as well as behavioural ones, returning a thinking mind to the acting body. Those who have proposed cognitive theories of personality point out that there are important individual differences in the way people think about and define any external situation. Cognitive theories stress the mental processes through which people turn their sensations and perceptions into organised impressions of reality. Like humanistic theories, cognitive theories emphasise that you participate in creating your own personality. For example, you actively *choose* your own environments to a great extent; you do not just react passively. You weigh alternatives and select the settings in which you act and are acted upon—you choose to enter situations that you expect to be reinforcing and to avoid those that are unsatisfying and uncertain. For example, you often choose to return to restaurants where you've had good meals before, rather than always trying someplace new.

Let's look now at more concrete embodiments of these ideas. We examine the theories of Walter Mischel, Albert Bandura and Nancy Cantor.

# MISCHEL'S COGNITIVE– AFFECTIVE PERSONALITY THEORY

**Walter Mischel** developed an influential theory of the cognitive basis of personality. Mischel emphasises that people actively participate in the cognitive organisation of their interactions with the environment. His approach emphasises the importance of understanding how behaviour arises as a function of interactions between persons and situations (Mischel, 2004). Consider this example:

> John's unique personality may be seen most clearly in that he is always very friendly when meeting someone for the first time, but that he also predictably becomes rather abrupt and unfriendly as he begins to spend more time with that person. Jim, on the other hand, is unique in that he is typically shy and quiet with people who he does not know well but becomes very gregarious once he begins to know someone well. (Shoda et al., 1993a, p. 1023)

If we were to average John's and Jim's overall friendliness, we would probably get about the same value on this trait—but that would fail to capture important differences in their behaviour. According to Mischel (1973, 2004), how you respond to a specific environmental input depends on the variables defined in **Table 13.4**. Do you see how each variable listed would affect the way in which a person would behave in particular situations? We have given you examples for each variable. Try to invent a situation in which you would produce behaviour different from the characters listed in the table, because you contrast on the particular variable. You may wonder what determines the nature of these variables for a specific individual. Mischel believes that they result from his or her history of observations and interactions with other people and with inanimate aspects of the physical environment (Mischel, 1973).

Mischel and his colleagues have demonstrated the importance of patterns of behaviour in their field studies of children's experiences in summer camp.

Would you feel comfortable making personality judgments about these children from this one snapshot? Why might you want to know their patterns of behaviour across different types of situations?

This project was carried out on a group of 6- to 12-year old children who were referred to a camp for children with social adjustment problems. The study focused on children's reactions to different psychological situations, such as having another child initiate positive social contact or being warned by an adult to cease some activity. Children's reactions were coded into categories such as 'talked pro-socially' or 'complied or gave in'. In addition, at the end of

## Table 13.4

Person variables in Mischel's cognitive–affective personality theory

| Variable | Definition | Example |
| --- | --- | --- |
| Encodings | The way you categorise information about yourself, other people, events, and situations. | As soon as Bob meets someone, he tries to figure out how wealthy he or she is. |
| Expectancies and beliefs | Your beliefs about the social world and likely outcomes for given actions in particular situations. Your beliefs about your ability to bring outcomes about. | Greg invites friends to the movies, but he never expects them to say 'yes'. |
| Affects | Your feelings and emotions, including physiological responses. | Cindy blushes very easily. |
| Goals and values | The outcomes and affective states you do and do not value; your goals and life projects. | Peter wants to be president of his college class. |
| Competencies and self-regulatory plans | The behaviours you can accomplish and plans for generating cognitive and behavioural outcomes. | Jan can speak English, French, Russian and Japanese and expects to work for the United Nations. |

the camp, counsellors were asked to label individual children as 'aggressive', 'withdrawn', or 'friendly'.

What information did they use to make these judgments? Consider the behaviour of complying or giving in. Children who were ultimately rated as *friendly* had complied in situations in which they had been given warnings by an adult. Children who were ultimately rated as *withdrawn* had complied in situations in which peers had tested them (Shoda et al., 1993b).

These results suggest that knowing the average rates at which children complied wouldn't tell you very much about their personalities. You would have to know in what situation the compliance took place to understand why one child was labelled as friendly and another as withdrawn. Mischel emphasises that your beliefs about other people's personalities come not from taking averages but from tracking the way different situations bring out different behaviours.

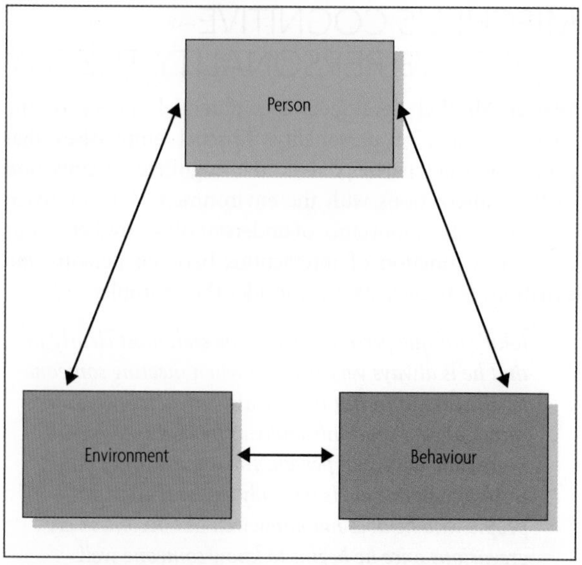

## BANDURA'S COGNITIVE SOCIAL-LEARNING THEORY

Through his theoretical writing and extensive research with children and adults, Albert Bandura (1986, 1999) has been an eloquent champion of a social-learning approach to understanding personality (recall from Chapter 6 his studies of aggressive behaviour in children). This approach combines principles of learning with an emphasis on human interactions in social settings. From a social-learning perspective, human beings are not driven by inner forces, nor are they helpless pawns of environmental influence. The social-learning approach stresses the cognitive processes that are involved in acquiring and maintaining patterns of behaviour and, thus, personality.

Bandura's theory points to a complex interaction of individual factors, behaviour and environmental stimuli. Each can influence or change the others, and the direction of change is rarely one way—it is *reciprocal*. Your behaviour can be influenced by your attitudes, beliefs or prior history of reinforcement as well as by stimuli available in the environment. What you do can have an effect on the environment, and important aspects of your personality can be affected by the environment or by feedback from your behaviour. This important concept, **reciprocal determinism**, implies that you must examine all components if you want to completely understand human behaviour, personality and social ecology (Bandura, 1999; see **Figure 13.7**). So, for example, if you don't generally think of yourself as an athlete, you may not choose to be active in track-and-field events, but if you live near a pool, you may nonetheless spend time swimming. If you are outgoing, you'll talk to others sitting around the pool and thereby create a more sociable atmosphere, which, in turn, makes it a more enjoyable environment. This is one instance of reciprocal determinism among person, place and behaviour.

You may recall from Chapter 6 that Bandura's social-learning theory emphasises observational learning as the

Figure 13.7

**Reciprocal determinism**
In reciprocal determinism, the individual, the individual's behaviour, and the environment all interact to influence and modify the other components.

process by which a person changes his or her behaviour based on observations of another person's behaviour. Through observational learning, children and adults acquire an enormous range of information about their social environment. Through observation, you learn what is appropriate and gets rewarded and what gets punished or ignored. Because you can use memory and think about external events, you can foresee the possible consequences of your actions without having to actually experience them. You may acquire skills, attitudes and beliefs simply by watching what others do and the consequences that follow.

As his theory developed, Bandura (1997) elaborated self-efficacy as a central construct. **Self-efficacy** is the belief that one can perform adequately in a particular situation. Your sense of self-efficacy influences your perceptions, motivation and performance in many ways. You don't even try to do things or take chances when you expect to be ineffectual. You avoid situations when you don't feel adequate. Even when you do, in fact, have the ability—and the desire—you may not take the required action or persist to complete the task successfully, if you think you lack what it takes.

Beyond actual accomplishments, there are three other sources of information for *self-efficacy judgments*:

- vicarious experience—your observations of the performance of others

- persuasion—others may convince you that you can do something, or you may convince yourself

- monitoring of your emotional arousal as you think about or approach a task—for example, anxiety suggests low expectations of efficacy; excitement suggests expectations of success.

**self-efficacy** The set of beliefs that one can perform adequately in a particular situation.

**reciprocal determinism** Albert Bandura's social-learning theory that a complex reciprocal interaction exists among the individual, his or her behaviour and environmental stimuli, and that each of these components affects the others.

Self-efficacy judgments influence how much effort you expend and how long you persist when faced with difficulty in a wide range of life situations (Bandura, 1997; Cervone, 2000). For example, how vigorously and persistently you study this chapter may depend more on your sense of self-efficacy than on actual ability (Zimmerman et al., 1992).

One important type of self-efficacy beliefs reflects people's judgments about their ability to regulate their own behaviour. Let's look at an example of the impact of *self-regulatory efficacy* on adolescents' likelihood to engage in violent conduct.

> Bandura and his colleagues (Caprara et al., 2002) predicted that those adolescents who had the *highest* levels of perceived self-regulatory efficacy would be the *least* likely to engage in violent conduct. To test this hypothesis, the researchers recruited 350 adolescents (170 boys and 180 girls) from high schools located near Rome, Italy. The students provided initial data when they were 16 years old. At that time, they provided perceptions of their perceived self-regulatory efficacy by responding to such items as 'How well can you resist peer pressure to use drugs?' The students also indicated their level of violent conduct by responding to such items as 'Have you ever participated in violent actions of "gangs"?' When the students were 18, they were asked a second time about their violent conduct. The researchers examined the patterns of data to see how well perceived self-efficacy predicted violence at both ages 16 and 18. Those students who believed they were most able to control their behaviour were, in fact, least likely to engage in violent activities across time. Although the girls had lower levels of violence as both 16- and 18-year-olds, both boys and girls showed the same impact of self-regulatory efficacy on violent conduct.

You can see from this study the strong correlation between what people believe they can accomplish (or prevent) and what they are actually able to do.

Bandura's theory of self-efficacy also acknowledges the importance of the environment. Expectations of failure or success—and corresponding decisions to stop trying or to persevere—may be based on perceptions of the supportiveness or unsupportiveness of the environment, in addition to perceptions of one's own adequacy or inadequacy. Such expectations are called *outcome-based expectancies*. **Figure 13.8** displays how the parts of Bandura's theory fit together. Behavioural outcomes depend both on people's perceptions of their own abilities and their perceptions of the environment.

## CANTOR'S SOCIAL INTELLIGENCE THEORY

Building on these earlier cognitive and social theories, **Nancy Cantor** and her colleagues have outlined a *social intelligence* theory of personality (Cantor & Kihlstrom, 1987; Kihlstrom & Cantor, 2000). **Social intelligence**

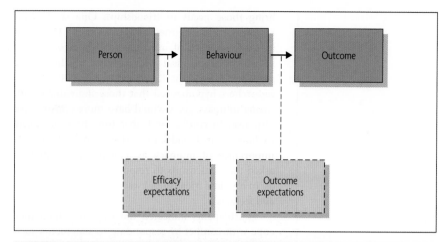

Figure 13.8

Bandura's self-efficacy model
This model positions efficacy expectations between the person and his or her behaviour; outcome expectations are positioned between behaviour and its anticipated outcomes.

refers to the expertise people bring to their experience of life tasks. The theory defines three types of individual differences:

- *Choice of life goals.* People differ as to which life goals or life tasks are most important to them. People's goals may also change over time.

- *Knowledge relevant to social interactions.* People differ with respect to the expertise they bring to tasks of social and personal problem solving.

- *Strategies for implementing goals.* People have different characteristic problem-solving strategies.

Can you see how these three dimensions interact to give rise to the different patterns of behaviour you would recognise as personality? You might, for example, have two friends—one of whom is more concerned about 'getting and keeping friends', whereas the other one gives more weight to 'getting good grades'. Or suppose two other friends both value getting good grades. Depending on what they know and how they are able to put that knowledge to use, the moment-by-moment decisions they make about how to behave could be very different. One may have been taught explicit strategies for studying, and the other muddles through without special help. The theory of social intelligence gives a new perspective on how personality predicts consistency: for a given period of time, consistency is found in people's goals, knowledge and strategies.

Let's examine concrete circumstances in which people's disparate goals yield different outcomes. Researchers have demonstrated that *intimacy goals* have an impact on relationship satisfaction.

> When people enter into friendships, they differ in the extent to which they have *intimacy* as a goal—some people strongly seek to foster interdependence and engage in self-disclosure, whereas other people don't

**social intelligence** A theory of personality that refers to the expertise people bring to their experience of life tasks.

bring those needs to friendships. One study with 80 participants (40 men and 40 women) examined how the strength of intimacy goals affects the way in which people deal with conflict in their close same-sex friendships (Sanderson et al., 2005). The researchers hypothesised that those individuals with strong intimacy goals would have more constructive responses to conflict and, therefore, be more likely to have their friendships endure. To measure the importance of intimacy as a goal, the researchers asked the participants to respond to statements such as 'In my close friendship, I want to share my thoughts and feelings'.

Participants indicated the ways in which they cope with conflict by responding to statements such as, 'My friend and I always express our feelings in an open and honest manner that prevents little problems from becoming big ones'. In keeping with the researchers' hypothesis, students with strong intimacy goals were most likely to endorse responses to conflicts that helped minimise those conflicts. Because of those constructive responses, students with strong intimacy goals also reported greater satisfaction with their friendships.

Do you see how this pattern could follow from the individuals' goals? People with stronger intimacy goals are highly motivated to behave in ways that will help preserve the friendships. In this case, you recognise personality in the consistent way in which people's goals lead them to behave.

## EVALUATION OF SOCIAL-LEARNING AND COGNITIVE THEORIES

One set of criticisms levelled against social-learning and cognitive theories is that they often overlook emotion as an important component of personality. In psychodynamic theories, emotions like anxiety play a central role. In social-learning and cognitive theories, emotions are perceived merely as by-products of thoughts and behaviour or are just included with other types of thoughts rather than being assigned independent importance. For those who feel that emotions are central to the functioning of human personality, this is a serious flaw. Cognitive theories are also attacked for not fully recognising the impact of unconscious motivation on behaviour and affect.

A second set of criticisms focuses on the vagueness of explanations about the way personal constructs and competencies are created. Cognitive theorists have often had little to say about the developmental origins of adult personality; their focus on the individual's perception of the current behaviour setting obscures the individual's history.

Despite these criticisms, cognitive personality theories have made major contributions to current thinking. Mischel's awareness of situation has brought about a better understanding of the interaction between what a person brings to a behaviour setting and what that setting brings out of the person. Bandura's ideas have led to improvements in the way teachers educate children and help them achieve as well as new treatments in the areas of health, business, and sports performance. Finally, Cantor's theory shifts the search for personality consistency to the level of life goals and social strategies.

Do these cognitive personality theories provide you with insights about your own personality and behaviours? You can start to see how you define yourself in part through interactions with the environment. We turn now to theories that can add even further to your definition of self.

### RECAP CHECKPOINT
#### Social-learning and cognitive theories

- Social-learning theorists focus on understanding individual differences in behaviour and personality as a consequence of different histories of reinforcement.
- Cognitive theorists emphasise individual differences in perception and subjective interpretation of the environment.
- Walter Mischel explored the origins of behaviours as interactions of persons and situations, where as Albert Bandura described the reciprocal determinism among people, environments, and behaviours.
- Lastly, Nancy Cantor's theory emphasised the impact of goals, knowledge and strategies on people's behaviour.

### CONCEPT QUESTIONS

1. In Walter Mischel's theory, what five types of variables explain individual differences?

2. What three components are involved in Albert Bandura's theory of reciprocal determinism?

3. How is social intelligence defined?

### CRITICAL THINKING
Recall the study that examined self-regulatory efficacy. Why was it important to use a longitudinal design for this study?

# SELF THEORIES

We have now arrived at theories of personality that are most immediately personal: they deal directly with how each individual manages his or her sense of *self*. What is your conception of your *self*? Do you think of your *self* reacting consistently to the world? Do you try to present a consistent *self* to your friends and family? What impact do positive and negative experiences have on the way you think about your *self*? We will begin our consideration of these questions with a brief historical review.

The concern for analysis of the self found its strongest early advocate in William James (1892). James identified three components of self-experience: the *material me* (the bodily self, along with surrounding physical objects), the *social me* (your awareness of how others view you), and the *spiritual me* (the self that monitors private thoughts and feelings). James believed that everything that you associate with your identity becomes, in some sense, a part of the self. This explains why people may react defensively when their friends or family members—a part of the self—have been attacked. The concept of self was also central to psychodynamic theories. Self-insight was an important part of the psychoanalytic cure in Freud's theory, and Jung stressed that to fully develop the self, one must integrate and accept all aspects of one's conscious and unconscious life.

How has the self been treated in contemporary theory? We will first describe cognitive aspects of the self: self-concepts and possible selves. We then examine the way that people present their selves to the world. Finally, we look at the important topic of how views of the self differ across cultures.

## DYNAMIC ASPECTS OF SELF-CONCEPTS

The **self-concept** is a dynamic mental structure that motivates, interprets, organises, mediates, and regulates intrapersonal and interpersonal behaviours and processes. The self-concept includes many components. Among them are your memories about yourself; beliefs about your traits, motives, values and abilities; the ideal self that you would most like to become; the possible selves that you contemplate enacting; positive or negative evaluations of yourself (self-esteem); and beliefs about what others think of you (Chen et al., 2006). In Chapter 7, we discussed *schemas* as 'knowledge packages' that embody complex generalisations about the structure of the environment. Your self-concept contains schemas about the self—*self-schemas*—that allow you to organise information about yourself, just as other schemas allow you to manage other aspects of your experience. However, self-schemas influence more than just the way you process information about yourself. Research indicates that these schemas, which you frequently use to interpret your own behaviour,

Imagine for a moment your different 'possible selves'. What effect might consideration of possible selves have on your behaviour?

influence the way you process information about other people as well (Krueger & Stanke, 2001; Mussweiler & Bodenhausen, 2002). Thus you interpret other people's actions in terms of what you know and believe about yourself.

Another important component of your cognitive sense of self may be the other *possible selves* to which you compare your current self-concept. **Hazel Markus** and her colleagues have defined **possible selves** as 'the ideal selves that we would very much like to become. They are also the selves we could become, and the selves we are afraid of becoming' (Markus & Nurius, 1986, p. 954). Possible selves play a role in motivating behaviour—they spur action by allowing you to consider what directions your 'self' could take, for better or for worse.

Consider a study that explored individuals' ideas about whether they are prepared to become parents.

A team of researchers developed an assessment device intended to measure the extent to which young adults could imagine themselves becoming parents (Bloom et al., 1999). The 683 university students who participated in the study responded on a scale of *not at all like me to very much like me* to statements such as 'In the future I see myself as the kind of person who would get married but choose not to have children'. To discourage students from guessing the study's purpose, the items relevant to parenting were dispersed into a longer questionnaire. After completing the questionnaire, each student was assigned a *parent possible-self score* (PPS). On average, men and women did not differ on these scores. However, the researchers defined subsets of both men and women who were particularly high and low on the scale. The individuals in those subsets rated their perceptions of videotaped infants whose behaviour ranged from happy to fussy. The high-PPS students gave consistently more favourable ratings to the infants than the low-PPS students did.

Can you think of reasons why a person's ability to envision him- or herself as a parent might have an impact on that person's interpretations of an infant's behaviour?

**possible selves** The ideal selves that a person would like to become, the selves a person could become, and the selves a person is afraid of becoming.

**self-concept** A person's mental model of his or her abilities and attributes.

Self-handicapping behaviour in action: instead of studying for tomorrow's exam, you fall asleep in the library, thereby enabling yourself to say, 'Well, I didn't really study' if you don't ace the test. Are there situations in which you resort to self-handicapping?

## SELF-ESTEEM AND SELF-PRESENTATION

We have already acknowledged that some people have a negative self-concept, which we could also characterise as low self-esteem. A person's **self-esteem** is a *generalised* evaluation of the self. Self-esteem can strongly influence thoughts, moods and behaviour (Baumeister et al., 2003). Low self-esteem may be characterised, in part, by less certainty about the self. When high- and low-self-esteem individuals were asked to rate themselves along a number of trait dimensions (such as logical, intellectual, and likeable), low-self-esteem participants, as you might expect, gave themselves overall lower ratings (Baumgardner, 1990). However, when they were also asked to provide upper and lower limits for their estimates, the low-self-esteem participants indicated larger ranges: they had a less precise sense of self than their high-self-esteem peers. Thus part of the phenomenon of low self-esteem may be feeling that you just don't know much about yourself. Lack of self-knowledge makes it difficult to predict that one will make a success of life's endeavours.

Evidence suggests that most people go out of their way to maintain self-esteem and to sustain the integrity of their self-concept (Vignoles et al., 2006). People engage in a variety of forms of self-enhancement. For example, when you doubt your ability to perform a task, you may engage in **self-handicapping** behaviour. You deliberately sabotage your performance! The purpose of this strategy is to have a ready-made excuse for failure that does not imply *lack of ability* (McCrea & Hirt, 2001). Thus, if you are afraid to find out whether you have what it takes to top a class at university, you might party with friends instead of studying for an important exam. That way, if you don't succeed, you can blame your failure on low effort, without finding out whether you really had the ability to make it.

A pair of researchers asked university students to indicate their agreement with statements that measured self-handicapping: 'I would do a lot better

if I tried harder'; 'I suppose I feel 'under the weather' more often than most'; 'I tend to put things off to the last moment.' Before their first exam, the students were asked what grade would make them happy. After the exam, they were given false feedback that their score was one-third grade below that 'happy' grade (for example, if they had desired a score of 8/10, they were told they got a 5/10). At that point, the researchers assessed the students' self-esteem. If self-handicapping protects self-esteem, we would expect high self-handicappers to suffer the least injury to self-esteem when they obtained the dissatisfying grade. That's exactly the pattern that the men in the study showed: high self-handicapping was associated with higher self-esteem. The women students, however, did not show any correlation between self-handicapping and self-esteem. The researchers speculated that men may have a stronger tendency to protect against threats to the self (Rhodewalt & Hill, 1995).

You should think about this study with respect to your own behaviours. Do you indulge in self-handicapping? Even if it protects your self-esteem (particularly if you are male), your grades are still likely to suffer! (By the way, after the study was completed, the researchers thoroughly debriefed the participants—which included explaining the purpose of the deception and giving them their real grades.)

The phenomenon of self-handicapping suggests, as well, that important aspects of self-esteem are related to *self-presentation*. Self-handicapping is more likely when people know that outcomes will be made public (Self, 1990). After all, how can someone think less well of you when your handicap is so obvious? Similar issues of self-presentation help explain behavioural differences between individuals with high and low self-esteem (Baumeister et al., 1989). People with high self-esteem present themselves to the world as ambitious, aggressive risk takers. People with low self-esteem present themselves as cautious and prudent.

In this section, we've emphasised that people engage in behaviours such as self-handicapping to maintain a high sense of self-esteem. For that reason, you might not be surprised to learn that high self-esteem is not a good predictor of performance in many settings (Baumeister et al., 2003). In fact, it's safer to assume that high self-esteem is a consequence of success. Thus making students feel better about themselves doesn't lead to better school performance. Rather, high self-esteem flows, in part, from success in school.

## THE CULTURAL CONSTRUCTION OF SELF

Our discussion so far has focused on constructs relevant to the self, such as self-esteem and possible selves, that apply quite widely across individuals. However, researchers on the self have also begun to study the way in which self-concepts and self-development are affected by differing cultural constraints. If you have grown up in a Western culture, you are likely to be pretty comfortable with the research we

**self-esteem** A generalised evaluative attitude towards the self that influences both moods and behaviour and that exerts a powerful effect on a range of personal and social behaviours.

**self-handicapping** The process of developing, in anticipation of failure, behavioural reactions and explanations that minimise ability deficits as possible attributions for the failure.

have reviewed so far: the theories and constructs match the ways that Western cultures conceptualise the *self*. However, the type of culture from which the Western self emerges—an *individualistic* culture—is in the minority with respect to the world's population, which includes about 70 percent *collectivist* cultures. Individualistic cultures emphasise individuals' needs, whereas collectivist cultures emphasise the needs of the group (Triandis, 1994, 1995). This overarching emphasis has important implications for how each member of these cultures conceptualises his or her *self*: Hazel Markus and Shinobu Kitayama (1991; Kitayama et al., 1995; Markus et al., 1997) have argued that each culture gives rise to different interpretations of the meaning of self—or different *construals* of self:

- Individualistic cultures encourage **independent construals of self**—'Achieving the cultural goal of independence requires construing oneself as an individual whose behaviour is organised and made meaningful primarily by reference to one's own internal repertoire of thoughts, feelings and action, rather than by reference to the thoughts, feelings and actions of others' (Markus & Kitayama, 1991, p. 226).

- Collectivist cultures encourage **interdependent construals of self**—'Experiencing interdependence entails seeing oneself as part of an encompassing social relationship and recognising that one's behaviour is determined, contingent on, and to a large extent organised by what the actor perceives to be the thoughts, feelings and actions of *others* in the relationship' (Markus & Kitayama, 1991, p. 227).

Researchers have documented the reality and implications of these distinctions in a number of ways.

One type of cross-cultural research on the self has used a measurement device called the *Twenty Statements Test* (TST) (Kuhn & McPartland, 1954). When they take this test, participants are asked to give 20 different answers to the question 'Who am I?' Take a moment to reflect on that question. As shown in **Table 13.5**, responses typically fall into six different categories. Culture has an impact on the categories that are most likely for people's responses. For example, one study had roughly 300 students from the United States and India perform the TST procedure (Dhawan et al., 1995). In keeping with their independent sense of self, about 65 percent of the responses of U.S. women and 64 percent of the responses of U.S. men fell into the category of *self-evaluations*. For the Indian students, 33 percent of women's responses and 35 percent of men's responses fell into this category. Thus the Indian students were about half as likely to produce self-evaluations. Note that differences between men and women overall were rather small—culture mattered more.

You might wonder how the export of Western culture affects the self-concepts of members of collectivist cultures. One study compared the TST responses of Kenyans who had virtually no exposure to Western culture—members of pastoral Samburu and Maasai tribes—to those who had moved to the Westernised capital city of Nairobi. Roughly 82 percent of the tribe members' responses on the TST

## Table 13.5

Categories of twenty statements test responses

| Category | Examples |
|---|---|
| Social identity | I'm a student. |
| | I am a daughter. |
| Ideological beliefs | I believe that all human beings are good. |
| | I believe in God. |
| Interests | I like playing the piano. |
| | I enjoy visiting new places. |
| Ambitions | I want to become a doctor. |
| | I want to learn more psychology. |
| Self-evaluations | I am honest and hardworking. |
| | I am a tall person. |
| | I worry about the future. |
| Other | I have noisy friends. |
| | I own a dog. |

**independent construals of self** Conceptualisation of the self as individual whose behaviour is organised by reference to one's own thoughts, feelings and actions rather than by the thoughts, feelings and actions of others.

**interdependent construals of self** Conceptualisation of the self as part of an encompassing social relationship.

were social responses; workers in Nairobi gave only 58 percent social responses, and students at the University of Nairobi gave only 17 percent social responses (Ma & Schoeneman, 1997). This pattern suggests that when a nation imports Western products, they may also import a Western sense of self.

This cultural difference has also been found between urban and rural Australian Aboriginal teenagers. Aboriginal children who grew up in large cities in Australia have been found to have some complications in defining 'Who am I?' when compared to Aboriginal teenagers who grew up in an isolated, more traditional and culturally driven environment, such as the outback in the Northern Territory of Australia (Money, et al., 1970). Debate about this has come from education theorists who believe that Aboriginal culture should be taught in all regions of Australia, both rural and urban, and be specific to the region that the Aboriginal person originates from (Fleming & Southwell, 2006). By recognising cultural difference, even between regions, a greater identity formation will be apparent and help in defining self-concept. This research, once again, suggests that culture is perhaps a stronger

In what ways is an individual's sense of self different when he or she is a member of a culture with an interdependent construal of self rather than an independent construal of self?

influence over the definition of the self, than that of individual assessment.

These studies illustrate that the cultures to which people belong have a strong impact on the way they construe their selves. You have already read about some consequences of these construals. In Chapter 10, you learned that culture affects moral judgments (Miller & Bersoff, 1992). You will encounter this distinction again later in the book when, for example, we consider the question of whether ideas about *love* are influenced by construals of the self (see Chapter 16). For now, consider a study that has particular relevance to theories about the self.

Earlier we reviewed evidence that people are concerned with *self-enhancement*—bringing about positive changes in self-esteem. However, people in different cultures have different interpretations of the *self* in self-enhancement. For that reason, a team of researchers predicted that students from the United States would be more likely to choose individualistic behaviours for self-enhancement, whereas students from Japan would choose collectivist behaviours (Sedikides et al., 2003). To test that idea, the researchers asked each student from the United States and Japan to spend 10 minutes imagining that he or she was part of a taskforce responsible for solving business problems. The students were asked to consider a range of issues and write down their ideas on those issues. After performing this exercise, the students made predictions about how likely it was that they would outperform the other (imaginary) taskforce members on a range of behaviours. Some of those behaviours were individualistic: Would they 'disagree with [their] group when [they] believe the group is wrong'? Some of those behaviours were collectivist: Would they 'avoid open confrontation with [their] group'? For each behaviour, the students gave responses ranging from −5 ('much less likely than the typical group member') to +5 ('much more likely than the typical group member'). As shown in **Table 13.6**, the students predicted that they would outperform their peers—the more positive numbers indicate more self-enhancement—with respect to those behaviours that were matched with their construals of self.

Over the next few days, you might try to experience both construals of self by trying to attend to how the events that happen around you have an impact both on your self as an individual and your self as a member of a larger social structure.

## EVALUATION OF SELF THEORIES

Self theories succeed at capturing people's own concepts of their personalities and the way they wish to be perceived by others. Furthermore, examinations of cross-cultural construals of the self have had great influence on the way psychologists assess the universality of their theories. However, critics of self theory approaches to personality argue against its limitless boundaries. Because so many things are relevant to the self and to the self-concept, it is not always clear which factors are most important for predicting behaviour. In addition, the emphasis on the self as a social construct is not entirely consistent with evidence that some facets of personality may be inherited. As with the other theories we have described, self theories capture some but not all of what you think of as personality.

For answers go to MyPsychLab!

**mypsychlab** *where learning comes to life!*

### RECAP CHECKPOINT
#### Self theories

- Self theories focus on the importance of the self-concept for a full understanding of human personality.

- The self-concept is a dynamic mental structure that motivates, interprets, organises, mediates and regulates personal and interpersonal behaviours and processes.

- People engage in behaviours such as self-handicapping to maintain self-esteem.

- Cross-cultural research suggests that individualistic cultures give rise to independent construals of self, whereas collectivist cultures give rise to interdependent construals of self.

### CONCEPT QUESTIONS

1. What role do possible selves play for motivation?

2. What is self-handicapping?

3. What does it mean to have an interdependent construal of self?

### CRITICAL THINKING

Consider the study that examined students' self-handicapping behaviours. Why did the researchers ask each individual student to provide the grade with which he or she would be happy?

## Table 13.6

Self-enhancement across cultures

| Culture | BEHAVIOURS | |
| --- | --- | --- |
| | Individualist | Collectivist |
| American | 1.28 | −0.45 |
| Japanese | 0.06 | 0.63 |

# CRITICAL THINKING *in your life*

## WHO ARE YOU ON THE INTERNET?

Suppose you had the opportunity to change something about your 'self.' Would you make the change? How could you learn in advance what the consequences of that change might be? Researchers have documented that many people turn to the Internet as a means to conduct 'identity experiments' (McKenna & Bargh, 2000; Valkenburg et al., 2005). When a person enters a chat room, she might decide to be a man rather than a woman, black rather than white, age 40 rather than 18, and a successful executive rather than a college sophomore. The Internet brings the concept of *possible selves* very vividly into many people's everyday lives. Let's focus on the functions those identity experiments might serve.

Consider a study that surveyed the Internet use of 600 students whose ages ranged from 9 to 18 years old (Valkenburg et al., 2005). Those students were asked whether they had 'ever pretended to be somebody else while communicating on the Internet' (p. 389). Among the 9- to 12-year-olds, 72 percent said 'yes'. The number fell to 53 percent for 13- to 14-year-olds and 28 percent for 15- to 18-year-olds. Recall from Chapter 10 that people establish their identities during adolescence. These data suggest that, in contemporary times, the Internet plays a role in the way that adolescents try out identities. The researchers also

asked the students why they had pretended to be somebody else. In fact, the most prominent motive the students reported was *self-exploration*: The students indicated that they wished to learn how it might feel to be someone else and how others might react to them if they were different.

Although 'identity experiments' become less common across the period of adolescence, the Internet's potential for self-exploration remains attractive in adult life. Something that many people find burdensome in 'real' life is that they feel as though they are defined rather narrowly: Repeated interactions with family, friends, bosses, and co-workers require them to remain consistent in a way that may be at odds with the person they wish to be; it is relatively difficult for people to expand into new realms of experience, given the constraints of their day-to-day social context. The Internet loosens up that social context (Bargh et al., 2003; McKenna & Bargh, 2000). People can use the anonymity of the Internet to express new interests or explore new ideas without fear of real-world consequences. Without making radical changes (e.g., claiming to be a woman rather than a man), a person can rehearse possible selves that may be closer to his or her ideal self.

Furthermore, the anonymity of the Internet allows people to reveal

more of their selves than they might otherwise be willing to disclose. Recall from Chapter 12 that people obtain positive health benefits when they make emotional disclosures (Pennebaker, 1997; Petrie et al., 2004). The Internet offers people a broad range of opportunities to engage in such disclosure. People can find specialised chat rooms or newsgroups that explicitly provide forums for such disclosure and social support for the content of the disclosures.

We have been focusing on the positive aspects of the Internet: People's ability to expand their sense of self and their ability to engage in self-disclosure with consequences for health and self-acceptance. There are, of course, some dangers. Anonymity can lead people to fragment their lives in ways that might lead to maladaptive behaviours (Reid, 1998). We also noted earlier that some researchers attribute a rise in the prevalence of shyness to the availability of the Internet. Still, as you think about your 'self', you can also think critically about the opportunities the Internet provides for you to engage, very literally, in self-exploration.

- Why is the anonymity of the Internet so important for 'identity experiments'?

- How might people use information they gather from Internet interactions in their real lives?

## COMPARING PERSONALITY THEORIES

There is no unified theory of personality that a majority of psychologists can endorse. Several differences in basic assumptions have come up repeatedly in our survey of the

various theories. It may be helpful to recap five of the most important differences in assumptions about personality and the approaches that advance each assumption.

1. *Heredity versus environment.* As you have learned throughout *Psychology and Life*, this difference is also referred to as *nature versus nurture*. What is more important to personality development: genetic and biological factors or environmental influences?

Trait theories have been split on this issue; Freudian theory depends heavily on heredity; humanistic, social-learning, cognitive and self theories all emphasise either environment as a determinant of behaviour or interaction with the environment as a source of personality development and differences.

2. *Learning processes versus innate laws of behaviour.* Should emphasis be placed on the view that personalities are modified through learning or on the view that personality development follows an internal timetable? Again, trait theories have been divided. Freudian theory has favoured the inner determinant view, whereas humanists postulate an optimistic view that experience changes people. Social-learning, cognitive and self theories clearly support the idea that behaviour and personality change as a result of learned experiences.

3. *Emphasis on past, present or future.* Trait theories emphasise past causes, whether innate or learned; Freudian theory stresses past events in early childhood; social-learning theories focus on past reinforcements and present contingencies; humanistic theories emphasise present reality or future goals; and cognitive and self theories emphasise past and present (and the future if goal setting is involved).

4. *Consciousness versus unconsciousness.* Freudian theory emphasises unconscious processes; humanistic, social-learning and cognitive theories emphasise conscious processes. Trait theories pay little attention to this distinction; self theories are unclear on this score.

5. *Inner disposition versus outer situation.* Social-learning theories emphasise situational factors; traits play up dispositional factors; and the others allow for an interaction between person-based and situation-based variables.

Each type of theory makes different contributions to the understanding of human personality. Trait theories provide a catalogue that describes parts and structures. Psychodynamic theories add a powerful engine and the fuel to get the vehicle moving. Humanistic theories put a person in the driver's seat. Social-learning theories supply the steering wheel, directional signals and other regulation equipment. Cognitive theories add reminders that the way the trip is planned, organised and remembered will be affected by the mental map the driver chooses for the journey. Finally, self theories remind the driver to consider the image his or her driving ability is projecting to backseat drivers and pedestrians.

To complete our discussion of personality, we now consider personality assessment. We will describe some of the ways in which psychologists obtain information about the range of personality attributes that make each individual unique.

For answers go to MyPsychLab!

## RECAP CHECKPOINT
### Comparing personality theories

- Personality theories can be contrasted with respect to the emphasis they put on heredity versus environment; learning processes versus innate laws of behaviour; the past, present or future; consciousness versus unconsciousness; and inner dispositions versus outer situations.

- Each theory makes different contributions to the understanding of human personality.

## CONCEPT QUESTIONS

1. In what ways do personality theories differ on the dimension of heredity versus environment?

2. Does Freud's theory of personality focus most directly on the past, present or future?

3. Which dimension of personality theories refers to people's awareness of the forces that shape their behaviours?

# ASSESSING PERSONALITY

Think of all the ways in which you differ from your best friend. Psychologists wonder about the diverse attributes that characterise an individual—set one person apart from others, or distinguish people in one group from those in another (for example, shy people from outgoing or depressed individuals from happy). Two assumptions are basic to these attempts to understand and describe human personality: first, that there are personal characteristics of individuals that give coherence to their behaviour and, second, that those characteristics can be assessed or measured. Personality tests must also meet the standards of reliability and validity (see Chapter 9). Personality tests that pursue these goals can be classified as being either *objective* or *projective*.

## OBJECTIVE TESTS

Objective tests of personality are those in which scoring and administration are relatively simple and follow well-defined rules. Some objective tests are scored, and even interpreted, by computer programs. The final score is usually a single number, scaled along a single dimension (such as *adjustment* versus *maladjustment)*, or a set of scores on different traits (such as impulsiveness, dependency, or extraversion) reported in comparison with the scores of a normative sample.

A *self-report inventory* is an objective test in which individuals answer a series of questions about their thoughts, feelings and actions. One of the first self-report inventories, the *Woodworth Personal Data Sheet* (written in 1917) asked questions such as 'Are you often frightened in the middle of the night?' (see DuBois, 1970). Today, a person taking a **personality inventory** reads a series of statements and indicates whether each one is true or typical for himself or herself.

The most frequently used personality inventory is the *Minnesota Multiphasic Personality Inventory*, or MMPI (Dahlstrom et al., 1975). It is used in many clinical settings to aid in the diagnosis of patients and to guide their treatment. After reviewing its features and applications, we will briefly discuss the *NEO Personality Inventory* (NEO-PI), which is used widely with non-patient populations.

The MMPI The MMPI was developed at the University of Minnesota during the 1930s by psychologist Starke Hathaway and psychiatrist J. R. McKinley (Hathaway & McKinley, 1940, 1943). Its basic purpose was to diagnose individuals according to a set of psychiatric labels. The first test consisted of 550 items, which individuals determined to be either true or false for themselves or to which they responded, 'Cannot say'. From that item pool, scales were developed that were relevant to the kinds of problems patients showed in psychiatric settings.

The MMPI scales were unlike other existing personality tests because they were developed using an *empirical* strategy rather than the intuitive, theoretical approach that dominated at the time. Items were included on a scale only if they clearly distinguished between two groups—for example, schizophrenic patients and a normal comparison group. Each item had to demonstrate its validity by being answered similarly by members within each group but differently between the two groups. Thus the items were not selected on a theoretical basis (what the content seemed to mean to experts) but on an empirical basis (Did they distinguish between the two groups?).

The MMPI has 10 *clinical scales*, each constructed to differentiate a special clinical group (such as individuals with schizophrenia) from a normal comparison group. The test also includes *validity scales* that detect suspicious response patterns, such as blatant dishonesty, carelessness, defensiveness, or evasiveness. When an MMPI is interpreted, the tester first checks the validity scales to be sure the test is valid and then looks at the rest of the scores. The pattern of the scores—which are highest, how they differ—forms the 'MMPI profile.' Individual profiles are compared with those common for particular groups, such as felons and gamblers.

In the mid-1980s, the MMPI underwent a major revision, and it is now called the *MMPI-2* (Butcher et al., 2001). The MMPI-2 has updated language and content to better reflect contemporary concerns, and new populations provided data for norms. The MMPI-2 also adds 15 new *content scales* that were derived using, in part, a theoretical method. For each of 15 clinically relevant topics (such as anxiety or family problems), items were selected on two bases: if they seemed theoretically related to the topic area and if they statistically formed a *homogeneous scale*, meaning that each scale measures a single, unified concept. The clinical and content scales of the MMPI-2 are given in **Table 13.7** and **Table 13.8**. You'll notice that

**personality inventory** A self-report questionnaire used for personality assessment that includes a series of items about personal thoughts, feelings and behaviours.

## Table 13.7

**MMPI-2 clinical scales**

*Hypochondriasis (Hs)*: Abnormal concern with bodily functions

*Depression (D)*: Pessimism; hopelessness; slowing of action and thought

*Conversion hysteria (Hy)*: Unconscious use of mental problems to avoid conflicts or responsibility

*Psychopathic deviate (Pd)*: Disregard for social custom; shallow emotions; inability to profit from experience

*Masculinity–femininity (Mf)*: Differences between men and women

*Paranoia (Pa)*: Suspiciousness; delusions of grandeur or persecution

*Psychasthenia (Pt)*: Obsessions; compulsions; fears; guilt; indecisiveness

*Schizophrenia (Sc)*: Bizarre, unusual thoughts or behaviour; withdrawal; hallucinations; delusions

*Hypomania (Ma)*: Emotional excitement; flight of ideas; overactivity

*Social introversion (Si)*: Shyness; disinterest in others; insecurity

## Table 13.8

**MMPI-2 content scales**

| | |
|---|---|
| Anxiety | Antisocial practices |
| Fears | Type A (workaholic) |
| Obsessiveness | Low self-esteem |
| Depression | Social discomfort |
| Health concerns | Family problems |
| Bizarre mentation (thoughts) | Work interference |
| Anger and cynicism | Negative treatment indicators (negative attitudes about doctors and treatment) |

most of the clinical scales measure several related concepts and that the names of the content scales are simple and self-explanatory.

The benefits of the MMPI-2 include its ease and economy of administration and its usefulness for the diagnosis of psychopathology (Butcher, 2004; Butcher & Rouse, 1996). In addition, the item pool can be used for many purposes. For example, you could build a creativity scale by finding creative and noncreative groups of individuals and determining the MMPI items that they answered differently. Over the years, psychologists have developed and validated hundreds of special-purpose scales in this way. For researchers, one of the most attractive characteristics of the MMPI is the enormous archives of MMPI profiles collected over 50 years. Because all of these people have been tested on the same items in a standardised way, they can be compared either on the traditional clinical scales or on special-purpose scales (like our new 'creativity' scale). These MMPI archives allow researchers to test hypotheses on MMPIs taken by people many years earlier, perhaps long before the construct being measured was even conceived.

However, the MMPI-2 is not without its critics. Its clinical scales have been criticised, for example, because they are *heterogeneous*—they measure several patterns at once rather than focusing on a specific clinical group. Researchers have also suggested that the changes from the original MMPI to the revised MMPI-2 were insufficient to recognise advances in personality theory; the test remains close to its empirical origins (Helmes & Reddon, 1993). Clinicians have also been concerned whether the MMPI-2 is equally valid for all racial and ethnic groups (Arbisi et al., 2002). As with any assessment device, researchers must carefully evaluate the reliability and validity of each particular use of the MMPI and MMPI-2 (Greene et al., 1997).

The MMPI was designed to assess individuals with clinical problems. In the next section, we'll describe devices more suited to assess personality in the general, non-patient population.

**The NEO-PI** The NEO Personality Inventory (NEO-PI) was designed to assess personality characteristics in non-clinical adult populations. It measures the five-factor model of personality we discussed earlier. If you took the NEO-PI, you would receive a profile sheet that showed your standardised scores relative to a large normative sample on each of the five major dimensions: Neuroticism, Extraversion, Openness, Agreeableness and Conscientiousness (Costa & McCrae, 1985). The recent NEO-PI-3 assesses 30 separate traits organised within the five major factors (McCrae et al., 2005). For example, the Neuroticism dimension is broken down into six facet scales: Anxiety, Angry hostility, Depression, Self-consciousness, Impulsiveness and Vulnerability. Much research has demonstrated that the NEO-PI dimensions are homogeneous, highly reliable, and show good criterion and construct validity (Furnham et al.,

1997; McCrae et al., 2004). The NEO-PI is being used to study personality stability and change across the life span as well as the relationship of personality characteristics to physical health and various life events, such as career success or early retirement.

A second inventory based on the five-factor model, the *Big Five Questionnaire (BFQ)*, was designed to have validity across different cultures. The scale was developed in Italy, but it shows similar psychometric characteristics for U.S. and Spanish populations, and appropriate norms are being established for French, German, Czech, Hungarian, and Polish translations (Barbaranelli et al., 1997; Caprara et al., 1993). Although the BFQ correlates highly with the NEO-PI, it differs in important ways. Factor 1 is labelled Energy or Activity rather than Extraversion (to reduce overlap with the social aspects of Agreeableness). The BFQ includes a scale to see if test takers' responses are biased toward socially desirable responses. It is simpler than the NEO-PI in having only two facets for each of the five factors. For example, Energy is composed of the facets of Dynamism and Dominance. The first is intra-personal; the second is interpersonal. As psychology becomes more global in its concerns, such assessment instruments that work equally well across language and national boundaries are essential for conducting meaningful cross-cultural research in personality and social psychology.

## PROJECTIVE TESTS

Have you ever looked at a cloud and seen a face or the shape of an animal? If you asked your friends to look, too, they may have seen a reclining nude or a dragon. Psychologists rely on a similar phenomenon in their use of projective tests for personality assessment.

As we just saw, objective tests take one of two forms: Either they provide test takers with a series of statements and ask them to give a simple response (such as 'true', 'false', or 'cannot say') or they ask test takers to rate themselves with respect to some dimension (such as 'anxious' versus 'non-anxious'). Thus the respondent is constrained to choose one of the predetermined responses. *Projective tests*, by contrast, have no predetermined range of responses. In a **projective test**, a person is given a series of stimuli that are purposely ambiguous, such as abstract patterns, incomplete pictures or drawings that can be interpreted in many ways. The person may be asked to describe the patterns, finish the pictures or tell stories about the drawings. Projective tests were first used by psychoanalysts, who hoped that such tests would reveal their patients' unconscious personality dynamics. Because the stimuli are ambiguous, responses to them are determined partly by what the person brings to the situation—namely, inner feelings, personal motives and conflicts from prior life experiences. These personal, idiosyncratic aspects, which are *projected* onto the stimuli, permit the personality assessor to make various interpretations.

**projective test** A method of personality assessment in which an individual is presented with a standardised set of ambiguous abstract stimuli and interprets their meanings; responses reveal inner feelings and conflicts.

Projective tests are among the assessment devices most commonly used by psychological practitioners (Butcher & Rouse, 1996). They have also been used more often outside the United States, such as in the Netherlands, Hong Kong, and Japan, than objective tests like the MMPI (Piotrowski et al., 1993). Objective tests often fail to be adequately translated or adequately standardised for non-U.S. populations. Projective tests are less sensitive to language variation. However, because projective tests are so widespread, critics have often worried that they are used in ways that are not valid. As we examine two of the most common projective tests, the Rorschach test and the Thematic Apperception Test (TAT), we will discuss those issues of validity.

**The Rorschach** In the Rorschach test, developed by Swiss psychiatrist **Hermann Rorschach** in 1921, the ambiguous stimuli are symmetrical inkblots (Rorschach, 1942). Some are black and white and some are coloured (see **Figure 13.9**). During the test, a respondent is shown an inkblot and asked, 'What might this be?' Respondents are assured that there are no right or wrong answers (Exner, 1974). Testers record verbatim what people say, how much time they take to respond, the total time they take per inkblot, and the way they handle the inkblot card. Then, in a second phase called an *inquiry*, the respondent is reminded of the previous responses and asked to elaborate on them.

The responses are scored on three major features: (1) the *location*, or part of the card mentioned in the response—whether the respondent refers to the whole stimulus or to part of it and the size of the details mentioned; (2) the *content* of the response—the nature of the object and activities seen; and (3) the *determinants*—which aspects of the card (such as its colour or shading) prompted the response. Scorers may also note whether responses are original and unique or popular and conforming.

You might think that ambiguous inkblots would give rise to an uninterpretable diversity of responses. In fact,

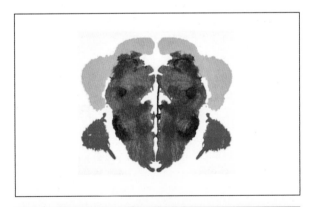

**Figure 13.9**

An inkblot similar to those used in the Rorschach Test
What do you see? Does your interpretation of this inkblot reveal anything about your personality?

researchers have devised a comprehensive scoring system for Rorschach responses that allows for meaningful comparisons among different test takers (Exner, 2003; Exner & Weiner, 1994). This scoring system specifies, for example, common categories of content response like *whole human* (the response mentions or implies a whole human form) and *blood* (the response mentions blood, either human or animal). Patterns of responses have been successfully related to normal personality characteristics as well as to psychopathology. Even so, some controversy remains about the validity of the scoring system and the Rorschach test (Exner, 2003; Garb et al., 2001).

**The TAT** In the Thematic Apperception Test (TAT), developed by **Henry Murray** in 1938, respondents are shown pictures of ambiguous scenes and asked to generate stories about them, describing what the people in the scenes are doing and thinking, what led up to each event, and how each situation will end. The person administering the TAT evaluates the structure and content of the stories as well as the behaviour of the individual telling them, in an attempt to discover some of the respondent's major concerns, motivations and personality characteristics. For example, an examiner might evaluate a person as conscientious if his or her stories concerned people who lived up to their obligations and if the stories were told in a serious, orderly way. Recall from Chapter 11 that the TAT has often been used to reveal individual differences in dominant needs, such as needs for power, affiliation, and achievement (McClelland, 1961). Over several decades of research, the TAT has proven to be a valid measure of the need for achievement (Spangler, 1992).

Let us offer some concluding remarks on the subject of personality assessment. Did you see the relationship between these personality assessment devices and the theories of personality we reviewed earlier? The conclusion we reached was that each of the types of theories illuminated best different aspects of human experience. We can reach much the same conclusions for personality tests: each has the potential to provide unique insights into an individual's personality. Clinicians most often use a combination of tests when they carry out a personality assessment. Under many circumstances, the profiles that arise from objective, even computer-based analyses may allow accurate predictions to be made for specific outcomes. Under other circumstances, clinical expertise and skilled intuition must supplement objective norms. In practice, the best predictions are made when the strengths of each approach are combined.

To close the chapter, we want you to consider a series of questions in light of what you have just learned: If psychologists studied you, what portrait of your personality would they draw? What early experiences might they identify as contributing to how you now act and think? What conditions in your current life exert strong influences on your thoughts and behaviours?

What makes you different from other individuals who are functioning in many of the same situations as you? You now can see that each type of personality theory provides a framework against which you can begin to form your answers to these questions. Suppose the time has really come to paint your psychological portrait. Where would you begin?

For answers go to MyPsychLab!

## RECAP CHECKPOINT
### Assessing personality

- Personality characteristics are assessed by both objective and projective tests.

- The most common objective test, the MMPI-2, is used to diagnose clinical problems.

- The NEO-PI and BFQ are newer objective personality tests that measure five major dimensions of personality.

- Projective tests of personality ask people to respond to ambiguous stimuli.

- Two important projective tests are the Rorschach test and the TAT.

## CONCEPT QUESTIONS

1. What is the purpose of the MMPI's 10 clinical scales?

2. What is the purpose of the NEO Personality Inventory (NEO-PI)?

3. What three major features do clinicians use to interpret Rorschach responses?

# SUMMARY

Chapter 13 takes a close look at how personality emerges and develops with individuals. It provides an overview of type and trait personality theories and a history of how these theories have been either dismissed or validated over the last century. The chapter examines the theory of 'the self' and its relationship to culture. Personality theories are contrasted against one another to demonstrate how each approach may compliment another or convey just how complex analysing personality can be with human beings. Personality mearsurement and assessment is also explained in relation to objective and projective testing.

# KEY TERMS

analytic psychology (p. 459)
anxiety (p. 457)
archetype (p. 459)
collective unconscious (p. 459)
consistency paradox (p. 451)
ego (p. 456)
ego defence mechanisms (p. 457)
five-factor model (p. 448)
fixation (p. 455)
id (p. 456)
independent construals of self (p. 469)
interdependent construals of self (p. 469)

libido (p. 453)
personality (p. 446)
personality inventory (p. 473)
personality types (p. 446)
possible selves (p. 467)
projective test (p. 474)
psychic determinism (p. 455)
psychobiography (p. 461)
psychodynamic personality theories
   (p. 453)
reciprocal determinism (p. 464)
repression (p. 457)

self-actualisation (p. 460)
self-concept (p. 467)
self-efficacy (p. 464)
self-esteem (p. 468)
self-handicapping (p. 468)
shyness (p. 454)
social intelligence (p. 465)
superego (p. 456)
traits (p. 448)
unconditional positive regard
   (p. 460)
unconscious (p. 455)

# PRACTICE TEST

1. William Sheldon predicted that_____ would be brainy, artistic and introverted.
   a. endomorphs
   b. ectomorphs
   c. mesomorphs
   d. polymorphs

2. Which of these factors is *not* a trait dimension in the five-factor model?
   a. creativeness
   b. neuroticism
   c. agreeableness
   d. extraversion

3. Which of these is a *nature* explanation for why people are shy?
   a. Many of the activities people carry out on the Internet are socially isolating.
   b. Some cultures put a greater emphasis on obedience to authority.
   c. Some children are more reserved with unfamiliar people from birth.
   d. Parents may withhold love if children are not successful.

4. According to Freud, at ages 4 to 5 children are in the
   _____ stage of development.
   a. genital          c. phallic
   b. oral             d. anal

5. You attend a lecture that is focusing on archetypes in
   the collective unconscious. The lecture seems to be
   about the ideas of
   a. Carl Jung.          c. Karen Horney.
   b. Sigmund Freud.      d. Alfred Adler.

6. One of the most important claims of humanistic
   theories of personality is that people strive for
   a. Superiority.        c. self-preservation.
   b. erogenous zones.    d. self-actualisation.

7. Humanistic theories are _____ because
   they emphasise an individual's subjective view of
   reality.
   a. holistic            c. phenomenological
   b. deterministic       d. dispositional

8. With respect to Walter Mischel's personality theory,
   which of these statements relates to the variable of
   goals and values?
   a. Bart wants to graduate from college before he
      turns 30.
   b. Reese thinks she can persuade her brother to lend
      her his car.
   c. Piper sweats a lot before she takes an exam.
   d. Vito can do multiplication without a calculator.

9. Jody's best friend Buffy is trying to convince him that
   he can get a new job. If Buffy is successful, that could
   have an impact on Jody's sense of
   a. self-efficacy.      c. reciprocal determinism.
   b. self-regulation.    d. libido.

10. Brian spends the whole night before he is going to
    compete in a triathlon reviewing the notes for his
    philosophy class. This might be an example of
    a. self-efficacy.      c. self-handicapping.
    b. psychic determinism. d. neuroticism.

11. Because Miriam lives in a _____ culture she
    is likely to have an _____ construal of self.
    a. collectivist; dependent
    b. collectivist; interdependent
    c. individualistic; interdependent
    d. collectivist; independent

12. In one study, the students *most* likely to engage
    in 'identity experiments' on the Internet were
    _____ year-olds.
    a. 9- to 12-           c. 15- to 18-
    b. 13- to 14-          d. 19- to 22-

13. Chad and Jeremy are both personality theorists. Chad
    believes that personalities are largely determined before
    birth. Jeremy believes that personalities arise from life
    experiences. The dimension on which they disagree is:
    a. learning processes versus innate laws of behaviour.
    b. consciousness versus unconsciousness.
    c. inner disposition versus outer situation.
    d. heredity versus environment.

14. Which personality theory puts the most emphasis on
    innate laws of behaviour?
    a. Humanistic theory      c. Self theory
    c. Social-learning theory d. Freudian theory

15. The personality test that most directly assesses the
    dimensions of the five-factor model is the:
    a. Rorschach.          c. TAT.
    b. NEO-PI.             d. MMPI-2.

16. If you wanted to measure need for achievement, your
    first choice might be the
    a. Rorschach.          c. MMPI-2.
    b. TAT.                d. NEO-PI.

## Essay Questions

1. How do traits and situations interact to affect
   predictions of behaviours?

2. How do humanistic theories give rise to a focus on life
   stories and psychobiography?

3. What theoretical ideas led to the development of
   projective personality tests?

# WEB LINKS

http://www.freudfile.org/
    Sigmund Freud – Life and Works

Are you ready for the test? MyPsychLab offers dozens of ways to deepen your understanding and test your recall of the material in this chapter—including video and audio clips, simulations and activities, self-assessments, practice tests and other study materials. Specific resources available for this chapter include:

The id, ego, and superego
Freud's five psychosexual stages of
    personality development
Mischel's theory of personality

Discover me
Self-concept

To access MyPsychLab, please visit **www.pearsoned.com.au/mypsychlab**

# How does this apply to me?

## NOW YOU HAVE READ CHAPTER 13—ARE YOU PREPARED FOR THE EXAM?

To enhance your understanding of any of the material in your *Psychology and Life* textbook, go to **MyPsychLab: www.pearsoned.com.au/mypsychlab**.

Complete pre- and post-tests, create your own individualised study plan, watch videos and animations and listen to audio glossaries—all of which will help you understand the themes of this chapter:

- Type and trait personality theories
- Psychodynamic theories
- Humanistic theories
- Social-learning and cognitive theories
- Self theories
- Comparing personality theories
- Assessing personality

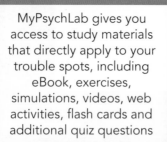

MyPsychLab gives you access to study materials that directly apply to your trouble spots, including eBook, exercises, simulations, videos, web activities, flash cards and additional quiz questions

Watch *Set In Your Ways*, a video about different personality types.

'MyPsychLab gave me the principles to focus on when I was studying.'

00:12/01:32

**EXPLORE**
Complete interactive 'drop and drag' activities to enhance your understanding of the key concepts.

'I clearly earned a better grade on my test after studying with MyPsychLab.'

## The Id, Ego and Superego

Drag and drop the term from the left-hand column to the corresponding place in the right-hand column.

|  | | Id | Ego | Superego |
|---|---|---|---|---|
| Adapt to reality while controlling the id and superego | Nature | | | |
| Conscious, preconscious, and unconscious | Level | Conscious, preconscious, and unconscious | | |
| Immediate gratification | | | | |
| Moralistic and idealistic | | | | |
| Perfection | Principle | | | |
| Pleasure | | | | |
| Reality | | | | |
| Represent right and wrong | Purpose | | | |
| Represents biological aspect | | | | |
| Represents psychological aspect | | | | |
| Represents societal and parental aspect | Aim | | | |
| Safety, compromise, and delayed gratification | | | | |
| Seek pleasure, and avoid pain | | | | |
| Unconscious | | | | |

Reset

THE ID, EGO AND SUPEREGO

FREUD'S PSYCHOSEXUAL STAGES

## Freud's Five Psychosexual Stages of Personality Development

Drag and drop the term from the left-hand column to the corresponding place in the right-hand column.

Genital

Latency

Oral

Phallic

**Descriptor**

[ ] ........ Activities such as feeding, thumb sucking, and cooling bring gratification

Anal ........ Child responds to some parental demands such as for bowel and bladder control

[ ] ........ Child experiences the Oedipus complex

[ ] ........ Development continues, but sexual urges are relatively quiet

[ ] ........ Child shakes off old dependencies

Reset

**What can you find in MyPsychLab?**

Self-directed tests * Videos * Simulations * eBook * Biographies * Audio glossary * Web links … and more—organised by chapter, section and learning objective.

mypsychlab™
where learning comes to life!

Psychological
Disorders

CHAPTER

14

# CHAPTER FOCUS POINTS

After studying this chapter you will have a better understanding of:

1. The nature of psychological disorders

2. Different types of anxiety disorders

3. Different types of mood disorders

4. How personality disorders are identified

5. The complexities of somatoform and dissociative disorders

6. What schizophrenia is

7. Psychological disorders of childhood

8. The stigma behind mental illness.

## CHAPTER CONTENTS

onsider these words, written by a 30-year-old woman who was receiving treatment for schizophrenia:

*I want to let you know what it is like to be a functional person with schizophrenia in these days and times and what someone with my mental illness faces. . . . I live pretty normal and no one can tell [I'm] mentally ill unless I tell them. . . . The delusions before I got my medicine picked any story line it chose, and changed it at will. As time went by before help, I felt it was taking over my whole brain, and I'd cry wanting my mind and life back.*

What are your reactions as you read this young woman's words, an excerpt from a letter to your authors?

If your reactions are similar to ours, you feel a mixture of sadness at her plight, of delight in her willingness to do all she can to cope with the many problems her mental illness creates, of anger toward those who stigmatise her because she may act differently at times, and of hope that, with medication and therapy, her condition may improve. These are but a few of the emotions that clinical and research psychologists and psychiatrists feel as they try to understand and treat mental disorders.

This chapter focuses on the nature and causes of psychological disorders: what they are, why they develop, and how we can explain their causes. The next chapter builds on this knowledge to describe the strategies used

**psychopathological functioning** Disruptions in emotional, behavioural or thought processes that lead to personal distress or block one's ability to achieve important goals.

**abnormal psychology** The area of psychological investigation concerned with understanding the nature of individual pathologies of mind, mood and behaviour.

What do you imagine the lives of people with mental illnesses are like?

to treat, and to prevent, mental illness. Research indicates that 1 in 5 Australians will suffer from a psychological disorder at some point in their lives (ABS, 2006). Thus many of you who read this text are likely to benefit directly from knowledge about psychopathology. Facts alone, however, will not convey the serious impact psychological disorders have on the everyday lives of individuals and families. Throughout this chapter, as we discuss categories of psychological disorders, try to envision the real people who live with such a disorder every day. We will share with you their words and lives, as we did at the start of the chapter. Let's begin now with a discussion of the concept of abnormality.

# THE NATURE OF PSYCHOLOGICAL DISORDERS

ave you ever worried excessively? Felt depressed or anxious without really knowing why? Been fearful of something you rationally knew could not harm you? Had thoughts about suicide? Used alcohol or drugs to escape a problem? Almost everyone will answer yes to at least one of these questions, which means that almost everyone has experienced the symptoms of a psychological disorder. This chapter looks at the range of psychological functioning that is considered unhealthy or abnormal, often referred to as *psychopathology* or *psychological disorder*. **Psychopathological functioning** involves disruptions in emotional, behavioural or thought processes that lead to personal distress or that block one's ability to achieve important goals. The field of **abnormal psychology** is the area of psychological investigation most directly concerned with understanding the nature of individual pathologies of mind, mood and behaviour.

We begin this section by exploring a more precise definition of abnormality and then look at problems of objectivity. We then examine how this definition evolved over hundreds of years of human history.

## DECIDING WHAT IS ABNORMAL

What does it mean to say someone is *abnormal* or *suffering from a psychological disorder*? How do psychologists and other clinical practitioners decide what is abnormal? Is it always clear when behaviour moves from the normal to the abnormal category? The judgment that someone has a mental disorder is typically based on the evaluation of the individual's *behavioural* functioning by people with some special authority or power. The terms used to describe these phenomena—*mental disorder, mental illness* or *abnormality*—depend on the particular perspective, training and cultural background of the evaluator, the situation, and the status of the person being judged.

Let's consider seven criteria you might use to label behaviour as 'abnormal' (*DSM-IV- TR*, 2000; Rosenhan & Seligman, 1989):

1. *Distress or disability.* An individual experiences personal distress or disabled functioning, which produces a risk of physical or psychological deterioration or loss of freedom of action. For example, a man who cannot leave his home without weeping would be unable to pursue ordinary life goals.

2. *Maladaptiveness.* An individual acts in ways that hinder goals, do not contribute to personal well-being, or interfere strongly with the goals of others and the needs of society. Someone who is drinking so heavily that she cannot hold down a job or who is endangering others through her intoxication is displaying maladaptive behaviour.

3. *Irrationality.* An individual acts or talks in ways that are irrational or incomprehensible to others. A man who responds to voices that do not exist in objective reality is behaving irrationally.

4. *Unpredictability.* An individual behaves unpredictably or erratically from situation to situation, as if experiencing a loss of control. A child who smashes his fist through a window for no apparent reason displays unpredictability.

5. *Unconventionality and statistical rarity.* An individual behaves in ways that are statistically rare and that violate social standards of what is acceptable or desirable. Just being statistically unusual, however, does not lead to a psychological judgment of abnormality. For example, possessing genius-level intelligence is extremely rare, but it is also considered desirable. Conversely, having extremely low intelligence is also rare but is considered undesirable; thus it has often been labelled abnormal.

6. *Observer discomfort.* An individual creates discomfort in others by making them feel threatened or distressed in some way. A woman walking down the middle of the footpath, having a loud conversation with herself, creates observer discomfort in other pedestrians trying to avoid her.

7. *Violation of moral and ideal standards.* An individual violates expectations for how one ought to behave with respect to societal norms. By this criterion, people might be considered abnormal by some if they did not wish to work or they did not believe in God. This criterion for abnormality also becomes relevant in legal situations, a topic we address in the Critical Thinking in Your Life box on page 514.

Can you see why most of these indicators of abnormality may not be immediately apparent to all observers? Consider just the last criterion. Are you mentally ill if you don't wish to work, even if that is abnormal with respect to the norms of society? Or consider a more serious symptom. It is 'bad' to have hallucinations in our culture because they are taken as signs of mental disturbance, but it is 'good' in cultures in which hallucinations are interpreted as mystical visions from spirit forces. Whose judgment is correct? At the end of this chapter, we will consider some negative consequences and dangers associated with such socially regulated judgments and the decisions based on them.

We are more confident in labelling behaviour as 'abnormal' when more than just one of the indicators is present and valid. The more extreme and prevalent the indicators are, the more confident we can be that they point to an abnormal condition. None of these criteria is a *necessary* condition shared by all cases of abnormality. For example, during his murder trial, a Stanford University postgraduate student who had killed his maths professor with a hammer, and then taped to his office door a note that read 'No office hours today', reported feeling neither guilt nor remorse. Despite the absence of personal suffering, we would not hesitate to label his overall behaviour as abnormal. It is also true that no single criterion, by itself, is a *sufficient* condition that distinguishes all cases of abnormal behaviour from normal variations in behaviour. The distinction between normal and abnormal is not so much a difference between two independent types of behaviours as it is a matter of the degree to which a person's actions resemble a set of agreed-upon criteria of abnormality. Mental disorder is best thought of as a *continuum* that varies between *mental health* and *mental illness*, as shown in **Figure 14.1**.

How comfortable do you feel with these ideas about abnormality? Although the criteria seem fairly clear-cut, psychologists still worry about the problem of objectivity.

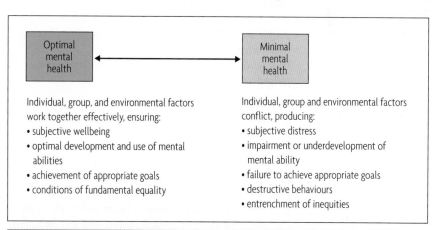

Figure 14.1

**Mental health continuum**
Because the distinction between *normal* and *abnormal* is relative, rather than absolute, it is useful to think of mental health as a continuum. At one end are behaviours that define optimal mental health; at the other end are behaviours that define minimal mental health. In between lie gradual increases in maladaptive behaviours.

Reprinted with permission from Rosenthal et al., *Archives of General Psychiatry*, Vol. 41, pp. 72–80, 1984. Copyright © 1984 by the American Medical Association.

# THE PROBLEM OF OBJECTIVITY

The decision to declare someone psychologically disordered or abnormal is always a *judgment* about behaviour: the goal for many researchers is to make these judgments *objectively*, without any type of bias. For some psychological disorders, like depression or schizophrenia, diagnosis often easily meets the standards of objectivity. Other cases are more problematic. As we have seen throughout our study of psychology, the meaning of behaviour is jointly determined by its *content* and by its *context*. The same act in different settings conveys very different meanings. A man kisses another man; it may signify a gay relationship in Australia, a ritual greeting in France, or a Mafia 'kiss of death' in Sicily. The meaning of a behaviour always depends on context.

Let's see why objectivity is such an important issue. History is full of examples of situations in which judgments of abnormality were made by individuals to preserve their moral or political power. Consider an 1851 report, entitled 'The Diseases and Physical Peculiarities of the Negro Race', published in a medical journal. Its author, Dr. Samuel Cartwright, had been appointed by the Louisiana Medical Association to chair a committee to investigate the 'strange' practices of African American slaves. 'Incontrovertible scientific evidence' was amassed to justify the practice of slavery. Several 'diseases' previously unknown to the white race were discovered. One finding was that blacks allegedly suffered from a sensory disease that made them insensitive 'to pain when being punished' (thus no need to spare the whip). The committee also invented the disease *drapetomania*, a mania to seek freedom—a mental disorder that caused certain slaves to run away from their masters. Runaway slaves needed to be caught so that their illness could be properly treated (Chorover, 1981)!

Once an individual has obtained an 'abnormal' label, people are inclined to interpret later behaviour to confirm that judgment. **David Rosenhan** (1973, 1975) and his colleagues demonstrated that it may be impossible to be judged 'sane' in an 'insane place.'

> Rosenhan and seven other sane people gained admission to different psychiatric hospitals by pretending to have a single symptom: hallucinations. All eight of these *pseudopatients* were diagnosed on admission as having either paranoid schizophrenia or bipolar disorder. Once admitted, they behaved normally in every way. Rosenhan observed, however, that when a sane person is in an insane place, he or she is likely to be judged insane, and any behaviour is likely to be reinterpreted to fit the context. If the pseudopatients discussed their situation in a rational way with the staff, they were reported to be using 'intellectualisation' defences, while their taking notes of their observations were evidence of 'writing behaviour'. The pseudopatients remained on the wards for almost 3 weeks, on average, and not one was identified by the staff as sane. When they were finally released—only with the help of

> spouses or colleagues—their discharge diagnosis was still 'schizophrenia' but 'in remission'. That is, their symptoms were no longer active.

Rosenhan's research demonstrates how judgments of abnormality rely on factors beyond behaviour itself.

In the view of psychiatrist **Thomas Szasz**, mental illness does not even exist—it is a 'myth' (1974, 2004). Szasz argues that the symptoms used as evidence of mental illness are merely medical labels that sanction professional intervention into what are social problems—deviant people violating social norms. Once labelled, these people can be treated either benignly or harshly for their problem 'of being different', with no threat of disturbing the existing status quo.

Few clinicians would go this far, in large part because the focus of much research and treatment is on understanding and alleviating personal distress. For most of the disorders we will describe in this chapter, individuals experience their own behaviour as abnormal, or poorly adapted to the environment. Even so, this discussion suggests that there can be no altogether objective assessments of abnormality. As we describe each type of psychological disorder, try to understand why clinicians believe the cluster of symptoms represents behaviour patterns that are more serious for the individual than mere violations of social norms.

# CLASSIFYING PSYCHOLOGICAL DISORDERS

Why is it helpful to have a classification system for psychological disorders? What advantages are gained by moving beyond a global assessment that abnormality exists to distinguish among different types of abnormalities? A **psychological diagnosis** is the label given to an abnormality by classifying and categorising the observed behaviour pattern into an approved diagnostic system. Such a diagnosis is in many ways more difficult to make than a medical diagnosis. In the medical context, a doctor can rely on physical evidence, such as X-rays, blood tests and biopsies, to inform a diagnostic decision. In the case of psychological disorders, the evidence for diagnosis comes from interpretations of a person's actions. In order to create greater consistency among clinicians and coherence in their diagnostic evaluations, psychologists have helped to develop a system of diagnosis and classification that provides precise descriptions of symptoms, as well as other criteria to help practitioners decide whether a person's behaviour is evidence of a particular disorder.

To be most useful, a diagnostic system should provide the following three benefits:

- *Common shorthand language.* To facilitate a quick and clear understanding among clinicians or researchers working in the field of psychopathology, practitioners seek a common set of terms with agreed-upon meanings. A diagnostic category, such as depression, summarises a large and complex collection of

**psychological diagnosis** The label given to psychological abnormality by classifying and categorising the observed behaviour pattern into an approved diagnostic system.

information, including characteristic symptoms and the typical course of the disorder. In clinical settings, such as clinics and hospitals, a diagnostic system allows mental health professionals to communicate more effectively about the people they are helping. Researchers studying different aspects of psychopathology or evaluating treatment programs must agree on the disorder they are observing.

- *Understanding of causality.* Ideally, a diagnosis of a specific disorder should make clear the causes of the symptoms. As is the case for physical illness, the same symptoms may arise for more than one disorder. A goal of a classification system is to indicate why practitioners should interpret particular patterns of symptoms as evidence for specific underlying disorders.

- *Treatment plan.* A diagnosis should also suggest what types of treatments to consider for particular disorders. Researchers and clinicians have found that certain treatments or therapies work most effectively for specific kinds of psychological disorders. For example, drugs that are quite effective in treating schizophrenia do not help and may even hurt people with depression. Further advances in knowledge about the effectiveness and specificity of treatments will make fast and reliable diagnosis even more important.

## Historical perspectives on classification

Throughout history, humans have feared psychological disorders, often associating them with evil. Because of this fear, people have reacted aggressively and decisively to any behaviours they perceived as bizarre or abnormal. People who have exhibited such behaviours have been imprisoned and made subject to radical medical treatments. Until the end of the 18th century, the mentally ill in Western societies were perceived as mindless beasts who could be controlled only with chains and physical discipline.

The Salem witchcraft trials were an outgrowth of a desperate attempt to affix blame for frighteningly bizarre behaviour among the Puritan colonists. The colonists theorised that the symptoms were the work of the devil, who, through the efforts of earthbound witches, had taken over the minds and bodies of young women.

In the latter part of the 18th century, a new perspective about the origins of abnormal behaviour emerged—people began to perceive those with psychological problems as *sick*, suffering from illness, rather than as *possessed* or *immoral.* As a result, a number of reforms were gradually implemented in the facilities for the insane. **Philippe Pinel** (1745–1826) was one of the first clinicians to use these ideas to attempt to develop a classification system for psychological difficulties based on the idea that disorders of thought, mood and behaviour are similar in many ways to the physical, organic illnesses. According to such a system, each disorder has a group of characteristic symptoms that distinguishes it from other disorders and from healthy functioning. Disorders are classified according to the patterns of observed symptoms, the circumstances surrounding the onset of the disturbance, the natural course of the disorder and its response to treatment. Such classification systems are modelled after the biological classification systems naturalists use and are intended to help clinicians identify common disorders more easily.

In 1896, **Emil Kraepelin** (1855–1926), a German psychiatrist, was responsible for creating the first truly comprehensive *classification system* of psychological disorders. Strongly motivated by a belief that there was a physical basis to psychological problems, he gave the process of psychological diagnosis and classification the flavour of medical diagnosis. That flavour remains today in the diagnostic system we now review.

*DSM-IV-TR* In Australia, the most widely accepted classification scheme comes from two professional publications: the *Diagnostic and Statistical Manual of Mental Disorders* (published by the American Psychiatric Association), and the *International Classification of Diseases* (published by the World Health Organisation). The most recent revision of the APA manual is known by clinicians and researchers as **DSM-IV-TR.** It classifies, defines and describes over 200 mental disorders but also includes as mental illness conditions generally excluded in Australian health care planning, particularly drug and alcohol disorders, and dementia.

To reduce the diagnostic difficulties caused by variability in approaches to psychological disorders, *DSM-IV-TR* emphasises the *description* of patterns of symptoms and courses of disorders rather than etiological theories or treatment strategies. The purely descriptive terms allow clinicians and researchers to use a common language to describe problems while leaving room for disagreement and continued research about which theoretical models best *explain* the problems.

The first version of *DSM*, which appeared in 1952 (*DSM-I*), listed several dozen mental illnesses. *DSM-II*, introduced in 1968, revised the diagnostic system to make it more compatible with another popular system, the World Health Organization's *International Classification of Diseases (ICD).* The fourth edition of the *DSM* (*DSM-IV*, 1994) emerged after several years of intense work by committees of scholars. To make their changes (from the *DSM-III-Revised*, which appeared in 1987), these

**DSM-IV-TR** The current diagnostic and statistical manual of the American Psychological Association that classifies, defines and describes mental disorders.

committees carefully scrutinised large bodies of research on psychopathology and also tested proposed changes for workability in actual clinical settings. *DSM-IV* is also fully compatible with the 10th edition of the *ICD*. *DSM-IV-TR* (2000) incorporated a review of the research literature that had accumulated since *DSM-IV*. Because the changes largely affected the supporting text, rather than the system of classification, the revision was termed a 'text revision' which yielded the name *DSM-IV-TR*.

To encourage clinicians to consider the psychological, social and physical factors that may be associated with a psychological disorder, *DSM-IV-TR* uses dimensions, or *axes,* that portray information about all these factors (see **Table 14.1**). Most of the principal clinical disorders are contained on Axis I. Included here are all disorders that emerge in childhood, except for mental retardation. Axis II lists mental retardation as well as personality disorders. These problems may accompany Axis I disorders. Axis III incorporates information about general medical conditions, such as diabetes, that may be relevant to understanding or treating an Axis I or II disorder. Axes IV and V provide supplemental information that can be useful when planning an individual's treatment or assessing the *prognosis* (predictions of future change). Axis IV assesses psychosocial and environmental problems that may explain patients' stress responses or their resources for coping with stress. On Axis V, a clinician evaluates the global level of an individual's functioning. A full diagnosis in the *DSM-IV-TR* system would involve consideration of each of the axes.

Throughout this chapter, we will provide estimates of the frequency with which individuals experience particular psychological disorders. These estimates arise from research projects in which mental health histories are obtained from large samples of the population. Figures are available for the prevalence of different disorders over 1-year and lifetime periods (Kessler et al., 2005a,

2005b). The figures we will generally cite come from the *National Comorbidity Study (NCS)*, which sampled 9,282 U.S. adults ages 18 and older (Kessler et al., 2005a). It is important to emphasise that often the same individuals have experienced more than one disorder simultaneously at some point in their life span, a phenomenon known as **comorbidity.** (*Morbidity* refers to the occurrence of disease. *Comorbidity* refers to the co-occurrence of diseases.) The NCS found that 45 percent of the people who had experienced one disorder in a 12-month period had actually experienced two or more. Researchers have begun to study intensively the patterns of comorbidity of different psychological disorders (Kessler et al., 2005b).

## Evolution of diagnostic categories

The diagnostic categories and the methods used to organise and present them have shifted with each revision of the *DSM*. These shifts reflect changes in the opinions of a majority of mental health experts about exactly what constitutes a psychological disorder and where the lines between different types of disorders should be drawn. They also reflect changing perspectives among the public about what constitutes *abnormality*.

In the revision process of each *DSM*, some diagnostic categories were dropped and others were added. For example, with the introduction of *DSM-III*, in 1980, the traditional distinction between *neurotic* and *psychotic* disorders was eliminated. **Neurotic disorders,** or *neuroses,* were originally conceived of as relatively common psychological problems in which a person did not have signs of brain abnormalities, did not display grossly irrational thinking, and did not violate basic norms; but he or she did experience subjective distress or a pattern of self-defeating or inadequate coping strategies. **Psychotic disorders,** or *psychoses,* were thought to differ in both quality and severity from neurotic problems. It was believed that psychotic behaviour deviated significantly

**comorbidity** The experience of more than one disorder at the same time.

**neurotic disorders** Mental disorders in which a person does not have signs of brain abnormalities and does not display grossly irrational thinking or violate basic norms but does experience subjective distress.

**psychotic disorders** Severe mental disorders in which a person experiences impairments in reality testing manifested through thought, emotional or perceptual difficulties.

## Table 14.1

The five axes of *DSM-IV-TR*

| Axis | Classes of information | Description |
|---|---|---|
| Axis I | Clinical disorders | These mental disorders present symptoms or patterns of behavioural or psychological problems that typically are painful or impair an area of functioning. Included are disorders that emerge in infancy, childhood or adolescence. |
| Axis II | (a) Personality disorders (b) Mental retardation | These are dysfunctional patterns of perceiving and responding to the world. |
| Axis III | General medical conditions | This axis codes physical problems relevant to understanding or treating an individual's psychological disorders on Axes I and II. |
| Axis IV | Psychosocial and environmental problems | This axis codes psychosocial and environmental stressors that may affect the diagnosis and treatment of an individual's disorder and the likelihood of recovery. |
| Axis V | Global assessment of functioning | This axis codes the individual's overall level of current functioning in the psychological, social, and occupational domains. |

from social norms and was accompanied by a profound disturbance in rational thinking and general emotional and thought processes. The *DSM-III* advisory committees felt that the terms *neurotic disorders* and *psychotic disorders* had become too general in their meaning to have much usefulness as diagnostic categories (however, they continue to be used by many psychiatrists and psychologists to characterise the general level of disturbance in a person).

Across the editions of the *DSM*, individual diagnoses have also come and gone. One of the best examples is *homosexuality*. You may recall from Chapter 11 that it was in 1973 that the American Psychiatric Association voted to remove homosexuality from the list of psychological disorders. Until that time, homosexuality appeared in the *DSM* as a bona fide mental illness. What changed the opinions of psychiatric experts was research data demonstrating the generally positive mental health of gay men and lesbians. Homosexuality is now simply considered a variant of sexual expression. It is relevant to a diagnosis in *DSM-IV-TR* only if an individual shows 'persistent and marked distress about sexual orientation' (*DSM-IV-TR*, 2000, p. 582). That diagnostic criterion could, of course, apply equally well to distressed heterosexuals.

Finally, critics of earlier editions of the *DSM* had been greatly concerned that no attention was paid to cultural variation in the incidence of psychological disorders. In *DSM-IV-TR*, the description of most disorders includes information about 'specific culture features'. Furthermore, an appendix describes about 25 *culture-bound syndromes*: 'recurrent, locality-specific patterns of aberrant behaviour and troubling experience that may or may not be linked to a particular *DSM-IV* diagnostic category' (*DSM-IV- TR*, 2000, p. 898). Here are some examples:

- *Boufée delirante.* 'A sudden outburst of agitated and aggressive behaviour, marked confusion, and psychomotor excitement' (p. 899); reported in West Africa and Haiti.

- *Koro.* 'An episode of sudden and intense anxiety that the penis (or, in females, the vulva and nipples) will recede into the body and possibly cause death' (p. 900); reported in south and east Asia.

- *Taijin kyofusho.* 'An individual's intense fear that his or her body, its parts or its functions, displease, embarrass, or are offensive to other people in appearance, odour, facial expressions, or movements' (p. 903); reported in Japan.

As we describe each major form of psychological disorder, it is important to bear in mind that not all cultures treat the same behaviours as normal or abnormal.

Before we turn to the causes of mental illness, we want to note a final aspect of classification that has evolved over time. Historically, people with mental illnesses were often labelled with the name of their disorder. For example, clinicians referred to people as 'schizophrenics' or 'phobics'. That didn't happen for physical illnesses—people with cancer were never known as 'cancerics.' Clinicians and researchers now take care to separate the person from the diagnosis. People have schizophrenic disorders or phobias, just as they have cancer or the flu. The hope is that appropriate treatments can alleviate each condition so they no longer apply to the person.

# THE AETIOLOGY OF PSYCHOPATHOLOGY

**Aetiology** refers to the factors that cause or contribute to the development of psychological and medical problems. Knowing why the disorder occurs, what its origins are, and how it affects thought and emotional and behavioural processes may lead to new ways of treating and, ideally, preventing it. An analysis of causality will be an important part of our discussion of each individual disorder. Here we introduce two general categories of causal factors: biological and psychological.

**aetiology** The causes of, or factor related to, the development of a disorder.

Biological approaches Building on the heritage of the medical model, modern biological approaches assume that psychological disturbances are directly attributable to underlying biological factors. Biological researchers and clinicians most often investigate structural abnormalities in the brain, biochemical processes and genetic influences.

The brain is a complex organ whose interrelated elements are held in delicate balance. Subtle alterations in its chemical messengers—the neurotransmitters—or in its tissue can have significant effects. Genetic factors, brain injury and infection are a few of the causes of these alterations. We have seen in earlier chapters that technological advances in brain-imaging techniques allow mental health professionals to view the structure of the brain and specific biochemical processes in living individuals without surgery. Using these techniques, biologically oriented researchers are discovering new links between psychological disorders and specific abnormalities in the brain. In addition, continuing advances in the field of behavioural genetics have improved researchers' abilities to identify the links between specific genes and the presence of psychological disorders. We will look to these different types of biological explanations throughout the chapter as we try to understand the nature of various forms of abnormality.

Psychological approaches Psychological approaches focus on the causal role of psychological or social factors in the development of psychopathology. These approaches perceive personal experiences, traumas, conflicts and environmental factors as the roots of psychological disorders. We will outline four dominant psychological models of abnormality: the psychodynamic, the behavioural, the cognitive and the sociocultural.

## *Psychodynamic*
Like the biological approach, the psychodynamic model holds that the causes of psychopathology are located inside the person. However, according to Sigmund Freud, who developed this model, the internal causal factors are psychological rather than biological. As we noted in earlier

chapters, Freud believed that many psychological disorders were simply an extension of 'normal' processes of psychic conflict and ego defence that all people experience. In the psychodynamic model, early childhood experiences shape both normal and abnormal behaviour.

In psychodynamic theory, behaviour is motivated by drives and wishes of which people are often unaware. Symptoms of psychopathology have their roots in *unconscious conflict* and thoughts. If the unconscious is conflicted and tension-filled, a person will be plagued by anxiety and other disorders. Much of this psychic conflict arises from struggles between the irrational, pleasure-seeking impulses of the *id* and the internalised social constraints imposed by the *superego*. The *ego* is normally the arbiter of this struggle; however, its ability to perform its function can be weakened by abnormal development in childhood. Individuals attempt to avoid the pain caused by conflicting motives and anxiety with *defence mechanisms*, such as repression or denial. Defences can become overused, distorting reality or leading to self-defeating behaviours. The individual may then expend so much psychic energy in defences against anxiety and conflict that there is little energy left to provide a productive and satisfying life.

## Behavioural

Because of their emphasis on observable responses, behavioural theorists have little use for hypothetical psychodynamic processes. These theorists argue that abnormal behaviours are acquired in the same fashion as healthy behaviours—through learning and reinforcement. They do not focus on internal psychological phenomena or early childhood experiences. Instead, they focus on the current behaviour and the current conditions or reinforcements that sustain the behaviour. The symptoms of psychological disorders arise because an individual has learned self-defeating or ineffective ways of behaving. By discovering the environmental contingencies that maintain any undesirable, abnormal behaviour, an investigator or clinician can then recommend treatment to change those contingencies and extinguish the unwanted behaviour. Behaviourists rely on both classical and operant conditioning models (recall Chapter 6) to understand the processes that can result in maladaptive behaviour.

## Cognitive

Cognitive perspectives on psychopathology are often used to supplement behavioural views. The cognitive perspective suggests that the origins of psychological disorders cannot always be found in the objective reality of stimulus environments, reinforcers and overt responses. What matters as well is the way people perceive or think about themselves and about their relations with other people and the environment. Among the cognitive variables that can guide—or misguide—adaptive responses are a person's perceived degree of control over important reinforcers, a person's beliefs in his or her ability to cope with threatening events, and interpretations of events in terms of situational or personal factors. The cognitive approach suggests that psychological problems are the result of distortions in perceptions of the reality of a situation, faulty reasoning or poor problem solving.

## Sociocultural

The sociocultural perspective on psychopathology emphasises the role culture plays in both the diagnosis and etiology of abnormal behaviour. We already gave you a taste of the impact of culture on diagnosis when we described the problem of objectivity. We suggested that behaviours are interpreted in different ways in different cultures: the threshold at which a certain type of behaviour will cause an individual problems in adjustment will depend, in part, on how that behaviour is viewed in its cultural context. With respect to aetiology, the particular cultural circumstances in which people live may define an environment that helps bring about distinctive types or subtypes of psychopathology. We gave you examples of such *culture-bound syndromes* in the section on classification.

We have now given you a general sense of the types of explanations researchers give for the emergence of mental illness. It is worth noting that contemporary researchers increasingly take an *interactionist* perspective on psychopathology, seeing it as the product of a complex interaction between a number of biological and psychological factors. For example, genetic predispositions may make a person vulnerable to a psychological disorder by affecting neurotransmitter levels or hormone levels, but psychological or social stresses or certain learned behaviours may be required for the disorder to develop fully.

Now that we have given you a basic framework for thinking about abnormality, we get to the core information that you will want to know—the causes and consequences of major psychological disorders, such as anxiety, depression and schizophrenia. For each category, we will begin by describing what sufferers experience and how they appear to observers. Then we will consider how each of the major biological and psychological approaches to etiology explains the development of these disorders.

There are many other categories of psychopathology that we will not have time to examine. However, the following bullet points outline the disorders not covered in this text:

- *Substance-use disorders* include both dependence on and abuse of alcohol and drugs. We discussed many issues of substance abuse in the broader context of states of consciousness (see Chapter 5).

- *Sexual disorders* involve problems with sexual inhibition or dysfunction and deviant sexual practices.

- *Eating disorders*, such as anorexia and bulimia, were discussed in Chapter 11.

As you read about the symptoms and experiences that are typical of the various psychological disturbances, you may begin to feel that some of the characteristics seem to apply to you—at least part of the time—or to someone you know. Some of the disorders that we will consider are not uncommon, so it would be surprising if they sounded completely alien. Many people have human frailties that appear on the list of criteria for a particular psychological disorder. Recognition of this familiarity can further your understanding of abnormal psychology, but remember that a diagnosis for any disorder depends on a number of criteria and requires the judgment of a trained mental health professional. Please resist the temptation to use this new knowledge to diagnose friends and family members as pathological. However, if the chapter leaves you uneasy about mental health issues, please note that most universities have counselling centres for students with such concerns.

## RECAP CHECKPOINT

### The nature of psychological disorders

- Abnormality is judged by the degree to which a person's actions resemble a set of indicators that include distress, maladaptiveness, irrationality, unpredictability, unconventionality, observer discomfort and violation of standards or societal norms.
- Objectivity is an important problem for discussions of mental illness.
- Classification systems for psychological disorders should provide a common shorthand for communicating about general types of psychopathologies and specific cases.
- The most widely accepted diagnostic and classification system is DSM-IV-TR.
- The biological approach to the etiology of mental illness concentrates on abnormalities in the brain, biochemical processes and genetic influences.
- Psychological approaches include psychodynamic, behavioural, cognitive and socio-cultural models.

## CONCEPT QUESTIONS

1. Jerry has such an overwhelming fear of spiders that he will not enter a room until someone he trusts assures him the room has no spiders in it. By what criteria might we decide that Jerry's behaviour is abnormal?

2. What are three important benefits provided by the classification of mental disorders?

3. Why does culture play a role in the diagnosis of psychopathology?

## CRITICAL THINKING

Consider the study in which David Rosenhan and seven other people were admitted to psychiatric hospitals. Why might they have chosen 'hallucinations' as their pretend symptom?

# ANXIETY DISORDERS

Everyone experiences anxiety or fear in certain life situations. For some people, however, anxiety becomes problematic enough to interfere with their ability to function effectively or enjoy everyday life. It has been estimated that 28.8 percent of the adult population has, at some time, experienced symptoms characteristic of the various **anxiety disorders** (Kessler et al., 2005a). Although anxiety plays a key role in each of these disorders, they differ in the extent to which anxiety is experienced, the severity of the anxiety and the situations that trigger the anxiety. We will review five major categories: generalised anxiety disorder, panic disorder, phobic disorder, obsessive-compulsive disorder and posttraumatic stress disorder. We then consider the causes of these disorders.

**anxiety disorders** Mental disorders marked by psychological arousal, feeling of tension, and intense apprehension without apparent reason.

## GENERALISED ANXIETY DISORDER

When a person feels anxious or worried most of the time for at least 6 months, when not threatened by any specific danger, clinicians diagnose **generalised anxiety disorder**. The anxiety is often focused on specific life circumstances, such as unrealistic concerns about finances or the wellbeing of a loved one. The way the anxiety is expressed—the specific symptoms—varies from person to person, but for a diagnosis of generalised anxiety disorder to be made, the patient must also suffer from at least three other symptoms, such as muscle tension, fatigue, restlessness, poor concentration, irritability or sleep difficulties. Among Australian. adults, approximately 5 percent have experienced generalised anxiety disorder (Kessler et al., 2005a).

Generalised anxiety disorder leads to impaired functioning because the person's worries cannot be controlled or put aside. With the focus of attention on the sources of anxiety, the individual cannot attend sufficiently to social or job obligations. These difficulties are compounded by the physical symptoms associated with the disorder.

**generalised anxiety disorder** An anxiety disorder in which an individual feels anxious most of the time for at least 6 months when not threatened by any specific danger or object.

For answers go to MyPsychLab!

## PANIC DISORDER

In contrast to the chronic presence of anxiety in generalised anxiety disorder, sufferers of **panic disorder** experience unexpected, severe *panic attacks* that may last only minutes. These attacks begin with a feeling of intense apprehension, fear or terror. Accompanying these feelings are physical symptoms of anxiety, including autonomic hyperactivity (such as rapid heart rate), dizziness, faintness, or sensations of choking or smothering. The attacks are unexpected in the sense that they are not brought about by something concrete in the situation. A panic disorder is diagnosed when an individual has recurrent unexpected panic attacks and also begins to have persistent concerns about the possibility of having more attacks. Panic disorder affects approximately 1.3% of all Australians (ABS, 2005).

In *DSM-IV-TR*, panic disorder must be diagnosed as occurring with or without the simultaneous presence of agoraphobia. **Agoraphobia** is an extreme fear of being in public places or open spaces from which escape may be difficult or embarrassing. Individuals with agoraphobia usually fear such places as crowded rooms, malls, buses and freeways. They are often afraid that, if they experience some kind of difficulty outside the home, such as a loss of bladder control or panic attack symptoms, help might not be available or the situation will be embarrassing to them. These fears deprive individuals of their freedom, and, in extreme cases, they become prisoners in their own homes.

Can you see why agoraphobia is related to panic disorder? For some (but not all) people who suffer from panic attacks, the dread of the next attack—the helpless feelings it engenders—can be enough to imprison them. The person suffering from agoraphobia may leave the safety of home but almost always with extreme anxiety.

## PHOBIAS

**Fear** is a rational reaction to an objectively identified external danger (such as a fire in one's home or a mugging attack) that may induce a person to flee or to attack in self-defence. In contrast, a person with a **phobia** suffers from a persistent and irrational fear of a specific object, activity, or situation that is excessive and unreasonable given the reality of the threat.

Many people feel uneasy about spiders or snakes (or even multiple-choice tests). These mild fears do not prevent people from carrying out their everyday activities. Phobias, however, interfere with adjustment, cause significant distress, and inhibit necessary action toward goals. Even a very specific, apparently limited phobia can have a great impact on one's whole life. *DSM-IV-TR* defines two categories of phobias: *social phobias* and *specific phobias* (see **Table 14.2**).

**panic disorder** An anxiety disorder in which sufferers experience unexpected, severe panic attacks that begin with a feeling of intense apprehension, fear or terror.

**fear** A rational reaction to an objectively identified external danger that may induce a person to flee or attack in self-defence.

**phobia** A persistent and irrational fear of a specific object, activity or situation that is excessive and unreasonable given the reality of the threat.

**agoraphobia** An extreme fear of being in public places or open spaces from which escape may be difficult or embarrassing.

Why might agoraphobia cause people to become 'prisoners' in their own homes?

### Table 14.2

#### Common phobias

Social phobias (fear of being observed doing something humiliating)
Specific phobias
Animal type
  Cats (ailurophobia)
  Dogs (cynophobia)
  Insects (insectophobia)
  Spiders (arachnophobia)
  Snakes (ophidiophobia)
  Rodents (rodentophobia)
Natural environment type
  Storms (brontophobia)
  Heights (acrophobia)
Blood–injection–injury type
  Blood (haemaphobia)
  Needles (belonephobia)
Situational type
  Closed spaces (claustrophobia)
  Railways (siderodromophobia)

**social phobia** A persistent, irrational fear that arises in anticipation of a public situation in which an individual can be observed by others.

**Social phobia** is a persistent, irrational fear that arises in anticipation of a public situation in which an individual can be observed by others. A person with a social phobia fears that he or she will act in ways that could be embarrassing. The person recognises that the fear is

What turns a harmless snake into a threatening object of phobia?

excessive and unreasonable yet feels compelled by the fear to avoid situations in which public scrutiny is possible. Social phobia often involves a self-fulfilling prophecy. A person may be so fearful of the scrutiny and rejection of others that enough anxiety is created to actually impair performance. Even when people with social phobias are successful in social circumstances, they do not allow that success to reflect positively on themselves (Wallace & Alden, 1997). Among Australian adults, 13 percent have experienced a social phobia (ABS).

**Specific phobias** occur in response to several different types of objects or situations. As shown in Table 14.2, specific phobias are further categorised into several subtypes. For example, an individual suffering from an *animal-type specific phobia* might have a phobic response to spiders. In each case, the phobic response is produced either in the presence of or in anticipation of the feared specific object or situation. Research suggests that between 5 and 12 percent of adults in the Australia have experienced a specific phobia (Kessler et al., 2005a).

## OBSESSIVE-COMPULSIVE DISORDER

Some people with anxiety disorders get locked into specific patterns of thought and behaviour. Consider the following case:

*Only a year or so ago, 17-year-old Jim seemed to be a normal adolescent with many talents and interests. Then, almost overnight, he was transformed into a lonely outsider, excluded from social life by his psychological disabilities. Specifically, he developed an obsession with washing. Haunted by the notion that he was dirty—in spite of what his senses told him—he began to spend more of his time cleansing himself of imaginary dirt. At first, his ritual washings were confined to weekends and evenings, but soon they began to consume all his time, forcing him to drop out of school. (Rapoport, 1989)*

Jim is suffering from a condition known as **obsessive-compulsive disorder (OCD)**, which has been estimated to affect 2–3 percent of Australians at some point during their lives (ABS 2006). *Obsessions* are thoughts, images or impulses (such as Jim's belief that he is unclean) that recur or persist despite a person's efforts to suppress them. Obsessions are experienced as an unwanted invasion of consciousness, they seem to be senseless or repugnant, and they are unacceptable to the person experiencing them. You probably have had some sort of mild obsessional experience, such as the intrusion of petty worries—'Did I really lock the door?'; or 'Did I turn off the oven?' The obsessive thoughts of people with obsessive-compulsive disorder are much more compelling, cause much more distress, and may interfere with their social or occupational functioning.

*Compulsions* are repetitive, purposeful *acts* (such as Jim's washing) performed according to certain rules or in a ritualised manner in response to an obsession. Compulsive behaviour is performed to reduce or prevent the discomfort associated with some dreaded situation, but it is either unreasonable or clearly excessive. Typical compulsions include irresistible urges to clean, to check that lights or appliances have been turned off, and to count objects or possessions.

At least initially, people with obsessive-compulsive disorder resist carrying out their compulsions. When they are calm, they view their compulsion as senseless. When anxiety rises, however, the power of the ritual compulsive behaviour to relieve tension seems irresistible. Part of the pain experienced by people with this mental problem is created by their frustration at recognising the irrationality or excessive nature of their obsessions without being able to eliminate them.

**obsessive-compulsive disorder (OCD)** A mental disorder characterised by obsessions—thoughts, images or impulses that persist despite efforts to suppress them—and compulsions—repetitive, purposeful acts performed in a ritualised manner.

**specific phobias** Phobias that occur in response to specific types of objects or situations.

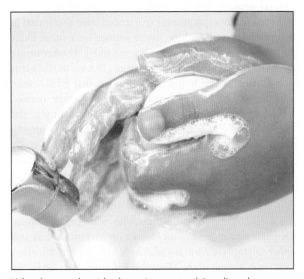

Why do people with obsessive-compulsive disorder engage in behaviours such as repetitive hand-washing?

# POSTTRAUMATIC STRESS DISORDER

In Chapter 12, we presented a discussion between two women who were still grappling with the after effects of rape. The conversation portrayed the two women's ongoing anxiety. One reported going through a 'long period of fear and anger' and having dreams of being assaulted in front of her dorm, with friends watching without coming to her rescue. The other, who had been raped while jogging, was still afraid to resume running: 'Every time I go jogging I have a perpetual fear. My pulse doubles. Of course I don't go jogging alone any more, but still the fear is there constantly.' These women suffer from posttraumatic stress disorder (PTSD), an anxiety disorder that is characterised by the persistent re-experience of traumatic events through distressing recollections, dreams, hallucinations or flashbacks. Individuals may develop PTSD in response to rape, life-threatening events or severe injury, and natural disasters. People develop PTSD both when they themselves have been the victim of the trauma and when they have witnessed others being victimised. People who suffer from PTSD are also likely to suffer simultaneously from other psychopathologies, such as major depression, substance-abuse problems and sexual dysfunction (Kilpatrick et al., 2003).

Research suggests that about 1.33 percent of the Australian public will experience PTSD at some point during their lifetime (ABS 2006). Surveys consistently reveal that around 80 percent of adults have experienced an event that could be defined as traumatic, such as a serious accident, a tragic death, or physical or sexual abuse (Green, 1994; Vrana & Lauterbach, 1994). One study with 1,824 Swedish adults found that 80.8 percent had experienced at least one traumatic event (Frans et al., 2005). In this sample, men had experienced more traumatic events than women, but women were twice as likely to develop PTSD. The researchers suggested that women's greater distress in response to traumatic events helped explain this difference. The gender differences between trauma symptoms experienced were also found in a similar Australian study, where women were more likely to be at risk to developing symptoms of PTSD after injury or abuse. Data was obtained from 10,641 participants across Australia with findings indicating that PTSD onset was more likely to occur with women who never married or who were divorced or separated. Interestingly, the likelihood of PTSD onset was found to be lower among those women aged over 55. The conclusion of the study suggests that being at risk for PTSD symptoms correlates more with those women who are not in supporting or lasting relationships (Creamer et al, 2001).

Much attention has focused on the prevalence of PTSD in the wake of traumas with widespread impact. Of particular interest is the impact on asylum seekers and other migrants to Australia who have been kept in detention centres as a result of the *Migration Reform Act* passed by the federal government in 1992. The Australian Psychological Society has 'categorically condemn[ed] the practice of detaining child asylum seekers and their families, on the grounds that it is not commensurate with psychological best practice concerning children's development and mental health and wellbeing' (HREOC 1998, 2004). Australian studies have supported this contention, and documented the prevalence of PTSD in asylum seeker 'communities'. In a 1998 study by Dr. Zachary Steel (2001) (and similar studies by Sultan and Sullivan, 2001) highlight the impact, particularly on children, of being confined to such hostile environments for long periods of time. In Steel's study, 86% of adult detainees and 50 percent of children were found to be suffering from PTSD. **Table 14.3** indicates the specific feelings of trauma felt by detainees once they were 'released' into the community by the grant of either Temporary Protection Visas or Permanent Citizenship.

Other tragic events in Australia, such as the massive bush fires experienced on 'Ash Wednesday' during 16th February 1983 and the Newcastle earthquake in 1989, left 18% of victims, respectively for each incident, with symptoms of PTSD.

Posttraumatic stress disorder severely disrupts sufferers' lives. How do researchers go about the complex task of exploring the origins of PTSD and other anxiety disorders? Understanding the origins gives hope to eliminating the psychological distress.

# CAUSES OF ANXIETY DISORDERS

How do psychologists explain the development of anxiety disorders? Each of the four etiological approaches we have outlined (biological, psychodynamic, behavioural and cognitive) emphasises different factors. Let's analyse how each adds something unique to the understanding of anxiety disorders.

## Biological

Various investigators have suggested that anxiety disorders have biological origins. One theory attempts to explain why certain phobias, such as those for spiders or heights, are more common than fears of other dangers, such as electricity. Because many fears are shared across cultures, it has been proposed that, at one time in the evolutionary past, certain fears enhanced our ancestors' chances of survival. Perhaps humans are born with a predisposition to fear whatever is related to sources of serious danger in the evolutionary past. This preparedness hypothesis suggests that we carry around an evolutionary tendency to respond quickly and 'thoughtlessly' to once-feared stimuli (Öhman & Mineka, 2001). However, this hypothesis does not explain types of phobias that develop in response to objects or situations that would not have had survival meaning over evolutionary history, like fear of needles or driving or elevators.

The ability of certain drugs to relieve and of others to produce symptoms of anxiety offers evidence of a biological role in anxiety disorders (Nutt & Malizia, 2001). For example, recall from Chapter 3 that when the level of the neurotransmitter GABA in the brain becomes low, people often experience feelings of anxiety. As we will see in Chapter 15, drugs that affect GABA levels are used as successful treatments for some types of anxiety disorders.

## Table 14.3

Living difficulties causing serious/very serious stress since release from detention (holders of temporary protection visas [TPVs]) or arrival in Australia (holders of permanent protection visas [PPVs])

| Living difficulties | TPV (n = 49) | PPV (n = 67) |
|---|---|---|
| **Protection concerns** | | |
| Worry about family in home country | 47 (96%) | 0 (0) |
| Separation from family | 47 (96%) | 5 (7%) |
| Fear of repatriation | 45 (92%) | 0 (0) |
| Unable to return home in an emergency | 48 (98%) | 0 (0) |
| Interviews by immigration officers | 36 (73%) | 1 (1%) |
| Conflict with immigration officers | 35 (71%) | 0 (0) |
| **Access to health and welfare** | | |
| Unemployment | 45 (92%) | 7 (10%) |
| Insufficient money to buy food, pay rent and buy necessities | 45 (92%) | 9 (13%) |
| Difficulty obtaining government welfare | 47 (96%) | 4 (6%) |
| Bad working conditions | 43 (92%) | 10 (10%) |
| Difficulty obtaining help from charities | 40 (82%) | 16 (24%) |
| Worry about not getting medical treatment | 38 (78%) | 1 (1%) |
| Poor access to emergency care | 37 (76%) | 1 (1%) |
| Poor access for long-term health problems | 34 (69%) | 1 (1%) |
| Poor access to dental care | 31 (63%) | 1 (1%) |
| Poor access to counselling | 16 (33%) | 1 (1%) |
| **Resettlement experiences** | | |
| Communication difficulties | 49 (100%) | 36 (54%) |
| Discrimination | 38 (78%) | 1 (1%) |
| Loneliness and boredom | 47 (96%) | 2 (3%) |
| Discrimination by other ethnic groups | 38 (78%) | 1 (1%) |
| Isolation | 45 (92%) | 10 (15%) |
| Conflict with other ethnic groups in Australia | 34 (69%) | 4 (6%) |
| Lack of access to preferred foods | 29 (59%) | 3 (4%) |

All contrasts between TPV and PPV holders significant at $P < 0.001$ using Fisher's exact test.

From Momartin et al. (2006). A comparison of the mental health of refugees with temporary versus permanent protection visas, 185: 357–361. © 2006 *Medical Journal of Australia*. Reproduced with permission.

Researchers are also using imaging techniques to examine the brain bases of these disorders. Consider a study of posttraumatic stress disorder.

Some people who suffer traumatic events develop PTSD; whereas others do not. A team of researchers used fMRI scans to explore differences in patterns of brain activity for individuals in those two categories (Lanius et al., 2003). The study focused on the brain activity that arose when the individuals recalled memories of sad, anxious and traumatic events. As shown in **Figure 14.2**, those individuals who had experienced a trauma but not developed PTSD showed more activity in areas of the brain (the thalamus and the anterior cingulate) that play a role in emotional processing compared to individuals whose traumatic experiences led to PTSD. These differences in brain activity applied for all three types of memories (i.e., sad, anxious and traumatic). The generality of the finding suggests that the traumatic experiences for the individuals who developed PTSD led to a broad disruption of the way in which their brains respond to emotional events.

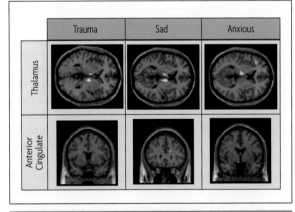

## Figure 14.2

Brain activity and emotional memories
The study compared individuals who developed PTSD in response to traumatic experiences with those who did not. Members from each group recalled emotional memories while undergoing fMRI scans. The figure shows more brain activity for the group of individuals without PTSD across memories of traumatic, sad and angry events.

This study illustrates why brain-imaging techniques can help deepen the understanding of the biological bases of anxiety disorders. Similar results have emerged for other disorders. For example, PET scans have revealed a difference in the function of GABA receptors between the brains of individuals who suffer from panic disorder and those of control individuals (Malizia et al., 1998). These differences may help explain the onset of panic disorder. MRI techniques have revealed very widespread abnormalities in OCD patients' brains with respect to a much lower volume of myelinated nerve fibres than in normal brains (Jenike et al., 1996). Researchers are trying to understand the relationship between these brain abnormalities and the symptoms of OCD.

Finally, family and twin studies suggest that there is a genetic basis for the predisposition to experience anxiety disorders (Hettema et al., 2005). For example, the probability that a pair of male identical twins both suffered from a social or specific phobia was consistently greater than the probability that both male fraternal twins were sufferers (Kessler et al., 2001). Still, it's important to remember that nature and nurture always interact. For example, recall from Chapter 13 that many aspects of personality are heritable. Research suggests that part of the influence of genes on PTSD arises because people with different personality traits make life choices that decrease or increase the probability that they will experience traumas (Stein et al., 2002).

## Psychodynamic

The psychodynamic model begins with the assumption that the symptoms of anxiety disorders come from underlying psychic conflicts or fears. The symptoms are attempts to protect the individual from psychological pain. Thus panic attacks are the result of unconscious conflicts bursting into consciousness. Suppose, for example, a child represses conflicting thoughts about his or her wish to escape a difficult home environment. In later life, a phobia may be activated by an object or situation that symbolises the conflict. A bridge, for example, might come to symbolise the path that the person must traverse from the world of home and family to the outside world. The sight of a bridge would then force the unconscious conflict into awareness, bringing with it the fear and anxiety common to phobias. Avoiding bridges would be a symbolic attempt to stay clear of anxiety about the childhood experiences at home.

In obsessive-compulsive disorders, the obsessive behaviour is seen as an attempt to displace anxiety created by a related but far more feared desire or conflict. By substituting an obsession that symbolically captures the forbidden impulse, a person gains some relief. For example, the obsessive fears of dirt experienced by Jim, the adolescent we described earlier, may have their roots in the conflict between his desire to become sexually active and his fear of 'dirtying' his reputation. Compulsive preoccupation with carrying out a minor ritualistic task also allows the individual to avoid the original issue that is creating unconscious conflict.

## Behavioural

Behavioural explanations of anxiety focus on the way symptoms of anxiety disorders are reinforced or conditioned. Investigators do not search for underlying unconscious conflicts or early childhood experiences, because these phenomena can't be observed directly. As we saw in Chapter 6, behavioural theories are often used to explain the development of phobias, which are seen as classically conditioned fears: Recall Little Albert, in whom John Watson and Rosalie Rayner instilled a fear of a white rat (see page 183). The behavioural account suggests that a previously neutral object or situation becomes a stimulus for a phobia by being paired with a frightening experience. For example, a child whose mother yells a warning when he or she approaches a snake may develop a phobia about snakes. After this experience, even thinking about snakes may produce a wave of fear. Phobias continue to be maintained by the reduction in anxiety that occurs when a person withdraws from the feared situation.

A behavioural analysis of obsessive-compulsive disorders suggests that compulsive behaviours tend to reduce the anxiety associated with obsessive thoughts—thus reinforcing the compulsive behaviour. For example, if a woman fears contamination by touching garbage, then washing her hands reduces the anxiety and is therefore reinforcing. In parallel to phobias, obsessive-compulsive disorders continue to be maintained by the reduction in anxiety that follows from the compulsive behaviours.

## Cognitive

Cognitive perspectives on anxiety concentrate on the perceptual processes or attitudes that may distort a person's estimate of the danger that he or she is facing. A person may either overestimate the nature or reality of a threat or underestimate his or her ability to cope with the threat effectively. For example, before delivering a speech to a large group, a person with a social phobia may feed his or her anxiety:

> What if I forget what I was going to say? I'll look foolish in front of all these people. Then I'll get even more nervous and start to perspire, and my voice will shake, and I'll look even sillier. Whenever people see me from now on, they'll remember me as the foolish person who tried to give a speech.

People who suffer from anxiety disorders may often interpret their own distress as a sign of impending disaster. Their reaction may set off a vicious cycle in which the person fears disaster, which leads to an increase in anxiety, which in turn worsens the anxiety sensations and confirms the person's fears (Beck & Emery, 1985).

Psychologists have tested this cognitive account by measuring *anxiety sensitivity*: individuals' beliefs that bodily symptoms—such as shortness of breath or heart palpitations—may have harmful consequences. People high in anxiety sensitivity are likely to agree with statements such as 'When I notice that my heart is beating rapidly, I worry that I might have a heart attack.' In one study, researchers assessed the anxiety sensitivity of a group of students who were about to undergo a stressful course of Air Force Academy basic cadet training. Approximately 20 percent of those students who measured above the 90th percentile on anxiety sensitivity experienced panic attacks during the 5-week course, compared to 6 percent for the rest of the group (Schmidt et al., 1997). These data suggest that some individuals may experience panic attacks because they interpret their bodily arousal in a fearful fashion.

Research has also found that anxious patients contribute to the *maintenance* of their anxiety by employing cognitive biases that highlight the threatening stimuli. For example, one study examined people's ability to name either body-related words (e.g., *dizzy, fainting,* and *breathless*) versus control words (e.g., *delicate, slow,* and *friendly*) when they were presented on a computer screen for only 1/100th of a second. Individuals who suffered from panic disorder showed much greater ability to recognise the body-related words than did the healthy controls (Pauli et al., 1997). Similarly, patients whose symptoms of obsessive-compulsive disorder focused on issues of cleanliness, watched a researcher touch a series of objects with a 'clean and unused' tissue or a 'dirty and already used' tissue. In a later memory test, these OCD patients showed greater ability to recall which objects were 'dirty' than which were 'clean' (Ceschi et al., 2003). Studies of this type confirm that people suffering from anxiety disorders focus their attention on aspects of the world that may help to sustain their anxiety.

Each of the major approaches to anxiety disorders may explain part of the etiological puzzle. Continued research of each approach will clarify causes and, therefore, potential avenues for treatment. Now that you have this basic knowledge about anxiety disorders, we'd like you to consider the next of the three major categories of abnormality we are covering in some detail—*mood disorders*.

# MOOD DISORDERS

There have almost certainly been times in your life when you would have described yourself as terribly depressed or incredibly happy. For some people, however, extremes in mood come to disrupt normal life experiences. A mood disorder is an emotional disturbance, such as severe depression or depression alternating with mania. Researchers estimate that 20.8 percent of adults have suffered from mood disorders (Kessler et al., 2005a). We will describe two major categories: major depressive disorder and bipolar disorder.

## MAJOR DEPRESSIVE DISORDER

Depression has been characterised as the 'common cold of psychopathology', both because it occurs so frequently and because almost everyone has experienced elements of the full-scale disorder at some time in his or her life. Everyone has, at one time or another, experienced grief after the loss of a loved one or felt sad or upset when failing to achieve a desired goal. These sad feelings are only one symptom experienced by people suffering from a **major depressive disorder** (see **Table 14.4**). Consider one

**major depressive disorder** A mood disorder characterised by intense feelings of depression over an extended time, without the manic high phase of bipolar depression.

### Table 14.4

Characteristics of major depressive disorder

| Characteristics | Example |
| --- | --- |
| Dysphoric mood | Sad, blue, hopeless; loss of interest or pleasure in almost all usual activities |
| Appetite | Significant weight loss (while not dieting) or weight gain |
| Sleep | Insomnia or hypersomnia (sleeping too much) |
| Motor activity | Markedly slowed down (motor retardation) or agitated |
| Guilt | Feelings of worthlessness; self-reproach |
| Concentration | Diminished ability to think or concentrate; forgetfulness |
| Suicide | Recurrent thoughts of death; suicidal ideas or attempts |

For answers go to MyPsychLab!

**mypsychlab** *where learning comes to life!*

individual's description of his struggle to carry out normal daily tasks while in the depths of depression:

> *It seemed to take the most colossal effort to do simple things. I remember bursting into tears because I had used up the cake of soap that was in the shower. I cried because one of the keys stuck for a second on my computer. I found everything excruciatingly difficult, and so, for example, the prospect of lifting the telephone receiver seemed to me like bench-pressing two hundred kilograms. The reality that I had to put on not just one but two socks and then two shoes so overwhelmed me that I wanted to go back to bed.*
> *(Solomon, 2001, pp. 85–86)*

This excerpt illustrates some vivid consequences of major depressive disorder.

People diagnosed with depression differ in terms of the severity and duration of their symptoms. Many individuals struggle with clinical depression for only several weeks at one point in their lives, whereas others experience depression episodically or chronically for many years. Estimates of the prevalence of mood disorders reveal that about 21 percent of females and 13 percent of males suffer a major depression at some time in their lives (Kessler et al., 1994).

Depression takes an enormous toll on those afflicted, on their families, and on society. A study undertaken on behalf of the World Health Organisation estimated the loss of healthy life years that could be attributed to physical and mental illnesses (Murray & Lopez, 1996). In this analysis, major depressive disorder ranked second (behind heart disease) in terms of the burden it places on people's lives around the world. In Australia, depression accounts for the majority of all mental hospital admissions, but it is still believed to be underdiagnosed and undertreated. Statistics indicate that only 50 percent of individuals sought treatment in the first year after a major depressive episode (Beyond Blue website: www.beyondblue.org.au).

This is further evidenced in a study conducted in Australia, which surveyed 1312 adults in various rural and urban community settings. The study found a longer period of time between onset of a major depressive episode and seeking treatment for those in rural and remote areas of Australia. This may be due to poor mental health services in these areas, but is thought to be more likely due to the stigma behind seeking mental health treatment in smaller country towns (Barney, et al. 2006).

## BIPOLAR DISORDER

**Bipolar disorder** is characterised by periods of severe depression alternating with manic episodes. A person experiencing a **manic episode** generally acts and feels unusually elated and expansive. However, sometimes the individual's predominant mood is irritability rather than elation, especially if the person feels thwarted in some way. During a manic episode, a person often experiences an inflated sense of self-esteem or an unrealistic belief that he or she possesses special abilities or powers. The person

What are some differences between the occasional feelings of unhappiness that most people feel and the symptoms of major depressive disorder?

may feel a dramatically decreased need to sleep and may engage excessively in work or in social or other pleasurable activities.

Caught up in a manic mood, the person shows unwarranted optimism, takes unnecessary risks, promises anything, and may give everything away. Consider this first-person account:

> *Manic depression is about buying a dozen bottles of tomato sauce and all eight bottles of Windex in stock at the 7/11 at 4:00 A.M., flying from Zurich to the Bahamas and back to Zurich in three days to balance the hot and cold weather, [and] carrying $20,000 in $100 bills in your shoes into the country on your way back from Tokyo. . . . It's about blips and burps of madness, moments of absolute delusion, bliss, and irrational and dangerous choices made in order to heighten pleasure and excitement and to ensure a sense of control. (Behrman, 2002)*

**bipolar disorder** A mood disorder characterised by alternating periods of depression and mania.

**manic episode** A component of bipolar disorder characterised by periods of extreme elation, unbounded euphoria without sufficient reason, and grandiose thoughts or feelings about personal abilities.

When the mania begins to diminish, people are left trying to deal with the damage and predicaments they created during their period of frenzy. Thus manic episodes almost always give way to periods of severe depression.

The duration and frequency of the mood disturbances in bipolar disorder vary from person to person. Some people experience long periods of normal functioning punctuated by occasional short manic or depressive episodes. A small percentage of unfortunate individuals go right from manic episodes to clinical depression and back again in continuous, unending cycles that are devastating to them, their families, their friends and their co-workers. While manic, they may gamble away life savings or give lavish gifts to strangers, acts that later add to guilt feelings when they are in the depressed phase. Bipolar disorder is rarer than major depressive disorder, occurring in about 3.9 percent of adults (Kessler et al., 2005a).

# CAUSES OF MOOD DISORDERS

What factors are involved in the development of mood disorders? We will address this question from the biological, psychodynamic, behavioural and cognitive perspectives. Note that, because of its prevalence, major depressive disorder has been studied more extensively than bipolar disorder. Our review will reflect that distribution of research.

## Biological

Several types of research provide clues to the contribution of biology to mood disorders. For example, the ability of different drugs to relieve manic and depressive symptoms provides evidence that different brain states underlie the two extremes of bipolar disorder. Reduced levels of two chemical messengers in the brain, serotonin and norepinephrine, have been linked to depression; increased levels of these neurotransmitters are associated with mania. However, the exact biochemical mechanisms of mood disorders have not yet been discovered (Nestler et al., 2002).

Researchers have begun to use brain-imaging techniques to understand the causes and consequences of mood disorders (Liotti et al., 2002; Strakowski et al., 2002). For example, researchers have used fMRI to demonstrate that the brains of people who suffer from bipolar disorder respond differently when they are in depressed versus manic states (Blumberg et al., 2003). **Figure 14.3** reports the data from 36 individuals with bipolar disorder. At the time of the study, 11 were in elevated moods, 10 were in depressed moods and 15 were in *euthymic* (or balanced) emotional states. All of the individuals performed the same cognitive task—naming the colours in which words were printed—while undergoing fMRI scans. Figure 14.3 indicates that particular regions of cortex were more active or less active depending on each individual's particular phase of bipolar disorder.

The contribution of biology to the etiology of mood disorders is also confirmed by evidence that the incidence of mood disorder is influenced by genetic factors (Johnson et al., 2002). Studies of twins show that when one identical twin is afflicted by a mood disorder, there is a 67 percent

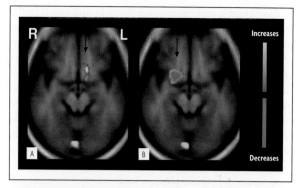

## Figure 14.3

Brain activity and bipolar disorder
Individuals with bipolar disorder underwent fMRI scans while performing a cognitive task. The brain response was different in an area known as the *caudal ventral prefrontal cortex* (cVPFC) depending on whether the individuals were experiencing elevated, depressed or balanced moods. As shown in A, individuals in depressed moods showed increased left cVPFC activity by comparison to those in balanced moods. As shown in B, individuals in elevated moods showed reduced right cVPFC activity by comparison to those in balanced moods.

chance that the second twin will also have the disorder; the figure for fraternal twins, who do not share identical genetic material, is only 20 percent (Ciaranello & Ciaranello, 1991; Gershon et al., 1987). You will see in the Psychology In Your Life box that researchers have begun to make progress identifying the actual genes that have an impact on individuals' predispositions to experience mood disorders.

Let's see now what the three major psychological approaches can add to your understanding of the onset of mood disorders.

## Psychodynamic

In the psychodynamic approach, unconscious conflicts and hostile feelings that originate in early childhood are seen to play key roles in the development of depression. Freud was struck by the degree of self-criticism and guilt that depressed people displayed. He believed that the source of this self-reproach was anger, originally directed at someone else, that had been turned inward against the self. The anger was believed to be tied to an especially intense and dependent childhood relationship, such as a parent–child relationship, in which the person's needs or expectations were not met. Losses, real or symbolic, in adulthood reactivate hostile feelings, now directed toward the person's own ego, creating the self-reproach that is characteristic of depression.

## Behavioural

Rather than searching for the roots of depression in the unconscious, the behavioural approach focuses on the effects of the amount of positive reinforcement and punishments a person receives (Lewinsohn, 1975; Lewinsohn et al., 1985). In this view, depressed feelings result when an individual receives insufficient positive reinforcements and experiences many punishments in the environment following a loss or other major life changes. Without sufficient positive reinforcement, a person begins to feel sad and withdraws. This state of sadness is initially reinforced by increased attention and sympathy from others (Biglan, 1991). Typically, however, friends who at first respond with support grow tired of the depressed person's negative moods and attitudes and begin to avoid him or her. This reaction eliminates another source of positive reinforcement, plunging the person further into depression. Research also shows that depressed people tend to underestimate positive feedback and overestimate negative feedback (Kennedy & Craighead, 1988; Nelson & Craighead, 1977).

## Cognitive

At the centre of the cognitive approach to depression are two theories. One theory suggests that negative *cognitive sets*—'set' patterns of perceiving the world—lead people to take a negative view of events in their lives for which they feel responsible. The second theory, the *explanatory style* model, proposes that depression arises from the belief that one has little or no personal control over significant life events. Each of these models explains some aspects of the experience of depression. Let's see how.

**Aaron Beck** (1983, 1985, 1988), a leading researcher on depression, has developed the theory of cognitive sets. Beck has argued that depressed people have three types of negative cognitions, which he calls the *cognitive triad* of depression: negative views of themselves, negative views of ongoing experiences, and negative views of the future. Depressed people tend to view themselves as inadequate or defective in some way, to interpret ongoing experiences in a negative way, and to believe that the future will continue to bring suffering and difficulties. This pattern of negative thinking clouds all experiences and produces the other characteristic signs of depression. An individual who always anticipates a negative outcome is not likely to be motivated to pursue any goal, leading to the *paralysis of will* that is prominent in depression.

In the explanatory style view, pioneered by Martin Seligman (see Chapter 11), individuals believe, correctly or not, that they cannot control future outcomes that are important to them. Seligman's theory evolved from research that demonstrated depression-like symptoms in dogs (and later in other species). Seligman and Maier (1967) subjected dogs to painful, unavoidable shocks: no matter what the dogs did, there was no way to escape the shocks. The dogs developed what Seligman and Maier called **learned helplessness**. Learned helplessness is marked by three types of deficits: *motivational deficits*—the dogs were slow to initiate known actions; *emotional deficits*—they appeared rigid, listless, frightened and distressed; and *cognitive deficits*—they demonstrated poor learning in new situations. Even when put in a situation in which they could, in fact, avoid shock, they did not learn to do so (Maier & Seligman, 1976).

Seligman believed that depressed people are also in a state of learned helplessness: They have an expectancy that nothing they can do matters (Abramson et al., 1978; Peterson & Seligman, 1984; Seligman, 1975). However, the emergence of this state depends, to a large extent, on how individuals explain their life events. As we discussed in Chapter 11, there are three dimensions of explanatory style: *internal-external*, *global-specific* and *stable-unstable*. Suppose that you have just received a poor grade on a psychology exam. You attribute the negative outcome on the exam to an internal factor ('I'm stupid'), which makes you feel sad, rather than to an external one ('The exam was really hard'), which would have made you angry. You could have chosen a less stable internal quality than intelligence to explain your performance ('I was tired that day'). Rather than attributing your performance to an internal, stable factor that has global or far-reaching influence (stupidity), you could even have limited your explanation to the psychology exam or course ('I'm not good at psychology courses'). Explanatory style theory suggests that individuals who attribute failure to internal, stable and global causes are vulnerable to depression. This prediction has been confirmed repeatedly (Peterson & Vaidya, 2001; Seligman, 1991).

Once people begin to experience the negative moods associated with major depressive disorder, ordinary cognitive processes make it more difficult for them to escape those moods. Recall from Chapter 12 that people have a general tendency toward mood-congruent processing: they are sensitised to process and retrieve information that is congruent with their current mood state. Research has demonstrated the impact of mood-congruent processing for people suffering from depression.

A team of researchers recruited 26 participants who were currently experiencing depression, 19 participants who had recovered from depression, and 29 control participants with no history of depression (Rottenberg et al., 2006). The participants underwent a structured interview in which they attempted to report their happiest and saddest life events. The interviewers allowed participants as much time as they needed to produce those memories. The interviews were videotaped. The mood-congruency hypothesis suggests that people with depression would have particular difficulty retrieving happy events. Research assistants who were unaware of each participant's depression status (i.e., currently depressed, recovered or control) evaluated each videotape to assess how much effort the interviewers expended to elicit happy and sad memories. As shown in **Figure 14.4**, participants who were currently depressed had particular difficulty retrieving happy memories. Further analyses demonstrated that depressed participants also generated happy memories that had the least specific content.

This research demonstrates that people with major depressive disorder find it difficult to remember anything happy about their lives. You can understand how this memory bias could help make depression feel inescapable.

In Chapter 15, we will see that insights generated from cognitive theories of depression have given rise to

**learned helplessness**
A general pattern of nonresponding in the presence of noxious stimuli that often follows after an organism has previously experienced noncontingent, inescapable aversive stimuli.

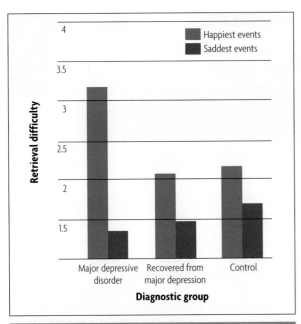

## Figure 14.4

**Mood-congurent processing in major depressive disorder**
Participants who were experiencing major depressive disorder had the most difficulty recalling the happiest events from their lives. Participants who had recovered from depression showed a retrieval pattern that was very much like control group participants who had never experienced depression.

From Rottenberg, Hildner & Gotlib, "Idiographic autobiographical memories in major depressive disorder," *Cognition and Emotion*, *20*(1), p. 124, by kind permission of Psychology Press, www.psychpress.co.uk/journals.asp, 2006.

successful forms of therapy. For now, there are two other important aspects of the study of depression that we will review: the large differences between the prevalence of depression in men and women and the link between depression and suicide.

## GENDER DIFFERENCES IN DEPRESSION

One of the central questions of research on depression is why women are afflicted twice as often as men (Kessler, 2003). Estimates of the prevalence of mood disorders reveal that about 21 percent of females and 13 percent of males suffer a major depression at some time in their lives (Kessler et al., 1994). One factor that contributes to this difference is, unfortunately, quite straightforward: On average, women experience more negative events and life stressors than men do (Hankin & Abramson, 2001; Nolen-Hoeksema, 2002). For example, women have a greater likelihood of experiencing physical or sexual abuse, and they are more likely to live in poverty while being the primary caregiver for children and elderly parents. Thus women's lives provide more of the types of experiences that lay the groundwork for serious depression.

Other gender differences explain why women may become more depressed once that groundwork has been laid. For example, women may be more likely to have the type of internal–global–stable explanatory style. There are also other cognitive factors at work. Research by **Susan Nolen-Hoeksema** (2002; Nolen-Hoeksema et al., 1999) points to the response styles of men and women once they begin to experience negative moods. According to this view, when women experience sadness, they tend to think about the possible causes and implications of their feelings. In contrast, men attempt actively to distract themselves from depressed feelings, either by focusing on something else or by engaging in a physical activity that will take their minds off their current mood state. This model suggests that it is the more thoughtful, *ruminative* response style of women, the tendency to focus obsessively on their problems, that increases women's vulnerability to depression. From a cognitive approach, paying attention to your negative moods can increase your thoughts of negative events, which eventually increases the quantity and/or the intensity of negative feelings. Men who ruminate are also at risk for depression. The gender difference emerges because more women ruminate (Nolen-Hoeksema et al., 1999).

There is a relationship between the gender differences in life experiences and the gender differences in cognitive styles. Researchers believe that women might, for example, explain negative events in ways different from men because they have more of them to explain (Hankin & Abramson, 2001). Suppose bad events happen to you with great frequency. Wouldn't you start to attribute those events to something about you rather than something about the world? This overall pattern suggests that the gender

What factors help explain why more women than men experience depression?

# PSYCHOLOGY *in your life*

## HOW CAN WE PINPOINT INTERACTIONS OF NATURE AND NURTURE?

Throughout this chapter, we have asserted that major types of mental illnesses have a genetic component. The majority of those claims have been based on methods that should be quite familiar to you by this point in *Psychology and Life*. Researchers, for example, compare the rate at which monozygotic and dizygotic twins share the same psychopathology to offer estimates of the heritability of each type of disorder (Coolidge et al., 2001; Hettema et al., 2001). However, in recent years, researchers have begun to move beyond calculations of heritability to pinpoint the actual differences in genetic material that predispose some individuals to experience mental illness. Let's consider a study that establishes an important relationship between genetic variation and life experiences in the etiology of depression.

A paper, just published in the *British Journal of Psychiatry* and based on landmark research from Brain Sciences UNSW, has found more than a fifth of the population has a genetic predisposition to depression in response to a series of stressful life events.

Brain Sciences UNSW represents researchers from the University of New South Wales (UNSW) and its affiliated research institutes and teaching hospitals, including the Prince of Wales Medical Research Institute, Black Dog Institute, Garvan Institute of Medical Research, St Vincent's Hospital and Prince of Wales Hospital.

The researchers based their findings on DNA samples of a group of 128 people who have been monitored for over 25 years for depression onset and major life events. Forty-two percent met criteria for lifetime major depression.

'We have been following a group of school teachers who graduated in 1978', said the lead author of the paper, UNSW Associate Professor of Psychiatry Kay Wilhelm, who is based at St Vincent's Hospital in Sydney. 'We've been catching up with them every five years since, to see if there has been any onset of depression and if there have been any major life events.'

'There is an 80 percent chance that those with the genetic predisposition will become depressed, if there are three or more negative life events in a year', said the geneticist on the paper, Professor Peter Schofield, who is Executive Director of the Prince of Wales Medical Research Institute (POWMRI).

'This contrasts with some people who have genetic resilience against depression', said Professor Schofield. 'Even in similar situations, there's only a thirty percent chance of them becoming depressed.'

There are three different genetic types in the population:

- 21 percent of people have the genotype that predisposes them to depression
- 26 percent of people have the genotype with resilience to depression
- 53 percent of people have a mix of the two genotypes.

The research also showed there was a 'tipping point' in regards to environmental factors.

'It's not just one negative life event, such as a health crisis', said Professor Mitchell, Head of the UNSW School of Psychiatry and Convenor of Brain Sciences UNSW. 'The critical issue here is when you're exposed to a series of life events during a period of a year. There is a threshold.'

'Our research is significant because there are social, psychological and genetic aspects to it', said Professor Schofield. 'While there is plenty of evidence surrounding the significance of family history of depression, until now there has been very little idea about the specific genes involved.'

'We already had a chart for each individual's life events and whether or not they had had a depressive episode', said Professor Wilhelm, who has tracked the teachers for most of her career with UNSW Professor Gordon Parker, from the Black Dog Institute. 'Now the genetic tests back that up. We are the first study to be able to look at the genetics and the five years leading up to the first depressive episode.'

'The research has some very significant implications', said Professor Wilhelm. 'Perhaps you could reduce the likelihood of depression amongst those with the vulnerable genotype, by training them up in terms of improving their coping styles and stress responses.

'Eventually you might be able to better identify those who are likely to be at risk, suggest psychological treatment at times and even work out the best kind of antidepressant to use, if the need arises.'

Based on media release from UNSW Media Unit, 1 March 2006. 'Nature, Nuture and the Risk of Depression' University of NSW. Accessed from <http://www.powmri.edu.au/pdf/Media%20Releases/DEPRESSION_GENETICS_FINAL.pdf>

differences in depression will endure as long as gender differences in life experiences endure.

## SUICIDE

'The will to survive and succeed had been crushed and defeated. . . . There comes a time when all things cease to shine, when the rays of hope are lost' (Shneidman, 1987, p. 57). This sad statement by a suicidal young man reflects the most extreme consequence of any psychological disorder—*suicide*. Although most depressed people do not commit suicide, analyses suggest that many suicides are attempted by those who are suffering from depression (Conner et al., 2001). In the general Australian population, the number of deaths officially designated as suicide is approximately 21 persons per 100,000 population, per year. In the Indigenous population, especially Aboriginals who live in the Northern Territory, the suicide rate per year is much higher and is estimated to be 66 persons per 100,000 population – more than 3 times higher than the general Australian population suicide statistics (Measey, et al., 2006). Indigenous males 25-44 years are in fact the most at risk group in the country (Trewen & Madden, ABS, 2005). Research into suicide rates in rural settings by Judd, Cooper, Fraser and Davis (2006) highlight that the reasons for this alarmingly high rate are a combination of 'compositional', 'contextual' and 'collective' variables,

Highly successful individuals, such as rugby league star Andrew Johns, are not immune to depression, which can sometimes lead to destructive behaviour such as alcohol and drug abuse. What has research revealed about the relationship between depression and drug abuse?

most notably the higher rates of alcoholism and cannabis use among these communities. Parker's 2002 study indicated that 56% of suicides in the Northern Territory were alcohol-related. Furthermore, ABS statistics show that Indigenous people are four times more likely than the general population to be hospitalised for misuse of psychoactive substances (ABS, 2005).

These variables formed the basis for a mental health program undertaken by the Indigenous Tiwi people in the Northern Territory. The program emphasises:

- community leadership
- information sessions on coping with life stress and substance misuse, and;
- crisis plans to deal with specific incidents of threatened suicide.

The Tiwi Mental Health Program has not yet been formally assessed, but early indications are that it has had some impact in terms of reducing suicidal behaviour in the Tiwi communities. This may inspire the rest of Australia to follow their lead. (Measey et al., 2006).

Many suicides are attributed to accidents or other causes, the actual rate is probably much higher. Because depression occurs more frequently in women, it is not surprising that women act, but typically it occurs as the final stage of a period of inner turmoil and outer distress. The majority of young suicide victims have talked to others about their intentions or have written about them. Thus talk of suicide should always be taken seriously (Marttunen et al., 1998). As is the case for adults, adolescents are very likely to attempt suicide when they are experiencing depression (Gutierrez et al., 2004). Feelings of hopelessness and isolation, as well as negative self-concepts, are also associated with suicide risk (Rutter & Behrendt, 2004). Furthermore, gay and lesbian youths are at even higher risk for suicide than are other adolescents (D'Augelli et al., 2005). These higher suicide rates undoubtedly reflect the relative lack of social support for homosexual orientation. Suicide is an extreme reaction that occurs especially when adolescents feel unable to cry out to others for help. Being sensitive to signs of suicidal intentions and caring enough to intervene are essential for saving the lives of both youthful and mature people who have come to see no exit for their troubles except total self-destruction.

### RECAP CHECKPOINT
#### Mood Disorders

- Major depressive disorder is the most common mood disorder; bipolar disorder is much rarer.
- People have genetic predispositions toward mood disorders.
- Mood disorders change the way people respond to life experiences.

- Women's higher level of major depressive disorder may reflect a greater tendency towards rumination.
- Suicides are most frequent among people suffering from depression.

## CONCEPT QUESTIONS

1. What experiences characterise bipolar disorder?

2. In Aaron Beck's theory, what types of negative cognitions make up the cognitive triad?

3. How does the ruminative response style help explain gender differences in depression?

4. What are some suicide risk factors for adolescents?

## CRITICAL THINKING

Recall the study on mood congruency in major depressive disorder. Why was it important that participants had no time pressure to produce their memories?

# PERSONALITY DISORDERS

A **personality disorder** is a long-standing (chronic), inflexible, maladaptive pattern of perceiving, thinking or behaving. These patterns can seriously impair an individual's ability to function in social or work settings and can cause significant distress. They are usually recognisable by the time a person reaches adolescence or early adulthood. Personality disorders are coded on Axis II of *DSM-IV-TR*. As shown in **Table 14.5**, *DSM-IV-TR* organises 10 types of personality disorders into three clusters.

Diagnoses of personality disorders have sometimes been controversial because of the overlap among the disorders: some of the same behaviours contribute to diagnoses of different disorders. In addition, researchers have tried to understand the relationship between normal and abnormal personalities. They ask, at what point does an extreme on a particular dimension of personality indicate a disorder (Livesley & Lang, 2005)? For example, most people are somewhat dependent on other people. When does dependence become sufficiently extreme to signal dependent personality disorder? As with other types of psychological disorders, clinicians must understand when and how personality traits become maladaptive—when and how those traits cause either the person or society to suffer. To illustrate that conclusion, we focus on *borderline personality disorder* and *antisocial personality disorder*.

# BORDERLINE PERSONALITY DISORDER

Individuals with **borderline personality disorder** experience great instability and intensity in personal relationships. These difficulties arise in part from difficulties controlling anger. The disorder leads people to have frequent fights and temper tantrums. In addition, people with this disorder display great impulsivity in their behaviours—particularly with respect to behaviours that can relate to self-harm, such as substance abuse or suicide attempts. *DSM-IV-TR* (2000) estimates the prevalence of borderline personality disorder as 2 percent in the general population.

One important component of borderline personality disorder is an intense fear of abandonment (Lieb et al., 2004). People engage in frantic behaviours to prevent abandonment such as frequent phone calls and physical clinging. However, because of their difficulty with emotional control, people are likely to engage in behaviours—angry outbursts and bouts of self-harm—that make it quite difficult to maintain relationships with them. One study that followed people with borderline personality disorder over the course of 2 years found impaired social functioning across the whole period (Skodol et al., 2005). This research suggests that borderline personality disorder remains stable over time.

## Causes of borderline personality disorder

As with other disorders, researchers have focused on both the nature and nurture of borderline personality disorder. Twin studies provide strong evidence in favour of a genetic contribution. For example, one study compared the rate of concordance for monozygotic versus dizygotic twins (Torgersen et al., 2000). When one MZ twin had borderline personality disorder, 35.3 percent of their siblings also had the disorder; for DZ twins, only 6.7 percent of their siblings also had the disorder. If you recall the discussion in Chapter 13 about the strong heritability of personality traits, you might not be surprised that disorders of those traits are also heritable.

Still, research suggests that environmental factors make a strong contribution in the etiology of borderline personality disorder (Lieb et al., 2004). One study compared the incidence of early traumatic events for 66 patients with the disorder to 109 healthy controls (Bandelow et al., 2005). The patients had considerably different lives. For example, 73.9 percent of the patients with borderline personality disorder reported childhood sexual abuse; only 5.5 percent of the controls did so. The patients reported, on average, that the abuse started at age 6 and lasted for 3½ years. That early trauma likely contributed to the incidence of the disorder. However, not all people who endure childhood sexual abuse develop borderline personality disorder—witness the 5.5 percent of control participants in this study who survived childhood sexual abuse but did not develop the disorder. It is likely that a combination of genetic risk and traumatic events explains the etiology of the disorder.

## Table 14.5

Personality disorders

| Disorder | Characteristics |
|---|---|
| **Cluster A: People's behaviour appears odd or eccentric** | |
| Paranoid | Distrust and suspiciousness about the motives of the individuals with whom they interact |
| Schizoid | Lack of desire to have social relationships; lack of emotionality in social situations |
| Schizotypal | Cognitive or perceptual distortions as well as discomfort in social relationships |
| **Cluster B: People's behaviour appears dramatic or erratic** | |
| Antisocial | Inability to respect the rights of others; irresponsible or unlawful behaviour that violates social norms |
| Borderline | Instability and intensity in personal relationships; impulsivity, particularly with respect to behaviours that include self-harm |
| Histrionic | Excessive emotionality and attention seeking; inappropriate sexual or seductive behaviour |
| Narcissistic | Grandiose sense of self-importance and a need for constant admiration; lack of empathy for others |
| **Cluster C: People's behaviour appears anxious or fearful** | |
| Avoidant | Avoid interpersonal contact because of risk of rejection; fear criticism and feel inadequate in social situations |
| Dependent | Need others to take responsibility for major areas of life; feel uncomfortable or helpless without support from other people |
| Obsessive-Compulsive | Preoccupied with rules and lists; perfectionism interferes with being able to complete tasks |

# ANTISOCIAL PERSONALITY DISORDER

**Antisocial personality disorder** is marked by a long-standing pattern of irresponsible or unlawful behaviour that violates social norms. Lying, stealing and fighting are common behaviours. People with antisocial personality disorder often do not experience shame or remorse for their hurtful actions. Violations of social norms begin early in their lives—disrupting class, getting into fights and running away from home. Their actions are marked by indifference to the rights of others. Roughly 3 percent of men and 1 percent of women have antisocial personality disorder (*DSM-IV-TR*, 2000).

Antisocial personality disorder is often comorbid with other pathologies. For example, in one study, about 25 percent of individuals who met criteria for opioid (e.g., opium, morphine and heroin) abuse were also diagnosed with antisocial personality disorder (Brooner et al., 1997). In addition, antisocial personality disorder also puts people at risk for suicide, even in the absence of major depressive disorder (Hills et al., 2005). This suicide risk is likely to be a product of the impulsivity and disregard for safety that characterises the disorder.

## Causes of antisocial personality disorder

Researchers have used twin studies to examine genetic components of specific behaviours associated with antisocial personality disorder. For example, one study examined the concordance in behaviours for 3,687 pairs of twins (Viding et al., 2005). Teachers responded to statements about each twin to indicate the presence of callous-unemotional traits (e.g., 'Does not show feelings

Why do people with antisocial personality disorder often have problems with the law?

**antisocial personality disorder** A disorder characterised by stable patterns of irresponsible or unlawful behaviour that violates social norms.

For answers go to MyPsychLab!

or emotions') and antisocial behaviour (e.g., 'Often fights with other children or bullies them'). The comparisons of MZ and DZ twins suggested that the tendency to display callous-unemotional traits had a strong genetic component. In addition, for twins who displayed high levels of those callous-emotional traits, genetics also made a strong contribution to antisocial behaviour.

Research has also focused on the environmental circumstances that give rise to personality disorders (Paris, 2003). Consider this study of the relationship between parenting practices and antisocial personality traits.

> A team of researchers assessed 742 men and women for personality traits that met *DSM-IV* criteria for antisocial personality disorder (Reti et al., 2002). The participants reported on their parents' behaviours toward them during childhood by completing the *Parental Bonding Instrument* (PBI). The PBI posed a range of questions to which participants responded on a 4-point scale. Some of the questions measured the extent to which parents showed caring for the child (e.g., 'Could make me feel better when I was upset'). Other questions measured the extent to which parents restricted the child's behaviour (e.g., 'Let me dress in any way I pleased'). A third type of question measured the extent to which parents allowed the child psychological freedom (e.g., 'Tried to control everything I did'). The researchers looked for relationships between the participants' responses on the PBI and the extent to which they showed antisocial personality traits. The researchers found that the people who reported low levels of parental care had high levels of antisocial personality traits. Also, those individuals who believed that their mothers had been particularly overprotective also had high levels of antisocial personality traits.

The researchers were quick to assert that correlation is not causation. It's possible that parenting behaviours brought about antisocial personality traits; it's also possible that children whose behaviour was influenced by antisocial traits negatively affected the way their parents behaved toward them. Still, the results suggest that researchers could observe family patterns to determine what children might be at risk to develop adult forms of antisocial personality disorder.

**somatoform disorder** A disorder in which people have physical illnesses or complaints that cannot be fully explained by actual medical conditions.

**hypochondriasis** A disorder in which individuals are preoccupied with having or getting physical ailments despite reassurances that they are healthy.

## RECAP CHECKPOINT
### Personality disorders

- Personality disorders are patterns of perception, thought or behaviour that are long standing and inflexible and impair an individual's functioning.

- Both borderline personality disorder and antisocial personality disorder arise because of genetic and environmental factors.

## CONCEPT QUESTIONS

1. What intense fear do people with borderline personality disorder have with respect to interpersonal relationships?

2. How do the early lives of people with borderline personality disorder compare to those of healthy controls?

3. Why are people with antisocial personality disorder at risk for suicide?

## CRITICAL THINKING
Consider the study that assessed the impact of parenting on antisocial personality traits. Why might the researchers have assessed the three different dimensions of parenting?

# SOMATOFORM AND DISSOCIATIVE DISORDERS

As we have reviewed various types of psychological disorders, you have seen how certain everyday experiences can, pushed to the limit, lead to disability or maladaptive behaviour. For example, everyone experiences anxiety, but for some people those experiences become so severe that they develop an anxiety disorder. Similarly, many people experience symptoms for physical illnesses that don't have any obvious causes; many people have days when they just 'don't feel like themselves.' However, when those types of experiences impair individuals' day-to-day life, they may indicate *somatoform disorders* or *dissociative disorders*. We review the symptoms and etiology of each type of disorder.

## SOMATOFORM DISORDERS

A person suffering from a **somatoform disorder** has physical illnesses or complaints that cannot be fully explained by actual medical conditions. To be diagnosed with one of these disorders, people must experience the illnesses or complaints to an extent that they cause sufficient distress to interfere with their everyday functioning. We will focus on *hypochondriasis*, *somatisation disorder* and *conversion disorder*.

Individuals with **hypochondriasis** believe they have physical illnesses despite assurance from medical practitioners that they do not. Even when they are currently healthy, they may be constantly fearful that they will contact physical illnesses. In addition, this preoccupation with being or getting ill causes sufficient distress so that individuals are impaired in their day-to-day lives. To assess the prevalence of hypochondriasis and other somatoform disorders, researchers often focus on people who present themselves for medical treatment. In that context, the question becomes what proportion of people have physical complaints that don't allow medical explanations. Research suggests that 4.7 percent of adults 18 and older who seek medical treatment meet *DSM-IV-TR* criteria for hypochondriasis (Fink et al., 2004).

Individuals with **somatisation disorder** present a long history of physical complaints over many years. Those complaints—which remain medically unexplained—must span several medical categories. To meet *DSM-IV-TR* criteria for the diagnosis, individuals must have experienced four pain symptoms (e.g., headaches or stomach aches), two gastrointestinal symptoms (e.g., nausea or diarrhoea), one sexual symptom (e.g., erectile dysfunction or excessive menstrual bleeding), and one neurological symptom (e.g., paralysis or double vision). Among adults seeking medical treatment, 1.5 percent meet criteria for somatisation disorder (Fink et al., 2004).

**Conversion disorder** is characterised by a loss of motor or sensory function that cannot be explained by damage to the nervous system or other physical damage. For example, individuals may experience paralysis or blindness without a medical cause. In addition, the onset of the physical symptoms must be preceded by psychological factors such as interpersonal conflict or emotional stressors. Historically, conversion disorder was called *hysteria*—and was believed to represent, in some eras, possession by the devil. Sigmund Freud helped bring about the contemporary understanding of conversion disorder. One of his most enduring insights was that psychological trauma could yield physical symptoms. Conversion disorder is present in 1.5 percent of adults seeking medical treatment (Fink et al., 2004).

**Causes of somatoform disorders** The defining characteristic of somatoform disorders is that individuals experience physical ailments that have no adequate medical explanation. Researchers have attempted to understand how that could be possible: How, for example, could individuals whose motor systems are intact experience paralysis? Studies have used neuroimaging techniques to discover the brain bases of conversion disorder (Black et al., 2004). Consider a study that demonstrated that individuals with conversion symptoms show different patterns of brain activity than individuals who are only pretending to have the symptoms.

This study focused on two men who had weakness in their left arms that was not the result of any neurological disorder (Spence et al., 2000). Those two men underwent PET scans while in a resting state and while they moved a joystick with their left hand. The researchers instructed a second pair of healthy individuals to pretend that they had the same symptoms. Those individuals carried out the same tasks, as did a group of six control participants who had no special instructions. The brain activity of the patients with conversion disorder was not different from the other groups while they were in a resting state. However, differences emerged when the task required participants to move their left hands. Both the patients and the pretenders showed diminished brain activity for this task—this result reflects the symptoms of the patients and the simulation of the pretenders. However, the areas in which brain activity decreased were different for the two groups. The patients with conversion symptoms were not merely pretending that they couldn't move their arms.

The particular brain region that was inactive for the patients plays an important role in the selection of voluntary actions. These data from this study point to a separation of awareness from intention: in the brain, conversion disorder makes these patients unaware that they have 'chosen' not to move their arms.

Researchers have also focused on cognitive processes that contribute to somatoform disorders (Brown, 2004). For example, an important aspect of hypochondriasis is an attentional bias in the way that individuals respond to bodily sensations. Suppose you wake up one morning with a scratchy throat. If you have an attention bias that makes it difficult to divert your thoughts from that scratchy throat, you might come to believe that you are seriously ill. In fact, one study demonstrated that people who experience a high level of anxiety about their health find it difficult to disengage their attention even from words such as *cancer*, *tumour* and *stroke* (Owens et al., 2004). The tight focus on symptoms and illness contributes to a vicious cycle: stress and anxiety have physical consequences (e.g., increased sweating and elevated heart rate) that can feel like the symptoms of illness—providing further proof that the health anxiety is appropriate. Someone who attributes all physical symptoms to illness may perceive a perilous pattern in the co-occurrence of a scratchy throat, excessive sweating and a swiftly beating heart. Thus the cognitive biases associated with somatoform disorders serve to exaggerate minor bodily sensations.

# DISSOCIATIVE DISORDERS

A **dissociative disorder** is a disturbance in the integration of identity, memory or consciousness. It is important for people to see themselves as being in control of their behaviour, including emotions, thoughts and actions. Essential to this perception of self-control is the sense of selfhood—the consistency of different aspects of the self and the continuity of identity over time and place. Psychologists believe that, in dissociated states, individuals escape from their conflicts by giving up this precious consistency and continuity—in a sense, disowning part of themselves. The forgetting of important personal experiences, a process caused by psychological factors in the absence of any organic dysfunction, called **dissociative amnesia**, is one example of dissociation. Psychologists have begun to document the degree to which such memory dissociation may accompany instances of sexual and physical childhood abuse (Draijer & Langeland, 1999). Other types of severe traumas—such as the firestorm that struck the suburbs of Oakland and Berkeley, California, in 1991, resulting in a loss of 25 lives and over a billion

**somatisation disorder** A disorder characterised by unexplained physical complaints in several categories over many years.

**conversion disorder** A disorder in which psychological conflict or stress brings about loss of motor or sensory function.

**dissociative disorder** A personality disorder marked by a disturbance in the integration of identity, memory or consciousness.

**dissociative amnesia** The inability to remember important personal experiences, caused by psychological factors in the absence of any organic dysfunction.

**dissociative identity disorder (DID)** A dissociative mental disorder in which two or more distinct personalities exist within the same individual; formerly multiple personality disorder.

dollars in damage—also produce dissociative symptoms (Koopman et al., 1996).

**Dissociative identity disorder (DID)**, formerly known as *multiple personality disorder*, is a dissociative mental disorder in which two or more distinct personalities exist within the same individual. At any particular time, one of these personalities is dominant in directing the individual's behaviour. Dissociative identity disorder is popularly known as *split personality*, and sometimes mistakenly called *schizophrenia*, a disorder, as we will see in the next section, in which personality often is impaired but is not split into multiple versions. In DID, each of the emerging personalities contrasts in some significant way with the original self—it might be outgoing if the person is shy, tough if the original personality is weak, and sexually assertive if the other is fearful and sexually naive. Each personality has a unique identity, name and behaviour pattern. In some cases, dozens of different characters emerge to help the person deal with a difficult life situation. Here is an excerpt from a first-person account of a woman who experiences DID (Mason, 1997, p. 44):

> Just as waves turn the ocean inside out and rearrange the water, different ones of us cycle in and out in an ebb and flow that is sometimes gentle, sometimes turbulent. A child colours with Crayola markers. She moves aside to make way for the administrator, who reconciles the bank statement. A moment later, the dead baby takes over and lies paralysed on the floor. She remains that way for a while, but no one gets upset—it's her turn. The live baby stops in her crawl, engrossed by a speck of dust. The cooker prepares meals for three days and packages each separately—we all have different likes and dislikes. A terrified one screams aloud, a wounded one moans, a grieving one wails.

Can you put yourself in this woman's place, and imagine what it would be like to have this range of 'individuals'—the child, the dead baby, the live baby, the cooker and so on—inside your one head?

**Causes of dissociative disorders** Some psychologists believe that multiple personalities develop to serve a vital survival function. DID victims may have been beaten, locked up or abandoned by those who were supposed to love them—those on whom they were so dependent that they could not fight them, leave them or even hate them. Instead, the psycho-dynamic perspective suggests that these victims have fled their terror symbolically through dissociation. They have protected their egos by creating stronger internal characters to help cope with the ongoing traumatic situation. Typically, DID victims are women who report being severely abused physically or sexually by parents, relatives or close friends for extended periods during childhood. One study obtained questionnaire data from 448 clinicians who had treated cases of dissociative identity disorders and major depressions (used for comparative purposes). As shown in **Table 14.6**, the dominant feature of the 355 DID cases is the almost universal reports of abuse, with incidents often starting around age 3

Table 14.6

Responses to inquiries regarding abuse: comparing dissociative identity disorder and depression

| Questionnaire item | DID (%) | Major depression (%) |
|---|---|---|
| Abuse incidence | 98 | 54 |
| Type(s) | | |
| Physical | 82 | 24 |
| Sexual | 86 | 25 |
| Psychological | 86 | 42 |
| Neglect | 54 | 21 |
| All of above | 47 | 6 |
| Physical and sexual | 74 | 14 |
| | (N = 355) | (N = 235) |

and continuing for more than a decade. Although the 235 comparison patients with depression disorder also had a high incidence of abuse, it was significantly less than that experienced by those with DID (Schultz et al., 1989).

Although these data—and personal accounts of the type we quoted earlier—seem compelling, many psychologists remain sceptical about the diagnosis of DID (Lilienfeld & Lynn, 2003). No solid data exist about the prevalence of this disorder (*DSM-IV-TR*, 2000). Sceptics have often suggested that therapists who 'believe' in DID may create DID—these therapists question their patients, often under hypnosis, in a way that encourages multiple personalities to 'emerge'.

Other psychologists believe that sufficient evidence has accumulated in favour of the DID diagnosis to indicate that it is not just the product of zealous therapists (Gleaves et al., 2001). The safest conclusion may be that of the group of people diagnosed with DID, some cases are genuine, whereas other cases emerge in response to therapists' demands.

## RECAP CHECKPOINT
### Somatoform and dissociative disorders

- Somatoform disorders such as hypochondriasis, somatisation disorder, and conversion disorder are characterised by circumstances in which physical illnesses or complaints cannot be fully explained by actual medical conditions.

- Dissociative disorders involve a disruption of the integrated functioning of memory, consciousness, or personal identity.

## CONCEPT QUESTIONS

1. Howard believes that his headaches prove he has a brain tumour, despite his doctor's assurances that he is fine. From which somatoform disorder might Howard suffer?

For answers go to MyPsychLab!

# SCHIZOPHRENIC DISORDERS

Everyone knows what it is like to feel depressed or anxious, even though most of us never experience these feelings to the degree of severity that constitutes a disorder. Schizophrenia, however, is a disorder that represents a qualitatively different experience from normal functioning. A **schizophrenic disorder** is a severe form of psychopathology in which personality seems to disintegrate, thought and perception are distorted and emotions are blunted. The person with a schizophrenic disorder is the one you most often conjure up when you think about madness or insanity.

For many of the people afflicted with schizophrenia, the disease is a life sentence without possibility of parole, endured in the solitary confinement of a mind that must live life apart. Although schizophrenia is relatively rare—approximately 0.7 percent of U.S. adults have suffered from schizophrenia at some point in their lives (Kessler et al., 1994)—this figure translates to around 2 million people affected by this most mysterious and tragic mental disorder. In Australia, the prevalence of schizophrenia is approximately 1 in 100, with most cases being diagnosed in a person's late teenage years or early 20's (SANE

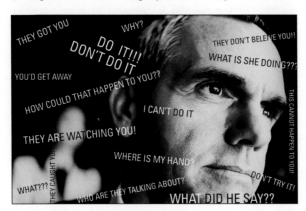

What patterns of thoughts may indicate that a person is experiencing schizophrenia?

Australia, 2007). Mark Vonnegut, son of novelist Kurt Vonnegut, was in his early 20s when he began to experience symptoms of schizophrenia. In *The Eden Express* (1975), he tells the story of his break with reality and his eventual recovery. Once, while pruning some fruit trees, his reality became distorted:

> *I began to wonder if I was hurting the trees and found myself apologising. Each tree began to take on personality. I began to wonder if any of them liked me. I became completely absorbed in looking at each tree and began to notice that they were ever so slightly luminescent, shining with a soft inner light that played around the branches. And from out of nowhere came an incredibly wrinkled, iridescent face. Starting as a small point infinitely distant, it rushed forward, becoming infinitely huge. I could see nothing else. My heart had stopped. The moment stretched forever. I tried to make the face go away but it mocked me. . . . I tried to look the face in the eyes and realised I had left all familiar ground. (1975, p. 96)*

Vonnegut's description gives you a glimpse at the symptoms of schizophrenia.

In the world of schizophrenia, *thinking* becomes illogical; associations among ideas are remote or without apparent pattern. *Hallucinations* often occur, involving imagined sensory perception—sights, smells, or, most commonly, sounds (usually voices)—that patients assume to be real. A person may hear a voice that provides a running commentary on his or her behaviour or may hear several voices in conversation. **Delusions** are also common; these are false or irrational beliefs maintained in spite of clear contrary evidence. *Language* may become incoherent—a 'word salad' of unrelated or made-up words—or an individual may become mute. *Emotions* may be flat, with no visible expression, or they may be inappropriate to the situation. *Psychomotor behaviour* may be disorganised (grimaces, strange mannerisms), or posture may become rigid. Even when only some of these symptoms are present, deteriorated functioning in work and interpersonal relationships is likely as the patient withdraws socially or becomes emotionally detached.

Psychologists divide the symptoms between a positive category and a negative category. During *acute* or *active phases* of schizophrenia, the positive symptoms—hallucinations, delusions, incoherence and disorganised behaviour—are prominent. At other times, the negative symptoms—social withdrawal and flattened emotions—become more apparent. Some individuals, such as Mark Vonnegut, experience only one or a couple of acute phases of schizophrenia and recover to live normal lives. Others, often described as chronic sufferers, experience either repeated acute phases with short periods of negative symptoms or occasional acute phases with extended periods of negative symptoms. Even the most seriously disturbed are not acutely delusional all the time.

**schizophrenic disorder** Severe form of psychopathology characterised by the breakdown of integrated personality functioning, withdrawal from reality, emotional distortions and disturbed thought processes.

**delusions** False or irrational beliefs maintained despite clear evidence to the contrary.

# MAJOR TYPES OF SCHIZOPHRENIA

Because of the wide variety of symptoms that can characterise schizophrenia, investigators consider it not a single disorder but rather a constellation of separate types. The five most commonly recognised subtypes are outlined in **Table 14.7**.

**Table 14.7**

Types of schizophrenic disorders

| Types of schizophrenia | Major symptoms |
| --- | --- |
| Disorganised | Inappropriate behaviour and emotions; incoherent language |
| Catatonic | Frozen, rigid or excitable motor behaviour |
| Paranoid | Delusions of persecution or grandeur |
| Undifferentiated | Mixed set of symptoms with thought disorders and features from other types |
| Residual | Free from major symptoms but evidence from minor symptoms of continuation of the disorder |

**Disorganised type** In this subtype of schizophrenia, a person displays incoherent patterns of thinking and grossly bizarre and disorganised behaviour. Emotions are flattened or inappropriate to the situation. Often, a person acts in a silly or childish manner, such as giggling for no apparent reason. Language can become so incoherent, full of unusual words and incomplete sentences, that communication with others breaks down. If delusions or hallucinations occur, they are not organised around a coherent theme.

> Mr. F. B. was a hospitalised patient in his late twenties. When asked his name, he said he was trying to forget it because it made him cry whenever he heard it. He then proceeded to cry vigorously for several minutes. Then, when asked about something serious and sad, Mr. P. B. giggled or laughed. When asked the meaning of the proverb 'When the cat's away, the mice will play,' Mr. P. B. replied, 'Takes less place. Cat didn't know what mouse did and mouse didn't know what cat did. Cat represented more on the suspicious side than the mouse. Dumbo was a good guy. He saw what the cat did, put himself with the cat so people wouldn't look at them as comedians.' (Zimbardo, personal communication, 1957).

Mr. F.B.'s mannerisms, depersonalised, incoherent speech, and delusions are the hallmarks of the disorganised type of schizophrenia.

**Catatonic type** The major feature of the catatonic type of schizophrenia is a disruption in motor activity. Sometimes people with this disorder seem frozen in a stupor. For long periods of time, the individual can remain motionless, often in a bizarre position, showing little or no reaction to anything in the environment. At other times, these patients show excessive motor activity, apparently without purpose and not influenced by external stimuli. The catatonic type is also characterised by extreme *negativism*, an apparently unmotivated resistance to all instructions.

**Paranoid type** Individuals suffering from this form of schizophrenia experience complex and systematised delusions focused around specific themes:

- *Delusions of persecution.* Individuals feel that they are being constantly spied on and plotted against and that they are in mortal danger.
- *Delusions of grandeur.* Individuals believe that they are important or exalted beings—millionaires, great inventors or religious figures such as Jesus Christ. Delusions of persecution may accompany delusions of grandeur—an individual is a great person but is continually opposed by evil forces.
- *Delusional jealousy.* Individuals become convinced—without due cause—that their mates are unfaithful. They contrive data to fit the theory and 'prove' the truth of the delusion.

Individuals with paranoid schizophrenia rarely display obviously disorganised behaviour. Instead, their behaviour is likely to be intense and quite formal.

**Undifferentiated type** This is the grab-bag category of schizophrenia, describing a person who exhibits prominent delusions, hallucinations, incoherent speech, or grossly disorganised behaviour that fits the criteria of more than one type or of no clear type. The hodgepodge of symptoms experienced by these individuals does not clearly differentiate among various schizophrenic reactions.

**Residual type** Individuals diagnosed as residual type have usually suffered from a major past episode of schizophrenia but are currently free of major positive symptoms such as hallucinations or delusions. The ongoing presence of the disorder is signalled by minor positive symptoms or negative symptoms like flat emotion. A diagnosis of residual type may indicate that the person's disease is entering *remission*, or becoming dormant.

# CAUSES OF SCHIZOPHRENIA

Different etiological models point to very different initial causes of schizophrenia, different pathways along which it develops, and different avenues for treatment. Let's look at the contributions several of these models can make to an understanding of the way a person may develop a schizophrenic disorder.

**Genetic approaches** It has long been known that schizophrenia tends to run in families (Bleuler, 1978;

Kallmann, 1946). Three independent lines of research—family studies, twin studies and adoption studies—point to a common conclusion: Persons related genetically to someone who has had schizophrenia are more likely to become affected than those who are not (Owen & O'Donovan, 2003). A summary of the risks of being affected with schizophrenia through various kinds of relatives is shown in **Figure 14.5**. Schizophrenia researcher **Irving Gottesman** (1991) pooled these data from about 40 reliable studies conducted in Western Europe between 1920 and 1987; he dropped the poorest data sets. As you can see, the data are arranged according to degree of genetic relatedness, which correlates highly with the degree of risk. For example, when both parents have suffered from schizophrenia, the risk for their offspring is 46 percent, as compared with 1 percent in the general population. When only one parent has had schizophrenia, the risk for the offspring drops sharply, to 13 percent. Note also that the probability that identical twins will both have schizophrenia is roughly three times greater than the probability for fraternal twins.

Researchers have also used adoption studies to demonstrate that the etiology of schizophrenia is greatly influenced by genetic factors (Kety et al., 1994). Consider a study that assessed the incidence of thought disorders in biological and adoptive relatives of patients with schizophrenia.

Participants with schizophrenia were drawn from a larger sample of individuals who had developed the disorder after having been adopted. A control sample was matched to the sample with schizophrenia on variables such as sex and age; participants in the control sample had experienced no psychiatric

hospitalisations. Tape recordings were made of the patients' and controls' speech, as well as the speech of their biological relatives—to assess the importance of genetics—and their adopted relatives—to assess the importance of environment. Based on these speech samples, each individual (that is, patients and relatives) was assigned a thought disorder score, using a set of categories specified by a measure called the Thought Disorder Index (TDI). Results are presented in **Table 14.8**—higher TDI scores indicate more disordered thought. The results indicate that the biological relatives of the adoptees with schizophrenia had higher levels of disordered thought than did the biological relatives of control adoptees. However, the adoptive relatives of both groups did not differ in their thought disorders. This pattern of data suggests that genetics matters more than environment in predicting who will experience thought disorders (Kinney et al., 1997).

Almost all the adoptees had been separated from their biological families shortly after birth. Therefore, whatever forces were leading to very high levels of thought disorder in the adoptees with schizophrenia and relatively high levels in their biological relatives cannot be attributed to environmental factors.

Although there is certainly a strong relationship between genetic similarity and schizophrenia risk, even in the groups with the greatest genetic similarity, the risk factor is less than 50 percent (see Figure 14.5). This indicates that, although genes play a role, environmental conditions may also be necessary to give rise to the

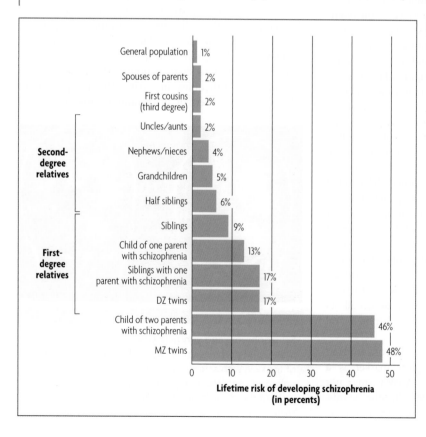

### Figure 14.5

**Genetic risk of developing schizophrenia**

The graph shows average risks for developing schizophrenia. Data were compiled from family and twin studies conducted in European populations between 1920 and 1987; the degree of risk correlates highly with the degree of genetic relatedness.

Except when the label indicates otherwise, the data reflect the relationship between an individual and someone who has been diagnosed with schizophrenia. For example, the D2 twin of someone diagnosed with schizophrenia has a 17 percent chance of sharing the diagnosis.

Table 14.8

Thought disorder scores for adoptees with schizophrenia, control adoptees and their relatives

| SCORES ON THE THOUGHT DISORDER INDEX | | | |
|---|---|---|---|
| | Adoptees with schizophrenia | Control adoptees | Difference |
| The adoptees themselves | 4.82 | 1.15 | 3.67 |
| All their biological relatives | 1.37 | 0.99 | 0.38 |
| Their biological siblings and half siblings | 1.44 | 0.82 | 0.62 |
| Their adoptive relatives | 1.11 | 1.31 | –0.20 |

**diathesis-stress hypothesis**
A hypothesis about the cause of disorders, such as schizophrenia, that suggests that genetic factors predispose an individual to a certain disorder and that environmental stress factors can cause the risk to manifest itself.

disorder. A widely accepted hypothesis for the cause of schizophrenia is the *diathesis-stress hypothesis*. According to the **diathesis-stress hypothesis**, genetic factors place the individual at risk, but environmental stress factors must impinge in order for the potential risk to be manifested as a schizophrenic disorder. Once we have considered other biological aspects of schizophrenia, we will review the types of environmental stressors that may speed the emergence of this disorder.

**Brain function and biological markers** Another biological approach to the study of schizophrenia is to look for abnormalities in the brains of individuals suffering from the disorder. Much of this research now relies on brain-imaging techniques that allow direct comparisons to be made between the structure and functioning of the brains of individuals with schizophrenia and normal control individuals. For example, as shown in **Figure 14.6**, magnetic resonance imaging has shown that the *ventricles*—the brain structures through which cerebrospinal fluid flows—are often enlarged in individuals with schizophrenia (Barkataki et al., 2006). MRI studies also demonstrate that individuals with schizophrenia have measurably thinner regions in frontal and temporal lobes of cerebral cortex; the loss of neural tissue presumably relates to the disorder's behavioural abnormalities (Kuperberg et al., 2003). Imaging techniques have also revealed that individuals with schizophrenia may have patterns of brain activity different from those of normal controls. For example, one study examined identical twins in which either one or both members of each pair had schizophrenia (Berman et al., 1992). Only those individuals who actually had schizophrenia showed lower activity in the frontal lobes of the brain. This research design allows 'genetics' to be held constant, to reveal this other biological aspect of the disorder.

Researchers continue to add to the list of *biological markers* for schizophrenia. A biological marker is a 'measurable indicator of a disease that may or may not be causal' (Szymanski et al., 1991, p. 99). In other words, a biological marker may be correlated with a disease,

although it does not bring the disease about. At present no known marker perfectly predicts schizophrenia, but markers have great potential value for diagnosis and research. For example, persons with schizophrenia are more likely than normal people to have an eye movement dysfunction when they scan the visual field. This biological marker can be quantified in individuals and is related to the presence of schizophrenia in families (Clementz & Sweeney, 1990; Lencer et al., 2000). Researchers continue to probe to find the specific elements of eye movements that most precisely set individuals with schizophrenia apart from patients with other mental disorders (Hong et al., 2006). Precise knowledge of biological markers may help researchers determine what groups of individuals are at risk for developing the disorder.

Given the wide range of symptoms of schizophrenia, you are probably not surprised by the comparably wide range of biological abnormalities that may be either causes or consequences of the disorder. What are the ways in which features of the environment may prompt people who are at risk to develop the disease?

## Family interaction as environmental stressor

If it is difficult to prove that a highly specific biological factor is a *sufficient* cause of schizophrenia, it is equally hard to prove that a general psychological one is a *necessary* condition. Sociologists, family therapists and psychologists have all studied the influence of family role relationships and communication patterns in the development of schizophrenia. The hope is to identify environmental circumstances that increase the likelihood of schizophrenia—and to protect at-risk individuals from those circumstances.

Research has provided evidence for theories that emphasise the influence of *deviations* in parental communication on the development of schizophrenia (Miklowitz & Tompson, 2003). These deviations include a family's inability to share a common focus of attention and parents' difficulties in taking the perspective of other family members or in communicating clearly and

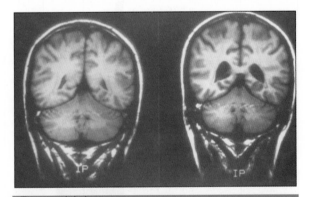

Figure 14.6

**Schizophrenia and ventricle size**
Male identical twins underwent MRI scans. The scan of the twin with schizophrenia (on the right) reveals enlarged ventricles compared to the scan of the twin without the disorder (on the left).
Photo courtesy of Drs. E. Fuller Torrey and Daniel Weinberger.

accurately. Studies suggest that the speech patterns of families with a member who has schizophrenia show less responsiveness and less interpersonal sensitivity than those of normal families.

Uncertainty remains over whether deviant family patterns are a cause of schizophrenia, a reaction to an individual's developing symptoms of schizophrenia, or both. To help answer this question, researchers undertake *prospective* studies: They measure family function to see which patterns predict who will develop schizophrenia, or experience relapses, in the future. For example, one study focused on the *empathy* skills of patients' relatives with respect to their ability to perceive the patients' mood states (Giron & Gomez-Beneyto, 1998). Over a 2-year period, the patients whose relatives had shown low levels of empathy were more likely to suffer relapses in their symptoms of schizophrenia. This study is consistent with other findings that family factors play an important role in influencing the functioning of an individual after the first symptoms appear.

To examine the role of family communication in schizophrenia, researchers have defined the concept of *expressed emotion*. Families are high on expressed emotion if they make a lot of critical comments about the patient, if they are emotionally over-involved with the patient (that is, if they are over-protective and intrusive), and if they have a generally hostile attitude toward the patient. One study gathered data on the families of 69 patients with schizophrenia who were living at home during a period in which they were considered stable. Each family was evaluated for the extent of its expressed emotion. When the patients' condition was assessed 9 months later, 50 percent of the patients from high-expressed emotion homes had experienced a relapse, whereas only 17 percent of patients from low-expressed-emotion homes had done so. Nonetheless, some aspects of expressed emotion were beneficial to the patients. Those patients whose families were emotionally over-involved had better social adjustment 9 months later. Perhaps the rigid family environment helped the patients make the difficult transition from hospitalisation to the outside world (King & Dixon, 1996).

This study replicates the general pattern that when parents reduce their criticism, hostility and intrusiveness toward an offspring with schizophrenia, the recurrence of acute symptoms and the need for rehospitalisation are also reduced (Wearden et al., 2000). The implication is that treatment should be for the entire family as a *system*, to change the operating style toward the disturbed child.

The number of explanations of schizophrenia that we have reviewed—and the questions that remain despite significant research—suggests how much there is to learn about this powerful psychological disorder. Complicating understanding is the likelihood that the phenomenon called schizophrenia is probably better thought of as a group of disorders, each with potentially distinct causes. Genetic predispositions, brain processes and family interactions have all been identified as participants in

at least some cases. Researchers must still determine the exact ways in which these elements may combine to bring about schizophrenia.

These four genetically identical women each experience a schizophrenic disorder, which suggests that heredity plays a role in the development of schizophrenia. For each of the Genain quadruplets, the disorder differs in severity, duration and outcome. In general, how do genetics and environment interact to produce instances of schizophrenia?

## RECAP CHECKPOINT
### Schizophrenic disorders

- Schizophrenia is a severe form of psychopathology characterised by extreme distortions in perception, thinking, emotion, behaviour and language.

- The five subtypes of schizophrenia are disorganised, catatonic, paranoid, undifferentiated and residual.

- Evidence for the causes of schizophrenia has been found in a variety of factors including genetics, brain abnormalities and family processes.

## CONCEPT QUESTIONS

1. Are social withdrawal and flattened emotions positive or negative symptoms of schizophrenia?

2. For what type of schizophrenic disorder would delusions of persecution or grandeur be symptoms?

3. What benefits follow from the discovery of biological markers for schizophrenic disorders?

## CRITICAL THINKING

Recall the study that examined expressed emotion and symptom relapse. Why was it important that all the participants with schizophrenia were stable at the time the researchers assessed expressed emotion?

For answers go to MyPsychLab!

In 1969 Australia was reeling from a spate of child kidnappings and murders during the past four years. Among them was Yvonne Elizabeth Tuohy, who had been abducted at Ski Beach, Warneet, and then molested, tortured and murdered. Local police arrested railway electrician Derek Ernest Percy for Yvonne's murder, and after meeting with prison psychiatrist Dr Allen Bartholomew, Percy pleaded not guilty on the ground of insanity. So just what does it mean for someone to be *insane*?

**Insanity** is not defined in *DSMIV-TR*; there is no accepted clinical definition of insanity. Rather, insanity is a concept that belongs to popular culture and to the legal system. The treatment of insanity in the law dates back to England in 1843, when Daniel M'Naghten was found not guilty of murder by reason of insanity. M'Naghten's intended victim was the British prime minister—M'Naghten believed that God had instructed him to commit the murder. (He accidentally killed the prime minister's secretary instead.) Because of M'Naghten's delusions, he was sent to a mental hospital rather than to prison. The anger surrounding this verdict—even Queen Victoria was infuriated—prompted the House of Lords to articulate a guideline, known as the *M'Naghten rule,* to limit claims of insanity. This rule specifies that a criminal must not 'know the nature and quality of the act he was doing; or, if he did know it, that he did not know what he was doing was wrong'. Does the M'Naghten rule seem a fair test of guilt or innocence?

With advances in the understanding of mental illness, researchers became more aware of circumstances in which a criminal might know right from wrong—a criminal might understand that what he or she was doing was illegal or immoral—but still might not be able to suppress the actions. Often, for example, people with phobias 'know' that a spider can do them no harm, but they are unable to suppress panic behaviours in the presence of the spider.

Did Percy go free? Not at all. he is serving an indefinite sentence—he has previously applied for a minimum term—an appeal that has failed because he is considered a danger to the community.. In fact, one of the public's main misconceptions of the insanity defence is that it allows murderers to go free (Borum & Fullero, 1999; Silver et al., 1994). Perhaps 90 percent of the individuals acquitted on insanity pleas spend time in psychiatric care after they are found not guilty. In cases like Percy's, the individual is released into the community only when he or she is judged by experts no longer to be dangerous—there is often no upper limit placed on psychiatric incarceration as there would be for prison incarceration. In Percy's case, how certain do you think a panel of psychiatrists and psychologists would have to feel before they would agree that Percy could go free?

In the 1980s , The Australian Law Reform Commission, with the assistance of Chief Justices, psychiatrists and various other private organisations, reviewed the defence, and in 1991 released a report which recommended that the defence of insanity be maintained. Despite the great attention that insanity pleas receive in the media—and, thus, the public's great awareness of them—such pleas are quite rare (Kirschner & Galperin, 2001). For example, one study found that in 60,432 indictments in the U.S. city of Baltimore, Maryland, only 190 defendants (0.31 percent) entered insanity pleas; of the 190 pleas, only 8 (4.2 percent) were successful (Janofsky et al., 1996). Thus, the likelihood that you will ever be asked to sit on a jury and judge another person as sane or insane is quite low.

- Why do people often experience 'outrage' when someone is found 'not guilty by virtue of Insanity'?

- How might the misconception arise that the insanity defence allows murderers to go free?

**insanity** The legal (not clinical) designation for the state of an individual judged to be legally irresponsible or incompetent.

# PSYCHOLOGICAL DISORDERS OF CHILDHOOD

Our discussion so far has largely focused on adults who suffer from psychopathology. It is important to note, however, that many individuals begin to experience symptoms of mental illness in childhood and adolescence. Researchers have recently intensified their study of the types of stressors that increase the risk of psychopathology in young lives (Grant et al., 2003). For example, the gender difference for the prevalence of depression begins to emerge around age 13 (Hankin & Abramson, 2001). Researchers seek to understand how boys' and girls' lives diverge, early on, to yield a relative disproportion of depressed girls versus depressed boys.

*DSM-IV-TR* also identifies a range of disorders that are 'usually first diagnosed in infancy, childhood or adolescence'. We discussed one of these disorders, *mental retardation*, in Chapter 9. Here, we focus on *attention-deficit hyperactivity disorder* and *autistic disorder*.

## ATTENTION-DEFICIT HYPERACTIVITY DISORDER

The definition of **attention-deficit hyperactivity disorder** (ADHD) refers to two clusters of symptoms (*DSM-IV-TR*, 2000). First, children must show a degree of *inattention* that is not consistent with their level of development. They might, for example, have difficulty paying attention in school or often lose items such as toys or school assignments. Second, children must show signs of *hyperactivity-impulsivity* that, once again, is not consistent with their developmental level. Hyperactive behaviours include squirming, fidgeting and excessive talking; impulsive behaviours include blurting out answers and interrupting. A diagnosis of ADHD requires that children have shown these patterns of behaviour for at least 6 months before age 7.

Researchers estimate the prevalence of ADHD to be 3 to 7 percent of school-age children in developed countries (Root & Resnick, 2003). The diagnosis of ADHD is complicated by the fact that many children are prone to episodes of inattention, hyperactivity or impulsiveness. For that reason, the diagnosis has sometimes been controversial: people have worried that children's normal disorderliness was being labelled as abnormal. However, there is now a large consensus among clinicians that some children's behaviour reaches a level at which it is maladaptive—the children are unable to control their behaviour or complete tasks.

As with the other disorders we've described, researchers have considered both the nature and nurture of ADHD. Twin and adoption studies have provided strong evidence for the heritability of the disorder (Biederman & Faraone, 2005). Researchers have started to document relationships between specific genes that affect the brain's neurotransmitter function and the symptoms of ADHD (Smoller et al., 2006). There are also important environmental variables associated with ADHD. For example, children who come from families with economic disadvantages or families with high levels of conflict are more likely to experience the disorder (Biederman et al., 2002). Some environmental variables have greater impact on children in different birth positions. For example, the eldest children in families that lack cohesion—families in which members are not committed to providing support to each other—are more at risk for ADHD than are younger siblings in such families (Pressman et al., 2006). Results of this sort suggest that parenting experience has an impact on the incidence of ADHD.

**attention-deficit hyperactivity disorder (ADHD)** A disorder of childhood characterised by inattention and hyperactivity-impulsivity.

## AUTISTIC DISORDER

Children with **autistic disorder** present severe disruption in their ability to form social bonds. They are likely to have greatly delayed and very limited development of spoken language as well as very narrow interests in the world. Consider a report on a child who was diagnosed with this disorder:

> [Audrey] seemed frightened by nearly any changes in her customary routine, including the presence of strange people. She either shrank from contact with other children or avoided them altogether, seemingly content to engage in nonfunctional play by herself for hours at a time. When she was with other children, she seldom engaged in reciprocal play or even copied any of their motor movements. (Meyer, 2003, p. 244)

Many children with autistic disorder also engage in repetitive and ritualistic behaviours: They might, for example, place objects in lines or symmetrical patterns (Greaves et al., 2006).

Estimates of the prevalence of autistic disorder (and related disorders) range from about 30 to 60 per 10,000 children (Fombonne, 2003; Yeargin-Allsopp et al., 2003). Because many of the symptoms of autistic disorder relate to language and social interaction, it has often been difficult to diagnose the disorder until parents notice that their children are failing to use language or interact. However,

**autistic disorder** A developmental disorder characterised by severe disruption of children's ability to form social bonds and use language.

What psychological disorders of childhood might lead to classroom disruptions?

recent research has begun to document behaviours in the first year of life that predict later diagnoses of autistic disorder (Zwaigenbaum et al., 2005). For example, children at risk for autistic disorder are less likely to smile in response to social smiles and respond to their names than are other children.

stigma The negative reaction of people to an individual or group because of some assumed inferiority or source of difference that is degraded.

Causes of autistic disorder As with ADHD, autistic disorder has a large genetic component. In fact, researchers have begun to identify the variations in the human genome that may predispose individuals to experience the disorder (Bartlett et al., 2005; Pericak-Vance, 2003). Researchers have also discovered brain markers of the disorder. For example, individuals with autistic disorder experience more rapid brain growth than do their peers (Cody et al., 2002; Courchesne et al., 2003). The ongoing question is how such brain abnormalities bring about the symptoms of the disorder.

Researchers have suggested that individuals who suffer from autistic disorder have an inability to develop an understanding of other people's mental states (Baron-Cohen, 2000). Under ordinary circumstances, children develop what has been called a *theory of mind*. At first, they interpret the world only from their own perspective. However, with rapid progress between ages 3 and 4, children develop an understanding that other people have different knowledge, beliefs and intentions than they do. Research suggests that individuals with autistic disorder lack the ability to develop this understanding. Without a theory of mind, it is quite difficult for people to establish social relationships. Individuals with autistic disorder find it virtually impossible to understand and predict other people's behaviour, making everyday life seem mysterious and hostile.

For answers go to MyPsychLab!

**mypsychlab**
where learning comes to life!

## RECAP CHECKPOINT
### Psychological disorders of childhood
- Children with ADHD display inattention and hyperactivity–impulsivity.
- Autistic disorder is characterised by severe disruption of children's ability to form social bonds and use language.

## CONCEPT QUESTIONS
1. What types of behaviours characterise ADHD?
2. Why has it been difficult to diagnose autistic disorder before age 2 or 3?
3. Why is theory of mind relevant to autistic disorder?

# THE STIGMA OF MENTAL ILLNESS

One of our most important goals for this chapter has been to demystify mental illness—to help you understand how, in some ways, abnormal behaviour is really ordinary. People with psychological disorders are often labelled as *deviant*. However, the deviant label is not true to prevailing realities: When 20 percent of the Australian adult population will experience some sort of psychiatric disorder in their lifetime (ARHRF, 2006), psychopathology is, at least statistically, relatively normal.

Even given the frequency with which psychopathology touches 'normal lives,' people who are psychologically disordered are often stigmatised in ways that most physically ill people are not. A **stigma** is a mark or brand of disgrace; in the psychological context, it is a set of negative attitudes about a person that places him or her apart as unacceptable (Clausen, 1981). The woman with schizophrenia we quoted at the beginning of the chapter had this to say: 'The patient and public, in my [opinion] needs to be educated about mental illness because people ridicule and mistreat, even misunderstand us at crucial times.' Another recovered patient wrote, 'For me, the stigma of mental illness was as devastating as the experience of hospitalisation itself. Repeated rejections, the awkwardness of others around me, and my own discomfort and self-consciousness propelled me into solitary confinement' (Houghton, 1980, pp. 7–8).

Cultural impact Australian Aboriginals and Torres Strait Islander (ATSI) people have suffered under a stigma of 'mad or bad' for decades. Like all other cultures, ATSI people do not wish to seek out help for mental health disorders in case it brings shame to them or their community.

Research suggests a similar case for Australians who come from non-English speaking backgrounds (NESB), particularly true for those from Middle Eastern backgrounds. The impact of stigma was investigated among 100 Moroccan families of patients with schizophrenia by Kadri, Manoudi, Berradda & Moussaoui (2004). Stigma associated with this schizophrenia affected 86.7% of family members' lives, while 72% suffered from psychological problems, sleep disturbances, relationship difficulties and reduced quality of life. Further analysis showed that 15% of families in the study felt that they were disadvantaged by others due to distrust, 29% suffered mockery and 41% maltreatment. Of the 100 families studied, approximately one-third stated that friends and neighbours avoided them while 29% of people were afraid of socialising with these families.

The importance of the family and honour (known as *sharaf* in Arabic) directly relates to the ongoing stigma of mental illness in NESB communities. In Arab cultures an individual's behaviour can be seen to reflect poorly on the family and their values, thus the decision to seek help often becomes a 'collective enterprise' (Al-Krenawi et al., 1999).

The Australian Transcultural Mental Health Network published a report on mental health in cross-cultural contexts, with a particular focus on NESB communities. They noted the major causes of stigma among these communities, detailed in **Table 14.9** below. They also argued the impacts of such stigma, most notably:

- Perpetuation of negative stereotypes
- Underutilisation of mental health services
- Worsening of mental illness in individuals.

Rooney (1997) advocates the need for more effective education through the [ethnic] media, combined with

## Table 14.9

Causes of stigma towards mental illness

| | |
|---|---|
| Culturally embedded attitudes | In NESB communities there are culturally embedded attitudes and beliefs that involve negative associations with mental illness. Subsequently the behaviour, feelings and attitudes of community members towards those living with a mental illness promotes the stigma of mental illness within NESB communities. These reactions include avoidance, ridicule, rejection, fear and viewing people with a mental illness as weak, incurable, bad or dangerous. These attitudes vary both between NESB groups and individuals reflecting a high degree of cultural diversity in communities. They occur in those who are better informed or well educated about mental illness as well as those who are less well informed. |
| Lack of knowledge about mental illness | Although people are better informed than they were (Ng, 1997), there is still a lack of understanding about how stressors, genes and psychological factors interact to cause mental illness (Rooney et al., 1997).<br><br>Education about the Bio-Psycho-Social Model of mental illness is needed in NESB communities. This will decrease the perception that mental illness is a punishment brought upon a person by their own actions or a sign of weakness, and promote tolerance and understanding of why people can develop a mental health problem. |
| Lack of knowledge about how to help those with a mental illness | Avoidance of a person with a mental illness also stems from not knowing how to help. If people were better informed about support, what role they can play to help a mentally ill person, and treatment options, they would be better equipped to help and be less fearful of becoming involved. |
| Fear | Fear of being stigmatised at a number of levels, including being unemployed, a migrant and having mental illness. The fear of having such a triple stigma that incorporates mental illness increases the reluctance of migrants to acknowledge that there is something wrong with their psychological wellbeing. Such fear is the negative side of people wishing to participate and become members of the new community in which they have arrived. |
| Community services | The role that community and health services have played in addressing mental illness 'back home' may also be assumed to exist within Australia. In some home countries, such as Romania, there is so much stigma surrounding mental illness that people may have assumed that the same stigma would exist in Australia. As agencies have not provided information to ethnic communities, members can only assume that the mental health system operates in similar fashion to that operating in their country of origin. |
| Lack of time, energy and cohesion in NESB communities | For some people from NESB groups, particularly recently arrived migrants, time and energy is low due to the strain of establishing themselves. People are often only just able to cope and are without the resources to help others.<br><br>In addition, certain NESB groups (e.g. Romanians in Perth) are not cohesive and lack support groups or networks to help those associated with mental illness, including those with the mental illness, their families, carers and friends. |

Table 14.9 *continued*

| Cultural traditions | For most NESB groups, there is a tradition of avoidance and marginalisation of the mentally ill which occurs regardless of the problem or reason. As part of the community's belief system, it is a behaviour that is learned and passed on within the community, especially while these beliefs are not discussed or challenged. |
|---|---|
| Stigma perpetuates stigma | People who have been stigmatised with a mental illness continue to be viewed and treated in a negative way which reinforces the role model of the public treatment and attitudes toward those with a mental illness. People living with mental illness are treated in a negative way and there are many consequences including lack of aid for problems, isolation and low self-esteem. The lack of assistance and marginalisation reinforces the negative attitudes within the community towards those with a mental illness. |
| By association | Anything associated with a mental illness has become stigmatised, from talking about it through to seeking help and through to contact with psychiatrists and hospitals. Consequently, people don't seek help, don't talk about it and avoid hospitals. |
| Lack of role models | There are limited role models in communities to show that openness, support and seeking help are positive things to do, or information to refute stigmatising attitudes. |

Source: Multicultural Mental Health Australia (MMHA)

community forums and workshops, to effectively tackle the ongoing stigma in NESB communities.

Negative attitudes toward the psychologically disturbed come from many sources: The mass media portray psychiatric patients as prone to violent crime; jokes about the mentally ill are acceptable; families deny the mental distress of one of their members; legal terminology stresses mental incompetence. People also stigmatise themselves by hiding current psychological distress or a history of mental health care.

Researchers have documented a number of ways in which the stigma of mental illness has a negative impact on people's lives (Farina et al., 1996; Wright et al., 2000). In one sample of 84 men who had been hospitalised for mental illness, 6 percent reported having lost a job because of their hospitalisation; 10 percent reported having been denied an apartment or room; 37 percent reported being avoided by others; and 45 percent reported that others had used their history of mental illness to hurt their feelings. Only 6 percent of the men reported no incidents of rejection (Link et al., 1997). This group of men went through a year-long course of treatment that resulted in considerable improvement in their mental health. Even so, at the end of that year, there were no changes in their perception of stigma: Despite their improvements in functioning, the patients did not expect to be treated any more kindly by the world. This type of research shows the great duality of many people's experience with mental disorders: seeking help—allowing one's problems to be labelled—generally brings both relief *and* stigma; treatment improves quality of life at the same time that stigma degrades it (Rosenfield, 1997).

An added difficulty is that people with mental illness often internalise expectations of rejections that may, in turn, bring about negative interactions (Link et al., 1997). Consider this classic experiment.

Twenty-nine men who had formerly been hospitalised for mental illness volunteered to participate in this study. They believed that the research concerned the difficulties ex-psychiatric patients have with finding jobs. The participants were informed that they would interact with a personnel trainee recruited from a business establishment. Half of the participants were told that the trainee knew of their status as ex-psychiatric patients; the other half were told that the trainee had been led to believe they had been medical or surgical patients at the hospital. In fact, the 'trainee' was a confederate of the experimenter who did not have any prior information about the participants' beliefs about his knowledge. That is, he did not know which participants thought that *he* knew that they were ex-patients. Therefore, any differences in the interactions during the time the participants and confederate spent together can be attributed to the participants' *expectations*. In fact, the participants who believed themselves to have been labelled as ex-psychiatric patients talked less during the session and performed less well on a cooperative task. Furthermore, the confederate rated members of this group as more 'tense and anxious' without, again, knowing which group each participant was in (Farina et al., 1971).

The important conclusion here is that people who believe that others have attached the 'mental illness' label to them may change their interactions in a way that brings about genuine discomfort: The expectation of rejection can create rejection; mental illness can be another of life's unfortunate self-fulfilling prophecies.

# PSYCHOLOGY *in your life*

## HOW HAS MENTAL ILLNESS BEEN PORTRAYED IN AUSTRALIAN AND NEW ZEALAND FILMS?

Without doubt, the American film industry has dominated when it comes to famous onscreen portrayals of mental illness and treatment, including:

- Jack Nicholson's Oscar-winning roles in *One Flew Over the Cuckoo's Nest* and as an OCD sufferer in *As Good As It Gets*
- *Silence of the Lambs* (with Anthony Hopkins in his Oscar-winning role as 'Hannibal the Cannibal' Lecter)
- *What About Bob?* starring Bill Murray and Richard Dreyfuss

Still, the Australian and New Zealand film industry has made a significant and incisive contribution to the portrayal of mental illness. Since 1974's *Between Wars*, local and worldwide audiences have been treated to a number of complex tales with psychiatric themes (a more detailed chronology of these films is provided below).

But what exactly has this contribution by the Australian and New Zealand film industry been? How has it affected people's perceptions of mental illness and treatment? We shall explore this in greater detail.

Australian and New Zealand films have traditionally provided a point of view of mental illness that is more compassionate and uplifting than the attitudes found in American film, particularly over the last two decades. There are several films that stand out as highlighting the complex nature of psychiatric illness, particularly: Domaradzki's *Struck by Lightning* and McKenzie's *On the Waves of the Adriatic*. These films are not about institutionalism and

treatment, but rather human triumph over adversity. Films like *Angel Baby*, *Cosi*, *Lilian's Story* and *Shine* (for which Geoffrey Rush won an Academy Award for Best Actor) all contain this central theme. *Angel Baby* director Michael Rymer famously stated that his film 'is not about crazy people. It's about people who have an illness'.

### Treatment

Australian and New Zealand films have sought to tackle a plethora of psychiatric treatments, from various angles, with varying degrees of success.

Electroconvulsive Therapy (ECT) with its billowing smoke

is associated with something nefarious in *Cosi*, whereas its treatment in *Shine* is relatively neutral. Similarly, medication has comic overtones in *Cosi* (for example, when Lewis is accidentally injected with a tranquiliser), whereas in *Angel Baby* when Kate cries out for her Stelazine it is anything but funny.

The impact of community groups has not been given much attention and when it has, the portrayal has not been positive. In *Cosi*, Errol states: 'Half-way houses, community care . . . come on, the Government cuts the cost and chucks them [the patients] on the street.'

A chronology of Australian and New Zealand films about mental illness and psychiatry

| Year | Title | Director |
|------|-------|----------|
| 1974 | *Between Wars* | Michael Thornhill |
| | *27A* | Esben Storm |
| 1984 | *Bliss* | Ray Lawrence |
| 1985 | *An Indecent Obsession* | Lex Marinos |
| | *Wrong World* | Ian Pringle |
| 1987 | *Pandemonium* | Haydn Keenan |
| | *Stroker* | John Laurie |
| | *Contagion* | Karl Zwicky |
| 1989 | *Sweetie* | Jane Campion |
| 1990 | *An Angel at my Table* | Jane Campion |
| | *On the Waves of the Adriatic* | Brian McKenzie |
| 1991 | *Struck by Lightning* | Jerzy Domaradzki |
| 1993 | *The Piano* | Jane Campion |
| 1994 | *Bad Boy Bubby* | Rolf de Heer |
| | *Heavenly Creatures* | Peter Jackson |
| | *Once Were Warriors* | Lee Tamahori |
| 1995 | *Angel Baby* | Michael Rymer |
| 1996 | *Cosi* | Mark Joffe |
| | *Lilian's Story* | Jerzy Domaradzki |
| | *Lust and Revenge* | Paul Cox |
| | *Shine* | Scott Hicks |

**Stigma**

The National Mental Health Policy and the Burdekin Report have both highlighted the need to closely monitor the stigma of mental illness, and to accurately educate the community about people suffering from its various forms. So, have Australian and New Zealand films been sensitive to this stigma, and portrayed mental illness in a way that is factually accurate?

The character-driven nature of many Australian and New Zealand films has gone some way towards humanising mental illness rather than something which is a burden on society. Real-life sufferers of mental illness like David Helfgott have received greater media coverage as a result of these films, most of it positive. It has highlighted how individuals can triumph over adversity in a factual and informative manner.

Simon Champ, chair of the Australian Mental Health Consumer Network, pointed out: 'There is plenty enough drama available if you care to accurately tune into the subjective experience of an individual or family who has survived mental illness.'

A final note on stigma: research suggests that people who have had prior contact with individuals with mental illnesses hold attitudes that are less affected by stigma (Couture & Penn, 2003). For example, students who read a vignette about a man named Jim who had recovered from schizophrenia were more optimistic about Jim's future prospects when the students had had prior contact with someone who suffered from a mental illness (Penn et al., 1994). Similarly, students' ratings of the dangerousness of patients with schizophrenia were lower when they had had prior contact (Penn et al., 1999). We hope that one consequence of reading this chapter and the next will be to help modify your beliefs about what it means to be mentally ill and what it means to be 'cured'—and to increase your tolerance and compassion for mentally ill individuals.

In making sense of psychopathology, you are forced to come to grips with basic conceptions of normality, reality and social values. In discovering how to understand, treat, and, ideally, prevent psychological disorders, researchers not only help those who are suffering and losing out on the joys of living, they also expand the basic understanding of human nature. How do psychologists and psychiatrists intervene to right minds gone wrong and to modify behaviour that doesn't work? We will see in the next chapter on therapies.

---

### RECAP CHECKPOINT

#### The stigma of mental illness

- Those with psychological disorders are often stigmatised in ways that most physically ill people are not.

- Although treatment for psychological disorders brings about positive changes, the stigma associated with mental illness has a negative impact on quality of life.

### CONCEPT QUESTIONS

1. In the context of mental illness, how does stigma function?

2. Why does treatment for mental illness often bring about both relief and stigma?

3. What types of experience reduce stigma?

### CRITICAL THINKING

Consider the study on ex-psychiatric patients' expectations of rejections. Why was it important that the accomplice not know which patients were in which group?

For answers go to MyPsychLab!

# SUMMARY

Chapter 14 has briefly outlined the major abnormal psychological disorders. It is by no means a complete review of the literature on each disorder presented. It is important to remember that the majority of mental health disorders are treatable, but as outlined in the chapter, a lot is yet to be discovered about the causes behind each disorder. Given this, treatment practices will continue to improve in the years to come, but the stigma behind mental health disorders is a hard fought battle across gender, age and cultural groups. Public education is the key to de-stigmatising psychological disorders.

# KEY TERMS

abnormal psychology (p. 484)
aetiology (p. 489)
agoraphobia (p. 492)
antisocial personality disorder (p. 505)
anxiety disorders (p. 491)
attention-deficit hyperactivity disorder (p. 515)
autistic disorder (p. 515)
bipolar disorder (p. 498)
borderline personality disorder (p. 504)
comorbidity (p. 488)
conversion disorder (p. 507)
delusions (p. 509)
diathesis-stress hypothesis (p. 512)

dissociative amnesia (p. 507)
dissociative disorder (p. 507)
dissociative identity disorder (DID) (p. 508)
*DSM-IV-TR* (p. 487)
fear (p. 492)
generalised anxiety disorder (p. 491)
hypochondriasis (p. 506)
insanity (p. 514)
learned helplessness (p. 500)
major depressive disorder (p. 497)
manic episode (p. 498)
mood disorder (p. 497)
neurotic disorders (p. 488)

obsessive-compulsive disorder (OCD) (p. 493)
panic disorder (p. 492)
personality disorder (p. 504)
phobia (p. 492)
psychological diagnosis (p. 486)
psychopathological functioning (p. 484)
psychotic disorders (p. 488)
schizophrenic disorder (p. 509)
social phobia (p. 492)
somatisation disorder (p. 507)
somatoform disorder (p. 506)
specific phobias (p. 493)
stigma (p. 516)

# PRACTICE TEST

1. Comorbidity refers to circumstances in which an individual
   a. cannot be accurately diagnosed using *DSM-IV-TR*.
   b. has a neurotic disorder that cannot be easily cured.
   c. has a psychotic disorder that includes a fear of death.
   d. experiences more than one psychological disorder at the same time.

2. Professor Hexter believes that unconscious conflicts often cause psychological disorders. Which approach to psychopathology does Professor Hexter use?
   a. psychodynamic      c. cognitive
   b. sociocultural       d. behavioural

3. For over a year, Jane has felt anxious or worried throughout the day. It sounds like Jane is suffering from
   a. panic disorder.
   b. generalised anxiety disorder.
   c. obsessive-compulsive disorder.
   d. agoraphobia.

4. Research with fMRI scans suggests that people who have developed PTSD have_____disruptions in brain areas devoted to_____.
   a. limited; planning for the future
   b. broad; emotional memories
   c. limited; emotional memories
   d. broad; planning for the future

5. What attribution style puts people at risk for depression?
   a. internal-specific-stable
   b. external-specific-unstable
   c. internal-global-stable
   d. external-global-unstable

6. When something bad happens, Chris spends a lot of time ruminating about the problem. Based on this behaviour, you think it is
   a. more likely that Chris is a man.
   b. equally likely that Chris is a man or a woman.
   c. likely that Chris will develop a specific phobia.
   d. more likely that Chris is a woman.

7. You are trying to assess the probability that Paula will develop major depressive disorder. You would be most concerned if she had the _____ form of a serotonin gene as well as _____ stressful life events.
   a. s/l; two             c. l/l; four
   b. s/s; three           d. s/l; three

8. Nadine alternates between yelling at Tricia and begging her to remain friends. Tricia is convinced that Nadine suffers from _____ personality disorder.
   a. schizotypal          c. borderline
   b. narcissistic         d. obsessive-compulsive

9. Although Peter routinely steals the purses of elderly women, he doesn't experience any remorse. This leads you to wonder whether Peter has _____ personality disorder.
   a. histrionic           c. antisocial
   b. dependent            d. narcissistic

10. To diagnose conversion disorder, you'd try to find _____ that preceded the appearance of symptoms.
    a. a serious physical illness
    b. psychological conflict or stress
    c. a visit to a medical doctor
    d. both pain and gastrointestinal complaints

11. Although Eve doesn't have any organic dysfunction, she often forgets important personal experiences. This could be an instance of
    a. dissociative amnesia.      c. somatisation disorder.
    b. hypochondriasis.           d. dependent personality disorder.

12. Which of these is a negative symptom of schizophrenia?
    a. hallucinations       c. delusions
    b. incoherent language  d. social withdrawal

13. While in remission from schizophrenia, Mark is living with his family. Mark is less likely to experience a relapse if his family is _____ on overall_____ .
    a. low; expressed emotion   c. low; empathy
    b. high; hostility          d. high; expressed emotion

14. What percentage of the Australian adult population will experience one or more forms of mental illness in their lifetime?
    a. 5 percent            c. 20 percent
    b. 10 percent           d. 30 percent

15. Which of these behaviours would *not* generally support a diagnosis of attention-deficit hyperactivity disorder?
    a. Manfred blurts out answers during class activities.
    b. Manfred loses his toys and school assignments.
    c. Manfred squirms and fidgets in the classroom.
    d. Manfred cries when other children tease him.

16. Professor Wyatt believes that 1-year-old Brian is at risk for autistic disorder. The professor might observe Brian to determine whether he
    a. fails to respond to his name.
    b. can walk without assistance.
    c. responds appropriately to loud noises.
    d. shows smooth pursuit with his eyes.

17. In a study of the stigma associated with mental illness, around _____ percent of the sample reported no incidents of rejection.
    a. 22                   c. 43
    b. 6                    d. 74

18. As part of an introductory psychology class, a lecturer has her students interview people who have recovered from psychological disorders. This exercise should
    a. prompt the students to be more affected by the stigma of mental illness.
    b. have no impact on the students' experience of stigma.
    c. prompt the students to be less affected by the stigma of mental illness.
    d. decrease the probability that students would seek treatment for mental illness.

## Essay Questions

1. Why is it not always possible to be objective about diagnoses of mental illness?

2. What are some benefits of a useful classification system for psychological disorders?

3. What life circumstances lead some people to contemplate suicide?

# WEB LINKS

www.anxietyaustralia.com.au
> Anxiety Treatment Australia

http://www.healthinsite.gov.au/topics/Mental_Health_of_Aboriginal_and_Torres_Strait_Islander_Peoples
> Mental Health of Aboriginal and Torres Strait Islanders

http://www.schizophrenia.org.au/
> Mental Illness Fellowship of Australia Inc

www.adhd.org.au/
> ADHD Australia Inc

http://www.mentalhealth.asn.au/resources/stigma.htm
> Mental Health Association of NSW (Stigma)

www.beyondblue.org.au
> beyondblue

Are you ready for the test? MyPsychLab offers dozens of ways to deepen your understanding and test your recall of the material in this chapter—including video and audio clips, simulations and activities, self-assessments, practice tests and other study materials. Specific resources available for this chapter include:

 Overview of the types of schizophrenia

 Anxiety and worry
Fear of flying
Social phobia
Schizophrenic disorder

 Learned helplessness: an experimental
procedure, parts I and II

To access MyPsychLab, please visit **www.pearsoned.com.au/mypsychlab**

# What type are you?

## NOW YOU HAVE READ CHAPTER 14—ARE YOU PREPARED FOR THE EXAM?

To enhance your understanding of any of the material in your *Psychology and Life* textbook, go to **MyPsychLab: www.pearsoned.com.au/mypsychlab**.

Complete pre- and post-tests, create your own individualised study plan, watch videos and animations and listen to audio glossaries—all of which will help you understand the themes of this chapter:

* The nature of psychological disorders
* Anxiety disorders
* Mood disorders
* Personality disorders
* Somatoform and dissociative disorders
* Schizophrenic disorders
* Psychological disorders of childhood
* The stigma of mental illness

Listen to the online AUDIO GLOSSARY for a complete list of definitions for key terms in Chapter 14, such as *dissociative amnesia*, *aetiology* and *agoraphobia*.

'MyPsychLab was a fantastic asset in preparing for exams.

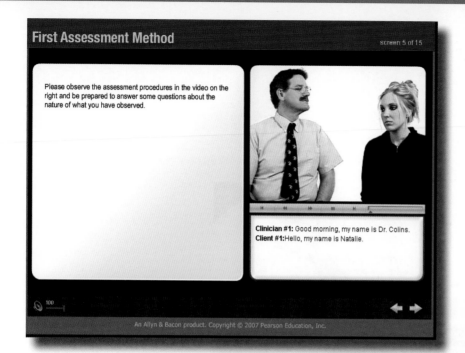

**First Assessment Method**

screen 5 of 15

Please observe the assessment procedures in the video on the right and be prepared to answer some questions about the nature of what you have observed.

**Clinician #1:** Good morning, my name is Dr. Colins.
**Client #1:** Hello, my name is Natalie.

An Allyn & Bacon product. Copyright © 2007 Pearson Education, Inc.

Watch, read and listen—then answer questions about **SIMULATIONS** on *clinical assessment methods ...*

*... and schizophrenia*

'The diagnostic tests helped me to know what topics I needed to study further and helped me prepare for my exam.'

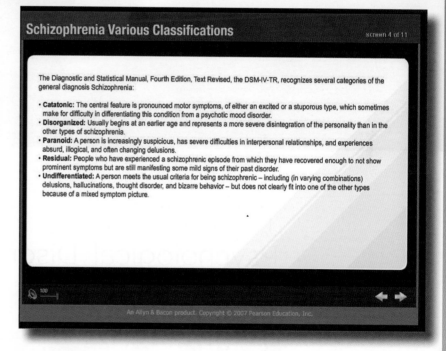

**Schizophrenia Various Classifications**

screen 4 of 11

The Diagnostic and Statistical Manual, Fourth Edition, Text Revised, the DSM-IV-TR, recognizes several categories of the general diagnosis Schizophrenia:

- **Catatonic:** The central feature is pronounced motor symptoms, of either an excited or a stuporous type, which sometimes make for difficulty in differentiating this condition from a psychotic mood disorder.
- **Disorganized:** Usually begins at an earlier age and represents a more severe disintegration of the personality than in the other types of schizophrenia.
- **Paranoid:** A person is increasingly suspicious, has severe difficulties in interpersonal relationships, and experiences absurd, illogical, and often changing delusions.
- **Residual:** People who have experienced a schizophrenic episode from which they have recovered enough to not show prominent symptoms but are still manifesting some mild signs of their past disorder.
- **Undifferentiated:** A person meets the usual criteria for being schizophrenic – including (in varying combinations) delusions, hallucinations, thought disorder, and bizarre behavior – but does not clearly fit into one of the other types because of a mixed symptom picture.

An Allyn & Bacon product. Copyright © 2007 Pearson Education, Inc.

**What can you find in MyPsychLab?**

Self-directed tests * Videos * Simulations * eBook * Biographies * Audio glossary * Web links ... and more—organised by chapter, section and learning objective.

mypsychlab™
*where learning comes to life!*

Therapies for
Psychological Disorders

CHAPTER
15

# CHAPTER FOCUS POINTS

After studying this chapter you will have a better understanding of:

1. The therapeutic context for psychological disorders

2. How psychodynamic therapies work

3. How behaviour therapies work

4. How cognitive therapies work

5. How humanistic therapies work

6. The process of group therapies

7. How biomedical therapies work

8. Implementation of treatment evaluations and prevention strategies for mental health.

# CHAPTER CONTENTS

As you read Chapter 14, you might at some points have felt overwhelmed by all the ways in which individuals can experience mental illness. Fortunately, psychologists and other providers of mental healthcare have worked intently to create therapies that address the full range of psychopathology. We will see in this chapter that researchers continue to generate innovations in therapeutic techniques. The more researchers learn about the causes and consequences of psychopathology—the research we described in Chapter 14—the better they are able to fine-tune their repertory of therapies.

In this chapter, we will examine the types of therapies that can help restore personal control to individuals with a range of disorders. We address a number of formidable questions: How has the treatment of psychological disorders been influenced by historical, cultural and social forces? How do theory, research and practice interact as researchers develop and test treatment methods? What can be done to influence a mind ungoverned by ordinary reason, to modify uncontrolled behaviour, to alter unchecked emotions and to correct abnormalities of the brain?

This chapter surveys the major types of treatments currently used by health-care providers: psychoanalysis, behaviour modification, cognitive alteration, humanistic therapies and drug therapies. We will examine the way these treatments work. We will also evaluate the validity of claims about the success of each therapy.

# THE THERAPEUTIC CONTEXT

There are different types of therapies for mental disorders, and there are many reasons some people seek help (and others who need it do not). The purposes or goals of therapy, the settings in which therapy occurs, and the kinds of therapeutic helpers also vary. Despite any differences between therapies, however, all are *interventions* into a person's life, designed to change the person's functioning in some way.

## GOALS AND MAJOR THERAPIES

The therapeutic process can involve four primary tasks or goals:

1. Reaching a *diagnosis* about what is wrong, possibly determining an appropriate psychiatric *(DSM-IV-TR)* label for the presenting problem and classifying the disorder.

2. Proposing a probable *aetiology* (cause of the problem)—that is, identifying the probable origins of the disorder and the functions being served by the symptoms.

3. Making a *prognosis*, or estimate, of the course the problem will take with and without any treatment.

4. Prescribing and carrying out some form of *treatment*—a therapy designed to minimise or eliminate the troublesome symptoms and, perhaps, their sources.

**Biomedical therapies** focus on changing the mechanisms that run the central nervous system. Practised largely by psychiatrists and physicians, these therapies try to alter brain functioning with chemical or physical interventions, including surgery, electric shock and drugs that act directly on the brain–body connection.

Psychological therapies, which are collectively called **psychotherapy**, focus on changing the faulty behaviours people have learned: the words, thoughts, interpretations and feedback that direct daily strategies for living. These therapies are practised by clinical psychologists as well as by psychiatrists. There are four major types of psychotherapies: psychodynamic, behavioural, cognitive, and existential-humanistic.

The *psychodynamic* approach views neurotic suffering as the outer symptom of inner, unresolved traumas and conflicts. Psychodynamic therapists treat mental disorder with a 'talking cure,' in which a therapist helps a person develop insights about the relation between the overt symptoms and the unresolved hidden conflicts that presumably caused them.

*Behaviour therapy* treats the behaviours themselves as disturbances that must be modified. Disorders are viewed as learned behaviour patterns rather than as the symptoms of mental disease. Behaviours are transformed in many ways, including changing reinforcement contingencies for desirable and undesirable responding, extinguishing conditioned responses and providing models of effective problem solving.

*Cognitive therapy* tries to restructure the way a person thinks by altering the often distorted self-statements a person makes about the causes of a problem. Restructuring cognitions changes the way a person defines and explains difficulties, often enabling the person to cope with the problems.

Therapies that have emerged from the *humanistic tradition* emphasise the patients' values. They are directed toward self-actualisation, psychological growth, the development of more meaningful interpersonal relationships and the enhancement of freedom of choice. They tend to focus more on improving the functioning of essentially healthy people than on correcting the symptoms of seriously disturbed individuals.

Although we have introduced each type of psychotherapy separately, it is important to note that many psychotherapists take an *integrative* approach to practice: they integrate different theoretical approaches to provide maximum benefit to their patients or clients. In many cases, psychotherapists begin their careers adhering to a particular theoretical orientation. However, as their careers unfold, they begin to mix together the most effective elements of different therapies (Norcross et al., 2005). Psychotherapists integrate across virtually every pair of orientations (e.g., cognitive and humanistic; behavioural and psychodynamic). However, the most prominent integrative therapies combine aspects of the cognitive and behavioural approaches (Goldfried, 2003; Norcross et al., 2005). Later in the chapter, we describe integrative cognitive behavioural therapies.

# THERAPISTS AND THERAPEUTIC SETTINGS

When psychological problems arise, most people initially seek out informal counsellors who operate in familiar settings. Many people turn to family members, close friends, personal physicians, lawyers, or favourite teachers for support, guidance and counsel. Those with religious affiliations may seek help from a clergy member. Others get advice and a chance to talk by opening up to bartenders, salesclerks, cabdrivers or other people willing to listen. In our society, these informal therapists carry the bulk of the daily burden of relieving frustration and conflict. When problems are limited in scope, informal therapists can often help.

Although more people seek out therapy now than in the past, people usually turn to trained mental health professionals only when their psychological problems become severe or persist for extended periods of time. When they do, they can turn to several types of therapists.

A **clinical social worker** is a mental health professional whose specialised training in a school of social work prepares him or her to work in collaboration with psychiatrists and clinical psychologists. Unlike many psychiatrists and psychologists, these counsellors are trained to consider the social contexts of people's problems, so these practitioners may also involve other family members in the therapy or at least become acquainted with clients' homes or work settings.

A **pastoral counsellor** is a member of a religious group who specialises in the treatment of psychological disorders. Often, these counsellors combine spirituality with practical problem solving.

A **clinical psychologist** is required to have concentrated his or her graduate school training in the assessment and treatment of psychological problems, completed a supervised internship in a clinical setting, and earned a Masters, PhD or PsyD. These psychologists tend to have a broader background in psychology, assessment and research than do psychiatrists.

A **counselling psychologist** also typically has obtained a Masters, PhD or PsyD. He or she usually provides guidance in areas such as vocation selection, school problems, drug abuse and marital conflict. Often, these counsellors work in community settings related to the problem areas—within a business, a school, a prison, the military service, or a neighbourhood clinic—and use interviews, tests, guidance and advising to help individuals solve specific problems and make decisions about future options.

A **psychiatrist** must have completed all medical school training for an MD degree and also have undergone some postdoctoral specialty training in mental and emotional disorders. Psychiatrists are trained more in the biomedical basis of psychological problems and they are currently the only therapists who can prescribe medical or drug-based interventions.

A **psychoanalyst** is a therapist with either an MD or a PhD degree who has completed specialised postgraduate training in the Freudian approach to understanding and treating mental disorders.

These different types of therapists practise in many settings: hospitals, clinics, schools and private offices. Some humanistic therapists prefer to conduct group sessions in their homes in order to work in a more natural environment. Community-based therapies, which take the treatment to the client, may operate out of local storefronts or houses of worship. Finally, there are therapists who practise in vivo therapy work with clients in the life setting that is associated with their problem. For example, they work in airplanes with clients who suffer from flying phobias or in shopping malls with people who have social phobias.

Psychotherapists have also begun to provide mental healthcare using email or the Internet (King & Moreggi, 1998; Taylor & Luce, 2003). In this type of computer-assisted therapy, individuals often interact with their therapists through exchanges of email. Researchers have been quick to point out both potential dangers and benefits of therapy on the Internet. On the dangers side, researchers worry that patients may be misdiagnosed if they present limited or distorted information without the extra scrutiny that is possible face to face (King & Moreggi, 1998). Furthermore, consumers rarely are able to verify the credentials of online therapists; in cyberspace anyone can claim to be an expert. Despite these dangers, email therapy may also provide unique opportunities for therapists and their clients. For example, some therapists believe that the relative anonymity of this form of therapy allows clients to reveal their most pressing problems and concerns more quickly and with less embarrassment; individuals may be more honest when they don't have to worry about their therapist's overt reactions to their difficult confessions (Grohol, 1998).

People who enter therapy are usually referred to as either patients or clients. The term **patient** is used by professionals who take a biomedical approach to the treatment of psychological problems. The term **client** is used by professionals who think of psychological disorders as 'problems in living' and not as mental illnesses. We will use the preferred term for each approach: *patient* for biomedical and psychoanalytic therapies and *client* for other therapies.

Whatever the form of the treatment, it's important that the individual seeking help enter into an effective therapeutic alliance. A *therapeutic alliance* is a mutual relationship that a client or patient establishes with a therapist: The individual and the therapist collaborate to bring about relief. Research suggests that the quality of the therapeutic alliance has an impact on psychotherapy's ability to bring about improved mental health (Goldfried & Davila, 2005; Joyce et al., 2003). When you enter into therapy, you should believe that you can establish a strong therapeutic alliance with your therapist.

Before looking at contemporary therapies and therapists in more detail, we will first consider the historical contexts in which treatment of the mentally ill was developed and then broaden the Western perspective with a look at the healing practices of other cultures.

**clinical social worker** A mental health professional whose specialised training prepares him or her to consider the social context of people's problems.

**pastoral counsellor** A member of a religious order who specialises in the treatment of psychological disorders, often combining spirituality with practical problem solving.

**clinical psychologist** An individual who has earned a doctorate in psychology and whose training is in the assessment and treatment of psychological problems.

**patient** The term used by those who take a biomedical approach to the treatment of psychological problems to describe the person being treated.

**client** The term used by clinicians who think of psychological disorders as problems in living, and not as mental illnesses, to describe those being treated.

**counselling psychologist** Psychologist who specialises in providing guidance in areas such as vocational selections, school problems, drug abuse and marital conflict.

**psychiatrist** An individual who has obtained a medical degree and also has completed specialty training in mental and emotional disorders; a psychiatrist may prescribe medications for the treatment of psychological disorders.

**psychoanalyst** An individual who has earned either a psychology or a medical degree and has completed postgraduate training in the Freudian approach to understanding and treating mental disorders.

# HISTORICAL PERSPECTIVES ON INSTITUTIONAL TREATMENT

What kind of treatment might you have received in past centuries if you were suffering from psychological problems? For much of history, chances are the treatment would not have helped and could even have been harmful. We will trace the institutional treatment of psychological disorders to the 21st century, in which *deinstitutionalisation*—the practice of moving people from psychiatric hospitals to other venues for treatment—has become an important issue.

**deinstitutionalisation** The movement to treat people with psychological disorders in the community rather than in psychiatric hospitals.

**History of treatment** Population increases and migration to big cities in 14th-century Western Europe created unemployment and social alienation. These conditions led to poverty, crime and psychological problems. Special institutions were soon created to warehouse society's three emerging categories of so-called misfits: the poor, criminals and the mentally disturbed.

In 1403, a London hospital—St. Mary of Bethlehem—admitted its first patient with psychological problems. For the next 300 years, mental patients of the hospital were chained, tortured and exhibited to an admission-paying public. Over time, a mispronunciation of Bethlehem—*bedlam*—came to mean chaos because of the horrible confusion reigning in the hospital and the dehumanised treatment of patients there (Foucault, 1975).

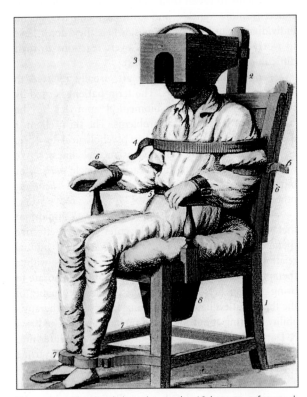

Treatment of mental disorders in the 18th century focused on banishing 'ill humours' from the body. Shown here is the 'tranquilising chair' advocated by Philadelphia physician Benjamin Rush. Why did attitudes towards the treatment of the mentally ill change?

It wasn't until the late 18th century that the perception of psychological problems as mental illness emerged in Europe. In 1792, the French physician Philippe Pinel received permission from the government installed after the French Revolution to remove the chains from some of the inmates in mental hospitals. In the United States, psychologically disturbed individuals were confined for their own protection and for the safety of the community, but they were given no treatment. However, by the mid-1800s, when psychology as a field of study was gaining some credibility and respectability, 'a cult of curability' emerged throughout the country. Spurred on by her firsthand experience working in prison settings, **Dorothea Dix** laboured continuously between 1841 and 1881 to improve the physical treatment of the mentally ill.

In the late 19th and early 20th centuries, many people argued that mental illness arose from the environmental stresses brought on by the turmoil of newly developing cities. To ease those stresses, the disturbed were confined to asylums in rural areas, far from the stress of the city, not only for protection but also for treatment (Rothman, 1971). Unfortunately, many of the asylums that were built became overcrowded. The humane goal of alleviating mental illness was replaced with the pragmatic goal of containing strange people in remote places. These large understaffed state mental hospitals became little more than human warehouses for disturbed individuals (Scull, 1993). Beginning in the 1960s, reformers began to agitate against these warehouses, in favour of the deinstitutionalisation of at least those mental patients who could thrive with outpatient treatment and appropriate community supports. Unfortunately, as we'll see next, many deinstitutionalised patients do not obtain adequate assistance in their communities.

**Deinstitutionalisation and homelessness** In the 1960s, about 30,000 people in Australia were residents in mental hospitals. More recently, that figure has fallen to approximately 8,000. This reduction for Australia is parallelled in other countries around the world (Fakhoury & Priebe, 2002). As we saw in Chapter 14, it isn't the case that the number of people affected by psychological disorders has fallen. Rather, the change reflects a process of deinstitutionalisation: Many people with disorders are now treated outside of hospital settings. Deinstitutionalisation arose from both social forces (i.e., the movement against the warehousing of people with mental illness) and genuine advances in treatment. For example, later in this chapter we will describe drug treatments that allowed people with schizophrenia to live outside of institutions.

Many people have been deinstitutionalised with the assumption that they will receive mental health care in some other setting. Unfortunately, that hasn't always proven to be the case. In fact, many people who leave psychiatric hospitals are not able to cope with their psychological disorders once they are in the community. One consequence is that people who leave institutions become homeless. For example, U.S. researchers found that 24 percent of a sample of 438 individuals with serious mental illnesses were homeless (Kuno et al., 2000). Among people who were admitted to a major state mental hospital in 1980, 15.3 percent were homeless. By 1996, that figure had risen to 20.2 percent and by 2003 to 29.2 percent (Appleby et al., 2006). Even when deinstitutionalised people are not homeless, ongoing mental health issues can cause substantial problems. For example, researchers examined the rate at which people with severe mental illness are the victims of violent crime such as robbery or assault (Teplin et al., 2005). In a sample of 936 men and women, 25.3 percent had experienced a violent crime—a rate 11 times higher than for individuals in the general population. The researchers suggested that the individuals' mental illnesses may prevent them from recognising risk or appropriately protecting themselves.

Another consequence of deinstitutionalisation is what has sometimes been called the 'revolving door': people leave institutions for only brief periods of time before needing help once again. For example, one large-scale U.S. study looked at 29,373 patients with schizophrenia who had been released from hospitals. The researchers found that 42.5 percent of the patients were readmitted within 30 days of their initial release (Lin et al., 2006). More generally, approximately 40 to 50 percent of psychiatric patients are readmitted within 1 year after their initial discharge (Bridge & Barbe, 2004). In many of these cases, individuals left institutional care with the symptoms of their psychological disorders at a level that could have allowed them to function in the outside world. Unfortunately, people often do not have appropriate community or personal resources to adhere to treatment outside the structure provided by an institution. In that sense, the problem is not so much with deinstitutionalisation as it is with the lack of community resources outside the institutions. Researchers have begun to focus attention on how community and educational programs can reduce the number of readmissions—and close the revolving door (Bridge & Barbe, 2004).

For answers go to MyPsychLab!

# PSYCHODYNAMIC THERAPIES

*Psychodynamic* therapies assume that a patient's problems have been caused by the psychological tension between unconscious impulses and the constraints of his or her life situation. These therapies locate the core of the disorder inside the disturbed person.

## FREUDIAN PSYCHOANALYSIS

**Psychoanalysis**, as developed by Sigmund Freud, is an intensive and prolonged technique for exploring unconscious motivations and conflicts in neurotic, anxiety-ridden individuals. As we saw in earlier chapters, Freudian theory views anxiety disorders as inabilities to resolve adequately the inner conflicts between the unconscious, irrational impulses of the *id* and the internalised social constraints imposed by the *superego*. The goal of psychoanalysis is to establish intra-psychic harmony that expands awareness of the forces of the *id*, reduces over-compliance with the demands of the *superego*, and strengthens the role of the *ego*.

Of central importance to a therapist is to understand the way a patient uses the process of *repression* to handle conflicts. Symptoms are considered to be messages from the unconscious that something is wrong. A psychoanalyst's task is to help a patient bring repressed thoughts to consciousness and to gain *insight* into the relationship between the current symptoms and the repressed conflicts. In this psychodynamic view, therapy succeeds and patients recover when they are 'released from repression' established in early childhood. Because a central goal of a therapist is to guide a patient towards discovering insights into the relationships between present symptoms and past origins, psychodynamic therapy is often called **insight therapy**.

Traditional psychoanalysis is an attempt to reconstruct long-standing repressed memories and then work through painful feelings to an effective resolution. Accordingly, it is a therapy that takes a long time (several years at least, with as many as five sessions a week). It also requires introspective patients who are verbally fluent, highly motivated to remain in therapy, and willing and able to undergo considerable

**psychoanalysis** The form of psychodynamic therapy developed by Freud which explores unconscious motivations and conflicts in neurotic, anxiety-ridden individuals.

**insight therapy** A technique by which the therapist guides a patient toward discovering insights between present symptoms and past origins.

Why is psychoanalytic therapy, originally practised in Freud's study, often called the 'talking cure'?

expense. (Newer forms of psychodynamic therapy are making therapy briefer in total duration.) Therapists in the psychodynamic tradition use several techniques to bring repressed conflicts to consciousness and to help a patient resolve them (Henry et al., 1994). These techniques include free association, analysis of resistance, dream analysis, and analysis of transference and counter-transference.

## Free association and catharsis

The principal procedure used in psychoanalysis to probe the unconscious and release repressed material is called **free association**. A patient, sitting comfortably in a chair or lying in a relaxed position on a couch, lets his or her mind wander freely and gives a running account of thoughts, wishes, physical sensations, and mental images. The patient is encouraged to reveal every thought or feeling, no matter how unimportant it may seem.

Freud maintained that free associations are *predetermined*, not random. The task of an analyst is to track the associations to their source and identify the significant patterns that lie beneath the surface of what are apparently just words. The patient is encouraged to express strong feelings, usually toward authority figures, that have been repressed for fear of punishment or retaliation. Any such emotional release, by this or other processes within the therapeutic context, is called **catharsis**.

## Resistance

A psychoanalyst attaches particular importance to subjects that a patient does *not* wish to discuss. At some time during the process of free association, a patient will show **resistance**—an inability or unwillingness to discuss certain ideas, desires or experiences. Such resistances are conceived of as *barriers* between the unconscious and the conscious. This material is often related to an individual's sexual life (which includes all things pleasurable) or to hostile, resentful feelings toward parents. When the repressed material is finally brought into the open, a patient generally claims that it is unimportant, absurd, irrelevant, or too unpleasant to discuss. The therapist believes the opposite. Psychoanalysis aims to break down resistances and enable the patient to face these painful ideas, desires and experiences.

## Dream analysis

Psychoanalysts believe that dreams are an important source of information about a patient's unconscious motivations. When a person is asleep, the superego is presumably less on guard against the unacceptable impulses originating in the id, so a motive that cannot be expressed in waking life may find expression in a dream. In analysis, dreams are assumed to have two kinds of content: *manifest* (openly visible) content that people remember upon awakening and *latent* (hidden) content—the actual motives that are seeking expression but are so painful or unacceptable that they are expressed in disguised or symbolic form. Therapists attempt to uncover these hidden motives by using **dream analysis**, a therapeutic technique that examines the content of a person's dreams to discover the underlying or disguised motivations and symbolic meanings of significant life experiences and desires.

## Transference and counter-transference

During the course of the intensive therapy of psychoanalysis, a patient usually develops an emotional reaction toward the therapist. Often, the therapist is identified with a person who has been at the centre of an emotional conflict in the past—most often a parent or a lover. This emotional reaction is called **transference**. Transference is called *positive transference* when the feelings attached to the therapist are those of love or admiration and *negative transference* when the feelings consist of hostility or envy. Often, a patient's attitude is ambivalent, including a mixture of positive and negative feelings. An analyst's task in handling transference is a difficult one because of the patient's emotional vulnerability; however, it is a crucial part of treatment. A therapist helps a patient to interpret the present transferred feelings by understanding their original source in earlier experiences and attitudes (Henry et al., 1994).

Personal feelings are also at work in a therapist's reactions to a patient. **Counter-transference** refers to what happens when a therapist comes to like or dislike a patient because the patient is perceived as similar to significant people in the therapist's life. In working through counter-transference, a therapist may discover some unconscious dynamics of his or her own. The therapist becomes a 'living mirror' for the patient and the patient, in turn, for the therapist. If the therapist fails to recognise the operation of counter-transference, the therapy may not be as effective (Winarick, 1997). Because of the emotional intensity of this type of therapeutic relationship and the vulnerability of the patient, therapists must be on guard about crossing the boundary between professional caring and personal involvement with their patients. The therapy setting is obviously one with an enormous power imbalance that must be recognised, and honoured, by the therapist.

# LATER PSYCHODYNAMIC THERAPIES

Freud's followers retained many of his basic ideas but modified certain principles and practices. In general, these therapists place more emphasis than Freud did on: (1) a patient's *current* social environment (less focus on the past); (2) the continuing influence of life experiences (not just childhood conflicts); (3) the role of social motivation and interpersonal relations of love (rather than of biological instincts and selfish concerns); (4) the significance of ego functioning and development of the self-concept (less on the conflict between id and superego).

In Chapter 13, we noted two other prominent theorists, Carl Jung and Alfred Adler. To get a flavour of more contemporary psychodynamic approaches, here we will examine the work of Harry Stack Sullivan and Melanie Klein (see Ruitenbeek, 1973, for a look at other members of the Freudian circle).

**Harry Stack Sullivan** (1953) felt that Freudian theory and therapy did not recognise the importance of social relationships and a patient's needs for acceptance, respect, and love. Mental disorders, he insisted, involve not only traumatic intra-psychic processes, but also troubled interpersonal relationships and even strong societal pressures. Anxiety and other mental ills arise out of insecurities in relations with parents and significant others. Therapy based on this interpersonal view involves observing a *patient's feelings* about the *therapist's attitudes*. The therapeutic interview is seen as a social setting in which each party's feelings and attitudes are influenced by the other's.

**Melanie Klein** (1975) defected from Freud's emphasis on the Oedipus conflict as the major source of psychopathology. Instead of oedipal sexual conflicts as the most important organising factors of the psyche, Klein argued that a *death instinct* preceded sexual awareness and led to an innate aggressive impulse that was equally important in organising the psyche. She contended that the two fundamental organising forces in the psyche are aggression and love, where love *unites* and aggression *splits* the psyche. On Klein's view, conscious love is connected to remorse over destructive hate and potential violence toward those we love. Thus Klein explained, 'one of the great mysteries that all people face [is] that love and hate—our personal heaven and hell—cannot be separated from one another' (Frager & Fadiman, 1998, p. 135). Klein pioneered the use of forceful therapeutic interpretations of both aggressive and sexual drives in analytic patients.

We already noted that psychoanalytic therapy often requires a long period of time to achieve its goals. Often, however, people are suffering from disorders that require more speedy remedies. Behaviour therapies, to which we turn next, provide the potential for swift relief from symptoms.

In what ways did the theories of Melanie Klein and Sigmund Freud differ?

## RECAP CHECKPOINT

### Psychodynamic therapies

- Psychodynamic therapies grew out of Sigmund Freud's psychoanalytic theory.

- Freud emphasised the role of unconscious conflicts in the aetiology of psychopathology.

- Psychodynamic therapy seeks to reconcile these conflicts.

- Free association, attention to resistance, dream analysis, transference and counter-transference are all important components of this therapy.

- Other psychodynamic theorists place more emphasis on the patient's current social situation and interpersonal relationships.

## CONCEPT QUESTIONS

For answers go to MyPsychLab!

1. Why is psychodynamic therapy also known as insight therapy?

2. What is transference?

3. What role did the death instinct play in Melanie Klein's theory?

# PSYCHOLOGY *in your life*

## ARE LIVES HAUNTED BY REPRESSED MEMORIES?

In 1994 the trial of a 65-year-old former teacher in Bunbury (Western Australia) sparked much media attention and widespread controversy about repressed memories of sexual abuse. During the trial, the man's two daughters, then adults, recalled 25 years of incestuous abuse which, they said, they had forgotten until consultation with psychologists had helped them 'recover' memories of their ordeal.

After evidence was heard, the jury in the Bunbury case acquitted the father on 15 charges and was unable to reach a decision on the remaining 27. This was purported to be the first case of repressed memory trial in Australia but there have been other charges, including the assault of a prisoner in Long Bay Jail.

How, in theory, had these memories remained hidden for so many years? The answer to this mystery finds its roots in Sigmund Freud's concept of repressed memories. As we just reminded you, Freud (1923) theorised that some people's memories of life experiences become sufficiently threatening to their psychological wellbeing that the individuals banish the memories from consciousness—they repress them. Clinical psychologists are often able to help clients take control of their lives by interpreting disruptive life patterns as the consequences of repressed memories; an important goal of therapy is to achieve catharsis with respect to these repressed memories.

But not all experiences of repressed memories remain in the therapist's office. In recent years, there has been an explosion of mass-media claims for the dramatic recovery of repressed memories. After long intervals of time, individuals report sudden vivid recollections of horrifying events, such as murders or childhood sexual abuse. Could all these claims be real? Our review of memory research in Chapter 7—particularly research on eyewitness memories—provided you with grounds for scepticism (Wells & Loftus, 2003). You might recall from that research that people will report as true memories information that was provided from an artificial source. They will do so even when, as witnesses, they have been specifically warned that they have been misled. Thus being in confident possession of a memory provides no assurance of the ultimate source of that memory.

In fact, the popular media have in recent years frequently provided reports of repressed memories that can serve as an 'artificial source.' What an individual saw on TV could be reborn as a personal memory if information about the TV as source somehow got lost. Thus media descriptions of repressed memories will potentially lead some individuals to 'recover' the same memories. Basically, the individual has lost access to the *source* of the memory but held on to the *content* (Johnson et al., 1993).

Clinicians also worry that therapists who believe in repressed memories may, through the mechanisms of psychotherapy, implant those beliefs in their patients (Lynn et al., 2003). For example, researchers have studied women who have ultimately retracted charges of childhood sexual abuse—these women had come to understand that their 'memories' of abuse could not have been real. These studies provide evidence that therapists often instigated the patients' efforts to find these memories—and verbally rewarded them when the 'memories' came to light (de Rivera, 1997). Cases of this sort have convinced clinicians that they must study the social forces that are at work in therapy to discover how the therapist's theory is translated into the patient's reality (Lynn et al., 1997).

Belief in the recovery of repressed memories may provide a measurable benefit for patients in psychotherapy. In fact, some portion of recovered memories are valid recollections of earlier traumatic experiences (Schooler & Eich, 2000; Williams, 1995). Even so, if you come to explore the question of whether repressed memories from your past can help explain present discomfort, you should ensure that you are not passively accepting someone else's version of your life. For George Franklin, doubts about his daughter's repressed memories led his verdict to be overturned.

# BEHAVIOUR THERAPIES

Whereas psychodynamic therapies focus on presumed inner causes, behaviour therapies focus on observable outer behaviours. Behaviour therapists argue that abnormal behaviours are acquired in the same way as normal behaviours—through a learning process that follows the basic principles of conditioning and learning. Behaviour therapies apply the principles of conditioning and reinforcement to modify undesirable behaviour patterns associated with mental disorders.

The terms **behaviour therapy** and **behaviour modification** are often used interchangeably. Both refer to the systematic use of principles of learning to increase the frequency of desired behaviours and/or decrease that of problem behaviours. The range of deviant behaviours and personal problems that typically are treated by behaviour therapy is extensive and includes fears, compulsions, depression, addictions, aggression and delinquent behaviours. In general, behaviour therapy works best with specific rather than general types of personal problems: it is better for a phobia than for unfocused anxiety.

The therapies that have emerged from the theories of conditioning and learning are grounded in a pragmatic, empirical research tradition. The central task of all living organisms is to learn how to adapt to the demands of the current social and physical environment. When organisms do not learn how to cope effectively, their maladaptive reactions can be overcome by therapy based on principles of learning (or relearning). The target behaviour is not assumed to be a symptom of any underlying process. The symptom itself is the problem. Psychodynamic therapists predicted that treating only the outer behaviour without confronting the true, inner problem would result in *symptom substitution*, the appearance of a new physical or psychological problem. However, research has shown that when pathological behaviours are eliminated by behaviour therapy, new symptoms are not substituted (Kazdin, 1982; Wolpe, 1986). 'On the contrary, patients whose target symptoms improved often reported improvement in other, less important symptoms as well' (Sloane et al., 1975, p. 219).

Let's look at the different forms of behaviour therapies that have brought relief to distressed individuals.

## COUNTERCONDITIONING

Why does someone become anxious when faced with a harmless stimulus, such as a nonpoisonous spider, a nonpoisonous snake, or social contact? The behavioural explanation is that the anxiety arises due to the simple conditioning principles we reviewed in Chapters 6 and 14: strong emotional reactions that disrupt a person's life 'for no good reason' are often conditioned responses that the person does not recognise as having been learned previously. In **counter-conditioning**, a new response is conditioned to replace, or 'counter', a maladaptive response. The earliest recorded use of behaviour therapy followed this logic. **Mary**

**Cover Jones** (1924) showed that a fear could be *unlearned* through conditioning. (Compare with the case of Little Albert in Chapter 6.)

> Her patient was Peter, a 3-year-old boy who, for some unknown reason, was afraid of rabbits. The therapy involved feeding Peter at one end of a room while the rabbit was brought in at the other end. Over a series of sessions, the rabbit was gradually brought closer until, finally, all fear disappeared and Peter played freely with the rabbit.

Following in Cover Jones's footsteps, behaviour therapists now use several counter-conditioning techniques, including systematic desensitisation, implosion, flooding and aversion therapy.

**Exposure therapies** The central component of **exposure therapy** is that individuals are made to confront the object or situation that causes anxiety. The therapeutic principle is that exposure permits counter-conditioning—people learn to remain relaxed in circumstances that once would have made them highly anxious. Individual exposure therapies differ with respect to the time course and circumstances in which people are exposed to their sources of anxiety.

For example, **Joseph Wolpe** (1958, 1973) observed that the nervous system cannot be relaxed and agitated at the same time because incompatible processes cannot be activated simultaneously. This insight was central to the *theory of reciprocal inhibition* that Wolpe applied to the treatment of fears and phobias. Wolpe taught his patients to *relax* their muscles and then to *imagine* visually their feared situation. They did so in gradual steps that moved from initially remote associations to direct images. Psychologically confronting the feared stimulus while being relaxed and doing so in a *graduated* sequence is the therapeutic technique known as **systematic desensitisation**.

Desensitisation therapy involves three major steps. First, the client identifies the stimuli that provoke anxiety and arranges them in a hierarchy ranked from weakest to strongest. For example, a student suffering from severe test anxiety constructed the hierarchy in **Table 15.1**. Note that she rated immediate anticipation of an examination (No. 14) as more stressful than taking the exam itself (No. 13). Second, the client is trained in a system of progressive deep-muscle relaxation. Relaxation training requires several sessions in which the client learns to distinguish between sensations of tension and relaxation and to let go of tension in order to achieve a state of physical and mental relaxation. Finally, the actual process of desensitisation begins: the relaxed client vividly imagines the weakest anxiety stimulus on the list. If it can be visualised without discomfort, the client goes on to the next stronger one. After a number of sessions, the most distressing situations on the list can be imagined without anxiety.

Systematic desensitisation represents a gradual course of exposure to stimuli that provoke anxiety. Therapists have explored a variety of other techniques, some of which

**behaviour therapy** See behaviour modification.

**behaviour modification** The systematic use of principles of learning to increase the frequency of desired behaviours and/or decrease the frequency of problem behaviours.

**exposure therapy** A behavioural technique in which clients are exposed to the objects or situations that cause them anxiety.

**systematic desensitisation** A behavioural therapy technique in which a client is taught to prevent the arousal of anxiety by confronting the feared stimulus while relaxed.

**counter-conditioning** A technique used in therapy to substitute a new response for a maladaptive one by means of conditioning procedures.

Table 15.1

Hierarchy of anxiety-producing stimuli for a test-anxious college student (in order of increasing anxiety)

1. A month before an examination.
2. Two weeks before an examination.
3. A week before an examination.
4. Five days before an examination.
5. Four days before an examination.
6. Three days before an examination.
7. Two days before an examination.
8. One day before an examination.
9. The night before an examination.
10. The examination paper face down.
11. Awaiting the distribution of examination papers.
12. Before the unopened doors of the examination room.
13. In the process of answering an examination paper.
14. On the way to the university on the day of an examination.

bring about exposure with less delay. For example, in a technique known as *flooding*, clients agree to be put directly into the phobic situation. A person with claustrophobia is made to sit in a dark closet, and a child with a fear of water is put into a pool. Researchers successfully treated a 21-year-old student's phobia of balloon pops by having him experience three sessions in which he endured hundreds of balloons being popped (Houlihan et al., 1993). In the third session, the student was able to pop the last 115 balloons himself. Another form of flooding therapy begins with the use of imagination. In this procedure, the client may listen to a tape that describes the most terrifying version of the phobic fear in great detail for an hour or two. Once the terror subsides, the client is then taken to the feared situation.

When exposure techniques were first created, therapists brought about exposure through mental imagery or actual contact. In recent years, clinicians have turned to virtual reality to provide exposure therapy (Glanz et al., 2003). Consider this study that compared virtual reality therapy to standard exposure therapy for individuals with *acrophobia*—a fear of heights.

> A team of researchers recruited 33 people suffering from acrophobia (Emmelkamp et al., 2002). Roughly half of the group (16 participants) received a standard form of exposure therapy. The researchers took them to actual physical locations that became successively more anxiety provoking with respect to the fear of heights—a mall with several levels, a fire escape and a roof garden. The participants experienced each location until their anxiety had diminished. The remainder of the participants visited the same locations—but as virtual environments. As with their peers who went out into the world, they remained in each virtual location until their

anxiety had diminished. To measure the effectiveness of each intervention, the researchers assessed the participants' lingering discomfort toward heights on measures such as an *attitudes toward heights questionnaire*. Both types of therapies yielded consistent and lasting relief for the participants. There were no differences in the effectiveness of the two types of therapies.

Exposure therapies have proved to be highly effective for alleviating phobias. Virtual reality techniques hold out the promise of providing powerful exposure experiences without the time and expense of venturing out into the real world.

Exposure therapy has also been used to combat obsessive-compulsive disorders. For example, one woman who was obsessed with dirt compulsively washed her hands over and over until they cracked and bled. She even thought of killing herself because this disorder totally prevented her from leading a normal life. Under the supervision of a behaviour therapist, she confronted the things she feared most—dirt and garbage—and eventually even touched them. She gave up washing and bathing her hands and face for 5 days. Note that behaviour therapy here has an added component, *response prevention*. Not only is the client exposed to what is feared (dirt and garbage), but she is also prevented from performing the compulsive behaviour that ordinarily reduces her anxiety (washing). The therapy teaches the woman to reduce anxiety without engaging her compulsion.

The latest version of exposure therapy for OCD has been developed in Australia and is known as Danger Ideation Reduction Therapy (D.I.R.T.). This particular treatment is targeted at treatment resistant OCD clients with contamination fears about germs. Treatment consists of weekly one-hour therapy sessions for 14 weeks. The trial of this treatment program found reduction in symptom severity, which was measured on all scales used to assess OCD symptoms. The Padua Inventory, a test to measure obsessive-compulsive disorder symptoms, had shown an 85% reduction; Activity checklist, used to measure how often a behaviour occurs, an 86% reduction; Y-BOCS, which is a secondary obsessive-compulsive disorder symptoms measure, and indicated an overall 41% reduction; and a 33% reduction on the Beck Depression Inventory (Govender, Drummond & Menzies, 2006). The unique aspect of this treatment is that it combines exposure therapy with cognitive therapy—another therapeutic approach that will be further outlined later in this chapter.

**Aversion therapy** The forms of exposure therapy we've described help clients deal directly with stimuli that are not really harmful. What can be done to help those who are *attracted* to stimuli that *are* harmful? Drug addiction, sexual perversions and uncontrollable violence are human problems in which deviant behaviour is elicited by tempting stimuli. **Aversion therapy** uses counter-conditioning procedures to pair these stimuli with strong noxious stimuli such as electric shocks or

**aversion therapy** A type of behavioural therapy used to treat individuals attracted to harmful stimuli.

nausea-producing drugs. In time, the same negative reactions are elicited by the tempting stimuli, and the person develops an aversion that replaces his or her former desire. For example, aversion therapy has been used with individuals who engage in *self-injurious behaviours*, such as hitting their heads or banging their heads against other objects. When an individual performs such a behaviour, he or she is given a mild electric shock. This treatment effectively eliminates self-injurious behaviours in some, but not all, patients (Duker & Seys, 1996).

In the extreme, aversion therapy resembles torture, so why would anyone submit voluntarily to it? Usually, people do so only because they realise that the long-term consequences of continuing their behaviour pattern will destroy their health or ruin their careers or family lives. They may also be driven to do so by institutional pressures, as has happened in some prison treatment programs. However, use of aversion therapy in institutional rehabilitation programs has become regulated by ethical guidelines and state laws. The hope is that, under these restrictions, it will be therapeutic rather than coercive.

## CONTINGENCY MANAGEMENT

Counter-conditioning procedures are appropriate when one response can be replaced with another. Other behaviour modification procedures rely on the principles of operant conditioning that arose in the research tradition pioneered by B. F. Skinner. **Contingency management** refers to the general treatment strategy of changing behaviour by modifying its consequences. The two major techniques of contingency management in behaviour therapy are *positive reinforcement strategies* and *extinction strategies*.

**Positive reinforcement strategies** When a response is followed immediately by a reward, the response tends to be repeated and to increase in frequency over time. This central principle of operant learning becomes a therapeutic strategy when it is used to modify the frequency of a desirable response as it replaces an undesirable one. Dramatic success has been obtained from the application of positive reinforcement procedures to behaviour problems.

You might recall from Chapter 6 a technique called *shaping* in which researchers reinforce successive approximations to a desired behaviour. Consider how shaping was used to improve the athletic performance of a 21-year-old university pole vaulter (Scott et al., 1997). The vaulter didn't sufficiently extend his arms (holding the pole) above his head before planting the pole to lift himself off. The research team used a photoelectric beam that beeped when the vaulter achieved the desired extension and broke the beam. In Chapter 6, we also described *token economies*, in which desired behaviours (e.g., practising personal care or taking medication) are explicitly defined, and token payoffs are given by institutional staff when the behaviours are performed. These tokens can later be exchanged for an

How might a behaviour therapist use virtual reality exposure therapy to help a client overcome a fear of flying?

array of rewards and privileges (Kazdin, 1994; Martin & Pear, 1999). These systems of reinforcement are especially effective in modifying patients' behaviours regarding self-care, upkeep of their environment and frequency of their positive social interactions.

In another approach, therapists differentially reinforce behaviours that are incompatible with the maladaptive behaviour. This technique has been used successfully with individuals in treatment for drug addiction.

Researchers recruited 142 individuals who were seeking treatment for cocaine and opioid (e.g., heroin) dependence into a 12 week study (Petry et al., 2005). All the participants received standard treatment of a series of counselling sessions that imparted strategies and skills for overcoming dependence. In addition to this standard treatment, one group of 53 participants received vouchers each time they produced a urine specimen that was drug free. The first time participants produced a negative urine specimen, they were given a voucher worth $1. The voucher amounts increased by $1.50 with each negative specimen. A positive specimen reset the voucher amount to $1. Another group of 51 participants was given the opportunity to win prizes, contingent on negative urine specimens. To win the prizes, participants pulled cards from an urn. The majority of the cards (62.8 percent) read 'good job, try again', but the remainder provided prizes that valued $1, $20 or $100. For the first negative specimen, participants got to pull one card from the urn. For each subsequent negative specimen, they earned an extra one pull. A positive specimen reduced participants back to a single pull. The researchers assessed the efficacy of each treatment program, for example, by measuring the average number of weeks participants in each group were continuously abstinent. For the group that only received standard treatment, that number was 4.6 weeks. For the voucher group, that number was 7.0 weeks, and for the prize group that number

**contingency management** A general treatment strategy involving changing behaviour by modifying its consequences.

was 7.8 weeks. Thus both contingency management treatments increased the likelihood that participants would abstain from drugs.

This study verifies that two different programs of contingency management—vouchers and prizes—can be used successfully to treat drug dependence. You might recognise the same philosophy at work here as the one that motivated the counter-conditioning procedures we described earlier: basic principles of learning are used to increase the probability of adaptive behaviours.

**Extinction strategies** Why do people continue to do something that causes pain and distress when they are capable of doing otherwise? The answer is that many forms of behaviour have multiple consequences—some are negative and some are positive. Often, subtle positive reinforcements keep a behaviour going despite its obvious negative consequences. For example, children who are punished for misbehaving may continue to misbehave if punishment is the only form of attention they seem to be able to earn.

Extinction strategies are useful in therapy when dysfunctional behaviours have been maintained by unrecognised reinforcing circumstances. Those reinforcers can be identified through a careful situational analysis, and then a program can be arranged to withhold them in the presence of the undesirable response. When this approach is possible, and everyone in the situation who might inadvertently reinforce the person's behaviour cooperates, extinction procedures work to diminish the frequency of the behaviour and eventually to eliminate the behaviour completely. Consider a classroom example. Researchers discovered that attention from their peers was reinforcing the disruptive behaviour of four elementary school children. By having their classmates provide attention to appropriate behaviours and ignore disruptive behaviours, the researchers were able to eliminate the children's patterns of misbehaviour (Broussard & Northup, 1997).

Even symptoms of schizophrenia can be maintained and encouraged by unintentional reinforcement. Consider the following circumstances. It is standard procedure in many psychiatric hospitals for the staff to ask patients frequently, as a form of social communication, 'How are you feeling?' Patients often misinterpret this question as a request for diagnostic information, and they respond by thinking and talking about their feelings, unusual symptoms and hallucinations. Such responding is likely to be counterproductive because it leads staff to conclude that the patients are self-absorbed and not behaving normally. In fact, the more bizarre the symptoms and verbalisations, the more attention the staff members may show to the patient, which reinforces continued expression of bizarre symptoms. In a classic study, dramatic decreases in symptoms were observed when hospital staff members were simply instructed to ignore the behaviour and to give attention to the patients only when they were behaving normally (Ayllon & Michael, 1959).

# SOCIAL-LEARNING THERAPY

The range of behaviour therapies has been expanded by social-learning theorists who point out that humans learn by observing the behaviour of other people. Often, you learn and apply rules to new experiences through symbolic means, such as watching other people's experiences in life, in a movie, or on TV. **Social-learning therapy** is designed to modify problematic behaviour patterns by arranging conditions in which a client will observe models being reinforced for a desirable form of responding. This vicarious learning process has been of special value in overcoming phobias and building social skills. We have noted in earlier chapters that this social-learning theory was largely developed through the pioneering research of Albert Bandura (1977, 1986). Here we will mention only two aspects of his approach: imitation of models and social-skills training.

**Imitation of models** Social-learning theory predicts that individuals acquire responses through observation. Thus it should be the case that people with phobias should be able to unlearn fear reactions through imitation of models. For example, in treating a phobia of snakes, a therapist will first demonstrate fearless approach behaviour at a relatively minor level, perhaps approaching a snake's cage or touching a snake. The client is aided, through demonstration and encouragement, to imitate the modelled behaviour. Gradually, the approach behaviours are shaped so that the client can pick up the snake and let it crawl freely over him or her. At no time is the client forced to perform any behaviour. Resistance at any level is overcome by having the client return to a previously successful, less threatening level of approach behaviour.

The power of this form of **participant modelling** can be seen in research comparing this technique with symbolic modelling, desensitisation and a control condition. In *symbolic modelling therapy*, individuals who had been trained in relaxation techniques watched a film in which several models fearlessly handled snakes; they could stop the film and try to relax whenever a scene made them feel anxious. In the control condition, no therapeutic intervention was used. As you can see in **Figure 15.1**, participant modelling was clearly the most successful of these techniques. Snake phobia was eliminated in 11 of the 12 individuals in the participant modelling group (Bandura, 1970).

**Social-skills training** A major therapeutic innovation encouraged by social-learning therapists involves training people with inadequate social skills to be more effective. Many difficulties arise for someone with a mental disorder, or even just an everyday problem, if he or she is socially inhibited, inept or unassertive. *Social skills* are sets of responses that enable people effectively to achieve their social goals when approaching or interacting with others. These skills include knowing *what* (content) to say and do in given situations in order to elicit a

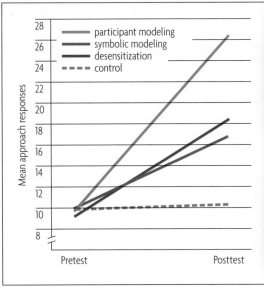

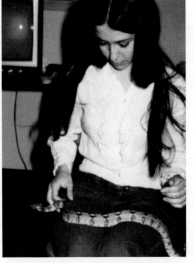

**Participant modelling therapy**
The subject shown in the photo first watched a model make a graduated series of snake-approach responses and then repeated them herself. She eventually was able to pick up the snake and let it crawl about on her. The graph compares the number of approach responses subjects made before and after receiving participant modelling therapy (most effective) with the behaviour of those exposed to two other therapeutic techniques and a control group.

Albert Bandura, from "Modeling Therapy." Reprinted by permission of Albert Bandura.

desired response (consequences), *how* (style) to say and do it, and *when* (timing) to say and do it. To help people acquire such skills, many social-learning therapists recommend **behavioural rehearsal**—visualising how one should behave in a given situation and the desired positive consequences. Rehearsal can be used to establish and strengthen any basic skill, from personal hygiene to work habits to social interactions.

Adult pathology is often preceded by deficits in social skills in childhood. Therefore, considerable research and therapy are directed at building competence in children (Alvord & Grados, 2005; Fraser et al., 2005). For example, one study provided an intervention based on guided imagery to increase the peer acceptance of social isolates.

The researchers observed 6- to 8-year-old boys and girls during recess and identified a group of children who were relatively isolated from their peers (Hernandez Guzman et al., 2002). A subset of the children received social-skills training that the researchers intended to increase the likelihood that they would engage in social play. The training involved guided imagery: The children were asked to imagine themselves approaching a peer ('You softly tell [David]: 'Would you play with me?'') and anticipating their peers' reactions. At first, the children were asked to imagine rejection ('Someone else calls [David] and he leaves'); over time, they visualised success ('OK, let's play.'). The researchers measured the students' percentage of socialisation—the extent to which they engaged in social play with their peers— before and after the intervention. As seen in **Table 15.2**, children who received social-skills training through guided imagery showed great improvement with respect to their untreated peers in the control group.

The treatment group continued to show an advantage over their peers 3 months after the end of the intervention, a month into the next school year.

**Children's socialisation with peers before and after guided imagery training for social skills**

|  | Pretest | Posttest |
|---|---|---|
| Treatment | 50.3 | 66.8 |
| Control | 57.0 | 48.3 |

Note: The figures are percentage socialisation (out of 100 percent).

**behavioural rehearsal**
Procedures used to establish and strengthen basic skills; requires the client to rehearse a desirable behaviour sequence mentally.

## GENERALISATION TECHNIQUES

An ongoing issue of concern for behaviour therapists is whether new behaviour patterns generated in a therapeutic setting will actually be used in the everyday situations faced by their clients (Kazdin, 1994). This question is important for all therapies, because any measure of treatment effectiveness must include maintenance of long-term changes that go beyond a therapist's couch, clinic or laboratory.

When essential aspects of a client's real-life setting are absent from the therapy program, behavioural changes accomplished through therapy may be lost over time after therapy terminates. To prevent this gradual loss, it has become common practice to build generalisation techniques into the therapeutic procedure itself. These techniques attempt to *increase* the similarity of target behaviours, reinforcers, models and stimulus demands between therapy and real-life settings. For example, behaviours are taught that are likely to be reinforced naturally in a person's environment, such as showing courtesy or consideration. Rewards are given on a partial reinforcement schedule to ensure that their effect will be maintained in the real world, where rewards are not always forthcoming. Expectation of tangible extrinsic rewards is gradually *faded out* while social approval and more naturally occurring consequences, including reinforcing self-statements, are incorporated.

Table 15.3

Comparison of psychoanalytic and behavioural approaches to psychotherapy

| Issue | Psychoanalysis | Behaviour therapy |
|---|---|---|
| Basic human nature | Biological instincts, primarily sexual and aggressive, press for immediate release, bringing people into conflict with social reality. | Similar to other animals, people are born only with the capacity for learning, which follows similar principles in all species. |
| Normal human development | Growth occurs through resolution of conflicts during successive stages. Through identification and internalisation, mature ego controls and character structures emerge. | Adaptive behaviours are learned through reinforcement and imitation. |
| Nature of psychopathology | Pathology reflects inadequate conflict resolutions and fixations in earlier development, which leave overly strong impulses and/or weak controls. Symptoms are defensive responses to anxiety. | Problematic behaviour derives from faulty learning of maladaptive behaviours. The *symptom* is the problem; there is no *underlying disease*. |
| Goal of therapy | Psychosexual maturity, strengthened ego functions, and reduced control by unconscious and repressed impulses are attained. | Symptomatic behaviour is eliminated and replaced with adaptive behaviours. |
| Psychological realm emphasized | Motives, feelings, fantasies and cognitions are experienced. | Therapy involves behaviour and observable feelings and actions. |
| Time orientation | The orientation is discovering and interpreting past conflicts and repressed feelings in light of the present. | Concerned only about client's reinforcement history. Present behaviour is examined and treated. |
| Role of unconscious material | This is primary in classical psychoanalysis and somewhat less emphasised by neo-Freudians. | There is no concern with unconscious processes or with subjective experience even in the conscious realm. |
| Role of insight | Insight is central; it emerges in 'corrective emotional experiences'. | Insight is irrelevant and/or unnecessary. |
| Role of therapist | The therapist functions as a *detective*, searching out basic root conflicts and resistances; detached and neutral, to facilitate transference reactions. | The therapist functions as a *trainer*, helping patients unlearn old behaviours and/or learn new ones. Control of reinforcement is important; interpersonal relationship is minor. |

Behaviour therapists, for example, used a fading procedure with a 7-year-old boy who frequently stole from his classmates (Rosen & Rosen, 1983). The boy was fined or awarded 'points' (which could be exchanged for reinforcers such as extra recess) when a check revealed whether he did or did not have other children's possessions. At first, these checks were made every 15 minutes. Over time, they were faded out to only once every 2 hours. Finally, the possession checks were eliminated. Even after the direct manipulation of reinforcers had been faded out, the boy did not return to stealing.

Before we move on to cognitive therapies, take a few minutes to review the major differences between the two psychotherapies outlined thus far—the psychoanalytic and the behavioural—as summarised in **Table 15.3**.

## RECAP CHECKPOINT
### Behaviour therapies
- Behaviour therapies use the principles of learning and reinforcement to modify or eliminate problem behaviours.
- Counter-conditioning techniques replace negative behaviours, like phobic responses, with more adaptive behaviours.
- Exposure is the common element in phobia-modification therapies.
- Contingency management uses operant conditioning to modify behaviour, primarily through positive reinforcement and extinction.
- Social-learning therapy uses models and social-skills training to help individuals gain confidence about their abilities.

## CONCEPT QUESTIONS
1. What is the basic principle of counter-conditioning?
2. What learning principle is at work when clinicians allow patients to earn vouchers?
3. What is likely to take place if someone undergoes social-learning therapy?
4. How does the therapist's role differ between psychoanalysis and behaviour therapy?

CRITICAL THINKING
Recall the study that used social-skills training to help children who were isolated from their peers. In the early part of the training, why might the researchers have asked the children to imagine themselves being rejected?

# COGNITIVE THERAPIES

**C**ognitive therapy attempts to change problem feelings and behaviours by changing the way a client thinks about significant life experiences. The underlying assumption of such therapy is that abnormal behaviour patterns and emotional distress start with problems in *what* people think (cognitive content) and *how* they think (cognitive process). Cognitive therapies focus on changing different types of cognitive processes and providing different methods of cognitive restructuring. We discussed some of these approaches in Chapter 12 as ways to cope with stress and improve health. In this section, we will describe two major forms of cognitive therapy: alteration of false belief systems and cognitive behavioural therapy.

## CHANGING FALSE BELIEFS

Some cognitive behaviour therapists have, as their primary targets for change, beliefs, attitudes and habitual thought patterns. These cognitive therapists argue that many psychological problems arise because of the way people think about themselves in relation to other people and the events they face. Faulty thinking can be based on (1) unreasonable attitudes ('Being perfect is the most important trait for a student to have'), (2) false premises ('If I do everything they want me to, then I'll be popular'), and (3) rigid rules that put behaviour on automatic pilot so that prior patterns are repeated even when they have not worked ('I must obey authorities'). Emotional distress is caused by cognitive misunderstandings and by failure to distinguish between current reality and one's imagination (or expectations).

**Cognitive therapy for depression** A cognitive therapist helps a patient to correct faulty patterns of thinking by substituting more effective problem-solving techniques. Aaron Beck (1976) has successfully pioneered cognitive therapy for the problem of depression. He states the formula for treatment in simple form: 'The therapist helps the patient to identify his warped thinking and to learn more realistic ways to formulate his experiences' (p. 20). For example, depressed individuals may be instructed to write down negative thoughts about themselves, figure out why these self-criticisms are unjustified, and come up with more realistic (and less destructive) self-cognitions.

Beck believes that depression is maintained because depressed patients are unaware of the negative automatic thoughts that they habitually formulate, such as 'I will never be as good as my brother'; 'Nobody would like me if they really knew me'; and 'I'm not smart enough to make it in this competitive school.' A therapist then uses four tactics to change the cognitive foundation that supports the depression (Beck & Rush, 1989; Beck et al., 1979):

- Challenging the client's basic assumptions about his or her functioning.
- Evaluating the evidence the client has for and against the accuracy of automatic thoughts.
- Re-attributing blame to situational factors rather than to the patient's incompetence.
- Discussing alternative solutions to complex tasks that could lead to failure experiences.

This therapy is similar to behaviour therapies in that it centres on the present state of the client.

One of the worst side effects of being depressed is having to live with all the negative feelings and lethargy associated with depression. Becoming obsessed with thoughts about one's negative mood brings up memories of all the bad times in life, which worsens the depressive feelings. By filtering all input through a darkly coloured lens of depression, depressed people see criticism where there is none and hear sarcasm when they listen to praise—further 'reasons' for being depressed. Cognitive therapy has proved successful at arresting depression's downward spiral (Hollon et al., 2006).

**Rational-emotive therapy** One of the earliest forms of cognitive therapy was the **rational-emotive therapy (RET)** developed by **Albert Ellis** (1962, 1995; Windy & Ellis, 1997). RET is a comprehensive system of personality change based on the transformation of irrational beliefs that cause undesirable, highly charged emotional reactions, such as severe anxiety. Clients may have core values *demanding* that they succeed and be approved, *insisting* that they be treated fairly, and *dictating* that the universe be more pleasant.

Rational-emotive therapists teach clients how to recognise the 'shoulds', 'oughts' and 'musts' that are controlling their actions and preventing them from choosing the lives they want. They attempt to break through a client's closed-mindedness by showing that an emotional reaction that follows some event is really the effect of unrecognised beliefs about the event. For example, failure to achieve orgasm during intercourse (event) is followed by an emotional reaction of depression and self-derogation. The belief that is causing the emotional reaction is likely to be 'I am sexually inadequate and may be impotent because I failed to perform as expected.' In therapy, this belief (and others) is openly disputed through rational confrontation and examination of

**cognitive therapy**
Psychotherapeutic treatment that attempts to change feelings and behaviours by changing the way a client thinks about or perceives significant life experiences.

**rational-emotive therapy (RET)** A comprehensive system of personality change based on changing irrational beliefs that cause undesirable, highly charged emotional reactions such as severe anxiety.

Suppose you were learning to knit. Assuming you wanted to get better at it over time, what would be the best internal message to give yourself about the activity?

alternative reasons for the event, such as fatigue, alcohol, false notions of sexual performance, or reluctance to engage in intercourse at that time or with that particular partner. This confrontation technique is followed by other interventions that replace dogmatic, irrational thinking with rational, situationally appropriate ideas.

Rational-emotive therapy aims to increase an individual's sense of self-worth and the potential to be self-actualised by getting rid of the system of faulty beliefs that block personal growth. As such, it shares much with humanistic therapies, which we consider later in the chapter.

## COGNITIVE BEHAVIOURAL THERAPY

You are what you tell yourself you can be, and you are guided by what you believe you ought to do. This is a starting assumption of **cognitive behavioural therapy**. This therapeutic approach combines the cognitive emphasis on changing false beliefs with the behavioural focus on reinforcement contingencies in the modification of performance (Goldfried, 2003). Unacceptable behaviour patterns are modified by *cognitive restructuring*—changing a person's negative self-statements into constructive coping statements.

A critical part of this therapeutic approach is the discovery by therapist and client of the way the client thinks about and expresses the problem for which therapy is sought. Once both therapist and client understand the kind of thinking that is leading to unproductive or dysfunctional behaviours, they develop new self-statements that are constructive and minimise the use of self-defeating ones that elicit anxiety or reduce self-esteem (Meichenbaum, 1977, 1985, 1993). For example, they might substitute the negative self-statement 'I was really boring at that party; they'll never ask me back' with constructive criticism: 'Next time, if I want to appear interesting, I will plan some provocative opening lines, practice telling a good joke, and be responsive to the host's stories.' Instead of dwelling on negatives in past situations

that are unchangeable, the client is taught to focus on positives in the future.

Cognitive behavioural therapy builds expectations of being effective. Therapists know that building these expectations increases the likelihood that people will behave effectively. Through setting attainable goals, developing realistic strategies for attaining them, and evaluating feedback realistically, you develop a sense of mastery and *self-efficacy* (Bandura, 1992, 1997). As we saw in Chapter 13, your sense of self-efficacy influences your perceptions, motivation and performance in many ways. Self-efficacy judgments influence how much effort you expend and how long you persist in the face of difficult life situations (Schwarzer, 1992). The modelling procedures we described earlier allow individuals to increase feelings of *behavioural* self-efficacy: They learn that they can carry out a certain range of behaviours. In contrast, therapy for *cognitive* self-efficacy changes the way clients think about their abilities. For example, in one study, students who believed that a decision-making task would *enhance* their abilities outperformed a second group who thought that the task would only gauge the abilities they already had (Wood & Bandura, 1989). In the study, types of thoughts like 'I can learn to do better' actually allowed the students to become better.

For answers go to MyPsychLab!

**cognitive behavioural therapy** A therapeutic approach that combines the cognitive emphasis on thoughts and attitudes with the behavioural emphasis on changing performance.

## RECAP CHECKPOINT
### Cognitive therapies

- Cognitive therapy concentrates on changing negative or irrational thought patterns about the self and social relationships.

- Cognitive therapy has been used successfully to treat depression.

- Rational-emotive therapy helps clients recognise that their irrational beliefs about themselves interfere with successful life outcomes.

- Cognitive behavioural therapy calls for the client to learn more constructive thought patterns in reference to a problem and to apply the new technique to other situations.

## CONCEPT QUESTIONS

1. What is the underlying assumption of cognitive therapy?

2. With respect to rational-emotive therapy, what is the origin of highly charged emotional reactions?

3. Why is increased self-efficacy a goal for cognitive behavioural therapy?

# HUMANISTIC THERAPIES

Humanistic therapies have at their core the concept of a whole person in the continual process of changing and of becoming. Although environment and heredity place certain restrictions, people always remain free to choose what they will become by creating their own values and committing to them through their own decisions. Along with this *freedom to choose*, however, comes the burden of responsibility. Because you are never fully aware of all the implications of your actions, you experience anxiety and despair. You also suffer from guilt over lost opportunities to achieve your full potential. Psychotherapies that apply the principles of this general theory of human nature attempt to help clients define their own freedom, value their experiencing selves and the richness of the present moment, cultivate their individuality, and discover ways of realising their fullest potential (self-actualisation).

In some cases, humanistic therapies also absorbed the lessons of *existentialist* approaches to human experience (May, 1975). This approach emphasises people's ability to meet or be overwhelmed by the everyday challenges of existence. Existential theorists suggest that individuals suffer from *existential crises*: problems in everyday living, a lack of meaningful human relationships, and an absence of significant goals. A clinical version of existential theory, which integrates its various themes and approaches, assumes that the bewildering realities of modern life give rise to two basic kinds of human maladies. Depressive and obsessive syndromes reflect a retreat from these realities; sociopathic and narcissistic syndromes reflect an exploitation of these realities (Schneider & May, 1995).

The humanistic philosophy also gave rise to the **human-potential movement**, which emerged in the United States in the late 1960s. This movement encompassed methods to enhance the potential of the average human being towards greater levels of performance and greater richness of experience. Through this movement, therapy originally intended for people with psychological disorders was extended to mentally healthy people who wanted to be more effective, more productive and happier human beings.

How might volunteer work help people to maximise their human potential?

Let's examine two types of therapies in the humanistic tradition: client-centred therapy and Gestalt therapy.

## CLIENT-CENTRED THERAPY

As developed by Carl Rogers (1951, 1977), *client-centred therapy* has had a significant impact on the way many different kinds of therapists define their relationships to their clients. The primary goal of **client-centred therapy** is to promote the healthy psychological growth of the individual. The approach begins with the assumption that all people share the basic tendency to self-actualise—that is, to realise their potential. Rogers believed that 'it is the inherent tendency of the organism to develop all its capacities in ways which seem to maintain or enhance the organism' (1959, p. 196). Healthy development is hindered by faulty learning patterns in which a person accepts the evaluation of others in place of those provided by his or her own mind and body. A conflict between the naturally positive self-image and negative external criticisms creates anxiety and unhappiness. This conflict, or *incongruence*, may function outside of awareness, so that a person experiences feelings of unhappiness and low self-worth without knowing why.

The task of Rogerian therapy is to create a therapeutic environment that allows a client to learn how to behave in order to achieve self-enhancement and self-actualisation. Because people are assumed to be basically good, the therapist's task is mainly to help remove barriers that limit the expression of this natural positive tendency. The basic therapeutic strategy is to recognise, accept and clarify a client's feelings. This is accomplished within an atmosphere of *unconditional positive regard*—nonjudgmental acceptance and respect for the client. The therapist allows his or her own feelings and thoughts to be transparent to the client. In addition to maintaining this genuineness, the therapist tries to experience the client's feelings. Such total empathy requires that the therapist care for the client as a worthy, competent individual—not to be judged or evaluated but to be assisted in discovering his or her individuality (Meador & Rogers, 1979).

The emotional style and attitude of the therapist are instrumental in *empowering* the client to attend once again to the true sources of personal conflict and to remove the distracting influences that suppress self-actualisation. Unlike practitioners of other therapies, who interpret, give answers or instruct, the client-centred therapist is a supportive listener who reflects and, at times, restates the client's evaluative statements and feelings. Client-centred therapy strives to be *nondirective* by having the therapist merely facilitate the client's search for self-awareness and self-acceptance.

Rogers believed that, once people are freed to relate to others openly and to accept themselves, individuals have the potential to lead themselves back to psychological health. This optimistic view and the humane relationship between therapist-as-caring-expert and client-as-person have influenced many practitioners.

client-centred therapy
A humanistic approach to treatment that emphasises the individual's healthy psychological growth based on the assumption that all people share the basic tendency of human nature toward self-actualisation.

human-potential movement
The therapy movement that encompasses those practices that release the potential of the average human being for greater levels of performance and richness of experience.

## GESTALT THERAPY

**Gestalt therapy** focuses on ways to unite mind and body to make a person whole (recall the Gestalt school of perception, described in Chapter 4). Its goal of self-awareness is reached by helping clients express pent-up feelings and recognise unfinished business from past conflicts that is carried into new relationships and must be completed for growth to proceed. **Fritz Perls** (1969), the originator of Gestalt therapy, asked clients to act out fantasies concerning conflicts and strong feelings and also to recreate their dreams, which he saw as repressed parts of personality. Perls said, 'We have to *re-own* these projected, fragmented parts of our personality, and re-own the hidden potential that appears in the dream' (1969, p. 67).

In Gestalt therapy workshops, therapists encourage participants to regain contact with their 'authentic inner voices' (Hatcher & Himelstein, 1996). Among the best known methods of Gestalt therapy is the *empty chair technique*. To carry out this technique, the therapist puts an empty chair near the client. The client is asked to imagine that a feeling, a person, an object, or a situation is occupying the chair. The client then 'talks' to the chair's occupant. For example, clients would be encouraged to imagine their mother or father in the chair and reveal feelings they might otherwise be unwilling to reveal. The clients can then imagine those feelings in the chair to 'talk' to the feelings about the impact they have on the clients' lives. This technique allows clients to confront and explore strong unexpressed feelings that may interfere with psychological wellbeing.

### RECAP CHECKPOINT

**Humanistic therapies**

- Humanistic therapies work to help individuals become more fully self-actualised.
- Therapists strive to be nondirective in helping their clients establish a positive self-image that can deal with external criticisms.
- Gestalt therapy focuses on the whole person — body, mind and life setting.

### CONCEPT QUESTIONS

1. What was the goal of the human-potential movement?

2. In client-centred therapy, what is meant by unconditional positive regard?

3. In Gestalt therapy, what is the purpose of the empty chair technique?

For answers go to MyPsychLab!

## GROUP THERAPIES

All the treatment approaches outlined thus far are primarily designed as one-to-one relationships between a patient or client and a therapist. Many people, however, now experience therapy as part of a group. There are several reasons why group therapy has flourished. Some advantages are practical. Group therapy is less expensive to participants and allows small numbers of mental health personnel to help more clients. Other advantages relate to the power of the group setting. The group (1) is a less threatening situation for people who have problems dealing on their own with authority; (2) allows group processes to be used to influence individual maladaptive behaviour; (3) provides people with opportunities to observe and practise interpersonal skills within the therapy session; and (4) provides an analogue of the primary family group, which enables corrective emotional experiences to take place.

Group therapy also poses some special problems (Motherwell & Shay, 2005). For example, some groups establish a culture in which little progress can be made—members create a norm of passivity and limited self-disclosure. In addition, the effectiveness of groups can change dramatically when members leave or join the groups. Both arrivals and departures can change the delicate balance that allows groups to function well as a unit. Therapists who specialise in group therapy must take care to address these group dynamics.

Some of the basic premises of group therapies differ from those of individual therapy. The social setting of group therapies provides an opportunity to learn how one comes across to others, how the self-image that is projected differs from the one that is intended or personally experienced. In addition, the group provides confirmation that one's symptoms, problems and 'deviant' reactions are not unique but often are quite common. Because people tend to conceal from others negative information about themselves, it is possible for many people with the same problem to believe 'It's only me'. The shared group experience can help to dispel this pluralistic ignorance in

What are some strengths of group therapies?

which many share the same false belief about their unique failings. In addition, the group of peers can provide social support outside the therapy setting.

## COUPLE AND FAMILY THERAPY

Much group therapy consists of strangers coming together periodically to form temporary associations from which they may benefit. Couple and family therapy brings meaningful, existing units into a therapy setting.

*Couple therapy* for marital problems seeks to clarify the typical communication patterns of the partners and then to improve the quality of their interaction (Snyder et al., 2006). By seeing a couple together, and often by videotaping and replaying their interactions, a therapist can help them appreciate the verbal and nonverbal styles they use to dominate, control or confuse each other. Each party is taught how to reinforce desirable responding in the other and withdraw reinforcement for undesirable reactions. They are also taught nondirective listening skills to help the other person clarify and express feelings and ideas. Couple therapy has been shown to reduce marital crises and keep marriages intact (Johnson, 2003).

In *family therapy*, the client is a whole nuclear family, and each family member is treated as a member of a *system* of relationships (Fishman & Fishman, 2003). A family therapist works with troubled family members to help them perceive what is creating problems for one or more of them. Consider circumstances in which a child has been diagnosed with an anxiety disorder. Research suggests that certain parenting practices may, unfortunately, maintain the child's anxiety (Wood et al., 2003). For example, if parents do not allow their children sufficient autonomy, the children may never gain enough self-efficacy to cope successfully with novel tasks. Under those circumstances, novel tasks will continue to provoke anxiety. Family therapy can focus on both the child's anxiety and the parent's behaviours that may maintain that anxiety.

Researchers recruited 40 children, ages 6 to 13, to participate in a treatment study (Wood et al., 2006). All the children had been diagnosed with an anxiety disorder (e.g., generalised anxiety disorder or social phobia). Half of the children underwent individual cognitive behavioural therapy that included skills training (e.g., strategies for coping with anxiety) as well as exposure to a hierarchy of feared situations. The other half of the children participated in similar activities, but their parents were also involved for much of the therapy sessions. In these family sessions, parents were taught skills, for example, to increase their children's autonomy and self-efficacy. The two groups of children were comparable in their levels of distress before treatment. At the end of therapy, both groups presented lower levels of anxiety. However, the group whose parents were included in the therapy showed greater improvement than their peers who received individual treatment.

This study illustrates the importance of the family therapy approach. By engaging the whole family, the therapeutic intervention changed environmental factors that may have helped maintain the children's levels of anxiety.

Family therapy can reduce tensions within a family and improve the functioning of individual members by helping clients recognise the positive as well as the negative aspects in their relationships. **Virginia Satir** (1967), a developer of family therapy approaches, noted that the family therapist plays many roles, acting as an interpreter and clarifier of the interactions that are taking place in the therapy session and as influence agent, mediator and referee. Most family therapists assume that the problems brought into therapy represent *situational* difficulties between people or problems of social interaction, rather than *dispositional* aspects of individuals. These difficulties may develop over time as members are forced into or accept unsatisfying roles. Nonproductive communication patterns may be set up in response to natural transitions in a family situation—loss of a job, a child's going to school, dating, getting married or having a baby. The job of the family therapist is to understand the structure of the family and the many forces acting on it. Then he or she works with the family members to dissolve 'dysfunctional' structural elements while creating and maintaining new, more effective structures (Fishman & Fishman, 2003).

## COMMUNITY SUPPORT GROUPS

A dramatic development in therapy has been the surge of interest and participation in mutual support groups and self-help groups. This is a growing phenomena in Australia with many well-known support groups already established since the 1980s and 1990s, such as Lifeline, Reach Out! and beyondblue. In partnership with the Royal Australian and New Zealand College of Psychiatrists (RANZCP), Beyondblue has also funded the development of an Australian Indigenous Mental Health website. The website currently provides information to Aboriginal health and allied health workers and the general public. Many more support groups are formed yearly in both rural and remote Australia to address issues related specifically to those areas, such as Indigenous mental health support and counselling for drought affected farming regions. There are now upwards of 2200 self-help groups in Australia, up from just 70 in 1985.

Support group sessions are typically free, especially when they are not directed by a health-care professional, and they give people a chance to meet others with the same problems who are surviving and sometimes thriving. The self-help concept applied to community group settings was pioneered by Alcoholics Anonymous (AA), which was founded in 1935. However, it was the women's consciousness-raising movement of the 1960s that helped extend self-help beyond the arena of alcoholism. Now support groups deal with four basic categories of problems: addictive behaviour, physical and mental disorders, life transition or other crises, and the traumas experienced by friends or relatives of those with serious problems.

For answers go to MyPsychLab!

In recent years, people have begun to turn to the Internet as another venue for self-help groups (Zuckerman, 2003). In general, Internet self-help groups engage the same range of issues as their physical counterparts (Davison et al., 2000). However, the Internet provides a particularly important meeting place for people who suffer from conditions that limit mobility, such as chronic fatigue syndrome and multiple sclerosis: An inability to attend meetings physically no longer denies people the benefits of self-help.

Researchers have begun to investigate what properties of self-help groups can make them most effective. Self-help groups appear to serve a number of functions for their members: For example, they provide people with a sense of hope and control over their problems, they engage social support for people's suffering, and they provide a forum for dispensing and acquiring information about disorders and treatments (Riessman, 1997; Schiff & Bargal, 2000). If you consider joining a self-help group, it is important to note that these groups have the most positive impact on people's feelings of wellbeing when they are satisfied with the group (Schiff & Bargal, 2000). For example, one study found that individuals who affiliated most strongly with AA after treatment for alcoholism showed the lowest levels of continuing substance abuse. Strong affiliation with AA apparently allowed these individuals to maintain their behavioural self-efficacy with respect to the control of their alcoholism (Morgenstern et al., 1997).

A valuable development in self-help is the application of group therapy techniques to the situations of terminally ill patients. The goals of such therapy are to help patients and their families live lives as fulfilling as possible during their illnesses, to cope realistically with impending death, and to adjust to the terminal illness (Kissane et al., 2004). One general focus of such support groups for the terminally ill is to help patients learn how to live fully until they 'say goodbye'.

The group therapies are our final examples of types of therapies that are based purely on psychological interventions. We will now analyse how biomedical therapies work to alter the brain in order to affect the mind.

## RECAP CHECKPOINT
### Group therapies
- Group therapy allows people to observe and engage in social interactions as a means to reduce psychological distress.
- Family and marital therapy concentrates on situational difficulties and interpersonal dynamics of the couple or family group as a system in need of improvement.
- Community and Internet self-help groups allow individuals to obtain information and feelings of control in circumstances of social support.

**psychopharmacology** The branch of psychology that investigates the effects of drugs on behaviour.

## CONCEPT QUESTIONS
1. How does group therapy help inform participants about the uniqueness of their problems?
2. What is a common goal for couple therapy?
3. Under what circumstances are Internet self-help groups particularly valuable?

## CRITICAL THINKING
Recall the study that used family therapy to treat children's anxiety disorders. Why was it important that the two groups of children had comparable anxiety levels before treatment began?

# BIOMEDICAL THERAPIES

The ecology of the mind is held in delicate balance. When something goes wrong with the brain, we see the consequences in abnormal patterns of behaviour and peculiar cognitive and emotional reactions. Similarly, environmental, social or behavioural disturbances, such as drugs and violence, can alter brain chemistry and function. Biomedical therapies most often treat mental disorders as problems in the brain. We will describe four biomedical approaches to alleviating the symptoms of psychological disorders: drug therapies, psychosurgery, electroconvulsive therapy (ECT), and repetitive transcranial magnetic stimulation (rTMS).

## DRUG THERAPY

In the history of the treatment of mental disorders, nothing has rivalled the revolution created by the discovery of drugs that can calm anxious patients, restore contact with reality in withdrawn patients and suppress hallucinations in psychotic patients. This new therapeutic era began in 1953 with the introduction of tranquilising drugs, notably *chlorpromazine*, into hospital treatment programs. Emerging drug therapies gained almost instant recognition and status as an effective way to transform patient behaviour. **Psychopharmacology** is the branch of psychology that investigates the effects of drugs on behaviour. Researchers in psychopharmacology work to understand the effect drugs have on some biological systems and the consequent changes in responding.

The discovery of *drug therapies* had profound effects on the treatment of severely disordered patients. No longer did mental hospital staff have to act as guards, putting patients in seclusion or strait-jackets; staff morale improved as rehabilitation replaced mere custodial care of the mentally ill (Swazey, 1974). Moreover, the drug therapy revolution had a great impact on the U.S. mental hospital population. Over half a million people were living in mental institutions in 1955, staying an average of several years. The introduction of chlorpromazine and other drugs reversed the steadily increasing numbers of patients. By the early 1970s, it was estimated that fewer than half the country's mental patients actually resided in mental hospitals; those who did were institutionalised for an average of only a few months.

The drugs we will describe that alleviate symptoms of various mental disorders are widely prescribed. As mental health care comes increasingly under the direction of health maintenance organisations (HMOs), cost-cutting practices are limiting the number of patients' visits to therapists for psychological therapies while substituting cheaper drug therapies. Researchers have documented great increases in prescriptions for drug therapies (Larkin et al., 2005; Thomas et al., 2006). For that reason, it is important to understand the positive and negative features of drug therapies.

Three major categories of drugs are used today in therapy programs: *antipsychotic*, *antidepressant* and *antianxiety* medications (see **Table 15.4**). As their names suggest, these drugs chemically alter specific brain functions that are responsible for psychotic symptoms, depression and extreme anxiety.

## Antipsychotic drugs

Antipsychotic drugs alter symptoms of schizophrenia such as delusions, hallucinations, social withdrawal and occasional agitation (Dawkins et al., 1999). Antipsychotic drugs work by reducing the activity of the neurotransmitter dopamine in the brain. The earliest drugs researchers developed, like *chlorpromazine* (marketed under the brand name *Thorazine)* and *haloperidol* (marketed as *Haldol*) blocked or reduced the sensitivity of dopamine receptors. Although those drugs functioned by decreasing the overall level of brain activity, they were not just tranquilisers. For many patients, they did much more than merely eliminate agitation. They also relieved or reduced the positive symptoms of schizophrenia, including delusions and hallucinations.

There were, unfortunately, negative side effects of these early antipsychotic drugs. Because dopamine plays a role in motor control, muscle disturbances frequently accompany a course of drug treatment. *Tardive dyskinesia* is a particular disturbance of motor control, especially of the facial muscles, caused by antipsychotic drugs. Patients who develop this side effect experience involuntary jaw, lip and tongue movements.

Over time, researchers created a new category of drugs, which are called *atypical* antipsychotic drugs, that create fewer motor side effects. The first member of this category, *Clozapine* (marketed as *Clozaril*), was approved in Australia in 1992. Clozapine both directly decreases dopamine activity and increases the level of serotonin activity, which inhibits the dopamine system. This pattern of activity blocks dopamine receptors more selectively, resulting in a lower probability of motor disturbance.

## Table 15.4

Drug therapies for mental illness

| Disorder | Type of therapy | Examples |
| --- | --- | --- |
| Schizophrenia (Thorazine) | Antipsychotic drug | chlorpromazine haloperidol (Haldol) clozapine (Clozaril) |
| Depression | Tricyclic antidepressant | imipramine (Tofranil) amitriptyline (Elavil) |
| | Selective serotonin reuptake inhibitor | fluoxetine (Prozac) paroxetine (Paxil) sertraline (Zoloft) |
| | Serotonin and norepinephrine reuptake inhibitor MAO inhibitor | milnacipran (Dalcipran) venlafaxine (Effexor) phenelzine (Nardil) isocarboxazid (Marplan) |
| Bipolar disorder | Mood stabiliser | lithium (Eshalith) |
| Anxiety disorders | Benzodiazepines | diazepam (Valium) alprazolam (Xanax) |
| | Antidepressant drug | fluoxetine (Prozac) |

Unfortunately, *agranulocytosis,* a rare disease in which the bone marrow stops making white blood cells, develops in 1 to 2 percent of patients treated with clozapine.

Researchers have created a range of atypical antipsychotic drugs that act in the brain in a fashion similar to clozapine. Large-scale studies suggest that each of these drugs is effective in relieving the symptoms of schizophrenia—but each also has the potential for side effects (Lieberman et al., 2005). For example, people who take these drugs are at risk for weight gain and diabetes (Nasrallah, 2005). Unfortunately, the side effects often prompt patients to discontinue the drug therapy. The rate of relapse when patients go off the drugs is quite high—three quarters have new symptoms within 1 year (Gitlin et al., 2001). Even patients who remain on the newer drugs such as clozapine have about a 15 to 20 percent chance of relapse (Leucht et al., 2003). Thus antipsychotic drugs do not cure schizophrenia—they do not eliminate the underlying psychopathology. Fortunately, they are reasonably effective at controlling the disorder's most disruptive symptoms.

## Antidepressant drugs

Antidepressant drugs work by increasing the activity of the neurotransmitters norepinephrine and serotonin (Holmes, 1994). Recall from Chapter 3 that nerve cells communicate by releasing neurotransmitters into synaptic clefts (the small gaps between neurons). *Tricyclics*, such as *Tofranil* and *Elavil*, reduce the reuptake (removal) of the neurotransmitters from the synaptic cleft (see **Figure 15.2**). Drugs such as *Prozac* are known as *selective serotonin reuptake inhibitors* (SSRIs) because they specifically reduce the reuptake of serotonin. The *monoamine oxidase* (MAO) *inhibitors* limit the action of the enzyme monoamine oxidase, which is responsible for breaking down (metabolising) norepinephrine. When MAO

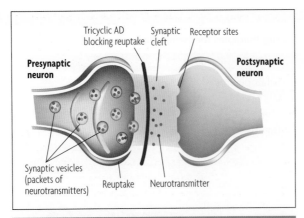

**Figure 15.2**

**The brain mechanisms of tricyclic antidepressants**
Tricyclic antidepressants block the reuptake
of noradrenaline and serotonin so that the
neurotransmitters remain in the synaptic cleft.

Butcher et al., *Abnormal Psychology*, 13/e, Allyn and Bacon, Boston,
p. 615. © 1991 by Pearson Education. Reprinted by permission.

is inhibited, more of the neurotransmitter is left available. Thus each type of drug leaves more neurotransmitters available to bring about neural signals.

Antidepressant drugs can be successful at relieving the symptoms of depression, although as many as 50 percent of patients will not show improvement (Hollon et al., 2002). (Those patients may be candidates for ECT or rTMS, which we discuss later.) Because antidepressant drugs affect important neurotransmitter systems in the brain, they have the potential for serious side effects. For example, people taking SSRIs such as *Prozac* may experience symptoms such as nausea, insomnia, nervousness and sexual dysfunction. Tricyclics and MAO inhibitors may cause dry mouth, difficulty sleeping and memory impairment. Research suggests that most of the major antidepressant drugs are roughly equal, across individuals, in their ability to bring relief (Hollon et al., 2002). For that reason, it is important for each individual to find the drug that yields the fewest side effects for him or her personally.

Researchers also continue to search for drugs that will help alleviate the symptoms of depression with fewer side effects. The newest class of drugs are called *serotonin and noradrenaline reuptake inhibitors*, or *SNRIs*. As that name suggests, these drugs, such as *Effexor* and *Dalcipran*, block the reuptake of both serotonin and noradrenaline. Clinical trials using these drugs indicate that they may be more effective than SSRIs (Stahl et al., 2005). However, researchers still must determine which SNRIs function without serious side effects.

*Lithium salts* have proven effective in the treatment of bipolar disorders (Schou, 2001). People who experience uncontrollable periods of hyperexcitement, when their energy seems limitless and their behaviour extravagant and flamboyant, are brought down from their state of manic excess by doses of lithium. Between 60 and 80 percent of patients treated with lithium have a good chance of

recovery (Walden et al., 1998). However, for those people suffering from bipolar disorders who cycle frequently between manic episodes and depression, lithium appears to be less effective than other treatments such as the drug *valproate*, which was originally developed as a drug to prevent seizures.

**Antianxiety drugs** Like antipsychotic and antidepressant drugs, antianxiety drugs generally have their effect by adjusting the levels of neurotransmitter activity in the brain. Different drugs are most effective at relieving different types of anxiety disorders (Spiegel et al., 2000). Generalised anxiety disorder is best treated with a *benzodiazepine*, such as *Valium* or *Xanax*, which increases the activity of the neurotransmitter GABA. Because GABA regulates inhibitory neurons, increases in GABA activity decrease brain activity in areas of the brain relevant to generalised anxiety responses. Panic disorders, as well as agoraphobia and other phobias, can be treated with antidepressant drugs, although researchers do not yet understand the biological mechanism involved. Obsessive-compulsive disorder, which may arise from low levels of serotonin, responds particularly well to drugs, like *Prozac*, that specifically affect serotonin function.

As with drugs that treat schizophrenia and mood disorders, benzodiazepines affect a major neurotransmitter system and therefore have a range of potential side effects (Rivas-Vazquez, 2003). People who begin a course of therapy may experience daytime drowsiness, slurred speech and problems with coordination. The drugs may also impair cognitive processes such as attention and memory (Stewart, 2005). Furthermore, people who begin treatment with benzodiazepines often experience drug tolerance—they must increase their dosage to maintain a stable effect (see Chapter 5). Discontinuation of treatment might also lead to withdrawal symptoms (O'Brien, 2005). Because of the potential for psychological and physical dependence, people should undertake treatment with antianxiety drugs in careful consultation with a healthcare provider.

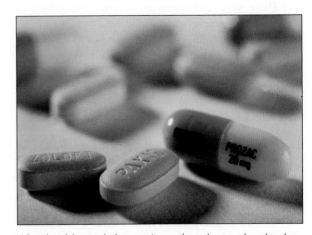

Why should people be cautious when they undertake drug therapies?

## PSYCHOSURGERY

The headline in the *Los Angeles Times* read, 'Bullet in the Brain Cures Man's Mental Problem' (2/23/1988). The article revealed that a 19-year-old man suffering from severe obsessive-compulsive disorder had shot a .22-caliber bullet through the front of his brain in a suicide attempt. Remarkably, he survived, his pathological symptoms were cured, and his intellectual capacity was not affected, although some of the underlying causes of his problems remained.

This case illustrates the potential effects of one of the most direct biomedical therapies: surgical intervention in the brain. Such intervention involves lesioning (severing) connections between parts of the brain or removing small sections of the brain. These therapies are often considered methods of last resort to treat psychopathologies that have proven intractable to other, less extreme forms of therapy. **Psychosurgery** is the general term for surgical procedures performed on brain tissue to alleviate psychological disorders.

The best known form of psychosurgery is the **prefrontal lobotomy**, an operation that severs the nerve fibres connecting the frontal lobes of the brain with the di-encephalon, especially those fibres of the thalamic and hypothalamic areas. The procedure was developed by neurologist **Egas Moniz**, who, in 1949, won a Nobel Prize for this treatment.

The original candidates for lobotomy were agitated patients with schizophrenia and patients who were compulsive and anxiety ridden. The effects of this psychosurgery were dramatic: a new personality emerged without intense emotional arousal and, thus, without overwhelming anxiety, guilt or anger. However, the operation permanently destroyed basic aspects of human nature. The lobotomy resulted in inability to plan ahead, indifference to the opinions of others, childlike actions and the intellectual and emotional flatness of a person without a coherent sense of self. (One of Moniz's own patients was so distressed by these unexpected consequences that she shot Moniz, partially paralysing him.) Because the effects of psychosurgery are permanent, its negative effects are severe and common, with positive results less certain. As such, its continued use is very limited.

## ECT AND rTMS

**Electroconvulsive therapy (ECT)** is the use of electric shock applied to the brain to treat psychiatric disorders such as schizophrenia, mania, and, most often, depression. The technique consists of applying weak electric current (75 to 100 volts) to a patient's temples for a period of time from 1/10 to a full second until a convulsion occurs. The convulsion usually runs its course in 45 to 60 seconds. Patients are prepared for this traumatic intervention by sedation with a short-acting barbiturate and muscle relaxant, which renders the patient unconscious and minimises the violent physical reactions (Abrams, 1992).

Electroconvulsive therapy has proven quite successful at alleviating the symptoms of serious depression (McCall et al., 2006; Sackheim et al., 2000). ECT is particularly important because it works quickly. Typically, the symptoms of depression are alleviated in a 3- or 4-day course of treatment, as compared with the 1- to 2-week time window for drug therapies. Even so, most therapists hold ECT as a treatment of last resort. ECT is often reserved for emergency treatment for suicidal or severely malnourished, depressed patients and for patients who do not respond to antidepressant drugs or can't tolerate their side effects.

If ECT is so effective, why has it so often been demonised? For example, in 1982, the citizens of Berkeley, California, voted to ban the use of electroconvulsive shock in any of their community mental health facilities (the action was later overturned on legal grounds). Scientific unease with ECT centres largely on the lack of understanding of how it works. The therapy was originated when clinicians observed that patients who suffered from

**electroconvulsive therapy (ECT)** The use of electroconvulsive shock as an effective treatment for severe depression.

**psychosurgery** A surgical procedure performed on brain tissue to alleviate a psychological disorder.

**prefrontal lobotomy** An operation that severs the nerve fibres connecting the frontal lobes of the brain with the diencephalons, especially those fibres in the thalamic and hypothalamic areas.

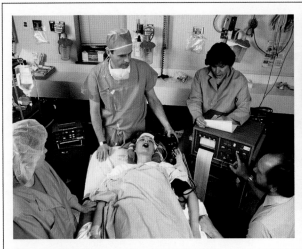
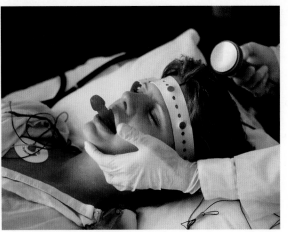

Electroconvulsive therapy has been very effective in cases of severe depression. Why does it remain controversial as a treatment?

# CRITICAL THINKING *in your life*

## DOES THERAPY AFFECT BRAIN ACTIVITY?

In this chapter, we've made a number of distinctions among types of therapies. However, our most basic distinction has been between psychological and biomedical approaches to treatment. It has often been the practice to use a computer analogy to motivate this distinction: If we think of the brain as a computer, we can say that mental illness may arise from either the brain's hardware or in the software that programs its actions. With respect to this analogy, biomedical treatments focus on changing the hardware, whereas psychological treatments focus on changing the software. However, cutting-edge research blurs the distinction between hardware and software: there is growing evidence that biomedical and psychological therapies produce many of the same changes in the brain.

Consider a study that examined the brain changes that accompanied treatment for social phobia (Furmark et al., 2002). Each of the 10 men and 8 women in the study met *DSM-IV* criteria for the disorder. The researchers placed them into one of three groups. One group of participants was given the drug citalopram (which has the prescription name *Celexa).* At the end of the 9-week treatment period, the researchers did blood assays to ensure that the participants had adhered to their drug regimen. A second group of participants received eight weekly sessions of therapy. In each 3-hour session, participants engaged in simulated exposure to feared situations and cognitive restructuring. The third group of participants was the control group. (After the period of the experiment, they began the drug regimen.)

To assess the impact of the drug and cognitive behavioural therapies, all the participants were asked to deliver brief speeches while they underwent PET scans. The situation was intended to be quite threatening for individuals with social phobia: An audience of six to eight people surrounded the scanner bed while the participants gave their 2½ minute speeches. With respect to behavioural measures (e.g., the extent to which participants experienced anxiety during their speeches), both treatment groups showed substantial and roughly equivalent improvement as compared to the control group. Moreover, as

hown in the figure, the PET scans demonstrated decreased brain activity (again, relative to the control group) in much the same locations in the brain. Of importance, the decreased activity was in areas of the brain (e.g., the amygdala) that play a role in emotional responses.

Researchers have found similar patterns for other disorders. For example, PET scans detected the same changes in brain function for patients who underwent either behavioural or drug therapy for obsessive-compulsive disorder (Baxter et al., 1992; Schwartz et al., 1996). Similarly, patients who experienced either a form of cognitive therapy or drug therapy for major depressive disorder showed similar brain changes (Brody et al., 2002).

In each of these cases, it hasn't been enough to show just that the two types of therapies affect the same areas of the brain. Researchers have also argued that changes in those areas are related to the relief that patients experience.

In light of these results, researchers can now shift their attention to *how:* How is it that psychotherapy can restore the brain's balance in the same systems affected by drugs? How, for example, can cognitive therapy have a similar impact on the brain's use of the neurotransmitter serotonin as does a drug that is specifically designated as a selective serotonin reuptake inhibitor (Brody et al., 2002)? These types of questions will help set the research agenda for the first part of the 21st century.

- Why was it important to ensure that the participants in the drug group adhered to the regimen?

- Why did the researchers put a real audience around the scanner?

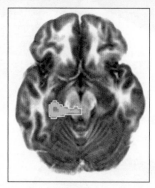

Cognitive behavioural group therapy (compared to control)

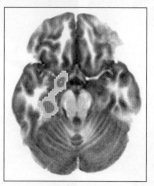

Drug therapy (compared to control)

both schizophrenia and epilepsy showed improvement in their symptoms of schizophrenia after epileptic seizures. The clinicians conjectured that the same effect could be obtained with artificially induced seizures. Although the conjecture proved correct in part—ECT is much more effective at alleviating depression than schizophrenia—researchers have yet to fit a definitive theory to this chance observation.

Critics have also worried about potential side effects of ECT (Breggin, 1979, 1991). ECT produces temporary disorientation and a variety of memory deficits. Patients often suffer amnesia for events in the period of time preceding the treatment; the amnesia becomes more severe the longer the course of treatment. Research has shown, however, that patients generally recover their specific memories within months of the treatment (Cohen et al., 2000). As a way of minimising even short-term deficits, ECT is now often administered to only one side of the brain so as to reduce the possibility of speech impairment. Such unilateral ECT is an effective antidepressant.

In recent years, researchers have explored an alternative to ECT called *repetitive transcranial magnetic stimulation (rTMS)*. As you might recall from Chapter 3, people who undergo rTMS receive repeated pulses of magnetic stimulation to the brain. As with ECT, researchers have not yet determined why rTMS can bring relief for major depressive disorder and other forms of psychopathology. However, evidence is mounting that rTMS can be just as effective as, for example, ECT (Grunhaus et al., 2003). Researchers are working to determine how variables such as the intensity of the magnetic stimulation affect rTMS's ability to bring relief (Loo & Mitchell, 2005; Padberg et al., 2002).

## RECAP CHECKPOINT

### Biomedical therapies

- Biomedical therapies concentrate on changing physiological aspects of mental illness.
- Drug therapies include antipsychotic medications for treating schizophrenia as well as antidepressants and antianxiety drugs.
- Psychosurgery is rarely used because of its radical, irreversible effects.
- Electroconvulsive therapy and repetitive transcranial magnetic stimulation (rTMS) can be effective with depressed patients.

## CONCEPT QUESTIONS

1. What advantages do atypical antipsychotic drugs have over early drug therapies for schizophrenia?
2. What do SNRIs do in the brain?
3. What are some effects of prefrontal lobotomies?
4. What is the rTMS procedure?

# TREATMENT EVALUATION AND PREVENTION STRATEGIES

Suppose you have come to perceive a problem in your life that you believe could be alleviated by interaction with a trained clinician. We have mentioned a great variety of types of therapies. How can you know which one of them will work best to relieve your distress? How can you be sure that *any* of them will work? In this section, we examine the projects researchers undertake to test the effectiveness of particular therapies and make comparisons between different therapies. The general goal is to discover the most efficient way to help people overcome distress. We also consider briefly the topic of *prevention*: How can psychologists intervene in people's lives to prevent mental illness before it occurs?

## EVALUATING THERAPEUTIC EFFECTIVENESS

British psychologist Hans Eysenck (1952) created a furore some years ago by declaring that psychotherapy does not work at all! He reviewed available publications that reported the effects of various therapies and found that patients who received no therapy had just as high a recovery rate as those who received psychoanalysis or other forms of insight therapy. He claimed that roughly two-thirds of all people with neurotic problems would recover spontaneously within 2 years of the onset of the problem.

Researchers met Eysenck's challenge by devising more accurate methodologies to evaluate the effectiveness of therapy. What Eysenck's criticism made clear was that researchers needed to have appropriate control groups. For a variety of reasons, *some* percentage of individuals in psychotherapy *does* improve without any professional intervention. This **spontaneous-remission effect** is one *baseline* criterion against which the effectiveness of therapies must be assessed. Simply put, doing something must be shown to lead to a greater percentage of improved cases than doing nothing.

Similarly, researchers generally try to demonstrate that their treatment does more than just take advantage of clients' own expectations of healing. You may recall

**spontaneous-remission effect** The improvement of some mental patients and clients in psychotherapy without any professional intervention.

For answers go to MyPsychLab!

our earlier discussions of *placebo* effects. In many cases, people's mental or physical health will improve because they expect that it will improve. The therapeutic situation helps bolster this belief by putting the therapist in the specific social role of *healer* (Frank & Frank, 1991). Although the placebo effects of therapy are an important part of the therapeutic intervention, researchers typically wish to demonstrate that their specific form of therapy is more effective than a **placebo therapy** (a neutral therapy that just creates expectations of healing) (Enserink, 1999).

In recent years, researchers have evaluated therapeutic effectiveness using a statistical technique called meta-analysis. **Meta-analysis** provides a formal mechanism for detecting the general conclusions to be found in data from many different experiments. In many psychological experiments, the researcher asks, 'Did most of my participants show the effect I predicted?' Meta-analysis treats experiments like participants. With respect to the effectiveness of therapy, the researcher asks, 'Did most of the outcome studies show positive changes?'

Consider **Figure 15.3**, which presents the results of meta-analyses of the research literature on treatments for depression (Hollon et al., 2002). The figure compares results for three types of psychotherapies and medications (averaged across different types of antidepressant drugs) to placebo treatments. We described psychodynamic and cognitive behavioural therapies earlier in the chapter. Interpersonal therapy focuses on a patient's current life and interpersonal relationships. As you can see,

across all the studies reviewed in the meta-analyses that contributed to this figure, interpersonal therapy, cognitive behavioural therapy and drug therapies had a consistently larger impact than did placebos. At least for treatment of depression, classic psychodynamic therapy did not fare well.

Note that these data reflect the impact of each type of treatment alone. Researchers have assessed the effectiveness of psychotherapy alone versus psychotherapy combined with drug therapy. One study found that combination therapy was most successful (Keller et al., 2000). Of 519 participants who completed a course of treatment, 55 percent of the participants who received only drug therapy met the study's criterion for symptom relief, as did 52 percent of the participants who received only psychotherapy. For participants who received both drug therapy and psychotherapy, 85 percent showed the same level of improvement.

Because of such findings, contemporary researchers are less concerned about asking *whether* psychotherapy works and more concerned about asking why it works and whether any one treatment is most effective for any particular problem and for certain types of patients (Goodheart et al., 2006). For example, much treatment evaluation has been carried out in research settings that afford reasonable control over patients (often, the studies exclude individuals who have more than one disorder) and procedures (therapists are rigorously trained to minimise differences in treatment). Researchers need to ensure that therapies that work in research settings also work out in community settings in which patients and therapists have more diversity of symptoms and experience (Hohmann & Shear, 2002). Another important issue for evaluation research is to assess the likelihood that individuals will complete a course of treatment. In almost all circumstances, some people choose to discontinue treatments (Klein et al., 2003; Wierzbicki & Pekarik, 1993). Researchers seek to understand who leaves treatment and why—with the ultimate hope of creating treatments to which most everyone can adhere.

**Figure 15.4** provides a general flowchart for the way theory, clinical observation and research all play a role in the development and evaluation of any form of treatment (for both mental and physical disorders). It shows the type of systematic research needed to help clinicians discover if their therapies are making the differences that their theories predict. On one side, you see clinical observation—clinicians' own experience with a new procedure. Often, new treatments first get tested without rigorous experimental control. On the other side of the figure, you see a theory being developed. The theory makes predictions about what should work, which may be confirmed in laboratory studies. These two types of insights—clinical and experimental—are combined to yield a new therapy.

In the final section of this chapter, we reflect on an important principle of life: whatever the effectiveness of treatment, it is often better to prevent a disorder than to heal it once it arises.

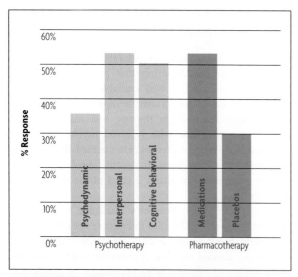

Figure 15.3

**Treatment evaluation for depression**
The figure displays the results from meta-analyses of treatments for depression. For each treatment, the figure presents the percentage of patients who typically respond to each category of treatment. For example, about 50 percent of patients taking antidepressant medication experience recognisable symptom relief whereas 50 percent do not.

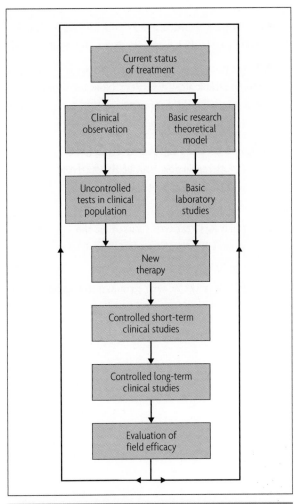

## Figure 15.4

**Building better therapies**
Flowchart of stages in the development of treatments for mental/physical disorders.

From Weissman et al., *American Journal of Psychiatry*, Vol. 136, p. 558, 1979. Copyright © 1979 American Psychiatric Association. Reprinted by permission.

## PREVENTION STRATEGIES

*Two friends were walking on a riverbank. Suddenly, a child is swept downstream in the current. One of the friends jumped in the river and rescued the child. Then the two friends resumed their stroll. Suddenly, another child appeared in the water. The rescuer jumped in and again pulled the victim to safety. Soon, a third drowning child swept by. The still-dry friend began to trot up the riverbank. The rescuer yelled, 'Hey, where are you going?' The dry one replied, 'I'm going to get the bastard that's throwing them in.' (Wolman, 1975, p.3)*

The moral of this story is clear: *Preventing* a problem is the best solution. The traditional therapies we have examined here share the focus of changing a person who is already distressed or disabled. They begin to do their work after the problem behaviours show up and after the suffering

How can prevention strategies encourage people to build 'mental hygiene' habits to minimise the need for treatment?

starts. By the time someone elects to go into therapy or is required to, the psychological disorder has 'settled in' and had its disruptive effects on the person's daily functioning, social life, job or career.

The goal of *preventing* psychological problems can be realised at several different levels. *Primary* prevention seeks to prevent a condition before it begins. Steps might be taken, for example, to provide individuals with coping skills so they can be more resilient or to change negative aspects of an environment that might lead to anxiety or depression (Boyd et al., 2006; Hudson et al., 2004). *Secondary* prevention attempts to limit the duration and severity of a disorder once it has begun. This goal is realised by means of programs that allow for early identification and prompt treatment. For example, based on the meta-analyses we described for depression, a mental health practitioner might recommend a combination of psychotherapy and drug therapy to optimise secondary prevention (Keller et al., 2000). *Tertiary* prevention limits the long-term impact of a psychological disorder by seeking to prevent a relapse. For example, we noted earlier that individuals with schizophrenia who discontinue drug therapy have a very high rate of relapse (Gitlin et al., 2001). To engage in tertiary prevention, mental health practitioners would recommend that their patients with schizophrenia continue their courses of antipsychotic drugs.

The implementation of these three types of prevention has signalled major shifts in the focus and in the basic paradigms of mental health care. The most important of these paradigm shifts are: (1) supplementing treatment with prevention; (2) going beyond a medical disease model to a public health model; (3) focusing on situations and ecologies that put people at risk and away from 'at-risk people'; and (4) looking for precipitating factors in life settings rather than for predisposing factors in people.

Preventing mental disorders is a complex and difficult task. It involves not only understanding the relevant causal factors, but overcoming individual, institutional and governmental resistance to change. A major research effort will be needed to demonstrate the long-range utility of prevention and the public health approach to psychopathology in order to justify the expense in the face of the many other problems that demand immediate solutions. The ultimate goal of prevention programs is to safeguard the mental health of all members of our society.

For answers go to MyPsychLab!

## RECAP CHECKPOINT

### Treatment evaluation and prevention strategies

- Research shows that many therapies work better than the mere passage of time or nonspecific placebo treatment.

- Evaluation projects are helping to answer the question of what makes therapy effective.

- Prevention strategies are necessary to stop psychological disorders from occurring and minimise their effects once they have occurred.

## CONCEPT QUESTIONS

1. What conclusions can be drawn from meta-analyses of treatments for depression?

2. Why has research focused on the probability that people will complete courses of treatment?

3. What is the goal of primary prevention?

# SUMMARY

Chapter 15 has provided a broad scope on the various types of treatment options currently in use for general and specific psychological disorders. By reviewing each approach to mental health treatment, it can be appreciated that treatments to date are effective, but sometimes only in part, as there are numerous variables that need to be accounted for when treating a client or patient. The biological, behavioural, cognitive and humanistic factors behind each individual make treatment options sometimes complex. However, as the chapter concludes, prevention and ongoing management of mental health problems are seen as the best strategy for maintaining quality of life and wellbeing when faced with a mental illness.

# KEY TERMS

aversion therapy (p. 536)
behaviour modification (p. 535)
behavioural rehearsal (p. 539)
behaviour therapy (p. 535)
biomedical therapies (p. 528)
catharsis (p. 532)
client (p. 529)
client-centred therapy (p. 543)
clinical psychologist (p. 529)
clinical social worker (p. 529)
cognitive behavioural therapy (p. 542)
cognitive therapy (p. 541)
contingency management (p. 537)
counselling psychologist (p. 529)

counter-conditioning (p. 535)
counter-transference (p. 532)
deinstitutionalisation (p. 530)
dream analysis (p. 532)
electroconvulsive therapy (ECT) (p. 549)
exposure therapy (p. 535)
free association (p. 532)
Gestalt therapy (p. 544)
human-potential movement (p. 543)
insight therapy (p. 531)
meta-analysis (p. 552)
participant modelling (p. 538)
pastoral counsellor (p. 529)
patient (p. 529)

placebo therapy (p. 552)
prefrontal lobotomy (p. 549)
psychiatrist (p. 529)
psychoanalysis (p. 531)
psychoanalyst (p. 529)
psychopharmacology (p. 546)
psychosurgery (p. 549)
psychotherapy (p. 528)
rational-emotive therapy (RET) (p. 541)
resistance (p. 532)
social-learning therapy (p. 538)
spontaneous-remission effect (p. 551)
systematic desensitisation (p. 535)
transference (p. 532)

# PRACTICE TEST

1. When Sonja begins treatment, her therapist focuses on her inner conflicts that he believes remain unresolved. It seems that Sonja's therapist takes a _____ approach.
   a. psychodynamic
   b. cognitive
   c. biological
   d. humanist

2. Which of these topics would you be *least* likely to hear about in a lecture on deinstitutionalisation?
   a. homelessness
   b. meta-analysis
   c. readmission rates
   d. violent crime

3. In psychodynamic therapy, _____ refers to a patient's inability or unwillingness to discuss certain topics.
   a. catharsis
   b. transference
   c. counter-transference
   d. resistance

4. Therapy that follows from the work of _____ focuses on the patient's feelings about the therapist's attitudes.
   a. Sigmund Freud
   b. Harry Stack Sullivan
   c. Melanie Klein
   d. Alfred Adler

5. Research on repressed memories suggests that
   a. recovered memories are never accurate.
   b. people's memories are not subject to therapists' influence.
   c. some memories of abuse are implanted by therapists.
   d. most memories are subject to repression.

6. If Roland undergoes _____ he should expect to have a strong noxious stimulus paired with stimuli to which he is attracted.
   a. systematic desensitisation
   b. behavioural rehearsal
   c. social-learning therapy
   d. aversion therapy

7. Every time Janice provides a urine sample that is drug free, she gets vouchers with which she can purchase items she enjoys. This treatment is a form of
   a. systematic desensitisation.
   b. contingency management.
   c. participant modelling.
   d. generalisation.

8. People can learn the process of _____ to change negative self-statements into positive coping statements.
   a. social learning        c. cognitive restructuring
   b. self-efficacy          d. catharsis

9. You hear a therapist talking about how hard he works to communicate unconditional regard. You suspect that he is a _____ therapist.
   a. Gestalt                c. behavioural
   b. client-centred         d. psychodynamic

10. In your Introductory Psychology class, you watch a movie clip of an individual in therapy addressing an empty chair as if it were his abusive boss. This clip demonstrates _____ therapy.
    a. Gestalt               c. aversion
    b. client-centred        d. social-learning

11. The particular focus of _____ therapy will often be on poor patterns of communication.
    a. Gestalt               c. couple
    b. client-centred        d. psychodynamic

12. _____drugs largely have their impact in the brain by changing the function of the neurotransmitters serotonin and noradrenaline.
    a. Antidepressant        c. Antipsychotic
    b. Antianxiety           d. Antimania

13. In clinical research, _____ proven effective at relieving the symptoms of depression.
    a. only ECT has          c. neither ECT nor rTMS have
    b. only rTMS has         d. both ECT and rTMS have

14. _____ therapy is the type of treatment *least* likely to provide relief from major depressive disorder.
    a. Placebo               c. Cognitive behavioural
    b. Interpersonal         d. Drug

15. When prevention efforts are intended to prevent relapse, it is called _____ prevention.
    a. primary               c. tertiary
    b. regulatory            d. secondary

16. You are looking at PET scans of the brain activity of two people who have undergone treatment for social phobia. One received cognitive behavioural therapy and one received drug therapy. You expect _____ to show differences in brain activity with respect to people who hadn't received treatment.
    a. only the person who received cognitive behavioural therapy
    b. only the person who received drug therapy
    c. neither person
    d. both people

## Essay Questions

1. Why do behaviour therapies target adaptive and maladaptive behaviours?

2. What features of self-help groups make them beneficial to mental health?

3. Why are therapies compared to placebos to evaluate their effectiveness?

# WEB LINKS

http://www.beyondblue.org.au
  Beyond Blue

www.lifeline.org.au/
  Lifeline Australia

www.aacbt.org/
  The Australian Association for Cognitive Behaviour Therapy

http://www.healthinsite.gov.au/topics/Treating_Mental_Illness
  Health In Site

Are you ready for the test? MyPsychLab offers dozens of ways to deepen your understanding and test your recall of the material in this chapter—including video and audio clips, simulations and activities, self-assessments, practice tests and other study materials. Specific resources available for this chapter include:

 Overview of clinical assessment methods

 Recent trends in treatment
Treating psychological disorders

 Drugs commonly used to treat psychiatric disorders
Key components of psychoanalytic, humanistic, behaviour and cognitive therapies
Psychotherapy practitioners and their activities

To access MyPsychLab, please visit **www.pearsoned.com.au/mypsychlab**

# Did you get it?

## YOU MADE IT TO CHAPTER 15—ARE YOU PREPARED FOR THE EXAM?

To enhance your understanding of any of the material in your *Psychology and Life* textbook, go to **MyPsychLab: www.pearsoned.com.au/mypsychlab**.

Complete pre- and post-tests, create your own individualised study plan, watch videos and animations and listen to audio glossaries—all of which will help you understand the themes of this chapter:

- The therapeutic context
- Psychodynamic theories
- Behaviour therapies
- Cognitive therapies
- Humanistic therapies
- Group therapies
- Biomedical therapies
- Treatment evaluation and prevention strategies

EXPLORE drugs commonly used to treat psychiatric disorders

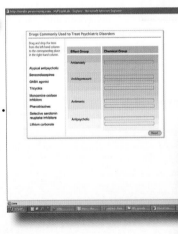

Watch a VIDEO on cognitive behaviour therapy

'I wish all textbooks had a site like MyPsychLab.'

Read the biographies of AARON BECK and his theories of MALADAPTIVE THINKING ...

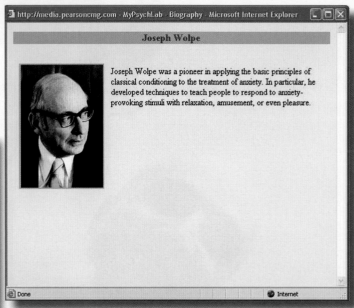

**Joseph Wolpe**

Joseph Wolpe was a pioneer in applying the basic principles of classical conditioning to the treatment of anxiety. In particular, he developed techniques to teach people to respond to anxiety-provoking stimuli with relaxation, amusement, or even pleasure.

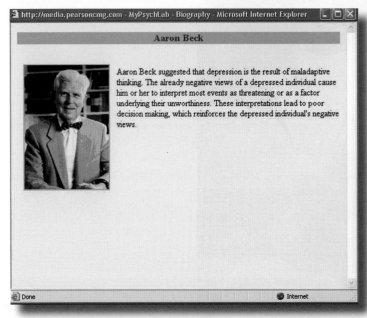

**Aaron Beck**

Aaron Beck suggested that depression is the result of maladaptive thinking. The already negative views of a depressed individual cause him or her to interpret most events as threatening or as a factor underlying their unworthiness. These interpretations lead to poor decision making, which reinforces the depressed individual's negative views.

... and JOSEPH WOLPE, a pioneer in applying CLASSICAL CONDITIONING for the treatment of anxiety.

## STUDY TIP

Check out Chapter 15 of your *Psychology and Life* eBook for a page-by-page reproduction of the textbook, complete the practice tests and interactive activities.

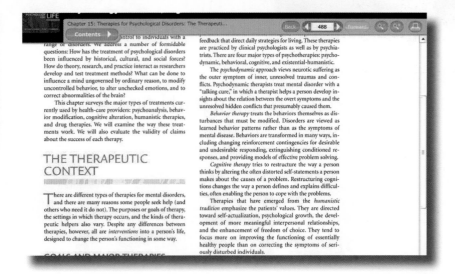

Chapter 15: Therapies for Psychological Disorders: The Therapeuti...

...ontrol to individuals with a range of disorders. We address a number of formidable questions: How has the treatment of psychological disorders been influenced by historical, cultural, and social forces? How do theory, research, and practice interact as researchers develop and test treatment methods? What can be done to influence a mind ungoverned by ordinary reason, to modify uncontrolled behavior, to alter unchecked emotions, and to correct abnormalities of the brain?

This chapter surveys the major types of treatments currently used by health-care providers: psychoanalysis, behavior modification, cognitive alteration, humanistic therapies, and drug therapies. We will examine the way these treatments work. We will also evaluate the validity of claims about the success of each therapy.

### THE THERAPEUTIC CONTEXT

There are different types of therapies for mental disorders, and there are many reasons some people seek help (and others who need it do not). The purposes or goals of therapy, the settings in which therapy occurs, and the kinds of therapeutic helpers also vary. Despite any differences between therapies, however, all are *interventions* into a person's life, designed to change the person's functioning in some way.

feedback that direct daily strategies for living. These therapies are practiced by clinical psychologists as well as by psychiatrists. There are four major types of psychotherapies: psychodynamic, behavioral, cognitive, and existential-humanistic.

The *psychodynamic* approach views neurotic suffering as the outer symptom of inner, unresolved traumas and conflicts. Psychodynamic therapists treat mental disorder with a "talking cure," in which a therapist helps a person develop insights about the relation between the overt symptoms and the unresolved hidden conflicts that presumably caused them.

*Behavior therapy* treats the behaviors themselves as disturbances that must be modified. Disorders are viewed as learned behavior patterns rather than as the symptoms of mental disease. Behaviors are transformed in many ways, including changing reinforcement contingencies for desirable and undesirable responding, extinguishing conditioned responses, and providing models of effective problem solving.

*Cognitive therapy* tries to restructure the way a person thinks by altering the often distorted self-statements a person makes about the causes of a problem. Restructuring cognitions changes the way a person defines and explains difficulties, often enabling the person to cope with the problems.

Therapies that have emerged from the *humanistic tradition* emphasize the patients' values. They are directed toward self-actualization, psychological growth, the development of more meaningful interpersonal relationships, and the enhancement of freedom of choice. They tend to focus more on improving the functioning of essentially healthy people than on correcting the symptoms of seriously disturbed individuals.

### What can you find in MyPsychLab?

Self-directed tests * Videos * Simulations * eBook * Biographies * Audio glossary * Web links … and more—organised by chapter, section and learning objective.

**mypsychlab**™
*where learning comes to life!*

Social Cognition and
Relationships

CHAPTER

16

# CHAPTER FOCUS POINTS

After studying this chapter you will have a better understanding of:

1. What social reality is and how it works

2. How attitudes are formed and changed

3. How prejudices can be formed and changed

4. How social relationships are formed and are evolving with the advent of the Internet.

## CHAPTER CONTENTS

Imagine circumstances in which you've done everything to get to a job interview on time, but nothing has gone your way. The electricity went off during the night, so your alarm didn't wake you. The friend who was supposed to give you a ride had a flat tire. When you tried to get money for a taxi, the ATM ate your card. When you finally get to the office, you know what the manager is thinking: 'Why would I give a job to someone this unreliable?' You want to protest, 'It's not me, it's the circumstances!' As you have contemplated this scenario, you have begun to enter the world of *social psychology*—that area of psychology that investigates the ways in which individuals create and interpret social situations.

**Social psychology** is the study of the ways in which thoughts, feelings, perceptions, motives and behaviour are influenced by interactions and transactions between people. Social psychologists try to understand behaviour within its social context. This social context is the vibrant canvas on which are painted the movements, strengths and vulnerabilities of the social animal. Defined broadly, the social context includes the real, imagined or symbolic presence of other people; the activities and interactions that take place between people; the features of the settings in which behaviour occurs; and the expectations and norms that govern behaviour in a given setting (Sherif, 1981).

In this chapter and the next, we explore several major themes of social psychological research. For much of this chapter we focus on **social cognition**, which is the processes by which people select, interpret and remember social information. We examine the ways in which people construct social reality and the ways in which attitudes are formed and changed. We then consider circumstances of prejudice, in which beliefs and attitudes have distressing consequences for social interactions. Finally, we consider the relationships of liking and loving. Throughout this chapter, we illustrate how research in social psychology has immediate applications to your life. As you will see, in Chapter 17, we extend our analysis of social psychology's relevance beyond the personal to societal concerns. In both chapters, abstract theory meets the stern test of practicality, as we attempt to answer this question: Does psychological knowledge make a difference in the everyday lives of people and society?

# CONSTRUCTING SOCIAL REALITY

To open the chapter, we asked you to imagine everything that could go wrong in advance of a job interview. When you finally arrive at the manager's office you have very different interpretations of the same event. You know you've been a victim of circumstances. However, at least in the short run, the manager judges you only by what is readily apparent: you are late and you are dishevelled. That's what we mean by *constructing social reality*. The manager considers the evidence you present and makes an interpretation of the situation. If you still wish to get the job, you'll have to get the manager to construct a new interpretation.

Let's look at one classic social psychological example in which people's beliefs led them to view the same situation from different vantage points and make contrary conclusions about what 'really happened'. The study concerned a football game that took place some years ago between two university football teams. An undefeated Princeton team played Dartmouth in the final game of the season. The game, which Princeton won, was rough, filled with penalties and serious injuries to both sides. After the game, the newspapers of the two schools offered very different accounts of what had happened.

A team of social psychologists, intrigued by the different perceptions, surveyed students at both university campuses, showed them a film of the game, and recorded their judgments about the number of infractions committed by each of the teams. Nearly all Princeton students judged the game as 'rough and dirty', none saw it as 'clean and fair', and most believed that Dartmouth players started the dirty play. In contrast, the majority of Dartmouth students thought both sides were equally to blame for the rough game, and many thought it was 'rough, clean, and fair'. Moreover, when the Princeton students viewed the game film, they 'saw' the Dartmouth team commit twice as many penalties as their own team. When viewing the same film, Dartmouth students 'saw' both sides commit the same number of penalties (Hastorf & Cantril, 1954).

This study makes clear that a complex social occurrence, such as a football game, cannot be observed in an objective, unbiased fashion. Social situations obtain significance when observers *selectively encode* what is happening in terms of what they expect to see and want to see. In the case of the football game, people *looked* at the same activity, but they *saw* two different games.

To explain how the Princeton and Dartmouth fans came to such different interpretations of the football

Why are fans who watch their favourite team play likely to perceive more instances of unfair play on the part of the opposing team?

**social psychology** The branch of psychology that studies the effect of social variables on individual behaviour, attitudes, perceptions and motives.

**social cognition** The process by which people select, interpret and remember social information.

game returns us to the realm of *perception*. Recall from Chapter 4 that you often must put prior knowledge to work to interpret ambiguous perceptual objects. The principle is the same for the football game—people bring past knowledge to bear on the interpretation of current events—but the objects for perceptual processing are people and situations. **Social perception** is the process by which people come to understand and categorise the behaviours of others. In this section, we will focus largely on two issues of social perception. First, we consider how people make judgments about the forces that influence other people's behaviour, their *causal attributions*. Next, we discuss how processes of social perception can sometimes bring the world in line with expectations.

## THE ORIGINS OF ATTRIBUTION THEORY

One of the most important inferential tasks facing all social perceivers is to determine the causes of events. You want to know the whys of life. Why did my girlfriend break off the relationship? Why did he get the job and not I? Why did my parents' divorce after so many years of marriage? All such whys lead to an analysis of possible causal determinants for some action, event or outcome. **Attribution theory** is a general approach to describing the ways the social perceiver uses information to generate causal explanations.

Attribution theory originated in the writings of Fritz Heider (1958). Heider argued that people continually make causal analyses as part of their attempts at general comprehension of the social world. People, he suggested, are all *intuitive psychologists* who try to figure out what people are like and what causes their behaviour, just as professional psychologists do. Heider believed that the questions that dominate most attributional analyses are whether the cause of a behaviour is found in the person (internal or *dispositional* causality) or in the situation (external or *situational* causality) and who is responsible for the outcomes. How do people make those judgments?

**Harold Kelley** (1967) formalised Heider's line of thinking by specifying the variables that people use to make their attributions. Kelley made the important observation that people most often make causal attributions for events under conditions of *uncertainty*. You rarely, if ever, have sufficient information to know for sure what caused someone to behave in a particular way. Kelley believed that people grapple with uncertainty by accumulating information from multiple events and using the *covariation principle*. The **covariation principle** suggests that people should attribute a behaviour to a causal factor if that factor was present whenever the behaviour occurred but was absent whenever it didn't occur. Suppose, for example, you are walking down a street and you see a friend pointing at a horse and screaming. What evidence would you gather to decide whether your friend is crazy (a dispositional attribution) or danger is afoot (a situational attribution)?

Kelley suggested that people make this judgment by assessing covariation with respect to three dimensions of information relevant to the person whose acts they are trying to explain: distinctiveness, consistency and consensus.

- *Distinctiveness* refers to whether the behaviour is specific to a particular situation—does your friend scream in response to all horses?

- *Consistency* refers to whether the behaviour occurs repeatedly in response to this situation—has this horse made your friend scream in the past?

- *Consensus* refers to whether other people also produce the same behaviour in the same situation—is everyone pointing and screaming?

Each of these three dimensions plays a role in the conclusions you draw. Suppose, for example, that your friend was the only one screaming. Would that make you more likely to make a dispositional or a situational attribution?

Thousands of studies have been conducted to refine and extend attribution theory beyond the solid foundation provided by Heider and Kelley (Försterling, 2001; Moskowitz, 2004). Many of those studies have concerned themselves with conditions in which attributions depart from a systematic search of available information. We will describe four types of circumstances in which bias may creep into your attributions.

## THE FUNDAMENTAL ATTRIBUTION ERROR

Suppose you have made an arrangement to meet a friend at 7 o'clock. It's now 7:30, and the friend still hasn't arrived. How might you be explaining this event to yourself?

- I'm sure something really important happened that made it impossible for her to be here on time.

- What a jerk! Couldn't she try a little harder?

We've given you a choice again between a situational and a dispositional attribution. Research has shown that people are more likely, on average, to choose the second type, the dispositional explanation (Ross & Nisbett, 1991). This tendency is so strong, in fact, that social psychologist **Lee Ross** (1977) labelled it the fundamental attribution error. The **fundamental attribution error (FAE)** represents the dual tendency for people to overestimate dispositional factors (blame or credit people) and to underestimate situational factors (blame or credit the environment) when searching for the cause of some behaviour or outcome

Let's look at a laboratory example of the FAE. Ross and his colleagues (1977) created an experimental version of a type of quiz game in which participants became questioners or contestants by the flip of a coin. After the coin flip, both the questioners- and contestants-to-be listened to the instructions: The experimenters asked the questioners to invent challenging questions based on their own personal knowledge. When the questioners were

**social perception** The process by which a person comes to know or perceive the personal attributes.

**attribution theory** A social-cognitive approach to describing the ways the social perceiver uses information to generate causal explanations.

**fundamental attribution error (FAE)** The dual tendency of observers to underestimate the impact of situational factors and to overestimate the influence of dispositional factors on a person's behaviour.

**covariation principle** A theory that suggests that people attribute a behaviour to a causal factor if that factor was present whenever the behaviour occurred but was absent whenever it did occur.

done, they posed those questions to the contestants. The contestant tried, often in vain, to answer the questions. At the end of the session, the questioner, the contestant and observers (other participants who had watched the game) rated the general knowledge of both questioner and contestant. The results are shown in **Figure 16.1**. As you can see, questioners seem to believe that both they and the contestants are average. Both contestants and observers, however, rate the questioner as much more knowledgeable than the contestant—and contestants even rate themselves to be a bit below average! Is this fair? It should be clear that the situation confers a great advantage on the questioner. (Wouldn't you prefer to be the one who gets to ask the questions?) The contestants' and observers' ratings ignore the way in which the situation allowed one person to look bright and the other to look dull. That's the fundamental attribution error.

You should be on a constant lookout for instances of the FAE. However, this may not always be easy: it often takes a bit of 'research' to discover the situational roots of behaviour. Situational forces are often invisible. You can't, for example, *see* social norms; you can only see the behaviours they give rise to. What can you do to avoid the FAE? Particularly in circumstances in which you are making a dispositional attribution that is negative ('What a jerk!'), you should take a step back and ask yourself, 'Could it be something about the situation that is bringing about this behaviour?' You might think of such an exercise as 'attributional charity'. Do you see why?

This advice may be particularly important to those of us who live in Western society because evidence suggests that the FAE is due, in part, to cultural sources (Miller, 1984). Recall the discussion in Chapter 13 of cultural differences in construals of the self. As we explained there, most Western cultures embody *independent construals of self*, whereas most Eastern cultures embody *interdependent construals of self* (Markus & Kitayama, 1991). Research demonstrates that, as a function of the culture of interdependence, members of non-Western cultures are less likely to focus on individual actors in situations. This is quite prevalent with the Aboriginal and Pacific Islander culture, where 'going walkabout' is considered to be a social experience widely accepted within a community. In other words, punctuality for an appointment is not viewed as important when compared to appreciating and understanding social and cultural experience, which is widely accepted within these communities. You might therefore say that some Eastern and indigenous cultures may account for cultural factors more than dispositional factors and therefore attribute someone being late to the community and/or situational factors rather than to an individual's temperament. Let's see how in Western society this cultural difference affects reporting of news events.

Researchers selected articles from newspapers in the United States (*New York Times*) and Japan (*Asahi Shimbun*) that reported on financial scandals such as the 1995 collapse of England's oldest bank, Barings. A research assistant, who was blind to the study's purpose, read each article to extract excerpts in which causal explanations were offered. For each excerpt, another pair of blind research assistants judged whether the

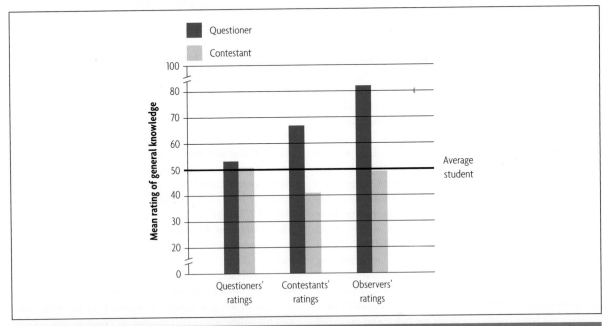

Figure 16.1

**Ratings of questioners' and contestants' general knowledge**
After the quiz game, questioners, contestants and observers rated each of the participant's general knowledge with respect to a rating of 50 for the average student. Questioners believed that both they and the contestants were average. However, both contestants and observers rated the questioner as much more knowledgeable than the contestant. Furthermore, contestants rated themselves to be a bit below average.

explanation offered was dispositional—it attributed blame to an individual—or situational—it attributed blame to an organisation. The patterns of attributions were strikingly different for the two sets of articles. U.S. writers tended to make stronger dispositional attributions, whereas Japanese writers made stronger situational attributions (Menon et al., 1999).

An impressive feature of this study is that it captures cultural attributional styles as they are written for newspaper articles. The study makes clear one way in which a cultural style of attribution is transmitted and maintained for all those who are exposed to the media in a particular culture.

## SELF-SERVING BIASES

One of the most startling findings in the quiz game study was the contestants' negative evaluation of their own abilities. This suggests that people will make the FAE even at their own expense. (In fact, you should recall from Chapter 14 that one theory of the origins of depression suggests that depressed people make too many negative attributions to themselves rather than to situational causes.) In many circumstances, however, people do just the opposite—their attributions err in the direction of being self-serving. A **self-serving bias** leads people to take credit for their successes while denying or explaining away responsibility for their failures. In many situations, people tend to make dispositional attributions for success and situational attributions for failure (Gilovich, 1991): 'I got the prize because of my ability'; 'I lost the competition because it was rigged.'

These patterns of attribution may be good for short-term self-esteem. However, it may often be more important to have an accurate sense of what causal forces are at work in your life outcomes. Consider how you do in your classes. If you get an A, what attributions do you make? How about if you get a C? Research has demonstrated that students tend to attribute high grades to their own efforts and low grades to factors external to themselves (McAllister, 1996). In fact, lecturers show the same pattern—they make attributions to themselves for students' successes but not their failures. Once again, can you see what impact this pattern of attributions might have on your Grade Point Average (GPA)? If you don't think about the external causes for your successes (for example, 'That first exam was easy'), you might fail to study enough the next time; if you don't think about the dispositional causes for failures (for example, 'I shouldn't have stayed so long at that party'), you also might never get around to studying hard enough. We emphasised earlier that you should strive to avoid the FAE when you think about others' behaviour. Similarly, you might examine attributions about your own behaviour to weed out (non-self-serving) self-serving biases.

People also indulge in self-serving biases when they are members of groups: They are more likely to attribute group successes to themselves and failures to other group members. You may be pleased, however, to learn that friendship puts limits on this effect.

Experimental participants were asked to engage in a task that measured creativity with either a friend or a stranger. After completing the task, each participant was given feedback on the success of his or her group relative to a large normative sample. Irrespective of their actual performance, half the participants were given *success* feedback (i.e., they were told their performance was in the 93rd percentile); half were given *failure* feedback (i.e., they were told their performance was in the 31st percentile). All the participants were then asked to rate who was more responsible for the test outcome on a scale that ranged from 1 (the other participant) to 10 (myself). As seen in **Figure 16.2**, participants who engaged in the task with a stranger made considerably stronger attributions to themselves for success than for failure (Campbell et al., 2000). Participants' attributions in circumstances of success and failure were more consistent when their partners had been their friends.

Next time you are engaged in a group activity, try to see how this experiment applies to the way in which you make attributions of responsibility to different members of the group.

Why does it matter so much what attributions you make? Recall the example of your tardy friend. Suppose

**self-serving bias** An attributional bias in which people tend to take credit for their successes and deny responsibility for their failures.

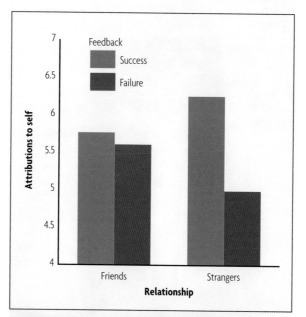

### Figure 16.2

**Patterns of attributions to friends and strangers**
Experimental participants were asked to rate who was responsible for their groups' success or failure on a task. With strangers, participants showed a pattern of self-serving biases: They made stronger attributions to themselves when the group had succeeded than when it had failed. Ratings were more consistent when the participants' partners were their friends.

that, because you don't seek information about the situation, you decide that she isn't actually interested in being your friend. Can that incorrect belief actually cause the person to be unfriendly toward you in the future? To address that question, we turn now to the power of beliefs and expectations in constructing social reality.

## EXPECTATIONS AND SELF-FULFILLING PROPHECIES

Can beliefs and expectations go beyond colouring the way you interpret experiences to actually shape social reality? Much research suggests that the very nature of some situations can be modified significantly by the beliefs and expectations people have about them. **Self-fulfilling prophecies** (Merton, 1957) are predictions made about some future behaviour or event that modify behavioural interactions so as to produce what is expected. Suppose, for example, you go to a party expecting to have a great time. Suppose a friend goes expecting it to be boring. Can you imagine the different ways in which the two of you might behave, given these expectations? These alternative ways of behaving may, in turn, alter how others at the party behave toward you. In that case, which of you is actually more likely to have a good time at the party?

How do self-fulfilling prophecies affect the likelihood that children will engage in underage drinking?

One of the most powerful demonstrations of self-fulfilling prophecies took its cue from a play by George Bernard Shaw. In Shaw's *Pygmalion* (popularised as the musical *My Fair Lady*), a street waif is transformed into a proper society lady under the intense training of her teacher, Professor Henry Higgins. The effect of social expectancy, or the *Pygmalion effect*, was recreated in a classic experiment by psychologist Robert Rosenthal in conjunction with school principal Leonore Jacobson.

> Primary school teachers were informed by researchers that their testing had revealed that some of their students were 'academic spurters'. The teachers were led to believe that these particular students were 'intellectual bloomers who will show unusual gains during the academic year'. In fact, there was no objective basis for that prediction; the names of these late bloomers were chosen randomly. However, by the end of that school year, 30 percent of the children arbitrarily named as spurters had gained an average of 22 IQ points! Almost all of them had gained at least 10 IQ points. Their gain in intellectual performance, as measured by a standard test of intelligence, was significantly greater than that of their control group classmates who had started out with the same average IQ (Rosenthal & Jacobson, 1968).

How did the teachers' false expectations get translated into such positive student performance? Rosenthal (1974) points to at least four processes that were activated by the teachers' expectations. First, the teachers acted more warmly and more friendly toward the 'late bloomers', creating a climate of social approval and acceptance. Second, they put greater demands—involving both quality and level of difficulty of material to be learned—on those for whom they had high hopes. Third, they gave more immediate and clearer feedback (both praise and criticism) about the selected students' performance. Finally, the teachers created more opportunities for the special students to respond in class, show their stuff, and be reinforced, thus giving them hard evidence that they were indeed as good as the teachers believed they were.

What is unusual, of course, about the situation in the classrooms is that the teachers were purposefully given false expectations. This methodology allowed Rosenthal and Jacobson to demonstrate the full potential for self-fulfilling prophecies. In most real-world situations, however, expectations are based on fairly accurate social perceptions (Jussim & Harber, 2005). Teachers, for example, expect certain students to do well because those students arrive in the classroom with better qualifications; and those students, typically, do show the best performance. Research has suggested, in fact, that self-fulfilling prophecies have the greatest effect on the lives of low-achieving students (Madon et al., 1997). When teachers expect them to do poorly, they may do even worse; when teachers expect them to do well, that has the potential to turn their school lives around.

Much of the research on self-fulfilling prophecies has focused on school success. However, researchers have found evidence in other domains that people's mistaken beliefs and expectations can have an influence on what actually happens. For example, research suggests that when parents overestimate the amount of alcohol their adolescents will consume, those expectations can become self-fulfilling prophecies (Madon et al., 2004). The impact of parents' beliefs was greatest when both parents overestimated their children's future alcohol consumption.

This has also been found with Aboriginal youth in Australia; however, other factors such as reducing access to alcohol in remote communities has also been suggested to be effective. More likely, a dual-strategy approach with parent education on how to talk to their children about drinking and a reduction in alcohol access would be of optimal benefit. However, it is critical that caretakers of children are less pessimistic about their drinking behaviour since access to alcohol will most likely always be present in a community—perhaps then a reduction in the prevalence of alcohol abuse will occur in rural Australia? Unfortunately, reports on this issue say the problem is even more complex than self-fulfilling prophecies perpetuated by the community, the parent or the individual (Gray et al, 2000), The complexities range from a lack of community and government programs to provide local community alcohol education programs, rehabilitation programs and policing and laws to control existing Aboriginal drinking behaviour. The key tool however, is considered to be direct parental education programs in regards to solving Indigenous drinking problems in rural and remote Australia.

As you consider these studies on self-fulfilling prophecies, you might wonder what behaviours teachers and mothers perform that allow their mistaken expectations to be confirmed. Let's see now how a person's choice of behaviours can affect the construction of social reality.

## BEHAVIOURS THAT CONFIRM EXPECTATIONS

Consider the primary school classroom experiment once again. We have already noted that the teachers performed a series of behaviours that enabled them, in the long run, to confirm their expectations. **Mark Snyder** (1984; Klein & Snyder, 2003) introduced the term **behavioural confirmation** to label the process by which someone's expectations about another person actually influence the second person to behave in ways that confirm the original hypothesis. For example, imagine you were about to interview someone, and you were told that the person was shy or introverted. Which of these questions might you select to ask (Snyder & Swann, 1978)?

- What would you do if you wanted to liven things up at a party?
- In what situations do you wish you could be more outgoing?
- What factors make it hard for you to really open up to people?
- In what situations are you most talkative?

Suppose you chose the second question—as many experimental participants did when they believed they were going to talk to someone introverted. Isn't it likely that even a very extraverted person could give you reasonable answers to the question? Thus an expectation—'I'm going to talk to someone who is an introvert'—leads to a behavioural choice—'I'm going to ask the kind of question you ask an introverted person'—which leads to potential confirmation of the expectation—'If he could give a good answer to this question, I guess he really is introverted.'

How powerful are the forces of behavioural confirmation? Suppose you learned that someone had formed an impression of you that could set the stage for behavioural confirmation. Under what circumstances might you labour to change that impression? Consider a study that provided participants with information about their partners' impressions.

> Researchers brought pairs of men and women into the laboratory (Stukas & Snyder, 2001). The men became the *perceivers* (i.e., they received impression information) and the women became the *targets* (i.e., the expectations were about them). (The participants were not aware that they had been cast in these roles.) Half of the perceivers were informed that their target was introverted and half that their target was extraverted. We'll focus on circumstances in which perceivers were led to believe the targets were introverts. The participants had a 10-minute conversation over an intercom. After that interaction, both perceivers and targets reported impressions of their partners. A few minutes later, the perceivers believed they were getting true feedback on what their partners thought about them. In fact, they were told (for the part of the experiment that is our focus) that their partners thought that they were introverted. For half of the targets, that account included a situational attribution: the partner thought that the target was behaving like an introvert only because of the situation. For the other half of the targets, that account included a dispositional attribution: the partner thought that the target was deep down an introvert. At this point, the pairs had a second 10-minute conversation, this time face to face. Raters later listened to the conversations and evaluated the targets' performance for introverted and extraverted behaviours. How did the targets behave, knowing that their partner thought they were introverts? In the presence of a situational attribution, the targets were likely to produce behaviours that confirmed that impression: they were, for example, shy and passive in their parts of the conversation. However, in the presence of a dispositional attribution, the targets were likely to produce behaviours that were so relatively extraverted—loud and outspoken— that they even struck the raters as rude!

This result might remind you of our earlier discussion of the fundamental attribution error. When the targets knew about a dispositional attribution that they apparently

**behavioural confirmation**
The process by which people behave in ways that elicit from others specific expected reactions and then use those reactions to confirm their beliefs.

disliked, they worked hard to provide behaviour to overcome that attribution.

The extent of behavioural confirmation also depends on the motivations the target has with respect to the interaction. In another study, male perceivers were led to believe—they were shown photographs—that the female targets at the other end of a phone conversation were either of normal weight or obese. In some cases, the women (whose actual weight was unrelated to the photographs) were asked to participate in the conversations to gain knowledge about the personality of the man to whom they were speaking; in other cases, the women's goal was to have a smooth and pleasant interaction with their male partner. In general, this latter situation produced behavioural confirmation: the *targets* were rated as producing behaviours that conformed to an obesity stereotype (for example, they were rated as less sociable and less happy). However, when the *targets* were motivated to obtain knowledge, behavioural confirmation was *not* found (Snyder & Haugen, 1995). This experiment suggests that the normal impulse to have smooth social interactions makes it *more* possible for people to remake the world in line with their own beliefs and attitudes, including stereotypes.

The research we have described in this section leads naturally to the question, How do attitudes and expectations arise? In the experiments we have reviewed, participants are typically told what to believe. But what happens in the real world, when you arrive at expectations on your own? In the next section, we consider the question of how attitudes are formed and changed—and we examine the links among beliefs, attitudes and action.

**attitude** The learned, relatively stable tendency to respond to people, concepts and events in an evaluative way.

## RECAP CHECKPOINT
### Constructing social reality

- Each person constructs his or her own social reality.
- Social perception is influenced by beliefs and expectations.
- Attribution theory describes the judgments people make about the causes of behaviours.
- Several biases, such as the fundamental attribution error, self-serving biases, and self-fulfilling prophecies, can creep into attributions and other judgments and behaviours.
- However, the influence of expectations is limited by accurate information you have about the world.

## CONCEPT QUESTIONS
1. What three dimensions did Harold Kelley suggest affect the attribution process?

2. Why might self-serving biases have a negative impact on a student's Grade Point Average?

3. What limits do ordinary classroom practices place on self-fulfilling prophecies?

4. What is meant by behavioural confirmation?

## CRITICAL THINKING
Recall the study that examined cross-cultural differences in causal explanations. Why might the researchers have focused on financial scandals?

# ATTITUDES, ATTITUDE CHANGE AND ACTION

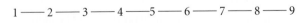

Have you already had a chance today to express an *attitude*? Has someone asked you, 'What do you think of my shirt?' or 'Was the chicken any good?' An **attitude** is a positive or negative evaluation of people, objects, and ideas. You may have favourable attitudes toward daycare workers, sports cars and tax cuts, and unfavourable attitudes toward telemarketers, contemporary art and astrology. This definition of attitude allows for the fact that many of the attitudes you hold are not overt; you may not be consciously aware that you harbour certain attitudes. Attitudes are important because they influence your behaviour and how you construct social reality. Recall the Princeton–Dartmouth football game. Those people who favoured Princeton 'saw' a different game from those people who favoured Dartmouth; attributions about events were made in line with their attitudes. What are the sources of your attitudes, and how do they affect your behaviours?

## ATTITUDES AND BEHAVIOURS
We have already defined attitudes as positive or negative evaluations. We'll begin this section by giving you an opportunity to make an evaluation. To what extent do you agree with this statement? (Circle a number.)

I enjoy movies that star Angelina Jolie.

1 —— 2 —— 3 —— 4 —— 5 —— 6 —— 7 —— 8 —— 9

Strongly                    Neutral                    Strongly
disagree                                                    agree

Let's say that you gave a rating of 3—you disagree somewhat. What is the origin of that judgment? We can

How does your attitude toward Angelina Jolie affect your willingness to watch her movies?

identify three types of information that give rise to your attitude:

- *Cognitive.* What thoughts do you have in response to 'Angelina Jolie'?
- *Affective.* What feelings does the mention of 'Angelina Jolie' evoke?
- *Behavioural.* How do you behave when, for example, you have the opportunity to see one of Angelina Jolie's movies?

Some combination of these types of information most likely guided your hand when you circled '3' (or some other number). Your attitudes also generate responses in the same three categories. If you believe yourself to have a somewhat negative attitude toward Angelina Jolie, you might say, 'She isn't a serious actor' (cognitive), 'She looked better when she first started out' (affective), or 'After *Sky Captain and The World of Tomorrow*, I'm going to wait to read her reviews' (behavioural).

It isn't too hard to measure an attitude, but is that attitude always an accurate indication of how people will actually behave? You know from your own life experiences that the answer is 'no': people will say they dislike Angelina Jolie but spend good money to see her anyway. At the same time, sometimes people's behaviours *do* follow their attitudes: they say they won't pay to see Angelina Jolie, and they don't. How can you determine when attitudes will or

will not predict behaviour? Researchers have worked hard to answer that question—to identify the circumstances in which the link is strongest between people's attitudes and how they act (Ajzen & Fishbein, 2005; Fazio & Roskos-Ewoldsen, 2005).

One property of attitudes that predicts behaviour is accessibility—the strength of the association between an attitude object and a person's evaluation of that object (Fazio, 1995). When we asked you about Angelina Jolie, did an answer rush to mind or did you have to consider the question for a while? The more quickly an answer rushed in, the more likely it is that your behaviour will be consistent with that attitude. But how do attitudes become more accessible? Research suggests that attitudes are more accessible when they are based on direct experience: You will have a more accessible attitude about Angelina Jolie movies if you've experienced several of them yourself rather than hearing or reading about them indirectly. Attitudes are also more accessible when they have been rehearsed more often: just as you might expect, the more often you've formulated an attitude about something (consider 'chocolate' versus 'kiwi'), the more accessible is the attitude. Rehearsal makes attitudes more accessible even when you've been lying.

Suppose someone asks you how you feel about Angelina Jolie and you decide to lie to be polite. What impact does lying have on your attitude and your subsequent behaviour? Researchers have tested the hypothesis that because lies make your *real* attitude more accessible, they actually make your behaviour more consistent with that real attitude (Johar & Sengupta, 2002). In the study, participants were asked to consider four brands of chocolate bars that were unfamiliar to them—the researchers imported them from foreign countries. After considering information associated with each chocolate bar, participants in one group were asked to indicate their true attitude toward each brand five times. Participants in a second group were asked to express the opposite of their true feelings—they were asked to lie five times. A third group served as a control group and did not express their opinions. At the end of the study, participants were asked to choose the chocolate bar they most wanted to sample. **Table 16.1** shows the correlations between the participants' true attitude ratings and the brands they selected. As you can see, for both true and false expressions of attitudes the correlation is higher than in the control condition. Thus lying made people's behaviours more consistent with what they really thought rather than with what they said.

Each time the participants prepared a lie, they had to examine mentally their true attitudes. That process of examination made their true attitudes more accessible.

Attitudes also are better predictors of behaviour when the attitudes and behaviours are measured at the same level of *specificity*. Consider the data presented in **Table 16.2**. In this study, the researchers were trying to predict the likelihood that members of an initial sample

## Table 16.1

### Accessibility improves attitude–behaviour correlations

| | Correlation between true attitude and behavioural choice |
|---|---|
| True expression of attitude | 0.61 |
| False expression of attitude | 0.54 |
| Control | 0.39 |

## Table 16.2

### Specificity improves attitude–behaviour correlations

| Attitude measured | Correlation with behaviour of using birth control |
|---|---|
| Attitude toward birth control | .08 |
| Attitude toward birth control pills | .32 |
| Attitude toward using birth control pills | .52 |
| Attitude toward using birth control pills during the next 2 years | .57 |

(left axis label: Specificity)

Note: Researchers were trying to predict the likelihood that women would use birth control pills in the next 2 years. The more specific the question the women were asked about their attitudes, the higher was the correlation with their actual behavior.

Why might someone be able to predict your vote from the speed with which you express an attitude?

of 270 women, ages 18 to 38, would use birth control pills. You can see in Table 16.2 that the more *specific* the question the women were asked about their attitudes was, the higher was the correlation with their actual specific behaviour (Davidson & Jaccard, 1979). (Recall that the closer a correlation is to 1 or −1, the stronger is the relationship.) The concept of specificity also applies to the specific *exemplars* you call to mind when you produce an attitude (Sia et al., 1997). Suppose, for example, we asked you to agree or disagree with the statement 'I trust politicians.' Your judgment would depend on which politician or politicians came to mind: Was it Winston Churchill, Bill Clinton, George W. Bush or Kevin Rudd? If we asked you the same question in a week, your judgment—your report of your general attitude— might change if some other set of politicians came to mind.

When your attitudes are based on different subsets of information, they may change radically over time: When you gave us your attitude about Angelina Jolie, were you thinking about the film *The Good Shepherd*, *Mr. & Mrs. Smith*, or *Lara Croft: Tomb Raider*? Only when the 'evidence' for your attitude remains stable over time can we expect to find a strong relationship between your evaluation (thoughts) and what you do (actions).

## PROCESSES OF PERSUASION

We've just seen that, under appropriate circumstances, attitudes can predict behaviour. That's good news for all the people who spend time and money to affect your attitudes. But quite often others *can't* affect your attitudes when they want to do so. You don't change brands of toothpaste each time you see a peppy new commercial with scads of pearly-toothed actors; you don't change your political affiliation each time a candidate looks into the camera and declares sincerely that he or she deserves your vote. Many people in your life indulge in **persuasion**— deliberate efforts to change your attitudes. For persuasion to take place, certain conditions must be met. Let's explore some of those conditions.

To begin, we introduce the **elaboration likelihood model**, a theory of persuasion that defines how likely it is that people will focus their cognitive processes to elaborate on a persuasive message (Petty et al., 2005). This model makes a critical distinction between *central* and *peripheral routes* to persuasion. The central route represents circumstances in which people think carefully about a persuasive communication so that attitude change depends on the strength of the arguments. This careful thought is called *high* elaboration. When someone is trying to convince you that gasoline should cost $5 a gallon, you are likely to process the information in this careful fashion. The peripheral route represents circumstances in which people do not focus critically on the message but respond to superficial cues in the situation. When a sexy model is placed in front of the product someone wishes you to buy, the seller is hoping you'll avoid critical thought. That absence of critical thought is called *low* elaboration. The central or peripheral route that people take depends in large part on their *motivation* with respect to the message: Are they willing and able to think carefully about the persuasive content; will they engage in high or low elaboration?

If you take a close look at the messages that surround you, you will quickly come to the conclusion that advertisers, for example, often count on you to take the peripheral route. Why do advertisers pay celebrities to sell their products? Do you really believe that Hollywood actors worry enormously about which long-distance phone service will produce bigger savings? Presumably, the advertisers hope that you won't evaluate the arguments too closely—instead, they hope you'll let yourself be persuaded by your general feelings of warmth towards the actor hawking the product.

Now ask yourself this question: Under what circumstances are you likely to feel sufficiently motivated to take the central route to persuasion? Researchers have undertaken an enormous amount of research to address that question (Petty et al., 2005). Let's consider a study that illustrates how difficult it is to persuade all of the people all of the time. The study starts with the observation that individuals often label themselves as a *morning person* or an *evening person*. Researchers hypothesised that people are more likely to have the energy and motivation to engage in elaborative processing— the central route to persuasion—when they encounter persuasive messages at their right time of day.

To test their hypothesis, the researchers recruited participants who self-identified their 'optimal' time of day as morning or evening (Martin & Marrington, 2005). The study had two sessions: one at 8:30 A.M. and one at 7:00 P.M. Each session included both morning people and evening people. At the start of the session, participants provided attitude ratings (on 9-point scales) on several social issues including the mercy killing of terminally ill people. Next, the participants read the same set of persuasive statements that argued against mercy killing. Finally, participants listed the thoughts they had while reading the statements and provided a second set of attitude ratings. When the participants' session matched their optimal time of day, they listed more thoughts that were focused on the persuasive statements. In addition, as shown in **Figure 16.3**, people showed more attitude change in the direction of the statements when they read the persuasive statements at the optimal time of day.

At their optimal time of day, participants were motivated to elaborate on the persuasive statements. Because the statements provided strong arguments against mercy killing, their attitudes changed in the direction of the statements. If the arguments had been weak, high elaboration should have prevented attitude change.

Another factor that influences your choice of central versus peripheral routes is the match between the type of

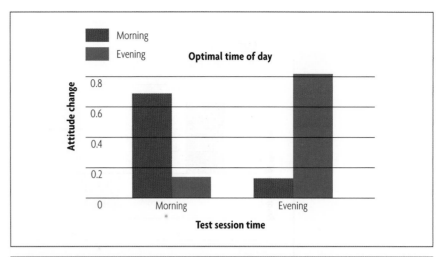

Figure 16.3

Persuasion at the optimal time of day
When participants read persuasive statements at their optimal time of day, they showed more attitude change in the direction of those statements.

Adapted from Martin & Marrington, *Personality and Individual Differences, 39*, 367-377, 2005.

attitude and the type of argument (Ajzen & Sexton, 1999). Earlier, we suggested that both cognitive and affective experiences give rise to attitudes. Research suggests that attitudes are more likely to change when advertisers match cognitive-based arguments to cognitive-based attitudes and affect-based arguments to affect-based attitudes.

What is the basis of your attitudes toward brands of *coffee*? You are likely to make evaluations based on your *cognitive* responses: How do they taste? How much do they cost? Now think about *greeting cards*. For greeting cards, you're more likely to be swayed by *affective* responses: Do they make you smile? Will they capture the right quality relationship? In one experiment, participants were exposed to either cognitive-based or affective-based advertisements for products, including coffee and greeting cards. A cognitive-based ad might read, 'The delicious, hearty flavour and aroma of Nescafé coffee come from a blend of the freshest coffee beans'; an emotion-based ad might read, 'The coffee you drink says something about the type of person you are. It can reveal your rare, discriminating taste.' After participants read each of a series of ads, they listed thoughts to indicate how favourably they felt toward the product. As you can see in **Figure 16.4**, there was a strong effect of the match: Participants produced more favourable thoughts when the type of message (for example, cognitive-based ads) matched the type of attitude (for example, cognitive-based attitudes) (Shavitt, 1990).

In your own efforts to change people's attitudes you should also be able to put this result to use: Does the attitude have a strong cognitive component or a strong

Why do advertisers pay celebrities to endorse their products?

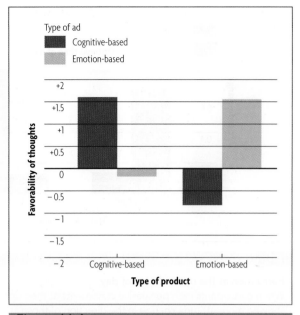

Type of ad
■ Cognitive-based
▢ Emotion-based

## Figure 16.4

**Emotion- and cognitive-based ads and products**
When the type of advertisement (emotion- or cognitive-based) matched the dimension of evaluation underlying the object—emotions for greeting cards and cognitions for coffee—people reacted more favorably to the product. (The favourability of thoughts was measured on a scale ranging from −3 to +3.)

From Shavitt, "The Role of Attitude Objects in Attitude Functions," *Journal of Personality and Social Psychology*, Vol. 63, No. 4, 1992. Copyright © 1992 American Psychological Association.

affective component? How can you tailor your persuasive message accordingly?

## PERSUASION BY YOUR OWN ACTIONS

In the last section, we described factors that influence people's ability to change others' attitudes. However, there are forces at work in a number of circumstances that cause people to bring about their *own* attitude change. Imagine a situation in which you've vowed not to eat any extra calories. You arrive at work, and there's a cake for your boss's birthday. You consume a piece. Did you break your vow? That is, should you have a negative attitude about your own behaviour? Aren't you likely to think what you did was okay? Why? We describe two analyses of self-persuasion, *dissonance theory* and *self-perception theory*.

**Dissonance theory** One of the most common assumptions in the study of attitudes is that people like to believe that their attitudes remain consistent over time. This striving for consistency was explored within the field of social psychology in the theory of *cognitive dissonance,* as developed by **Leon Festinger** (1957). **Cognitive dissonance** is the state of conflict someone experiences *after* making a decision, taking an action, or being exposed to information that is contrary to prior

**cognitive dissonance** The theory that the tension-producing effects of incongruous cognitions motivate individuals to reduce such tension.

beliefs, feelings or values. Suppose, for example, you chose to buy a car against a friend's advice. Why might you be overly defensive about the car? It is assumed that when a person's cognitions about his or her behaviour and relevant attitudes are dissonant—they do not follow one to the next—an aversive state arises that the person is motivated to reduce. Dissonance-reducing activities modify this unpleasant state. In the case of your car, being defensive—overstating its value—makes you feel better about going against your friend's advice. (Dissonance also might lead you to think less well of your friend.)

Dissonance has motivational force—it impels you to take action to reduce the unpleasant feeling (Wood, 2000). The motivation to reduce dissonance increases with the magnitude of the dissonance created by a cognitive inconsistency. In other words, the stronger the dissonance, the greater the motivation to reduce it. In a classic dissonance experiment, university students told a lie to other students and came to believe in their lie when they got a small, rather than a large, reward for doing so.

Stanford University students participated in a very dull task and were then asked (as a favour to the experimenter because his assistant hadn't shown up) to lie to another participant by saying that the task had been fun and interesting. Half the participants were paid $20 to tell the lie; the others were paid only $1. The $20 payment was sufficient external justification for lying, but the $1 payment was an inadequate justification. The people who were paid $1 were left with dissonant cognitions: 'The task was dull' and 'I chose to lie by telling another student it was fun and interesting without a good reason for doing so.'

To reduce their dissonance, these $1 participants changed their evaluations of the task. They later expressed the belief that they found 'it really was fun and interesting—I might like to do it again'. In comparison the participants who lied for $20 did not change their evaluations—the task was still a bore; they had only lied 'for the money' (Festinger & Carlsmith, 1959).

As this experiment shows, under conditions of high dissonance, an individual acts to justify his or her behaviour after the fact and engages in self-persuasion. This analysis says that the way to change attitudes is first to change behaviour. Ancient biblical scholars knew this principle. They urged rabbis not to insist that people believe before praying but to get them to pray first—and then they would come to believe.

Hundreds of experiments and field studies have shown the power of cognitive dissonance to change attitudes and behaviour (Crano & Prislin, 2006). Recently, however, researchers have begun to question whether dissonance effects generalise to other cultures. Consider again the way the concept of *self* changes from culture to culture. As we noted earlier, North Americans typically view themselves as *independent*, distinct from others in the environment;

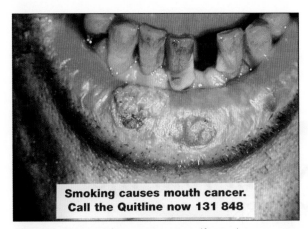

Smoking causes mouth cancer.
Call the Quitline now 131 848

What messages might you give yourself to reduce cognitive dissonance if you were aware of the adverse effects of smoking but continued to smoke?

members of Asian cultures typically view themselves as *interdependent*, fundamentally interconnected with others. Does the cultural concept of the self affect the experience of cognitive dissonance?

> Groups of Canadian and Japanese participants examined a list of entrées for a Chinese restaurant (Hoshino-Browne et al., 2005). Out of list of 25 dishes, they chose the 10 that they most liked (in one condition) or that they thought a friend would most like (in a second condition). Next, they rank-ordered those 10 dishes from most to least desirable—again, with respect either to their own or to a friend's preferences. The experimenters then asked the participants to choose between two coupons for free food. The coupons named the participants' fifth- and sixth-ranked choices (for them or their friend). Finally, participants were asked to go through and rate their top 10 choices once again. How might those ratings change from the first to the second time? According to dissonance theory, when you make a tough choice—like the one between your fifth- and sixth-ranked alternatives—you should adjust your attitudes to feel better about the outcome of the choice: 'If I chose kung pao chicken [originally no. 5], it really must be a better choice than mu shu pork [originally no. 6].' However, cross-cultural research on the self suggests that Canadian participants should experience more dissonance with respect to their own choices (because of their independent senses of self), whereas Japanese participants should experience more dissonance with respect to their choices for their friends (because of their interdependent senses of self). The data confirmed those expectations: Canadian participants' attitudes changed considerably more for self-judgments; Japanese participants' attitudes changed considerably more for friend judgments.

This research suggests that people experience cognitive dissonance—they seek to maintain consistency within their self-concept—in ways that are specific to their particular senses of self. If you are ever in circumstances in which you must make decisions jointly with members of other cultures, you will want to reflect on the culture's impact on the way you all think and act after the decision has been made.

### Self-perception theory

Dissonance theory describes one way in which people, at least in Western cultures, allow their behaviours ('I chose that CD') to have an impact on their attitudes ('I must like it much better than my other option'). *Self-perception theory*, developed by Daryl Bem (1972), identifies other circumstances in which behaviours inform attitudes. According to **self-perception theory**, you infer what your internal states (beliefs, attitudes, motives and feelings) are or should be by perceiving how you are acting now and recalling how you have acted in the past in a given situation. You use that self-knowledge to reason backward to the most likely causes or determinants of your behaviour. For example, the self-perceiver responds to the question, 'Do you like psychology?' by saying, 'Sure, I'm taking the basic course and it's not required, I do all the readings, I pay attention during lectures, and I'm getting a good grade in the course.' In other words, you answer a question about personal preferences by a behavioural description of relevant actions and situational factors—rather than undertaking an intense search of thoughts and feelings.

Self-perception theory lacks the motivational components of dissonance theory. Because self-perception fills in missing attitudes—you look to your behaviour to learn how you feel—self-perception processes occur mainly when you are in ambiguous situations and dealing with unfamiliar events (Fazio, 1987). In these situations, you have a need to discover how you feel about some novel object of attitudinal scrutiny—if you find yourself applauding during your first Angelina Jolie movie, you may infer a favourable attitude toward her. One flaw in the process of gaining self-knowledge through self-perception is that people are often insensitive about the extent to which their behaviour is influenced by situational forces. You can see this if we return a final time to the Quiz Game experiment. Recall that the participants who laboured unsuccessfully as contestants rated their own general knowledge relatively low. Imagine what it must have been like to be in their position. Over and over you would hear yourself saying, 'I don't know the answer to that question.' Can you see how observation of this behaviour—the process of self-perception—could give rise to a negative self-evaluation?

Let's return to the attitudes you might express toward yourself if you eat a slice of cake at your boss's birthday party. According to dissonance theory, you need to resolve the inconsistency between your vow ('I won't consume any extra calories') and your behaviour (eating a piece of cake). There are many things you can do to avoid feeling bad: perhaps you'd reason, 'I can't afford to have my boss be angry at me by declining a piece of cake.' Similarly, according to self-perception theory, you look at your behaviour to calculate your attitude. If you think, 'Because I ate cake, my boss's birthday must have been very important,' you'll also escape any negative impact on your self-esteem. Self-persuasion can sometimes be useful!

**self-perception theory** The idea that people observe themselves in order to figure out the reasons they act as they do.

compliance A change in
behaviour consistent with
a communication source's
direct requests.

## COMPLIANCE

In this section so far, we have discussed what attitudes are and how they might be changed. It should be clear to you, however, that most often what people want you to do is change your *behaviour*: People wish to bring about **compliance**—a change in behaviour consistent with their direct requests. When advertisers spend a lot of money for TV commercials, they don't just want you to feel good about their products—they want you

# CRITICAL THINKING *in your life*
## DO LATE-NIGHT TV ADS REALLY WORK?

If you've spent any time watching late-night (or early-morning) television, you've certainly been subjected to the types of advertisements that attempt to sell you sets of knives or CDs that you really don't need. If you pay close attention to these ads, you'll often see that they are structured to take strong advantage of the quirks of human compliance (Cialdini, 2001).

Let's look at one particular method that researchers have called the *That's-Not-All* (TNA) technique (Burger, 1986; Burger et al., 1999). Suppose you have been offered five CDs of 'The Greatest Hits of the '70s' for three easy payments of only $29.95. However, before you can make your decision the announcer adds, 'But that's not all: Act now and we'll also include—at no extra cost— a bonus CD with 12 more songs!' Does the addition of the extra CD make it more likely that you'll accept the offer? It probably should—you're getting more for the same money. Suppose, however, that you'd been offered the six CDs (for three easy payments of only $29.95) all at the same time, without the 'that's not all.' You'd be getting exactly the same amount of merchandise (six CDs) for the same money. Would you be equally likely to make the purchase?

Here's another common version of the TNA technique. They offer you the five CDs for three easy payments of $29.95 but then, before you can respond, they announce that (for a limited

time only) the price has been reduced to three payments of $24.95. Again, compare this to circumstances in which they always offer you the merchandise at the lower price. Would you be equally likely to make the purchase?

If you think about both these variations, you'll probably guess correctly that the TNA staging has a major impact on people's compliance. Consider a study that was framed as a psychology club bake sale (Burger, 1986). When community members approached the table to ask prices, they were told one of two things. In one condition (which, for the study, was the control condition), they were told that a cupcake with two biscuits was 75¢. In a second condition (the TNA condition), potential customers were told that the cupcake was 75¢. However, before they could respond, they were told 'wait a second' and told that the deal also included two biscuits. In the control condition, 40 percent of the potential customers closed the deal. In the TNA condition, the success rate was 73 percent. Remember, everyone was getting the same overall deal—what mattered quite a bit was the way in which the deal unfolded in time.

Why does that's-not-all work? One explanation is the reciprocity norm that we have already described: The seller has done something for you (added to the deal) and now you should do something for him or her (buy the product).

Another explanation points to the type of anchoring phenomenon we described in Chapter 8. The original deal serves as an anchor point against which you decide whether you are at all interested. If you have some interest, then the added bonus seals the deal. For that reason, that's-not-all doesn't work if the original deal isn't sufficiently attractive (Burger et al., 1999). For example, in one study university students were asked to make a donation of $5 to a charity. In the control condition, they were told directly that if they donated $5 they would receive a mug. In the TNA condition, they were first asked to make the donation but, before they could respond, they were told 'you'll get the mug too.' In the control condition, 63 percent of the students agreed to the donation; in the TNA condition, only 23 percent of the students agreed. That's-not-all fails in this case because the initial offer ('Give $5' with no mention of the mug) strikes most students as unreasonable.

In light of this research, you can watch late-night advertisements with a trained eye. How often are they using the TNA technique? How well have the advertisers done in framing an initial offer that doesn't immediately make you say no?

- Why is timing critical for that's-not-all to be effective?

- How might you use that's-not-all successfully to increase donations?

to march into a store and buy them. Similarly, doctors want you to follow their medical advice. Social psychologists have extensively studied the way in which individuals bring about compliance with their requests (Cialdini, 2001). We will describe some of those techniques and note how wily salespeople often use them to get you to do things you might not otherwise have done.

Reciprocity One of the rules that dominates human experience is that when someone does something for you, you should do something for that person as well—this is called the **reciprocity norm**. Laboratory research has shown that even very small favours can lead participants to do much larger favours in return (Regan, 1971). Salespeople use reciprocity against you by appearing to do you a favour: 'I'll tell you what, I'll take $5 off the price' or 'Here's a free sample just for agreeing to talk to me today'. This strategy puts you in a position of psychological distress if you don't return the favour and buy the product.

Another compliance technique that arises from the reciprocity norm has often been called the *door-in-the-face technique*: When people say 'no' to a large request, they will often say 'yes' to a more moderate request.

> In one experiment, students were asked to spend 2 hours every week for 2 years as counsellors for juvenile delinquents. They all said 'no'. Next, they were asked if they would serve as chaperones for some of the delinquents on a trip to the zoo. When they had previously said 'no' to the large request, 50 percent of the students agreed to this smaller request. When a different group of students was approached, who had never been asked the large request, only 17 percent of them agreed to serve as chaperones (Cialdini et al., 1975).

How does this technique invoke the reciprocity norm? When people making requests go from the large to the moderate request, they have done something for you. Now you must do something for them—or risk violating the norm. You agree to the smaller request!

Commitment The door-in-the-face technique moves you from a large to a moderate request. Salespeople also know that if they can get you to *commit* yourself to some small concession, they can probably also get you to commit to something larger. In experiments, people who agreed to small requests (for example, signing petitions) were more likely subsequently to agree to a bigger request (for example, putting large signs on their lawn) (Freedman & Fraser, 1966). This is often called the *foot-in-the-door technique*: Once people get a foot in the door, they can use your sense of commitment to increase your later compliance. Salespeople use this technique against you by getting you to make a decision and then subtly changing the deal: 'I know this is the car you want to buy, but my manager will only let me give you a $200 discount'; 'I know you're the sort of

How do salespeople exploit the reciprocity norm when they offer you a free sample?

person who buys quality goods, so I know you won't mind paying a little extra'. This strategy makes you feel inconsistent or foolish if you don't go through with the purchase.

Scarcity People dislike feeling that they can't have something (or, from another perspective, people like to have things others can't). Participants, for example, give higher ratings to the taste of chocolate chip biscuits that come from a jar with just two biscuits than to those that come from a jar of ten (Worchel et al., 1975). How does the principle of *scarcity* apply in the marketplace? Salespeople know that they can increase the likelihood of your purchase if they make goods seem scarce: 'This is the last one I have, so I'm not sure you should wait until tomorrow'; 'I have another customer who's planning to come back and get this.' This strategy makes you feel as if you are missing a critical opportunity by not buying now.

In explaining these compliance techniques, we have provided a couple of examples of things you might *want* to do: You might want to volunteer your time or sign petitions for good causes. However, you can see that much of the time people use these techniques to get you to do things you probably *wouldn't* want to do. How can you defend yourself against wily salespeople and their kin? Try to catch them using these strategies—and resist their efforts. Try to ignore meaningless favours. Try to avoid foolish consistency. Try to detect false claims of scarcity. Always take time to think and reason before acting. Your knowledge of social psychology can make you an all-round wiser consumer.

In this section we have described attitudes and behaviours and the relationships between them. However, we have not yet touched on circumstances in which attitudes in the form of *prejudice* may lead to destructive behaviours. We turn now to the topic of prejudice and document both how it comes about and procedures that may be effective to reduce or eliminate it.

**reciprocity norm** Expectation that favours will be returned— if someone does something for another person that person should do something in return.

**mypsych**lab

What can you do if you want to increase the actions of other people in your community towards recycling?

**prejudice** The word prejudice refers to prejudgment. It is viewed as an unreasonable attitude that is unusually resistant to rational influence and is likely to be socially destructive.

## RECAP CHECKPOINT
### Attitudes, attitude change and action

• Attitudes are positive or negative evaluations of objects, events, or ideas.

• Not all attitudes accurately predict behaviours; they must be highly accessible or highly specific.

• According to the elaboration likelihood model, the central route to persuasion relies on careful analyses of arguments, whereas the peripheral route relies on superficial features of persuasive situations.

• The match between the basis for an attitude and the type of argument also affects the argument's effectiveness.

• Dissonance theory and self-perception theory consider attitude formation and change that arise from behavioural acts.

• To bring about compliance, people can exploit reciprocity, commitment and scarcity.

## CONCEPT QUESTIONS
1. What three components define attitudes?
2. What cognitive process discriminates the central and peripheral routes to persuasion?
3. Why does culture have an impact on processes of cognitive dissonance?
4. Why does the door-in-the-face technique engage the reciprocity norm?

## CRITICAL THINKING
Recall the study that examined the effect of lying on attitudes. Why was it important for the experimenters to use chocolate bars with which the participants were unfamiliar?

# PREJUDICE

Of all human weaknesses, none is more destructive to the dignity of the individual and the social bonds of humanity than prejudice. Prejudice is the prime example of social reality gone awry—a situation created in the minds of people that can demean and destroy the lives of others. **Prejudice** is a learned attitude toward a target object, involving negative feelings (dislike or fear), negative beliefs (stereotypes) that justify the attitude and a behavioural intention to avoid, control, dominate, or eliminate those in the target group. Nazi leaders, for example, passed laws to enforce their prejudiced beliefs that Jews were subhuman and trying to bring about the downfall of Aryan culture. A false belief qualifies as prejudice when it resists change even in the face of appropriate evidence of its falseness. People display prejudice, for example, when they assert that Aboriginal Australians are all uneducated

How did Kenneth Clark (second from left) contribute to the end of segregated schooling?

and lazy despite many hardworking Aboriginal people working across Australia in diverse workplaces such as government, medicine, science, art and the environment. Prejudiced attitudes serve as biasing filters that influence the way individuals are perceived and treated once they are categorised as members of a target group.

Social psychology has always put the study of prejudice high on its agenda in an effort to understand its complexity and persistence and to develop strategies to change prejudiced attitudes and discriminatory behaviour (Allport, 1954; Nelson, 2006). In fact, the United States of America Supreme Court's 1954 decision to outlaw segregated public education was, in part, based on research, presented in federal court by social psychologist **Kenneth Clark**, that showed the negative impact on black children of their separate and unequal education (Clark & Clark, 1947). In this section, we will describe the progress social psychologists have made in their efforts to understand the origins and effects of prejudice, as well as their efforts to help reverse its effects.

## ORIGINS OF PREJUDICE

One of the sad truths from the study of prejudice is that it is easy to get people to show negative attitudes toward people who do not belong to the same 'group'. **Social categorisation** is the process by which people organise their social environment by categorising themselves and others into groups. The simplest and most pervasive form of categorising consists of an individual determining whether people are like him or her. This categorisation develops from a 'me versus not me' orientation to an 'us versus them' orientation: People divide the world into **in-groups**—the groups with which they identify as members—and **out-groups**—the groups with which they do not identify. These cognitive distinctions result in an **in-group bias**, an evaluation of one's own group as better than others (Nelson, 2006). People defined as part of the out-group almost instantly are candidates for hostile feelings and unfair treatment.

The most minimal of distinctive cues is sufficient to trigger the formation of bias and prejudice against those in an out-group.

> In a series of experiments in Holland, participants were randomly divided into two groups: a blue group and a green group. According to the participants' group membership, they were given either blue or green pens and asked to write on either blue or green paper. The experimenter addressed participants in terms of their group colour. Even though these colour categories had no intrinsic psychological significance and assignment to the groups was completely arbitrary, participants gave a more positive evaluation of their own group than of the other. Furthermore, this in-group bias, based solely on colour identification, appeared even before the group members began to work together on an experimental task (Rabbie, 1981).

What is at work even in this 'colour' experiment is the very swift action of social categorisation.

Many experiments have examined the consequences of in-group versus out-group status (Hewstone et al., 2002). This research points to the conclusion that, for the most part, people show favouritism toward those people who are members of their own group rather than bias against members of the other group. For example, people typically rate members of their in-group more highly (on pleasantness, diligence, and so on) than they do members of the out-group. However, that's because they have positive feelings toward the in-group and neutral feelings toward the out-group. Thus, one can have an in-group bias without also having the negative feelings that constitute prejudice.

Unfortunately, in some circumstances people's feelings about out-groups are guided by learned prejudices. In those cases, in-group bias may become more purposeful. Prejudice easily leads to **racism**—discrimination against people based on their skin colour or ethnic heritage—and **sexism**—discrimination against people based on their sex. The instant tendency toward defining 'us' against 'them' becomes even more powerful when the perception grows that resources are scarce and that goods can be given only to one group, at the expense of the other. In fact, people who express high and low degrees of prejudice show different patterns of brain activity when they make judgments about members of an out-group.

> Researchers recruited groups of students who, on a self-report scale, revealed themselves to be high and low in prejudice toward African Americans (Chiu et al., 2004). The students viewed photographs that showed black and white individuals with either happy or angry expressions. For each face, students responded to the question, 'Would you like to work with this person?' At the beginning of each trial, the students were given a warning to tell them which type of face would appear next (e.g., angry white, happy black). The researchers used scalp electrodes to record the students' brain activity after the warning: they wished to demonstrate differences in the way the high- and low-prejudice students prepared to make their judgments. In fact, the patterns of brain activity were quite distinct. For example, when low-prejudice students anticipated angry black faces they appeared to be marshalling brain resources so as to assess each face individually—and not give stereotyped responses to those faces. By contrast, high-prejudice students engaged less brain effort and made swift responses of 'No, I wouldn't want to work with this person'.

This experiment supports the idea that high-prejudice individuals do little to evaluate members of an out-group as anything but members of a category to which stereotypes apply. Lets look at an Australian study that measured predictions of young Australian attitudes toward Aboriginals, Asians and Arabs.

> The participants interviewed were 139 Anglo-Saxon volunteer university students (60 male, 79 female). The survey findings highlighted the fact that attitudes were

**racism** Discrimination against people based on their skin colour or ethnic heritage.

**sexism** Discrimination against people because of their sex.

**social categorisation** The process by which people organise the social environment by categorising themselves and others into groups.

**in-groups** The groups with which people identify as members.

**out-groups** The groups with which people do not identify.

**in-group bias** An evaluation of one's own group as better than others.

significantly positive towards Aboriginals compared with attitudes towards Asians and Arabs. However, Asian stereotypes were distinctively positive compared to the two other target groups. Analysis of the results indicated the importance of emotional stakes as crucial components of racial attitudes in Australia. The implications of these findings suggest that attitude change programs, which have traditionally been based on simply changing cognitive aspects of attitudes (e.g., knowledge structures, facts about racial groups) should also take into consideration the roles of affective features of attitudes (e.g., anxiety, distrust, frustration evoked by racial groups) (**Islam & Jahjah, 2001**). Essentially, the study revealed that as much as we wish to reduce prejudice through education and practice of political correctness in society, true reduction in prejudiced behaviour comes when a person spends time with a differing racial group in close proximity and gains valued and experience from their relationships with cross-cultural groups.

Researchers have also developed an explicit measure of *non-prejudice* that captures the idea that people without prejudice are less likely to focus on the differences among individuals (Phillips & Ziller, 1997). People who fall high on the *universal orientation scale* tend to endorse statements such as 'When I meet someone I tend to notice similarities between myself and the other person' and reject statements such as 'I can tell a great deal about a person by knowing his or her gender'. Thus some people appear to have a fundamental ability to overcome the tendency to experience the world in terms of in-groups and out-groups.

We have seen so far that people's categorisation of the world into 'us' and 'them' can swiftly lead to prejudice. Let's look at the way in which prejudice functions through applications of stereotypes.

## EFFECTS OF STEREOTYPES

We can use the power of social categorisation to explain the origins of many types of prejudice. To explain how prejudice affects day-to-day interactions, we must explore the memory structures that provide important support for prejudice. **Stereotypes** are generalisations about a group of people in which the same characteristics are assigned to all members of a group. You are no doubt familiar with a wide range of stereotypes. What beliefs do you have about men and women? Jews, Muslims, and Christians? Aboriginals, Maoris, Islanders, Asians, Middle Eastern people and Whites? How do those beliefs affect your day-to-day interactions with members of those groups? Do you avoid members of some of these groups based on your beliefs?

Because stereotypes so powerfully encode *expectations,* they frequently contribute to the types of situations we described earlier in this chapter, in which people construct their own social reality. Consider the potential role stereotypes play to generate judgments about what 'exists' in the environment. People are prone to fill in

**stereotypes** Generalisations about a group of people in which the same characteristics are assigned to all members of a group.

How does prejudice arise, and why is it so difficult to eradicate?

'missing data' with information from their stereotypes: 'I'm not going to get in a car with Hiroshi—all Asians are terrible drivers.' Similarly, people may knowingly or unknowingly use stereotypical information to produce *behavioural confirmation.* If, for example, you reason that Jewish friends are likely to be cheapskates, you may never give them opportunities to prove otherwise. Worse than that, to maintain consistency, people are likely to discount information that is inconsistent with their stereotyped beliefs.

What happens when you are presented with information, some of which supports your beliefs and some of which contradicts them? In one study, researchers classified students as having high or low prejudice toward homosexuals. Each student subsequently read a pair of scientific studies about homosexuality. One of those studies concluded that, consistent with the stereotype, homosexuality is associated with cross-gender behaviours. The other study came to the stereotype-inconsistent conclusion that homosexuality is not associated with cross-gender behaviours. When the high- and low-prejudice students evaluated the *quality* of each study, they gave consistently higher ratings to the study that supported their point of view. For example, high-prejudice students found more merit in the study that supported the cross-gender stereotype. Furthermore, as a consequence of reading a pair of studies that were intended to exactly balance each other out, the students on average reported that their beliefs had shifted further in the direction of their original attitudes (Munro & Ditto, 1997).

This experiment suggests why information alone can typically not reduce prejudice: People tend to devalue information that is inconsistent with their prior stereotype. (We will see in the next section more successful methods for overcoming prejudice.)

Let us remind you about another effect of stereotypes that we introduced in the context of intelligence testing. Recall that in Chapter 9, we discussed racial differences among IQ scores. In that section, we reviewed evidence that suggests that members of stereotyped groups suffer

Why might prejudiced beliefs affect the brain responses that underlie judgments about these faces?

from what Claude Steele and his colleagues have called *stereotype threat* (Steele, 1997; Steele & Aronson, 1995, 1998). Stereotype threat occurs when people are placed in situations to which negative aspects of stereotypes are relevant. For example, in Chapter 9, we provided evidence that African Americans' performance on aptitude tests is impaired when they believe the outcome of the test is relevant to the stereotype of black underachievement. We remind you of this result here to emphasise the forces that sustain negative stereotypes—and the way they deform the lives of people who are stereotyped.

Even if you do not believe yourself to be a prejudiced person, you still are likely aware of the stereotypes that exist in contemporary society. Knowledge of these stereotypes might prompt you to use them in some ways, below the level of conscious awareness (Crandall & Eshleman, 2003; Payne, 2005). Even people whose explicit beliefs are not prejudiced may produce automatic acts of prejudice as a function of the messages they have unknowingly internalised from many sources in their current and earlier environments. Consider your best friends: Do they belong to the same ethnic group as you do? If so, why might this be the case?

We have come to the rather troubling conclusion that prejudice is easy to create and difficult to remove. Even so, from the earliest days of social psychology, researchers have attempted to reverse the march of prejudice. Let's now sample some of those efforts.

## REVERSING PREJUDICE

One of the classic studies in social psychology was also the first demonstration that arbitrary 'us' versus 'them'

divisions could lead to great hostility. In the summer of 1954, **Muzafer Sherif** and his colleagues (1961/1988) brought two groups of boys to a summer camp at Robbers Cave State Park in Oklahoma. The two groups were dubbed the 'Eagles' and the 'Rattlers.' Each group forged its own camp bonds—for example, the boys hiked, swam, and prepared meals together—in ignorance of the other group for about a week. The groups' introduction to each other consisted of a series of competitive activities like baseball, football and a tug-of-war. From this beginning, the rivalry between the groups grew violent. Group flags were burned, cabins were ransacked, and a near riot-like food fight broke out. What could be done to reduce this animosity?

> The experimenters tried a propaganda approach, by complimenting each group to the other. That did not work. The experimenters tried bringing the groups together in noncompetitive circumstances. That did not work either. Hostility seethed even when the groups were just watching a movie in the same place. Finally, the experimenters hit on a solution. What they did was to introduce problems that could be solved only through *cooperative action* on *shared goals*. For example, the experimenters arranged for the camp truck to break down. Both groups of boys were needed to pull it back up a steep hill. In the face of mutual dependence, hostility faded away. In fact, the boys started to make 'best friends' across group boundaries.

The Robbers Cave experiment disproved the idea that simple contact between hostile groups alone will reduce prejudice (Allport, 1954). The boys did not like each other any better just by being in each others' company. Instead, the experiment provided evidence for the **contact hypothesis**—a program combating prejudice must foster personal interaction in the pursuit of shared goals (Dovidio et al., 2003; Pettigrew & Trupp, 2006). Take a moment to consider how you might apply these lessons to situations that matter to you. Suppose, for example, that you are managing employees who cannot get along. What intervention might you design?

Social psychologist **Elliot Aronson** and his colleagues (1978) developed a program anchored in the Robbers Cave philosophy to tackle prejudice in newly desegregated classrooms in Texas and California. The research team created conditions in which fifth-grade students had to depend on one another rather than compete against one another to learn required material. In a strategy known as the *jigsaw technique*, each pupil is given part of the total material to master and then share with other group members. Performance is evaluated on the basis of the overall group presentation. Thus every member's contribution is essential and valued.

Interracial conflict has decreased in **jigsaw classrooms**—classes in which jig-sawing has united formerly hostile white, Latino, and African American students in a common-fate team (Aronson, 2002; Aronson & Gonzalez, 1988). Consider the story of one young boy named Carlos. Carlos, who had been ignored because his primary language was not English, was assigned a vital part of the team assignment on Joseph Pulitzer. The other teammates had to figure out how to get him to share the information he was responsible for providing. In response to his teammates' patience and encouraging comments, Carlos felt needed, developed affection for the group

members, and also discovered that learning was fun. Both his self-esteem and his grades increased. (We are happy to report that Carlos went on to Harvard Law School after graduating from a Texas college.)

Although most of our examples have looked at prejudice within the developed nations like Australia and the United States, virtually every society defines in-groups and out-groups. Researchers have carried out studies around the world to determine what types of contact between people lead to reduced prejudice. A review of 515 studies on the contact hypothesis—studies carried out all over the world—strongly supported the conclusion that contact with out-group members lowers prejudice (Pettigrew & Tropp, 2006). However, it is not just contact with out-group members that is important—it is continuous close contact. A study conducted by Hill and Augoustinos (2001) discovered that most prejudice reduction programs are only successful during the actual program. In a study that looked at reducing anti-racism toward Aboriginal Australians in a large public service organisation, the program showed improvement in race attitudes whilst people were partaking in the intervention. However, a 3 month follow up of those who took part in the program found that prejudice attitudes had returned towards the Aboriginal Australians, sometimes more strongly than before the intervention to reduce the initial prejudice.

Let's consider another concrete example of the effects of contact with people from a different out-group.

Although Germany was reunited in October 1990, the inhabitants of the former East and West Germany still show important differences: when social scientists assess the level of prejudice and violence toward foreigners, the data consistently show that

In the intergroup competition phase of the Robbers Cave experiment, the 'Eagles' and 'Rattlers' pulled apart—but in the end, they pulled together. What general conclusions about contact and prejudice can be drawn from this study?

**contact hypothesis** The prediction that contact between groups will reduce prejudice only if the contact includes features such as cooperation towards shared goals.

**jigsaw classrooms** Classrooms that use a technique known as jigsawing, in which each pupil is given part of the total material to master and then share with other group members.

East Germans are much more hostile. Researchers tested the hypothesis that an important force that contributes to the ongoing hostility arises from East Germany's historic isolation (Wagner et al., 2003): Fewer foreigners reside in East Germany, providing fewer opportunities for the type of contact that reduces prejudice. A study with 2,893 East and West German participants confirmed this hypothesis. Each participant provided information about his or her level of prejudice by responding to statements such as 'Foreigners living in Germany are a problem for the social system'. Each participant also indicated his or her level of personal contact by responding to questions such as 'Are there any foreigners among your friends?' Those individuals who had more foreign friends reported, on average, lower levels of prejudice. Because the inhabitants of East Germany had fewer opportunities to have foreign friends, their prejudice levels remained relatively high.

Why is friendship so effective? Friendships allow people to learn about out-group members: They may come to identify and empathise with out-group members. Friendships may also foster a process of *deprovincialisation*: When people learn more about out-group social norms and customs, they may become less 'provincial' about the correctness of their in-group processes (Pettigrew, 1997).

Social psychology has no great solution to end prejudice all at once. It does, however, provide a set of ideas to eliminate prejudice's worst effects slowly but surely, in each small locality. It is worth taking a moment to contemplate the prejudices you have enforced or endured—to see how you might begin to make adjustments in your own small locality.

We have just considered circumstances in which psychological forces drive individuals apart. In the final section of this chapter, we examine the opposite situations in which people are drawn together in relationships of liking and loving.

For answers go to MyPsychLab!

## RECAP CHECKPOINT

### Prejudice

- Even arbitrary, minimal cues can yield prejudice when they define an in-group and an out-group.

- Stereotypes affect the way in which people evaluate behaviours and information in the world.

- Researchers have eliminated some of the effects of prejudice by creating situations in which members of different groups must cooperate to reach shared goals.

- Cross-cultural studies also suggest that friendship plays an important role in eliminating prejudice.

## CONCEPT QUESTIONS

1. What is the relationship between in-group bias and prejudice?

2. How does the process of behavioural confirmation support stereotypes?

3. What has research demonstrated about the impact of contact between members of different groups?

## CRITICAL THINKING

Consider the study on brain processes and prejudice. Why might the experimenters have used happy and angry faces to study judgments based on stereotypes?

# SOCIAL RELATIONSHIPS

How do you choose the people with whom you share your life? Why do you seek the company of your friends? Why are there some people for whom your feelings move beyond friendship to feelings of romantic love? Social psychologists have developed a variety of answers to these questions of *interpersonal attraction*. (But don't worry, no one yet has taken all the mystery out of love!)

## LIKING

Have you ever stopped to examine how and why you acquired each of your friends? The first part of this answer is straightforward: People tend to become attracted to others with whom they are in close *proximity*—you see and meet them because they live or work near you. This factor probably requires little explanation, but it might be worth noting that there is a general tendency for people to like objects and people just by virtue of *mere exposure*: As we explained in Chapter 12, the more you are exposed to something or someone, the more you like it (Zajonc, 1968). This mere exposure effect means that, on the whole, you will come to like more and more the people who are nearby. As we shall see in the Psychology in Your Life box, however, the computer age is giving a new meaning to the idea of proximity. Many people now maintain relationships over networks of computers. Although a friend may be geographically quite distant, daily messages appearing on a computer screen can make the person seem psychologically very close. Let's look now at other factors that can lead to attraction and liking.

Why does proximity—in physical space or cyberspace—affect liking?

### Physical attractiveness

For better or worse, *physical attractiveness* often plays a role in the kindling of friendship. There is a strong stereotype in Western culture that physically attractive people are also good in other ways. A review of a large number of studies documented the impact of physical attractiveness on a whole range of judgments (Langlois et al., 2000). For example, people rate both children and adults as more socially competent when they are attractive. In addition, attractive children receive higher competence ratings in school, and attractive adults receive higher competence ratings in their occupations. In light of the social basis of the stereotype, it might not surprise you that physical attractiveness plays a role in liking.

> In one study, researchers randomly assigned incoming University of Minnesota 1st year students to couples as blind dates for a large dance. The researchers collected a variety of information about each student along dimensions of intelligence and personality. On the night of the dance and in later follow-ups the students were asked to evaluate their dates and indicate how likely they were to see the individual again. The results were clear, and very similar for both men and women. Beauty mattered more than high IQs, good social skills or good personalities. Only those matched by chance with beautiful or handsome blind dates wanted to pursue the relationship further (Walster et al., 1966).

Physical attractiveness appears to predict liking in different cultures as well. For example, Chinese 10th- to 12th-graders accorded greater status to their classmates who were physically attractive (Dong et al., 1996). However, as we noted in Chapter 12, cultures differ with respect to their standards for physical beauty. African Americans, for example, associate fewer negative personality traits with obesity than do Anglo-Americans (Hebl & Heatherton, 1998; Jackson & McGill, 1996).

### Similarity

A famous adage on *similarity* suggests that 'Birds of a feather flock together'. Is this correct? Research evidence suggests that, under many circumstances, the answer is yes. Similarity on dimensions such as beliefs, attitudes, and values fosters friendship. Why might that be so? People who are similar to you can provide a sense of personal validation, because a similar person makes you feel that the attitudes, for example, you hold dear are, in fact, the right ones (Byrne & Clore, 1970). Furthermore, dissimilarity often leads to strong repulsion (Rosenbaum, 1986). When you discover that someone holds opinions that are different from yours, you may evoke from memory past instances of interpersonal friction. That will motivate you to stay away—and if you stay away from dissimilar people, only the similar ones will be left in your pool of friends.

If you are living in a dormitory while you attend university, you can look around you to see similarity at work. Do you perceive successfully matched roommates to be similar? Researchers have looked at the similarity of roommates on a variety of dimensions. For example, one study assessed the *communication traits* of pairs of roommates: How similar were they on dimensions such as their willingness to communicate? Roommates who were similar at the positive ends of the trait dimensions (for example, they were both willing to communicate) liked each other more than mismatched pairs or pairs that were both unwilling to communicate (Martin & Anderson, 1995).

### Reciprocity

Finally, you tend to like people whom you believe like you. Do you recall our discussion of salespeople's use of *reciprocity*? The rule that you should give back what you receive applies to friendship as well. People give back 'liking' to people whom they believe have given 'liking' to them (Backman & Secord, 1959; Kenny & La Voie, 1982). Furthermore, because of the way your beliefs can affect your behaviours, believing that someone likes or dislikes you can help bring that relationship about (Curtis & Miller, 1986). Can you predict how you would act towards someone you believe likes you? Toward someone you believe dislikes you? Suppose you act with hostility towards someone you think doesn't like you. Do you see how your belief could become a self-fulfilling prophecy? When we look out at the social world, our judgments about which acquaintances are united by a 'liking' relationship tend to be heavily guided by reciprocity. That is, if we know that Person A particularly likes Person B, we infer that Person B has the same feelings toward Person A (Kenny et al., 1996).

The evidence we have reviewed suggests that most of your friends will be people you encounter frequently, and people with whom you share the bonds of similarity and reciprocity. But what have researchers found about more intense relationships people call 'loving'?

# LOVING

Many of the same forces that lead to liking also get people started on the road to love—in most cases, you will first like the people you end up loving. (However, some people report loving certain relatives that they don't particularly like as individuals.) What special factors have social psychologists learned about loving relationships?

**The experience of love** What does it mean to experience *love*? Take a moment to think how you would define this important concept. Do you think your definition would agree with your friends' definitions? Researchers have tried to answer this question in a variety of ways, and some consistency has emerged. People's conceptualisations of love cluster into three dimensions (Aron & Westbay, 1996):

- *Passion*—sexual passion and desire
- *Intimacy*—honesty and understanding
- *Commitment*—devotion and sacrifice.

Would you characterise all your loving relationships as including all three dimensions? You're probably thinking, 'not *all* of them'. In fact, it is important to make a distinction between 'loving' someone and being 'in love' with someone (Meyers & Berscheid, 1997). Most people report themselves to 'love' a larger category of people than the group with whom they are 'in love'—who among us hasn't been heartbroken to hear the words, 'I love you, but I'm not *in* love with you'? Being 'in love' implies something more intense and special—this is the type of experience that includes sexual passion.

Although it is possible to state some general features of loving relationships, your knowledge of the world has probably led you to the correct generalisation that there are individual differences in the way that people experience love. Researchers have been particularly interested in understanding individual differences in people's ability to sustain loving relationships over an extended period of time. In recent years, attention has often focused on *adult attachment style* (Fraley et al., 2005; Fraley & Shaver, 2000). Recall from Chapter 10 the importance of the quality of a child's attachment to his or her parents for smooth social development. Researchers began to wonder how much impact that early attachment might have later in life, as the children grew up to have committed relationships and children of their own.

What are the types of attachment styles? **Table 16.3** provides three statements about close relationships (Hazan & Shaver, 1987; Shaver & Hazan, 1994). Please take a moment to note which statement fits you best. When asked which of these statements best describes them, the

| Table 16.3 |
| --- |
| **Styles of adult attachment for close relationships** |

**Statement 1:**

I find it relatively easy to get close to others and am comfortable depending on them. I don't often worry about being abandoned or about someone getting too close to me.

**Statement 2:**

I am somewhat uncomfortable being close to others; I find it difficult to trust them completely, difficult to allow myself to depend on them. I am nervous when anyone gets too close, and often, love partners want me to be more intimate than I feel comfortable being.

**Statement 3:**

I find that others are reluctant to get as close as I would like. I often worry that my partner doesn't really love me or won't want to stay with me. I want to get very close to my partner, and this sometime scares people away.

majority of people (55 percent) choose the first statement; this is a *secure* attachment style. Sizeable minorities select the second statement (25 percent, an *avoidant* style) and the third (20 percent, an *anxious-ambivalent* style). Attachment style has proven to be an accurate predictor of relationship quality (Mikulincer et al., 2002; Tidwell et al., 1996). Compared with individuals who chose the other two styles, securely attached individuals had the most enduring romantic relationships as adults. Attachment style also predicts the ways in which individuals experience jealousy in relationships (Sharpsteen & Kirkpatrick, 1997). For example, people with an anxious style tend to experience jealousy more frequently and more intensely than do people with a secure attachment style.

Let us make one final distinction. Many loving relationships start out with a period of great intensity and absorption, which is called *passionate* love. Over time, there is a tendency for relationships to migrate toward a state of lesser intensity but greater intimacy, called *companionate love* (Berscheid & Walster, 1978). When you find yourself in a loving relationship, you may do well to anticipate that transition—so that you don't misinterpret a natural change as a process of falling 'out of love'. In fact, people who report higher levels of companionate love also generally experience greater satisfaction with their lives (Kim & Hatfield, 2004). Even so, the decline of passionate love may not be as dramatic as the stereotype of long-committed couples suggests. Researchers find a reasonable level of passionate love as much as 30 years into a relationship (Aron & Aron, 1994). When you enter a loving relationship, you can have high hopes that the passion will endure in some form, even as the relationship grows to encompass other needs.

Note that experiences of romantic relationships are also influenced by cultural expectations (Wang & Mallinckrodt, 2006). At various moments in this chapter, we've alluded to the cultural dimension of independence versus interdependence: Cultures with independent construals of self value the person over the collective; interdependent cultures put greater value on shared cultural goals rather than on individual ones. How does this apply to your love life? If you choose a life partner based on your own feelings of love, you are showing preference for your personal goals; if you choose a partner with an eye to how that individual will mesh with your family's structure and concerns, you are being more attuned to collective goals. Cross-cultural research has led to the very strong generalisation that members of independent cultures put much greater emphasis on love (Dion & Dion, 1996). Consider the question, 'If a man (woman) had all the other qualities you desired, would you marry this person if you were not in love with him (her)?' Only 3.5 percent of a sample of male and female undergraduates in the United States answered yes; 49 percent of a comparable group of students in India answered yes (Levine et al., 1995). Members of independent cultures are also more *demanding* of their potential partners. Because people in these cultures have stronger ideas about personal fulfilment within relationships, they also expect more from marriage partners (Hatfield & Sprecher, 1995).

Companionate feelings for someone you were once passionate about do not signal 'falling out of love': On the contrary, they are a natural outgrowth of romance and a vital ingredient to most long-term partnerships.

## What factors allow relationships to last?

It seems likely that everyone reading this book—and certainly everyone *writing* this book—has been in a relationship that didn't last. What happened? Or, to put the question in a more positive light, what can researchers say about the types of situations, and people in those situations, that are more likely to lead to long-term loving relationships?

One theory conceptualises people in close relationships as having a feeling that the 'other' is included in their 'self' (Aron et al., 2004). Consider the series of diagrams given in **Figure 16.5**. Each of the diagrams represents a way you could conceptualise a close relationship. If you are in a romantic relationship, can you say which of the diagrams seems to capture most effectively the extent of interdependence between you and your partner? Research has shown that people who perceive the most overlap between self and other—those people who come to view the other as included within the self—are most likely to remain committed to their relationships over time (Aron et al., 1992; Aron & Fraley, 1999).

What other factors contribute to the likelihood that someone will remain in a relationship? *Interdependence theory* examines people's needs with respect to their social interactions (Rusbult & Van Lange, 2003). This perspective suggests that commitment is based on a series of judgments (Drigotas & Rusbult, 1992, p. 65):

- The degree to which each of several needs is important in the individual's relationship. Important needs are intimacy, sex, emotional involvement, companionship and intellectual involvement.

- The degree to which each of those needs is satisfied in that relationship.

- For each need, whether there is anyone other than the current partner with whom the individual has an important relationship.

- The degree to which each need is satisfied by the alternative relationship.

As you might expect, this model predicts that people are more likely to stay in a relationship when the relationship satisfies important needs that cannot be satisfied by anyone else. Thus if *companionship* is very important to you—you enjoy spending leisure time with other people—and a person with whom you share a relationship provides more companionship than anyone else you know, you're likely to feel committed to that relationship. This will be true even if your partner is not your first choice on dimensions that matter less. The dependence model also offers insight into why people will stay in relationships in which they have been physically abused (Choice & Lamke, 1999). In a sample of 100 women at a shelter for battered women, the women who saw themselves as having few alternatives—often for economic reasons—were still committed to returning to their relationships (Rusbult & Martz, 1995). Thus people may be quite unhappy in a relationship and yet depend on the relationship.

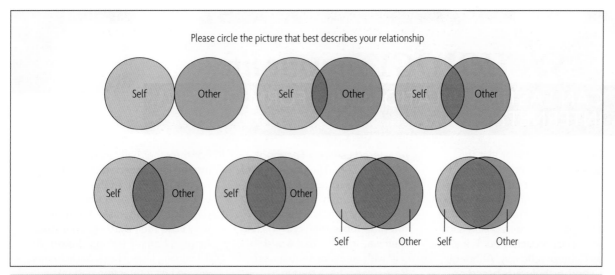

Please circle the picture that best describes your relationship

**Figure 16.5**

**The inclusion of other in the self (IOS) scale**

If you are in a romantic relationship, which diagram best captures the interdependence of you and your partner? Research with the IOS scale suggests that people who most perceive the other as included with the self are most likely to stay committed to their relationships.

From IOS Scale, *Journal of Personality and Social Psychology, 63*(4), 1992. Copyright © 1992 American Psychological Association. Reprinted with permission. The use of APA information does not imply endorsement by APA.

Throughout this chapter, we've seen how individuals construct and respond to aspects of their social worlds. We've seen, for example, how your attitudes are forged in the social cauldron and how those attitudes can lead to the very different outcomes of prejudice and love. We've encouraged you to examine your behaviours, to see the way in which your interpretation of social setting helps to explain important aspects of your day-to-day experiences. In the next chapter, we will see how the same types of forces control your own behaviour and the behaviours of larger groups of people.

## RECAP CHECKPOINT

### Social relationships

- Interpersonal attraction is determined in part by proximity, physical attractiveness, similarity, and reciprocity.
- Loving relationships are defined with respect to passion, intimacy and commitment.
- Adult attachment style affects the quality of relationships.
- A person's commitment to a loving relationship is related to the level of closeness and interdependence.

## CONCEPT QUESTIONS

1. What effect does similarity have on liking?

2. Which adult attachment style is generally associated with the highest quality relationships?

3. How does interdependence theory predict which relationships are likely to last?

## CRITICAL THINKING

Recall the study that examined the impact of physical attractiveness on people's liking for randomly assigned dates. Why was it important to assess the impact of physical attractiveness both on the night of the date and in later follow-ups?

For answers go to MyPsychLab!

# PSYCHOLOGY *in your life*

## CAN LASTING RELATIONSHIPS FORM ON THE INTERNET?

Does anyone doubt that the advent of the Internet has had a broad impact on how people initiate and conduct their close relationships? The phenomenon of social interaction online and its impact on behaviour is known as *Cyberpsychology*, Although Cyberpsychology is based on the research principles of social psychology, it uniquely looks at how information communication technology (the Internet, mobile phones and other electronic communication mediums) are affecting individuals across cultures and their relationships with one another. Consider that the average teenager today seeks to make friends through social networking sites such as *MySpace* or *Facebook*. It is likely that conversations online may lead to sharing of personal feelings and beliefs. This personal disclosure may even lead to intense emotions such as trust, affection, perhaps and even love—and yet neither person has met the other in a face-to-face setting (Suler, 2007)Clearly, until late in the 20th century, this is not the type of relationship most people would have had in mind for forming intimate relationships Let's explore the impact of the Internet on relationships.

Studies have shown that social interaction is one of Internet users' most frequent activities. Over the last few years, social networking sites such as *MySpace* and *Facebook* have shown astonishing growth. For example, as measured by the number of pages viewed and the time spent on the site, *MySpace* has ranked second for Web popularity (behind Yahoo) (Walker, 2006). At one U.S. midwestern university, 20,247 out of 25,741 enrolled students were registered users on *Facebook* (Bugeja, 2006). The popularity of these sites suggests that large numbers of relationships now begin in cyberspace. But how often do those relationships find their way into the real world, and with what consequences? Researchers have begun to address those questions (Bargh & McKenna, 2004).

Consider a study that involved 568 individuals (59 percent women and 41 percent men) who had made postings to newsgroups (McKenna et al., 2002). In that sample, 63 percent had spoken on the telephone with an acquaintance they'd made on the Internet; 54 percent had met face-to-face with an Internet acquaintance. A follow-up study 2 years later showed that many of the relationships formed over the Internet were still going strong. In fact, 15 percent of the sample had become engaged to someone they'd met on the Internet, and 10 percent had married an Internet partner.

We noted earlier that *proximity* is an important ingredient for liking: You need to meet people before they can become your friends or romantic partners. The studies we've just cited indicate that the Internet provides an important new mechanism to establish psychological proximity in the absence of geographic proximity. In fact, some evidence suggests that relationships get off to a better start when they begin on the Internet rather than face to face (Bargh et al., 2002). In one study using college students, participants interacted on two occasions with the same partner. For half of the pairs, both interactions were face to face.

For the other half, an Internet interaction preceded the face-to-face meeting. At the end of the second interaction, the participants were asked how much they liked their partners on a scale ranging from –7 (strong dislike) to +7 (strong like). Those participants whose first interaction had taken place over the Internet reported consistently greater liking for their partners (with a mean of 4.70) than did their peers who had met only face to face (with a mean of 2.45).

Why might that be? The researchers speculated that the initial Internet interaction allowed participants to be less affected by surface features of their partners such as physical attractiveness. Furthermore, the momentary anonymity of the Internet likely encouraged people to be more self-disclosing, which also may increase liking. Internet contacts that evolve into face-to-face relationships are more careful and honest about the information they disclose (Gibbs et al., 2006).

The studies we've cited here suggest that the Internet may be a positive force for many or most people's social and romantic lives. It has already been found to be a great help to those with social phobias by engaging people and work through their fears (King and Poulos, 1998; Campbell, et al, 2006), However, it's important to acknowledge that, for some people, the use or overuse of the Internet decreases real-life social activity (Caplan, 2005). In addition, there is growing awareness that sexual predators lurk on many social networking sites (Dombrowski et al., 2004). These problems confirm the reality that the Internet has radically changed the way that social lives unfold.

# SUMMARY

Chapter 16 explores the behaviour behind how people form social opinions and actions. It specifically identifies the theories behind the Fundamental Attribution Error—i.e. how we formulate untrue opinions about people and social events; actions that increase persuasion of others; and how prejudice and stereotypes can form, as well as ways of reversing these negative behaviours. Lastly, we reviewed how people develop friendships and loving relationships and how proximity to form these relationships is translating to the online world via the Internet.

# KEY TERMS

attitude (p. 568)
attribution theory (p. 563)
behavioural confirmation (p. 567)
cognitive dissonance (p. 572)
compliance (p. 574)
contact hypothesis (p. 580)
covariation principle (p. 563)
elaboration likelihood model (p. 570)
fundamental attribution error (FAE)
   (p. 563)

in-group bias (p. 577)
in-groups (p. 577)
jigsaw classrooms (p. 580)
out-groups (p. 577)
persuasion (p. 570)
prejudice (p. 576)
racism (p. 577)
reciprocity norm (p. 575)
self-fulfilling prophecy (p. 566)
self-perception theory (p. 573)

self-serving bias (p. 565)
sexism (p. 577)
social categorisation (p. 577)
social cognition (p. 562)
social perception (p. 563)
social psychology (p. 562)
stereotypes (p. 578)

# PRACTICE TEST

1. Becky wants to help her friend Tom avoid the fundamental attribution error. She suggests that he focus on _____ causes of behaviours.
   a. situational
   b. dispositional
   c. instinctive
   d. consistent

2. Which of these statements is *not* consistent with a self-serving bias?
   a. I lost because the other guy was probably cheating.
   b. I lost because it was too hot in the room.
   c. I won because I'm a genius.
   d. I won because I got lucky.

3. Self-fulfilling prophecies may be modest in the real world because
   a. most students perform better than their teachers expect them to perform.
   b. teachers usually have accurate expectations about how students will perform.
   c. teachers do not modify their behaviours in line with their expectations.
   d. students do not allow teachers to treat them differently from their classmates.

4. Bruce is about to interview Joan for a job. When he meets her, his first impression is that she is shy. The first question Bruce asks Joan is, 'Have you ever had trouble working as part of a group?' It appears that Bruce may be engaging in the process of
   a. self-fulfilling prophecy.
   b. covariation.
   c. behavioural confirmation.
   d. reality construction.

5. You are trying to assess Tim's attitude toward coffee. Which of these statements is most relevant to the behavioural bases of Tim's attitude?
   a. 'I love the smell of coffee beans.'
   b. 'I remember my grandparents drinking coffee.'
   c. 'I can't start the day without a cup of coffee.'
   d. 'I think coffee drinkers are the safest drivers.'

6. When a company hires a celebrity to endorse a product, they are likely hoping that most consumers will follow the _____ route to persuasion and engage in _____ elaboration.
   a. peripheral; low
   b. central; high
   c. peripheral; high
   d. central; low

7. Sam chooses desserts for himself and for his friend Randy. Suppose both desserts turn out to be duds. If Sam has an _____ sense of self, you'd expect him to experience the most cognitive dissonance with respect to the dessert he chose for_____.
   a. independent; Randy
   b. interdependent; himself
   c. interdependent; Randy
   d. dependent; himself

8. When you walk into an appliance store, there's a big sign taped to a refrigerator reading 'We only have two left!!!' The store is trying to get people to buy the refrigerator by using
   a. reciprocity.
   b. commitment.
   c. self-perception.
   d. scarcity.

9. Research has demonstrated that the that's-not-all technique is reasonably successful. The_____ provides one explanation for its success.
   a. fundamental attribution error
   b. scarcity principle
   c. elaboration likelihood model
   d. reciprocity norm

10. Felicia gets a high score on a measure of non-prejudice. With which statement is she most likely to agree?
    a. I can tell a great deal about a person by knowing his or her gender.
    b. When I meet someone I tend to notice similarities between myself and the other person.
    c. I am uncomfortable when I meet people from different racial groups.
    d. When I meet people, it's important for them to reveal their sexuality.

11. Oliver is trying to change his friend Stan's stereotype that women aren't as funny as men. They watch a TV special with a series of women doing comedy routines. Do you think Stan's stereotype will change?
    a. Yes, because he will appreciate Oliver's effort on his behalf.
    b. No, because he will discount information that is inconsistent with his stereotype.
    c. No, because he will convince Stan that the stereotype is true.
    d. Yes, because he will learn a new stereotype from the TV special.

12. Jigsaw classrooms represent an application of _____ in educational settings.
    a. stereotype threat
    b. self-fulfilling prophecies
    c. the contact hypothesis
    d. behavioural confirmation

13. Which of these statements suggests that Carmen is exploiting similarity to get Perry to like her more?
    a. 'Did you know that we're both Libras?'
    b. 'I really enjoy spending time with you.'
    c. 'Would you like me to get you the newspaper?'
    d. 'Your new haircut looks terrific.'

14. Which statement is *not* correct?
    a. Companionate love is associated with life satisfaction.
    b. Most relationships have more passionate love at the outset.
    c. Companionate love is characterised by less intensity but greater intimacy.
    d. There is little passionate love in long-term relationships.

15. To explain why relationships last, interdependence theory focuses on the
    a. needs that relationships satisfy.
    b. inclusion of other within the self.
    c. balance of companionate and passionate love.
    d. individuals' adult attachment styles.

16. Because Candice has_____interest in starting face-to-face relationships with the people she meets online, the information she shares is usually_____.
    a. low; true
    b. high; true
    c. low; careful
    d. high; careless

## Essay Questions

1. What does it mean to say that people construct social reality?

2. What properties of attitudes increase the correlations between attitudes and behaviours?

3. What impact do stereotypes have on people's behaviour?

# WEB LINKS

http://www.facebook.com
    Facebook

http://www.myspace.com
    MySpace

http://www.rsvp.com.au
    RSVP

Are you ready for the test? MyPsychLab offers dozens of ways to deepen your understanding and test your recall of the material in this chapter—including video and audio clips, simulations and activities, self-assessments, practice tests and other study materials. Specific resources available for this chapter include:

 Unconscious stereotyping

 Elaboration likelihood model
Cognitive dissonance & attitude change

 Infomercial example
Attraction
Social influence

To access MyPsychLab, please visit **www.pearsoned.com.au/mypsychlab**

# How do you like to study?

## NOW YOU HAVE READ CHAPTER 16—ARE YOU PREPARED FOR THE EXAM?

To enhance your understanding of any of the material in your *Psychology and Life* textbook, go to **MyPsychLab: www.pearsoned.com.au/mypsychlab**.

Complete pre- and post-tests, create your own individualised study plan, watch videos and animations and listen to audio glossaries—all of which will help you understand the themes of this chapter:

- Constructing social reality
- Attitudes, attitude change, and action
- Prejudice
- Social relationships

Use RESEARCH NAVIGATOR to find out more about key concepts covered in Chapter 16

EXPLORE the *Elaboration Likelihood Model*

Elaboration likelihood model

According to the elaboration likelihood model, attitude change occurs one of two ways: The first way is called the *central route*, and emphasizes conscious and thoughtful consideration of arguments regarding a particular issue. For example, when presented with scientific evidence on how smoking can be detrimental to health, people may be convinced that the scientific arguments are too strong to refute.

CENTRAL ROUTE

Important message is logical and convincing. → Message receives close attention. → ATTITUDE CHANGE

'MyPsychLab was a fantastic asset in preparing for exams.'

Read Susan Saulny's article entitled *Goodbye, Therapist. Hello, Anxiety?* in the **eTHEMES section**. Be sure to answer the questions linked to the article.

'The diagnostic tests helped me to know what topics I needed to study further and helped me prepare for my exam.'

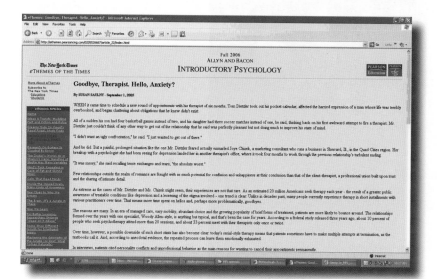

*STUDY TIP*

Take a MyPsychLab EXAM on content covered in Chapter 16!

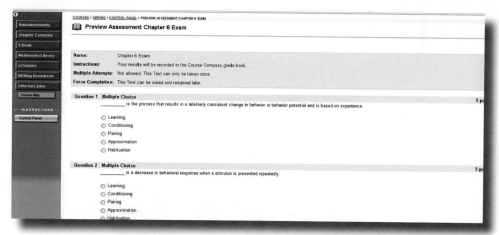

**What can you find in MyPsychLab?**

Self-directed tests * Videos * Simulations * eBook * Biographies * Audio glossary * Web links … and more—organised by chapter, section and learning objective.

# Social Processes, Society and Culture

# CHAPTER 17

# CHAPTER FOCUS POINTS

After studying this chapter you will have a better understanding of:

1. How the power given in a situation affects behaviour

2. What leads people to being altruistic and social

3. How aggression manifests and escalates

4. How conflict and peace can be influenced by psychology.

## CHAPTER CONTENTS

We have come to the moment in *Psychology and Life* when we consider the most extreme consequences of the way in which social forces act on human behaviour. Some of the content of this chapter will be quite disturbing with respect to the potential it reveals for destructive and inhumane acts. We consider the power of situations, aggressive behaviour, and the circumstances that can lead to acts of genocide. At the same time, we describe the innate drive of the human species to be pro-social—to perform altruistic acts of generosity with no expectation of reward. Ultimately, we hope that this chapter strikes an optimistic note by suggesting how the insights generated through social science research can help relieve some of the world's tension.

Students often find the topics discussed in this chapter both provocative and disconcerting. We hope you will have the opportunity to discuss and debate the full implications with your classmates. You should finish the chapter with an understanding of how the social psychological forces acting on each individual can, as individuals join together in groups, produce some of the most intimidating moments of world history.

# THE POWER OF THE SITUATION

Throughout *Psychology and Life*, we have seen that psychologists who strive to understand the causes of behaviour look in many different places for their answers. Some look to genetic factors and others to biochemical and brain processes; still others focus on the causal influence of the environment. Social psychologists believe that the primary determinant of behaviour is the nature of the social situation in which that behaviour occurs. They argue that social situations exert significant control over individual behaviour, often dominating personality and a person's past history of learning, values and beliefs. In this section, we will review both classic research and recent experiments that together explore the effect of subtle but powerful situational variables on people's behaviour.

## ROLES AND RULES

What *social roles* are available to you? A **social role** is a socially defined pattern of behaviour that is expected of a person when functioning in a given setting or group. Different social situations make different roles available. When you are at home, you may accept the role of 'child' or 'sibling'. When you are in the classroom, you accept the role of 'student'. At other times still, you are a 'best friend' or 'lover'. Can you see how these different roles immediately make different types of behaviours more or less appropriate and also available to you?

To open or not to open? How do people learn the etiquette for giving and receiving gifts in different cultures?

Situations are also characterised by the operation of **rules**, behavioural guidelines for specific settings. Some rules are *explicitly* stated in signs (DON'T SMOKE; NO EATING IN CLASS) or are explicitly taught to children (Respect the elderly; Never take candy from a stranger). Other rules are *implicit*—they are learned through transactions with others in particular settings. How loud you can play your music, how close you can stand to another person, when you can call your teacher or boss by a first name, and what is the suitable way to react to a compliment or a gift—all of these actions depend on the situation. For example, the Japanese do not open a gift in the presence of the giver, for fear of not showing sufficient appreciation; foreigners not aware of this unwritten rule will misinterpret the behaviour as rude instead of sensitive. Next time you get in an elevator, try to determine what rules you have learned about that situation. Why do people usually speak in hushed tones or not at all?

Ordinarily, you might not be particularly aware of the effects of roles and rules, but one classic social psychological experiment, the *Stanford Prison Experiment*, put these forces to work with startling results (Haney & Zimbardo, 1977; Zimbardo, 1975; replicated in Australia by Lovibond et al., 1979).

On a summer Sunday in California, a siren shattered the serenity of college student Tommy Whitlow's morning. A police car screeched to a halt in front of his home. Within minutes, Tommy was charged with a felony, informed of his constitutional rights, frisked, and handcuffed. After he was booked and fingerprinted, Tommy was blindfolded and transported to the Stanford County Prison, where he was stripped, sprayed with disinfectant and issued a smock-type uniform with an ID number on the front and back. Tommy became prisoner 647. Eight other college students were also arrested and assigned numbers.

Tommy and his cellmates were all volunteers who had answered a newspaper ad and agreed to be participants in a 2-week experiment on prison life. By random flips of a coin, some of the volunteers had

**social role** A socially defined pattern of behaviour that is expected of a person who is functioning in a given setting or group.

been assigned to the role of prisoners; the rest became guards. All had been selected from a large pool of student volunteers who, on the basis of extensive psychological tests and interviews, had been judged as law-abiding, emotionally stable, physically healthy and 'normal-average'. The prisoners lived in the jail around the clock; the guards worked standard 8-hour shifts.

What happened once these students had assumed their randomly assigned roles? In guard roles, college students who had been pacifists and 'nice guys' behaved aggressively—sometimes even sadistically. The guards insisted that prisoners obey all rules without question or hesitation. Failure to do so led to the loss of a privilege. At first, privileges included opportunities to read, write or talk to other inmates. Later on, the slightest protest resulted in the loss of the 'privileges' of eating, sleeping and washing. Failure to obey rules also resulted in menial, mindless work such as cleaning toilets with bare hands, doing push-ups while a guard stepped on the prisoner's back, and spending hours in solitary confinement. The guards were always devising new strategies to make the prisoners feel worthless.

As prisoners, psychologically stable students soon behaved pathologically, passively resigning themselves to their unexpected fate. Less than 36 hours after the mass arrest, Prisoner 8412, one of the ringleaders of an aborted prisoner rebellion that morning, began to cry uncontrollably. He experienced fits of rage, disorganised thinking and severe depression. On successive days, three more prisoners developed similar stress-related symptoms. A fifth prisoner developed a psychosomatic rash all over his body when the Parole Board rejected his appeal.

Because of the dramatic and unexpectedly severe emotional and behavioural effects observed, those five prisoners with extreme stress reactions were released early from this unusual prison, and the psychologists were forced to terminate their 2-week study after only 6 days. Although Tommy Whitlow said he wouldn't want to go through it again, he valued the personal experience because he learned so much about himself and about human nature. Fortunately, he and the other students were basically healthy, and they readily bounced back from this highly charged situation. Follow-ups over many years revealed no lasting negative effects. The participants had all contributed to an important lesson: The power of the simulated prison situation had created a new *social reality*—a real prison—in the minds of the jailers and their captives.

By the conclusion of the Stanford Prison Experiment, guards' and prisoners' behaviour differed from each other in virtually every observable way (see **Figure 17.1**). However, the figure doesn't completely reveal the extremes of the guards' behaviour. On many occasions, the guards stripped their prisoners naked. The guards hooded and chained their prisoners. They denied them food and

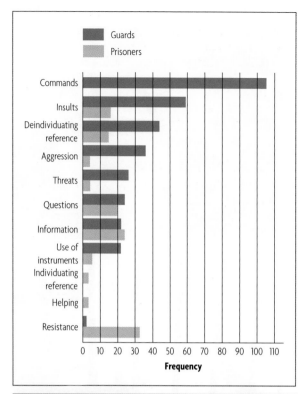

**Figure 17.1**

**Guard and prisoner behaviour**
During the Stanford Prison Experiment, the randomly assigned roles of prisoners and guards drastically affected participants' behaviour. The observations recorded in the six-day interaction profile show that across 25 observation periods, the prisoners engaged in more passive resistance, while the guards became more dominating, controlling and hostile.

bedding. Does this list of behaviours sound familiar? They are among the abuses the guards committed in 2003 at the Abu Ghraib prison in Iraq. The Stanford Prison Experiment helps shed light on this scandal: situational forces can lead ordinary people to exhibit horrendous behaviours (Fiske et al., 2004; Zimbardo, 2004).

A critical feature of the Stanford Prison Experiment is that only chance, in the form of random assignment, decided the participants' roles as guards or prisoners. Those roles created status and power differences that were validated in the prison situation. No one taught the participants to play their roles. Without ever visiting real prisons, all the participants learned something about the interaction between the powerful and the powerless (Banuazizi & Movahedi, 1975). A guard type is someone who limits the freedom of prisoner types to manage their behaviour and make them behave more predictably. This task is aided by the use of *coercive rules*, which include explicit punishment for violations. Prisoners can only *react* to the social structure of a prison-like setting created by those with power. Rebellion or compliance are the only options of the prisoners; the first choice results in punishment, and the second results in a loss of autonomy and dignity.

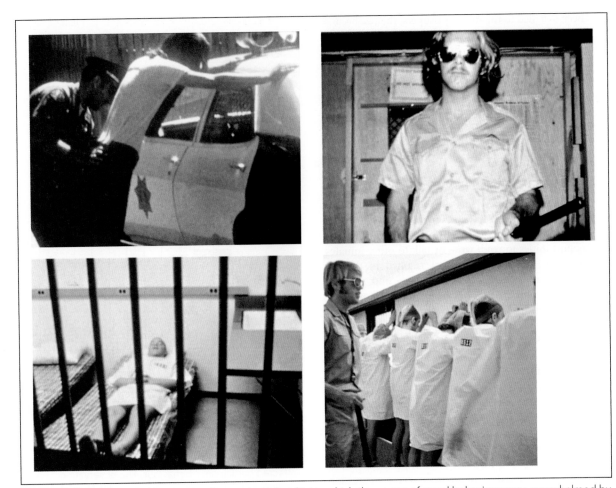

The Stanford Prison Experiment created a new 'social reality' in which the norms of good behaviour were overwhelmed by the dynamics of the situation. Why did the student guards and inmates adopt their roles so powerfully?

The student participants had already experienced such power differences in many of their previous social interactions: parent–child, teacher–student, doctor–patient, boss–worker, male–female. They merely refined and intensified their prior patterns of behaviour for this particular setting. Each student could have played either role. Many students in the guard role reported being surprised at how easily they enjoyed controlling other people. Just putting on the uniform was enough to transform them from passive university students into aggressive prison guards. What sort of person do *you* become when you slip in and out of different roles? Where does your sense of personal self end and your social identity begin?

## SOCIAL NORMS

In addition to the expectations regarding role behaviours, groups develop many expectations for the ways their members *should* act. The specific expectations for socially appropriate attitudes and behaviours that are embodied in the stated or implicit rules of a group are called **social norms**. Social norms can be broad guidelines; if you are a member of the Liberal Party in Australia, you may be expected to hold conservative political beliefs, whereas members of the Labor Party will advocate more socialist

views. Social norms can also embody specific standards of conduct. For example, if you are employed as a waiter or a waitress, you will be expected to treat your customers courteously no matter how unpleasant and demanding they are to you.

Belonging to a group typically involves discovering the set of social norms that regulates desired behaviour in the group setting. This adjustment occurs in two ways: You notice the *uniformities* in certain behaviours of all or most members, and you observe the *negative consequences* when someone violates a social norm.

Norms serve several important functions. Awareness of the norms operating in a given group situation helps orient members and regulate their social interaction. Each participant can anticipate how others will enter the situation, how they will dress, and what they are likely to say and do, as well as what type of behaviour will be expected of them to gain approval. You often feel awkward in new situations precisely because you may be unaware of the norms that govern the way you ought to act. Some tolerance for deviating from the standard is also part of the norm—wide in some cases, narrow in others. For example, shorts and a T-shirt might be marginally acceptable attire for a religious ceremony; a bathing suit would almost certainly deviate too far from the norm.

**social norms** The expectation a group has for its members regarding acceptable and appropriate attitudes and behaviours.

The guards in the above photo appear to be enjoying the prisoners at Abu Ghraib. How does social psychological research explain some aspects of their behaviours?

Group members are usually able to estimate how far they can go before experiencing the coercive power of the group in the form of ridicule, re-education, and rejection.

# CONFORMITY

When you adopt a social role or bend to a social norm, you are, to some extent, *conforming* to social expectations. **Conformity** is the tendency for people to adopt the behaviour and opinions presented by other group members. Why do you conform? Are there circumstances under which you ignore social constraints and act independently? Social psychologists have studied two types of forces that may lead to conformity:

- **Informational influence** processes—wanting to be correct and to understand the right way to act in a given situation.
- **Normative influence** processes—wanting to be liked, accepted and approved of by others.

We will describe classic experiments that illustrate each type of influence.

## Informational influence: Sherif's autokinetic effect

Many life situations in which you must make decisions about behaviours are quite ambiguous. Suppose, for example, you are dining at an elegant restaurant with a large group of people. Each place at the table is set with a dazzling array of silverware. How do you know which fork to use when the first course arrives? Typically, you would look to other members of the party to help you make an appropriate choice. This is *informational influence*.

A classic experiment, conducted by Muzafer Sherif (1935), demonstrated how informational influence can lead to **norm crystallisation**—norm formation and solidification.

Participants were asked to judge the amount of movement of a spot of light, which was actually stationary but that appeared to move when viewed in total darkness with no reference points. This is a perceptual illusion known as the *autokinetic effect*. Originally, individual judgments varied widely. However, when the participants were brought together in a group consisting of strangers and stated their judgments aloud, their estimates began to converge. They began to see the light move in the same direction and in similar amounts. Even more interesting was the final part of Sherif's study—when alone in the same darkened room after the group viewing, these participants continued to follow the group norm that had emerged when they were together.

Once norms are established in a group, they tend to perpetuate themselves. In later research, these autokinetic group norms persisted even when tested a year later and without former group members witnessing the judgments (Rohrer et al., 1954). Norms can be transmitted from one generation of group members to the next and can continue to influence people's behaviour long after the original group that created the norm no longer exists (Insko et al., 1980). How do we know that norms can have trans-generational influence? In autokinetic effect studies, researchers replaced one group member with a new one after each set of autokinetic trials until all the members of the group were new to the situation. The group's autokinetic norm remained true to the one handed down to them across several successive generations (Jacobs & Campbell, 1961). Do you see how this experiment captures the processes that allow real-life norms to be passed down across generations?

## Normative influence: The Asch effect

What is the best way to demonstrate that people will sometimes conform because of *normative influence*—their desire to be liked, accepted, and approved of by others? One of the most important early social psychologists, **Solomon Asch**

When individuals become dependent on a group—such as a religious cult—for basic feelings of self-worth, they are prone to extremes of conformity. Twenty thousand identically dressed couples were married in this service conducted by the Reverend Sun Myung Moon. In August 1995, Moon simultaneously married 360,000 'Moonie' couples who were linked by satellite in 500 worldwide locations. Why do people find comfort in such large-scale conformity?

**normative influence** Group effects that arise from individuals' desire to be liked, accepted and approved of by others.

**norm crystallisation** The convergence of the expectations of a group of individuals into a common perspective as they talk and carry out activities together.

**conformity** The tendency for people to adopt the behaviours, attitudes and values of other members of a reference group.

**informational influence** Group effects that arise from individuals' desire to be correct and right and to understand how best to act in a given situation.

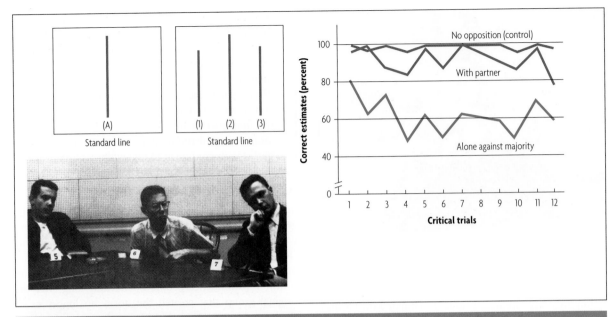

Figure 17.2

**Conformity in the Asch experiments**

In this photo from Asch's study, it is evident that the naive participant, Number 6, is distressed by the unanimous majority's erroneous judgment. The typical stimulus array is shown at the top left. At top right, the graph illustrates conformity across 12 critical trials when solitary participants were grouped with a unanimous majority, as well as their greater independence when paired with a dissenting partner. A lower percentage of correct estimates indicates the greater degree of an individual's conformity to the group's false estimate.

(1940, 1956), created circumstances in which participants made judgments under conditions in which the physical reality was absolutely clear—but the rest of a group reported that they saw that reality differently. Male university students were led to believe they were in a study of simple visual perception. They were shown cards with three lines of differing lengths and asked to indicate which of the three lines was the same length as the standard line (see **Figure 17.2**). The lines were different enough so that mistakes were rare, and their relative sizes changed on each series of trials.

The participants were seated next to last in semicircles of six to eight other students. Unknown to the participants, the others were all experimental confederates—accomplices of the experimenter—who were following a prearranged script. On the first three trials, everyone in the circle agreed on the correct comparison. However, the first confederate to respond on the fourth trial matched two lines that were obviously different. So did all members of the group up to the participant. That student had to decide if he should go along with everyone else's view of the situation and conform or remain independent, standing by what he clearly saw. That dilemma was repeated for the naive participant on 12 of the 18 trials. The participants showed signs of disbelief and obvious discomfort when faced with a majority who saw the world so differently. What did they do?

Roughly one fourth of the participants remained completely independent—they never conformed.

However, between 50 and 80 percent of the participants (in different studies in the research program) conformed with the false majority estimate at least once, and a third of the participants yielded to the majority's wrong judgments on half or more of the critical trials.

Asch describes some participants who yielded to the majority most of the time as 'disoriented' and 'doubt-ridden'; he states that they 'experienced a powerful impulse not to appear different from the majority' (1952, p. 396). Those who yielded underestimated the influence of the social pressure and the frequency of their conformity; some even claimed that they really had seen the lines as the same length, despite their obvious discrepancy.

In other studies, Asch varied three factors: the size of the unanimous majority, the presence of a partner who dissented from the majority, and the size of the discrepancy between the correct physical stimulus comparison and the majority's position. He found that strong conformity effects were elicited with a unanimous majority of only three or four people. However, giving the naive participant a single ally who dissented from the majority opinion had the effect of sharply reducing conformity, as can be seen in Figure 17.2. With a partner, the participant was usually able to resist the pressures to conform to the majority (Asch, 1955, 1956).

How should we interpret these results? Asch himself was struck by the rate at which participants did *not* conform (Friend et al., 1990). He reported this research as studies in 'independence'. In fact, two-thirds of the time, participants gave the correct, nonconforming answer. However, most descriptions of Asch's experiment have emphasised the one-third conformity rate. Accounts of this experiment also often fail to note that not all participants were alike: the number of individuals who never conformed, about 25 percent, was roughly equal to the number who always or almost always conformed. Thus Asch's experiment teaches two complementary lessons. On the one hand, we find that people are not entirely swayed by normative influence—they assert their independence on a majority of occasions (and some people always do). On the other hand, we find that people will sometimes conform, even in the most unambiguous situations. That potential to conform is an important element of human nature.

## Conformity in everyday life

Although you've almost certainly never faced the exact circumstances of the Asch experiment, you can no doubt recognise conformity situations in your everyday life. Many of these situations are easy to spot. You might notice, for example, that you are wearing clothes that you find rather silly because someone has declared them to be fashionable. (Certainly that's true of *other* people.) Also, as we noted in Chapter 10, adolescents often conform with their peer groups with respect to risky behaviours such as drug use.

There are also subtler instances of conformity that may not be immediately apparent to you. Consider a study that examined how long it took people to provide either majority or minority answers to questions about both important and mundane topics.

When was the last occasion on which you offered an opinion that differed from the majority around you? In what ways did you find it difficult? A series of studies demonstrated that people with minority opinions took consistently more times to voice their opinions (Bassili, 2003). In an initial study, interviews called 714 students at the University of Toronto and asked them to respond to statements such as 'We should be tolerant of groups that do not share basic Canadian values.' For that statement, 88 percent of the students responded 'agree' with an average response time of 2.71 seconds. Almost all the other students, 11 percent, said 'disagree' (the rest gave other responses) with an average response time of 4.59 seconds. Thus participants took 1.88 seconds longer to give a minority opinion. In a sample of 191 Indiana University students, the same pattern emerged for attitudes toward activities (for example, sewing and swimming) and objects (for example, snakes and chocolate chip cookies). A majority of 76 percent of the sample took on average 1.28 seconds to say that they like dentists, whereas a minority 24 percent took on average 1.72 seconds to say they dislike them.

Bear in mind that participants were not offering these opinions in a particularly public fashion. In the first study, they were giving their response to a single interviewer who did not offer any sort of feedback; in the second study they were pushing 'like' or 'dislike' keys on a computer. Even so, when they gave opinions that failed to conform to the majority, they hesitated to do so.

## Minority influence and nonconformity

Given the power of the majority to control resources and information, it is not surprising that people regularly conform to groups. As we've just seen, majority power even extends to how long it takes people to offer their opinions in private. Yet you know that sometimes individuals persevere in their personal views. How can this happen? How do people escape group domination, and how can anything new (counter-normative) ever come about? Are there any conditions under which a small minority can turn the majority around and create new norms?

Whereas researchers in the United States have concentrated their studies on conformity, in part because conformity is intertwined with the democratic process, some European social psychologists have instead focused on the power of the few to change the majority. **Serge Moscovici** of France pioneered the study of minority influence. In one study where participants were given colour-naming tasks, the majority correctly identified the colour patches, but two of the experimenter's confederates consistently identified a green colour as blue. Their consistent minority opposition had no immediate effect on the majority, but, when later tested alone, some of the participants shifted their judgments by moving the boundary between blue and green toward the blue side of the colour continuum (Moscovici, 1976; Moscovici & Faucheux, 1972). Eventually, the power of the many may be undercut by the conviction of the dedicated few (Moscovici, 1980, 1985).

You can conceptualise these effects with respect to the distinction we introduced earlier between normative influence and informational influence (Crano & Prislin, 2006; Wood et al., 1994). Minority groups have relatively little normative influence: members of the majority are typically not particularly concerned about being liked or accepted by the minority. Conversely, minority groups do have informational influence: Minorities can encourage group members to understand issues from multiple perspectives (Peterson & Nemeth, 1996). Unfortunately, this potential for informational influence may only infrequently allow minorities to overcome majority members' normative desire to distance themselves from deviant or low-consensus views (Wood, 2000).

In society, the majority tends to be the defender of the status quo. Typically, the force for innovation and change comes from the minority members or from individuals who are either dissatisfied with the current system or able to visualise new options and create alternative ways of dealing with current problems. The conflict between the entrenched majority view and the dissident minority perspective is an essential precondition of innovations that can lead to positive social change.

## DECISION MAKING IN GROUPS

If you've ever tried to make a decision as part of a group, you know that it can be quite torturous. Imagine, for example, that you have just seen a movie with a bunch of friends. Although you thought the movie was 'OK,' by the end of a post-movie discussion you find yourself agreeing that it was 'an incredible piece of trash'. Is this change after group discussion typical? Are the judgments groups make consistently different from individuals' judgments? Researchers in social psychology have documented specific forces that operate when groups make decisions (Kerr & Tindale, 2004). We will focus on *group polarisation* and *groupthink*.

Your post-movie experience is an example of **group polarisation**: Groups show a tendency to make decisions that are more extreme than the decisions that would be made by the members acting alone. Suppose, for example, you asked each member of the movie group to provide an attitude rating toward the movie; subsequently, as a group you agree on a single value to reflect your group attitude. If the group's rating is more extreme than the average of the individuals' ratings, that would be an instance of polarisation. Depending on the initial group tendency—toward caution or risk—group polarisation will tend to make a group more cautious or more risky.

Researchers have suggested that two types of processes underlie group polarisation: the *information-influence* model and the *social comparison* model (Liu & Latané, 1998). The information-influence model suggests that group members contribute different information to a decision. If you and your friends each have a different reason for disliking a movie a little bit, all that information taken together would provide the evidence that you should actually dislike the movie a lot. The social comparison model suggests that group members strive to capture their peers' regard by representing a group ideal that is a bit more extreme than the group's true norm. Thus, if you come to decide that everyone was unhappy with a movie, you could try to present yourself as particularly astute by stating a more extreme opinion. If everyone in a group tries to capture the group's esteem in that same fashion, polarisation will result.

Group polarisation is one consequence of a general pattern of thought called *groupthink*. **Irving Janis** (1982) coined the term **groupthink** for the tendency of a decision-making group to filter out undesirable input so that a consensus may be reached, especially if it is in line with the leader's viewpoint. Janis's theory of groupthink emerged from his historical analysis of the Bay of Pigs invasion of Cuba in 1960. This disastrous invasion was approved by President Kennedy after cabinet meetings in which contrary information was minimised or suppressed by those advisers to the president who were eager to undertake the invasion. From his analysis of this event, Janis outlined a series of features that he believed would predispose groups to fall prey to groupthink: He suggested, for example, that groups that were highly cohesive, insulated from experts, and operated under directed leadership would make groupthink decisions.

To test Janis's ideas, researchers have turned both to further historical analyses and laboratory experiments (Henningsen et al., 2006). This body of research suggests that groups are particularly vulnerable to groupthink when they embody a collective desire to maintain a shared positive view of a group (Turner & Pratkanis, 1998). Group members must understand that dissent often improves the quality of a group decision even if it may detract, on the surface, from the group's positive feel.

The next time you are involved in a group enterprise, see if you can detect these processes at work.

## SITUATIONAL POWER: 'CANDID CAMERA' REVELATIONS

Social psychologists have attempted to demonstrate the power of social norms and social situations by devising experiments that reveal the ease with which smart, independent, rational, good people can be led into behaving in ways that are less than optimal. Although social psychologists have shown the serious consequences of situational power such as the social roles that turn ordinary students into aggressive prison guards, it is equally possible to demonstrate this principle with humour. Indeed, the classic *Candid Camera* television show, created by intuitive social psychologist **Allen Funt**, did just that. Funt showed how human nature follows a situational script to the letter. Millions in his TV audiences laughed when a diner stopped eating a hamburger whenever a DON'T EAT counter light flashed; when pedestrians stopped and waited at a red

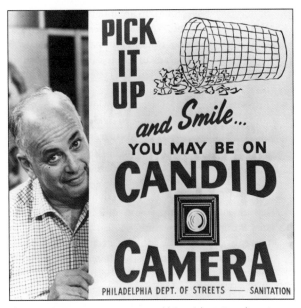

If you came upon an overturned bin with a sign directing you to Pick It Up, would you obey it?

**group polarisation** The tendency for groups to make decisions that are more extreme than the decisions that would be made by the members acting alone.

**groupthink** The tendency of a decision-making group to filter out undesirable input so that a consensus may be reached, especially if it is in line with the leader's viewpoint.

street light above the *footpath* on which they were walking; when highway drivers turned back after seeing a road sign that read DELAWARE IS CLOSED; and when customers jumped from one white tile to another in response to a store sign that instructed them not to walk on black tiles. One of the best *Candid Camera* illustrations of the subtle power of implicit situational rules to control behaviour is the 'elevator caper'. A person riding a rigged elevator first obeyed the usual silent rule to face the front, but when a group of other passengers all faced the rear, the hapless victim followed the new emerging group norm and faced the rear as well.

We see in these 'slice-of-life' episodes the minimal situational conditions needed to elicit unusual behaviours in ordinary people. You laugh because people who appear similar to you behave foolishly in response to small modifications in their commonplace situations. You implicitly distance yourself from them by assuming you would not act that way. The lesson of much social psychological research is that, more than likely, you would behave exactly as others have if you were placed in the same situation. Poet John Donne wrote, 'No man is an island, entire of itself; every man is a piece of the continent.' People are all interconnected by the situations and norms and rules they share. The wise reply to someone who asks how *you* would act if you were in a situation in which people behaved in evil, foolish or irrational ways is, 'I don't know. It depends on how powerful the situation is.'

We have reached the important conclusion that situations play a substantial role in determining people's behaviour. In the next two sections we will revisit that conclusion with respect to positive and negative behaviours—altruism and aggression. We will also see how other factors, such as our genetic inheritance, play a role in determining who might help and who might do harm within particular situations.

## RECAP CHECKPOINT
### The power of the situation

- Human thought and action are affected by situational influences.
- Being assigned to play a social role, even in artificial settings, can cause individuals to act contrary to their beliefs, values, and dispositions.
- Social norms shape the attitudes and behaviours of group members.
- Classic research by Sherif and Asch illustrated the informational and normative forces that lead to conformity.
- Minority influence may arise as a consequence of informational influence.

## CONCEPT QUESTIONS

1. What did the Stanford Prison Experiment demonstrate about social roles?

2. Why are groups able to have normative influence?

3. What type of influence are minorities able to exert in a group?

4. How can you recognise circumstances of group polarisation?

## CRITICAL THINKING

Consider the study that looked at conformity in line judgments. Why was it important that the group members all gave the correct answer on the first few trials?

# ALTRUISM AND PRO-SOCIAL BEHAVIOUR

You see the same images after almost every tragedy: People risk their own lives to try to save the lives of others. Recall, for example, the horror of the World Trade Center attack. People from all the over the country converged on Ground Zero with the hope of finding and aiding survivors. Such tragedies show the human species' potential for **pro-social behaviours**, behaviours that are carried out with the goal of helping other people. Beyond that, these tragedies often demonstrate **altruism**—the pro-social behaviours a person carries out without considering his or her own safety or interests. Much of what defines a *culture* or *society* is people's willingness to help each other. As members of a culture or society, people cooperate and make sacrifices for the good of other members. We begin this section by considering why it is that people are willing to perform acts of altruism.

**pro-social behaviours** Behaviours that are carried out with the goal of helping other people.

**altruism** Prosocial behaviours a person carries out without considering his or her own safety or interests.

## THE ROOTS OF ALTRUISM

Let's start with a concrete example of altruism, reported in a daily newspaper (Porstner, 1997):

> A Bay Shore man pulled in front of and stopped a swerving car on the Southern State Parkway in Lindenhurst Thursday, saving a Connecticut man whom police said may have suffered a seizure.
>
> 'I just got up real close in front of him and just slowed down so he would hit me', said [the driver, age] 25. 'That was the only way I could get his moving car to a stop.'

What response do you have to this report? Can you imagine risking your own life—or, at least, your own car—to save someone else's life? As this event unfolded, what do you imagine the Bay Shore driver might have been thinking to himself? Do you believe he calculated costs and benefits before he acted?

When you consider examples like this courageous driver, it seems fairly natural to conclude that there is some basic human motive to be altruistic. In fact, the existence of altruism has sometimes been controversial. To understand why, you must think back to the discussion of evolutionary forces we presented in Chapters 3 and 11. According to the evolutionary perspective, the main goal of life is to reproduce so that one can pass on one's genes. How, in that context, does altruism make sense? Why should you risk your life to aid others? There are two answers to this question, depending on whether the 'others' are family members or strangers.

For family members, altruistic behaviours makes some sense because—even if you imperil your own survival—you aid the general survival of your gene pool (Burnstein, 2005). In fact, when asked about who they might aid in life-or-death situations, people are relatively sensitive to their genetic overlap.

reciprocal altruism The idea that people perform altruistic behaviours because they expect that others will perform altruistic behaviours for them in turn.

University students from the United States and Japan were asked to consider scenarios in which they could only save one of three individuals in grave peril. For example, in one scenario the three individuals were sleeping in a rapidly burning house. In each scenario, the individuals differed with respect to their imagined *kinship* with the students. Some were close relatives, such as brothers (0.5 overlap in genes); others were more distant, such as cousins (0.125 overlap). The students were asked to indicate which individual they would be most likely to save. As you can see in **Figure 17.3**, the closer the kinship, the more likely people were to 'save' that individual. The figure also shows a comparison condition in which the situation wasn't life or death: the students were asked how they would deal with more everyday decisions, like choosing someone for whom they would run an errand. The results still show the effects of kinship, but the relationship is not quite as strong. That is, the 'life-or-death' scenarios yield more extreme evaluations of kinship than the 'everyday' scenarios. The results were the same for both Japanese and U.S. students (Burnstein et al., 1994).

Students in this study didn't actually have to rescue anyone from a burning house, yet you can see how kinship affected their choices. However, more recent research suggests that people's impulses are not influenced directly by kinship. Rather, they are most likely willing to help individuals to whom they feel emotionally close (Korchmaros & Kenny, 2006). For most people, their closest emotional attachments are also to their closest kin. Thus patterns of helping based on emotional closeness indirectly help people's gene pools to survive.

But how about nonkin? The focus on emotional closeness suggests why people might engage in altruistic behaviours toward their closest friends. But why, for example, was the driver willing to risk his own survival to help a stranger? To explain altruism toward acquaintances and strangers, theorists have explored the concept of **reciprocal altruism** (Trivers, 1971). This concept suggests that people perform altruistic behaviours because they, in some sense, expect that others will perform altruistic behaviours for them: I will save you when you are drowning with the expectation that you would save me, in the future, when I am drowning. Thus expectations of reciprocity endow altruism with survival value. You have already become acquainted with this concept in other guises. In Chapter 16, for example, we

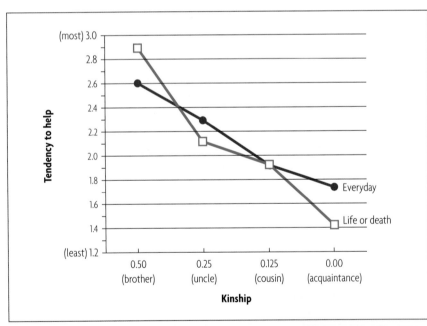

**Figure 17.3**

**Tendency to help kin**
Students were asked to indicate which relatives, of differing degrees of kinship, they were most likely to save in life-or-death and everyday circumstances. Although closeness had an effect on both types of judgments, it mattered more for life-or-death situations.

From E. Brunstein et al., *Journal of Personality and Social Psychology, 67*, 773-789. Copyright © 1994 American Psychological Association. Adapted with permission. The use of APA information does not imply endorsement by APA.

What social forces prompt people like the Rural Fire Service members to put their lives in jeopardy for the sake of others?

introduced the *norm of reciprocity* to explain one way in which people can bring about compliance. When someone does a favour for you, you are in a state of psychological distress until you can return the favour—this distress, apparently, has its roots in evolution because it helps increase survival. Because of these evolutionary underpinnings, altruism is not unique to the human species. In fact, anthropologists have identified patterns of reciprocal altruism among a variety of species, such as vampire bats, capuchin monkeys and chimpanzees, that function in social groups (Hattori et al., 2005; Nielsen, 1994).

Note, however, that the concept of reciprocal altruism cannot explain all facets of cooperation in social species. For example, the guy who stopped the stranger's car surely didn't expect that the stranger would perform a similarly altruistic act in return. To explain acts of this sort, researchers suggest that *indirect reciprocity* is at work: People perform altruistic behaviours because they believe that, in the future, they will become the recipients of altruistic acts. To put it somewhat more plainly, 'I scratch your back and someone else will scratch mine' (Nowak & Sigmund, 2005, p. 1291). An important component of this concept of indirect reciprocity is that people gain the reputation of being altruistic and trustworthy. For example, in one study participants played a game that gave them several opportunities to behave altruistically by making monetary donations to other players (Wedekind & Braithwaite, 2002). As the game unfolded, the players' 'image scores' were posted as a concrete index of their reputations. In a second phase of the study—in a different game—players with the best reputations for being altruistic were themselves the most likely to be rewarded by altruistic actions. Results of this sort suggest that there is long-term value in having a reputation for being a trustworthy source of altruism. In fact, people sometimes compete to obtain the most favourable reputation (Barclay, 2004). More generally, expectations of indirect reciprocity suggest why people are willing to incur the costs of altruistic acts.

## MOTIVES FOR PRO-SOCIAL BEHAVIOUR

In the last section, we suggested that altruism—a motive to sacrifice for others—has an innate basis. We now consider altruism in the context of other motives for pro-social behaviour. Researcher **C. Daniel Batson** (1994) suggests that there are four forces that prompt people to act for the public good:

- *Altruism.* Acting in response to a motive to benefit others, as in the case of the driver who saved another person's life.
- *Egoism.* Performing pro-social behaviours ultimately in one's own self-interest; someone might perform a helping behaviour to receive a similar favour in return (for example, compliance with a request) or to receive a reward (for example, money or praise).

- *Collectivism.* Performing pro-social behaviours to benefit a particular group; people might perform helping behaviours to improve circumstances for their families, fraternities or sororities, political parties, and so on.
- *Principlism.* Performing pro-social behaviours to uphold moral principles; someone might act in a pro-social manner because of a religious or civic principle.

You can see how each of these motives might apply in different situations.

Although each motive may lead people to perform behaviours in the service of others, they also sometimes can act in competition (Batson & Powell, 2003). Suppose, for example, that you must decide how to allocate a scarce resource to several people. You might be thinking, 'I'd give the same amount to all individuals' because the principle of *justice* suggests that each person should have equal access to resources. Suppose, however, that other motives come into play that lead you to favour one individual over the others.

> Participants in an experiment were asked to allocate raffle tickets either to a whole group or to individuals within the group. If the tickets were given to the whole group, each member would get the same number of tickets—a *justice* outcome. However, in one condition of the experiment, the participants read an autobiographical message from someone they were led to believe was a group member; the message revealed that that person had just been dumped by a long-time romantic partner. How does this information affect people's distributions of raffle tickets? When the participants were encouraged to try to imagine how the student would feel, they gave extra tickets to the dumped individual. *Empathy*—the participants' emotional identification with the student—won out over *justice* (Batson et al., 1999).

Batson and his colleagues have provided several demonstrations in favour of the *empathy-altruism hypothesis*: When you feel empathy towards another

What pro-social motive explains why people band together to protect the environment on Clean-up Australia Day?

individual, those feelings evoke an altruistic motive to provide help. In the experiment we just described, the immediate altruistic goal proved stronger for some participants than the more abstract goal of justice. In a similar fashion, empathy can give rise to altruistic behaviours that favour an individual over the collective good (Batson et al., 1995).

You can see why it's important to consider each behaviour in light of the full situation. What looks at first like *anti*social behaviour—for example, violating principles of justice—may turn out, from a different vantage point, to be *pro*-social behaviour. A social psychology lesson we emphasised in the first section of this chapter was how much people's behaviours are constrained by situations. We have just had a first hint of such constraints for pro-social behaviour. Next, we describe a classic program of research that demonstrated fully how much people's willingness to help—their ability to follow through on pro-social motives—depends on characteristics of the situation.

## THE EFFECTS OF THE SITUATION ON PRO-SOCIAL BEHAVIOUR

This program of research began with a tragedy. From the safety of their apartment windows, 38 respectable, law-abiding citizens in the suburb of Queens in New York City, for more than half an hour watched a killer stalk and stab a woman in three separate attacks. Two times the sound of the bystanders' voices and the sudden glow of their bedroom lights interrupted the assailant and frightened him off. Each time, however, he returned and stabbed the victim again. Not a single person telephoned the police during the assault; only one witness called the police after the woman was dead (Rosenthal, 1964). This newspaper account of the murder of Kitty Genovese shocked a nation that could not accept the idea of such apathy or hard-heartedness on the part of its responsible citizenry.

But is it fair to pin the label of 'apathy' or 'hard-hearted' on these bystanders? Or can we explain their inaction in terms of situational forces? To make the case for situational forces, **Bibb Latané** and **John Darley** (1970) carried out a classic series of studies. Their goal was to demonstrate that **bystander intervention**—people's willingness to help strangers in distress—was very sensitive to precise characteristics of the situation. They ingeniously created in the laboratory an experimental analogue of the bystander-intervention situation.

The participants were male university students. Each student, placed in a room by himself with an intercom, was led to believe that he was communicating with one or more students in an adjacent room. During the course of a discussion about personal problems, he heard what sounded like one of the other students having an epileptic seizure and gasping for help. During the 'seizure,' it was impossible for the participant to talk to the other students or to find out what, if anything, they were doing about the

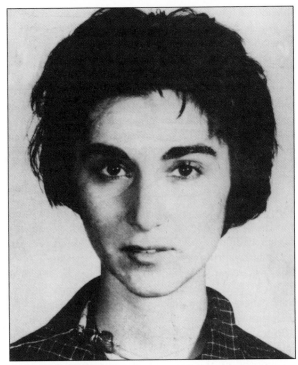

The murder of Kitty Genovese, in a pleasant Queens neighborhood, shocked the nation. Why did so many responsible citizens fail to intervene when they heard her cries for help?

emergency. The dependent variable was the speed with which the participant reported the emergency to the experimenter.

It turned out that the likelihood of intervention depended on the number of bystanders the participant thought were present. The more people he thought were present, the slower he was in reporting the seizure, if he did so at all. As you can see in **Figure 17.4**, everyone in a two-person situation intervened within 160 seconds, but nearly 40 percent of those who believed they were part of a larger group never bothered to inform the experimenter that another student was seriously ill (Darley & Latané, 1968).

This result arises from a **diffusion of responsibility**. When more than one person *could* help in an emergency situation, people often assume that someone else *will* or *should* help—so they back off and don't get involved.

Diffusion of responsibility is only one of the reasons that bystanders may fail to help. Let's explore more of the facets of many emergency situations.

Bystanders must notice the emergency In the seizure study, the situation was rigged so that participants had to notice what was going on. In many real-life circumstances, however, people who are pursuing their own agendas—they may, for example, be on their way to work or an appointment—may not even notice that there is a situation in which they can help. In one dramatic experiment, students at the Princeton Theological Seminary thought they were going to be evaluated on their sermons,

**diffusion of responsibility**
In emergency situations, the larger the number of bystanders, the less responsibility any one of the bystanders feels to help.

**bystander intervention**
Willingness to assist a person in need of help.

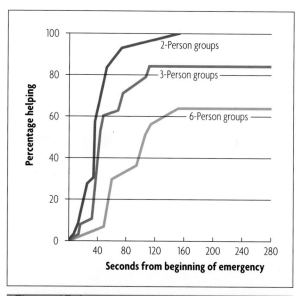

**Figure 17.4**

**Bystander Intervention in an Emergency**
The more people present, the less likely that any one bystander will intervene. Bystanders act most quickly in two-person groups.

From Darley & Latané, *Journal of Personality and Social Psychology*, 8(4), 1968. Copyright © 1968 American Psychological Association. Reprinted with permission.

one of which was to be about the parable of the Good Samaritan—a New Testament figure who takes time to help a man lying injured by the roadside.

> The seminarians had to deliver their lectures in a different building from the one in which they were initially briefed. Some were randomly assigned to a *late* condition, in which they had to hurry to make the next session, others to an *on-time* condition, and a third group to an *early* condition. When each seminarian walked down an alley between the two buildings, he came upon a man slumped in a doorway, coughing and groaning. On their way to deliver a sermon about the Good Samaritan, these seminary students now had the chance to practise what they were about to preach. Did they? Of those who were in a hurry because they were late, only 10 percent helped. If they were on time, 45 percent helped the stranger. Most bystander intervention came from those who were early—63 percent of these seminarians acted as Good Samaritans (Darley & Batson, 1973).

How should we evaluate the 'late' seminarians? Perhaps the seminarians were so caught up in their own concerns that they failed to even 'notice' the emergency situation. Perhaps they noticed, but in their hurry, they did not pay careful enough attention to determine how serious the situation was. In either case, you see that helping behaviour depends on taking the time to evaluate a situation accurately.

### Bystanders must label events as an emergency

Many situations in life are ambiguous. You don't want

to embarrass yourself by trying to give mouth-to-mouth resuscitation to someone who is merely asleep. To decide if a situation is an emergency, you typically see how other people are responding (Latané & Darley, 1970). (Recall the earlier discussion of informational influence in Chapter 16.) Consider this first-person account from one of your authors who was attending a lecture at which the speaker appeared to be on the brink of fainting:

> The speaker is flustered and his rapid delivery is clearly slowing down. Is it to emphasise his final points or because he is about to collapse? Maybe he needs to sit down, but how can I tell without interrupting him? What if I am reading the situation wrong, and then everyone will think I'm a fool? But suppose I am right and he passes out before finishing, and falls off the stage? He will surely get hurt smashing down into the seats. I'll know that I could have prevented his accident and did not.

You can see here how hard it is, even for someone with a firm grasp on the psychological forces at work in such a situation, to commit himself to action when no one else seems to be labelling the situation as an emergency. Here's how the situation ended:

> I stood up in front of the speaker and put my arms up toward him. He looked down at me in total confusion. I imagined what my students and colleagues were thinking of my seemingly bizarre behaviour as I wrapped my arms around the honoured guest speaker, moments before he finished his distinguished lecture. Just then, the speaker went limp, unconscious and fell on me. We crashed back into the first-row seats.

The decision to intervene, as you can see, proved to be prudent. However, from this brief account, you can see how very stressful it is to make a personal decision to define a situation as an emergency.

**Bystanders must feel responsibility** We have already seen that an important factor in non-intervention is the diffusion of responsibility. If you find yourself in a situation in which you need help, you should do everything you can to cause bystanders to focus responsibility on themselves and overcome this force. Point directly toward someone and say, 'You! I need your help.' Consider two studies that involved apparent crimes. In the first study, New Yorkers watched as a thief snatched a women's suitcase in a fast-food restaurant when she left her table. In the second, beachgoers watched as a thief snatched a portable radio from a beach blanket when the owner left it for a few minutes.

> In each experiment, the would-be theft victim (the experimenter's accomplice) asked the soon-to-be observer of the crime either, 'Do you have the time?' or 'Will you please keep an eye on my bag (radio) while I'm gone?' The first interaction elicited no personal responsibility, and the bystanders simply stood by idly as the thefts unfolded. However, of those

who agreed to watch the victim's property, almost every bystander intervened. They called for help, and some even tackled the runaway thief on the beach (Moriarty, 1975).

These experiments suggest that the act of requesting a favour forges a special human bond that involves other people in ways that materially change the situation. This is another instance in which it would be wrong to make an attribution of apathy when people fail to stop the theft. The social psychological power of the small commitment—'Will you watch this for me?'—turned almost every bystander into someone who cared enough to help.

# CRITICAL THINKING *in your life*
## HOW CAN YOU GET PEOPLE TO VOLUNTEER?

Suppose you become a leader in an organisation. It's very likely that you'll want to recruit volunteers to help with the organisation's activities. To do so, it should help to have an understanding of why people undertake volunteer work and what sustains their interest in the work.

Let's begin with the question of why people volunteer. Researchers have identified several motives that prompt people to get involved (Omoto & Snyder, 2002). For example, people volunteer to express personal values related to altruism, to expand their range of experiences, and to strengthen social relationships. If volunteer positions do not meet these needs, people may not wish to participate. To recruit volunteers, you may need to understand the motives of the people you wish to attract.

People also volunteer because they are required to do so. To increase levels of community service, some schools have instituted mandatory volunteer programs. Unfortunately, these mandatory programs can shift people's causal attributions from an internal locus of control (e.g., 'I volunteer because it's important to me') to an external locus of control (e.g., 'I volunteer because I'm required to do so'). When that happens, people become less likely to volunteer in the future (Stukas et al., 1999). People must be sensitive to this possibility when they mandate volunteer activities.

Once people begin to volunteer, what leads them to remain in their positions over time? To answer this question, researchers have engaged in longitudinal studies in which they track volunteers over time. For example, one study followed 238 volunteers in Florida over the course of a year (Davis et al., 2003). The volunteers participated in organisations such as the St. Petersburg Free Clinic and the Center Against Spouse Abuse. One of the most important factors that influenced the participants' satisfaction as volunteers was the amount of distress they experienced in their volunteer positions. Although this result may not surprise you, it leads to important practical advice. The researchers note that attention should be given to 'training methods that would prepare volunteers for distressing situations or provide them with strategies for coping with the distress they do experience' (p. 259).

Another study of 302 volunteers at a hospice focused on individual differences in the extent to which people view 'volunteer' as an important social role (Finkelstein et al., 2005). Recall from earlier in the chapter that people's behaviour is often highly influenced by social roles. This study addressed the hypothesis that those people for whom the role of volunteer was most part of their personal identity would also be most likely to continue volunteer work.

Participants indicated the extent to which the social role mattered by responding to statements such as 'Volunteering for Hospice is an important part of who I am'. Consistent with the researchers' expectations, they found a positive correlation between the strength of role identity and the length of time people continued to volunteer. These results, once again, lead to concrete advice: 'Once an individual begins volunteering, retention efforts might focus on cultivating a volunteer role identity. . . . Items (e.g., T-shirts, licence plate holders) that allow volunteers to be recognised publicly for their contributions can help strengthen role identity' (p. 416).

We have offered this analysis from the perspective of a person who wishes to encourage others to volunteer. However, you can also use these analyses to scrutinise your own behaviour. What motives apply to your experiences of volunteering? Are you ready to cope with distress? To what extent do you embrace 'volunteer' as a respected social role? You can address these questions to increase the personal and societal benefits of your volunteer activities.

- Why is it appropriate to use longitudinal designs to study volunteer behaviours?

- Why might T-shirts and licence plate holders help strengthen role identity?

In this section, we have discussed pro-social behaviours—those circumstances in which people come to each others' aid. We suggested that the motivation to help may be part of each human's genetic inheritance. However, human nature presents a mixture of pro-social and antisocial impulses. In the next section, we move to another type of behaviour—*aggression*—that may also be encoded in the human genome.

## RECAP CHECKPOINT

### Altruism and prosocial behaviour

- Researchers have tried to explain why people engage in pro-social behaviours, particularly altruistic behaviours that do not serve their own interests.

- Evolutionary explanations focus on kinship and reciprocity.

- People also engage in pro-social behaviours to serve their self-interest, to benefit particular communities and to uphold social principles.

- Bystander intervention studies show that situations largely determine who is likely or unlikely to help in emergencies.

### CONCEPT QUESTIONS

1. What sets altruistic behaviours apart from other types of pro-social behaviours?

2. What is meant by reciprocal altruism?

3. What four motives explain pro-social behaviours?

4. Why does diffusion of responsibility occur?

### CRITICAL THINKING

Consider the study that demonstrated a tendency to help kin. Why does the cross-cultural comparison provide important support for the study's conclusions?

# AGGRESSION

To introduce the concept of altruism, we quoted a newspaper article about a heroic act. Unfortunately, newspapers are much more likely to contain reports on acts of **aggression**: a person's behaviours that cause psychological or physical harm to another individual. These were some headlines from a single issue of *The Sydney Morning Herald*, 17 December, 2007:

- Overtaking bid kills five
- Father jailed for raping daughter
- Terror suspect 'backs killing infidels'
- News anchor accused of punching cop in face
- Inner-city stabbing: one dead

Just from this brief sample, you can see the many ways in which people aggress against one another. You can see why, consequently, it is so important to psychologists that they understand the causes of aggression. The ultimate goal, of course, is to try to use psychological knowledge to help reduce societal levels of aggression.

## EVOLUTIONARY PERSPECTIVES

In the section on pro-social behaviour, we posed a puzzle of evolution: Why is it that people would risk their own lives to benefit others? The existence of aggressive behaviours, however, has posed no similar puzzle. In evolutionary terms, animals commit aggressive behaviours to ensure themselves access to desired mates and to protect the resources that allow themselves and their offspring to survive. In his classic book *On Aggression*, Konrad Lorenz (1966) documented a range of aggressive activity in the animal kingdom. In the course of his review, Lorenz also documented the mechanisms that keep aggression in check: 'A raven can peck out the eye of another with one thrust of its beak, a wolf can rip the jugular vein of another with a single bite. There would be no more ravens and no more wolves if reliable inhibitions did not prevent such actions' (p. 240). On Lorenz's view, this is what sets the human species apart: he argued that humans do not have appropriately evolved mechanisms to *inhibit* their aggressive impulses. Lorenz believed that these inhibitory mechanisms failed to evolve because, until the invention of artificial weapons, humans could not do each other much harm. When weapons appeared, Lorenz suggested that the human species' 'position was very nearly that of a dove which, by some unnatural trick of nature, has suddenly acquired the beak of a raven' (p. 241).

Research in response to Lorenz's work has contradicted his assessment of human aggression in two ways (Lore & Schultz, 1993). First, field research with a variety of animal species suggests that many other species commit the same range of aggressive acts as do humans. For example, even seemingly mild-mannered chimpanzees gang up on and kill their own kind (Goodall, 1986). Aggression in other species is not particularly good news for humans—it just seems that we're no worse—but it does suggest less of an evolutionary discontinuity. Second, research suggests that humans have more inhibitory control over their use of aggression than Lorenz suggested. In fact, humans make choices with respect to their display of aggression conditioned on their social environments. As we will see later in this section, cultures specify norms for circumstances in which aggression is acceptable or required. We will suggest there that cultures themselves play a critical role in determining the extent to which people are 'able' to inhibit aggression.

For answers go to MyPsychLab!

**aggression** Behaviours that cause psychological or physical harm to another individual.

Why do so many species of animals engage in aggressive behaviours? What did Konrad Lorenz believe makes human aggression unique?

Evolutionary analysis suggests that a drive for survival may have endowed many or most species with an innate predisposition toward some forms of violence. For humans, however, it is nonetheless the case that different members of the species are more or less likely to perform aggressive behaviours. We next consider those individual differences in aggression.

## INDIVIDUAL DIFFERENCES

Why are some individuals more aggressive than others? In the context of Lorenz's evolutionary claims, you can see why one hypothesis that researchers have pursued is that there is a genetic component to individual differences in rates of aggression. Researchers have sought an answer to the genetics of aggression using many of the methodologies we've illustrated in earlier chapters. They have, for example, compared the similarity of identical (monozygotic, MZ) and fraternal (dizygotic, DZ) twins with respect to aggressive personalities; in other cases, they have estimated the contributions of nature and nurture by examining children raised in adoptive homes. These studies typically demonstrate a strong genetic component for aggressive behaviour (DiLalla, 2002; Miles & Carey, 1997). For example, MZ twins consistently show higher correlations for aggressiveness than do DZ twins (Arsenault et al., 2003). However, research suggests that genetics may play a stronger and weaker role for different types of aggression.

Researchers collected data on 234 6-year-old twins to assess genetic and environmental contributions to individual differences in *physical* and *social* aggression (Brendgen et al., 2005). Physical aggression represents circumstances in which children get into fights or hit, bite or kick other children. Social aggression represents circumstances in which children spread nasty rumours or try to make others dislike particular classmates. To assess the twins' behaviours for both types of aggression, the researchers obtained ratings from the twins' teachers and their peers. These ratings provided converging evidence that the MZ and DZ twins differed with respect to their similarity levels of aggression. The comparison between MZ and DZ twins suggested that 50 to 60 percent of the variation in physical aggression could be explained by genetic factors. For social aggression, 20 percent of the variation was explained by genetics.

Why might genetics have less influence over social aggression? The researchers speculated that children's inclination to use social aggression might follow from the type of parenting they receive: parents who use shame or guilt to manipulate their children may provide models for the children's later classroom behaviour. Overall, this study supports the conclusion that some individuals have a greater genetic predisposition toward aggression than do others.

Researchers have also focused attention on brain and hormonal differences that may mark a predisposition toward aggressive behaviour. As we saw in Chapter 12, several brain structures, such as the amygdala and portions of cortex, play roles in the expression and regulation of emotion. With respect to aggression, it is critical that brain pathways function effectively so that individuals can control the expression of negative emotion. If, for example, people experience inappropriate levels of activation in the amygdala, they may not be able to inhibit the negative emotions that lead to aggressive behaviours (Davidson et al., 2000).

Researchers have begun to document relationships between gene variations and amygdala structure. For example, a gene called *MAOA* has been implicated as a genetic marker for individual differences in aggression. The *low expressive* variant put people at greater risk than the *high expressive* variant. Brain scans using fMRI revealed that individuals with the low expressive variant have amygdalas with smaller volume than those with the high expressive variant of the gene (Meyer-Lindenberg et al., 2006).

Attention has also focused on the neurotransmitter serotonin. Research suggests that inappropriate levels of serotonin may impair the brain's ability to regulate negative emotions and impulsive behaviour (Enserink, 2000). For example, one study demonstrated that men with higher life histories of aggression showed decreased response in the serotonin system to a drug (fenfluramine) that typically has a considerable impact on that system (Manuck et al., 2002). Recall from Chapter 14 that researchers have begun to explore consequences of variations in the actual genes that underlie serotonin function. In this study as well, the researchers showed that a particular genetic variation was likely to affect serotonin function in a way that put people at risk for high levels of aggressive behaviour.

Finally, studies suggest that some individual differences in aggression may reflect muted stress responses. For example, one project related levels of the stress hormone *cortisol* to the aggressive behaviour of 7- to 12-year-old boys: The most aggressive boys had the most muted stress response (McBurnett et al., 2000). These results suggest that some individuals may not experience the types of physiological stress responses that inhibit most people from behaving in a dramatically aggressive fashion: Their bodies do not experience the negative consequences of negative behaviours and emotions.

Personality research on aggression has pointed to the importance of differentiating categories of aggressive behaviours: People with different personality profiles are likely to engage in different types of aggression. One important distinction separates *impulsive aggression* from *instrumental aggression* (Little et al., 2003; Ramírez & Andreu, 2006). **Impulsive aggression** is produced in reaction to situations and is emotion driven: people respond with aggressive acts in the heat of the moment. If you see people get into a fistfight after a car accident, that is impulsive aggression. **Instrumental aggression** is goal directed (the aggression serves as the *instrument* for some goal) and cognition based: people carry out acts of aggression, with premeditated thought, to achieve specific aims. If you see someone knock an elderly woman down to steal her purse, that is instrumental aggression. Research has confirmed that those individuals with high propensities toward one or the other of these types of violence have distinct sets of personality traits (Caprara et al., 1996). For example, individuals who reported a propensity toward impulsive aggression were likely, in general, to be characterised as high on the factor of *emotional responsivity*. That is, they were likely, in general, to report highly emotional responses to a range of situations. By contrast, individuals who reported a propensity toward instrumental aggression were likely to score high on the factor of *positive evaluation of violence*. These individuals believed that many forms of violence are justified, and they also did not accept moral responsibility for aggressive behaviours. You learn from this analysis that not all types of aggression arise from the same underlying personality factors.

Most people are not at the extremes of either impulsive or instrumental aggression: They do not lose their tempers at the least infraction or purposefully commit acts of violence. Even so, in some situations, even the most mild-mannered individuals will perform aggressive acts. We look now at the types of situations that may often provide the triggering conditions for aggression.

# SITUATIONAL INFLUENCES

Take a moment now to think back to the last time you engaged in aggressive behaviour. It may not have been physical aggression: you may just have been verbally abusive toward some other individual, with the intent of causing psychological distress. How would you explain why that particular situation gave rise to aggression? Did you have a long history of conflict with the individual or was it just a onetime interaction? Were you inclined toward an aggressive act because of something very specific or were you just feeling frustrated at that moment? These are some of the questions researchers have asked when they've examined the links between situations and aggression. When we've asked our own students to think about their aggressive acts, they've given us a variety of answers, as you will see in what follows.

## Frustration-aggression hypothesis

> *I'd been having a really bad day. I needed to register late for a course. I couldn't find anyone to help me. When I was told for the thousandth time, 'You've got to go to a different office', I got so angry I practically kicked a hole in the door.*

This anecdote provides an instance of a general relationship captured by the **frustration-aggression hypothesis** (Dollard et al., 1939). According to this hypothesis, *frustration* occurs in situations in which people are prevented or blocked from attaining their goals; a rise in frustration then leads to a greater probability of aggression. The link between frustration and aggression has obtained a high level of empirical support (Berkowitz, 1993, 1998). For example, children who are frustrated in their expectation that they will be allowed to play with highly attractive toys act aggressively toward those toys when they finally have an opportunity to play (Barker et al., 1941). Researchers have used this relationship to explain aggression at both the personal and societal levels.

Do you recognise this news story? A man gets fired from a job and goes back to kill the boss who fired him, as well as several co-workers. Could this count as an instance of frustration (that is, the frustrated goal of earning a living) leading to aggression? To provide a general answer to this question, a team of researchers examined the relationship between San Francisco's unemployment rate and the rate at which people in that city were committed for being 'dangerous to others.' This analysis allows for predictions across a whole community: What unemployment rate is likely to lead to the highest levels of violence? The researchers found that violence increased as unemployment increased, but only to a certain point. When unemployment got too high, violence began to fall again. Why might that be? The researchers speculated that people's fears that they too might lose their jobs helped inhibit frustration-driven tendencies toward violence (Catalano et al., 1997, 2002).

**frustration-aggression hypothesis** According to this hypothesis, frustration occurs where people are prevented or blocked from attaining their goals; a rise in frustration leads to a greater probability of aggression.

**impulsive aggression** Cognition-based and goal-directed aggression carried out with premeditated thought to achieve specific aims.

**instrumental aggression** Cognition-based and goal-directed aggression carried out with premeditated thought to achieve specific aims.

This study suggests how individual and societal forces interact to produce a net level of violence. We can predict a certain level of aggression based on the frustration each individual experiences in an economy with rising unemployment. However, as people realise that expressions of aggression may imperil their own employment, violence is inhibited. You can probably recognise these forces in your day-to-day experiences: There are many situations in which you might feel sufficiently frustrated to express aggression, but you also understand that an expression of aggression will work against your long-term best interest.

Frustration doesn't always lead to aggression. When, for example, the frustration is brought about unintentionally—suppose a child spills juice on his mother's new dress—people are less likely to become aggressive than when the action is intentional (Burnstein & Worchel, 1962). At the same time, other situations that are not frustrating with respect to goals, but bring about negative emotional states, can also lead to aggression. We see such a situation in another student anecdote.

## Temperature and aggression

*It was a hot summer day, and the air conditioning in my car was broken. This guy cut me off. I chased after him and tried to run him off the road.*

Is there a relationship between temperature and aggression? Consider the data plotted in **Figure 17.5**. This figure is taken from a study that examined the effects of temperature on assaults for a 2-year period in Minneapolis, Minnesota; the plot is based on 36,617 reported assaults (Bushman et al., 2005). As you can see, for the hours 9:00 p.m. to 2:59 a.m., there is a strong relationship between how cold or hot it is and how likely it is that people will commit assaults.

Why might this be so? An explanation of these data relies on both societal and psychological forces. At a societal level, you probably guessed that it's more likely that people will commit assault when they are more likely to be out and about. That is, in warmer weather, people are more likely to be outdoors and, therefore, are also more likely to be 'available' as assault victims. You can also

Why do some types of day-to-day experiences make even the calmest people contemplate aggressive acts?

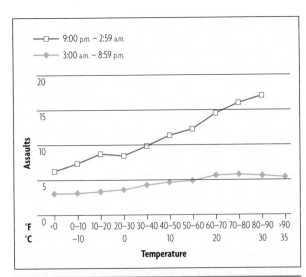

### Figure 17.5

**Temperature and aggression**
The figure presents average number of assaults (in a three-hour period) as a function of the temperature in that period. For the times of day in which people do not have sleep, school, work or family obligations, aggression rises steadily as the temperature warms up.

From B. Bushman, M.C. Wang, & C.A.Anderson, "Is the Curve Relating Temperature to Aggression Linear or Curvilinear?" *Journal of Personality and Social Psychology, 89*(1), 62–66. Copyright © 2005 American Psychological Association. Reprinted with permission.

provide the same analysis for time of day: in the 9:00 p.m. to 2:59 a.m. hours, people are typically less constrained by work or other responsibilities. Furthermore, by the late evening hours, people may have been drinking alcohol or using other substances that lower their inhibition for aggression (Ito et al., 1996). By contrast, during the hours of 3:00 a.m. to 8:59 p.m., people are typically involved in sleep, school, work and family obligations—which makes it more difficult for them to be involved in assaults.

Given all these societal explanations for increased aggression, do we also need to invoke psychology? The answer is yes. Another important component of an explanation for the data in Figure 17.5 is the way in which people cope with and interpret the discomfort associated with high temperatures. Recall the discussion of appraisal and emotions in Chapter 12. Suppose on a 35° day you're having a conversation with someone that makes you feel hot and uncomfortable. Do you attribute the emotion to the temperature or to your adversary? To the extent that you misattribute your emotion to another person, rather than to the situation, you're more likely to become aggressive toward that person. (You might recognise this from Chapter 16 as a dangerous consequence of the fundamental attribution error.) Why does heat matter most in the late evening and early morning? As the day goes on, it may become harder to remember 'I'm feeling this way because it's hot' and not just conclude 'I'm feeling this way because this jerk is making me crazy'.

A third student anecdote illustrates how situations elicit hostility that gets amplified over time.

## Direct provocation and escalation

*I was sitting in the library trying to get some work done. These two women were having a really loud conversation that was bothering a lot of people. I asked them to quiet down, and they pretty much ignored me. I asked again about five minutes later, and they only started talking louder. Finally, I told them they were both stupid, ugly jerks and that if they didn't shut up I was going to pick them up and throw them out of the library. That worked.*

It's not going to surprise you that *direct provocation* will also give rise to aggression. That is, when someone behaves in a way that makes you angry or upset—and you think that behaviour was intentional—you are more likely to respond with some form of physical or verbal aggression (Johnson & Rule, 1986). The effects of direct provocation are consistent with the general idea that situations that produce negative affect will lead to aggression. The intentionality of the act matters because you are less likely to interpret an unintentional act in a negative way. (Recall that we made the similar observation that frustration is less likely to lead to aggression when it is brought about unintentionally.)

Researchers have looked at issues of provocation to assess the causes of extreme violence in schools.

Researchers reviewed 15 instances of shootings that occurred in schools between 1995 and 2001 (Leary et al., 2003). The most publicised of these was the incident at Columbine High School in 1999 that led to the deaths of 12 students and one teacher. All told, in that 6-year period students killed nearly 40 individuals including, in some cases, themselves. The researchers examined extensive reports of the 15 incidents to determine the extent to which the perpetrators had been the victims of either chronic teasing, rejection or bullying or an acute episode of humiliation or romantic rejection. These factors were present in 12 of the 15 incidents. For example, the perpetrators at Columbine left behind videotapes in which they recounted the teasing and ostracism they believed they had endured. In several of the incidents, the perpetrator's victims were drawn from the group of peers who had mistreated them.

Note that these data in no way *excuse* the killer's actions—they only help to *explain* them. In most of these situations, there were other causal forces in play. For example, in 10 of the 15 incidents, the perpetrators had shown previous signs of psychological distress such as depression and animal abuse. Still, it's important to keep in mind that provocation can lead to extreme acts of aggression.

A second characteristic of the anecdote with which we opened this section, beyond provocation, is *escalation*: Because less intense responses to the provocation had no effect, the student's response became more aggressive over time. Researchers have demonstrated that aggressive responses will, in fact, escalate in the face of a persistent annoyance. For example, in one study, participants were unable to get members of a group to share resources (Mikolic et al., 1997). (The group members were privately instructed by the experiments not to cooperate.) Over the course of the session, the participants' verbal remarks progressed from *demanding statements* ('We need it now'), through *angry statements* ('I'm really getting annoyed with you'), all the way to *abusive statements* (for example, 'You guys are total jerks'). In fact, the strength of the responses followed a very orderly sequence of escalation. The experimenters suggested that people have learned an *escalation script*. This memory structure encodes cultural norms for the sequence with which people should ratchet up the aggressiveness of their responses to continuing provocation. Can you see how the escalation script also refers back to the relationship between frustration and aggression? The failures of the initial attempts to change the situation likely lead to feelings of frustration that also will increase the likelihood of more intense aggression.

We've now considered some of the situational forces that may lead you to produce psychological or physical aggression. It's important to note that our examples all refer to impulsive aggression rather than to instrumental aggression. As we explained earlier, instrumental aggression refers to circumstances in which people use aggression to achieve an end—for example, when muggers use physical force to commit their crimes. That type of aggression must be explained as a component of a larger theory of criminality. We have been concerned here largely with circumstances in which ordinary individuals find themselves committing impulsive aggressive acts. In the next section, we will see, even so, that cultural differences constrain levels of both individual and criminal aggression.

## CULTURAL CONSTRAINTS

We have seen so far that aggressive behaviours are part of your evolutionary inheritance and that certain situations are more likely to evoke aggressive behaviour. Even so, several types of data suggest that the probability that an individual will display aggression is highly constrained by cultural values and norms (Bond, 2004). Let's see why culture has an impact on individuals' aggressive behaviours.

**Construals of the self and aggressive behaviour** To begin an examination of culture and aggression, we return to a distinction in cultural construals of the self that has loomed large in several places in *Psychology and Life*: As explained earlier, most Western cultures embody *independent construals of self,* whereas most Eastern cultures embody *interdependent construals of self* (Markus & Kitayama, 1991). What are the consequences for aggressive behaviour? Studies have shown that if you think of yourself as fundamentally interconnected with other members of your culture, you will be less likely to respond aggressively—an act of aggression, after all, would be an act against your 'self' (Bergeron & Schneider, 2005). For example, in one study Japanese and U.S. preschoolers,

Why might Gandhi's philosophy of nonviolent resistance have been particularly appropriate for the culture of India?

are used to protect property or redress personal insults (Cohen & Nisbett, 1994).

Researchers arranged for male university students—northerners and southerners—to endure a mild insult: while the participant walked down a hallway, an experimental confederate bumped each participant with his shoulder and called him an 'asshole.' (Students in the control group did not experience this event.) The researchers predicted that southerners would react more dramatically than their northern peers to the bump and insult. One measure the researchers used to gauge the students' reactions was based on the game of 'chicken' in which two people drive toward each other until one swerves out of the way. In this case, a second confederate marched directly at each approaching participant. The researchers measured how close each participant got to the confederate before he changed path. As you can see in **Figure 17.6**, the mild insult had a dramatic effect on southern students' behaviour. Without an insult, they were actually more polite than the northerners—they 'gave way' sooner. However, when southerners had been bumped, they turned away considerably later (Cohen et al., 1996).

Many people in the United States share the general sense that southern culture is more polite than northern culture—you'd rather ask directions from someone

average age roughly 4½ years, were asked to use dolls to act out endings to stories involving conflicts (Zahn-Waxler et al., 1996). The U.S. children scored considerably higher both on measures of aggressive verbalisations— U.S. children were more likely to say things such as 'I hate —and aggressive behaviours—U.S. children were more likely to act out behaviours with the dolls such as pushing and hitting. This experiment suggests that the Japanese children have already internalised the cultural norm of interdependence that weighs against bringing harm to others. The U.S. children, by contrast, show evidence for an independent self that must be protected from others' insults.

Although we have identified this major cultural divide between independence and interdependence, it is also possible to find more fine-grained cultural differences nested within this overarching perspective. For example, **Richard Nisbett** (Nisbett & Cohen, 1996) and his colleagues have extensively studied regional attitudes and behaviours within the United States with respect to uses of aggression. One consistent difference that has emerged is that southern behaviour is guided by a *culture of honour*, in which 'even small disputes become contests for reputation and social status' (Cohen et al., 1996, p. 945). The culture of honour doesn't sanction all forms of aggression—only those aggressive behaviours that

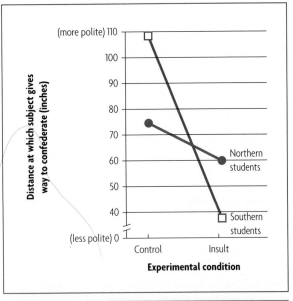

### Figure 17.6

**The effects of insults on northerners and southerners**
Northern and southern students in the experimental group suffered a minor insult. Although southerners were more polite without an insult, they became considerably less likely to give way in a game of 'chicken' after they had been insulted.

From Cohen et al., 'Insult Agression and Southern Culture and Honor,' *Journal of Personality and Social Psychology, 70,* 945–960. Copyright © American Psychological Association. Reprinted with permission.

in Richmond than someone in New York City. This experiment echoes that belief, in the sense that southerners in the control group made way for the confederate earlier than did their northern peers. However, this general aura of politeness broke down quite quickly when an attack had been made on the students' sense of honour. Thus, even within the overarching independent construal of self that characterises most U.S. citizens, southern men react more sharply when that sense of self is challenged and their 'honour' is on the line (Nisbett & Cohen, 1996; Vandello & Cohen, 2004).

**Norms of aggressive behaviour** Another important cultural factor is the relative availability of aggressive models in the environment. In Chapter 6, we discussed research suggesting that children very readily adapt aggressive behaviours from watching adult models. For example, children who watched adult models punching, hitting and kicking a large plastic BoBo doll later showed a greater frequency of the same behaviours than did children in control conditions who had not observed the aggressive models (Bandura et al., 1963). We also suggested in Chapter 6 that television in the United States beams an enormous number of aggressive models directly into children's homes—exposure to violence is highly related to adult levels of aggression (Comstock & Scharrer, 1999; Huesmann et al., 2003).

Researchers have developed the *general aggression model* to explain the relationship between exposure to violent media (television, movies, and so on) and aggressive behaviour. This model suggests that people acquire a general set of aggression-related knowledge structures through their experiences of media violence: on this view, 'each violent media episode is essentially one more trial to learn that the world is a dangerous place, that aggression is an appropriate way to deal with conflict and anger, and that aggression works' (Bushman & Anderson, 2002, p. 1680). Consider a study that examined the short-term impact of violent video games.

> Researchers asked 224 college undergraduates to play either violent video games (for example, Mortal Kombat) or non-violent video games (for example, 3D Pinball) (Bushman & Anderson, 2002). After playing for 20 minutes, the participants were asked to complete what they believed to be an unrelated task. The participants read incomplete stories and indicated what they thought would happen next. For example, in one story, Todd was rear-ended when he braked quickly at a yellow light. Participants wrote answers to the question, 'What happens next?' Those students who played the violent video games gave consistently more aggressive outcomes for the stories. For example, participants suggested that Todd would kick out a window or stab or shoot the other driver.

This study illustrates that those students who had just played violent video games versus non-violent video games were ready to provide much more aggressive responses. In general, children and young adults who play video games have higher levels of aggressive behaviours and aggression-related thoughts and feelings (Anderson & Bushman, 2001).

> With the increasing popularity of violent video games across all cultures, aggression theories suggest that interactive violent media (violent video games) are perhaps more impacting on increasing aggressive behaviour than non-interactive aggressive media (e.g. TV and movies). An Australian study investigated this hypothesis by inviting 150 University of Sydney students to watch a 2-hour episode of the war mini-series *Band of Brothers* which depicted 6 June 1944 D-Day invasion of Normandy, France. Subjects were asked to rate how they felt about the violence they witnessed in the program at the end of the viewing, with most showing feelings of heightened aggression, but also reporting feelings of sadness and empathy for casualties they saw on film. One week later, subjects were asked to play a violent video game that was similar to the episode they watched on TV. After playing the game for more than 1 hour, both male and female participants were asked the same questions about their feelings of aggression. Each reported higher aggression levels than when they watched the D-Day invasion episode of *Band of Brothers*. They also reported little to no remorse for their actions of killing characters in the war game. Perhaps this is due to the fact that animation does not substitute for the reality of actually killing a living human being, but when asked to recall that what they were playing in the video game happened in real-life history, each subject still reported little remorse for killing German soldiers in the game (Toh & Campbell, 2008).

Exposure to these games—and other violent media—makes the world seem more dangerous. In that context, aggression becomes an appropriate response to a dangerous world.

Unfortunately, for many children the world does present real dangers. Children may be exposed to aggressive acts in their homes. We noted in Chapter 6 that children who are physically punished often begin themselves to use aggression as a tactic for controlling others' behaviours. In addition, many children in Australia grow up in inner-city communities in which violence is daily and chronic. Researchers have only begun to explore the consequences of exposure to violence for children's mental health and their inclination to aggressive behaviour (Bingenheimer et al., 2005).

We end this section on cultural norms for aggressive behaviour by noting that those norms can be quite local and quite stable. Consider two adjacent Zapotec villages in the state of Oaxaca, Mexico (Scott, 1992). One of the villages is violent and the other non-violent: the violent village has a murder rate five times as great as the non-violent village. The villages have been on the same spots since at least the 1500s; they are highly similar with respect to religion and economics. More or less, the only explanation for their differing characters is the stability of culture: one way or another each village has acquired a characteristic level of violence, and that has stayed stable over time. This is a salient real-world example of the processes of norm transmission and preservation we described earlier in this chapter. Similarly, with its modern modes of mass communication, Australia has become a very large village that preserves norms of aggressive behaviour.

In this section we have described far too many reasons why people might engage in aggressive behaviour. We turn now to aggression on a broader scale. We examine the forces that bring groups of people into conflict and interventions that might help alleviate some of those conflicts.

**peace psychology** An interdisciplinary approach to the prevention of nuclear war and the maintenance of peace.

For answers go to MyPsychLab!

## RECAP CHECKPOINT
### Aggression

- From an evolutionary perspective, aggressive behaviours arose because people needed to ensure their ability to preserve their genes.

- Individual differences in aggressive behaviour are reflected both in genetic analyses and in brain and hormone function.

- Different personality profiles predict propensities toward either impulsive or instrumental aggression.

- Although there are inhibitions to aggressive behaviour, situations arise that prompt people to respond aggressively.

- Frustration can lead to aggression; ongoing irritation will escalate the level of aggression.

- Different cultures provide different norms for aggressive behaviour depending, in part, on cultural construals of the self.

### CONCEPT QUESTIONS

1. What claim did Karl Lorenz make about human aggression?

2. Why do researchers believe that genetic factors play a role in aggression?

3. What is the relationship between frustration and aggression?

4. Why do experiences of violent media affect aggressive thoughts and behaviours?

### CRITICAL THINKING

Recall the experiment that assessed the impact of violent video games. Why was it important that participants believed the task in which they provided endings for stories was unrelated to their video game playing?

# THE PSYCHOLOGY OF CONFLICT AND PEACE

We begin this final section on a sombre note. In these early years of the 21st century, the globe is still littered with instances of catastrophic violence born from religious, racial and cultural prejudice. What can be done? In the opening chapter of *Psychology and Life*, we characterised psychologists as a 'rather optimistic group' because they believe that the theories and results of psychology can be used to better people's lives. In these final sections of *Psychology and Life*, we wish to carry through on that optimistic message. Although we will begin by documenting more of the psychological forces that can lead to devastating behaviours, that discussion will generate insights that can form the basis for constructive change. Our endpoint will be a discussion of **peace psychology**, a multidisciplinary effort to use social science knowledge to further the cause of world peace. This is the note of optimism on which we wish you to end your first experience of psychology.

We begin with perhaps the most classic study in the social psychological canon—research carried out by Stanley Milgram in an effort to understand some of the vast horrors of World War II.

## OBEDIENCE TO AUTHORITY

What made thousands of Nazis willing to follow Hitler's orders and send millions of Jews to the gas chambers? Did character defects lead them to carry out orders blindly? Did they have no moral values? How can we explain the willingness of cult members to take their own lives and the lives of others? How about you? Are there any conditions under which you would blindly obey an order from your religious leader to poison others and then commit suicide? Could you imagine being part of the massacre of hundreds of innocent citizens of the Vietnamese village of My Lai by U.S. soldiers who were following the orders of their superiors (Hersh, 1971; Opton, 1970, 1973)? Your answer—as ours used to be—is most likely, 'No! What kind of person do you think I am?' After reading this section, we hope you may be more willing to answer, 'Maybe. I don't know for sure'. Depending on the power of the social forces operating, you might do what other human beings have done in those situations, however horrible and alien their actions may seem—to you and to them—outside that setting.

The most convincing demonstration of situational power over individual behaviour was created by Stanley Milgram, a student of Solomon Asch. Milgram's research (1965, 1974) showed that the blind obedience of Nazis during World War II was less a product of dispositional characteristics (their unusual personality or German national character) than it was the outcome of situational forces that could engulf anyone. Milgram's program of obedience research is one of the most controversial because of its significant implications for real-world phenomena and the ethical issues it raises.

### The obedience paradigm

To separate the variables of personality and situation, Milgram used a series of 19 separately controlled laboratory experiments involving more than 1,000 participants. Milgram's first experiments were conducted at Yale University, with male residents of New Haven and surrounding communities who received payment for their participation. In later variations, Milgram took his obedience laboratory away from the university. He set up a storefront research unit in Bridgeport, Connecticut, recruiting through newspaper ads a broad cross-section of the population, varying widely in age, occupation and education and including members of both sexes.

Milgram's basic experimental paradigm involved individual participants delivering a series of what they thought were extremely painful electric shocks to another person. These volunteers thought they were participating in a scientific study of memory and learning. They were led to believe that the educational purpose of the study was to discover how punishment affects memory, so that learning could be improved through the proper balance of reward and punishment. In their *social roles* as *teachers*, the participants were to punish each error made by someone playing the role of *learner*. The major rule they were told to follow was to increase the level of shock each time the learner made an error until the learning was errorless. The white-coated experimenter acted as the *legitimate authority* figure—he presented the rules, arranged for the assignment of roles (by a rigged drawing of lots), and ordered the teachers to do their jobs whenever they hesitated or dissented. The dependent variable was the final level of shock—on a shock machine that went up to 450 volts in small, 15-volt steps—that a teacher gave before refusing to continue to obey the authority.

### The test situation

The study was staged to make a participant think that, by following orders, he or she was causing pain and suffering and perhaps even killing an innocent person. Each teacher had been given a sample shock of 45 volts to feel the amount of pain it caused. The learner was a pleasant, mild-mannered man, about 50 years old, who mentioned something about a heart condition but was willing to go along with the procedure. He was strapped into an 'electric chair' in the next room and communicated with the teacher via an intercom. His task was to memorise pairs of words, giving the second word in a pair when he heard the first one. The learner soon began making errors—according to a prearranged schedule—and the teacher began shocking the learner. The protests of the victim rose with the shock level. At 75 volts, he began to moan and grunt; at 150 volts, he demanded to be released from the experiment; at 180 volts, he cried out that he could not stand the pain any longer. At 300 volts, he insisted that he would no longer take part in the experiment and must be freed. He yelled out about his heart condition and screamed. If a teacher hesitated or protested delivering the next shock, the experimenter said, 'The experiment requires that you continue' or 'You have no other choice, you *must* go on.'

As you might imagine, the situation was stressful for the participants. Most participants complained and protested, repeatedly insisting they could not continue. Women participants often were in tears as they dissented. That the experimental situation produced considerable conflict in the participants is readily apparent from their protests:

- 180 volts delivered: 'He can't stand it! I'm not going to kill that man in there! You hear him hollering? He's hollering. He can't stand it. What if something happens to him? . . . I mean, who is going to take the responsibility if anything happens to that gentleman?' [The experimenter accepts responsibility.] 'All right.'

- 195 volts delivered: 'You see he's hollering. Hear that. Gee, I don't know.' [The experimenter says, 'The experiment requires that you go on.'] 'I know it does, sir, but I mean—huh—he don't know what he's in for. He's up to 195 volts' (Milgram, 1965, p. 67).

Even when there was only silence from the learner's room, the teacher was ordered to keep shocking him more and more strongly, all the way up to the button that was marked 'Danger: Severe Shock XXX (450 volts).'

### To shock or not to shock?

When 40 psychiatrists were asked by Milgram to predict the performance of

Milgram's obedience experiment: the 'teacher' (participant) with experimenter (authority figure), the shock generator, and the 'learner' (the experimenter's confederate). What aspects of the situation affected the likelihood that the teachers would continue to the maximum shock level?

participants in this experiment, they estimated that most would not go beyond 150 volts (based on a description of the experiment). In their professional opinions, fewer than 4 percent of the participants would still be obedient at 300 volts, and only about 0.1 percent would continue all the way to 450 volts. The psychiatrists presumed that only those few individuals who were *abnormal* in some way, sadists who enjoyed inflicting pain on others, would blindly obey orders to continue up to the maximum shock.

The psychiatrists based their evaluations on presumed *dispositional* qualities of people who would engage in such abnormal behaviour; they were, however, overlooking the power of this special situation to influence the thinking and actions of most people caught up in its social context. The remarkable and disturbing conclusion is just how wrong these experts were: *The majority of participants obeyed the authority fully.* No participant quit below 300 volts. Sixty-five percent delivered the maximum 450 volts to the learner. Note that most people *dissented* verbally, but the majority did not *disobey* behaviourally. From the point of view of the victim, that's a critical difference. If you were the victim, would it matter much that the participants said they didn't want to continue hurting you (they dissented), if they then shocked you repeatedly (they obeyed)?

The results of the Milgram studies were so unexpected that researchers worked hard to rule out alternative interpretations of the results. One possibility was that the participants did not really believe the 'cover story' of the experiment. They might have believed that the victim was not really getting hurt. This alternative was ruled out by a study that made the effects of being obedient vivid, immediate and direct for the participants. College students thought they were training a puppy by shocking him each time he made a mistake. The students actually saw the puppy jump and heard him squeal each time they pressed a button to activate an electrified grid beneath his paws. How many people would continue to shock the puppy and watch him suffer? Even under these vivid circumstances, three fourths of all students delivered the maximum shock possible (Sheridan & King, 1972).

Another alternative explanation for participants' behaviour is that the effect is limited to the *demand characteristics* of the experimental situation. **Demand characteristics** are cues in an experimental setting that influence participants' perceptions of what is expected of them and systematically influence their behaviour. Suppose Milgram's participants guessed that his results would be more interesting if they kept giving shocks—so they played along. Further research showed that obedience to authority does not rely on the demands of an unusual experimental setting. It can happen in any natural setting.

A team of researchers performed the following field study to test the power of obedience in the natural setting of a hospital. A nurse (the participant) received a call from a staff doctor whom she had not met. He told her to administer some medication to a patient so that it could take effect by the time he arrived. He would sign the drug order after he got to the ward. The doctor ordered a dose of 20 milligrams of a drug called *Astroten*. The label on the container of Astroten stated that 5 milligrams was the usual dose and warned that the maximum dose was 10 milligrams.

Would a nurse administer an excessive dose of a drug on the basis of a telephone call from an unfamiliar person when doing so was contrary to standard medical practice? When this dilemma was *described* to 12 nurses, 10 *said* they would disobey. However, what the nurses *did* was another, by now familiar, story. When another group of them was actually in the situation, almost every nurse obeyed. Twenty-one of 22 had started to pour the medication (actually a harmless substance) before a physician researcher stopped them (Hofling et al., 1966).

These results suggest that Milgram's findings cannot be attributed solely to participants responding to the demands of the experiment.

**Why do people obey authority?** Milgram's research suggests that, to understand why people obey authority, you need to look closely at the psychological forces at work in the situation. We saw earlier how often situational factors constrain behaviours; in Milgram's research, we see an especially vivid instance of that general principle. Milgram and other researchers manipulated a number of aspects of the experimental circumstances to demonstrate that the obedience effect is overwhelmingly due to situational variables and not personality variables. **Figure 17.7** displays the level of obedience found in different situations. Obedience is quite high, for example, when a peer first models obedience, when a participant acts as an *intermediary bystander* assisting another person who actually delivers the shock, or when the victim (the learner) is physically remote from the teacher. Obedience is quite low when the learner demands to be shocked, when two authorities give contradictory commands, or when the authority figure is the victim. These findings all point to the idea that the *situation*, and not differences among individual participants, largely controlled behaviour.

Would you risk your life to defy authority in defence of your beliefs, as this young Chinese student did in a student-led rebellion?

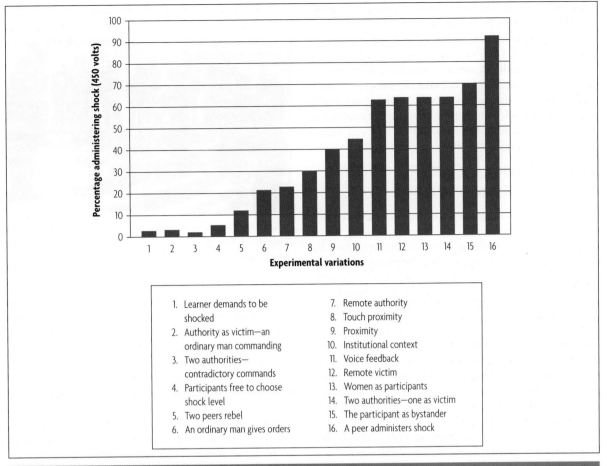

**Figure 17.7**

**Obedience in Milgram's Experiments**
The graph shows a profile of weak to strong obedience effects across Milgram's many experimental variations.

From *The Obedience Experiments*, A.G. Miller, 'Obedience in Milgram's Experiments.' Copyright © 1986 Praeger. Reproduced with permission.

Two reasons people obey authority in these situations can be traced to the effects of *normative* and *informational* sources of influence, which we discussed earlier: people want to be liked (normative influence), and they want to be right (informational influence). They tend to do what others are doing or requesting in order to be socially acceptable and approved. In addition, when in an ambiguous, novel situation—like the experimental situation—people rely on others for cues as to what is the appropriate and correct way to behave. They are more likely to do so when experts or credible communicators tell them what to do. A third factor in the Milgram paradigm is that participants were probably confused about *how* to *disobey*; nothing they said in dissent satisfied the authority. If they had a simple, direct way out of the situation—for example, by pressing a 'quit' button—it is likely more would have disobeyed (Ross, 1988). Finally, obedience to authority in this experimental situation is part of an *ingrained habit* that is learned by children in many different settings—obey authority without question (Brown, 1986). This heuristic usually serves society well when authorities are legitimate and deserving of obedience. The problem is that the rule gets over applied.

Blind obedience to authority means obeying any and all authority figures simply because of their ascribed status, regardless of whether they are unjust or just in their requests and commands.

**The Milgram experiments and you** What is the personal significance to you of this obedience research? What choices will you make when faced with moral dilemmas throughout your life? Take a moment to reflect on the types of obedience to authority situations that might arise in your day-to-day experience. Suppose you were a sales clerk would you cheat customers if your boss encouraged such behaviour? Suppose you were a member of parliament, would you vote along party lines, rather than vote with your conscience?

Milgram's obedience research challenges the myth that evil lurks in the minds of evil people—the bad 'they' who are different from the good 'us' or 'you,' who would never do such things. Our purpose in recounting these findings is not to debase human nature, but to make clear that even normal, well-meaning individuals are subject to the potential for frailty in the face of strong situational and social forces.

Finally, we wish to add a note on heroism. Suppose the majority of people who are comparable to you yield to powerful group forces. In our view, if you are able to resist, that qualifies you as heroic. The hero is the person who can act mindfully, out of conscience, when others are all conforming, or who can take the moral high road when others are standing by silently, allowing evil deeds to go unchallenged. Perhaps your knowledge of situational forces that make possible the 'banality of evil' can nudge you in the direction of heroism.

## THE PSYCHOLOGY OF GENOCIDE AND WAR

We have seen so far that the human species has a distinct predilection to obey authority. However, it takes more than an appreciation of this feature of human nature to explain why at some times and in some places one group undertakes purposeful violence toward another group. In this section, we will analyse some of the historical and psychological forces that lead populations to pursue the path of highly organised aggression.

**Genocide** At many times in human history, groups have initiated campaigns of **genocide**—the systematic destruction of other groups. Psychologist **Ervin Staub** (1989, 2000) has studied campaigns of genocide throughout history and has offered an account of the sets of cultural and psychological forces that make campaigns of terror possible:

The starting point is often severely difficult life conditions for members of a society—harsh economic circumstances, political upheaval, and so on.

Under these conditions of difficulty, people will intensify the ordinary impulse to define in-groups and out-groups that we described in Chapter 16. In this case, out-groups become *scapegoats* for the ills of society. In many instances, as in Nazi Germany, the scapegoating becomes part of the cultural or political ideology shared by the nation's leaders and citizens.

Because the scapegoat group is blamed for society's ills, it becomes easy to justify violence against them. These incidents of violence lead to *just world thinking* (Lerner, 1980): Perpetrators and bystanders come to believe—because we live in a just world—that the victims must have done something to bring the violence upon themselves. Thus Germans of the Nazi era came to believe that the Jews deserved their fate because of the imagined harm they had done to the German state.

The violence also comes to justify itself—to stop the violence would mean to admit that it had been wrong to begin with. Furthermore, when regimes carry out organised violence without sanctions from other nations, the world community's passivity is taken as evidence of the justice of the regime's actions. This was the case with the 'ethnic cleansing' massacres that followed the dissolution of Yugoslavia in 1991—although images of the massacres were widely transmitted, the world community took no action for several years.

Consider the case of Cambodia (Hinton, 1996). The situation began with difficult life conditions: Starting in

In Salman, Iraq, soldiers and forensic experts examine a mass grave found early in 2007. What sequence of events may create a context for mass murders?

the late 1960s, the country suffered economic hardships as well as bombings by the United States as war spread to Cambodia from its neighbour Vietnam. A new regime began to identify scapegoats, and the scapegoats became the targets of extreme violence: The communists who captured the city of Phnom Penh in 1975 identified a number of ideological enemies who needed to be eliminated to put a new society into place. Former military and political leaders were arrested and often executed. The definition of 'class enemies' swiftly became broader, however, as teachers, students, bureaucrats and professionals were denounced as potential traitors. The killing gathered momentum because it was in service to such a powerful ideology and a clearly defined goal: the country must be rid of its internal enemies. Finally, as has most often been the case, the world community did not intervene.

**Concepts and images of the 'enemy'** We have suggested that an important way station on the path to genocide is scapegoating. We can see the same process at work, even when the endpoint is not systematic murder. Consider the attitudes of young Australians towards Muslims. In a survey of 551 Victorian school children from years 10 and 11, 40 per cent of respondents said that Muslims were 'unclean', while a similar number said they 'acted strangely' (Ata, 2006). Prejudice and willingness to discriminate do not arise spontaneously; they require societal circumstances that foster the belief that an 'enemy' is consuming scarce resources. This sets the context for violence.

When regimes scapegoat the 'enemy', they often also *dehumanise* them—they attempt to convince people to conceive of the group as nonhuman objects to be hated and destroyed. This process of dehumanisation is also particularly critical to the conduct of war. Although most cultures oppose individual aggression as a crime, nations train millions of soldiers to kill. The challenge for leaders is to convert the act of murder into patriotism (Harle, 2000). Part of this mass social influence involves dehumanising the soldiers of the other side into 'the enemy.' This dehumanisation is accomplished by political rhetoric and by the media, in their vivid depictions of the enemy.

**genocide** The systematic destruction of one group of people, often an ethnic or racial group, by another.

Figure 17.8

Faces of the enemy
How does military psychology convert killing into patriotism? Note how in each of these caricatures the designated enemy is given monstrous and dehumanised characteristics.

According to army veterans, a soldier's most important weapon in war is not a gun but this internalised view of the hated 'enemy' (see **Figure 17.8**). Thus young soldiers become psychologically programmed to be wartime killers by these distorted images of anyone their government decides to label as the enemy.

In many cases, the images will not be literal representations but rather the mental images that politicians invoke to rally populations and send troops off to war. For example, in the lead-up to the war in Iraq in 2003, the Bush Administration in and U.S. and the Howard government in Australia worked to frame its citizens' conception of Saddam Hussein (Altheide & Grimes, 2005). Perhaps the most famous image from this period emerged in George W. Bush's State of the Union address in 2002, in which he characterised Iraq as part of an 'axis of evil'. Leaders in the Arab world use the same psychological forces when they refer to the United States as the 'Great Satan' (Beeman, 2005).

Leaders often invoke the lessons of history to sway their citizens. For example, Saddam Hussein has been likened to Adolf Hitler to make the case for military action (Voss et al., 1992). Research suggests that such references to history are effective to persuade some, but not all, people.

Participants in a study were asked to read an account of a conflict between two fictitious countries, Afslandia and Bagumba, about disputed territory (Beer et al., 1987; Bourne et al., 2003). Some participants also read brief texts that put the conflict in a historical context. One group read a text that described the human suffering of soldiers during World War I. A second group read a text that described the process of appeasement that enabled Hitler to gain power in World War II. The control group just read the basic text describing Afslandia and Bagumba. After reading their materials, all three groups selected what they believed to be appropriate reactions from a set that varied in their conflict level from 1 (for example, 'Afslandia accepts the Bagumban head of state as its own head of state') to 15 (for example, 'Afslandia firebombs 5 of Bagumba's major cities'). The researchers predicted that the historical material would have a different impact on participants' judgments depending on their personality characteristics. For that reason, participants also gave self-reports that indicated whether they were relatively high in dominance ('dominant, assertive, aggressive, stubborn, competitive, bossy') versus relatively low in dominance ('submissive, humble, mild, easily led, accommodating'). **Figure 17.9** shows that historical material had opposite effects on people who were more or less dominant. High dominant individuals tended to recommend that the nations react at higher levels of conflict whereas low dominant individuals tended to recommend lower levels of conflict.

Note that in control circumstances—without the historical contexts—the high and low dominance groups were more or less the same in their responses. It was the contemplation of the lessons of history that drove their responses apart. The historical context, apparently, helped participants develop their own inclinations toward aggression or submission.

**Why will people go to war?** When countries' leaders contemplate going to war, they do so with virtually certain knowledge that there will be negative consequences. Modern warfare no longer spares civilians (Roblyer, 2005). One of the great innovations of World War II was to target civilian populations to break 'the will of the people'. Even when a war is fought at great distance, as the Gulf War was for citizens of the Australia, wars inevitably produce

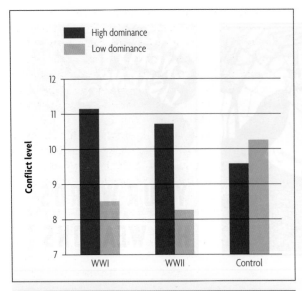

**Figure 17.9**

**Recommendations for responses to conflicts**

Participants were asked to recommend how two fictitious countries should react to a dispute over territory. Depending on the participants' personalities with respect to the dimension of dominance, material that provided a historical context led participants to recommend reactions with either higher or lower levels of conflict.

casualties on both sides. How does a country or other group determine that a cause is of sufficient importance that the loss of life is warranted? Most often this type of question is answered in a history class: countries go to war, we have learned, to protect their territory, their people, or their economic interests. In this section, however, we briefly discuss some of the more psychological factors that lead individuals to choose to participate in war.

We can ask, for example, why it is that people will sacrifice their lives for their nations. That may be the ultimate act of altruism—to give up one's life in service of some cause. Recall from earlier in the chapter that the evolutionary perspective identifies the desire to protect family members (that is, to preserve one's genes) as one important root of altruism. Some researchers have suggested that people have internalised an association between 'family' and 'nation' (Stern, 1995): talk about our 'motherland' or 'fatherland' and being 'sons' or 'daughters' of our country. Is this association sufficient to explain why people will die for their countries? Do people who march off to war construct a 'social reality' in which they believe that, ultimately, they are protecting the interests of their literal family? You can see why this is an important question for psychologists to address.

We can acquire additional insight into psychological aspects of war making by examining the circumstances that prompted the Serbians to undertake the aggressive acts in 1992 that led to sustained war in Bosnia (Oberschall, 2001). The Serbians, apparently, feared that they would become a persecuted minority after the disintegration of Yugoslavia in 1991. We have already seen how reasonable a fear this may be for a minority in times of strife. Here is the testimony of one Bosnian Serb policeman, recorded by a British journalist (Glenny, 1994; cited in White, 1996, p. 111):

> He confirmed the countless observations I had made while talking with local fighters of all nationalities—he was not a man of evil. On the contrary, he explained how he found it very difficult to shoot at the other side of the village, because he knew everybody who lived there. But the war had somehow arrived and he had to defend his home. The man was confused and upset by events, but he now perceived the Green Berets [Muslims] and Ustashas [Croats] as a real threat to his family.
> 'We cannot let them form an Islamic state here', he said with genuine passion. 'Are you sure they want to?' I asked him. 'Of course they want to. I don't understand why you people outside don't see that we are fighting for Europe against a foreign religion.'

In the context of this anticipated persecution, it was easy for Serbians to think of themselves as innocent even while they began to undertake aggressive action. From their psychological standpoint, they weren't the aggressors but the victims. As the conflict unfolded, Serbian leaders such as Slobodan Milosevic fanned the Serbian people's 'persecution mania' to maintain the belief that they were right to make war. In the long run, the Serbians turned to massacres—'ethnic cleansing'—to remove all possible 'persecutors' from their midst. We see how willing people are to go to war to protect themselves from enemies real, imagined, or created by their leaders.

What this analysis suggests is that, at least in modern times, countries rarely go to war with the goal of domination or conquest. Rather, countries come to believe—even when the rest of the world characterises them as aggressors—that they are protecting interests that are important to their survival and identity (Eidelson & Eidelson, 2003). Countries, of course, are made up of millions of individuals. Enough of those individuals must sufficiently internalise the values at stake to be willing to sacrifice their lives. Whatever the 'real' causes of war revealed by historical analysis, it is these individual, psychological forces that prompt people to endure war's hardships.

In this section so far, we have seen some of the ways in which psychological forces create the context that makes war—and atrocities committed in the context of wars—seem entirely reasonable. As the last topic of *Psychology and Life*, we turn to the efforts *peace psychologists* make to use psychological forces to promote peaceful coexistence.

## PEACE PSYCHOLOGY

It is time now to turn these analyses around, to see how we can harness social psychology to wage peace instead of war. Psychology is uniquely equipped to study the question of how to help resolve the dilemmas of national and international disharmony. The Australian Psychology Society includes an interest group called Psychologists for Peace (PFP). Its members are psychologists and others who are concerned about the prevalence of war and conflict in our world and are interested in applying their professional skills to issues relating to promoting peace and preventing war. We provide two examples of how applications of psychology can serve these goals.

**Analysing forms of leadership and government** Some of the earliest research on what we now call *peace psychology* was inspired by world historical events culminating in World War II. Social psychologists sought to understand how leaders and forms of government emerge to exert considerable power on group behaviour. What psychological constraints explain the emergence of Adolf Hitler in Germany and Benito Mussolini in Italy? These leaders forged individuals into mindless masses with unquestioning loyalty to fascist ideologies. Their authoritarian regimes threatened democracies and freedom everywhere. Modern social psychology developed out of this crucible of fear, prejudice, and war. Early social psychologists focused on understanding the nature of the *authoritarian personality* behind the fascist mentality (Adorno et al., 1950), the effects of propaganda and persuasive communications (Hovland et al., 1949), and the impact of group atmosphere and leadership styles on group members (Lewin et al., 1939).

The pioneering figure in social psychology and peace was **Kurt Lewin**, a German refugee who escaped Nazi oppression. Lewin could not help but wonder how his nation could succumb totally to the tyranny of an autocratic, fascist dictator. He witnessed the spectacle of rallies of tens of thousands of people shouting allegiance to their *Führer*. This was a frightening testimony to the dynamic power of groups to transform the minds and actions of individuals and the power of an individual to affect the masses. Lewin investigated **group dynamics**—the ways in which leaders directly influenced their followers and the ways in which group processes changed the behaviour of individuals.

In 1939, Lewin and his colleagues designed an experiment to investigate the effects of different leadership styles on group function. They wanted to find out if people are happier or more productive under autocratic or under democratic leadership. To assess the effects of different leadership styles, the researchers created three experimental groups, gave them different types of leaders, and observed the groups in action. The participants were four small groups of 10-year-old boys, who met after school. The group leaders were men trained to play each of the three leadership styles as they rotated from one to another group. When they acted as *autocratic leaders*, the men were to make all decisions and work assignments but not participate in the group activity. As *democratic leaders*, they were to encourage and assist group decision making and planning. Finally, when they acted as *laissez-faire leaders*, their job was to allow complete freedom with little leader participation.

The results of this experiment suggested a number of generalisations. First, *autocratic* leaders produced a mixed bag of effects on their followers—some positive and some quite negative. At times, the boys worked very hard, but typically only when the leader—acting as boss—was watching them. What most characterised the boys in the autocratic groups was their high level of aggression. These boys showed up to *30 times more hostility* when under autocratic leaders than they did under the other types of leaders. They demanded more attention, were more likely to destroy their own property, and showed more scapegoating behaviour—using weaker individuals as displaced targets for their frustration and anger.

As for the *laissez-faire groups*, not much good resulted. They were the most inefficient of all, doing the least amount of work and of the poorest quality. In the absence of any social structure, they simply fooled around. However, when the same groups were *democratically run*, members worked the most steadily and were most efficient. The boys showed the highest levels of interest, motivation and originality under democratic leadership. When discontent arose, it was likely to be openly expressed. Almost all the boys preferred the democratic group to the others. Democracy promoted more group loyalty and friendliness. There were more mutual praise, more friendly remarks, more sharing, and, overall, more playfulness (Lewin et al., 1939).

Democracy proved superior psychologically to the other forms of group atmosphere, as well as more productive. Democratic leaders also generated the healthiest reactions from group members; autocratic-leader groups generated the most destructive individual reactions.

What was true in Lewin's classroom seems also to be true in the real world. Consider the finding that authoritarian leadership leads to increased hostility. We can find a real-world correlate to that finding in analyses that relate type of government to instances of *democide*—genocide and other forms of mass murder (Rummel, 1994). If you examine **Figure 17.10**, you see that totalitarian governments—such as communist Russia and China—have been responsible for vast numbers of deaths; authoritarian governments—such as Idi Amin's reign in Uganda—have been responsible for fewer deaths, but democratic governments, though certainly not innocent of bloodshed, have produced fewest of all. Figure 17.10 also provides a comparison to the number of deaths caused by battles in war. Note that the great majority of deaths caused by authoritarian and totalitarian regimes were victims not of war but of other programs of mass murder. Ideological considerations aside, the world suffers least when democratic systems of government are in place to ensure that power cannot be used according to the whims of a small elite, with deadly consequences.

The overall conclusion we can draw from research on forms of leadership is that democracy works best. We derive that insight from research on groups quite small (groups of young boys) and quite large (whole countries). You should also apply this insight to the smallest and largest groups in your own life!

**group dynamics** The study of how group processes change individual functioning.

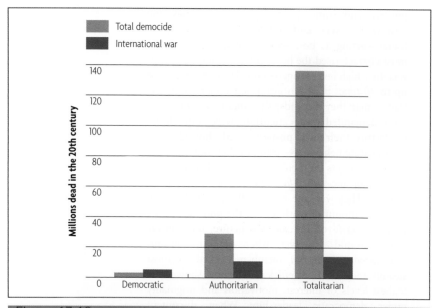

Figure 17.10

**Types of regimes and democide**

Totalitarian regimes are most likely to commit democide (genocide and other forms of mass murder). The comparison to war dead demonstrates that vastly more people are murdered by governments outside the context of war.

**Fostering contact to facilitate conflict resolution** Many of the antagonisms that give rise to conflict and violence are quite ancient. The Serbs who waged war in Bosnia, for example, traced their fear of persecution back to the Battle of Kosovo Field in 1389. What can be done in these situations? The main approach peace psychologists take is the same one we described for healing other types of prejudices: people must be brought together in cooperative settings that can foster mutual trust and shared goals.

There have been various approaches to conflict resolution in Australia over the past three decades when it comes to the issue of 'Reconciliation' between the wider Australian public and our Indigenous population, particularly in the 1990s. In 1991, the Commonwealth Parliament voted unanimously to establish the Council for Aboriginal Reconciliation and a formal reconciliation process, with the target of achieving reconciliation by 2001—the Centenary of Federation. In his famous speech in Redfern (an inner-city suburb of Sydney) in 1992, the Australian Prime Minister Paul Keating said 'The council's mission is to forge a new partnership built on justice and equity and an appreciation of the heritage of Australia's Indigenous people'. In that same year, the landmark *Mabo* case was decided in the High Court, and the *Native Title Act* passed in 1993, recognising that Australia was not *terra nullius* (meaning 'land belonging to no one') in 1788 when the First Settlement arrived.

During the last year of its 10-year existence (it ended in December 2000), the Council launched a *Roadmap for Reconciliation* at Corroboree 2000, held at the Sydney Opera House. The roadmap called for a national strategy and community partnerships including:

- Business and community groups to make commitments to overcome disadvantage
- The design and delivery of services in a way that is driven by local Indigenous people, strengthens local communities, and forges social coalitions and equal partnerships, drawing on and building the skills and resources of the community.
- Service providers, ATSIC and governments identify and eliminate systemic discrimination and racism, beginning with a review of their own practices.
- Governments adopt funding arrangements that are flexible and sufficient to meet local needs, and enable the pooling of funds across agencies and between the different levels of government.
- Employers link performance-based salaries in all sectors to improvements in Indigenous outcomes, where appropriate (Council for Aboriginal Reconciliation, 2000).

Unfortunately there is still some way to go before Reconciliation is achieved in Australia. The previous Howard Coalition Government's refusal to say 'sorry' to the Aboriginal community has made relations tenuous and conflict resolution difficult, although the new Prime Minister, Kevin Rudd, immediately committed his Labor Government by putting a motion before federal parliament to apologise to the Aboriginal people of Australia. The motion included a proposal for a policy commission to close the gap between Indigenous and non-indigenous Australian in 'life expectancy, educational achievement and economic opportunity'.

On 13 February 2008, Mr Rudd delivered a historic 361-word address to parliament, saying 'sorry' to all Australian Aboriginals, particularly the Stolen Generations and their families and communities, for laws and policies which had 'inflicted profound grief, suffering and loss

In 2008 Prime Minister Kevin Rudd officially apologised to Indigenous Australians for past wrong-doings. What sort of opportunities does this landmark gesture open for Reconciliation in Australia?

on these/our fellow Australians'. The speech was met with a rousing applause from the members of parliament, and is seen as a vital first step towards further reconciliation.

We turn to another of the world's major trouble spots, the Middle East, to describe the program of Israeli—Palestinian workshops conducted by psychologist **Herbert Kelman** (1997, 2005) and his colleagues. Over several years, Kelman's group has invited Palestinians and Israelis to participate in meetings in which they engaged in *interactive problem solving* with respect to the ongoing conflicts in their regions, such as the fate of settlements in occupied territories. The participants in this process were promised privacy and confidentiality as well as open and analytical discussion. They were encouraged to have appropriate expectations: no pressure was created to produce agreement among all the participants. Third-party members were present to facilitate conversation but did not mediate between the parties.

Kelman's group initiated these workshops at a time when it was still nearly unheard of for Palestinians and Israelis to meet at all. The workshops presented environments in which participants could have opportunities for direct interaction that could potentially foster mutual understanding. Moreover, graduates of the workshop could bring the insights they had gained into the broader, real-world political arena—along with a first approximation of the types of relationships and dialogue that are required for progress toward peace.

The situation in the Middle East has, unfortunately, not come to an end. There are militant groups in each region with political, economic and religious agendas that encourage violence and segregation over peace and integration. This continuing reality reminds us that change often comes in small increments. Nations and groups modify their responses only when education toward peace takes firm hold among their people (Staub, 2003). Insights from psychological research have helped produce some concrete programs for that education toward peace. The results are sufficiently important and encouraging to keep psychologists—that 'rather optimistic group'—diligently at work.

## RECAP CHECKPOINT
### The Psychology of Conflict and Peace

- Milgram's studies on obedience are a powerful testimony to the influence of the situational factors that can lead ordinary people to sanction and participate in organised aggression.
- Some of the same processes that foster prejudice can, in the long run, lead to mass murder and genocide.
- Leaders create images of the enemy as less than human.

- People sacrifice themselves for their country in response to fears and threats to their families and communities.
- Peace psychologists look for ways to help resolve competition and hostilities among nations.
- Democratic societies are least likely to commit mass murder.
- Programs fostering interaction between traditional 'enemies' may help to prepare the way for peace.

## CONCEPT QUESTIONS

1. How did psychiatrists' predictions compare to participants' actual behaviour in Milgram's experiments?
2. What role does scapegoating play in setting the stage for genocide?
3. What role does personality play in the way that people use history to make judgments about aggression in conflicts?
4. In Kurt Lewin's research, what leadership style provoked the most aggression?

## CRITICAL THINKING
Recall the study in which nurses received instructions to give a dangerous dose of a drug. Why was it important to measure both what nurses predicted they would do and what they actually did?

For answers go to MyPsychLab!

# A PERSONAL ENDNOTE

We have come to the end of our journey through *Psychology and Life*. As you think back, we hope you will realise just how much you have learned on the way. Yet we have barely scratched the surface of the excitement and challenges that await the student of psychology. We hope you will pursue your interest in psychology and that you may even go on to contribute to this dynamic enterprise as a scientific researcher or a clinical practitioner or by applying psychological knowledge to the solution of social and personal problems.

Playwright Tom Stoppard reminds us that 'every exit is an entry somewhere else'. We'd like to believe that the entry into the next phase of your life will be facilitated by what you have learned from *Psychology and Life* and from your Introductory Psychology course. In that next journey, may you infuse new life into the psychology of human endeavours while strengthening the connections among all the people you encounter.

# PSYCHOLOGY *in your life*

## HOW MIGHT RECONCILIATION BE POSSIBLE?

In this chapter, you have seen how psychological forces contribute to the bitter and violent conflicts that have plagued human history. When those conflicts end, is it possible to heal the hostility between groups? Can the lessons of psychology be applied to bring about *reconciliation*—mutual acceptance—between groups who sought each others' oppression or eradication? Recent evidence allows a cautious 'yes' in answer to these questions.

In the transition from apartheid to democracy, South Africa provides the most prominent national attempt to achieve reconciliation. Established in 1948, apartheid was a system of institutionalised racism through which the country's white minority exercised violent control over the black majority. After years of international pressure and sanctions, the government ended apartheid beginning in 1990. Established in 1995, the *Truth and Reconciliation Commission* provided a forum in which both the victims and perpetrators of violence testified about their experiences under apartheid. The testimony was often numbing as the scope of human rights atrocities became increasingly clear. Still, this nationwide experiment appears to have been a success. Ordinary South Africans (i.e., those who did not participate directly in the activities of the commission) who accepted that the commission generated truth also expressed greater levels of reconciliation (Gibson, 2006). That is, they were more likely to report interracial and political tolerance as well as support for human rights.

Why might the process have had this positive impact? An important

reason is that the testimony revealed—and the commission's report confirmed—that atrocities had been committed on all sides of the conflict. Recall from Chapter 16 that people experience cognitive dissonance when they are exposed to new information that contradicts their prior beliefs. The Truth and Reconciliation Commission provided new information that caused South Africans to have 'doubt about the goodness and morality of [their] cause' (Gibson, 2006, p. 414). The resulting cognitive dissonance may have led South Africans to change their beliefs in the direction of reconciliation.

When the South African model is unworkable, reconciliation can be achieved by other means. Ervin Staub and his colleagues have developed an intervention that they intended to achieve reconciliation through work with local communities (Staub et al., 2005). Their intervention focused on Rwanda where, in 1994, Hutus carried about a program of genocide against Tutsis and politically moderate Hutus, resulting in the deaths of perhaps 750,000 to 1 million people. Political change brought an end to the violence. Staub and his colleagues hoped to contribute to psychological change, to transform the context from which the violence emerged.

The intervention began when the researchers provided community workers with a 9-day training program. The program's intention was to help community workers understand the psychological consequences of trauma (e.g. posttraumatic stress disorder),

the cultural origins of genocide, and techniques for establishing empathy between individuals. At the end of the training program, the community workers bore the responsibility of communicating these core lessons to members of their groups—both Tutsis and Hutus.

To document the effectiveness of the program, Staub and his colleagues compared three groups. In the first condition, community members participated in groups in which the leaders integrated materials from the training sessions with their own treatment techniques (of whatever sort). In the second condition, leaders used just their own treatment techniques in group sessions. The third condition was a control condition in which community members did not participate in group treatment. Two months into the treatment, the researchers collected data to assess participants' trauma symptoms and attitudes toward members of the other group (i.e., Tutsis or Hutus). The results were quite promising. Individuals who participated in the groups that integrated the training material reported substantially lower trauma symptoms and stronger indications of reconciliation than participants in the other conditions.

These data from South Africa and Rwanda confirm that reconciliation is possible. Unfortunately, many people at many times may not be willing or able to begin this process. Still, it is important to understand how and why reconciliation can occur when the opportunity arises.

# SUMMARY

Chapter 17 gives an in-depth review of social psychology views of the qualities that make us human—altruism, pro-social behaviour and aggression. The power of social situations is highlighted and discussed in relation to why we seek conformity in groups and have the potential to abuse control if provided with a leadership or 'power' role. Debate on why we seek to help strangers is discussed from an egoism and genetic standpoint. Further, the reasons why aggression manifests and can influence world events is debated, as are strategies such as reconciliation for providing steps toward creating peace.

# KEY TERMS

aggression (p. 607)
altruism (p. 601)
bystander intervention (p. 604)
conformity (p. 597)
demand characteristics (p. 616)
diffusion of responsibility (p. 604)
frustration-aggression hypothesis
   (p. 609)

genocide (p. 618)
group dynamics (p. 621)
group polarisation (p. 600)
groupthink (p. 600)
impulsive aggression (p. 609)
informational influence (p. 597)
instrumental aggression (p. 609)
norm crystallisation (p. 597)

normative influence (p. 597)
peace psychology (p. 614)
pro-social behaviours (p. 601)
reciprocal altruism (p. 602)
rules (p. 594)
social norms (p. 596)
social role (p. 594)

# PRACTICE TEST

1. In the Stanford Prison Experiment, the guards often acted in abusive ways toward the prisoners. This result suggests that
   a. people seek situations in which they can indulge their aggressive impulses.
   b. some people are well suited to take on the role of guards.
   c. only aggressive people are willing to assume the role of prison guard.
   d. social roles have an important influence on how people behave.

2. Solomon Asch's experiments on conformity demonstrate the impact of_____ in group situations.
   a. norm crystallisation    c. normative influence
   b. social rules    d. informational influence

3. After testing a new brand of ice cream, each member of a group separately indicates that he or she has a mildly negative attitude. The members then begin a discussion to determine the group's overall attitude. Because of _____ , you would expect that overall attitude to be more _____ than the individual attitudes.
   a. group polarisation; negative
   b. groupthink; negative
   c. groupthink; positive
   d. group polarisation; positive

4. You need to guess how likely it is that Charlie will act altruistically toward Grace. If you can ask Charlie one question, which would be most useful?
   a. Is Grace your sister?
   b. Have you ever given help to a stranger?
   c. Is Grace your cousin?
   d. How emotionally close do you feel toward Grace?

5. Because Molly's past behaviours have inspired trust in those around her, she is likely to be the recipient of altruistic behaviours. This is an example of
   a. reciprocal altruism.
   b. direct reciprocity.
   c. indirect reciprocity.
   d. delayed reciprocity.

6. When Terry performs pro-social behaviours he is largely looking out for his own self-interest. It sounds like his main motive is
   a. egoism.         c. altruism.
   b. principlism.    d. collectivism.

7. Which of these conditions is typically *least* important with respect to bystander intervention?
   a. Bystanders must notice the emergency.
   b. Bystanders must label events as an emergency.
   c. Bystanders must feel responsibility in the situation.
   d. Bystanders must consider themselves to be helpful people.

8. If you want to increase the likelihood that people will continue to volunteer in the future, which of these measures would you *not* want to try?
   a. Give people T-shirts to recognise their volunteer work.
   b. Have people start to volunteer as a mandatory assignment.
   c. Help people cope with distressing aspects of the volunteer work.
   d. Determine the motives people have for volunteering.

9. In a classroom setting, you have been observing a highly aggressive 6-year-old child named Clark. You are asked to predict how aggressive another child, Bruce, is likely to be. You would have the most confidence in your prediction if Bruce is Clark's
   a. adopted brother.    c. DZ twin.
   b. MZ twin.            d. best friend.

10. According to the frustration-aggression hypothesis, in which of these situations is Brett most likely to act in an aggressive fashion?
    a. Brett has an important job interview, but he's stuck in a traffic jam.
    b. Brett's girlfriend yelled at him all morning for being mean to her.
    c. Brett doesn't like the song that's playing on his car radio.
    d. Brett thinks his boss has been monitoring the Websites he visits.

11. In response to continuing provocation, Jill first makes angry statements but then moves to abusive statements. Her behaviour is consistent with the concept of the
    a. culture of honour.
    b. positive evaluation of aggression.
    c. independent construal of self.
    d. escalation script.

12. Which of these four people would you expect to show the highest level of aggression?
    a. A southern U.S. student, after an insult.
    b. A northern U.S. student, after an insult.
    c. A southern U.S. student, without an insult.
    d. A northern U.S. student, without an insult.

13. In Milgram's experiments on obedience, many people protested that they didn't want to give any more shocks. After that happened,
    a. the experimenter told them the study was over.
    b. most participants asked to leave the experiment.
    c. most participants continued to administer shocks.
    d. the experimenter asked them to shock at a lower level.

14. When people believe that the victims of aggression must have done something to deserve their treatment, that is an example of
    a. scapegoating.         c. demand characteristics.
    b. just world thinking.  d. legitimate authority.

15. In Kurt Lewin's experiment, the groups with the _____ leaders got the least amount of work done.
    a. autocratic       c. laissez-faire
    b. democratic       d. aggressive

16. A key component of reconciliation is that members of formerly hostile groups
    a. agree to tell the truth.
    b. have opportunities to settle scores.
    c. deal with their traumatic experiences.
    d. express mutual acceptance.

## Essay Questions

1. How do social norms define acceptable attitudes and behaviours?

2. What role do psychological factors play in the relationship between temperature and aggression?

3. In what ways have researchers attempted to foster peace through interpersonal contact?

# WEB LINKS

www.altruism.org.au
   Altruism Australia

www.actnow.com.au/Groups/Australian_Altruism_Foundation.aspx
   Australian Altruism Foundation

http://www.worldpeace.org.au
   World Peace Society of Australia

http://www.reconciliation.org.au
   Reconciliation Australia

Are you ready for the test? MyPsychLab offers dozens of ways to deepen your understanding and test your recall of the material in this chapter—including video and audio clips, simulations and activities, self-assessments, practice tests and other study materials. Specific resources available for this chapter include:

 Helping a stranger

 Bystander intervention

 Stanford prison experiment
'We' versus 'they'
The power of the situation

To access MyPsychLab, please visit **www.pearsoned.com.au/mypsychlab**

# Will It Be On The Test?

## YOU HAVE MADE IT TO THE FINAL CHAPTER—ARE YOU PREPARED FOR THE EXAM?

To enhance your understanding of any of the material in your *Psychology and Life* textbook, go to **MyPsychLab: www.pearsoned.com.au/mypsychlab**.

Complete pre- and post-tests, create your own individualised study plan, watch videos and animations and listen to audio glossaries—all of which will help you understand the themes of this chapter:

- The power of the situation
- Altruism and prosocial behaviour
- Aggression
- The psychology of conflict and peace

Do you know what *altruism* means? Check out the AUDIO GLOSSARY!

Watch a simulation about *helping a stranger*.

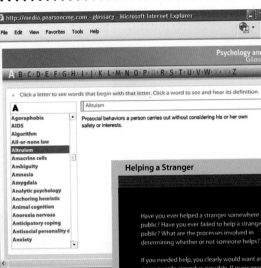

'MyPsychLab gave me the principles to focus on when I was studying.'

VIDEOS

http://abavtooldev.pearsoncmg.com - Universal Media Player - Microsoft Internet Explorer

00:03/01:59

'I clearly earned a better grade on my test after studying with MyPsychLab.'

WATCH A VIDEO ON **BULLYING**

AND THE [IN]FAMOUS
**STANFORD PRISON EXPERIMENT!**

Day 1

00:07/08:10

**What can you find in MyPsychLab?**

Self-directed tests * Videos * Simulations * eBook * Biographies * Audio glossary
* Web links … and more—organised by chapter, section and learning objective.

mypsychlab
where learning comes to life!

**abnormal psychology** The area of psychological investigation concerned with understanding the nature of individual pathologies of mind, mood and behaviour.

**absolute threshold** The minimum amount of physical energy needed to produce a reliable sensory experience operationally defined as the stimulus level at which a sensory signal is detected half the time.

**accommodation** 1. The process by which the ciliary muscles change the thickness of the lens of the eye to permit variable focusing on near and distant objects. 2. According to Piaget, the process of restructuring or modifying cognitive structures so that new information can fit into them more easily; this process works in tandem with assimilation.

**acquisition** The stage in a classical conditioning experiment during which the conditioned response is first elicited by the conditioned stimulus.

**action potential** The nerve impulse activated in a neuron that travels down the axon and causes neurotransmitters to be released into a synapse.

**acute stress** A transient state of arousal with typically clear onset and offset patterns.

**addiction** A condition in which the body requires a drug in order to function without physical and psychological reactions to its absence; often the outcome of tolerance and dependence.

**aetiology** The causes of, or factor related to, the development of a disorder.

**aggression** Behaviours that cause psychological or physical harm to another individual.

**agoraphobia** An extreme fear of being in public places or open spaces from which escape may be difficult or embarrassing.

**AIDS** Acronym for acquired immune deficiency syndrome, a syndrome caused by a virus that damages the immune system and weakens the body's ability to fight infection.

**algorithm** A step-by-step procedure that always provides the right answer for a particular type of problem.

**all-or-none law** The rule that the size of the action potential is unaffected by increases in the intensity of stimulation beyond the threshold level.

**altruism** Prosocial behaviours a person carries out without considering his or her own safety or interests.

**amacrine cells** Cells that integrate information across the retina; rather than sending signals toward the brain, amacrine cells link bipolar cells to other bipolar cells and ganglion cells to other ganglion cells.

**ambiguity** Property of perceptual object that may have more than one interpretation.

**amnesia** A failure of memory caused by physical injury, disease, drug use, or psychological trauma.

**amygdala** The part of the limbic system that controls emotion, aggression and the formation of emotional memory.

**analytic psychology** A branch of psychology that views the person as a constellation of compensatory internal forces in a dynamic balance.

**anchoring heuristic** An insufficient adjustment up or down from an original starting value when judging the probable value of some event or outcome.

**animal cognition** The cognitive capabilities of nonhuman animals; researchers trace the development of cognitive capabilities across species and the continuity of capabilities from nonhuman to human animals.

**anorexia nervosa** An eating disorder in which an individual weighs less than 85 percent of her or his expected weight but still expresses intense fear of becoming fat.

**anosmia** A complete lack of ability to smell. Anosmia can be permanent or temporary and is most often the result of head trauma or nasal and sinus diseases.

**anticipatory coping** Efforts made in advance of a potentially stressful event to overcome, reduce or tolerate the imbalance between perceived demands and available resources.

**antisocial personality disorder** A disorder characterised by stable patterns of irresponsible or unlawful behaviour that violates social norms.

**anxiety** An intense emotional response caused by the preconscious recognition that a repressed conflict is about to emerge into consciousness.

**anxiety disorders** Mental disorders marked by psychological arousal, feeling of tension, and intense apprehension without apparent reason.

**archetype** A universal, inherited, primitive, and symbolic representation of a particular experience or object.

**assimilation** According to Piaget, the process whereby new cognitive elements are fitted in with old elements or modified to fit more easily; this process works in tandem with accommodation.

**association cortex** The parts of the cerebral cortex in which many high-level brain processes occur.

**attachment** Emotional relationship between a child and the regular caregiver.

**attention** A state of focused awareness on a subset of the available perceptual information.

**attention-deficit hyperactivity disorder (ADHD)** A disorder of childhood characterised by inattention and hyperactivity-impulsivity.

**attitude** The learned, relatively stable tendency to respond to people, concepts and events in an evaluative way.

**attributions** Judgments about the causes of outcomes.

**attribution theory** A social-cognitive approach to describing the ways the social perceiver uses information to generate causal explanations.

**audience design** The process of shaping a message depending on the audience for which it is intended.

**auditory cortex** The area of the temporal lobes that receives and processes auditory information.

**auditory nerve** The nerve that carries impulses from the cochlea to the cochlear nucleus of the brain.

**autistic disorder** A developmental disorder characterised by severe disruption of children's ability to form social bonds and use language.

**automatic processes** Processes that do not require attention; they can often be performed along with other tasks without interference.

**autonomic nervous system (ANS)** The subdivision of the peripheral nervous system that controls the body's involuntary motor responses. by connecting the sensory receptors to the central nervous system (CNS) and the CNS to the smooth muscle, cardiac muscle, and glands.

**availability heuristic** A judgment based on the information readily available in memory.

**aversion therapy** A type of behavioural therapy used to treat individuals attracted to harmful stimuli; an attractive stimulus is paired with a noxious stimulus in order to elicit a negative reaction to the target stimulus.

**axon** The extended fibre of a neuron through which nerve impulses travel from the soma to the terminal buttons.

**basic level** The level of categorisation that can be retrieved from memory most quickly and used most efficiently.

**basilar membrane** A membrane in the cochlea that when set into motion stimulates hair cells that produce the neural effects of auditory stimulation.

**behaviour** The actions by which an organism adjusts to its environment.

**behaviour analysis** The area of psychology that focuses on the environmental determinants of learning and behaviour.

**behavioural data** Observational reports about the behaviour of organisms and the conditions under which the behaviour occurs or changes.

**behaviour modification** The systematic use of principles of learning to increase the frequency of desired behaviours and/or decrease the frequency of problem behaviours.

**behaviour therapy** See behaviour modification.

**behavioural confirmation** The process by which people behave in ways that elicit from others specific expected reactions and then use those reactions to confirm their beliefs.

**behavioural measures** Overt actions and reactions that are observed and recorded, exclusive of self-reported behaviour.

**behavioural neuroscience** A multidisciplinary field that attempts to understand the brain processes that underlie behaviour.

**behavioural rehearsal** Procedures used to establish and strengthen basic skills; as used in social-skills training programs, requires the client to rehearse a desirable behaviour sequence mentally.

**behaviourism** A scientific approach that limits the study of psychology to measurable or observable behaviour.

**behaviourist perspective** The psychological perspective primarily concerned with observable behaviour that can be objectively recorded and with the relationships of observable behaviour to environmental stimuli.

**belief-bias effect** A situation that occurs when a person's prior knowledge, attitudes or values distort the reasoning process by influencing the person to accept invalid arguments.

**between-groups design** A research design in which different groups of participants are randomly assigned to experimental conditions or to control conditions.

**biofeedback** A self-regulatory technique by which an individual acquires voluntary control over nonconscious biological processes.

**biological constraints on learning** Any limitations on an organism's capacity to learn that are caused by the inherited sensory, response, or cognitive capabilities of members of a given species.

**biological perspective** The approach to identifying causes of behaviour that focuses on the functioning of the genes, the brain, the nervous system, and the endocrine system.

**biomedical therapies** Treatments for psychological disorders that alter brain functioning with chemical or physical interventions such as drug therapy, surgery, or electroconvulsive therapy.

**biopsychosocial model** A model of health and illness that suggests links among the nervous system, the immune system, behavioural styles, cognitive processing and environmental domains of health.

**bipolar cells** Nerve cells in the visual system that combine impulses from many receptors and transmit the results to ganglion cells.

**bipolar disorder** A mood disorder characterised by alternating periods of depression and mania.

**borderline personality disorder** A disorder defined by instability and intensity in personal relationships as well as turbulent emotions and impulsive behaviours.

**bottom-up processing** Perceptual analyses based on the sensory data available in the environment; results of analysis are passed upward toward more abstract representations.

**brain stem** The brain structure that regulates the body's basic life processes.

**brightness** The dimension of colour space that captures the intensity of light.

**Broca's area** The region of the brain that translates thoughts into speech or signs.

**bulimia nervosa** An eating disorder characterised by binge eating followed by measures to purge the body of excess calories.

**bystander intervention** Willingness to assist a person in need of help.

**Cannon–Bard theory of emotion** A theory stating that an emotional stimulus produces two co-occurring reactions—arousal and experience of emotion—that do not cause each other.

**case study** Intensive observation of a particular individual or small group of individuals.

**catharsis** The process of expressing strongly felt but usually repressed emotions.

**central nervous system (CNS)** The part of the nervous system consisting of the brain and spinal cord.

**centration** A thought pattern common during the beginning of the preoperational stage of cognitive development; characterised by the child's inability to take more than one perceptual factor into account at the same time.

**cerebellum** The region of the brain attached to the brain stem that controls motor coordination, posture and balance as well as the ability to learn control of body movements.

**cerebral cortex** The outer surface of the cerebrum.

**cerebral hemispheres** The two halves of the cerebrum connected by the corpus callosum.

**cerebrum** The region of the brain that regulates higher cognitive and emotional functions.

**child-directed speech** A special form of speech with an exaggerated and high-pitched intonation that adults use to speak to infants and young children.

**chronic stress** A continuous state of arousal in which an individual perceives demands as greater than the inner and outer resources available for dealing with them.

**chronological age** The number of months or years since an individual's birth.

**chunking** The process of taking single items of information and recoding them on the basis of similarity or some other organising principle.

**circadian rhythm** A consistent pattern of cyclical body activities, usually lasting 24 to 25 hours and determined by an internal biological clock.

**classical conditioning** Learning in which a behaviour (conditioned response) is elicited by a conditioned stimulus whose power is acquired through an association with a biologically significant stimulus (unconditioned stimulus).

**client** The term used by clinicians who think of psychological disorders as problems in living, and not as mental illnesses, to describe those being treated.

**client-centred therapy** A humanistic approach to treatment that emphasises the healthy psychological growth of the individual based on the assumption that all people share the basic tendency of human nature toward self-actualisation.

**clinical psychologist** An individual who has earned a doctorate in psychology and whose training is in the assessment and treatment of psychological problems.

**clinical social worker** A mental health professional whose specialised training prepares him or her to consider the social context of people's problems.

**cochlea** The primary organ of hearing; a fluid-filled coiled tube located in the inner ear.

**cognition** Processes of knowing, including attending, remembering and reasoning; also the content of the processes, such as concepts and memories.

**cognitive appraisal** The cognitive interpretation of a stressor.

**cognitive appraisal theory of emotion** A theory stating that the experience of emotion is the joint effect of physiological arousal and cognitive appraisal, which serves to determine how an ambiguous inner state of arousal will be labelled.

**cognitive behavioural therapy** A therapeutic approach that combines the cognitive emphasis on thoughts and attitudes with the behavioural emphasis on changing performance.

**cognitive development** The development of processes of knowing, including imagining, perceiving, reasoning and problem solving.

**cognitive dissonance** The theory that the tension-producing effects of incongruous cognitions motivate individuals to reduce such tension.

**cognitive map** A mental representation of physical space.

**cognitive neuroscience** A multidisciplinary field that attempts to understand the brain processes that underlie higher cognitive functions in humans.

**cognitive perspective** The perspective on psychology that stresses human thought and the processes of knowing, such as attending, thinking, remembering, expecting, solving problems, fantasizing, and consciousness.

**cognitive processes** Higher mental processes, such as perception, memory, language, problem solving and abstract thinking.

**cognitive psychology** The study of higher mental processes, such as attention, language use, memory, perception, problem solving and thinking.

**cognitive science** The interdisciplinary field of study of the approach systems and processes that manipulate information.

**cognitive therapy** A type of psychotherapeutic treatment that attempts to change feelings and behaviours by changing the way a client thinks about or perceives significant life experiences.

**collective unconscious** The part of an individual's unconscious that is inherited, evolutionarily developed, and common to all members of the species.

**comorbidity** The experience of more than one disorder at the same time.

**complementary colours** Colours opposite each other on the colour circle; when additively mixed, they create the sensation of white light.

**compliance** A change in behaviour consistent with a communication source's direct requests.

**concepts** Mental representations of kinds or categories of items and ideas.

**conditioned reinforcers** In classical conditioning, formerly neutral stimuli that have become reinforcers.

**conditioned response (CR)** In classical conditioning, a response elicited by some previously neutral stimulus that occurs as a result of pairing the neutral stimulus with an unconditioned stimulus.

**conditioned stimulus (CS)** In classical conditioning, a previously neutral stimulus that comes to elicit a conditioned response.

**cones** Photoreceptors concentrated in the centre of the retina that are responsible for visual experience under normal viewing conditions for all experiences of colour.

**conformity** The tendency for people to adopt the behaviours, attitudes and values of other members of a reference group.

**confounding variable** A stimulus other than the variable an experimenter explicitly introduces into a research setting that affects a participant's behaviour.

**consciousness** A state of awareness of internal events and the external environment.

**conservation** According to Piaget, the understanding that physical properties do not change when nothing is added or taken away, even though appearances may change.

**consistency paradox** The observation that personality ratings across time and among different observers are consistent while behaviour ratings across situations are not consistent.

**construct validity** The degree to which a test adequately measures an underlying construct.

**contact comfort** Comfort derived from an infant's physical contact with the mother or caregiver.

**contact hypothesis** The prediction that contact between groups will reduce prejudice only if the contact includes features such as cooperation towards shared goals.

**contextual distinctiveness** The assumption that the serial position effect can be altered by the context and the distinctiveness of the experience being recalled.

**contingency management** A general treatment strategy involving changing behaviour by modifying its consequences.

**control procedures** Consistent procedures for giving instructions, scoring responses, and holding all other variables constant except those being systematically varied.

**controlled processes** Processes that require attention; it is often difficult to carry out more than one controlled process at a time.

**convergence** The degree to which the eyes turn inward to fixate on an object.

**conversion disorder** A disorder in which psychological conflict or stress brings about loss of motor or sensory function.

**Coolabah Dynamic Assessment Method** A tool for identifying the learning potential of gifted Aboriginal students who underperform in the classroom.

**coping** The process of dealing with internal or external demands that are perceived to be threatening or overwhelming.

**corpus callosum** The mass of nerve fibres connecting the two hemispheres of the cerebrum.

**correlational coefficient (r)** A statistic that indicates the degree of relationship between two variables.

**correlational methods** Research methodologies that determine to what extent two variables, traits or attributes are related.

**counselling psychologist** Psychologist who specialises in providing guidance in areas such as vocational selections, school problems, drug abuse and marital conflict.

**counterconditioning** A technique used in therapy to substitute a new response for a maladaptive one by means of conditioning procedures.

**countertransference** Circumstances in which a psychoanalyst develops personal feelings about a client because of perceived similarity of the client to significant people in the therapist's life.

**covariation principle** A theory that suggests that people attribute a behaviour to a causal factor if that factor was present whenever the behaviour occurred but was absent whenever it did occur.

**creativity** The ability to generate ideas or products that are both novel and appropriate to the circumstances.

**criterion validity** The degree to which test scores indicate a result on a specific measure that is consistent with some other criterion of the characteristic being assessed; also known as predictive validity.

**cross-sectional design** A research method in which groups of participants of different chronological ages are observed and compared at a given time.

**crystallised intelligence** The facet of intelligence involving the knowledge a person has already acquired and the ability to access that knowledge; measured by vocabulary, arithmetic and general information tests.

**cutaneous senses** The skin senses that register sensations or pressure, warmth and cold.

**dark adaptation** The gradual improvement of the eyes' sensitivity after a shift in illumination from light to near darkness.

**date rape** Unwanted sexual violation by social acquaintance in the context of a consensual dating situation.

**debriefing** A procedure conducted at the end of an experiment in which the researcher provides the participant with as much information about the study as possible and makes sure that no participant leaves feeling confused, upset or embarrassed.

**decision aversion** The tendency to avoid decision-making; the tougher the decision, the greater the likelihood of decision aversion.

**decision making** The process of choosing between alternatives; selecting or rejecting available options.

**declarative memory** Memory for information such as facts and events.

**deductive reasoning** A form of thinking in which one draws a conclusion that is intended to follow logically from two or more statements or premises.

**deinstitutionalisation** The movement to treat people with psychological disorders in the community rather than in psychiatric hospitals.

**delusions** False or irrational beliefs maintained despite clear evidence to the contrary.

**demand characteristics** Cues in an experimental setting that influence the participants' perception of what is expected of them and that systematically influence their behaviour within that setting.

**dendrites** The branched fibres of neurons that receive incoming signals.

**dependent variable** In an experimental setting, a variable that the researcher measures to assess the impact of a variation in an independent variable.

**descriptive statistics** Statistical procedures that are used to summarise sets of scores with respect to central tendencies, variability and correlations.

**determinism** The doctrine that all events—physical, behavioural and mental—are determined by specific causal factors that are potentially knowable.

**developmental age** The chronological age at which most children show a particular level of physical or mental development.

**developmental psychology** The branch of psychology concerned with interaction between physical and psychological processes and with stages of growth from conception throughout the entire life span.

**diathesis-stress hypothesis** A hypothesis about the cause of disorders, such as schizophrenia, that suggests that genetic factors predispose an individual to a certain disorder but that environmental stress factors must impinge in order for the potential risk to manifest itself.

**dichotic listening** An experimental technique in which a different auditory stimulus is simultaneously presented to each ear.

**difference threshold** The smallest physical difference between two stimuli that can still be recognised as a difference; operationally defined as the point at which the stimuli are recognised as different half of the time.

**diffusion of responsibility** In emergency situations, the larger the number of bystanders, the less responsibility any one of the bystanders feels to help.

**discriminative stimuli** Stimuli that act as predictors of reinforcement, signalling when particular behaviours will result in positive reinforcement.

**dissociative amnesia** The inability to remember important personal experiences, caused by psychological factors in the absence of any organic dysfunction.

**dissociative disorder** A personality disorder marked by a disturbance in the integration of identity, memory or consciousness.

**dissociative identity disorder (DID)** A dissociative mental disorder in which two or more distinct personalities exist within the same individual; formerly known as multiple personality disorder.

**distal stimulus** In the processes of perception, the physical object in the world, as contrasted with the proximal stimulus, the optical image on the retina.

**divergent thinking** An aspect of creativity characterised by an ability to produce unusual but appropriate responses to problems.

**DNA (deoxyribonucleic acid)** The physical basis for the transmission of genetic information.

**double-blind control** An experimental technique in which biased expectations of experimenters are eliminated by keeping both participants and experimental assistants unaware of which participants have received which treatment.

**dream analysis** The psychoanalytic interpretation of dreams used to gain insight into a person's unconscious motives or conflicts.

**dream work** In Freudian dream analysis, the process by which the internal censor transforms the latent content of a dream into manifest content.

**drives** Internal states that arise in response to a disequilibrium in an animal's physiological needs.

**DSM-IV-TR** The current diagnostic and statistical manual of the American Psychological Association that classifies, defines and describes mental disorders.

**echoic memory** Sensory memory that allows auditory information to be stored for brief durations.

**ego** The aspect of personality involved in self-preservation activities and in directing instinctual drives and urges into appropriate channels.

**ego defence mechanisms** Mental strategies (conscious or unconscious) used by the ego to defend itself against conflicts experienced in the normal course of life.

**egocentrism** In cognitive development, the inability of a young child at the preoperational stage to take the perspective of another person.

**elaboration likelihood model** A theory of persuasion that defines how likely it is that people will focus their cognitive processes to elaborate upon a message and therefore follow the central and peripheral routes to persuasion.

**elaborative rehearsal** A technique for improving memory by enriching the encoding of information.

**electroconvulsive therapy (ECT)** The use of electroconvulsive shock as an effective treatment for severe depression.

**electroencephalogram (EEG)** A recording of the electrical activity of the brain.

**emotion** A complex pattern of changes, including physiological arousal, feelings, cognitive processes and behavioural reactions, made in response to a situation perceived to be personally significant.

**emotional intelligence** The abilities to perceive, appraise and express emotions accurately; to use emotions to facilitate thinking and analysis; to use emotional knowledge effectively and regulate emotions to promote emotional and intellectual growth.

**encoding** The process by which a mental representation is formed in memory.

**encoding specificity** The principle that subsequent retrieval of information is enhanced if cues received at the time of recall are consistent with those present at the time of encoding.

**endocrine system** The network of glands that manufacture and secrete hormones into the bloodstream.

**engram** The physical memory trace for information in the brain.

**episodic memories** Long-term memories for auto-biographical events and the contexts in which they occurred.

**EQ** The emotional intelligence counterpart of IQ.

**equity theory** A cognitive theory of work motivation that proposes that workers are motivated to maintain fair and equitable relationships with other relevant persons; also, a model that postulates that equitable relationships are those in which the participants' outcomes are proportional to their inputs.

**evolutionary perspective** The approach to psychology that stresses the importance of behavioural and mental adaptiveness, based on the assumption that mental capabilities evolved over millions of years to serve particular adaptive purposes.

**evolutionary psychology** The study of behaviour and mind using the principles of evolutionary theory.

**excitatory inputs** Information entering a neuron that signals it to fire.

**exemplars** Members of categories that people have encountered.

**expectancy effects** Results that occur when a researcher or observer subtly communicates to participants the kind of behaviour he or she expects to find, thereby creating that expected reaction.

**expectancy theory** A cognitive theory of work motivation that proposes that workers are motivated when they expect their efforts and job performance to result in desired outcomes.

**experience-sampling method** An experimental method that assists researchers in describing the typical contents of consciousness; participants are asked to record what they are feeling and thinking whenever signalled to do so.

**experimental methods** Research methodologies that involve the manipulation of independent variables in order to determine their effects on the dependent variables.

**explicit uses of memory** Conscious effort to encode or recover information through memory processes.

**exposure therapy** A behavioural technique in which clients are exposed to the objects or situations that cause them anxiety.

**extinction** In conditioning, the weakening of a conditioned association in the absence of a reinforcer or unconditioned stimulus.

**face validity** The degree to which test items appear to be directly related to the attribute the researcher wishes to measure.

**fear** A rational reaction to an objectively identified external danger that may induce a person to flee or attack in self-defence.

**fight-or-flight response** A sequence of internal activities triggered when an organism is faced with a threat; prepares the body for combat and struggle or for running away to safety recent evidence suggests that the response is characteristic only of males.

**figure** Object like regions of the visual field that are distinguished from background.

**five-factor model** A comprehensive descriptive personality system that maps out the relationships among common traits, theoretical concepts and personality scales; informally called the Big Five.

**fixation** A state in which a person remains attached to objects or activities more appropriate for an earlier stage of psychosexual development.

**fixed-interval (FI) schedule** A schedule of reinforcement in which a reinforcer is delivered for the first response made after a fixed period of time.

**fixed-ratio (FR) schedule** A schedule of reinforcement in which a reinforcer is delivered for the first response made after a fixed number of responses.

**fluid intelligence** The aspect of intelligence that involves the ability to see complex relationships and solve problems.

**formal assessment** The systematic procedures and measurement instruments used by trained professionals to assess an individual's functioning, aptitudes, abilities or mental states.

**foundational theories** Frameworks for initial understanding formulated by children to explain their experiences of the world.

**fovea** Area of the retina that contains densely packed cones and forms the point of sharpest vision.

**frame** A particular description of a choice; the perspective from which a choice is described or framed affects how a decision is made and which option is ultimately exercised.

**free association** The therapeutic method in which a patient gives a running account of thoughts, wishes, physical sensations and mental images as they occur.

**frequency distribution** A summary of how frequently each score appears in a set of observations.

**frequency theory** The theory that a tone produces a rate of vibration in the basilar membrane equal to its frequency; with the result that pitch can be coded by the frequency of the neural response.

**frontal lobe** Region of the brain located above the lateral fissure and in front of the central sulcus; involved in motor control and cognitive activities.

**frustration-aggression hypothesis** According to this hypothesis, frustration occurs in situations in which people are prevented or blocked from attaining their goals; a rise in frustration then leads to a greater probability of aggression.

**functional fixedness** An inability to perceive a new use for an object previously associated with some other purpose. adversely affects problem solving and creativity.

**functional MRI (fMRI)** A brain-imaging technique that combines benefits of both MRI and PET scans by detecting magnetic changes in the flow of blood to cells in the brain.

**functionalism** The perspective on mind and behaviour that focuses on the examination of their functions in an organism's interactions with the environment.

**fundamental attribution error (FAE)** The dual tendency of observers to underestimate the impact of situational factors and to overestimate the influence of dispositional factors on a person's behaviour.

*g* According to Spearman, the factor of general intelligence underlying all intelligent performance.

**ganglion cells** Cells in the visual system that integrate impulses from many bipolar cells in a single firing rate.

**Gate-control theory** A theory about pain modulation that proposes that certain cells in the spinal cord act as gates to interrupt and block some pain signals while sending others to the brain.

**gender** A psychological phenomenon that refers to learned sex-related behaviours and attitudes of males and females.

**gender identity** One's sense of maleness or femaleness; usually includes awareness and acceptance of one's biological sex.

**gender roles** Sets of behaviours and attitudes associated by society as being male or female and expressed publicly by the individual.

**general adaptation syndrome (GAS)** The pattern of nonspecific adaptational physiological mechanisms that occurs in response to continuing threat by almost any serious stressor.

**generalised anxiety disorder** An anxiety disorder in which an individual feels anxious and worried most of the time for at least 6 months when not threatened by any specific danger or object.

**generativity** A commitment beyond one's self and one's partner to family, work, society and future generations; typically, a crucial state in development in one's 30s and 40s.

**genes** The biological units of heredity; discrete sections of chromosomes responsible for transmission of traits.

**genetics** The study of the inheritance of physical and psychological traits from ancestors.

**genocide** The systematic destruction of one group of people, often an ethnic or racial group, by another.

**genome** The genetic information for an organism stored in the DNA of its chromosomes.

**genotype** The genetic structure an organism inherits from its parents.

**Gestalt psychology** A school of psychology that maintains that psychological phenomena can be understood only when viewed as organised, structured wholes, not when broken down into primitive perceptual elements.

**Gestalt theory** Therapy that focuses on ways to unite mind and body to make a person whole.

**glia** The cells that hold neurons together and facilitate neural transmission, remove damaged and dead neurons and prevent poisonous substances in the blood from reaching the brain.

**goal-directed selection** A determinant of why people select some parts of sensory input for further processing; it reflects the choices made as a function of one's own goals.

**ground** The backdrop of background areas of the visual field against which figures stand out.

**group dynamics** The study of how group processes change individual functioning.

**group polarization** The tendency for groups to make decisions that are more extreme than the decisions that would be made by the members acting alone.

**groupthink** The tendency of a decision-making group to filter out undesirable input so that a consensus may be reached, especially if it is in line with the leader's viewpoint.

**habituation** A decrease in a behavioural response when a stimulus is presented repeatedly.

**hallucinations** False perceptions that occur in the absence of objective stimulation.

**health** A general condition of soundness and vigour of body and mind; not simply the absence of illness or injury.

**health promotion** The development and implementation of general strategies and specific tactics to eliminate or reduce the risk that people will become ill.

**health psychology** The field of psychology devoted to understanding the ways people stay healthy, the reasons they become ill and the ways they respond when they become ill.

**heredity** The biological transmission of traits from parents to offspring.

**heritability** The relative influence of genetics—versus environment—in determining patterns of behaviour.

**heritability estimate** A statistical estimate of the degree of inheritance of a given trait or behaviour, assessed by the degree of similarity between individuals who vary in their extent of genetic similarity.

**heuristics** Cognitive strategies, or 'rules of thumb', often used as shortcuts in solving a complex inferential task.

**hierarchy of needs** Maslow's view that basic human motives form a hierarchy and that the needs at each level of the hierarchy must be satisfied before the next level can be achieved.

**hippocampus** The part of the limbic system that is involved in the acquisition of explicit memory.

**HIV** Human immunodeficiency virus, a virus that attacks white blood cells (T lymphocytes) in human blood, thereby weakening the functioning of the immune system; HIV causes AIDS.

**homeostasis** The body's ability to maintain internal equilibrium by adjusting its physiological processes, such as temperature, heart rate and blood pressure.

**horizontal cells** The cells that integrate information across the retina; rather than sending signals toward the brain, horizontal cells connect receptors to each other.

**hormones** The chemical messengers manufactured and secreted by the endocrine glands that regulate metabolism and influence body growth, mood and sexual characteristics.

**hue** The dimension of colour space that captures the qualitative experience of the colour of light.

**human behaviour genetics** The area of study that evaluates the genetic component of individual differences in behaviours and traits.

**humanistic perspective** A psychological model that emphasises an individual's phenomenal world and inherent capacity for making rational choices and developing to maximum potential.

**human-potential movement** The therapy movement that encompasses those practices and methods that release the potential of the average human being for greater levels of performance and richness of experience.

**hypnosis** An altered state of awareness characterised by deep relaxation, susceptibility to suggestions and changes in perception, memory, motivation and self-control.

**hypnotisability** The degree to which an individual is responsive to standardised hypnotic suggestion.

**hypochondriasis** A disorder in which individuals are preoccupied with having or getting physical ailments despite reassurances that they are healthy.

**hypothalamus** The brain structure that regulates motivated behaviour (such as eating and drinking) and homeostasis.

**hypothesis** A tentative and testable explanation of the relationship between two (or more) events or variables.

**iconic memory** Memory system in the visual domain that allows large amounts of information to be stored for very brief durations.

**id** The primitive, unconscious part of the personality that represents the internalisation of society's values, standards and morals.

**identification and recognition** Two ways of attaching meaning to percepts.

**illusion** An experience of a stimulus pattern in a manner that is demonstrably incorrect but shared by others in the same perceptual environment.

**implicit uses of memory** Availability of information through memory processes without conscious effort to encode or recover information.

**imprinting** A primitive form of learning in which some infant animals physically follow and form an attachment to the first moving object they see and/or hear.

**impulsive aggression** Cognition-based and goal-directed aggression carried out with premeditated thought to achieve specific aims.

**incentives** External stimuli or rewards that motivate behaviour although they do not relate directly to biological needs.

**independent construals of self** Conceptualisation of the self as individual whose behaviour is organised by reference to one's own thoughts, feelings and actions rather than by the thoughts, feelings and actions of others.

**independent variable** In an experimental setting, a variable that the researcher manipulates with the expectation of having an impact on values of the dependent variable.

**inductive reasoning** A form of reasoning in which a conclusion is made about the probability of some state of affairs, based on the available evidence and past experience.

**inferences** Missing information filled in on the basis of a sample of evidence or on the basis of prior beliefs and theories.

**inferential statistics** Statistical procedures that allow researchers to determine whether the results they obtain support their hypotheses or can be attributed to chance variation.

**informational influence** Group effects that arise from individuals' desire to be correct and right and to understand how best to act in a given situation.

**in-group bias** An evaluation of one's own group as better than others.

**in-groups** The groups with which people identify as members.

**inhibitory inputs** Information entering a neuron that signals it not to fire.

**insanity** The legal (not clinical) designation for the state of an individual judged to be legally irresponsible or incompetent.

**insight therapy** A technique by which the therapist guides a patient toward discovering insights between present symptoms and past origins.

**insomnia** The chronic inability to sleep normally; symptoms include difficulty in falling asleep, frequent waking, inability to return to sleep, and early-morning awakening.

**instincts** Preprogrammed tendencies that are essential to a species' survival.

**instinctual drift** The tendency for learned behaviour to drift toward instinctual behaviour over time.

**instrumental aggression** Cognition-based and goal-directed aggression carried out with premeditated thought to achieve specific aims.

**intelligence** The global capacity to profit from experience and to go beyond given information about the environment.

**intelligence quotient (IQ)** An index derived from standardised tests of intelligence; originally obtained by dividing an individual's mental age by chronological age and then multiplying by 100; now directly computed as an IQ test score.

**interdependent construals of self** Conceptualisation of the self as part of an encompassing social relationship. recognising that one's behaviour is determined, contingent on, and, to a large extent organised by what the actor perceived to be the thoughts, feelings, and actions of others.

**interferences** Missing information filled on the basis of a sample of evidence or on the basis of prior beliefs and theories.

**internal consistency** A measure of reliability; the degree to which a test yields similar scores across its different parts, such as odd versus even items.

**internalisation** According to Vygotsky, the process through which children absorb knowledge from the social context.

**interneurons** Brain neurons that relay messages from sensory neurons to other interneurons or to motor neurons.

**intimacy** The capacity to make a full commitment—sexual, emotional and moral—to another person.

**ion channels** The portions of neurons' cell membranes that selectively permit certain ions to flow in and out.

**James–Lange theory of emotion** A peripheral-feedback theory of emotion stating that an eliciting stimulus triggers a behavioural response that sends different sensory and motor feedback to the brain and creates the feeling of a specific emotion.

**jigsaw classrooms** Classrooms that use a technique known as jigsawing, in which each pupil is given part of the total material to master and then share with other group members.

**job burnout** The syndrome of emotional exhaustion, depersonalisation and reduced personal accomplishment, often experienced by workers in high-stress jobs.

**judgment** The process by which people form opinions, reach conclusions and make critical evaluations of events and people based on available material; also, the product of the mental activity.

**just noticeable difference (JND)** The smallest difference between two sensations that allows them to be discriminated.

**kinaesthetic sense** The sense concerned with bodily position and movement of the body parts relative to one another.

**language-making capacity** The innate guidelines or operating principles that children bring to the task of learning a language.

**language production** What people say, sign and write, as well as the processes they go through to produce these messages.

**latent content** In Freudian dream analysis, the hidden meaning of a dream.

**law of effect** A law of learning where the power of a stimulus to evoke a response is strengthened when the response is followed by a reward and weakened when it is not followed by a reward.

**learned helplessness** A general pattern of nonresponding in the presence of noxious stimuli that often follows after an organism has previously experienced non-contingent, inescapable aversive stimuli.

**learning** A process based on experience that results in a relatively permanent change in behaviour or behavioural potential.

**learning disorder** A disorder defined by a large discrepancy between individuals' measured IQ and their actual performance.

**learning-performance distinction** The difference between what has been learned and what is expressed in overt behaviour.

**lesions** Injuries to or destruction of brain tissue.

**levels-of-processing theory** A theory that suggests that the deeper the level at which information was processed the more likely it is to be retained in memory.

**libido** The psychic energy that drives individuals toward sensual pleasures of all types, especially sexual ones.

**life-change units (LCUs)** In stress research, the measure of the stress levels of different types of change experienced during a given period.

**lightness constancy** The tendency to perceive the whiteness, greyness or blackness of objects as constant across changing levels of illuminations.

**limbic system** The region of the brain that regulates emotional behaviour, basic motivational urges and memory, as well as major physiological functions.

**longitudinal design** A research design in which the same participants are observed repeatedly, sometimes over many years.

**long-term memory (LTM)** Memory processes associated with the preservation of information for retrieval at any later time.

**loudness** A perceptual dimension of sound influenced by the amplitude of a sound wave: sound waves in large amplitudes are generally experienced as loud and those with small amplitudes as soft.

**lucid dreaming** The theory that conscious awareness of dreaming is a learnable skill that enables dreamers to control the direction and content of their dreams.

**magnetic resonance imaging (MRI)** A technique for brain imaging that scans the brain using magnetic fields and radio waves.

**major depressive disorder** A mood disorder characterised by intense feelings of depression over an extended time, without the manic high phase of bipolar depression.

**manic episode** A component of bipolar disorder characterised by periods of extreme elation, unbounded euphoria without sufficient reason, and grandiose thoughts or feelings about personal abilities.

**manifest content** In Freudian dream analysis, the surface content of a dream which is assumed to mask the dream's actual meaning.

**maturation** The continuing influence of heredity throughout development, the age-related physical and behavioural changes characteristic of a species.

**mean** The arithmetic average of a group of scores; the most commonly used measure of central tendency.

**measure of central tendency** A statistic such as a mean, median or mode that provides one score as representative of a set of observations.

**measures of variability** A statistic such as a range or standard deviation that indicates how tightly the scores in a set of observations cluster together.

**median** The score in a distribution above and below which lie 50% of the other scores; a measure of central tendency.

**meditation** A form of consciousness alteration designed to enhance self-knowledge and wellbeing through reduced self-awareness.

**medulla** The region of the brain stem that regulates breathing, waking and heartbeat.

**memory** The mental capacity to encode, store and retrieve information.

**menarche** The onset of menstruation.

**mental age** In Binet's measure of intelligence, the age at which a child is performing intellectually, expressed in terms of the average age at which normal children achieve a particular score.

**mental retardation** Condition in which individuals have IQ scores of 70 to 75 or below and also demonstrate limitations in the ability to bring adaptive skills to bear on life tasks.

**mental set** The tendency to respond to a new problem in the manner used to respond to a previous problem.

**meta-analysis** A statistical technique for evaluating hypotheses by providing a formal mechanism for detecting the general conclusions found in data from many different experiments.

**metamemory** Implicit or explicit knowledge about memory abilities and effective memory strategies; cognition about memory.

**mnemonics** Strategies or devices that use familiar information during the encoding of new information to enhance subsequent access to the information in memory.

**mode** The score appearing most frequently in a set of observations; a measure of central tendency.

**mood disorder** A mood disturbance such as severe depression or depression alternating with mania.

**morality** A system of beliefs and values that ensures that individuals will keep their obligations to others in society and will behave in ways that do not interfere with the rights and interests of others.

**motivation** The process of starting, directing and maintaining physical and psychological activities; includes mechanisms involved in preferences for one activity over another and the vigour and persistence of responses.

**motor cortex** The region of the cerebral cortex that controls the action of the body's voluntary muscles.

**motor neurons** The neurons that carry messages away from the central nervous system towards the muscles and glands.

**narcolepsy** A sleep disorder characterised by an irresistible compulsion to sleep during the daytime.

**natural selection** Darwin's theory that favourable adaptations to features of the environment allow some members of a species to reproduce more successfully than others.

**need for achievement (n Ach)** An assumed basic human need to strive for achievement of goals that motivates a wide range of behaviour and thinking.

**negative punishment** A behaviour is followed by the removal of an appetitive stimulus, decreasing the probability of that behaviour.

**negative reinforcement** A behaviour is followed by the removal of an aversive stimulus, increasing the probability of that behaviour.

**neurogenesis** The creation of new neurons.

**neuromodulator** Any substance that modifies or modulates the activities of the postsynaptic neuron.

**neuron** A cell in the nervous system specialised to receive, process and/or transmit information to other cells.

**neuroscience** The scientific study of the brain and of the links between brain activity and behaviour.

**neurotransmitters** The chemical messengers released from neurons that cross the synapse from one neuron to another, stimulating the postsynaptic neuron.

**neurotic disorders** Mental disorders in which a person does not have signs of brain abnormalities and does not display grossly irrational thinking or violate basic norms but does experience subjective distress; a category dropped from *DSM-III*.

**nonconscious** Not typically available to consciousness or memory.

**non-REM (NREM) sleep** The period during which a sleeper does not show rapid eye movement; characterised by less dream activity than during REM sleep.

**norm crystallisation** The convergence of the expectations of a group of individuals into a common perspective as they talk and carry out activities together.

**normal curve** The symmetrical curve that represents the distribution of scores on many psychological attributes; allows researchers to make judgments of how unusual an observation or result is.

**normative influence** Group effects that arise from individuals' desire to be liked, accepted and approved of by others.

**normative investigations** Research efforts designed to describe what is characteristic of a specific age or developmental stage.

**norms** Standards based on measurements of a large group of people; used for comparing the scores of an individual with those of others within a well-defined group.

**object permanence** The recognition that objects exist independently of an individual's action or awareness; an important cognitive acquisition of infancy.

**observational learning** The process of learning new responses by watching the behaviour of another.

**observer bias** The distortion of evidence because of the personal motives and expectations of the viewer.

**obsessive-compulsive disorder (OCD)** A mental disorder characterised by obsessions—thoughts, images or impulses that persist despite efforts to suppress them—and compulsions—repetitive, purposeful acts performed in a ritualised manner.

**occipital lobe** Rearmost region of the brain; contains primary visual cortex.

**oestrogen** The female sex hormone, produced by the ovaries, that is responsible for the release of eggs from the ovaries as well as for the development and maintenance of female reproductive structures and secondary sex characteristics.

**olfactory bulb** The centre where odour-sensitive receptors send their signals, located just below the frontal lobes of the cortex.

**operant** Behaviour emitted by an organism that can be characterised in terms of the observable effects it has on the environment.

**operant conditioning** Learning in which the probability of a response is changed by a change in its consequences.

**operant extinction** When a behaviour no longer produces predictable consequences, its return to the level of occurrence it had before operant conditioning.

**operational definition** A definition of a variable or condition in terms of the specific operation or procedure used to determine its presence.

**opponent-process theory** The theory that all colour experiences arise from three systems, each of which includes two 'opponent' elements (red v green, blue v yellow and black v white).

**optic nerve** The axons of the ganglion cells that carry information from the eye towards the brain.

**organisational psychologists** Psychologists who study various aspects of the human work environment, such as communication among employees, socialisation or enculturation of workers, leadership, job satisfaction, stress and burnout, and overall quality of life.

**out-groups** The groups with which people do not identify.

**over-regularisation** A grammatical error, usually appearing during early language development, in which rules of the language are applied too widely, resulting in incorrect linguistic forms.

**pain** The body's response to noxious stimuli that are intense enough to cause, or threaten to cause, tissue damage.

**panic disorder** An anxiety disorder in which sufferers experience unexpected, severe panic attacks that begin with a feeling of intense apprehension, fear or terror.

**parallel forms** Different versions of a test used to assess test reliability; the change of forms reduces effects of direct practice, memory, or the desire of an individual to appear consistent on the same items.

**parallel processes** Two or more mental processes that are carried out simultaneously.

**parasympathetic division** The subdivision of the autonomic nervous system that monitors the routine operation of the body's internal functions and conserves and restores body energy.

**parental investment** The time and energy parents must spend raising their offspring.

**parenting practices** Specific parenting behaviours that arise in response to particular parental goals.

**parenting styles** The manner in which parents rear their children; an authoritative parenting style, which balances demandingness and responsiveness, is seen as the most effective.

**parietal lobe** Region of the brain behind the frontal lobe and above the lateral fissure; contains somatosensory cortex.

**partial reinforcement effect** The behavioural principle that states that responses acquired under intermittent reinforcement are more difficult to extinguish than those acquired with continuous reinforcement.

**participant modelling** A therapeutic technique in which a therapist demonstrates the desired behaviour and a client is aided, through supportive encouragement, to imitate the modelled behaviour.

**pastoral counsellor** A member of a religious order who specialises in the treatment of psychological disorders, often combining spirituality with practical problem solving.

**patient** The term used by those who take a biomedical approach to the treatment of psychological problems to describe the person being treated.

**peace psychology** An interdisciplinary approach to the prevention of nuclear war and the maintenance of peace.

**perceived control** The belief that one has the ability to make a difference in the course of the consequences of some event or experience; often helpful in dealing with stressors.

**perception** The processes that organise information in the sensory image and interpret it as having been produced by properties of objects or events in the external, three-dimensional world.

**perceptual constancy** The ability to retain an unchanging percept of an object despite variations in the retinal image.

**perceptual organisation** The processes that put sensory information together to give the perception of a coherent scene over the whole visual field.

**peripheral nervous system (PNS)** The part of the nervous system composed of the spinal and cranial nerves that connect the body's sensory receptors to the CNS and the CNS to the muscles and glands.

**personality** The psychological qualities of an individual that influence a variety of characteristic behaviour patterns across difference situations and over time.

**personality disorder** A chronic, inflexible, maladaptive pattern of perceiving, thinking, and behaving that seriously impairs an individual's ability to function in social or other settings.

**personality inventory** A self-report questionnaire used for personality assessment that includes a series of items about personal thoughts, feelings and behaviours.

**personality types** Distinct patterns of personality characteristics used to assign people to categories; qualitative differences, rather than differences in degree, used to discriminate among people.

**persuasion** Deliberate efforts to change attitudes.

**PET scans** Brain images produced by a device that obtains detailed pictures of activity in the living brain by recording the radioactivity emitted by cells during different cognitive or behavioural activities.

**phenotype** The observable characteristics of an organism resulting from the interaction between the organism's genotype and its environment.

**pheromones** Chemical signals released by organisms to communicate with other members of the species that often serve as long-distance sexual attractors.

**phi phenomenon** The simplest form of apparent motion, the movement illusion in which one or more stationary lights going on and off in succession are perceived as a single moving light.

**phobia** A persistent and irrational fear of a specific object, activity or situation that is excessive and unreasonable given the reality of the threat.

**phonemes** Minimal units of speech in any given language that make a meaningful difference in speech and production and reception; *r* and *l* are two distinct phonemes in English but variations of one in Japanese.

**photoreceptors** Receptor cells in the retina that are sensitive to light.

**physical development** The bodily changes, maturation and growth that occur in an organism, starting with conception and continuing across the life span.

**physiological dependence** The process by which the body becomes adjusted to or dependent on a drug.

**pitch** Sound quality of highness or lowness primarily dependent on the frequency of the sound wave.

**pituitary gland** Located in the brain, the gland that secretes growth hormone and influences the secretion of hormones by other endocrine glands.

**place theory** The theory that different frequency tones produce maximum activation at different locations along the basilar membrane, with the result that pitch can be coded by the place at which activation occurs.

**placebo control** An experimental condition in which treatment is not administered; it is used in cases where a placebo effect might occur.

**placebo effect** A change in behaviour in the absence of an experimental manipulation.

**placebo therapy** A therapy interdependent of any specific clinical procedures that results in client improvement.

**plasticity** Changes in the performance of the brain; may involve the creation of new synapses or changes in the function of existing synapses.

**pons** The region of the brain stem that connects the spinal cord with the brain and links parts of the brain to one another.

**population** The entire set of individuals to which generalisations will be made based on an experimental sample.

**positive punishment** A behaviour is followed by the presentation of an aversive stimulus, decreasing the probability of that behaviour.

**positive reinforcement** A behaviour is followed by the presentation of an appetitive stimulus, increasing the probability of that behaviour.

**possible selves** The ideal selves that a person would like to become, the selves a person could become, and the selves a person is afraid of becoming components of the cognitive sense of self.

**posttraumatic stress disorder (PTSD)** An anxiety disorder characterised by the persistent re-experience of traumatic events through distressing recollections, dreams, hallucinations or dissociative flashbacks. develops in response to rapes, life-threatening events, severe injury, and natural disasters.

**preconscious memories** Memories that are not currently conscious but that can easily be called into consciousness when necessary.

**predictive validity** See criterion validity.

**prefrontal lobotomy** An operation that severs the nerve fibres connecting the frontal lobes of the brain with the diencephalons, especially those fibres in the thalamic and hypothalamic areas best known form of psychosurgery.

**prejudice** The word prejudice refers to prejudgment. It is viewed as an unreasonable attitude that is unusually resistant to rational influence and is likely to be socially destructive.

**preoperational stage** The period between ages two and seven during which a child learns to use language. During this stage, children do not yet understand concrete logic. They also cannot mentally manipulate information and are normally unable to take the point of view of other people.

**primacy effect** Improved memory for items at the start of a list.

**primary reinforcers** Biologically determined reinforcers such as food and water.

**priming** In the assessment of implicit memory, the advantage conferred by prior exposure to a word or situation.

**proactive interference** Circumstances in which past memories make it more difficult to encode and retrieve new information.

**problem solving** Thinking that is directed toward solving specific problems and that moves from an initial state to a goal state by means of a set of mental operations.

**problem space** The elements that make up a problem; the initial state, the incomplete information or unsatisfactory conditions the person starts with; the goal state, the set of information or state the person wishes to achieve; and the set of operations, the steps the person takes to move from the initial state to the goal state.

**procedural memory** Memory for how things get done; the way perceptual, cognitive, and motor skills are acquired, retained and used.

**projective test** A method of personality assessment in which an individual is presented with a standardised set of ambiguous abstract stimuli and interprets their meanings; responses reveal inner feelings and conflicts.

**prosocial behaviours** Behaviours that are carried out with the goal of helping other people.

**prototype** The most representative example of a category.

**proximal stimulus** The optical image on the retina; contrasted with the distal stimulus, the physical object in the world.

**psychiatrist** An individual who has obtained a medical degree and also has completed specialty training in mental and emotional disorders; a psychiatrist may prescribe medications for the treatment of psychological disorders.

**psychic determinism** The assumption that mental and behavioural reactions are determined by previous experiences.

**psychoactive drugs** Chemicals that affect mental processes and behaviour by temporarily changing conscious awareness of reality.

**psychoanalysis** The form of psychodynamic therapy developed by Freud; an intensive prolonged technique for exploring unconscious motivations and conflicts in neurotic, anxiety-ridden individuals.

**psychoanalyst** An individual who has earned either a psychology or a medical degree and has completed postgraduate training in the Freudian approach to understanding and treating mental disorders.

**psychobiography** The use of psychological (especially personality) theory to describe and explain an individual's course through life.

**psychodynamic personality theories** Theories of personality that share the assumption that personality is shaped by and behaviour is motivated by inner forces.

**psychodynamic perspective** A psychological model in which behaviour is explained in terms of past experiences and motivational forces; actions are viewed as stemming from inherited instincts, biological drives, and attempts to resolve conflicts between personal needs and social requirements.

**psychological assessment** The use of specified procedures to evaluate the abilities, behaviours and personal qualities of people.

**psychological dependence** The psychological need or craving for a drug.

**psychological diagnosis** The label given to psychological abnormality by classifying and categorising the observed behaviour pattern into an approved diagnostic system.

**psychology** The scientific study of the behaviour of individuals and their mental processes.

**psychometric function** A graph that plots the percentage of detections of a stimulus (on the vertical axis) for each stimulus intensity (on the horizontal axis).

**psychometrics** The field of psychology that specialises in mental testing.

**psychoneuroimmunology** The research area that investigates interactions between psychological processes, such as responses to stress, and the functions of the immune system.

**psychopathological functioning** Disruptions in emotional, behavioural or thought processes that lead to personal distress or block one's ability to achieve important goals.

**psychopharmacology** The branch of psychology that investigates the effects of drugs on behaviour.

**psychophysics** The study of the correspondence between physical stimulation and psychological experience.

**psychosocial stages** Proposed by Erik Erikson, successive developmental stages that focus on an individual's orientation toward the self and others; these stages incorporate both the sexual and social aspects of a person's developmental and the social conflicts that arise from the interaction between the individual and the social environment.

**psychosomatic disorders** Physical disorders aggravated by or primarily attributable to prolonged emotional stress or other psychological causes.

**psychosurgery** A surgical procedure performed on brain tissue to alleviate a psychological disorder.

**psychotherapy** Any of a group of therapies used to treat psychological disorders that focus on changing faulty behaviours, thoughts, perceptions and emotions that may be associated with specific disorders.

**psychotic disorders** Severe mental disorders in which a person experiences impairments in reality testing manifested through thought, emotional or perceptual difficulties; no longer used as diagnostic category after *DSM-III*.

**puberty** The process through which sexual maturity is attained.

**punisher** Any stimulus that when made contingent upon a response decreases the probability of that response.

**racism** Discrimination against people based on their skin colour or ethnic heritage.

**range** The difference between the highest and the lowest scores in a set of observations; the simplest measure of variability.

**rapid eye movements (REM)** A behavioural sign of the phase of sleep during which the sleeper is likely to be experiencing dreamlike mental activity.

**rational-emotive therapy (RET)** A comprehensive system of personality change based on changing irrational beliefs that cause undesirable, highly charged emotional reactions such as severe anxiety.

**reasoning** The process of thinking in which conclusions are drawn from a set of facts; thinking directed toward a given goal or objective.

**recall** A method of retrieval in which an individual is required to reproduce the information previously presented.

**recency effect** Improved memory for items at the end of a list.

**receptive field** The area of the visual field to which a neuron in the visual system responds.

**reciprocal altruism** The idea that people perform altruistic behaviours because they expect that others will perform altruistic behaviours for them in turn.

**reciprocal determinism** Albert Bandura's social-learning theory that a complex reciprocal interaction exists among the individual, his or her behaviour and environmental stimuli and that each of these components affects the others.

**reciprocity norm** Expectation that favours will be returned—if someone does something for another person that person should do something in return.

**recognition** A method of retrieval in which an individual is required to identify stimuli as having been experienced before.

**reconstructive memory** The process of putting information together based on general types of stored knowledge in the absence of a specific memory representation.

**reflex** An unlearned response elicited by specific stimuli that have biological relevance for an organism.

**refractory period** The period of rest during which a new nerve impulse cannot be activated in a segment of an axon.

**reinforcement contingency** A consistent relationship between a response and the changes in the environment that it produces.

**reinforcer** Any stimulus that when made contingent upon a response increases the probability of that response.

**relative motion parallax** A source of information about depth in which the relative distances of objects from a viewer determine the amount and direction of their relative motion in the retinal image.

**relaxation response** A condition in which muscle tension, cortical activity, heart rate, and blood pressure decrease and breathing slows.

**reliability** The degree to which a test produces similar scores each time it is used; stability or consistency of the scores produced by an instrument.

**repetitive transcranial magnetic stimulation (rTMS)** A technique for producing temporary inactivation of brain areas using repeated pulses of magnetic stimulation.

**representative sample** A subset of a population that closely matches the overall characteristics of the population with respect to the distribution of males and females, racial and ethnic groups, and so on.

**representativeness heuristic** A cognitive strategy that assigns an object to a category on the basis of a few characteristics regarded as representative of that category.

**repression** The basic defence mechanism by which painful or guilt-producing thoughts, feelings or memories are excluded from conscious awareness.

**resistance** The inability or unwillingness of a patient in psychoanalysis to discuss certain ideas, desires or experiences.

**response bias** The systematic tendency as a result of nonsensory factors for an observer to favour responding in a particular way.

**resting potential** The polarisation of cellular fluid within a neuron, which provides the capability to produce an action potential.

**reticular formation** The region of the brain stem that alerts the cerebral cortex to incoming sensory signals and is responsible for maintaining consciousness and awakening from sleep.

**retina** The layer at the back of the eye that contains photoreceptors and converts light energy to neutral responses.

**retinal disparity** The displacement between the horizontal positions of corresponding images in the two eyes.

**retrieval** The recovery of stored information from memory.

**retrieval cues** Internally or externally generated stimuli available to help with the retrieval of a memory.

**retroactive interference** Circumstances in which the formation of new memories makes it more difficult to recover older memories.

**reversal theory** Theory that explains human motivation in terms of reversals from one to the other opposing metamotivational states.

**rods** Photoreceptors concentrated in the periphery of the retina that are most active in dim illumination; rods do not produce sensation of colour.

**rules** Behavioural guidelines for acting in certain ways in certain situations.

**sample** A subset of a population selected as participants in an experiment.

**saturation** The dimension of colour space that captures the purity and vividness of colour sensations.

**schedules of reinforcement** In operant conditioning, the patterns of delivering and withholding reinforcement.

**schemas** General conceptual frameworks or clusters of knowledge regarding objects, people and situations; knowledge packages that encode generalisations about the structure of the environment.

**schemes** Piaget's term for cognitive structures that develop as infants and young children learn to interpret the world and adapt to their environment.

**schizophrenic disorder** Severe form of psychopathology characterised by the breakdown of integrated personality functioning, withdrawal from reality, emotional distortions and disturbed thought processes.

**scientific method** The set of procedures used for gathering and interpreting objective information in a way that minimises error and yields dependable generalisations.

**selective optimisation with compensation** A strategy for successful ageing in which one makes the most gains while minimising the impact of losses that accompany normal ageing.

**selective social interaction theory** The view that suggests that as people age they become more selective in choosing social partners who satisfy their emotional needs.

**self-actualisation** A concept in personality psychology referring to a person's constant striving to realise his or her potential and to develop inherent talents and capabilities.

**self-concept** A person's mental model of his or her abilities and attributes.

**self-efficacy** The set of beliefs that one can perform adequately in a particular situation.

**self-esteem** A generalised evaluative attitude towards the self that influences both moods and behaviour and that exerts a powerful effect on a range of personal and social behaviours.

**self-fulfilling prophecy** A prediction made about some future behaviour or event that modifies interactions so as to produce what is expected.

**self-handicapping** The process of developing, in anticipation of failure, behavioural reactions and explanations that minimise ability deficits as possible attributions for the failure.

**self-perception theory** The idea that people observe themselves in order to figure out the reasons they act as they do; people infer what their internal states are by perceiving how they are acting in a given situation.

**self-report measures** The self-behaviours that are identified through a participant's own observations and reports.

**self-serving bias** An attributional bias in which people tend to take credit for their successes and deny responsibility for their failures.

**semantic memories** Generic, categorical memories, such as the meanings of words and concepts.

**sensation** The process by which stimulation of a sensory receptor gives rise to neutral impulses that result in an experience or awareness of conditions inside or outside the body.

**sensory adaptation** A phenomenon in which receptor cells lose their power to respond after a period of unchanged stimulation; allows a more rapid reaction to new sources of information.

**sensory memory** The initial memory processes involved in the momentary preservation of fleeting impressions of sensory stimuli.

**sensorimotor stage** The period between birth and age two during which an infants knowledge of the world is limited to their sensory perceptions and motor activities.

**sensory neurons** The neurons that carry messages from sense receptors towards the central nervous system.

**sensory receptors** Special cells that convert physical signals into cellular signals that are processed by the nervous system.

**serial position effect** A characteristic of memory retrieval in which the recall of beginning and end items on a list is often better than recall of items appearing in the middle.

**serial processes** Two or more mental processes that are carried out in order one after the other.

**set** A temporary readiness to perceive or react to a stimulus in a particular way.

**sex chromosomes** Chromosomes that contain the genes that code for the development of male or female characteristics.

**sex differences** Biologically based characteristics that distinguish males from females.

**sexism** Discrimination against people because of their sex.

**sexual arousal** The motivational state of excitement and tension brought about by physiological and cognitive reactions to erotic stimuli.

**sexual scripts** Socially learned programs of sexual responsiveness.

**shape constancy** The ability to perceive the true shape of an object despite variations in the size of the retinal image.

**shaping by successive approximations** A behavioural method that reinforces responses that successively approximate and ultimately match the desired response.

**short-term memory (STM)** Memory processes associated with preservation of recent experiences and with retrieval of information from long-term memory; short-term memory is of limited capacity and stores information for only a short length of time without rehearsal.

**shyness** An individual's discomfort and/or inhibition in interpersonal situations that interferes with pursuing an interpersonal professional goal.

**signal detection theory** A systematic approach to the problem of response bias that allows an experimenter to identify and separate the roles of sensory stimuli and the individual's criterion level in producing the final response.

**significant difference** A difference between experimental groups or conditions that would have occurred by chance less than an accepted criterion; in psychology, the criterion most often used is a probability of less than 5 times out of 100, or $p < .05$.

**size constancy** The ability to perceive the true size of an object despite variations in the size of its retinal image.

**sleep apnoea** A sleep disorder of the upper respiratory system that causes the person to stop breathing while asleep.

**social categorisation** The process by which people organise the social environment by categorising themselves and others into groups.

**social cognition** The process by which people select, interpret and remember social information.

**social development** The ways in which individuals' social interactions and expectations change across the life span.

**social intelligence** A theory of personality that refers to the expertise people bring to their experience of life tasks.

**social-learning theory** The learning theory that stresses the role of observation and the imitation of behaviours observed in others.

**social-learning therapy** A form of treatment in which clients observe models' desirable behaviours being reinforced.

**social norms** The expectation a group has for its members regarding acceptable and appropriate attitudes and behaviours.

**social perception** The process by which a person comes to know or perceive the personal attributes.

**social phobia** A persistent, irrational fear that arises in anticipation of a public situation in which an individual can be observed by others.

**social psychology** The branch of psychology that studies the effect of social variables on individual behaviour, attitudes, perceptions and motives; also studies group and intergroup phenomena.

**social role** A socially defined pattern of behaviour that is expected of a person who is functioning in a given setting or group.

**social support** Resources, including material aid, socioemotional support and informational aid, provided by others to help a person cope with stress.

**socialisation** The lifelong process whereby an individual's behavioural patterns, values, standards, skills, attitudes and motives are shaped to conform to those regarded as desirable in a particular society.

**sociobiology** A field of research that focuses on evolutionary explanations for the social behaviour and social systems of humans and other animal species.

**sociocultural perspective** The psychological perspective that focuses on cross-cultural differences in the causes and consequences of behaviour.

**soma** The cell body of a neuron containing the nucleus and cytoplasm.

**somatic nervous system** The subdivision of the peripheral nervous system that connects the central nervous system to the skeletal muscles and skin.

**somatisation disorder** A disorder characterised by unexplained physical complaints in several categories over many years.

**somatoform disorder** A disorder in which people have physical illnesses or complaints that cannot be fully explained by actual medical conditions.

**somatosensory cortex** The region of the parietal lobes that processes sensory input from various body areas.

**somnambulism** A disorder that causes sleepers to leave their beds and wander while still remaining asleep; also known as sleepwalking.

**sound localisation** The auditory processes that allow the spatial origins of environmental sounds.

**specific phobias** Phobias that occur in response to specific types of objects or situations.

**split-half reliability** A measure of the correlation between test takers' performance on different halves (e.g., odd- and even-numbered items) of a test.

**spontaneous recovery** The reappearance of an extinguished conditioned response after a rest period.

**spontaneous-remission effect** The improvement of some mental patients and clients in psychotherapy without any professional intervention; a baseline criterion against which the effectiveness of therapies must be assessed.

**standard deviation (SD)** The average difference of a set of scores from their mean; a measure of variability.

**standardisation** A set of uniform procedures for treating each participant in a test, interview or experiment, or for recording data.

**stereotypes** Generalisations about a group of people in which the same characteristics are assigned to all members of a group.

**stereotype threat** The threat associated with being at risk for confirming a negative stereotype of one's group.

**stigma** The negative reaction of people to an individual or group because of some assumed inferiority or source of difference that is degraded.

**stimulus discrimination** A conditioning process in which an organism learns to respond differently to stimuli that differ from the conditioned stimulus on some dimension.

**stimulus-driven capture** A determinant of why people select some parts of sensory input for further processing; occurs when features of stimuli—objects in the environment—automatically capture attention, independent of the local goals of a perceiver.

**stimulus generalisation** The automatic extension of conditioned responding to similar stimuli that have never been paired with the unconditioned stimulus.

**storage** The retention of encoded material over time.

**stress** The pattern of specific and nonspecific responses an organism makes to stimulus events that disturb its equilibrium and tax or exceed its ability to cope.

**stress moderator variables** Variables that change the impact of a stressor on a given type of stress reaction.

**stressor** An internal or external event or stimulus that induces stress.

**structuralism** The study of the structure of mind and behaviour; the view that all human mental experience can be understood as a combination of simple elements or events.

**superego** The aspect of personality that represents the internalisation of society's values, standards, and morals.

**sympathetic division** The subdivision of the autonomic nervous system that deals with emergency response and the mobilisation of energy.

**synapse** The gap between one neuron and another.

**synaptic transmission** The relaying information from one neuron to another across the synaptic gap.

**systematic desensitisation** A behavioural therapy technique in which a client is taught to prevent the arousal of anxiety by confronting the feared stimulus while relaxed.

**taste-aversion learning** A biological constraint on learning in which an organism learns in one trial to avoid a food whose ingestion is followed by illness.

**temperament** A child's biologically based level of emotional and behavioural response to environmental events.

**temporal lobe** Region of the brain found below the lateral fissure; contains auditory cortex.

**tend-and-befriend response** A response to stressors that is hypothesised to be typical for females. Stressors prompt females to protect their offspring and join social groups to reduce vulnerability.

**terminal buttons** The bulblike structures at the branched endings of axons that contain vesicles filled with neurotransmitters.

**test–retest reliability** A measure of the correlation between the scores of the same people on the same test given on two different occasions.

**testosterone** The male sex hormone secreted by the testes that stimulates production of sperm and is also responsible for the development of male secondary sex characteristics.

**thalamus** The brain structure that relays sensory impulses to the cerebral cortex.

**Thematic Apperception Test (TAT)** A projective test in which pictures of ambiguous scenes are presented to an individual who is encouraged to generate stories about them.

**theory** An organised set of concepts that explains a phenomenon or set of phenomena.

**think-aloud protocols** Reports made by experimental participants of the mental processes and strategies they use while working on a task.

**three-term contingency** The means by which organisms learn that, in the presence of some stimuli but not others, their behaviour is likely to have a particular effect on the environment.

**timbre** The dimension of auditory sensation that reflects the complexity of a sound wave.

**tolerance** A situation that occurs with continued use of a drug in which an individual requires greater dosages to achieve the same effect.

**top-down processing** Perceptual processes in which information from an individual's past experience, knowledge, expectations, motivations and background influence the way a perceived object is interpreted and classified.

**traits** Enduring personal qualities or attributes that influence behaviour across situations.

**transduction** Transformation of one form of energy into another; for example, light is transformed into neutral impulses.

**transfer-appropriate processing** The perspective that suggests that memory is best when the type of processing carried out at encoding matches the processes carried out at retrieval.

**transference** The process by which a person in psychoanalysis attaches to a therapist feelings formerly held toward some significant person who figured in past emotional conflict.

**trichromatic theory** The theory that there are three types of colour receptors that produce the primary colour sensations of red, green and blue.

**Type A behaviour pattern** A complex pattern of behaviours and emotions that includes excessive emphasis on competition, aggression, impatience and hostility; hostility increases the risk of coronary heart disease.

**Type B behaviour pattern** As compared to Type A behaviour pattern, a less competitive, less aggressive, less hostile pattern of behaviour and emotion.

**unconditional positive regard** Complete love and acceptance of an individual by another person, such as a parent for a child, with no conditions attached.

**unconditioned response (UCR)** In classical conditioning, the response elicited by an unconditioned stimulus without prior training or learning.

**unconditioned stimulus (UCS)** In classical conditioning, the stimulus that elicits an unconditioned response.

**unconscious** The domain of the psyche that stores repressed urges and primitive impulses.

**validity** The extent to which a test measures what it was intended to measure.

**variable** In an experimental setting, a factor that varies in amount and kind.

**variable-interval (VI) schedule** A schedule of reinforcement in which a reinforcer is delivered for the first response made after a variable period of time whose average is predetermined.

**variable-ratio (VR) schedule** A schedule of reinforcement in which a reinforcer is delivered for the first response made after a variable number of responses whose average is predetermined.

**vestibular sense** The sense that tells how one's own body is oriented in the world with respect to gravity.

**visual cortex** The region of the occipital lobes in which visual information is processed.

**volley principle** An extension of frequency theory, which proposes that when peaks in a sound wave come too frequently for a single neuron to fire at each peak, several neurons fire as a group at the frequency of the stimulus tone.

**Weber's law** An assertion that the size of a difference threshold is proportional to the intensity of the standard stimulus.

**wellness** Optimal health, incorporating the ability to function fully and actively over the physical, intellectual, emotional, spiritual, social and environmental domains of health.

**within-groups design** A research design that uses each participant as his or her own control; for example, the behaviour of an experimental participant before receiving treatment might be compared to his or her behaviour after receiving treatment.

**working memory** A memory resource that is used to accomplish tasks such as reasoning and language comprehension; consists of the phonological loop, visuospatial sketchpad, and central executive.

**zygote** The single cell that results when a sperm fertilises an egg.

# REFERENCES

Abrams, R. (1992). *Electroconvulsive therapy.* New York: Oxford University Press.

Abramson, L.Y., Seligman, M.E.P. & Teasdale, J.D. (1978). Learned helplessness in humans: Critique and reformulation. *Journal of Abnormal Psychology,* 87, 32–48, 49–74.

Adams, J.L. (1986). *Conceptual blockbusting* (3rd ed.). New York: Norton.

Adams, J.S. (1965). Inequity in social exchange. In L. Berkowitz (Ed.), *Advances in experimental social psychology* (2, pp. 267–299). New York: Academic Press.

Ader, R. & Cohen, N. (1981). Conditioned immuno-pharmacological responses. In R. Ader (Ed.), *Psychoneuroimmunology* (pp. 281–319). New York: Academic Press.

Ader, R. & Cohen, N. (1993). Psychoneuroimmunology: Conditioning and stress. *Annual Review of Psychology.* 44, 53–85.

Adler, A. (1929). *The practice and theory of individual psychology.* New York: Harcourt, Brace & World.

Adolphs, R. & Damasio, A.R. (2001). The interaction of affect and cognition: A neurobiological perspective. In J.P. Forgas (Ed.), *Handbook of affect and social cognition* (pp. 27–49). Mahwah, NJ: Erlbaum.

Adolphs, R., Tranel, D., Damasio, H. & Damasio, A. (1994). Impaired recognition of emotion in facial expressions following bilateral damage to the human amygdala. *Nature,* 372, 669–672.

Adolphs, R., Tranel, D., Hamann, S., Young, A.W., Calder, A.J., Phelps, E.A., Anderson, A., Lee, G.P. & Damasio, A.R. (1999). Recognition of facial emotion in nine individuals with bilateral amygdala damage. *Neuropsychologia,* 37, 1111–1117.

Adorno, T.W., Frenkel-Brunswick, E., Levinson, D.J. & Sanford, R.N. (1950). *The authoritarian personality.* New York: Harper.

Aghajanian, G.K. & Marek, G.J. (1999). Serotonin and hallucinogens. *Neuropsychopharmacology,* 21 (Suppl.), 16S–23S.

Ahmed, S.H. & Koob, G.F. (2004). Changes in response to a dopamine receptor antagonist in rats with escalating cocaine intake. *Psychopharmacology,* 172, 450–454.

Ainsworth, M.D.S., Blehar, M., Waters, E. & Wall, S. (1978). *Patterns of attachment.* Hillsdale, NJ: Erlbaum.

Ajzen, I. & Fishbein, M. (2005). The influence of attitudes on behavior. In D. Albarracin, B.T. Johnson & M.P. Zanna (Eds.), *The handbook of attitudes* (pp. 173–221). Mahwah, NJ: Erlbaum.

Ajzen, I. & Sexton, J. (1999). Depth of processing, belief congruence, and attitude-behavior correspondence. In S. Chaiken & Y. Trope (Eds.), *Dual-process theories in social psychology* (pp. 117–138). New York: Guilford.

Akmajian, A., Demers, R.A., Farmer, A.K. & Harnish, R.M. (1990). *Linguistics.* Cambridge, MA: The MIT Press.

Al-Krenawi, A. & Graham J.R. (1999). Gender and Biomedical/Traditional Mental Health Utilization Among the Bedouin-Arabs of the Negev. *Culture Medicine and Psychiatry,* 23(2).

Allen, J.P. & Land, D. (1999). Attachment in adolescence. In J. Cassidy & P.R. Shaver (Eds.), *Handbook of attachment: Theory, research, and clinical applications.* New York: Guilford Press.

Allen, J.P., Porter, M.R. & McFarland, F.C. (2006). Leaders and followers in adolescent close relationships: Susceptibility to peer influence as a predictor of risky behavior, friendship instability, and depression. *Development and Psychopathology,* 18, 155–172.

Allison, D.B., Heshka, S., Neale, M.C., Lykken, D.T. & Heymsfield, S.B. (1994). A genetic analysis of relative weight among 4,020 twin pairs, with an emphasis on sex effects. *Health Psychology,* 13, 362–365.

Allport, G.W. (1937). *Personality: A psychological interpretation.* New York: Holt, Rinehart & Winston.

Allport, G.W. (1954). *The nature of prejudice.* Cambridge, MA: Addison-Wesley.

Allport, G.W. (1961). *Pattern and growth in personality.* New York: Holt, Rinehart & Winston.

Allport, G.W. (1966). Traits revisited. *American Psychologist,* 21, 1–10.

Allport, G.W. & Odbert, H.S. (1936). Trait-names, a psycholexical study. *Psychological Monographs,* 47(1, Whole No. 211).

Altheide, D.L. & Grimes, J.N. (2005). War programming: The propaganda project and the Iraq war. *The Sociological Quarterly,* 46, 617–643.

Alvord, M.K. & Grados, J.J. (2005). Enhancing resilience in children: A proactive approach. *Professional Psychology: Research and Practice,* 36, 238–245.

Amabile, T.M. (1983). *The social psychology of creativity.* New York: Springer-Verlag.

American Association on Mental Retardation. (1992). *Mental retardation: Definition, classification, and systems of supports* (9th ed.). Washington, DC: American Association on Mental Retardation.

American Psychological Association. (2002). Ethical principles of psychologists and code of conduct. *American Psychologist,* 57, 1060–1073.

American Psychological Association. (2003a). Summary report of journal operations, 2001. *American Psychologist,* 57, 659–660.

American Psychological Association. (2003b). Summary report of journal operations, 2002. *American Psychologist,* 58, 663–664.

American Psychological Association. (2006). Summary report of journal operations, 2005. *American Psychologist,* 61, 559.

Amoore, J.E. (1991). Specifics anosmias. In T.V. Getchell, R.L. Doty, L.M. Bartoshuk, and J.B. Snows (Eds.), *Smell and taste in health and disease.* New York: Raven Press. 655–664.

Amos Tversky, Eldar Shafir (1992) Choice under conflict: The Dynamics of Deferred Decision *Psychological Science* 3 (6),1992.

Andersen, B., Kiecolt-Glaser, J.K. & Glaser, R. (1994). A biobehavioral model of cancer stress and disease course. *American Psychologist,* 49, 389–404.

Anderson, A.D. & Phelps, E.A. (2001). Lesions of the human amygdala impair enhanced perception of emotionally salient events. *Nature,* 411, 305–309.

Anderson, A.E. & DiDomenico, L. (1992). Diet vs. shape content of popular male and female magazines: A dose-response relationship to the incidence of eating disorders? *International Journal of Eating Disorders,* 11, 283–287.

Anderson, C.A. & Bushman, B.J. (2001). Effects of violent video games on aggressive behavior, aggressive cognition, aggressive affect, physiological arousal, and prosocial behavior: A meta-analytic review of the scientific literature. *Psychological Science,* 12, 353–359.

Anderson, J.R. (1987). Skill acquisition: Compilation of weak-method problem-solutions. *Psychological Review,* 94, 192–210.

Anderson, J.R. (1996). ACT: A simple theory of complex cognition. *American Psychologist,* 51, 355–365.

Anderson, V.L., Levinson, E.M., Barker, W. & Kiewra, K.R. (1999). The effects of meditation on teacher perceived occupational stress, state and trait anxiety, and burnout. *School Psychology Quarterly,* 14, 3–25.

Angier, N. (1999). *Woman: An intimate geography.* Boston: Houghton Mifflin.

Anliker, J.A., Bartoshuk, L., Ferris, A.M. & Hooks, L.D. (1991). Children's food preferences and genetic sensitivity to the bitter taste of 6-*n*-propylthiouracil (PROP). *American Journal of Clinical Nutrition,* 54, 316–320.

Appelbaum, P.S. (1994). *Almost a revolution: Mental health law and the limits of change.* New York: Oxford University Press.

Appleby, D.C. (2006). Defining, teaching, and assessing critical thinking in introductory psychology. In D.S. Dunn & S.L. Chew (Eds.), *Best practices for teaching introduction to psychology* (pp. 57–69). Mahwah, NJ: Erlbaum.

Appleby, L., Luchins, D.J. & Freels, S. (2006). Homeless admissions and immigration in a state mental hospital. *Psychiatric Services,* 57, 144.

Apter, M.J. (1989). *Reversal theory: Motivation, emotion, and personality.* London: Routledge.

Apter, M.J. (Ed.). (2001). *Motivational styles in everyday life: A guide to reversal theory.* Washington, DC: American Psychological Association.

Apter, M.J. & Batler, R. (1997). Gratuitous risk: A study of parachuting. In S. Svebak & M.J. Apter (Eds.), *Stress & health: A reversal theory perspective* (pp. 119–129). Washington, DC: Taylor & Francis.

Arbisi, P.A., Ben-Porath, Y.S. & McNulty, J. (2002). A comparison of MMPI-2 validity in African American and Caucasian psychiatric inpatients. *Psychological Assessment,* 14, 3–15.

Arias, E. & Smith, B.L. (2003). Deaths: Preliminary data for 2001. *National Vital Statistics Reports,* 51(5), 1–48.

Arkin, R.M. (Ed.). (1990). Centennial celebration of the principles of psychology. *Personality and Social Psychology Bulletin,* 16(4).

Armour, B.S., Woollery, T., Malarcher, A., Pechacek, T.F., & Husten, C. (2005). Annual smoking attributable mortality, years of potential life lost, and productivity losses—United States, 1997–2001. *Morbidity and Mortality Weekly Report,* 54, 626–628.

Armstrong, J.E., Hutchinson, I., Laing, D.G. & Jinks, A.L. (2007). Facial electromyography: responses of children to odor and taste stimuli. *Chemical Senses,* 32, 611–621.

Arnett, J.J. (1999). Adolescent storm and stress reconsidered. *American Psychologist,* 54, 317–326.

Aron, A. & Aron, E.N. (1994). Love. In A.L. Weber & J.H. Harvey (Eds.), *Perspectives on close relationships* (pp. 131–152). Boston: Allyn & Bacon.

Aron A. & Fraley B (1999). Relationship closeness as including other in the self : Cognitive underpinnings and measures, *Social Cognition,* Vol. 17, 2, 140–160.

Aron, A., Mashek, D., McLaughlin-Volpe, T., Wright, S., Lewandowski, G. & Aron, E.N. (2004). Including close others in the cognitive structure of self. In M.W. Baldwin (Ed.), *Interpersonal cognition* (pp. 206–232). New York: Guilford Press.

Aron, A. & Westbay, L. (1996). Dimensions of the prototype of love. *Journal of Personality and Social Psychology,* 70, 535–551.

Aronson, E. & Gonzalez, A. (1988). Desegregation, Jigsaw, and the Mexican-American Experience. In P. A. Katz & D. A. Taylor, (Eds.), *Eliminating Racism: Profiles in Controversy.* New York: Plenum Press.

Aronson, E. (2002). Building empathy, compassion, and achievement in the jigsaw classroom. In J. Aronson (Ed.), *Improving academic achievement: Impact of psychological factors on education* (pp. 209–225). San Diego, CA: Academic Press.

Aruguete, M.S., DeBord, K.A. & Yates, A. & Edman, J. (2005). Ethnic and gender differences in eating attitudes among black and white college students. *Eating Behaviors,* 6, 328–336.

Aserinsky, E. & Kleitman, N. (1953). Regularly occurring periods of eye mobility and concomitant phenomena during sleep. *Science,* 118, 273–274.

Australian Bureau of Statistics 2006, *Deaths, Australia, 2005,* cat. no. 3302.0, ABS, Canberra.

Australian Bureau of Statistics 2006, *Marriages, Australia, 2005*, cat. no. 3306.0.55.001, ABS, Canberra.

Australian Bureau of Statistics (2006). Mental Health in Australia 2004–2005. Accessed 9 November 2007 from <http://www.abs.gov.au/ausstats/abs@.nsf/mf/4824.0.55.001>

Australian Bureau of Statistics 2005. *Suicides: Australia 2005*, cat. no. 3309.0.55.001, ABS, Canberra.

Australian Institute of Health and Welfare (2000). Overweight and Obesity: Australian Diabetes, Obesity and Lifestyle Study. Accessed from <http://www.aihw.gov.au/riskfactors/overweight.cfm>

Australian Institute of Health and Welfare (2004). *Australia's Health 2004.* Canberra: AIHW.

Australian Institute of Health and Welfare (2007). Child Protection Australia 2005–06. Child welfare series no. 40. cat. no. CWS 28. Canberra: AIHW.

Australian Psychological Society Ltd (2003). *Code of ethics.* Accessed 28 September 2007 from <http://www.psychology.org.au>

Australian Research Centre in Sex, Health and Society (2003). Survey published in *Australian and NZ Journal of Public Health*, 27(2).

Australian Rotary Health Research Fund (2006). Mental Health Awareness. Accessed 10 April 2008 from <http://www.arhrf.org.au>.

Ayllon, T. & Michael, J. (1959). The psychiatric nurse as a behavioral engineer. *Journal of the Experimental Analysis of Behavior*, 2, 323–334.

Baars, B.J. (1992). A dozen completing-plans techniques for inducing predictable slips in speech and action. In B.J. Baars (Ed.), *Experimental slips and human error: Exploring the architecture of volition* (pp. 129–150). New York: Plenum Press.

Baars, B.J. (1997). *In the theater of consciousness.* New York: Oxford University Press.

Baars, B.J. & McGovern, K. (1994). Consciousness. *Encyclopedia of Human Behavior*, 1, 687–699.

Baars, B.J. & McGovern, K. (1996). Cognitive views of consciousness: What are the facts? How can we explain them? In M. Velmans (Ed.), *The science of consciousness* (pp. 63–95). London: Routledge.

Baars, B.J., Cohen, J., Bower, G.H. & Berry, J.W. (1992). Some caveats on testing the Freudian slip hypothesis. In B.J. Baars (Ed.), *Experimental slips and human error: Exploring the architecture of volition* (pp. 289–313). New York: Plenum Press.

Baars, B.J., Motley, M.T. & MacKay, D.G. (1975). Output editing for lexical status in artificially elicited slips of the tongue. *Journal of Verbal Learning and Verbal Behavior*, 14, 382–391.

Backman, C.W. & Secord, P.F. (1959). The effect of perceived liking on interpersonal attraction. *Human Relations*, 12, 379–384.

Baddeley, A.D. (1986). *Working memory.* New York: Oxford University Press.

Baddeley, A.D. (1992). Working memory. *Science*, 255, 556–559.

Baddeley, A.D. (1994). The magical number seven: Still magic after all these years? *Psychological Review*, 101, 353–356.

Baddeley, A.D. & Andrade, J. (2000). Working memory and the vividness of imagery. *Journal of Experimental Psychology: General*, 129, 126–145.

Bahrick, H.P., Bahrick, P.O. & Wittlinger, R.P. (1975). Fifty years of memory for names and faces: A cross-sectional approach. *Journal of Experimental Psychology: General*, 104, 54–75.

Bailey, M.B. & Bailey, R.E. (1993). "Misbehavior": A case history. *American Psychologist*, 48, 1157–1158.

Balch, W.R. & Lewis, B.S. (1996). Music-dependent memory: The roles of tempo change and mood mediation. *Journal of Experimental Psychology: Learning, Memory, and Cognition*, 22, 1354–1363.

Balda, R.P., Kamil, A.C., Bednekoff, P.A. & Hile, A.G. (1997). Species differences in spatial memory performance on a three-dimensional task. *Ethology*, 103, 47–55.

Baldwin, A.L. & Baldwin, C.P. (1973). Study of mother–child interaction. *American Scientist*, 61, 714–721.

Ball, L.J., Phillips, P., Wade, C.N. & Quayle, J.D. (2006). Effects of belief and logic on syllogistic reasoning: Eye-movement evidence for selective processing models. *Experimental Psychology*, 53, 77–86.

Ballenger, J.C. (1999). Current treatments of the anxiety disorders in adults. *Biological Psychiatry*, 46, 1579–1594.

Baltes, P.B. (1993). The aging mind: Potential and limits. *The Gerontologist*, 33, 580–594.

Baltes, P.B. & Kunzmann, U. (2003). Wisdom. *Psychologist*, 16, 131–133.

Baltes, P.B., Smith, J. & Staudinger, U.M. (1992). Wisdom and successful aging. In T.B. Sonderegger (Ed.), *The Nebraska Symposium on Motivation: Vol. 39. The psychology of aging* (pp. 123–167). Lincoln: University of Nebraska Press.

Baltes, P.B. & Staudinger, U.M. (1993). The search for a psychology of wisdom. *Current Directions in Psychological Science*, 2, 75–80.

Baltes, P.B. & Staudinger, U.M. (2000). Wisdom: A metaheuristic (pragmatic) to orchestrate mind and virtue toward excellence. *American Psychologist*, 55, 122–136.

Bandelow, B., Krause, J., Wedekind, D., Broocks, A., Hajak, G. & Rüther, E. (2005). Early traumatic life events, parental attitudes, family history, and birth risk factors in patients with borderline personality disorder and healthy controls. *Psychiatry Research*, 134, 169–179.

Bandura, A. (1970). Modeling therapy. In W.S. Sahakian (Ed.), *Psychopathology today: Experimentation, theory and research.* Itasca, IL: Peacock.

Bandura, A. (1977). *Social learning theory.* Englewood Cliffs, NJ: Prentice-Hall.

Bandura, A. (1986). *Social foundations of thought and action: A social cognitive theory.* Englewood Cliffs, NJ: Prentice-Hall.

Bandura, A. (1992). Exercise of personal agency through the self-efficacy mechanism. In R. Schwarzer (Ed.), *Self-efficacy: Thought control of action* (pp. 3–38). Washington, DC: Hemisphere.

Bandura, A. (1997). *Self-efficacy: The exercise of control.* New York: Freeman.

Bandura, A. (1999). Social cognitive theory of personality. In L.A. Pervin & O.P. John (Eds.), *Handbook of personality: Theory and research* (2nd edn, pp. 154–196). New York: Guilford Press.

Bandura, A., Ross, D. & Ross, S.A. (1963). Imitation of film-mediated aggressive models. *Journal of Abnormal and Social Psychology,* 66, 3–11.

Banks, W.C. (1990). *In Discovering Psychology, Program 16* [PBS video series]. Washington, DC: Annenberg/CPB Program.

Banuazizi, A. & Movahedi, S. (1975). Interpersonal dynamics in a simulated prison: A methodological analysis. *American Psychologist,* 30, 152–160.

Banyai, E.I. & Hilgard, E.R. (1976). Comparison of active-alert hypnotic induction with traditional relaxation induction. *Journal of Abnormal Psychology,* 85, 218–224.

Barbaranelli, C., Caprara, G.V. & Maslach, C. (1997). Individuation and the Five Factor Model of personality traits. *European Journal of Psychological Assessment,* 13, 75–84.

Barclay, P. (2004). Trustworthiness and competitive altruism can also solve the "tragedy of the commons." *Evolution and Human Behavior,* 25, 209–220.

Bargh, J.A., Fitzsimons, G.M. & McKenna, K.Y.A. (2003). The self, online. In S.J. Spencer, S. Fein, M.P. Zanna & J.M. Olson (Eds.), *Motivated social perception: The Ontario symposium* (Vol. 9, pp. 195–213). Mahwah, NJ: Erlbaum.

Bargh, J.A. & McKenna, K.Y.A. (2004). The Internet and social life. *Annual Review of Psychology,* 55, 573–590.

Bargh, J.A., McKenna, K.Y.A. & Fitzsimons, G.M. (2002). Can you see the real me? Activation and expression of the "true self" on the Internet. *Journal of Social Issues,* 58, 33–48.

Bar-Hillel, M. & Neter, E. (1993). How alike is it versus how likely is it: A disjunction fallacy in probability judgments. *Journal of Personality and Social Psychology,* 65, 1119–1131.

Barinaga, M. (1993). Carbon monoxide: Killer to brain messenger in one step. *Science,* 259, 309.

Barkataki, I., Kumari, V., Das, M., Taylor, P. & Sharma, T. (2006). Volumetric structural brain abnormalities in men with schizophrenia and antisocial personality disorder. *Behavioural Brain Research,* 169, 239–247.

Barker, L.M., Best, M.R. & Domjan, M. (Eds.). (1978). *Learning mechanisms in food selection.* Houston: Baylor University Press.

Barker, R., Dembo, T. & Lewin, D. (1941). Frustration and aggression: An experiment with young children. *University of Iowa Studies in Child Welfare,* 18(1).

Barling, N.R. & Raine, S.J. (2005). Some effects of hypnosis on negative affect and immune system response. Humanities & Social Sciences Papers. Accessed from <http://epublications.bond.edu.au/bss_pbs/46>

Barney, L.J., Griffiths, K.M., Jorm, A.F. & Christensen, H. (2006). Stigma about depression and its impact on help-seeking intentions. *Australian and New Zealand Journal of Psychiatry,* 40 (1), 51–54.

Barondes, S.H. (1994). Thinking about Prozac. *Science,* 263, 1102–1103.

Baron-Cohen, S. (2000). Theory of mind and autism: A fifteen year review. In S. Baron-Cohen, H. Tager-Flusberg & D.J. Cohen (Eds.), *Understanding other minds: Perspectives from developmental cognitive neuroscience* (pp. 3–20). Oxford: Oxford University Press.

Barrett, L.F., Tugade, M.M. & Engle, R.W. (2004). Individual differences in working memory capacity and dual-process theories of mind. *Psychological Bulletin,* 130, 553–573.

Barry, R.J. (2004). Stimulus significance effects in habituation of the phasic and tonic orienting reflex. *Integrative Physiological and Behavioral Science,* 39, 166–179.

Bartlett, C.W., Gharani, N., Millonig, J.H. & Brzustowicz, L.M. (2005). Three autism candidate genes: A synthesis of human genetic analysis with other disciplines. *International Journal of Developmental Neuroscience,* 23, 221–234.

Bartlett, F.C. (1932). *Remembering: A study in experimental and social psychology.* Cambridge, UK: Cambridge University Press.

Barton, N. (2000). The rapid origin of reproduction isolation. *Science,* 290, 462–463.

Bartoshuk, L. (1990, August–September). Psychophysiological insights on taste. *Science Agenda,* pp. 12–13.

Bartoshuk, L.M. (1993). The biological basis of food perception and acceptance. *Food Quality and Preference,* 4, 21–32.

Bartoshuk, L.M. & Beauchamp, G.K. (1994). Chemical senses. *Annual Review of Psychology,* 45, 419–449.

Bassii, J.N. (2003). The minority slowness effect: Subtle inhibitions in the expression of views not shared by others. *Journal of Personality and Social Psychology,* 84, 26 1–276.

Basso, E.B. (1987). The implications of a progressive theory of dreaming. In B. Tedlock (Ed.), *Dreaming: Anthropological and psychological interpretations* (pp. 86–104). Cambridge, UK: Cambridge University Press.

Batson, C.D. (1994). Why act for the public good? Four answers. *Personality and Social Psychology Bulletin,* 20, 603–610.

Batson, C.D., Ahmad, N., Yin, J., Bedell, S.J., Johnson, J.W., Templin, C.M. & Whiteside, A. (1999). Two threats to the common good: Self-interested egoism and empathy-induced altruism. *Personality and Social Psychology Bulletin,* 25, 3–16.

Batson, C.D., Klein, T.R., Highberger, L. & Shaw, L.L. (1995). Immorality from empathy-induced altruism: When compassion and justice conflict. *Journal of Personality and Social Psychology,* 68, 1042–1054.

Batson, C.D. & Powell, A.A. (2003). Altruism and prosocial behavior. In T. Millon & M.J. Lerner (Eds.), *Handbook of psychology: Personality and social psychology* (5, pp. 463–484). New York: Wiley.

Baudry, M., Davis, J.L. & Thompson, R.F. (Eds.). (1999). *Advances in synaptic plasticity.* Cambridge, MA: MIT Press.

Baumeister, R.F. (2000). Gender differences in erotic plasticity: The female sex drive as socially flexible and responsive. *Psychological Bulletin, 126*, 347–374.

Baumeister, R.F., Campbell, J.D., Krueger, J.I. & Vohs, K.D. (2003). Does high self-esteem cause better performance, interpersonal success, happiness, or healthy lifestyles? *Psychological Science in the Public Interest, 4*, 1–44.

Baumeister, R.F., Tice, D.M. & Hutton, D.G. (1989). Self-presentational motivations and personality differences in self-esteem. *Journal of Personality, 57*, 547–579.

Baumeister, R.F. & Twenge, J.M. (2002). Cultural suppression of female sexuality. *Review of General Psychology, 6*, 166–203.

Baxter, L.R., Schwartz, J.M., Bergman, K.S., Szuba, M.P., Guze, B.H., Mazziotta, J.C., Alazraki, A., Selin, C.E., Ferng, H.K., Munford, P. & Phelps, M.E. (1992). Caudate glucose metabolic rate changes with both drug and behavior therapy for obsessive-compulsive disorder. *Archives of General Psychiatry, 49*, 681–689.

Bayley, N. (1956). Individual patterns of development. *Child Development, 27*, 45–74.

Beck, A.T. (1976). *Cognitive therapy and emotional disorders.* New York: International Universities Press.

Beck, A.T. (1983). Cognitive theory of depression: New perspectives. In P.J. Clayton & J.E. Barrett (Eds.), *Treatment of depression: Old controversies and new approaches* (pp. 265–290). New York: Raven Press.

Beck, A.T. (1985). Cognitive therapy. In H.I. Kaplan & J. Sandock (Eds.), *Comprehensive textbook of psychiatry* (4th ed.). Baltimore: Williams & Wilkins.

Beck, A.T. (1988). Cognitive approaches to panic disorders: Theory and therapy. In S. Rachman & J.D. Maser (Eds.), *Panic: Psychological perspectives.* New York: Guilford Press.

Beck, A.T. & Emery, G. (1985). *Anxiety disorders and phobias: A cognitive perspective.* New York: Basic Books.

Beck, A.T. & Rush, A.J. (1989). Cognitive therapy. In H.I. Kaplan & B. Sadock (Eds.), *Comprehensive textbook of psychiatry* (Vol. 5). Baltimore: Williams & Wilkins.

Beck, A.T., Rush, A.J., Shaw, B.F. & Emery, G. (1979). *Cognitive therapy of depression.* New York: Guilford Press.

Becker, M.W., Pashler, H. & Anstis, S.M. (2000). The role of iconic memory in change-detection tasks. *Perception, 29*, 273–286.

Becker, S.W. & Eagly, A.H. (2004). The heroism of women and men. *American Psychologist, 59*, 163–178.

Beeman, W.O. (2005). *The "great satan" vs. the "mad mullahs": How the United States and Iran demonize each other.* Westwood, CT: Greenwood.

Beer, F.A., Healy, A.F., Sinclair, G.P. & Bourne, L.E., Jr. (1987). War cues and foreign policy acts. *American Political Science Review, 81*, 701–715.

Behrman, A. (2002). *Electro boy.* New York: Random House.

Beiser, M. & Gotowiec, A. (2000). Accounting for native/non-native differences in IQ scores. *Psychology in the Schools, 37*, 237–252.

Bell, D.C. (2001). Evolution of parental caregiving. *Personality and Social Psychology Review, 5*, 216–229.

Bell, S.T., Kurioff, P.J. & Lottes, I. (1994). Understanding attributions of blame in stranger rape and date rape situations: An examination of gender, race, identification, and students' social perceptions of rape victims. *Journal of Applied Social Psychology, 24*, 1719–1734.

Bem, D. (2000). The exotic-becomes-erotic theory of sexual orientation. In J. Bancroft (Ed.), *The role of theory in sex research* (pp. 67–81). Bloomington: Indiana University Press.

Bem, D.J. (1972). Self-perception theory. In L. Berkowitz (Ed.), *Advances in experimental social psychology* (6, pp. 1–62). New York: Academic Press.

Bem, D.J. (1996). Exotic becomes erotic: A developmental theory of sexual orientation. *Psychological Review, 103*, 320–335.

Bem, S.L. (1974). The measurement of psychological androgyny. *Journal of Consulting and Clinical Psychology, 42*, 155–162.

Bendeich, M. (1996). RTRS—Hobart man charged with massacre murder a loner. *Reuters News.* 30 April. Accessed 12 November 2007 from <http://www.factiva.com>

Benedetti, F., Mayberg, H.S., Wager, T.D., Stohler, C.S. & Zubieta, J.K. (2005). Neurobiological mechanisms of the placebo effect. *Journal of Neuroscience, 25*, 10390–10402.

Benedict, R. (1938). Continuities and discontinuities in cultural conditioning. *Psychiatry, 1*, 161–167.

Benedict, R. (1959). *Patterns of culture.* Boston: Houghton Mifflin. Benenson, J.F., Apostoleris, N.H. & Parnass, J. (1997). Age and sex differences in dyadic and group interaction. *Developmental Psychology, 33*, 538–543.

Benenson, J.F. & Heath, A. (2006). Boys withdraw from one-on-one interactions, whereas girls withdraw more in groups. *Developmental Psychology, 42*, 272–282.

Benhamou, S. & Poucet, B. (1996). A comparative analysis of spa- tial memory processes. *Behavioural Processes, 35*, 113–126.

Benjamin, A.S. (2005). Response speeding mediates the contributions of cue familiarity and target retrievability to metamnemonic judgments. *Psychonomic Bulletin & Review, 12*, 874–879.

Benjet, C. & Kazdin, A.E. (2003). Spanking children: The controversies, findings, and new directions. *Clinical Psychology Review, 23*, 197–224.

Benson, H. & Stuart, E.M. (Eds.). (1992). *The wellness book.* New York: Simon & Schuster.

Bergeron, N. & Schneider, B.H. (2005). Explaining cross-national differences in peer-directed aggression: A quantitative synthesis. *Aggressive Behavior, 31*, 116–137.

Bergman, E.T. & Roediger, H.L., III. (1999). Can Bartlett's repeated reproduction experiments be replicated? *Memory & Cognition, 27,* 937–947.

Berkowitz, L. (1993). *Aggression: Its causes, consequences, and control.* New York: McGraw-Hill.

Berkowitz, L. (1998). Affective aggression: The role of stress, pain, and negative affect. In R.G. Geen & E. Donnerstein (Eds.), *Human aggression: Theories, research, and implications for public policy* (pp. 49–72). San Diego, CA: Academic Press.

Berkowitz, S.J. (2003). Children exposed to community violence: The rationale for early intervention. *Clinical Child and Family Psychology Review, 6,* 293–302.

Berlin, B. & Kay, P. (1969). *Basic color terms: Their universality and evolution.* Berkeley: University of California Press.

Berlyne, D.E. (1960). *Conflict, arousal, and curiosity.* New York: McGraw-Hill.

Berman, A.L. & Jobes, D.A. (1991). *Adolescent suicide: Assessment and intervention.* Washington, DC: American Psychological Association.

Berman, K.F., Torrey, E.F., Daniel, D.G. & Weinberger, D.R. (1992). Regional cerebral blood flow in monozygotic twins discordant and concordant for schizophrenia. *Archives of General Psychiatry, 49,* 927–934.

Bernard, L.L. (1924). *Instinct.* New York: Holt, Rinehart & Winston.

Berndt, T.J. (1992). Friendship and friends' influence in adolescence. *Current Directions in Psychological Science, 1,* 156–159.

Bernstein, I.L. (1991). Aversion conditioning in response to cancer and cancer treatment. *Clinical Psychology Review, 11,* 185–191.

Berscheid, E. & Walster, E.H. (1978). *Interpersonal attraction* (2nd ed.). Reading, MA: Addison-Wesley.

Bickerton, D. (1990). *Language and species.* Chicago: University of Chicago Press.

Biederman, J. & Faraone, S.V. (2005). Attention-deficit hyperactivity disorder. *The Lancet, 366,* 237–248.

Biederman, J., Faraone, S.V. & Monteaux, M.C. (2002). Differential effect of environmental adversity by gender: Rutter's index of adversity in a group of boys and girls with and without ADHD. *American Journal of Psychiatry, 159,* 1556–1562.

Biehl, M., Matsumoto, D., Ekman, P., Hearn, V., Heider, K., Kudoh, T. & Ton, V. (1997). Matsumoto and Ekman's Japanese and Caucasian facial expressions of emotion (JACFEE): Reliability data and cross-national differences. *Journal of Nonverbal Behavior, 21,* 3–21.

Biglan, A. (1991). Distressed behavior and its context. *Behavior Analyst, 14,* 157–169.

Bilder, R.M., Volavka, J., Lachman, H.M. & Grace, A.A. (2004). The Catechol-O-Methyltransferase polymorphism: Relations to the tonic-phasic dopamine hypothesis and neuropsychiatric phenotypes. *Neuropsychopharmacology, 29,* 1943–1961.

Billings, A.G. & Moos, R.H. (1982). Family environments and adaptation: A clinically applicable typology. *American Journal of Family Therapy, 20,* 26–38.

Binet, A. (1911). *Les idées modernes sur les enfants.* Paris: Flammarion.

Bingenheimer, J.B., Brennan, R.T. & Earls, F.J. (2005). Firearm violence exposure and serious violent behavior. *Science, 308,* 1323–1326.

Bionic Ear Institute (2006). About the Bionic Ear. 14 July. Accessed 25 October 2007 from <http://www.bionicear.org/bei/AboutHistory.html>

Bitterman, M.E. (1960). Toward a comparative psychology of learning. *American Psychologist, 15,* 704-712.

Bitterman, M.E. (1965). Phyletic differences in learning. *American Psychologist, 20,* 396-410.

Bizo, L.A. & McMahon, C.V. (2007). Temporal generalization and peak shift in humans. *Learning and Behavior, 35,* 123–130.

Black, D.N., Seritan, A.L., Taber, K.H. & Hurley, R.A. (2004). Conversion hysteria: Lessons from functional imaging. *Journal of Neuropsychiatry and Clinical Neurosciences, 16,* 245–251.

Blake, R. & Sekuler, R. (2006). *Perception* (5th ed.). New York: McGraw-Hill.

Bleich, A., Gelkopf, M. & Solomon, Z. (2003). Exposure to terrorism, stress-related mental health symptoms, and coping behaviors among a nationally representative sample in Israel. *JAMA, 290,* 612–620.

Bleuler, M. (1978). The long-term course of schizophrenic psychoses. In L.C. Wynne, R.L. Cromwell & S. Mattysse (Eds.), *The nature of schizophrenia: New approaches to research and treatment* (pp. 631–636). New York: Wiley.

Blood, A.J. & Zatorre, R.J. (2001). Intensely pleasurable responses to music correlate with activity in brain regions implicated in reward and emotion. *Proceedings of the National Academy of Sciences, 98,* 11818–11823.

Bloom, K., Delmore-Ko, P., Masataka, N. & Carli, L. (1999). Possible self as parent in Canadian, Italian, and Japanese young adults. *Canadian Journal of Behavioural Science, 31,* 198–207.

Blos, P. (1965). *On adolescence: A psychoanalytic interpretation.* New York: The Free Press.

Blumberg, H.P., Leung, H.C., Skudlarski, P., Lacadie, C.M., Fredericks, C.A., Harris, B.C., Charney, D.S., Gore, J.C., Krystal, J.H. & Peterson, B.S. (2003). A functional magnetic resonance imaging study of bipolar disorder. *Archives of General Psychiatry, 60,* 601–609.

Blyth, F.M., March, L.M., Brnabic, A.J.M., Jorm, L.R., Williamson, M. & Cousins, M.J. (2001). Chronic pain in Australia: a prevalence study. *Pain, 89,* 127–34.

Bock, K. (1990). Structure in language: Creating form in talk. *American Psychologist, 45,* 1221–1236.

Bock, K. (1996). Language production: Methods and methodologies. *Psychonomic Bulletin & Review, 3,* 395–421.

Bock, K. & Levelt, W. (1994). Language production: Grammatical encoding. In M.A. Gernsbacher (Ed.), *Handbook of psycholinguistics* (pp. 945–984). San Diego, CA: Academic Press.

Boldizar, J.P., Perry, D.G. & Perry L.C. (1989). Outcome Values and Aggression. *Child Development*, 60(3) Jun., 571–579.

Bond, Charles F., Pitre, Urvashi, Van Leeuwen, Marilyn D. (1991). Encoding operations and the next-in-line effect. *Personality and Social Psychology Bulletin*. 17(4), Aug, 435–441.

Bond, L. (1995). Unintended consequences of performance assessment: Issues of bias and fairness. *Educational Measurement: Issues and Practices*, 14(4), 21–24.

Bond, M.H. (2004). Culture and aggression—from context to coercion. *Personality and Social Psychology Review*, 8, 62–78.

Bonney, K.R. & Wynne, C.D.L. (2004). Studies of learning and problem solving in two species of Australian marsupials. *Neuroscience & Biobehavioral Reviews*, 28, 583–594.

Bostrom, N. (2005). In defense of posthuman dignity. *Bioethics*, 19, 202–214.

Boutin, P. & Frougel, P. (2005). GAD2: A polygenic contribution to genetic susceptibility for common obesity? *Pathologie Biologie*, 53, 305–307.

Bovbjerg, D.H., Montgomery, G.H. & Raptis, G. (2005). Evidence for classically conditioned fatigue responses in patients receiving chemotherapy treatment for breast cancer. *Journal of Behavioral Medicine*, 28, 231–237.

Bowd, A.D. & Shapiro, K.J. (1993). The case against laboratory animal research in psychology. *Journal of Social Issues*, 49, 133–142.

Bowden, E.M. & Beeman, M.J. (1998). Getting the right idea: Semantic activation in the right hemisphere may help solve insight problems. *Psychological Science*, 9, 435–440.

Bower, G.H. (1981). Mood and memory. *American Psychologist*, 36, 129–148.

Bower, G.H. (1991). Mood congruity of social judgments. In J.P. Forgas (Ed.), *Emotional & social judgments* (pp. 31–54). Oxford, UK: Pergamon Press.

Bowers, J.S. & Marsolek, C.J. (Eds.). (2003). *Rethinking implicit memory*. London: Oxford University Press.

Bowlby J. (1973). *Attachment and Loss, Vol 2*, New York: Basic Books.

Boyd, R.C., Diamond, G.S. & Bourolly, J.N. (2006). Developing a family-based depression prevention program in urban community mental health clinics: A qualitative investigation. *Family Process*, 45, 187–203.

Bradley, M.M. (1994). Emotional Memory: A Dimensional Analysis. In S. Van Goozen, N.E. Van de Poll, & J.A. Sergeant, (Eds.), *Emotions: Essays on Current Issues in the Field of Emotion Theory* (pp. 97–134). Hillsdale, NJ: Erlbaum.

Braginsky, Benjamin M. & Braginsky, Dorothea D. (1967) Schizophrenic patients in the psychiatric interview: An experimental study of their effectiveness at manipulation. *Journal of Consulting Psychology*. 31(6), Dec, 543–547.

Brainerd, C.J. (1996). Piaget: A centennial celebration. *Psychological Science*, 7, 191–195.

Bramlett, M.D. & Mosher, W.D. (2001). *First marriage dissolution, divorce, and remarriage: United States*. Washington, DC: Centers for Disease Control and Prevention.

Braun, K.A., Ellis, R. & Loftus, E.F. (2002). Make my memory: How advertising can change our memories of the past. *Psychology & Marketing*, 19, 1–23.

Breggin, P.R. (1979). *Electroshock: Its brain disabling effects*. New York: Springer.

Breggin, P.R. (1991). *Toxic psychiatry*. New York: St. Martin's Press. Bregman, A.S. (1981). Asking the "what for" question in auditory perception. In M. Kobovy & J. Pomerantz (Eds.), *Perceptual organization* (pp. 99–118). Hillsdale, NJ: Erlbaum.

Breland, K. & Breland, M. (1951). A field of applied animal psychology. *American Psychologist*, 6, 202–204.

Breland, K. & Breland, M. (1961). A misbehavior of organisms. *American Psychologist*, 16, 681–684.

Brendgen, M., Dionne, G., Girard, A., Boivin, M., Vitaor, F. & Pérusse, D. (2005). Examining genetic and environmental effects on social aggression: A study of 6-year-old twins. *Child Development*, 76, 930–946.

Brennan, A. (1997). Ethics, codes, and animal research. In L.F.M. van Zutphen and M. Balls (Eds.), *Animal alternatives, welfare and ethics*. London: Elsevier Science. pp. 43–54.

Breslin (2000). Human gustation. In T.E. Finger, W.L. Silver & D. Restrepo (Eds.), *The neurobiology of taste and smell* (2nd edn, pp. 423–461). New York: Wiley-Liss, Inc.

Bretherton, I. (1996). Internal working models of attachment relationships as related to resilient coping. In G.G. Noam & K.W. Fischer (Eds.), *Development and vulnerability in close relationships* (pp. 3–27). Mahwah, NJ: Erlbaum.

Bridge, J.A. & Barbe, R.P. (2004). Reducing hospital readmission in depression and schizophrenia: Current evidence. *Current Opinion in Psychiatry*, 17, 505–511.

Briones, T.L., Klintsova, A.Y. & Greenough, W.T. (2004). Stability of synaptic plasticity in the adult rat visual cortex induced by complex environment exposure. *Brain Research*, 1018, 130–135.

Broadbent, D.E. (1958). *Perception and communication*. London: Pergamon Press.

Brody, A.L., Saxena, S., Stoessel, P., Gillies, L.A., Fairbanks, L.A., Alborzian, S., Phelps, M.E., Huang, S.C., Wu, H.M., Ho, M.L., Ho, M.K., Au, S.C., Maidment, K. & Baxter, L.R., Jr. (2002). Regional brain metabolic changes in patients with major depression treated with either paroxetine or interpersonal therapy. *Archives of General Psychiatry*, 58, 631–640.

Broman, S.H., Nichols, P.I. & Kennedy, W.A. (1975). *Preschool IQ: Prenatal and early developmental correlates*. Hillsdale, NJ: Erlbaum.

Bronfenbrenner, U. (1999). Environments in developmental perspective: Theoretical and operational models. In S.L. Friedman & T.D. Wachs (Eds.), *Measuring environment across the lifespan: Emerging methods and concepts* (pp. 3–28). Washington, DC: American Psychological Association.

Bronfenbrenner, U. & Ceci, S.J. (1994). Nature–nurture reconceptualized in developmental perspective: A bioecological model. *Psychological Review*, 101, 568–586.

Brooner, R.K., King.V.L., Kidorf, M., Schmidt, C.W. & Bigelow, G.E. (1997). Psychiatric and substance abuse comorbidity among treatment-seeking opioid abusers. *Archives of General Psychiatry*, 54, 71–80.

Broughton, W.A. & Broughton, R.J. (1994). Psychosocial impact of narcolepsy. *Sleep*, 17(Suppl. 8), S45–S49.

Broussard, C. & Northup, J. (1997). The use of functional analysis to develop peer interventions for disruptive classroom behavior. *School Psychology Quarterly*, 12, 65–76.

Brown, F.B. & Klute, C. (2003). Friendships, cliques, and crowds. In G.R. Adams & M.D. Berzonsky (Eds.), *Blackwell handbooks of developmental psychology* (pp. 330–348). Malden, MA: Blackwell Publishing.

Brown, J.D. (1998). *The self*. New York: McGraw-Hill.

Brown, N.R. & Siegler, R.S. (1992). The role of availability in the estimation of national populations. *Memory & Cognition*, 20, 406–412.

Brown, R. (1976). Reference: In memorial tribute to Eric Lenneberg. *Cognition*, 4, 125–153.

Brown, R. (1986). *Social psychology: The second edition*. New York: The Free Press.

Brown, R.J. (2004). Psychological mechanisms in medically unexplained symptoms: An integrative conceptual model. *Psychological Bulletin*, 130, 793–8 12.

Brownell, K.D. & Rodin, J. (1994). The dieting maelstrom: Is it possible and advisable to lose weight? *American Psychologist*, 49, 781–791.

Buboltz, W.C., Jr., Soper, B., Brown, F. & Jenkins, S. (2002). Treatment approaches for sleep difficulties in college students. *Counselling Psychology Quarterly*, 15, 229–237.

Buchner, A. & Wippich, W. (2000). On the reliability of implicit and explicit memory measures. *Cognitive Psychology*, 40, 227–259.

Buckner, J.C., Mezzacappa, E. & Beardslee, W.R. (2003). Characteristics of resilient youths living in poverty: The role of self-regulatory processes. *Development and Psychopathology*, 15, 139–162.

Bugeja, M.J. (2006, January 23). Facing the Facebook. *Chronicle of Higher Education*.

Bukowski W.M., Newcomb A.F. & Hartup W.W. (1996). *The Company They Keep: Friendships in Adolescence*. Cambridge: Cambridge University Press

Burger, J.M. (1986). Increasing compliance by improving the deal: The that's-not-all technique. *Journal of Personality and Social Psychology*, 51, 277–283.

Burger, J.M., Reed, M., DeCesare, K., Rauner, S. & Rozolis, J. (1999). The effects of initial request size on compliance: More about the that's-not-all technique. *Basic and Applied Social Psychology*, 21, 243–249.

Burnett, R.C., Medin, D.L., Ross, N.O. & Blok, S.V. (2005). Ideal is typical. *Canadian Journal of Experimental Psychology*, 59, 3–10.

Burnstein, E. (2005). Altruism and genetic relatedness. In D.M. Buss (Ed.), *The handbook of evolutionary psychology* (pp. 528–551). Hoboken, NJ: Wiley.

Burnstein, E., Crandall, C. & Kitayama, S. (1994). Some neoDarwinian decision rules for altruism: Weighing cues for inclusive fitness as a function of the biological importance of the decision. *Journal of Personality and Social Psychology*, 67, 773–789.

Burnstein, E. & Worchel, P. (1962). Arbitrariness of frustration and its consequences for aggression in a social situation. *Journal of Personality*, 30, 528–540.

Bushman, B.J. & Anderson, C.J. (2002). Violent video games and hostile expectations: A test of the general aggression model. *Personality and Social Psychology Bulletin*, 28, 1679–1686.

Bushman, B.J., Wang, M.C. & Anderson, C.A. (2005). Is the curve relating temperature to aggression linear or curvilinear? Assaults and temperature in Minneapolis reexamined. *Journal of Personality and Social Psychology*, 89, 62–66.

Buss, D.M. (2000). The evolution of happiness. *American Psychologist*, 55, 15–23.

Buss, D.M. (2004). *Evolutionary psychology: The new science of mind* (2nd edn). Boston: Allyn & Bacon.

Butcher, J.N. (2004). Personality assessment without borders: Adaptation of the MMPI-2 across cultures. *Journal of Personality Assessment*, 83, 90–104.

Butcher, J.N., Graham, J.R., Ben-Porath, Y.S., Tellegen, A., Dahlstrom, W.G. & Kaemmer, B. (2001). *Minnesota Multiphasic Personality Inventory-2 (MMPI-2): Manual for administration and scoring* (2nd edn). Minneapolis: University of Minnesota Press.

Butcher, J.N. & Rouse, S.V. (1996). Personality: Individual differences and clinical assessment. *Annual Review of Psychology*, 47, 87–111.

Bykov, K.M. (1957). *The cerebral cortex and the internal organs*. New York: Academic Press.

Byrne, D. & Clore, G.L. (1970). A reinforcement model of evaluative processes. *Personality: An International Journal*, 1, 103–128.

Cabeza, R. (2002). Hemispheric asymmetry reduction in older adults: The HAROLD model. *Psychology and Aging*, 17, 85–100.

Cabeza, R., Daselaar, S.M., Dolcos, F., Prince, S.E., Budde, M. & Nyberg, L. (2004). Task-independent and task-specific age effects on brain activity during working memory, visual attention and episodic retrieval. *Cerebral Cortex*, 14, 364–375.

Cabeza, R. & Nyberg, L. (2000). Imaging cognition II: An empirical review of 275 PET and fMRI studies. *Journal of Cognitive Neuroscience*, 12, 1–47.

Cahill, L., Uncapher, M., Kilpatrick, L., Alkire, M.T. & Turner, J. (2004). Sex-related hemispheric lateralization of amygdale function in emotionally influenced memory: An fMRI investigation. *Learning & Memory*, 11, 261–266.

Cahn, B.R. & Polich, J. (2006). Meditation states and traits: EEG, ERP, and neuroimaging studies. *Psychological Bulletin, 132,* 180–211.

Cairns, E. & Darby, J. (1998). The conflict in Northern Ireland: Causes, consequences, and controls. *American Psychologist, 53,* 754–760.

Cameron, C.L., Cella, D.C., Herndon, E.E., II, Kornblith, A.B., Zucerkman, E., Henderson, E., Weiss, R.B., Cooper, M.R., Silver, R.T., Leone, L., Canellos, G.P., Peterson, B.A. & Holland, J.C. (2001). Persistent symptoms among survivors of Hodgkin's disease: An explanatory model based on classical conditioning. *Health Psychology, 20,* 71–75.

Campbell, A.J., Cumming, S. & Hughes, I. (2006). Internet Use by the Socially Fearful: Addiction or Therapy? *Cyberpsychology and Behavior, 9 (1),* 69–81.

Campbell, W.K., Sedikides, C., Reeder, G.D. & Elliot, A.J. (2000). Among friends? An examination of friendship and the self-serving bias. *British Journal of Social Psychology, 39,* 229–239.

Campfield, L.A., Smith, F.J. & Burn, P. (1998). Strategies and potential molecular targets for obesity treatment. *Science, 280,* 1383–1387.

Campos, J.J., Bertenthal, B.I. & Kermoian, R. (1992). Early experience and emotional development: The emergence of wariness of heights. *Psychological Science, 3,* 61–64.

Camras, L.A., Oster, H., Campos, J., Campos, R., Ujiie, T., Miyake, K., Wang, L. & Meng, Z. (1998). Production of emotional facial expressions in European American, Japanese, and Chinese infants. *Developmental Psychology, 34,* 616–628.

Camras, L.A., Oster, H., Campos, J.J., Miyake, K. & Bradshaw, D. (1992). Japanese and American infants' responses to arm restraint. *Developmental Psychology, 28,* 578–583.

Canli, T., Desmond, J.E., Zhao, Z. & Gabrieli, J.D.E. (2002). Sex differences in the neural basis of emotional memories. *Proceedings of the National Academy of Sciences, 99,* 10789–10794.

Canli, T., Desmond, J.E., Zhao, Z., Glover, G. & Gabrieli, J.D.E. (1998). Hemispheric asymmetry for emotional stimuli detected with fMRI. *NeuroReport, 9,* 3233–3239.

Canli, T., Sivers, H., Whitfield, S.L., Gotlib, I.H. & Gabrieli, J.D.E. (2002). Amygdala response to happy faces as a function of extraversion. *Science, 296,* 2191.

Cannon, W.B. (1927). The James–Lange theory of emotion: A critical examination and an alternative theory. *American Journal of Psychology, 39,* 106–124.

Cannon, W.B. (1929). *Bodily changes in pain, hunger, fear, and rage* (2nd edn). New York: Appleton-Century-Crofts.

Cannon, W.B. (1934). Hunger and thirst. In C. Murchison (Ed.), *A handbook of general experimental psychology.* Worcester, MA: Clark University Press.

Cannon, W.B. & Washburn, A.L. (1912). An explanation of hunger. *American Journal of Physiology, 29,* 441–454.

Cantor, N. & Kihlstrom, J.R. (1987). *Personality and social intelligence.* Englewood Cliffs, NJ: Prentice Hall.

Caplan, S.E. (2005). A social skill account of problematic Internet use. *Journal of Communication, 55,* 721–736.

Caprara, G.V., Barbaranelli, C., Borgoni, L. & Perugini, M. (1993). The Big Five Questionnaire: A new questionnaire for the measurement of the five factor model. *Personality and Individual Differences, 15,* 281–288.

Caprara, G.V., Barbaranelli, C. & Zimbardo, P.G. (1996). Understanding the complexity of human aggression: Affective, cognitive, and social dimensions of individual differences in pro-pensity toward aggression. *European Journal of Personality, 10,* 133–155.

Caprara, G.V., Regalia, C. & Bandura, A. (2002). Longitudinal impact of perceived self-regulatory efficacy on violent conduct. *European Psychologist, 7,* 63–69.

Carazo, P., Sanchez, E., Font, E. & Desbiis, E. (2004). Chemosensory cues allow male *Tenebrio molitor* beetles to assess the reproductive status of prospective mates. *Animal Behaviour, 68,* 123–129.

Carducci, B.J. & Zimbardo, P.G. (1995, November/December). Are you shy? *Psychology Today, 28,* 34–40.

Carey, S. (1978). The child as word learner. In M. Hale, J. Bresnan & G.A. Miller (Eds.), *Linguistic theory and psychological reality* (pp. 265–293). Cambridge, MA: MIT Press.

Carey, S. (1985). *Conceptual change in childhood.* Cambridge, MA: MIT Press.

Carlsmith, J.M. & Gross, A. (1969). Some effects of guilt on compliance. *Journal of Personality and Social Psychology, 11,* 232–240.

Carlson, M., Charlin, V. & Miller, N. (1988). Positive mood and helping behavior: A test of six hypotheses. *Journal of Personality and Social Psychology, 55,* 211–229.

Caron, S.L. & Moskey, E.G. (2002). Changes over time in teenage sexual relationships: Comparing the high school class of 1950, 1975, and 2000. *Adolescence, 37,* 515–526.

Carstensen, L.L. (1991). Selectivity theory: Social activity in life-span context. In K.W. Schaie (Ed.), *Annual review of geriatrics and gerontology* (11). New York: Springer.

Carstensen, L.L. (1998). A life-span approach to social motivation. In J. Heckhausen & C.S. Dweck (Eds.), *Motivation and self-regulation across the life span* (pp. 341–364). New York: Cambridge University Press.

Carstensen, L.L. & Freund, A.M. (1994). The resilience of the aging self. *Developmental Review, 14,* 81–92.

Carstensen, L.L. & Pasupathi, M. (1993). Women of a certain age. In S. Matteo (Ed.), *American women in the nineties: Today's critical issues* (pp. 66–78). Boston: Northeastern University Press.

Carter, J.H. (1982). The effects of aging on selected visual functions: Color vision, glare sensitivity, field of vision, and accommodation. In R. Sekuler, D. Kline & K. Dismukes (Eds.), *Aging and human visual function* (pp. 121–130). New York: Liss.

Caspi, A., Sugden, K., Moffitt, T.E., Taylor, A., Craig, I.W., Harrington, H., McClay, J., Mill, J., Martin, J., Braithwaite, A. & Poulton, R. (2003). Influence of life stress on depression: Moderation by a polymorphism in the 5-HTT gene. *Science, 301*, 386–389.

Cassel, J.-C., Riegert, C., Rutz, S., Koenig, J., Rothmaier, K., Cosquer, B., Lazarus, C., Birthelmer, A., Jeltsch, H., Jones, B.C. & Jackisch, R. (2005). Ethanol, 3,4-methylenedioxymethamphetamine (ecstasy and their combination: Long-term behavioral, neuro-chemical and neuropharmacological effects in the rat. *Neuropsychopharmacology, 30*, 1870–1882.

Catalan, J., Burgess, A., Pergami, A., Hulme, N., Gazzard, B. & Phillips, R. (1996). The psychological impact on staff of caring for people with serious diseases: The case of HIV infection and oncology. *Journal of Psychosomatic Research, 42*, 425–435.

Catalano, R., Novaco, R. & McConnell, W. (1997). A model of the net effect of job loss on violence. *Journal of Personality and Social Psychology, 72*, 1440–1447.

Catalano, R., Novaco, R.W. & McConnell, W. (2002). Layoffs and violence revisited. *Aggressive Behavior, 28*, 233–247.

Caterina, M.J., Leffler, A., Malmberg, A.B., Martin, W.J., Trafton, J., Petersen-Zeitz, K.R., Koltzenburg, M., Basbaum, A.I. & Julius, D. (2000). Impaired nociception and pain sensation in mice lacking the capsaicin receptor. *Science, 288*, 306–313.

Cattell, R.B. (1963). Theory of fluid and crystallized intelligence: A critical experiment. *Journal of Educational Psychology, 54*, 1–22.

Cattell, R.B. (1979). *Personality and learning theory.* New York: Springer.

Ceci, S.J. (1999). Schooling and intelligence. In S.J. Ceci & W.M. Williams (Eds.), *The nature-nurture debate: The essential readings* (pp. 168–175). Oxford, UK: Blackwell.

Cervone, D. (2000). Thinking about self-efficacy. *Behavior Modification, 24*, 30–56.

Ceschi, G., van der Linden, M., Dunker, D., Perroud, A. & Brédart, S. (2003). Further exploration memory bias in compulsive washers. *Behaviour Research and Therapy, 41*, 73 7–748.

Chaffey G. (2002). Identifiying High Academic Potential in Australian Aboriginal Children Using Dynamic Testing. *Australasian Journal of Gifted Education,* 12(1). June.

Chamberlain, K. & Zika, S. (1990). The minor events approach to stress: Support for the use of daily hassles. *British Journal of Psychology, 81*, 469–481.

Champoux, M., Boyce, W.T. & Suomi, S.J. (1995). Biobehavioral comparisons between adopted and nonadopted rhesus monkey infants. *Journal of Developmental and Behavioral Pediatrics, 16*, 6–13.

Chan, A.Y. & Wethington, E. (1998). Factors promoting marital resilience among interracial couples. In H.I. McCubbin, E.A. Thompson, A.I. Thompson & J.E. Fromer (Eds.), *Resiliency in Native American and immigrant families* (pp. 7 1–87). Thousand Oaks, CA: Sage.

Chao, S.J. & Cheng, P.W. (2000). The emergence of inferential rules: The use of pragmatic reasoning schemas by preschoolers. *Cognitive Development, 15*, 39–62.

Chapman, P.D. (1988). *Schools as sorters: Lewis M. Terman, applied psychology, and the intelligence testing movement, 1890–1930.* New York: New York University Press.

Chase, W.G. & Ericsson, K.A. (1981). Skilled memory. In J.R. Anderson (Ed.), *Cognitive skills and their acquisition.* Hillsdale, NJ: Erlbaum.

Chaudhari, N., Landin, A.M. & Roper, S.D. (2000). A metabotropic glutamate receptor variant functions as a taste receptor. *Nature Neuroscience, 3*, 113–119.

Chaves, J.F. (1999). Applying hypnosis in pain management: Implications of alternative theoretical perspectives. In I. Kirsch, A. Capafons, E. Cardeña-Buelna & S. Amigó (Eds.), *Clinical hypnosis and self-regulation: Cognitive-behavioral perspectives* (pp. 227–247). Washington, DC: American Psychological Association.

Chen, S., Boucher, H.C. & Tapias, M.P. (2006). The relational self revealed: Integrative conceptualization and implications for interpersonal life. *Psychological Bulletin, 132*, 151–179.

Chen, Z., Mo, L. & Honomichl, R. (2004). Having the memory of an elephant: Long-term retrieval and the use of analogues in problem solving. *Journal of Experimental Psychology: General, 133*, 415–433.

Cheney, D.L. & Seyfarth, R.M. (1990). *How monkeys see the world.* Chicago: University of Chicago Press.

Cheng, P.W. & Holyoak, K.J. (1985). Pragmatic reasoning schemas. *Cognitive Psychology, 17*, 391–416.

Cherry, E.C. (1953). Some experiments on the recognition of speech, with one and with two ears. *Journal of the Acoustical Society of America, 25*, 975–979.

Chess, S. & Thomas, A. (1984). *Origins and evolution of behavior disorders.* New York: Brunner/Mazel.

Chiu, P., Ambady, N. & Deldin, P. (2004). Contingent negative variation to emotional in- and out-group stimuli differentiates high-and low-prejudiced individuals. *Journal of Cognitive Neuroscience, 16*, 1830–1839.

Choice, P. & Lamke, L.K. (1999). Stay/leave decision-making processes in abusive dating relationships. *Personal Relationships, 6*, 351–367.

Chomsky, N. (1965). *Aspects of a theory of syntax.* Cambridge, MA: MIT Press.

Chomsky, N. (1975). *Reflections on language.* New York: Pantheon Books.

Chorover, S. (1981, June). *Organizational recruitment in 'open' and 'closed' social systems: A neuropsychological perspective.* Conference paper presented at the Center for the Study of New Religious Movements, Berkeley, CA.

Christensen, A.J., Moran, P.J., Lawton, W.J., Stallman, D. & Voights, A.L. (1997). Monitoring attentional style and medical regimen adherence in hemodialysis patients. *Health Psychology, 16,* 256–262.

Church, C., Visser, A. & Johnson, L.S. (2004). A path to peace or persistence? The "single identity" approach to conflict resolution in Northern Ireland. *Conflict Resolution Quarterly, 21,* 273–293.

Cialdini, R.B. (2001). *Influence: Science and practice* (4th ed.). Boston: Allyn & Bacon.

Cialdini, R.B., Vincent, J.E., Lewis, S.K., Catalan, J., Wheeler, D. & Darby, B.L. (1975). Reciprocal concessions procedure for inducing compliance: The door-in-the-face technique. *Journal of Personality and Social Psychology, 31,* 206–2 15.

Ciaranello, R.D. & Ciaranello, A.L. (1991). Genetics of major psychiatric disorders. *Annual Review ofMedicine, 42,* 151–158.

Cicchetti, D. & Carlson, V (Ed.) (1989). *Child Maltreatment: Theory and Research on the Causes and Consequences of Child Abuse and Neglect.* Boston: Cambridge University Press.

Claar, R.L. & Blumenthal, J.A. (2003). The value of stress-management interventions in life-threatening medical conditions. *Current Directions in Psychological Science, 12,* 133–137.

Clapperton, B.K., Mathews, L.R., Fawkes, M.S. & Pearson, A.J. (1996). *The Journal of Wildlife Management, 60,* 195–201.

Clark, B. (1992). *Growing Up Gifted,* 5th edn. New Jersey: Prentice Hall.

Clark, E.V. (2003). *First language acquisition.* Cambridge, UK: Cambridge University Press.

Clark G.M. (2003). Cochlear implants: Fundamentals and Applications. New York: Springer-Verlag.

Clark, H.H. (1996). *Using language.* Cambridge, UK: Cambridge University Press.

Clark, H.H. & Clark, E., V. (1977). *Psychology and language: An introduction to psycholinguistics.* New York: Harcourt Brace Jovanovich.

Clark, H.H. & Van Der Wege, M.M. (2002). Psycho-linguistics. In H. Pashler & D. Medin (Eds.), *Stevens' handbook of experimental psychology: Vol. 3. Memory and cognitive processes* (pp. 209–259). New York: Wiley.

Clark, K. & Clark, M. (1947). Racial identification and preference in Negro children. In T.M. Newcomb & E.L. Hartley (Eds.), *Readings in social psychology* (pp. 169–178). New York: Holt.

Clark, N.M. & Becker, M.H. (1998). Theoretical models and strategies for improving adherence and disease management. In S.A. Shumaker & E.B. Schron (Eds.), *The handbook of health behavior change* (pp. 5–32). New York: Springer.

Clark, Y. (2000) The construction of aboriginal identity in people separated from their families, community, and culture: Pieces of a jigsaw. *Australian Psychologist, 35,* 150–157.

Clarke-Stewart, K.A. (1991). A home is not a school: The effects of child care on children's development. *Journal of Social Issues, 47,* 105–123.

Clarke-Stewart, K.A. (1993). *Daycare.* Cambridge, MA: Harvard University Press.

Clausen, J.A. (1981). Stigma and mental disorder: Phenomena and mental terminology. *Psychiatry, 44,* 287–296.

Clementz, B.A. & Sweeney, J.A. (1990). Is eye movement dysfunction a biological marker for schizophrenia? A methodological review. *Psychological Bulletin, 108,* 77–92.

Clopton, N.A. & Sorell, G.T. (1993). Gender differences in moral reasoning: Stable or situational? *Psychology of Women Quarterly, 17,* 85–101.

Coates, H. (2003). Diagnostic tests: Newborn hearing screening. *Australian Prescriber, 26*(4), 82–84.

Coates, T.J. & Szekeres, G. (2004). A plan for the next generation of HIV prevention research: Seven key policy investigative challenges. *American Psychologist, 59,* 747–757.

Cody, H., Pelphrey, K. & Piven, J. (2002). Structural and functional magnetic resonance imaging of autism. *International Journal of Developmental Neuroscience, 20,* 421–438.

Coe, C.L. (1999). Psychosocial factors and psycho-neuroimmunology within a lifespan perspective. In D.P. Keating & C. Hertzman (Eds.), *Developmental health and the wealth of nations: Social, biological, and educational dynamics* (pp. 201–219). New York: Guilford Press.

Cogan, J.C., Bhalla, S.K., Sefa-Dedeh, A. & Rothblum, E.D. (1996). A comparison study of United States and African students on perceptions of obesity and thinness. *Journal of Cross-Cultural Psychology, 27,* 98–113.

Cohen, D. & Nisbett, R.E. (1994). Self-protection and the culture of honor: Explaining southern violence. *Personality and Social Psychology Bulletin, 20,* 551–567.

Cohen, D., Nisbett, R.E., Bowdle, B.R. & Schwarz, N. (1996). Insult, aggression, and the southern culture of honor: An "experimental ethnography." *Journal of Personality and Social Psychology, 70,* 945–960.

Cohen, D., Taieb, O., Flament, M., Benoit, N., Chevret, S., Corcos, M., Fossati, P., Jeammet, P., Allilaire, J.F. & Basquin, M. (2000). Absence of cognitive impairment at long-term follow-up in adolescents treated with ECT for severe mood disorder. *American Journal of Psychiatry, 157,* 460–462.

Cohen, S., Tyrrell, D.A.J. & Smith, A.P. (1993). Negative life events, perceived stress, negative affect, and susceptibility to the common cold. *Journal of Personality and Social Psychology, 64,* 131–140.

Colado, M.I., O'Shea, E. & Green, A.R. (2004). Acute and longterm effects of MDMA on cerebral dopamine biochemistry and function. *Psychopharmacology, 173,* 249–263.

Coles, C. (1994). Critical periods for prenatal alcohol exposure. *Alcohol Health & Research World, 18,* 22–29.

Collins, M.A. & Amabile, T.M. (1999). Motivation and creativity. In R.J. Sternberg (Ed.), *Handbook of creativity* (pp. 297–312). Cambridge, UK: Cambridge University Press.

Collins, W.A., Maccoby, E.E., Steinberg, L., Hetherington, E.M. & Bornstein, M.H. (2000). Contemporary research on parenting: The case for nature and nurture. *American Psychologist*, 55, 218–232.

Comstock, G. & Scharrer, E. (1999). *Television: What's on, who's watching, and what it means*. San Diego, CA: Academic Press.

Congdon, E. & Canli, T. (2006). The endophenotype of impulsivity: Reaching consilience through behavioral, genetic, and neuroimaging approaches. *Behavioral and Cognitive Neuroscience*, 4, 1–20.

Conner, K.R., Duberstein, P.R., Conwell, Y., Seidlitz, L. & Caine, E.D. (2001). Psychological vulnerability to completed suicide: A review of empirical studies. *Suicide and Life-Threatening Behavior*, 31, 367–385.

Conway, A.R., Kane, M.J., Bunting, M.F., Hambrick, D.Z., Wilhelm, O. & Engle, R.W. (2005). Working memory span tasks: A methodological review and user's guide. *Psychonomic Bulletin & Review*, 12, 769–786.

Coolidge, F.L., Thede, L.L. & Jang, K.L. (2001). Heritability of personality disorders in childhood: A preliminary investigation. *Journal of Personality Disorders*, 15, 33–40.

Cooper, S (2003), Gifted Indigenous Programs: Positive Steps Forward to Unmasking Potential in Minority Cultures, *Gifted*. Submitted Paper.

Coren, S., Ward, L.M. & Enns, J.T. (1999). *Sensation and perception* (5th ed.). Fort Worth, TX: Harcourt Brace.

Coren, S., Ward, L.M. & Enns, J.T. (2004). *Sensation and Perception* (6th ed.). New Jersey: Wiley.

Corina, D.P. & McBurney, S.L. (2001). The neural representation of language in users of American Sign Language. *Journal of Communication Disorders*, 34, 455–471.

Corr, P.J. & Gray, J.A. (1996). Attributional style as a personality factor in insurance sales performance in the UK. *Journal of Occupational and Organizational Psychology*, 69, 83–87.

Correy S. (2005). Constituting Sociality: The social relevance of traditional ownership in post-Mabo Aboriginal Australia. MPhil. Australia.

Corso, J.F. (1977). Auditory perception and communication. In J.E. Birren & K.W. Schaie (Eds.), *Handbook of the psychology of aging* (pp. 535–553). New York: Van Nostrand Reinhold.

Costa, P.T., Jr. & McCrae, R.R. (1985). *The NEO Personality Inventory manual*. Odessa, FL: Psychological Assessment Resources.

Costa, P.T., Jr. & McCrae, R.R. (1992). Four ways five factors are basic. *Personality and Individual Differences*, 13, 653–665.

Council for Aboriginal Reconciliation (2000). National Strategies to Advance Reconciliation. *Roadmap for Reconciliation*. Accessed from <http://www.austlii.edu.au/au/other/IndigLRes/car/2000/10/index.htm>

Council, J.R. & Green, J.P. (2004). Examining the absorption-hypnotizability link: The roles of acquiescence and consistency motivation. *International Journal of Clinical and Experimental Hypnosis*, 52, 364–377.

Courchesne, R., Carper, R. & Akshoomoff, N. (2003). Evidence of brain overgrowth in the first year of life in autism. *JAMA*, 290, 337–344.

Couture, S. & Penn, D. (2003). Interpersonal contact and the stigma of mental illness: A review of the literature. *Journal of Mental Health*, 12, 291–306.

Cowan, C.P. & Cowan, P. (2000). *When partners become parents: The big life change for couples*. Mahwah, NJ: Erlbaum.

Cowan, C.P. & Cowan, P.A. (1988). Changes in marriage during the transition to parenthood. In G.Y. Michaels & W.A. Goldberg (Eds.), *The transition to parenthood: Current theory and research*. Cambridge, UK: Cambridge University Press.

Cowan, C.P., Cowan, P.A., Heming, G., Garrett, E., Coysh, W.S., Curtis-Boles, H. & Boles, A.J., III. (1985). Transitions to parenthood: His, hers, and theirs. *Journal of Family Issues*, 6, 451–481.

Cowan, N. (2001). The magical number 4 in short-term memory: A reconsideration of mental storage capacity. *Behavioral and Brain Sciences*, 24, 87–185.

Cowan, P. & Cowan, C.P. (1998). New families: Modern couples as new pioneers. In M.A. Mason, A. Skolnick & S.D. Sugarman (Eds.), *All our families: New policies for a new century*. New York: Oxford University Press.

Cowan, W.M. (1979, September). The development of the brain. *Scientific American*, 241, 106–117.

Cowles, J.T. (1937). Food tokens as incentives for learning by chimpanzees. *Comparative Psychology Monographs*, 74, 1–96.

Craik, F.I.M. (1994). Memory changes in normal aging. *Current Directions in Psychological Science*, 3, 155–158.

Craik, F.I.M. & Lockhart, R.S. (1972). Levels of processing: A framework for memory research. *Journal of Verbal Learning and Verbal Behavior*, 11, 671–684.

Crandall, C.S. & Eshleman, A. (2003). A justification-suppression model of the expression and experience of prejudice. *Psychological Bulletin*, 129, 414–446.

Crano, W.D. & Prislin, R. (2006). Attitudes and persuasion. *Annual Review of Psychology*, 57, 345–3 74.

Creamer, M., Burgess, P., & McFarlane, C. (2001). Post-traumatic stress disorder: findings from the Australian National Survey of Mental Health and Well-being. *Psychological Medicine*, 31, 1237–1247.

Crockett, L.J. & Silbereisen, R.K. (Eds.). (2000). *Negotiating adolescence in times of social change*. New York: Cambridge University Press.

Crowder, R.G. (1992). Eidetic imagery. In L.R. Squire (Ed.), *Encyclopedia of learning and memory* (pp. 154–156). New York: Macmillan.

Crowder, R.G. & Morton, J. (1969). Precategorical acoustic storage (PAS). *Perception and Psychophysics*, 8, 815–820.

Cryder, C.H., Kilmer, R.P., Tedeschi, R.G. & Calhoun, L.G. (2006). An exploratory study of posttraumatic growth in children following a natural disaster. *American Journal of Orthopsychiatry, 76*, 65–69.

Cummins, D.D. (1996). Evidence of deontic reasoning in 3- and 4-year-old children. *Memory & Cognition, 24,* 823–829.

Cummins, D.D. (1999). Cheater detection is modified by social rank: The impact of dominance on the evolution of cognitive functions. *Evolution and Human Behavior, 20,* 229–248.

Curt, G.A., Breitbart, W., Cella, D., Groopman, J.E., Horning, S.J., Itri, L.M., Johnson, D.H., Miaskowski, C., Scherr, S.L., Portenoy, R.K. & Vogelzang, N.J. (2000). Impact of cancer-related fatigue on the lives of patients: New findings from the Fatigue Coalition. *Oncologist, 5,* 353–360.

Curtis, R.C. & Miller, K. (1986). Believing another likes or dislikes you: Behaviors making the beliefs come true. *Journal of Personality and Social Psychology, 51,* 284–290.

Cutting, J.C. & Bock, K. (1997). That's the way the cookie bounces: Syntactic and semantic components of experimentally elicited idiom blends. *Memory & Cognition, 25,* 57–7 1.

Cutting, J.C. & Proffitt, D. (1982). The minimum principle and the perception of absolute, common and relative motions. *Cognitive Psychology, 14,* 211–246.

Czeisler, C.A., Duffy, J.F., Shanahan, T.L., Brown, E.N., Mitchell, J.F., Rimmer, D.W., Ronda, J.M., Silva, E.J., Allan, J.S., Emens, J.S., Dijk, D.J. & Kronauer, R.E. (1999). Stability, precision, and near-24-hour period of the human circadian pacemaker. *Science, 284,* 2177–2181.

Dahlstrom, W.G., Welsh, H.G. & Dahlstrom, L.E. (1975). *An MMPI handbook, Vol. 1: Clinical interpretation.* Minneapolis: University of Minnesota Press.

Damasio, H., Grabowski, T., Frank, R., Galaburda, A.M. & Damasio, A.R. (1994). The return of Phineas Gage: Clues about the brain from the skull of a famous patient. *Science, 264,* 1102–1105.

Daneman, M. & Carpenter, P.A. (1980). Individual differences in working memory and reading. *Journal of Verbal Learning and Verbal Behavior, 19,* 450–466.

Darley, J.M. & Batson, C.D. (1973). From Jerusalem to Jericho: A study of situational and dispositional variables in helping behavior. *Journal of Personality and Social Psychology, 27,* 100–108.

Darley, J. & Latané, B. (1968). Bystander intervention in emergencies: Diffusion of responsibility. *Journal of Personality and Social Psychology, 8,* 377–383.

Darling, N. & Steinberg, L. (1993). Parenting style as context: An integrative model. *Psychological Bulletin, 113,* 487–496.

Darnton, R. (1968). *Mesmerism and the end of the Enlightenment in France.* Cambridge, MA: Harvard University Press.

Darwin, C. (1965). *The expression of emotions in man and animals.* Chicago: University of Chicago Press. (Original work published 1872)

D'Augelli, A.R., Grossman, A.H., Salter, N.P., Vasey, J.J., Starks, T. & Sinclair, K.O. (2005). Predicting the suicide attempts of lesbian, gay, and bisexual youth. *Suicide and Life-Threatening Behavior, 35,* 646–660.

D'Augelli, A.R., Grossman, A.H. & Starks, M.T. (2005). Parents' awareness of lesbian, gay, and bisexual youths' sexual orientation. *Journal of Marriage and Family, 67,* 474–482.

D'Augelli, A.R., Hershberger, S.L. & Pilkington, N.W. (2001). Suicidality patterns and sexual orientation-related factors among lesbian, gay, and bisexual youths. *Suicide and Life-Threatening Behavior, 31,* 250–264.

D'Augelli, A.R., Pilkington, N.W. & Hershberger, S.L. (2002). Incidence and mental health impact of sexual orientation victimization of lesbian, gay, and bisexual youths in high school. *Social Psychology Quarterly, 17,* 148–167.

Davidson, A.R. & Jaccard, J.J. (1979). Variables that moderate the attitude-behavior relation: Results of a longitudinal survey. *Journal of Personality and Social Psychology, 37,* 1364–1376.

Davidson, G., Sanson, A. & Gridley, H. (2000). Australian psychology and Australia's Indigenous people: A decade of action. *Australian Psychologist, 35,* 88–91.

Davidson, R.J., Jackson D.C. & Kalin, N.H. (2000a). Emotion, plasticity, context, and regulation: Perspectives for affective neuroscience. *Psychological Bulletin, 126,* 890–909.

Davidson, R.J., Putnam, K.M. & Larson, C.L. (2000b). Dysfunction in the neural circuitry of emotion regulation? A possible prelude to violence. *Science, 289,* 591–594.

Davis, M.H., Hall, J.A. & Meyer, M. (2003). The first year: Influences on the satisfaction, involvement, and persistence of new community volunteers. *Personality and Social Psychology Bulletin, 29,* 248–260.

Dawson, D. & Reid, K. (1997). Fatigue, alcohol and performance impairment. Nature, 388, 266.

Dawkins, K., Lieberman, J.A., Lebowitz, B.D. & Hsiao, J.K. (1999). Antipsychotics: Past and future. *Schizophrenia Bulletin, 25,* 395–405.

De Bellis, M.D., Keshavan, M.S., Beers, S.R., Hall, J., Frustaci, K., Masalehdan, A., Noll, J. & Boring, A.M. (2001). Sex differences in brain maturation during childhood and adolescence. *Cerebral Cortex, 11,* 552–557.

De Cock, R. & Matthysen, E. (2005). Sexual communication by pheromones in a firefly, *Phosphaenus hemipterus* (Coleoptera: Lampyridae). *Animal Behaviour, 70,* 807–818.

DeCasper, A.J. & Prescott, P.A. (1984). Human newborns' perception of male voices: Preference, discrimination, and reinforcing value. *Developmental Psychology, 17,* 481–491.

Deckro, G.R., Ballinger, K.M., Hoyt, M., Wilcher, M., Dusek, J., Myers, P., Greenberg B., Rosenthal, D.S. & Benson, H. (2002). The evaluation of a mind/body intervention to reduce psychological distress and perceived stress in college students. *Journal of American College Health,* 50, 281–287.

Dehaene, S. & Akhavein, R. (1995). Attention, automaticity, and levels of representation in number processing. *Journal of Experimental Psychology: Learning, Memory, and Cognition,* 21,314–326.

Dejin-Karlsson, E., Hsonson, B.S., Oestergren, P.-O., Sjoeberg, O. & Karel, M. (1998). Does passive smoking in early pregnancy increase the risk of small-for-gestational age infants? *American Journal of Public Health,* 88, 1523–1527.

Delaney, A.J. & Sah, P. (1999). GABA receptors inhibited by benzodiazepines mediate fast inhibitory transmission in the central amygdala. *Journal of Neuroscience,* 19, 9698–9704.

Delprato, D.J. & Midgley, B.D. (1992). Some fundamentals of B.F. Skinner's behaviorism. *American Psychologist,* 47, 1507–1520.

Dement, W.C. & Vaughan, C. (1999). *The promise of sleep.* New York: Delacorte Press.

Dennett, D.C. (1987). Consciousness. In R.L. Gregory (Ed.), *The Oxford companion to the mind* (pp. 160–164). New York: Oxford University Press.

Department of Education, Science and Training (DEST) (2000). *National Indigenous English Literacy and Numeracy Strategy,* Canberra, DEST.

DePaulo, B.M., Ansfield, M.E., Kirkendol, S.E. & Boden, J.M. (2004). Serious lies. *Basic and Applied Social Psychology,* 26, 147–167.

DePaulo, B.M., Lindsay, J.J., Malone, B.E., Muhlenbruck, L., Charlton, K. & Cooper, H. (2003). Cues to deception. *Psychological Bulletin,* 129, 74–118.

de Rivera, J. (1997). The construction of false memory syndrome: The experience of retractors. *Psychological Inquiry,* 8, 271–292.

Dew, M.A., Hoch, C.C., Buysse, D.J., Monk, T.H., Begley, A.E., Houck, P.R., Hall, M., Kupfer, D.J., & Reynolds, C.F. (2003). Healthy older adults' sleep predicts all-cause mortality at 4 to 19 years of follow-up. *Psychosomatic Medicine,* 65, 63–73.

Dewsbury, D.A. (1981). Effects of novelty on copulatory behavior: The Coolidge effect and related phenomena. *Psychological Bulletin,* 89, 464–482.

Dhawan, N., Roseman, I.J., Naidu, R.K., Thapa, K. & Rettek, S.I. (1995). Self-concepts across two cultures: India and the United States. *Journal of Cross-Cultural Psychology,* 26, 606–62 1.

Dietrich, A. (2004). The cognitive neuroscience of creativity. *Psychonomic Bulletin & Review,* 11, 1011–1026.

Digman, J.M. (1990). Personality structure: Emergence of the five-factor model. *Annual Review of Psychology,* 41, 417–440.

DiLalla, L.F. (2002). Behavior genetics of aggression in children: Reviews and future directions. *Developmental Review,* 22, 593–622.

Di Marzo, V., Fontana, A., Cadas, H., Schinelli, S., Cimino, G., Schwartz, J.C. & Piomelli, D. (1994). Formation and inactivation of endogenous cannabinoid anadamide in central neurons. *Nature,* 372, 686–691.

Dineen, B.R., Ash, S.R. & Noe, R.A. (2002). A web of applicant attraction: Person-organization fit in the context of Web-based recruitment. *Journal of Applied Psychology,* 87, 723–734.

Dion, K.K. & Dion, K.L. (1996). Cultural perspectives on romantic love. *Personal Relationships,* 3, 5–17.

DiPietro, J.A., Hodgson, D.M., Costigan, K.A. & Johnson, T.R.B. (1996). Fetal antecedents of infant temperament. *Child Development,* 67, 2568–2583.

Dirkzwager, A.J.E., Bramsen, I. & van der Ploeg, H.M. (2003). Social support, coping, life events, and posttraumatic stress symptoms among former peacekeepers: A prospective study. *Personality and Individual Differences,* 34, 1545–1559.

Dishman, R.K. & Buckworth, J. (1997). Adherence to physical activity. In W.P. Morgan (Ed.), *Physical activity and mental health* (pp. 63–80). Washington, DC: Taylor & Francis.

Dixon, R.A. (1999). Concepts and mechanisms of gains in cognitive aging. In D.C. Park & N. Schwarz (Eds.), *Cognitive aging: A primer* (pp. 23–41). Philadelphia: Psychology Press.

Dixon, R.A. (2003). Themes in the aging of intelligence: Robust decline with intriguing possibilities. In R.J. Sternberg, J. Lautrey & T.I. Lubart (Eds.), *Models of intelligence: International perspectives* (pp. 151–167). Washington, DC: American Psychological Association.

Dollard, J., Doob, L.W., Miller, N., Mower, O.H. & Sears, R.R. (1939). *Frustration and aggression.* New Haven: Yale University Press.

Dollard, J. & Miller, N.E. (1950). *Personality and psychotherapy.* New York: McGraw-Hill.

Dombrowski, S.C., LeMasney, J.W., Ahia, C.E. & Dickson, S.A. (2004). Protecting children from online sexual predators: Technological, psychoeducational, and legal considerations. *Professional Psychology: Research and Practice,* 35, 65–73.

Domhoff, G.W. (1996). *Finding meanings in dreams: A quantitative approach.* New York: Plenum.

Domhoff, G.W. (1999). Drawing theoretical implications from descriptive empirical findings on dream content. *Dreaming,* 9, 201–210.

Domhoff, G.W. (2005). Refocusing the neurocognitive approach to dreams: A critique of the Hobson versus Solms debate. *Dreaming,* 15, 3–20.

Domjan, M. & Purdy, J.E. (1995). Animal research in psychology. *American Psychologist,* 50, 496–503.

Dong, Q., Weisfeld, G., Boardway, R.H. & Shen, J. (1996). Correlates of social status among Chinese adolescents. *Journal of Cross-Cultural Psychology,* 27, 476–493.

Dorrian, J., Hussey, F. & Dawson, D. (2007). Train driving efficiency and safety: examining the cost of fatigue. Journal of Sleep Research, 16, 1–11.

Dovidio, J.F., Gaertner, S.L. & Kawakami, K. (2003). Intergroup contact: The past, present, and the future. *Group Processes & Intergroup Relations*, 6, 5–21.

Downing, P.E., Jiang, Y., Shuman, M. & Kanwisher, N. (2001). A cortical area selective for visual processing of the human body. *Science*, 293, 2470–2473.

Draijer, N. & Langeland, W. (1999). Childhood trauma and perceived parental dysfunction in the etiology of dissociative symptoms in psychiatric inpatients. *American Journal of Psychiatry*, 156, 379–385.

Drayna, D., Manichaikul, A., deLange, M., Snieder, H. & Spector, T. (2001). Genetic correlates of musical pitch recognition in humans. *Science*, 291, 1969–1972.

Dressel, U., Allen, T. L, Pippal, J.B., Rohde, P.R., Lau, P. & Muscat, G.E.O. (2003). The Peroxisome Proliferator-Activated Receptor ß/δ Agonist, GW501516, Regulates the Expression of Genes Involved in Lipid Catabolism and Energy Uncoupling in Skeletal Muscle Cells. *Molecular Endocrinology* 17 (12): 2477–2493.

Drigotas, S.M. & Rusbult, C.E. (1992). Should I stay or should I go? A dependence model of breakups. *Journal of Personality and Social Psychology*, 62, 62–87.

Drinkwater, Betty A. (1976). Verbal thinking and learning skills of Australian Aboriginal children. *Topics in Culture Learning*. 4, 10–12.

*DSM-IV*. (1994). *Diagnostic and statistical manual of mental disorders* (4th ed.). Washington, DC: American Psychiatric Association.

*DSM-IV-TR*. (2000). *Diagnostic and statistical manual of mental disorders* (4th edn, Text revision). Washington, DC: American Psychiatric Association.

DuBois, P.H. (1970). *A history of psychological testing*. Boston: Allyn & Bacon.

Dudycha, G.J. (1936). An objective study of punctuality in relation to personality and achievement. *Archives of Psychology*, 204, 1–53.

Duker, P.C. & Seys, D.M. (1996). Long-term use of electrical aversion treatment with self-injurious behavior. *Research in Developmental Disabilities*, 17, 293–301.

Duncker, D. (1945). On problem solving. *Psychological Monographs*, 58 (No. 270).

Durkin, S.J. & Paxton, S.J. (2002). Predictors of vulnerability to reduced body image satisfaction and psychological well-being in response to exposure to idealized female media images in adolescent girls. *Journal of Psychosomatic Research*, 53, 995–1005.

Dutton, D.G. & Aron, A.P. (1974). Some evidence for heightened sexual attraction under conditions of high anxiety. *Journal of Personality and Social Psychology*, 30, 510–517.

Dweck, C.S. (1975). The role of expectations and attributions in the alleviation of learned helplessness. *Journal of Personality and Social Psychology*, 31, 674–685.

Ebbinghaus, H. (1973). *Psychology: An elementary text-book*. New York: Arno Press. (Original work published 1908)

Eckensberger, L.H. & Zimba, R.F. (1997). The development of moral judgment. In J.W. Berry, P.R. Dasen & T.S. Saraswathi (Eds.), *Handbook of cross-cultural psychology: Vol. 2. Basic processes and human development* (pp. 299–338). Boston: Allyn & Bacon.

Edinger, J.D., Fins, A.I., Glenn, D.M., Sullivan, R.J., Jr., Bastian, L.A., Marsh, G.R., Dailey, D., Hope, T.V., Young, M., Shaw, E. & Vasilas, D. (2000). Insomnia and the eye of the beholder: Are there clinical markers of objective sleep disturbances among adults with and without insomnia complaints? *Journal of Consulting and Clinical Psychology*, 68, 593–596.

Eich, E. (1995). Searching for mood dependent memory. *Psychological Science*, 6, 67–75.

Eich, E. & Macaulay, D. (2000). Fundamental factors in mood-dependent memory. In J.P. Forgas (Ed.), *Feeling and thinking: The role of affect in social cognition* (pp. 109–130). New York: Cambridge University Press.

Eich, E., Macaulay, D. & Ryan, L. (1994). Mood dependent memory for events of the personal past. *Journal of Experimental Psychology: General*, 123, 201–215.

Eidelson, R.J. & Eidelson, J.I. (2003). Dangerous ideas: Five beliefs that propel groups toward conflict. *American Psychologist*, 58, 182–192.

Ekman, P. (1972). Universal and cultural differences in facial expressions of emotion. In J. Cole (Ed.), *Nebraska symposium on motivation.* Lincoln: University of Nebraska Press.

Ekman, P. (1984). Expression and the nature of emotion. In K.R. Scherer & P. Ekman (Eds.), *Approaches to emotion*. Hillsdale, NJ: Erlbaum.

Ekman, P. (1994). Strong evidence for universals in facial expressions: A reply to Russell's mistaken critique. *Psychological Bulletin*, 115, 268–287.

Ekman, P. & Friesen, W.V. (1971). Constants across cultures in the face and emotion. *Journal of Personality and Social Psychology*, 17, 124–129.

Ekman, P. & Friesen, W.V. (1986). A new pan-cultural facial expression of emotion. *Motivation and Emotion*, 10, 159–168.

Elbert, T., Pantev, C., Wienbruch, C., Rockstroh, B. & Taub, E. (1995). Increased cortical representation of the fingers of the left hand in string players. *Science*, 270, 305–307.

Elkin, A.P. (1977). *Aboriginal Men of High Degree* (2nd edn). University of Queensland Press, Brisbane.

Ellis, A. (1962). *Reason and emotion in psychotherapy*. New York: Lyle Stuart.

Ellis, A. (1995). *Better, deeper, and more enduring brief therapy: The rational emotive behavior therapy approach.* New York: Brunner/ Mazel.

Elms, A.C. (1988). Freud as Leonardo: Why the first psychobiography went wrong. *Journal of Personality*, 56, 19–40.

Elsabagh, S., Hartley, D.E., Ali, O., Williamson, E.M. & File, S.E. (2005). Differential cognitive effects of *Ginkgo biloba* after acute and chronic treatment in healthy young volunteers. *Psychopharmacology*, 179, 437–446.

Emmelkamp, P.M.G., Krijn, M., Hulsbosch, A.M., de Vries, S., Schuemie, M.J. & van der Mast, C.A.P.G. (2002). Virtual reality treatment versus exposure in vivo: A comparative evaluation in acrophobia. *Behaviour Research and Therapy*, 40, 509–516.

Endler, N.S., Macrodimitris, S.D. & Kocovski, N.L. (2000). Controllability in cognitive and interpersonal tasks: Is control good for you? *Personality & Individual Differences*, 29, 951–962.

Enserink, M. (1999). Can the placebo be the cure? *Science*, 284, 238–240.

Enserink, M. (2000). Searching for the mark of Cain. *Science*, 289, 575–579.

Epley, N. & Gilovich, T. (2006). The anchoring-and-adjustment heuristic. *Psychological Science*, 17, 311–318.

Epstein, L.H., Nandley, E.A., Dearing, K.K., Cho, D.D., Roemmich, J.N., Paluch, R.A., Raja, S., Pak, Y. & Spring, B. (2006). Purchases of food in youth: Influence of price and income. *Psychological Science*, 17, 82–89.

Ericsson, K.A. & Chase, W.G. (1982). Exceptional memory. *American Scientist*, 70, 607–615.

Ericsson, K.A. & Simon, H.A. (1993). *Protocol analysis: Verbal reports as data* (rev. edn). Cambridge, MA: MIT Press.

Erikson, E. (1963). *Childhood and society*. New York: Norton.

Esler, W.P. & Wolfe, M.S. (2001). A portrait of Alzheimer secretases–new features and familiar faces. *Science*, 293, 1449–1454.

Espie, C.A. (2002). Insomnia: Conceptual issues in the development, persistence, and treatment of sleep disorder in adults. *Annual Review of Psychology*, 53, 2 15–243.

Estrada, C.A., Isen, A.M. & Young, M.J. (1994). Positive affect improves creative problem solving and influences reported source of practice satisfaction in physicians. *Motivation and Emotion*, 18, 285–299.

Evans, E., Hawton, K., Rodham, K. & Deeks, J. (2005). The prevalence of suicidal phenomena in adolescents: A systematic review of population-based studies. *Suicide and Life Threatening Behavior*, 35, 239–250.

Evans, J. St.B.T., Newstead, S.E., Allen, J.L. & Pollard, P. (1994). Debiasing by instruction: The case of belief bias. *European Journal of Cognitive Psychology*, 6, 263–285.

Evans M. & Farley A. (1998). Institutional characteristics and the relationship between students' first year university and final year secondary school academic performance. Working Paper, 18, Department of Econometrics and Business Statistics, Monash University, p. 3.

Evans-Pritchard, E.E. (1937). *Witchcraft, oracles and magic among the Azande*. Oxford, UK: Oxford University Press.

Exner, J.E., Jr. (1974). *The Rorschach: A comprehensive system*. New York: Wiley.

Exner, J.E., Jr. (2003). *The Rorschach: A comprehensive system* (4th edn). New York: Wiley.

Exner, J.E., Jr. & Weiner, I.B. (1994). *The Rorschach: A comprehensive system: Vol. 3. Assessment of children and adolescents* (2nd edn). New York: Wiley.

Eysenck, H.J. (1952). The effects of psychotherapy: An evaluation. *Journal of Consulting Psychology*, 16, 319–324.

Eysenck, H.J. (1973). *The inequality of man*. London: Temple Smith.

Eysenck, H.J. (1990). Biological dimensions of personality. In L.A. Pervin (Ed.), *Handbook of personality theory and research* (pp. 244–276). New York: Guilford Press.

Fagot, B.I. & Hagan, R. (1991). Observations of parent reactions to sex-stereotyped behaviors: Age and sex effects. *Child Development*, 62, 617–628.

Fakhoury, W. & Priebe, S. (2002). The process of deinstitutionalization: An international overview. *Current Opinion in Psychiatry*, 15, 187–192.

Fantz Robert L. (1963) Pattern Vision in Newborn Infants *Science*, Vol. 140, no. 3564, pp. 296 – 297.

Farina, A., Fischer, E.H., Boudreau, L.A. & Belt, W.E. (1996). Mode of target presentation in measuring the stigma of mental disorder. *Journal of Applied Social Psychology*, 26, 2147–2156.

Farina, A., Gliha, D., Boudreau, L.A., Allen, J.G. & Sherman, M. (1971). Mental illness and the impact of believing others know about it. *Journal of Abnormal Psychology*, 77, 1–5.

Fazio, R.H. (1987). Self-perception theory: A current perspective. In M.P. Zanna, J.M. Olson & C.P. Herman (Eds.), *Social influence: The Ontario Symposium* (5, pp. 129–150). Hillsdale, NJ: Erlbaum.

Fazio, R.H. (1995). Attitudes as object-evaluation associations: Determinants, consequences, and correlates of attitude accessibility. In R.E. Petty & J.A. Krosnick (Eds.), *Attitude strength: Antecedents and consequences* (pp. 247–282). Mahwah, NJ: Erlbaum.

Fazio, R.H. & Roskos-Ewoldsen, D.R. (2005). Acting as we feel: When and how attitudes guide behavior. In T.C. Brock & M.C. Green (Eds.), *Persuasion: Psychological insights and perspectives* (2nd edn) (pp. 41–62). Thousand Oaks, CA: Sage.

Feather, N.T. (1961). The relationship of persistence at a task to expectation of success and achievement related motives. *Journal of Abnormal and Social Psychology*, 63, 552–561.

Fechner, G.T. (1966). *Elements of psychophysics* (H.E. Adler, Trans.). New York: Holt, Rinehart & Winston. (Original work published 1860)

Fernald, A. & Morikawa, H. (1993). Common themes and cultural variations in Japanese and American mothers' speech to infants. *Child Development*, 64, 637–656.

Fernandez-Ballesteros, R. (2002). Social support and quality of life among older people in Spain. *Journal of Social Issues*, 58, 645–659.

Ferster, C.B. & Skinner, B.F. (1957). *Schedules of reinforcement*. New York: Appleton-Century-Crofts.

Festinger, L. (1957). *A theory of cognitive dissonance.* Stanford, CA: Stanford University Press.

Festinger, L. & Carlsmith, J.M. (1959). Cognitive consequences of forced compliance. *Journal of Abnormal and Social Psychology,* 58, 203–211.

Fields, R.D. & Stevens-Graham, B. (2002). New insights into neuro-glia communication. *Science,* 298, 556–562.

Filik, R., Paterson, K.V. & Liversedge, S.P. (2005). Parsing with focus particles in context: Eye movements during the processing of relative clause ambiguities. *Journal of Memory and Language,* 53, 473–495.

Findlay, M. (2007). Introduction, *Futures*: Available online at www.ecoversity.org.au.

Finger, T.E. (1987). Gustatory nuclei and pathways in the central nervous system. In T.E. Finger & W.L. Silver (Eds.). *Neurobiology of taste and smell* (pp. 331–353). Florida: Krieger Publishing Company.

Finger, T.E. & Simon, S.A. (2000). Cell biology of taste epithelium. In T.E. Finger, W.L. Silver & D. Restrepo (Eds.), *The neurobiology of taste and smell* (2nd edn, pp. 287–314). New York: Wiley-Liss, Inc.

Fink, P., Hansen, M.S. & Oxhøj, M.L. (2004). The prevalence of somatoform disorders among internal medical inpatients. *Journal of Psychosomatic Research,* 56, 413–418.

Finkelstein, M.A., Penner, L.A. & Brannick, M.T. (2005). Motive, role identity, and prosocial personality as predictors of volunteer activity. *Social Behavior and Personality,* 33, 403–418.

Fiorito, G. & Scotto, P. (1992). Observational learning in *Octopus vulgaris. Science,* 256, 545–547.

Fisher, B.S., Cullen, F.T. & Turner, M.G. (2000). *The sexual victimization of college women.* Washington, DC: National Institute of Justice.

Fisher, S. & Greenberg, R. (1996). *Freud scientifically appraised.* New York: Wiley.

Fishman, H.C. & Fishman, T. (2003). Structural family therapy. In G.P. Sholevar & L.D. Schwoeri (Eds.), *Textbook of family and couples therapy: Clinical applications* (pp. 35–54). Washington, DC: American Psychiatric Publishing.

Fiske, S.T., Harris, L.T. & Cuddy, A.J.C. (2004). Why ordinary people torture enemy prisoners. *Science,* 306, 1482–1483.

Fitch, W.T. & Hauser, M.D. (2004). Computational constraints on syntactic processing in a nonhuman primate. *Science,* 303, 377–380.

Flavell, J.H. (1985). *Cognitive development* (2nd ed.). Englewood Cliffs, NJ: Prentice Hall.

Flavell, J.H. (1996). Piaget's legacy. *Psychological Science,* 7, 200–203.

Fleming, I. (1959). From a view to a kill. In *For your eyes only* (pp. 1–30). New York: Charter Books.

Fleming, R. & Southwell, B. (2006). An investigation of some factors in the education of Indigenous Australians. The Australian Association for Research in Education. Accessed from <http://www.aare.edu.au/05pap/fle05489.pdf>

Foa, E.B. & Riggs, D.S. (1995). Posttraumatic stress disorder following assault: Theoretical considerations and empirical findings. *Current Directions in Psychological Science,* 4, 61–65.

Folkman, S. (1984). Personal control and stress and coping processes: A theoretical analysis. *Journal of Personality and Social Psychology,* 46, 839–852.

Fombonne, E. (2003). The prevalence of autism. *JAMA,* 289, 87–89.

Ford, C.S. & Beach, F.A. (1951). *Patterns of sexual behavior.* New York: Harper & Row.

Foreshew, J. (2007). Australian researcher in $40m bid to develop bionic eye. *The Australian,* 23 October. Accessed 12 November 2007 from <http://www.factiva.com>

Forgas, J.P. (1995). Mood and judgment: The affect infusion model (AIM). *Psychological Bulletin,* 117, 39–66.

Forgas, J.P. (1999). Feeling and speaking: Mood effects on verbal communication strategies. *Personality and Social Psychology Bulletin,* 25, 850–863.

Forgas, J.P. (Ed.). (2000). *Feeling and thinking: The role of affect in social cognition.* New York: Cambridge University Press.

Försterling, F. (2001). *Attributions: An introduction to theories, research and applications.* New York: Psychology Press.

Foucault, M. (1975). *The birth of the clinic.* New York: Vintage Books.

Foulkes, D. (1962). Dream reports from different states of sleep. *Journal of Abnormal and Social Psychology,* 65, 14–25.

Fowler, H. (1965). *Curiosity and exploratory behavior.* New York: Macmillan.

Frager, R. & Fadiman, J. (1998). *Personality and personal growth.* New York: Longman.

Fraley, R.C., Brumbaugh, C.C. & Marks, M.J. (2005). The evolution and function of adult attachment: A comparative and phylogenetic analysis. *Journal of Personality and Social Psychology,* 89, 731–746.

Fraley, R.C. & Shaver, P.R. (2000). Adult romantic attachment: Theoretical developments, emerging controversies, and unanswered questions. *Review of General Psychology,* 4, 132–154.

Frank, J.D. & Frank, J.B. (1991). *Persuasion and healing: A comparative study ofpsychotherapy* (3rd edn). Baltimore: Johns Hopkins University Press.

Frank, M.E. & Nowlis, G.H. (1989). Learned aversions and taste qualities in hamsters. *Chemical Senses,* 14, 379–394.

Franklin, N. & Tversky, B. (1990). Searching imagined environments. *Journal of Experimental Psychology: General,* 119, 63–76.

Frans, Ö., Rimmö, P.A., Åberg, L. & Fredrikson, M. (2005). Trauma exposure and post-traumatic stress disorder in the general population. *Acta Psychiatrica Scandinavica,* 111, 291–299.

Fraser, M.W., Galinsky, M.J., Smokowski, P.R., Day, S.H., Terzian, M.A., Rose R.A. & Guo, S. (2005). Social information-processing skills training to promote social competence and prevent aggressive behavior in the third grade. *Journal of Consulting and Clinical Psychology, 73,* 1045–1055.

Free TV Australia (2004). *Commercial television industry code of practice* Mosman, NSW: Free TV Australia.

Freedman, J.L. & Fraser, S.C. (1966). Compliance without pressure: The foot-in-the-door technique. *Journal of Personality and Social Psychology, 4,* 195–202.

Freedman, M.S., Lucas, R.J., Soni, B., von Schantz, M., Muñoz, M., David-Gray, Z. & Foster, R. (1999). Regulation of mammalian circadian behavior by non-rod, non-cone, ocular photoreceptors. *Science, 284,* 502–507.

Freud, A. (1946). *The ego and the mechanisms of defense.* New York: International Universities Press.

Freud, A. (1958). Adolescence. *Psychoanalytic Study of the Child, 13,* 255–278.

Freud, S. (1915). Instincts and their vicissitudes. In S. Freud, *The collected papers.* New York: Collier.

Freud, S. (1923). *Introductory lectures on psycho-analysis* (J. Riviera, Trans.). London: Allen & Unwin.

Freud, S. (1957). Leonardo da Vinci and a memory of his childhood. In J. Strachey (Ed. and Trans.), *The standard edition of the complete psychological works of Sigmund Freud* (11, pp. 59–137). London: Hogarth Press. (Original work published 1910)

Freud, S. (1965). *The interpretation of dreams.* New York: Avon. (Original work published 1900)

Freund, A.M. & Baltes, P.B. (1998). Selection, optimization, and compensation as strategies of life management: Correlations with subjective indicators of successful aging. *Psychology and Aging, 13,* 531–543.

Friedman, M. & Rosenman, R.F. (1974). *Type A behavior and your heart.* New York: Knopf.

Friedman, R., Myers, P., Krass, S. & Benson, H. (1996). The relaxation response: Use with cardiac patients. In R. Allan & S.S. Scheidt (Eds.), *Heart and mind: The practice of cardiac psychology* (pp. 363–384). Washington, DC: American Psychological Association.

Friend, R., Rafferty, Y. & Bramel, D. (1990). A puzzling misinterpretation of the Asch 'conformity' study. *European Journal of Social Psychology, 20,* 29–44.

Fromkin, V.A. (Ed.). (1980). *Errors in linguistic performance: Slips of the tongue, pen, and hand.* New York: Academic Press.

Fromm, E. & Shor, R.E. (Eds.). (1979). *Hypnosis: Developments in research and new perspectives* (2nd ed.). Hawthorne, NY: Aldine.

Furman, W. & Buhrmester, D. (1992). Age and sex differences in perceptions of networks of personal relationships. *Child Development, 63,* 103–115.

Furmark, T., Tillfors, M., Marteinsdottir, I., Fischer, H., Pissiota, A., Långström, B. & Fredrikson, M. (2002). Common changes in cerebral blood flow in patients with social phobia treated with citalopram or cognitive-behavioral therapy. *Archives of General Psychiatry, 59,* 425–433.

Furnham, A., Crump, J. & Whelan, J. (1997). Validating the NEO Personality Inventory using assessor's ratings. *Personality & Individual Differences, 22,* 669–675.

Gackenbach, J. & LaBerge, S. (Eds.). (1988). *Conscious mind, sleeping brain: Perspectives on lucid dreaming.* New York: Plenum Press.

Gaines, S.O., Jr. & Agnew, C.R. (2003). Relationship maintenance in intercultural couples: An interdependence analysis. In D. Canary & M. Dainton (Eds.), *Maintaining relationships through communication: Relational, contextual, and cultural variations* (pp.231–253). Mahwah, NJ: Erlbaum.

Gallo, L.C. & Matthews, K.A. (2003). Understanding the association between socioeconomic status and physical health: Do negative emotions play a role? *Psychological Bulletin, 129,* 10–51.

Galton, F. (1907). *Inquiries into human faculty and its development.* London: Dent Publishers. (Original work published 1883)

Ganis, F., Thompson, W.L. & Kosslyn, S.M. (2004). Brain areas underlying visual imagery and visual perception: An fMRI study. *Cognitive Brain Research, 20,* 226–241.

Garb, H.N., Wood, J.M., Nezworski, M.T., Grove, W.M., & Stejskal, W.J. (2001). Toward a resolution of the Rorschach controversy. *Psychological Assessment, 13,* 433–448.

Garcia, J. (1990). Learning without memory. *Journal of Cognitive Neuroscience, 2,* 287–305.

Garcia, J. (1993). Misrepresentations of my criticisms of Skinner. *American Psychologist, 48,* 1158.

Garcia, J. & Koelling, R.A. (1966). The relation of cue to consequence in avoidance learning. *Psychonomic Science, 4,* 123–124.

Garcia, M.M., Shaw, D.S., Winslow, E.B. & Yaggi, K.E. (2000). Destructive sibling conflict and the development of conduct problems in young boys. *Developmental Psychology, 36,* 44–53.

Gardner, H. (1983). *Frames of mind.* New York: Basic Books. Gardner, H. (1993). *Creating minds.* New York: Basic Books.

Gardner, H. (1999). *The disciplined mind.* New York: Simon & Schuster.

Gardner, M. & Steinberg, L. (2005). Peer influence on risk taking, risk preference, and risky decision making in adolescence and adulthood: An experimental study. *Developmental Psychology, 41,* 625–635.

Gardner, R., Jr. (2000, June 12). Parenting: Is AOL worse than TV? *New York, 33,* 38–41.

Gardner, R.A. & Gardner, B.T. (1969). Teaching sign language to a chimpanzee. *Science, 165,* 664–672.

Gassió, R., Artuch, R., Vilaseca, M.A., Fusté, E., Boix, C., Sans, A. & Campistol, J. (2005). Cognitive functions in classic phenylketonuria and mild hyperphenylalaninaemia: Experience in a paediatric population. *Developmental Medicine & Child Neurology, 47,* 443–448.

Gatchel, R.J. & Oordt, M.S. (2003). Acute and chronic pain conditions. In R.J. Gatchel & M.S. Oordt (Eds.), *Clinical health psychology and primary care: Practical advice and clinical guidance for successful collaboration* (pp. 117–134). Washington, D.C.: American Psychological Association.

Gazzaniga, M.S. (1985). *The social brain.* New York: Basic Books.

Gegenfurtner, K.R. & Sperling, G. (1993). Information transfer in iconic memory experiments. *Journal of Experimental Psychology: Human Perception and Performance, 19,* 845–866.

Gelman, S.A. (2003). *Origins of essentialism in everyday thought.* London: Oxford University Press.

Gelman, S.A. & Raman, L. (2002). Folk biology as a window into cognitive development. *Human Development, 45,* 61–68.

Gelman, S.A. & Wellman, H.M. (1991). Insides and essences: Early understandings of the non-obvious. *Cognition, 38,* 213–244.

Gentner, D. & Goldin-Meadow, S. (Eds.), *Language in mind: Advances in the study of language and thought.* Cambridge, MA: MIT Press.

Gergen, K.J., Gulerce, A., Lock, A. & Misra, G. (1996). Psychological science in a cultural context. *American Psychologist, 51,* 496–503.

Gerrig, R.J. & O'Brien, E.J. (2005). The scope of memory-based processing. *Discourse Processes, 39,* 225–242.

Gershoff, E.T. (2002). Corporal punishment by parents and associated child behaviors and experiences: A meta-analytic and theoretical review. *Psychological Bulletin, 128,* 539–579.

Gershon, E.S., Berrettini, W., Nurnberger, J., Jr. & Goldin, L. (1987). Genetics of affective illness. In H.Y. Meltzer (Ed.), *Psychopharmacology: The third generation ofprogress* (pp. 481–491). New York: Raven Press.

Giambra, L.M. & Arenberg, D. (1993). Adult age differences in forgetting sentences. *Psychology and Aging, 8,* 451–462.

Gibbons, A. (2002). Hot spots of brain evolution. *Science, 296,* 837.

Gibbs, J.L., Ellison, N.B. & Heino, R.D. (2006). Self-presentation in online personals: The role of anticipated future interaction, self-disclosure, and perceived success in Internet dating. *Communication Research, 33,* 152–177.

Gibson, E.J. & Walk, R.D. (1960). The 'visual cliff', *Scientific American, 202,* 67–71.

Gibson, J.J. (1979). *An ecological approach to visual perception.* Boston: Houghton Mifflin.

Gibson, J.L. (2006). The contributions of truth to reconciliation. *Journal of Conflict Resolution, 50,* 409–432.

Gidron, Y., Davidson, K. & Bata, I. (1999). The short-term effects of a hostility-reduction intervention on male coronary heart disease patients. *Health Psychology, 18,* 416–420.

Gilligan, C. (1982). *In a different voice: Psychological theory and women's development.* Cambridge, MA: Harvard University Press.

Giligan, S. & Bower, G.H. (1984). Cognitive consequences of emotional arousal. In C. Izard, J. Kagan & R. Zajonc (Eds.), *Emotions, cognitions, and behavior* (pp. 547–588). Cambridge, UK: Cambridge University Press.

Giovich, T. (1991). *How we know what isn't so: The fallibility of human reason in everyday life.* New York: The Free Press.

Giron, M. & Gomez-Beneyto, M. (1998). Relationship between empathic family attitude and relapse in schizophrenia: A two-year follow-up prospective study. *Schizophrenia Bulletin, 24,* 619–627.

Gitlin, M., Nuechterlein, K., Subotnik, K.L., Ventura, J., Mintz, J., Fogelson, D.L., Bartzokis, G. & Aravagiri, M. (2001). Clinical outcome following neuroleptic discontinuation in patients with remitted recent-onset schizophrenia. *American Journal of Psychiatry, 158,* 1835–1842.

Glanz, K., Rizzo, A. & Graap, K. (2003). Virtual reality for psychotherapy: Current reality and future possibilities. *Psychotherapy: Theory, Research, Practice, Training, 40,* 55–67.

Glaser, R., Kiecolt-Glaser, J.K., Marucha, P.T., MacCallum, R.C., Laskowski, B.F. & Malarkey, W.B. (1999). Stress-related changes in proinflammatory cytokine production in wounds. *Archives of General Psychiatry, 56,* 450–456.

Gleaves, D.H., May, M.C. & Cardeña, E. (2001). An examination of the diagnostic validity of dissociative identity disorder. *Clinical Psychology Review, 21,* 577–608.

Glusman, G., Yania, I., Rubin, I. & Lancet, D. (2001). The complete human olfactory subgenome. *Genome Research, 11,* 685–702.

Gobet, F. & Simon, H.A. (1996). The roles of recognition processes and look-ahead search in time-constrained expert problem solving: Evidence from grand-master-level chess. *Psychological Science, 7,* 52–55.

Goddard, H.H. (1914). *The Kallikak family: A study of the heredity of feeble-mindedness.* New York: Macmillan.

Goldfried, M.R. (2003). Cognitive-behavior therapy: Reflections on the evolution of a therapeutic orientation. *Cognitive Therapy and Research, 27,*53–69.

Goldfried, M.R. & Davila, J. (2005). The role of relationship and technique in therapeutic change. *Psychotherapy: Theory, Research, Practice, Training, 42,* 421–430.

Goldin-Meadow, S. (2003). *The resilience of language: What gesture creation in deaf children can tell us about how all children learn language.* New York: Psychology Press.

Goldin-Meadow, S. & Mylander, C. (1990). Beyond the input given: The child's role in the acquisition of language. *Language, 66,* 323–355.

Goldstein, E.B. (1999). *Sensation & perception* (5th edn). Pacific Grove, CA: Brooks/Cole.

Goldstein, E.B. (2007). *Sensation and perception* (7th edn). Belmont CA: Thomson Wadsworth.

Goldstein, J.M., Seidman, L.J., Horton, N.J., Makris, N., Kennedy, D.N., Caviness, V.S., Jr., Faraone, S.V. & Tsuang, M.T. (2001). Normal sexual dimorphism of the human brain assessed by in vivo magnetic resonance imaging. *Cerebral Cortex*, 11, 490–497.

Goldstrom, I.D., Campbell, J., Rogers, J.A., Lambert, D.B., Black-low, B., Henderson, M.J. & Manderscheid, R.W. (2006). National estimates for mental health support groups, self-help organizations, and consumer-operated services. *Administration and Policy in Mental Health and Mental Health Services Research*, 33, 92–103.

Goodall, J. (1986). *The chimpanzees of Gombe: Patterns of behavior.* Cambridge, MA: Harvard University Press.

Goodall, J. (1990). *Through a window: My thirty years with the chimpanzees of Gombe.* Boston: Houghton Mifflin.

Gooden, D.R. & Baddeley, A.D. (1975). Context-dependent memory in two natural environments: On land and under water. *British Journal of Psychology*, 66, 325–331.

Goodheart, C.D., Kadzin, A.E. & Sternberg, R.J. (2006). *Evidence-based psychotherapy: Where practice and research meet.* Washington, DC: American Psychological Association.

Gorfein, D.S. (Ed.). (2001). *On the consequences of meaning selection: Perspectives on resolving lexical ambiguity.* Washington, DC: American Psychological Association.

Goshen-Gottstein, Y., Moscovitch, M. & Melo, B. (2000). Intact implicit memory for newly formed verbal associations in amnesic patients following single study trials. *Neuropsychology*, 14, 570–578.

Gottesman, I.I. (1991). *Schizophrenia genesis: The origins of madness.* New York: Freeman.

Gottfredson, L.S. (1997). Mainstream science on intelligence: An editorial with 52 signatories, history, and bibliography. *Intelligence*, 24, 13–23.

Gottfredson, L.S. (2002). Where and why gmatters: Not a mystery. *Human Performance*, 15, 25–46.

Gottman, J.M. (1994). *What predicts divorce?* Hillsdale, NJ: Erlbaum.

Gottman, J.M. & Levenson, R.W. (2000). The timing of divorce: Predicting when a couple will divorce over a 14-year period. *Journal of Marriage and the Family*, 62, 737–745.

Gould, E. & Gross, C.G. (2002). Neurogenesis in adult mammals: Some progress and problems. *Journal of Neuroscience*, 22, 619–623.

Gould, S.J. (2002). *The structure of evolutionary theory.* Cambridge, MA: Belknap Press.

Govender, S., Drummond, L.M. & Menzies, R.G. (2006). Danger Ideation Reduction Therapy for the Treatment of Severe, Chronic and Resistant Obsessive-Compulsive Disorder. Behavioural & Cognitive Psychotherapy. Accessed from <http://journals.cambridge.org/abstract_S1352465806003018>

Grady, C.L., McIntosh, A.R. & Craik, F.I.M. (2005). Task-related activity in prefrontal cortex and its relation to recognition memory performance in young and old adults. *Neuropsychologia*, 43, 1466–1481.

Grady, C.L., Springer, M.V., Hongwanishkul, D., McIntosh, A.R. & Winocur, G. (2006). Age-related changes in brain activity across the adult lifespan. *Journal of Cognitive Neuroscience*, 18, 227–241.

Grant, B.R. & Grant, P. (1989). *Evolutionary dynamics of a natural population.* Princeton: Princeton University Press.

Grant, K.E., Compas, B.E., Stuhlmacher, A.F., Thurm, A.E., McMahon, S.D. & Halpert, J.A. (2003). Stressors and child and adolescent psychopathology: Moving from markers to mechanisms of risk. *Psychological Bulletin*, 129, 447–466.

Grant, L. & Evans, A. (1994). *Principles of behavior analysis.* New York: HarperCollins.

Grant, P.R. & Grant, B.R. (2002). Unpredictable evolution in a 30-year study of Darwin's finches. *Science*, 296, 707–711.

Gray, D., Saggers, S., Sputore, B. & Bourbon, D. (2000). What works? A review of evaluated alcohol misuse interventions among Aboriginal Australians. *Addiction*, 95 (1), 11–22.

Gray, G.C., Smith, T.C., Kang, H. & Knoke, J.D. (2000). Are Gulf War Veterans Suffering War-related Illnesses? Federal and Civilian Hospitalizations Examined, June 1991 to December 1994. *American Journal of Epidemiology.* 151(1), 63–71.

Gray, M.R. & Steinberg, L. (1999). Unpacking authoritative parenting: Reassessing a multidimensional construct. *Journal of Marriage and the Family*, 61, 574–587.

Greaves, N., Prince, E., Evans, D.W. & Charman, T. (2006). Repetitive and ritualistic behaviour in children with Prader-Willi syndrome and children with autism. *Journal of Intellectual Disability Research*, 50, 92–100.

Green, A.R., Sanchez, V., O'Shea, E., Saadat, K.S., Elliott, J.M. & Colado, M.I. (2004). Effect of ambient temperature and a prior neurotoxic dose of 3,4-methylenedioxymethamphetamine (MDMA) on the hyperthermic response of rats to a single or repeated ('binge' ingestion) low does of MDMA. *Psychopharmacology*, 173, 264–269.

Green, B.L. (1994). Psychosocial research in traumatic stress: An update. *Journal of Traumatic Stress*, 7, 341–362.

Green, D.M. & Swets, J.A. (1966). *Signal detection theory and psychophysics.* New York: Wiley.

Greene, J.D., Sommerville, R.B., Nystrom, L.E., Darley, J.M. & Cohen, J.D. (2001). An fMRI investigation of emotional engagement in moral judgment. *Science*, 293, 2105–2108.

Greene, R.L., Gwin, R. & Staal, M. (1997). Current status of MMPI–2 research: A methodologic overview. *Journal of Personality Assessment*, 68, 20–36.

Greenfield, P.M. (1997). You can't take it with you: Why ability assessments don't cross cultures. *American Psychologist*, 52, 1115–1124.

Greeno, C.G. & Wing, R.R. (1994). Stress-induced eating. *Psychological Bulletin*, 115, 444–464.

Greenwald, A.G., Spangenber, E.R., Pratkanis, A.R. & Eskenazi, J. (1991). Double-blind tests of subliminal self-help audiotapes. *Psychological Science, 2,* 119–122.

Grice, H.P. (1968). Utterer's meaning, sentence-meaning, and word-meaning. *Foundations of Language, 4,* 1–18.

Grice, H.P. (1975). Logic and conversation. In P. Cole & J.L. Morgan (Eds.), *Syntax and semantics: Vol. 3. Speech acts* (pp. 41–58). New York: Academic Press.

Grieger, T.A., Waldrep, D.A., Lovasz, M.M. & Ursano, R.J. (2005). Follow-up of Pentagon employees two years after the terrorist attack of September 11, 2001. *Psychiatric Services, 56,* 1374–1378.

Griffin, A.S. & Evans, C.S. (2003). The role of differential reinforcement in predator avoidance learning. *Behavioural Processes,* 61, 87-94.

Griffin, K., Friend, R., Eitel, P. & Lobel, M. (1993). Effects of environmental demands, stress, and mood on health practices. *Journal of Behavioral Medicine,* 16, 1–19.

Grigorenko, E.L. (2000). Heritability and intelligence. In R.J. Sternberg (Ed.), *Handbook of intelligence* (pp. 53–91). Cambridge, UK: Cambridge University Press.

Grigorenko, E.L., Meier, E., Kipka, J., Mohatt, G., Yanez, E. & Sternberg, R.J. (2004). Academic and practical intelligence: A case study of the Yup'ik in Alaska. *Learning and Individual Differences,* 14, 183–207.

Grohol, J.M. (1998). Future clinical directions: Professional development, pathology, and psychotherapy on-line. In J. Gackenbach (Ed.), *Psychology and the Internet: Intrapersonal, interpersonal, and transpersonal implications* (pp. 111–140). San Diego, CA: Academic Press.

Gross, C.G. (2000). Neurogenesis in the adult brain: Death of a dogma. *Nature Reviews Neuroscience,* 1, 67–73.

Grunhaus, L., Schreiver, S., Dolberg, O.T., Polak, D. & Dannon, P.N. (2003). A randomized controlled comparison of electroconvulsive therapy and repetitive transcranial magnetic stimulation in severe and resistant nonpsychotic major depression. *Biological Psychiatry,* 53, 324–331.

Grüsser, S.M., Thalemann, C.N., Platz, W., Gölz, J. & Partecke, G. (2006). A new approach to preventing relapse in opiate addicts: A psychometric evaluation. *Biological Psychiatry,* 71, 231–235.

Guilford, J.P. (1961). Factorial angles to psychology. *Psychological Review,* 68, 1–20.

Guilford, J.P. (1985). The Structure-of-Intellect model. In B.B. Wolman (Ed.), *Handbook of intelligence.* New York: Wiley.

Guilleminault, C., Poyares, D., Aftab, F. & Palombini, L. (2001). Sleep and wakefulness in somnambulism: A spectral analysis study. *Journal of Psychosomatic Research,* 51, 411–416.

Gur, R.C., Gunning-Dixon, F., Bilker, W.B. & Gur, R.E. (2002). Sex differences in temporo-limbic and frontal brain volumes of healthy adults. *Cerebral Cortex,* 12, 998–1003.

Gura, T. (2000). Tracing leptin's partners in regulating body weight. *Science,* 287, 1738–1741.

Gura, T. (2003). Obesity drug pipeline not so fat. *Science,* 299, 849–852.

Gutierrez, P.M., Watkins, R. & Collura, D. (2004). Suicide risk screening in an urban high school. *Suicide and Life-Threatening Behavior,* 34, 421–428.

Haas, S.M. (2003). Relationship maintenance in same-sex couples. In D. Canary & M. Dainton (Eds.), *Maintaining relationships through communication: Relational, contextual, and cultural variations* (pp. 209–230). Mahwah, NJ: Erlbaum.

Haas, S.M. & Stafford, L. (1998). An initial examination of maintenance behaviors in gay and lesbian relationships. *Journal of Social and Personal Relationships,* 15, 846–855.

Habib, R., Nyberg, L. & Tulving, E. (2003). Hemispheric asymmetries of memory: the HERA model revisited. *TRENDS in Cognitive Sciences,* 7, 241–245.

Haddock, G. (2002). It's easy to like or dislike Tony Blair: Accessibility experiences and the favourabiity of attitude judgments. *British Journal of Psychology,* 93, 257–267.

Haier, R.J., Jung, R.E., Yeo, R.A., Head, K. & Alkire, M.T. (2004). Structural variation and general intelligence. *NeuroImage,* 23, 425–433.

Haines, B.A., Metalsky, G.I., Cardamone, A.L. & Joiner, T. (1999). Interpersonal and cognitive pathways in to the origins of attributional style: A developmental perspective. In T.E. Joiner & J.C. Coyne (Eds.), *The interactional nature of depression; Advances in interpersonal approaches* (pp. 65–92). Washington, DC: American Psychological Association.

Hall, D. & Suboski, M.D. (1995). Visual and olfactory stimuli in learned release of alarm reactions by zebra danio fish (*Brachydanio rerio*). *Neurobiology of Learning and Memory,* 63, 229–240.

Hall, G.S. (1904). *Adolescence: Its psychology and its relations to physiology, anthropology, sociology, sex, crime, religion and education* (Vols. 1 and 2). New York: D. Appleton.

Hamer, D.H. (1996). The heritability of happiness. *Nature Genetics,* 14, 125–126.

Hamilton, M. & Rajaram, S. (2001). The concreteness effect in implicit and explicit memory tests. *Journal of Memory and Language,* 44, 96–117.

Han, J.-S. (2004). Acupuncture and endorphins. *Neuroscience Letters,* 361, 258–261.

Haney, C. & Zimbardo, P.G. (1977). The socialization into criminality: On becoming a prisoner and a guard. In J.L. Tapp & F.L. Levine (Eds.), *Law, justice and the individual in society: Psychological and legal issues* (pp. 198–223). New York: Holt, Rinehart & Winston.

Hankin, B.L. & Abramson, L.Y. (2001). Development of gender differences in depression: An elaborated cognitive vulnerability-transactional stress model. *Psychological Bulletin,* 127, 773–796.

Hansen, J.-I.C. & Dik, B.J. (2005). Evidence of 12-year predictive and concurrent validity for SII Occupational Scale scores. *Journal of Vocational Behavior, 67*, 365–378.

Harder, J.W. (1991). Equity theory versus expectancy theory: The case of major league baseball free agents. *Journal of Applied Psychology, 76*, 458–464.

Hardy, J. & Selkoe, D.J. (2002). The amyloid hypothesis of Alzheimer's disease: Progress and problems on the road to therapeutics. *Science, 297*, 353–356.

Hargadon, R., Bowers, K.S. & Woody, E.Z. (1995). Does counter-pain imagery mediate hypnotic analgesia? *Journal of Abnormal Psychology, 104*, 508–516.

Hariri, A.R., Mattay, V.S., Tessitore, A., Kolachana, B., Fera, F., Goldman, D., Egan, M.F. & Weinberger, D.R. (2002). Serotonin transporter genetic variation and the response of the human amygdala. *Science, 297*, 400–403.

Harle, V. (2000). *The enemy with a thousand faces: The tradition of the other in Western political thought and history.* Westport, CT: Praeger.

Harlow, H.F. (1965). Sexual behavior in the rhesus monkey. In F. Beach (Ed.), *Sex and behavior.* New York: Wiley.

Harlow, H.F., Harlow, M.K. & Meyer, D.R. (1950). Learning motivated by a manipulation drive. *Journal of Experimental Psychology, 40*, 228–234.

Harlow, H.F. & Zimmerman, R.R. (1958). The development of affectional responses in infant monkeys. *Proceedings of the American Philosophical Society, 102*, 501–509.

Harlow, J.M. (1868). Recovery from the passage of an iron bar through the head. *Publications of the Massachusetts Medical Society, 2*, 327–347.

Harmon, L.W., Hansen, J.C., Borgen, F.H. & Hammer, A.L. (1994). *Strong Interest Inventory applications and technical guide.* Palo Alto, CA: Consulting Psychologists Press.

Harris, B. (1979). Whatever happened to Little Albert? *American Psychologist, 34*, 151–160.

Harris, J., Lack, L., Wright, H., Gradisar, M. & Brooks, A. (2007). Intensive Sleep Retraining treatment for chronic primary insomnia: a preliminary investigation. *Journal of Sleep Research, 16*, 276–284.

Harris, L.M. & Cumming, S.R. (2003). An examination of the relationship between anxiety and performance on prospective and retrospective memory tasks. *Australian Journal of Psychology. 55*(1), Apr, 51–55.

Harris, L.M. & Menzies, R.G. (1999). Mood and prospective memory. *Memory. 7*(1), Jan, 117–127.

Harrison, L.M., Kastin, A.J. & Zadina, J.E. (1998). Opiate tolerance and dependence: Receptors, G-proteins, and antiopiates. *Peptides, 19*, 1603–1630.

Harrison, Y. & Horne, J.A. (1996). Long-term sleep extension—Are we really chronically sleep deprived? *Psychophysiology, 33*, 22–30.

Hart, J.T. (1965). Memory and the feeling-of-knowing experience. *Journal of Educational Psychology, 56*, 208–216.

Hartshorne, H. & May, M.A. (1928). *Studies in the nature of character: Vol. 1. Studies in deceit.* New York: Macmillan.

Hartsuiker, R.J., Corley, M. & Martensen, H. (2005). The lexical bias effect is modulated by context, but the standard monitoring account doesn't fly: Related reply to Baars et al. (1975). *Journal of Memory and Language, 52*, 58–70.

Hartsuiker, R.J., Schriefers, H.J. & Kikstra, G.M. (2003). Morphophonological influences on the construction of subject-verb agreement. *Memory & Cognition, 31*, 1316–1326.

Hartup, W.H. (1996). The company they keep: Friendships and their developmental significance. *Child Development, 67*, 1–13.

Hastorf, A.H. & Cantril, H. (1954). They saw a game: A case study. *Journal ofAbnormal and Social Psychology, 49*, 129–134.

Hatcher, C. & Himelstein, P. (Eds.). (1996). *The handbook of Gestalt therapy.* Northvale, NJ: Jason Aronson.

Hatchett, L., Friend, R., Symister, P. & Wadhwa, N. (1997). Interpersonal expectations, social support, and adjustment to chronic illness. *Journal of Personality and Social Psychology, 73*, 560–573.

Hatfield, E. & Sprecher, S. (1995). Men's and women's preferences in marital partners in the United States, Russia, and Japan. *Journal of Cross-Cultural Psychology, 26*, 728–750.

Hathaway, S.R. & McKinley, J.C. (1940). A multiphasic person-laity schedule (Minnesota): I. Construction of the schedule. *Journal of Psychology, 10*, 249–254.

Hathaway, S.R. & McKinley, J.C. (1943). *Minnesota Multiphasic Inventory manual.* New York: Psychological Corporation.

Hattori, Y., Kuroshima, H. & Fujita, K. (2005). Cooperative problem solving by tufted capuchin monkeys (*Cebus paella*): Spontaneous division of labor, communication, and reciprocal altruism. *Journal of Comparative Psychology, 119*, 335–342.

Hauser, M.D., Chomsky, N. & Fitch, W.F. (2002). The faculty of language: What is it, who has it, and how did it evolve? *Science, 298*, 1569–1579.

Hayes, Brett K; Taplin, John E; Longstaff, Mitchell. (2002) Prior knowledge and exemplar similarity in category learning: Further evidence for their integration. *European Journal of Cognitive Psychology. 14*(4), Oct, 549–571.

Hazan, C. & Shaver, P. (1987). Romantic love conceptualized as an attachment process. *Journal of Personality and Social Psychology, 52*, 511–524.

Hazeltine, E. & Ivry, R.B. (2002). Can we teach the cerebellum new tricks? *Science, 296*, 1979–1980.

Healey, J. (Ed.).(2001), *S.A.'s greats. The men and women of the north terrace plaques.* Adelaide: Historical Society of South Australia.

Hearst, E. (1988). Fundamentals of learning and conditioning. In R.C. Atkinson, R.J. Herrnstein, G. Lindzey & R.D. Luce (Eds.), *Stevens' handbook of experimental psychology: Vol. 2. Learning and cognition* (2nd edn, pp. 3–109). New York: Wiley.

Hebl, M.R. & Heatherton, T.F. (1998). The stigma of obesity in women: The difference is black and white. *Personality and Social Psychology Bulletin,* 24, 417–426.

Hegelson, V.S. (2003). Cognitive adaptation, psychological adjustment, and disease progression among angioplasty patients: 4 years later. *Health Psychology,* 22, 30–38.

Heider, F. (1958). *The psychology of interpersonal relationships.* New York: Wiley.

Hektner, J.M. & Csikszentmihalyi, M. (2002). The experience sampling method: Measuring the context and the content of lives. In R.B. Bechtel & A. Churchman (Eds.), *Handbook of environmental psychology* (pp. 233–243). New York: Wiley.

Heller, M.A., Bracket, D.D., Salik, S.S., Scroggs, E. & Green, S. (2003). Objects, raised lines, and the haptic horizontal-vertical illusion. *Quarterly Journal of Experimental Psychology,* 56A, 891–907.

Helmes, E. & Reddon, J.R. (1993). A perspective on developments in assessing psychopathology: A critical review of the MMPI and MMPI–2. *Psychological Bulletin,* 113, 453–471.

Helmuth, L. (2002). Long-awaited technique spots Alzheimer's toxin. *Science,* 297, 752–753.

Henningsen, D.D., Henningsen, M.L.M., Eden, J. & Cruz, M.G. (2006). Examining the symptoms of groupthink and retrospective sensemaking. *Small Group Research,* 37, 36–64.

Henry, W.P., Strupp, H.H., Schacht, T.E. & Gaston, L. (1994). Psychodynamic approaches. In A.E. Bergin & S.L. Garfield (Eds.), *Handbook of psychotherapy and behavior change* (4th ed., pp. 467–508). New York: Wiley.

Henshall, T. et al. (1980) *Ngurrju Maninja Kurlangu. Yapa Nyurnu Kurlangu. Bush Medicine*, Warlpiri Literature Production Centre Inc, Yuendumu.

Herek, G.M. (2002). Gender gaps in public opinion about lesbians and gay men. *Public Opinion Quarterly,* 66, 40–66.

Herek, G.M. & Capitanio, J.P. (1996). "Some of my best friends": Intergroup contact, concealable stigma, and heterosexuals' attitudes toward gay men and lesbians. *Personality and Social Psychology Bulletin,* 22, 412–424.

Hernández-Guzmán, L., González, S. & López, F. (2002). Effect of guided imagery on children's social performance. *Behavioural and Cognitive Psychotherapy,* 30, 471–483.

Hernnstein, R.J. & Murray, C. (1994). *The bell curve.* New York: The Free Press.

Hersh, S.M. (1971). *My Lai 4: A report on the massacre and its aftermath.* New York: Random House.

Hertzog, C., Dixon, R.A. & Hultsch, D.F. (1990). Relationships between metamemory, memory predictions, and memory task performance in adults. *Psychology and Aging,* 5, 215–227.

Herz, R.S. (1997). The effects of cue distinctiveness on odor-based context-dependent memory. *Memory & Cognition,* 25, 375–380.

Hess, T.M. (2005). Memory and aging in context. *Psychological Bulletin,* 131, 383–406.

Hettema, J.M., Neale, M.C. & Kendler, K.S. (2001). A review and meta-analysis of the genetic epidemiology of anxiety disorders. *American Journal of Psychiatry,* 158, 1568–1578.

Hettema, J.M., Prescott, C.A., Myerse, J.M., Neale, M.C. & Kendler, K.S. (2005). The structure of genetic and environmental risk factors for anxiety disorders in men and women. *Archives of General Psychiatry,* 62, 182–189.

Hewstone, M., Rubin, M. & Willis, H. (2002). Intergroup bias. *Annual Review of Psychology,* 53, 575–604.

Hickok, G., Love-Geffen, T. & Klima, E.S. (2002). Role of the left hemisphere in sign language comprehension. *Brain & Language,* 82, 167–178.

Higgie, M., Chenoweth, S. & Blows, M.W. (2000). Natural selection and the reinforcement of mate recognition. *Science,* 290, 519–521.

Hilgard, E.R. (1986). *Psychology in America: A historical survey.* San Diego, CA: Harcourt Brace Jovanovich.

Hilgetag, C.C., O'Neill, M.A. & Young, M.P. (1996). Indeterminate organization of the visual system. *Science,* 271, 776–777.

Hill, M.E. & Augoustinos, M. (2001). Stereotype change and prejudice reduction: short- and long-term evaluation of a cross-cultural awareness programme. *Journal of Community & Applied Social Psychology,* 11 (4), 243–262.

Hills, A.L., Cox, B.J., McWilliams, L.A. & Sareen, J. (2005). Suicide attempts and externalizing psychopathology in a nationally representative sample. *Comprehensive Psychiatry,* 46, 334–339.

Hinton, A.L. (1996). Agents of death: Explaining the Cambodian genocide in terms of psychosocial dissonance. *American Anthropologist,* 98, 818–831.

Ho, C. (2006), Migration as feminisation? Chinese women's experiences of work and family in Australia. Journal of Ethnic and Migration Studies, 32, 497–514.

Hobara, M. (2005). Beliefs about appropriate pain behavior: Cross-cultural and sex differences between Japanese and EuroAmericans. *European Journal of Pain,* 9, 389–393.

Hobson, J.A. (1988). *The dreaming brain.* New York: Basic Books.

Hobson, J.A. & McCarley, R.W. (1977). The brain as a dream state generator: An activation-synthesis hypothesis of the dream process. *American Journal of Psychiatry,* 134, 1335–1348.

Hochner, B., Shomrat, T & Fiorito, G. (2006). The octopus: A model for a comparative analysis of the evolution of learning and memory mechanisms. *Biological Bulletin,* 210, 308-317.

Hoek, H.W. & van Hoeken, D. (2003). Review of the prevalence and incidence of eating disorders. *International Journal of Eating Disorders,* 34, 383–396.

Hoffman, M.L. (1986). Affect, cognition, and motivation. In R. Sorrentino & E. Higgins (Eds.), *Handbook of motivation and cognition: Foundations of social behavior* (pp. 244–280). New York: Guilford Press.

Hofling, C.K., Brotzman, E., Dalrymple, S., Graves, N. & Pierce, C.M. (1966). An experimental study in nurse–physician relationships. *Journal of Nervous and Mental Disease*, 143(2), 171–180.

Hoge, C.W., Castro, C.A., Messer, S.C., McGurk, D., Cotting, D.I. & Koffman, R.L. (2004). Combat duty in Iraq and Afghanistan, mental health problems, and barriers to care. *New England Journal of Medicine*, 351, 13–22.

Holahan, C.J., Moos, R.H. & Bonin, L. (1997). Social support, coping, and psychological adjustment: A resource model. In G.R. Pierce, B. Lakey, I.G. Sarason & B.R. Sarason (Eds.), *Sourcebook of social support and personality* (pp. 3–18). New York: Plenum.

Holahan, C.K. & Sears, R.R. (1995). The gifted group in later maturity. Stanford, CA: Stanford University Press.

Holden, C. (1998). No last word on language origins. *Science*, 282, 1455–1458.

Holen, Michael C. & Oaster, Thomas R. (1976). Serial position and isolation effects in a classroom lecture simulation. *Journal of Educational Psychology*. 68(3), Jun, 293–296.

Hollon, S.D., Stewart, M.O. & Strunk, D. (2006). Enduring effects for cognitive behavior therapy in the treatment of depression and anxiety. *Annual Review of Psychology*, 57, 285–315.

Hollon, S.D., Thase, M.E. & Markowitz, J.C. (2002). Treatment and prevention of depression. *Psychological Science in the Public Interest*, 3, 39–77.

Holmbeck, G.N. & O'Donnell, D. (1991). Discrepancies between perceptions of decision making and behavioral autonomy. In R.L. Paikoff (Ed.), *Shared views in the family during adolescence* (pp. 51–69). San Francisco: Jossey-Bass.

Holmes, D.S. (1994). *Abnormal psychology*. New York: HarperCollins. Holmes, T.H. & Rahe, R.H. (1967). The social readjustment rating scale. *Journal of Psychosomatic Research*, 11(2), 213–218.

Holtgraves, T. & Skeel, J. (1992). Cognitive biases in playing the lottery: Estimating the odds and choosing the numbers. *Journal of Applied Social Psychology*, 22, 934–952.

Holyoak, K.J. & Spellman, B.A. (1993). Thinking. *Annual Review of Psychology*, 44, 265–3 15.

Holyoak, K.J. & Thagard, P. (1997). The analogical mind. *American Psychologist*, 52, 35–44.

Hong, L.E., Mitchell, B.D., Avila, M.T., Adami, H., McMahon, R.P. & Thaker, G.K. (2006). Familial aggregation of eye-tracking endophenotypes in families of schizophrenic patients. *Archives of General Psychiatry*, 63, 259–264.

Hooker, C. & Chapman, S. (2006). Deliberately personal: Tobacco control debates and deliberative democracy in New South Wales. *Critical Public Health,* Vol. 16(1), Mar, 35–46.

Hopson, J.L. (1979). *Scent signals: The silent language of sex.* New York: Morrow.

Horgen, K.B. & Brownell, K.D. (2002). Comparison of price change and health message interventions in promoting healthy food choices. *Health Psychology*, 21, 505–512.

Horne, J. & Ostberg, O. (1976). A self-assessment questionnaire to determine morningness-eveningness in human circadian rhythms. *International Journal of Chronobiology*, 4, 97–110.

Horney, K. (1937). *The neurotic personality of our time.* New York: Norton.

Horney, K. (1939). *New ways in psychoanalysis.* New York: Norton. Horney, K. (1945). *Our inner conflicts: A constructive theory of neurosis.* New York: Norton.

Horney, K. (1950). *Neurosis and human growth.* New York: Norton.

Horton, J.E., Crawford, H.J., Harrington, G. & Downs, J.H., III. (2004). Increased anterior corpus callosum size associated positively with hypnotizability and the ability to control pain. *Brain,* 127, 1741–1747.

Horton, K.E. & Caldwell, C.A. (2006). Visual co-orientation and expectations about attentional orientation is pileated gibbons (*Hylobates pileatus*). *Behavioural Processes,* 72, 65–73.

Horton, W.S. & Gerrig, R.J. (2005a). Conversational common ground and memory processes in language production. *Discourse Processes,* 40, 1–35.

Horton, W.S. & Gerrig, R.J. (2005b). The impact of memory demands on audience design during language production. *Cognition,* 96, 127–142.

Hoshino-Browne, E., Zanna, A.S., Spencer, S.J., Zanna, M.P., Kitayama, S. & Lackenbauer, S. (2005). On the cultural guises of cognitive dissonance: The case of Easterners and Westerners. *Journal of Personality and Social Psychology*, 89, 294–310.

Hosking, K. & Rachinger, D. (2006) *Careers for Psychology Graduates.* Parkville, Victoria, Australia: Graduate Careers Australia.

Houghton, J. (1980). One personal experience: Before and after mental illness. In J.G. Rabkin, L. Gelb & J.B. Lazar (Eds.), *Attitudes toward the mentally ill: Research perspectives* (pp. 7–14). Rockville, MD: National Institutes of Mental Health.

Houlihan, D., Schwartz, C., Miltenberger, R. & Heuton, D. (1993). The rapid treatment of a young man's balloon (noise) phobia using in vivo flooding. *Journal of Behavior Therapy and Experimental Psychiatry,* 24, 233–240.

Hovland, C.I., Lumsdaine, A.A. & Sheffield, F.D. (1949). *Experiments on mass communication.* Princeton, NJ: Princeton University Press.

Hudson, D., Foster, T.M. & Temple, W. (1999). Fixed-ratio schedule performance of possum (*Trichosurus vulpecula*). *New Zealand Journal of Psychology,* 28, 80–86.

Hudson, J.L., Flannery-Schroeder, E. & Kendall, P. (2004). Primary prevention of anxiety disorders. In D.J.A. Dozois & K.S. Dobson (Eds.), *The prevention of anxiety and depression: Theory, research, and practice* (pp. 101–130). Washington, DC: American Psychological Association.

Huesmann, L.R., Moise-Titus, J., Podolski, C.L. & Eron, L.D. (2003). Longitudinal relations between children's exposure to TV violence and their aggressive and violent behavior in young adulthood: 1977–1992. *Developmental Psychology*, 39, 201–221.

Huey, R.B., Gilchrist, G.W., Carlson, M.L., Berrigan, D. & Serra, L. (2000). Rapid evolution of a geographic cline in size in an introduced fly. *Science*, 287, 308–309.

Hull, C.L. (1943). *Principles of behavior: An introduction to behavior theory.* New York: Appleton-Century-Crofts.

Hull, C.L. (1952). *A behavior system: An introduction to behavior theory concerning the individual organism.* New Haven: Yale University Press.

Hultsch, D.F., Hertzog, C., Dixon, R.A. & Small, B.J. (1998). *Memory change in the aged.* Cambridge, UK: Cambridge University Press.

Human Rights and Equal Opportunities Commission (1998). *Those Who've Come Across the Seas.* The report of the Commission's Inquiry into the detention of unauthorised arrivals. Canberra, ACT: HRECO.

Human Rights and Equal Opportunities Commission. (2004). *A last resort? The national inquiry into children in immigration detention.* Canberra, ACT: HREOC.

Hume, D. (1951). In L.A. Selby-Bigge (Ed.), *An enquiry concerning human understanding.* London: Oxford University Press. (Original work published 1748).

Hurvich, L.M. & Jameson D. (1974). Opponent processes as a model of neural organization. *American Psychologist*, 29, 88–102.

Huston, A.C. (2005). The effects of welfare reform and poverty policies on children and families. In D.B. Pillemer & S.H. White (Eds.), *Developmental psychology and social change: Research, history, and policy* (pp. 83–103). New York: Cambridge University Press.

Hyde, J.S. (2005). The genetics of sexual orientation. In J.S. Hyde (Ed.), *Biological substrates of human sexuality* (pp. 9–20). Washington, DC: American Psychological Association.

Hyde, J.S. & Durik, A.M. (2000). Gender differences in erotic plasticity—evolutionary or sociocultural forces? Comment on Baumeister (2000). *Psychological Bulletin*, 126, 375–379.

Indigenous Australia (2007). Food Rules and Laws. Accessed from <http://indigenousaustralia.frogandtoad.com.au/food3.html>

Insko, C.A., Thibaut, J.W., Moehle, D., Wilson, M., Diamond, W.D., Gilmore, R., Solomon, M.R. & Lipsitz, A. (1980). Social evolution and the emergence of leadership. *Journal of Personality and Social Psychology*, 39, 431–448.

Irvine, J.T. (1990). Registering affect: Heteroglossia in the linguistic expression of emotion. In C.A. Lutz & L. Abu-Lughod (Eds.), *Language and the politics of emotions* (pp. 126–161). Cambridge, UK: Cambridge University Press.

Isen, A.M. (1984). Toward understanding the role of affect in cognition. In R. Wyer & T. Srull (Eds.), *Handbook of social cognition* (pp. 174–236). Hillsdale, NJ: Erlbaum.

Isen, A.M., Daubman, D.A. & Nowicki, G.P. (1987). Positive affect facilitates creative problem solving. *Journal of Personality and Social Psychology*, 52, 1122–1131.

Ishii-Kuntz, M. (1990). Social interaction and psychological wellbeing: Comparison across stages of adulthood. *International Journal of Aging and Human Development*, 30, 15–36.

Islam, M.R. & Jahjah, M. (2001). Predictors of young Australians' attitudes toward Aboriginals, Asians and Arabs. *Social Behavior and Personality*, 29 (6), 569–579.

Ito, T.A., Miller, N. & Pollock,V.E. (1996). Alcohol and aggression: A meta-analysis on the moderating effects of inhibitory cues, triggering events, and self-focused attention. *Psychological Bulletin*, 120, 60–82.

Iyengar, S.S., Wells, R.E. & Schwartz, B. (2006). Doing better but feeling worse: Looking for the "best" job undermines satisfaction. *Psychological Science*, 17, 143–150.

Izard, C.E. (1993). Four systems for emotion activation: Cognitive and noncognitive processes. *Psychological Review*, 100, 68–90.

Izard, C.E. (1994). Innate and universal facial expressions: Evidence from developmental and cross-cultural research. *Psychological Bulletin,* 115, 288–299.

Jackson, L.A. & McGill, O.D. (1996). Body type preferences and body characteristics associated with attractive and unattractive bodies by African Americans and Anglo Americans. *Sex Roles,* 35, 295–307.

Jackson, R.S., Creemers, J.W.M., Ohagi, S., Raffin-Sanson, M.L., Sanders, L., Montague, C.T., Hutton, J.C. & O'Rahilly, S. (1997). Obesity and impaired prohormone processing associated with mutations in the human prohormone convertase 1 gene. *Nature Genetics*, 16, 303–306.

Jacobs, R.C. & Campbell, D.T. (1961). The perpetuation of an arbitrary tradition through several generations of a laboratory micro-culture. *Journal of Abnormal and Social Psychology,* 62, 649–658.

Jacobsen, P.B., Bovbjerg, D.H., Schwartz, M.D., Andrykowski, M.A., Futterman, A.D., Gilewski, T., Norton, L. & Redd, W.H. (1993). Formation of food aversions in cancer patients receiving repeated infusions of chemotherapy. *Behaviour Research and Therapy,* 31, 739–748.

Jaffee, S. & Hyde, J.S. (2000). Gender differences in moral orientation: A meta-analysis. *Psychological Bulletin,* 126, 703–726.

Jahnke, J.C. (1965). Primacy and recency effects in serial-position curves of immediate recall. *Journal of Experimental Psychology, 70,* 130–132.

James, S.E. & Murphy, B.C. (1998). Gay and lesbian relationships in a changing social context. In C.J. Patterson & A.R. D'Augelli (Eds.), *Lesbian, gay, and bisexual identities in families: Psychological perspectives* (pp. 99–121). New York: Oxford University Press.

James, W. (1882). Subjective effects of nitrous oxide. *Mind, 7,* 186–208.

James, W. (1892). *Psychology.* New York: Holt.

James, W. (1902). *The varieties of religious experience.* New York: Longmans, Green.

James, W. (1950). *The principles of psychology* (2 vols.). New York: Holt, Rinehart & Wilson. (Original work published 1890)

Janis, I. (1982). *Groupthink* (2nd ed.). Boston: Houghton Mifflin.

Janis, I.L. & Frick, F. (1943). The relationship between attitudes toward conclusions and errors in judging logical validity of syllogisms. *Journal of Experimental Psychology, 33,* 73–77.

Janofsky, J.S., Dunn, M.H., Roskes, E.J., Briskin, J.K. & Rudolph, M.S.L. (1996). Insanity defense pleas in Baltimore City: An analysis of outcome. *American Journal of Psychiatry, 153,* 1464–1468.

Janowitz, H.D. & Grossman, M.I. (1950). Hunger and appetite: Some definitions and concepts. *Journal of the Mount Sinai Hospital, 16,* 231–240.

Jedrej, M.C. (1995). *Ingessana: The religious institutions of a people of the Sudan–Ethiopia borderland.* Leiden: Brill.

Jenike, M.A., Breiter, H.C., Baer, L., Kennedy, D.N., Savage, C.R., Olivares, M.J., O'Sullivan, R.L., Shera, D.M., Rauch, S.C., Keuthen, N., Rosen, B.R., Caviness, V.S. & Fiipek, P.A. (1996). Cerebral structural abnormalities in obsessive-compulsive disorder. *Archives of General Psychiatry, 53,* 625–632.

Jensen, A.R. (1962). Spelling errors and the serial position effect. *Journal of Educational Psychology, 53,* 105–109.

Jo, H., Chen, Y.J., Chua, S.C., Jr., Talmage, D.A. & Role, L.W. (2005). Integration of endocannabinoid and leptin signaling in an appetite-related neural circuit. *Neuron, 48,* 1055–1066.

Joh, A.S. & Adolph, K. E (2006). Learning from falling. *Child Development, 77,* 89–102.

Johar, G.V. & Sengupta, J. (2002). The effects of dissimulation on the accessibility and predictive power of weakly held attitudes. *Social Cognition, 20,* 257–293.

Johnson, J.R. & Vickers, Z.M. (1993). The effects of flavor and macronutrient composition of preloads on liking, hunger, and subsequent intake in humans. *Appetite, 21,* 15–31.

Johnson, M.K., Hashtroudi, S. & Lindsay, D.S. (1993). Source monitoring. *Psychological Bulletin, 114,* 3–28.

Johnson, S.M. (2003). The revolution in couple therapy: A practitioner-scientist perspective. *Journal of Marital and Family Therapy, 29,* 365–384.

Johnson, T.D. & Gottlieb, G. (1981). Visual preferences of imprinted ducklings are altered by the maternal call. *Journal of Comparative and Physiological Psychology, 95*(5), 665–675.

Johnson, T.E. & Rule, B.G. (1986). Mitigating circumstances, information, censure, and aggression. *Journal of Personality and Social Psychology, 50,* 537–542.

Johnson, W., McGue, M., Gaist, D., Vaupel, J.W. & Christensen, K. (2002). Frequency and heritability of depression symptomatology in the second half of life: Evidence from Danish twins over 45. *Psychological Medicine, 32,* 1175–1185.

Johnson-Laird, P.N. & Wason, P.C. (1977). A theoretical analysis of insight into a reasoning task. In P.N. Johnson-Laird & P.C. Wason (Eds.), *Thinking* (pp. 143–157). Cambridge, UK: Cambridge University Press.

Jones, E. (1953). *The life and works of Sigmund Freud.* New York: Basic Books.

Jones, M.C. (1924). A laboratory study of fear: The case of Peter. *Pedagogical Seminary and Journal of Genetic Psychology, 31,* 308–315.

Joyce, A.S., Ogrodniczuk, J.S., Piper, W.E. & McCallum, M. (2003). The alliance as mediator of expectancy effects in short-term individual therapy. *Journal of Consulting and Clinical Psychology, 71,* 672–679.

Joyce, L. (1990). Losing the connection. *Stanford Medicine,* pp. 19–21.

Judd, F., Cooper, A.M., Fraser, C., Davis, J. (2006). Rural suicide: People or place effect. *Australian and New Zealand Journal of Psychiatry, 40,* 208-216.

Judge, T.A. & Cable, D.M. (1997). Applicant personality, organizational culture, and organization attraction. *Personnel Psychology, 50,* 359–392.

Jung, C.G. (1959). The concept of the collective unconscious. In *The archetypes and the collective unconscious, collected works* (9 Part (1), pp. 54–74.). Princeton, NJ: Princeton University Press. (Original work published 1936)

Jung, C.G. (1973). *Memories, dreams, reflections* (rev. edn, A. Jaffe, Ed.). New York: Pantheon Books.

Jusczyk, P.W. (2003). Chunking language input to find patterns. In D.H. Rakison & L.M. Oakes (Eds.), *Early category and concept development.* London: Oxford University Press.

Jusczyk, P.W. & Aslin, R.N. (1995). Infants' detection of the sound patterns of words in fluent speech. *Cognitive Psychology, 29,* 1–23.

Jussim, L. & Harber, K.D. (2005). Teacher expectations and self-fulfilling prophecies: Knowns and unknowns, resolved and unresolved controversies. *Personality and Social Psychology Review, 9,* 131–155.

Kabat-Zinn, J. (1990). *Full catastrophe living: Using the wisdom of your body and mind to face stress, pain, and illness.* New York: Dell.

Kadri, N., Manoudi, F., Berrada, S. & Moussaoui, D. (2004). Stigma impact on Moroccan families of patients with schizophrenia. *Canadian Journal of Psychiatry*, 49(9), 625–9.

Kagan, J. (1994). *Galen's prophesy: Temperament in human nature.* New York: Basic Books.

Kagan, J. & Snidman, N. (1991). Infant predictors of inhibited and uninhibited profiles. *Psychological Science*, 2, 40–44.

Kagan, J. & Snidman, N. (2004). *The long shadow of temperament.* Cambridge, MA: Belknap Press.

Kahneman, D. (1991). Judgment and decision making: A personal view. *Psychological Science*, 2, 142–145.

Kahneman, D. (1992). Reference points, anchors, norms, and mixed feelings. *Organizational Behavior and Human Decision Processes*, 51, 296–312.

Kahneman, D. & Frederick, S. (2002). Representativeness revisited: Attribute substitution in intuitive judgment. In T. Giovich, D. Griffin & D. Kahneman (Eds.), *Heuristics and biases: The psychology of intuitive judgment* (pp. 49–81). Cambridge: Cambridge University Press.

Kahneman, D. & Tversky, A. (1973). On the psychology of prediction. *Psychological Review*, 80, 237–251.

Kallmann, F.J. (1946). The genetic theory of schizophrenia: An analysis of 691 schizophrenic index families. *American Journal of Psychiatry*, 103, 309–322.

Kamil, A.C. & Balda, R.P. (1990). Spatial memory in seed-caching corvids. In G.H. Bower (Ed.), *The psychology of learning and motivation* (26, pp. 1–25). San Diego: Academic Press.

Kamil, A.C., Balda, R.P., Olson, D.P. & Good, S. (1993). Returns to emptied cache sites by Clark's nutcrackers, *Nucifraga columbiana*: A puzzle revisited. *Animal Behaviour*, 45, 241–252.

Kamin, L.J. (1969). Predictability, surprise, attention, and conditioning. In B.A. Campbell & R.M. Church (Eds.), *Punishment and aversive behavior* (pp. 279–296). New York: Appleton-CenturyCrofts.

Kammrath, L.K., Mendoza-Denton, R. & Mischel, W. (2005). Incorporating *if . . . then . . .* personality signatures in person perception: Beyond the person-situation dichotomy. *Journal of Personality and Social Psychology*, 88, 605–618.

Kangas, M., Henry, J.L. & Bryant, R.A. (2005). Predictors of post-traumatic stress disorder following cancer. *Health Psychology*, 24, 579–585.

Kantrowitz, B. & McGinn, D. (2000, June 19). When teachers are cheaters. *Newsweek*, pp. 48–49.

Kaplan, C.A. & Simon, H.A. (1990). In search of insight. *Cognitive Psychology*, 22, 374–419.

Kaplan, R.M. (2000). Two pathways to prevention. *American Psychologist*, 55, 382–396.

Karin-D'Arcy, M.R. & Povinelli, D.J. (2002). Do chimpanzees know what each other see? A closer look. *International Journal of Comparative Psychology*, 15, 21–54.

Kassebaum, N.L. (1994). Head Start: Only the best for America's children. *American Psychologist*, 49, 1123–1126.

Kazdin, A.E. (1982). The token economy: A decade later. *Journal of Applied Behavior Analysis*, 15, 431–445.

Kazdin, A.E. (1994). *Behavior modification in applied settings* (5th ed.). Pacific Grove, CA: Brooks/Cole.

Kazdin, A.E. & Benjet, C. (2003). Spanking children: Evidence and issues. *Current Directions in Psychological Science*, 12, 99–103.

Kearins, J. (1976) Skills of desert Aboriginal children. In G.E. Kearney & D.W. McElwain (Eds.), *Aboriginal cognition, refrospect and prospect.* Canberra: Australian Institute of Aboriginal Studies.

Kearins, Judith M. (1981). Visual spatial memory in Australian Aboriginal children of desert regions. *Cognitive Psychology.* 13(3) Jul. 434–460.

Keiger, D. (1993, November). Touched with fire. *Johns Hopkins Magazine*, pp. 38, 40–44.

Keller, M.B., McCullough, J.P., Klein, D.N., Arnow, B., Dunner, D.L., Gelenberg, A.J., Markowitz, J.C., Nemeroff, C.B., Russell, J.M., Thase, M.E., Trivedi, M.H. & Zajecka, J. (2000). A comparison of nefazodone, the cognitive behavioral-analysis system of psychotherapy, and their combination for the treatment of chronic depression. *New England Journal of Medicine*, 342, 1462–1470.

Kelley, H.H. (1967). Attribution theory in social psychology. In D. Levine (Ed.), *Nebraska symposium on motivation* (Vol. 15). Lincoln: University of Nebraska Press.

Kelman, H.C. (1997). Group processes in the resolution of international conflicts: Experiences from the Israeli–Palestinian case. *American Psychologist*, 52, 212–220.

Kelman, H.C. (2005). Building trust among enemies: The central challenge for international conflict resolution. *International Journal of Intercultural Relations*, 29, 639–650.

Kempermann, G. (2002). Why new neurons? Possible functions for adult hippocampal neurogenesis. *Journal of Neuroscience*, 22, 635–638.

Kendler, H.H. (1987). *Historical foundations of modern psychology.* Chicago: Dorsey Press.

Kendler, K.S., Myers, J., Prescott, C.A. & Neale, M.C. (2001). The genetic epidemiology of irrational fears and phobias in men. *Archives of General Psychiatry*, 58, 257–265.

Kendler, K.S., Thornton, L.M., Gilman, S.E. & Kessler, R.C. (2000). Sexual orientation in a U.S. national sample of twin and nontwin sibling pairs. *American Journal of Psychiatry*, 157, 1843–1846.

Kendler, K.S., Thornton, L.M. & Pedersen, N.L. (2000). Tobacco consumption in Swedish twins reared apart and reared together. *Archives of General Psychiatry*, 57, 886–892.

Kennedy, R.E. & Craighead, W.E. (1988). Differential effects of depression and anxiety on recall of feedback in a learning task. *Behavior Therapy*, 19, 437–454.

Kenny, D.A., Bond, C.F., Jr., Mohr, C.D. & Horn, E.M. (1996). Do we know how much people like one another? *Journal of Personality and Social Psychology*, 71, 928–936.

Kenny, D.A. & La Voie, L. (1982). Reciprocity of interpersonal attraction: A confirmed hypothesis. *Social Psychology Quarterly*, 45, 54–58.

Kensinger, E.A., Garoff-Eaton, R.J. & Schacter, D.L. (2006). Memory for specific visual details can be enhanced by negative arousing content. *Journal of Memory and Language*, 54, 99–112.

Kerr, N.L. & Tindale, R.S. (2004). Group performance and decision making. *Annual Review of Psychology*, 55, 625–655.

Kessel, N. (1989). Genius and mental disorder: A history of ideas concerning their conjunction. In P. Murray (Ed.), *Genius: The history of an idea* (pp. 196–212). London: Basil Blackwell.

Kessler, R.C. (2003). Epidemiology of women and depression. *Journal of Affective Disorders*, 74, 5–13.

Kessler, R.C., Berglund, P., Demler, O., Jin, R., Merikangas, K.R. & Walters, E.E. (2005a). Lifetime prevalence and age-of-onset distributions of *DSM-IV* disorders in the National Comorbidity Survey Replication. *Archives of General Psychiatry*, 62, 593–602.

Kessler, R.C., Chiu, W.T., Demler, O. & Walters, E.E. (2005b). Prevalence, severity, and comorbidity of 12-month *DSM-IV* disorders in the National Comorbidity Survey Replication. *Archives of General Psychiatry*, 62, 617–627.

Kessler, R.C., McGonagle, K.A., Zhao, S., Nelson, C.B., Hughes, M., Eshleman, S., Wittchen, H.U. & Kendler, K.S. (1994). Lifetime and 12-month prevalence of *DSM-III-R* psychiatric disorders in the United States. *Archives of General Psychiatry*, 51, 8–19.

Kety, S.S., Wender, P.H., Jacobsen, B., Ingraham, L.J., Jansson, L., Faber, B. & Kinney, D.K. (1994). Mental illness in the biological and adoptive relatives of schizophrenic adoptees: Replication of the Copenhagen study in the rest of Denmark. *Archives of General Psychiatry*, 51, 442–455.

Kiecolt-Glaser, J.K., Marucha, P.T., Malarkey, P.T., Mercado, A.M. & Glaser, R. (1995). Slowing of wound healing by psychological stress. *Lancet*, 346, 1194–1196.

Kiecolt-Glaser, J.K., McGuire, L., Robles, T.F. & Glaser, R. (2002). Psychoneuroimmunology: Psychological influences on immune function and health. *Journal of Consulting and Clinical Psychology*, 70, 537–547.

Kihlstrom, J.F. & Cantor, N. (2000). Social intelligence. In R.J. Sternberg (Ed.), *Handbook of intelligence* (pp. 359–369). New York: Cambridge University Press.

Killen, M. & Hart, D. (Eds.). (1999). *Morality in everyday life: Developmental perspectives.* New York: Cambridge University Press.

Kilpatrick, D.G., Ruggiero, K.J., Acierno, R., Saunders, B.E., Resnick, H.S. & Best, C.L. (2003). Violence and risk of PTSD, major depression, substance abuse/dependence, and comorbidity: Results from a national survey of adolescents. *Journal of Consulting and Clinical Psychology*, 71, 692–700.

Kilpatrick, L A., Zald, D.H., Pardo, J.V. & Cahill, L.F. (2006). Sex-related differences in amygdale functional connectivity during resting conditions. *NeuroImage*, 30, 452–461.

Kim, J. & Hatfield, E. (2004). Love types and subjective well-being: A cross-cultural study. *Social Behavior and Personality*, 32, 173–182.

Kimura, D. (1999). *Sex and cognition.* Cambridge, MA: MIT Press.

King, S. & Dixon, M.J. (1996). The influence of expressed emotion, family dynamics, and symptom type on the social adjustment of schizophrenic young adults. *Archives of General Psychiatry*, 53, 1098–1104.

King, S.A. & Moreggi, D. (1998). Internet therapy and self-help groups—The pros and cons. In J. Gackenbach (Ed.), *Psychology and the Internet: Intrapersonal, interpersonal, and transpersonal implications* (pp. 77–109). San Diego, CA: Academic Press.

King, S.A. & Poulos, S.T. (1998). Using the Internet to treat Generalized Social Phobia and Avoidant Personality Disorder. *CyberPsychology and Behavior*, 1, 1, 29–36.

Kinney, D.K., Holzman, P.S., Jacobsen, B., Jansson, L., Faber, B., Hildebrand, W., Kasell, E. & Zimbalist, M.E. (1997). Thought disorder in schizophrenic and control adoptees and their relatives. *Archives of General Psychiatry*, 54, 475–479.

Kinsey, A.C., Martin, C.E. & Pomeroy, W.B. (1948). *Sexual behavior in the human male.* Philadelphia: Saunders.

Kinsey, A.C., Pomeroy, W.B., Martin, C.E. & Gebhard, R.H. (1953). *Sexual behavior in the human female.* Philadelphia: Saunders.

Kintner, C. (2002). Neurogenesis in embryos and in adult neural stem cells. *Journal of Neuroscience*, 22, 639–643.

Kintsch, W. (1974). *The representation of meaning in memory.* Hillsdale, NJ: Erlbaum.

Kirkham, T.C. (2005). Endocannabinoids in the regulation of appetite and body weight. *Behavioural Pharmacology*, 16, 297–313.

Kirsch, I. & Lynn, S.J. (1995). The altered state of hypnosis: Changes in the theoretical landscape. *American Psychologist*, 50, 846–858.

Kirschner, S.M. & Galperin, G.J. (2001). Psychiatric defenses in New York County: Pleas and results. *Journal of the American Academy of Psychiatry and the Law*, 29, 194–201.

Kisilevsky, B.S. & Low, J.A. (1998). Human fetal behavior: 100 years of study. *Developmental Review*, 18, 1–29.

Kisilevsky, B.S., Hains, S.M.J., Lee, K., Xie, X., Huang, H., Ye, H.H., Zhang, K. & Wang, Z. (2003). Effects of experience on fetal voice recognition. *Psychological Science*, 14, 220–224.

Kissane, D.W., Grabsch, B., Clarke, D.M., Christie, G., Clifton, D., Gold, S., Hill, C., Morgan, A., McDermott, F. & Smith, G.C. (2004). Supportive-expressive group therapy: The transformation of existential ambivalence into creative living while enhancing adherence to anticancer therapies. *Psycho-Oncology*, 13, 755–768.

Kitamura, C., Thanavishuth, C., Burnham, D. & Luksaneeyanawin, S. (2002). Universality and specificity in infant-directed speech: Pitch modifications as a function of infant age and sex in a tonal and non-tonal language. *Infant Behavior & Development*, 372–392.

Kitayama, S., Markus, H.R. & Lieberman, C. (1995). The collective construction of self-esteem: Implications for culture, self, and emotion. In J.A. Russell, J. Fernandez-Dols, T. Manstead & J. Wellenkamp (Eds.), *Everyday conceptions of emotion* (pp. 523–550). Dordrecht: Kluwer.

Klein, E.B., Stone, W.N., Hicks, M.W. & Pritchard, I.L. (2003). Understanding dropouts. *Journal of Mental Health Counseling*, 89–100.

Klein, K.E. & Wegmann, H.M. (1974). The resynchronization of human circadian rhythms after transmeridian flights as a result of flight direction and mode of activity. In L.E. Scheving, F. Halberg & J.E. Pauly (Eds.), *Chronobiology* (pp. 564–570). Tokyo: Igaku.

Klein, M. (1975). *The writings of Melanie Klein* (Vols. 1–4). London: Hogarth Press and the Institute of Psychoanalysis.

Klein, O. & Snyder, M. (2003). Stereotypes and behavioral confirmation: From interpersonal to intergroup perspectives. In M.P. Zanna (Ed.), *Advances in experimental social psychology* (Vol. 35, pp. 153–234). New York: Academic Press.

Klich, L. Z; Davidson, G.R. (1983) A cultural difference in visual memory: On le voit, on ne le voit plus. *International Journal of Psychology.* Vol. 18(3–4), Aug, 189–201.

Knee, C.R. & Boon, S.D. (2001). When the glass is half-empty: Framing effects and evaluations of a romantic partner's attributes. *Personal Relationships*, 8, 249–263.

Knickmeyer, R., Baron-Cohen, S., Raggatt, P. & Taylor, K. (2005). Foetal testosterone, social relationships, and restricted interests in children. *Journal of Child Psychology and Psychiatry*, 46, 198–2 10.

Knox, C. & Quirk, P. (2000). *Peace building in Northern Ireland, Israel, and South Africa: Transition, transformation, and reconciliation.* New York: St. Martin's Press.

Kogen, J. (Writer), Wolodarsky, W. (Writer) & Reardon, J. (Director) (1992). Bart's friend falls in love [Television series episode]. In G. Meyer, R. Sakai & D. Silverman (Producers), *The Simpsons.* Los Angeles: 20th Century Fox Television.

Kohlberg, L. (1964). Development of moral character and moral ideology. In M.L. Hoffman & L.W. Hoffman (Eds.), *Review of child development research* (Vol. 1). New York: Russell Sage Foundation.

Kohlberg, L. (1981). *The philosophy of moral development.* New York: Harper & Row.

Köhler, W. (1947). *Gestalt psychology.* New York: Liveright.

Kolb, B. (1989). Development, plasticity, and behavior. *American Psychologist*, 44, 1203–1212.

Koopman, C., Classen, C. & Spiegel, D. (1996). Dissociative responses in the immediate aftermath of the Oakland/Berkeley firestorm. *Journal of Traumatic Stress*, 9, 521–540.

Korchmaros, J.D. & Kenny, D.A. (2006). An evolutionary and close-relationship model of helping. *Journal of Social and Personal Relationships*, 23, 21–43.

Koren, G., Nulman, I., Rovet, J., Greenbaum, R., Loebstein, M. & Einarson, T. (1998). Long-term neurodevelopmental risks in children exposed in utero to cocaine: The Toronto adoption study. In J.A. Harvey & B.E. Kosofsky (Eds.), *Cocaine: Effects on the developing brain* (pp. 306–313). New York: New York Academy of Sciences.

Koriat, A. & Fischoff, B. (1974). What day is today? An inquiry into the process of time orientation. *Memory & Cognition*, 2, 201–205.

Koriat, A. & Levy-Sadot, R. (2001). The combined contributions of cue-familiarity and accessibility heuristics to feelings of knowing. *Journal of Experimental Psychology: Learning, Memory, and Cognition*, 27, 34–53.

Kortegaard, L.S., Hoerder, K., Joergensen, J., Gillberg, C. & Kyvik, K.O. (2001). A preliminary population-based twin study of self-reported eating disorder. *Psychological Medicine*, 31, 361–365.

Kosslyn, S.M. (1980). *Image and mind.* Cambridge, MA: Harvard University Press.

Kosslyn, S.M., Pascual-Leone, A., Felician, O., Camposano, S., Keenan, J.P., Thompson, W.L., Ganis, G., Sukel, K.E. & Alpert, N.M. (1999). The role of area 17 in visual imagery: Convergent evidence from PET and rTMS. *Science*, 284, 167–170.

Kotovsky, K., Hayes, J.R. & Simon, H.A. (1985). Why are some problems hard? Evidence from Tower of Hanoi. *Cognitive Psychology*, 17, 248–294.

Kotovsky, K. & Simon, H.A. (1990). What makes some problems really hard: Explorations in the problem space of difficulty. *Cognitive Psychology*, 22, 143–183.

Kraepelin, E. (1921). *Manic-depressive disorder and paranoia.* London: Churchill Livingstone.

Kraut, R., Patterson, M., Lundmark, V., Kiesler, S., Mukopadhyay, T. & Scherlis, W. (1998). Internet paradox: A social technology that reduces social involvement and psychological well being? *American Psychologist*, 53, 1017–1031.

Krohne, H.W. & Slangen, K.E. (2005). Influence of social support on adaptation to surgery. *Health Psychology*, 24, 101–105.

Krueger, J. & Stanke, D. (2001). The role of self-referent and other-referent knowledge in perceptions of group characteristics. *Personality & Social Psychology Bulletin*, 27, 878–888.

Kruger, J., Wirtz, D. & Miller, D.T. (2005). Counterfactual thinking and the first instinct fallacy. *Journal of Personality and Social Psychology, 88,* 725–735.

Kuest, J. & Karbe, H. (2002). Cortical activation studies in aphasia. *Current Neurology and Neuroscience Reports, 2,* 511–515.

Kuhn, M.H. & McPartland, T.S. (1954). An empirical investigation of self-attitudes. *American Sociological Review, 19,* 68–76.

Kujawski, J.H. & Bower, T.G.R. (1993). Same-sex preferential looking during infancy as a function of abstract representation. *British Journal of Developmental Psychology, 11,* 201–209.

Kuno, E., Rothbard, A.B., Averyt, J. & Culhane, D. (2000). Homelessness among persons with serious mental illness in an enhanced community-based mental health system. *Psychiatric Services, 51,* 1012–1016.

Kuperberg, G.R., Broome, M.R., McGuire, P.K., David, A.S., Eddy, M., Ozawa, F., Goff, D., West, W.C., Williams, S.C.R., van der Kouwe, A.J.W., Salat, D.H., Dale, A.M. & Fischl, B. (2003). Regionally localized thinning of the cerebral cortex in schizophrenia. *Archives of General Psychiatry, 60,* 878–888.

LaBerge, S. & DeGracia, D.J. (2000). Varieties of lucid dreaming experience. In R.G. Kunzendorf & B. Wallace (Eds.), *Individual differences in conscious experience* (pp. 269–307). Amsterdam: John Benjamins.

LaBerge, S. & Levitan, L. (1995). Validity established of Dream-Light cues for eliciting lucid dreaming. *Dreaming: Journal of the Association for the Study ofDreams, 5,* 159–168.

LaBerge, S., Nagle, L., Dement, W. & Zarcone, V. (1981). Lucid dreaming verified by volitional communication during REM sleep. *Perceptual & Motor Skills, 52,* 727–732.

LaBerge, S. & Rheingold, H. (1990). *Exploring the world of lucid dreaming.* New York: Ballantine Books.

Lachman, M.E. (2004). Development in midlife. *Annual Review of Psychology, 55,* 305–331.

Lachman, R., Lachman, J.L. & Butterfield, E.C. (1979). *Cognitive psychology and information processing.* Hillsdale, NJ: Erlbaum.

Lampinen, J.M., Copeland, S.M. & Neuschatz, J.S. (2001). Recollections of things schematic: Room schemas revisited. *Journal of Experimental Psychology: Learning, Memory, and Cognition, 27,* 1211–1222.

Lander, E.S. & Weinberg, R.A. (2000). Genomics: Journey to the center of biology. *Science, 287,* 1777–1782.

Lang, F.R. & Carstensen, L.L. (1994). Close emotional relationships in late life: Further support for proactive aging in the social domain. *Psychology and Aging, 9,* 315–324.

Langlois, J.H., Kalakanis, L., Rubenstein, A.J., Larson, A., Hallam, M. & Smoot, M. (2000). Maxims or myths of beauty? A meta-analytic and theoretical review. *Psychological Bulletin, 126,* 390–423.

Lanius, R.A., Williamson, P.C., Hopper, J., Densmore, M., Boksman, K., Gupta, M.A., Neufeld, R.W.J., Gati, J.S. & Menon, R.S. (2003). Recall of emotional states in posttraumatic stress disorder: An fMRI investigation. *Biological Psychiatry, 53,* 204–210.

Larkin, G.L., Claassen, C.A., Emond, J.A., Pelletier, A.J. & Camargo, C.A. (2005). Trends in U.S. emergency department visits for mental health conditions, 1992 to 2001. *Psychiatric Services, 56,* 671–677.

Larner, A.J., Moss, J., Rossi, M.L. & Anderson, M. (1994). Congenital insensitivity to pain: A 20-year follow up. *Journal of Neurology, Neurosurgery & Psychiatry, 57,* 973–974.

Lashley, K.S. (1929). *Brain mechanisms and intelligence.* Chicago: University of Chicago Press.

Lashley, K.S. (1950). In search of the engram. In *Physiological mechanisms in animal behavior: Symposium of the Society for Experimental Biology* (pp. 454–482). New York: Academic Press.

Latané, B. & Darley, J.M. (1970). *The unresponsive bystander: Why doesn't he help?* New York: Appleton-Century-Crofts.

Lau, I.Y., Chiu, C. & Hong, Y. (2001). I know what you know: Assumptions about others' knowledge and their effects on message construction. *Social Cognition, 19,* 587–600.

Laumann, E.O. & Gagnon, J.H. (1995). A sociological perspective on sexual action. In R.G. Parker & J.H. Gagnon (Eds.), *Conceiving sexuality: Approaches to sex research in a postmodern world* (pp. 183–213). New York: Routledge.

Lauronen, E., Veijola, J., Isohanni, I., Jones, P.B., Nieminen, P. & Isohanni, M. (2004). Links between creativity and mental disorder. *Psychiatry, 6,* 81–98.

Lay, C.H. (1986). At last my research article on procrastination. *Journal of Research in Personality, 20,* 474–495.

Lazar, S.W., Kerr, C.E., Wasserman, R.H., Gray, J.R., Greve, D.N., Treadway, M.T., McGarvey, M., Quinn, B.T., Dusek, J.A., Benson, H., Rauch, S.L., Moore, C.I. & Fischl, B. (2005). Meditation experience is associated with increased cortical thickness. *NeuroReport, 16,* 1893–1897.

Lazareva, O.F., Freiburger, K.L. & Wasserman, E.A. (2004). Pigeons concurrently categorize photographs at both basic and superordinate levels. *Psychonomic Bulletin & Review, 11,* 1111–1117.

Lazarus, R.S. (1981, July). Little hassles can be hazardous to your health. *Psychology Today,* pp. 58–62.

Lazarus, R.S. (1984a). On the primacy of cognition. *American Psychologist, 39,* 124–129.

Lazarus, R.S. (1984b). Puzzles in the study of daily hassles. *Journal of Behavioral Medicine, 7,* 375–389.

Lazarus, R.S. (1991). Cognition and motivation in emotion. *American Psychologist, 46,* 352–367.

Lazarus, R.S. (1993). From psychological stress to the emotions: A history of changing outlooks. *Annual Review of Psychology, 44,* 1–21.

Lazarus, R.S. (1995). Vexing research problems inherent in cognitivemediational theories of emotion—and some solutions. *Psychological Inquiry,* 6, 183–196.

Lazarus, R.S. & Folkman, S. (1984). *Stress, appraisal, and coping.* New York: Springer.

Lazarus, R.S. & Lazarus, B.N. (1994). *Passion and reason: Making sense of our emotions.* New York: Oxford University Press.

Leaper, C. (2000). The social construction and socialization of gender during development. In P.H. Miller & E.K. Scholnick (Eds.), *Toward a feminist developmental psychology* (pp. 127–152). New York: Routledge.

Leary, M.R., Kowalski, R.M., Smith, L. & Phillips, S. (2003). Teasing, rejection, and violence: Case studies of the school shootings. *Aggressive Behavior,* 29, 202–214.

Leary, M.R., Tchividjian, L.R. & Kraxberger, B.E. (1994). Self-presentation can be hazardous to your health: Impression management and health risk. *Health Psychology,* 13, 461–470.

Lee, M., Zimbardo, P. & Bertholf, M. (1977, November). Shy murderers. *Psychology Today,* pp. 68–70, 76, 148.

Leger, D. (1992). *Biological foundations of behavior: An integrative approach.* New York: HarperCollins.

Leiter, M.P. & Maslach, C. (2005). *Banishing burnout: Six strategies for improving your relationship with work.* San Francisco: JosseyBass.

Lencer, R., Malchow, C.P., Trillenberg-Krecker, K., Schwinger, E. & Arolt, V. (2000). Eye-tracking dysfunction (ETD) in families with sporadic and familial schizophrenia. *Biological Psychiatry,* 47, 391–401.

Lennon, R.T. (1985). Group tests of intelligence. In B.B. Wolman (Ed.), *Handbook of intelligence* (pp. 825–847). New York: Wiley.

Lerner, M. (1980). *The belief in a just world: A fundamental delusion.* New York: Plenum Press.

Leucht, S., Barnes, T.R.E., Kissling, W., Engel, R.R., Correll, C. & Kane, J.M. (2003). Relapse prevention in schizophrenia with new-generation antipsychotics: A systematic review and exploratory meta-analysis of randomized, controlled trials. *American Journal of Psychiatry,* 160, 1209–1222.

LeVay, S. & Valente, S.M. (2002). *Human sexuality.* Sunderland, MA: Sindauer Associates.

Levenson, R.W., Carstensen, L.L. & Gottman, J.M. (1993). Longterm marriage: Age, gender, and satisfaction. *Psychology and Aging,* 8, 301–313.

Levenson, R.W., Ekman, P., Heider, K. & Friesen, W.V. (1992). Emotion and autonomic nervous system activity in the Minangkabau of West Sumatra. *Journal of Personality and Social Psychology,* 62, 972–988.

Leventhal, H. (1980). Toward a comprehensive theory of emotion. In L. Berkowitz (Ed.), *Advances in experimental social psychology* (Vol. 13, pp. 139–207). New York: Academic Press.

Leventhal, T. & Brooks-Gunn, J. (2000). The neighborhoods they live in: The effects of neighborhood on child and adolescent outcomes. *Psychological Bulletin,* 126, 309–337.

Levine, R., Sato, S., Hashimoto, T. & Verma, J. (1995). Love and marriage in eleven cultures. *Journal of Cross-Cultural Psychology,* 26, 544–571.

Levine, S.B. (1998). *Sexuality in mid-life.* New York: Plenum.

Levi-Strauss, C. (1963). The effectiveness of symbols. In C. Levi-Strauss (Ed.), *Structural anthropology.* New York: Basic Books.

Levy, B. & Langer, E. (1994). Aging free from negative stereotypes: Successful memory in China and among the American deaf. *Journal of Personality and Social Psychology,* 66, 989–997.

Levy, G.D. & Fivush, R. (1993). Scripts and gender: A new approach for examining gender-role development. *Developmental Review,* 13, 126–146.

Levy, J.A. (1994). Sex and sexuality in later life stages. In A. Rossi (Ed.), *Sexuality across the life course* (pp. 287–309). Chicago: University of Chicago Press.

Lewin, K., Lippitt, R. & White, R.K. (1939). Patterns of aggressive behavior in experimentally created 'social climates.' *Journal of Social Psychology,* 10, 271–299.

Lewinsohn, P.M. (1975). The behavioral study and treatment of depression. In M. Hersen, R.M. Eisler & P.M. Miller (Eds.), *Progress in behavior modification* (pp. 19–64). New York: Academic Press.

Lewinsohn, P.M., Hoberman, H.M., Teri, L. & Hautzinger, M. (1985). An integrative theory of depression. In S. Reiss & R. Bootzin (Eds.), *Theoretical issues in behavior therapy* (pp. 331–359). San Diego, CA: Academic Press.

Lewis, R.J., Derlega, V.J., Clarke, E.G. & Kuang, J.C. (2006). Stigma consciousness, social constraints, and lesbian wellbeing. *Journal of Counseling Psychology,* 53, 48–56.

Liang, C.T.H. & Alimo, C. (2005). The impact of white heterosexual students' interactions on attitudes toward lesbian, gay and bisexual people: A longitudinal study. *Journal of College Student Development,* 46, 237–250.

Liao, S.M. (2005). The ethics of using genetic engineering for sex selection. *Journal of Medical Ethics,* 31, 116–118.

Lieb, K., Zanarini, M.C., Schmahl, C., Linehan, M.M. & Bohus, M. (2004). Borderline personality disorder. *The Lancet,* 364, 453–461.

Lieberman, J.A., Stroup, T.S., McEvoy, J.P., Swartz, M.S., Rosenheck, A., Perkins, D.O., Keefe, R.S.E., Davis, S.M., Davis, C.E., Lebowitz, B.D., Severe, J. & Hsiao, J.K. (2005). Effectiveness of antipsychotic drugs in patients with chronic schizophrenia. *New England Journal of Medicine,* 353, 1209–1223.

Lilienfeld, S.O. & Lynn, S.J. (2003). Dissociative identity disorder: Multiple personalities, multiple controversies. In S.O. Lilienfeld, J. Lynn & J.M. Lohr (Eds.), *Science and pseudoscience in clinical psychology* (pp. 109–142). New York: Guilford Press.

Lima, S.L., Rattenborg, N.C., Lesku, J.A. & Amlaner, C.J. (2005). Sleeping under risk of predation. *Animal Behaviour, 70,* 723–736.

Lin, H., Tian, W., Chen, C., Liu, T., Tsai, S. & Lee, H. (2006). The association between readmission rates and length of stay for schizophrenia: A 3-year population based study. *Schizophrenia Research, 83,* 211–214.

Lindsay, D.S. (1990). Misleading suggestions can impair eyewitnesses' ability to remember event details. *Journal of Experimental Psychology: Learning, Memory, and Cognition, 16,* 1077–1083.

Lindsay, D. Stephen, Allen, B.P., Chan, J.C.K. & Dahl, L.C. (2004). Eyewitness suggestibility and source similarity: Intrusions of details from one event into memory reports of another event. *Journal of Memory and Language, 50,* 96–111.

Link, B.G., Struening, E.L., Rahav, M., Phelan, J.C. & Nuttbrock, L. (1997). On stigma and its consequences: Evidence from a longitudinal study of men with dual diagnoses of mental illness and substance abuse. *Journal of Health and Social Behavior, 38,* 177–190.

Liotti, M., Mayberg, H.S., McGinnis, S., Brannan, S.L. & Jerabek, P. (2002). Unmasking disease-specific cerebral blood flow abnormalities: Mood challenge in people with remitted unipolar depression. *American Journal of Psychiatry, 159,* 1830–1840.

Lipkus, I.M., Barefoot, J.C., Williams, R.B. & Siegler, I.C. (1994). Personality measures as predictors of smoking initiation and cessation in the UNC Alumni Heart Study. *Health Psychology, 13,* 149–155.

Lipp, O.V., Oughton, N. & LeLievre, J. (2003). Evaluative learning in human Pavlovian conditioning: Extinct, but still there? *Learning and Motivation, 34,* 219–239.

Little, T.D., Jones, S.M., Henrich, C.C. & Hawley, P.H. (2003). Disentangling the 'whys' from the 'whats' of aggressive behavior. *International Journal of Behavioral Development, 27,* 122–123.

Liu, J.H. & Latané, B. (1998). Extremitization of attitudes: Does thought- and discussion-induced polarization cumulate? *Basic and Applied Social Psychology, 20,* 103–110.

Liu, W., Vichienchom, K., Clements, M., DeMarco, S.C., Hughes, C., McGucken, E., Humayun, M.S., de Juan, E., Weiland, J.D. & Greenberg, R. (2000). A neuro-stimulus chip with telemetry unit for retinal prosthetic device. *IEEE Journal of Solid-State Circuits, 35,* 1487–1497.

Livesley, W.J. & Lang, K.L. (2005). Differentiating normal, abnormal, and disordered personality. *European Journal of Personality, 19,* 257–268.

Lloyd-Jones, T.J. & Luckhurst, L. (2002). Effects of plane rotation, task, and complexity on recognition of familiar and chimeric objects. *Memory & Cognition, 30,* 499–510.

Locke, J. (1975). *An essay concerning human understanding.* Oxford, UK: P.H. Nidditch. (Original work published 1690)

Lockhart, R.S. & Craik, F.I.M. (1990). Levels of processing: A retrospective commentary on a framework for memory research. *Canadian Journal of Psychology, 44,* 87–122.

Loehlin, J.C. (2000). Group differences in intelligence. In R.J. Sternberg (Ed.), *Handbook of intelligence* (pp. 176–193). Cambridge, UK: Cambridge University Press.

Loftus, E.F. (1979). *Eyewitness testimony.* Cambridge, MA: Harvard University Press.

Loftus, E.F. (2005). Planting misinformation in the human mind: A 30-year investigation of the malleability of memory. *Learning & Memory, 12,* 361–366.

Loftus, E.F., Miller, D.G. & Burns, H.J. (1978). Semantic integration of verbal information into a visual memory. *Journal of Experimental Psychology: Human Learning and Memory, 4,* 19–31.

Loftus, E.F. & Palmer, J.C. (1974). Reconstruction of automobile destruction: An example of the interaction between language and memory. *Journal of Verbal Learning and Verbal Behavior, 13,* 585–589.

Logan, G.D. (2002). Parallel and serial processes. In H. Pashler & J. Wixted (Eds.), *Stevens' handbook of experimental psychology: Vol 4. Methodology in experimental psychology* (pp. 271–300). New York: Wiley.

Logue, A.W. (1991). *The psychology of eating & drinking: An introduction* (2nd edn). New York: Freeman.

Loo, C.K. & Mitchell, P.B. (2005). A review of the efficacy of transcranial magnetic stimulation (TMS) treatment for depression, and current and future strategies to optimize efficacy. *Journal of Affective Disorders, 88,* 255–267.

Loomis, A.L., Harvey, E.N. & Hobart, G.A. (1937). Cerebral states during sleep as studied by human brain potentials. *Journal of Experimental Psychology, 21,* 127–144.

Lore, R.K. & Schultz, L.A. (1993). Control of human aggression: A comparative perspective. *American Psychologist, 48,* 16–25.

Lorenz, K. (1966). *On aggression.* New York: Harcourt, Brace & World.

Lourenço, O. & Machado, A. (1996). In defense of Piaget's theory: A reply to 10 common criticisms. *Psychological Review, 103,* 143–164.

Lovibond, P.F., Been, S., Mitchell, C.J., Bouton, M.E. & Frohardt, R. (2003). Forward and backward blocking of causal judgment is enhanced by additivity of effect magnitude. *Memory and Cognition, 31,* 133–142.

Lovibond, S.H., Adams, M. & Adams, W.G. (1979). The effects of three experimental prison environments on the behavior of nonconflict volunteer subjects. *Australian Psychologist, 14,* 273–285.

Lubart, T.I. (1994). Creativity. In R.J. Sternberg (Ed.), *Handbook of perception and cognition: Vol. 2. Thinking and problem solving* (pp. 289–332). Orlando, FL: Academic Press.

Lucas, R.E., Clark, A.E., Georgellis, Y. & Diener, E. (2003). Reexamining adaptation and the set point model of happiness: Reactions to changes in marital status. *Journal of Personality and Social Psychology, 84*, 527–539.

Luchins, A.S. (1942). Mechanization in problem solving. *Psychological Monographs, 54* (No. 248).

Luo, M., Fee, M.S. & Katz, L.C. (2003). Encoding pheromonal signals in the accessory olfactory bulb of behaving mice. *Science, 299*, 1196–1201.

Luong, A. & Rogelberg, S.G. (2005). Meetings and more meetings: The relationship between meeting load and daily well-being of employees. *Group Dynamics: Theory, Research, and Practice, 9*, 58–67.

Lutchmaya, S., Baron-Cohen, S. & Raggatt, P. (2002). Foetal testosterone and vocabulary size in 18- and 24-month-old infants. *Infant Behaviour and Development, 24*, 418–424.

Luzzo, D.A., James, T. & Luna, M. (1996). Effects of attributional retraining on the career beliefs and career exploration behavior of college students. *Journal of Counseling Psychology, 43*, 415–422.

Lykken, D. & Tellegen, A. (1996). Happiness is a stochastic phenomenon. *Psychological Science, 7*, 186–189.

Lynch, J.W., Kaplan, G.A. & Shema, S.J. (1997). Cumulative impact of sustained economic hardship on physical, cognitive, psychological, and social functioning. *New England Journal of Medicine, 337*, 1889–1895.

Lynn, S.J. & Kirsch, I. (2006). *Essentials of clinical hypnosis: An evidence-based approach.* Washington, DC: American Psychological Association.

Lynn, S.J., Lock, T., Loftus, E.F., Krackow, E. & Lilienfeld, S.O. (2003). The remembrance of things past: Problematic memory recovery techniques in psychotherapy. In S.O. Lilienfeld, S.J. Lynn & J.M. Lohr (Eds.), *Science and pseudoscience in clinical psychology* (pp. 205–239). New York: Guilford Press.

Lynn, S.J., Stafford, J., Malinoski, P. & Pintar, J. (1997). Memory in the hall of mirrors: The experience of 'retractors' in psychotherapy. *Psychological Inquiry, 8*, 307–312.

Lyons, N. (1983). Two perspectives: On self, relationships, and morality. *Harvard Educational Review, 53*, 125–146.

Lytton, H. & Romney, D.M. (1991). Parents' differential socialization of boys and girls: A meta-analysis. *Psychological Bulletin, 109*, 267–296.

Lyubomirsky, S., King, L. & Diener, E. (2005). The benefits of frequent positive affect: Does happiness lead to success? *Psychological Bulletin, 131*, 803–855.

Ma, V. & Schoeneman, T.J. (1997). Individualism versus collectivism: A comparison of Kenyan and American self-concepts. *Basic and Applied Social Psychology, 19*, 261–273.

Macchi Cassia, V., Turati, C. & Simion, F. (2004). Can a nonspecific bias toward top-heavy patterns explain newborns' face preference? *Psychological Science, 15*, 379–383.

Maccoby, E.E. (1998). *The two sexes: Growing up apart, coming together.* Cambridge, MA: Harvard University Press.

Maccoby, E.E. & Martin, J.A. (1983). Socialization in the context of the family: Parent–child interaction. In E.M. Hetherington (Ed.), *Handbook of child psychology: Vol. 4. Socialization, personality, and social development* (pp. 1–101). New York: Wiley.

MacDonald, M.C. (1993). The interaction of lexical and syntactic ambiguity. *Journal of Memory and Language, 32*, 692–715.

MacGregor, J.N., Ormerod, T.C. & Chronicle, E.P. (2001). Information processing and insight: A process model of performance on the nine-dot and related problems. *Journal of Experimental Psychology: Learning, Memory, and Cognition, 27*, 176–201.

MacLeod, C. & Campbell, L. (1992). Memory accessibility and probability judgments: An experimental evaluation of the availability heuristic. *Journal of Personality and Social Psychology, 63*, 890–902.

Macmillan, D., Gresham, F. & Siperstein, G. (1993). Conceptual and psychometric concerns about the 1992 AAMR definition of mental retardation. *Amercican Journal on Mental Retardation, 98*, 325–335.

MacPhail, E. (1992). *Brain and intelligence in vertebrates.* Oxford: Oxford University Press.

Madon, S., Fuyll, M., Spoth, R. & Willard, J. (2004). Self-fulfilling prophecies: The synergistic accumulative effect of parents' beliefs on children's drinking behaviors. *Psychological Science, 15*, 837–845.

Madon, S., Jussim, L. & Eccles, J. (1997). In search of the powerful self-fulfilling prophecy. *Journal of Personality and Social Psychology, 72*, 791–809.

Maguen, S., Floyd, F.J., Bakeman, R. & Armistead, L. (2002). Developmental milestones and disclosure of sexual orientation among gay, lesbian, and bisexual youths. *Applied Developmental Psychology, 23*, 219–233.

Mahay, J., Laumann, E. O & Michaels, S. (2001). Race, gender, and class in sexual scripts. In E.O. Laumann & R.T. Michael (Eds.), *Sex, love, and health in America* (pp. 197–238). Chicago: University of Chicago Press.

Mahowald, M.W. & Schenck, C.H. (2005). Insights from studying human sleep disorders. *Nature, 437*, 1279–1285.

Maier, N.R.F. (1931). Reasoning in humans: II. The solution of a problem and its appearance in consciousness. *Journal of Comparative Psychology, 12*, 181–194.

Maier, S.F. & Seligman, M.E.P. (1976). Learned helplessness: Theory and evidence. *Journal of Experimental Psychology, 105*, 3–46.

Malinowski, B. (1927). *Sex and repression in savage society.* London: Routledge & Kegan Paul.

Malizia, A.L., Cunningham, V.J., Bell, C.J., Liddle, P.F., Jones, T. & Nutt, D.J. (1998). Decreased brain GABA-sub(A)-benzodiazepine receptor binding in panic disorder: Preliminary results from a quantitative PET study. *Archives of General Psychiatry, 55*, 715–720.

Malizia, A.L. & Nutt, D.J. (1995). Psychopharmacology of benzodiazepines: An update. *Human Psychopharmacology: Clinical and Experimental, 10* (Suppl. 1), S1–S14.

Mandel, D.R., Jusczyk, P.W. & Pisoni, D.B. (1995). Infants' recognition of the sound patterns of their own names. *Psychological Science*, 5, 314–317.

Manoussaki, D., Dimitriadis, E.K. & Chadwick, R.S. (2006). Cochlea's graded curvature effect on low frequency waves. *Physical Review Letters*, 96, 088701.

Manuck, S.B., Flory, J.D., Muldoon, M.F. & Ferrell, R.E. (2002). Central nervous system serotonergic responsivity and aggressive disposition in men. *Physiology & Behavior*, 77, 705–709.

Marcus, A.D. (1990, December 3). Mists of memory cloud some legal proceedings. *Wall Street Journal*, p. B1.

Margot, P., Sanson, A., Smart, D. & Oberklaid, F. (2000). Pathways from Infancy to Adolescence: Australian Temperament Project 1983–2000. *Australian Institute of Family Studies—Commonwealth of Australia*. National Library of Australia.

Markovitz, H. & Nantel, G. (1989). The belief-bias effect in the production and evaluation of logical conclusions. *Memory & Cognition*, 17, 11–17.

Markowitsch, H.J. (2000). Neuroanatomy of memory. In E. Tulving & F.I.M. Craik (Eds.), *The Oxford handbook of memory* (pp. 465–484). Oxford, UK: Oxford University Press.

Markus, H. & Nurius, P. (1986). Possible selves. *American Psychologist*, 41, 954–969.

Markus, H.R. & Kitayama, S. (1991). Culture and the self: Implications for cognition, emotion, and motivation. *Psychological Review*, 98, 224–253.

Markus, H.R., Mullally, P.R. & Kitayama, S. (1997). Selfways: Diversity in modes of cultural participation. In U. Neisser & D.A. Jopling (Eds.), *The conceptual self in context* (pp. 13–61). Cambridge, UK: Cambridge University Press.

Marshall, G.D. & Zimbardo, P.G. (1979). Affective consequences of inadequately explained physiological arousal. *Journal of Personality and Social Psychology*, 37, 970–988.

Marshall, S.J. & Biddle, S.J.H. (2001). The transtheoretical model of behavior change: A meta-analysis of applications to physical activity and exercise. *Annals of Behavioral Medicine*, 23, 229–246.

Martin, G. & Pear, J. (1999). *Behavior modification: What it is and how to do it* (6th ed.). Upper Saddle River, NJ: Prentice Hall.

Martin, M.M. & Anderson, C.M. (1995). Roommate similarity: Are roommates who are similar in their communication traits more satisfied? *Communication Research Reports*, 12, 46–52.

Martin, I. & Levy, A.B. (1978). Evaluative conditioning. *Advances in Behavior Research and Therapy*, 1, 57–102.

Martin, P.Y. & Marrington, S. (2005). Morningness-eveningness orientation, optimal time-of-day and attitude change: Evidence for the systematic processing of a persuasive communication. *Personality and Individual Differences*, 39, 367–377.

Martin, R.J., White, B.D. & Hulsey, M.G. (1991). The regulation of body weight. *American Scientist*, 79, 528–541.

Martin-Fardon, R., Lorentz, C.U., Stuempfig, N.D. & Weiss, F. (2005). Priming with BTCP, a dopamine reuptake blocker, reinstates cocaine-seeking and enhances cocaine cue-induced reinstatement. *Pharmacology, Biochemistry, and Behavior*, 92, 46–54.

Marttunen, M.J., Henriksson, M.M., Isometsae, E.T., Heikkinen, M.E., Aro, H.M. & Loennqvist, J.K. (1998). Completed suicide among adolescents with no diagnosable psychiatric disorder. *Adolescence*, 33, 669–681.

Marx, B.P. & Gross, A.M. (1995). Date rape: An analysis of two contextual variables. *Behavior Modification*, 19, 451–463.

Marx, J. (2001). New leads on the "how" of Alzheimer's. *Science*, 293, 2192–2194.

Marx, J. (2003). Cellular warriors in the battle of the bulge. *Science*, 299, 846–849.

Maslach, C. (1979). Negative emotional biasing of unexplained arousal. *Journal of Personality and Social Psychology*, 37, 953–969.

Maslach, C., Schaufeli, W.B. & Leiter, M.P. (2001). Job burnout. *Annual Review of Psychology*, 52, 397–422.

Maslow, A.H. (1968). *Toward a psychology of being* (2nd ed.). Princeton, NJ: Van Nostrand.

Maslow, A.H. (1970). *Motivation and personality* (rev. edn). New York: Harper & Row.

Mason, L.E. (1997, August 4). Divided she stands. *New York*, pp. 42–49.

Mason, M.A., Skolnick, A. & Sugarman, S.D. (Eds.). (1998). *All our families: New policies for a new century*. New York: Oxford University Press.

Masten, A.S. (2001). Ordinary magic: Resilience processes in development. *American Psychologist*, 56, 227–238.

Masters, W.H. & Johnson, V.E. (1966). *Human sexual response*. Boston: Little, Brown.

Masters, W.H. & Johnson, V.E. (1970). *Human sexual inadequacy*. Boston: Little, Brown.

Masters, W.H. & Johnson, V.E. (1979). *Homosexuality in perspective*. Boston: Little, Brown.

Mattson, S.N., Schoenfeld, A.M. & Riley, E.P. (2001). Teratogenic effects of alcohol on the brain. *Alcohol Research & Health*, 25, 185–191.

Maurer, D., Lewis, T.L., Brent, H.P. & Levin, A.V. (1999). Rapid improvement in the acuity of infants after visual input. *Science*, 286, 108–110.

May, R. (1975). *The courage to create*. New York: Norton.

Mayer, J.D. & Salovey, P. (1997). What is emotional intelligence? In P. Salovey & D. Sluyter (Eds.), *Emotional development and emotional intelligence: Educational implications* (pp. 3–31). New York: Basic Books.

Mayer, J.D., Salovey, P. & Caruso, D.R. (2004). Emotional intelligence: Theory, findings, and implications. *Psychological Inquiry*, 15, 197–215.

Mazurski, E.J., Bond, N.W., Siddle, D.A.T. & Lovibond, P.F. (1996). Conditioning with facial expressions of emotion: Effects of CS sex and age. *Psychophysiology*, 33, 416–425.

McAdams, D.P. (1988). Biography, narrative, and lives: An introduction. *Journal of Personality*, 56, 1–18.

McAdams, D.P. (2001). The psychology of life stories. *Review of General Psychology*, 5, 100–122.

McAdams, D.P. & de St. Aubin, E. (1992). A theory of generativity and its assessment through self-report, behavioral acts, and narrative themes in autobiography. *Journal of Personality and Social Psychology*, 62, 1003–1015.

McAdams, D.P. & de St. Aubin, E. (Eds.). (1998). *Generativity and adult development: How and why we care for the next generation.* Washington, DC: American Psychological Association.

McAllister, H.A. (1996). Self-serving bias in the classroom: Who shows it? Who knows it? *Journal of Educational Psychology*, 88, 123–131.

McBurnett, K., Lahey, B.B., Rathouz, P.J. & Loeber, R. (2000). Low salivary cortisol and persistent aggression in boys referred for disruptive behavior. *Archives of General Psychiatry*, 57, 38–43.

McCall, W.V., Prudic, J., Olfson, M. & Sackeim, H. (2006). Health-related quality of life following ECT in a large community sample. *Journal of Affective Disorders*, 90, 269–274.

McClelland, D.C. (1961). *The achieving society.* Princeton, NJ: Van Nostrand.

McClelland, D.C. (1971). *Motivational trends in society.* Morristown, NJ: General Learning Press.

McClelland, D.C., Atkinson, J.W., Clark, R.A. & Lowell, E.L. (1953). *The achievement motive.* New York: Appleton-CenturyCrofts.

McClelland, D.C., Atkinson, J.W., Clark, R.A. & Lowell, E.L. (1976). *The achievement motive* (2nd edn). New York: Irvington.

McClelland, D.C. & Franz, C.E. (1992). Motivational and other sources of work accomplishments in midlife: A longitudinal study. *Journal of Personality*, 60, 679–707.

McClelland, J.L. & Elman, J.L. (1986). The TRACE model of speech perception. *Cognitive Psychology*, 18, 1–86.

McCrae, R.R. & Costa, P.T., Jr. (1997). Personality trait structure as a human universal. *American Psychologist*, 52, 509–5 16.

McCrae, R.R. & Costa, P.T., Jr. (1999). A five-factor theory of personality. In L.A. Pervin & O.P. John (Eds.), *Handbook of personality: Theory and research* (2nd edn, pp. 139–153). New York: Guilford Press.

McCrae, R.R., Costa, P.T., Jr. & Martin, T.A. (2005). The NEO-PI-3: A more readable revised NEO Personality Inventory. *Journal of Personality Assessment*, 84, 261–270.

McCrae, R.R., Costa, P.T., Jr., Martin, T.A., Oryol, V.E., Rukavishnikov, A.A., Senin, I.G., Hřebíčková, M. & Urbánek, T. (2004). Consensual validation of personality traits across cultures. *Journal of Research in Personality*, 38, 179–201.

McCrae, R.R., Costa, P.T., Jr., Ostendorf, F., Angleitner, A., Hřebíčková, M., Avia, M.D., Sanz, J., Sanchez-Bernardos, M.L., Kusdil, M.E., Woodfield, R.,

Saunders, P.R. & Smith, P.B. (2000). Nature over nurture: Temperament, personality, and life span development. *Journal of Personality and Social Psychology*, 78, 173–186.

McGeough, P. & Simpson, L. (1996). Young, rich and out of control: The portrait of a lone gunman. *The Sydney Morning Herald*, 30 April. Accessed 12 November 2007 from <http://www.factiva.com>

McGregor, H.A. & Elliott, A.J. (2002). Achievement goals as predictors of achievement-relevant processes prior to task engagement. *Journal of Educational Psychology*, 94, 381–395.

McGue, M., Elkins, I., Walden, B. & Iacono, W.G. (2005). Perceptions of the parent-adolescent relationship: A longitudinal investigation. *Developmental Psychology*, 41, 971–984.

McKenna, K.Y.A. & Bargh, J.A. (1998). Coming out in the age of the Internet: Identity "demarginalization" through virtual group participation. *Journal of Personality and Social Psychology*, 75, 681–694.

McKenna, K.Y.A. & Bargh, J.A. (2000). Plan 9 from cyberspace: The implications of the Internet for personality and social psychology. *Personality and Social Psychology Review*, 4, 57–75.

McNally, G.P. & Westbrook, R.F. (2006). Predicting danger: The nature, consequences, and mechanisms of predictive fear learning. *Learning and Memory*, 13, 245–253.

McNeil, B.J., Pauker, S.G., Sox, H.C., Jr. & Tversky, A. (1982). On the elicitation of preferences for alternative therapies. *New England Journal of Medicine*, 306, 1259–1262.

McPherson, K.S. (1985). On intelligence testing and immigration legislation. *American Psychologist*, 40, 242–243.

Mead, M. (1928). *Coming of age in Samoa.* New York: Morrow. Mead, M. (1939). *From the South Seas: Studies of adolescence and sex in primitive societies.* New York: Morrow.

Meador, B.D. & Rogers, C.R. (1979). Person-centered therapy. In R.J. Corsini (Ed.), *Current psychotherapies* (2nd ed., pp. 131–184). Itasca, IL: Peacock.

Measey, M.L., Li, S.Q., Parker, R. & Wang, Z. (2006). Suicide in the Northern Territory, 1981–2002, *Medical Journal of Australia*, 185 (6), 315–319.

Meece, J.L., Anderman, E.M. & Anderman, L.H. (2006). Classroom goal structure, student motivation, and academic achievement. *Annual Review of Psychology*, 57, 487–503.

Meichenbaum, D. (1977). *Cognitive-behavior modification: An integrative approach.* New York: Plenum.

Meichenbaum, D. (1985). *Stress inoculation training.* New York: Pergamon Press.

Meichenbaum, D. (1993). Changing conceptions of cognitive behavior modification: Retrospect and prospect. *Journal of Consulting and Clinical Psychology*, 61, 202–204.

Meier, R.P. (1991). Language acquisition by deaf children. *American Scientist*, 79, 60–70.

Melzack, R. (1973). *The puzzle of pain.* New York: Basic Books. Melzack, R. (1980). Psychological aspects of pain. In J.J. Bonica (Ed.), *Pain.* New York: Raven Press.

Melzach, R. (1999). From the gate to the neuromatrix. *Pain Supplement,* 16, S121–S126.

Menaker, M. (2003). Circadian photoreception. *Science,* 299, 213–214.

Menon, T., Morris, M.W., Chiu, C. & Hong, Y. (1999). Culture and construal of agency: Attribution to individual versus group dispositions. *Journal of Personality and Social Psychology,* 76, 701–717.

Merton, R.K. (1957). *Social theory and social structures.* New York: The Free Press.

Mesquita, B. & Frijda, N.H. (1992). Cultural variations in emotions: A review. *Psychological Bulletin,* 112, 179–204.

Metcalfe, J. (2000). Metamemory: Theory and data. In E. Tulving & F.I.M. Craik (Eds.), *The Oxford handbook of memory* (pp. 197–211). Oxford, UK: Oxford University Press.

Meyer, R.G. (2003). *Case studies in abnormal behavior* (6th ed.). Boston: Allyn & Bacon.

Meyer-Lindenberg, A., Buckholtz, J.W., Kolachana, B., Hariri, A.R., Pezawas, L., Blasi, G., Wabnitz, A., Honea, R., Verchinski, B., Callicott, J.H., Egan, M., Mattay, V. & Weinberger, D.R. (2006). Neural mechanisms of genetic risk for impulsivity and violence in humans. *Proceedings of the National Academy of Sciences,* 103, 6269–6274.

Meyers, S.A. & Berscheid, E. (1997). The language of love: The difference a preposition makes. *Personality and Social Psychology Bulletin,* 23, 347–362.

Michael, R.T., Gagnon, J.H., Laumann, E.O. & Kolata, G. (1994). *Sex in America: A definitive survey.* Boston: Little, Brown.

Middlebrooks, J.C. & Green, D.C. (1991). Sound localization by human listeners. *Annual Review of Psychology,* 42, 135–159.

Miklowitz, D.J. & Tompson, M.C. (2003). Family variables and interventions in schizophrenia. In G.P. Sholevar & L.D. Schwoeri (Eds.), *Textbook of family and couples therapy: Clinical applications* (pp. 585–617). Washington, DC: American Psychiatric Publishing.

Mikolic, J.M., Parker, J.C. & Pruitt, D.G. (1997). Escalation in response to persistent annoyance: Groups versus individuals and gender effects. *Journal of Personality and Social Psychology,* 72, 151–163.

Mikulincer, M., Florian, V., Cowan, P.A. & Cowan, C.P. (2002). Attachment security in couple relationships: A systematic model and its implications for family dynamics. *Family Process,* 41, 405–434.

Miles, D.R. & Carey, G. (1997). Genetic and environmental architecture of human aggression. *Journal of Personality and Social Psychology,* 72, 207–217.

Milgram, S. (1965). Some conditions of obedience and disobedience to authority. *Human Relations,* 18, 56–76.

Milgram, S. (1974). Obedience to authority. New York: Harper & Row.

Miller, G.A. (1956). The magic number seven plus or minus two: Some limits in our capacity for processing information. *Psychological Review,* 63, 81–97.

Miller, J.G. (1984). Culture and the development of everyday social explanation. *Journal of Personality and Social Psychology,* 46, 961–978.

Miller, J.G. & Bersoff, D.M. (1992). Culture and moral judgment: How are conflicts between justice and interpersonal responsibilities resolved? *Journal of Personality and Social Psychology,* 62, 541–554.

Miller, J.G., Bersoff, D.M. & Harwood, R.L. (1990). Perceptions of social responsibilities in India and in the United States: Moral imperatives or personal decisions? *Journal of Personality and Social Psychology,* 58, 33–47.

Miller, K.A., Fisher, P.A., Fetrow, B. & Jordan, K. (2006). Trouble on the journey home: Reunification failures in foster care. *Children and Youth Services Review,* 28, 260–274.

Miller, M.A. & Rahe, R.H. (1997). Life changes scaling for the 1990s. *Journal of Psychosomatic Research,* 43, 279–292.

Miller N.E. (1978). Biofeedback and visceral learning. *Annual Review of Psychology,* 29, 373–404.

Miller, N.E. (1985). The value of behavioral research on animals. *American Psychologist,* 40, 423–440.

Mindell, J.A. (1997). Children and sleep. In M.R. Pressman & W.C. Orr (Eds.), *Understanding sleep: The evaluation and treatment of sleep disorders* (pp. 427–439). Washington, DC: American Psychological Association.

Miniño, A.M., Heron, M. & Smith, B.L. (2006). *Deaths: Preliminary data for 2004.* Washington, DC: National Center for Health Statistics.

Mischel, W. (1973). Toward a cognitive social learning reconceptualization of personality. *Psychological Review,* 80, 252–283.

Mischel, W. (2004). Toward an integrative science of the person. *Annual Review of Psychology,* 55, 1–22.

Mischel, W. & Shoda, Y. (1995). A cognitive-affective system theory of personality: Reconceptualizing situations, dispositions, dynamics, and invariance in personality structure. *Psychological Review,* 102, 246–268.

Mischel, W. & Shoda, Y. (1999). Integrating dispositions and processing dynamics within a unified theory of personality: The cognitive-affective personality system. In L.A. Pervin & O.P. John (Eds.), *Handbook of personality: Theory and research* (2nd ed., pp. 197–218). New York: Guilford Press.

Mitchell, C.J. & Lovibond, P.F. (2002). Backward and forward blocking in human electrodermal conditioning: Blocking requires an assumption of outcome additivity. *Quarterly Journal of Experimental Psychology,* 55, 311–329.

Mitchell, K.J. & Johnson, M.K. (2000). Source monitoring: Attributing mental experiences. In E. Tulving & F.I.M. Craik (Eds.), *The Oxford handbook of memory* (pp. 179–195). London: Oxford University Press.

Mohamed, F.B., Faro, S.H., Gordon, N.J., Platek, S.M., Ahmad, H. & Williams, J.M. (2006). Brain mapping of decpetoin and truth telling about an ecologically valid situation: Functional MR imaging and polygraph investigation—initial experience. *Radiology, 238*, 679–688.

Moncrieff, R.W. (1951). *The chemical senses.* London: Leonard Hill.

Money, J., Cawte.J.E., Bianchi, G.N. & Nurcombe, B. (1970). Sex training and traditions in Arnhem Land. *British Journal of Medicine, 43*, 383–399.

Montague, C.T., Farooqi, I.S., Whitehead, J.P., Soos, M.A., Rau, H., Wareham, N.J., Sewter, C.P., Digby, J.E., Mohammed, S.N., Hurst, J.A., Cheetham, C.H., Earley, A.R., Barnett, A.H., Prins, J.B. & O'Rahilly, S. (1997). Congenital leptin deficiency is associated with severe early-onset obesity in humans. *Nature, 387*, 903–908.

Moore-Ede, M.C. (1993). *The twenty-four-hour society: Understanding human limits in a world that never stops.* Reading, MA: Addison-Wesley.

Morgan, A.H., Hilgard, E.R. & Davert, E.C. (1970). The heritability of hypnotic susceptibility of twins: A preliminary report. *Behavior Genetics, 1*, 213–224.

Morgenstern, J., Labouvie, E., McCrady, B.S., Kahler, C.W. & Frey, R.M. (1997). Affiliation with Alcoholics Anonymous after treatment: A study of its therapeutic effects and mechanisms of action. *Journal of Consulting and Clinical Psychology, 65*, 768–777.

Moriarty, T. (1975). Crime, commitment and the responsive bystander: Two field experiments. *Journal of Personality and Social Psychology, 31*, 370–376.

Morin, S.F. & Rothblum, E.D. (1991). Removing the stigma: Fifteen years of progress. *American Psychologist, 46*, 947–949.

Morphy, H. (1999). Australian Aboriginal Concepts of Time, in Lippincott, K. (ed) *The Story of Time.* London: Merrell Holberton in association with National Maritime Museum, pp. 264–267.

Morris, J.A., Jordan, C.L. & Breedlove, S.M. (2004). Sexual differentiation of the vertebrate nervous system. *Nature Neuroscience, 7*, 1034–1039.

Morris, J.S., Frith, C.D., Perrett, D.I., Rowland, D., Young, A.W., Calder, A.J. & Dolan, R.J. (1996). A differential neural response in the human amygdala to fearful and happy facial expressions. *Nature, 383*, 812–815.

Moscovici, S. (1976). *Social influence and social change.* New York: Academic Press.

Moscovici, S. (1980). Toward a theory of conversion behavior. In L. Berkowitz (Ed.), *Advances in experimental social psychology* (Vol. 13, pp. 209–239). New York: Academic Press.

Moscovici, S. (1985). Social influence and conformity. In G. Lindzey & E. Aronson (Eds.), *The handbook of social psychology* (3rd edn, pp. 347–412). New York: Random House.

Moscovici, S. & Faucheux, C. (1972). Social influence, conformity bias, and the study of active minorities. In L. Berkowitz (Ed.), *Advances in experimental social psychology* (Vol. 6). New York: Academic Press.

Moskowitz, B.A. (1978). The acquisition of language. *Scientific American, 239*(11), 92–108.

Moskowitz, G.B. (2004). *Social cognition: Understanding self and others.* New York: Guilford Press.

Motherwell, L. & Shay, J.J. (2005). (Eds.). *Complex dilemmas in group therapy.* New York: Brunner-Routledge.

Motley, M.T. & Baars, B.J. (1979). Effects of cognitive set upon laboratory-induced verbal (Freudian) slips. *Journal of Speech and Hearing Research, 22*, 421–432.

Mumme, D.L. & Fernald, A. (2003). The infant as onlooker: Learning from emotional reactions observed in a television scenario. *Child Development, 74*, 221–237.

Munn, N.D. (1973), *Warlpiri Iconography.* New York: Cornell University Press.

Munro, G.D. & Ditto, P.H. (1997). Biased assimilation, attitude polarization, and affect in reactions to stereotype-relevant scientific information. *Personality and Social Psychology Bulletin, 23*, 636–653.

Munsterberg, H. (1908). *On the witness stand.* New York: McClure.

Murata, P.J., McGlynn, E.A., Siu, A.L. & Brook, R.H. (1992). *Prenatal care.* Santa Monica, CA: The Rand Corporation.

Murphy, G.L. (2002). *The big book of concepts.* Cambridge, MA: MIT Press.

Murphy, M.C. & Archer, J. (1996). Stressors on the college campus: A comparison of 1985–1993. *Journal of College Student Development, 37*, 20–28.

Murray, C.J.L. & Lopez, A.D. (Eds.) (1996). *The global burden of disease and injury series.* Cambridge, MA: Harvard University Press.

Murray, H.A. (1938). *Explorations in personality.* New York: Oxford University Press.

Mussweiler, T. & Bodenhausen, G.V. (2002). I know you are, but what am I? Self-evaluative consequences of judging in-group and out-group members. *Journal of Personality and Social Psychology, 82*, 19–32.

Myers, R.S. & Roth, D.L. (1997). Perceived benefits of and barriers to exercise and stage of exercise adoption in young adults. *Health Psychology, 16*, 277–283.

Nasrallah, H.A. (2005). Factors having impact on the tolerability of antipsychotic agents. *Journal of Clinical Psychiatry, 66*, 131–133.

National Clearinghouse on Child Abuse and Neglect Information (2005). Foster care: Numbers and trends. Retrieved from <nccanch.acf.hhs.gov/pubs/factsheets/foster.cfm>

National Health and Medical Research Council (2003). *Values and Ethics: Guidelines for ethical conduct in Aboriginal and Torres Strait Islander health research.* Canberra: Australian Government.

National Health and Medical Research Council (2004). Australian code of practice for the care and use of animals for scientific purposes (7th edn). Canberra: Australian Government Printer.

National Health and Medical Research Council & Australian Research Council. (2007). *Australian Code for the Responsible Conduct of Research.* Canberra: Australian Government.

National Health and Medical Research Council, Australian Research Council & Australian Vice-chancellors Committee (2007). *National Statement on Ethical Conduct in Human Research.* Canberra: Australian Government.

National Institute on Aging. (2005). *Alzheimer's Disease fact sheet.* Retrieved from <www.nia.nih.gov/Alzheimers/ Publications/ adfact.htm>

National Sleep Foundation. (2000). *2000 omnibus sleep in America poll.* Retrieved from <www.sleepfoundation. org/publications/ 2000poll.html>

National Sleep Foundation. (2003). *2003 sleep in America poll.* Retrieved from <www.sleepfoundation.org/ polls/2003SleepPollExecSumm.pdf>

National Sleep Foundation. (2005). Summary findings of the 2005 *Sleep in America* poll. Available at <www. sleepfoundation.org/_content/hottopics/2005summary _of_findings.pdf>

Natsoulas, T. (1998). Consciousness and self-awareness. In M. Ferrari & R.J. Sternberg (Eds.), *Self-awareness: Its nature and development* (pp. 12–33). New York: Guilford Press.

Neath, I. & Crowder, R.G. (1990). Schedules of presentation and temporal distinctiveness in human memory. *Journal of Experimental Psychology: Learning, Memory, and Cognition, 16*, 316–327.

Neath, I., Brown, G.D.A., McCormack, T., Chater, N. & Freeman, R. (2006). Distinctiveness models of memory and absolute identification: Evidence for local, not global, effects. *Quarterly Journal of Experimental Psychology, 59*, 121–135.

Neath, I. & Surprenant, A.M. (2003). *Human memory: An introduction to research, data, and theory* (2nd edn). Belmont, CA: Wadsworth.

Neisser, U. (1967). *Cognitive psychology.* New York: Appleton-Century-Crofts.

Neisser, U., Boodoo, G., Bouchard, T.J., Jr., Boykin, A.W., Brody, N., Ceci, S.J., Halpern, D.F., Loehlin, J.C., Perloff, R., Sternberg, R.J. & Urbina, S. (1996). Intelligence: Knowns and unknowns. *American Psychologist, 51*, 77–101.

Nelson, R.E. & Craighead, W.E. (1977). Selective recall of positive and negative feedback, self-control behaviors and depression. *Journal of Abnormal Psychology, 86*, 379–388.

Nelson, T.D. (2006). *The psychology ofprejudice* (2nd edn). Boston: Allyn & Bacon.

Nelson, T.O. (1996). Consciousness and metacognition. *American Psychologist, 51*, 102–116.

Nestler, E.J., Gould, E., Manji, H., Bucan, M., Duman, R.S., Gershenfeld, H.K., Hen, R., Koester, S., Lederhendler, I., Meaney, M.J., Robbins, T., Winsky, L. & Zalcman, S. (2002). Preclinical models: Status of basic research in depression. *Biological Psychiatry, 52*, 503–528.

Nettlebeck, T. & Wilson, C. (2005). Intelligence and IQ: What teachers should know. *Educational Psychology, 25*, 609–630.

Néveus, T., Cnattingius, S., Olsson, U. & Hetta, J. (2001). Sleep habits and sleep problems among a community sample of schoolchildren. *Acta Paediatr, 90*, 1450–1455.

Newcomb, T.M. (1929). *The consistency of certain extrovert-introvert behavior traits in 50 problem boys* (Contributions to Education, No. 382). New York: Columbia University Press.

Newell, A. & Simon, H.A. (1972). *Human problem solving.* Englewood Cliffs, NJ: Prentice Hall.

Newman, T.K., Syagailo, Y.V., Barr, C.S., Wendland, J.R., Champoux, M., Grassele, M., Suomi, S.J., Higley, J.D. & Lesch, K.-P. (2005). Monoamine oxidase A gene promoter variation and rearing experiences influence aggressive behavior in rhesus monkeys. *Biological Psychiatry, 57*, 167–172.

Ng, C. (1997). The stigma of mental illness in Asian cultures. *Australian and New Zealand Journal of Psychiatry, 31*: 382–390.

Niaura, R., Todaro, J.F., Stoud, L., Sprio, A., III, Ward, K.D. & Weiss, S. (2002). Hostility, the metabolic syndrome, and incident coronary heart disease. *Health Psychology, 21*, 588–593.

Nicoll, C., Russell, S. & Katz, L. (1988, May 26). Research on animals must continue. *San Francisco Chronicle,* p. A25.

Nie, N.H. & Erbring, L. (2000). *Internet and society: A preliminary report.* Stanford, CA: Stanford Institute for the Quantitative Study of Society.

Nielsen, F. (1994). Sociobiology and sociology. *Annual Review of Sociology, 20*, 267–303.

Nielsen, T.A. & Stenstrom, P. (2005). What are the memory sources of dreaming? *Nature, 437*, 1286–1289.

Nisbett, R.E. (1995). Race, IQ, and scientism. In S. Fraser (Ed.), *The Bell Curve wars: Race, intelligence, and the future ofAmerica* (pp. 36–57). New York: Basic Books.

Nisbett, R.E. (1998). Race, genetics, and IQ. In C. Jencks & M. Phillips (Eds.), *The black–white test score gap* (pp. 86–102). Washington, DC: Brookings Institution Press.

Nisbett, R.E. & Cohen, D. (1996). *Culture of honor: The psychology of violence in the South.* Boulder, CO: Westview Press.

Noack, P. (2004). The family context of preadolescents' orientations toward education: Effects of maternal orientations and behavior. *Journal of Educational Psychology, 96*, 714–722.

Nolen-Hoeksema, S. (2002). Gender differences in depression. In I.H. Gotlib & C.L. Hammen (Eds.), *Handbook of depression* (pp. 492–509). New York: Guilford Press.

Nolen-Hoeksema, S., Larson, J. & Grayson, C. (1999). Explaining the gender difference in depressive symptoms. *Journal of Personality and Social Psychology, 77*, 1061–1072.

Norcross, J.C., Karpiak, C.P. & Lister, K.M. (2005). What's an integrationist? A study of self-identified and (occasionally) eclectic psychologists. *Journal of Clinical Psychology,* 61, 1587–1594.

Norman, G.J., Velicer, W.F., Fava, J.L. & Prochaska, J.O. (1998). Dynamic topology clustering within the stages of change for smoking cessation. *Addictive Behaviors,* 23, 139–153.

Norman, G.J., Velicer, W.F., Fava, J.L. & Prochaska, J.O. (2000). Cluster subtypes within stage of change in a representative sample of smokers. *Addictive Behaviors,* 25, 183–204.

Norman, W.T. (1963). Toward an adequate taxonomy of personality attributes: Replicated factor structure in peer nomination personality ratings. *Journal of Abnormal and Social Psychology,* 66, 574–583.

Norman, W.T. (1967). *2,800 personality trait descriptors: Normative operating characteristics for a university population* (Research Rep. No. 08310-1-T). Ann Arbor: University of Michigan Press.

Nosofsky, R.M. & Stanton, R.D. (2005). Speeded classification in a probabilistic category structure: Contrasting exemplar-retrieval, decision-boundary, and prototype models. *Journal of Experimental Psychology: Human Perception and Performance,* 31, 608–629.

Novick, L.R. & Bassok, M. (2005). Problem solving. In K.J. Holyoak & R.G. Morrison (Eds.), *Cambridge handbook of thinking and reasoning* (pp. 321–349). New York: Cambridge University Press.

Nowak, M.A. & Sigmund, K. (2005). Evolution of indirect reciprocity. *Nature,* 437, 1291–1298.

NSW Statewide Ophthalmology Service (2006). *Revised Vision Surveillance and Vision Screening Protocols NSW Health Personal Health Records,* Sydney, NSW Health.

Nutt, D.J. & Malizia, A.L. (2001). New insights into the role of the GABA-sub(A)-benzodiazepine receptor in psychiatric disorder. *British Journal of Psychiatry,* 179, 390–396.

Nyberg, L. & Cabeza, R. (2000). Brain imaging of memory. In E. Tulving & F.I.M. Craik (Eds.), *The Oxford handbook of memory* (pp. 501–519). Oxford, UK: Oxford University Press.

Oaksford, M. & Chater, N. (1994). A rational analysis of the selection task as optimal data selection. *Psychological Review,* 101, 608–631.

Oaksford, M., Chater, N., Grainger, B. & Larking, J. (1997). Optimal data selection in the reduced array selection task (RAST). *Journal of Experimental Psychology: Learning, Memory, and Cognition,* 23, 441–458.

Oberschall, A. (2001). From ethnic cooperation to violence and war in Yugoslavia. In D. Chirot & M.E.P. Seligman (Eds.), *Ethnopolitical warfare: Causes, consequences, and possible solutions* (pp. 119–150). Washington, DC: American Psychological Association.

O'Brien, C.P. (2005). Benzodiazepine use, abuse, and dependence. *Journal of Clinical Psychiatry,* 66 (Suppl. 2), 28–33.

O'Connor, M.G. & Lafleche, G. (2005). Amnesic syndromes. In P.J. Snyder, P.D. Nussbaum & D.L. Robins (Eds.), *Clinical neuropsychology: A pocket handbook for assessment* (2nd edn) (pp. 463–488). Washington, DC: American Psychology Association.

Ogden, C.L., Carroll, M.D., Curtin, L.R., McDowell, M.A., Tabak, C.J. & Flegal, K.M. (2006). Prevalence of overweight and obesity in the United States, 1999–2004. *Journal of The American Medical Association,* 295, 1549–1555.

Ohayon, M.M., Guilleminault, C. & Priest, R.G. (1999). Night terrors, sleepwalking, and confusional arousals in the general population: Their frequency and relationship to other sleep and mental disorders. *Journal of Clinical Psychiatry,* 60, 268–276.

Öhman, A. & Mineka, S. (2001). Fears, phobias, and preparedness: Toward an evolved module of fear and fear learning. *Psychological Review,* 108, 483–522.

Oishi, S. (2003). The experiencing and remembering of well-being: A cross-cultural analysis. *Personality and Social Psychology Bulletin,* 28, 1398–1406.

Olson, D.J., Kamil, A.C., Balda, R.P. & Nims, P.J. (1995). Performance of four seed-caching corvid species in operant tests of nonspatial and spatial memory. *Journal of Comparative Psychology,* 109, 173–181.

Olszewski-Kubiius, P. & Lee, S.Y. (2004). The role of participation in in-school and outside-of-school activities in the talent development of gifted students. *Journal of Secondary Gifted Education,* 15, 107–123.

Olton, D.S. (1992). Tolman's cognitive analyses: Predecessors of current approaches in psychology. *Journal of Experimental Psychology: General,* 121, 427–428.

Omoto, A.M. & Snyder, M. (2002). Considerations of community: The context and process of volunteerism. *American Behavioral Scientist,* 45, 846–867.

Opton, E.M., Jr. (1970). Lessons of My Lai. In N. Sanford & C. Comstock (Eds.), *Sanctions for evil.* San Francisco: Jossey-Bass.

Opton, E.M., Jr. (1973). "It never happened and besides they deserved it." In W.E. Henry & N. Stanford (Eds.), *Sanctions for evil* (pp. 49–70). San Francisco: Jossey-Bass.

Orbuch, T.L., Veroff, J., Hassan, H. & Horrocks, J. (2002). Who will divorce: A 14-year longitudinal study of black couples and white couples *Journal of Social and Personal Relationships,* 19, 179–202.

O'Regan, J.K. (1992). Solving the "real" mysteries of visual perception: The world as an outside memory. *Canadian Journal of Psychology,* 46, 461–488.

Ornstein, R.E. (1991). *The evolution of consciousness.* New York: Simon & Schuster.

Orr, W.C. (1997). Obstructive sleep apnea: Natural history and varieties of clinical presentation. In M.R. Pressman & W.C. Orr (Eds.), *Understanding sleep: The evaluation and treatment of sleep disorders* (pp. 267–281). Washington, DC: American Psychological Association.

Oster, H. (1997). Facial expression as a window on sensory experience and affect in newborn infants. In P. Ekman & E. Rosenberg (Eds.), *What the face reveals: Basic and applied studies of spontaneous expression using the facial action coding system (FACS)* (pp. 320–327). New York: Oxford University Press.

Owen, M.J. & O'Donovan, M.C. (2003). Schizophrenia and genetics. In R. Plomin, J.C. DeFries, I.W. Craig & P. McGuffin (Eds.), *Behavioral genetics in the postgenomic era* (pp. 463–480). Washington, DC: American Psychological Association.

Owens, K.M.B., Asmundson, G.J.G., Hadjistavropoulos, T. & Owens, T.J. (2004). Attentional bias toward illness threat in individuals with elevated health anxiety. *Cognitive Therapy and Research,* 28, 57–66.

Ozer, D.J. & Reise, S.P. (1994). Personality assessment. *Annual Review of Psychology,* 45, 357–388.

Padberg, R., Zwanzger, P., Keck, M.E., Kathmann, N., Mikhaiel, P., Ella, R., Rupprecht, P., Thoma, H., Hampel, H., Toschi, N. & Möller, H.J. (2002). Repetitive transcranial magnetic stimulation (rTMS) in major depression: Relation between efficacy and stimulation intensity. *Neuropsychopharmacology,* 27, 638–645.

Paivio, A. (1995). Imagery and memory. In M.S. Gazzaniga (Ed.), *The cognitive neurosciences* (pp. 977–986). Cambridge, MA: MIT Press.

Paller, K.A. & Voss, J.L. (2004). Memory reactivation and consolidation during sleep. *Learning & Memory,* 11, 664–670.

Palmer, T. (Executive Producer) (2007). *Media Watch* [Television broadcast 5 November]. Sydney, Australia: Australian Broadcasting Corporation.

Paolini, S., Hewstone, M., Cairns, E. & Voci, A. (2004). Effects of direct and indirect cross-group friendships on judgments of Catholics and Protestants in Northern Ireland: The mediating role of an anxiety-reduction mechanism. *Personality and Social Psychology Bulletin,* 30, 770–786.

Paris, J. (2003). *Personality disorders over time: Precursors, course, and outcome.* Washington, DC: American Psychiatric Publishing.

Parker R. & Ben-Tovim, D. (2002). A study of factors affecting suicide in Aboriginal and 'other' populationsin the Top End of the Northern Territory through an audit of coronial records. *Australian and New Zealand Journal of Psychiatry,* 36 (3), 404–410.

Parr, W.V. & Siegert, R. (1993). Adults' conceptions of everyday memory failures in others: Factors that mediate the effects of target age. *Psychology and Aging,* 8, 599–605.

Parsons, L.M. & Osherson, D. (2001). New evidence for distinct right and left brain systems for deductive versus probabilistic reasoning. *Cerebral Cortex,* 11, 954–965.

Pasternak, T., Bisley, J.W. & Calkins, D. (2003). Visual processing in the primate brain. In M. Gallager &

R.J. Nelson (Eds.), *Handbook of psychology: Biological psychology* (Vol. 3, pp. 139–185). New York: Wiley.

Patterson, C.J. (2002). Lesbian and gay parenthood. In M.H. Bornstein (Ed.), *Handbook of parenting: Vol. 3. Being and becoming a parent* (2nd edn, pp. 317–338). Mahwah, NJ: Erlbaum.

Patterson, G.R. (2002). The early development of coercive family process. In J.B. Ried, G.R. Patterson & J.J. Snyder (Eds.), *Antisocial behavior in children and adolescents: A developmental analysis and the Oregon model for intervention* (pp. 25–44). Washington, DC: American Psychological Association.

Pauli, P., Dengler, W., Wiedemann, G., Montoya, P., Flor, H., Birbaumer, N. & Buchkremer, G. (1997). Behavioral and neuropsychological evidence for altered processing of anxiety-related words in panic disorder. *Journal ofAbnormal Psychology,* 106, 213–220.

Paus, T. (2005). Mapping brain maturation and cognitive development during adolescence. *Trends in Cognitive Sciences,* 9, 60–68.

Pavlov, I.P. (1927). *Conditioned reflexes* (G.V. Anrep, Trans.). London: Oxford University Press.

Pavlov, I.P. (1928). *Lectures on conditioned reflexes: Twenty-five years of objective study of higher nervous activity (behavior of animals)* (Vol. 1, W.H. Gantt, Trans.). New York: International Publishers.

Payne, B.K. (2005). Conceptualizing control in social cognition: How executive functioning modulates the expression of automatic stereotyping. *Journal of Personality and Social Psychology,* 89, 488–503.

Pederson, D.R. & Moran, G. (1996). Expressions of the attachment relationship outside of the strange situation. *Child Development,* 67, 915–927.

Penick, S., Smith, G., Wienske, K. & Hinkle, L. (1963). An experimental evaluation of the relationship between hunger and gastric motility. *American Journal of Physiology,* 205, 421–426.

Penn, D.L., Guynan, K., Daily, T., Spaulding, W.D., Garbin, C.P. & Sullivan, M. (1994). Dispelling the stigma of schizophrenia: What sort of information is best? *Schizophrenia Bulletin,* 20, 567–578.

Penn, D.L., Kommana, S., Mansfield, M. & Link, B.G. (1999). Dispelling the stigma of schizophrenia: II. The impact of information on dangerousness. *Schizophrenia Bulletin,* 25, 437–446.

Pennebaker, J.W. (1990). *Opening up: The healing power of confiding in others.* New York: Morrow.

Pennebaker, J.W. (1997). Writing about emotional experiences as a therapeutic process. *Psychological Science,* 8, 162–166.

Peracchi, K.A. & O'Brien, E.J. (2004). Character profiles and the activation of predictive inferences. *Memory & Cogntion,* 32, 1044–1052.

Pericak-Vance, M.A. (2003). The genetics of autistic disorder. In R. Plomin, J.C. DeFries, I.W. Craig & P. McGuffin (Eds.), *Behavioral genetics in the postgenomic era* (pp. 267–288). Washington, DC: American Psychological Association.

REFERENCES

Perkins, D.N. (1988). Creativity and the quest for mechanism. In R.J. Sternberg & E.E. Smith (Eds.), *The psychology of human thought* (pp. 309–336). Cambridge, UK: Cambridge University Press.

Perls, F.S. (1969). *Gestalt therapy verbatim.* Lafayette, CA: Real People Press.

Pervin, L.A. (1994). A critical analysis of current trait theory. *Psychological Inquiry,* 5, 103–113.

Peterson, C. & Seligman, M.E.P. (1984). Causal explanations as a risk factor for depression: Theory and evidence. *Psychological Review,* 91, 347–374.

Peterson, C., Seligman, M.E.P. & Valliant, G.E. (1988). Pessimistic explanatory style is a risk factor for physical illness: A thirty-five year longitudinal study. *Journal of Personality and Social Psychology,* 55, 23–27.

Peterson, C. & Vaidya, R.S. (2001). Explanatory style, expectations, and depressive symptoms. *Personality and Individual Differences,* 31, 1217–1223.

Peterson, D. & Goodall, J. (1993). *Visions of Caliban: On chimpanzees and people.* Boston: Houghton Mifflin.

Peterson, L.R. & Peterson, M.J. (1959). Short-term retention of individual verbal items. *Journal of Experimental Psychology,* 58, 193–198.

Peterson, R.S. & Nemeth, C.J. (1996). Focus versus flexibility: Majority and minority influence can both improve performance. *Personality and Social Psychology Bulletin,* 22, 14–23.

Petrie, K.J., Booth, R.J. & Pennebaker, J.W. (1998). The immunological effects of thought suppression. *Journal of Personality and Social Psychology,* 75, 1264–1272.

Petrie, K.J., Fontanilla, I., Thomas, M.G., Booth, R.J., & Pennebaker, J.W. (2004). Effect of written emotional expression on immune function in patients with human immunodeficiency virus infection: A randomized trial. *Psychosomatic Medicine,* 66, 272–275.

Petrinovich, L.F. (1998). *Darwinian dominion: Animal welfare and human interests.* Cambridge, MA: MIT Press.

Petry, N.M., Alessi, S.M., Marx, J., Austin, M. & Tardif, M. (2005). Vouchers versus prizes: Contingency management treatment of substance abusers in community settings. *Journal of Consulting and Clinical Psychology,* 73, 1005–1014.

Pettigrew, T.F. (1997). Generalized intergroup contact effects on prejudice. *Personality and Social Psychology Bulletin,* 23, 173–185.

Pettigrew, T.F. & Tropp, L.R. (2006). A meta-analytic test of inter-group contact theory. *Journal of Personality and Social Psychology,* 90, 751–783.

Petty, R.E., Cacioppo, J.T., Strathman, A.J. & Priester, J.R. (2005). To think of not to think: Exploring two routes to persuasion. In T.C. Brock & M.C. Green (Eds.), *Persuasion: Psychological insights and perspectives* (2nd ed., pp. 81–116). Thousand Oaks, CA: Sage.

Pfeifer, M., Goldsmith, H.H., Davidson, R.J. & Rickman, M. (2002). Continuity and change in inhibited and uninhibited children. *Child Development,* 73, 1474–1485.

Phillips, D.P. (1993). Representation of acoustic events in primary auditory cortex. *Journal of Experimental Psychology: Human Perception and Performance,* 19, 203–216.

Phillips, S.T. & Ziller, R.C. (1997). Toward a theory and measure of the nature of nonprejudice. *Journal of Personality and Social Psychology,* 72, 420–432.

Piaget, J. (1929). *The child's conception of the world.* New York: Harcourt, Brace.

Piaget, J. (1954). *The construction of reality in the child.* New York: Basic Books.

Piaget, J. (1965). *The moral judgment of the child* (M. Gabain, Trans.). New York: Macmillan.

Piaget, J. (1977). *The development of thought: Equilibrium of cognitive structures.* New York: Viking Press.

Piccione, C., Hilgard, E.R. & Zimbardo, P.G. (1989). On the degree of stability of measured hypnotizability over a 25-year period. *Journal of Personality and Social Psychology,* 56, 289–295.

Pich, E.M., Pagliusi, S.R., Tessari, M., Talabot-Ayer, D., van Juijsduijnen, R.H. & Chaimulera, C. (1997). Common neural substrates for the addictive properties of nicotine and cocaine. *Science,* 275, 83–85.

Pierucci-Lagha, A., Covault, J., Feinn, R., Nellissery, M., Hernandez-Avila, C., Oncken, C., Morrow, A.L., & Kranzler, H.R. (2005). *GABRA2* alleles moderate the subjective effects of alcohol, which are attenuated by finasteride. *Neuropsychopharmacology,* 30, 1193–1203.

Pilcher, J.J. & Walters, A.S. (1997). How sleep deprivation affects psychological variables related to college students' cognitive performance. *Journal of American College Health,* 46, 121–126.

Pilkonis, P.A. & Zimbardo, P.G. (1979). The personal and social dynamics of shyness. In C.E. Izard (Ed.), *Emotions in personality and psychopathology* (pp. 131–160). New York: Plenum Press.

Pines, A. & Zimbardo, P.G. (1978). The personal and cultural dynamics of shyness: A comparison between Israelis, American Jews and Americans. *Journal of Psychology and Judaism,* 3, 81–101.

Pinker, S. (1994). *The language instinct: How the mind creates language.* New York: Morrow.

Piotrowski, C., Keller, J.W. & Ogawa, T. (1993). Projective techniques: An international perspective. *Psychological Reports,* 72, 179–182.

Pitts, D.G. (1982). The effects of aging on selected visual functions: Dark adaptation, visual acuity, stereopsis, and brightness contrast. In R. Sekuler, D. Kline & K. Dismukes (Eds.), *Aging and human visual function* (pp. 131–159). New York: Liss.

Plante, T.G. & Sykora, C. (1994). Are stress and coping associated with WISC-III performance among children? *Journal of Clinical Psychology,* 50, 759–762.

Plomin, R., DeFries, J.C., Craig, I.W. & McGuffin, P. (2003). Behavioral genetics. In R. Plomin, J.C. DeFries, I.W. Craig & P. McGuffin (Eds.), *Behavioral genetics in the postgenomic era* (pp. 3–15). Washington, DC: American Psychological Association.

Plomin, R. & Petrill, S.A. (1997). Genetics and intelligence: What's new? *Intelligence,* 24, 53–77.

Plomin, R. & Spinath, F.M. (2004). Intelligence: Genetics, genes, and genomics. *Journal of Personality and Social Psychology,* 86, 112–129.

Plous, S. (1996a). Attitudes toward the use of animals in psychological research and education: Results from a national survey of psychology majors. *Psychological Science,* 7, 352–358.

Plous, S. (1996b). Attitudes toward the use of animals in psychological research and education:Results from a national survey of psychologists. *American Psychologist,* 51, 1167–1180.

Polivy, J. & Herman, C.P. (1999). Distress and eating: Why do dieters overeat? *International Journal of Eating Disorders,* 26, 153–164.

Poppen, P.J. (1995). Gender and patterns of sexual risk taking in college students. *Sex Roles,* 32, 545–555.

Porstner, D. (1997, July 26). Man stops car with own. *Newsday,* p. A32.

Porter, L.W. & Lawler, E.E. (1968). *Managerial attitudes and performance.* Homewood, IL: Irwin.

Poucet, B. (1993). Spatial cognitive maps in animals: New hypotheses on their structure and neural mechanisms. *Psychological Review,* 100, 163–182.

Poulos, C.X. & Cappell, H. (1991). Homeostatic theory of drug tolerance: A general model of physiological adaptation. *Psychological Review,* 98, 390–408.

Povinelli, D.J. & Prince, C.G. (1998). When self met other. In M. Ferrari & R.J. Sternberg (Eds.), *Self-awareness: Its nature and development.* New York: Guilford Press.

Powley, T. (1977). The ventromedial hypothalamic syndrome, satiety, and a cephalic phase hypothesis. *Psychological Review,* 84, 89–126.

Pratt, M.W., Golding, G., Hunter, W. & Norris, J. (1988). From inquiry to judgment: Age and sex differences in patterns of adult moral thinking and information-seeking. *International Journal of Aging and Human Development,* 27, 109–124.

Premack, D. (1965). Reinforcement theory. In D. Levine (Ed.), *Nebraska symposium on motivation* (pp. 128–180). Lincoln: University of Nebraska Press.

Premack, D. (1971). Language in chimpanzee? *Science,* 172, 808–822.

Pressman, L.J., Loo, S.K., Carpenter, E.M., Asarnow, J.R., Lynn, D., McCracken, J.T., McGough, J.J., Lubke, G.H., Yang, M.H. & Smalley, S.L. (2006). Relationship of family environment and parental psychiatric diagnosis to impairment in ADHD. *Journal of the American Academy of Child and Adolescent Psychiatry,* 45, 346–354.

Price, D.D. (2000). Psychological and neural mechanisms of the affective dimension of pain. *Science,* 288, 1769–1772.

Price, R. (1980). *Droodles.* Los Angeles: Price/Stern/Sloan. (Original work published 1953)

Prosser, D., Johnson, S., Kuipers, E., Szmukler, G., Bebbington, P. & Thornicroft, G. (1997). Perceived sources of work stress and satisfaction among hospital and community mental health staff, and their relation to mental health, burnout, and job satisfaction. *Journal of Psychosomatic Research,* 43, 51–59.

Putnam, D.E., Finney, J.W., Barkley, P.L. & Bonner, M.J. (1994). Enhancing commitment improves adherence to a medical regimen. *Journal of Consulting and Clinical Psychology,* 62, 191–194.

Quine, W.V.O. (1960). *Word and object.* Cambridge, MA: The MIT Press.

Rabbie, J.M. (1981). The effects of intergroup competition and cooperation on intra- and intergroup relationships. In J. Grzelak & V. Derlega (Eds.), *Living with other people: Theory and research on cooperation and helping.* New York: Academic Press.

Rachlin, H. (1990). Why do people gamble and keep gambling despite heavy losses? *Psychological Science,* 1, 294–297.

Rahman, Q. & Wilson, G.D. (2003). Born gay? The psychobiology of human sexual orientation. *Personality and Individual Differences,* 34, 1337–1382.

Rainnie, D.G., Grunze, H.C.R., McCarley, R.W. & Greene, R.W. (1994). Adenosine inhibition of mesopontine cholinergic neurons: Implications for EEG arousal. *Science,* 263, 689–692.

Rajaram, S. & Coslett, H.B. (2000). New conceptual associative learning in amnesia: A case study. *Journal of Memory and Language,* 43, 291–315.

Rajaram, S. & Roediger, H.L., III (1993). Direct comparison of four implicit memory tests. *Journal of Experimental Psychology: Learning, Memory, and Cognition,* 19, 765–776.

Ramírez, J.M. & Andreu, J.M. (2006). Aggression, and some related psychological constructs (anger, hostility, and impulsivity): Some comments from a research project. *Neuroscience and Biobehavioral Reviews,* 30, 276–291.

Rand, C.S. & Kuldau, J.M. (1992). Epidemiology of bulimia and symptoms in a general population: Sex, age, race, and socioeconomic status. *International Journal of Eating Disorders,* 11, 37–44.

Randall, C.L. (2001). Alcohol and pregnancy: Highlights from three decades of research. *Journal of Studies on Alcohol,* 62, 554–561.

Ranganath, C., Cohen, M.X. & Brozinsky, C.J. (2005). Working memory maintenance contributes to long-term memory formation: Neural and behavioral evidence. *Journal of Cognitive Neuroscience,* 17, 994–1010.

Rao, S.C., Rainer, G. & Miller, E.K. (1997). Integration of what and where in the primate prefrontal cortex. *Science,* 276, 821–824.

Rapoport, J.L. (1989). The biology of obsessions and compulsions. *Scientific American,* March. 83–89.

Rapp, B. & Goldrick, M. (2000). Discreteness and interactivity in spoken word production. *Psychological Review,* 107, 460–499.

Rasmussen, T. & Milner, B. (1977). The role of early left-brain injury in determining lateralization of cerebral speech functions. *Annals of the New York Academy of Sciences, 299, 355–369.*

Ratcliff, R. & Mckoon, G. (1978). Priming in item recognition: Evidence for the propositional structure of sentences. *Journal of Verbal Learning and Verbal Behavior, 17, 403–418.*

Ratner, C. (2000). A cultural-psychological analysis of emotions. *Culture and Psychology, 6, 5–39.*

Rau, H., Bührer, M. & Wietkunat, R. (2003). Biofeedback of R-wave-to-pulse interval normalizes blood pressure. *Applied Psychophysiology and Biofeedback, 28, 37–46.*

Ray, W.J., Keil, A., Mikuteit, A., Bongartz, W. & Elbert, T. (2002). High resolution EEG indicators of pain responses in relation to hypnotic susceptibility and suggestion. *Biological Psychology, 60, 17–36.*

Raynor, H.A. & Epstein, L.H. (2001). Dietary variety, energy regulation, and obesity. *Psychological Bulletin, 127, 325–341.*

Raz, A. (2005). Attention and hypnosis: Neural substrates and genetic associations of two converging processes. *International Journal of Clinical and Experimental Hypnosis, 53, 237–258.*

Redfern, P., Minors, D. & Waterhouse, J. (1994). Circadian rhythms, jet lag, and chronobiotics: An overview. *Chronobiology International, 11, 253–265.*

Reed, S.B., Kirsch, I., Wickless, C., Moffitt, K.H. & Taren, P. (1996). Reporting biases in hypnosis: Suggestion of compliance? *Journal of Abnormal Psychology, 105, 142–145.*

Regan, R.T. (1971). Effects of a favor and liking on compliance. *Journal of Experimental Social Psychology, 7, 627–639.*

Regier, D.A., Narrow, W.E., Rae, D.S., Manderscheid, R.W., Locke, B.Z. & Goodwin, F.K. (1993b). The de facto US mental and addictive disorders service system: Epidemiologic Catchment Area prospective 1-year rates of disorders and services. *Archives of General Psychiatry, 50, 85–94.*

Reid, E. (1998). The self and the Internet: Variations on the illusion of one self. In J. Gackenbach (Ed.), *Psychology and the Internet: Intrapersonal, interpersonal, and transpersonal implications* (pp. 29–42). San Diego, CA: Academic Press.

Reid, J.B., Patterson, G.R. & Snyder, J.J. (Eds.). (2002). *Antisocial behavior in children and adolescents: A developmental analysis and the Oregon model for intervention.* Washington, DC: American Psychological Association.

Renzulli, J.S. (2005). The three-ring conception of giftedness: A developmental model for promoting creative productivity. In R.J. Sternberg & J.E. Davidson (Eds.), *Conceptions of giftedness* (2nd edn) (pp. 246–279). New York: Cambridge University Press.

Rescorla, R.A. (1966). Predictability and number of pairings in Pavlovian fear conditioning. *Psychonomic Science, 4, 383–384.*

Rescorla, R.A. (1988). Pavlovian conditioning: It's not what you think it is. *American Psychologist, 43, 151–160.*

Reti, I.M., Samuels, J.F., Eaton, W.W., Bienvenu, O.J., III, Costa, P.T., Jr. & Nestadt, G. (2002). Adult antisocial personality traits are associated with experiences of low paternal care and maternal overprotection. *Acta Psychiatrica Scandinavica, 106, 126–133.*

Reyna, C. & Weiner, B. (2001). Justice and utility in the classroom: An attributional analysis of the goals of teachers' punishment and intervention strategies. *Journal of Educational Psychology, 93, 309–319.*

Reynolds, A.J., Temple, J.A., Robertson, D.L. & Mann, E.A. (2001). Long-term effects of an early childhood intervention on educational achievement and juvenile arrest: A 15-year follow up of low-income children in public schools. *Journal of the American Medical Association, 285, 2339–2346.*

Reynolds, J.S. & Perrin, N.A. (2004). Mismatches in social support and psychosocial adjustment. *Health Psychology, 23, 425–430.*

Rhodewalt, F. & Hill, S.K. (1995). Self-handicapping in the classroom: The effects of claimed self-handicaps on responses to academic failure. *Basic and Applied Social Psychology, 16, 397–416.*

Ribeiro, S.C., Kennedy, S.E., Smith, Y.R., Stohler, C.S. & Zubieta, J.K. (2005). Interface of physical and emotional stress regulation through the endogenous opioid system and μ-opioid receptors. *Progress in Neuro-Psychopharmacology & Biological Psychiatry, 29, 1264–1280.*

Richards, M.H., Crowe, P.A., Larson, R. & Swarr, A. (1998). Developmental patterns and gender differences in the experience of peer companionship during adolescence. *Child Development, 69, 154–163.*

Riemann, R., Angleitner, A. & Strelau, J. (1997). Genetic and environmental influences on personality: A study of twins reared together using the self- and peer report NEO-FFI scales. *Journal of Personality, 65, 449–475.*

Riessman, F. (1997). Ten self-help principles. *Social Policy, 27, 6–11.*

Rinck, M., Hähnel, A., Bower, G.H. & Glowalla, U. (1997). The metrics of spatial situation models. *Journal of Experimental Psychology: Learning, Memory, and Cognition, 23, 622–637.*

Ritchie, P.L.-J. (2004). Annual report of the International Union of Psychological Science (IUPsyS). *International Journal of Psychology, 39, 231–240.*

Rivas-Vazquez, R.A. (2003). Benzodiazepines in contemporary clinical practice. *Professional Psychology: Research and Practice, 34, 424–428.*

Roberson, D., Davidoff, J., Davies, I.R.L. & Shapiro, L.R. (2005). Color categories: Evidence for the cultural relativity hypothesis. *Cognitive Psychology, 50, 378–411.*

Roberts, A.H., Kewman, D.G., Mercier, L. & Hovell, M. (1993). The power of nonspecific effects in healing: Implications for psychosocial and biological treatments. *Clinical Psychology Review, 13, 375–391.*

Roblyer, D.A. (2005). Beyond precision: Morality, decision making, and collateral casualties. *Peace and Conflict: Journal of Peace Psychology,* 11, 17–39.

Rodd, J.M., Davis, M.H. & Johnsrude, I.S. (2005). The neural mechanisms of speech comprehension: fMRI studies of semantic ambiguity. *Cerebral Cortex,* 15, 1261–1269.

Roediger, H.L., III, Gallo, D.A. & Geraci, L. (2002). Processing approaches to cognition: The impetus from the levels-of-processing framework. *Memory,* 10, 319–332.

Roese, N.J. & Summerville, A. (2005). What we regret most . . . and why. *Personality and Social Psychology Bulletin,* 31, 1273–1285.

Rogers, C.R. (1947). Some observations on the organization of personality. *American Psychologist,* 2, 358–368.

Rogers, C.R. (1951). *Client-centered therapy: Its current practice, implications and theory.* Boston: Houghton Mifflin.

Rogers, C.R. (1959). A theory of therapy, personality, and interpersonal relationships, as developed in the client-centered framework. In S. Koch (Ed.), *Psychology: A study of a science* (Vol. 3). New York: McGraw-Hill.

Rogers, C.R. (1977). *On personal power: Inner strength and its revolutionary impact.* New York: Delacorte.

Rogers, M. & Smith, K. (1993). Public perceptions of subliminal advertising: Why practitioners shouldn't ignore this issue. *Journal of Advertising Research,* 33(2), 10–18.

Rogers, S. (1993). How a publicity blitz created the myth of subliminal advertising. *Public Relations Quarterly,* 37, 12–17.

Rogoff, B. (1990). *Apprenticeship in thinking: Cognitive development in social context.* New York: Oxford University Press.

Rogoff, B. (2003). *The cultural nature of human development.* London: Oxford University Press.

Rogoff, B. & Chavajay, P. (1995). What's become of research on the cultural basis of cognitive development? *American Psychologist,* 50, 859–877.

Rohrer, J.H., Baron, S.H., Hoffman, E.L. & Swinder, D.V. (1954). The stability of autokinetic judgment. *Journal of Abnormal and Social Psychology,* 49, 595–597.

Roid, G. (2003). *Stanford-Binet intelligence scale* (5th ed.). Itasca, IL: Riverside Publishing.

Rolls, E.T. (1994). Neural processing related to feeding in primates. In C.R. Legg & D. Booth (Eds.), *Appetite: Neural and behavioural bases* (pp. 11–53). Oxford, UK: Oxford University Press.

Rolls, E.T. (2000). Memory systems in the brain. *Annual Review of Psychology,* 51, 599–630.

Rolls, E.T. & Baylis, L.L. (1994). Gustatory, olfactory and visual convergence within the primate orbitofrontal cortex. *Journal of Neuroscience,* 14, 5437–5452.

Romer, M., Lehrner, J., Wymelbeke, V.V., Jiang, T., Deecke, L. & Brondel, L. (2006). Does modification of olfacto-gustatory stimulation diminish sensory-specific satiety in humans? *Physiology & Behavior,* 87, 469–477.

Rooney, R., O'Neil, K., Bakshi, L. & Tan-Quigley, A., (1997). Investigation of stigma and mental illness amongst non-English speaking background communities and development of approaches to its reduction: http:ariel.unimelb.edu.au/%7Eatmhn/www.research.stigma1.html.

Root, R.W., II & Resnick, R.J. (2003). An update on the diagnosis and treatment of attention-deficit/hyperactivity disorder in children. *Professional Psychology: Research and Practice,* 34, 34–41.

Rorschach, H. (1942). *Psychodiagnostics: A diagnostic test based on perception.* New York: Grune & Stratton.

Rosch, E. & Mervis, C.B. (1975). Family resemblances: Studies in the internal structure of categories. *Cognitive Psychology,* 7, 573–605.

Rosch, E.H. (1973). Natural categories. *Cognitive Psychology,* 4, 328–350.

Rosch, E.H. (1978). Principles of categorization. In E. Rosch & B.B. Lloyd (Eds.), *Cognition and categorization* (pp. 27–48). Hillsdale, NJ: Erlbaum.

Rosch, E.H., Mervis, C.B., Gray, W.D., Johnson, D.M. & BoyesBraem, P. (1976). Basic objects in natural categories. *Cognitive Psychology,* 8, 382–439.

Rose, A.J. & Rudolph, K.D. (2006). A review of sex-differences in peer relationship processes: Potential trade-offs for the emotional and behavioral development of girls and boys. *Psychological Bulletin,* 132, 98–131.

Rosen, H.S. & Rosen, L.A. (1983). Eliminating stealing: Use of stimulus control with an elementary student. *Behavior Modification,* 7, 56–63.

Rosenbaum, M.E. (1986). The repulsion hypothesis: On the non-development of relationships. *Journal of Personality and Social Psychology,* 51, 1156–1166.

Rosenfield, S. (1997). Labeling mental illness: The effects of received services and perceived stigma on life satisfaction. *American Sociological Review,* 62, 660–672.

Rosenhan, D.L. (1973). On being sane in insane places. *Science,* 179, 250–258.

Rosenhan, D.L. & Seligman, M.E.P. (1989). *Abnormal psychology* (2nd edn). New York: Norton.

Rosenkoetter, L.I. (1999). The television situation comedy and children's prosocial behavior. *Journal of Applied Social Psychology,* 29, 979–993.

Rosenthal, A.M. (1964). *Thirty-eight witnesses.* New York: McGraw-Hill.

Rosenthal, R. (1966). *Experimenter effects in behavioral research.* New York: Appleton-Century-Crofts.

Rosenthal, R. (1974). *On the social psychology of the self-fulfilling prophecy: Further evidence for Pygmalion effects and their mediating mechanisms.* New York: MSS Modular Publications.

Rosenthal, R. (1994). Science and ethics in conducting, analyzing, and reporting psychological research. *Psychological Science,* 5, 127–134.

Rosenthal, R. & Fode, K.L. (1963). The effect of experimenter bias on the performance of the albino rat. *Behavioral Science,* 8, 183–189.

Rosenthal, R. & Jacobson, L.F. (1968). *Pygmalion in the classroom: Teacher expectations and intellectual development.* New York: Holt.

Rosenzweig, M.R. (1996). Aspects of the search for neural mechanisms of memory. *Annual Review of Psychology,* 47, 1–32.

Rosenzweig, M.R. (1999). Effects of differential experience on brain and cognition throughout the life span. In S.H. Broman & J.M. Fletcher (Eds.), *The changing nervous system: Neurobehavioral consequences of early brain disorders* (pp. 25–50). New York: Oxford University Press.

Ross, B.H. & Kennedy, P.T. (1990). Generalizing from the use of earlier examples in problem solving. *Journal of Experimental Psychology: Learning, Memory, and Cognition,* 16, 42–55.

Ross, L. (1977). The intuitive psychologist and his shortcomings. In L. Berkowitz (Ed.), *Advances in experimental social psychology* (Vol. 10, pp. 173–220). New York: Academic Press.

Ross, L. (1988). Situational perspectives on the obedience experiments. [Review of the obedience experiments: A case study of controversy in social science]. *Contemporary Psychology,* 33, 101–104.

Ross, L., Amabile, T. & Steinmetz, J. (1977). Social roles, social control and biases in the social perception process. *Journal of Personality and Social Psychology,* 37, 485–494.

Ross, L. & Nisbett, R.E. (1991). *The person and the situation: Perspectives of social psychology.* New York: McGraw-Hill.

Rossell, S.L., Bullmore, E.T., Williams, S.C.R. & David, A.S. (2001). Brain activation during automatic and controlled processing of semantic relations: A priming experiment using lexical decision. *Neuropsychologia,* 39, 1167–1176.

Rothman, D.J. (1971). *The discovery of the asylum: Social order and disorder in the new republic.* Boston: Little, Brown.

Rottenberg, J., Hildner, J.C. & Gotlib, I.H. (2006). Idiographic autobiographical memories in major depressive disorder. *Cognition and Emotion,* 20, 114–128.

Rotter, J.B. (1954). *Social learning and clinical psychology.* Englewood Cliffs, NJ: Prentice-Hall.

Roussi, P. (2002). Discriminative facility in perceptions of control and its relation to psychological distress. *Anxiety, Stress & Coping: An International Journal,* 15, 179–191.

Rowe, D.C. (1997). A place at the policy table? Behavior genetics and estimates of family environmental effects on IQ. *Intelligence,* 24, 133–158.

Rozin, P. & Fallon, A.E. (1987). A perspective on disgust. *Psychological Review,* 94, 23–41.

Rozin, P., Kabnick, K., Pete, E., Fischler, C. & Shields, C. (2003). The ecology of eating: Smaller portion sizes in France than in the United States help explain the French paradox. *Psychological Science,* 14, 450–454.

Rozin, P., Millman, L. & Nemeroff, C. (1986). Operation of the laws of sympathetic magic in disgust and other domains. *Journal of Personality and Social Psychology,* 50, 703–712.

Rubin, D.C. & Kontis, T.C. (1983). A schema for common cents. *Memory & Cognition,* 11, 335–341.

Rubin, J.Z., Provenzano, F.J. & Luria, Z. (1974). The eye of the beholder: Parents' views on sex of newborns. *American Journal of Orthopsychiatry,* 44, 512–519.

Ruch, R. (1937). *Psychology and life.* Glenview, IL: Scott, Foresman. Rucker, C.E., III & Cash, T.F. (1992). Body images, body-size perceptions, and eating behaviors among African-American and white college women. *International Journal of Eating Disorders,* 12, 291–299.

Ruitenbeek, H.M. (1973). *The first Freudians.* New York: Jason Aronson.

Rummel, R.J. (1994). Power, genocide and mass murder. *Journal of Peace Research,* 31, 1–10.

Runco, M.A. (1991). *Divergent thinking.* Norwood, NJ: Ablex. Rundle, H.D., Nagel, L., Boughman, J.W. & Schluter, D. (2000). Natural selection and parallel speciation in sympatric sticklebacks. *Science,* 287, 306–308.

Rural Health Education Foundation (2005). *Growing Healthy Aboriginal Kids—The Early Years 1–5.* Television Broadcast on the Rural Health Education Foundation Satelite Network on 30 September 2005. Accessed from <http://www.rhef.com.au/programs/509b/509b.html>

Rusbult, C.E. & Martz, J.M. (1995). Remaining in an abusive relationship: An investment model analysis of nonvoluntary dependence. *Personality and Social Psychology Bulletin,* 21, 558–571.

Rusbult, C.E. & Van Lange, P.A.M. (2003). Interdependence, interaction, and relationships. *Annual Review of Psychology,* 54, 351–375.

Russell, A., Hart, C., Robinson, C. & Olsen, S. (2003). Children's sociable and aggressive behaviour with peers: A comparison of the US and Australia, and contributions of temperament and parenting styles. *International Journal of Behavioral Development,* 27 (1), 74–86.

Russo, F.A. & Thompson, W.F. (2005). An interval size illusion: The influence of timbre on the perceived size of melodic intervals. *Perception & Psychophysics,* 67, 559–568.

Russo, N.F. & Denmark, F.L. (1987). Contributions of women to psychology. *Annual Review of Psychology,* 38, 279–298.

Rutter, P.A. & Behrendt, A.E. (2004). Adolescent suicide risk: Four psychosocial factors. *Adolescence,* 39, 295–302.

Ryan, L., Hatfield, C. & Hofstetter, M. (2002). Caffeine reduces time-of-day effects on memory performance in older adults. *Psychological Science,* 13, 68–7 1.

Ryckman, R.M., Graham, S.S., Thornton, B., Gold, J.A. & Lindner, M.A. (1998). Physical size stereotyping as a mediator of attributions of responsibility in an alleged date-rape situation. *Journal of Applied Social Psychology,* 28, 1876–1888.

Ryff, C.D. (1989). In the eye of the beholder: Views of psychological well-being among middle-aged and older adults. *Psychology and Aging,* 4, 195–210.

Saarinen, T.F. (1987). *Centering of mental maps of the world: Discussion paper.* Tucson: University of Arizona, Department of Geography and Regional Development.

Sackheim, H.A., Prudic, J., Devanand, D.P., Nobler, M.S., Lisanby, S.H., Peyser, S., Fitzsimons, L., Moody, B.J., & Clark, J. (2000). A prospective, randomized, double-blind comparison of bilateral and right unilateral electroconvulsive therapy at different stimulus intensities. *Archives of General Psychiatry,* 57, 425–434.

Sagi, A., Koren-Karie, N., Gini, M., Ziv, Y. & Joels, T. (2002). Shedding further light on the effects of various types and quality of early child care on infant-mother attachment relationship: The Haifa Study of Early Child Care. *Child Development,* 73, 1166–1186.

Sak, U. (2004). A synthesis of research on psychological types of gifted adolescents. *Journal of Secondary Gifted Education,* 15, 70–79.

Salthouse, T.A. (1996). The processing-speed theory of adult age differences in cognition. *Psychological Review,* 103, 403–428.

Salzinger, S., Ng-Mak, D.S., Feldman, R.S., Kam, C.M., & Rosario, M. (2006). Exposure to community violence: Processes that increase the risk for inner-city middle school children. *Journal of Early Adolescence,* 26, 232–266.

Samuda, R.J. (1998). *Psychological testing of American minorities* (2nd edn). Thousand Oaks, CA: Sage.

Samuel, A.G. (1981). Phonemic restoration: Insights from a new methodology. *Journal of Experimental Psychology: General,* 110, 474–494.

Samuel, A.G. (1991). A further examination of attentional effects in the phonemic restoration illusion. *Quarterly Journal of Experimental Psychology: Human Experimental Psychology,* 43A, 679–699.

Samuel, A.G. (1997). Lexical activation produces potent phonemic percepts. *Cognitive Psychology,* 32, 97–127.

Sanderson, C.A., Rahm, K.B. & Beigbeder, S.A. (2005). The link between pursuit of intimacy goals and satisfaction in close same-sex friendships: An examination of the underlying processes. *Journal of Social and Personal Relationships,* 22, 75–98.

Sandstrom, M.J. & Cramer, P. (2003). Girls' use of defense mechanisms following peer rejection. *Journal of Personality,* 71, 605–627.

SANE Australia (2007). Schizophrenia. Accessed 12 November 2007 from <http://www.sane.org/information/factsheets/schizophrenia.html>

Sapir, E. (1964). *Culture, language, and personality.* Berkeley: University of California Press. (Original work published 1941)

Sapolsky, R.M. (1994). *Why zebras don't get ulcers: A guide to stress, stress-related disease, and coping.* New York: Freeman.

Satir, V. (1967). *Conjoint family therapy* (rev. edn). Palo Alto, CA: Science and Behavior Books.

Savage-Rumbaugh, S., Shanker, S.G. & Taylor, T.J. (1998). *Apes, language, and the human mind.* New York: Oxford University Press.

Scarborough, E. & Forumoto, L. (1987). *Untold lives: The first generation of women psychologists.* New York: Columbia University Press.

Scarr, S. (1998). American child care today. *American Psychologist,* 53, 95–108.

Scarr, S. & Eisenberg, M. (1993). Child care research: Issues, perspectives, and results. *Annual Review of Psychology,* 44, 613–644.

Schab, F.R. (1990). Odors and the remembrance of things past. *Journal of Experimental Psychology: Learning, Memory, and Cognition,* 16, 648–655.

Schachter, S. (1971a). Some extraordinary facts about obese humans and rats. *American Psychologist,* 26, 129–144.

Schachter, S. (1971b). *Emotion, obesity and crime.* New York: Academic Press.

Schaeken, W., De Booght, G., Vandierendonck, A. & d'Ydewalle, G. (Eds.). (2000). *Deductive reasoning and strategies.* Mahwah, NJ: Erlbaum.

Schaie, K.W. (2005). *Developmental influences on adult intelligence: The Seattle longitudinal study.* New York: Oxford University Press.

Schaufeli, W.B., Maslach, C. & Marek, T. (1993). *Professional burnout: Recent developments in theory and research.* Washington, DC: Taylor & Francis.

Schiff, M. & Bargal, D. (2000). Helping characteristics of self-help and support groups: Their contribution to participants' subjective well-being. *Small Group Research,* 31, 275–304.

Schlenger, W.E., Caddell, J.M., Ebert, L., Jordan, B.K., Rourke, K.M., Wilson, D., Thalji, L., Dennis, J.M., Fairbank, J.A. & Kulka, R.A. (2002). Psychological reactions to terrorist attacks: Findings from the National Study of Americans' reactions to September 11. *JAMA,* 288, 581–588.

Schlitz, M. (1997). *Dreaming for the community: Subjective experience and collective action among the Anchuar Indians of Ecuador.* Research proposal. Marin, CA: Institute of Noetic Sciences.

Schmidt, L.A. & Trainor, L.J. (2001). Frontal brain electrical activity (EEG) distinguishes *valence* and *intensity* of musical emotions. *Cognitive and Emotion,* 15, 487–500.

Schmidt, N.B., Lerew, D.R. & Jackson, R.J. (1997). The role of anxiety sensitivity in the pathogenesis of panic: Prospective evaluation of spontaneous panic attacks during acute stress. *Journal of Abnormal Psychology,* 106, 355–364.

Schmitt, D.P. (2003). Universal sex differences in desire for sexual variety: Tests from 52 nations, 6 continents, and 13 islands. *Journal of Personality and Social Psychology,* 85, 85–104.

Schneider, K. & May, R. (1995). *The psychology of existence: An integrative, clinical perspective.* New York: McGraw-Hill.

Scholnick, E.K., Nelson, K., Gelman, S.A. & Miller, P.H. (1999). *Conceptual development: Piaget's legacy.* Mahwah, NJ: Erlbaum.

Schooler, J.W. & Eich, E. (2000). Memory for emotional events. In E. Tulving & F.I.M. Craik (Eds.), *The Oxford handbook of memory* (pp. 379–392). Oxford, UK: Oxford University Press.

Schou, M. (2001). Lithium treatment at 52. *Journal of Affective Disorders, 67,* 21–32.

Schroeder, D.A., Penner, L.A., Dovido, J.F. & Piiavin, J.A. (1995). *The psychology of helping and altruism.* New York: McGraw-Hill.

Schultz, R., Braun, R.G. & Kluft, R.P. (1989). Multiple personality disorder: Phenomenology of selected variables in comparison to major depression. *Dissociation, 2,* 45–51.

Schwartz, B., Ward, A., Monterosso, J., Lyubomirsky, S., White, K. & Lehman, D.R. (2002). Maximizing versus satisficing: Happiness is a matter of choice. *Journal of Personality and Social Psychology, 83,* 1178–1197.

Schwartz, J.M., Stoessel, P.W., Baxter, L.R., Martin, K.M. & Phelps, M.E. (1996). Systematic changes in cerebral glucose metabolic rate after successful behavior modification treatment of obsessive-compulsive disorder. *Archives of General Psychiatry, 53,* 109–113.

Schwartz, S. (1987). Pavlov's heirs: classic psychology experiments that changed the way we view ourselves. North Ryde: Angus & Robertson.

Schwarz, N., Bless, H., Wänke, M. & Winkielman, P. (2003). Accessibility revisited. In G.V. Bodenhausen & A.J. Lambert (Eds.), *Foundations of social cognition: A festschrift in honor of Robert S. Wyer* (pp. 51–77). Mahwah, NJ: Erlbaum.

Schwarzer, R. (Ed.). (1992). *Self-efficacy: Thought control of action.* Washington, DC: Hemisphere.

Schweinhart, L.J. (2004). *The High/Scope Perry preschool study through age 40: Summary, conclusions, and frequently asked questions.* Retrieved from <www.highscope.org/Research/PerryProject/ PerryAge40SumWeb.pdf>

Schützwohl, A. (2006). Sex differences in jealousy: Information search and cognitive preoccupation. *Personality and Individual Differences, 40,* 285–292.

Scott, D., Scott, L.M. & Goldwater, B. (1997). A performance improvement program for an international-level track and field athlete. *Journal ofApplied Behavior Analysis, 30,* 573–575.

Scott, J.P. (1992). Aggression: Functions and control in social systems. *Aggressive Behavior, 18,* 1–20.

Scull, A. (1993). *A most solitary of afflictions: Madness and society in Britain 1700–1900.* London: Yale University Press.

Scutter S.D. and Goold M. (1995). Burnout in recently qualified physiotherapists in South Australia. *Australian Journal of Physiotherapy, 41:* 115–118.

Searle, J.R. (1979). Literal meaning. In J.R. Searle (Ed.), *Expression and meaning* (pp. 117–136). Cambridge, UK: Cambridge University Press.

Sears, S.R., Stanton, A.L. & Danoff-Burg, S. (2003). The yellow brick road and the Emerald City: Benefit finding, positive reappraisal coping, and posttraumatic growth in women with early-stage breast cancer. *Health Psychology, 22,* 487–497.

Sedikides, C., Gaertner, L. & Toguchi, Y. (2003). Pancultural self-enhancement. *Journal of Personality and Social Psychology, 84,* 60–79.

Segerstrom, S.C., Taylor, S.E., Kemeny, M.E. & Fahey, J.L. (1998). Optimism is associated with mood, coping and immune change in response to stress. *Journal of Personality and Social Psychology, 74,* 1646–1655.

Seidenberg, M.S. & Petitto, L.A. (1979). Signing behavior in apes: A critical review. *Cognition, 7,* 177–215.

Seidler, R.D., Purushotham, A., Kim S.G., Ugurbil, K., Willingham, D. & Ashe, J. (2002). Cerebellum activation associated with performance change but no motor learning. *Science, 296,* 2043–2046.

Sekuler, R. & Blake, R. (2001). *Perception* (4th edn). New York: McGraw-Hill.

Self, E.A. (1990). Situational influences on self-handicapping. In R.L. Higgins, C.R. Snyder & S. Berglas (Eds.), *Self-handicapping: The paradox that isn't* (pp. 37–68). New York: Plenum Press.

Selfridge, O.G. (1955). Pattern recognition and modern computers. *Proceedings of the Western Joint Computer Conference.* New York: Institute of Electrical and Electronics Engineers.

Seligman, M.E.P. (1975). *Helplessness: On depression, development, and death.* San Francisco: Freeman.

Seligman, M.E.P. (1991). *Learned optimism.* New York: Norton.

Seligman, M.E.P. & Maier, S.F. (1967). Failure to escape traumatic shock. *Journal of Experimental Psychology, 74,* 1–9.

Seligman, M.E.P., Steen, T.A., Park, N. & Peterson, C. (2005). Positive psychology progress: Empirical validation of interventions. *American Psychologist, 60,* 410–421.

Selye, H. (1976a). *Stress in health and disease.* Reading, MA: Butterworth.

Selye, H. (1976b). *The stress of life* (2nd edn). New York: McGraw-Hill.

Serpell, R. (2000). Intelligence and culture. In R.J. Sternberg (Ed.), *Handbook of intelligence* (pp. 549–577). Cambridge, UK: Cambridge University Press.

Serpell, R. & Boykin, A.W. (1994). Cultural dimensions of cognition: A multiplex, dynamic system of constraints and possibilities. In R.J. Sternberg (Ed.), *Handbook ofperception and cognition: Vol. 2. Thinking and problem solving* (pp. 369–408). Orlando, FL: Academic Press.

Serrano, J.M., Iglesias, J. & Loeches, A. (1992). Visual discrimination and recognition of facial expressions of anger, fear, and surprise in 4- to 6-month-old infants. *Developmental Psychobiology, 25,* 411–425.

Serrano, J.M., Iglesias, J. & Loeches, A. (1995). Infants' responses to adult static facial expressions. *Infant Behavior and Development, 18,* 477–482.

Shafir, E. (1993). Choosing versus rejecting: Why some options are both better and worse than others. *Memory & Cognition,* 21, 546–556.

Shapiro, K.F. (1998). *Animal models of human psychology: Critique of science, ethics, and policy.* Seattle, WA: Hogrefe & Huber.

Shapiro, S.L., Schwartz, G.E. & Bonner, G. (1998). Effects of mindfulness-based stress reduction on medical and premedical students. *Journal of Behavioral Medicine,* 21, 581–599.

Sharpsteen, D.J. & Kirkpatrick, L.A. (1997). Romantic jealousy and adult romantic attachment. *Journal of Personality and Social Psychology,* 72, 627–640.

Shaver, P.R. & Hazan, C. (1994). Attachment. In A.L. Weber & J.H. Harvey (Eds.), *Perspectives on close relationships* (pp. 110–130). Boston: Allyn & Bacon.

Shavitt, S. (1990). The role of attitude objects in attitude functions. *Journal of Experimental Social Psychology,* 26, 124–148.

Sheehan, E.P. (1993). The effects of turnover on the productivity of those who stay. *Journal of Social Psychology,* 133, 699–706.

Sheehy, R. & Horan, J.J. (2004). Effects of stress inoculation training for 1st-year law students. *International Journal of Stress Management,* 11, 41–55.

Sheets, V.L. & Lugar, R. (2005). Sources of conflict between friends in Russia and the United States. *Cross-Cultural Research,* 39, 380–398.

Sheldon, W. (1942). *The varieties of temperament: A psychology of constitutional differences.* New York: Harper.

Shepard, R.N. (1978). Externalization of mental images and the act of creation. In B.S. Randhawa & W.E. Coffman (Eds.), *Visual learning, thinking, and communicating.* New York: Academic Press.

Shepard, R.N. (1984). Ecological constraints on internal representation: Resonant kinematics of perceiving, imagining, thinking and dreaming. *Psychological Review,* 91, 417–447.

Shepard, R & Cooper, L. (1982). *Mental images and their transformations.* Cambridge, MA: MIT Press.

Shepard, R.N. & Jordan, D.S. (1984). Auditory illusions demonstrating that tones are assimilated to an internalized musical scale. *Science,* 226, 1333–1334.

Sher, K.J., Bartholow, B.D. & Wood, M.D. (2000). Personality and substance use disorders: A prospective study. *Journal of Consulting and Clinical Psychology,* 68, 818–829.

Sheridan, C.L. & King, R.G. (1972). Obedience to authority with an authentic victim. Proceedings from the 80th Annual Convention. *American Psychological Association, Part I,* 7, 165–166.

Sherif, C.W. (1981, August). *Social and psychological bases of social psychology.* The G. Stanley Hall Lecture on social psychology, presented at the annual convention of the American Psychological Association, Los Angeles, 1961.

Sherif, M. (1935). A study of some social factors in perception. *Archives of Psychology,* 27(187).

Sherif, M., Harvey, O.J., White, B.J., Hood, W.R. & Sherif, C.W. (1988). *The Robbers Cave experiment: Intergroup conflict and cooperation.* Middletown, CT: Wesleyan University Press. (Original work published 1961)

Shettleworth, S.J. (1993). Where is the comparison in comparative cognition? *Psychological Science,* 4, 179–184.

Shiffrar, M. (1994). When what meets where. *Current Directions in Psychological Science,* 3, 96–100.

Shiffrin, R.M. (2003). Modeling memory and perception. *Cognitive Science,* 27, 341–378.

Shiffrin, R.M. & Schneider, W. (1977). Controlled and automatic human information processing: II. Perceptual learning, automatic attending, and a general theory. *Psychological Review,* 84, 127–190.

Shimamura, A.P., Berry, J.M., Mangels, J.A., Rusting, C.L. & Jurica, P.J. (1995). Memory and cognitive abilities in university professors: Evidence for successful aging. *Psychological Science,* 6, 271–277.

Shneidman, E.S. (1987). At the point of no return. *Psychology Today,* March. 54–59.

Shoda, Y., Mischel, W. & Wright, J.C. (1993a). The role of situational demands and cognitive competencies in behavior organization and personality coherence. *Journal of Personality and Social Psychology,* 65, 1023–1035.

Shoda, Y., Mischel, W. & Wright, J.C. (1993b). Links between personality judgments and contextualized behavior patterns: Situation-behavior profiles of personality prototypes. *Social Cognition,* 11, 399–429.

Sia, T.L., Lord, C.G., Blessum, K.A., Ratcliff, C.D. & Lepper, M.R. (1997). Is a rose always a rose? The role of social category exemplar change in attitude stability and attitude-behavior consistency. *Journal of Personality and Social Psychology,* 72, 501–514.

Siegel, B. (1988). *Love, medicine, and miracles.* New York: Harper & Row.

Siegel, J.M. (2005). Clues to the functions of mammalian sleep. *Nature,* 437, 1264–1271.

Siegel, S. (1984). Pavlovian conditioning and heroin overdose: Reports by overdose victims. *Bulletin of the Psychonomic Society,* 22, 428–430.

Siegel, S. (2005). Drug tolerance, drug addiction, and drug anticipation. *Current Directions in Psychological Science,* 14, 296–300.

Siegel, S., Hinson, R.E., Krank, M.D. & McCully, J. (1982). Heroin "overdose" death: The contribution of drug-associated environmental cues. *Science,* 216, 436–437.

Silver, E., Cirincione, C. & Steadman, H.J. (1994). Demythologizing inaccurate perceptions of the insanity defense. *Law & Human Behavior,* 18, 63–70.

Silverman, A.B., Reinherz, H.Z. & Giaconia, R.M. (1996). The long-term sequelae of child and adolescent abuse: A longitudinal community study. *Child Abuse & Neglect,* 20, 709–723.

Simkin, L.R. & Gross, A.M. (1994). Assessment of coping with high-risk situations for exercise relapse among healthy women. *Health Psychology,* 13, 274–277.

Simmons, J.A., Ferragamo, M.J. & Moss, C.F. (1998). Echo-delay resolution in sonar images of the big brown bat, *Eptesicus fuscus. Proceedings of the National Academy of Sciences of the United States,* 95, 12647–12652.

Simon, H.A. (1973). The structure of ill-structured problems. *Artificial Intelligence,* 4, 181–202.

Simon, H.A. (1979). *Models of thought* (Vol. 1). New Haven: Yale University Press.

Simon, H.A. (1989). *Models of thought* (Vol. 2). New Haven: Yale University Press.

Simons, D.J. (1996). In sight, out of mind: When object representations fail. *Psychological Science,* 7, 301–305.

Simons, D.J. & Ambinder, M.S. (2005). Change blindness: Theory and consequences. *Current Directions in Psychological Science,* 14, 44–48.

Sims, M., Guilfoyle, A. & Parry, T. (2005). What Children's Cortisol Levels Tell Us about Quality in Childcare Centres. *Australian Journal of Early Childhood,* 30 (2), 29–39.

Sinclair, R.C., Hoffman, C., Mark, M.M., Martin, L.L. & Pickering, T.L. (1994). Construct accessibility and the misattribution of arousal: Schachter and Singer revisited. *Psychological Science,* 5, 15–19.

Singer, D.G. & Singer, J.L. (1990). *The house of make-believe.* Cambridge, MA: Harvard University Press.

Singer, L.T., Arendt, R., Minnes, S., Farkas, K., Salvator, A., Kirchner, H.L. & Kliegman, R. (2002). Cognitive and motor outcomes of cocaine-exposed infants. *Journal of the American Medical Association,* 287, 1952–1960.

Singer, T., Verhaegen, P., Ghisletta, P., Lindenberger, U. & Baltes, P.B. (2003). The fate of cognition in very old age: Six-year longitudinal findings in the Berlin Aging Study (BASE). *Psychology & Aging,* 18, 318–331.

Sireteanu, R. (1999). Switching on the infant brain. *Science,* 286, 59–61.

Skinner, B.F. (1938). *The behavior of organisms.* New York: AppletonCentury-Crofts.

Skinner, B.F. (1953). *Science and human behavior.* New York: Macmillan.

Skinner, B.F. (1966). What is the experimental analysis of behavior? *Journal of the Experimental Analysis of Behavior,* 9, 213–218.

Skinner, B.F. (1972). *Beyond freedom and dignity.* Toronto: Bantam Books.

Skinner, B.F. (1990). Can psychology be a science of mind? *American Psychologist,* 45, 1206–1210.

Skodol, A.E., Pagano, M.E., Bender, D.S., Shea, M.T., Gunderson, G., Yen, S., Stout, R.L., Morey, L.C., Sanislow, C.A., Grilo, C.M., Zanarini, M.C. & McGlashan, T.H. (2005). Stability of functional impairment in patients with schizotypal, borderline, avoidant, or obsessive-compulsive personality disorder over two years. *Psychological Medicine,* 35, 443–451.

Slaski, M. & Cartwright, S. (2002). Health, performance and emotional intelligence: An exploratory study of retail managers. *Stress and Health,* 18, 63–68.

Sloane, R.B., Staples, F.R., Cristol, A.H., Yorkston, N.J. & Whipple, (1975). *Psychotherapy versus behavior therapy.* Cambridge, MA: Harvard University Press.

Slobin, D.I. (1982). Universal and particular in the acquisition of language. In E. Wanner & L. Gleitman (Eds.), *Language acquisition: The state of the art* (pp. 128–170). Cambridge, UK: Cambridge University Press.

Slobin, D.I. (1985). Crosslinguistic evidence for the language-making capacity. In D. Slobin (Ed.), *The crosslinguistic study of language acquisition: Vol. 2. Theoretical issues* (pp. 1157–1256). Hillsdale, NJ: Erlbaum.

Slobin, D.I. (2003). Language and thought online: Cognitive consequences of linguistic relativity. In D. Gentner & S. Goldin-Meadow (Eds.), *Language in mind: Advances in the study of language and thought* (pp. 157–191). Cambridge, MA: MIT Press.

Slobin, D.I. & Aksu, A. (1982). Tense, aspect, and modality in the use of the Turkish evidential. In P.J. Hopper (Ed.), *Tense-aspect: Between semantics & pragmatics* (pp. 185–200). Amsterdam: Benjamins.

Sloman, S.A., Hayman, C.A.G., Ohta, N., Law, J. & Tulving, E. (1988). Forgetting in primed fragment completion. *Journal of Experimental Psychology: Learning, Memory, and Cognition,* 14, 223–239.

Slovic, P. (1995). The construction of preference. *American Psychologist,* 50, 364–371.

Smetana, J.G., Campione-Barr, N. & Metzger, A. (2006). Adolescent development in interpersonal and societal contexts. *Annual Review of Psychology,* 57, 255–284.

Smith, C.T., Nixon, M.R. & Nader, R.S. (2004). Posttraining increases in REM sleep intensity implicate REM sleep in memory processing and provide a biological marker of learning potential. *Learning & Memory,* 11, 714–719.

Smith, J. & Baltes, P.B. (1990). Wisdom-related knowledge: Age/cohort differences in response to life-planning problems. *Developmental Psychology,* 26, 494–505.

Smith, S.L. & Donnerstein, E. (1998). Harmful effects of exposure to media violence: Learning of aggression, emotional desensitization, and fear. In R.G. Geen & E. Donnerstein (Eds.), *Human aggression: Theories, research, and implications for public policy* (pp. 167–202). San Diego, CA: Academic Press.

Smith, T.W. & Ruiz, J.M. (2002). Psychosocial influences on the development and course of coronary heart disease: Current status and implications for research and practice. *Journal of Consulting and Clinical Psychology,* 70, 548–568.

Smits, T., Storms, G., Rosseel, Y. & De Boeck, P. (2002). Fruits and vegetables categorized: An application of the generalized context model. *Psychonomic Bulletin & Review,* 9, 836–844.

Smoller, J.W., Biederman, J., Arbeitman, L., Doyle, A.E., Fagerness, J., Perlis, R.H., Sklar, P. & Faraone, S.V. (2006). Association between the 5HT1B receptor gene (*HTR1B*) and the inattentive subtype of ADHD. *Biological Psychiatry,* 59, 460–467.

Smutzer, G.S., Doty, R.L., Arnold, S.E. & Trojanowski, J.Q. (2003). Olfactory system neuropathology in Alzheimer's disease, Parkinson's disease, and schizophrenia. In R.L. Doty (Ed.), *Handbook of Olfaction and Gustation* (2nd edn, pp. 503–524). New York: Marcel Dekker.

Snyder, D.K., Castellani, A.M. & Whisman, M.A. (2006). Current status and future directions in couple therapy. *Annual Review of Psychology, 57*, 317–344.

Snyder, M. (1984). When beliefs create reality. In L. Berkowitz (Ed.), *Advances in experimental social psychology* (Vol. 18, pp. 247–305). New York: Academic Press.

Snyder, M. & Haugen, J.A. (1995). Why does behavioral confirmation occur? A functional perspective on the role of the target. *Personality and Social Psychology Bulletin, 21*, 963–974.

Snyder, M. & Swann, W.B., Jr. (1978). Hypothesis-testing processes in social interaction. *Journal of Personality and Social Psychology, 36*, 1202–1212.

Sokolov Ye.N.(1963). *Perception and the conditioned reflex*

Solomon, A. (2001). *The noonday demon*. New York: Scribner.

Sommer, W., Heinz, A., Leuthold, H., Matt, J. & Schweinberger, S.R. (1995). Metamemory, distinctiveness, and event-related potentials in recognition memory for faces. *Memory & Cognition, 23*, 1–11.

Sommerville, J.A., Woodward, A.L. & Needham, A. (2005). Action experience alters 3-month-old infants' perception of others' actions. *Cognition, 96*, B1–B11.

Sonnad, S.S., Moyer, C.A., Patel, S., Helman, J.I., Garetz, S.L. & Chervin, R.D. (2003). A model to facilitate outcome assessment of obstructive sleep apnea. *International Journal of Technology Assessment in Health Care, 19*, 253–260.

Sonnadara, R.R. & Trainor, L.J. (2005). Perceived intensity effects in the octave illusion. *Perception & Psychophysics, 67*, 648–658.

Spangler, W.D. (1992). Validity of questionnaire and TAT measures of need for achievement: Two meta-analyses. *Psychological Bulletin, 112*, 140–154.

Spearman, C. (1927). *The abilities of man*. New York: Macmillan.

Spence, M.J. & DeCasper, A.J. (1987). Prenatal experience with low-frequency maternal-voice sounds influences neonatal perception of maternal voice samples. *Infant Behavior and Development, 10*, 133–142.

Spence, M.J. & Freeman, M.S. (1996). Newborn infants prefer the maternal low-pass filtered voice, but not the maternal whispered voice. *Infant Behavior and Development, 19*, 199–212.

Spence, S.A., Crimlisk, H.L., Cope, H., Ron, M.A. & Grasby, P.M. (2000). Discrete neurophysiological correlates in prefrontal cortex during hysterical and feigned disorder of movement. *The Lancet, 355*, 1243–1244.

Sperling, G. (1960). The information available in brief visual presentations. *Psychological Monographs, 74*, 1–29.

Spetch, M.L. & Cheng, K. (1998). A step function in pigeons temporal generalization in the peak shift task. *Animal Learning & Behavior, 26*, 103–118.

Spiegel, D., Bloom, J.R., Kraemer, H.C. & Gottheil, E. (1989). Effect of psychosocial treatment on survival of patients with metastatic breast cancer. *The Lancet, 2*, 888–891.

Spiegel, D.A., Wiegel, M., Baker, S.L. & Greene, K.A.I. (2000). Pharmacological management of anxiety disorders. In D.I. Mostofsky & D.H. Barlow (Eds.), *The management of stress and anxiety in medical disorders* (pp. 36–65). Boston: Allyn & Bacon.

Spielman, A.J. & Glovinsky, P.B. (1997). The diagnostic interview and differential diagnosis for complaints of insomnia. In M.R. Pressman & W.C. Orr (Eds.), *Understanding sleep: The evaluation and treatment of sleep disorders* (pp. 125–160). Washington, DC: American Psychological Association.

Spivey, M.J., Tanenhaus, M.K., Eberhard, K.M. & Sedivy, J.C. (2002). Eye movements and spoken language comprehension: Effects of visual context on syntactic ambiguity resolution. *Cognitive Psychology, 45*, 447–481.

Springer, M.V., McIntosh, A., Wincour, G. & Grady, C.L. (2005). The relation between brain activity during memory tasks and years of education in young and older adults. *Neuropsychology, 19*, 181–192.

Stahl, S.M. (1998). Getting stoned without inhaling: Anandamide is the brain's natural marijuana. *Journal of Clinical Psychiatry, 59*, 566–567.

Stahl, S.M., Grady, M.M., Moret, C. & Briley, M. (2005). SNRIs: Their pharmacology, clinical efficacy, and tolerability in comparison with other classes of antidepressants. *CNS Spectrums, 109*, 732–747.

Stams, G.J. J.M., Juffer, F. & van Ijzendoorn, M.H. (2002). Maternal sensitivity, infant attachment, and temperament in early childhood predict adjustment in middle childhood: The case of adopted children and their biologically unrelated parents. *Developmental Psychology, 38*, 806–821.

*Stanford Daily*. (1982). Rape is no accident, say campus assault victims. (February 2, pp. 1, 3, 5).

Starace, F., Massa, A., Amico, K.R. & Fisher, J.D. (2006). Adherence to antiretroviral therapy: An empirical test of the information-motivation-behavioral skills model. *Health Psychology, 25*, 153–162.

Staub, E. (1989). *The roots of evil: The origins of genocide and other group violence*. New York: Cambridge University Press.

Staub, E. (2000). Genocide and mass killing: Origins, prevention, healing and reconciliation. *Political Psychology, 21*, 367–382.

Staub, E. (2003). Notes on cultures of violence, cultures of caring and peace, and the fulfillment of basic human needs. *Political Psychology, 24*, 1–21.

Staub, E., Pearlman, L.A., Gubin, A. & Hagengimana, A. (2005). Healing, reconciliation, forgiving and the prevention of violence after genocide or mass killing: An intervention and its experimental evaluation in Rwanda. *Journal of Social and Clinical Psychology, 24*, 297–334.

Steel, Z. & Silove, D. (2001). The mental health implications of detaining asylum seekers. *Medical Journal of Australia, 175*, 596–599.

Steele, C.M. (1997). A threat in the air: How stereotypes shape intellectual identity and performance. *American Psychologist, 6*, 613–629.

Steele, C.M. & Aronson, J. (1995). Stereotype threat and the intellectual test performance of African Americans. *Journal of Personality and Social Psychology, 69*, 797–811.

Steele, C.M. & Aronson, J. (1998). Stereotype threat and the test performance of academically successful African Americans. In C. Jencks & M. Phillips (Eds.), *The black–white test score gap* (pp. 401–427). Washington, DC: Brookings Institution Press.

Stein, M.B., Jang, K.L., Taylor, S., Vernon, P.A. & Livesley, W.J. (2002). Genetic and environmental influences on trauma exposure and posttraumatic stress disorder symptoms: A twin study. *American Journal of Psychiatry, 159*, 1675–1681.

Steiner, J.E., Glaser, D., Hawilo, M.E. & Berridge, K.C. (2001). Comparative expression of hedonic impact: affective reactions to taste by human infants and other primates. *Neuroscience & Biobehavioral Reviews, 25*, 53–74.

Stemler, S.E., Elliott, J.G., Grigorenko, E.L. & Sternberg, R.J. (2006). There's more to teaching practical intelligence than instruction: Seven strategies for dealing with the practical side of teaching. *Educational Studies, 32*, 101–118.

Stern, M. & Karraker, K.H. (1989). Sex stereotyping of infants: A review of gender labeling studies. *Sex Roles, 20*, 501–522.

Stern, P.C. (1995). Why do people sacrifice for their nations? *Political Psychology, 16*, 217–235.

Stern, W. (1914). The psychological methods of testing intelligence. *Educational Psychology Monographs* (No. 13).

Sternberg, R.J. (1986). *Intelligence applied.* San Diego: Harcourt Brace Jovanovich.

Sternberg, R.J. (1994). Intelligence. In R.J. Sternberg (Ed.), *Handbook of perception and cognition: Vol. 2. Thinking and problem solving* (pp. 263–288). Orlando, FL: Academic Press.

Sternberg, R.J. (1999). The theory of successful intelligence. *Review of General Psychology, 3*, 292–316.

Sternberg, R.J. & Grigorenko, E.L. (2000). *Teaching for successful intelligence.* Arlington Heights, IL: Skylight Training and Publishing.

Sternberg, R.J. & Grigorenko, E.L. (2003). Teaching for successful intelligence: Principles, procedures, and practices. *Journal for the Education of the Gifted, 27*, 207–228.

Sternberg, R.J., Grigorenko, E.L. & Kidd, K.K. (2005). Intelligence, race, and genetics. *American Psychologist, 60*, 46–59.

Sternberg, R.J. & Lubart, T.I. (1996). Investing in creativity. *American Psychologist, 51*, 677–688.

Sternberg, R.J. & Lubart, T.I. (1999). The concept of creativity: Prospects and paradigms. In R.J. Sternberg (Ed.), *Handbook of creativity* (pp. 3–15). Cambridge, UK: Cambridge University Press.

Sternberg, R.J. & O'Hara, L.A. (1999). Creativity and intelligence. In R.J. Sternberg (Ed.), *Handbook of creativity* (pp. 251–272). Cambridge, UK: Cambridge University Press.

Stevens, J.A., Fonlupt, P., Shiffrar, M. & Decety, J. (2000). New aspects of motion perception: Selective neural encoding of apparent human movements. *Neuroreport, 11*, 109–115.

Stevenson, H.W., Chen, C. & Lee, S.Y. (1993). Mathematics achievement of Chinese, Japanese, and American children: Ten years later. *Science, 259*, 53–58.

Stewart, S.A. (2005). The effects of benzodiazepines on cognition. *Journal of Clinical Psychiatry, 66* (Suppl. 2), 9–13.

Stone, A.A., Neale, J.M., Cox, D.S., Napoli, A., Valdimarsdottir, H. & Kennedy-Moore, E. (1994). Daily events are associated with a secretory immune response to an oral antigen in men. *Health Psychology, 13*, 440–446.

Stone, R. (2000). Stress: The invisible hand in Eastern Europe's death rates. *Science, 288*, 1732–1733.

Story, L.B. & Bradbury, T.N. (2004). Understanding marriage and stress: Essential questions and challenges. *Clinical Psychology Review, 23*, 1139–1162.

Strakowski, S.M., DelBello, M.P., Zimmerman, M.E., Getz, G.E., Mills, N.P., Ret, J., Shear, P. & Adler, C.M. (2002). Ventricular and periventricular structural volumes in first versus multiple-episode bipolar disorder. *American Journal of Psychiatry, 159*, 1841–1847.

Strassberg, Z., Dodge, K.A., Pettit, G.S. & Bates, J.E. (1994). Spanking in the home and children's subsequent aggression toward kindergarten peers. *Development and Psychopathology, 6*, 445–461.

Strauch, I. (2005). REM dreaming in transition from late childhood to adolescence: A longitudinal study. *Dreaming, 15*, 155–169.

Strauch, I. & Lederbogen, S. (1999). The home dreams and waking fantasies of boys and girls between ages 9 and 15: A longitudinal study. *Dreaming, 9*, 153–161.

Straus, M.A. & Stewart, J.H. (1999). Corporal punishment by American parents: National data on prevalence, chronicity, severity, and duration, in relation to child and family characteristics. *Clinical Child and Family Psychology Review, 2*, 55–70.

Striegel-Moore, R.H., Dohm, F.A., Kraemer, H.C., Taylor, C.B., Daniels, S., Crawford, P.B. & Schreiber, G.B. (2003). Eating disorders in white and black women. *American Journal of Psychiatry, 160*, 1326–1331.

Stukas, A.A., Snyder, M. & Clark, E.G. (1999). The effects of "mandatory volunteerism" on intentions to volunteer. *Psychological Science*, 10, 59–64.

Stukas, A.A., Jr. & Snyder, M. (2001). Targets' awareness of expectations and behavioral confirmation in ongoing interactions. *Journal of Experimental Social Psychology*, 38, 31–40.

Stunkard, A.J., Harris, J.R., Pedersen, N.L. & McClearn, G.E. (1990). The body mass index of twins who have been reared apart. *New England Journal of Medicine*, 322, 1483–1487.

Substance Abuse and Mental Health Service Administration. (2003). *The national survey on drug use and health*. Retrieved from <http://www.samhsa.gov/oas/nhsda/2k1nhsda/vol2/toc.htm>

Substance Abuse and Mental Health Service Administration. (2005). *The national survey on drug use and health*. Available at <http://www.samhsa.gov/nhsda.htm>

Suedfeld, P. & Steel, G.D. (2000). The environmental psychology of capsule habitats. *Annual Review of Psychology*, 51, 227–253.

Suler, J. (2007). The Psychology of Cyberspace. Accessed from <http://www-usr.rider.edu/~suler/psycyber/psycyber.html>

Sullivan, H.S. (1953). *The interpersonal theory of psychiatry*. New York: Norton.

Sulloway, F.J. (1996). *Born to rebel: Birth order, family dynamics, and creative lives*. New York: Pantheon.

Suomi, S.J. (1999). Developmental trajectories, early experiences, and community consequences: Lessons from studies with rhesus monkeys. In D.P. Keating & C. Hertzman (Eds.), *Developmental health and the wealth of nations: Social, biological, and educational dynamics* (pp. 185–200). New York: Guilford Press.

Sultan A. & O'Sullivan K. (2001). Psychological disturbances in asylum seekers held in long-term detention: a participant-observer account. *Medical Journal of Australia*, 175, 593–596.

Suzuki, L.A. & Valencia, R.R. (1997). Race-ethnicity and measured intelligence: Educational implications. *American Psychologist*, 52, 1103–1114.

Suzuki, M., Hagino, H., Nohara, S., Zhou, S., Kawasaki, Y., Takahashi, T., Matsui, M., Seto, H., Ono, T. & Kurachi, M. (2005). Male-specific volume expansion of the human hippocampus during adolescence. *Cerebral Cortex*, 15, 187–193.

Swazey, J.P. (1974). *Chlorpromazine in psychiatry: A study of therapeutic innovation*. Cambridge, MA: MIT Press.

Szasz, T.S. (1974). *The myth of mental illness* (rev. ed.). New York: Harper & Row.

Szasz, T.S. (2004). *Faith in freedom: Libertarian principles and psychiatric practices*. Somerset, NJ: Transaction Publishers.

Szymanski, S., Kane, J.M. & Leiberman, J.A. (1991). A selective review of biological markers in schizophrenia. *Schizophrenia Bulletin*, 17, 99–111.

Tacon, A.M., McComb J., Caldera, Y. & Patrick R. (2003). Mindfulness, meditation, anxiety reduction and heart disease: A pilot study. *Family & Community Health*, 26(1), 25.

Taft, R. & Day, R.H. (1988). Psychology in Australia. *Annual Review of Psychology*, 39, 375-400.

Tanofsky-Kraff, M., Wilfley, D.E. & Spurrell, E. (2000). Impact of interpersonal and ego-related stress on restrained eaters. *International Journal of Eating Disorders*, 27, 411–418.

Taylor, C.B. & Luce, K.H. (2003). Computer- and internet-based psychotherapy interventions. *Current Directions in Psychological Science*, 12, 18–22.

Taylor, M.G. (1996). The development of children's beliefs about social and biological aspects of gender differences. *Child Development*, 67, 1555–1571.

Taylor, S.E., Klein, L.C., Lewis, B.P., Gruenewald, T.L., Gurung, R.A.R. & Updegraff, J.A. (2000). Biobehavioral responses to stress in females: Tend-and-befriend, not fight-or-flight. *Psychological Review*, 107, 411–429.

Tedeschi, R.G. & Calhoun, L.G. (2004). Posttraumatic growth: Conceptual foundations and empirical evidence. *Psychological Inquiry*, 15, 1–18.

Tedlock, B. (1992). The role of dreams and visionary narratives in Mayan cultural survival. *Ethos*, 20, 453–476.

Templin, M. (1957). Certain language skills in children: Their development and interrelationships. *Institute of Child Welfare Monograph*, Series No.26. Minneapolis: University of Minnesota Press.

Tennen, H. & Affleck, G. (2002). Benefit-finding and benefit-reminding. In C.R. Snyder & S.J. Lopez (Eds.), *The handbook of positive psychology* (pp. 584–594). New York: Oxford University Press.

Teplin, L.A., McClelland, G.M., Abram, K.M. & Weiner, D.A. (2005). Crime victimization in adults with severe mental illness. *Archives of General Psychiatry*, 62, 911–921.

Terman, L.M. (1916). *The measurement of intelligence*. Boston: Houghton Mifflin.

Terman, L.M. (1925) *Genetic studies of genius: Vol. 1. Mental and physical traits of a thousand gifted children*. Stanford, CA: Stanford University Press.

Terman, L.M. & Merrill, M.A. (1937). *Measuring intelligence*. Boston: Houghton Mifflin.

Terman, L.M. & Merrill, M.A. (1960). *The Stanford-Binet intelligence scale*. Boston: Houghton Mifflin.

Terman, L.M. & Merrill, M.A. (1972). *Stanford-Binet intelligence scale—manual for the third revision, Form L-M*. Boston: Houghton Mifflin.

Terrace, H.S. & Metcalfe, J. (2005). *The missing link in cognition: Origins of self-reflective consciousness*. Oxford: Oxford University Press.

Tetlock, P.E. (2005). *Expert political judgment: How good is it? How can we know?* Princeton, NJ: Princeton University Press.

Theeuwes, J., Kramer, A.F., Hahn, S. & Irwin, D.E. (1998). Our eyes do not always go where we want them to go: Capture of the eyes by new objects. *Psychological Science, 9*, 379–385.

Thomas, A. & Chess, S. (1977). *Temperament and development.* New York: Brunner/Mazel.

Thomas, A.K. & Loftus, E.F. (2002). Creating bizarre false memories through imagination. *Memory & Cognition, 30*, 423–431.

Thomas, C.P., Conrad, P., Casler, R. & Goodman, E. (2006). Trends in the use of psychotropic medicines among adolescents, 1994 to 2001. *Psychiatric Services, 57*, 63–69.

Thomas, E. & Wingert, P. (2000). Bitter lessons. *Newsweek*, June 19. 50–52.

Thomas, E.L. & Robinson, H.A. (1972). *Improving reading in every class: A sourcebook for teachers.* Boston: Allyn & Bacon.

Thompson, S.C., Nanni, C. & Levine, A. (1994). Primary versus secondary and central versus consequence-related control in HIV-positive men. *Journal of Personality and Social Psychology, 67*, 540–547.

Thoresen, C.E. & Powell, L.H. (1992). Type A behavior pattern: New perspectives on theory, assessment, and intervention. *Journal of Consulting and Clinical Psychology, 60*, 595–604. Thorndike, E.L. (1898). Animal intelligence. *Psychological Review Monograph Supplement, 2*(4, Whole No. 8).

Thorndike, R.L., Hagen, E.P. & Sattler, J.M. (1986). *Stanford-Binet intelligence scale* (4th ed.). Chicago: Riverside.

Tice, D.M. & Baumeister, R.F. (1997). Longitudinal study of procrastination, performance, stress, and health: The costs and benefits of dawdling. *Psychological Science, 8*, 454–458.

Tidwell, M.C.O., Reis, H.T. & Shaver, P.R. (1996). Attachment, attractiveness, and social interaction: A diary study. *Journal of Personality and Social Psychology, 71*, 729–745.

Timberlake, W. & Allison, J. (1974). Response deprivation: An empirical approach to instrumental performance. *Psychological Review, 81*, 146–164.

Todd, J.T. & Morris, E.K. (1992). Case histories in the great power of steady misrepresentation. *American Psychologist, 47*, 1441–1453.

Todd, J.T. & Morris, E.K. (1993). Change and be ready to change again. *American Psychologist, 48*, 1158–1159.

Todrank, J. & Bartoshuk, L.M. (1991). A taste illusion: Taste sensation localized by touch. *Physiology & Behavior, 50*, 1027–1031.

Toh, M. & Campbell, A.J. (2008). The role of interactivity and personality in video game aggression. *Journal of Personality and Social Psychology.*

Tolman, E.C. (1948). Cognitive maps in rats and men. *Psychological Review, 55*, 189–208.

Tolman, E.C. & Honzik, C.H. (1930). "Insight" in rats. *University of California Publications in Psychology, 4*, 215–232.

Tombu, M. & Jolicœur, P. (2005). Testing the predictions of the central capacity sharing model. *Journal of Experimental Psychology: Human Perception and Performance, 31*, 790–802.

Tomkins, S. (1962). *Affect, imagery, consciousness* (Vol. 1). New York: Springer.

Tomkins, S. (1981). The quest for primary motives; Biography and autobiography of an idea. *Journal of Personality and Social Psychology, 41*, 306–329.

Tomoyasu, N., Bovbjerg, D.H. & Jacobsen, P.B. (1996). Conditioned reactions to cancer chemotherapy: Percent reinforcement predicts anticipatory nausea. *Physiology & Behavior, 59*, 273–276.

Torgersen, S., Lygren, S., Øien, P.A., Skre, I., Onstad, S., Edvardsen, J., Tambs, K. & Kringlen, E. (2000). A twin study of personality disorders. *Comprehensive Psychiatry, 41*, 416–425.

Torrance, E.P. (1974). *The Torrance tests of creative thinking: Technical-norms manual.* Bensenville, IL: Scholastic Testing Services.

Trainor, L.J., Austin, C.M. & Desjardins, R.N. (2000). Is infant-directed speech prosody a result of the vocal expression of emotion? *Psychological Science, 11*, 188–195.

Travis, J. (2005). Saving the mind faces high hurdles. *Science, 309*, 731–734.

Trewin D & Madden R. (2005). The health and welfare of Australia's Aboriginal and Torres Strait Islander peoples. Canberra: Australian Bureau of Statistics. (ABS Cat. No. 4704.0.)

Triandis, H.C. (1990). Cross-cultural studies of individualism and collectivism. In J. Berman (Ed.), *Nebraska Symposium on Motivation, 1989* (pp. 41–133). Lincoln: University of Nebraska Press.

Triandis, H.C. (1994). *Culture and social behavior.* New York: McGraw-Hill.

Triandis, H.C. (1995). *Individualism and collectivism.* Boulder, CO: Westview.

Trivers, R.L. (1971). The evolution of reciprocal altruism. *Quarterly Review of Biology, 46*, 35–57.

Tsang, C.D., Trainor, L.J., Santesso, D.L., Tasker, S.L. & Schmidt, L.A. (2001). Frontal EEG responses as a function of affective musical features. In R.J. Zatorre & I. Peretz (Eds.), *Annals of the New York Academy of Sciences: Vol. 930. The Biological foundations of music* (pp. 439–442). New York: New York Academy of Sciences.

Tsoh, J.Y., McClure, J.B., Skaar, K.L., Wetter, D.W., Cinciripini, P.M., Prokhorov, A.V., Friedman, K. & Gritz, E. (1997). Smoking cessation 2: Components of effective intervention. *Behavioral Medicine, 23*, 15–27.

Tsuzuki, M., Asada, Y., Akiyama, S., Macer, N. & Macer, D.R.J. (1998). Animal experiments and bioethics in high schools in Australia, Japan and New Zealand, *Journal of Biological Education, 32*(2), 119–126.

Tulving, E. (1972). Episodic and semantic memory. In E. Tulving & W. Donaldson (Eds.), *Organization of memory.* New York: Academic Press.

Tulving, E. & Thomson, D.M. (1973). Encoding specificity and retrieval processes in episodic memory. *Psychological Review, 80*, 352–373.

Tupes, E.G. & Christal, R.C. (1961). *Recurrent personality factors based on trait ratings* (Tech. Rep. No. ASD-TR–61–97). Lackland Air Force Base, TX: U.S. Air Force.

Turk, D.C. & Okifuji, A. (2003). Psychological factors in chronic pain: Evolution and revolution. *Journal of Consulting and Clinical Psychology, 70,* 678–690.

Turner, C.F., Villarroel, M.A., Chromy, J.R., Eggleston, E. & Rogers, S.M. (2005). Same-gender sex among U.S. adults: Trends across the twentieth century and during the 1990s. *Public Opinion Quarterly, 69,* 439–462.

Turner, M.E. & Pratkanis, A.R. (1998). A social identity maintenance model of groupthink. *Organizational Behavior and Human Decision Processes, 73,* 210–235.

Tversky, A. & Kahneman, D. (1973). Availability: A heuristic for judging frequency and probability. *Cognitive Psychology, 5,* 207–232.

Tversky, A. & Kahneman, D. (1981). The framing of decisions and the psychology of choice. *Science, 211,* 453–458.

Tversky, A. & Shafir, E. (1992). Choice under conflict: The dynamics of deferred decision. *Psychological Science, 3,* 358–361.

Tyler, L.E. (1965). *The psychology of human differences* (3rd edn). New York: Appleton-Century-Crofts.

Tynan, B.J. (1979). *Medical Systems in Conflict. A Study of Power.* Government Printer of the Northern Territory, Darwin.

Underwood, B.J. (1948). Retroactive and proactive inhibition after five and forty-eight hours. *Journal of Experimental Psychology, 38,* 28–38.

Underwood, B.J. (1949). Proactive inhibition as a function of time and degree of prior learning. *Journal of Experimental Psychology, 39,* 24–34.

U.S. Department of Agriculture. (2005). *Dietary guidelines for Americans.* Retrieved from <http://www.health.gov/dietaryguidelines/ dga2005/document>

U.S. Department of Health and Human Services. (2000). *Reducing tobacco use: A report of the Surgeon General.* Atlanta, GA: U.S. Department of Health and Human Services.

U.S. Department of Health and Human Services. (2005). *Child maltreatment 2003.* Washington, DC: U.S. Government Printing Office. Retrieved from <www.acf.hhs.gov/programs/cb/pubs/ cm03/index.htm>

Urban, J., Carlson, E., Egeland, B. & Stroufe, L.A. (1991). Patterns of individual adaptation across childhood. *Development and Psychopathology, 3,* 445–460.

Urbszat, D., Herman, C.P. & Polivy, J. (2002). Eat, drink, and be merry, for tomorrow we diet: Effects of anticipated deprivation on food intake in restrained and unrestrained eaters. *Journal of Abnormal Psychology, 111,* 396–401.

Vaillant, G.E. (1977). *Adaptation to life.* Boston: Little, Brown. Valkenburg, P.M., Schouten, A.P. & Peter, J. (2005). Adolescents' identity experiments on the internet. *New Media & Society, 7,* 383–402.

Vandello, J.A. & Cohen, D. (2004). When believing is seeing: Sustaining norms of violence in cultures of honor. In M. Schaller & C.S. Crandall (Eds.), *The psychological foundations of culture* (pp. 281–304). Mahwah, NJ: Erlbaum.

Vandewaters, K. & Vickers, Z. (1996). Higher-protein foods produce greater sensory-specific satiety. *Physiology & Behavior, 59,* 579–583.

van Dijk, E. & Zeelenberg, M. (2005). On the psychology of 'if only': Regret and the comparison between factual and counterfactual outcomes. *Organizational Behavior and Human Decision Processes, 97,* 152–160.

van IJzendoorn, M.H. & Kroonenberg, P.M. (1988). Cross-cultural patterns of attachment: A meta-analysis of the Strange Situation. *Child Development, 59,* 147–156.

van Leeuwen, M.T., Blyth, F.M., March, L.M., Nicholas, M.K. & Cousins, M.J. (2006). Chronic pain and reduced work effectiveness: The hidden cost to Australian employers. *European Journal of Pain, 10,* 161–166.

Van Vianen, A.E.M. (2000). Person-organization fit: The match between newcomers' and recruiters' preferences for organizational culture. *Personnel Psychology, 53,* 113–149.

Vaughan, E. & Seifert, M. (1992). Variability in the framing of risk issues. *Journal of Social Issues, 48*(4), 119–135.

Viding, E., Blair, J.R., Moffitt, T.E. & Plomin, R. (2005). Evidence for substantial genetic risk for psychopathy in 7-year-olds. *Journal of Child Psychology and Psychiatry, 46,* 592–597.

Vignoles, V.L., Regalia, C., Manzi, C., Golledge, J. & Scabini, E. (2006). Beyond self-esteem: Influence of multiple motives on identity construction. *Journal of Personality and Social Psychology, 90,* 308–333.

von Hecker, U. & Dutke, S. (2004). Integrative social perception: Individuals low in working memory benefit more from external representations. *Social Cognition, 22,* 336–365.

Vonnegut, M. (1975). *The Eden express.* New York: Bantam.

Voss, J.F., Kennet, J., Wiley, J. & Schooler, T.Y.E. (1992). Experts at debate: The use of metaphor in the U.S. Senate debate on the Gulf crisis. *Metaphor and Symbolic Activity, 7,* 197–214.

Vrana, S. & Lauterbach, D. (1994). Prevalence of traumatic events and post-traumatic psychological symptoms in a nonclinical sample of college students. *Journal of Traumatic Stress, 7,* 289–302.

Vroom, V.H. (1964). *Work and motivation.* New York: Wiley.

Vu, H., Kellas, G., Metcalf, K. & Herman, R. (2000). The influence of global discourse on lexical ambiguity resolution. *Memory & Cognition, 28,* 236–252.

Vu, H., Kellas, G. & Paul, S.T. (1998). Sources of constraint on lexical ambiguity resolution. *Memory & Cognition, 26,* 979–1001.

Wagner, U., van Dick, R., Pettigrew, T.F. & Christ, O. (2003). Ethnic prejudice in East and West Germany: The explanatory power of intergroup contact. *Group Processes & Intergroup Relations, 6,* 23–37.

Walden, J., Normann, C., Langosch, J., Berger, M. & Grunze, H. (1998). Differential treatment of bipolar disorder with old and new antiepileptic drugs. *Neuropsycho biology*, 38, 181–184.

Walk, R.D. (1990). Jacqueline Jarret Goodnow. In A.N. O'Connell & N.F. Russo (Eds.), *Women in psychology: A bio-bibliographic sourcebook* (pp. 134–142). New York: Greenwood Press.

Walker, L. (2006). New trends in online traffic. *Washington Post*, April 4. p. D01.

Walker, M.P. & Stickgold, R. (2006). Sleep, memory, and plasticity. *Annual Review of Psychology*, 57, 139–166.

Wallace, S.T. & Alden, L.E. (1997). Social phobia and positive social events: The price of success. *Journal of Abnormal Psychology*, 106, 416–424.

Wallach, M.A. & Kogan, N. (1965). *Modes of thinking in young children.* New York: Holt, Rinehart & Winston.

Walster, E., Aronson, V., Abrahams, D. & Rottman, L. (1966). Importance of physical attractiveness in dating behavior. *Journal of Personality and Social Psychology*, 5, 508–516.

Walther, E. (2002). Guilty by mere association: Evaluative conditioning and the spreading attitude effect. *Journal of Personality and Social Psychology*, 82, 919–934.

Wang, C. & Mallinckrodt, B.S. (2006). Differences between Taiwanese and U.S. cultural beliefs about ideal adult attachment. *Journal of Counseling Psychology*, 53, 192–204.

Wang, P.S., Berglund, P., Olfson, M., Pincus, H.A., Wells, K.B. & Kessler, R.C. (2005). Failure and delay in initial treatment contact after first onset of mental disorders in the national comorbidity survey replication. *Archives of General Psychiatry*, 62, 603–613.

Wang, S., Baillargeon, R. & Brueckner, L. (2004). Young infants' reasoning about hidden objects: Evidence from violation-ofexpectation tasks with test trials only. *Cognition*, 93, 167–198.

Wann, D.L., Royalty, J.L. & Rochelle, A.R. (2002). Using motivation and team identification to predict sport fans' emotional responses to team performance. *Journal of Sport Behavior*, 25, 207–216.

Wann, D.L., Schrader, M.P. & Wilson, A.M. (1999). Sport fan motivation: Questionnaire validation, comparisons by sport, and relationship to athletic motivation. *Journal of Sport Behavior*, 22, 114–139.

Ward, C.D. & Cooper, R.P. (1999). A lack of evidence in 4-monthold human infants for paternal voice preference. *Developmental Psychobiology*, 35, 49–59.

Warker, J.A. & Dell, G.S. (2006). Speech errors reflect newly learned phonotactic constraints. *Journal of Experimental Psychology: Learning, Memory & Cognition*, 32, 387–398.

Warren, R.M. (1970). Perceptual restoration of missing speech sounds. *Science*, 167, 392–393.

Wasserman, E.A. (1993). Comparative cognition: Beginning the second century of study of animal intelligence. *Psychological Bulletin*, 113, 211–228.

Wasserman, E.A. (1994). Animal learning and comparative cognition. In I.P. Levin & J.V. Hinrichs (Eds.), *Experimental psychology: Contemporary methods and applications* (pp. 117–164). Dubuque, IA: Brown & Benchmark.

Watson, J.B. (1913). Psychology as the behaviorist views it. *Psychological Review*, 20, 158–177.

Watson, J.B. (1919). *Psychology from the standpoint of a behaviorist.* Philadelphia: Lippincott.

Watson, J.B. & Rayner, R. (1920). Conditioned emotional reactions. *Journal of Experimental Psychology*, 3, 1–14.

Watson, R.J., McDonald J. & Pearce D.C. (2006). An exploration of national calls to Lifeline Australia: social support or urgent suicide intervention? *British Journal of Guidance and Counselling*, 34(4), Nov, 471–482(12).

Watterlond, M. (1983). The holy ghost people. Reprinted in A.L. Hammond & P.G. Zimbardo (Eds.), *Readings on human behavior: The best of* Science *'80–'86* (pp. 48–55). Glenview, IL: Scott, Foresman.

Watts, M.W. (1996). Political xenophobia in the transition from socialism: Threat, racism and ideology among East German youths. *Political Psychology*, 17, 97–126.

Wax, M.L. (2004). Dream sharing as social practice. *Dreaming*, 14, 83–93.

Wearden, A.J., Tarrier, N., Barrowclough, C., Zastowny.T.R. & Rahill, A.A. (2000). A review of expressed emotion research in health care. *Clinical Psychology Review*, 20, 633–666.

Wechsler, D. (1997). *Manual for the Wechsler Adult Intelligence Scale-III.* San Antonio, TX: Psychological Corporation.

Wechsler, D. (2002). *WPPSI-III manual.* San Antonio, TX: Psychological Corporation.

Wechsler, D. (2003). *WISC-IV manual.* San Antonio, TX: Psychological Corporation.

Wedekind, C. & Braithwaite, V.A. (2002). The long-term benefits of humangenerosity in indirect reciprocity. *Current Biology*, 12, 1012–1015.

Weekes, P. (2007). The blind will see: bionic eyes to help restore sight. *The Age*, 18 February. Accessed 12 November 2007 from <http://www.theage.com.au/news/national/the-blind-will-see-bionic-eyes-to-help-restore-sight/2007/02/17/1171405502417.html>

Weiner, B. (2006). *Social motivation,justice, and the moral emotions: An attributional approach.* Mahwah, NJ: Erlbaum.

Weiner, J. (1994). *The beak of the finch.* New York: Knopf.

Weinfield, N.S., Ogawa, J.R. & Sroufe, L.A. (1997). Early attachment as a pathway to adolescent peer competence. *Journal of Research on Adolescence*, 7, 24 1–265.

Weisberg, R.W. (1986). *Creativity: Genius and other myths.* New York: Freeman.

Wellman, H.M. & Inagaki, K. (1997). *The emergence of core domains of thought.* San Francisco: Jossey-Bass.

Wells, G.L. & Loftus, E.F. (2003). Eyewitness memory for people and events. In A.M. Goldstein (Ed.), *Handbook ofpsychology: Forensic psychology* (Vol. 11, pp. 149–160). New York: Wiley.

Werker, J.F. (1991). The ontogeny of speech perception. In I.G. Mattingly & M. Studdert-Kennedy (Eds.), *Modularity and the motor theory of speech perception* (pp. 91–109). Hillsdale, NJ: Erlbaum.

Werker, J.F. & Lalond, F.M. (1988). Cross-language speech perception: Initial capabilities and developmental change. *Developmental Psychology, 24,* 672–683.

Werker, J.F. & Tees, R.C. (1999). Influences on infant speech processing: Toward a new synthesis. *Annual Review of Psychology, 50,* 509–535.

Wertheim, E.H., Paxton, S.J., Schutz, H.K. & Muir, S.L. (1997). Why do adolescent girls watch their weight? An interview study examining sociocultural pressures to be thin. *Journal of Psychosomatic Research, 42,* 345–355.

Westen, D. (1998). The scientific legacy of Sigmund Freud: Toward a psychodynamically informed psychological science. *Psychological Bulletin, 124,* 333–371.

Wever, E.G. (1949). *Theory of hearing.* New York: Wiley.

White, L. & Edwards, J.N. (1990). Emptying the nest and parental well-being: An analysis of national panel data. *American Sociological Review, 55,* 235–242.

White, R.K. (1996). Why the Serbs fought: Motives and misperceptions. *Peace and Conflict: Journal of Peace Psychology, 2,* 109–128.

Whorf, B.L. (1956). In J.B. Carroll (Ed.), *Language, and reality: Selected writings of Benjamin Lee Whorf.* Cambridge, MA: MIT Press.

Wierzbicki, M. & Pekarik, G. (1993). A meta-analysis of psychotherapy dropout. *Professional Psychology: Research & Practice, 24,* 190–195.

Wiggins, J.S. (1973). *Personality and prediction: Principles of personality assessment.* Reading, MA: Addison-Wesley.

Wiggins, J.S. & Pincus, A.L. (1992). Personality: Structure and assessment. *Annual Review of Psychology, 43,* 473–504.

Williams, L.M. (1995). Recovered memories of abuse in women with documented child sexual victimization histories. *Journal of Traumatic Stress, 8,* 649–673.

Williams, W.M., Blythe, T., White, N., Li, J., Gardner, H. & Sternberg, R.J. (2002). Practical intelligence for school: Developing metacognitive sources of achievement in adolescence. *Developmental Review, 22,* 162–210.

Williams, W.M. & Ceci, S.J. (1997). Are Americans becoming more or less alike? Trends in race, class, and ability differences in intelligence. *American Psychologist, 52,* 1226–1235.

Williamson, G.M., Clark, M.S., Pegalis, L.J. & Behan, A. (1996). Affective consequences of refusing to help in communal and exchange relationships. *Personality and Social Psychology Bulletin, 22,* 34–47.

Williamson, P., McLeskey, J., Hoppey, D. & Rentz, T. (2006). Educating students with mental retardation in general education classrooms. *Exceptional Children, 72,* 347–361.

Wilson, J. (1990). Stoneman, Ethel Turner (1890–1973). In *Australian dictionary of biography* (Vol. 12, p. 103). Melbourne: Melbourne University Press.

Wilson, R.I. & Nicoll, R.A. (2002). Endocannabinoid signaling in the brain. *Science, 296,* 678–682.

Wilson, S.I. & Edlund, T. (2001). Neural induction: Toward a unifying mechanism. *Nature Neuroscience, 4,* 1161–1168.

Wilson, T.D., Houston, C.E., Etling, K.M. & Brekke, N. (1996). A new look at anchoring effects: Basic anchoring and its antecedents. *Journal of Experimental Psychology: General, 125,* 387–402.

Winarick, K. (1997). Visions of the future: The analyst's expectations and their impact on the analytic process. *American Journal of Psychoanalysis, 57,* 95–109.

Windy, D. & Ellis, A. (1997). *The practice of rational emotive behavior therapy.* New York: Springer.

Winner, E. (2000). The origins and ends of giftedness. *American Psychologist, 55,* 159–169.

Wismer Fries, A.B., Ziegler, T.E., Kurian, J.R., Jacoris, S. & Pollak, S.D. (2005). Early experience in humans is associated with changes in neuropeptides critical for regulating social behavior. *Proceedings of the National Academy of Sciences, 102,* 17237–17240.

Witt, J.K. & Proffitt, D.R. (2005). See the ball, hit the ball: Apparent ball size is correlated with batting average. *Psychological Science, 16,* 937–938.

Witt, S.D. (1997). Parental influence of children's socialization to gender roles. *Adolescence, 32,* 253–259.

Witte, K. & Noltemeier, B. (2002). The role of information in mate-choice copying in female sailfin mollies (*Poecilia latipinna*). *Behavioral Ecology and Sociobiology, 52,* 194–202.

Wolcott, S. & Strapp, C.M. (2002). Dream recall frequency and dream detail as mediated by personality, behavior, and attitude. *Dreaming, 12,* 27–44.

Wolfe, J.M. (2003). Moving towards solutions to some enduring con- troversies in visual search. *Trends in Cognitive Science, 7,* 70–76.

Wolfe, J.M., Friedman-Hill, S.R. & Bilsky, A.B. (1994). Parallel processing of part-whole information in visual search tasks. *Perception & Psychophysics, 55,* 537–550.

Wolfe, J.M., Kluender, K.R., Levi, D.M., Bartoshuk, L.M., Herz, R.S., Klatzky, R.L. & Lederman, S.J. (2006). *Sensation and Perception.* Sunderland, Massachusetts, USA: Sinaur Associates, Inc.

Wolfson, A.R. & Carskadon, M.A. (1998). Sleep schedules and daytime functioning in adolescents. *Child Development, 69,* 875–887.

Wolman, C. (1975). Therapy and capitalism. *Issues in Radical Therapy, 3*(1).

Wolpe, J. (1958). *Psychotherapy by reciprocal inhibition.* Stanford, CA: Stanford University Press.

Wolpe, J. (1973). *The practice of behavior therapy* (2nd ed.). New York: Pergamon Press.

Wolpe, J. (1986). Misconceptions about behaviour therapy: Their sources and consequences. *Behaviour Change*, 3, 9–15.

Wood, J.J., McLeod, B.D., Sigman, M., Hwang, W.C., & Chu, B.C. (2003). Parenting and childhood anxiety: Theory, empirical findings, and future directions. *Journal of Child Psychology and Psychiatry*, 44, 134–151.

Wood, J.J., Piacentini, J.C., Southam-Gerow, M., Chu, B.C. & Sigman, M. (2006). Family cognitive behavioral therapy for child anxiety disorders. *Journal of the American Academy of Child and Adolescent Psychiatry*, 45, 314–321.

Wood, J.M., Bootzin, R.R., Rosenhan, D., Nolen-Hoeksema, S. & Jourden, F. (1992). Effects of the 1989 San Francisco earthquake on frequency and content of nightmares. *Journal of Abnormal Psychology*, 101, 219–224.

Wood, N. & Cowan, N. (1995a). The cocktail party phenomenon revisited: How frequent are attention shifts to one's name in an irrelevant auditory channel? *Journal of Experimental Psychology: Learning, Memory, and Cognition*, 21, 255–260.

Wood, N. & Cowan, N. (1995b). The cocktail party phenomenon revisited: Attention and memory in the classic selective listening procedure of Cherry (1953). *Journal of Experimental Psychology: General*, 124, 243–262.

Wood, R.E. & Bandura, A. (1989). Impact of conceptions of ability on self-regulatory mechanisms and complex decision making. *Journal of Personality and Social Psychology*, 56, 407–415.

Wood, W. (2000). Attitude change: Persuasion and social influence. *Annual Review of Psychology*, 51, 539–570.

Wood, W., Lundgren, S., Ouellette, J.A., Busceme, S. & Blackstone, T. (1994). Minority influence: A meta-analytic review of social influence processes. *Psychological Bulletin*, 115, 323–345.

Woods, S.C., Seeley, R.J., Porte, D., Jr. & Schwartz, M.W. (1998). Signals that regulate food intake and homeostasis. *Science*, 280, 1378–1383.

Worchel, S., Lee, J. & Adewole, A. (1975). Effects of supply and demand on ratings of object value. *Journal of Personality and Social Psychology*, 32, 906–914.

Workman, B. (1990). Father guilty of killing daughter's friend, in '69. *San Francisco Examiner-Chronicle*, December 1, pp. 1, 4.

Wright, E.R., Gronfein, W.P. & Owens, T.J. (2000). Deinstitutionalization, social rejection, and the self-esteem of former mental patients. *Journal of Health and Social Behavior*, 41, 68–90.

Wynne, C.D.L. & McLean, I.G. (1999). The comparative psychology of marsupials. *Australian Journal of Psychology*, 51, 111-116.

Wysocki, C.J., Dorries, K.M. & Beauchamp, G.K. (1989). Ability to perceive androstenone can be acquired by ostensibly anosmic people. *Proceedings of the National Academy of Sciences USA*, 86, 7976–7978.

Yang, Y., Raine, A., Lencz, T., Bihrle, S., Lacasse, L. & Coletti, P. (2005). Prefrontal white matter in pathological liars. *British Journal of Psychiatry*, 187, 320–325.

Yantis, S. (1993). Stimulus-driven attentional capture. *Current Directions in Psychological Science*, 2, 156–161.

Yantis, S. & Jonides, J. (1996). Attentional capture by abrupt onsets: New perceptual objects or visual masking? *Journal ofExperimental Psychology: Human Perception and Performance*, 22, 1505–1513.

Yeargin-Allsopp, M., Rice, C., Karapurkar, T., Doernberg, N., Boyle, C. & Murphy, C. (2003). Prevalence of autism in a US Metropolitan area. *JAMA*, 289, 49–55.

Yoon, C., May, C.P. & Hasher, L. (1999). Aging, circadian arousal patterns, and cognition. In D.C. Park & N. Schwarz (Eds.), *Cognitive aging: A primer* (pp. 151–172). Philadelphia: Psychology Press.

Zadra, A. & Donderi, D.C. (2000). Nightmares and bad dreams: Their prevalence and relationship to well-being. *Journal of Abnormal Psychology*, 109, 273–281.

Zahn-Waxler, C., Friedman, R.J., Cole, P.M., Mizuta, I. & Hiruma, N. (1996). Japanese and United States preschool children's responses to conflict and distress. *Child Development*, 67, 2462–2477.

Zajonc, R.B. (1968). Attitudinal effects of mere exposure. *Journal of Personality and Social Psychology. Monograph Supplement*, 9 (2, Part 2), 1–27.

Zajonc, R.B. (2000). Feeling and thinking: Closing the debate over the independence of affect. In J.P. Forgas (Ed.), *Feeling and thinking: The role of affect in social cognition* (pp. 31–58). New York: Cambridge University Press.

Zajonc, R.B. (2001). Mere exposure: A gateway to the subliminal. *Current Directions in Psychological Science*, 10, 224–228.

Zaslow, M.J. (1991). Variation in child care quality and its implications for children. *Journal of Social Issues*, 47, 125–138.

Zeanah, C.H., Smyke, A.T., Koga, S.F. & Carlson, E. (2005). Attachment in institutionalized and community children in Romania. *Child Development*, 76, 1015–1028.

Zeineh, M.M., Engel, S.A., Thompson, P.M. & Bookheimer, S.Y. (2003). Dynamics of the hippocampus during encoding and retrieval of face-name pairs. *Science*, 299, 577–580.

Zelazo, P.D., Helwig, C.C. & Lau, A. (1996). Intention, act, and outcome in behavioral prediction and moral judgment. *Child Development*, 67, 2478–2492.

Zelinski, E.M., Gilewski, M.J. & Schaie, K.W. (1993). Individual differences in cross-sectional and 3-year longitudinal memory performance across the adult life span. *Psychology and Aging*, 8, 176–186.

Zenderland, L. (1998). *Measuring minds: Henry Herbert Goddard and the origins of American intelligence testing.* Cambridge, UK: Cambridge University Press.

Zentall, T.R., Sutton, J.E. & Sherburne, L.M. (1996). True imitative learning in pigeons. *Psychological Science, 7,* 343–346.

Zhang, Y., Proenca, R., Maffel, M., Barone, M., Leopold, L. & Friedman, J.M. (1994). Positional cloning of the mouse *obese* gene and its human homologue. *Nature,* 372, 425–432.

Zimbardo, P.G. (1975). On transforming experimental research into advocacy for social change. In M. Deutsch & H. Hornstein (Eds.), *Applying social psychology: Implications for research, practice and training.* Hillsdale, NJ: Erlbaum.

Zimbardo, P.G. (1991). *Shyness: What it is, what to do about it* (rev. edn). Reading, MA: Addison-Wesley. (Original work published 1977)

Zimbardo, P.G. (2004, May 9). Power turns good soldiers into 'bad apples'. *Boston Globe,* p. D11.

Zimbardo, P.G. & Leippe, M. (1991). *The psychology of attitude change and social influence.* New York: McGraw-Hill.

Zimbardo, P.G. & Montgomery, K.D. (1957). The relative strengths of consummatory responses in hunger, thirst, and exploratory drive. *Journal of Comparative and Physiological Psychology,* 50, 504–508.

Zimbardo, P.G. & Radl, S.L. (1999). *The shy child* (2nd edn). Los Altos, CA: Malor Press.

Zimmerman, B.J., Bandura, A. & Martinez-Pons, M. (1992). Self-motivation for academic attainment: The role of self-efficacy beliefs and personal goal setting. *American Educational Research Journal,* 29, 663–676.

Zubrick, S.R., Lawrence, D.M., Silburn, S.R., Blair, E., Milroy, H., Wilkes, T., Eades, S., D'Antoine, H., Read, A., Ishiguchi, P. & Doyle, S. (2004). *The Western Australian Aboriginal Child Health Survey: The Health of Aboriginal Children and Young People.* Telethon Institute for Child Health Research, Perth.

Zuckerman, M. (1988). Sensation seeking, risk taking, and health. In M.P. Janisse (Ed.), *Individual differences, stress, and health psychology* (pp. 72–88). New York: Springer-Verlag.

Zwaan, R.A. & Radvansky, G.A. (1998). Situation models in language comprehension and memory. *Psychological Bulletin,* 123, 162–185.

Zwaigenbaum, L., Bryson, S., Rogers, T., Roberts, W., Brian, J. & Szatmari, P. (2005). Behavioral manifestations of autism in the first year of life. *International Journal of Developmental Neuroscience,* 23, 143–152.

# NAME INDEX

Curtis, R.C. 582
Cutting, J.C. 128, 255
Czeisler, C.A. 150

Dahlstrom, W.G. 473
Dali, S. 97, *97*
Damasio, A.R. 413
Damasio, H. 78
Darley, J.M. 604, 605
Darling, N. 349
Darwin, C. 13, 54–5, *55*, 56, 199, 290, 404
D'Augelli, A.R. 389–90, 503
Davey, C. 18–19
Davidson, A.R. 570
Davidson, G. 608
Davidson, G.R. 212
Davidson, R.J. 86, 409
Davila, J. 529
da Vinci, L. 461
Davis, J. 503
Davis, M.H. 606
Dawkins, K. 547
Dawson, D. 154
Day, R.H. 9
De Bellis, M.D. 356
DeCasper, A.J. 328
Deckro, G.R. 434
DeCock, R. 118, 383
DeGracia, D.J. 159
Dehaene, S. 251
Dejin-Karlsson, E. 327
Delaney, A.J. 165
Dell, G.S. 255
Delprato, D.J. 175
Dement, W.C. 155
Denmark, F.L. 18
Dennett, D.C. 146
DePaulo, B.M. 262
de Rivera, J. 534
Descartes, R. 61
de St Aubin, E. 354, 461
Dew, M.A. 152
Dewey, J. 10
Dewsbury, D.A. 383
Dhawan, N. 469
DiDomenico, L. 380
Dietrich, A. 314
Digman, J.M. 449
Dik, B.J. 8
DiLalla, L.F. 608
Di Marzo, V. 164
Dineen, B.R. 8
Dion, K.K. 584
Dion, K.L. 584
Dirkzwager, A.J.E. 426
Dishman, R.K. 436
Ditto, P.H. 578
Dix, D. 530
Dixon, M.J. 513
Dixon, R.A. 324, 337
Dollard, J. 462, 609
Domhoff, G.W. 156, 158
Domjan, M. 43
Donderi, C.D. 158
Donders, F.C. 249
Dong, Q. 582
Donne, J. 601

Donnerstein, E. 202
Donovan, M.C. 511
Dorrian, J. 154
Dovidio, J.F. 580
Downing, P.E. 107
Draijer, N. 507
Drayna, D. 60
Drummond, L.M. 536
DuBois, P.H. 473
Dudycha, G.J. 451
Duker, P.C. 537
Duncker, D. 271
Durik, A.M. 386
Durkin, S.J. 380
Dutke, S. 218
Dutton, D.G. 410
Dweck, C.S. 374

Eagly, A.H. 41
Ebbinghaus, H. 8, 225, 226
Eckensberger, L.H. 359
Edinger, J.D. 154
Edlund, T. 84
Edwards, J.N. 353
Eich, E. 413, 534
Eidelson, J.I. 620
Eidelson, R.J. 620
Einstein, A. 263
Eisenberg, M. 344
Ekman, P. 405, 406
Elbert, T. 84
Elkin, A.P. 429
Elliott, A.J. 396
Ellis, A. 541
Elman, J.L. 134
Emery, G. 496
Emmelkamp, P.M.G. 536
Endler, N.S. 426
Enserink, M. 552, 608
Epley, N. 278
Epstein, L.H. 376, 378
Erbring, L. 454
Ericsson, K.A. 146, 216, 269
Erikson, E. *344*, 345–6, 351, 352
Eshleman, A. 579
Esler, W.P. 237
Espie, C.A. 154
Estrada, C.A. 413
Evans, A. 176
Evans, C.S. 198
Evans, J. 271
Evans, M. 293
Exner, J.E. 475
Eysenck, H. *448*, 448–9, 551

Fadiman, J. 460, 533
Fagot, B.I. 357
Fakhoury, W. 530
Fallon, A.E. 182–3
Fantz, R. 328
Faraday, M. 263
Faraone, S.V. 515
Farina, A. 518
Farley, A. 293
Fatt, J. 307, *307*
Faucheux, C. 599
Fawkes, M.S. 196
Fazio, R.H. 569, 573

Feather, N.T. 391
Fechner, G. 99
Fernald, A. 34, 341
Fernandez-Ballesteros, R. 352
Ferster, C.B. 194
Festinger, L. 374, 572
Field, A. 307
Fields, R.D. 63
Findlay, M. 156
Finger, T.E. 120
Fink, P. 507
Finkelstein, M.A. 606
Fiorito, G. 198, 201
Fischoff, B. 222
Fishbein, M. 569
Fisher, B.S. 388
Fisher, S. 156
Fishman, H.C. 545
Fishman, T. 545
Fiske, S.T. 595
Fitch, W.T. 259
Fivush, R. 358
Flavell, J.H. 333, 335
Fleming, I. 264
Fleming, R. 469
Foa, E.B. 421
Folkman, S. 423, 424
Fombonne, E. 515
Ford, C.S. 383
Forgas, J. 412
Forumoto, L. 18
Foster, T.M. 198
Fösterling, F. 563
Foucault, M. 530
Foulkes, D. 155
Fowler, H. 371
Frager, R. 460, 533
Fraley, B. 584
Fraley, R.C. 583
Frank, J.B. 552
Frank, M.E. 120, 552
Franklin, G. 534
Franklin, N. 265
Franz, C.E. 391, 392
Fraser, C. 503
Fraser, M.W. 539
Fraser, S.C. 575
Frederick, S. 278
Freedman, J.L. 575
Freedman, M.S. 150
Freeman, M.S. 328
Freud, A. *11*, 18, 345–6, 351
Freud, S. 11, *11*, 14, 146, 155–6, 157, 349, 373, 453, 455–9, 461, 467, 472, 489–90, 499, 507, 531–3, 534
Freund, A.M. 339, 361
Frick, F. 271
Friedman, M. 436–7
Friedman, R. 434
Friend, R. 598
Friesen, W.V. 405, 406
Frijda, N.H. 407
Froghardt, R. 182
Fromkin, V.A. 255
Fromm, E. 160
Frougel, P. 379
Funt, A. 600
Furman, W. 352

ambiguity resolution *256–7*, 256–8
bases of general intelligence 300, *300*
brain function and schizophrenia 512, *512*
central responses in eating 377
extraversion and amygdala activity 450, *450*
in foetuses 326–7, *326–7*
gender differences 356
hemispheric lateralisation *80–1*, 80–3
impact of meditation on 162
individual differences relating to aggression 608
interventions in the 69–71
memory structures and processes *238*, 238–9, 240, 495, *495*
panic disorder sufferers 496
reasoning tasks 274, *274*
recording and imaging brain activity 72, *72*, 239–40, *240–1*
during sleep 152, 157
structures and functions 74–80, *76–9*
techniques for *72*
visual processing 107, 264, *265*
*see also* brain imaging; consciousness
brain imaging 257
Brain Sciences NSW 502
brain stem 74–6, *76*, 115
breast cancer patients 428
breastfeeding, and intelligence 301
brightness (colour) 110
British English 261
British Psychological Society 9, 18
Broca's aphasia 80
Broca's area 69, 78, *78*
*Bufo marinus* 198–9
bulimia nervosa 380–1
Burdekin Report 520
burnout 437–8
Bush Administration 619
bushfires 494
bystander intervention 604–6, *605*

caffeine 163, 167
Cambodia 618
cancer treatment 185, 197–8
*Candid Camera* (television show) *600*, 600–1
cane toads 198–9
cannabinoids 164, 379
cannabis 163, 164
Cannon–Bard theory of emotion 409, *410*
capsaicin 125
carbon monoxide 68
cardinal traits 448
Caroline Island 302
case studies, as a research method 41
cataplexy 154
catatonic schizophrenia 510
catecholamines 67
categorical perception 261
categories 200, 230–1
categorisation *233–4*
catharsis 532

caudal ventral prefrontal cortex *499*
causal attributions 563
cause and effect 28, 30, 32, 35, 45
celebrities, use of to sell products 570, *571*
Celexa 550
central executive (memory) 217
central nervous system 72–3, *73–4*, 409
central responses, in eating 377
central route, to persuasion 570, 571
central sulcus 78, *78*
central traits 448
centration 334
cerebellum 75, *76*, 238, *238*
cerebral cortex 75, *76*, 77, 78, 238, *238*
cerebral hemispheres 77, *78*, 80–2, *81*
cerebrum 75, 77–80
change blindness *127*, 128
chat rooms 471
cheating scandals 315
chemotherapy 185, 197–8
Chicagocentric world view *266*
child detainees 494
child-directed speech 341
children
    abuse of 350, 504, 508
    behaviour problems in 190
    childhood development 328–9, *329*, 332–7, 346–50
    effect of child care on development 348
    effect of stress on intellectual development 422
    psychological disorders 514–16
    whether to smack 193
chillis 125
chimpanzees 259–60, 607
'chimp-o-mat' 191, *191*
China, civil service testing 290
chlorpromazine 546, 547
choice, freedom of 543
cholesterol 379
chromosomes 58, *59*
chronic stress 416
chronic stressors 422
chronological age 295, 296, 324
chunk 216
chunking 216
cigarettes 163
circadian rhythms 150
citalopram 550
civilians, war waged against 619–20
civil service testing 290
classical conditioning 176–85, *177–9*, 197–8, 199, 238
classification systems, for psychological disorders 486–9
client-centred therapy 543
clients 529
clinical disorders 488
clinical neuropsychologists *18*
clinical psychologists 17, *18*, 528, 529
clinical scales (MMPI) 473–4
clinical social worker 529
cliques 352
closure, law of 127
clozapine 547

Clozaril 547
cocaine 163, 165, 167, 327, 537–8
cochlea *114*, 114–15
cochlear implants 115–16
cochlear nucleus 115
cocktail party phenomenon 126
coercion model, of antisocial behaviour 190
coercive rules 595
cognition
    in animals *199*, 199–200, *201*
    cognitive approach to motivation 373–4
    cognitive deficits 500
    cognitive development over the lifespan 332–9
    cognitive influences on learning 199–202
    combining visual and verbal representations 264–6
    current views on early development 335–7
    defined 199, 248
    effect of emotions on 412–14
    effect of stress on 422
    gender differences 356
    Piaget's research on 332–6
    social influences on development 336–7
    stages of cognitive development 333–4
    study of 249–51
    use of working memory in 217
    visual cognition 263–6, *263–6*
    *see also* intelligence; language; problem solving; reasoning
cognitive-affective personality theory 463–4
cognitive appraisal, of demands 423, 424
cognitive appraisal theories, of emotion 409–11, *410*
cognitive behavioural therapy 542, 550, 552, *552*
cognitive content 541
cognitive dissonance 572–3
cognitive maps *199*, 199–200, 202
cognitive model, of psychopathology 490
cognitive neuroscience 13
cognitive perspective 12–13, 14, 15, 496–7, 500
cognitive processes 248, 541
cognitive psychology 17, 248, *248*
cognitive psychotherapy 528
cognitive restructuring 542
cognitive science 5, 17, 248, *248*
cognitive sets 500
cognitive strategies, for stress 425–6
cognitive theories, of personality 462–6, 472
cognitive therapies 541–2
cognitive triad 500
cohorts 325
collective unconscious 459
collectivist cultures 303, 469, 470, 584, 603
colour, and language 260–1

instinctual behaviours 372–3, 472
instinctual drift 195–6
institutional treatment, of mental
    illness 530, 530–1
institutions, children raised in 350
instrumental aggression 609
instrumentality 394–5
insults 612, 612
intellect, model of 300, 300
intellectual disability 297–8
intelligence
    with age 337, 339
    defined 293
    extremes of 297, 297–8
    politics of 304–12
    relation to breastfeeding 301
    relation to environment 308–10
    relation to heredity 306, 306–8
    relation to social class 309, 309
    testing of 290–1, 294–8, 304–12,
        315–16
    theories of 299–304
    see also creativity
intelligence quotients 295–7, 297, 306,
    306–8
interactive problem solving 623
interdependence 573
interdependence theory 584
interdependent construals of self 469,
    564, 611–12
interference 225–6, 226
intermarriage 308
intermediary bystanders 616
internal consistency, in tests 292
internal control orientation 392–3,
    393, 500
internal drives 371
internalisation 336–7
internal working model 347
International Classification of
    Diseases 487
International Union of Psychological
    Science 18
internet 46, 471, 529, 546
interneurons 62, 63
interpersonal attraction 581
interpersonal defences 460
interpersonal intelligence 302, 303
interpersonal responsibility, versus
    justice 360, 360
interpersonal therapy 552, 552
interposition cues 130, 130
The Interpretation of Dreams
    (Freud) 156
interracial conflict 580
interracial couples 353
interval schedules 192
interventions 7, 528
interviews 39–40
intimacy 345, 352–3, 354, 465–6, 583
intrapersonal intelligence 302
intrapsychic defences 460
intrapsychic events 453
introspection 9–10, 146, 175
introversion 346, 454, 473, 567
intuitive psychologists 563
ion channels 64–5
ions 64

IQ tests 295–8, 297, 304–12, 311, 422,
    578–9
Iraq War 619
iris 103, 103, 104
irrationality 485
isolation 345, 457
Israelis 623

James–Lange theory of emotion 409,
    410
Japan 303, 470
jealousy 386, 387, 510, 583
jet lag 150
Jews 576, 618
jigsaw classrooms 580
jigsaw technique 580
JNDs 102, 102
job burnout 437–8
John Hopkins University 9
judgements, impact of emotions on
    413
judgments 275–9
justice 360, 360, 603–4
just noticeable differences 102, 102
just world thinking 618

Kalapalo Indians 157
Kallikak family 305
Kanzi (bonobo) 259
K complex 151
'Kim's game' 306, 306–8
kinaesthaesis 121
kinaesthetic sense 121–2, 302
kinship 602, 602
knowledge acquisition 300
knowledge compilation 211

laissez-faire leaders 621
language
    acquisition of 340–3
    describing colour in 260–1
    effect on thought and culture 260–1
    evolution of 57, 259–60
    left hemisphere of brain 274
    production of 252–5
    relation to intelligence 308
    role of auditory cortex in
        comprehension of 80
    structure of 10, 259
    unconscious processes in 146
    understanding of 255–9
    use of 252–61
language-making capacity 342
Lardil people 157
latency 455, 456
latent content, of dreams 156, 532
lateral fissure 78
lateral hypothalamus 377
lateralisation, hemispheric 80–2, 81
Latinos 305
law of effect 186
LCUs 419
leadership, analysis of 621
learned helplessness 500
learning
    in Australian animal species 198–9
    biological constraints on 195
    cognitive influences on 199–202

comparing theories 472
defined 174–5
instinctual drift 195–6
observational learning 201–2
taste-aversion learning 196–9, 197
theories of 462
see also classical conditioning; operant
    conditioning
learning-performance distinction 174
left hemisphere, of brain 80–2, 274
left visual field 80, 81
legitimate authority figures 615
lens (eye) 103, 103, 104
leptin 379
lesbian youth 503
lesions 70–1
levelling (memory) 234
level of analysis 5–6
levels-of-processing theory 223
lexical ambiguity 256, 256
lexical meaning 340
lexicon 276
libido 453, 459
lies 262
life-change units 419
life-changing events 419
lifecycle, sleep patterns over 152
Lifeline Australia 427, 545
life-or-death situations 602, 602
life span development 324
    see also developmental psychology
life stories 461
light, and circadian rhythms 150
lightness constancy 133, 133
likes and dislikes 8, 183, 581–3
limbic system 74, 76, 76–80, 77, 408
linear perspective 130, 131
linguistic intelligence 302
linguistic relativity 260
listeners 252
lithium salts 548
lobes, of the brain 78, 78
loci, method of 227, 227
locomotion 328–9, 330
locus of control 393, 392–3
logical-mathematical intelligence 302
longitudinal research design 324–5,
    325, 606
long-term memory 212, 218–25,
    230–6
loudness 113
love, and loving 583–5
low elaboration 570
low monitors 433
low span 217
LSD 68, 163, 164
lucid dreaming 159
lysergic acid diethylamide 68, 163,
    164

Mabo case 148–9, 622
madness, and creativity 314
magnetic resonance imaging 72, 72
maintenance rehearsal 215
major depressive disorder 497–8, 501
majority, power of 599
major life events, stress of 418–19
maladaptiveness 485

NCS   488
near point (vision)   104
Necker Cube   97, *97*
needs   *374*, 374–5, 391–2, 584
negative afterimages   *110*, 110–11
negative correlations   35, *35*
negative punishment   188, 189
negative reinforcement   188, 189
negative thinking   500
negative transference   532
negativism   510
negativistic states   372
neglect, of children   350
neo-Freudian theorists   11
NEO Personality Inventory   473, 474
NEO-PI   473–4
nerve deafness   115
nervous system   61–8, 72–4, *73–4*
   *see also* brain
NESB communities, mental illness
   in   516–18
neurogenesis   84
neuromatrix theory of pain   122
neuromodulators   68, 164
neurons   61–6, *62*, 84
neuroscience   13, 61
neuroses   488
neurotic disorders   488–9
neuroticism   449, 474
neurotransmitters   *66*, 66–8, 70, 165–6,
   379, 494, 547–8, 608–9
neutral stimuli   188
New Guinea   405–6
New Zealand   198
next-in-line effect   227
ngangkari   157
nicotine   163, 167
nicotine replacement therapy   432
nightmares   158
nitric oxide   68
nodes of Ranvier   *62*, 65
noise   113–14
nonadrenaline   68
nonconformity   598
nonconscious processes   145
nondirective therapy   543
non-English speaking communities,
   mental illness in   516–18
non-prejudice   578
nonprocrastinators   *420*, 420–1
non-REM sleep   150–5, *152*
nonviolent resistance   *612*
noradrenaline   416
norepinephrine   165, 166, 416, 499,
   547
normal distribution   291
normative influences   597–8, 617
normative investigations   324
normative populations   293
norm crystallisation   597
norm of reciprocity   575, 603
norms   293, 596–7, 613
NREM sleep   150–5, *152*
nucleus   *59*
number processing   251

obedience to authority   42, 614–18, *615*,
   *617*

obesity   378–80, 436, 582
objectivity, in observation   6, 29–31, 32,
   35, 486
object permanence   333, *336*
observation
   in behaviourism   175
   filters in   30
   objectivity in   6, 29–31, 32, 35
   observer bias   29–30, *30*
   observer discomfort   485
   as a research method   *40*, 40–1
   subjectivity in   6
observational learning   201–2, 464
obsessions   493, 543
obsessive-compulsive disorder   493, 496,
   497, 536, 548
obsessiveness   473
occipital cortex   *265*
occipital lobe   78, *78*
occlusion   130
OCD   493, 496, 497, 536, 548
octopuses   198, 201
*Octpus cyaneus*   198
odours   117–18, 221
Oedipus complex   455
oestrogen   83, 383
olefactory bulb   117, *118*
olefactory cilia   117
olefactory receptors   117–18, *118*
*On Aggression* (Lorenz)   607
One Nation Party   291
open-ended questions   39
openness to experience   449, 474
operant   186
operant chamber   187, *187*, 194
operant conditioning   186–95, 199,
   537
operant extinction   188
operational definitions   30
operationalisation   30
operation (intellect)   300, *300*
opiates   163, 164–5, 184
opioid abuse   505, 537–8
opossums   198
opponent-process theory   111–12
optic chiasma   105
optic disk   104
optic nerve   105, *105*, 106
optic tracts   106, *106*
optimism   393, 437
oral contraceptives   387
oral stage   455
organisational psychology   394–5
orgasms   384, 385, *385*
orienting response   177
*The Origin of the Species*   55
orphanages   350
'other' and 'self'   584, *585*
otitis media   115
outcome-based expectancies   465
out-groups   577, 618
ovaries   83, *83*
over-regularisation   343
ovulation   384

Pacific Islanders   564
Padua Inventory   536
pain   122, 125, 161, 407

Pain Management Research
   Institute   122
painting, levels of analysis of   5
pain withdrawal reflex   62–3, *63*
Palestinians   623
pancreas   83, *83*
panic attacks   492
panic disorders   492, 496, 548
papillae   *119*
parachuting   372
paradoxical sleep   151
parallel forms, in tests   292
parallel process   250, *250*
paralysis   73
paralysis of will   500
paranoia   473
paranoid delusions   167
paranoid schizophrenia   510
parasympathetic division   74, *74*, 408
parasympathetic nervous system   *75*
paratelic states   372
parathyroid gland   *83*
Parental Bonding Instrument   506
parental investment   386
parentese   341
parenting styles   *349*, 349–50, 357, 506,
   608
parents, prospective   467
parietal cortex   *265*
parietal lobe   78, 78–9
Parkinson's disease   68
partial reinforcement effect   192
partial reinforcement schedule   192
partial-report procedure   213
participant modelling   538, *539*
participatory education   309
passion   583
passionate love   583
the past   472
pastoral counsellors   529
pathological liars   262
patient adherence, to treatment
   433–4
patients   529, 533
patriotism   620
pattern recognition   106
Pavlovian conditioning   176–7
PBI   506
PCP   163, 164
Peabody Picture Vocabulary Test
   301
peace psychology   614, 620–3
peer relationships   351–2, *352*, 357
peer review   46
peg-word method   227
penis size   384
perceived control   426
perception
   ambiguity in   96–7, *97*
   attentional processes   123–6
   defined   94
   depth perception   128–31
   illusions   97–9, *98*
   influence of context and
      expectations   *135*, 135–6
   influence of expectations on   567
   motion perception   128
   perceptual constancies   131–4

principles of perceptual
   grouping   126–7
proximal and distant stimuli   95,
   95–6
social perception   563
spatial integration   127, 127–8
stages of   94
temporal integration   127, 127–8
percepts   94
perceptual constancy   131–4
perceptual copresence   253
perceptual organisation   94, 96
perceptual set   136
performance   31, 31, 174
performance-approach goals   396
performance-avoidance goals   396
performance components, of
   intelligence   300–1
Performance IQ   296
peripheralist theory   409
peripheral nervous system   72–4, 73–4
peripheral responses, in eating   376–7
peripheral route, to persuasion   570,
   571
persecution, delusions of   510
personal achievement, motivation
   for   391–6
personal constructions of reality   148
personality
   comparing personality theories
      471–2
   defined   446
   development of   354
   Freudian theory of   456
   humanistic theories   460–1
   objective tests of   472–4
   personality disorders   504–6
   personality psychologists   17
   personality types   432, 446–7, 452–3
   projective tests of   472, 474–6
   psychodynamic theories   453–9
   relation to health   436–7
   social learning and cognitive
      theories   462–6
   theory overview   446
   trait theories   447–53, 448–9, 609
personality disorders   488
personality inventories   473
personality structures   448, 453, 456,
   459
personnel psychology   8
person–organisation fit   8
persuasion   464, 570–4, 621
pessimism   393
PET scans   72, 72, 86, 237, 239, 240
phallic stage   455, 459
pharmacotherapy   552, 552
phencyclidine   163
phenomenological approach, to
   psychology   461
phenotypes   56, 57
phenylketonuria   298
pheromones   118, 383
phi phenomenon   128
phlogeny   198
phobias   197, 492–3, 496, 535–6, 538,
   539, 548
phonemes   134, 340, 341

phonemic restoration   134–5, 135
phonetics   340
phonological loop (memory)   217
phonology   340
'photographic memory'   214
photoreceptors   104, 105, 108, 111
physical abuse   508, 584, 613
physical attractiveness   582
physical development   326–31
physicians   528
physiological arousal   31, 31
physiological dependence   164
pictorial cues   130
PIFS   304
pigeons, in research   198, 200, 201,
   201
pinna   114, 115
pitch   113
pitch perception   60, 116
pituitary gland   82–3, 83, 416, 417
pixels   108
PKU   298
placebo controls   33
placebo effects   32–3, 37, 42, 68, 160,
   552
placebo therapy   552, 552
place recognition   106
place theory   116
plaques   237
plasticity   83–4
plateau phase   385, 385
pleasure principle   456, 459
plieated gibbons   260
Poggendorf illusion   98
polarisation, of cells   64
politeness, and moods   412
political forecasting   283
pons   75, 76
Ponzo illusion   130, 131
population (research)   33–4
porpoises   117
positive correlations   35, 35
positive emission topography   72, 72
Positive Parenting Program   190
positive psychology   427
positive punishment   188, 189
positive reappraisal coping   428
positive reinforcement   188, 189,
   537–8
positive transference   532
possible selves   467, 471
possums   196, 198
posterior pituitary gland   83
post event information   235
postsynaptic membrane   65–6, 66
posttraumatic growth   428
post-traumatic stress disorder   421,
   426, 494–5
PPARd   379
PPVT-R   301
practical intelligence   302
practical intelligence for school
   curriculum   304
pragmatic reasoning   273
pragmatics   340
preconscious memories   145
predictions   7, 28, 283
predictive validity   293

preferences, and emotions   182–3
prefrontal cortex   86
prefrontal lobotomy   549
pregnancy   298, 327–8
prejudice   576–81, 618
prenatal development   326–7, 326–7
preoperational stage   333–4
the present   472
presynaptic membrane   65, 66
preventative medicine   430, 431
prewiring, for survival   327–8
primacy effect   221
primary appraisal   423
primary prevention   553
primary reinforcers   190–1
priming   224, 224
Princeton Theological Seminary   604
Principles of Physiological Psychology
   (Wundt)   9
principlism   603
proactive interference   226, 226
problem, defined   269
problem-directed coping   424
problem solving   267–71, 268, 270
problem space   269
procedural memory   211–12, 239
process, in observation   40
procrastinators   420, 420–1
product (intellect)   300, 300
products, in observation   40
prognosis   528
progressive education   10
projection   457
projective tests, of personality   472,
   474–6
propaganda   618–19, 619, 621
propositions   258
prosocial behaviour   201, 202, 412,
   601–7
prospective studies   513
prototypes   232
provocation   611
proximal stimuli   95, 95–6
proximity, law of   126
proximity, of friends   581
Prozac   68, 547, 548
pseudopatients   486
Psilocybe mushroom   163
psychasthenia   473
psychedelics   164
psychiatrists   17, 528, 529
psychic determinism   455–6
psychic energy   453
psychoactive drugs   163–7
psychoanalysis   18, 540
psychoanalysts   529
psychobiographies   461
psychobiology   13
psychodynamic perspective
   on aggression   15
   on anxiety disorders   496
   features of   11, 14
   on mood disorders   499
   on psychopathology   489–90
   on therapy   18, 528, 531–4
psychoeuroimmunology   434–5, 435
psychological assessment   290–8,
   315–16

psychological dependence 164
psychological diagnoses 486–7
psychological disorders
  anxiety disorders 491–7
  biological approaches 489
  childhood disorders 514–16
  classifying 486–9
  deciding what is abnormal 484–5
  diagnosis of 486–7
  mood disorders 497–503
  personality disorders 504–6
  portrayal of in films 519
  preventative strategies 553–4
  problem of objectivity 486
  psychological approaches 489–91
  somatoform disorders 506–7
  stigma of mental illness 516–20
psychological laboratories 9
Psychologists for Peace 620–1
psychology
  as a career 8, 17, *18*
  current perspectives 11–15
  defined 4, 144
  goals of 5–7
  history of 8–10
  professional societies 18
  reasons for studying 4
  what psychologists do 17–19
*Psychology from the Standpoint of a*
  *Behaviourist* (Watson) 175
*Psychology* (James) 144
psychometric function 100, *100*
psychometrics 299
psychometric theories, of
  intelligence 299–300
psychopathic deviate 473
psychopathological functioning 484
psychopathology 484, 489–91
psychopharmacology 17, 546
psychophysics 99–102
psychoses 488
psychosexual development 453, 455
psychosocial maturity 354–5
psychosocial stages 345–6
psychosomatic disorders 418
psychosurgery 549
psychotherapy
  behaviour therapies 528, 535–40
  cognitive therapies 541–2
  evaluating effectiveness of 552, *552*
  humanistic therapies 528, 529
  overview of 528
  psychodynamic therapies 18, 528,
    531–4
psychotic disorders 488–9
PTSD 421, 426, 494–5
puberty 330
pubescent growth spurt 329
publication, of research 28–9
public health 430–3
public verifiability 29
punishers 188
punishment 188, 193
pupil dilation 120
pupil (eye) 103, *103*, 104
pure tones 113
Pygmalion effect 566
*Pygmalion* (Shaw) 566

quadriplegics *194*
questionnaires 39
questions, phrasing of 280
quokkas 198

race, as a construct 307
racism 291, 305–6, 577
radical behaviourism 175
random assignment 33
rape 388
rape victims 421–2
rapid eye movements 150–1, *151*
rapport, in interviews 39
rational-emotive therapy 541–2
rationalisation 457
ratio schedules 192
rats, in research 196–200, *197, 199*
Reach Out! 545
reaction formation 457
reaction time 249
reality, constructions of 148
reality principle 456
real-world reasoning 272, *272*
reappraisal 425
reasoning 268, 271–4, *274*, 413
rebellion 595
recall 219, 221, *222*, 226–7, 276–7
recency effect 221, 222
receptive fields (cells) 106, *106*
receptor molecules 66
reciprocal altruism 602–3
reciprocal determinism 464, *464*
reciprocity, between friends 582
reciprocity norm 575, 603
recognition 94, *96*, 133–6, 219, 221
reconciliation 622–3, 624
reconstructive memory 234–6
recruiting, use of intelligence tests
  in 295
reference points 280
reflex 177
refractory period 65
regression 457
regret 281
rehabilitation psychologists 17
rehearsal 215
reinforcement 187–95, 201, 539
reinforcement contingencies 187,
  190–1
reinforcement histories 462
reinforcers 187–92
relative motion parallax 129
relative refractory period 65
relative size 130, *130*
relaxation 434
relaxation response 434
relaxation training 535
reliability 39, 291–2, 293
religious ecstasy 162
*Remembering...*(Bartlett) 234
remission 510
REM sleep 150–5, *151–2, 157, 158, 159*
repeated measures designs 34
repetitive transcranial magnetic
  stimulation 71, *71*, 551
reporting, of news events 564–5
representativeness heuristic 277–8,
  *278*

representative samples 34
repressed memories 534
repression 146, 456–7, 531–2
reproduction 383, 385
reproductive functions 331
research
  on animals 43–5, 196–200, *197, 199*,
    259–60, 607
  application of 17
  behavioural measures 40–2
  correlational methods 35, 35–6
  critical thinking skills 45–6
  ethics in 40, 42–5
  experimental methods 32–5
  process of 28–9, *29*
  psychological measurement in 39–42
  reliability and validity of data 39
  subliminal influences 36–7, *37*
  white middle-class American bias
    14
residual schizophrenia 510
resistance, in psychoanalysis 532
resistance, to stressors 418, *419*
resolution phase 385, *385*
response bias 101
response deprivation theory 191–2
response prevention 536
response selection 249
responsibility 370–1
responsiveness 349, *349*
resting metabolic rate 379
resting potentials 64, *64*
restrained eating 378–9, *380*
restructuring, of cognitions 425
RET 541–2
retention interval 219
reticular formation 75, *76*
retinal disparity 128–9, *129*
retinas *103*, 104, *105*, 108, *108*
retrieval cues 219–20
retrieval (memory) 212, 223–5, 239–40,
  *240–1*, 500, *501*
retroactive interference 226, *226*
retrograde amnesia 239
reversal theory 372
reversibility 334
review boards 42
'the revolving door' 531
rewards 539
right hemisphere, of brain 80–2, 274
right visual field 80, *81*
risk-gain assessment 42
risk taking 314, 352, *352*, 433
*Roadmap for Reconciliation* 622
Robbers Cave State Park
  experiment 579, *580*
rod cells 104, *105*, 109
Rohypnol 163, 165
role confusion 345
roles, of gender 356–8
romantic relationships 583–5
roofies 165
Rorschach test 475
rote learning 10, 225
Royal Australian and New Zealand
  College of Psychiatrists 545
Royal Victorian Eye and Ear
  Hospital 108, 115

rTMS  71, *71*, 548, 551
rubella  298, 327
Rudd government  622–3
rules  594–6
rumination  501
Rwanda  624

saccule  *114*, 121
safety needs  374, *374*
sailfin mollies  384, *384*
Salem witchcraft trials  *487*
salespeople  393
salinity  120
saliva  120
samples, for research  33–4
Sarah (chimpanzee)  259
satiety  376
satisficers  281–2
saturation (colour)  110
scapegoats  618, 621
scarcity  575
schedules of reinforcement  192, *192*, 194, 198
schemas  231–2, 467
schemes  332
schizophrenic disorders
  causes of  509–13
  classification of  473
  distinguished from DID  508
  drug therapy for  68, 547, 548
  ECT for  549, 551
  internet information about  46
  personal anecdote of sufferer  484
  stigma associated with  516
  symptoms of  509
  types of  509
  unintentional reinforcement of  538
school psychologists  17
schools, violence in  611
scientific concepts  336
scientific method  4, 28–9
Seconal  163
secondary appraisal  423
secondary gains  190
secondary prevention  553
secondary sexual characteristics  82–3
secondary traits  448
secrets  435, 458, 471
secure attachment style  583
segregation, in US schools  577
selective advantage  56, *57*
selective opitmisation with
  compensation  339, 361
selective serotonin reuptake
  inhibitors  547–8
selective social interaction theory  354
self-actualisation  12, *12*, 459, 460, 461, 543
self-actualisation needs  374, 375
'self' and 'other'  584, *585*
self-concept  467
self-efficacy  464–5, *465*, 542, 545
self-enhancement  470
self-esteem  468, 473
self-evaluations  469
self-exploration  471
self-fulfilling prophecies  566–7, 582
self-handicapping  468

self-help groups  545–6
self-injurious behaviours  537
self-perception theory  573
self-presentation  468
self-preservation  453
self-regard  460
self-regulatory efficacy  465
self-report inventory  473
self-report measures  39–40, 41
self-schemas  467
self, sense of  144
self-serving biases  565, *565–6*
self theories  467–70, 472
semantic memories  220
semantics  340
semicircular canals  *114*, 121
Senegal  407
sensation  94, *96*, 99–102
sensation seeking  432
sensorimotor intelligence  332
sensorimotor stage  333
sensory adaption  100
sensory cortex  79, *79*, 84
sensory memory  213–14, 238
sensory neurons  62, *63*
sensory receptors  94, 103
sentence meaning  252
sentence structures  *256*, 256–7
September 11, 2001  421, 601
Serbians  620, 622
serial position effect  221–2, *222*, 228
serial process  250, *250*
serial recall  221, *222*
serotonin  68, 164, 165, 166, 499, 547, 608–9
serotonin and norepinephrine reuptake
  inhibitors  547–8
set learning  198
set of operations  269
set (perception)  136
sex chromosomes  59
sex differences  355–6
sex flushes  385
sexism  577
sexual behaviours
  arousal and response  383, 384–5, 410
  cultural norms  383
  evolution of  385–7, *387*
  homosexuality  353, 388–90, *390*, 489, 578
  infidelity  386, *387*
  motivation for  383
  non-human sexual behaviour  383–4, *384*
  perversions  536
  to protect oneself from AIDS  432–3
  psychological origins of problems 385
  research into  384–5
  risk taking  388
  sexual abuse  508, 534
  sexual disorders  490
  sexual drives  453, 455, 459, 533
  sexual norms  387–8
  sexual revolution (1960s)  386
  thinking about sex  383
sexual functions  331

sexual scripts  387–8
'S.F.' (subject)  216
shadowing  125
shamans  156, 167
shape constancy  132, *132*
shaping  187, 194–5, 537
shaping by successive
  approximations  194
sharpening (memory)  234
*Shine* (film)  314
short-term memory  213–17, *215*
shuttlebox  180–1, *181*
shyness  6–7, 346, 454
sibling conflict  36
signal detection theory  101, *101*
similarity, between friends  582
similarity, law of  127
simple cells  106
simultaneous conditioning  178, *179*
sine waves  112, *113*
situational forces
  assumptions about in therapy for
    couples  545
  in attribution theory  563–5, 567
  effect on obedience to authority  614, 616
  effect on pro-social behaviour 604–5
  and the expression of
    aggression  609–11, *610*
  in Heider's theory  374
  in personality theories  461, 472
  power of  594–601, 614, 616
size constancy  131–2, *132*
skin receptors  *63*
slavery  486
sleep  35, 150–5, *151–2*
sleep apnoea  154
sleep cycles  150–1, *151*
sleep deprivation  153, 155
sleep disorders  153–4
sleep spindles  151, *151*
sleepwalking  154
SLIP technique  149, 255
smacking, of children  193
smell  117–19, *118*, 221
smell testing  120
smoking  6, 327, 431–2
snakes, phobia of  538, *539*
SNRIs  547–8
social categorisation  577
social class, and IQ  309, *309*
social cognition  562
social comparison model  600
social Darwinism  291
social development  344–55
social discomfort  473
social experience  349
social imitation  462
social influences, on cognitive
  development  336–7
social intelligence theory  465–6
social introversion  473
socialisation  346, 349, 357, 539
social isolates, peer acceptance of  539
social learning  201
social learning theory  374, 462–6, 472, 538–9, *539*

social learning therapy   538–9
social norms   596–7
social obligations   412
social perception   563
social phobias   454, 492–3, 545, 550
social psychologists   17
social psychology   562, 577, 581
Social Readjustment Rating Scale   419,
   420
social reality, construction of   562–8
social relationships   533, 581–6
social roles   594–6, 606, 615
social science, psychology as a   4
social-skills training   538–9
social support   426–7, 435
social variables   459
social workers   529
sociobiology   61
sociocultural model, of
   psychopathology   490
sociocultural perspective   14, 15
socioeconomic status   309
sociopathic syndromes   543
soma   62, 62, 64
somatic nervous system   73–4, 74
somatisation disorder   507
somatoform disorders   506–7
somatosensory cortex   79, 79, 84
somnambulism   154
sound   112–14
sound localisation   116, 116–17
sound shadows   116
source traits   448
sourness   120
South Africa, reconciliation in   624
South Australian Department of
   Education   18
spatial integration   127, 127–8
spatial intelligence   302
spatial memory   200
spatial mental models   265, 266
speakers   252
speaker's meaning   252
species, survival of   82
specific anosmia   118–19
specificity   569–70
specific phobias   493
speech   81, 149, 341
speech errors   254
speech execution   254
speech processes   255
speech representations   255
speech signals   115
sperm   82
spinal column   72
spinal cord   72–3, 76
spleen   416
split-brain patients   80–2
split-half reliability   292
split personality   508
spontaneous recovery   179, 188
spontaneous-remission effect   551
spoonerisms   254–5
Spoonerisms of Laboratory-Induced
   Predisposition   149, 255
sports psychologists   17, 18
S–R connection   186
SRRS   419, 420

SSRIs   547–8
stability   392–3, 500
standardisation   30, 293–5
standardised assessment tests   315
Stanford-Binet Intelligence Scale
   295–6
Stanford Prison experiment   594–5,
   595, 596
Stanford University   18
State Psychological Clinic, WA   18
statistical rarity   485
statistical relationships, in
   psychometrics   299
statistics   277
   see also appendix
stem cells   84
stereotypes   383, 517, 577–9, 582
stereotype threat   311–12, 312, 579
stereotype vulnerability   311
stigmas   516
stimulants   165, 167
stimuli   103
stimulus categorisation   249
stimulus discrimination   180
stimulus-driven capture   123–4, 124
stimulus generalisation   179–80, 180
stimulus–response connection   186
stimulus-response connections   238
stirrup   114, 115
STM   213–17, 215
St Mary of Bethlehem hospital,
   London   530
'stolen generations'   148, 622–3
stomach cramps   376
storage (memory)   212
storm-and-stress theory   351
Strange Situation Test   347
'streaming'   290
stress
   coping with   423–7
   defined   415
   effect on healing   434, 435
   model of   416
   muted stress responses   609
   physiological stress reactions   416–18,
      418
   positive effects of   427–8
   psychological stress reactions
      418–23
'stress hormones'   418
stress inoculation   425
stress inoculation training   426
stress moderator variables   423
stressors   415, 434
striatum   238, 238
Strong Interest Inventory   8
structural ambiguity   256–7
structuralism   9–10
structure of intellect model   300, 300
Student Stress Scale   420
A Study of Thinking (Goodnow)   19
subiculum   240, 241
subjective reality   13
subjective workloads   423
subjectivity, in observation   6
sublimation   457
subliminal messages   36–7, 37, 45
subnormality   298

substance-abuse disorders   490
subtractive colour mixture   111
suicide   503
superego   456, 457, 490, 531, 532
supertasters   125
survey questions, effect on attitudes
   of   38, 38
surveys   39
survival of the fittest   56, 57, 147
sweetness   120
Sydney Children's Hospital   120
Sydney Diocese Catholic Education
   Office   311
syllogisms   271
symapthetic states   372
symbolic modelling therapy   538
symbols, in dreams   156
sympathetic division   74, 74, 408
sympathetic nervous system   75
synapses   65–6
synaptic clefts   66, 66, 547
synaptic transmission   65–6, 66
synaptic vesicles   66, 66
syntax   340
syntheses   7, 94
syphilis   298
systematic desensitisation   535–6

taboos   146
tammar wallabies   198
tangible support   426
tardive dyskinesia   547
target tracking   120
taste   119, 119–20
taste adaption   120
taste-aversion learning   196–9, 197
taste buds   119, 119, 125
taste receptors   119, 119–20
taste testing   120
TAT   391, 392, 458, 475
TDI   511, 512
technology   40, 108, 108, 115–16, 454
telegraphic speech   343
television, violence on   201–2, 202,
   613
telic states   372
temperament   346, 446
temperature, and aggression   610,
   610
temporal cortex   265
temporal integration   127, 127–8
temporal lobe   78, 78
temporally contiguous responses   180
tend-and-befriend response   417
tendons   121
tension reduction   371, 462
tension systems   453
teonanacatl   163
terminal buttons   62, 62
terra nullius   622
tertiary prevention   553
testes   83, 83
testosterone   82–3, 356, 384
test-retest reliability   291
texture gradients   130–1, 131
thalamus   75, 76, 117–18, 120, 238
Thanatos   453, 455
That's-Not-All technique   574

Wolof people   407
'womb envy'   459
women   18, 344, 417, 501, 503
Woodworth Personal Data Sheet
   473
word fragment completion   223, *224*
word identification   224, *224*
word meanings   341–2
words, perception of   341
word stem completion   223, *224*
workaholics   473
working memory   217–18

working memory span   217
World Health Organization   487, 498
World Trade Center attack   421, 601
World War II   619
World Wide Web   *see* Internet
WPPSI-III   296

Xanax   67, 548
X chromosomes   59, 111

*yarda*   429
Yawulyu ceremonies   430

Y-BOCS   536
Y chromosomes   59
*yinawaru*   430
yoga   434
Yugoslavia   618, 620
Yup'ik Eskimo people   302

Zapotec villages, Mexico   613
Zen   434
Zöllner illusion   *98*
zygotes   326